THE LAW OF GUARANTIES

A Jurisdiction-by-Jurisdiction Guide to U.S. and Canadian Law

Jeremy S. Friedberg, Brian D. Hulse, and James H. Prior,
Editors

Commercial Finance Committee
Uniform Commercial Code Committee

AMERICAN BAR ASSOCIATION
Business Law Section

Cover design by Jill Tedhams/ABA Publishing.

Page layout by Quadrum Solutions.

Printed in the United States of America.

17 16 15 14 13   5 4 3 2 1

Library of Congress Cataloging-in-Publication Data

The Law of Guaranties: A Jurisdiction-by-Jurisdiction Guide to U.S. and Canadian Law / Jeremy S. Friedberg, Brian D. Hulse, and James H. Prior, editors.

pages cm

ISBN 978-1-61438-805-0 (alk. paper)

1. Suretyship and guaranty—United States—States. I. Jeremy S. Friedberg, Brian D. Hulse, and James H. Prior, editors of compilation.

KF1045.L39 2013

346.7307'4-dc23

2013003734

Contents

Preface

We are pleased to present the first edition of *The Law of Guaranties, A Jurisdiction-by-Jurisdiction Guide to U.S. and Canadian Law.* This book is the product of a joint task force of the Commercial Finance Committee and the Uniform Commercial Code Committee of the ABA's Business Law Section.

The Law of Guaranties is a unique resource for commercial lenders and their lawyers. It collects detailed information about the laws of guaranty of all 50 states, the District of Columbia, Puerto Rico, Canada and applicable Federal statutes updated as of late 2012. *The Law of Guaranties* represents a tremendous effort on the part of many experienced and devoted lawyers over an extended period of time, often by individuals who are leaders of the bar.

Our sincere gratitude is due to each of our authors and to the American Bar Association's talented and committed staff members, who brought the project to fruition.

Special thanks are in order for Penelope L. Christophorou of Cleary Gottlieb Steen & Hamilton LLP. Penny was the original inspiration for this project when she was the chair of the Uniform Commercial Code Committee of the ABA's Business Law Section. Penny was responsible for the first draft of the template used to create the chapters in this book.

We hope you find *The Law of Guaranties* to be useful and welcome your input and suggestions for future editions.

Jeremy S. Friedberg
Leitess Friedberg PC
Baltimore, Maryland

Brian D. Hulse
Davis Wright Tremaine LLP
Seattle, Washington

James H. Prior
Porter, Wright, Morris, & Arthur LLP
Columbus, Ohio

Co-Chairs, Joint Task Force on Survey of Laws of Guaranties

Foreword

Anyone remotely familiar with the law of guaranty knows that the Restatement (Third) of the Law of Suretyship and Guaranty (ALI 1996) is an indispensable text. It provides a wonderful summary of what the law is generally, along with the reasons underlying each rule. Unfortunately, no area of law is truly as uniform as any restatement makes it seem, and that is certainly true with respect to the law of guaranty. Hence the need for this book.

In the pages that follow, the reader will learn about the key cases, statutes, and nuances of the law of guaranty in each jurisdiction within the United States and Canada. That makes this book an essential tool for both transactional lawyers and litigators. The former can use it when drafting or negotiating a guaranty, particularly one that may be governed by the law of a jurisdiction with which the lawyer is not intimately familiar. For as this book ably demonstrates, choice of law matters. Litigators will find this book useful in preparing to enforce or escape liability under a guaranty. By organizing the material by jurisdiction, and providing what is in essence a basic law review article about the law in that locality, this book refers users to what they need to know, even if they were unaware they needed to know it.

That is something of a Herculean task. Yet the editors have obtained the assistance of notable and experienced practitioners in each jurisdiction. These authors have produced a work that belongs on the shelf of every commercial lawyer. That is evidenced most clearly by the highlights and practice pointers in each section. Those highlights and practice pointers reveal how varied – and occasionally surprising – the law of guaranty is. For example,

Anti-deficiency statutes. In Nebraska, guarantors do not get the benefit of the three-month statute of limitations applicable to an action for a deficiency against a principal obligor following a non-judicial foreclosure of real property. In Utah, they do.

Attorney's fees. In Nebraska, a contractual provision providing for attorney's fees in connection with a lawsuit to enforce a contract is void as against public policy. The same is true in the Dakotas.

Community property. The rules vary widely about whether the community property of a guarantor can be reached if the guarantor's spouse has not signed the guaranty. In Arizona, the guarantor has no recourse to community property. In Idaho, the guarantor does. In Washington, it depends on whether the guaranteed obligation benefitted the community. And in New Mexico, the law is unclear on this point. Of course, the federal Equal Credit Opportunity Act and Regulation B (detailed in the chapter on federal law) limit a creditor's ability to simply require both spouses to sign the guaranty, so an understanding of the marital property laws of the applicable jurisdiction are critical when the guarantor is an individual.

Continuing guaranties. Kentucky apparently restricts the use of continuing guaranties because it requires that a guaranty agreement either expressly reference the instrument being guaranteed or specify both a maximum liability and a termination date. In Alabama, in contrast, a clause in a guaranty agreement requiring the express written consent of the obligee before the guarantor may revoke a continuing guaranty is enforceable.

Secured transactions. Washington State has non-uniform versions of U.C.C. §§ 9-602 and 9-624, which allow secondary guarantors to waive several otherwise non-waivable rights under Article 9.

This brief glimpse should be sufficient to show that this book will appeal to novices and experts alike.

December 2012

Stephen L. Sepinuck
Professor
Director, Commercial Law Center
Gonzaga University School of Law

Alabama State Law of Guaranties

Haskins W. Jones
Laura J. Biddy
Johnston Barton Proctor & Rose LLP
Colonial Brookwood Center
569 Brookwood Village, Suite 901
Birmingham, Alabama 35209
telephone: (205) 458-9400
facsimile: (205) 458-9500
e-mail: hjones@johnstonbarton.com
www.johnstonbarton.com

JohnstonBarton
ATTORNEYS

Contents

Alabama State Law of Guaranties

Definitions: For purposes of this article, the following defined terms are used:

"Guarantor" means a person who is secondarily liable on an obligation, and only bound if the principal obligor fails to pay the obligee.[1]

"Guaranty Agreement" means the contract pursuant to which the guarantor agrees to be secondarily liable for the underlying obligations of the principal obligor to the obligee if the principal obligor defaults in the payment of the underlying obligation.

"Obligee" means the person to whom the principal obligor owes the underlying obligation.

"Primary Obligor" means the person who incurs the underlying obligation to the obligee.

"Underlying Obligation" means the obligations of the principal obligor to the obligee.

ALABAMA LAW HIGHLIGHTS

- In Alabama, generally, the express written terms of the guaranty agreement are enforceable. Alabama courts, in the absence of fraud or other basic contractual defenses, have enforced guaranty agreements in accordance with their terms.
- The Alabama Supreme Court has upheld a contractual provision in a guaranty agreement requiring the express written consent of the obligee before the guarantor could revoke his continuing guaranty. The Court found that provided the guaranty agreement was validly formed and no defenses existed, such term was enforceable.[2]

Restatement of Suretyship and Guaranty

- Alabama Courts have cited to the Restatement of Suretyship and Guaranty.[3]

---

1. Alabama courts have noted the distinction between sureties and guarantors based on a surety being primarily liable, along with the principal obligor, on the underlying obligation, while a guarantor is secondarily liable, and is not required to make good on the underlying obligation until the principal obligor fails to satisfy the underlying obligation. Valley Mining Corp., Inc. v. Metro Bank, 383 So.2d 158, 162 (Ala. 1980). Courts will look to the substance of the transaction to determine if the party is a surety or a guarantor. SouthTrust Bank of Alabama, N.A. v. Webb-Stiles Co., Inc., 931 So.2d 706, 708 (Ala. 2005) (citing Gambill v. Fox Typewriter Co, 66 So. 655, 656 (Ala. 1914)). In some cases, surety law is applied to obligations of guarantor under a guaranty agreement. *See infra* footnote 70 and accompanying text.
2. *See infra* footnotes 35 and 36 and accompanying text.
3. *See* Hous. Auth. v. Hartford Accident & Indem. Co., 954 So.2d 577, 581(Ala. 2006), and *Webb-Stiles*, 931 So.2d at 712, (each citing to the Restatement (Third) of Suretyship and Guaranty (1996)).

§ 1 Nature of the Guaranty Arrangement

1.1 Creation of Guaranty Arrangement—Evidenced by Contract

The construction and interpretation of guaranty agreements are governed by the law of contracts.[4] "[W]hen the terms of the guaranty are clear and certain, its construction and legal effect are questions of law for the court."[5] Determining whether the terms of a contract are ambiguous is a question of law, to be determined by the court, but the determination of the meaning of ambiguous terms is a factual determination for the jury.[6] Ambiguous language in a guaranty agreement is construed more strongly against the guarantor.[7]

1.2 Choice of Law

Alabama recognizes the principle of "*lex loci contractus* which states that a contract is governed by the laws of the state where it is made except where the parties have legally contracted with reference to the laws of another jurisdiction."[8] Alabama will recognize the law of another state provided that the law of the state chosen has a reasonable relationship to the parties or the transaction, and such choice of law is not contrary to the public policy of the State of Alabama.[9]

§ 2 State Law Requirements for Entering into a Guaranty Agreement; Authority

2.1 Individuals

The age of majority in Alabama is 19.[10] An individual signing a personal guaranty is liable on a guaranty regardless of whether such individual read or even understood the terms of the guaranty agreement.[11] Absent fraud or

---

4. Government Street Lumber Co., Inc. v. AmSouth Bank, N.A., 553 So.2d 68, 75 (Ala. 1989).
5. Robbins Tire & Rubber Credit Union v. Donald B. Hunt and Diana G. Brickley, 669 So.2d 969, 970 (Ala. Civ. App. 1995) (quoting Moody v. Schloss & Kahn, Inc., 600 So.2d 1045, 1047 (Ala. Civ. App. 1992)); *but see* Crawford v. Chattanooga Savings Bank, 78 So. 58, 60 (Ala. 1917) (stating that a guarantor is a form of surety).
6. Colonial Bank of Alabama v. Coker, 482 So.2d 286, 291 (Ala. 1985).
7. Dill v. Blakeney, 568 So.2d 774, 778 (Ala. 1990) (citing Sales Corp. v. U.S. Fidelity & Guaranty Co., 110 So. 277, 278 (Ala. 1926)); *Crawford*, 78 So. at 60 (stating "[w]here language is susceptible of two meanings, it should be taken most strongly against guarantor, and in favor of party who has parted with his property").
8. Cherry, Bekaert & Holland v. Brown, 582 So.2d 502, 506 (Ala. 1991).
9. *Id.* at 506-07.
10. Ala. Code § 26-1-1.
11. First Nat'l Bank of Mobile v. Horner, 494 So.2d 419, 420 (Ala. 1986) (holding that evidence that the guarantor did not know that she was signing a guaranty agreement was inadmissible, in the absence of allegations of fraud, mistake, or ambiguity, when the guarantor's signature was accompanied by a notary acknowledgment that the guarantor was informed of the contents of the instrument and that she voluntarily signed the guaranty agreement).

mistake, a guarantor may generally not allege that he did not understand the terms of the guaranty agreement.[12] Evidence of a contemporaneous oral statement that personal guaranty agreements would not be enforced against the guarantor is not a sufficient allegation of fraud where the oral statements did not misrepresent or conceal the contents of the agreements.[13] The mere fact that the obligee sued on the guaranty agreements and such alleged statements were false does not necessarily prove that the statements were false at the time they were made.[14] The guarantor must show that the obligee had a present intent to deceive.[15]

Merely adding a title to an individual's signature, such as "/s/John Doe, President," is not sufficient to indicate that no personal liability is to attach to the person executing the guaranty agreement. To determine whether a guaranty agreement is ambiguous with respect to the capacity of the person signing the document, Alabama courts look for consistency between the signature block and the main body of the contract.[16] In general, Alabama courts have not found ambiguity where a guarantor added a title after his signature to guaranty agreements indicating that the guarantor was to be individually liable.[17]

2.2 Husband and Wife

Alabama is an equitable division of property state, meaning that marital assets and liabilities are divided equitably between spouses upon divorce, either by a court of equity or by mutual agreement of the parties.[18] A couple's divorce decree should address each marital debt and which spouse will be liable for it.[19] Generally, if a guaranty agreement has been entered into by one spouse only, a subsequent divorce should not affect the guarantor's liability under that guaranty agreement.[20]

---

12. *Id.*
13. *See* Dobbins v. Dicus Oil Company, Inc., 495 So.2d 587, 589 (Ala. 1986) (citing Blake v. Coates, 294 So.2d 433 (Ala. 1974)).
14. *See* Mulvaney v. Secor Bank, 599 So.2d 1161, 1162 (Ala. 1992).
15. *Id.*
16. Marriott Int'l, Inc. v. deCelle, 722 So.2d 760 (Ala. 1998) (reversing trial court's grant of guarantor's motion to dismiss by finding that the guaranty agreement was ambiguous where body of contract indicated that the guarantor was individually guaranteeing the underlying obligations of the principal obligor and the signature block indicated that the guarantor was signing as officer of the principal obligor).
17. *See* Moody v. Schloss Kahn, 600 So.2d 1045, 1047 (Ala. Civ. App. 1992) (affirming trial court's grant of the obligee's motion for summary judgment by finding that signature of president of the principal obligor to an individual guaranty agreement, where he wrote president after his name, was not sufficient to create ambiguity in the contract, and the addition of the title to his signature was not sufficient to defeat his personal liability under the guaranty agreement); *see also* Shipp v. First Alabama Bank of Gadsden, N.A., 473 So.2d 1014, 1018 (holding that without more, merely signing a guaranty and adding a title does not indicate that an individual is signing in a representative capacity); Maske v. Chrysler First Commercial Corporation, 602 So.2d 388 (Ala. 1992) (finding that the addition of a title to guarantor's signature was merely a description of the guarantor, and not an indication that the guarantor was signing in a representative capacity).
18. Rick Fernambucq & Gary Pate, *Family Law in Alabama Practice and Procedure*, § 8.01[1] (3rd edition, 2002).
19. *Id. See also* Green v. SouthTrust Bank of Sand Mountain, 519 So.2d 1289 (Ala. 1987) (The Alabama Supreme Court found that a guaranty agreement executed by a husband and wife was not enforceable against the wife after her divorce from her husband, when the former wife went in person to the bank, provided a copy of her divorce decree to the bank, and indicated she was no longer liable for the husband's debts pursuant to said decree, and the bank made subsequent loans to the husband for use in his business.).
20. *See* Allen v. Allen, 465 So.2d 424, 426 (Ala. Civ. App. 1985).

2.3 Entities

Generally, Alabama Code § 10A-1-2.11 grants corporations, limited or general partnerships, limited liability companies, business trusts, real estate investment trusts, joint ventures, joint stock companies, cooperatives, associations, banks, insurance companies, credit unions, savings and loan associations, or other organizations, regardless of whether the organization is for profit, nonprofit, domestic, or foreign, the ability to enter into guaranty agreements.[21]

Since a guaranty agreement is strictly construed in accordance with its terms, a guaranty agreement will generally not extend to the obligations of a successor entity where the obligee has notice of the new entity as the principal obligor.[22]

§ 3 Signatory's Authority to Execute a Guaranty Agreement

Alabama does not have any particular law on point regarding the authority of a person who executes a guaranty agreement to bind a guarantor; however, in general, "Alabama law is well settled on the principle that in order for an agent to act on a principal's behalf regarding a matter controlled by the statute of frauds, the agent's authority must be in writing. Moreover, any contract made by an agent without written authority is *void* if the contract itself is one that has to be in writing."[23]

§ 4 Consideration

Guaranty agreements, as all contracts, require consideration to be enforceable. If a guaranty agreement is made prior to or at the same time that the principal obligor contracts with the obligee, as part of the same transaction, the consideration between the principal obligor and the obligee is sufficient consideration for the guaranty agreement.[24] When a guaranty agreement is entered into after the underlying obligation has been undertaken by the principal obligor to the obligee, and the guarantor was not a party to that original transaction, such contract requires separate consideration.[25] A promise by the

---

21. Ala. Code § 10A-1-1.03(64).
22. *See* Dozier v. Paterson Co., Inc., 648 So.2d 610, 612 (Ala. Civ. App. 1994) (holding that a guaranty agreement executed by an individual guaranteeing a partnership's credit arrangement with a supplier did not extend to the debts of the corporation subsequently formed for operation of the business, when supplier had notice of formation of new corporation).
23. Hight v. Byars, 569 So.2d 387, 388 (Ala. 1990); *see* discussion at Section 7.5 infra regarding guaranty agreements and Alabama's statute of frauds.
24. Colonial Bank of Alabama v. Coker, 482 So.2d 286, 291 (Ala. 1985) (quoting Shur-Gain Feed Division William Davies Co., Inc. v. Huntsville Production Credit Ass'n, 372 So.2d 1317, 1320 (Ala. Civ. App. 1979).
25. Medley v. SouthTrust Bank of the Quad Cities, 500 So.2d 1075, 1078 (Ala. 1986) (citing Clark v. McGinn, 105 So.2d 668, 671 (Ala. 1958)).

guarantor to guarantee future debt from the principal obligor to the obligee is sufficient consideration for such a guaranty agreement.[26] Generally, a guaranty agreement where a guarantor promises to pay an existing debt is not supported by sufficient consideration, but an extension of time of payment of the underlying obligation or a renewal of the underlying obligation is sufficient consideration for a guarantor's promise to guarantee payment of such underlying obligation.[27]

§ 5 Notice of Acceptance

An offer of guaranty, such as a letter of credit, must be accepted and notice given to the guarantor before said guaranty is binding.[28] A bilateral guaranty agreement, signed by both the guarantor and the obligee, reciting that a consideration has been received for the agreement's execution, even if nominal, is a complete and binding contract, and no acceptance is required.[29] Parties may waive notice of acceptance of the guaranty, either by the express or implied terms of the guaranty agreement.[30]

§ 6 Interpretation of Guaranties

6.1 General Principles

A guaranty is to be construed solely on the terms in the agreement, as "[it] is fundamental that the liability of a guarantor will not be extended by implication beyond the terms of his contract."[31]

6.2 Guaranty of Payment versus Guaranty of Collection

A guaranty agreement guaranteeing the payment of the underlying obligation is an absolute guaranty, whereas a guaranty agreement guaranteeing the collection of the underlying obligation is a conditional guaranty, and is therefore not immediately enforceable against the guarantor until the obligee has exercised all reasonable efforts to collect from the primary obligor.[32]

26. *Id.* at 1078.
27. Grant v. SouthTrust Bank of Baldwin County, 512 So.2d 914, 916 (Ala. 1987) (holding that a guaranty agreement executed by the guarantors 60 days after extension of credit by the obligee to the principal obligor was supported by sufficient consideration, namely the extension or renewal of the principal obligor's debt, when loan was refinanced two years later).
28. Shows v. Steiner, Lobman & Frank, 57 So. 700, 701 (Ala. 1911).
29. Phillips-Boyd Pub. Co. v. McKinnon, 73 So. 43 (Ala. 1916); Huckaby v. McConnon & Co., 105 So. 886, 888 (Ala. 1925).
30. *Phillips-Boyd*, 73 So. at 45-46.
31. *Government Street,* 553 So.2d at 75; Medley v. SouthTrust Bank of the Quad Cities, 500 So.2d 1075, 1081 (Ala. 1986) (quoting Russell v. Garrett, 93 So. 711, 715 (Ala. 1922), that the guarantor "has a right to stand upon the very terms of his contract, and if he does not assent to any variation of it, and a variation is made, it is fatal").
32. Shur-Gain Feed Division William Davies Co., Inc. v. Huntsville Production Credit Ass'n, 372 So.2d 1317, 1320 (Ala. Civ. App. 1979).

6.3 Language Regarding the Revocation of Guaranty Agreements; Continuing Guaranties

6.3.1 *Generally*

A continuing guaranty is an offer by the guarantor to guarantee future obligations of the principal obligor and may be revoked by the guarantor at any time, and the guarantor will not be liable for any credit extended to the principal obligor after the obligee's receipt of notice of the revocation.[33] The method of revocation of a continuing guaranty is governed by the guaranty agreement.[34]

In 2007, the Alabama Supreme Court upheld a contractual provision in a guaranty agreement requiring the express written consent of the obligee before the guarantor could revoke his continuing guaranty.[35] The Court found that provided the guaranty agreement was validly formed and no defenses existed, such term was enforceable.[36]

Mere knowledge on the part of the obligee that a guarantor is no longer a principal of the principal obligor is not sufficient notice of a revocation of a continuing guaranty agreement.[37] A guarantor must give notice as provided in the continuing guaranty agreement.[38]

6.3.2 *Duration*

A continuing guaranty unlimited in duration is valid for a reasonable time.[39] A guaranty agreement which provides for a specific and exclusive method of revocation by the guarantor is valid until revoked.[40]

These principles can lead to conflicting results. For example, the Alabama Court of Civil Appeals implied a reasonable time standard and held that a guaranty agreement was no longer enforceable nine years after a principal of the principal obligor entered into a guaranty agreement in favor of a supplier. The court found that since the principal obligor stopped doing business with the obligee for that nine-year period, it was unreasonable for the obligee to rely on the guaranty agreement. Alternatively, the Alabama Court of Civil Appeals held that a continuing guaranty agreement entered into by a former

---

33. Barnett Millworks, Inc. v. Guthrie, 974 So.2d 952, 955-56 (Ala. 2007) (citing Green v. SouthTrust Bank of Sand Mountain, 519 So.2d 1289, 1291 (Ala. 1987)).
34. *See* Lightsey v. Orgill Bros. & Co, Inc., 454 So.2d 1002, 1005 (Ala. Civ. App. 1984); *see also Barnett Millworks*, 974 So.2d at 957.
35. *Barnett Millworks*, 974 So.2d at 957.
36. *Id.*
37. *See* Bledsoe v. Cargill, 452 So.2d, 1334, 1336 (Ala. Civ. App. 1984); *see also* Sharer v. Bend Millwork Systems, Inc., 600 So.2d 223, 227 (Ala. 1992).
38. *But see* discussion at Section 6.3(b) infra, where Alabama courts have held that a continuing guaranty agreement with no express termination date shall be enforceable for a reasonable time.
39. William R. Hubbell Steel Corp. v. Epperson, 679 So.2d 1131 (Ala. Civ. App. 1996) (holding that it was unreasonable to enforce a guaranty agreement where a guarantor was liable for debts nine years after his execution of the guaranty, and debts were incurred several years after the principal obligor initially transacted business with the obligee).
40. Sherman Industries, Inc. v. Alexander, 980 So.2d 991, 995-96 (Ala. Civ. App. 2007).

shareholder of the principal obligor is still effective even when the current shareholders entered into new guaranty agreements intended to replace the old guaranty agreements, as the guarantor/former shareholder failed to consent to the substitution of the new guaranty agreements, was not a party to the substitution, nor did he revoke his continuing guaranty agreement as provided in the original guaranty agreement.[41]

6.4 Assignment

In general, contracts are freely assignable provided that a duty is not personal.[42] A duty is personal if such duty was intended to be personal by the terms of the contract.[43] An obligee may restrict the assignment of the guaranty agreement by the guarantor by prohibiting assignment completely, or by prohibiting assignment without the obligee's prior consent. The Alabama Supreme Court has held that there is no implied duty of good faith or commercial reasonableness when the express terms of the contract contradict those principles.[44]

With respect to guaranty agreements, Alabama recognizes the general rule that along with the assignment of the underlying obligation, any security for the payment of that underlying obligation, including any guaranty agreements, is contemporaneously assigned along with the debt.[45]

§ 7 Defenses of the Guarantor

7.1 Discharge of Underlying Obligation

Alabama has adopted the general principle that a guarantor is discharged from his or her liability on the underlying obligation to the extent the underlying obligation has been paid or satisfied.[46] If the underlying obligation is with respect to an open account, payments on such account are applied to the oldest debt first.[47]

---

41. Bledsoe v. Cargill, Inc., 452 So.2d 1334, 1336-37 (Ala. Civ. App. 1984).
42. Sisco v. Empiregas, Inc. of Belle Mina, 286 Ala. 72, 77 (Ala. 1970).
43. *Id.*
44. Shoney's LLC v. MAC East, LLC, 27 So.3d 1216, 1223 (Ala. 2009) (holding that there was no implied duty of good faith on the part of the sublessor in exercising its consent to assignment of the sublease by the subtenant, where the terms of the sublease explicitly granted the sublessor the right to withhold consent to assignment in its sole discretion).
45. LPP Mortgage, Ltd. v. Boutwell, 36 So.3d 497, 501 (Ala. 2009) (holding that even though the guaranty agreements were not explicitly assigned to the purchaser of a promissory note, a general assignment in the mortgage assignment of "all documents, agreement, instruments and other collateral that evidence, secure or otherwise relate to Assignor's right, title or interest in and to the Mortgage and/or the Note...", physical delivery of the guaranty agreements to the purchaser, and application of the general rule indicated that the guaranties were in fact assigned to the new purchaser).
46. Shur-Gain Feed Division William Davies Co., Inc. v. Huntsville Production Credit Ass'n, 372 So.2d 1317, 1320 (Ala. Civ. App. 1979).
47. *Id.* at 1320-21.

7.2 Defenses of the Principal Obligor

An unconditional guaranty agreement, even though unlimited, is still limited to the total of the underlying obligations of the principal obligor.[48]

Defenses and claims of the principal obligor, even if valid, are not available to the guarantor as defenses under an unconditional guaranty agreement.[49]

7.3 Novation

Some guarantors have argued that their guaranty agreement is no longer valid due to a novation of the guaranty agreement by a subsequent guaranty. In general, this claim has had little success in Alabama courts if the original guarantor is not a party to the replacement guaranty.[50]

A subsequent guaranty agreement may serve as a novation of a prior guaranty agreement if the following elements are met: "(1) there must have been a previous valid obligation; (2) there must be an agreement of the parties thereto to a new contract or obligation; (3) there must be an agreement that it is an extinguishment of the old contract or obligation; and (4) the new contract or obligation must be a valid one between the parties thereto."[51] The key factor in determining if a novation has occurred is the intent of the parties.[52]

The Alabama Supreme Court has held that a novation is only effective if it includes the guarantor and the replacement guarantor as parties thereto, to evidence the consent to the extinguishment of the obligation of the guarantor.[53]

7.4 Running of Statute of Limitations as to Underlying Obligation

A surety may use any defense of the principal obligor, except those personal to the principal obligor, including running of the statute of limitations.[54]

---

48. Ex parte Kaschak, 681 So.2d 197, 201 (Ala. 1996) (overruling the Alabama Court of Civil Appeals which held that a termination of a lease agreement and discharge of a tenant from its obligations did not release the guarantor from liability for rent due after termination of the lease. The Alabama Supreme Court held that the lessor could only recover against the guarantor for amounts owed by the tenant on the underlying lease agreement).
49. PR Leasing Co., Inc. v. Cowin Equipment Co., Inc., 611 So.2d 232, 234 (Ala. 1992) (quoting Government Street Lumber Co. v. AmSouth Bank, N.A., 553 So.2d 68, 79 (Ala. 1989) which held that a guaranty agreement was clear and unambiguous where the guarantor waived any defenses of the principal obligor against the obligee; the guarantor could not raise those defenses in the action brought by the obligee against the guarantor).
50. *See Pilalas*, 549 So.2d at 95; *see also* Bledsoe v. Cargill, Inc., 452 So.2d 1334, 1337 (Ala. Civ. App. 1984).
51. Medley v. SouthTrust Bank of the Quad Cities, 500 So.2d 1075, 1081 (Ala. 1986) (citing Warrior Drilling & Engineering Co. v. King, 446 So.2d 31, 33 (Ala. 1984)).
52. *Id.*
53. Safeco Insurance Co. of America v. Graybar Electric Co., Inc., 59 So.3d 649, 656 (Ala. 2010) (holding that a settlement agreement did not serve as a novation and the surety bond issuer was not released from its obligations as surety when the principal obligor and the obligee entered into a settlement agreement, as the settlement agreement did not include the surety as a party, did not release the principal obligor from its obligations to pay, and stated that it was not intended to benefit any third-party); *see also Bledsoe*, 452 So.2d at 1336.
54. *See* Housing Authority of the City of Huntsville v. Hartford Accident and Indemnity Co., 954 So.2d 577, 580-81 (Ala. 2006); *see also* McKerall v. Kaiser, 60 So.3d 288, 293 (Ala. 2010) (holding that the obligee's claim against the guarantor of a promissory note was barred by the statute of limitations for enforcement of the note).

7.5 Statute of Frauds (Alabama Code § 8-9-2)

Alabama law requires that agreements for a person to "answer for the debt, default or miscarriage of another" be in writing and signed by the party to be charged, or such agreement is void.[55] Alabama courts distinguish between a collateral promise to pay, such as a guaranty agreement, which is subject to Alabama's statute of frauds, and an original promise to pay, such as a promise by a third-party directly to the primary obligor to discharge the primary obligor's debt to the obligee, which is not.[56]

7.6 Guaranty Agreement is Void

7.6.1 Generally

Generally, if the underlying obligation between the obligee and the principal obligor is void, the guaranty agreement guaranteeing such obligation is void. If the obligation is merely voidable at the option of the principal obligor, then the obligations of the guarantor pursuant to the guaranty agreement are void to the extent the principal obligor has exercised his, her, or its option.[57]

7.6.2 Fraud

A guaranty agreement is voidable at the option of the guarantor if the obligee has made a fraudulent representation or concealment which affects the liability or potential obligation of the guarantor.[58] Absent fraud in the inducement or mistake, a guarantor cannot avoid his or her obligations under a guaranty by claiming ignorance of its terms or that he or she failed to read the guaranty agreement.[59] "If the circumstances are such that a reasonably prudent person who exercised ordinary care would have discovered the facts, [the guarantor] should not be entitled to prevail on [an] affirmative defense of fraud."[60]

A guarantor is charged with exercising due care in executing the guaranty agreement and ensuring that he or she understands the guaranty agreement's terms.[61]

In general, when the obligee and the guarantor have solely a debtor-creditor relationship, the obligee has no duty to disclose any facts to the

55. Ala. Code § 8-9-2(3).
56. Spafford v. Crescent Credit Corp., 497 So.2d 160 (Ala. Civ. App. 1986); Stewart v. State Farm Mut. Auto. Ins. Co., 605 So.2d 1214, 1216 (Ala. 1992).
57. Scharnagel v. Furst, 112 So. 102 (Ala. 1927).
58. Associates Financial Services Co., Inc. v. First Nat'l Bank of Mobile, 292 So.2d 112, 116 (Ala. 1974).
59. Government Street Lumber Co., Inc. v. AmSouth Bank, N.A., 553 So.2d 68, 75 (Ala. 1989); Williams v. Bank of Oxford, 523 So.2d 367, 369 (Ala. 1988).
60. First Nat'l Bank of Mobile v. Horner, 494 So.2d 419 (Ala. 1986).
61. *Williams* 523 So.2d at 370.

guarantor.[62] In certain instances, a bank may have a fiduciary duty to disclose certain facts to a guarantor if a guarantor has a special relationship with the bank in which the guarantor entrusts the bank and relies on the bank for certain financial advice.[63]

7.6.3 *Mistake*

Generally, a unilateral mistake made by the guarantor at the time the guaranty agreement is entered into that has a material adverse effect on the guarantor is voidable, so long as the guarantor did not bear the risk of the mistake, enforcement of the guaranty agreement would be unconscionable, and the obligee caused the mistake or had reason to know of the mistake.[64] Further, a guarantor's allegation that he or she did not understand the terms of the guaranty agreement, or even that he or she did not know that he or she was executing a guaranty agreement is not sufficient to void the guarantor's obligations under the guaranty agreement.[65]

7.6.4 *Unconscionability*

An unconscionable contract or provision is one "such as no man in his sense and not under delusion would make on the one hand, and as no honest and fair man would accept on the other."[66]

If a court determines that a guaranty agreement is unconscionable, it may void the entire contract, refuse to enforce the unconscionable provisions, or limit the application of the contract to avoid an unconscionable outcome.[67]

Courts are hesitant to exercise the remedy of rescission of a contract due to unconscionability; the remedy is reserved generally "for the protection of the unsophisticated and uneducated."[68]

---

62. *Associates*, 292 So.2d at 116 (In this case, the obligee and the principal obligor knew that security for loan to the principal obligor did not exist at the time guarantor was induced to enter into guaranty, which effectively increased guarantor's liability to the obligee. The obligee's employee and the principal obligor were engaged in fraud with respect to documentation of collateral for the floor plan financing arrangement. The court noted that facts of this case were extraordinary to overcome the general principle that when the obligee is not physically present at the execution of the guaranty agreement, the obligee is freed from the good faith duty of disclosure of facts materially increasing the guarantor's risks of which the obligee has knowledge.).
63. *Williams* 523 So.2d at 369 (citing Faith, Hope and Love, Inc. v. First Alabama Bank, 496 So.2d 708 (Ala. 1986)); *see also* Hackney v. First Alabama Bank, 555 So.2d 97, 100 (Ala. 1989).
64. Hackney v. First Alabama Bank, 555 So.2d 97, 101 (Ala. 1989).
65. *See* First Nat'l Bank of Mobile v. Horner, 494 So.2d 419 (Ala. 1986) (finding that testimony that the guarantor did not understand that she was executing a guaranty agreement was inadmissible in the face of an acknowledgment by a notary public that the guarantor was informed of contents of instrument, in the absence of mistake, fraud, or ambiguity); *see also Williams*, 523 So.2d at 370 (holding that affidavit of the guarantors stating that they did not read nor understand the terms of their guaranty agreements was not sufficient to provide an issue of material fact sufficient to overturn trial court's grant of bank's motion for summary judgment against the guarantors).
66. Layne v. Garner, 612 So.2d 404, 408 (Ala. 1992) (holding that a provision in a guaranty agreement requiring the underlying obligation to be paid in full before any guarantor sought an action against his coguarantors as not unconscionable. The guarantor did not lack meaningful choice or bargaining power, and the term was not unreasonably favorable to the obligee, nor was it oppressive or patently unfair).
67. Crestline Center v. Hinton, 567 So.2d 393 (Ala. Civ. App. 1990).
68. *Layne*, 612 So.2d at 408.

§ 8 Waiver of Defenses by the Guarantor

Alabama law provides that a guarantor may not waive in a guaranty agreement the "notification of the disposition of collateral and of the right to raise the issue of commercial reasonableness in the disposition of collateral" under Alabama's Article 9 of the Uniform Commercial Code.[69]

§ 9 Rights Provided to Secondary Obligor

9.1 Rights Against the Principal Obligor

Alabama Code Section 8-3-42(1) provides that a surety is entitled to a summary judgment against the principal obligor by motion and upon three days' notice thereof in the circuit court when the surety satisfied a judgment against him and the judgment has been satisfied, either wholly or in part. Alabama courts have applied this law of sureties to that of guarantors without distinction between a surety and a guarantor.[70]

9.2 Rights Against Coguarantors—Contribution

Alabama Code Section 8-3-42(2) also provides that a surety who has paid the debt of the principal obligor may seek contribution from his, her, or its cosureties and may similarly file a motion for summary judgment.

In general, if not specifically prohibited by the guaranty agreement, a guarantor may seek contribution from his, her, or its coguarantors before payment in full of the guaranteed indebtedness.[71] A guarantor who has paid more than his or her allocable portion of the underlying obligation has a statutory right to contribution from his or her coguarantors.[72] The right to contribution from coguarantors can generally only be waived by an agreement among the coguarantors, and not in any agreement between the guarantor and the principal obligor or between the guarantor and the obligee. Such waiver must be fully and clearly established by the evidence.[73] Separate guaranty agreements that contain waiver of contribution language may be enforceable among coguarantors if the guaranty agreements can be read together as a single contract.[74]

---

69. Prescott v. Thompson Tractor Co., 495 So.2d 513, 517 (Ala. 1986).
70. *See* Layne v. Garner, 612 So.2d 404, 405-06 (Ala. 1992); *see also* Moody v. Hinton, 603 So.2d 912, 914-15 (Ala. 1992), and Harris v. Shelton, 837 So.2d 276, 278 (Ala. Civ. App. 2001, overturned on other grounds by Ex parte Harris, 837 So.2d 283 (Ala. 2002)).
71. *Layne*, 612 So.2d at 405 (Ala. 1992) (holding that a guarantor's lawsuit seeking contribution from his coguarantors was premature when the guaranty agreement specifically prohibited the exercise or enforcement of any right of contribution unless and until all of the indebtedness shall have been fully paid and discharged).
72. *Harris v. Shelton*, 837 So.2d 276 (relying on Alabama Code Sections 8-3-9, 8-3-42(2)(a) and *Layne*, 612 So.2d at 407).
73. *Harris*, 837 So.2d at 278.
74. Ex parte Harris, 837 So.2d at 288 (adopting the rule that "in the absence of anything to indicate a contrary intention, instruments executed at the same time, by the same contracting parties, for the same purpose, and in the course of the same transaction will be considered and construed together, because they are, in the eyes of the law, one contract or instrument").

A release of a coguarantor of liability under a guaranty agreement by the obligee does not act as an accord and satisfaction nor a novation releasing other coguarantors who are joint and severally liable under the same guaranty agreement.[75]

§ 10 Enforcement of Guaranty Agreements

An absolute guaranty by the guarantor gives the obligee the right to pursue its remedy against the principal obligor or the guarantor at the obligee's option.[76] A guarantor's obligation is to the obligee, not the principal obligor, so the principal obligor has no authority to release the guarantor from its obligations under a guaranty agreement.[77]

The Alabama Supreme Court held that for recovery under a guaranty agreement, the obligee must show "proof of existence of the guaranty agreement, default on the underlying contract by debtor, and nonpayment of the amount due from the guaranty under the terms of the guaranty. However, to recover under a conditional guaranty or continuing guaranty, an additional element, notice to the guarantor of the debtor's default, must be proved."[78] This element is trumped by the Alabama Court's general principle that the terms of the guaranty agreement control, and if the guarantor expressly waives this notice of default requirement, then this element is not required.[79] The courts have noted that the purpose of the obligee's notice to the guarantor of the principal obligor's default is to protect the guarantor from additional harm. In some instances, as when the principal obligor is insolvent, the Alabama Supreme Court has noted that no notice to the guarantor is required.[80]

An absolute and unconditional guaranty, coupled with a waiver of notice of default of the principal obligor, is the guarantor's unconditional promise to pay upon default of the principal obligor.[81]

No presentation or demand is required to be made on an absolute guaranty.[82]

§ 11 Revival and Reinstatement of Guaranty Agreements

Alabama does not have any particular law on point regarding the revival and reinstatement of guaranty agreements.

75. Pilalas v. Baldwin County Savings and Loan Ass'n, 549 So.2d 92 (Ala. 1989).
76. Colonial Bank of Alabama v. Coker, 482 So.2d 286, 290 (Ala. 1985).
77. Barnett Bank of Pensacola v. Marable, 385 So.2d 66, 67 (Ala. Civ. App. 1980).
78. Delro Industries, Inc. v. Evans, 514 So.2d 976, 979 (Ala. 1987).
79. *See* Sharer v. Bend Millwork Systems, Inc., 600 So.2d 223, 226 (Ala. 1992) (holding that a guarantor's waiver of notice of nonperformance in a written guaranty agreement was effective, and proof of such notice was not required for the obligee to sustain its action against the guarantor).
80. *Delro Industries*, 514 So.2d at 979.
81. Huckaby v. McConnon & Co., 105 So. 886, 888 (Ala. 1925).
82. Union Indemnity Co. v. Goodman, 114 So. 108, 110 (Ala. 1932).

Alaska State Law of Guaranties

Joseph L. Reece
Garrett Parks

Davis Wright Tremaine LLP
701 West Eighth Avenue, Suite 800
Anchorage, AK 99501
Phone: (907) 257-5300
Fax: (907) 257-5399
josephreece@dwt.com
garrettparks@dwt.com
http://www.dwt.com

Contents

Alaska State Law of Guaranties

ALASKA LAW HIGHLIGHTS

1. Individuals signing obligations in an official or corporate capacity in Alaska should exercise extreme care to expressly disclaim any personal liability for the underlying obligation. See § 2.4 and § 7.3.6 below.
2. A shareholder agreement imposing an obligation on each of the shareholders to bear a proportionate burden of repaying any debt on which the corporation defaulted can create enforceable guaranties running from each shareholder to the corporate creditors. See § 6 below.
3. Creditors taking a guaranty from an individual in Alaska need to know whether the guarantor has a community property agreement effective under the Alaska Community Property Act.
4. Coguarantors should understand that they have joint and several liability on their guaranty, with a right of contribution from their coguarantors. See § 10.1 below.
5. In Alaska, a creditor is not required to prove reliance, and can prevail against a guarantor based only on the existence of a valid contract between them.

Introduction

Alaska is a comparatively young state, having been admitted to the union only in 1959, and therefore has a smaller body of case law compared to most other jurisdictions in the United States. As a result, cases applying and interpreting the law of guaranties in Alaska, as in many other areas of law, is relatively sparse. For this reason, as a general rule, Alaska courts "construe guarantees under traditional contract principles."[1] When faced with issues of first impression, courts in Alaska frequently turn to the Restatements of the Law for guidance, and have done so in interpreting guaranties and suretyship issues.[2]

This survey will discuss guaranties in the context of commercial transactions. It will not discuss insurance, performance bonds, or product warranties.

1. Crook v. Mortensen-Neal, 727 P.2d 297, 304 (Alaska 1986).
2. *See, e.g.*, Estate of Arbow v. Alliance Bank, 790 P.2d 1343, 1346 (Alaska 1990); Still v. Cunningham, 94 P.3d 1104, fn. 10 (Alaska 2004).

§ 1 Nature of the Guaranty Arrangement

1.1 Guaranty Relationships

Alaska law recognizes the formation of a guaranty obligation as a contract under traditional contract principles.

> "A guaranty is a contract between two or more persons, founded upon consideration, by which one person promises to answer to another for the debt, default or miscarriage of a third person, and, in a legal sense, has relation to some other contract or obligation with reference to which it is a collateral undertaking." Like any other contract, its formation is governed by principles of mutual assent, adequate consideration, definiteness and a meeting of the minds.[3]

Although there are not a large number of cases construing guaranties under Alaska law, the Alaska cases that have dealt with the subject apply a considerably expansive scope in construing the existence of guaranties. For example, under traditional contract law, a guaranty obligation cannot exist unless there is an underlying primary obligation. Alaska courts have construed the condition for an underlying primary obligation broadly, finding that even an obligation created by the application of promissory estoppel is sufficient to create the required foundation for a guaranty.[4] In some circumstances, even an agreement to provide additional security for an obligation owed by others can create a guaranty obligation binding the guarantor for the entire obligation.[5]

1.2 Other Suretyship Relationships

Alaska law recognizes certain suretyship obligations and obligations of accommodation parties to financial transactions, creating obligations very similar to guaranties.[6] Alaska cases sometimes use the terms guarantor and surety interchangeably.[7] Alaska has also adopted the Uniform Commercial Code provision defining "surety" to include "a guarantor or other secondary obligor."[8]

An accommodation party, on the other hand, is defined as:

> one who has signed the instrument as maker, drawer, acceptor, or indorser, without receiving value therefor, and for the purpose of lending his name to some other person.[9]

---

3. *Crook*, 727 P.2d at 304 (*quoting* Timi v. Prescott State Bank, 553 P.2d 315, 324 (Kan. 1976), *and referencing*, 38 C.J.S. Guaranty § 8, p. 1143).
4. *Crook*, 727 P.2d at 304.
5. Johnson v. Schaub, 867 P.2d 812, 819 (Alaska 1994).
6. *See* State v. McKinnon, 667 P.2d 1239 (Alaska 1983).
7. *Still*, 94 P.3d at 1112.
8. ALASKA STAT. § 45.01.211(b)(42).
9. Hartley v. Hollman, 376 P.2d 1005, 1006 n. 3 (Alaska 1962) (internal citation omitted).

The relationship of an accommodation party to the other parties is therefore distinct from that of a guarantor or surety, but the nature of the obligation is very similar.

§ 2 State Law Requirements for an Entity to Enter into a Guaranty

2.1 Corporations

The Alaska Corporations Code gives a for-profit corporation properly formed under Alaska law the power to enter into guaranties subject to any limitations in its articles of incorporation, and subject to certain other limitations.

> Subject to the limitations in its articles of incorporation, the provisions of this chapter and other applicable law, a corporation has all the powers of a natural person in carrying out its business activities, including, without limitation, the power to... (8) make contracts and guarantees, incur liabilities,....[10]

Alaska Statute 10.06.485(d) provides that if a corporation acts as a guarantor on a loan to a director, officer, or employee, the guaranty is treated as a loan for purposes of restrictions on loans to directors, officers, and employees.

The Alaska Nonprofit Corporation Act does not expressly grant the power to enter into guaranties, but does give a nonprofit corporation the power to "make contracts" and "incur liabilities," as well as a general provision granting it the power to "have and exercise all powers necessary or convenient to effect the purposes for which the corporation is organized."[11]

2.2 Partnerships

Alaska adopted the Revised Uniform Partnership Act in 2000, effective January 1, 2001.[12] The Uniform Partnership Act does not expressly authorize a partnership to enter into a guaranty obligation, but neither does it forbid such activity. Section 32.06.965 of the Act provides that "[u]nless displaced by particular provisions of this chapter, the principles of law and equity supplement this chapter." It is entirely reasonable to conclude that a partnership has the power to guarantee obligations consistent with its business needs, provided that the partnership agreement does not forbid entering into such obligations.

10. Alaska Stat. § 10.06.010.
11. Alaska Stat. § 10.20.011 (8), (17).
12. Alaska Stat. § 32.06.201 et seq.

2.3 Limited Liability Companies

The Alaska Revised Limited Liability Company Act, Alaska Stat. 10.50.010 et seq., does not expressly grant an Alaska limited liability company (LLC) power to enter into a guaranty obligation or forbid it from doing so. However, there is no reason to think that the LLC would be treated any differently than a corporation or partnership under Alaska law, with respect to entering into a guaranty.

2.4 Individuals

Individual persons of course have the power to bind themselves to guaranty obligations, and they also may have the authority, as an officer or agent of a corporation or other legal entity, to bind the corporation or other legal entity to guaranty obligations. Under Alaska law, however, a designation of corporate capacity or position after a signature on a guaranty does not automatically relieve the signer of individual liability. Alaska courts have recognized that there is a split of authority on this issue in other jurisdictions, but have adopted the line of reasoning that holds:

> where a writing in the nature of the contract is signed by a person, and contains apt words to bind him personally, the fact that to such signature is added such words as "trustee," "agent," "treasurer," "president," and the like does not change the character of the person so signing, but is considered as merely descriptive of him… If it appears from the contract that he pledged his own credit or bound himself personally, the addition of such words as "president" and the like will be considered as mere *descriptio personae.*[13]

Individuals signing obligations in an official or corporate capacity must therefore exercise extreme care to expressly disclaim any personal liability for the underlying obligation.

Alaska is not a community property state, but permits its citizens to enter into a community property agreement.[14] Assets of individual guarantors to which a creditor has recourse will be governed in part by the existence or nonexistence of a community property agreement if only one spouse signs the guaranty. If there is no community property agreement, or if a guaranty was in existence prior to the effective date of the community property agreement,[15] the creditor has access to all property of the guarantor, subject to normal exemptions under federal and state law. If there is a community property agreement that became effective prior to the existence of the guaranty, the creditor's recourse may be limited by the terms of the community property agreement. The Alaska Community Property Act gives the spouses wide latitude in fash-

13. Beck v. Haines Terminal & Hwy. Co., 843 P.2d 1229, 1231 (Alaska 1992).
14. Alaska Stat. 34.77.010 et seq.
15. Alaska Stat. 34.77.070(f).

ioning their community property agreement, permitting them to determine the rights and obligations of each with regard to their property.[16]

2.5 Trusts

Alaska's trust administration statute is found at Alaska Statute 13.36.005 through 13.36.390. The general and specific powers of the trustee are found at Alaska Statute 13.36.107 and .109.

Generally, when a trustee of a trust makes a contract, the trustee may be held personally liable on the contract "if the contract does not exclude the trustee's personal liability."[17] A presumption against personal liability is created with "the addition of the word 'trustee' or the words 'as trustee' after the signature of a trustee to a contract."[18] This presumption may only be rebutted by "clear and convincing evidence" of contrary intent.[19]

§ 3 Signatory's Authority to Execute the Guaranty

Authority to execute a guaranty for a business entity such as a corporation, limited liability company, partnership, and other business entities, is governed by the same principles that would govern the authority to sign any other contract or agreement.

§ 4 Consideration; Sufficiency of Past Consideration

As in other jurisdictions, consideration is a requirement under Alaska law to create an enforceable contract. However, there is no Alaska case law specifically construing consideration or the sufficiency of past consideration in the context of guaranties. Traditional contract principles would therefore apply, and Alaska courts would likely be guided by the Restatement in applying requirements for consideration.

§ 5 Notice of Acceptance

As noted earlier, Alaska courts construe guaranties under traditional contract principles. Alaska law acknowledges that acceptance of an offer of a guaranty

16. Alaska Stat. 334.77.090(d).
17. Alaska Stat. 13.36.175(e).
18. *Id.*
19. *Id.*

is a necessary element in creating an enforceable obligation.[20] Acceptance must also be in exact compliance with the terms of the offer.[21]

§ 6 Interpretation of Guaranties

Alaska courts will not interpret an agreement to constitute a guaranty without a clear indication of intent on the part of the party purportedly guaranteeing an obligation.[22] In the context of landlord-tenant law, the Alaska Supreme Court found that even where a landlord knowingly acquiesced in and ultimately benefited from the work performed, a landlord is not a guarantor of contracts entered into between his tenants and third parties unless the landlord expressly undertakes that liability.[23]

Conditional guaranties will not be enforced absent the occurrence of the event or action on which the guaranty was conditioned.[24] Intent of the parties plays a major role in interpreting such agreements.

There is one Alaska case in which the Alaska Supreme Court departed from its usually strict construction of requirements for creation of a guaranty obligation. In *Estate of Arbow,* the court found that, even in the absence of express guaranties provided to the lender, enforceable guaranties were created when shareholders of the borrower entered into a shareholder agreement among themselves imposing an obligation on each of the shareholders to bear a proportionate burden of repaying any debt on which the corporation defaulted.[25]

§ 7 Defenses of the Guarantor

Because Alaska courts construe guaranties under general contract principles,[26] the general defenses available in a breach of contract action are available in an action related to a guaranty. It is also noteworthy that the Alaska Supreme Court frequently looks to and relies on the principles set forth in the Restatement (Third) of Suretyship and Guaranty (1996).

A guarantor may always raise the defense that the guaranty was induced by fraud or material misrepresentations made by the obligee.[27] When the guarantor succeeds with such a defense, the guaranty is voidable. Unilateral mistake related to a basic assumption of the guaranty is also a basis to void a guaranty when the mistake is known to the other party or due to the fault

20. *Crook,* 727 P.2d at 305.
21. *Id.* (citing Thrift Shop, Inc. v. Alaska Mut. Sav. Bank, 398 P.2d 657 (Alaska 1965)).
22. Donnybrook Bldg. Supply v. Interior City, 798 P.2d 1263, 1267 (Alaska 1990).
23. Frontier Rock & Sand v. Heritage Ventures, 607 P.2d 364, 368 (Alaska 1980).
24. *Estate of Arbow,* 790 P.2d at 1345.
25. *Id.* at 1345-1346.
26. *Crook,* 727 P.2d at 304.
27. *Still,* 94 P.3d at 1110 (citing Restatement (Third) Suretyship and Guaranty § 12(1) (1996)).

of the other party.[28] Notably, these defenses "are not precluded by the parole evidence rule."[29]

7.1 Defenses of the Primary Obligor

7.1.1 *General*

Generally, a guarantor may assert the defenses of the obligor.[30] This is because it would be unfair to permit:

> A creditor who has behaved improperly toward the principal from recovering against the [guarantor] when it could not recover against the principal. However, the guarantor's status entitles him only to prevent such an unfair result by the defensive use of the principal's claim. Once the claim against the guarantor has been nullified by full set-off he no longer bears any risks or suffers any injury from the creditor's wrongdoing. Thus, affirmative recovery by the guarantor would exceed the scope of the [guarantor] relationship and would actually usurp claims belonging only to the principal.[31]

7.2 Suretyship Defenses

7.2.1 *Modification of the Underlying Obligation, including Release*

Guarantors will not be relieved of their obligations if they agree in advance to extensions or modifications of the underlying obligation.[32]

7.3 Other Defenses

7.3.1 *Failure to Fulfill a Condition Precedent*

Under Alaska law, "conditional guarantees are unenforceable absent the occurrence of the condition."[33]

7.3.2 *Modification, Revocation, or Termination of the Guaranty*

Revocation or termination of a continuing guaranty does not relieve a guarantor of its obligations as a secondary obligor with respect to the obligations

28. *Id.* (citing Restatement (Second) of Contracts § 153 (1981) and Restatement (Third) Suretyship and Guaranty § 12(3)).
29. *Id.*
30. Arctic Contractors, Inc. v. State, 573 P.2d 1385, 1387 n.5 (Alaska 1978).
31. *Id.* (citing L. Simpson, Handbook of the Law of Suretyship § 70, at 319-326 (1950)).
32. *Still*, 94 P.3d at 1111-1112.
33. *Estate of Arbow*, 790 P.2d at 1345.

incurred prior to termination or revocation.[34] A guarantor's consent to future extensions expressed in a guaranty is binding.[35]

7.3.3 *Failure to Pursue the Primary Obligor*

A guarantor will not succeed in raising the defense of failure to pursue the primary obligor in the event that the obligee proceeds directly against the guarantor. "[I]t is well settled that a creditor upon default of the principal debtor may proceed immediately against an absolute guarantor without making a formal demand on the debtor for payment and without first having proceeded against the debtor."[36]

7.3.4 *Statute of Limitations*

In Alaska, "courts construe guarantees under traditional contract principles."[37] Alaska Statute 09.10.053 imposes a three-year statute of limitations on contract actions.[38] Also noteworthy is that Alaska's 10-year statute of repose does not apply to actions resulting from the breach of an express guaranty.[39]

7.3.5 *Statute of Frauds*

Alaska Statute 09.25.010 provides that an agreement, promise, or undertaking to answer for the debt of another is unenforceable "unless it or some note or memorandum of it is in writing."[40] Thus, the general rule in Alaska is that a guaranty must be in writing.[41] However, the statute of frauds does not apply when the guarantor's main purpose or objective is to benefit his own pecuniary or business position.[42] The primary inquiry to determine whether the statute of frauds applies is "whether the promise is only an assumption of another's liability or a new and primary obligation of the promisor.[43]

7.3.6 *Defenses particular to Guarantors that are Natural Persons and their Spouses*

Under Alaska law, when an individual signs a guaranty that contains words to bind him personally, it is irrelevant that the signature also contains a cor-

34. *Still*, 94 P.3d at 1112-13 (citing Restatement (Third) Suretyship and Guaranty § 16).
35. *Id.* (citing Restatement (Third) Suretyship and Guaranty § 48(1)).
36. Kupka v. Morey, 541 P.2d 740, 753 (Alaska 1975) (citing Texas Water Sup. Corp. v. Reconstruction Fin., 204 F.2d 190 (5th Cir. 1953) and Terry v. Tubman, 92 U.S. 156 (1875)).
37. *Crook*, 727 P.2d at 304.
38. Alaska Stat. § 09.10.053.
39. *See* Alaska Stat. § 09.10.055(b)(1)(D) (Ten-year statute of repose does not apply when "personal injury, *death*, or property damage result[ed] from . . . breach of an express warranty or guarantee.")
40. Alaska Stat. § 09.25.010(a)(3).
41. *See* Merdes v. Underwood, 742 P.2d 245, 251 (Alaska 1987).
42. *Id.* (citing Restatement (Second) Contracts § 116 (1981)).
43. *Id.* at n. 11 (quoting Farr & Stone Ins. Brokers, Inc. v. Lopez, 61 Cal.App.3d 618, 132 Cal.Rptr. 641, 642 (1976)).

porate designation.[44] Liability will still be imposed on the guarantor in his individual capacity.[45]

The rationale for this approach is that: "a written collateral undertaking given to secure a corporate debt will be rendered meaningless if the primary debtor is found to be the sole party liable thereunder."[46] This means that individuals signing obligations in their official or corporate capacity must exercise extreme care to expressly disclaim any personal liability for the underlying obligation.

7.4 Right of Set-off

Alaska follows the general rule of set-off that applies to sureties for guarantors. A guarantor, therefore, may set off the obligee's claim against the obligor in three instances: (1) when the guarantor has taken an assignment of the claim or the obligor has consented to the guarantor's use of the claim; (2) where both the obligor and guarantor are joined as defendants; or (3) where the obligor is insolvent.[47] A guarantor who does assert the counterclaims of the obligor is limited in its recovery to the amount of set-off.[48]

§ 8 Waiver of Defenses by the Guarantor

8.1 Defenses that cannot be Waived

There is no Alaska law on this topic.

8.2 Catch-all Waivers

There is no Alaska law on this topic.

8.3 Specific Waivers

A guarantor that consents to "any modification or renewal" of the agreement guaranteed waives its right to be exonerated as a result of the modification or renewal.[49] Moreover:

> Where the contract between the guarantee and principal debtor limits the obligation of the former to extend credit to the latter up to a specified amount, such limitation does not modify or condition the contract by which the guarantor agrees to guarantee the payment of all credits extended to the debtor, and the liability of the guarantor is

44. *Beck*, 843 P.2d at 1231.
45. *Id.* (quoting Ricker v. B-W Acceptance Corp., 349 F.2d 892, 894 (10th Cir. 1965) and *Williston on Contracts* § 299 at 393-94) (holding the designation "General Manager" was merely descriptive).
46. *Id.* (quoting Dann v. Team Bank, 788 S.W.2d 182, 184 (Tex. App. 1990)).
47. *Arctic Contractors, Inc.*, 573 P.2d 1385, 1386-87 (Alaska 1978).
48. *Id.* at 1387.
49. *Beck*, 843 P.2d at 1231.

not limited to such amount or discharged by the extension of more credit than the amount so specified.[50]

§ 9 Third-party Pledgors—Defenses and Waiver Thereof

There is no Alaska law on this topic.

§ 10 Jointly and Severally Liable Guarantors—Contribution and Reduction of Obligations upon Payment by a Co-obligor

10.1 Contribution

While Alaska courts recognize the general rule that coguarantors should share the cost of performance of their obligations based on their respective contributions, courts also have held that a single guarantor is liable to the obligee for the entire amount of the obligation.[51] Should a guarantor pay the obligee more than its proportional share of the guaranty, the guarantor then "has a right to contribution from co-guarantors."[52] In other words, where a coguarantor contributes more than its proportional share, it is entitled to seek proportional reimbursement from other coguarantors.[53]

10.2 Reduction of Obligations upon Payment of Co-obligor

There is no Alaska law on this topic.

10.3 Liability of Parent Guarantors owning less than 100 percent of Primary Obligor

There is no Alaska law on this topic.

50. *Id.* at 1231-32 (citing Mo. Farmers Ass'n, Inc. v. Coleman, 676 S.W.2d 855, 858 n.1 (Mo. Ct. App. 1984) (quoting 38 C.J.S. *Guaranty* § 56 at 1211)).
51. *Still*, 94 P.3d at 1112.
52. *Id.* (citing the Restatement (Third) Suretyship and Guaranty §§ 55, 57 (1996)).
53. *Estate of Arbow*, 790 P.2d at 1345-46, (quoting the Restatement of Security § 149 (1941) which provides: "A surety who in the performance of his own obligation discharges more than his proportionate share of the principal's duty is entitled to contribution from a courtesy.")

§ 11 Reliance

The Alaska Supreme Court has never expressed reliance as a requirement for the validity of a personal guaranty.[54] Indeed, the Court has expressly declined to adopt a reliance requirement, holding that "[r]equiring a creditor to prove reliance, in addition to the existence of a valid contract, is unduly burdensome and serves no valid purpose."[55]

§ 12 Subrogation

There is no Alaska law on this topic.

§ 13 Indemnification

Alaska has expressly affirmed the right to enforce indemnity obligations generally, both under contract and common law.[56] Although no Alaska case has directly addressed an obligor's duty to indemnify a guarantor, the indemnification obligation has been clearly implied in Alaska cases.[57]

§ 14 Enforcement of Guaranties

14.1 Limitations on Recovery

A guarantor is limited in its recovery to the amount of set-off.[58]

14.2 Enforcement of Guaranties of Payment versus Guaranties of Performance

There is no Alaska law on this topic.

54. *Beck*, 843 P.2d at 1231.
55. *Id.*
56. Fairbanks N. Star Borough v. Roen Design, 727 P.2d 758, 761 (Alaska 1986).
57. *See, e.g.* Arctic Contractors, Inc. v. State, 573 P.2d 1385 (Alaska 1978).
58. *Arctic Contractors, Inc.*, 573 P.2d at 1387 n.5.

14.3 Exercising Rights under a Guaranty Where the Underlying Obligation is also Secured by a Mortgage

Alaska Statute 34.20.100 provides:

> When a sale is made by a trustee under a deed of trust, as authorized by AS 34.20.070 – 34.20.130, no other or further action or proceeding may be taken nor judgment entered against the maker or the surety or guarantor of the maker, on the obligation secured by the deed of trust for a deficiency.[59]

The antideficiency statute applies only to nonjudicial foreclosure sales and not to judicial foreclosures.[60]

14.4 Litigating Guaranty Claims: Procedural Considerations

There is no Alaska law on this topic.

§ 15 Revival and Reinstatement of Guaranties

There is no Alaska law on this topic.

§ 16 Conflicts of Law—Choice of Law

Alaska courts generally honor an express contractual choice of law provision agreed to by the parties to a contract and apply the substantive law of the chosen jurisdiction. Under Alaska's choice of law rules:

> A choice of law clause in a contract will generally be given effect unless (i) the chosen state has no substantial relationship with the transaction or there is no other reasonable basis for the parties' choice, or (ii) the application of the law of the chosen state would be contrary to a fundamental public policy of a state that has a materially greater interest in the issue and would otherwise provide the governing law.[61]

59. Alaska Stat. § 34.20.100.
60. *See id.; see also* Hull v. Alaska Fed. Sav. & Loan Ass'n, 658 P.2d 122 (Alaska 1983).
61. Peterson v. Ek, 93 P.3d 458, 465 n.11 (Alaska 2004) (citing Restatement (Second) of Conflict of Laws § 187 (1971)). Although there is no Alaska case law construing choice of law principles specifically in the context of a guaranty, the Alaska Supreme Court has applied the Restatement principles in the context of common law indemnity. Palmer G. Lewis Co. v. ARCO Chemical Co., 904 P.2d 1221, 1227 (Alaska 1995).

Alaska has generally followed the most significant relationship test of the *Restatement (Second) Conflict of Laws* (1971) when resolving contractual choice-of-law problems in which the parties did *not* make an express choice of law.[62]

62. *See, e.g.*, Lakeside Mall, Ltd. v. Hill, 826 P.2d 1137, 1140 n. 8 (Alaska 1992).

Arizona State Law of Guaranties

Jeffrey H. Verbin
Brynn Hallman
Greenberg Traurig, LLP
2375 E. Camelback Rd. Suite 700
Phoenix, AZ 85016
Phone: (602) 445-8202
e-mail: verbinj@gtlaw.com
www.gtlaw.com

GT GreenbergTraurig

Contents

Arizona State Law of Guaranties

ARIZONA LAW HIGHLIGHTS

1. Arizona contracts are generally interpreted using basic principles of contract law. A guarantor's liability is strictly construed based upon the express terms of the contract. See § 6 below.
2. A guarantor under a guaranty of payment is jointly and severally liable for the primary obligor's breach. On the other hand, a guarantor under a guaranty of collection is only jointly liable. See § 6.3 below.
3. Arizona is a community property state, and as a result, a guaranty must be signed by both spouses in order to bind the marital community. A guaranty signed by only one spouse is enforceable against the separate property of the signing spouse, but not against the separate property of the nonsigning spouse or the marital community. See § 7.1 below.
4. Modification of the primary obligation without an uncompensated guarantor's consent discharges the guarantor. See § 7.2 below.
5. A guarantor is entitled to the protections set forth in Arizona's antideficiency statutes. See § 14.3 below.
6. If a lender fails to bring an action for a "deficiency judgment" against a guarantor within 90 days after the date of a trustee's sale, the trustee's deed will be deemed to be in full satisfaction of the guarantor's obligation and the lender will be prohibited from bringing an action against the guarantor. See § 14.4 below.

Introductory Note: In order to standardize our discussion of the law of guaranties, we use the following vocabulary to refer to the various parties to a guaranty and their respective obligations.

"Guarantor" means a person who, by contract, agrees to satisfy an underlying obligation of another to an obligee upon the primary obligor's default on that underlying obligation.

"Guaranty" means the contract by which the guarantor agrees to satisfy the underlying obligation of a primary obligor to an obligee in the event the primary obligor defaults on the underlying obligation.

"Obligee" means the person to whom the underlying obligation is owed.

"Primary Obligor" means the person who incurs the underlying obligation to the obligee.

"Underlying Obligation" means the obligation or obligations incurred by the primary obligor and owed to the obligee.

Introduction and sources of law

Arizona statutes and case law offer relatively light treatment of the law of guaranties. For issues of first impression, Arizona usually applies the law of the Restatement.[1] Until recently, the primary treatise related to the law of guaranties on which Arizona courts relied was the Restatement of Security (1941).[2] However, for issues of first impression, Arizona courts now look to the Restatement (Third) of Suretyship and Guaranty (1996).[3] This survey is limited to those issues on which the Arizona Revised Statutes ("A.R.S.") or Arizona case law offer guidance. For those issues on which Arizona statue or case law are silent, reliance upon the Restatement (Third) of Suretyship and Guaranty (1996) is appropriate to the extent it is generally persuasive.

§ 1 Nature of the Guaranty Obligation

A contract of guaranty is a collateral promise by a guarantor to answer for the payment of some debt or the performance of some duty in the case of a default by a primary obligor who, pursuant to an underlying obligation to an obligee, is liable for such payment or performance.[4]

1.1 Guaranty

A guaranty is a contract of secondary liability under which Arizona statute gives the guarantor the right to demand that an action is first brought against the primary obligor for its default under the underlying obligation.[5] If there is no obligation by the primary obligor under the underlying obligation, there is no obligation by the guarantor under the secondary contract of guaranty.[6]

A guaranty contract is separately enforceable and independent of the obligation of the primary obligor.[7]

In determining whether a contract of guaranty exists, Arizona courts look to substance over form. Arizona courts consider the character of the obligation, rather than the labels used by the parties.[8] The use of "technical words" such as "surety" or "guaranty" in the contract is not controlling in characterizing the contract.[9]

1. Indian Village Shopping Center Investment Co. v Kroger Co., 854 P.2d 155, 156 (Ariz. Ct. App. 1993).
2. *Id.*
3. *See, e.g.*, Data Sales Co., Inc. v. Diamond Z Mfg., 74 P.3d 268 (Ariz. Ct. App. 2003).
4. Dykes v. Clem Lumber Co., 118 P.2d 454, 455 (Ariz. 1941).
5. A.R.S. § 12-1641. The remedies in § 12-1641 are expressly granted to "a person bound by a surety," but Arizona statute extends these remedies to "guarantors . . . whether created by express contract or operation of law." A.R.S. § 12-1646.
6. Howard v. Associated Grocers, 601 P.2d 593, 595 (Ariz. 1979).
7. Provident Nat'l Assur. Co. v. Sbrocca, 885 P.2d 152, 154 (Ariz. Ct. App. 1994).
8. McClellan Mortgage Co. v. Storey, 704 P.2d 826, 829 (Ariz. Ct. App. 1985).
9. Dayton Rubber Mfg. Co. of DE v. Sabra, 31 F.2d 9, 10 (9th Cir. 1929).

1.2 Suretyship

While Arizona distinguishes between contracts of guaranty and contracts of surety,[10] the distinction is muddled such that courts use the terms interchangeably.[11] Arizona case law has developed in reliance on the fact that the term "guaranty" was used in the Restatement of Security (1941) as a synonym for "suretyship."[12] Moreover, the remedies provided to sureties by Arizona statute extend to guarantors.[13]

§ 2 State Law requirements to Enter a Guaranty

Generally, corporations, partnerships, limited liability companies, and state-chartered banks may issue a guaranty, unless otherwise prohibited by law or the entity's controlling document.

2.1 Corporations

Arizona statute provides that a corporation may "make contracts and guarantees" unless its articles of incorporation provide otherwise.[14]

2.2 Partnerships

The Revised Uniform Partnership Act, A.R.S. §§ 29-1001 *et seq.*, does not expressly authorize a partnership to issue a guaranty. However, Arizona case law provides examples of instances in which a partnership issues a guaranty.[15]

2.3 Limited Liability Companies

Arizona statute provides that a domestic limited liability company may "[m]ake contracts, including contracts of guaranty, suretyship and indemnification" unless its articles of organization deny, limit, or otherwise lawfully reduce its authority to do so.[16]

---

10. McClellan Mortgage, 704 P.2d at 828-829. A surety "is a party to an original obligation which binds him as well as his principal," while a guarantor is not party to the original obligation, but instead bound by a contract that is "collateral" to the primary obligation (citing Security Ins. Co. v. Johns-Manville Sales Corp., 442 P.2d 555, 558 (Ariz. Ct. App. 1968)). Id. at 828-29.
11. *See* Western Coach Corp. v. Roscoe, 650 P.2d 449, 453 (Ariz. 1982).
12. Indian Village, 854 P.2d at 156 (citing the Restatement of Security (1941), § 82, cmt. g).
13. A.R.S. § 12-1646.
14. *Id.* § 10-302(7).
15. *See* First Interstate Bank v. Tatum & Bell, 821 P.2d 1384 (Ariz. Ct. App. 1991); *see also* Chase Bank of Arizona v. Acosta, 880 P.2d 1109 (Ariz. Ct. App. 1994), review granted, review denied as improvidently granted, 880 P.2d 1152 (Ariz. 1995).
16. A.R.S. §§ 26-610(A)(6); 26-610(B).

2.4 State-chartered Banks

Under A.R.S. § 6-184, an Arizona corporation with a banking permit may, unless prohibited by law: (i) "exercise the powers derived from its existence as an Arizona corporation"[17]; (ii) "exercise any power and engage in any activity which it could exercise or engage in if it were a national banking association with a banking office in [Arizona]"[18]; and (iii) "directly ... engage in any lawful activity which is reasonably related or incidental to banking."[19]

§ 3 Signatory's Authority to Execute a Guaranty

The ability of a signatory to execute a binding guaranty on behalf of the entity for which he or she signs depends on a combination of statutory authority, controlling documents of the entity, and common law principles of agency.

3.1 Corporations

As a general rule, a "corporation acts through its officers, agents, or employees and is liable for the actions of such persons acting within the scope of their agency."[20] A corporation will not be bound on a contract, even if entered on the corporation's behalf, if the executing party did not have authority to act on the corporation's behalf.[21]

The actual authority of a corporate officer to take a particular action may be set forth in the bylaws or prescribed by the board of directors, to the extent consistent with the bylaws.[22] The actual authority may also stem from the position that an officer holds within the corporation.[23] While the title of an officer is not determinative of his or her authority, "when he is clothed with titles implying general powers (i.e., president, chief executive officer, and chairman of the board), the business public and courts may fairly presume he is what the corporation holds him out to be."[24]

A "corporation may be bound where its agent acts without or in excess of his actual authority" if the agent acts within the scope of apparent authority with which the corporation has clothed him.[25] That is, when a corporation "holds out" an officer as having certain authority, and as a result a third party reasonably relies on the existence of such authority, the corporation in effect gives the officer apparent authority to act and to bind the corporation, regardless of a lack of actual authority.[26]

17. *Id.* § 6-184(A)(1).
18. *Id.* § 6-184(A)(2).
19. *Id.* § 6-184(A)(3).
20. SEC v. Jenkins, 718 F.Supp.2d 1070 (D. Ariz. 2010).
21. GM Development Corp. v. Community American Mortgage Corp., 795 P.2d 827, 833 (Ariz. Ct. App. 1990).
22. A.R.S. § 10-841.
23. *See* Harper v. Independence Development Co., 108 P. 701 (Ariz. 1910).
24. *GM Development*, 795 P.2d at 833.
25. O'Malley Inv. & Realty Co. v. Trimble, 422 P.2d 740, 748-49 (Ariz. Ct. App. 1967).
26. Anchor Equities, Ltd. v. Joya, 773 P.2d 1022, 1025-26 (Ariz. Ct. App. 1989).

3.2 Partnerships

Partners in a partnership function as agents of the partnership.[27] A partnership is bound by the actions of its partners so long as the underlying act was actually or apparently carried out in the ordinary course of the partnership business or in business of the kind carried out by the partnership.[28] However, the partnership will not be bound by a partner's actions if the partner lacked authority to act on behalf of the partnership in the particular matter and the other party had actual or constructive knowledge of that lack of authority.[29]

If the action was outside the ordinary course of the partnership business, the action will bind the partnership only if such action was authorized by the other partners.[30] Further, a partner may not bind a partnership by his or her guaranty in partnership's name of the debts of a third party, unless his or her action is approved in advance or ratified by other partners, or agreement is reasonably made in the due course of partnership business.[31]

A partner's authority may be expanded or limited either by a partnership agreement or by a statement of partnership authority filed with the secretary of state.[32] A grant of authority extended in a statement of partnership with respect to transactions other than real property transfers is conclusive in favor of a person who gives value without knowledge of the partner's lack of authority.[33] However, a similar limitation on partner's authority contained in the statement of partnership authority alone will not serve as constructive knowledge on behalf of the contracting party.[34]

3.3 Limited Liability Companies

The authority to bind a limited liability company (LLC) to a guaranty executed on its behalf depends on whether the LLC is organized as member-managed or manager-managed, as set forth in its articles of organization.

If the LLC is member-managed, then each member acts as the entity's agent "for the purpose of carrying on its business in the usual way," unless the articles of organization provide otherwise.[35] Therefore, any member's act "for apparently carrying on in the usual way the business" of the entity will bind the LLC, unless the other side knows that the member lacks authority.[36]

If the LLC is manager-managed, then a member is not an agent of the LLC solely by virtue of the membership in the LLC, unless the operating agreement otherwise delegates authority to such member.[37] On the other hand, each manager in a manager-managed LLC is an agent of the LLC "for the purpose

27. A.R.S. § 29-1021(1); *see also* Indigo Co. v. City of Tucson, 804 P.2d 129 (Ariz. Ct. App. 1991) (finding that partners are agents of partnership for purpose of its business).
28. A.R.S. § 29-1021(1).
29. *Id.* § 29-1021(1).
30. *Id.* § 29-1021(2).
31. Wolff v. First Nat'l. Bank, 53 P.2d 1077, 1080 (Ariz. 1936).
32. A.R.S. § 29-1023(A)(1).
33. *Id.* § 29-1023(D)(1).
34. *Id.* § 29-1023(F).
35. A.R.S. § 29-654(A)(1).
36. *Id.* 29-654(A)(2).
37. *Id.* 29-654(B)(1).

of carrying on its business in the usual way."[38] Similar to a member-managed LLC, a manager's act will bind the LLC when such act appears to be carried on in the usual way of the LLC's business.[39]

In cases where the act of the member or manager does not appear to be executed to carry out the business of the LLC in the usual way, such act will not bind the LLC unless it is actually authorized by the LLC in that particular matter.[40]

3.4 Banks

Arizona statute does not address the issue of who may validly execute a guaranty on behalf of an Arizona-chartered bank.

3.5 Individuals

From time to time, an issue may arise where it is unclear whether an individual has issued a guaranty in his or her personal capacity or on behalf of an entity which he or she represents. To resolve this question, a court may look to the instrument granting the guaranty, together with the general business practices underlying the transaction in question.[41] On the other hand, when in a signature block the corporate name is followed by the name of a corporate officer who affixes his or her corporate title to his or her name, the signature binds the corporation, not the individual.[42]

See Section 7.1 below for a discussion of community property issues relevant to guaranties by individuals.

§ 4 Consideration; Sufficiency of Past Consideration

Like any contract, a contract of guaranty is subject to the principles of contract law that require adequate consideration.

Consideration is required to create a valid contract of guaranty.[43] The consideration for the contract of guaranty may be sufficient even if the benefit flows from the obligee to the primary obligor, rather than directly to the guarantor.[44]

Forbearance may be sufficient consideration. Forbearance by an obligee to seize property of the primary obligor or enforce a lien against the primary obligor has been held to be sufficient consideration to support an oral

38. *Id.* 29-654(B)(2).
39. *Id.* 29-654(B)(3).
40. *Id.* 29-654(C).
41. Hofman Co. v. Meisner, 497 P.2d 83 (Ariz. Ct. App. 1972) (superseded by statute on an unrelated point of law) (finding that a corporation's president granted a personal guaranty where the language of the instrument unambiguously provided for a grant of a personal guaranty, in part due to the general business practice of extending credit to small corporate businesses only upon the personal guaranty of its officers).
42. Kitchell Corp. v. Hermansen, 446 P.2d 934, 937-38 (Ariz. Ct. App. 1968).
43. *See, e.g.*, Phil Bramsen Distributor, Inc. v. Mastroni, 726 P.2d 610, 615 (Ariz. Ct. App. 1986).
44. Crown Life Ins. Co. v. Howard, 822 P.2d 483, 485-86 (Ariz. Ct. App. 1991).

promise of guaranty when the forbearance enables the guarantor to obtain an advantage or benefit.[45] In that case, the main purpose of the guaranty was to obtain a substantial benefit for the guarantor, and "not to answer for the debt of another."[46]

§ 5 Notice of Acceptance

Whether the obligee must give notice to the guarantor of its acceptance of the guaranty depends on whether the guaranty is a secondary obligation or, despite its label as a "guaranty," whether the contract is actually a primary obligation.

Generally, because a guaranty is a secondary obligation, the guaranty is an offer by the guarantor to the obligee; the obligee must accept the offer and give notice of its acceptance to the guarantor before the contract of guaranty is valid.[47] However, if the contract is absolute in its terms such that the guarantor must pay unconditionally upon the default of the primary obligor, the obligation of the "guarantor" is a primary obligation and notice of acceptance is not necessary.[48]

§ 6 Interpretation of Guaranties

Contracts of guaranty are interpreted by Arizona courts much the same as other contracts. The express language of the guaranty may determine the rights of the parties against each other.

6.1 General Principles

The general rule is that a contract of guaranty "will be strictly construed to limit the liability of the guarantor."[49]

Notwithstanding a strict construction of a guaranty to limit the liability of a guarantor, clear and unambiguous language in a contract of guaranty "must be given effect as written."[50] For example, where the express language of a guaranty provided for a continuing guaranty by a corporation's stockholders, the mistaken understanding of one guarantor that his or her liability was limited was not controlling given that the express language of the guaranty unambiguously guaranteed future debts of the primary obligor.[51]

---

45. Yarbro v. Neil B. McGinnis Equip. Co., 420 P.2d 163, 166-67 (Ariz. 1966).
46. *Id.* at 167.
47. *Dayton Rubber*, 31 F.2d at 10.
48. *Id.*
49. Consolidated Roofing & Supply Co., Inc. v. Grimm, 682 P.2d 457, 460 (Ariz. Ct. App. 1984).
50. *Id.* at 460.
51. *Id.* at 460-61.

6.2 Scope of Liability

The guaranty may provide for greater liability than that of the primary obligor.[52] While a primary obligor may not be held liable for the deficiency under a nonrecourse promissory note, a guarantor who guarantees repayment of the nonrecourse note implicitly consents to liability greater than that of the primary obligor under the note.[53]

6.3 Guaranty of Payment versus Guaranty of Collection

A guaranty of payment is a guarantor's agreement to be jointly and severally liable for the primary obligor's breach.[54] A guarantor under a guaranty of payment agrees to perform without requiring the obligee to first exhaust its remedies against the primary obligor.[55] Where the terms of one guaranty provided that it was "absolute, unconditional and irrevocable" and given to secure "due and punctual performance and payment," an Arizona court found a guaranty of payment rather than a guaranty of collection.[56]

On the other hand, a guarantor under a guaranty of collection is only jointly liable.[57] The guarantor under a guaranty of collection is liable only if the obligee attempted to collect from the primary obligor, but was unsuccessful because the primary obligor is "insolvent or cannot otherwise pay the underlying obligation."[58]

As discussed below in Section 7.1.1, A.R.S. § 12-1641 gives the guarantor the right to demand that an action is first brought against the primary obligor,[59] unless otherwise waived.

6.4 Continuing Guaranties (Future Obligations)

A guarantor may contract to be liable for the future obligations of the primary obligor.[60] Such a "continuing guaranty" may contemplate future obligations of the primary obligor without limit, but will be strictly construed to limit the liability of the guarantor.[61] In effect, a continuing guaranty is an offer of guarantee "accepted serially by each extension of credit."[62]

Arizona also has examined the issue of future obligations in the context of a guaranty of a lease that included a lease renewal term. In order for a guaranty of a lease "to continue into a successive term, the 'express terms' of the lease must show that it is of a continuing nature."[63] In this instance, the guaranty terminated at the expiration of the original lease term because the

52. *Provident Nat'l. Assur.*, 885 P.2d at 154.
53. *Id.* at 155-56.
54. Tenet HealthSystem TGH, Inc. v. Silver, 52 P.3d 786, 789-90 (Ariz. Ct. App. 2002).
55. *Id.* (citing the Restatement (Third) of Suretyship & Guaranty § 15(b), cmt. d (1996)).
56. *Id.* at 789-90.
57. *Id.* (citing the Restatement (Third) of Suretyship & Guaranty § 15(b), cmt. d (1996)).
58. *Id.*
59. A.R.S. § 12-1641.
60. *Consolidated Roofing*, 682 P.2d at 460.
61. *Id.* at 460-61.
62. Georgia-Pacific Corp., Williams Furniture Div. v. Levitz, 716 P.2d 1057, 1059 (Ariz. Ct. App. 1986).
63. Westcor Co. Ltd. Partnership v. Pickering, 794 P.2d 154, 157 (Ariz. Ct. App. 1990).

guaranty did not expressly state that it applied generally to renewal periods or specifically to the renewal period contemplated by the lease, nor did the guaranty expressly state a period of effectiveness.[64]

§ 7 Defenses of the Guarantor

Contracts of guaranty are subject to the defenses typically available to challenge the enforceability of a contract, such as the defenses to formation noted above. The enforceability of a guaranty and the extent of the guarantor's liability are also subject to additional statutory and common law defenses specific to guaranties.

7.1 Statutory Remedies

7.1.1 Statutory Remedies specific to Guarantors

When an obligee wishes to bring an action on the guaranty, a guarantor may request that an action is first brought against the primary obligor.[65] This request by the guarantor must be given in writing to the obligee.[66] If the obligee fails to bring the requested action against the primary obligor within 60 days after receiving notice of the guarantor's request, the guarantor's liability is discharged.[67]

7.1.2 Statute of Limitations

An action on a guaranty is not necessarily governed by the same statute of limitations that governs an action on the underlying obligation.[68]

The statute of limitations for an action for debt evidenced by or founded on a contract in writing executed in Arizona is six years after the cause accrues.[69] This six-year statute of limitation applies to a contract of guaranty executed in Arizona, even if an action on the underlying obligation is barred by a shorter statute of limitation. For example, the underlying obligation may be governed by Arizona's four-year statute of limitation applicable to a contract for the sale of goods or a three-year statute of limitation applicable to claims on an open account.[70] A guarantor is not released or discharged merely because the obligee is barred from bringing an action on the underlying obligation.[71]

64. *Id.* at 156.
65. A.R.S. § 12-1641.
66. *Id.*
67. *Id.*
68. Flori Corp. v Fitzgerald, 810 P.2d 599, 600-01 (Ariz. Ct. App. 1990).
69. A.R.S. § 12-548(A)(1).
70. *Id.* §§ 12-544(4); 12-543(2).
71. *Flori,* 810 P.2d at 600; Intern'l Harvester Co. v. Fuoss, 758 P.2d 649, 650 (Ariz. Ct. App. 1988).

7.1.3 Marital Joinder required to bind Community Property

Arizona is a community property state. In order to bind the marital community, Arizona statute requires the signature of both spouses to "any transaction of guaranty, indemnity or suretyship."[72] A guaranty signed by only one spouse is not enforceable against the separate property of the nonsigning spouse or the marital community, even if the guaranty is for a business that benefits the marital community.[73] Although the marital community is not liable under a guaranty that lacks the signature of both spouses, the separate property of the signing spouse is liable on the guaranty.[74]

Careful attention to the joinder of the spouse is essential. First, both spouses must join in the guaranty and sign the same document.[75] Confirmation of the joinder in a separate document will not meet the statutory standard.[76] Second, the creditor cannot *require* the spouse to be a coguarantor on the guaranty with the guarantor because of their marital status (which would bind both the spouse's marital community property as well as the spouse's sole and separate property). If the creditor requires the spouse to be a coguarantor resulting in the spouse's sole and separate property becoming liable, the creditor probably has violated the federal Equal Credit Opportunity Act,[77] which is applicable to many commercial lending transactions. The joinder should consist of a statement on the guaranty that the spouse is joining in the guaranty solely to commit the marital community of the guarantor and the guarantor's spouse as required by applicable law and that the sole and separate property of the guarantor's spouse shall not be liable on the guaranty.

Nonetheless, the spouse can be required to be a coguarantor if the spouse otherwise holds a position such as a senior officer, director, shareholder, or member of the borrower that the creditor requires to guaranty the obligation.

Some uncertainty exists in the context of a general partner's ability to bind community property. One court held that a general partner that issued a guaranty without the consent of his spouse nonetheless bound the community because he executed the guaranty as a general partner.[78] This holding is difficult to reconcile with the otherwise consistent interpretation in other Arizona case law that A.R.S. § 25-214(C) prevents a spouse from unilaterally binding the obligations of the marital community.

Generally, however, the joinder requirement in A.R.S. § 25-214(C) shields the marital community from liability under a guaranty signed by only one spouse. In one case in which only a husband had signed a guaranty, the obligee obtained a judgment against the husband for his obligation under the guaranty and, in settlement, took a promissory note signed by only the husband.[79] The court looked to the origin of the obligation and rejected the creditor's argument

72. A.R.S. § 25-214(C)(2).
73. Vance-Koepnick v. Koepnick, 3 P.3d 1082, 1083 (Ariz. Ct. App. 1999). See also Rackmaster Systems, Inc. v. Maderia, 193 P.3d 314, 317 (Ariz. Ct. App. 2008).
74. *Consolidated Roofing*, 682 P.2d at 463.
75. *Id.*
76. *Id.*
77. 15 USCA § 1691 et seq.
78. *Chase Bank of Arizona*, 880 P.2d at 1117.
79. Zork Hardware Co. v. Gottlieb, 821 P.2d 272, 273 (Ariz. Ct. App. 1991).

that promissory notes are not subject to the joinder requirement and, therefore, the marital community should be liable for the promissory note.[80]

7.1.4 Deficiency against a Guarantor following Foreclosure

Arizona is a deed of trust state, which permits nonjudicial foreclosure of a deed of trust by a trustee pursuant to its power of sale.[81] Following a trustee's sale of the primary obligor's property, an obligee has 90 days to commence an action for a deficiency judgment against a guarantor.[82] If an obligee fails to maintain an action within this time, "the proceeds of the sale, regardless of amount, shall be deemed to be in full satisfaction of the obligation and no right to recover a deficiency in any action shall exist.[83] Where an obligee receives property through a trustee's sale in accordance with Arizona statutes, a guarantor is entitled to a "fair market value credit" of the value of the real property that secures the underlying obligation.[84]

If provided for by the terms of the contract of guaranty, an obligee may commence an action against a guarantor even if no trustee's sale is held.[85] In the event a trustee's sale is held, the obligee then becomes subject to the 90-day statute of limitation within which it must bring a deficiency claim against a guarantor.[86]

Guarantors of mortgages or deeds of trust foreclosed judicially also are entitled to the "fair market value credit."[87]

7.2 Common Law Remedies

7.2.1 Release of Primary Obligor

Generally, the guarantor is released from liability where the primary obligor has become discharged by a rule of law.[88] Where there is no underlying obligation on the part of the primary obligor, there is nothing to guarantee.[89]

The release of a primary obligor from the underlying obligation without the consent of the guarantor releases the guarantor from its obligation under the guaranty.[90] A guarantor, however, may waive discharge by release of the primary obligor by specific agreement in the guaranty to remain liable upon such a release.[91]

80. *Id.*
81. A.R.S. § 33-807.
82. *Id.* § 33-814(A) thru (C).
83. *Id.* § 33-814(D).
84. *Id.* § 33-814(A).
85. *Id.* § 33-814(C); see Crown Life, 822 P.2d at 485.
86. A.R.S. § 33-814(C).
87. *Id.* § 12-1566.
88. *Howard,* 601 P.2d at 595.
89. *Dykes,* 118 P.2d at 455.
90. *Howard,* 601 P.2d at 595.
91. *Id.*

7.2.2 *Modification without Consent*

A modification of the underlying obligation without the consent of an *uncompensated* guarantor discharges the guarantor if the modification could, under any circumstances, increase the risk to the guarantor, regardless of whether the risk *actually* increases in the transaction at issue.[92] A guarantor is considered uncompensated if the guarantor is not in the business of guaranteeing obligations, regardless of whether the guarantor is an equity owner in the primary obligor.[93]

Reformation of a mutual mistake in the underlying obligation is not an alteration of the underlying obligation and, accordingly, does not discharge the guarantor of its liability, regardless of consent to the reformation.[94]

7.2.3 *Misrepresentation*

The standard defenses of contract law, such as mistake and misrepresentation, are available to a guarantor. Arizona courts have recognized the general business practice of "extending credit to small corporate businesses, only upon the personal guarantee of its officers."[95] In light of this general business practice, an Arizona court found no misrepresentation or mistake and enforced a personal guaranty of a corporate officer for an obligation of the corporation where, without carefully reading the contract, the officer signed a credit application that included a personal guaranty.[96]

If the obligee has knowledge of facts that materially increase the risk that a guarantor assumes and has reason to believe that the guarantor is unaware of those facts and has a reasonable opportunity to inform the guarantor, the guarantor has a defense to its liability under the contract of guaranty.[97]

7.2.4 *Insolvency of the Primary Obligor known to the Obligee*

Where an obligee suspected that a primary obligor was nearly insolvent, but nevertheless continued to extend credit to the primary obligor, a guarantor who had sold his ownership stake in the primary obligor six months before the extension of credit, but failed to provide written notice of the revocation of his guaranty, was not liable under the continuing guaranty.[98]

7.2.5 *Conditions Precedent*

A written guaranty may be subject to conditions precedent. A guarantor may argue that the condition precedent did not occur and, therefore, the guarantor is not liable under the guaranty.[99]

---

92. *Indian Village,* 854 P.2d at 156-57 (citing the RESTATEMENT OF SECURITY (1941), §§ 128; 82, cmt. i).
93. *Id.*
94. *Phil Bramsen Distributor,* 726 P.2d at 615.
95. *Hofmann,* 497 P.2d at 86-87.
96. *Id.*
97. *Georgia-Pacific Corp.,* 716 P.2d at 1059.
98. *Id.* at 1059.
99. *See* Anderson v. Preferred Stock Food Markets, Inc., 854 P.2d 1194 (Ariz. Ct. App. 1993).

In considering an oral condition precedent, one Arizona court held that a written guaranty that is fully executed and unconditional on its face may be subject to oral conditions precedent that do not vary or contradict the terms of the written agreement.[100]

7.2.6 *Application of Payment*

A guarantor does not have the right to control how payments made by a primary obligor on its indebtedness should be applied by the obligee.[101]

7.2.7 *Right to Set-Off against Obligee*

A guarantor may set off a claim it has against the obligee against its liability under the contract of guaranty, but any such claim is an affirmative defense for which the guarantor has the burden of proof. [102]

§ 8 Waiver of Defenses by Guarantor

8.1 Right to Waive Statutory Defenses and Common Law "Suretyship Defenses"

Guarantors may waive the statutory defenses enacted for their benefit.[103] Guarantors also may waive the common law rights, collectively known as "suretyship defenses," that prevent the obligee from impairing or destroying a guarantor's rights or ability to enforce them.[104] It is "well settled" that these rights can be waived by contract.[105]

In a 2003 case of first impression regarding the waivers permitted under the Restatement (Third) of Suretyship and Guaranty (1996), the Court of Appeals of Arizona noted that "parties to a commercial transaction may generally structure their agreements as they see fit."[106] The list of defenses that may be waived in advance by express terms in the contract of guaranty pursuant to § 48 of the Restatement (Third) of Suretyship and Guaranty (1996) is not exhaustive.[107] Thus, the guarantor's agreement to waive its defenses regarding modification of the underlying obligation was not against public policy or unconscionable.[108]

In another instance, a guarantor was permitted to expressly waive the requirement that the obligee first proceed against the primary obligor before

100. *Anderson*, 854 P.2d at 1200.
101. Valley Nat'l. Bank of Phoenix v. Shumway, 163 P.2d 676, 679 (Ariz. 1945).
102. *Consolidated Roofing*, 682 P.2d at 462.
103. Austad v. U.S., 386 F.2d 147 (9th Cir. 1967); *McClellan*, 704 P.2d at 829.
104. *Data Sales Co.*, 74 P.3d at 272.
105. *Id.* (citations omitted).
106. *Id.* at 273.
107. *Id.*
108. *Id.* at 274.

proceeding against the guarantor.[109] In yet another case, the guarantor was permitted to waive the requirement that the obligee first exhaust any security held from the primary obligor before proceeding against the guarantor.[110]

8.2 Limitation on Waiver

A guarantor may not waive all defenses. A party is not free to waive basic principles of contract law, such as unconscionability, good faith and fair dealing, and the statute of frauds.[111]

§ 9 Third-party Pledgors—Defenses and Waivers Thereof

Arizona law does not address the issue of third-party pledgors. However, a third-party pledgor who pledges collateral to support the primary obligor's obligations to a third party arguably stands in the relation of a guarantor to the primary obligor to the extent of the pledge. It seems logical, therefore, that the pledgor can avail itself of the defenses of a guarantor and may also waive such defenses.

§ 10 Joint Liability and Joint and Several Liability of Guarantors—Contribution and Reduction of Obligations upon Payment by a Co-obligor

Coguarantors are liable to each other for their ratable proportion of the amount for which they are liable under the contract of guaranty.[112] If "one [guarantor] has paid more than his share of the sum, he is entitled to demand contribution from the other or others and may maintain suit to enforce the right."[113]

§ 11 Reliance

Arizona law does not specifically hold that reliance upon the presence of a guaranty constitutes sufficient consideration when an obligee extends credit to a primary obligor. However, general contract interpretation principles in Arizona do provide that where traditional consideration is lacking, reliance,

109. First Nat'l Bank of Arizona v. Bennett Venture, Ltd., 637 P.2d 1065, 1068-90 (Ariz. Ct. App. 1981).
110. *Id.*
111. *Data Sales Co.*, 74 P.3d at 274 (citing Restatement (Third) of Suretyship & Guaranty, § 6 cmt. b, § 48 cmt. a (1996)).
112. A.R.S. § 12-1644.
113. Western Coach Corp. v. Roscoe, 650 P.2d 449, 454-55 (Ariz. 1982).

under the doctrine of promissory estoppel, may require enforcement if injustice cannot otherwise be avoided.

Arizona courts follow the RESTATEMENT (SECOND) OF CONTRACTS in defining causes of action based on reliance.[114] The RESTATEMENT § 90 (1981) provides that, "[a] promise which the promisor should reasonably expect to induce action or forbearance on the part of the promisee or a third person and which does induce such action or forbearance is binding if injustice can be avoided only by enforcement of the promise." However, affirmative promissory estoppel claims are not particularly favored in Arizona.[115]

§ 12 Indemnification

Two distinct actions support a guarantor's indemnification from a primary obligor: (i) an implied promise of reimbursement; or (ii) the guarantor's rights as subrogee to the obligee.[116]

A guarantor that has been compelled to satisfy the obligation of the primary obligor has a right of action against the primary obligor for reimbursement.[117] "Compelled to pay" includes one who is under a legal obligation to do so, such as a guarantor that is obligated to make payments pursuant to its liability under a contract of guaranty.[118]

§ 13 Subrogation

When a guarantor is compelled to pay a judgment in full or in part, the judgment is not discharged, remains in force against the primary obligor, and is considered assigned to the guarantor together with all rights of the obligee to the extent the guarantor made payment.[119]

A guarantor may not take possession of the collateral securing the underlying obligation until it has made payment in full and has become subrogated to the rights of the obligee.[120] To permit the guarantor to take possession of collateral without paying off the full underlying obligation would impair the obligee's security interest in the collateral.[121]

An obligee must be mindful of the guarantor's rights against the primary obligor. The right of subrogation substitutes the guarantor in place of the obligee such that the guarantor can exercise any of the obligee's rights against

114. *See* Schade v. Diethrich, 158 Ariz. 1, 11 760 P.2d 1050, 1060 (1988).
115. *Id.*
116. Mobile Discount Corp. v. LuBean, 656 P.2d 639, 641 (Ariz. Ct. App. 1982).
117. A.R.S. § 12-1643(A)-(B); Dykes, 18 P.2d at 455.
118. *Mobile,* 656 P.2d at 641.
119. A.R.S. § 12-1643(A).
120. Western Coach Corp. v. Rexrode, 634 P.2d 20, 23-24 (Ariz. Ct. App. 1981).
121. Poling v. Morgan, 829 F.2d 882, 885-86 (9th Cir. 1987)

the primary obligor.[122] An obligee risks destroying or impairing a guarantor's subrogation rights by modifying the underlying obligation or releasing the primary obligor or collateral without the consent of the guarantor. Any waiver by a guarantor of its subrogation rights "should only be by the most unequivocal language in the guarantee agreement."[123] A guarantor is released from liability to the extent its subrogation rights have been impaired by the obligee, but the guarantor remains otherwise liable under the contract of guaranty.[124]

§ 14 Limitations on Enforcement of Guaranties

14.1 Failure to Join a Spouse

As discussed in Section 7.1.3, a guaranty signed by only one spouse does not effectively encumber the couple's community property interests in the real property.[125]

14.2 Modification without Consent

Modification of the original obligation without the consent of an uncompensated guarantor discharges the guarantor, as discussed in Section 7.2.2 above.

14.3 Antideficiency Statute Relating to Certain Types of Residential Property

Under Arizona's "Anti-Deficiency Statute,"[126] a lender is prevented from taking any steps to collect a deficiency or pursuing a deficiency judgment following the foreclosure of certain types of residential property. The antideficiency language neither specifies, nor exempts, guarantors, and logically, seems to prohibit a deficiency action against anyone.

14.4 90-day Statute of Limitation

If a lender fails to bring an action for a "deficiency judgment" against a guarantor within 90 days after the date of a trustee's sale, the trustee's deed will be deemed to be in full satisfaction of the guarantor's obligation and the lender will be prohibited from bringing an action against the guarantor.[127] See Section 7.1.4 above for a further discussion of the 90-day rule.

---

122. *See* D.W. Jaquays & Co. v. First Security Bank, 419 P.2d 85, 88-89 (Ariz. 1966).
123. *Id.* at 89.
124. *Id.*
125. In re Janis, 151 B.R. 936 (Bankr. D. Ariz. 1992).
126. A.R.S. § 33-729(A) (relating to mortgages); A.R.S. § 33-814 (relating to deeds of trust).
127. *Id.* § 33-814(G).

14.5 Fair Market Value Defense

If the proceeds of the sale of the underlying property are insufficient to satisfy the obligation, the lender may pursue the guarantor for the deficiency. However, Arizona law provides that if the obligation is greater than the bid price at a sheriff's sale[128] or trustee's sale,[129] the debtor must be credited with the fair market value of the property as of the date of the foreclosure sale. The fair market value credit is available not only to the primary obligor, but also to the guarantor and any other person directly, indirectly, or contingently liable on the debt.[130] A lender may require that the fair market value defense be waived in the guaranty; however, Arizona courts have not ruled on whether such waiver is effective. Under the RESTATEMENT (THIRD) OF PROPERTY (MORTGAGES), which Arizona courts generally follow, mortgage documents purporting to waive such a statutory fair market value protection are ineffective.[131]

14.6 Duty to Mitigate

A guarantor might allege that the lender failed to mitigate its damages, for example, by allowing a short sale. However, in Arizona, a deficiency defendant is not entitled to a damages defense based on what the lender allegedly may have realized by mitigating damages.[132]

§ 15 Revival and Reinstatement of Guaranties

Arizona does not appear to have any law specific to the reinstatement of guaranties in a situation where a guaranty has been discharged, for example, by a payment in full, but the payment is later avoided in bankruptcy and recovered by the creditor. However, there is no reason to believe that Arizona would not follow the general rule adopted by the Ninth Circuit that the guaranty obligation would be revived in such a case.[133]

§ 16 Guaranties of less than the Entire Primary Obligation

Guarantors often provide guaranties that are less expansive than the primary obligation. Common examples of such guaranties are (a) guaranties limited

128. *Id.* § 33-725(B).
129. *Id.* §§ 33-814(A); 12-1566(C).
130. *Id.* §§ 12-1566(A) (relating to a judicial foreclosure); 33-814(A), (C) and 12-1566(A) (relating to post-trustee's sale deficiency actions).
131. RESTATEMENT (THIRD) OF PROPERTY (MORTGAGES) § 8.4(c), cmt. b and Reporter's Note to cmt. b.
132. Life Investors Ins. Co. of Am. v. Horizon Resources Bethany, Ltd., 182 Ariz. 429, 898 P.2d 478 (Ariz. Ct. App. 1995).
133. *See, e.g.*, In re SNTL Corp., 571 F.3d 826, 835-36 (9th Cir. 2009) and cases cited therein.

to a specified dollar amount or percentage of the primary obligation ("Partial Guaranties"); (b) guaranties of losses to the creditor arising from certain actions of the primary obligor that are prohibited by the loan documents or by law, such as misapplication of rents of encumbered property, waste, etc. ("Carveout Guaranties"); (c) springing guaranties under which a loan becomes fully recourse to the guarantor if certain events occur such as a bankruptcy filing by the primary obligor or a prohibited transfer of the financed property ("Springing Guaranties"); and (d) completion guaranties by which the guarantor guaranties a construction lender that the contemplated project will be completed by a specified date, in accordance with approved plans and specifications, with all costs paid, and without liens ("Completion Guaranties"). Arizona has little law specifically addressing these types of limited guaranties.

§ 17 Conflict of Laws—Choice of Law

Arizona courts will recognize a choice of law clause contained within a guaranty, and apply another state's law if the guaranty so provides.[134]

134. Desarrollo Inmobiliario y Negocios Industriales De Alta Tecnologia De Hermosillo, S.A. De C.V. v. Kader Holdings Co. Ltd., 229 Ariz. 367, 276 P.3d 1, 6 (App. 2012).

Arkansas State Law of Guaranties

Jeb Joyce
Timothy W. Grooms
Quattlebaum, Grooms, Tull & Burrow PLLC[1]
111 Center Street, Suite 1900
Little Rock, AR 72201
Phone (501) 379-1700
Fax: (501) 379-1701
www.QGTB.com

QGTB
QUATTLEBAUM, GROOMS, TULL & BURROW PLLC

Contents

---

1. Provided by Jeb H. Joyce and Timothy W. Grooms. Thank you to Patrick Murphy, Ryan O'Quinn, Geoffrey Treece and Meghan Vernetti of the firm, who contributed valuable time and effort to this survey.

Arkansas State Law of Guaranties

ARKANSAS LAW HIGHLIGHTS

MARITAL PROPERTY

Arkansas presumes any transfer to a married couple is a transfer to them as tenants by the entirety. *Kinghorn v. Hughes,* 761 S. W. 2d 930, 932 (1988). A tenancy by the entirety protects one spouse against the unilateral impairment of his or her property rights by the other spouse. *Id.* Thus, a guaranty, and any subsequent judgment stemming therefrom, cannot be enforced against property held as tenants by the entirety if such guaranty was only executed by one spouse. An obligee of a guaranty should, where possible under other applicable law, require the signature of both spouses. Arkansas also recognizes dower and curtesy interests in the property of a spouse. Ark. Code Ann 28-11-101, et seq. These rights must be waived or conveyed by the spouse to be extinguished.

Introduction: Arkansas courts have cited to the *Restatement (Third) of Suretyship and Guaranty* in cases involving guaranties.[2]

Introductory Note: In order to standardize our discussion of the law of guaranties, we use the following vocabulary to refer to the various parties to a guaranty and their obligations.

"Guarantor" means a person who, by contract, agrees to satisfy an underlying obligation of another to an obligee upon the primary obligor's default on that underlying obligation. We do not draw a distinction between guarantors and sureties.[3]

"Guaranty" means the contract by which the guarantor agrees to satisfy the underlying obligation of a primary obligor to an obligee in the event the primary obligor defaults on the underlying obligation.

"Obligee" means the person to whom the underlying obligation is owed.

"Primary Obligor" means the person who incurs the underlying obligation to the obligee.

"Underlying Obligation" means the obligation or obligations incurred by the primary obligor and owed to the obligee.

---

2. B.S.G. Foods, Inc. v. Multifoods Distribution Group, Inc., 54 S.W.3d 553, 559 (2001).
3. *See, e.g.,* Ark. Code Ann. § 4-1-201 (39); *see also* Restatement (Third) of Suretyship And Guaranty § 1 cmt. c (1996).

§ 1 Nature of the Guaranty Arrangement

Under Arkansas law, a guaranty involves an independent contract with the obligee.[4]

1.1 Guaranty Relationships

A guaranty is a contract of "secondary liability" under which the guarantor has an obligation to pay only upon default by the primary obligor.[5] The relationship between the primary obligor and the guarantor arises as a matter of law, and it is based in the notion that, while the guarantor is liable to the obligee, it is the principal obligor who ultimately should bear the underlying obligation.[6] However, a guaranty need not be strictly an obligation to "pay" in the event of a default by the primary obligor. Arkansas courts have recognized "performance" or "completion" guaranties through which the guarantor has an obligation to effect performance other than payment in the event of a default by the primary obligor.[7]

Under Arkansas law, no "technical words" are needed to create a guaranty obligation; rather, a court will look to substance over form and whether there exists intent to bind a party in the capacity of a guarantor.[8]

1.2 Other Suretyship Relationships

While not the focus of this survey, we note that a suretyship relationship may also arise because of the pledge of collateral.[9]

§ 2 State Law Requirements for an Entity to Enter a Guaranty

Partnerships, limited liability companies (LLCs), corporations, and banks can all grant guaranties in furtherance of their business activities. Such grants are generally permitted by the appropriate Arkansas statute. Additionally, corporations, partnerships, and LLCs can sometimes grant guaranties even when not in furtherance of their business activities.

4. First Commercial Bank, N.A. v. Walker, 969 S.W.2d 146, 152 (Ark. 1998).
5. First American Nat'l Bank v. Coffey-Clinton, Inc., 633 S.W.2d 704, 705 (Ark. 1982).
6. *Id.*
7. *See* Exchange Bank & Trust Co. v. Texarkana School Dist. No. 7, Miller County, U.S. Fidelity & Guaranty Co., Intervenor, 301 S.W.2d 453 (1957).
8. *See* Stewart, Gwynne & Co., v. Sharp County Bank, 76 S.W. 1064 (Ark. 1903); Ouachita Val. Bank v. De Motte, 291 S.W. 984 (Ark. 1927); and Pharis Tire & Rubber Co. v. May, 94 S.W.2d 1040 (Ark. 1936).
9. *See* Restatement (Third) of Suretyship and Guaranty § 1 (noting that a person is a surety when "pursuant to contract . . . an obligee has recourse against [that] person . . . *or against that person's property* with respect to an obligation . . . of another person . . . to the obligee" (emphasis added)).

2.1 Corporations

Under the Business Corporation Act of 1987, an Arkansas corporation may, within the scope of its general corporate powers, give a guaranty, provided that its articles of incorporation or bylaws do not prevent it from doing so.[10] If so authorized, the guaranty may even be secured by corporate property or income.[11]

An Arkansas corporation may execute a guaranty to benefit a director only if the guaranty is approved by a shareholder vote conducted pursuant to statutory requirements (requiring a majority of the votes represented by the outstanding voting shares of all classes, voting as a single voting group, and excluding any shares held by or under the control of the benefitted director).[12] Certain corporations existing before 1987 may grant such guaranties without a vote.[13]

2.2 Partnerships

Arkansas' Uniform Partnership Act[14] neither expressly empowers a partnership to issue a guaranty nor expressly regulates or prohibits such activity. Additionally, Arkansas' Uniform Limited Partnership Act[15] neither expressly empowers a limited partnership to issue a guaranty nor expressly regulates or prohibits such activity.

2.3 Limited Liability Companies

Arkansas' Small Business Entity Tax Pass Through Act, which governs LLCs, neither expressly empowers a LLC to issue a guaranty nor expressly regulates or prohibits such activity.[16]

2.4 Banks and Trust Companies

An Arkansas state bank is not authorized to be an accommodation guarantor.[17] An accommodation guaranty by a state bank is void and *ultra vires*.[18] A state bank can execute a valid guaranty agreement if such action is necessary or advisable to protect an economic interest of the bank. [19]

Note also that guaranties offered by state banks may also be significantly affected by federal law. First, federal law prohibits a state-chartered bank from engaging in activities in which a national bank may not engage under federal

---

10. Ark. Code Ann. §§ 4-26-204 (b)(3); 4-27-202; 4-27-206; 4-27-302 (7).
11. Ark. Code Ann. § 4-27-302 (7).
12. Ark. Code Ann. § 4-27-832 (a).
13. Ark. Code Ann. §§ 4-26-204 (b)(3).
14. Ark. Code Ann. §§ 4-46-101 et seq.
15. Ark. Code Ann. §§ 4-47-101 et seq.
16. Ark. Code Ann. §§ 4-32-101 et seq.
17. Ark. ST. Bank Dept. § 47-101.5.
18. *Id.*
19. *Id.*, citing Bank of Morrilton v. Skipper, Tucker & Co., 263 S.W. 54 (1924), and Wasson v. American Can Co., 72 S.W.2d 241 (1934).

law. The situations under which a national bank may become a guarantor are governed by federal law. See National Bank as Guarantor or Surety on Indemnity Bond, 12 C.F.R. § 7.1017 (2010).

2.5 Individuals

Confusion can sometimes arise in the case of corporate officers or directors signing guaranties in closely held corporations or other organizations. In such instances, a case-by-case inquiry determines whether an individual intended to be personally bound or, instead, only issued a guaranty on behalf of a partnership or corporation and thus only in an official employment capacity.[20] When an individual signs his title as well as his name, this is not dispositive proof of an intention not to issue a personal guaranty.[21]

Special issues arise with marital property as a potential resource of creditors when enforcing a guaranty executed by only one spouse. Arkansas recognizes a form of ownership called a "tenancy by the entirety."[22] Each spouse in a tenancy by the entirety is protected against the impairment of his or her property rights through the sole act of the other spouse.[23] Thus, a guaranty executed by only one spouse does not extend to the marital property of that spouse held in a tenancy by the entirety. Arkansas also has statutory dower and curtesy rights for spouses.[24] An individual has a dower or curtesy interest in any real property owned by his or her spouse in fee simple during their marriage.[25] The nonconveying spouse generally must waive his or her dower or curtesy right to extinguish it. The dower or curtesy interest is, however, inchoate and, as such, is only effective upon the death of the spouse owning the land in fee simple.[26]

While a business corporation must have "authority" to execute a guaranty, an individual guarantor must have the "capacity" to enter into the guaranty. Incapacity can be a defense against the enforcement of a guaranty issued by an individual.[27]

§ 3 Signatory's Authority to Execute a Guaranty

Generally, an obligee of a guaranty has a duty to make inquiry into the authority of the executor of a guaranty when the executor is an agent of the guarantor.

20. *See* Cleveland Chemical Co. of Arkansas, Inc. v. Keller, 716 S.W.2d 204 (Ark. 1986).
21. *Id.; see also* United Fasteners, Inc. v. First State Bank of Crossett, 691 S.W.2d 126 (Ark. 1985).
22. Kinghorn v. Hughes, 761 S.W.2d 930 (1988).
23. *Id.* at 932.
24. Ark. Code Ann. § 28-11-101, et seq.
25. Ark. Code Ann. § 28-11-301(a).
26. *Id.*
27. *See* Lillian H. Ashton Trust v. Caraway, 370 S.W.3d 278 (2009); First Nat'l Bank v. Nakdimen, 163 S.W.785 (1914) (a guaranty is a type of contract).

3.1 Corporations

For an obligee to rely on a guaranty of a corporation, the guaranty must be executed by an officer with actual or apparent authority to act in such capacity.[28] An obligee cannot enforce a guaranty if he or she had notice that the officer who signed for the corporation lacked authority to do so.[29] Where an obligee relies on the doctrine of apparent authority, that obligee bears a duty to "make inquiry and use due diligence to learn the nature and extent of such authority."[30]

Generally, an officer of a corporation has authority to act on behalf of the corporation only "(1) where the board of directors or the by-laws have conferred upon the officer the authority; (2) where the corporation, through its directors, has permitted the officer to habitually do such an act in the course of its business – in other words, has clothed them with the apparent authority to so act; (3) where the directors have ratified the unauthorized acts of its officer; or (4) where the corporation has received the proceeds or any benefit from the transaction."[31] The directors of the corporation are the only agents with general authority to act on behalf of the corporation.[32] Thus an officer, having no general grant of authority, must be given special authority to bind the corporation to a guaranty.[33]

3.2 Partnerships

Arkansas Code Annotated § 4-46-301 grants a partner the authority to bind the partnership when such partner undertakes an act "for apparently carrying on in the ordinary course the partnership business or business of the kind carried on by the partnership," unless such partner has no such authority and the person with whom the partner was dealing has notice of such a lack of authority.[34] If a partner's action is not "apparently for carrying on of the business of the partnership," the partner must be authorized by the other partners to bind the partnership.[35] A partner's authority may also be expanded or restricted, sometimes conclusively, through a "statement of partnership authority" filed with the Arkansas Secretary of State.[36] Those persons dealing with partners most likely have a duty of inquiry as to whether a signatory has the appropri-

28. "[T]he corporation is liable (1) where the board of directors or the by-laws have conferred upon the president and secretary the authority to issue negotiable paper; (2) where the corporation, through its directors, has permitted these officers to habitually do such an act in the course of its business, – in other words, has clothed them with the apparent authority to so act; (3) where the directors have ratified the unauthorized acts of its officers; (4) where the corporation has received the proceeds or any benefit from the transaction." City Electric St. Ry. Co. v. First Nat'l Exch. Bank, 62 Ark. 33, 91-92 (1896).
29. Southern Equipment & Tractor Co. v. K & K Mines, Inc, 613 S.W.2d 596 (1981).
30. U.S. Bedding Co. v. Andre, 150 S.W. 413, 414 (1912).
31. *Id.*
32. Anderson-Tully Co. v. Gillett Lumber Co., 244 S.W.26 (1922).
33. *Id.*
34. Ark. Code Ann. § 4-46-301.
35. Ark. Code Ann. § 4-46-301(2).
36. Ark. Code Ann. §§ 4-46-301; 4-46-303; 4-46-105.

ate authority to bind the partnership.[37] Under Arkansas law, there exists no indication that the authority of a partner is examined differently in the context of guaranties.

Under Arkansas' codification of the Uniform Limited Partnership Act, a general partner has the same powers as a partner in a general partnership.[38] A limited partner has no right or power to act for or bind the limited partnership.[39]

3.3 Limited Liability Companies

Under the Small Business Entity Tax Pass Through Act, if the articles of organization filed with the Arkansas Secretary of State provide for a member-managed LLC, every member is an agent of that company and can sign instruments "for apparently carrying on in the usual way the business or affairs of the limited liability company of which he or she is a member" unless that person has no actual authority to act in such way and his counterparty has knowledge of such lack of authority[40] If the articles provide for a manager-managed LLC, no member has authority, solely by reason of being a member, to bind the LLC to a guaranty.[41] Thus, each manager of a manager-managed LLC, and member of a member-managed LLC, can bind the LLC if such guaranty is for apparently carrying on in the usual way the business or affairs of the LLC unless such manager or member has no actual authority and the counterparty knows of this lack of authority.

§ 4 Consideration; Sufficiency of Past Consideration

Standard contract principles apply to the analysis of consideration for a contract of guaranty. For valid consideration to exist, there must be a benefit to the principal debtor or guarantor, or some detriment to the obligee. Past consideration is insufficient consideration for a guaranty.

Sufficient consideration is required to create a valid contract of guaranty.[42] The inquiry into sufficient consideration is based on standard contract law principles.[43] The consideration is sufficient to create an enforceable guaranty so long as there is a benefit to the principal obligor or guarantor, or a detriment to the obligee.[44]

37. Ark. Code Ann. § 4-46-301(1) ("Each partner is an agent of the partnership for the purposes of its business"); U.S. Bedding Co. v. Andre, 150 S.W. 413, 414 (1912) ("A person dealing with an agent is at once put upon notice of the limitations of his authority, and must ascertain what that authority is").
38. Ark. Code Ann. § 4-47-402(a).
39. Ark. Code Ann. § 4-47-302.
40. Ark. Code Ann. § 4-32-301(a).
41. Ark. Code Ann. § 4-32-301(b)(1).
42. Marsh v. Nat'l Bank of Commerce of El Dorado, 822 S.W.2d 404 (1992) (citing First Nat'l Bank v. Nakdimen, 163 S.W. 785 (1914)).
43. *Id.* at 408.
44. Shamburger v. Union Bank of Benton, 650 S.W.2d 596 (1983).

Past consideration under Arkansas law will not serve as sufficient consideration for a guaranty.[45] Thus, a guaranty of preexisting debt must be based on new and additional consideration to be valid.[46]

§ 5 Notice of Acceptance

Notice of acceptance may not be required, if credit is extended to the primary obligor based upon the guaranty or if the guaranty is absolute.

Under guaranty law, generally, the obligee must notify the guarantor of its acceptance of the guaranty.[47] However, under Arkansas law, if notice of acceptance is not "required by the terms of the guarantee," the extension of credit by the obligee will "constitute[] acceptance . . . of the guarantor's offer of surety."[48] Notice of acceptance also will not be required where the guaranty is "absolute."[49] Commonly, the guarantor waives the notification of acceptance requirement in the guaranty agreement.

§ 6 Interpretation of Guaranties

Courts in Arkansas are guided by the principle of strictly construing the obligations of the guarantor. In addition, certain terms have become words of art in the context of guaranties. In other regards, courts will interpret a guaranty in the same manner by which they would interpret the language of any other contract.

6.1 General Principles

Under Arkansas law, a guarantor is entitled to strict construction of his undertaking and cannot be held liable beyond strict terms of his contract.[50] In ascertaining the meaning of the language of a contract of guaranty, the same rules of construction control as apply in case of other contracts; in accordance with such rules, it is important, if possible, to determine and give effect to intention of parties as ascertained by fair and reasonable interpretation of terms used and language employed, read in light of attendant circumstances and purposes for which guaranty was made.[51]

45. First Nat'l Bank v. Nakdimen, 163 S.W. 785 (1914).
46. *Id.*
47. Peter A. Alces, The Law of Suretyship and Guaranty § 3:27 (Thompson West 1996).
48. Davis v. Wells, 104 U.S. 159, 163 (1881).
49. Murphy v. Continental Supply Co., 65 S.W.2d 11 (1933).
50. Lee v. Vaughn, 534 S.W.2d 221, 223 (Ark. 1976); Gulf Refining Co. v. Williams Roofing Co., 186 S.W.2d 790, 794 (Ark. 1945).
51. McCaleb v. Nat'l Bank of Commerce of Pine Bluff, 752 S.W.2d 54, 56 (Ark. App. Ct. 1988); Ouachita Valley Bank v. De Motte, 291 S.W. 984 (Ark. 1927).

6.2 Guaranty of Payment versus Guaranty of Collection

Under Arkansas law, a guaranty is a collateral undertaking by one person to answer for the payment of debt of another, and the undertaking of principal debtor is independent of the promise of guarantor; upon default of the principal debtor and satisfaction of conditions precedent to liability, the promise of the guarantor becomes absolute. For a guarantor to become liable under a guaranty of payment, there need only be a failure of the primary obligor to make payment.[52]

If the language of the guaranty is clear and unambiguous evidencing an absolute guaranty of the payment of the debt, and not conditional, then the contract is an original undertaking to pay the debt, and liability of the guarantor immediately matures upon the failure of the principal debtor to pay; and it is not essential before the obligee is entitled to sue the guarantor that suit be commenced against the principal debtor and the claim reduced to judgment.[53]

Arkansas case law does not specifically distinguish between guaranteeing payment and guaranteeing collection. While signing on an instrument and signing a separate guaranty are two separate events, perhaps a look at the Arkansas Code with respect to accommodation parties could provide some insight on the issue. With respect to signing on a promissory note, if the language unambiguously states that the guarantor is guaranteeing collection only rather than payment of the obligation, the guarantor is obliged to pay the amount due only if (1) execution of judgment against the principal has been returned unsatisfied, (2) the principal is insolvent or in an insolvency proceeding, (3) the principal cannot be served with process or (4) it is otherwise apparent that payment cannot be obtained from the principal.[54]

6.3 Language Regarding the Revocation of Guaranties

A guaranty that is revocable by its terms may not be revoked with respect to transactions entered into by the primary obligor prior to the revocation.[55]

A guarantor may revoke the guaranty with regard to future liability upon reasonable notice listed in the terms of the guaranty. Furthermore, even if the terms of the guaranty specify that the notice must be in writing, a verbal revocation of the guaranty, if accepted and acted upon, will relieve the guarantor.[56]

6.4 "Continuing"

Under Arkansas law, where the guaranty contains a limitation as to the amount for which the guarantor will be bound, but contains no limitation as to time, and there is nothing in the circumstances surrounding the execution of the

---

52. First American Nat'l Bank v. Coffey-Clifton, Inc., 633 S.W.2d 704, 705 (Ark. 1982).
53. Bank of Morrilton v. Skipper, Tucker & Co., 263 S.W. 54, 55 (Ark. 1924).
54. *See* Ark. Code Ann. § 4-3-419(d); U.C.C. § 3-419(d).
55. Ouachita Valley Bank v. De Motte, 291 S.W. 984, 986 (Ark. 1927).
56. Olson v. Swift Co., 182 S.W. 903 (Ark. 1916).

contract to evince a contrary intention, it will, in general, be construed to be a continuing guaranty and operative until revoked.[57]

Under Arkansas law, if a guaranty agreement specifically provides that it will not be affected by renewal or extension of the obligation guaranteed, that provision will be honored and the guarantor will remain liable on any renewal or extension of such obligation.[58] On the other hand, if a guaranty is limited to a specific contract, such guaranty will not be a continuing guaranty so that the guarantor will be liable for additional debt accruing under a new or renewal contract.[59] A guaranty that is continuing will remain in full force until it is revoked as to future transactions.[60]

6.5 "Absolute and Unconditional"

Under Arkansas law, if a guaranty agreement specifically provides that it is an "absolute and unconditional" guaranty, then the liability of the guarantor becomes fixed upon the failure of the primary obligor to pay. While the terms of the guaranty will control, from and after the date of the default of the primary obligor, the obligee may exercise all remedies against the guarantor, for all amounts guaranteed.[61]

§ 7 Defenses of the Guarantor; Set-off

The defenses that may be available to a guarantor can be grouped into three categories: (1) defenses of the primary obligor; (2) "suretyship defenses;" and (3) other defenses.

7.1 Defenses of the Primary Obligor

7.1.1 General

Generally, a guarantor is not liable to the creditor unless the debtor is also bound under the principal contract.[62] Thus, where the principal contract is contrary to law, void, or invalid, the guarantor is not liable on the contract of guaranty.[63] Arkansas courts do not appear to have directly addressed when defenses personal to the principal may be used by the guarantor to defeat an action seeking to hold him liable on the contract of guaranty. However, the Arkansas Court of Appeals has explained in dictum that it is not a defense to liability under a guaranty that the principal obligation is merely unenforceable against the debtor due to some matter of defense that is personal to the debtor.[64]

57. First Nat'l Bank v. Waddell, 85 S.W. 417, 418 (Ark. 1905).
58. Germer v. Missouri Portland Cement Co., 783 S.W.2d 359, 360 (Ark. 1990).
59. Aluminum Cooking Utensil Co. v. Chastain, 167 S.W. 495, 496 (Ark. 1914).
60. Spears v. El Dorado Foundry, Mach. & Supply Co., 414 S.W.2d 622, 623 (Ark. 1967).
61. Bank of Morrilton v. Skipper, Tucker & Co., 263 S.W. 54 (Ark. 1924).
62. Dean Leasing, Inc. v. Van Buren County, 767 S.W.2d 316, 318 (1989).
63. *Id.* at 319.
64. *Id.*, 767 S.W.2d 316, 318.

Accordingly, at least when sued alone in Arkansas, a guarantor presumably may not successfully defend an action brought on the guaranty agreement on the basis that the principal obligation was obtained through fraud practiced on the debtor, that the principal obligation was not in writing (and, therefore, did not conform to the requirements of the statute of frauds), that the principal obligation was subject to the defense of usury (where usury does not have the effect of rendering the obligation invalid), that the creditor was guilty of a breach of warranty, or that the debtor was under a disability, such as coverture, infancy, or incompetency.[65]

7.1.2 When guarantor may assert primary obligor's defense

When the primary obligor and the guarantor are sued in the same action and the primary obligor asserts a defense personal to him, the guarantor may also assert the defense personal to the guarantor to defeat a claim on the contract of guaranty.[66] For example, defenses by a boat dealer and guarantors that the manufacturer charged usurious interest and that the guaranties were unenforceable because of usury were used successfully to defeat the manufacturer's enforcement of the contract of guaranty with regard to the usurious interest.[67]

When the primary obligor and the guarantor are sued in the same action, the guarantor may successfully defeat liability on the guaranty agreement when the guaranty agreement lacked mutuality.[68] For example, when the obligee retains the right to revoke the primary obligor's credit sales at any time, rendering it entirely optional with the obligee as whether to perform its obligation to the primary obligor, the guaranty agreement is not binding on the guarantor.[69]

7.1.3 Defenses that may not be raised by guarantor

See generally Section 7.1.1 *supra.*

7.1.4 Defenses that may always be raised by guarantor

See generally Section 7.1.2 *supra.*

7.2 "Suretyship" Defenses

A guarantor, like a surety, is a favorite of the law, and her liability is not to be extended by implication beyond the expressed terms of the agreement or its plain text.[70] A guarantor is entitled to have her undertaking strictly construed

65. *Id.* (quoting 38 Am. Jur. 2d *Guaranty* § 52 (1968)).
66. Taylor's Marine, Inc. v. Waco Manufacturing, Inc., 792 S.W.2d 286 (1990).
67. *Id.*
68. *See* Helena Chemical Co. v. Carey, 220 S.W.3d 235, 237 (2005) (discussing the trial court's reasoning in dictum).
69. *See id.*
70. Helena Chemical Co. v. Carey, 220 S.W.3d 235, 237 (2005).

and she cannot be held liable beyond the strict terms of her contract.[71] A guarantor who pleads release has the burden of proving that release.[72]

7.2.1 Change in identity of principal obligor

Not all changes in the identity of the principal obligor will serve to release the guarantor. Arkansas courts hold that, as a matter of law, a guarantor of a partnership obligation is released from his obligation by the subsequent change in ownership of the partnership.[73] Similarly, as a matter of law, a guarantor is discharged when the principal debtor changes the form of his business from a sole proprietorship to a partnership and credit is extended to that partnership without the knowledge or consent of the guarantor.[74] However, a guarantor of a corporate debt is not released simply by virtue of a change in ownership, particularly where the change is brought about by the sale of the guarantor's interest in the corporation.[75] The question of whether the guarantor has been discharged depends on the facts and whether there has been a material alteration of the surety contract.[76]

7.2.2 Modification of the underlying obligation, including release

In Arkansas, whether a guarantor's obligation is governed by the Uniform Commercial Code (UCC) or common law will determine whether a modification of the underlying obligation will affect a guarantor's obligations.

A guarantor's obligation may be fixed by the Arkansas UCC.[77] When the obligation of the surety is fixed by the UCC, the guarantor must show (1) that there was a modification "in any respect" of the obligation of a party and (2) the modification was fraudulently made.[78] "No other alteration discharges a party" under the UCC.[79] However, even if there is no evidence of a fraudulent modification, the question of a guarantor's discharge is not completely answered. Arkansas Code Annotated § 4-3-605 specifies changes in the legal relationship between debtor and creditor that discharge the guarantor. If the obligee "grants a principal obligor an extension of the time at which one or more payments are due on the instrument," the guarantor "is discharged to the extent that the extension would otherwise cause the secondary obligor a loss."[80] If the obligee agrees to a modification of the obligation of the principal obligor, the guarantor "is discharged from any unperformed portion of its obligation to

71. *Id.*
72. Continental Ozark, Inc. v. Lair, 779 S.W.2d 187, 189 (1989). *But see* Arkansas Industrial Development Commission v. Fabco of Ashdown, Inc., 847 S.W.2d 13 (1993).
73. Gazette Publishing Co. v. Cole, 262 S.W. 985, 986-87 (1924). *See also* Continental Ozark, Inc. v. Lair, 779 S.W.2d 187, 188-89 (1989).
74. Helena Chemical Co. v. Carey, 220 S.W.3d 235, 237-38 (2005). *See also* Gazette Publishing Co. v. Cole, 262 S.W. 985, 987 (1924).
75. Continental Ozark, Inc. v. Lair, 779 S.W.2d 187, 189 (1989).
76. *Id.*
77. *See generally* ARK. CODE ANN. §§ 4-1-101 et seq.
78. *See* ARK. CODE ANN. §§ 4-3-407(a) and (b).
79. ARK. CODE ANN. § 4-3-407(b).
80. ARK. CODE ANN. § 4-3-605(b)(2).

the extent the modification would otherwise cause the [guarantor] a loss."[81] If the obligee "releases the obligation of a principal obligor in whole or in part," the guarantor "is discharged to the same extent as the principal obligor from any unperformed portion of its obligation on the instrument."[82] Even if the guarantor is not discharged under this rule, the guarantor "is discharged to the extent of the value of the consideration for the release, and to the extent that the release would otherwise cause the [guarantor] a loss."[83] The burden of proof both with respect to the occurrence of the acts alleged to harm the guarantor and the loss or prejudice caused by those acts rests with the guarantor.[84] However, if the guarantor demonstrates prejudice caused by an impairment of its recourse, and the circumstances of the case indicate that the amount of loss is not reasonably susceptible of calculation or requires proof of facts that are not ascertainable, it is presumed that the act impairing recourse caused a loss or impairment equal to the liability of the guarantor on the instrument.[85] In that event, the burden of persuasion as to any lesser amount of the loss is on the person entitled to enforce the instrument.[86]

Under the common law analysis, Arkansas courts apply the well-settled principle of the law of guaranty that a material alteration in the obligation assumed, made without the assent of the guarantor, discharges him from liability as guarantor.[87] An alteration is material, however, only if "the guarantor is placed in the position of being required to do more than his original undertaking."[88] In determining whether an alteration is material, Arkansas courts look to see whether the surety has been placed in a position different from that which it promised to guarantee.[89] Whether or not the guarantor has been prejudiced by the alteration is irrelevant.[90]

When the obligee substantially increases the risk to the guarantor by increasing the credit limit extended to the principal obligor over time, this may constitute a material alteration resulting in a discharge of the guarantor's liability on the guaranty contract.[91] The guarantor may be released in such circumstances even when the guaranty agreement provides that the guarantor unconditionally guarantees payment "to cover the present balance, together with any and all future indebtedness."[92]

The substitution of a promissory note for a franchise agreement may constitute a material change in both the form and substance of the original understanding, thereby extinguishing any liability the guarantors may have had for the payment of royalties arising from the franchise agreement.[93]

---

81. Ark. Code Ann. § 4-3-605(c)(2).
82. Ark. Code Ann. § 4-3-605(a)(2).
83. Ark. Code Ann. § 4-3-605(a)(3).
84. Ark. Code Ann. § 4-3-605(h).
85. Ark. Code Ann. § 4-3-605(i).
86. Ark. Code Ann. § 4-3-605(i).
87. Helena Chemical Co. v. Carey, 220 S.W.3d 235, 237 (2005).
88. *Id.; see also* Finagin v. Arkansas Development Finance Authority, 139 S.W.3d 797, 804 (2003).
89. Finagin v. Arkansas Development Finance Authority, 139 S.W.3d 797, 804 (2003).
90. Inter-Sport, Inc. v. Wilson, 661 S.W.2d 367, 368 (1983).
91. *See* Helena Chemical Co. v. Carey, 220 S.W.3d 235, 238 (2005).
92. Helena Chemical Co. v. Carey, 220 S.W.3d 235, 236 (2005).
93. Inter-Sport, Inc. v. Wilson, 661 S.W.2d 367, 368 (1983).

The substitution of interest-bearing notes, payable in 90 days, for an open account, payable on demand, may discharge liability of the guarantor of the open account.[94]

Under both the UCC and the common law, if, however, the guaranty agreement specifically provides that it will not be affected by renewals or extensions of the obligation guaranteed, that provision will be honored.[95] Where the guaranty contract contains a provision that authorizes a change in the terms of the principal contract, a change within the scope of that authorization does not discharge the guarantor.[96]

The general rule is that a release of the principal debtor terminates the guarantor's liability and discharges the guarantor's obligation on the contract of guaranty unless the right of right of recourse against the guarantor is expressly reserved in the guaranty agreement.[97]

7.2.3 Release or impairment of security for the underlying obligation

In Arkansas, whether a guarantor's obligation is governed by the UCC or common law will determine what effect the release or impairment of the security for the underlying obligation will have on the guarantor's obligations.

When a guarantor's obligation is fixed by the UCC and the principal obligor's obligation is secured by an interest in collateral and the obligee impairs the value of the interest in collateral, the obligation of the guarantor is discharged to the extent of the impairment.[98] Impairing the value of an interest in collateral includes failure to obtain or maintain perfection or recordation of the interest in collateral, release of collateral without substitution of collateral of equal value or equivalent reduction of the underlying obligation, failure to perform a duty to preserve the value of collateral owed, under chapter 9 or other law, to a debtor or other person secondarily liable, and failure to comply with applicable law in disposing of or otherwise enforcing the interest in collateral.[99] The burden of proof both with respect to the occurrence of the acts alleged to harm the guarantor and the loss or prejudice caused by those acts rests with the guarantor.[100] However, if the guarantor demonstrates prejudice caused by an impairment of its recourse, and the circumstances of the case indicate that the amount of loss is not reasonably susceptible of calculation or requires proof of facts that are not ascertainable, it is presumed that the act impairing recourse caused a loss or impairment equal to the liability of the guarantor on the instrument.[101] In that event, the burden of persuasion as to any lesser amount of the loss is on the person entitled to enforce the instrument.[102]

---

94. *See* Spears v. El Dorado Foundry, Machine & Supply Co., 414 S.W.2d 622 (1967).
95. *See* Morrilton Security Bank v. Kelemen, 16 S.W.3d 567, 568 (2000); Ark. Code Ann. § 4-3-407(b).
96. *See* Morrilton Security Bank v. Kelemen, 16 S.W.3d 567, 569 (2000); Smith v. Elder, 849 S.W.2d 513, 519 (1993); Ark. Code Ann. § 4-3-407(b).
97. *See generally* 38 Am. Jur. 2d Guaranty § 67.
98. Ark. Code Ann. § 4-3-605(d).
99. Ark. Code Ann. § 4-3-605(d)
100. Ark. Code Ann. § 4-3-605(h).
101. Ark. Code Ann. § 4-3-605(i).
102. Ark. Code Ann. § 4-3-605(i).

Arkansas courts have explained that under the common law a creditor in possession of collateral is held to a high standard of care.[103] A surety must prove two elements in order to be entitled to discharge: "that the holder of the note was responsible for the loss or impairment of the collateral, and the extent to which the impairment results in loss."[104] However, Arkansas courts have also explained a creditor is not obligated to preserve the right of recourse in collateral of a surety.[105] A creditor has *no* duty to repossess collateral to protect, or for the benefit of, a guarantor.[106] Thus, a creditor not in possession of the collateral is not required to protect the collateral for the benefit of the guarantors.[107]

The obligee may, in the absence of a special pledge to a particular debt, apply the proceeds of collateral to debts of the principal on which the surety or guarantor is not bound, in preference to debts on which he is bound, assuming that both classes of debts are covered by the collateral.[108] However, after credit is made by the obligee to the debt for which the guarantor is bound, the guarantor is discharged *pro tanto*, and cannot be affected by a subsequent change of application by the obligee or principal obligor.[109]

Under both the UCC and the common law, a guarantor may waive in advance its defense based on the release or impairment of collateral.[110] An absolute and unconditional guaranty, which contains a term providing that the delay or omission of the holder in exercising any right or power with respect to the indebtedness does not affect the liability of the guarantor, waives any defense based on impairment of collateral.[111]

7.3 Other Defenses

7.3.1 Failure to fulfill a condition precedent

In Arkansas, guarantors may raise a defense of failure to fulfill a condition precedent provided for in the guaranty agreement.[112] Relying on the well-settled principle that a guarantor is entitled to have his undertaking strictly construed and that he cannot be held liable beyond the strict terms of his contract, the failure to fulfill a condition precedent in the guaranty agreement may release the guarantor whether or not he is prejudiced thereby.[113]

---

103. *See* Finagin v. Arkansas Development Finance Authority, 139 S.W.3d 797, 805 (2003).
104. Myers v. First State Bank of Sherwood, 732 S.W.2d 459 (1987), opinion supplemented by 741 S.W.2d 624 (1987).
105. *Id.*
106. *Id.*
107. *Id.*
108. Holt v. Gregory, 244 S.W.2d 951, 953 (1952).
109. *See* Kelley Brothers Lumber Co. v. Leming, 248 S.W.2d 358 (1952).
110. *See* Finagin v. Arkansas Development Finance Authority, 139 S.W.3d 797, 805 (2003); Smith v. Elder, 849 S.W.2d 513, 519 (1993); Ark. Code Ann. § 4-3-605(f).
111. Smith v. Elder, 312 Ark. 384, 395, 849 S.W.2d 513, 519 (1993).
112. Arkansas Industrial Development Commission v. Fabco of Ashdown, Inc., 847 S.W.2d 13 (1993).
113. *Id.*

7.3.2 *Modification of the guaranty*

Under Arkansas law, there must be additional consideration when the parties to a contract enter into an additional contract.[114] If no benefit is received by the obligee except which he was entitled to under the original contract, and the other party to the contract parts with nothing except that which he was already bound for, there is no consideration for the additional contract concerning the subject matter of the original one.[115]

A guarantor cannot unilaterally terminate his contract of guaranty of an existing obligation.[116]

7.3.3 *Failure to pursue primary obligor*

Under an absolute, unconditional guaranty of payment, the liability of a guarantor immediately matures upon the failure of the principal debtor to pay and it is not essential before the obligee is entitled to sue the guarantor that suit be commenced against the principal debtor and the claim reduced to judgment.[117] The parties may also contractually agree that the obligee does not have to exhaust any remedies available to it against the primary obligor or collateral securing the obligation in order to collect against the guarantor.

7.3.4 *Statute of limitations*

In Arkansas, the statute of limitations on most written contracts is five years.[118] There are exceptions to the general rule. For example, the statute of limitations to enforce an obligation, duty, or right arising under the UCC is three years after the cause of action accrues.[119] Another exception is that an action for breach of any contract for the sale of goods must be commenced within four years after the cause of action has accrued.[120]

The statute of limitations begins to run when a complete and present cause of action first arises.[121] The true test in determining when a cause of action arises or accrues is to establish a time when a plaintiff could have first maintained the action to a successful conclusion.[122] One's ignorance of the existence of his cause of action does not prevent the statute of limitations from running, unless his ignorance is due to fraudulent concealment or misrepresentation on the part of the one seeking to invoke the statute.[123]

A cause of action to cancel a written instrument arises when the ground for its cancelation first occurs.[124] Thus, a party seeking to cancel an instrument purporting to release a guarantor from his obligations must be brought

---

114. *See* Crookham & Vessels, Inc. v. Larry Moyer Trucking, Inc., 699 S.W.2d 414, 416 (1985).
115. Crookham & Vessels, Inc. v. Larry Moyer Trucking, Inc., 699 S.W.2d 414, 416 (1985).
116. *See* Meek v. U.S. Rubber Tire Co., 425 S.W.2d 323, 325 (1968).
117. *See* Bank of Morrilton v. Skipper, Tucker & Co., 263 S.W.54, 55-56 (1924).
118. ARK. CODE ANN. § 16-56-111.
119. ARK. CODE ANN. § 4-4-111.
120. ARK. CODE ANN. § 4-2-725(1).
121. Hedlund v. Hendrix, 837 S.W.2d 488, 489 (1992).
122. *Id.*
123. *Id.*
124. *Id.*

within five years of execution of the release.[125] A cause of action on a guaranty agreement executed after the principal obligation has become due arises at the time of the execution of the guaranty agreement.[126]

If a guarantor seeks to recover against the principal obligor pursuant to a written agreement, the guarantor's cause of action is governed by a five-year statute of limitations.[127] However, if a guarantor seeks to recover against the principal obligor pursuant to an implied agreement, the guarantor's cause of action is governed by a three-year statute of limitations.[128] The statute of limitations does not begin to run as between the principal and surety until the surety has been called upon to make good the default of the principal.[129] Thus, the fact that the statute of limitations might bar any claim of the obligee against the principal does not necessarily bar the guarantor from bringing a claim against the principal after he has been called to satisfy the principal's obligations.[130] Where, for example, the running of the period of limitations has barred recovery from the principal, but not from the guarantor, the nonliability of the former does not impair the guarantor's right against the principal.[131] Thus, where no claim is asserted by the obligee against the principal, but judgment is obtained against the guarantor, who pays the judgment after the right of action by the obligee against the principal is barred by the statute of limitations, the guarantor may recover from the principal.[132]

7.3.5 Statute of frauds

In Arkansas, an oral undertaking to answer for the debt of another without any new consideration is a collateral understanding and not enforceable under the statute of frauds.[133] However, an oral contract is considered original and enforceable when the agreement is based on new consideration or benefit moving to the promisor.[134] When considering whether the undertaking is collateral or original, courts look to the words of the promise, the situation of the parties, and the circumstances surrounding the transaction.[135] The determination of whether an undertaking is collateral or original is one of fact.[136]

125. *Id.*
126. Smith v. Farmers' & Merchants' Bank, 35 S.W.2d 347, 348-49 (1931).
127. Hendrickson v. Carpenter, 199 S.W.3d 100, 103 (2004).
128. *See* Hendrickson v. Carpenter, 199 S.W.3d 100, 102-03 (2004).
129. McDonald v. Mueller, 183 S.W. 751, 753 (1916); Pierce v. Stirling, 279 S.W.2d 840, 842-43 (1955); *cf.* Ray & Sons Masonry Contractors, Inc. v. U.S. Fidelity & Guaranty Co., 114 S.W.3d 189, 198 (2003).
130. Pierce v. Stirling, 279 S.W.2d 840, 842-43 (1955).
131. *Id.*
132. *Id.*
133. *See* Ark. Code Ann. § 4-59-101(a)(2); Capel v. Allstate Insurance Co., 77 S.W.3d 533, 541 (2002); Barnett v. Hughey Auto Parts, Inc., 631 S.W.2d 623, 625 (1982).
134. *See* Capel v. Allstate Insurance Co., 77 S.W.3d 533, 541 (2002); Barnett v. Hughey Auto Parts, Inc., 631 S.W.2d 623, 625 (1982).
135. Capel v. Allstate Insurance Co., 77 S.W.3d 533, 541 (2002); Barnett v. Hughey Auto Parts, Inc., 631 S.W.2d 623, 625 (1982).
136. Capel v. Allstate Insurance Co., 77 S.W.3d 533, 541 (2002); Barnett v. Hughey Auto Parts, Inc., 5 Ark. App. 1, 4, 631 S.W.2d 623, 625 (1982).

The statute of frauds does not apply when a guarantor is sued upon its own obligation outside the statute of frauds.[137] Arkansas courts have long recognized that a promise is not within the statute of frauds where the main purpose of the promisor was to serve some purpose of his own, even though the effect is to be responsible for the debt of another.[138]

7.3.6 Defenses particular to guarantors that are natural persons and their spouses

Research did not reveal any Arkansas cases on point.

7.3.7 Release of coguarantors

The general rule in Arkansas is that a release to one of several obligors may serve as a release as to all obligors.[139] This rule generally applies with regard to a single debt or obligation incurred by a group or joint and several liability.[140] However, guaranty agreements that are individual pro rata guaranties, rather than joint and several guaranties, may create individual liability.[141] Under such circumstances, the release as to one guarantor may not serve to release all guarantors.[142]

7.3.8 Impairment of a guarantor's right of recourse against third-party in possession of collateral

As a matter of law, if the obligee fails to preserve a guarantor's right of recourse against a third party by discharging with prejudice its claim against all parties in possession of collateral, the guarantor is discharged of his obligation on the guaranty agreement.[143]

7.4 Assignment of Guarantee Agreement to Another Obligee

Traditionally, guaranties were divided into two classes, general and special.[144] A general guaranty is addressed to persons generally and may be enforced by anyone to whom it is presented.[145] A special guaranty is one addressed to particular persons and may not be enforced by any person other than to whom it is addressed.[146] However, Arkansas courts have curtailed the significance of any substantive difference between general and special guaranties by holding

137. *See* Forever Green Athletic Fields, Inc. v. Lasiter Construction, Inc., 2011 Ark. App. 347 (2011).
138. *See id.*
139. Finagin v. Arkansas Development Finance Authority, 139 S.W.3d 797, 803 (2003).
140. *Id.*
141. *Id.*
142. *Id.*
143. *See* Myers v. First State Bank of Sherwood, 741 S.W.2d 624, 625 (1987); Moore v. Luxor, 742 S.W.2d 916, 919-20 (1988).
144. B.S.G. Foods, Inc. v. Multifoods Distribution Group, Inc., 54 S.W.3d 553, 556 (2001).
145. *Id.*, 54 S.W.3d at 556-57.
146. *Id.* at 557.

that the rights under a special guaranty are generally assignable unless: the assignment is prohibited by statute, public policy, or the terms of the assignment; the assignment would materially alter the guarantor's risks, burdens, or duties, or the guarantor executed the contract because of personal confidence in the obligee.[147] Thus, a guaranty agreement addressed to a particular obligee may be enforced by the obligee's assigns even though the guaranty agreement does not contain "successors and assigns" language indicating that it can be enforced by the obligee's successor or assigns.[148]

7.5 Right of Set-off

In Arkansas, "any demand, right, or cause of action, regardless of how it may have arisen, may be asserted by way of setoff in any action to the extent of the plaintiff's demand."[149] Likewise, "[j]udgments for the recovery of money may be set off against each other, having due regard to the legal and equitable rights of all persons interested in both judgments."[150] On the other hand, judgments assigned to the defendant *after suit* has been commenced against him shall not be allowed to be set off against the demands of the plaintiff.[151]

§ 8 Waiver of Defenses by the Guarantor

8.1 Defenses that cannot be Waived

Generally, because of the combined private and public interests involved, individual parties are not entirely free to waive statutory and constitutional defenses.[152] For example, Arkansas courts have held that an express agreement, made at the time of the original contract, never to plead the statute of limitations as a defense, is generally regarded as against public policy and void.[153]

8.2 "Catch-all" Waivers

Arkansas courts analyze clauses in guaranty agreements waiving "all defenses" using the same analysis Arkansas courts apply to all other exculpatory contracts.[154] An exculpatory contract is one in which a party seeks to absolve himself in advance for the consequences of his own negligence.[155] Such con-

147. *Id.* at 557.
148. *Id.* at 559.
149. ARK. CODE ANN. § 16-56-102.
150. ARK. CODE ANN. § 16-65-603(a).
151. ARK. CODE ANN. § 16-63-206(c).
152. *See* First Nat'l Bank of Eastern Arkansas v. Arkansas Development Finance Authority, 146-47, 870 S.W.2d 400, 402-03 (1994).
153. *Id. But see* Slade v. Horn, 185 S.W.2d 924, 924-25 (1945).
154. *See* Finagin v. Arkansas Development Finance Authority, 139 S.W.3d 797, 806 (2003). In *Finagin,* the Arkansas Supreme Court examined the following release clause from the guarantor's agreement as an exculpatory contract: "No setoff, counterclaim, reduction, diminution of an obligation, or any defense of any kind or nature which the guarantor has or may have against the [obligee] or the trustee shall be available hereunder to the guarantor against the [obligee]." *Id.*
155. *Id.*

tracts are not invalid per se and are upheld in Arkansas.[156] When reviewing exculpatory contracts, Arkansas courts apply two rules of construction. First, they are to be strictly construed against the party relying on them.[157] Second, to be enforceable, the contract must clearly set out what negligent liability is to be avoided.[158] Additionally, the court is not restricted to the literal language of the contract, and, therefore, will also consider the facts and circumstances surrounding the execution of the release in order to determine the intent of the parties.[159]

An exculpatory clause may be enforced: (1) when the party is knowledgeable of the potential liability that is released; (2) when the party is benefiting from the activity which may lead to the potential liability that is released; and (3) when the contract that contains the clause was fairly entered into.[160] Therefore, Arkansas courts will enforce a waiver of defenses provision of a guaranty agreement when the guarantors are shareholders in the primary obligor, there is no evidence to suggest that the guarantors are unsophisticated business people or that the guaranty agreements were entered into unfairly, and the guaranty agreements were entered into in the course of businesses dealing at arms' length.[161]

Catch-all waivers may not provide the obligee all of the protection that their broad language may indicate. Arkansas courts have held that although a guaranty agreement contained a boilerplate clause waiving "any and all notice of non-payment and dishonor, demand, notice, protest and notice of protest and . . . notice of the acceptance of this guaranty," the guarantor was released because the obligee failed to comply with the requirements of notice and commercial reasonableness under the UCC.[162]

8.3 Use of Specific Waivers

It appears that no defense requires an explicit waiver in Arkansas. Specific waivers may address the particular concerns of the parties. However, Arkansas courts have sometimes narrowly construed contract clauses limiting them to the precise words that were used.[163] Therefore, caution should be taken in drafting specific waivers to not unnecessarily limit their application by drafting them too narrowly.

156. *Id.*
157. *Id.*
158. *Id.*
159. *Id.*
160. *Id.*
161. *Id.*
162. *See* First Nat'l Bank of Wynne v. Hess, 743 S.W.2d 825 (1988).
163. *See, e.g.*, Buffington v. Diamond Transport & Drilling, LLC, 2011 Ark. App. 76 (construing a governing law and venue provision to mandate that Louisiana state law would govern the agreement but not to mean that the parties agreed to be heard only in one particular venue).

§ 9 Third-party Pledgors—Defenses and Waiver Thereof

Arkansas courts have generally likened third-party pledgors to guarantors.[164] Whether this means that a third-party pledgor may enjoy all of the same defenses of a guarantor remains to be established in Arkansas courts. However, a third-party pledgor arguably stands in the same position of that of a guarantor to the extent of the pledge. It appears likely that a third-party pledgor may avail himself of the same rights and defenses enjoyed by guarantors generally in Arkansas courts.

§ 10 Jointly and Severally Liable Guarantors—Contribution and Reduction of Obligations upon Payment by a Co-obligor

10.1 Contribution

The right of contribution among coguarantors is well settled in Arkansas.[165] A party is entitled to contribution when he is jointly and severally liable for a debt and subsequently pays the entire obligation.[166] The right of contribution accrues, and the three-year statute of limitations for an implied contract of contribution begins to run, when one guarantor pays more than his share of the common liability.[167] Thus, the remedy of contribution is not available to a c-guarantor until he has satisfied more than his pro rata share of the debt.[168]

The equitable doctrine of exoneration, which gives a surety in certain situations the right to call upon his cosureties for exoneration before any payment is made, has not been recognized by Arkansas courts.[169]

164. *See* Ryder Truck Rental, Inc. v. Sutton, 807 S.W.2d 909, 912 (1991) (discussing whether the requirement of a surety or sureties on supersedeas bonds under Ark. R. Civ. P. 62(d) and Ark. R. App. P. 8 can be satisfied by the pledge of property and explaining that "the pledge of property is a *kind* of surety"); Chicago Building & Manufacturing Co. v. Stoker, 136 S.W. 183, 186 (1911) (likening subscribers to stock subscriptions in future corporation to guarantors).

165. *See* Hendrickson v. Carpenter, 199 S.W.3d 100, 102-03 (2004); Wroten v. Evans, 21 Ark. App. 134, 136, 729 S.W.2d 422, 424 (1987).

166. Hendrickson v. Carpenter, 199 S.W.3d 100, 102 (2004); Wroten v. Evans, 729 S.W.2d 422, 424 (1987).

167. *Id.*

168. *Id.*

169. Wroten v. Evans, 729 S.W.2d 422, 424 (1987).

10.2 Reduction of Obligations upon Payment of Co-obligor

A guarantor's obligations to the obligee under the guaranty agreement are reduced by any payments received by the obligee towards the underlying obligation.[170]

10.3 Liability of Parent Guarantors owning less than 100 percent of Primary Obligor

Arkansas courts do not appear to have addressed the liability of a parent corporation that has guaranteed the obligations of the primary obligor when the parent corporation owns less than 100 percent of the primary obligor. A parent corporation is ordinarily not liable for the debts of its subsidiary.[171] However, courts will ignore the corporate form of a subsidiary where fairness demands it.[172] Within the parameters of these rules, Arkansas courts should interpret the parent corporation's obligations under the guaranty agreement according to the terms set forth in the guaranty agreement.[173] "A guarantor is entitled to have her undertaking strictly construed and she cannot be held liable beyond the strict terms of her contract."[174]

§ 11 Reliance

Reliance is not a requisite to enforce a guaranty agreement in Arkansas.[175] Whether or not the guarantor relied on the identity of the principal obligor may become an issue with regard to whether or not a change in the principal obligor constituted a material change relieving the guarantor of his obligation.[176] Reliance is an essential element to establish a claim for common defenses such as fraud[177] or promissory estoppel.[178]

170. This principal is so well-settled in Arkansas that there appears to be a lack of judicial precedent on point. However, *see* Lindel Square Limited Partnership v. Savers Federal Savings and Loan Association, 766 S.W.2d 41 (1989), *appeal after remand,* 799 S.W.2d 569 (1999), wherein the parties and the court appear to have assumed without question that the monies the obligee received from the sale of collateral reduced the guarantors' indebtedness.
171. *See* Rounds & Porter Lumber Co. v. Burns, 225 S.W.2d 1, 2-3 (1949).
172. Woodyard v. Arkansas Diversified Ins. Co., 594 S.W.2d 13, 17 (1980).
173. *Cf.* Miller v. Addison Products Co., No. CA 91-138, 1992 WL 51212 (Ark. App. Mar. 11, 1992) (holding that guaranty agreement, specifying that president and CEO of parent corporation would guaranty the debts of parent corporation, did not obligate president and CEO to be liable for the debts of the parent corporation's subsidiary corporation).
174. Helena Chemical Co. v. Carey, 220 S.W.3d 235, 237 (2005).
175. *See* McCaleb v. Nat'l Bank of Commerce of Pine Bluff, 752 S.W.2d 54, 56 (1988) ("In ascertaining the meaning of the language of a contract of guaranty, the same rules of construction control as apply to other contracts.")
176. *See* § 7.2.1.
177. Tyson Foods, Inc. v. Davis, 66 S.W.3d 568, 577 (2002).
178. Fairpark, LLC v. Heathcare Essential, Inc., 2011 Ark. App. 146, _ S.W.3d _ .

§ 12 Subrogation

Subrogation is an equitable remedy that rests upon principles of unjust enrichment and attempts to accomplish complete and perfect justice among the parties.[179] In Arkansas, the elements of subrogation are as follows: "1) a party pays in full a debt or an obligation of another or removes an encumbrance of another, 2) for which the other is primarily liable, 3) although the party is not technically bound to do so, 4) in order to protect his own secondary rights, to fulfill a contractual obligation, or to comply with the request of the original debtor, 5) without acting as a volunteer or an intermeddler."[180] Under subrogation, the payor who is the subrogee steps into the shoes of the payee and becomes subrogated to whatever rights the payee had against the wrongdoer.[181]

§ 13 Triangular Set-off in Bankruptcy

The bankruptcy court in *In re Fairfield Plantation, Inc.*[182] held that the mutuality requirement contained in section 553(a) of the Bankruptcy Code precludes triangular set-off in bankruptcy cases. Mutuality requires that the debts involved be between the same parties standing in the same capacity.

§ 14 Indemnification—Whether the Primary Obligor has a Duty

In the ordinary relation between principal obligor and guarantor, there is an implied contract of indemnity; indemnity may be permitted where the principal obligor/indemnitor has breached a duty of his own owed to the guarantor/indemnitee.[183] The doctrine of indemnity is based upon equitable principles of restitution which permit one who is compelled to pay money, which in justice ought to be paid by another, to recover the sums to be paid unless the payor is barred by the wrongful nature of his own conduct."[184]

An indemnitee is entitled to recover reimbursement for all expenses reasonably incurred by him in connection with the obligation, including attorney's

179. Hendrickson v. Carpenter, 199 S.W.3d 100, 103 (2004).
180. St. Paul Fire & Marine Insurance Co. v. Murray Guard, Inc., 37 S.W.3d 180, 183 (2001).
181. *Id.*
182. 147 Bankr. 946, 952 (1992).
183. *See* McDonald v. Mueller, 183 S.W. 751, 753 (1916); Pierce v. Stirling, 279 S.W.2d 840, 842 (1955); Larson Machine, Inc. v. Wallace, 600 S.W.2d 1, 12 (1980).
184. Larson Machine, Inc. v. Wallace, 600 S.W.2d 1, 12 (1980).

fees and costs.[185] However, attorney's fees expended by the indemnitee in an action on the indemnity agreement against the indemnitor are not recoverable.[186]

An indemnity contract set out in writing is controlled by a five-year statute of limitations in Arkansas. A three-year statute of limitations applies to oral contracts for indemnity.[187] A cause of action accrues the moment the right to commence an action comes into existence, and the statute of limitations commences to run from that time.[188] An action on a contract for indemnity accrues when the indemnitee is subjected to damage on account of its own liability.[189] To be subjected to damage, there must be a loss.[190] An indemnitor's obligation to reimburse against loss does not become due until after the indemnitee has paid damages to a third party.[191] Therefore, the fact that the underlying obligation is barred by the statute of limitations does not necessarily prevent the claims of the guarantor/indemnitee for indemnity against the principal obligor/indemnitor.[192]

In a suit brought by the obligee against the guarantor, the failure of the guarantor to pursue his right for indemnity against the principal obligor by third-party pleading would not preclude the guarantor from subsequently maintaining such an action.[193] However, in a suit brought by the obligee against the guarantor, the indemnitee/guarantor may pursue a third-party complaint for indemnity against the indemnitor/principal obligor to avoid a multiplicity of actions.[194]

§ 15 Enforcement of Guaranties

15.1 Limitations on Recovery

See Article 6 *supra*.

15.2 Enforcement of Guaranties of Payment versus Guaranties of Performance

See Section 6.2 *supra*.

185. *See* U.S. Fidelity and Guaranty Co. v. Love, 538 S.W.2d 558, 559 (1976); Arkansas Transport Co. v. Hartford Accident & Indemnity Co., No. CA 89-456, 1990 WL 160394, at *4 (Ark. App. Oct. 17, 1990).
186. U.S. Fidelity and Guaranty Co. v. Love, 538 S.W.2d 558, 559 (1976).
187. Ray & Sons Masonry Contractors, Inc. v. U.S. Fidelity and Guaranty Co., 114 S.W.3d 189, 198 (2003).
188. *Id.*
189. *Id.*
190. *Id.*
191. *Id.*
192. Pierce v. Sterling, 279 S.W.2d 840, 842 (1955).
193. Larson Machine, Inc. v. Wallace, 600 S.W.2d 1, 12 (1980).
194. *Id.*

15.3 Exercising Rights under a Guaranty Where the Underlying Obligation is also Secured by a Mortgage

As previously discussed in Section 7.3.3 *supra*, an obligee does not have to exhaust any remedies available to it against the primary obligor or collateral securing the obligation in order to collect against a guarantor. An obligee may elect to enforce the guaranty agreement directly against a guarantor and not to dispose of any collateral securing the mortgage, unless the guaranty agreement indicates otherwise.

15.4 Litigating Guaranty Claims: Procedural Considerations

As previously discussed in Section 7.3.3 *supra*, an obligee does not have to exhaust any remedies available to it against the primary obligor or collateral securing the obligation in order to collect against the guarantor.

As previously discussed in Section 14 *supra*, the guarantor may pursue a third-party claim for indemnification against the principal obligor when the guarantor is sued by the obligee on the guaranty agreement, or the guarantor may wait and bring a separate lawsuit against the principal obligor for indemnification thereafter.

§ 16 Revival and Reinstatement of Guaranties

For all practical purposes, a guarantor's liability under a guaranty agreement is more likely to be governed by the particular language employed in the guaranty agreement than any rule of law. This is true whether the guarantor attempts to revoke his guaranty or the guaranty agreement contains an expiration date. Guaranty agreements often contain language providing that a revocation or termination of the guaranty agreement will not be effective as to indebtedness existing or committed for at the time of actual receipt of such notice by the obligee, or as to any renewals, extensions, and refinancings thereof. Such provisions are generally binding on the guarantor.[195] A guarantor may bind himself to pay such obligations as might arise or accrue prior to the expiration date, even though the obligation might not be payable until long after the expiration of the guaranty agreement.[196] Of course, a guarantor may limit his liability to obligations that actually become due and payable during the effective dates of the guaranty agreement.[197] A guarantor is generally bound by the clear wording of his agreement.[198]

195. *See generally* § 7.2 *supra.*
196. *See, e.g.*, American Indemnity Co. v. Reed, 87 S.W.2d 1 (1935); Fidelity & Deposit Co. of Maryland v. Frazier, 81 S.W.2d 915 (1935).
197. *See, e.g.*, American Indemnity Co. v. Reed, 87 S.W.2d 1 (1935); McMillan et al. v. Farmers' Bonded Warehouse, 272 S.W. 867 (1925).
198. *See* Lindell Square Limited Partnership v. Savers Federal Savings and Loan Ass'n, 766 S.W.2d 41, 45 (1989), *appeal after remand* 799 S.W.2d 569 (1999); Morrilton Security Bank v. Kelemen, 16 S.W.3d 567, 568 (2000).

§ 17 Choice of Law Rules Applicable to Guaranties

Arkansas choice of law is governed by common law and by statute. When a transaction bears a reasonable relationship to this state and also to another state or nation, the parties may agree that the law either of this state or of such other state or nation shall govern their rights and duties. Under Arkansas law, where one of the following provisions specifies the applicable law, that provision governs and a contrary agreement is effective only to the extent permitted by the law (including the conflict of laws rules) so specified:

- Rights of creditors against sold goods;
- Applicability of the chapter on leases;
- Applicability as to bank deposits and collections;
- Governing law in the chapter on funds transfers;
- Letters of credit;
- Applicability of the chapter on investment securities; and
- Law governing perfection, the effect of perfection or nonperfection, and the priority of security interests and agricultural liens.[199]

Where a guaranty is executed in another state and is to be performed in that same state, that state's law should govern any suit brought against a guarantor.[200]

199. *See* ARK. CODE ANN. § 4-1-301.
200. Lee v. Vaughn, 534 S.W.2d 221, 222 (Ark. 1976).

California State Law of Guaranties

Robert A. Zadek
Shadi J. Enos
Buchalter Nemer P.C.
55 Second Street, Suite 1700
San Francisco, California 94105-3493
Phone: (415) 227-0900
Fax: (415) 227-0770
www.buchalter.com

BuchalterNemer
A Professional Law Corporation

Contents

California State Law of Guaranties

Introduction: This chapter is intended to provide an overview of the guaranty and suretyship laws in California, particularly in the context of commercial lending transactions. As an abstract, the chapter offers a summary of germane concepts but does not purport to cover all nuances and variations that may arise in particular guaranty relationships.

To begin our discussion, we provide definitions of the following key terms in an effort to establish a consistent vernacular throughout the chapter and familiarize the reader with the basic concepts of suretyship law:

"Guarantor" means a person "who promises to answer for the debt, default, or miscarriage of another or hypothecates property as security therefore."[1]

"Guaranty" means a written contract between the guarantor and the obligee, pursuant to which the guarantor agrees to "answer for the debt, default, or miscarriage"[2] of the primary obligor.

"Obligee" means the person to whom the underlying obligation is owed.

"Primary Obligor" means the person who is liable for the underlying obligation to the obligee and whose default under such obligation would trigger the guarantor's obligation.

"Surety" means a guarantor. The California Civil Code abolished the distinction between a guarantor and a surety in 1939 and the terms are used interchangeably.[3]

"Underlying Obligation" means the obligation owed by the primary obligor to the obligee for which the guarantor promises to answer upon default of the primary obligor.

Example of Terms: The following is an example illustrating the interplay of the above-listed terms. It is not meant to demonstrate the complex dynamics that can exist in commercial lending facilities, but rather to acquaint the reader with the terminology.

> Borrower enters into a credit agreement with Lender for a $100 million working capital facility. Parent Holdco of Borrower promises Lender that if Borrower does not pay the principal, interest, and fees owed under the facility when due, Parent Holdco will make the payments. In this example, Borrower is the primary obligor, Lender is the obligee, and Parent Holdco is the guarantor or surety. The principal, interest, and fees owed to Lender are collectively referred to as the underlying obligation.

1. Cal. Civ. Code § 2787 (West 2012).
2. Cal. Civ. Code § 2787 (West 2012).
3. Cal. Civ. Code § 2787 (West 2012).

§ 1 Nature of the Guaranty Arrangement

In its simplest form, the California laws of guaranty and suretyship govern the rights and duties of three parties: the obligee, the primary obligor, and the guarantor. California generally follows the *Restatement of the Law Third, Suretyship and Guaranty (1996)*[4] (the "Restatement of Suretyship"), but the state has adopted some meaningful deviations. While courts continue to acknowledge the persuasive importance of the Restatement of Suretyship, a large part of California law is derived from judicial decisions. Accordingly, a practitioner in California will need to analyze both statutory law and case law.

1.1 Guaranty Relationships

Under a guaranty, the guarantor's liability is "secondary to, and derivative of the liability of the principal for that obligation."[5] Accordingly, the surety's obligation is triggered only when the primary obligor defaults.[6] If the primary obligor defaults, the surety's obligation will be coterminous with that of the principal obligor both in terms of amount owed and burden.[7]

To determine whether a suretyship relationship exists, California courts will not look for any particular form of agreement or language; rather, the courts will look to the specific intent of the parties to create a suretyship contract.[8] Part of this specific intent requirement is that a guarantor makes its promise to the obligee as opposed to the primary obligor.[9] While the specifics of suretyship contract formation will be discussed more fully in sections V and VI *supra*, it is important to initially note that courts will require a guaranty to be in writing and to be signed by the bound parties.[10]

1.2 Other Suretyship Relationships

The scope of this survey is limited to consensual contractual relationships rather than guaranties created by legal incident or prescribed by statute.

4. The UCC Committee of the Business Law Section of the State Bar of California, *California Commentary on the Restatement of the Law Third, Suretyship and Guaranty*, 34 Loy. L.A. L. Rev. 231 (2000).
5. Morgan Creek Residential v. Kemp, 153 Cal. App. 4th 675, 685 (citing the California Supreme Court as its authority).
6. American Contractors Indem. Co. v. Saladino, 115 Cal. App. 4th 1262, 1268 (2d Dist. 2004) ("In the absence of default, the surety has no obligation."); *see also* Schmitt v Ins. Co. of N. Am., 230 Cal. App. 3d 245, 257 (4th Dist. 1991).
7. Cal. Civ. Code § 2809 (West 2012) ("The obligation of a surety must be neither larger in amount nor in other respects more burdensome than that of the principal; and if in its terms it exceeds it, it is reducible in proportion to the principal obligation.").
8. Superior Wholesale Elec. Co. v. Cameron, 264 Cal. App. 2d 488 (2d Dist. 1968) (citing Cal. Jur. 2d, Suretyship and Guaranty § 23).
9. King v. Smith, 33 Cal. 2d 71 (1948).
10. Cal. Civ. Code § 2793 (West 2012); Rose v. Feldman, 67 Cal. 100, 101 (1885).

§ 2 State Law Requirements for an Entity to Enter a Guaranty

In California, legal entities, such as corporations, limited liability companies (LLCs), and partnerships, are generally afforded the same rights as natural persons to enter into guaranties. For example, section 207(g) of the California Corporations Code provides that it is within the scope of a corporation's general powers "to assume obligations [and] enter into contracts, including contracts of guaranty or suretyship."[11] Section 17003 of the same code permits LLCs to issue guaranties unless the articles of organization of a particular company provide otherwise.[12] While California law governing partnerships does not expressly authorize partnerships to issue guaranties,[13] courts regularly enforce such guaranties.[14]

§ 3 Community Property Considerations

California is among a handful of states that impose community property laws.[15] Community property laws determine whether a particular spouse or the marital community is vested with right of control or ownership over the couple's property.[16] Community property laws apply to the real or personal property of a married couple, regardless of where such property is located, so long as it was acquired during the marriage and while the couple was domiciled in California.[17] Guaranties executed by persons in their individual capacities have the potential to create recourse to marital property that is not separately owned by a guarantor.

To avoid any conflicts with community property laws and ensure that a guarantor will be able to fulfill its duty to make full payment on the underlying obligation, prudent obligees will require the spouse of a guarantor acting in his/her individual capacity to acknowledge that the marital property is subject to the guaranty. This acknowledgment is included to estop the spouse from later claiming that his/her portion of the marital property may not be used to satisfy the underlying obligations. The language below is typical of a California spousal consent:

11. Cal. Corp. Code § 207(g) (West 2012) ("Subject to the provisions of Section 315, [a corporation may] assume obligations, enter into contracts, including contracts of guaranty or suretyship, ...").
12. Cal. Corp. Code § 17003 (West 2012).
13. Cal. Corp. Code § 15901.05 (West 2012).
14. *See, e.g.*, Jans v. Nelson, 83 Cal. App. 4th 848 (5th Cir. 2000).
15. *See* www.irs.gov/publications/p501/ar02.html for a list of community property states.
16. Cal. Fam. Code § 700 et seq.
17. Cal. Fam. Code § 760.

SAMPLE LANGUAGE: SPOUSAL CONSENT

"I, the undersigned and the spouse of __________, an individual, hereby acknowledge that my spouse has entered into that certain Guaranty in favor of obligee with respect to certain obligations of Primary Obligor, to make prompt and full payment and performance of the indebtedness described in the Guaranty on the terms set forth therein. I further acknowledge that all community property in which my spouse and I have an interest may be subject to any claim brought by the obligee in exercising its rights under the Guaranty. I hereby consent to the Guaranty to the extent required by applicable law to accomplish this purpose. I have read the Guaranty, understand its terms and conditions, and to the extent that I have felt it necessary, have retained independent legal counsel to advise me concerning the legal effect of the Guaranty and this Spousal Consent to Guaranty. I understand and acknowledge that obligee is relying on the validity and accuracy of this Spousal Consent to Guaranty in making financial accommodations to Primary Obligor. I also acknowledge that I have been advised to obtain independent counsel to represent my interests with respect to the Guaranty and this Spousal Consent to Guaranty."

§ 4 Choice of Law Considerations

Because parties entering into commercial loan transactions seek predictability in the enforcement of the underlying agreements, they often include a choice of law provision in the guaranty which expressly identifies the state law that will govern. While California courts generally enforce such provisions and apply the chosen state law, there are a number of cases where the courts have upset the parties' expectations and applied a different state law. For example, in *Mencor Enters. v. Hets Equities Corp.*, 190 Cal. App. 3d 432 (1987), the court refused to enforce a choice of law provision selecting Colorado state law on the basis that the loan agreement violated California's usury law and was thus contrary to California's public policy interests.[18] The California courts struggle with the issue of whether a choice of law provision should be enforced or disregarded and have consequently adopted a multitude of approaches to evaluating this issue.[19]

Some courts, though less commonly, apply the "modern choice-of-law theory" which emphasizes state sovereignty and governmental interests over

18. Mencor Enters. v. Hets Equities Corp., 190 Cal. App. 3d 432, 464 (1987). For a thorough discussion of the California cases voiding choice of law provisions see Mark J. Kelson, *Choice-of-Law, Venue, and Consent-to-Jurisdiction Provisions in California Commercial Lending Agreements: Can Good Draftsmanship Overcome Bad Choice-of-Law Doctrine*, 23 Loy. L.A. L. Rev. 1337 (1990).

19. Mark J. Kelson, *Choice-of-Law, Venue, and Consent-to-Jurisdiction Provisions in California Commercial Lending Agreements: Can Good Draftsmanship Overcome Bad Choice-of-Law Doctrine*, 23 Loy. L.A. L. Rev. 1337 (1990).

contractual freedom.[20] Other courts apply the more common "autonomy principle," echoed in section 187 of the Restatement (Second) of the Conflict of Laws,[21] which stresses adherences to the parties' choice of law selection.[22] Even when the Restatements approach is applied, however, there have been cases where the California courts have utilized "exceptions to circumvent the wishes of the parties in regard to choice of law." Accordingly, obligees and guarantors must recognize the risk that a choice of law provision may not be enforced by a California court.

§ 5 Consideration; Sufficiency of Past Consideration

In determining whether a guaranty has been properly formed, courts will require evidence that the general rules of contract formation have been satisfied. In this aspect, the laws of suretyship overlap considerably with the laws of contract, so much so that the Reporter Notes to the Restatement of Suretyship officially recognize the contribution of the Restatement of Contract.[23]

The threshold consideration for almost all contracts is whether sufficient consideration exists. While consideration remains an element of guaranty formation, California courts generally presume the existence of consideration in suretyship agreements[24] but allow the presumption to be rebutted by a challenging party.[25] There are a few instances, however, where consideration is not presumed and must be demonstrated. For example, when the guaranty is created after the underlying obligation is in place, parties must demonstrate consideration independent of the underlying obligation.[26] However, courts may find new consideration exists where the obligee forbears on its rights to any remedies it might have with respect to the underlying obligation. For example, a lender forbearing on its right to sue a debtor[27] or providing a maturity extension to the debtor[28] may constitute sufficient consideration. It must be demonstrated, however, that the obligee's forbearance was pursuant to an agreement (whether express or implied) with the parties and that the exercise of such remedies would have maintained a substantive right.[29]

20. *Id.*
21. Restatement (Second) of Conflict of Laws § 187 (1971).
22. Mark J. Kelson, *Choice-of-Law, Venue, and Consent-to-Jurisdiction Provisions in California Commercial Lending Agreements: Can Good Draftsmanship Overcome Bad Choice-of-Law Doctrine*, 23 Loy. L.A. L. Rev. 1337, 1383 (1990).
23. Peter A. Alces, *The Law of Suretyship and Guaranty*, p. 94 (West 2011).
24. Cal. Civ. Code § 2793 (West 2012) (stating that a guaranty "need not express a consideration.").
25. *See, e.g.*, In re Thomson's Estate, 165 Cal. 290 (1913) and Pierce v. Wright, 117 Cal. App. 2d 718 (1st Dist. 1953).
26. Pacific States Sav. & Loan v Stowell, 7 Cal. App. 2d. 280, 281 (1935) (citing Cal. Civ. Code § 2792 and stating that "a guaranty of antecedent debt of another must be supported by consideration distinct from the original obligation.").
27. In re Estate of Thomson, 165 Cal. 290, 296 (1913).
28. Drovers' Nat. Bank v. Browne, 88 Cal. App. 716 (2d Dist. 1928).
29. In re Estate of Thomson, 165 Cal. 290, 296 (1913).

§ 6 Notice of Acceptance

Generally, the rules of offer and acceptance apply to a guaranty as they would to any other contract.[30] However, California courts will not require evidence that the obligee expressly accepted the guarantor's offer unless the guarantor required express acceptance.[31] Rather, implied acceptance will be sufficient. For example, a lender may be deemed to have accepted a guarantor's offer of suretyship if the lender advances funds to a borrower after the guarantor extended its offer of guaranty.[32] Implied acceptance is only permitted, however, where the obligee was aware of the existence of the offer and advanced the funds in reliance on the offer.[33]

Furthermore, notice of acceptance is not required under the California Civil Code in cases where the suretyship obligation is absolute.[34] An absolute suretyship obligation is one where the guarantor unconditionally promises to answer for the underlying obligation if the principal obligor defaults. The guarantor need not use the term absolute or even unconditional for the guaranty to be deemed absolute. In fact, one court has held that a guaranty was absolute because the guarantor promised that upon the default of the primary obligor, it "[would] well and truly pay the said rent or any arrears thereof."[35]

§ 7 Interpretation of Guaranties

7.1 General Principles

As with the formation of a guaranty, the California laws of contract also apply to the interpretation of a guaranty.[36] Generally, contract interpretation is a question of law, whether such interpretation is made directly from the language of the contract or from extrinsic evidence.[37] The interpretation becomes an issue of fact rather than law when varying evidence is presented to clarify the meaning of a term or provision.[38]

Courts will favor an interpretation of the contract that best gives effect to the parties' mutual intentions[39] and the purpose of the guaranty at the time to which the contract was entered.[40] To ascertain the parties' mutual intentions, the court will first look to the language of the agreement[41] unless "through

30. *See, e.g.*, California Bank v. Kenoyer, 2 Cal. App. 2d 367 (1934); R.H. Herron Co. v. Flack, 46 Cal. App. 374 (1920).
31. Cal. Civ. Code § 2795 (West 2012).
32. Hickey Pipe & Supply Co. v. Fitzgerald, 3 Cal. App. 2d 389 (1934).
33. Skaggs-Stone, Inc. v. La Batt, 182 Cal. App. 2d 142 (1960).
34. Cal. Civ. Code § 2795 (West 2012).
35. Thorpe v. Story, 10 Cal. 2d 104, 107-18 (1937).
36. Cal. Civ. Code § 2837 (West 2012); Standard Oil Co. v. Houser, 101 Cal. App. 2d 480, 487 (1950).
37. In re Estate of Thomson Estate, 165 Cal. 290, 296 (1913).
38. In re Estate of Thomson Estate, 165 Cal. 290, 296 (1913); United California Bank v. THC Fin. Corp., 557 F.2d 1351, 1360 (9th Cir. 1977).
39. Airlines Reporting Corp. v. United States Fidelity & Guaranty Co., 31 Cal. App. 4th 1458 (1995).
40. Bank of America Nat. Trust & Sav. Ass'n v. Waters, 209 Cal. App. 2d 635 (1962).
41. Standard Oil Co. of Cal. v. Houser, 101 Cal. App. 2d 480 (1950).

fraud, mistake, or accident, a written contract fails to express the real intention of the parties, [in such case the] intention is to be regarded, and the erroneous parts of the writing disregarded."[42] Furthermore, in construing the obligations of the guarantor where the contract is ambiguous, California Civil Code section 2799 requires the court to accept the terms that do not impose any risk greater to the guarantor than it would have incurred "under those terms which are most common in similar contracts at the place where the principal contract is to be performed."[43]

7.2 Guaranty of Payment versus Guaranty of Collection

California distinguishes between guaranties of payment and guaranties of collection.[44] A guaranty of payment is one where the guarantor is required to answer for the underlying obligation as soon as the primary obligor defaults. Whereas, in a guaranty of collection, the guarantor is not required to answer for the underlying obligation until the primary obligor defaults and recovery from the primary obligor cannot be obtained[45] because "(1) execution of judgment against the [primary obligor] has been returned unsatisfied, (2) the [primary obligor] is insolvent or in an insolvency proceeding, (3) the [primary obligor] cannot be served with process, or (4) it is otherwise apparent that payment cannot be obtained from the [primary obligor]."[46]

7.3 Language Regarding the Revocation of Guaranties

Section 2815 of the California Civil Code permits a guarantor to revoke a continuing guaranty with respect to future transactions so long as any continuing consideration has been renounced.[47] A guarantor who gives notice of its revocation pursuant to section 2815 essentially "freezes" its liability to those debts acquired by the primary obligor up to the date of the notice.[48] All obligee advances made to the primary obligor after the notice will not be the responsibility of the guarantor.[49]

As a corollary to this law, new advances made without the objection of the guarantor will be deemed new consideration and as such strip the guarantor of its ability to revoke the guaranty with respect to those advances.[50]

Another situation in which a guarantor cannot revoke is where the contract specifies a duration for the underlying obligation and the guarantor is meant to act as a surety to the underlying obligation for such time period. While the guarantor may not be permitted to revoke the guaranty in this instance, it may seek a written release from the obligee. Additionally, the court in *Nielsen v. Davidson* held that a guaranty cannot be revoked after it has "been

42. Cal. Civ. Code § 1640 (West 2012).
43. Cal. Civ. Code § 2799 (West 2012).
44. Cal. U. Com. Code § 3419(d) (West 2012).
45. Menefee v. Robert A. Klein & Co., 121 Cal. App. 294 (1932).
46. Cal. U. Com. Code § 3-419(d) (West 2012).
47. Cal. Civ. Code § 2815 (West 2012); Sharp v. Miller, 57 Cal. 415 (1881).
48. Pearl v. General Motors Acceptance Corp., 13 Cal. App. 4th 1023, 1030 (4th Dist. 1993).
49. *Id.*
50. Valentine v. Donohoe-Kelly Banking Co., 133 Cal. 191 (1901).

acted upon and the object for which it was executed has been obtained" by the principal obligor.[51]

Another case in which courts have held a guaranty cannot be revoked is when the guarantor has waived its rights under section 2815. In enacting section 2815, the California legislature was attempting to protect guarantors "from seemingly unending continuing guarantees of loans to debtors which frequently were beyond the control of the Guarantors."[52] Nonetheless, the California courts have held that if a guarantor is not deterred by the prospect of being responsible for future (and even unforeseen) advances to the primary obligor, public policy demands the guarantor be permitted to contract freely and expressly waive its rights under section 2815.[53]

The consequences of a section 2815 waiver is that a guarantor may be required to answer for debt that is completely unrelated to the debt which prompted the guarantor to initially become a guarantor. Imagine, for example, the scenario where a lender and a borrower enter into a working capital facility for the borrower's company, which the guarantor agrees to irrevocably guaranty all past and future debts of the company to the lender. Then, the borrower decides to take out a separate loan with the bank for an independent reason (say, to purchase a jet). If the guarantor waived its right to section 2815, it could be on the hook for the jet loan as well as the original working capital facility.

See section IX *supra* for an expanded discussion on the waiver of suretyship rights.

7.4 "Continuing"

In an ongoing lender-borrower relationship, the lender will typically require the guarantor to enter into an analogous ongoing relationship, known as a continuing guaranty. A continuing guaranty is "a guaranty relating to a future liability of the principal, under successive transactions, which either continues his liability or from time to time renews it after it has been satisfied...."[54]

To determine whether a guaranty is continuing, courts will first look to the language of the contract and only consider parol evidence where the terms are ambiguous.[55] Courts have consistently held that a guaranty will not be deemed continuing unless the parties clearly intended so.[56] Where there is doubt as to the parties' intent, courts will presume the suretyship was not intended to be continuing.[57]

51. Nielson v. Davidson, 66 Cal. App. 442, 444 (1924).
52. Pearl v. General Motors Acceptance Corp., 13 Cal. App. 4th 1023, 1030 (4th Dist. 1993).
53. Id.
54. Cal. Civ. Code § 2814 (West 2012).
55. Berg Metals Corp. v. Wilson, 170 Cal. App. 2d 559, 569 (2d Dist. 1959).
56. Carson v. Reid, 137 Cal. 253, 256-57 (1902).
57. *Id.*

7.5 "Absolute and Unconditional"

California law further categorizes guaranties as either absolute or conditional. An absolute guaranty is one in which the guarantor's performance is not subject to any conditions beyond default of the principal obligation.[58] Conversely, in the case of a conditional guaranty, performance of the guarantor explicitly requires not only default on the part of the principal obligor but also the fulfillment of specified conditions precedent.[59] For example, the obligee may be required to exhaust its remedies against the principal obligor or exhaust any security to which it is entitled, prior to calling upon the guarantor. The California Civil Code provides that guaranty is unconditional unless its terms require conditions precedent to guarantor's liability.[60]

§ 8 Defenses of the Guarantor; Set-off

A guarantor's defenses can be categorized as follows: (1) defenses of the primary obligor; (2) "suretyship defenses"; and (3) other defenses. As a threshold matter, California courts have held that a guarantor's defense arises only after the obligee becomes aware of the guarantor's existence.[61] Prior to the obligee's awareness of the guarantor, the only defenses an obligee may face are those presented by the primary obligor.[62]

8.1 Defenses of the Primary Obligor

8.1.1 General

Subject to exceptions set forth in sections VIII.A.2 and VIIIA.3 below, a guarantor is only liable if the underlying obligation is enforceable against the primary obligor.[63] If the underlying obligation is deemed to be unenforceable, courts have held there can be no consideration for the guaranty[64] and consequently the guaranty is unenforceable. The California Civil Code further provides that the guarantor "is not liable if for any other reason there is no liability upon the part of the principal at the time of the execution of the contract, or the liability of the principal thereafter ceases, unless the Surety has assumed liability with knowledge of the existence of the defense."[65]

58. Bank of America Nat. Trust & Savings Ass'n v. McRae, 81 Cal. App. 2d 1 (1947).
59. *Id.*
60. Cal. Civ. Code § 2806 (West 2012).
61. Westinghouse Credit Corp. v. Wolfer 10 Cal. App. 3d 63, 68 (2d Dist. 1970).
62. *Id.*
63. Thomas Haverty Co. v. Pacific Indemnity Co., 215 Cal. 555 (1932).
64. Taylor v. Exnicious, 197 Cal. 442 (1925).
65. Cal. Civ. Code § 2810 (West 2012).

8.1.2 When Guarantor May assert Primary Obligor's Defense

The logical extension to the principle that a guarantor's liability is coextensive with the primary obligor's liability is that a guarantor is generally permitted to raise the same defenses that the primary obligor would be permitted to raise against the obligee.[66] For example, a surety may raise the defense that the contract between the obligee and the primary obligor is unenforceable because of illegality,[67] want of consideration,[68] fraud, duress,[69] or improper execution.[70]

At least one court has held, however, that a guarantor cannot successfully raise the primary obligor's defense that the contract between the obligee and the primary obligor was not faithfully performed.[71] The court reasoned that since the obligation of the guarantor was independent of the performance of the underlying contract, the guarantor's duty was unaffected by the less than perfect performance of the contract.[72]

Even if a guarantor is permitted to raise a defense held by a primary obligor, the guarantor may freely and proactively waive such defense. See section IX *supra* for an expanded discussion on the waiver of defenses.

8.1.3 Defenses that May not be Raised by Guarantor

California statutory law prohibits a guarantor from raising the primary obligor's personal disability as a defense to the guaranty even in cases where the disability would render the contract unenforceable against the primary obligor.[73] Additionally, a guarantor may not object on the basis that the primary obligor filed bankruptcy after the date of the guaranty.[74]

8.2 "Suretyship" Defenses

8.2.1 Change in Identity of Principal Obligor

Generally, the release of the primary obligor discharges the guarantor.[75] One exception to the general rule, as set forth in California Civil Code section 2824, states that a guarantor who has been indemnified by the primary obligor remains liable to the obligee to the extent of the indemnity, even if the obligee, without the guarantor's assent, modified the contract or released the principal obligor.[76]

---

66. United States Leasing Corp. v. DuPont, 69 Cal. 2d 275, 290 (1968).
67. Wells v. Comstock, 46 Cal. 2d 528 (1956).
68. Wezel v. Cale, 175 Cal. 208 (1917).
69. *Id.*
70. City Nat'l Bank v. Lemco Mfg. Co., 57 Cal. App. 566, 567 (1922).
71. Los Angeles Stone Co. v. National Surety Co., 178 Cal. 247, 250 (Cal. 1918) ("The obligation of the surety does not depend upon the validity of the contract or the faithful performance thereof by the contractor.").
72. Los Angeles Stone Co. v. National Surety Co., 178 Cal. 247, 250 (Cal. 1918).
73. Cal. Civ. Code § 2810 (West 2012).
74. Superior Wholesale Elec. Co. v. Cameron, 264 Cal. App. 2d 488 (2d Dist. 1968) ("The surety remains fully liable when the obligation of the principal is discharged in bankruptcy.").
75. Superior Wholesale Elec. Co. v. Cameron, 264 Cal. App. 2d 488 (2d Dist. 1968); Bloom v. Bender, 48 Cal. 2d 793 (1957).
76. Cal. Civ. Code § 2824 (West 2012).

Another exception is that a guarantor's obligations are not released if the guarantor agrees to remain liable in spite of the primary obligor's being released from its obligations.[77] While the guarantor may provide such consent at the time of or after the primary obligor is released from its obligations, the more likely scenario is that the guarantor will provide such consent proactively in the guaranty.[78] For example, in *Bloom v. Bender*, the court held that a guarantor remained liable to the obligee after the primary obligor had been released because the guaranty stated that the suretyship obligations would "not be affected by . . . the acceptance of any settlement or composition offered . . ." even though such agreement was executed prior to the guarantor's knowledge of the release.[79]

California statutes have further eroded the general rule by providing that a guarantor is not discharged of its obligations unless there is some act or omission by the obligee.[80] Since a bankruptcy does not require the intervention or omission of the obligee, a guarantor will remain liable on the underlying obligations even if a primary obligor is released in accordance with bankruptcy laws.[81]

In addition, if the principal obligor dies prior to the full performance of the underlying obligation, the guarantor will remain liable where the underlying obligations were not specific to the principal obligor.[82] The obligations will be deemed specific to the primary obligor if, for example, the "character, credit and substance of the [primary obligor] was an inducement to the contract."[83] Since a guaranty of payment does not require services personal to the primary obligor, the death of the principal obligor would not release the guarantor.[84]

8.2.2 *Modification of the Underlying Obligation, Including Release*

California statutory law permits the guarantor to assert the defense of exoneration by modification of the underlying obligation.[85] To successfully assert such a defense, the guarantor must demonstrate that the principal obligation has been altered or the remedies of the obligee against the principal obligor have been impaired or suspended in some way without the guarantor's consent.[86] While the guarantor need not show that the alteration was prejudicial to the surety,[87] it must show that the changes altered the "meaning, nature, or subject matter of the contract."[88] Courts have held, for example, that absent the

77. Bloom v. Bender, 48 Cal. 2d 793 (1957).
78. *Id.*
79. *Id.*
80. Cal. Civ. Code § 2825 (West 2012).
81. Bloom v. Bender, 48 Cal. 2d 793 (1957).
82. Albany v. United States Fidelity & Guaranty Co., 38 Cal. App. 466 (1918).
83. Central Contra Costa Sanitary Dist. v. National Surety Corp., 112 Cal. App. 2d 61, 67-68 (1952) (citing Estate of Burke, 198 Cal. 163, 167 (1926)).
84. Turner v. Fidelity & Deposit Co., 187 Cal. 76 (1921).
85. Cal. Civ. Code § 2819 (West 2012).
86. Wexler v. McLucas, 48 Cal. App. 3d Supp. 9, 12-14 (Dep't Super. Ct. 1975).
87. Turner v. Fidelity & Deposit Co., 187 Cal. 76 (1921).
88. Cal. Jur. 3d, Suretyship and Guaranty, Alteration Must Be Act of Creditor For Surety to Be Exonerated § 45 (West Supp. 2011).

guarantor's consent, a change in the date, time, or place of payment, amount of principal, or rate of interest of a promissory note is sufficient to exonerate a surety's obligation.[89] Conversely, a change is not sufficient if it only varies the form[90] or if it is made to further the intent of the parties.[91]

Even if a surety is able to demonstrate the foregoing, the surety is only exonerated to the extent it is not indemnified by the principal obligor.[92] Where a surety has been indemnified by the principal obligor, an exception applies that requires the surety to remain liable to the obligee to the extent of the indemnity.[93] This exception applies even if the obligee modified the underlying obligation without the guarantor's consent.[94] The California courts have made it clear, however, that the guarantor must have "*received* the indemnified amount, physical collateral or a lien on property . . . [and that a] mere agreement to indemnify . . . is insufficient to trigger the exception."[95]

Section 2822 of the California Civil Code further narrows the applicability of the modification defense by providing that a guarantor is not exonerated if the obligee accepts partial payment from the primary obligor on the underlying obligation without the guarantor's prior consent.[96]

The statutes also provide that "a promise by a creditor is for any cause void, or voidable by the creditor at the creditor's option, does not prevent it from altering the obligation or suspending or impairing the Surety's remedy."[97]

As with the defense set forth in section VIII.B.1 *infra*, consent of the guarantor prohibits the application of the defense.[98] Also like the defense in section VIII.B.1, the guarantor may provide its consent in advance of, at the time of, or even after the alteration at issue.[99]

8.2.3 Release or Impairment of Security for the Underlying Obligation

A guarantor is "entitled to the benefit of every security for the performance of the principal obligation held by the creditor, or by a co-surety at the time of entering into the contract of suretyship, or acquired by him afterwards, whether the Surety was aware of the security or not."[100] Consequently, if the obligee releases security without the guarantor's consent, the guarantor will

89. Southern Cal. First Nat. Bank v. Olsen, 41 Cal. App. 3d 234 (2d Dist. 1974).
90. Cal. Jur. 3d, Suretyship and Guaranty, Alteration Must Be Act of Creditor For Surety to Be Exonerated § 45 (West Supp. 2011).
91. First Nat. Bank of Redondo v. Spalding, 177 Cal. 217 (1918).
92. Cal. Civ. Code § 2819 (West 2012).
93. Cal. Civ. Code § 2824 (West 2012).
94. Cal. Civ. Code § 2824 (West 2012).
95. Texaco Refining & Marketing, Inc. v. Aetna Cas. & Sur. Co., Inc., 895 F.2d 637 (9th Cir. 1990) (referencing the Law of Suretyship § 6.25, at 148; Conners, *California Surety and Fidelity Bond Practice* § 25.13, at 352 (1969)).
96. Cal. Civ. Code §§ 2819, 2822(b) (West 2012).
97. Cal. Civ. Code § 2820 (West 2012).
98. Krueger v. Bank of America, 145 Cal. App. 3d 204 (2d Dist. 1983).
99. Bloom v. Bender, 48 Cal. 2d 793 (1957); Southern Cal. First Nat. Bank v. Olsen, 41 Cal. App. 3d 234 (2d Dist. 1974).
100. Cal. Civ. Code § 2849 (West 2012).

be discharged.[101] Nonetheless, a guarantor may, by express agreement, waive its benefit to any security put forth by the primary obligor.[102]

8.2.4 The Gradsky Defense

The *Gradsky* defense is an estoppel-based defense which arose not from the statutes but from the courts in the famous case *Union Bank v. Gradsky.*[103] In 1968, the *Gradsky* court held that an obligee was estopped from recovering a deficiency judgment against a guarantor because the obligee elected to non-judicially foreclose on the primary obligor's property.[104] The court reasoned that since the obligee elected "to pursue a remedy which destroys both the security and the possibility of the Surety's reimbursement from the [primary obligor], the [obligee] is thereafter estopped from pursuing the Guarantor . . . ."[105] Accordingly, the *Gradsky* defense can be summarized as the "impairment of the right of recourse against the principal obligor will result in the complete exoneration of the secondary obligor."[106]

The *Gradsky* case is perhaps as notable for the creation of a new defense as it was for the expansion of the waivers that followed shortly after the court decision. After *Gradsky*, lenders began including waivers to estop guarantors from asserting that their rights were impermissibly impaired by the lender. Typical language used in subsequent contracts included: "Guarantor authorizes bank at its sole discretion . . . to . . . exercise any right or remedy it may have with respect to . . . any collateral . . . [and] Guarantor shall be liable to Bank for any deficiency resulting from the exercise by it of any such remedy, even though any rights which Guarantor may have against others might be . . . destroyed."[107] Opposition to this new waiver arose in *Cathay Bank v. Lee.*[108] The *Cathay* court held that such language was an insufficient waiver as it only addressed the guarantor's rights and "[did] not provide the [guarantor] with any actual awareness of the *Gradsky* defense"[109] or related statutory provisions such as section 580d of the California Code of Civil Procedure.

The combined effect of the two seminal cases, *Gradsky* and *Cathay Bank*, caused a sea change in the California lending world. No longer was an obligee safe to rely on a guarantor's written, express waiver of defenses. To remedy the uncertainty that followed *Gradsky* and *Cathay Bank,* the California legislature enacted section 2856 of the California Civil Code which expressly laid out which defenses a guarantor was permitted to waive and even provided safe harbor language for the wary obligee. See section IX *supra* for an expanded

101. Eppinger v. Kendrick, 114 Cal. 620 (1896).
102. Brunswick Corp. v. Hays, 16 Cal. App. 3d 134 (2d Dist. 1971); Wiener v. Van Winkle, 273 Cal. App. 2d 774 (2d Dist. 1969).
103. Union Bank v. Gradsky, 265 Cal. App. 2d 40 (1968).
104. Cathay Bank v. Lee, 14 Cal. App. 4th 1533 (1993) (citing Union Bank v. Gradsky, 265 Cal. App. 2d 40 (1968)).
105. Union Bank v. Gradsky, 265 Cal. App. 2d 40 (1968).
106. The UCC Committee of the Business Law Section of the State Bar of California, *California Commentary on the Restatement of the Law Third, Suretyship and Guaranty*, 34 Loy. L.A. L. Rev. 231, 290 (2000).
107. Cathay Bank v. Lee, 18 Cal. Rptr. 2d 420 (Ct. App. 1993).
108. *Id.*
109. *Id.*

discussion on how a guarantor may waive the *Gradsky* defense under current California law.

8.2.5 *Sumitomo* Defense—Voiding the Obligation due to Misrepresentation

In 1968, the California Supreme Court held that with a revocable continuing guaranty, an obligee has a duty to disclose to the guarantor information it reasonably believes will materially increase the guarantor's risk in excess of the amount of risk the guarantor intended to assume, if (i) the obligee believed the guarantor was unaware of such facts, and (ii) the obligee had a reasonable opportunity to inform the guarantor of such facts.[110] Where the obligee fails to convey such material information, the guarantor may raise the defense of a material misrepresentation, which if proved, serves to void the guarantor's obligation.[111]

Since section 2856 of the California Civil Code does not expressly state that a guarantor may waive its rights to notice of any adverse change in the financial condition of the primary obligor or of any other fact that might increase the guarantor's risk under a guaranty, there is some uncertainty as to whether a "waiver" would be enforced. Nonetheless, out of abundance of caution, most commercial guaranties will require the guarantor to waive such right.

The approach that is more likely to be enforced, however, is an estoppel against the guarantor based on the argument that the guarantor agreed to assume responsibility of keeping abreast of the primary obligor's financial condition. Accordingly, most guaranties also include a covenant similar to the below:

> "Guarantor acknowledges and agrees that it has the sole responsibility for, and has adequate means of, obtaining from [Primary Obligor] and any other Guarantor such information concerning the financial condition, business, and operations of [Primary Obligor] and any such other Guarantor as the Guarantor requires, and that [Obligee] has no duty, and Guarantor is not relying on [Obligee] at any time, to disclose to Guarantor any information relating to the business, operations, or financial condition of [Primary Obligor] or any other Guarantor (the Guarantor waiving any duty on the part of the [Obligee] to disclose such information and any defense relating to the failure to provide the same)."

8.2.6 Performance of the Underlying Obligation

The guarantor is exonerated if the underlying obligation is performed or if an offer to perform has been made.[112] If the obligee accepts partial satisfaction of the underlying obligation, the guarantor is released only to the extent of the

110. *See* Sumitomo Bank v. Iwasaki, 70 Cal. 2d 81, 84 (1968).
111. *See* Sumitomo Bank v. Iwasaki, 70 Cal. 2d 81, 84 (1968).
112. Cal. Civ. Code § 2839 (West 2012).

accepted partial satisfaction.[113] However, the California Civil Code provides that "if the surety is liable upon only a portion of an [underlying] obligation and the principal [obligor] provides partial satisfaction of the [underlying obligation], the principal may designate the portion of the [underlying obligation] that is to be satisfied."[114] It further provides that "an agreement by a creditor to accept from the principal [obligor] a sum less than the balance owed on the original obligation, without the prior consent of the surety and without any other change to the underlying agreement between the [obligee] and principal [obligor], does not exonerate the surety for the lesser sum agreed upon by the [obligee] and principal [obligor]."[115]

8.2.7 Release of Co-surety

California Civil Code section 1543 provides that the release of a joint debtor does not release the underlying obligation of any other joint debtor, except where such joint debtors are merely guarantors. The courts have nonetheless interpreted this statute to mean that where guarantors are jointly liable, a release of one guarantor does not release the obligations of any other co-guarantor.[116] California Code of Civil Procedure section 877 provides that where a co-obligor mutually subject to contribution rights pursues a settlement in good faith prior to a verdict or judgment, the co-obligors will not be discharged from liability but their claims will be reduced by the amount of the settlement or the consideration paid for it, whichever is higher.[117] On the other hand, the same provision provides that the settling obligor is discharged from liability for contribution.[118]

8.3 Other Defenses

8.3.1 Modification of the Guaranty

A guarantor and an obligee are free to enter into a contract to release the guarantor from the original guaranty.[119] However, California Civil Code section 2821 cautions obligees by providing that "the rescission of an agreement altering the original obligation of [the primary obligor], or impairing the remedy of the [obligee] does not restore the liability of the surety who has been exonerated by such agreement."[120]

113. Cal. Civ. Code § 2822(a) (West 2012).
114. Cal. Civ. Code § 2822(a) (West 2012).
115. Cal. Civ. Code § 2822(b) (West 2012).
116. Oil Tool Exchange, Inc. v. Schuh, 67 Cal. App. 2d 288, 296 (1944) (citing Brown v. Pacific Coast Agency, 53 Cal. App. 788 , 791 (1st Dist. 1921)).
117. Cal. Civ. Code § 1543 (West 2012); Code Civ. Proc. § 877 (West 2012).
118. Cal. Code Civ. Proc. § 877 (West 2012).
119. Cox v. Miller, 15 Cal. App. 2d 494 (3d Dist. 1936).
120. Cal. Civ. Code § 2821 (West 2012).

8.3.2 *Failure to Pursue Primary Obligor*

A guarantor may require the obligee to pursue the primary obligor.[121] Alternatively, a guarantor may require the obligee to pursue any remedy the obligee is entitled to pursue that would lighten the guarantor's burden if the guarantor is not able to pursue such remedy. If the obligee fails to proceed against the primary obligor or such other remedy as the guarantor requested, the guarantor is exonerated to the extent it is prejudiced.[122] Likewise, the guarantor is entitled to have the obligee first seek satisfaction of the underlying obligation from the primary obligor's property before looking to the guarantor's pledged property.[123]

8.3.3 *Statute of Limitations*

California Code of Civil Procedure imposes, with certain exceptions, a four-year statute of limitations on written contractual obligations.[124] The courts have ruled, however, that a guarantor is not exonerated merely because the statute of limitations has run against the primary obligor.[125] They have also held that tolling of the statute of limitations as to the primary obligor is ineffective as to a guarantor.[126]

With respect to the statute of limitations as it applies to a coguarantor's cause of action against the primary obligor, the California Supreme Court held that "where, at the time a paying cosurety received a promissory note from another cosurety as a contribution payment, the statute of limitations had expired on the paying cosurety's cause of action for reimbursement against the principal obligor, the statute of limitations had also expired on the reimbursement claim of the cosurety tendering the promissory note."[127]

8.3.4 *Statute of Frauds*

The California Civil Code requires that, absent an applicable exception, a contract that creates a secondary obligation, such as a guaranty, be in writing and signed by the secondary obligor.[128] One exception to the statute of frauds is provided in section 2794(4) of the California Civil Code. Pursuant to section 2794(4), a contract to answer for the obligation of another is not within the statute of frauds if the promise is made in connection with consideration advantageous to the promisor.[129]

---

121. Cal. Code Civ. Proc. § 877 (West 2012).
122. Cal. Civ. Code § 2845 (West 2012).
123. Cal. Civ. Code § 2850 (West 2012).
124. Cal. Code. Civ. Proc. § 337 (West 2012).
125. *See, e.g.*, Regents of the Univ. of Cal. v. Hartford Accident & Indem. Co., 21 Cal. 3d 624, 639 (1978).
126. 231 Cal. App. 3d 967, 971 (1991) ("[A] payment by a principal debtor will not operate to toll the statute of limitations as to a guarantor.").
127. The UCC Committee of the Business Law Section of the State Bar of California, *California Commentary on the Restatement of the Law Third, Suretyship and Guaranty*, 34 Loy. L.A. L. Rev. 231, 315 (2000) (citing In Stone v. Hammell, 83 Cal. 547, 551, 23 P. 703, 704 (1890)).
128. *See* Cal. Civ. Code § 2793 (West 2012).
129. *See* Cal. Civ. Code § 2794(4) (West 2012); Farr & Stone Ins. Brokers, Inc. v. Lopez, 61 Cal. App. 3d 618, 621 (1976); *see also* Cal. Civ. Code § 2794(1).

Another exception is one in which a guarantor receives consideration under circumstances that render it the principal obligor.[130] A holder of a financial instrument who transfers it and enters into a promise respecting such instrument is deemed to have made an original obligation that is not within the statute of frauds.[131]

Likewise, the statutes provide that an original obligation will be deemed to have been made when a holder of an instrument for the payment of money transfers such instrument and enters into a promise respecting such transfer. In this case, the new obligation will be deemed outside the statute of frauds.[132] The courts have also clarified that a guaranty does not exist within the statute of frauds where the guarantor made the promise to answer for the underlying obligation to the primary obligor in lieu of the obligee.[133]

8.4 Right of Set-off

California permits guarantors the right of set-off as a defense to payment. The right to set-off arises when the obligee is indebted to the guarantor pursuant to a contract separate from the underlying obligation and guarantor's debt owed to the obligee can be reduced by the reciprocal debt. The right of setoff is an equitable defense that is typically waived in commercial lending guaranties. Below is sample language that may be used in a guaranty to waive the right of set-off:

> "To the fullest extent permitted by applicable law, Guarantor hereby waives any right to assert against [Obligee], any defense (legal or equitable), set-off, counterclaim, or claim which such Guarantor may now or at any time hereafter have against [Primary Obligor] or any other party liable to [Obligee].
>
> Guarantor shall make all payments hereunder without set-off or counterclaim and free and clear of and without deduction for any taxes, levies, imposts, duties, charges, fees, deductions, withholdings, compulsory loans, restrictions, or conditions of any nature now or hereafter imposed or levied by any jurisdiction or any political subdivision thereof or taxing or other authority therein. The obligations of the Guarantor under this paragraph shall survive the payment in full of the [Underlying Obligations] and termination of this Guaranty."

§ 9 Waiver of Defenses by the Guarantor

As noted in section VIII.B.4 *infra*, California law pertaining to a guarantor's ability to waive its defenses has not always left the parties with a clear

130. Cal. Civ. Code § 2794(2) (West 2012).
131. *See* Cal. Civ. Code § 2794(6) (West 2012).
132. *See* Cal. Civ. Code § 2794(6) (West 2012).
133. King v. Smith, 33 Cal. 2d 71, 74 (1948).

understanding of what rights and in what manner these rights may be waived. However, in the wake of *Gradsky* and *Cathay Bank*, the California legislature adopted statutory regulations to provide clarity and certainty to guaranty law.

First, California Civil Code section 2856 provides that a guarantor may waive all defenses, whether arising under statutory or common law.[134] Accordingly, a guarantor may waive, among other things:

a. the rights afforded to it pursuant to sections 2787 to 2855, inclusive, namely the rights of subrogation, reimbursement, indemnification, and contribution and any of certain other statutory rights and defenses;[135]
b. the *Gradsky* defense; and
c. the rights or defenses that are based upon the application of sections 580a, 580b, 580d, or 726 of the Code of Civil Procedure to the principal's note or other obligation (namely, the rights and defenses that arise because the underlying obligation is secured by real property).

The validity of a waiver executed before January 1, 1997, will be determined by the application of the law that existed on the date that the waiver was executed.[136]

Next, with respect to how the guarantor must waive its rights and defenses, there is no required formula or mode of expression under current California law.[137] However, because some courts (most notably, *Cathay Bank*) prior to enactment of the expanded section 2856 deviated from the then predominant legal line of reasoning that no particular form of language was required for a guarantor to waive its defenses,[138] obligees began requiring explicit and lengthy waivers.[139] In enacting section 2856, the legislature essentially overruled the precedent set by *Cathay Bank* and made clear that a guarantor may "use any . . . language to express an intent to waive all rights and defenses of the surety by reason of any election of remedies by the creditor."

This expanded section 2856 provides guidance by stating that the following language would be sufficient, but not necessary, to waive the *Gradsky* defense: "The Guarantor waives all rights and defenses arising out of an election of remedies by the creditor, even though that election of remedies, such as a nonjudicial foreclosure with respect to security for a guaranteed obligation, has destroyed the Guarantor's rights of subrogation and reimbursement against the principal by the operation of section 580d of the Code of Civil Procedure or otherwise." Most guaranties now contain waivers permitted by section 2856.

134. *See* Cal. Civ. Code § 2856.
135. Cal. Civ. Code §§ 2787 to 2855 (West 2012).
136. Cal. Civ. Code § 2856(f) (West 2012).
137. *See* Cal. Civ. Code § 2856 (West 2012) and Mead v. Sanwa Bank Cal., 61 Cal. App. 4th 561, 571 (4th Dist. 1998).
138. *See, e.g.*, Bloom v. Bender, 48 Cal. 2d 793, 804 (1957); Union Bank v. Ross, 54 Cal. App. 3d 290, 294 (1976); Brunswick Corp. v. Hays, 16 Cal. App. 3d 134, 138-39 (1971).
139. *See, e.g.*, Cathay Bank v. Lee, 14 Cal. App. 4th 1533 (1993).

9.1 Defenses that cannot be Waived

Although California maintains broad waiver provisions for guarantors, there *are* limits. One limit is imposed by a body of law entirely separate from the suretyship and guaranty laws—the California Commercial Code (the "UCC"). Section 9-602 of the UCC prohibits debtors and obligors (including guarantors[140]) from waiving or varying certain enumerated rights in transactions governed by the UCC.[141] While section 9-602 expressly prohibits the enumerated waivers, the comments to the UCC clarify that the parties are free to settle claims even if such settlement includes a waiver that would have been prohibited by 9-602.[142]

Since the list of section 9-602 nonwaivable and nonvariable rights is expansive and is addressed in 13 different subsections, this chapter will not provide a comprehensive recital; rather, it will highlight a few key provisions that may not be waived. For example, section 9-602 prohibits the guarantor from waiving (i) the secured party's obligation to collect and enforce collateral in a commercially reasonable manner,[143] (ii) the guarantor's right to a response to requests for accounting, lists of collateral, and statement of account,[144] and (iii) the guarantor's rights to special methods of calculating surplus or deficiencies.[145] Section 9-602 does permit, however, the waivers listed in section 9-624.

Section 9-624 provides the following limited number of waivers a guarantor may make by entering into an authenticated agreement with the obligee after default of the primary obligor: (i) "the right to notification of disposition of collateral under section 9-611";[146] (ii) "the right to require disposition of collateral under section 9-620(e)";[147] and (iii) "the right to redeem collateral under section 9-623," except with respect to consumer-goods transactions.[148]

See also section VIII.B.5 *infra* addressing whether a *Sumitomo* defense may be waived.

§ 10 Third-party Pledgors—Defenses and Waiver Thereof

Under California law, a guarantor is not limited to a person who agrees to answer for the debt of another; it also includes a person who "hypothecates

140. Cal. U. Com. Code § 9102(a)(59) (West 2012) (defining an obligor to include any person who "owed payment or other performance of the obligation" or "is otherwise accountable in whole or in part for payment or other performance of the obligation").
141. Cal. U. Com. Code § 9602 (West 2012).
142. Cal. U. Com. Code § 9602, cmt. 3 (West 2012).
143. Cal. U. Com. Code § 9602(3) (West 2012).
144. Cal. U. Com. Code § 9602(2) (West 2012).
145. Cal. U. Com. Code § 9602(4)-(5) (West 2012).
146. Cal. U. Com. Code § 9624(a) (West 2012).
147. Cal. U. Com. Code § 9624(b) (West 2012).
148. Cal. U. Com. Code § 9624(c) (West 2012).

property as security" for another's debt.[149] Accordingly, a third-party pledgor is necessarily a guarantor. As a guarantor, a third-party pledgor is entitled to the full panoply of defenses discussed above.

§ 11 Scope of a Guaranty

Under California law, contracting parties are permitted great flexibility to narrow or expand the scope of a guaranty. For example, a guarantor can contractually limit the circumstances under which he may be liable by imposing prerequisites on the obligee. The guarantor can also limit the amount of his potential liability and the time frame under which he remains liable.[150]

11.1 Conditional Guaranties

An unconditional guaranty is one in which the liability of the guarantor is not contingent on the prior occurrence of some event or happening. Rather, the formation of the guaranty alone is sufficient to establish the guarantor's obligation. A guaranty will be presumed unconditional unless it calls for a "condition precedent to the liability of the surety."[151] A common example of such condition precedent is the requirement that the obligee seek satisfaction from the primary obligor prior to seeking satisfaction against the guarantor.

11.2 Carve-out Guaranties

Another way to narrow the scope of the guaranty is to limit the portion of the underlying obligation that is covered by the guaranty. For example, a guarantor may only guaranty 50 percent (in lieu of 100 percent) of a borrower's debt. So long as such carve-out is incorporated in the terms of the guaranty, California law will permit the limitation.

11.3 Continuing and Limited Guaranties

A guaranty can also be limited in terms of its temporal applicability. A continuing guaranty not only applies to a present underlying obligation but to any future liability of the primary obligor "under successive transactions, which either continue [the guarantor's] liability or from time to time renew it after it has been satisfied."[152] The issue of whether a guaranty is continuing or limited is determined by the language of agreement or by use of parol evidence if the language is ambiguous.[153] California courts have held that where "it is evident that the object is to give a standing credit to the principal, to be used

149. Cal. Civ. Code § 2787 (West 2012); *see also* Pearl v. Gen. Motors Acceptance Corp., 13 Cal. App. 4th 1023, 1028 (1993).
150. Berg Metals Corp. v. Wilson, 170 Cal. App. 2d 559, 569 (Cal. App. 2d Dist. 1959).
151. Cal. Civ. Code § 2806 (West 2012).
152. Cal. Civ. Code § 2814 (West 2012).
153. Berg Metals Corp. v. Wilson, 170 Cal. App. 2d 559, 569 (Cal. App. 2d Dist. 1959).

from time to time either indefinitely or for a certain period, it is deemed a continuing guaranty."[154] The intent of the parties to create a continuing guaranty, however, must be clear.

A continuing guaranty is not synonymous with an irrevocable guaranty. Pursuant to California Civil Code section 2815, a guarantor may revoke a continuing guaranty with respect to future transaction "unless there is a continuing consideration as to such transactions which he does not renounce."[155] The practical implication of section 2815 in a commercial finance context is that without a waiver of section 2815, a guarantor of a revolving line of credit, for example, may revoke its guaranty at any time with respect to future extensions of credit.

§ 12 Jointly and Severally Liable Guarantors—The Guarantors' Rights to Collect from Coguarantors

Where there are multiple guarantors, the guarantors can be jointly, severally, or jointly and severally liable to the obligee.[156] California statutes provide that where there is ambiguity as to which liability arrangement has been mutually agreed by all parties, it will be presumed that the guarantors are jointly and not severally liable.[157] In contrast, the parties will be presumed to be jointly and severally liable when either (i) "all the parties who unite in a promise receive some past or present benefit from the consideration;"[158] or (ii) when "a promise is made in the singular number but executed by several persons."[159]

12.1 Contribution from Coguarantor

Section 2848 of the California Civil Code permits the guarantor, upon satisfying the underlying obligation, to require contribution from any coguarantor. The statute requires the contribution to be provided by the coguarantors regardless of when they become guarantors of the underlying obligation.[160] Accordingly, a coguarantor may not protest its obligation of contribution on the basis that it became a guarantor subsequent to the guarantor who paid the underlying obligation. Furthermore, a co-surety cannot protest its obligation by arguing the guarantor must first seek reimbursement from the primary obligor; the obligation of contribution is primary.[161]

154. *Id.*
155. Pearl v. General Motors Acceptance Corp., 13 Cal. App. 4th 1023, 1028 (Cal. App. 4th Dist. 1993)
156. Cal. Civ. Code § 1430 (West 2012).
157. Cal. Civ. Code § 1431 (West 2012).
158. Cal. Civ. Code § 1659 (West 2012).
159. Cal. Civ. Code § 1660 (West 2012).
160. Cal. Civ. Code § 2848 (West 2012).
161. Taylor v. Reynolds, 53 Cal. 686 (1879).

Absent an agreement among the coguarantors allocating contribution, courts will presume contribution is to be shared equally among the sureties.[162] If one guarantor provides a greater portion of the underlying obligation than its required share, this guarantor may obtain contributions from the coguarantors.[163] Accordingly, a co-surety's obligations do not arise until a guarantor satisfies the underlying obligation in full or at least in an amount that exceeds its required share.

Even if a co-surety's obligations arise, the parties are free to contractually alter the obligations owed or to entirely release a coguarantor. Absent an agreement to the contrary, courts will impose the aforementioned contribution laws.

12.2 Subrogation against Coguarantors

A guarantor that has satisfied the underlying obligation is entitled to security held by the obligee when the guaranty was executed or at any point thereafter even if the guarantor did not know such security existed.[164] Accordingly, a guarantor can step into the shoes of the obligee and enforce the obligee's rights to any security as the subrogee thereunder and collect sums owed to the guarantor by a co-surety.

§ 13 The Guarantor's Rights to collect from Primary Obligor

Upon satisfying the underlying obligation, a guarantor's remedies against the primary obligor can be categorized into two categories: reimbursement and subrogation.

13.1 Reimbursement by the Primary Obligor

A guarantor may seek reimbursement from the primary obligor for the amount it has disbursed in connection with the underlying obligation, including necessary costs and expenses.[165] The guarantor is not required to commence legal proceedings to collect such reimbursement but may do so if the primary obligor does not pay.[166] The guarantor's rights to reimbursement do not extend to third parties. Rather, a guarantor seeking repayment of funds from a third party must rely on its rights of subrogation described below in section XII.B.

A threshold requirement for reimbursement is evidence that the guarantor was compelled to satisfy the underlying obligation. Courts have consistently held that if a guarantor voluntarily pays the underlying obligation without

162. Nieder v. Ferreira, 189 Cal. App. 3d 1485 (2d Dist. 1987).
163. Overholser v. Glynn, 267 Cal. App. 2d 800 (1968).
164. Cal. Civ. Code § 2849 (West 2012).
165. Cal. Civ. Code § 2847 (West 2012).
166. Cal. Civ. Code § 2847 (West 2012).

being legally compelled, the guarantor cannot seek reimbursement from the primary obligor.[167]

Assuming a guarantor has a right to reimbursement against the primary obligor, the guarantor is permitted to assign the right "and may be able to purchase the creditor's claim against the principal, instead of paying it, provided that the surety cannot both pay the claim against the principal and purchase it, since the payment will extinguish it, and there will then remain nothing to purchase."[168]

13.2 Subrogation against the Primary Obligor

The guarantor's more robust remedy to collect against the primary obligor is its ability to subrogate to the rights of the obligee. When the guarantor subrogates to the rights of the obligee, it steps into the obligee's shoes and is entitled to the remedies which the obligee had against the primary obligor in order to recoup the sums expensed by the guarantor.[169] The remedy of demanding repayment (reimbursement) is only the beginning of the subrogee's tools for collection. Because the guarantor is entitled to the benefit of every security for performance of the underlying obligation held by the obligee, the guarantor can look to collateral and other security for repayment. In fact, the guarantor can look to repayment from collateral even if that was acquired after the guaranty was executed and even if the guarantor was not aware of the security.[170]

Another benefit of subrogation is that the surety is also entitled to be subrogated to the rights of the principal obligor or the obligee against any third person.[171] For the guarantor to be subrogated into the shoes of the obligee, the payment of the underlying obligation must have been made under compulsion and not voluntarily.[172]

Accordingly, the guarantor's rights under subrogation, including the right to demand reimbursement, look to collateral, and look to third parties, thereby entitles the guarantor to a broad range of options for repayment.

§ 14 Enforcement of Guaranties

14.1 Limitations on Recovery

The obligee's recovery against a guarantor is limited to the amount specified in the guaranty.[173] Actual damages must be alleged and proved before there can be a recovery on a guaranty.[174] Whether the courts will uphold a provision in the guaranty providing for a fixed sum of damages as permitted liquidated

167. Schiltz v. Thomas, 61 Cal. App. 635 (1923).
168. Cal. Jur. 3d, Suretyship and Guaranty, Effect of Payment by Surety § 89 (West Supp. 2011).
169. Cal. Civ. Code § 2848 (West 2012).
170. Cal. Civ. Code § 2849 (West 2012).
171. *See* Cal. Jur. 3d, Suretyship and Guaranty, Subrogation § 97 (West Supp. 2011).
172. Schlitz v. Thomas, 61 Cal. App. 635 (1923).
173. Kane v. Mendenhall, 5 Cal. 2d 749 (1936).
174. Jack v. Sinsheimer, 125 Cal. 563 (1899).

damages or strike the provision as penalty is determined under the general rules of contract relating to liquidated damages.[175] Recovery is further limited in that punitive damages are only available in actions for breach of an obligation not arising from a contract.[176] Absent an independent tort, punitive damages are not available against a surety for breach of a suretyship contract.

14.2 Exercising Rights under a Guaranty Where the Underlying Obligation is also Secured by a Mortgage

Absent an express waiver, guarantors of obligations secured by California real property may seek protection under both statutory and case law. California Civil Code sections 2845 and 2850 provide that a surety has the right to demand the obligor proceed first against the security encumbered by the deed of trust. Additionally, California Civil Code sections 2809 and 2787 mandate that the guarantor's burden may not exceed the primary obligor's burden. Although no statute expressly provides the following, the logical extension of sections 2809 and 2787 is that a guarantor should be privy to the same defenses as a primary obligor, including access to California's antideficiency and one-action rules.

As discussed in section VIII.B.4 *infra*, the courts have provided protection to guarantors in the Gradsky decision. Under *Gradsky*, an obligee is estopped from enforcing a deficiency judgment against a guarantor where the obligee elects a more burdensome remedy (such as a nonjudicial trustee's sale) that impairs the guarantor's rights when the obligee could have elected an alternative, less burdensome remedy (such as a judicial foreclosure).

The California Civil Code permits, however, a guarantor to waive its antideficiency, one-action, or other statutorily provided protection.

§ 15 Revival and Reinstatement of Guaranties

On occasion, payments that are initially believed to satisfy the underlying obligation are subsequently treated as if such payments were never made and consequently as if the debt owed to the obligee was never fulfilled. Most commonly, this situation arises in an insolvency proceeding when a bankruptcy court declares a payment by the primary obligor or guarantor (or even a set-off by the obligee) to be a fraudulent transfer or preferential and the payment is avoided or set aside. To prevent the obligee from being left without satisfaction of its debt, the obligee usually negotiates to include a revival clause in the loan documents that reinstates the primary obligor's duty to pay any debt that has been set aside. The issue becomes, however, whether an analogous revival provision in a guaranty or a release of guaranty is enforceable against a guarantor.

175. Cal. Jur 3d, Suretyship and Guaranty, Damages §§ 151 et seq.
176. Cal. Civ. Code § 3291(a) (West 2012).

The Bankruptcy Appellate Panel (B.A.P.) for the Ninth Circuit recently opined that a "return of a preferential payment by a creditor generally revives the liability of a Guarantor" in spite of its finding that no Ninth Circuit or California case expressly provided such.[177] Rather, the B.A.P. relied upon, among other persuasive authorities, the Restatement of Suretyship which states that "[w]hen a secondary obligation is discharged in whole or part by performance by the principal obligor or another secondary obligor . . . the secondary obligation revives to the extent that the Obligee, under a legal duty to do so, later surrenders that performance or collateral, or the value thereof, as a preference or otherwise."[178] Obligees should be cautious, however, to draft the revival clauses broad enough to require reinstatement of the underlying obligation under a multitude of circumstances where a payment is refunded and not limit the case to a judicial finding of invalidation. For example, the revival language should also contemplate the return of payment as a result of a settlement entered into with the obligee. A sample guaranty revival language is provided below.

"Notwithstanding anything contained herein, this Guaranty shall continue in full force and effect or be revived, as the case may be, if any payment by or on behalf of the Primary Obligor or any Guarantor is made, or Obligee exercises its right of set-off, in respect of the Underlying Obligations and such payment or the proceeds of such set-off or any part thereof is subsequently invalidated, declared to be fraudulent or preferential, set aside or required (including pursuant to any settlement entered into by Obligee in its discretion) to be repaid to a trustee, receiver, or any other party, in connection with any proceeding under any insolvency proceeding or otherwise, all as if such payment had not been made or such set-off had not occurred and whether the Obligee is in possession of or has released this Guaranty and regardless of any prior revocation, rescission, termination, or reduction. The obligations of each Guarantor under this section shall survive termination of this Guaranty."

177. Centre Insurance Company v. SNTL Corp. (In re SNTL Corp), No. CC-06-1350, slip. op. (B.A.P. 9th Cir. Dec. 19, 2007) (relying on Tenth Circuit dicta and the Restatement (Third) of Suretyship & Guaranty § 70 (1996)).

178. Centre Insurance Company v. SNTL Corp. (In re SNTL Corp), No. CC-06-1350, slip. op. (B.A.P. 9th Cir. Dec. 19, 2007) (citing Restatement (Third) of Suretyship & Guaranty § 70 (1996)).

Colorado State Law of Guaranties

Beat U. Steiner
Paul Kyed
Erik Lemmon
Jeremy Syz
Rob Thomas
Holland & Hart LLP
555 17th Street, Suite 3200
Denver, CO 80202
Phone: 303-295-8000
Fax: 303-295-8261
bsteiner@hollandhart.com
www.hollandhart.com

HOLLAND&HART LLP

Contents

Colorado State Law of Guaranties

COLORADO LAW HIGHLIGHTS

Colorado guaranties are not significantly different from guaranties used in other states, and guaranties prepared under the laws of other states are generally enforceable under Colorado law.

A unique provision of Colorado guaranties is the addition of an express waiver of the provisions of Colo. Rev. Stat. §§ 3-58-102 and 103 relating to the release of joint debtors, if the guaranty is made by more than one debtor. *See* § 9 below.

Introductory Note: In order to standardize our discussion of the law of guaranties, we use the following vocabulary to refer to the various parties to a guaranty and their obligations.

"Guarantor" means a person who, by contract, agrees to satisfy an underlying obligation of another to an obligee upon the primary obligor's default on that underlying obligation.

"Guaranty" means the contract by which the guarantor agrees to satisfy the underlying obligation of a primary obligor to an obligee in the event the primary obligor defaults on the underlying obligation.

"Obligee" means the person to whom the underlying obligation is owed. For example, the lender under a loan agreement would be an obligee vis-à-vis the borrower.

"Primary Obligor" means the person who incurs the underlying obligation to the obligee. For example, the borrower under a loan agreement would be a primary obligor.

"Underlying Obligation" means the obligation or obligations incurred by the primary obligor and owed to the obligee. For example, the borrower's obligation to make payments to a lender of principal and interest on a loan constitutes an underlying obligation.

Introduction and Sources of Law

Colorado law is not distinctive from the laws of other states as to guaranties. Guaranty agreements prepared by Colorado lawyers do not differ substantially from guaranties used in other states. Guaranty agreements in use in other states are generally enforceable under Colorado law.

The only distinguishing feature of a Colorado guaranty is the addition of a waiver of the effect of Colo. Rev. Stat. §§ 13-50-102 and 103 (discussed in § 8.3 and §

9 below), which is typical even though the enforceability of such a waiver has not been established by law. This survey reflects matters related to guaranties that have been addressed in reported decisions of Colorado courts and of federal courts applying Colorado law.

Colorado courts occasionally cite to the Restatement (Third) of Suretyship and Guaranty (1995)[1] and to its predecessor, the Restatement of Security (1941)[2] as a source of law.

§ 1 Nature of the Guaranty Arrangement

A guaranty is a collateral promise to answer for the debt or obligation of another.[3]

An endorsement on a note is a guaranty of the note.[4]

A guarantor is treated as a debtor for purposes of Article 9 of the Uniform Commercial Code (UCC).[5]

1.1 Guaranty Relationships

An early Colorado case stated that there is a marked distinction between a contract of guaranty and one of suretyship. A surety is primarily liable on a contract; that is to say, a surety is bound with the principal on the identical contract under which the liability of the principal accrues, while the guarantor is only bound for the performance of a prior or collateral contract, by which the principal is alone obligated; that is, the contract of the guarantor is separate and distinct from that of the principal, so that the liability of a guarantor does not attach until default by the principal. In other words, the obligation of a surety is primary, and that of a guarantor secondary.[6] In *Cone v. Eldridge*, the treatment of the obligation as a guaranty meant that the underlying obligation was not extinguished when the guarantors paid the obligee; as a result, the guarantors could acquire the notes evidencing the underlying obligation jointly. While the distinction has been softened or eliminated in other states[7], more recent Colorado cases have not addressed the distinction, leaving the earlier case as good law, although perhaps of little practical significance. The distinction has not been eliminated statutorily in Colorado. For purposes of the

1. Edmonds v. W. Sur. Co., 962 P.2d 323 (Colo. App. 1998); Helmsman Mgmt. Servs., Inc. v. Colo. Dep't of Labor & Emp't, 31 P.3d 895, 895 (Colo. App. 2000).
2. Alie v. Futterman, 924 P.2d 1063 (Colo. App. 1995); C.I.I.S. Partners v. Miller, 762 P.2d 700 (Colo. App. 1988); Gerard Ins. Co. of Am. v. City of Colorado Springs, 638 P.2d 752 (Colo. 1981); Alzado v. Blinder Robinson & Co., Inc., 752 P.2d 544 (Colo. 1988).
3. FBS AG Credit, Inc. v. Estate of Walker, 906 F. Supp. 1427, 1430 (D. Colo. 1995) (citing Yama v. Sigman *et al.*, 165 P.2d 191 (Colo. 1945)).
4. Cripple Creek State Bank v. Rollestone, 202 P. 115, 116 (Colo. 1921).
5. *FBS AG Credit, Inc.*, 906 F. Supp. at 1430.
6. Cone v. Eldridge, 119 P. 616, 618 (Colo. 1911).
7. *See* Restatement (Third) of Suretyship & Guaranty § 1 (1996).

UCC as in effect in Colorado, however, the term "surety" includes a guarantor or other secondary obligor.[8]

1.2 Suretyship Relationships

A surety bond is a written contract guaranteeing the performance of an obligation by another.[9] Surety bonds should be interpreted according to the standards that govern the construction of contracts in general.[10]

A special relationship exists between a commercial surety and an obligee that is nearly identical to that involving an insurer and an insured.[11] When an obligee requests that a principal obtain a commercial surety bond to guarantee the principal's performance, the obligee is protecting itself from the losses that would result if the principal defaults on its original obligation.[12] If the principal defaults, the commercial surety must assume or correct any flaws in performance pursuant to the terms of the original contract, thereby eliminating the obligee's risk of loss in the venture.[13] As with insurers, commercial sureties must proceed with payment of claims made pursuant to a surety bond in good faith.[14] Colorado common law recognizes a cause of action in tort for a commercial surety's failure to act in good faith when processing claims made by an obligee pursuant to the terms of a performance bond.[15]

§ 2 State Law Requirements for a Person or Entity to Enter into a Guaranty

Individuals, corporations, partnerships, and limited liability companies all can grant guaranties. Such grants by entities are generally permitted by the appropriate Colorado statute.

2.1 Corporations

Pursuant to the Colorado Business Corporation Act, unless otherwise provided in a corporation's articles of incorporation, every corporation has the same powers as an individual to do all things necessary and convenient to carry its business and affairs, including the power to make contracts and guaranties.[16]

A guaranty by a corporation of an obligation of a director of the corporation or of an obligation of an entity in which a director of the corporation is a

8. *See* Colo. Rev. Stat. § 4-1-201(39) (2011).
9. *Helmsman Mgmt. Servs., Inc.*, 31 P.3d at 897.
10. *Id.*
11. Transamerica Premier Ins. Co. v. Brighton Sch. Dist. 27J, 940 P.2d 348, 352 (Colo. 1997).
12. *Transamerica Premier Ins. Co.*, 940 P.2d at 352.
13. *Id.* at 353.
14. *Id.*
15. *Id.*
16. Colo. Rev. Stat. § 7-103-102(1)(g) (2011).

director or officer or has a financial interest is considered a "conflicting interest transaction" under the Colorado Business Corporation Act.[17]

2.2 Nonprofit Corporations

Unless otherwise provided in a nonprofit corporation's articles of incorporation, every nonprofit corporation has the same powers as an individual to do all things necessary or convenient to carry out its affairs, including the power to make contracts and guaranties.[18]

A nonprofit corporation may not guarantee the obligation of a director or officer of the nonprofit corporation.[19]

2.3 Partnerships

Colorado statutes neither expressly empower a partnership to issue a guaranty nor expressly regulate or prohibit such activity.[20]

2.4 Limited Liability Companies

Each limited liability company formed and existing under the Colorado Limited Liability Company Act has the statutory authority to make contracts and guaranties.[21]

2.5 Individuals

When a person is charged with executing a signed document, for the purposes of affecting the individual with certain legal consequences, the act which suffices to charge the individual is any act by which the individual adopts and makes the individual's own the terms of the writing. It is therefore, in general, immaterial whether the individual has written the body of the document or not, if he has signed it. It is even immaterial whether he has signed it, if he has otherwise acknowledged or adopted it. Hence, proof of the signature of the document is sufficient to charge him.[22]

Colorado is not a community property state, so there is no general practice to require the signature of a spouse on a guaranty.

17. Colo. Rev. Stat. § 7-108-501(1)(a)(II) (2011).
18. Colo. Rev. Stat. § 7-123-102(1)(g) (2011).
19. Colo. Rev. Stat. § 7-123-102(1)(h) (2011).
20. Colo. Rev. Stat. §§ 7-60-101 to -154, 7-61-101 to -130, 7-62-101 to -1201, 7-64-101 to -1206 (2011).
21. Colo. Rev. Stat. § 7-80-104(1)(f) (2011).
22. Gates v. Am. Nat'l Bank of Denver, 479 P.2d 285, 287 (Colo. 1971) (citing 7 J. Wigmore, Evidence § 2134 (3d ed. 1940)).

§ 3 Signatory's Authority to Execute a Guaranty

When a guaranty is regular on its face, it may be presumed to have been properly executed.[23]

A person who signs a negotiable instrument, without indicating that he is signing it in a representative capacity, is personally bound.[24]

3.1 Corporations

As to corporations governed by the Colorado Business Corporations Act, the following applies:

Subject to any provision stated in the articles of incorporation, all corporate powers shall be exercised by or under the authority of, and the business and affairs of the corporation managed under the direction of, the board of directors or such other persons as the articles of incorporation provide shall have the authority and perform the duties of a board of directors.[25]

Directors of a corporation are agents of the corporation and occupy a quasi-fiduciary duty to the corporation.[26] Within the limits of their legal authority, directors of a corporation possess a large amount of discretionary power that, if exercised with reason, is not subject to control by either the stockholders or the courts.[27]

Each officer shall have the authority and shall perform the duties stated with respect to the officer's office in the bylaws or, to the extent not inconsistent with the bylaws, prescribed with respect to that office by the board of directors or by an officer authorized by the board of directors.[28]

Typically, a guaranty is signed by an officer of a corporation who has the authority to sign on behalf of the corporation, as granted in the bylaws or by the board of directors.

3.2 Nonprofit Corporations

As to nonprofit corporations, the following applies:

Subject to any provision stated in the articles of incorporation, all corporate powers shall be exercised by or under the authority of, and the business and affairs of the nonprofit corporation managed under the direction of, the board of directors or such other persons as the articles of incorporation provide shall have the authority and perform the duties of a board of directors.[29]

---

23. *FBS AG Credit, Inc.*, 906 F. Supp. at 1431 (citing *Gates*, 479 P.2d at 287).
24. Ford Motor Credit Co. v. Bob Jones Enters., Inc., 240 F. Supp. 667, 669-71 (D. Colo. 1965).
25. Colo. Rev. Stat. § 7-108-101(2) (2011).
26. Herald Co. v. Seawell, 472 F.2d 1081, 1094 (10th Cir. 1972).
27. *Herald Co.*, 472 F.2d at 1094.
28. Colo. Rev. Stat. § 7-108-302 (2011).
29. Colo. Rev. Stat. § 7-128-101(2) (2011).

To the extent the articles of incorporation provide that other persons shall have the authority and perform the duties of the board of directors, the directors shall be relieved to that extent from such authority and duties.[30]

Each officer shall have the authority and shall perform the duties stated with respect to officer's office in the bylaws or, to the extent not inconsistent with the bylaws, prescribed with respect to that office by the board of directors or by an officer authorized by the board of directors.[31]

Typically, a guaranty is signed by an officer of a nonprofit corporation who has the authority to sign on behalf of the nonprofit corporation, as granted in the bylaws or by the board of directors.

3.3 Partnerships

As to partnerships governed by the Uniform Partnership Law,[32] the following applies:

(1) Subject to the effect of a statement of partnership authority under section 7-64-303 [of the Colorado Revised Statutes], every partner is an agent of the partnership for the purpose of its business, and the act of every partner, including the execution in the partnership name of any instrument for apparently carrying on in the usual way the business of the partnership of which the partner is a member, binds the partnership, unless the partner so acting has in fact no authority to act for the partnership in the particular matter and the person with whom the partner is dealing has knowledge of the fact that the partner has no such authority.

(2) An act of a partner that is not apparently for the carrying on of the business of the partnership in the usual way does not bind the partnership unless authorized by the other partners.

As to partnerships governed by the Colorado Uniform Partnership Act (1997),[33] the following applies:

(1) Subject to the effect of a statement of partnership authority under section 7-64-303 [of the Colorado Revised Statutes]:

(a) Each partner is an agent of the partnership for the purposes of its business. An act of a partner, including the execution of an instrument in the partnership name, for apparently carrying on in the ordinary course the partnership business or business of the kind carried on by the partnership binds the partnership, unless the partner had no authority to act for the partnership

30. *Id.*
31. Colo. Rev. Stat. § 7-128-302 (2011).
32. Colo. Rev. Stat. §§ 7-60-101 to -154 (2011), applicable to partnerships formed before January 1, 1998, and limited partnerships formed under Colo. Rev. Stat. §§ 7-62-101 to -1201 (2011), except partnerships that have elected to be governed by the Colorado Uniform Partnership Act (1997).
33. Colo. Rev. Stat. §§ 7-64-101 to -1206 (2011), applicable to partnerships formed after January 1, 1998, or that have elected to be governed by its provisions.

in the particular matter and the person with whom the partner was dealing had notice that the partner lacked authority.

(b) An act of a partner which is not apparently for carrying on in the ordinary course the partnership business or business of the kind carried on by the partnership binds the partnership only if the act was authorized by the other partners.[34]

As to limited partnerships, a limited partner does not participate in the control of the business solely by acting as surety for the limited partnership or guaranteeing or assuming one or more specific obligations of the limited partnership.[35]

3.4 Limited Liability Companies

(1) If the articles of organization provide that management of the limited liability company is vested in one or more managers:

(a) A member is not an agent of the limited liability company and has no authority to bind the limited liability company solely by virtue of being a member; and

(b) Each manager is an agent of the limited liability company for the purposes of its business and an act of a manager, including the execution of an instrument in the name of the limited liability company, for apparently carrying on in the ordinary course the business of the limited liability company or business of the kind carried on by the limited liability company binds the limited liability company, unless the manager had no authority to act for the limited liability company in the particular matter and the person with whom the manager was dealing had notice that the manager lacked authority.

(2) If the articles of organization provide that management of the limited liability company is vested in the members, each member is an agent of the limited liability company for the purposes of its business and an act of a member, including the execution of an instrument in the name of the limited liability company, for apparently carrying on in the ordinary course the business of the limited liability company or business of the kind carried on by the limited liability company binds the limited liability company, unless the member had no authority to act for the limited liability company in the particular matter and the person with whom the member was dealing had notice that the member lacked authority.[36]

The authority of members and managers may be limited by provisions of the operating agreement that governs the limited liability company.

---

34. Colo. Rev. Stat. § 7-64-301 (2011).
35. Colo. Rev. Stat. § 7-62-303(2)(d) (2011).
36. Colo. Rev. Stat. § 7-80-405 (2011).

§ 4 Consideration; Sufficiency of Past Consideration

A contract of guaranty requires adequate consideration.[37] Consideration is not presumed, but must be established by evidence.[38] Where an endorsement [and, presumably, a guaranty] is made after delivery of the note, the intent to become liable to the payee must be shown by a preponderance of the evidence.[39] A valuable consideration, however small or nominal, if given or stipulated for in good faith, is, in the absence of fraud, sufficient consideration.[40] An incidental benefit, however, is not sufficient.[41]

Legal consideration may be in the form of either a detriment suffered by the creditor[42] or a benefit conferred on the principal debtor.[43] The obligee's forbearance from taking action against the primary obligor may be adequate consideration even if the guarantor receives no immediate benefit from the guaranty.[44] The extension of time for the payment of the underlying obligation can constitute consideration for a guaranty.[45] Where the guarantors of rental payments under a previously executed lease received a waiver of the provision of the lease that prevented the tenant from assigning the lease to anyone, in return for executing the guaranty, the guaranty was found to be supported by present consideration.[46]

A guaranty executed subsequent to the original undertaking must rest upon a new and adequate consideration in order to bind the guarantor.[47] However, the fact that guaranty contracts were signed subsequent to delivery of notes does not show lack of consideration for guaranties where obligee as holder did not release funds until notes were guaranteed by the guarantor.[48] In such case the act relates back to the inception of the original contract and is supported by the same consideration.[49]

The guaranty of a note given in payment of an antecedent obligation requires no consideration.[50]

---

37. *Cripple Creek State Bank*, 202 P. at 116.
38. *Id.*
39. *Id.*
40. Davis v. Wells, 104 U.S. 159, 168 (1881).
41. *Cripple Creek State Bank*, 202 P. at 117.
42. Farmers Elevator Co. v. First Nat'l Bank, 488 P.2d 238, 239 (Colo. App. 1971) (citing Colo. State Bank of Denver v. Rothberg, 474 P.2d 634, 636 (1970), for the proposition that "legal consideration may be in the form of a legal detriment incurred by the promisee by reason of its reliance on a guaranty contract where the guarantor knew or had reason to know that such detriment would result from the guaranty.").
43. Ransom Distrib. Co. v. Lazy B. Ltd., 532 P.2d 364, 365 (Colo. App. 1974).
44. *See* Linger v. Rocky Mountain Bank & Trust Co., 486 P.2d 29, 31 (Colo. App. 1971) (citing *Colo. State Bank of Denver*, 474 P.2d 634). On petition for certiorari, the Supreme Court stated, "In denying the petition for writ of certiorari to review the opinion of the Court of Appeals, the Supreme Court does not necessarily approve the statement in that opinion that '[t]he Bank's forbearance from action against the Club, as a legal detriment, was sufficient consideration to support the guaranty contract.'" *Linger*, 486 P.2d at 31.
45. State Bank of Greeley v. Owens, 502 P.2d 965 (Colo. App. 1972) (citing Wheelock v. Hondius, 222 P. 404 (Colo. 1924)).
46. Burkhardt v. Bank of Am. Nat'l Trust & Sav. Ass'n, 256 P.2d 234, 235-36 (Colo. 1953).
47. Jain v. Griffin, 32 P. 80, 81 (Colo. App. 1893).
48. *Colo. State Bank of Denver*, 474 P.2d at 635-36.
49. *Colo. State Bank of Denver*, 474 P.2d at 636 (citing Loveland v. Sigel-Campion Live Stock Co., 234 P. 168 (Colo. 1925)).
50. *State Bank of Greeley*, 502 P.2d at 966 (citing *Wheelock*, 222 P. 404).

§ 5 Notice of Acceptance

Notice of acceptance of an unconditional, absolute continuing guaranty is not required, absent an express contractual provision to the contrary.[51]

One who guaranties the payment of a debt to be created in the future and uncertain in amount and time is entitled to notice that his guaranty is accepted, and credit was given on the faith thereof.[52] Until notice is given of the acceptance, the guarantor may withdraw.[53]

A mere offer to guarantee requires notice of acceptance.[54] However, notice to guarantor of acceptance of an actual guaranty is unnecessary.[55] The test applied by Colorado courts in determining whether a guaranty is in fact an offer of guaranty, or an absolute guaranty, is whether there is mutual assent.[56] A Colorado court, relying on the Supreme Court decision in *Davis Sewing Machine Co. v. Richards,*[57] has held that "if the guaranty is signed by the guarantor at the request of the other party, or if the latter's agreement to accept is contemporaneous with the guaranty, or if the receipt from him of a valuable consideration, however small, is acknowledged in the guaranty, the mutual assent is proved, and the delivery of the guaranty to him or for his use completes the contract. But if the guaranty is signed by the guarantor without any previous requests of the other party, and in his absence, for no consideration moving between them except future advances to be made to the principal debtor, the guaranty is in legal effect an offer or proposal on the part of the guarantor, needing an acceptance by the other party to complete the contract."[58]

Under a contract containing an offer or proposal, which becomes binding upon the signer only after notice of acceptance of the same, it is not necessary that the notice be given directly by the obligee.[59] Guarantor's knowledge or information from any source that the obligee is acting under and extending credit on the strength of the guaranty is tantamount to direct notice and acceptance thereof thus sufficient to bind the guarantor.[60]

51. *Gates*, 479 P.2d at 287.
52. Asmussen v. Post Printing & Publ'g Co., 143 P. 396, 398-99 (Colo. App. 1914).
53. *Asmussen*, 143 P. at 421-23.
54. Taylor v. Hake, 20 P.2d 546, 549 (Colo. 1933).
55. *Taylor*, 20 P.2d at 549.
56. *Asmussen*, 143 P. at 400.
57. 115 U.S. 524 (1885).
58. *Asmussen*, 143 P. at 430.
59. *Id.* at 420-21.
60. *Id.* at 420-21; *Taylor*, 20 P.2d at 549.

§ 6 Interpretation of Guaranties

6.1 General Principles

A guarantor, like a surety, is a favorite of the law.[61] Guaranty agreements are to be strictly construed in favor of the guarantor.[62] A guaranty must be strictly construed and cannot be extended.[63] The liability of a guarantor cannot be enlarged beyond the strict intent of the instrument.[64] The mere use of the word "guarantee" will not imply a personal agreement in the absence of mutual assent and consideration.[65]

A guaranty may be narrower than the contract between the primary obligor and the obligee.[66]

When one enters into a guaranty to pay the debt of another, the guarantor has the right to make the terms and to set forth the conditions upon which he assumes the burden of guaranteeing the debt.[67] The language employed in a guaranty should have a reasonable interpretation according to the intent of the parties disclosed in the instrument read in the light of surrounding circumstances and the purpose thereof.[68]

As with contracts generally, in construing a guaranty, Colorado courts are required to give effect to the intentions of the parties, which must be deduced from the instrument as a whole. [69] A contract, including a guaranty contract, must be construed as a whole and effect given, if possible, to every provision.[70]

When a printed form of contract is furnished by a party and is ambiguous, it will receive a construction most strongly against the one drawing the same and in favor of the other party, when such construction is reasonable and fair.[71]

The extent of a guarantor's liability is determined by the language of the instrument itself,[72] and *absent language to the contrary*, it is usually equal to that of the primary obligor.[73]

---

61. Cooper Invs. v. Conger, 775 P.2d 76, 79 (Colo. App. 1989) (citing *Burkhardt*, 256 P.2d 234).
62. Highlands Ranch Univ. Park LLC v. UNO of Highlands Ranch, Inc., 129 P.3d 1020, 1024 (Colo. App. 2005); *FBS AG Credit, Inc.*, 906 F. Supp. at 1431 (citing First Interstate Bank of Denver, N.A. v. Colcott Partners IV, 833 P.2d 876, 878 (Colo. App. 1992)).
63. *Yama*, 165 P.2d at 193 (citing Sutton, Steele & Steele MFG., Mill & Mining Co. v. McCullough, 174 P. 302 (Colo. 1918)); Wilcoxson v. McMullin, 63 P.2d 880 (Colo. 1936); Walter E. Heller & Co. v. Wilkerson, 627 P.2d 773 (Colo. App. 1980); *First Interstate Bank of Denver*, 833 P.2d at 878.
64. *Sutton, Steele & Steele Mfg., Mill & Mining Co.*, 174 P. at 303-04.
65. Roemmich v. Lutheran Hosps. & Homes Soc. of Am., 934 P.2d 873, 876 (Colo. App. 1996).
66. *Sutton, Steele & Steele Mfg., Mill & Mining Co.*, 174 P. at 303-04.
67. *FBS AG Credit, Inc.*, 906 F. Supp. at 1430-31 (citing *Yama*, 165 P.2d at 193).
68. *Highlands Ranch Univ. Park LLC*, 129 P.3d at 1024; Valley Nat'l Bank of Ariz. v. Foreign Car Rental, Inc., 404 P.2d 272, 275 (Colo. 1965); *First Interstate Bank, N.A.*, 833 P.2d at 878; *C.I.I.S. Partners*, 762 P.2d at 702.
69. *Highlands Ranch Univ. Park LLC*, 129 P.3d at 1024 (citing Rohn v. Weld Cnty. Bank, 395 P.2d 1003 (Colo. 1964)).
70. Gandy v. Park Nat'l Bank, 615 P.2d 20 (Colo. 1990).
71. *Asmussen*, 143 P. at 421-23.
72. *FBS AG Credit, Inc.*, 906 F. Supp. at 1431 (citing Cont'l Bank v. Dolan, 564 P.2d 955 (Colo. App. 1977)).
73. *Highlands Ranch Univ. Park LLC*, 129 P.3d at 1024; *First Interstate Bank of Denver, N.A.*, 833 P.2d at 878 (citing *Cont'l Bank*, 564 P.2d 955(italics in original)).

The language of a guaranty is determinative of the parties' intent, and its interpretation is a question of law.[74] If a guaranty is not ambiguous, it is error to resort to the language of documents relating to the underlying transaction to construe the guaranty as to any limiting conditions.[75]

In Colorado, every contract imposes upon each party a duty of good faith and fair dealing in its performance and in its enforcement.[76] This duty is applicable to contracts of guaranty.[77]

6.2 Guaranty of Payment versus Guaranty of Collection

Where the performance under a guarantee is conditioned only on default by the debtor, the creditor may proceed directly against the guarantor without first proceeding against his debtor.[78]

6.3 General vs. Special Guaranties

Guaranties generally fall into one of two classifications, that is, 'general' or 'special.' A 'general' guaranty is such that it may be accepted by the public generally and according to its written terms, anyone to whom it is presented may enforce or comply with its terms and the liability of the guarantor attaches. A 'special' guaranty is addressed to a particular person, who alone may have the benefits thereof and to whom the guarantor only is liable.[79]

"Where a guaranty, not connected with a negotiable instrument, is so drawn as to be personal and as to have force and effect only as to the person to whom it is given, that is, where it is a special guaranty, no person except the one specified can secure any advantage from the guaranty, and likewise it cannot be transferred or assigned to any other person, until after a right of action has arisen thereon, in which case such right of action may be assigned." [80]

6.4 Language Regarding the Revocation of Guaranties

Unless specifically provided for in clear and unequivocal terms, a continuing guaranty does not cover renewals, after revocation, of obligations that were covered by the guaranty at the time of revocation.[81]

6.5 "Continuing"

A continuing guaranty is one not limited to a particular transaction or specific transactions, but is intended to cover all future transactions.[82]

---

74. *Highlands Ranch Univ. Park LLC*, 129 P.3d at 1024.
75. W. States Leasing Co. v. Adturn, Inc., 500 P.2d 1190 (Colo. App. 1972).
76. Ruff v. Yuma Cnty. Transp. Co., 690 P.2d 1296, 1298 (Colo. App 1984).
77. *See FBS AG Credit, Inc.*, 906 F. Supp. at 1431-32.
78. Prather v. Roto Ignition Sales, Inc., 468 P.2d 29, 31-32 (Colo. 1970) (citing *Jain*, 32 P. 80).
79. *Burkhardt*, 256 P.2d at 235-36.
80. *Id.* (citation omitted).
81. *Gandy*, 615 P.2d at 22.
82. *Valley Nat'l Bank of Ariz.*, 404 P.2d at 275.

6.6 "Absolute and Unconditional"

It is typical in a guaranty to state that the guaranty is absolute and unconditional.

Contracts of guaranty are classified as absolute or conditional.[83] An absolute guaranty is one by which the guarantor unconditionally promises payment or performance of the principal contract on default of the principal debtor or obligor.[84]

The conditional guaranty contemplates, as a condition to liability on the part of the guarantor, the happening of some contingent event other than the default of the primary obligor or the performance of some act on the part of the obligee. Where the guaranty is conditional, the obligation of the guarantor may not be enforced unless the event has occurred or the act has been performed.[85] Where, either by the express terms of the guaranty or by necessary implication, the guarantor's liability depends on the performance of certain conditions or stipulations other than the principal's default, mere default on the part of the principal is not sufficient to fix the liability on the guarantor; it is also necessary that there be proper performance on the part of the obligee of the conditions or stipulations; otherwise, the guarantor will not be liable.[86]

When a guaranty is absolute and unconditional by its terms, the fact that the underlying obligation is nonrecourse does not prevent recovery under the guaranty.[87]

6.7 "Liable as a Primary Obligor and not Merely as Surety"

"A surety is primarily liable on his contract; that is to say, he is bound with the principal on the identical contract under which the liability of the principal accrues, while the guarantor is only bound for the performance of a prior or collateral contract, by which the principal is alone obligated; that is, the contract of the guarantor is separate and distinct from that of his principal, so that the liability of a guarantor does not attach until default by his principal. In other words, the obligation of a surety is primary, and that of a guarantor secondary."[88]

6.8 Choice of Law

It is typical in a guaranty to state what jurisdiction's law governs the interpretation and enforcement of the guaranty.

Colorado requires resolution of conflicts under the principles set forth in Restatement (Second) of Conflict of Laws, §§ 187 and 188 (1971).[89] However,

---

83. *Yama*, 165 P.2d at 193.
84. *Id.* (citation omitted)*; see also FBS AG Credit, Inc.*, 906 F. Supp. at 1430.
85. *Yama*, 165 P.2d at 193.
86. *Id.* (citation omitted).
87. *See First Interstate Bank, N.A.*, 833 P.2d at 878.
88. Cone v. Eldridge, 119 P. 616, 618 (Colo. 1911).
89. *FBS AG Credit, Inc.*, 906 F. Supp. at 1429 (citing Wood Bros. Homes, Inc. v. Walker Adjustment Bureau, 601 P.2d 1369 (Colo. 1979)).

those principles apply only "in the absence of an effective choice of law by the parties."[90] The parties' choice of law is effective "unless there is no reasonable basis for their choice or unless applying the law of the state so chosen would be contrary to the fundamental policy of a state whose law would otherwise govern."[91] "Merely not recognizing a claim or theory of recovery is not a substantial conflict that warrants a court's rejection of a contractually designated choice of law." [92]

§ 7 Defenses of the Guarantor; Set-off

7.1 Defenses of the Primary Obligor

7.1.1 General

As a general rule, when a creditor sues a guarantor and does not name the primary obligor in the action, the guarantor is not entitled to raise defensively the claims of the primary obligor against the creditor.[93] The rationale behind this rule is to protect the claims of the primary obligor, since the guarantor may not be in the best position to assert them.[94]

7.1.2 When Guarantor may assert Primary Obligor's Defense

A guarantor may assert the independent claims of the primary obligor defensively if (1) the surety has taken an assignment of the claim or the primary obligor has consented to the guarantor's use of the claim, (2) both the primary obligor and the guarantor are joined as defendants, or (3) the primary obligor is insolvent.[95] Guaranties typically contain waivers to avoid this result.

7.1.3 Defenses that may not be Raised by Guarantor

The presence of a forged signature on a guaranty instrument is not itself sufficient to eliminate the liability of other guarantors, especially when the guarantor was not induced to sign the guaranty in reliance on the forged signature. When a forged signature is placed on a guaranty after the guarantor has signed, the guarantor is not relieved of liability.[96]

Even though under certain circumstances a guarantor's liability is coextensive with that of the primary obligor, when fraud is committed by an obligee on the primary obligor, the option to affirm or rescind the agreement belongs only to the primary obligor and not to the guarantor. Thus, a claim seeking

90. *Id.*; Restatement (Second) of Conflict of Laws §§ 187-88 (1971).
91. *FBS AG Credit, Inc.*, 906 F. Supp. at 1429 (quoting Hansen v. GAB Bus. Serv., Inc., 876 P.2d 112, 113 (Colo. App. 1994)); *see Wood Bros. Homes, Inc.*, 601 P.2d at 1372 n.4.
92. *FBS AG Credit, Inc.*, 906 F. Supp. at 1429 (quoting *Hansen*, 876 P.2d at 113).
93. First Tex. Serv. Corp. v. Roulier, 750 F. Supp. 1056, 1060 (D. Colo.1990).
94. *First Tex. Serv. Corp.*, 750 F. Supp. at 1061.
95. *Id.* (citing Cont'l Grp., Inc. v. Justice, 536 F. Supp. 658, 661 (D. Del. 1982) (citing Restatement of Security § 133(2) (1941)) (now addressed in Restatement of Suretyship and Guaranty § 35 (1995)).
96. First Nat'l Bank of Cedaredge v. Aspinwall, 613 P.2d 341, 342-43 (Colo. App. 1980).

avoidance of a contract based on fraud is not available to the guarantor once the primary obligor elects to affirm the underlying transaction.[97]

7.1.4 *Defenses that may always be Raised by Guarantor*

A guarantor is always entitled to assert personal defenses to the separate guaranty contract.[98]

7.2 "Suretyship" Defenses

A guarantor, like a surety, is favored in the law and the guarantor's liability is not to be extended by implication beyond the express limits or terms of the instrument, or its plain intent.[99] A person who enters into a contract of guaranty agrees to undertake a specific risk, and courts are reluctant to increase the guarantor's burden by extending the limits of the guaranty beyond the terms of the written instrument.[100]

7.2.1 *Change in Identity of Primary Obligor*

The guarantor should never be held liable for the nonperformance of a primary obligor unless there is reasonable ground to believe that the guarantor contemplated the person in default as primary obligor.[101] But if the person in default is identified and was in fact contemplated as primary obligor, the guarantor should be liable even though the primary obligor is slightly misdescribed or incorrectly named in the guaranty.[102]

7.2.2 *Modification of the Underlying Obligation, Including Release*

In general, when an obligee has chosen to materially alter the primary obligor's obligation to the guarantor's detriment, without the guarantor's consent, that alteration discharges the guarantor's liability.[103]

An alteration is material if it changes the nature of the primary obligor's obligation either by imposing some new obligation ... or by taking away some obligation already imposed.[104] A change in the rate of interest materially alters the primary obligor's obligation and an increase in the interest rate is materially detrimental to a guarantor.[105] An extension in time for payment is generally regarded as having the same result.

97. Alien Inc. v. Futterman, 924 P.2d 1063, 1068 (Colo. App. 1995).
98. *See Alien, Inc.*, 924 P.2d at 1067.
99. Nat'l State Bank of Boulder v. Burns, 525 P.2d 504, 506 (Colo. App. 1974).
100. *Nat'l State Bank of Boulder*, 525 P.2d at 506.
101. *Id.* (applying the law of suretyship, as described in L. Simpson, Handbook on the Law of Suretyship § 19 (1950), to a guarantor).
102. *Id.*
103. *Cooper Invs.*, 775 P.2d at 78 (citing *C.I.I.S. Partners*, 762 P.2d 700; Jackson v. First Nat'l Bank of Greeley, 474 P.2d 640 (1970)).
104. *Cooper Invs.*, 775 P.2d at 78 (citing A. Stearns, Law of Suretyship § 6.3 (1951)).
105. *Id.* at 79.

A compromise settlement of the underlying obligation, without the consent of the guarantor, discharges the guaranty.[106]

Where a guaranty, by its terms, is absolute and will not be affected or impaired by any modification, extension, or amendment of the underlying agreement, a change in the underlying agreement is of no consequence with regard to the guarantor's liability.[107]

Colorado follows the general rule that a guarantor will be discharged to the extent of modifications of the primary obligor's liability if such modifications were not contemplated by the guarantor.[108] The consent of a guarantor to an alteration is binding whether it is expressed as part of the initial obligation or is given later, either before or subsequent to the alteration.[109] Such consent need not be evidenced by a writing.[110] However, a guarantor's consent will be strictly construed, and a guarantor's consent to an extension or renewal of a promissory note neither contemplates nor authorizes an increase in the rate of interest and will not be deemed to be a consent by the guarantor to an increase in the interest rate.[111]

However, Colorado also recognizes that a guaranty agreement may authorize changes in the terms of the principal agreement without affecting the liability of the guarantor, provided that a court will strictly construe the terms of the authorization, and will only enforce the guaranty to the extent any modification was expressly consented to.[112] In applying this rule, the Colorado Supreme Court determined that a purported "amendment" to a lease that substituted different leased premises and increased the rent payable under the lease, in fact created a new lease, and held the guarantor of the original lease was not liable under a guaranty that related to the original lease.[113]

Whether a party's consent to an increased risk can be implied from silence depends on the circumstances of the particular case. An increase in the risk assumed by a surety in effect alters the terms of the initial suretyship agreement. Mere silence by a surety in the face of activity by the primary obligor and the obligee is not ordinarily regarded as acquiescence in or consent to any changes in the original arrangements. Such change should not be presumed in the absence of evidence that the surety not only knew of the extent of the additional risk to be assumed but also had no objection to assuming such additional risk. [114]

An obligee's release of a guarantor, without the consent of the remaining coguarantors, discharges the remaining coguarantors to the extent of their contributive share.[115] However, if the discharge of a guarantor's obligation results from operation of law, it generally has no effect upon the obligations

106. *See Jackson*, 474 P.2d 640.
107. First Commercial Corp. v. Geter, 547 P.2d 1291 (Colo. App. 1976).
108. Green Shoe Mfg. v. Farber, 712 P.2d 1014, 1016 (1986); *C.I.I.S. Partners*, 762 P.2d at 702.
109. *Cooper Invs.*, 775 P.2d at 79 (citing *C.I.I.S. Partners*, 762 P.2d 700).
110. *Id.*
111. *Id.*
112. *Green Shoe Mfg.*, 712 P.2d at 1016.
113. *Id.*
114. Haberl v. Bigelow, 855 P.2d 1368 (Colo. 1993).
115. *Cooper Invs.*, 775 P.2d at 80.

of the remaining coguarantors.[116] Hence, if an obligee and a primary obligor alter the obligation to the detriment of coguarantors, some of whom consent while others do not, those not consenting are discharged, but those consenting remain bound.[117] Guaranties typically contain waivers to avoid this result.

A mistake in reaching a stipulated settlement related solely to the primary obligor's liability does not necessarily provide a basis for relief to a guarantor.[118]

7.2.3 Release or Impairment of Security for the Underlying Obligation

If the obligee proceeds against the collateral and fails to do so in a commercially reasonable manner as required under the UCC, the guarantor has the same rights as the primary obligor, and those rights are not waived even though the guaranty, by its terms, is absolute and unconditional and provides that the primary obligor may proceed directly against the guarantor in the event of the primary obligor's default without having first to proceed against the collateral.[119]

7.3 Other Defenses

7.3.1 Failure to Fulfill a Condition Precedent

Where a contract of guaranty provides that notice of default of the primary obligor must be given to the guarantor, such notice must be given for the guarantor to be liable.[120] However, where an unambiguous absolute guaranty is silent as to notice and the maximum amount guaranteed is determinable at the time the guarantee is entered into, there is no basis to imply a requirement of notice.[121]

7.3.2 Modification of the Guaranty

The giving of a note does not, of itself, satisfy a guaranty obligation but merely further evidences the indebtedness.[122] It is, of course, possible for the parties to contract to release a guaranty by the giving of a note, but the intention to do so must be apparent.[123] To bring about a discharge, it would have to be apparent that an accord and satisfaction had been intended by the delivery of the subsequent note.[124]

---

116. *Id.* (citing L. Simpson, Handbook of Law of Suretyship § 79 (1951); Restatement of Security § 134 (1941)).
117. *Cooper Invs.*, 775 P.2d at 80.
118. *First Interstate Bank of Denver, N.A.*, 833 P.2d at 877-78.
119. *Walter E. Heller & Co.*, 627 P.2d at 775 (applying Illinois law). *But see FBS AG Credit, Inc.*, 906 F. Supp. at 1432.
120. *W. States Leasing Co*, 500 P.2d at 1191 (citing *Yama*, 165 P.2d 191).
121. *Id.*
122. *Ford Motor Credit Co,* 240 F. Supp. at 669-70.
123. *Id.* at 669.
124. *Id.*

7.3.3 *Failure to Pursue Primary Obligor*

Where the performance under the guaranty is conditioned only upon the default of the primary obligor, it is not necessary for the obligee to obtain judgment against the primary obligor before proceeding against the guarantor.[125] Nor is an action against the primary obligor necessary.[126]

Where the guaranty of a note payable to a bank was conditioned on "every effort to collect" the underlying obligation, the guaranty never becomes effective or is canceled, and the guarantor released, if the bank fails to use the diligence to collect the underlying obligation that a reasonable man would employ under the circumstances were there no guaranty.[127] Certainly this would require obtaining payment, or security covering all or any portion of the debt reasonably possible even though the primary obligor was execution proof.[128]

7.3.4 *Statute of Limitations*

The statute of limitations to collect a liquidated debt, an unliquidated, determinable amount of money due, or rent is six years from the time the cause of action accrues.[129] The cause of action accrues on the date the debt, obligation, money owed, or performance becomes due.[130]

7.3.5 *Statute of Frauds*

Under certain circumstances, a guaranty will fall within the statute of frauds, and thus will require a writing to evidence the agreement.[131] Under the Colorado Statute of Frauds, "Every special promise to answer for the debt, default, or miscarriage of another person" is void unless the agreement or some note or memorandum thereof is in writing and subscribed by the party charged therewith.[132] The statute does not bar enforcement of an oral promise that is "original" and not "collateral."[133]A promise is collateral if the leading object of the promise is to become a surety or guarantor for the debt of another; a promise is original when the performance of the agreement directly benefits the promisor.[134] An unconditional promise to pay the debt of another is an original promise and is not within the Statute of Frauds.[135]

The purpose of this section of the Statute of Frauds is to protect third parties from fraudulently being held to answer as surety for another party's debt.[136]

---

125. *Linger*, 486 P. 2d at 31 (citing *Prather*, 468 P.2d 29; *Jain*, 32 P. 80).
126. *First Commercial Corp.*, 547 P.2d at 1293.
127. *Wilcoxson*, 63 P.2d at 881 (citation omitted).
128. *Id.*
129. Colo. Rev. Stat. § 13-80-103.5 (2011).
130. Colo. Rev. Stat. § 13-80-108(4) (2011).
131. Moffat Cnty. State Bank v. Told, 800 P.2d 1320 (Colo. 1990).
132. Colo. Rev. Stat. § 38-10-112(1)(b) (2011).
133. Idealco, Inc. v. Gunnin, 746 P.2d 69, 70 (Colo. App. 1987) (citing Cramblitt v. Chateau Motel, Inc., 472 P.2d 183 (Colo. App. 1970)).
134. *Idealco*, 746 P.2d at 70.
135. *Moffat Cnty. State Bank*, 800 P.2d at 1322 (citing Spelts v. Anderson, 185 P. 468, 469 (1919); Tuttle v. Welty, 102 P. 1069, 1070 (1909)).
136. *Id.* (citing Walker v. Bruce, 97 P. 250, 252 (Colo. 1908)).

The Statute of Frauds does not bar proof of an oral agreement intended to constitute a novation of a guaranty.[137]

7.3.6 Defenses particular to Guarantors that are Natural Persons and their Spouses

There are no defenses particular to natural persons and their spouses.

7.4 Right of Set-off

Generally, a guarantor and primary obligor should be afforded the same right to offset damages because, unless otherwise agreed, a guarantor's liability is coextensive with that of the primary obligor.[138]

When the guarantor raises the claims of the primary obligor defensively against a creditor (see Section 7.1.2), the guarantor's right to assert the principal's claims defensively is in the nature of set-off against the creditor's claim on the guaranty; the guarantor may not recover affirmatively.[139] Thus, if the guarantor's recovery on his or her counterclaims exceeds his or her liability under the guaranty, the guarantor may not recover this excess.[140]

§ 8 Waiver of Defenses by the Guarantor

8.1 Defenses that cannot be Waived

A guarantor is an "obligor" for purposes of the provisions of Article 9 of the Uniform Commercial Code requiring the disposition of collateral in a commercially reasonable manner, and a guarantor cannot waive those provisions.[141] The parties can, however, agree on standards to measure the fulfillment of this requirement, so long as the standards are not unreasonable.[142]

8.2 "Catch-all" Waivers

Broad waiver language will be treated narrowly and with skepticism by Colorado courts. Like any other contract, the language of a guaranty is to be reasonably interpreted according to the intention of the parties as disclosed by facts and circumstances surrounding its execution.[143] Guarantee agreements are to be strictly construed in favor of the guarantor.[144] At a minimum, the words "absolute and unconditional" should be included to preserve the argument that all defenses were waived.

137. *Id. at* 1323.
138. *Highlands Ranch Univ. Park, LLC*, 129 P.3d at 1027.
139. *First Tex. Serv. Corp.*, 750 F. Supp. at 1060.
140. *Id.* (citing *Cont'l Grp., Inc.*, 536 F. Supp. at 662)
141. Colo. Rev. Stat. §§ 4-9-602(7), -610, -624 (2011).
142. Colo. Rev. Stat. § 4-9-603(a) (2011).
143. *Valley Nat'l Bank of Ariz.*, 404 P.2d at 274-75.
144. *Walter E. Heller & Co.*, 627 P.2d at 775.

8.3 Use of Specific Waivers

Colorado guaranties contain all of the waivers typically found in guaranties governed by the laws of other states. Among such waivers, guarantors typically waives all presentments, demands for payment or performance, notices of nonpayment or nonperformance, notices of default, protests, notices of protest, notices of dishonor, notice of acceptance of the guaranty, and all other notices whatever.

In addition, it is common practice in Colorado guaranties, when there are multiple guarantors, to include, in the guaranty agreement, a waiver of the provisions of C.R.S. §§13-50-102 and 103,[145] although the enforceability of the waiver is uncertain as there is no case law in Colorado addressing such a waiver.

It is typical in a guaranty for the guarantor to waive trial by jury and, if a particular court is specified for actions on the guaranty, waiver of any objection to the laying of venue or based on the grounds of *forum non conveniens.*

8.4 Defenses requiring an Explicit Waiver

In the absence of an explicit waiver, it is presumed that Colo. Rev. Stat. §§ 13-50-102 and 103 apply.

8.5 Third-party Pledgors—Defenses and Waiver thereof

Colorado has no reported cases relating specifically to the defenses of third-party pledgors.

§ 9 Jointly and Severally Liable Guarantors—Contribution and Reduction of Obligations upon Payment by a Co-obligor

Joint obligations are addressed by the following Colorado statutes:

C.R.S. § 13-50-101: All joint obligations and covenants shall be taken and held to be joint and several obligations and covenants.[146]

C.R.S. 13-50-102: A creditor of joint debtors may release one or more of such debtors, and such release shall operate as a full discharge of such debtor so released, but such release shall not release or discharge or affect the liability of the remaining debtor. Such release shall be taken and held to be a payment on the indebtedness of the full proportionate share of the debtor so released. [147]

---

145. *See infra* § 9.
146. *See* Bennett v. Morse, 39 P. 582 (Colo. App. 1894).
147. This section and §§ 13-50-101 and -103 did not apply where the defendant guarantors expressly agreed that the release of coguarantors would not affect defendants' liability in any way. United States v. Immordino, 386 F. Supp. 611 (D. Colo. 1974), *aff'd*, 534 F.2d 1378 (10th Cir. 1976).

C.R.S. 13-50-103: In case one or more joint debtors are released, no one of the remaining debtors shall be liable for more than his proportionate share of the indebtedness, unless he is the principal debtor and the debtor released was his surety, in which case the principal debtor is liable for the whole of the remainder of the indebtedness.

C.R.S. 13-50-104: Nothing in sections 13-50-102 to 13-50-104 affects or changes the right of a surety who has paid his proportionate share of an indebtedness of recovering the same from his principal debtor.

9.1 Contribution

"Contribution is an equitable doctrine based on principles of fundamental justice. It arises . . . when any burden ought, from the relationship of the parties . . . to be equally borne and each party is in *aequali jure*, contribution is due if one has been compelled to pay more than his share. The right to contribution is not dependent on contract, joint action, or original relationship between the parties; it is based on principles of fundamental justice and equity (footnotes omitted)."[148]

When there is an express agreement that a set of guarantors assume responsibility for the entire underlying obligation on default of the primary obligor, with full knowledge and understanding that some or all of the other coguarantors could be released from the guaranties, there is not necessarily a right of contribution.[149]

9.2 Reduction of Obligations upon Payment of Co-obligor

An obligee's release of a guarantor, without the consent of the remaining coguarantors, discharges the remaining coguarantors to the extent of their contributive share.[150] The release applies, however, only to the extent that the coguarantors are injured by the release.[151]

There is no release when a guarantor specifically consented to the release of one or more of his coguarantors,[152] nor when the guaranty is unconditional and absolute by its terms.[153] It is typical to include a consent to such releases in a guaranty.

Moreover, if the discharge of a guarantor's obligation results from operation of law, it generally has no effect upon the obligations of the remaining coguarantors.[154] Hence, if an obligee and a principal debtor alter the obligation to the detriment of coguarantors, some of whom consent while others do not, those not consenting are discharged, but those consenting remain bound.[155]

148. *Immordino*, 386 F. Supp at 616 (quoting Vickers Petroleum Co. v. Biffle, 239 F.2d 602, 606 (10th Cir. 1956)).
149. *Id.* at 614-16.
150. *Cooper Invs.*, 775, P.2d at 80.
151. *Immordino*, 386 F. Supp at 615-16.
152. *Id.*
153. *Id.*
154. *Cooper Invs.*, 775 P.2d at 80 (citing L. Simpson, Handbook on the Law of Suretyship § 19 (1950); Restatement of Security § 134 (1941)).
155. *Id.* at 80.

9.3 Liability of Parent Guarantors Owning less than 100 percent of Primary Obligor

There are no reported cases on the liability of parent guarantors owning less than 100 percent of a primary obligor, but guaranties of parent guarantors owning less than 100 percent of a primary obligor are generally regarded as being enforceable.

§ 10 Reliance

Legal consideration for a guaranty may be in the form of a legal detriment incurred by the obligee by reason of its reliance on a guaranty contract where the guarantor knew or had reason to know that such detriment would result from the guaranty.[156] For example, if an obligee's loan to a primary obligor is made in reliance on the execution of a guaranty agreement and the guarantor knew or had reason to know of the obligee's reliance on the guaranty agreement, then sufficient consideration exists for the guaranty.[157] Likewise, if an obligee relies on a guaranty and refrains from taking action against the primary obligor for the primary obligor's past debts, the obligee's forbearance from action constitutes sufficient consideration for the guaranty, notwithstanding the fact that the guarantor derived no immediate benefit from the guaranty.[158]

An extension of credit to a primary obligor in reliance upon a guaranty is sufficient consideration for the guaranty as to both past and future obligations, even though the benefit to the primary obligor constitutes the whole consideration.[159]

§ 11 Subrogation

One who is secondarily liable, upon discharge of the underlying obligation, has the right to be put in place of the one who has received payment while the underlying obligation still exists.[160]

Subrogation is an equitable doctrine allowing for the "substitution of another person in the place of a creditor, so that the person in whose favor it is exercised succeeds to the rights of the creditor in relation to the debt."[161] Therefore, a guarantor who is secondarily liable, upon discharging the underlying obligation, has the right to be put in the place of the one who has received payment while the primary obligation still exists.[162] Subrogation may apply

156. *Colo. State Bank of Denver*, 474 P.2d at 636.
157. *Farmers Elevator Co.*, 488 P.2d at 239.
158. *Linger*, 486 P.2d at 30.
159. *Ford Motor Credit Co.*, 615 F.2d at 898.
160. Cobbey v. Peterson, 3 P.2d 298 (Colo. 1931).
161. Behlen Mfg. Co. v. First Nat'l Bank of Englewood, 472 P.2d 703, 707 (Colo. App. 1970).
162. *Cobbey*, 3 P.2d at 352.

when 1) the guarantor makes the payment to protect its own interest, 2) the guarantor did not act as a volunteer, 3) the guarantor was not primarily liable for the debt paid, 4) the guarantor paid off the entire obligation, and 5) subrogation would not prejudice an intervening lienholder or lienholders.[163]

A guarantor's subrogation rights extend to all of the rights the obligee has against the primary obligor, including the right to dispose of collateral.[164] However, if the guarantor fails to satisfy the entire obligation, it may not seek subrogation for the partial obligation satisfied. Partial subrogation is not permitted because it has the effect of "dividing the security between the original obligee and the subrogee, imposing unexpected burdens and potential complexities of division of the security."[165]

A guarantor's right to subrogation may be waived, but such waivers must be evidenced "by the most unequivocal language in the guaranty agreement."[166]

§ 12 Triangular Set-off in Bankruptcy

Courts across the country are split as to whether a guaranty agreement creates mutuality for the purposes of bankruptcy setoffs.[167] However, at least one Colorado case has recognized the possibility of mutuality between a creditor, a creditor's wholly owned subsidiary, and the debtor when the parties enter into an express contract recognizing each party's right to set off the other's debts.[168] In that case, the court ultimately declined to find mutuality between the debtor, the creditor, and the creditor's wholly owned subsidiary because there was no evidence of an express written agreement between the parties to treat the creditor and the subsidiary as one entity.[169] However, this "contract exception" to the requirement of mutuality in bankruptcy setoffs has been heavily criticized in other jurisdictions.[170]

---

163. Land Title Ins. Corp. v. Ameriquest Mortg. Co., 207 P.3d 141, 145 (Colo. 2009).
164. May v. Women's Bank, N.A., 807 P.2d 1145, 1148 (Colo. 1991).
165. Hicks v. Londre, 125 P.3d 452, 457 (Colo. 2005).
166. *Behlen Mfg. Co.*, 472 P.2d at 707-08.
167. *Compare* Bloor v. Shapiro, 32 B.R. 993, 1001-02 (S.D.N.Y. 1983) ("Where, however, as here, the defendant has assumed a third party's obligations to the bankrupt, and where the bankrupt had agreed that the defendant is entitled to assert the bankrupt's liabilities to the third party, these liabilities become debts owed by the bankrupt to the defendant; such debts may be asserted by the defendant as off-sets against the bankrupt's claims.") *with* In re Ingersoll, 90 B.R. 168, 172 (Bankr. W.D.N.C. 1987) (although the guaranty at issue created an absolute promise that essentially made the guarantor a comaker of an obligation to the bankrupt obligee, "it does not change the fact that the debts are between different parties in different capacities and, thus, not subject to offset.").
168. *See* In re Balducci Oil Co., 33 B.R. 847, 853 (Bankr. D. Colo. 1983).
169. *Id.*
170. *See, e.g.*, In re Lehman Bros. Inc., 458 B.R. 134 (Bankr. S.D.N.Y. 2011); In re SemCrude, L.P., 399 B.R. 388 (Bankr. D. Del. 2009).

§ 13 Indemnification—Whether the Primary Obligor has a Duty

The Court of Appeals for the Tenth Circuit has generally stated that "it is well settled in the law that one who guarantees the debt of another and is required to pay the same is entitled to reimbursement from the principal debtor."[171] "This principle is so well settled that no citation of authority is necessary."[172]

Further, the law raises an implied promise on the part of the primary obligor to repay the guarantor who guarantees an obligation at the request or consent of the primary obligor.[173] Once the guarantor pays the debt, it has a right of action against the primary obligor for reimbursement even in the absence of any express promise in that regard.[174] However, some jurisdictions hold that if a guarantor binds itself at the request of the obligee or otherwise voluntarily guarantees the obligation without the request or consent of the primary obligor, then the guarantor is not entitled to indemnity for any amounts paid to the obligee pursuant to its guaranty.[175] Colorado courts do not appear to have decided the issue of whether a primary obligor's duty to indemnify depends on whether the primary obligor requested or consented to the guaranty, or whether the duty attaches regardless of whether the guarantor binds itself at the behest of either the primary obligor or the obligee.

§ 14 Enforcement of Guaranties

14.1 Limitations on Recovery

The obligee cannot collect more than the amount of the debt owed.

14.2 Enforcement of Guaranties of Payment versus Guaranties of Performance

There are no reported cases distinguishing the enforcement of guaranties of payment versus guaranties of performance.

---

171. United States v. Hendler, 225 F.2d 106, 108 (10th Cir. 1955), *disapproved of on other grounds,* United States v. Plesha, 352 U.S. 202 (1957).
172. *Id.*
173. 38A C.J.S. Guaranty § 156 (2008).
174. *Id.*
175. *See id.*; Van Shaick v. Lawyers' Title & Guar. Co., 268 N.Y.S. 554, 565 (N.Y. Sup. 1933).

14.3 Exercising Rights under a Guaranty Where the Underlying Obligation is also Secured by a Mortgage or Where the Guaranty is Secured by a Mortgage

Colorado does not have a single-action rule. Accordingly, an obligee can sue on a guaranty while at the same time proceeding with the foreclosure of real property securing the underlying debt. Colorado has no antideficiency legislation, but an obligee cannot collect more than the amount of the debt owed. Colorado also has legislation and cases that hold that an obligor may plead as a defense to a deficiency action that the obligee's bid in the foreclosure was less than the obligor's good faith estimate of the fair market value of the property being sold less the amount of unpaid real property taxes and all amounts secured by liens against the property being sold that are senior to the deed of trust or other lien being foreclosed and certain costs; provided that the obligor need not bid more than the amount due to the holder.[176]

Under Colorado's unique Public Trustee system,[177] the original "evidence of debt"[178] must be presented to the Public Trustee in order to obtain a release of,[179] or to foreclose,[180] a deed of trust (which is the customary instrument in Colorado to secure a lien on real property). Certain banking and other institutions identified as "qualified holders"[181] are relieved of this obligation[182] and a corporate surety bond may be substituted if the original evidence of debt is lost.[183] A guaranty generally will meet the statutory definition of an "evidence of debt," although it is not listed in the statute as an example of an "evidence of debt." Because the amount payable under a guaranty generally is not stated in the guaranty and in a performance guaranty may not be a readily determinable amount, foreclosure of a deed of trust secured by a guaranty may be more difficult than foreclosure of the typical deed of trust secured by a promissory note. If the Public Trustee will not foreclose a deed of trust for any reason, the deed of trust may be foreclosed judicially.[184]

Generally, any lien upon property created by a mortgage or deed of trust ceases to be a lien 15 years after the date on which the final payment or performance of the obligation secured thereby is due as shown by such mortgage or deed of trust recorded in the office of the county clerk and recorder of the county wherein the property is located.[185] If the date on which the final payment or performance is due cannot be determined from the information contained in the recorded mortgage or deed of trust, such date shall, for the

176. Colo. Rev. Stat. § 38-38-106(6) (2011); *see also* First Nat'l Bank of Se. Denver v. Blanding, 885 P.2d 324 (Colo. App. 1994); Bank of Am. v. Kosovich, 878 P.2d 65 (Colo. App. 1994).
177. *See* Colo. Rev. Stat. §§ 38-37-100.5 to -113 (2011).
178. Defined in Colo. Rev. Stat. § 38-38-100.3(8) (2011) as follows: "'Evidence of debt' means a writing that evidences a promise to pay or a right to the payment of a monetary obligation, such as a promissory note, bond, negotiable instrument, a loan, credit, or similar agreement, or a monetary judgment entered by a court of competent jurisdiction."
179. *See* Colo. Rev. Stat. § 38-39-102 (2011).
180. *See* Colo. Rev. Stat. § 38-38-101(1)(b) (2011).
181. *See* Colo. Rev. Stat. § 38-39-100.3(28) (2011).
182. *See* Colo. Rev. Stat. § 38-38-101(b)(II) (2011).
183. *See* Colo. Rev. Stat. § 38-38-101(b)(I) (2011).
184. *See* Colo. Rev. Stat. § 38-39-101 (2011).
185. *See* Colo. Rev. Stat. § 38-39-201 (2011).

purpose of Colo. Rev. Stat. § 38-39-201, be considered to be the date of the recorded instrument or, if the instrument is undated, the date the instrument was first recorded, notwithstanding anything in any other instrument or any unrecorded instrument to the contrary. Thus, a deed of trust or mortgage that secures a guaranty and that does not state the maturity date of the obligation will remain a lien only for 15 years from the date of recording of the mortgage or deed of trust.

14.4 Litigating Guaranty Claims: Procedural Considerations

Fraud is an affirmative defense that must be pled with particularity.[186]

A sufficient evidentiary foundation for admission of a guaranty into evidence is established if the guaranty is regular on its face, was in the possession of the obligee as part of the obligee's records, and the obligee extended credit in reliance on it. Evidence of the genuineness of the signatures and evidence of the circumstances surrounding the negotiation of the guaranty and its delivery to the obligee is not required.[187]

§ 15 Revival and Reinstatement of Guaranties

There are no reported cases specifically on the revival and reinstatement of guaranties.

186. *Alien, Inc.*, 924 P.2d at 1068.
187. *Gates*, 479 P.2d at 287.

Connecticut State Law of Guaranties

Michael F. Maglio
Robinson & Cole LLP
280 Trumbull Street
Hartford, CT 06103-3597
(860) 275-8274
(860) 275-8299
mmaglio@rc.com
www.rc.com

James C. Schulwolf
Shipman & Goodwin LLP
One Constitution Plaza
Hartford, CT 06103
Telephone: (860) 251-5949
Fax: (860) 251-5311
jschulwolf@goodwin.com
www.shipmangoodwin.com

R. Jeffrey Smith
Bingham McCutchen LLP
One State Street
Hartford, CT 06103
Telephone: 860-240-2759
Fax: 860-240-2575
jeff.smith@bingham.com
www.bingham.com

Thomas J. Welsh
Brown & Welsh, P.C.
530 Preston Avenue, Suite 220
Meriden, CT 06450
Telephone: (203) 235-1651
Telefax: (203) 235-9600
TJWelsh@BrownWelsh.com

Contents

Connecticut State Law of Guaranties[1]

Practice Pointer: **Both the Restatement (Third) of Suretyship and Guaranty** and the **Restatement (Third) of Contracts** have been cited by Connecticut courts as authority with approval. See *Lestorti v. DeLeo*, 298 Conn. 466, 475 (fn 8) (Conn. Supreme Ct. 2010) ("[w]e have previously relied on the Restatement (Third) of Suretyship and Guaranty to fill gaps in and support our common law (citations omitted)"... [w]e also frequently have relied on the Restatement (Second) of Contracts (citations omitted)"). Introductory Note: In order to standardize our discussion of the law of guaranties, we use the following vocabulary to refer to the various parties to a guaranty and their obligations.

"Guarantor" means a person who, by contract, agrees to satisfy an underlying obligation of a principal obligor to an obligee upon the principal obligor's default on that underlying obligation. We do not draw a distinction between guarantors and sureties, as the distinction in Connecticut between the two is often unclear and not helpful.[2]

"Guaranty" means the contract by which the guarantor agrees to satisfy the underlying obligation of a principal obligor to an obligee in the event the principal obligor defaults on the underlying obligation.

"Obligee" means the person to whom the underlying obligation is owed. For example, the lender under a loan agreement would be an obligee with respect to the borrower.

"Principal Obligor" means the person who incurs the underlying obligation to the obligee. For example, the borrower under a loan agreement would be a principal obligor.

"Underlying Obligation" means the obligation or obligations incurred by the principal obligor and owed to the obligee. For example, the borrower's obligation to make payments to a lender of principal and interest on a loan constitutes an underlying obligation.

---

1. By: Michael F. Maglio, Esq., Robinson & Cole LLP, Hartford, CT, James C. Schulwolf, Esq., Shipman & Goodwin LLP, Hartford, CT, R. Jeffrey Smith, Esq., Bingham McCutchen, LLP, Hartford, CT, and Thomas J. Welsh, Esq., Brown & Welsh, P.C., Meriden, CT. The authors are the officers and are members of the Commercial Finance Committee of the Connecticut Bar Association. The authors express their appreciation to Travis Searles, an associate attorney at Robinson & Cole, LLP, Olga Kamensky, a student associate at Bingham McCutchen, LLP, and Karun Ahuja at Shipman & Goodwin LLP, for their assistance with this outline.
2. *See, e.g.,* Bronx Derrick Tool Co. v. Porcupine Co., 117 Conn. 314, 167 A. 829 (1933) in which an agreement was construed as an "agreement to indemnify" and not a "conditional guaranty," allowing recovery by a creditor without exhausting remedies against the steel erection company that failed to pay for the use of equipment; and Regency Savings Bank v. Westmark Partners, 59 Conn. App. 160, 164, 756 A.2d 299 (2000) stating that a guaranty "is simply a species of contract"; *see also* Restatement (Third) of Suretyship & Guar. § 1 cmt. c (1996) [. . . Although there are important differences between the two mechanisms that should not be obscured, these differences relate to the duties contractually imposed on the secondary obligor by the secondary obligation and not to the nature of the rights inherent in suretyship status. . . . ". The Connecticut Uniform Commercial Code provides that the term "surety" includes the term guarantor in Conn. Gen. Stat. § 42a-1-201(39).

§ 1 Nature of the Guaranty Arrangement

Connecticut law of guaranty and suretyship is largely case law extending over a century, with many cited cases dating from the mid-1800s. Under Connecticut law, a contract of guaranty is a promise to answer for the debt, default, or miscarriage of another and is a collateral undertaking and presupposes some contract or transaction to which it is collateral.[3] Suretyship, in general, including a guaranty, is a three-party relationship where the surety undertakes to perform to an obligee if the principal obligor fails to do so.[4] It is a three-party separate engagement for the performance of an undertaking of another and there exist two different obligations—one obligation is that of the principal obligor, and the other that of the guarantor. The principal obligor is not a party to the guaranty, and the guarantor is not a party to the underlying obligation. The undertaking of the principal obligor is independent of the promise of the guarantor, and the responsibility imposed by the contract of guaranty differs from that which is created by the contract to which the guaranty is collateral. The fact that both contracts are written on the same paper or instrument does not affect the independence or separateness of the one from the other.

1.1 Guaranty Relationships

A guaranty is a contract of secondary liability. The contract of a guarantor is his own separate contract; it is in the nature of a contract by him that the thing guaranteed to be done by the principal shall be done, and is not merely an engagement jointly with the principal to do the thing.[5] A guarantor, not being a joint contractor with his principal, is not bound to do what the principal has contracted to do; rather, the guarantor has to answer for the consequences of his principal obligor's default pursuant to the guaranty agreement. Since, however, the guarantor's contract is ancillary to that of the principal obligor, suretyship law will permit the guarantor to assert defenses or discharge of the principal obligor unless the very purpose of that guaranty was to shift the risk of the particular event from the obligee to the guarantor.[6] The principal obligor, however, has an obligation under law to perform its underlying agree-

3. Regency Sav. Bank v. Westmark Partners, 59 Conn. App 160, 756 A.2d 299 (2000), on remand 2001 WL 399921, affirmed in part, reversed in part 70 Conn. App. 341, 798 A.2d 476 (2001). Wolthausen v. Trimpert, 93 Conn. 260, 105 A. 687 (1919) (need for underlying contract for guaranty) and Star Contracting Corp v. Manway Const. Co., Inc., 32 Conn Sup. 64, 337 A.2d 669 (Conn. Super. 1973) (need for underlying obligation for surety contract).
4. Elm Haven Const. Ltd. Partnership v. Neri Const., LLC, 281 F. Supp.2d 406, (D. Conn, 2003) affirmed 376 F.3d 96 (2nd Cir., 2004).
5. The undertaking of the parties is a matter of agreement and the court will not rewrite commercially sophisticated agreements. Bank of Boston Connecticut v. Schlesinger, 220 Conn. 152, 159, 595 A.2d 872 (1991). In Monroe Ready Mix Concrete, Inc. v. Westcor Development Corp., 183 Conn. 348, 439 A.2d 362 (1981) the Connecticut Supreme Court pointed out that, in discussing continuing guaranties, the New York Court of Appeals lamented that "[p]recedents do not help much in the construction of such instruments" and that "[t]he interpretation of continuing guaranties, as of other contracts, is principally a question of the intention of the contracting parties . . . to be determined by the trier of facts." (citations omitted)
6. American Oil Company v. Valenti et al, 179 Conn. 349 (1979); Cadle Company of Connecticut, Inc. v. C.F.D. Development Corporation, 44 Conn. App. 409, certification granted in part 241 Conn. 901, 693 A.2d 303, appeal dismissed, 243 Conn. 667, 706 A.2d 975 (1997).

ment with the obligee and to reimburse the guarantor that pays the obligee pursuant to a guaranty.[7]

Although, under Connecticut law, no "technical words" are needed to create a guaranty obligation, a court will look to the substance of the agreement of the parties to determine whether sufficient facts exist to fairly presume the intent of the parties to create guarantor liability.[8] Indefinite agreements showing no intent to constitute an enforceable contract will not be sufficient to constitute an enforceable guaranty.[9]

1.2 Other Suretyship Relationships

While not the focus of this survey, we note that a suretyship relationship may also arise because of the pledge of collateral.[10] As such, a guaranty-type relationship arises, to the extent of the collateral pledged, when a person supplies collateral for a loan in order to induce the obligee to lend to the principal obligor or where one party mortgages property to an obligee to secure the debt of another.[11]

§ 2 State Law Requirements for an Entity to Enter a Guaranty[12]

Partnerships, limited liability companies, and corporations can all grant guaranties in furtherance of their business activities. Such grants are generally permitted by the appropriate Connecticut statute.[13]

---

7. Note the principal obligor's duty of performance and reimbursement to the guarantor under RESTATEMENT (THIRD) OF SURETYSHIP & GUAR. §§ 21 and 22. *Also see, for example*, In re Metal Center, Inc., 31 B.R. 458 (Bankr. D. CT 1983) (reimbursement of guarantor) and Smith v. Mitsubishi Motors Credit of America, 247 Conn. 342, 721 A.2d 1197 (1998) (surety's right of reimbursement from principal obligor).
8. Finnican v. Feigenspan, 81 Conn. 378, 71 A. 497 (1908) and later cases. In fact, in Associated Catalog Merchandisers, Inc. v. Chagnon, 210 Conn. 734, 557 A.2d 525, appeal after remand 212 Conn. 322, 561 A.2d 436 (1989), the court found an installment promissory note evidenced a continuing guaranty when viewed with the course of performance by the parties over years.
9. *See* Glazer v. Dress Barn, Inc., 274 Conn. 33, 873 A.2d 929 (2005).
10. *See* Rowan v. Sharps' Rifle Mfg. Co., 33 Conn. 1 (1865); RESTATEMENT (THIRD) OF SURETYSHIP AND GUARANTY § 1 (noting that a person is a surety when "pursuant to contract . . . an obligee has recourse against [that] person . . . *or against that person's property* with respect to an obligation . . . of another person . . . to the obligee" (emphasis added)). *See also* § 9 infra.
11. Under RESTATEMENT (THIRD) OF SURETYSHIP & GUAR. § 2(c) the secondary obligation may be created by "contract granting the obligee a security interest in property of the secondary obligor to secure the underlying obligation."
12. For the purposes of this survey, we assume that a guaranty will not constitute "financial guaranty insurance" within the meaning of Part IIb. of Chapter 698 of the Connecticut General Statutes (§ 38a-*et seq.*) (the "Insurance Law"). *See* Conn. Gen. Stat. § 38a-92a (defining financial guaranty insurance). Under the Insurance Law, "[e]ach financial guaranty insurance corporation may transaction financial guaranty insurance business in this state if licensed to do so . . ." Conn. Gen. Stat.§ 38a-92b. In addition, the Insurance Law limits the underlying obligations for which even a licensed corporation may issue financial guaranty insurance. *See* Conn. Gen. Stat. § 38a-92g.
13. This article does not consider whether such a guaranty would be considered an obligation that would be considered the incurring of an obligation that would be a fraudulent transfer under Chapter 923a of the Connecticut General Statutes. While no Connecticut case has been found stating that a guaranty was in violation of this statute, counsel should be aware to check for such cases in the future.

2.1 Corporations

Under the Connecticut Business Corporation Act, a Connecticut business corporation may, within the scope of its general corporate powers, make contracts or guarantees, unless its certificate of incorporation provides otherwise.[14] A Connecticut business corporation is also expressly authorized by this statute to secure any of its obligations by mortgage or pledge of any of its property.

Transactions by corporations, or any subsidiary or other entity in which the corporation has a controlling interest, including guaranty transactions, with directors (or their relatives or entities in which they have an interest) may be challenged as directors' conflicting interest transactions unless they either (a) are disclosed and approved by disinterested directors or stockholders of the corporation or (b) the transaction is found to have been fair to the corporation.[15]

The statutes governing Connecticut nonstock corporations have similar statutory provisions.[16]

2.2 Partnerships and Limited Liability Partnerships

Connecticut has adopted the Uniform Partnership Act[17] which neither expressly empowers a partnership to issue a guaranty nor expressly regulates or prohibits such activity. An act of a partner that is not apparently for carrying on in the ordinary course the partnership business binds the partnership only if the act was authorized by the other partners.[18]

Connecticut limited partnerships, under Chapter 610 of the Connecticut General Statutes (Conn. Gen. Stat. §34-9 *et seq.*), and Connecticut limited liability partnerships, under Part XI of Chapter 614 of the Connecticut General Statutes (Conn. Gen. Stat. §34-406, *et seq.),* have the same general authorization provisions and limitation to actions in the ordinary course of the entity's business as for Connecticut general partnerships.

2.3 Limited Liability Companies

The Connecticut Limited Liability Company Act[19] generally permits limited liability companies to issue guaranties unless the articles of organization of a particular company provide otherwise.[20]

---

14. Conn. Gen. Stat. § 33-647(7). Application of Conn. Gen. Stat. § 33-649 would also limit challenges to a guaranty to a third party on the grounds that a corporation did not have the power to act.
15. Part VIII(F) of Chapter 601 of the Connecticut General Statutes (Conn. Gen. Stat. § 33-781 *et seq.*).
16. *See* Conn. Gen. Stat. § 33-1036(7) (power to guaranty), § 33-1038 (Ultra Vires transactions) and Part VII(F) of Chapter 602 of the Connecticut General Statutes (Directors' conflicting interest transactions).
17. Chapter 614 of the Connecticut General Statutes (Conn. Gen. Stat. § 34-300 *et seq.*).
18. Conn. Gen. Stat. § 34-322(2). Obligees are advised to obtain the consent of all general partners to guaranty or loan transactions unless clearly to the partnership or for its benefit.
19. Chapter 613 of the Connecticut General Statutes (Conn. Gen. Stat. § 34-100 *et seq.*).
20. Conn. Gen. Stat. § 34-124(d)(3).

2.4 Statutory Trusts

Statutory trusts were adopted in Connecticut in 1996.[21] No specific authorization is provided in the governing statutes for guarantees by statutory trusts. However, Conn. Gen Stat. §34-502b provides that " . . . a statutory trust may be sued for debts and other obligations or liabilities contracted or incurred by the trustees . . . in the performance of their . . . duties under the governing instrument of the statutory trust . . . "

2.5 Banks and Trust Companies

Under Chapter 665 of the Connecticut General Statutes, a Connecticut state-chartered bank has no authority to issue guarantees. The situations under which a national bank may become a guarantor are governed by federal law. *See* National Bank as Guarantor or Surety on Indemnity Bond, 12 C.F.R. § 7.1017 (2010).

2.6 Individuals

Confusion can sometimes arise in the case of corporate officers or directors signing guaranties in closely held corporations or other organizations. In such instances, a case-by-case inquiry determines whether an individual intended to be personally bound or, instead, only issued a guaranty on behalf of a partnership or corporation and thus only in an official employment capacity.

While a business corporation must have "authority" to execute a guaranty, an individual guarantor must have the "capacity" to enter into the guaranty. Incapacity can be a defense against the enforcement of a guaranty issued by an individual.[22]

Another consideration with individual guaranties is marital property. Connecticut is not a community property state and under Conn. Gen. Stat. §46b-36 each spouse can enter into contracts and deal with their property to the same extent as if he or she were unmarried. Under this statute, a spouse's earnings in Connecticut are treated as the individual property of that spouse. Aside from the duty of mutual support, neither spouse has any interest in the property of the other. Put another way, a creditor does not have recourse to the property of a nonsigning spouse under a guaranty signed by the other spouse.

§ 3 Signatory's Authority to Execute a Guaranty

Generally, the obligee has a duty of reasonable inquiry when it has some notice that the signor of the guaranty does not have authority to bind the guarantor.

---

21. *See* Chapter 615 of the Connecticut General Statutes (Conn. Gen. Stat. § 34-501 *et. seq.*).
22. *See* Restatement (Third) of Suretyship & Guar. (1996) § 10 (Capacity).

3.1 Corporations

For an obligee to rely on a guaranty, the guaranty must be signed by an officer with actual or apparent authority to act in such capacity.[23] An obligee cannot enforce a guaranty if the obligee had notice that the officer who signed for the corporation lacked authority to do so. Where an obligee-plaintiff invokes the doctrine of apparent authority, that obligee bears a duty to demonstrate that it acted in good faith based on the actions or inadvertences of the principal.[24]

Corporate officers do not have inherent authority to commit the corporation by virtue of their office *per se*. The corporation is generally only liable if it is shown that the acts are so related to the duties of the office that they may reasonably be held to have been done in the prosecution of the business of the corporation and while acting in the course of their employment.[25] If a corporation's guaranty bears some reasonable relationship to the corporation's business, evidence that a signing officer was charged with the general management of the corporation's business can provide apparent authority to execute a guaranty.[26] However, under Connecticut law, apparent authority is not limitless; the potential obligee dealing with an agent and seeking to impose liability on the principal has the burden to "demonstrate that it acted in good faith based on the actions or inadvertences of the principal."[27] For this reason, obligees are advised to make reasonable inquiry of the actual authority of a corporate officer to execute a guaranty on behalf of a corporation.

3.2 Partnerships and Limited Liability Partnerships

Under the Uniform Partnership Act as adopted in Connecticut, an act of a partner that is not apparently for carrying on the partnership business in the ordinary course binds the partnership only if the act was authorized by the other partners.[28] When carrying out the business of the partnership, however, it is settled law that a general partner has the authority to bind the partnership.[29]

---

23. One dealing with a person known to be an agent of a corporation is "put on inquiry as to the scope of his authority" and the corporation will not be obligated as principal, unless the agent . . . was acting within the scope of the authority expressly or impliedly conferred upon him ..., or unless the corporation is estopped from denying that the agent was so acting, or unless there has been a subsequent ratification of the agent's act." Adams v. Herald Pub. Co., 82 Conn. 448 at 451, 74 A. 755 (1909).
24. Newtown Associates v. Northeast Structures, 15 Conn. App. 633 at 638-639, 546 A.2d 310 (1988) and cases cited therein.
25. Lettieri v. American Savings Bank, 182 Conn. 1 at 7, 437 A.2d 822 (mortgage loan not authorized by corporation but upheld due to apparent authority conferred on president of corporation by past conduct of the corporation relied upon in good faith by lender).
26. *See, e.g.,* Host America Corp. v. Ramsey, 107 Conn. App. 849, 947 A.2d 957, certification denied 289 Conn. 904, 957 A.2d 870 (2008) (corporate president had apparent authority to execute employment agreements) in which the two elements of apparent authority are recited, namely (1) acts or inadvertences of the principal (not of the agent) that causes or allows third persons to believe the agent possesses this authority and (2) the third party dealing with the agent must have, acting in good faith, reasonably believed under all of the circumstances that the agent had the necessary authority to bind the principal. *See also* Lettieri v. American Savings Bank, *supra.*
27. *See* Newtown Associates v. Northeast Structures, Inc., 15 Conn. App. 633 at 638-639, 546 A.2d 310 (1988) and cases cited therein.
28. Conn. Gen. Stat. § 34-322(2). Obligees are advised to obtain the consent of all general partners to guaranty or loan transactions unless clearly to the partnership or for its benefit.
29. Hirschfeld v. Hirschfeld, 50 Conn. App. 280, 719 A.2d 41, certification denied 247 Conn. 929, 719 A.2d 1168 (1998) and cases cited therein. [The specific statute section cited in this case and prior cited cases was repealed but was enacted as part of the Uniform Partnership Act adopted by Connecticut in Conn. Gen. Stat. § 34-322.]

Actual authority may also be provided in the partnership agreement.[30] Under the same principles of agency noted above in the discussion of agents of corporations, those dealing with partners are advised to inquire as to whether a signatory has the appropriate authority to bind the partnership.[31] The consequence of finding that the general partner had no authority and that the obligee was aware of that fact is that the action of the general partner does not bind the partnership or its property.

Under the Uniform Limited Partnership Act as adopted in Connecticut, a general partner has the same powers as a partner in a general partnership.[32] Therefore, the foregoing principles are also applicable to the authority of the general partner of a Connecticut limited partnership.

3.3 Limited Liability Companies

The Connecticut Limited Liability Company Act provides that, in the case of a member-managed LLC, every member is an agent of that company and can sign instruments pursuant to carrying on in the usual way of business unless that person has no actual authority to act in such way and his counterparty has knowledge of that fact.[33] In the case of a manager-managed LLC, no member has authority to bind the LLC. Each manager of a manager-managed LLC can bind the LLC if such guaranty is "for apparently carrying on in the usual way the business of the [LLC]" unless the manager has no actual authority and the counterparty knows of this lack of authority.[34] Note, however, that any act of a member or a manager that is *not* "apparently carrying on in the usual way the business of the [LLC]" does not bind the LLC or its property unless actually authorized pursuant to the operating agreement.[35] Therefore, practitioners dealing with Connecticut limited liability companies are advised to investigate and determine whether guaranties are expressly authorized in the operating agreement or if additional approvals are needed to give the manager(s) and/or members(s) executing such guaranties the express authority to do so.

3.4 Statutory Trusts

The Connecticut Statutory Trust Act provides that the statutory trust may be sued and its property is subject to attachment and execution for debts and other obligations or liabilities contracted or incurred by the trustees in the performance of their duties under the governing instrument.[36] Conn. Gen. Stat. §34-517 provides that the business and affairs of a statutory trust shall

30. *See* Standish v. Sotavento Corp., 58 Conn. App. 789, 755 A.2d 910, certification denied 254 Conn. 935, 761 A.2d 762 (2000) (upholding revolving credit agreement and mortgage).
31. Although no cases have been noted where the issue of whether a guaranty is "for apparently carrying on in the ordinary course the partnership business," it is likely that a guaranty would not be considered in the "ordinary course."
32. Conn. Gen. Stat. § 34-17(a).
33. Conn. Gen. Stat. § 34-130(a).
34. Conn. Gen. Stat. § 34-130(b).
35. Conn. Gen. Stat. § 34-130(c). Although no case has been found on this point, it might be argued that guaranties of third-party obligations are not "usual" in the business of most LLCs.
36. Conn. Gen. Stat. § 34-502b.

be managed "by or under the direction of" its trustees. Wide latitude is provided in this statute for the governing instrument of a statutory trust to alter the "rights, duties and obligations" of the trustees. Although no case has been found relating to this statute, parties dealing with Connecticut statutory trusts are advised to review the governing instruments of these statutory trusts to determine whether guaranties are permitted and any conditions or necessary authorizations to allow the trustees to execute them.[37] Connecticut's adoption of Uniform Commercial Code (UCC) Article 9 was amended in 2003 to specifically permit security interests to be granted in deposit accounts of statutory trusts (other than a payroll or trust account labeled as such).[38]

3.5 Banks and Trust Companies

A case-by-case inquiry of the powers provided for in a bank's or trust company's corporate governance documents is necessary to determine who may validly execute a guaranty on behalf of a bank or trust company.

§ 4 Consideration; Sufficiency of Past Consideration

Standard contract principles apply to the analysis of consideration for a contract of guaranty. The principal agreement is sufficient consideration for an accompanying guaranty.[39]

Consideration is required to create a valid contract of guaranty.[40] The inquiry into sufficient consideration is based on standard contract law principles. The benefit or obligation that forms the consideration need not flow directly to the guarantor from the obligee; the consideration flowing from the obligee to the principal obligor is sufficient to support a contemporaneous guaranty.[41] Note that some cases have indicated that some length of time between consideration of the underlying obligation and a guaranty does not necessarily render them noncontemporaneous.[42] Where, however, a guaranty

37. Since the only restriction appears to be whether the action is performed by the trustees "in the performance of their duties under the governing instrument," review of the governing instruments and any and all amendments is advisable.
38. Conn. Gen. Stat. § 42a-9-109(d)(16).
39. Murphy v. Schwaner, 84 Conn. 420, 80 A. 295 (1911) (guaranty lease payments). However, *see* Superior Wire and Paper Products, Ltd. v. Talcott Tool and Mach., Inc., 184 Conn. 10 at 20, 441 A.2d 43 (1981), in which the Supreme Court noted that "the modern law of contracts . . . makes guaranties enforceable on the basis of reliance" citing Restatement (Second) of Contracts § 89C (Tent. Ed. 1973).
40. Allen v. Rundle, 45 Conn. 528 (1878).
41. Superior Wire and Paper Products, Ltd. v. Talcott Tool and Mach., Inc., 184 Conn. 10, 441 A.2d 43 (1981) (shipments of steel goods after or contemporaneously with execution of guaranty was consideration for guaranty to induce further shipments). The court held that whether the further shipments were made contemporaneously with the execution of the guaranty or at some time thereafter is "legally irrelevant to the issue of inducement."
42. *See, e.g.,* Garland v. Gaines, 73 Conn. 662, 49 A. 19, 84 Am. St. Rep. 182 (1901) (guaranty of lease not signed until after lease executed, but landlord did not allow tenant to occupy the premises until the guaranty was executed); Connecticut Bank & Trust Co. v. Wilcox, 201 Conn. 570 at 575, 518 A.2d 928 (1986) ("Both our case law and the modern law of contract eschew any requirement of contemporaneity between a continuing guaranty and the obligations secured thereby" where notes evidencing the guaranteed debt were executed several months after the continuing guaranty agreements were executed.).

is given after the execution of the principal contract, a new consideration is necessary to support the guaranty.[43]

It is a long-standing rule in Connecticut that forbearance in requiring immediate payment or filing suit or otherwise exercising remedies is sufficient consideration to support a guaranty of the prior debt.[44]

§ 5 Notice of Acceptance

Notice of acceptance is not required if the guaranty is absolute.

A mere offer to guaranty payment of a prospective debt the incurrence of which is dependent upon future executory acts by the obligee of which the guarantor would have no knowledge is not binding until notice of acceptance is communicated by the obligee to the guarantor.[45] Notice of acceptance is not required where the guaranty is "absolute"[46] or is given in exchange for the consideration given by the obligee in a simultaneous transaction.[47] Commonly, a guarantor waives notice of acceptance in its guaranty agreement. Under Connecticut law, such a waiver is enforceable.[48]

§ 6 Interpretation of Guaranties

In Connecticut, a guaranty is "a species of contract"[49] and, accordingly, courts will interpret a guaranty in the same manner by which they would interpret the language of any other contract.

---

43. Cowles v. Peck, 55 Conn. 251, 10 A. 569, 3 Am. St. Rep. 44 (1887).
44. Barnard v. Norton, 1 Kirby 193 (1786) (forbearance from immediately suing and attaching property); Sage v. Wilcox, 6 Conn. 81 (1826) (forbearance to sue maker of note for one year); Breed v. Hillhouse, 7 Conn. 522 (1829) (delay in payment of a note); Swift v. Lundin, 98 Conn. 78, 118 A. 444 (1922) (forbearance to require payment on delivery); Matter of Autoworld Enterprises, 131 B.R. 1 (Bankr. D. Conn. 1991) (forbearance on collection of payment of notes, although no specified time period of forbearance).
45. *See* Craft v. Isham, 13 Conn. 28 (1838); The New-Haven County Bank v. Mitchell, 15 Conn. 206 (1842).
46. Craft v. Isham, 13 Conn. 28 (1838) ("the undertaking of the defendant was absolute, that the note should be paid within the time limited; and it was correctly held, that no notice [of acceptance] was necessary." (citations omitted)).
47. *See, e.g.,* The New-Haven County Bank v. Mitchell, 15 Conn. 206, at 219 (1842) (notice of acceptable not required where "delivery of the guaranty in question was not an incipient step in the formation of the contract, but the result of a previous negotiation and agreement, and constituted the very consummation of the contract"); White v. Reed, 15 Conn. 457, 463 (1843)("where the guaranty and the acceptance of it are simultaneous, and parts of the same transaction, no subsequent notice of acceptance is necessary" (citing The New-Haven County Bank v. Mitchell, 15 Conn. 206)); Hartford-Aetna National Bank v. Anderson, 92 Conn. 643 at 647 (1918)(no notice of acceptance required where guaranty "was delivered to the bank, not as an offer originating with the guarantor, but in answer to the requirement of the bank that [the debtor] should procure [the guaranty] to be signed by a responsible guarantor").
48. *See* § 8 *infra.*
49. JSA Financial Corporation v. Quality Kitchen Corporation of Delaware, et al, 113 Conn. App. 52 at 47 (2009); Garofalo v. Squillante, 60 Conn. App. 687,694 (2000), cert. denied 255 Conn. 929 (2001).

6.1 General Principles

Like any other contract, Connecticut courts will construe a guaranty to give effect to the intent of the parties,[50] ascertaining such intent by a "fair and reasonable construction of the written words"[51] that are given their "common, natural and ordinary meaning and usage."[52] To that end, Connecticut courts give effect to terms that are clear and unambiguous as a matter of law and will not "torture words to import ambiguity when the ordinary meaning leaves no room for ambiguity."[53] Ambiguity must arise from the contract itself and not simply from one party's subjective interpretation of the disputed language.[54] A presumption that the language used in a guaranty is definitive arises when the guaranty is between sophisticated parties and is commercial in nature.[55]

6.2 Guaranty of Payment versus Guaranty of Collection

A guaranty of the payment of a debt is distinguished from a guaranty of the collection of a debt. A guaranty of payment is an absolute unconditional promise to satisfy the underlying obligation while a guaranty of collection is a mere promise to satisfy the underlying obligation only if payment cannot by reasonable diligence be obtained from the principal obligor.[56]

Under a guaranty of payment, the liability of the guarantor to satisfy the underlying obligation becomes absolute upon default and without any requirement on the part of the obligee to demand payment from or otherwise proceed against the principal obligor.[57]

Under a guaranty of collection, the liability of the guarantor to satisfy the underlying obligation is not determined upon default, but rather is conditioned upon the obligee having first used every reasonable effort to collect the underlying debt from the principal obligor.[58] Since a guaranty of collection is, in essence, a guaranty of the principal obligor's solvency,[59] the requirement to use reasonable efforts does not impose an obligation on an obligee to sue an insolvent debtor or file a proof of claim in the bankruptcy case involving such debtor's estate.[60]

---

50. *See, e.g.*, Tallmadge Bros., Inc. v. Iroquois Gas Transmission System, L.P., 252 Conn. 479 at 498 (2000) ("A contract must be construed to effectuate the intent of the parties, which is determined from the language used interpreted in the light of the situation of the parties and the circumstances connected with the transaction.").
51. *Id.*
52. United Illuminating Co. v. Wisvest-Connecticut, LLP, 259 Conn. 665, 670 (2002).
53. *Id.*
54. *See, e.g.*, United Illuminating Co. v. Wisvest-Connecticut, LLP, 259 Conn. 665, 671 (2002) ("if the language of the contract is susceptible to more than one reasonable interpretation, the contract is ambiguous").
55. *Id.* at 670.
56. Cowles v. Peck, 55 Conn. 251 (1887); Beardsley v. Hawes et al, 71 Conn. 39 (1898).
57. *See* Perry v. Cohen, 126 Conn. 457 (1940); TD Bank, N.A. v. School Street Plaza, LLC et al, 2012 Conn. Super. LEXIS 154 (2012).
58. Beitler et al v. Rudkin, 104 Conn. 404 (1926) (citing Cowles v. Peck, 55 Conn. 251 (1887)).
59. *Id.* at 408-409.
60. *Id.*

A court will look to the intent of the parties as expressed in the plain language of the guaranty to determine whether it is one of payment or one of collection.[61]

6.3 "Continuing"

A continuing guaranty is one that contemplates a future course of action during an indefinite period of time or is intended to cover a series of transactions or a succession of credits, or if its purpose is to give the principal obligor a standing credit to be used by him from time to time.[62] While the use of the word "continuing" helps to make clear that a guaranty is meant to be continuing,[63] courts in Connecticut have interpreted a guaranty as continuing even where the word "continuing" has not been used, as long as the language of the guaranty clearly indicates that a continuing guaranty was intended by the parties.[64]

6.4 Language Regarding the Revocation of Guaranties

A continuing guaranty is ordinarily effective until revoked by the guarantor or extinguished by operation of law.[65] In order to revoke a continuing guaranty, the guarantor must usually give notice of revocation to the obligee.[66] However, although Connecticut case law "eschews any requirement of contemporaneity between a continuing guaranty and the obligations secured thereby,"[67] a continuing guaranty imposes liability on the guarantor only for a period of time that is "reasonable in light of all the circumstances of the particular case"[68] even if unlimited in duration by its terms.

---

61. *See, e.g.*, Heritage Bank v. Southbury Lighting, et al, 1992 Conn. Super LEXIS 1538 (1992) (holding that a statement in a guaranty that the guarantor "unconditionally and absolute guarantees . . . payment" was sufficient alone to impose "primary liability on the guarantor"); Cowles v. Peck, 55 Conn. 457 (1997) (holding that the words "I guarantee the within note good till paid" was not an absolute guaranty).
62. Associated Catalog Merchandisers, Inc. v. Chagnon et al., 210 Conn. 734 (1989); Connecticut Bank and Trust v. Wilcox, 201 Conn. 570 (1986); White v. Reed, 15 Conn. 457 (1843).
63. *See, e.g.*, L. Suzio Concrete Company, Inc. v. Birmingham Construction Services Company, Inc., et al, 79 Conn. App. 211 (2003).
64. *Compare* Connecticut National Bank v. Foley et al., 188 Conn. App. 667 (1989) (holding that a guaranty stating that the guarantor was "responsible for everything the borrower owes [the Bank] *now and in the future*" was a continuing guaranty) with White v. Reed, 15 Conn. 457 (1843) (holding that a writing stating that "for any sum that my son George Reed may become indebted to you . . . I will hold myself accountable" was not a continuing guaranty).
65. Associated Catalog Merchandisers, Inc. v. Chagnon et al., 210 Conn. 734 (1989).
66. *Id.*
67. Connecticut Bank and Trust v. Wilcox, 201 Conn. 570 at 575 (1986).
68. Monroe Ready Mix Concrete, Inc. v. Westcor Development Corporation, 183 Conn. 348 at 351 (1981). As to what constitutes a reasonable period of time for a continuing guaranty to remain effective, *compare* Connecticut National Bank v. Foley et al., 188 Conn. App. 667 (1989) (upholding trial court's finding that 14 months between the execution of the guaranty and the execution of a note by the obligor was not unreasonable); with Monroe Ready Mix Concrete, Inc. v. Westcor Development Corporation, 183 Conn. 348 (1981) (upholding trial court's finding that a nearly three-year delay between the execution of the guaranty and the extension of credit was unreasonable); and L. Suzio Concrete Company, Inc. v Birmingham Construction Services Company, Inc., et al, 79 Conn. App. 211 (2003) (upholding the trial court's finding that it was not unreasonable to impose liability for a guaranty executed seven years prior to the initial extension of credit since credit was extended continuously through such period).

6.5 "Absolute" and "Unconditional"

An "absolute" guaranty is a contract by which the guarantor promises to pay or perform the underlying obligation subject to no condition other than the default of the principal obligor.[69] Guaranties of payment are considered as absolute and unconditional in nature while guaranties of collection are considered as conditional in nature.[70] Guaranties that are "given absolutely and unconditionally" are frequently discussed by Connecticut courts in the context of determining the nature and extent of suretyship waiver clauses.

§ 7 Defenses of the Guarantor

7.1 Defenses or Discharge of the Principal Obligor

7.1.1 General

Connecticut courts follow the general rules of suretyship law that permit a guarantor, absent an effective waiver,[71] to assert the defenses or the discharge of the principal obligor as a defense to liability unless the very purpose of the guaranty is to "shift the risk of this event from the creditor to the surety,"[72] as in the event of bankruptcy or infancy of the principal obligor.[73] In determining such purpose, Connecticut courts inquire whether the conduct of the obligee "unreasonably and without authorization materially altered the risk"[74] that the guarantor can properly be understood to have assumed by virtue of its guaranty. The test "weighs heavily against automatic discharge"[75] of a guarantor under an absolute guaranty.

7.1.2 Defenses that may not be raised by Guarantor

The insolvency of the principal obligor is not a defense that the guarantor may raise unless the guaranty is conditioned on the solvency of the principal obligor.[76] A guarantor also may not raise the principal obligor's incapacity as a defense to liability under the guaranty.[77]

69. *See* Perry v. Cohen, 126 Conn. 457 (1940); TD Bank, N.A. v. School Street Plaza, LLC et al., 2012 Conn. Super. LEXIS 154 (2012).
70. *See* § 6.2 *supra*.
71. See § 8 infra. Under Connecticut law, a party to a contract may waive any defenses or rights it has against another party to the contract and such waiver will be enforced if it is clear and unambiguous. *See, e.g.,* Terracino et al v. Gordon and Hiller et al, 121 Conn. App. 795, 803 (2010)("a guarantor expressly may waive his rights to the protection that the common law or statutory law presumptively affords him."); Connecticut National Bank v. Douglas, 221 Conn, 530 at 545 (1992)("[b]oth the common law and the Uniform Commercial Code recognize that a guarantor may expressly waive his rights with respect to collateral that secures the debt that he has guaranteed.").
72. American Oil Company v. Valenti et al, 179 Conn. 349, 353 (1979); Cadle Company of Connecticut, Inc. v. C.F.D. Development Corporation, 44 Conn. App. 409, 414 (1997).
73. *Id.*
74. American Oil Company v. Valenti et al, 179 Conn. 349, 354 (1979).
75. *Id.*
76. *Id.* at 353.
77. *Id.*

7.2 "Suretyship" Defenses

In general, absent an effective waiver,[78] if an obligee acts in such a manner as to increase a guarantor's risk of loss by increasing its potential cost of performance or decreasing its potential ability to cause the principal obligor to bear the cost of performance, such guarantor's duties are discharged to the extent of the impairment.[79]

7.2.1 Modification of the Underlying Obligation, including Release

Under Connecticut law, modifications to the underlying obligation may permit the guarantor to raise a defense to liability. The relevant inquiry focuses on whether "the modification creates a substituted contract or imposes risks on the secondary obligor fundamentally different from those imposed pursuant to the transaction prior to modification."[80] However, a guarantor will not be permitted to raise such a defense if it had consented in advance to the modification in question.[81]

7.2.2 Release or Impairment of Security for the Underlying Obligation

When an obligee has a security interest in collateral to secure an underlying obligation that is guaranteed by a guarantor, the liability of the guarantor can be reduced to the extent that the security interest is impaired.[82] A guarantor may, however, waive in advance its defense based on the release or impairment of collateral, both under the common law and under Section 42a-3-605(i) of Connecticut's Uniform Commercial Code.[83]

7.2.3 Discharge of Coguarantor, including Release

The discharge or release of a coguarantor does not impair or release the obligations of any other guarantor, even if the rights of the coguarantor to recourse

78. *See* § 8 *infra*.
79. *See* Lestorti v. Deleo, et al, 298 Conn. 466, 479 (2010) (citing provisions of The Restatement (Third) of Suretyship and Guaranty).
80. Freidman v. Millpit Corporation et al, 49 Conn. App. 354, 358 n.3 (1998).
81. *See* JSA Financial Corporation v. Quality Kitchen Corporation of Delaware et al., 113 Conn. App. 52 at 60 (2009) (holder of guaranteed note was free to modify the terms of its repayment without the consent or knowledge of the guarantor where the express terms of the guaranty at issue provided that any such modification would not "in any way release the [guarantor] from or reduce [his] liability" thereunder.).
82. Connecticut National Bank v. Douglas, 221 Conn. 530 (1992); TD Bank, N.A. V. ARS Partners Poplar Plains, LLC, 2010 Conn. Super. LEXIS 232 (2010); Vigil v. Timoney, 1994 Conn. Super. LEXIS 10 (1994).
83. Connecticut National Bank v. Douglas, 221 Conn. 530 (1992). See also § 8.1 infra.

against the released guarantor are not expressly preserved.[84] In addition, a guarantor will not be permitted to raise such a defense if it had consented in advance to such release or discharge.[85]

7.3 Other Defenses

7.3.1 Good Faith and Fair Dealing

A guarantor may raise as a defense to its liability under its guaranty the obligee's breach of its duty of good faith and fair dealing to the principal obligor.[86] Reasoning that the duty of good faith and fair dealing is implicit in every contract, the Connecticut Appellate Court has held that shifting the risk of loss that might result from an obligee's breach of such duty could not reasonably be "the very purpose" of a guaranty.[87]

7.3.2 Failure to pursue Principal Obligor

Only when the underlying guaranty is a guaranty of collection and the principal obligor is solvent is an obligee required to first pursue the principal obligor.[88] Thus, the running of the statute of limitations against the principal obligor or an obligee's decision to allow a disciplinary nonsuit to stand against a principal obligor is no defense to a guarantor's liability under a guaranty of payment.[89]

7.3.3 Statute of Limitations

Connecticut General Statutes § 52-576 imposes, with certain exceptions, a six-year statute of limitations on contractual obligations.[90] One such exception applies to contracts for the sale of goods that are governed by Article 2

---

84. *See* Lestorti v. Deleo, et al, 298 Conn. 466, 479 at 481 (2010) ("a guarantor's duties are not discharged when the creditor releases a coguarantor or allows the statute of limitations to expire as to a coguarantor"). Under Connecticut law, a "secondary obligor's right of recourse against the principal obligor is automatically preserved" under an implied contract theory to the right of contribution. *Id. See also*, § 10.1 *infra.* Thus, under Connecticut law, contrary to the rules set forth in §§ 38 and 39 of the RESTATEMENT (THIRD) OF SURETYSHIP & GUARANTY which require the express preservation of such rights, an obligee's failure to preserve the rights of a guarantor to recourse against a coguarantor does not relieve such guarantor from liability under its guaranty. Lestorti v. Deleo, et al, 298 Conn. 466 at 482 (2010).
85. *Id.* at 482-483 (guarantor contractually agreed to a release of a coguarantor where its guaranty provided that the creditor "could, 'without impairing or releasing the obligations of [any] [g]uarantor .... [a]dd, release, settle, modify or discharge the obligation of any ... guarantor ... for any of the [l]iabilities' or '[t]ake any other action which might constitute a defense available to, or a discharge of ... any other ... guarantor'...").
86. *See* Cadle Company of Connecticut, Inc. v. C.F.D. Development Corporation, 44 Conn. App. 409 at 414 (1997), appeal dismissed Cadle Company of Connecticut, Inc. v. C.F.D. Development Corporation, 243 Conn. 667 (1998).
87. *Id.* The holding in the Connecticut Appellate Court case may be of questionable value in the context of an absolute and unconditional guaranty. On appeal, the Connecticut Supreme Court refused to "reexamine the thorny relationship between a guarantor's broadly phrased undertaking to ensure payment of a debt and such guarantor's access to suretyship defenses" because of "procedural irregularities at trial." Cadle Company of Connecticut, Inc. v. C.F.D. Development Corporation, 243 Conn. 667 at 669 (1998).
88. *See* § 6.2 *supra.*
89. American Oil Company v. Valenti et al, 179 Conn. 349 at 354 (1979).
90. C.G.S.A. § 52-576 (2012).

of the Connecticut Uniform Commercial Code, which imposes a four-year statute of limitations.[91]

However, even where the underlying obligation is a contract for the sale of goods governed by the Uniform Commercial Code, the six-year statute of limitations applicable to contracts generally applies to the guaranty.[92] While in many cases the statutes of limitations for the guaranty and the underlying obligation may lapse concurrently, the running of the statute of limitations against the principal obligor is no defense to a guarantor's liability under a guaranty of payment.[93]

In the case of a continuing guaranty, the statute of limitations does not commence to run in favor of a guarantor until a default has occurred in the payment by the principal obligor and a cause of action has accrued against the guarantor.[94] A statute of limitations defense to payment on a guaranty is lost if the guarantor unequivocally acknowledges his debt or, under certain circumstances, makes a partial payment.[95] Although, as a general rule, a payment made by a principal obligor that tolls the statute of limitations is ineffective as to a guarantor if the payment is made without the guarantor's knowledge or consent,[96] such knowledge or consent is not necessary if the terms of the guaranty disclaim any requirement for the same.[97]

7.3.4 Statute of Frauds

The statute of frauds[98] guaranty provision bars an action to enforce any agreement "against any person upon any special promise to answer for the debt, default or miscarriage of another"[99] unless the agreement or a memorandum of the agreement is made in writing and signed by the party to be charged therewith or his agent. Thus, a guaranty which does not satisfy the requirements of the statute of frauds is not enforceable unless the undertaking is an original undertaking rather than a collateral one.[100] A guaranty is an original undertaking "if . . . there is a benefit to the promisor which he did not before, and would not otherwise, enjoy and in addition the act is done upon his request

---

91. *See* C.G.S.A. § 42a-2-725 (2012).
92. Associated Catalog Merchandisers, Inc. v. Chagnon et al, 210 Conn. 734 (1989).
93. American Oil Company v. Valenti et al, 179 Conn. 349 at 354-355 (1979).
94. Associated Catalog Merchandisers, Inc. v. Chagnon et al, 210 Conn. 734 at 745-46 (1989).
95. *See* Zapolsky v. Sacks et al, 191 Conn. 194 (1983); JSA Financial Corporation v. Quality Kitchen Corporation of Delaware et al., 113 Conn. App. 52 (2009).
96. JSA Financial Corporation v. Quality Kitchen Corporation of Delaware et al., 113 Conn. App. 52 at 59 (2009).
97. *Id.*
98. C.G.S.A. § 52-550 (2012).
99. C.G.S.A. § 52-550(a)(2) (2012).
100. *See* Otto Contracting Company, Inc. v. S. Schinella & Son, Inc., et al, 179 Conn. 704 at 710 (1980); Kerin Agency, Inc. v. West Haven Painting and Decorating, Inc., et al, 38 Conn. App. 329 at 331 (1995). In *Otto*, the Connecticut Supreme Court noted that "the 'main purpose' or 'leading object' rule, which defines when an undertaking is original rather than collateral, is an exception of long standing to the statute of frauds' guaranty provision." *Id. See, also,* Bartolotta v. Calvo, 112 Conn. 385 at 389 (1930) ("the distinction between a contract that falls with the condemnation of the statute of frauds and one which does not is that the former is a collateral undertaking to answer in case of a default on the part of the obligor in the contract, upon which still rests primary liability to perform, whereas in the latter the obligation assumed is a primary one that the contract shall be performed").

and credit."[101] Whether a guaranty falls under the statute of frauds is a question of fact.[102] In order to be in compliance with the statute of frauds, the essential terms of a guaranty must be clear and unambiguous. [103]

7.3.5 Commercially Reasonable Collateral Disposition

While a waiver of suretyship defenses may waive the guarantor's right to challenge the impairment of collateral before a default,[104] the waiver does not apply in the post-default context, where Article 9's provisions on commercial reasonableness apply. Thus, a guarantor may raise as a defense to its liability under its guaranty the obligee's failure to act in a commercially reasonable manner with respect to the disposition of collateral governed by Article 9 of the UCC.[105]

§ 8 Waiver of Defenses by the Guarantor

A guarantor may waive defenses based on a section 42a-3-605 discharge of liability.[106] A guarantor may also expressly waive common law defenses to its liability[107] and its right to assert any defenses that the principal obligor could have asserted against the obligee.[108] In general, a waiver in a guaranty waives defenses that would, absent the waiver, discharge the secondary obligation in actions by an obligee against the guarantor.[109]

A guarantor may not waive its defense of lack of commercial reasonableness by a secured obligee in disposing and redeeming secured collateral, and accounting for its proceeds.[110]

101. Otto Contracting Company, Inc. v. S. Schinella & Son, Inc., et al, 179 Conn. 704 at 711 (1980). *See also* Kerin Agency, Inc. v. West Haven Painting and Decorating, Inc., et al, 38 Conn. App. 329 at 333 (1995) ("it is not necessary . . . that the promisor receive any benefit from his promise. It is enough that the promise induced the extension of credit (citations omitted).").
102. Otto Contracting Company, Inc. v. S. Schinella & Son, Inc., et al, 179 Conn. 704 at 711 (1980).
103. *See* Yellow Book Sales and Distribution Company, Inc. v. Valle, 133 Conn. App. 75 (2012).
104. *See* § 7.2.2 *supra.*
105. *See* Connecticut Nat'l Bank v. Douglas, 221 Conn. 530 at 546-47, 606 A.2d 684 at 692 (1992); Morris et al v. Shawmut Bank, 1997 Conn. Super. LEXIS 3247 (1997).
106. "A party is not discharged . . . if . . . the instrument or a separate agreement of the party provides for waiver of discharge under this section either specifically or by general language indicating that parties waive defenses based on suretyship or impairment of collateral." Conn. Gen. Stat. § 42a-3-605(i); *see also* Merrill Lynch Bus. Fin. Services, Inc. v. Psychiatric Services Inst., LLC, CV010457220S, 2002 WL 31460439 (Conn. Super. Ct. Oct. 11, 2002) (upholding a waiver of defenses in a guaranty). The term "surety" includes a guarantor. Conn. Gen. Stat. § 42a-1-201(39).
107. Connecticut Nat'l Bank v. Douglas, 221 Conn. 530, 544-45, 606 A.2d 684, 691 (1992); Terracino v. Gordon & Hiller, 121 Conn. App. 795, 796 (2010). American Oil Company v. Valenti et al, 179 Conn. 349, 353 (1979); Cadle Company of Connecticut, Inc. v. C.F.D. Development Corporation, 44 Conn. App. 409, 414 (1997).
108. Barclays Bus. Credit, Inc. v. Freyer, CV 960152347S, 1997 WL 255248, at *3 (Conn. Super. Ct. May 6, 1997). A guarantor may assert any defenses that the principal obligor can rightfully assert against the obligee. Restatement (Third), Suretyship and Guaranty § 34 (1996).
109. Barclays Bus. Credit, Inc. v. Freyer, CV 960152347S, 1997 WL 255248, at *3 (Conn. Super. Ct. May 6, 1997) (citing Restatement (Third), Suretyship and Guaranty § 48 (1996)).
110. Conn. Gen. Stat. § 42a-9-501(3); Connecticut Nat'l Bank v. Douglas, 221 Conn. 530, 546-47, 606 A.2d 684, 692 (1992).

Under Connecticut law, jury trial waivers are presumptively enforceable.[111] To rebut this presumption, the party seeking to avoid the waiver must show, by a preponderance of the evidence, that it clearly did not intend to waive the right to a jury trial.[112] The evidence may be apparent on the face of the agreement if the waiver is in fine print or buried in a large document.[113] The evidence may also be of an "inequality of bargaining power, that the party was not represented by counsel, or other evidence indicating a lack of intent to be bound by the waiver provision."[114]

8.1 Waiver of Impairment of Collateral Claim

A waiver of a claim for impairment of collateral must be sufficiently specific and broad.[115] An unspecific waiver will not be enforced. In *TD Bank, N.A. v. ARS Partners Poplar Plains, LLC,* CV095026521, 2010 WL 745757 (Conn. Super. Ct. Feb. 2, 2010), the court did not enforce a waiver provision regarding impairment of collateral, finding that [u]nlike the waiver provisions in *Connecticut National Bank [v. Douglas,* 221 Conn. 530,] there is no reference to the collateral underlying the subject loans, to the protection or collection of the collateral, or to a waiver of a claim that the collateral has been impaired to the detriment of the defendant guarantors. In fact, the language at issue wholly fails to discuss the defendant guarantors' waiver of any rights they may have to challenge the plaintiff's conduct concerning the secured collateral.[116]

§ 9 Third-party Pledgors—Defenses and Waiver Thereof

Collateral pledged by a third party as a security for an underlying obligation stands in the position of a guarantor.[117] Any defenses that would discharge a guarantor would discharge such collateral.[118] It would seem to follow, given the state of the law, that a third-party pledgor may waive these defenses.

111. *L & R Realty v. Connecticut Nat'l Bank,* 246 Conn. 1, 14, 715 A.2d 748, 755 (1998).
112. *Id.*
113. *Id.* Obligees are advised to make such jury trial waivers conspicuous, or separately consented to or acknowledged, in order to avoid such defenses.
114. *Id.*
115. *See* Connecticut Nat'l Bank v. Douglas, 221 Conn. 530, 545, 606 A.2d 684, 691 (1992) (enforcing a guarantor's waiver of claims relating to a secured obligee's alleged impairment of collateral because the language of guaranty was sufficiently specific).
116. TD Bank, N.A. v. ARS Partners Poplar Plains, LLC, CV095026521, 2010 WL 745757, at *4 (Conn. Super. Ct. Feb. 2, 2010).
117. *See* Rowan v. Sharps' Rifle Mfg. Co., 33 Conn. 1 (1865).
118. *See Id.*

§ 10 Jointly and Severally Liable Guarantors

Two or more persons with the same liability on an instrument are jointly and severally liable unless otherwise provided in the instrument.[119]

A guarantor who pays a debt is entitled to reimbursement from the principal obligor and is entitled to enforce the instrument against the principal obligor.[120] A principal obligor who pays a debt, however, has no right of recourse against, and is not entitled to contribution from, a guarantor of the debt.[121]

A jointly and severally liable coguarantor who pays a debt is entitled to receive contribution from the other coguarantors of the same debt.[122]

10.1 Contribution

As between guarantors, each coguarantor of the same debt is liable to the other guarantors only for a contributive share of the total outstanding debt owed.[123] The right of contribution between coguarantors is based on the theory of implied contract.[124] Coguarantors impliedly promise to contribute their share, if necessary, to meet the common obligation.[125]

The discharge of one coguarantor's direct liability by the obligee will not relieve that coguarantor from its liability to contribute to the other coguarantors.[126] The coguarantors are the only parties to the implied contract.[127] The obligee is not a party.[128] The obligee has nothing to do with the right of contribution and cannot impair it.[129]

The right of contribution is an existing obligation running from the inception of the relationship.[130] Enforcement of the right of contribution does not accrue until the actual payment in full of the common debt to the obligee.[131]

A coguarantor is not entitled to contribution unless it pays more than its contributive share.[132] Each coguarantor is a principal obligor to the extent of its contributive share, and a secondary obligor as to the remainder.[133]

A coguarantor is also not entitled to contribution if it voluntarily pays more than its share[134]—the payment must be compulsory.[135] Payment is compulsory

119. "Except as otherwise provided in the instrument, two or more persons who have the same liability on an instrument as makers, drawers, acceptors, endorsers who endorse as joint payees, or anomalous endorsers are jointly and severally liable in the capacity in which they sign." Conn. Gen. Stat. § 42a-3-116(a).
120. Conn. Gen. Stat. § 42a-3-419(e).
121. *Id.*
122. Conn. Gen. Stat. § 42a-3-116(b).
123. Terracino v. Gordon & Hiller, 121 Conn. App. 795, 796 (2010) (citing Restatement (Third), Suretyship and Guaranty §§ 55-57 (1996)).
124. Lestorti v. DeLeo, 298 Conn. 466, 473 (2010).
125. *Id.*
126. Conn. Gen. Stat. § 42a-3-116(c); Lestorti v. DeLeo, 298 Conn. 466, 473 (2010).
127. Lestorti v. DeLeo, 298 Conn. 466, 473 (2010).
128. *Id.*
129. *Id.*
130. *Id.*
131. *Id.*
132. *Id.* at 475.
133. *Id.*
134. Gay v. Ward, 67 Conn. 147, 34 A. 1025, 1028 (1895).
135. Waters v. Waters, 110 Conn. 342, 148 A. 326, 328 (1930).

if it can be "shown that the payment was one which was demanded and could have been enforced by suit, the [co-guarantor] being legally liable."[136]

A coguarantor against whom judgment is recovered may compel contribution from the other coguarantors after paying the obligee.[137]

§ 11 Reliance

In Connecticut, the modern law of contracts can make guaranties enforceable on the basis of reliance.[138] However, it is arguable that a lack of consideration may remain a viable defense to an action on a guaranty.[139]

§ 12 Subrogation

Subrogation allows a guarantor who pays a debt to "step into the shoes" of an obligee and "assume [the obligee's] legal rights against a third party to prevent that party's unjust enrichment."[140] The guarantor will have no rights beyond those possessed by the obligee.[141]

When a guarantor pays a debt, the guarantor is subrogated to all the rights and remedies of the obligee, including the right to the debt itself, even without a formal assignment of the debt.[142] The guarantor will also have the same priority with respect to the perfected security interest as that of the obligee.[143]

Subrogation is an equitable remedy used to enforce a legal right and "compel the ultimate discharge of a debt or obligation by one who in good conscience ought to pay it."[144] The right of subrogation arises at the time of payment by the guarantor.[145]

The right of subrogation does not extend to bringing a legal malpractice action against the obligee's attorney.[146]

---

136. *Id.*
137. Lestorti v. DeLeo, 298 Conn. 466, 473 (2010).
138. Superior Wire & Paper Products, Ltd. v. Talcott Tool & Mach., Inc., 184 Conn. 10, 20, 441 A.2d 43, 48 (1981) (citing Restatement (Second), Contracts § 89C (1973).
139. In the unreported case of Connecticut Nat. Bank v. Ealahan Elec. Co., the court stated that the "*Superior Wire* court did not adopt the 'modern law of contracts' interpretation it referred to, but, instead, based its holding on the ground that there was consideration to support the guaranty at issue." Connecticut Nat'l Bank v. Ealahan Elec. Co., 519422, 1992 WL 335729, at * 2 (Conn. Super. Ct. Nov. 6, 1992) (denying the plaintiff's motion to strike on the basis of lack of consideration). In the later case of Martin Printing, Inc. v. Andres J. Sone et. al., 89 Conn App 336 at 348 (2005), the court concluded that a guaranty may be enforceable if it is supported by consideration.
140. Rathbun v. Health Net of the Northeast., Inc., 133 Conn. App. 202, 211 (2012).
141. Connecticut Sav. Bank v. First Nat'l Bank & Trust Co., 138 Conn. 298, 305, 84 A.2d 267, 270 (1951).
142. In re Mr. R's Prepared Foods, Inc., 251 B.R. 24, 29 (Bankr. D. Conn. 2000).
143. *Id.*
144. Balboa Ins. Co. v. Bank of Boston Connecticut, 702 F. Supp. 34, 36 (D. Conn. 1988) (quoting Hartford Accid. and Indem. Co. v. Chung, 37 Conn.Supp. 587, 594, 429 A.2d 158, 162 (Appell. Sess. 1981)).
145. In re William P. Bray Co., 127 F. Supp. 627, 628 (D. Conn. 1954).
146. Cont'l Cas. Co. v. Pullman, Comley, Bradley & Reeves, 929 F.2d 103, 107 (2d Cir. 1991) ("[W]e are persuaded that the Connecticut Supreme Court would not permit a subrogee excess insurer to file legal malpractice claims against the insured's attorney."); W. Sur. Co. v. Peitrzkiewicz, FSTCV106007722S, 2011 WL 4447242, at *5 (Conn. Super. Ct. Sept. 6, 2011).

12.1 Partial Subrogation

As a general rule, subrogation can be used only after full payment of the debt to the obligee.[147] This rule against partial subrogation does not apply if the obligee acquiesces in the subrogation.[148] The rule against partial subrogation also does not apply if an obligee objects to partial subrogation but subrogation would not work to the detriment of the obligee.[149] An obligee must object to partial subrogation and the objection must be made to protect the obligee's interests for the rule against partial subrogation to apply.

12.2 Payment and Performance Bonds

Subrogation applies to guaranties of payment and performance bonds. Under Connecticut law, a surety[150] has priority to undisbursed contract proceeds when the surety becomes subrogated to the rights of a contractor.[151] A surety seeking reimbursement for a debt paid under a performance and payment bond also has priority over an assignee obligee[152]: "When a surety performs its obligations under a performance and payment bond, it stands in the shoes of the contractor. Thus, if the contractor has the right to the retained funds, the surety accedes to those rights when it meets its obligations under the bonds."[153]

§ 13 Triangular Set-off in Bankruptcy

Triangular set-off may be permissible in Connecticut.

Where a principal obligor has a claim against the obligee unrelated to the underlying obligation, which could be set-off against the underlying obligation, the guarantor may use that claim to reduce its duty to the obligee, either by consent of the principal obligor, to the extent that the claim is uncontested by the obligee, or if the principal obligor is made a party to the obligee's action to enforce the guaranty.[154]

---

147. Grant Thornton v. Syracuse Sav. Bank, 961 F.2d 1042, 1047 (2d Cir. 1992) (citing Sav. Bank of Manchester v. Kane, 35 Conn. Supp. 82, 84, 396 A.2d 952, 953 (Com. Pl. 1978) and affirming denial of partial subrogation).
148. *Id.*
149. *See Id.*
150. Under Connecticut law, the term "surety" includes a guarantor. Conn. Gen. Stat. § 42a-1-201(39).
151. Amwest Sur. Ins. Co. v. United States, CIV. 3:92CV221(PCD), 1995 WL 452992, at *1 (D. Conn. May 10, 1995) (citing Employers' Liab. Assur. Corp. v. Crandall, 22 Conn. Supp. 404, 173 A.2d 926 (Com. Pl. 1961) and Balboa Ins. Co. v. Bank of Boston Connecticut, 702 F. Supp. 34, 36 (D. Conn. 1988)).
152. Balboa Ins. Co. v. Bank of Boston Connecticut, 702 F. Supp. 34, 36 (D. Conn. 1988).
153. *Id.* at 37.
154. *See* Restatement (Third) of Suretyship & Guaranty, § 35 (1996). In matters of suretyship and guaranty the Connecticut Supreme Court "is likely to follow the Restatement, at least in the absence of authority to the contrary. *See, e.g.,* Cadle Co. of Connecticut, Inc. v. C.F.D. Development Corp., 243 Conn. 667, 706 A.2d 975 (Conn. 1998); *see also* Southington v. Commercial Union Ins. Co., 71 Conn. App. 715, 805 A.2d 76 (Conn. App. 2002)." *See* Lestorti v. DeLeo, 298 Conn. 466 (2010), 968 A.2d 941, 945 (Conn. App. 2009), reversed on other grounds by Lestorti v. DeLeo, 4 A.3d 269, 276 (Conn. 2010).

§ 14 Indemnification—Whether the Principal Obligor has a Duty

The principal obligor with notice of the guaranty generally has a duty of reimbursement to the guarantor once the underlying obligation is discharged.

A guarantor is entitled to reimbursement from a principal obligor who has notice of the guaranty.[155] The principal obligor has a duty of reimbursement to the extent that the guarantor performs on the guaranty or makes a settlement with the obligee that discharges the principal obligor's obligation.[156] The duty to reimburse does not arise in certain situations: where bankruptcy law relieves the principal obligor of this duty; where the principal obligor lacked capacity to enter a contractual obligation; where a defense available to the principal obligor is not available to the guarantor; where the obligee's release of the principal obligor discharges the duty; or if at the time of performance or settlement the guarantor had notice of a defense, unless it was a reasonable business decision to perform or settle despite this defense.[157]

The scope of the indemnification can be altered by contract.[158] Where the guarantor makes a voluntary payment on a debt that the principal obligor objects to, there may not be a duty of indemnification.[159] However, where an obligee obtains a judgment against a guarantor, "the issue of the validity of the underlying debt must be litigated and established before the imposition of such liability, and would have a binding effect upon the principal obligor in a claim over by the guarantor."[160]

§ 15 Enforcement of Guaranties

15.1 Limitations on Recovery

The enforcement of some guaranties is subject to the Statute of Frauds, and additional limits in certain cases.

In order to recover on a guaranty there must be a written agreement in compliance with the Statute of Frauds.[161] However, "[t]he suretyship provision [of the Statute of Frauds] does not apply to a promise unless the promisee is

155. *See* Smith v. Mitsubishi Motors Credit Corp., 721 A.2d 1187, 1190 (Conn. 1998).
156. *See* Restatement (Third) of Suretyship & Guaranty, § 22(1). The Connecticut courts have relied on this section of the Restatement to fill in gaps and support the state's common law. Lestorti, 4 A.3d at 276.
157. *See* Restatement (Third) of Suretyship & Guaranty, § 24. See also Lestorti, 968 A.2d at 945.
158. *See* Bentz v. Halsey, 736 A.2d 931, 937 (Conn. App. 1999).
159. *See* In re Metal Center, Inc., 31 B.R. 458, 462 (Bankr. D. Conn. 1983). ("While it might be argued that voluntary payment by a guarantor does not bind the principal debtor where the principal debtor has objected to the underlying debt, the result is different where the creditor obtains a judgment against the guarantor. Under those circumstances, the issue of the validity of the underlying debt must be litigated and established before the imposition of such liability, and would have a binding effect upon the principal debtor in a claim over by the guarantor.")
160. *Id.*
161. *See* 73-75 Main Ave., LLC v. PP Door Enterprise, Inc., 991 A.2d 650, 660 (Conn. App. 2010). *See also* Conn. Gen. Stat. § 52-550(a)(2) (1991). *See also* § 7.3.4 *supra*.

the obligee. Moreover, the obligee-promisee must know or have reason to know of the secondary obligor's suretyship status."[162] A guaranty is voidable by the guarantor if the guarantor's assent is induced by a justifiably relied upon fraudulent or material misrepresentation by the obligee, or by the principal obligor or a third person as long as the obligee did not materially rely on the guaranty in good faith and with no knowledge of the misrepresentation.[163]

The amount an obligee can recover may be limited in certain circumstances. For example, where the underlying obligation was covered by an uninsured motorist policy, the obligee's potential recovery from a state guaranty fund was reduced by the full amount of the policy limit, even if the actual amount recovered was below that limit.[164]

15.2 Exercising Rights under a Guaranty Where the Underlying Obligation is also Secured by a Mortgage

Foreclosure on a mortgage securing an underlying obligation does not prevent enforcement of a deficiency judgment against the guarantor where the contract didn't explicitly shield the guarantor from this risk.

In the case of a foreclosure on a mortgage securing a promissory note, a subsequent deficiency judgment was enforceable against the guarantors of the note, where the note and mortgage deed protected the borrower against a deficiency judgment, but the language of the guarantee did not afford the guarantors such protection.[165]

15.3 Litigating Guaranty Claims: Procedural Considerations

To enforce a deficiency claim against a guarantor of a mortgage loan, the foreclosure complaint must name and be served upon the guarantor, assuming the guarantor can be served in Connecticut; open-end mortgages securing open-end loans or letters of credit must meet certain requirements.

The foreclosure of a mortgage must name and be served upon all parties who could have been served in Connecticut at the commencement of the foreclosure in order to preserve the right to enforce deficiency judgments against potentially liable parties.[166] Connecticut General Statutes § 49-1 "prohibits the foreclosing mortgagee from maintaining a separate action on the underlying mortgage debt, note or obligation against any person liable except those upon whom personal service could not have been made at the outset of the foreclosure."[167]

---

162. *See* Restatement (Third) of Suretyship & Guaranty, cmt. (g). *See also id.* at § 11(1), 3(a); Lestorti, 968 A.2d at 945.
163. *See* Restatement (Third) of Suretyship & Guaranty, § 12. *See also* Lestorti, 968 A.2d at 945.
164. *See* Robinson v. Gailno, 880 A.2d 127, 137 (Conn. 2005).
165. *See* Regency Savings Bank v. Westmark Partners, 756 A.2d 299, 303 (Conn. App. 2000).
166. *See* Conn. Gen. Stat. § 49-1 (1957).
167. *See, e.g.*, TD Bank N.A. v. Northern Expansion, No. CV 09-6001534 S, 2010 Ct. Sup. 22614, 22619 (Conn. Super. Ct. Nov. 22, 2010).

An open-end mortgage securing a guaranty of an open-end loan or reimbursement obligations in respect of a letter of credit must meet the requirements of Connecticut General Statutes § 49-4b, which include entitling the deed "Open-End Mortgage" and stating in the deed the name and address of the principal obligor, the full amount authorized and maximum term of the loan, and certain additional information.[168]

15.4 Choice of Law and Venue

Under Connecticut law, courts will generally give effect to an express choice of law chosen by the parties to a contract, including a guaranty.[169] The Connecticut Supreme Court, adopting the approach set out in the Restatement (Second) of Conflict of Laws § 187, has enunciated Connecticut's rule for enforcement of contractual choice of law provisions as follows: the law of the state chosen by the parties to govern their contractual rights and duties will be applied, even if the particular issue is one that the parties could not have resolved by an explicit provision in their agreement directed to that issue, unless either (a) the chosen state has no substantial relationship to the parties or the transaction, and there is no other reasonable basis for the parties' choice, or (b) application of the law of the chosen state would be contrary to a fundamental policy of a state that has a materially greater interest than the chosen state in the determination of the particular issue and that, under the rule of § 188 [of the Restatement (Second) of Conflict of Laws (1971)], would be the state of the applicable law in the absence of an effective choice of law by the parties.[170]

In the absence of an effective choice of law by the parties to a contract, the Connecticut Supreme Court has adopted the "most significant relationship" approach taken in the Restatement (Second) of Conflict of Laws § 188.[171] It should be noted, however, that an effective choice of law provision in a contract which designates the laws of a state other than Connecticut may not preclude the assertion of Connecticut law-based tort claims arising out of or relating to the contract.[172]

Under Connecticut law, courts will also uphold forum selection clauses unless enforcement would be "unreasonable, unfair, unjust."[173]

---

168. *See* Conn. Gen. Stat. § 49-4b (1997). *See also* Mundaca Investment Corporation v. Homespun, et al., No. 31 99 46, 1996 Ct. Sup. 5325-VVV, 5325-WWW - 5235-XXX (Conn. Super. Ct. Sept. 18, 1996).
169. *See* Wells Fargo Bank, N.A. v. Lambot, 2009 Conn. Super. LEXIS 1085 (2009).
170. *See* Elgar v. Elgar, 238 Conn. 839, 679 A.2d 937 (1996).
171. *See* Reichhold Chemicals, Inc. v. Hartford Accident and Indem. Co., 252 Conn. 774, 750 A.2d. 1051 (2000).
172. *Compare* Travel Servs. Network, Inc. v. Presidential Fin. Corp. of Massachusetts, 959 F. Supp. 135, 146-47 (D. Conn. 1997) (holding that "broadly-worded choice-of-law provisions in a contract may govern not only interpretation of the contract in which it is contained, but also tort claims arising out of or relating to the contract") with Blakesee Arpaia Chapman, Inc. v. Helmsman Mgmt Servs, Inc., 31 Conn. L. Rptr. 214 (Conn. Super. 2002) (holding that a provision in a contract stating that "this Agreement shall be construed under and governed by the law of the State of Massachusetts" is "narrowly worded and does not govern tort as well as contract disputes").
173. *See* Reiner, Reiner and Bendett, P.C v. The Cadle Company, 278 Conn. 92 (2006) (citing with approval the holding of the U.S. Supreme Court in Bremen v. Zapata Off-Shore Co., 407 U.S. 1 (1972)); Royal Bank of Scotland, PLC v. Lexham Farmington I, LLC, 2011 Conn. Super. LEXIS 510 (2011).

§ 16 Revival and Reinstatement of Guaranties

Guaranties may be revived to the extent that the obligee later surrenders the performance or collateral pursuant to a legal duty to do so.

A guarantor's obligation may be revived to the extent that the obligee surrenders the performance or collateral pursuant to a legal duty to do so, such as in a preference action.[174] Where the obligee returns the performance voluntarily, however, the guaranty is not revived.[175]

174. *See* North American Bank & Trust Co. v. Biebel, No. CV 03-0522575S, 2005 Ct. Sup. 11952-r, 11952-s (Conn. Super. Ct. Aug. 16, 2005); *See also* Restatement (Third) of Suretyship & Guaranty, § 70; Lestorti, 968 A.2d at 945.

175. *See* Restatement (Third) of Suretyship & Guaranty, § 70, cmt. c. *See also* Lestorti, 968 A.2d at 945.

Delaware State Law of Guaranties

Cynthia D. Kaiser
Thomas A. Barr

Richards, Layton & Finger PA
One Rodney Square
920 North King Street
Wilmington, Delaware 19801
302-651-7700
302-498-7701
kaiser@rlf.com
www.rlf.com

Contents

Delaware State Law of Guaranties

TIP—Delaware courts have cited to the Restatement of Security on several occasions. *See, e.g., Collins v. Throckmorton*, 425 A.2d 146, 150 (Del. 1979) (quoting it as "stat[ing] the general rule governing contribution rights among co-guarantors"). A Westlaw search indicated a single case in which the Restatement (Third) of Suretyship and Guaranty was cited. *Travelers Cas. and Sur. Co. of America v. Colonial School Dist.*, 2001 WL 287482 (Del. Ch. Mar. 16, 2001). Generally, Delaware courts appear receptive to secondary authority on the law of guaranties.

Introductory Note: In order to standardize our discussion of the law of guaranties, we use the following vocabulary to refer to the various parties to a guaranty and their obligations.

"Guarantor" means a person who, by contract, agrees to satisfy an underlying obligation of another to an obligee upon the primary obligor's default on that underlying obligation. Generally, we will use "guarantor" synonymously with "surety."[1] We will specifically identify those instances where Delaware courts draw a distinction.

"Guaranty" means the contract by which the guarantor agrees to satisfy the underlying obligation of a primary obligor to an obligee in the event the primary obligor defaults on the underlying obligation.

"Obligee" means the person to whom the underlying obligation is owed. For example, the lender under a loan agreement would be an obligee vis-à-vis the borrower.

"Primary Obligor" means the person who incurs the underlying obligation to the obligee. For example, the borrower under a loan agreement would be a primary obligor.

"Underlying Obligation" means the obligation or obligations incurred by the primary obligor and owed to the obligee. For example, the borrower's obligation to make payments to a lender of principal and interest on a loan constitutes an underlying obligation.

1. Recent Delaware cases have acknowledged the distinction between these terms. *See, e.g.*, Trader v. Wilson, No. Civ.A. 01A-06-002, 2002 WL 499888, at *4 n.8 (Del. Super. Feb. 1, 2002).

§ 1 Nature of the Guaranty Arrangement

Under Delaware law, a guaranty involves "two different obligations."[2] The first is the underlying obligation owed by the primary obligor to the obligee. The second, owed by the guarantor to the obligee, is created by the guaranty and is "collateral" to the first.[3] Where the primary obligor defaults and the guarantor satisfies the underlying obligation to the obligee, then the guarantor is subrogated to the rights of the obligee against the primary obligor with respect to the underlying obligation.

1.1 Guaranty Relationships

The relationship between the guarantor and the obligee is contractual.[4] Consequently, whether such a relationship has been formed is subject to general contract principles of formation[5] and interpretation.[6] Delaware courts will determine whether a party is a guarantor by looking to the contract as whole to ascertain the objective intent of the contracting parties.[7] Neither the use of particular words such as "guaranty" nor labeling a party a "guarantor" is itself determinative, although these may evince the parties' intent to enter into a contract of guaranty.[8]

A prerequisite to a guarantor's obligation to "answer for the payment of some debt or performance of some obligation" to the obligee is default by the primary obligor.[9] Additional conditions precedent to performance or liability may be imposed by contract[10] or implied by law.[11] Obligees are expected to

---

2. FinanceAmerica Private Brands, Inc. v. Harvey E. Hall, Inc., 380 A.2d 1377, 1379 (Del. Super. 1977).
3. *Id.*
4. FinanceAmerica Private Brands, Inc. v. Harvey E. Hall, Inc., 380 A.2d 1377, 1379 (Del. Super. 1977); *see* Pellaton v. Bank of New York, 592 A.2d 473, 476-78 (Del. 1991) (holding guarantor's failure to read the guaranty was not a defense and discussing how alleged ambiguities may be resolved applying general contract principles); *see also, e.g., 8 Del. C. § 122* ("Every corporation created under this chapter shall have power to … Make contracts, *including* contracts of guaranty and suretyship …") (emphasis added).
5. *See* Industr. Am., Inc. v. Fulton Industr., Inc., 285 A.2d 412, 415 (Del. 1971) (applying the "basic" rule of contracts that "overt manifestation of assent not subjective intent – controls formation of a contract" with respect to whether an offer of guaranty was accepted).
6. Cooling v. Springer, 30 A.2d 466, 469 (Del. Super. 1943); *see also* Wilmington Trust Co. v. Keith, C.A. No. 00C-11-016, 2002 WL 1748622, at * 4 (Del. Super. June 26, 2002).
7. *See* Chestnut Hill Plaza Holdings Corp. v. Parkway Cleaners, Inc., C.A. No. N10C–09–161 DCS, 2011 WL 1885256, at *5 (Del. Super. May 17, 2011); Citizens Bank v. Gupta, No. Civ. A. 02J-05-068, 2004 WL 1965924, at *2 (Del. Super. Aug. 26, 2004).
8. W. T. Rawleigh Co. v. Warrington, 199 A. 666, 670 (Del. Super. 1938); *see also* Chestnut Hill Plaza Holdings Corp. v. Parkway Cleaners, Inc., C.A. No. N10C–09–161 DCS, 2011 WL 1885256, at *5 (Del. Super. May 17, 2011).
9. FinanceAmerica Private Brands, Inc. v. Harvey E. Hall, Inc., 380 A.2d 1377, 1379 (Del. Super. 1977); *see also* In re Explorer Pipeline Company, 781 A.2d 705, 716 (Del. Ch. 2001) ("[The defendant] is not a guarantor, as that term is commonly understood, because it does not have any obligation to pay what materializes upon the default of the primary obligor and because it does not have any obligation to pay off the borrowed money.").
10. *See* Ajax Rubber Co., Inc. v. Gam, 151 A. 828, 829 (Del. Super. 1923); *see also* Gaylords, Inc. v. Tollin, No. Civ. A. 80C-JN23, 1984 WL 547850, at *2 (Del. Super. Jan. 31, 1984) (finding that by the terms of the guaranty "prosecution of the civil claims against [the primary obligor] or the determination that there was no reasonable hope of recovery were the conditions precedent to [the guarantor's] liability").
11. Ajax Rubber Co., Inc. v. Gam, 151 A. 831, 833 (Del Super. 1924); Gaylords, Inc.,1984 WL 547850, at *3 (Del. Super. Jan. 31, 1984).

"strictly follow the specific provisions of the guaranty agreement on how, when, and where to demand" satisfaction from the guarantor.[12]

Between the primary obligor and the guarantor, it is the primary obligor "who has the primary obligation to discharge the debt."[13] However, where the primary obligor has defaulted and the guarantor has paid the obligee, the guarantor is "ordinarily subrogated to all of [obligee's] rights and remedies, of every nature, against the principal, for its collection."[14] The Delaware Court of Chancery has indicated that the guarantor is then regarded as the "purchaser, and the equitable assignee of the debt."[15]

1.2 Other Suretyship Relationships

The Restatement of the Law (Third) of Suretyship and Guaranty applies to secondary obligors having "suretyship status."[16] It defines this term broadly, including parties that grant security interests in personal property.[17] No Delaware authority has used this term; consequently, this survey does not examine any other "suretyship relationships" aside from those discussed in § 1.1.

§ 2 State Law Requirements for an Entity to Enter a Guaranty

Generally, Delaware entities are specifically, statutorily authorized to enter into contracts of guaranty. This authorization may be limited by a particular entity's organizational documents. In the case of a Delaware corporation, there is an additional requirement that the guaranty be "necessary or convenient to the conduct, promotion or attainment of [its] business."18 Practically speaking, this does not provide a significant obstacle where the guarantor corporation is related to the primary obligor.

2.1 Corporations

In 1967, Delaware's General Corporation Law expressly granted Delaware corporations the specific power to enter into contracts of guaranty, provided that the guaranty is "necessary or convenient to the conduct, promotion or attainment of the business of the contracting corporation."[19] It also made explicit that a Delaware corporation may validly be formed in order "to engage in any

12. Sunrise Ventures, LLC v. Rehoboth Canal Ventures, LLC, C.A. No. 4119-VCS, 2010 WL 363845, at *13 n. 73 (Del. Ch. Jan. 27, 2010).
13. VandePoele v. Brennan, Civil Action No. 204-01-1984, 1985 WL 444625, *1 (Del. Com. Pl. Sept. 10, 1985).
14. Leiter v. Carpenter, 22 A.2d 393, 395 (Del. Ch. 1941).
15. *Id.*
16. Restatement (Third) of Suretyship & Guaranty § 1 (1996).
17. Restatement (Third) of Suretyship & Guaranty § 1 (1996).
18. 8 Del. C. § 122(13); Folk on the Delaware General Corporation Law, § 122.1.
19. *Id.*

lawful activity."[20] With certain narrow exceptions, Delaware abolished the doctrine of *ultra vires* in that same year.[21] Subsequently there "have been no reported decisions ... in which a corporate guarantee given to support extension of credit to a related entity has been denied enforcement on the grounds of *ultra vires*."[22] However, as with corporate powers generally, the corporation's certificate of incorporation and bylaws may circumscribe the corporation's exercise of its power to enter into guaranties.[23] Similarly, the specific grant of power is limited by the fiduciary duties of the board.[24]

In 1983, the Delaware General Corporation Law was amended to provide additional guidance with respect to guaranties involving a guarantor and primary obligor within the same corporate "family."[25] A guaranty is "deemed to be necessary or convenient to the conduct, promotion or attainment of the business of" the guarantor where it was so for the primary obligor, if the primary obligor falls into one of the following three categories: (1) the primary obligor wholly owns the guarantor, (2) the primary obligor is a wholly owned subsidiary of the guarantor, or (3) the primary obligor is wholly owned by the same corporate parent that wholly owns the guarantor.[26] Thus, where such a relationship exists between the guarantor and the primary obligor, the guaranty is "conclusively presumed to be necessary to the business" of the guarantor.[27] In each case, the parent may own the wholly owned subsidiary either directly or indirectly.[28] The 1983 amendment did not affect the power of corporations to guaranty the debt of unaffiliated entities or affiliates that have a "less than wholly-owned subsidiary" relationship.[29]

Additionally, a Delaware corporation may "guarantee any obligation of ... any officer or other employee of the corporation or of its subsidiary, including any officer or employee who is a director of the corporation or its subsidiary, whenever, in the judgment of the directors, such ... guaranty ... may reasonably be expected to benefit the corporation."[30]

2.2 Partnerships

Under Delaware's Revised Uniform Partnership Act ("DRUPA"), "a [general] partnership shall, subject to such standards and restrictions, if any, as are set forth in its partnership agreement, have the power and authority to make

20. Giancarlo v. OG Corp., Civil Action No. 10669, 1989 WL 72022, at *2 (Del. Ch. June 23, 1989).
21. Balotti and Finkelstein, The Delaware Law of Business Corporations and Business Organizations (3d Edition), § 2.3; Drexler, Black, and Sparks, Delaware Corporation Law and Practice, § 11.05.
22. Drexler, Black, and Sparks, Delaware Corporation Law and Practice, § 11.03[3].
23. *See* 8 Del. C. §§ 102(b)(1), 109(b); *see also* Jones Apparel Group, Inc. v. Maxwell Shoe Co., Inc., 883 A.2d 837 (Del. Ch. 2004) (suggesting that 8 Del. C. § 143 could be modified in the charter despite not including "magic language" to that effect).
24. Folk on the Delaware General Corporation Law, § 122.1.
25. Drexler, Black, and Sparks, Delaware Corporation Law and Practice, § 11.03[3].
26. 8 Del. C. § 122(13).
27. Balotti and Finkelstein, The Delaware Law of Business Corporations and Business Organizations (3d Edition), § 2.1.
28. 8 Del. C. § 122(13).
29. Balotti and Finkelstein, The Delaware Law of Business Corporations and Business Organizations (3d Edition), § 2.1; Drexler, Black, and Sparks, Delaware Corporation Law and Practice, § 11.03[3].
30. 8 Del. C. § 143.

contracts of guaranty and suretyship."[31] General contract principles apply to the interpretation and construction of any such standard or restriction on the authority and power of the general partnership to enter into guaranties.[32]

2.2a Limited Partnerships

Under Delaware's Revised Uniform Limited Partnership Act ("DRULPA"), "a limited partnership shall, subject to such standards and restrictions, if any, as are set forth in its partnership agreement, have the power and authority to make contracts of guaranty and suretyship."[33] General contract principles apply to the interpretation and construction of any such standard or restriction on the authority and power of the limited partnership to enter into guaranties.[34]

2.3 Limited Liability Companies

Under Delaware's Limited Liability Company Act ("LLC Act"), "a limited liability company shall, subject to such standards and restrictions, if any, as are set forth in its limited liability company agreement, have the power and authority to make contracts of guaranty and suretyship."[35] General contract principles apply to the interpretation and construction of any such standard or restriction on the authority and power of the limited liability company to enter into guaranties.[36]

2.4 Banks and Trust Companies

Delaware's Corporation Law for State Banks and Trust Companies ("DCLBTC") provides that banks and trust companies created or established under that chapter "shall have power to... act as guarantor or surety for the debt or obligation of another."[37] A Delaware bank must be formed as a corporation.[38] However, a Delaware trust company may be formed as either a corporation or a limited liability company ("LLC").[39] The power to enter into guaranties of a Delaware bank or trust company formed as a corporation can be circumscribed by its articles of association and bylaws.[40] The power to enter into guaranties of a Delaware trust company formed as a LLC can be circumscribed by its LLC agreement, which is comprised solely of its articles

31. 6 Del. C. § 15-202(e).
32. *See* Grunstein v. Silva, C.A. No. 3932-VCN, 2011 WL 378782, at *9 (Del. Ch. Jan. 31, 2011).
33. 6 Del. C. § 17-106(c).
34. *See* Schuss v. Penfield Partners, L.P., Civil Action No. 3132-VCP, 2008 WL 2433842, at *6 (Del.Ch. June 13, 2008) ("Limited partnership agreements are contracts the courts construe like any other contract."); *see generally* Elf Atochem North America, Inc. v. Jaffari , 727 A.2d 286, 290 (Del. 1999).
35. 6 Del. C. § 18-106(c).
36. Arbor Place, L.P. v. Encore Opportunity Fund, L.L.C., No. CIV.A. 18928 2002 WL 205681, at *3 (Del. Ch. 2002) ("It is undisputed that the LLC Agreements are contracts to be construed like any other contract."; *see generally* Elf Atochem North America, Inc. v. Jaffari , 727 A.2d 286, 290 (Del. 1999).
37. 5 Del. C. § 761.
38. *See* 5 Del. C. § 706.
39. *See* 5 Del. C. § 706.
40. *See* 5 Del. C. §§ 723(b), 741.

of association and bylaws.[41] Unless inconsistent with the express provisions of the DCLBTC, banks and trust companies organized as corporations are also subject to Delaware's General Corporation Law.[42] Similarly, with the same proviso, trust companies organized as LLCs are subject to the LLC Act.[43]

The DCLBTC also provides for the creation of limited purpose trust companies.[44] Limited purpose trust companies may also enter into guaranties so long as they are "necessary or incidental to the performance of trust company powers."[45]

Delaware's Corporation Law for State Savings Banks provides that Delaware savings banks "shall have power to... act as guarantor or surety for the debt or obligation of another."[46] Like Delaware banks generally, a savings bank's power to enter into guaranties can be circumscribed by its articles of association and bylaws.[47]

2.5 Individuals

6 Del. C. § 2705 provides that "[a]ny person who has attained 18 years of age shall have full capacity to contract; provided such person has not been declared legally incompetent to contract for reasons other than age." Under Delaware law, mental capacity is a prerequisite to enter into a valid contract.[48] Unless adjudicated incompetent, adults are presumed to have the capacity to contract.[49] "Lack of contractual capacity will be found [due to mental incompetence] if [the party] was incapable of understanding the nature and effect of the transaction or [the party's] mental faculties were so impaired as to render [the party] unable to properly, intelligently, and fairly preserve [the party's] rights."[50]

In the case of a valid contract of guaranty, a question may arise regarding whether a natural person who has signed a guaranty did so in his individual capacity or as the agent for a business entity. This issue appears to most frequently arise under Delaware law in cases involving Delaware entities where at least one of the alleged guarantors owned a substantial interest in the entity and also executed the underlying obligation on behalf of the primary obligor.[51] Whether a person signing the contract did so in a personal

---

41. *See* 5 Del. C. §§ 706(c), 723(b), 741.
42. 5 Del. C. § 702.
43. 5 Del. C. § 702.
44. 5 Del. C. § 744.
45. 5 Del. C. § 775(a).
46. 5 Del. C. § 1661(a)(15).
47. 5 Del. C. § 1602; *see* 5 Del. C. §§ 723(b), 741.
48. Barrows v. Bowen, Civ. A. No 1454-S, 1994 WL 198724, at *4 (Del. Ch. May 10, 1994).
49. Barrows v. Bowen, Civ. A. No 1454-S, 1994 WL 198724, at *4 (Del. Ch. May 10, 1994); cf. Doe v. Cedars Academy, LLC, C.A. 09C-09-136-JRS, 2010 WL 5825343, at *4 n.37 (Del. Super. Oct. 27, 2010) ("A person does not have the capacity to contract until he or she reaches the age of majority.").
50. McAllister v. Schettler, 521 A.2d 617, 621 (Del Ch. 1986).
51. *See*, e.g., Chestnut Hill Plaza Holdings Corp. v. Parkway Cleaners, Inc., C.A. No. N10C–09–161 DCS, 2011 WL 1885256, at *5 (Del. Super. May 17, 2011); Citizens Bank v. Gupta, No. Civ. A.02J-05-068, 2004 WL 1965924, at *2 (Del. Super. Aug. 26, 2004); Auth Sausage Co. v. Dutch Oven II, Inc., No 1-17-078, 2001 WL 209817, at *2 (Del. Super. Jan. 16, 2001); Alpha Affiliates, Inc. v. McGrath, No. Civ. A. 97–494 MMS, 1997 WL 782011, at *5 (D. Del. Dec. 10, 1997).

capacity is determined by the shared, objective intent of the parties, looking to the agreement as whole.[52]

The difficulty in these cases stems from the fact that the signers were alleged to have entered into agreements with the obligees in more than one capacity, often in the same writing.[53] Where a contract discloses the principal and the signer is acting within his actual or apparent authority, "[i]t is established law that an agent is not a party to a contract and is not liable for its nonperformance."[54] In this circumstance, there is no affirmative requirement for the signer to disclaim personal liability.[55]

§ 3 Signatory's Authority to Execute a Guaranty

Unless specifically addressed by statute, whether a signatory has authority to execute a guaranty on behalf of another will be determined applying general agency law principles. Thus, generally, an obligee who reasonably should have known that a signatory may not have such authority is duty bound to inquire further. Failure to do so may render the guaranty unenforceable against the alleged principal. Relevant statutory authorizations and restrictions on the ability of Delaware entities to delegate such authority are set forth below.

3.1 Agency Law Generally

Business entities as nonnatural persons can only operate through their agents.[56] The question may arise of whether an obligee will be prevented from recovering from an entity acting as guarantor because the alleged guarantor's agent did not have actual authority to enter into a contract of guaranty. As discussed *supra*, a contract of guaranty is a species of contract.[57] Whether one is party to a contract purportedly signed on its behalf by another is a question of agency law.[58]

---

52. *See* Chestnut Hill Plaza Holdings Corp. v. Parkway Cleaners, Inc., C.A. No. N10C–09–161 DCS, 2011 WL 1885256, at *5 (Del. Super. May 17, 2011); Citizens Bank v. Gupta, No. Civ.A.02J-05-068, 2004 WL 1965924, at *2 (Del. Super. Aug. 26, 2004); Auth Sausage Co. v. Dutch Oven II, Inc., No 1-17-078, 2001 WL 209817, at *2 (Del.Super. Jan. 16, 2001); Alpha Affiliates, Inc. v. McGrath, No. Civ.A. 97–494 MMS, 1997 WL 782011, at *5 (D. Del. Dec. 10, 1997).
53. *See* Chestnut Hill Plaza Holdings Corp. v. Parkway Cleaners, Inc., C.A. No. N10C–09–161 DCS, 2011 WL 1885256, at *5 (Del. Super. May 17, 2011); Auth Sausage Co. v. Dutch Oven II, Inc., No 1-17-078, 2001 WL 209817, at *2 (Del.Super. Jan. 16, 2001); Alpha Affiliates, Inc. v. McGrath, No. Civ.A. 97–494 MMS, 1997 WL 782011, at *5 (D. Del. Dec. 10, 1997).
54. American Ins. Co. v. Material Transit, Inc., 446 A.2d 1101, 1105 (Del. Super. Ct. 1982); *see generally* Cencom Cable Income Partners II, Inc., L.P. v. Wood, 752 A.2d 1175, 1180 (Del. Ch. 1999) ("It is a general principle of contract law that only a party to a contract may be sued for breach of that contract.").
55. *See* Pennsylvania House, Inc. v. Kaufman's of Delaware, Inc., No. 97J-10-039, 1998 WL 442701, at *1-2 (Del. Super. Ct. May 20, 1998).
56. *See* Hessler, Inc. v. Farrell, 226 A.2d 708, 712 (1967).
57. A.G. Barr v. Agribusiness Partners Intern, 2003 WL 1873848, 2 n.11 (Del. Super. Apr. 14, 2003) ("The general rules of pleading in contract actions govern the pleadings of the parties in an action to enforce a contract of guaranty.")
58. *See* Citadel Engineering, Inc. v. American Aerospace Corp., 2011 WL 1632184, at 3 n.1 (Del. Super. 2011) (citing the Restatement (Third) of Agency, § 6.01 (2006); Jack J. Morris Associates v. Mispillion Street Partners, LLC 2008 WL 3906755, at *3 (Del. Super. 2008); *see also* Dweck v. Nasser, 959 A.2d 29, 39 (Del. Ch. 2008).

Under Delaware law, agency is a question of fact, which the party asserting, e.g., the obligee in the guaranty context, has the burden of proving.[59] Unless an issue of agency is specifically addressed by statute, Delaware courts will apply general principles of agency law to determine the liability of business entity principals.[60]

Unlike the rule for the liability of agents, the rule with respect to liability of principals is essentially the same whether the principal was "disclosed," i.e., its identity and existence were made known to the third party in the contract; "partially disclosed," i.e., only its existence was made known to the third party; or "undisclosed."[61] An undisclosed principal may be sued for a contract made in its agent's name, unless the agent made the contract under seal, so long as the agent was actually or apparently authorized to do so.[62] A disclosed principal is a party to a contract, and thus may be held liable for its breach, where its agent was "acting with actual or apparent authority" in making the contract on its behalf.[63] The same is true in the case of a partially disclosed principal.[64]

Actual authority includes that authority expressly granted, either orally or in writing.[65] It also includes "implied authority" to (i) "do what is necessary, usual, and proper to accomplish or perform the agent's express responsibilities," or (ii) to act in a manner in which the agent reasonably "believes the principal wishes the agent to act," taking into account the principal's objectives and the circumstances.[66] Generally, the other party to the contract's knowledge or reliance on the agent's actual authority is immaterial to "the validity of a contract entered into on one side by an agent for his principal."[67]

Apparent authority is authority that the principal has not actually granted, but that the "principal knowingly or negligently permits the 'agent' to exercise or which [the principal] holds him out as possessing."[68] In the case of alleged apparent authority, the third party must demonstrate (i) it reasonably relied on indicia of the alleged agent's authority, and (ii) that indicia of authority "originated with the principal."[69] For this reason, "one dealing with an agent does so at his peril."[70] Under Delaware law, if one reasonably should have known "that the agent is exceeding his authority [one] is duty bound to ascertain the

59. Billops v. Magness Const. Co., 391 A.2d 196, 198-99 (Del. 1978).
60. *See* Harris v. Dependable Used Cars, Inc., 1997 WL 358302, at *1 (Del. Super. 1997); *see also* Pennsylvania House, Inc. v. Kauffman's of Delaware, Inc., 1998 WL 442701, at *1 (Del. Super. May 20, 1998) (applying general principles of agency law because "Title 6 is silent on this issue").
61. *See* McCabe v. Williams, 45 A.2d 503, 506 (1944); Chalik v. Levy, 42 A.2d 16, 18 (Del. Ch. 1945).
62. Chalik v. Levy, 42 A.2d 16, 18 (Del. Ch. 1945).
63. *See* Citadel Engineering, Inc. v. American Aerospace Corp., 2011 WL 1632184, at 3 (Del. Super. 2011) (citing Restatement (Third) Agency); *see also* American Insurance Co. v. Material Transit Inc., Del.Super., 446 A.2d 1101 (1982) (citing Restatement (Second) Agency § 320) ("[W]here the principal is disclosed, only the principal is liable for a breach thereof, not the agent.").
64. Jack J. Morris Associates v. Mispillion Street Partners, LLC 2008 WL 3906755, at *3 (Del. Super. 2008) ("A disclosed or partially disclosed principal is a party to a contract, when executed by an authorized agent.").
65. Dweck v. Nasser, 959 A.2d 29, 39 (Del. Ch. 2008).
66. Dweck v. Nasser, 959 A.2d 29, 39 (Del. Ch. 2008) (citing the Restatement (Third) of Agency § 2.01 (2006)).
67. Zeeb v. Atlas Powder Co., 87 A.2d 123, 126 (Del.1952).
68. Finnegan Const. Co. v. Robino-Ladd Co., 354 A.2d 142, 144 (Del. Super. 1976); *see also* Dweck v. Nasser, 959 A.2d 29, 39 (Del. Ch. 2008).
69. Billops v. Magness Const. Co., 391 A.2d 196, 198-99 (Del. 1978).
70. Limestone Realty Co. v. Town & Country Fine Furniture & Carpeting, Inc., 256 A.2d 676, 678 -679 (Del.Ch. 1969).

extent of the authority."[71] Failure to act with "ordinary prudence and reasonable diligence" after one is put on such inquiry notice might render the offer made by the supposed agent unacceptable.[72] *A fortiori*, "[i]t is an established principle of Delaware law that apparent authority cannot be asserted by a party who knew, at the time of the transaction, that the agent lacked actual authority."[73]

3.2 Corporations

Delaware corporations are managed "by or under the direction of a board of directors."[74] The board has broad power to delegate its authority to officers and other agents.[75] Moreover, with exceptions not relevant to their powers to execute contracts, Delaware corporations are largely free to assign duties and responsibilities to officers in their bylaws or by board resolutions consistent with the bylaws irrespective of their titles.[76] Nevertheless, Delaware courts have relaxed the traditional rule that certain officers have "very little or no authority merely by virtue of [their] office[s]."[77] With respect to the office of president, Delaware courts have concluded that "the office itself ... confers ... the requisite authority to make contracts in the usual and ordinary course of business."[78] However, the Delaware Superior Court has held that the general rule is that guaranteeing the debt of an entity in which the corporation has "no apparent interest" is not within the ordinary course of business.[79]

In the case of an officer who is also appointed "general manager" of a corporation, the Delaware Superior Court has held that the officer has the "implied authority to do anything that the corporation could do in the general scope and operation of its business."[80] That is, the officer has the "common law powers" of general manager.[81] However, like the president, an officer who is also general manager "would have ... no implied authority to enter into [an] unusual and extraordinary contract."[82]

One commentator has noted that the practical value of the liberalization of the traditional limit on *ex officio* implicit authority of officers to enter into contracts has been mitigated by the difficulty of determining in advance what falls within the "ordinary course of business" of a particular entity.[83] That same commentator has noted that "prudence suggests that persons contracting with

71. Limestone Realty Co. v. Town & Country Fine Furniture & Carpeting, Inc., 256 A.2d 676, 678-679 (Del.Ch. 1969); Whittington v. Dragon Group L.L.C., Civil Action No. 2291-VCP, 2010 WL 692584, at *5 (Del. Ch. Feb. 15, 2010).
72. Limestone Realty Co. v. Town & Country Fine Furniture & Carpeting, Inc., 256 A.2d 676, 678-679 (Del.Ch. 1969).
73. Rudnitsky v. Rudnitsky, 2000 WL 1724234, at *6 (Del. Ch. 2000).
74. 8 Del. C. § 141(a).
75. Balotti, § 4.10[A].
76. Drexler § 14.02.
77. Italo-Petroleum Corp. of America v. Hannigan, 14 A.2d 401, 406 (Del. 1940).
78. Folk § 142.6.
79. Atlantic Refining Co. v Ingalls & Co., Inc., 185 A. 885, 886 (Del. Super. 1936).
80. Phoenix Finance Corp. v. Iowa-Wisconsin Bridge Co., 41 Del. 130, 140, 16 A.2d 789, 793 (Del. Super. 1940).
81. Folk § 142.6.
82. Colish v. Brandywine Raceway Ass'n, 119 A.2d 887, 891 (Del. Super. 1955).
83. Drexler § 14.02 (citing Colish v. Brandywine Raceway Ass'n, 119 A.2d 887, 891 (Del. Super. 1955)).

a corporation obtain, where feasible, evidence of board approval for sizeable transactions even tenuously outside the ordinary course of business."[84]

With respect to delegation to agents not specifically discussed, Delaware courts should apply the general principles of agency law discussed *supra*.[85]

3.3 Partnerships

Under DRUPA, generally the "act of a partner, including the execution of an instrument in the partnership name, for apparently carrying on in the ordinary course the partnership's business, purposes or activities or business, purposes or activities of the kind carried on by the partnership binds the partnership."[86] The exception is where (i) the partner had no actual authority and (ii) the other party to the agreement had notice that this partner lacked authority.[87] The act "of a partner which is *not* apparently for carrying on in the ordinary course the partnership's business, purposes or activities or business, purposes or activities of the kind carried on by the partnership binds the partnership *only* if the act was authorized by the other partners."[88]

A Delaware court "may consider the partnership's stated purposes, the precedent set by the partnership's prior 'custom or course of dealing' and 'the general custom' of analogous partnerships" in determining whether an act is in the "ordinary course" of the partnership's business.[89] As with corporations, it may not always be clear whether a challenged transaction will be found to be within the "ordinary course" of the partnership's business.[90]

Additionally, under DRUPA, the partnership may state the limits upon the actual authority of "some or all partners to enter into transactions on behalf of the partnership" in its filed statement of partnership existence.[91] However, Section 15-303 of DRUPA provides that "a person not a partner is not deemed to know of [this] limitation on the authority of a partner merely because the limitation is contained in a statement."[92] However, there is some authority for the proposition that more sophisticated parties and parties familiar with the partnership may not be able to rely on "apparent authority" without inquiring

84. Drexler § 14.02.
85. *See* Harris v. Dependable Used Cars, Inc., No. CIV. A. 96C-10-023, 1997 WL 358302, 1 (Del. Super. 1997) (suggesting that application of general principles of agency law with respect to contract liability is the default which may be altered by statute in case involving a corporation as alleged principal); Colish v. Brandywine Raceway Ass'n, 119 A.2d 887, 891 (Del.Super.1955) (noting that Delaware courts had acknowledged the "doctrine of apparent authority" to bind a principal in the corporate context).
86. 6 Del. C. § 15-301.
87. 6 Del. C. § 15-301.
88. 6 Del. C. § 15-301 (emphasis added).
89. Rudnitsky v. Rudnitsky, 2000 WL 1724234, at *6 (Del. Ch. Nov. 14, 2000).
90. *See, e.g.*, Abt .v Harmony Mill Limited Partnership, C.A. No. 12435, Chandler, V.C., Mem. Op. at 6 (Dec. 18, 1992); Rudnitsky v. Rudnitsky, 2000 WL 1724234, at *6 (Del. Ch. Nov. 14, 2000) (citing Abt for proposition that where the stated purpose of a partnership was to own and operate a building, a contract to compensate a third party for services in finding investors for a partnership, was not "carrying on the business of the partnership").
91. 6 Del. C. § 15-303(a)(2).
92. 6 Del. C. § 15-303(d).

further into the authority of the partner that supposedly executed the agreement on behalf of the partnership.[93]

Consequently, as with corporations, when there is the possibility that a transaction will be found to be outside of the "ordinary business" of the partnership, further assurances should be sought by the contracting party from the partnership with respect to the actual authority of the person that will execute the contract of guaranty. With respect to delegation to alleged nonpartner agents, Delaware courts should apply the general principles of agency law discussed *supra*.[94]

3.3a Limited Partnerships

Under DRULPA, unless limited by its limited partnership agreement, general partners in a Delaware limited partnership have the same rights and powers as they would in a general partnership under Delaware's Uniform Partnership Act ("DUPA").[95] Thus, under the default rule, "every [general] partner is an agent of the partnership for the purpose of its business, and the act of every [general] partner for apparently carrying on in the usual way of business of the partnership of which he is a member binds the partnership."[96] The exception is where (i) the general partner does not have actual authority to bind the limited partnership in this particular matter, and (ii) the party with whom the general partner is dealing knows the general partner lacks actual authority.[97] However, a general partner's act that is "not apparently for the carrying on of the business of the partnership in the usual way does not bind the partnership" unless the other partners have authorized the act.[98] As with the forms of business entities discussed *supra*, it may not always be clear whether a challenged transaction will be found to be within the "ordinary course" of the limited partnership's business.[99] Thus, when there is the possibility that a transaction will be found to be outside of the "ordinary business" of the limited partnership, further assurances should be sought by the contracting party from the limited partnership with respect to the actual authority of the person who will execute the contract of guaranty.

Under DRULPA, a general partner "has the power and authority to delegate to [one] or more other persons the general partner's rights and powers to manage and control the business and affairs of the limited partnership."[100]

---

93. Rudnitsky v. Rudnitsky, 2000 WL 1724234, at *6-7 (Del. Ch. Nov. 14, 2000) (finding that two parties could not claim (and questioning the credibility of the claim of the third) not to have notice that the partner lacked actual authority noting that the parties claiming to have entered into the mortgage with the partnership were attorneys familiar with agency and partnership law and further that each had some exposure to the specifics of this particular partnership).
94. *See* Rudnitsky v. Rudnitsky, 2000 WL 1724234, at *6 n.15 (noting that agency law continued to apply under the Uniform Partnership Act and that DRUPA preserved the "premise" of its predecessor) (Del. Ch. Nov. 14, 2000); Pennsylvania House, Inc. v. Kauffman's of Delaware, Inc., 1998 WL 442701, at *1 (Del. Super. May 20, 1998) ("Because Title 6 is silent on this issue, the court must look to principals of agency law to determine the rights and liabilities of partners with respect to each other and to third persons ....".).
95. Lubaroff and Altman, § 4.16.
96. *Id.*
97. *Id.*
98. *Id.*
99. *See, e.g.*, Abt v. Harmony Mill Ltd. P'ship, C.A. No. 12435, Chandler, V.C., Mem. Op. at 6 (Dec. 18, 1992).
100. 6 Del. C. § 17-403.

One prominent commentator has suggested the mandatory inclusion of the names of general partners in the certificate of limited partnership places persons dealing with a limited partnership on notice that those who are not listed as general partners in the certificate "do not have the rights [and] powers ... of a general partner."[101] With respect to delegation to alleged nongeneral partner agents, Delaware courts should apply the general principles of agency law discussed *supra*.[102]

3.4 Limited Liability Companies

Under the LLC Act, "the management of a LLC shall be vested in its members," with the decision of members representing a majority of ownership controlling.[103] This default provision may be altered in the LLC agreement.[104] The LLC agreement may vest management, in whole or in part, to one or more managers.[105] "Unless otherwise provided in a [LLC] agreement, each member and manager has the authority to bind the [LLC]."[106] The LLC agreement can eliminate this authority.[107] However, this agreement need not be filed.[108] Additionally, the certificate of formation may, but need not, contain limitations on the ability of managers or members to bind the LLC.[109] Consequently, inclusion of this information in the certificate of formation does not necessarily put a third party on notice of the limitation.[110] Unless restricted by the LLC agreement, managers and members may delegate their "rights and powers to manage and control the business and affairs" of the LLC to one or more persons."[111] General agency law principles should apply to whether a LLC is bound by the acts of these agents, as this has not specifically been addressed by Delaware statute.[112]

3.5 Banks and Trust Companies

The DCLBTC does not expressly address the principal-agent relationship. The DCLBTC does provide, however, that banks and trust companies organized as corporations are subject to Delaware's General Corporation Law

101. Lubaroff and Altman, § 3.13.
102. *See* Rudnitsky v. Rudnitsky, 2000 WL 1724234, at *6 n.15 (citing the Restatement (Second) of Partnership for the proposition that agency law continued to apply under DUPA); Pennsylvania House, Inc. v. Kauffman's of Delaware, Inc., 1998 WL 442701, at *1 (Del. Super. May 20, 1998).
103. 6 Del. C. § 18-402.
104. *Id.*
105. *Id.*
106. *Id.*
107. Symonds & O'Toole on Delaware Limited Liability Companies, § 9.04[A][iv].
108. *See generally* Symonds & O'Toole § 2.01.
109. *See* 6 Del. C. § 18-201.
110. 6 Del. C. § 18-207.
111. 6 Del. C. § 18-407.
112. *See* Harris v. Dependable Used Cars, Inc., No. CIV. A. 96C-10-023, 1997 WL 358302, 1 (Del. Super. 1997) (suggesting that application of general principles of agency law with respect to contract liability is the default which may be altered by statute in case involving a corporation as alleged principal); Pennsylvania House, Inc. v. Kauffman's of Delaware, Inc., 1998 WL 442701, at *1 (Del. Super. May 20, 1998) (applying general principles of agency law because "Title 6 is silent on this issue"); Thomas v. Hobbs, No. C.A. 04C-02-010 RFS, 2005 WL 1653947, *2 (Del. Super. April 27, 2005) (citing to "well established principle of agency law"" in a case involving the LLC Act).

unless expressly inconsistent with the DCLBTC.[113] Similarly, the DCLBTC provides that trust companies organized as LLCs are subject to the LLC Act with the same proviso.[114] As noted *supra*, Delaware courts have applied general agency principles as the default unless altered by statute, including in a case dealing with a national bank operating in Delaware.[115] Consequently, the general principles of agency law discussed at the outset of this section would apply in determining whether a state bank, trust company, or limited purpose trust company is liable for a guaranty executed by its alleged agent, with the statutory exceptions noted *supra* in the subsections dealing with Delaware corporations and LLCs respectively.

The same would be the case for Delaware savings banks as Delaware's Corporation Law for State Savings Banks does not appear to address this issue, and it provides that state savings banks are governed by both Delaware's General Corporation Law and the DCLBTC "where the same are not inconsistent with the express provisions of this chapter."[116]

§ 4 Consideration; Sufficiency of Past Consideration

Standard contract principles apply to the analysis of consideration for a contract of guaranty. The principal agreement is sufficient consideration for an accompanying guaranty. A subsequent contract of guaranty made separately from the underlying obligation must be supported by separate consideration to be enforceable.

As with all contracts, consideration is required to create a valid contract of guaranty.[117] An offer to guaranty an underlying obligation that is not supported by consideration may be withdrawn by the offeror.[118] Under Delaware law, consideration "can consist of either a benefit to the promiser or a detriment to the promisee."[119] However, under Delaware law a contract under seal

113. 5 Del. C. § 702.
114. *Id.*
115. *See* Edge of the Woods, Ltd. P'ship v. Wilmington Savings Fund Society, No. C.A. 97C-09-281-JEB, 2000 WL 305448, at *5 (Del. Super. Feb. 7, 2000) (applying the general rule "in a breach of contract action involving a disclosed principal, on the principal is liable for breach contract" to a national bank operating in Delaware and governed in part under Title 5); *see generally* Harris v. Dependable Used Cars, Inc., No. CIV. A. 96C-10-023, 1997 WL 358302, 1 (Del. Super. 1997) (suggesting that application of general principles of agency law with respect to contract liability is the default which may be altered by statute in case involving a corporation as alleged principal); Pennsylvania House, Inc. v. Kauffman's of Delaware, Inc., 1998 WL 442701, at *1 (Del. Super. May 20, 1998) (applying general principles of agency law because "Title 6 is silent on this issue"); Thomas v. Hobbs, No. C.A. 04C-02-010 RFS, 2005 WL 1653947, *2 (Del. Super. April 27, 2005) (citing to "well established principle of agency law" and citing to its application in a case dealing with a corporation as alleged principal in a case dealing with a LLC).
116. 5 Del. C. § 1602.
117. Banco Credito y Ahorro Ponceno v. Scott, 250 A.2d 387, 388 (Del. Super. 1969); *see also* Lyons v. DBHI, LLC, C.A. No. U607-12-063, 2010 WL 335634, at *2 (Del. Com. Pl. Jan. 27, 2010) (finding that the defendant's alleged contract of guaranty was a "gratuitous promise" due to lack of consideration).
118. *See* Danby v. Osteopathic Hospital Ass'n of Delaware, 104 A.2d 903, 906 (Del. 1954).
119. First Mortgage Co. of Pa. v. Fed. Leasing Corp., 456 A.2d 794, 795–96 (Del. 1982).

essentially operates as a consideration substitute, as it "precludes challenges to the validity of a contract on the ground of lack of consideration."[120]

The inquiry into the sufficiency of consideration is governed by standard contract law principles.[121] The benefit or detriment that forms the consideration need not flow directly to the guarantor from the obligee.[122] The consideration flowing from the obligee to the principal obligor is sufficient to support a contemporaneous guaranty.[123] However, where the contract of guaranty is a separate, subsequent agreement from the underlying obligation, it requires separate consideration.[124]

§ 5 Notice of Acceptance

Generally, reasonable notice of acceptance is required where a guaranty is revocable. This requirement may be waived. Conversely, notice of acceptance is generally not required where a guaranty is irrevocable.

Under Delaware law, the general rule is that so long as a guarantor is free to revoke a guaranty, reasonable notice of acceptance is required to bind the guarantor.[125] This is true whenever there is an unaccepted offer of guaranty.[126] Likewise, notice of acceptance should be given with respect to those transactions under a continuing guaranty which are not yet binding on the guarantor.[127] However, notice of acceptance may be waived.[128]

Under Delaware law, "notice of acceptance" is not required where the offer of guaranty is no longer revocable.[129] For this reason, it is said that an "absolute guaranty" does not require "notice of acceptance."[130] This includes where the obligee acts simultaneously with the offer of guaranty, e.g., "in the case of goods then sold and delivered to a third party on the credit of the [offer of] guaranty."[131] Similarly, if an offer of guaranty may be accepted by performance, there is ordinarily no requirement of notice of acceptance where

---

120. Monroe Park v. Metro. Life Ins. Co., 457 A.2d 734, 737 (Del. 1983); *see, e.g.*, Leiter v. Carpenter, 22 A.2d 393 (Del. Ch. 1941) (dealing with a contract of guaranty made under seal).
121. *See* Banco Credito y Ahorro Ponceno v. Scott, 250 A.2d 387, 388 (Del. Super. 1969); Lyons v. DBHI, LLC, C.A. No. U607-12-063, 2010 WL 335634, at *2 (Del. Com. Pl. Jan. 27, 2010).
122. *See* Banco Credito y Ahorro Ponceno v. Scott, 250 A.2d 387, 388 (Del. Super. 1969).
123. *See* Banco Credito y Ahorro Ponceno v. Scott, 250 A.2d 387, 388 (Del. Super. 1969) (describing this area of law as "well settled" in suretyship and applying the principle to a guaranty); W. T. Rawleigh Co. v. Warrington, 199 A. 666, 668 (Del.Super. 1938) ("When, however, the suretyship contract, though not under seal, is made at the same time as the principal contract, and both contracts form parts of the same transaction, there need not be any consideration other than that moving between the obligee and the obligor under the principal contract.").
124. *See* Banco Credito y Ahorro Ponceno v. Scott, 250 A.2d 387, 388 (Del. Super. 1969); W. T. Rawleigh Co. v. Warrington, 199 A. 666, 668 (Del.Super. 1938).
125. *See* Farmers' Bank v. Tatnall, 31 A. 879, 879-880 (Del. 1885); Wanamaker v. Benn, 50 A. 512, 512 (Del. Super. 1901); Taylor v. McClung, 2 Houst. 24 (Del. Super. 1858).
126. *See* Farmers' Bank v. Tatnall, 31 A. 879, 879-880 (Del. 1885); Wanamaker v. Benn, 50 A. 512, 512 (Del. Super. 1901); Taylor v. McClung, 2 Houst. 24 (Del. Super. 1858).
127. *See, e.g.*, Ajax Rubber Co. v. Gam, 105 A. 834, 834 (Del. Super. 1919); *see generally* Danby v. Osteopathic Hospital Ass'n of Delaware, 101 A.2d 308, 312 (Del. Ch. 1953) (describing the functional nature of continuing guaranties).
128. *See* Am. Jur. 2d § 28; cf. W.T. Rawleigh Co. v. Warrington, 199 A. 666, 670 (Del. Super. 1938).
129. Farmers' Bank v. Tatnall, 31 A. 879, 879-880 (Del. 1885).
130. *Id.*
131. *Id* at 879, 880.

the offeror is reasonably expected to become aware that the offeree has taken action in reliance on the offer.[132] However, a guarantor can make notice of acceptance a prerequisite to acceptance.[133]

Subject to the restriction set forth in § 8.1, notice of acceptance may be (and frequently is) waived by guarantors.[134]

§ 6 Interpretation of Guaranties

Delaware courts will interpret a guaranty in the same manner they would interpret the language of any other contract. Delaware courts strictly construe guaranty contracts. In the case of ambiguity, ambiguous terms and provisions are construed against the drafter.

6.1 General Principles

Delaware courts will apply general rules of contract interpretation to contracts of guaranty.[135] Delaware follows the "objective theory" of contract.[136] A Delaware court's "ultimate goal in contract interpretation is to determine the parties' shared intent."[137] Delaware courts consider "the most objective indicia of that intent [to be] the words found in the written instrument."[138] As discussed *supra*, intent controls determination of: (1) whether a party is a guarantor,[139] and (2) the scope of a guaranty's coverage.[140]

Where the intent of the parties is reasonably clear, "there is no room for construction."[141] Where it is not, a Delaware court may consider extrinsic evidence, including parol evidence, to resolve the ambiguity.[142] Delaware will construe ambiguous terms and provisions in a guaranty against the drafting

132. *See* Industrial America, Inc. v. Fulton Indus., Inc., 285 A.2d 412, 416 (Del. 1971); Am. Jur. 2d *Guaranty* § 28 ("Notice of acceptance is required ... where the guarantor cannot reasonably anticipate that a creditor will act in reliance on the offer, but not otherwise.").

133. *See* Am. Jur. 2d § 28; Sunrise Ventures, LLC v. Rehoboth Canal Ventures, LLC, C.A. No. 4119-VCS, 2010 WL 363845, at *13 n.73 (Del. Ch. Jan. 27, 2010).

134. Peter A. Alces, The Law of Suretyship and Guaranty § 3:27 (Thomson West 1996) ("[W]aiver is the rule rather than the exception. However, when such a waiver is not present in the guarantee, the common law doctrine applies."); Restatement (Third) of Suretyship & Guaranty § 8 cmt (2006).

135. *See* Pellaton v. Bank of New York, 592 A.2d 473, 477-78 (Del. 1991) (applying general rules of contract interpretation to resolve whether the language of guaranty was ambiguous); Medek v. Medek, No. Civ. A. 2559-VCP, 2009 WL 2005365, *8-9 (Del. Ch. July 1, 2009).

136. Medek v. Medek, No. Civ. A. 2559-VCP, 2009 WL 2005365, *8 (Del. Ch. July 1, 2009).

137. Medek v. Medek, No. Civ. A. 2559-VCP, 2009 WL 2005365, *8 (Del. Ch. July 1, 2009); *see also* Cooling v. Springer, 30 A.2d 466, 469 (Del. Super. 1943).

138. Medek v. Medek, No. Civ. A. 2559-VCP, 2009 WL 2005365, *8 (Del. Ch. July 1, 2009).

139. *See* W. T. Rawleigh Co. v. Warrington, 199 A. 666, 670 (Del. Super. 1938); *see also* Chestnut Hill Plaza Holdings Corp. v. Parkway Cleaners, Inc., C.A. No. N10C–09–161 DCS, 2011 WL 1885256, at *5 (Del. Super. May 17, 2011).

140. *See* FinanceAmerica Private Brands, Inc. v. Harvey E. Hall, Inc., 380 A.2d 1377, 1379-80 (Del. Super. 1977); *see also* Wilmington & N. R.R Co. v. Delaware Valley Ry. Co., Inc., C.A. No. 97C-09-297-WTQ, 1999 WL 463705, at *5-6 (Del. Super. 1999).

141. Cooling v. Springer, 30 A.2d 466, 469 (Del. Super. 1943); Wilmington Trust Co. v. Keith, C.A. No. 00C-11-016, 2002 WL 1748622, at * 4 (Del. Super. June 26, 2002).

142. *See* Pellaton v. Bank of New York, 592 A.2d 473, 477-78 (Del. 1991); Medek v. Medek, No. Civ. A. 2559-VCP, 2009 WL 2005365, *8-9 (Del. Ch. July 1, 2009) (discussing the types of extrinsic evidence that might be used to resolve ambiguities in a guaranty).

party.[143] In the case of ambiguity, guaranty contracts are "strictly construed."[144] That is, the guarantor "cannot be held liable beyond the strict terms of his contract."[145]

However, "compensated sureties ... are denied the benefit of the rule of *strictissmi juris*."[146] A "compensated surety" is "ordinarily defined as one who is engaged in the business of executing surety contracts for an actuarially computed premium."[147] However, there is also a well-established line of cases that treats shareholders and directors who act as sureties for corporate debts as occupying the position of compensated sureties although the contract may in fact be an infrequent, even singular business affair.[148]

6.2 "Absolute and Unconditional"

An absolute and unconditional guaranty is one in which the guarantor's liability to the obligee for the underlying obligation arises upon the default of the primary obligor without more.[149] Thus, for example, there is no requirement that the obligee give the guarantor notice of default, which is generally a requirement implied by law in the case of conditional guaranties.[150] Nor is the guarantor's liability contingent upon the failure of the obligee to obtain satisfaction from the primary obligor after due diligence.[151] The court will look to the parties' shared, objective intent to determine whether a guaranty is "absolute and unconditional."[152] The "absolute and unconditional" guarantor's liability is "governed by the same rules of law by which the liability of one who has broken an ordinary contract is determined."[153]

6.3 Guaranty of Payment versus Guaranty of Collection

A guaranty of collection is a species of conditional guaranty.[154] The condition precedent to the guarantor of collection's liability is the failure of the obligee to collect the debt from the primary obligor "by the use of due diligence."[155] No Delaware case has established what constitutes "due diligence" in this context.

143. *See* Kuhn Const., Inc. v. Diamond State Port Corp., 993 A.2d 393, 397 (Del. 2010); Fed. Deposit Ins. Corp. v. Bloom, No. 29 C.A. 1977, 1986 WL 221, at * 6 (Del. Super. May 21, 1986) (A guaranty will be "interpreted most strongly against the party in which has prepared and offered it for execution.").
144. Fed. Deposit Ins. Corp. v. Bloom, No. 29 C.A. 1977, 1986 WL 221, at * 6 (Del. Super. May 21, 1986).
145. Garfield Trust Co. v. Teichmann, 95 A.2d 18, 22 (N.J. Super. 1953) (Cited with approval in Fed. Deposit Ins. Corp. v. Bloom, No. 29 C.A. 1977, 1986 WL 221, at * 6 (Del. Super. May 21, 1986).
146. Gellis v. S. Gellis & Co., Inc., 322 A.2d 287, 292 (Del. Ch. 1974); *see also* Kent County Levy Court v. International Underwriters, Inc., C.A. No. 745(k), 1985 WL 149635, at *3 (Del. Ch. July 31, 1985) ("Where the terms of the undertaking are set forth in a written contract of suretyship the usual standards of contract interpretation apply, unless the surety is uncompensated.").
147. Gellis v. S. Gellis & Co., Inc., 322 A.2d 287, 292 (Del. Ch. 1974).
148. *Id.*
149. Ajax Rubber Co., Inc. v. Gam, 151 A. 828, 829 (Del. Super. 1923).
150. *Id.* at 831, 832.
151. *Id.* at 828, 830.
152. *Id.* at 828, 829.
153. Ajax Rubber Co., Inc. v. Gam, 151 A. 831, 832 (Del Super. 1924).
154. Ajax Rubber Co., Inc. v. Gam, 151 A. 828, 830 (Del. Super. 1923); *see also* Gaylords, Inc. v. Tollin, No. Civ. A. 80C-JN23, 1984 WL 547850, at *2 (Del. Super. Jan. 31, 1984).
155. *See* Ajax Rubber Co., Inc. v. Gam, 151 A. 828, 830 (Del. Super. 1923); *see also* Gaylords, Inc. v. Tollin, No. Civ. A. 80C-JN23, 1984 WL 547850, at *2 (Del. Super. Jan. 31, 1984).

However, *American Jurisprudence*, which has been cited with approval by Delaware courts with respect to the law of guaranties generally,[156] indicates that the guarantor's liability is conditioned upon the obligee "exhausting its remedies" against the primary obligor.[157]

A guaranty of payment is a type of absolute guaranty.[158] With this type of guaranty, "it is neither necessary for the [obligee] to allege and prove diligence" in obtaining payment from the primary obligor nor is it required for the obligee "to allege facts to excuse such failure" before the obligee may seek satisfaction of the underlying obligation from the guarantor.[159] Simply, the guarantor's liability arises upon the default of the primary obligor.[160]

As with the interpretation of guaranties generally, a Delaware court will resolve the specific question of whether a guaranty is one of payment or collection by giving effect to the objective, shared intent of the parties looking to the contract as a whole.[161]

6.4 "Continuing" Guaranties

"A continuing guaranty, as generally defined, is one which is not limited to a single transaction, but which contemplates a future course of dealing covering a series of transactions, and generally for an indefinite time."[162] In the case of a continuing guaranty, the guarantor's promise with respect to future transactions operates as an offer.[163] Thus a guarantor may limit its liability to that amount already accepted by the obligee by effectively revoking its promise to guaranty future transactions prior to the obligee's acceptance.[164] General contract principles govern whether the guarantor's offer to guarantee future transactions is accepted or is revoked.[165] The parties may circumscribe their respective rights, e.g., with respect to revocation or notice of acceptance, by contract.[166]

As with other categorizations of guaranties, whether a guaranty is a "continuing guaranty" is determined by the shared, objective intent of the parties.[167] The use of the word "continuing" is not itself determinative.[168] The inquiry

156. *See, e.g,* Gaylords, Inc. v. Tollin, No. Civ. A. 80C-JN23, 1984 WL 547850, at *3 (Del. Super. Jan. 31, 1984).
157. 38 AM. JUR. 2D *Guaranty* § 16 (2010).
158. *See* Ajax Rubber Co., Inc. v. Gam, 151 A. 828, 829 (Del. Super. 1923).
159. Ajax Rubber Co., Inc. v. Gam, 151 A. 828, 829 (Del. Super. 1923).
160. *See* Ajax Rubber Co., Inc. v. Gam, 151 A. 828, 829 (Del. Super. 1923).
161. *See* Ajax Rubber Co., Inc. v. Gam, 151 A. 828, 829 (Del. Super. 1923) ("There is nothing in the guaranty to indicate that [the guarantor's] liability was conditioned upon failure of the [obligee] to collect from the principal debtor."); Gaylords, Inc. v. Tollin, No. Civ. A. 80C-JN23, 1984 WL 547850, at *2 (Del. Super. Jan. 31, 1984).
162. Cooling v. Springer, 30 A.2d 466, 469 (Del. Super. 1943).
163. *See* Danby v. Osteopathic Hospital Ass'n of Delaware, 101 A.2d 308, 312 (Del. Ch. 1953).
164. *Id.*
165. *See* Danby v. Osteopathic Hospital Ass'n of Delaware, 101 A.2d 308, 312 (Del. Ch. 1953); *see also* Gupta v. Citizens Bank, 860 A.2d 810 (Table), at *2 (Del. May 4, 2004) (noting that the guarantors' revocation was ineffective because the lower court found it had not been received and that they failed to mention the letter at the closing of the loan).
166. *See* Cooling v. Springer, 30 A.2d 466, 470 (Del. Super. 1943); Ajax Rubber Co., Inc. v. Gam, 151 A. 831, 832 (Del. Super. 1924).
167. Cooling v. Springer, 30 A.2d 466, 469 (Del. Super. 1943).
168. *See* Cooling v. Springer, 30 A.2d 466, 469 (Del. Super. 1943); *see* Danby v. Osteopathic Hospital Ass'n of Delaware, 101 A.2d 308, 312 (Del. Ch. 1953).

focuses on whether the guaranty offer is "divisible."[169] That is whether the guaranty offer is in essence a series of offers inviting separate acceptances by the obligee, e.g., by making future advances to the primary obligor.[170] Each would in practical effect be a separate underlying obligation.[171] Or, whether the parties intended to irrevocably bind the guarantor from the outset to be liable as a guarantor with respect to a single underlying obligation, the parameters of which may not be fixed.[172] For example, an obligee might agree to lend a primary obligor up to $50,000 at a fixed rate within a set period of time at the primary obligor's option, so long as the guarantor agreed to be bound from the first advancement to guarantee this and all additional advancements up to an aggregate of $50,000.[173]

It important to keep in mind that the distinction between "continuing" and "limited" guaranties relates *solely* to the number of transactions that are covered by a guaranty. For example, parties "may plainly ... indicate" that a guaranty limited to a single transaction may continue beyond the original term of the transaction, e.g., through a series of renewals prior to expiration.[174] Similarly, a continuing guaranty can be limited to a certain dollar amount.[175]

6.5 "Special Guaranties" versus "General Guaranties"

A "general guaranty," i.e., an "instrument of guaranty addressed to all persons generally, or 'to whom it may concern,'" may be enforced "by anyone to whom it was presented who acts upon it."[176] A "special guaranty" is one "addressed to a particular person, firm, or corporation."[177] Whether a guaranty is "special" is determined by the shared, objective intent of the parties.[178] The "majority rule [is] once a guaranty is correctly categorized as special, it is not assignable absent a specific assignability provision or other special circumstances."[179]

In *FinanceAmerica Private Brands, Inc.*, the Delaware Superior Court applied but did not adopt the "majority rule."[180] It mentioned the following two minority rules, without foreclosing the possibility of their future application: (1) after determining that it is dealing with a "special guaranty," the court does not discharge the guarantor's obligation if the guarantor's undertaking was not materially altered by the transfer of the primary obligor's assets,"[181] (2) even after labeling the guaranty "special," the court considers the contract and the surrounding circumstances to determine whether the guaranty was intended to be transferrable with the collateral contract.[182]

169. *See* Danby v. Osteopathic Hospital Ass'n of Delaware, 101 A.2d 308, 312 (Del. Ch. 1953).
170. *Id.*
171. *Id.*
172. *Id.*
173. *Id.*
174. Cooling v. Springer, 30 A.2d 466, 470 (Del. Super. 1943).
175. *Id.*
176. FinanceAmerica Private Brands, Inc. v. Harvey E. Hall, Inc., 380 A.2d 1377, 1379 (Del. Super. 1977).
177. *Id.*
178. *Id.*
179. *Id.* at 1377, 1380.
180. *Id.* at 1377, 1380-81.
181. *Id.* at 1377, 1381.
182. *Id.*

Under Delaware law, a special guaranty is assignable by operation of law to and enforceable by a successor entity of the obligee following a merger.[183] The Delaware Supreme Court has explained that the pertinent sections of the Delaware Code, e.g., 8 Del. C. § 259, "provide[] the 'special circumstance' lacking in *FinanceAmerica* to make a special guaranty assignable."[184]

6.6 Language Regarding the Revocation of Guaranties

Whether a guaranty is revocable turns on general contract principles.[185] Prior to acceptance, a promise of guaranty is revocable like any other contract offer—upon effective notice to the offeree.[186] Once there is a validly formed contract, attempts at revocation generally constitute breach.[187]

Thus, in the case of a contract of limited guaranty, an attempt at revocation generally would constitute a breach.[188] However, the contract of limited guaranty might provide otherwise. For example, a limited guaranty might provide for extensions of the expiration of the underlying obligation of the single transaction. This contract might validly permit the guarantor to revoke the guaranty beyond the expiration of the original period prior to the acceptance of the extension by the primary obligor.[189]

With respect to a continuing guaranty, each subsequent transaction essentially operates as an offer to enter into a contract of guaranty, the acceptance of which is typically the advance of money by the obligee to the primary obligor.[190] Consequently, a guarantor may not effectively withdraw its guaranty with respect to those transactions under the continuing guaranty that have already been accepted.[191] However, with respect to future advances, i.e., unaccepted offers to guarantee a greater underlying obligation, the guarantor may revoke the offer, thus limiting the scope of its liability.[192] As discussed *supra*, whether a contract of guaranty envisioning several advancements is a limited or continuing guaranty turns on the objective, shared intent of the parties.

---

183. Deascanis v. Brosius-Eliason Co., 533 A.2d 1254 (Table), at * 2 (Del. 1987).
184. Deascanis v. Brosius-Eliason Co., 533 A.2d 1254 (Table), at * 2 (Del. 1987). Portions of the Delaware Code dealing with partnerships, limited partnerships, limited liability companies, etc. each contain sections nearly identical to 8 Del. C. § 259, which deals with mergers under Delaware's General Corporation Law. *See, e.g,* 6 Del. C. § 17-211(h) (dealing with mergers under the chapter dealing with limited partnerships).
185. *See* Danby v. Osteopathic Hospital Ass'n of Delaware, 101 A.2d 308, 312 (Del. Ch. 1953).
186. *See* Danby v. Osteopathic Hospital Ass'n of Delaware, 104 A.2d 903, 906 (Del. 1954) (It is the "undoubted general rule that unless an offer of guaranty-or for that matter, any other offer-is supported by consideration, or until it has been accepted or acted upon, it may be withdrawn.").
187. *See* Danby v. Osteopathic Hospital Ass'n of Delaware, 104 A.2d 903, 906 (Del. 1954); Danby v. Osteopathic Hospital Ass'n of Delaware, 101 A.2d 308, 312 (Del. Ch. 1953); Ajax Rubber Co., Inc. v. Gam, 151 A. 831, 832 (Del Super. 1924).
188. *Id.*
189. *See* Cooling v. Springer, 30 A.2d 466, 470 (Del. Super. 1943).
190. *See* Danby v. Osteopathic Hospital Ass'n of Delaware, 101 A.2d 308, 312 (Del. Ch. 1953).
191. *See id.*
192. *See id.*

§ 7 Defenses of the Guarantor; Set-off

The defenses that may be available to a guarantor can be grouped into three categories: (1) defenses of the primary obligor; (2) "suretyship defenses"; and (3) other defenses.

7.1 Defenses of the Primary Obligor

7.1.1 General

Although they do not speak with one voice, the Restatement (Third) of Suretyship and Guaranty, *American Jurisprudence* ("Am. Jur."), and *Corpus Juris Secundum* ("C.J.S.") are generally in agreement that a guarantor may raise at least some of the primary obligor's defenses against the obligee by virtue of its status as guarantor.[193] However, under Delaware law, whether and to what extent a guarantor by virtue of this status may assert the primary obligor's defenses against the obligee is unclear.

In *Anguilla RE, LLC,* the Delaware Superior Court recited as the general rule that a "guarantor, when sued by the principal's creditor pursuant to a guaranty agreement, *cannot rely on an independent cause of action existing in favor of the principal* against the creditor as a defense or counterclaim."[194] The court noted that courts have recognized three exceptions: "(1) the guarantor has taken an assignment of the independent claim or the principal has consented to the guarantor's use of the claim; (2) both principal and guarantor are joined as defendants; or (3) the principal is insolvent."[195] However, even in these circumstances "the guarantor may not recover affirmatively."[196] There was no discussion of the availability of the principal's other defenses. In *First Federal Savings Bank (of Delaware)*, the Delaware Superior Court only assumed for purposes of "disposing of th[e] motion" before it that the defendants "would be able as guarantors ... to assert the defenses" of the primary obligor before holding that the defendants had clearly waived any such rights.[197] No published Delaware decision further explicates this issue with respect to guarantors.

The Delaware Superior Court has held that a surety could preclude liability by raising the principal's defenses because "a surety on a bond is not liable unless the principal is liable."[198] However, it did not clarify what, if any,

193. *See* Restatement (Third) of Suretyship and Guaranty § 34 (noting that with the exception of incapacity or discharge in bankruptcy, a guarantor "may raise as a defense to the secondary obligation any defense of the principal obligor to the underlying obligation"); 38 Am. Jur. 2d *Guaranty* § 36 ("As a general rule, a guaranty agreement is not enforceable if the underlying obligation on which the guaranty is based is void.... [or] illegal."); 38A C.J.S. *Guaranty* §§ 17, 103 ("In general, the guarantor may set up any defense that would have been available to the principal obligor, against the guarantee, at least where they are both sued in the same action.").

194. Anguilla RE, LLC v. Lubert-Adler Real Estate Fund IV, L.P., C.A. No. N11C-10-061 MMJ CCLD, 2012 WL 1408857, at *4 (Del. Super. Mar. 28, 2012).

195. *Id.*

196. *Id.*

197. First Federal Savings Bank (of Delaware) v. CPM Energy Systems Corp., C.A. No. 88C-MY-249, 1991 WL 35689, at *3 & n.2 (Del. Super. Mar. 12, 1991).

198. Tilcon Delaware v. Delaware State Univ., No. CIV. A. 96L-11-010, 1997 WL 358645, at *2 (Del. Super. May 14, 1997).

restrictions are placed on the surety's ability to assert them.[199] Moreover, as noted at the outset, recent Delaware decisions have acknowledged the distinction between sureties and guarantors.[200]

Clear drafting can mitigate problems arising from the limited case law on this issue. Delaware has enunciated a strong public policy in favor of freedom of contract.[201] Absent a showing of illegality or other violation of public policy, a Delaware court will enforce a contract according to its terms.[202] Consequently, parties to a guaranty could provide either that a guarantor is or is not liable where the primary obligor would have had any valid defense to liability on the underlying obligation.[203]

However, there still may be instances in which a guarantor is collaterally estopped from raising the primary obligor's defenses. Generally, "[u]nder the doctrine of collateral estoppel, if a court has decided an issue of fact necessary to its judgment, that decision precludes relitigation of the issue in a suit on a different cause of action involving a party to the first case."[204] However, the Delaware Supreme Court has held a guarantor "need not participate in prior litigation to the time of final judgment in order to be controlled by it."[205] Noting, for example, that a guarantor is collaterally estopped "as to issues ... decided against the principal, or issues which could have been raised, even though suit against [the guarantor] was dismissed before trial."[206]

---

199. *Id.*

200. *See, e.g.,* Trader v. Wilson, No. Civ.A. 01A-06-002, 2002 WL 499888, at *4 n.8 (Del. Super. Feb. 1, 2002).

201. Libeau v. Fox, 880 A.2d 1049, 1056 (Del. Ch. 2005), *aff'd in pertinent part,* 892 A.2d 1068 (Del. 2006) ("When parties have ordered their affairs voluntarily through a binding contract, Delaware law is strongly inclined to respect their agreement, and will only interfere upon a strong showing that dishonoring the contract is required to vindicate a public policy interest even stronger than freedom of contract. Such public policy interests are not to be lightly found, as the wealth-creating and peace-inducing effects of civil contracts are undercut if citizens cannot rely on the law to enforce their voluntarily-undertaken mutual obligations."); State v. Tabasso, 28 A.2d 248, 252 (Del. Gen. Sess. 1942) ("[F]reedom of contract shall not lightly be interfered with. [It] is the rule and restraints on this freedom the exception, and to justify this exception unusual circumstances should exist.").

202. Bunting v. Citizens Financial Group, Inc., No. C.A. 05C-03-013-ESB, 2007 WL 2122137, at *5 (Del. Super. 2007) ("Contracts may be unenforceable if they are either illegal per se or violate public policy."); *see* Lincoln Nat. Life Ins. Co. v. Joseph Schlanger 2006 Ins. Trust, 28 A.3d 436, 441 (Del. 2011) ("Under Delaware common law, contracts that offend public policy or harm the public are deemed void, as opposed to voidable"); Della Corp. v. Diamond, 210 A.2d 847, 849-50 (Del. 1965) (making clear that Delaware courts will not enforce "any term of the illegal agreement"); *see generally* Nationwide General Ins. Co. v. Seeman, 702 A.2d 915, 919 (Del. Supr. 1997) ("The public policy of this State is not only expressed in legislative enactments but also evolves as a matter of common law."); Kelly v. Bell, 254 A.2d 62, 70 (Del. Ch. 1969) ("In sum, an agreement or promise will not be condemned as being against public policy unless it is clearly contrary to what the legislature or judicial decision has declared to be public policy.").

203. *See* Sunrise Ventures, LLC v. Rehoboth Canal Ventures, LLC, C.A. No. 4119-VCS, 2010 WL 363845, at *13 & n. 73 (Del. Ch. Jan. 27, 2010) ("When seeking payment of a guaranty, a lender must strictly follow the specific provisions of the guaranty agreement on how, when, and where to demand payment."); Gaylords, Inc. v. Tollins, at *2 (Del. Super. 1984) (finding that the language of the guaranty provided that "prosecution of civil claims against [the primary obligor] or determination that there was no reasonable hope of recovery were conditions precedent to [the guarantor's] liability").

204. Messick v. Star Enterprise, 655 A.2d 1209, 1211 (Del. 1995); Tyndall v. Tyndall, 238 A.2d 343, 346 (Del. 1968) ("Under that doctrine, where a question of fact essential to the judgment is litigated and determined by a valid and final judgment, the determination is conclusive between the same parties in a subsequent case on a different cause of action. In such situation, a party is estopped from relitigating the issue again in the subsequent case.").

205. E.B.R. Corp. v. PSL Air Lease Corp., 313 A.3d 893, 895 (Del. 1973).

206. *Id.*

7.1.2 When Guarantor May Assert Primary Obligor's Defense

Assuming a guarantor can assert the defenses of the primary obligor against the obligee by virtue of its status as guarantor in some instances, we are unaware of any explication of *when* it may do so or *if* the consent of the primary obligor is required under Delaware law, aside from the discussion in *Anguilla RE, LLC* discussed in 7.1.1. Under New York law, for example, a guarantor generally cannot assert the defenses or claims of the primary obligor without its consent.[207]

7.1.3 Defenses that May not be Raised by Guarantor

The Restatement (Third) of Suretyship and Guaranty, Am. Jur., and C.J.S. are generally in agreement that a guarantor may neither raise the incapacity of the primary obligor nor the discharge of the primary obligor's debts in bankruptcy as a defense to liability under the guaranty.[208] The latter two go further, suggesting that the guarantor generally may not raise the primary obligor's "personal defenses" as a defense to liability under the guaranty.[209]

Delaware courts have acknowledged the general rule with respect to the nonavailability of the primary obligor's bankruptcy as a defense.[210] Otherwise, there appears to be no Delaware authority directly on point.

7.2 "Suretyship" Defenses

7.2.1 Change in Identity of Principal Obligor

The general rule is that a change in the identity of the principal obligor that "significantly alter[s] the nature of the guarantor's undertaking and result[s] in increased risk to the guarantor" will release the guarantor unless the guarantor "consents thereto, or the guaranty provides for a change in status."[211]

However, under Delaware law, the extent to which a change in the identity of the principal obligor will discharge the guarantor's obligation to the obligee is unclear. In an unpublished opinion in 2010, the Delaware Superior Court found "no relevant Delaware case law" when confronted with the question of whether the incorporation of the primary obligor, formerly an unincorporated sole proprietorship operated by the guarantor, revoked the guarantor's obligations under his personal guaranty.[212]

207. *See, e.g.*, Cinema North Corp. v. Plaza at Latham Assocs., 867 F.2d 135, 139 (2d Cir. 1989).

208. *See* Restatement (Third) of Suretyship and Guaranty § 34; 38 Am. Jur. 2d *Guaranty* § 37; 38A C.J.S. *Guaranty* § 103.

209. *See* 38 Am. Jur. 2d *Guaranty* § 37 ("It is not a defense to liability under a guaranty that the primary obligation is merely unenforceable against the debtor due to some matter of defense that is personal to the debtor."); 38A C.J.S. *Guaranty* § 103 ("[T]he guarantor cannot assert as a defense matters affecting the liability of the principal which are personal to the principal, such as the principal's infancy, bankruptcy or incapacity.").

210. *See* Chrysler Financial Corp. v. Fruit of the Loom, Inc., C.A. 91C-08-108-1-CV, 1993 WL 19659, at * 5 (Del Super. Jan. 12, 1993) (noting that courts have uniformly ruled this way); Mellon Bank (DE) Nat'l Ass'n v. Mattson, Civ. A. No. 90C-12-38, 1991 WL 190310, at *2 (Del. Super. Sept. 11, 1991) ("follow[ing]" the rule that "confirmation of a reorganization plan [under Chapter 11 of the U.S. Bankruptcy Code] does not affect the creditor's claim against guarantors or co-debtors").

211. 38A C.J.S. *Guaranty* § 85; *see generally* Am. Jur. 2d *Guaranty*, § 71.

212. 84 Lumber Co. v Derr, C.A. No. S08L-11-014 RFS, 2010 WL 2977949, at * 4 (Del. Super. July 29, 2010).

Finding the case of law of sister states "instructive," the Court's inquiry focused on four considerations: (1) whether the guarantor's obligation was intended to be a "continuing" one; (2) whether there was a material change in the relationship between the obligee and the guarantor by virtue of the incorporation; (3) whether the original principal continued to control the business after incorporation; and (4) whether the guarantor's risk was increased as a result of the incorporation.[213] The Superior Court found that the guaranty was "continuing" for this purpose because it did not specify the duration of the guaranty.[214] It did not elaborate on the second or third considerations. With respect to the fourth, the Court suggested that a mere expectation that the business might grow after incorporation would be sufficient to revoke the guarantor's personal liability.[215]

The lack of clarity with respect to the default rule can be obviated by clear drafting indicating whether the parties intend for the guaranty to continue after a change in the primary obligor.[216]

7.2.2 *Change in Identity of the Obligee*

As discussed *supra*, a special guaranty is generally nonassignable and only enforceable by the party to whom it was addressed, unless it contains a "specific assignability provision."[217] However, the Delaware Superior Court specifically left open the possibility that "special circumstances" in future cases might permit the enforcement of a special guaranty by an assignee of the original obligee.[218] The Delaware Supreme Court has identified succession by merger to the original obligee as one such "special circumstance."[219] Again, the lack of clarity with respect to the default rule can be obviated by clear drafting indicating whether the parties intend for the guaranty to continue after a change in the principal obligor.[220]

However, the foregoing does not prevent the obligee from assigning the right to payment on the underlying obligation.[221] In this circumstance, the guarantor "continues to guarantee the transferred debt."[222]

---

213. *Id.*
214. *Id.*
215. 84 Lumber Co. v Derr, C.A. No. S08L-11-014 RFS, 2010 WL 2977949, at * 4 (Del. Super. July 29, 2010).
216. *See* Fed. Deposit Ins. Corp. v. Bloom, No. 29 C.A. 1977, 1986 WL 221, at * 6 (Del. Super. May 21, 1986); *see generally* Libeau v. Fox, 880 A.2d 1049, 1056, (Del. Ch. 2005), *aff'd in pertinent part*, 892 A.2d 1068 (Del. 2006).
217. FinanceAmerica Private Brands, Inc. v. Harvey E. Hall, Inc., 380 A.2d 1377, 1380 (Del. Super. 1977).
218. *Id.*
219. Deascanis v. Brosius-Eliason Co., 533 A.2d 1254 (Table), at * 2 (Del. 1987) (8 Del. C. § 259 "provides the 'special circumstance' lacking in *FinanceAmerica* to make a special guaranty assignable."). Portions of the Delaware Code dealing with partnerships, limited partnerships, limited liability companies, etc. each contain sections nearly identical to 8 Del. C. § 259, which deals with mergers under Delaware's General Corporation Law. *See, e.g.*, 6 Del. C. § 17-211(h) (dealing with mergers under the chapter dealing with limited partnerships).
220. *See* FinanceAmerica Private Brands, Inc. v. Harvey E. Hall, Inc., 380 A.2d 1377, 1380 (Del. Super. 1977) ("I find the special guaranty is addressed to specific named obligees and was intended only for their benefit. Therefore, such guaranty is non-assignable."); *see also* Fed. Deposit Ins. Corp. v. Bloom, No. 29 C.A. 1977, 1986 WL 221, at * 6 (Del. Super. May 21, 1986); *see generally* Libeau v. Fox, 880 A.2d 1049, 1056, (Del. Ch. 2005), *aff'd in pertinent part*, 892 A.2d 1068 (Del. 2006).
221. FinanceAmerica Private Brands, Inc. v. Harvey E. Hall, Inc., 380 A.2d 1377, 1380 (Del. Super. 1977).
222. *Id.*

7.2.3 *Actions by the Creditor that Increase the Risk of the Guarantor*

Under Delaware law, "[i]t is a firmly established legal principle that an act or omission by a creditor which increases a surety's or guarantor's risk, or injures his rights will discharge the surety's obligation."[223] For example, in *Fed. Deposit Ins. Co. v. Bloom,* the primary obligor was developing properties that were already subject to certain mortgages.[224] Pursuant to a loan agreement, the obligee loaned money to the primary obligor for this development, including money to be disbursed upon the demand of the primary obligor to pay off those mortgages.[225] This agreement required the defendants to become sureties for the loaned money.[226] The primary obligor was offered an opportunity to discharge the mortgages at a discount, but the obligee wrongfully refused to disburse the funds.[227] Consequently, the Delaware Superior Court held that "the defendants are discharged of their obligations under the Suretyship Agreement ... because [this breach of the underlying loan agreement] increased the defendants' risk and injured their rights."[228]

For an additional example, in *S & S Builders, Inc. v. Di Mondi*, the Delaware Supreme Court indicated "if a creditor, even by mistake, advises a guarantor that the claim, the payment of which has been guaranteed by him, has been paid and the guarantor as a result ... in some ... manner changes his position to his disadvantage, the guarantor is thereby released from any liability under the guaranty."[229] However, the rule was inapplicable in that case, as the guarantor's change in position resulted from its own action.[230]

7.2.4 *Modification of the Underlying Obligation*

Delaware follows the general rule that "a guarantor cannot be held liable beyond the strict terms of his contract."[231] It generally follows from this rule that "a guarantor will be released from his undertaking by any material alteration of the original obligation or duty to which the guaranty relates, unless he consents thereto."[232] For example, this would occur in the case of limited guaranty where the obligee extends the primary obligor's time for

223. Fed. Deposit Ins. Corp. v. Bloom, No. 29 C.A. 1977, 1986 WL 221, at * 4 (Del. Super. May 21, 1986); *see also* S & S Builders, Inc. v Di Mondi, 126 A.2d 826, 830 (Del. 1956); *see generally* 38A C.J.S. § 81 ("[I]t may be stated as a general rule that any act or omission on the part of the [primary obligor] in breach of his duty under the guaranty, that increases the guarantor's risk or otherwise injures his rights and remedies, discharges the guarantor from his liability under the guaranty, at least to the extent of the injury so occasioned").
224. Fed. Deposit Ins. Corp. v. Bloom, No. 29 C.A. 1977, 1986 WL 221, at *1 (Del. Super. May 21, 1986).
225. *Id.*
226. *Id.*
227. Fed. Deposit Ins. Corp. v. Bloom, No. 29 C.A. 1977, 1986 WL 221, at *2, *5 (Del. Super. May 21, 1986).
228. Fed. Deposit Ins. Corp. v. Bloom, No. 29 C.A. 1977, 1986 WL 221, at *11 (Del. Super. May 21, 1986).
229. S & S Builders, Inc. v Di Mondi, 126 A.2d 826, 830 (Del. 1956).
230. *Id.*
231. 38A C.J.S. § 86; Garfield Trust Co. v. Teichmann, 95 A.2d 18, 22 (N.J. Super. 1953) (noting that a guarantor "cannot be held liable beyond the strict terms of his contract.") (Cited with approval in Fed. Deposit Ins. Corp. v. Bloom, No. 29 C.A. 1977, 1986 WL 221, at * 6 (Del. Super. May 21, 1986); 38 Am. Jur. § 71.
232. 38A C.J.S. § 86; cf Elysian Federal Savings Bank v. Sullivan, Civ. A. No. 10964, 1990 WL 20737, at *4-5 (Del. Ch. Mar. 2, 1990) (declining to discharge the guarantors' obligations "because equity regards substance rather than form" and consequently finding that the restructuring of the underlying obligation was essentially a renewal and extension provided for in the continuing guaranty).

performance.[233] However, in the case of the "compensated surety," liability will only be discharged for an alteration that was not only material, but also prejudicial."[234] In either case, under Delaware law, "sureties or guarantors may consent in advance to alterations in the underlying obligation between the creditor and the principal."[235]

7.2.5 Release of the Primary Obligor

Am. Jur. and C.J.S. give as the general rule that the release of the primary obligor without the consent of the guarantor releases the guarantor from liability under the guaranty unless: (i) the guarantor agrees to remain liable, or (ii) the obligee reserves the right to proceed against the guarantor in the release.[236] Although no Delaware case has directly addressed this issue in the guaranty context, a Delaware court should follow the rule that, absent the consent of the guarantor, the guarantor is released if the primary obligor is released.

The Delaware Court of Chancery has recited the general rule in the surety context, citing to Section 122 of the Restatement of Security, which generally uses the terms "surety" and "guarantor" interchangeably.[237] However, comment b to Section 122 clarifies that the general rule does not apply "where the surety and principal are not bound jointly, but the obligation of the surety is to answer for the duty of the principal," i.e., in the case of a guaranty.[238] In this case, "the termination of the principal's duty is also the termination of the surety's obligation" irrespective of any purported reservation by the obligee.[239] Moreover, the release of the primary obligor clearly is an act by the obligee that increases the risk of the guarantor being held liable for the underlying obligation, as it ensures the primary obligor will not pay its own debt.[240] That Delaware courts should follow the Restatement of Security's position follows from Delaware authority that an extension of time by the obligee to the primary

---

233. *See* Cooling v. Springer, 30 A.2d 466, 469 (Del. Super. 1943); Equitable Trust Co. v. Shaw, 194 A. 24, 28 (Del. Ch. 1937) ("It is of course one of the elementary principles of the law of suretyship that if the creditor extends the enforceability of the obligation, the surety is discharged unless he has assented thereto."); 38A C.J.S. § 89.
234. Gellis v. S. Gellis & Co., Inc., 322 A.2d 287, 292 (Del. Ch. 1974).
235. Fed. Deposit Ins. Corp. v. Bloom, No. 29 C.A. 1977, 1986 WL 221, at * 6 (Del. Super. May 21, 1986).
236. 38A C.J.S. *Guaranty* § 98 ("Where the principal debtor has not made complete payment or has not completely performed the guaranteed contract, but the effect of the creditor's acts is nevertheless to release or discharge him, the guarantor is also discharged, unless the [obligee's] right of recourse against the guarantor is expressly reserved in the contract releasing the principal."); 38 Am. Jur. *Guaranty* § 67.
237. In re Int'l Ins. Corp., 48 A.2d 529, 551 (Del. Ch. 1946) ("When a creditor releases his principal from liability, a surety is similarly released, unless the surety agrees that his liability shall survive, or unless, in the release itself, the creditor reserves his right to proceed against the surety.") (citing to Restatement of Security § 122); Restatement of Security § 82 comment g ("The term 'guaranty' is used in this Restatement as a synonym for suretyship. 'Guarantor' is used as a synonym for surety.").
238. Restatement of Security § 122 comment b.
239. Restatement of Security § 122 comment b.
240. Fed. Deposit Ins. Corp. v. Bloom, No. 29 C.A. 1977, 1986 WL 221, at * 4 (Del. Super. May 21, 1986); *see also* S & S Builders, Inc. v Di Mondi, 126 A.2d 826, 830 (Del. 1956); *see generally* 38A C.J.S. § 81.

obligor to satisfy the underlying obligation without the consent of the guarantor discharges the guarantor's obligation under the guaranty.[241]

Parties to a contract of guaranty can obviate the lack of clarity with respect to the default rule by clearly indicating in their agreement whether they intend the guaranty to continue if the obligee releases the primary obligor.[242]

7.2.6 *Release or Impairment of Security for the Underlying Obligation*

Under Delaware law, a surety's liability is reduced *pro tanto*, where the obligee "has security from the [primary obligor] and knows of the surety's obligation" if the primary obligor: "(a) surrenders or releases the security, or (b) willfully or negligently harms it, or (c) fails to take reasonable action to preserve its value at a time when the surety does not have an opportunity to take such action."[243]

The Delaware Superior Court, finding no Delaware cases on point, enunciated this rule citing the Restatement of Security, which generally uses "surety" and "guarantor" interchangeably.[244] The Restatement of Security's rationale is that the surety is "entitled" to the obligee's rights in the security upon performance of the underlying obligation.[245] Thus, where the obligee reduces the value of its rights in the security its right to the obligation of the surety should be similarly reduced.[246] This is consistent with Delaware's view, equally applicable to guarantors, that a surety who satisfies the primary obligor's obligation has equitably purchased the creditor's rights vis-à-vis the primary obligor.[247] Consequently, a Delaware court should follow the same rule in the guaranty context.

---

241. Cooling v. Springer, 30 A.2d 466, 469 (Del. Super. 1943); Equitable Trust Co. v. Shaw, 194 A. 24, 28 (Del. Ch. 1937) ("It is of course one of the elementary principles of the law of suretyship that if the creditor extends the enforceability of the obligation, the surety is discharged unless he has assented thereto."); 38A C.J.S. § 89. The Restatement (Third) of Suretyship and Guaranty indicated that the "traditional reservation of rights doctrine has outlived whatever usefulness it may have had." Restatement (Third) of Suretyship and Guaranty § 38 comment a. However, in its place it would permit an obligee to release from or extend the time for performance of "a duty to pay money pursuant to an underlying obligation" if (i) the obligee expressly retains its rights against the guarantor and (ii) the guarantor's rights against the primary obligor are unaffected by the release or extension. Restatement (Third) of Suretyship and Guaranty § 38. At least with respect to extension of time for performance, this solution is clearly inconsistent with Delaware law. *See* Cooling v. Springer, 30 A.2d 466, 469 (Del. Super. 1943); Equitable Trust Co. v. Shaw, 194 A. 24, 28 (Del. Ch. 1937); *see generally* Fed. Deposit Ins. Corp. v. Bloom, No. 29 C.A. 1977, 1986 WL 221, at * 4 (Del. Super. May 21, 1986).
242. *See* Fed. Deposit Ins. Corp. v. Bloom, No. 29 C.A. 1977, 1986 WL 221, at * 6 (Del. Super. May 21, 1986) (noting that parties to a contract of guaranty may consent in advance to alterations of the underlying obligation); 38A C.J.S. *Guaranty* § 98 ("Of course, the guaranty may provide, by its terms, that the guarantor remains liable despite the release of the principal … obligor."); 38A C.J.S. *Guaranty* § 98 (providing for reservation of rights in the contract of guaranty); *see generally* Libeau v. Fox, 880 A.2d 1049, 1056, (Del. Ch. 2005), *aff'd in pertinent part*, 892 A.2d 1068 (Del. 2006).
243. Sussex Finance Co. v. Goslee, 82 A.2d 743, 747 (Del. Super. 1951).
244. Sussex Finance Co. v. Goslee, 82 A.2d 743, 747 (Del. Super. 1951) (citing Restatement of Security § 132); Restatement of Security § 82 comment g ("The term 'guaranty' is used in this Restatement as a synonym for suretyship. 'Guarantor' is used as a synonym for surety.").
245. Restatement of Security § 132 comment b.
246. Restatement of Security § 132 comment b.
247. Leiter v. Carpenter, 22 A.2d 393, 396 (Del. Ch. 1941) ("But, so far as the primary debtor is concerned, the surety or guarantor making the payment, and who relies on the right of subrogation, is regarded as a purchaser, and the equitable assignee of the debt.").

Subject to the limitations set forth in 8.1 below, this defense may be (and frequently is) waived.

7.3 Other Defenses

7.3.1 Failure to Fulfill a Condition Precedent

A guarantor may plead nonoccurrence of a condition precedent as a defense.[248] As discussed *supra*, an absolute contract of guaranty is one in which the guarantor's liability arises upon the default of the primary obligor without more.[249] Conversely, a conditional contract of guaranty is one in which the liability of the guarantor is conditioned upon the happening of some contingency in addition to the default of the primary obligor.[250] "Whether a provision in a contract constitutes a condition precedent depends on the intention of the parties, and the Court must first look to the contractual language and also to the circumstances surrounding its execution."[251] Where a condition precedent has not been fulfilled, the guarantor is not liable.[252] Obligees must strictly comply with the conditions in the guaranty before they may obtain satisfaction from the guarantor.[253] However, Delaware requires that defendants plead with particularity "to deny the performance of or occurrence of a condition precedent."[254]

---

248. *See* Del. Ch. R. Civ. P. 9(c); Del. Super. R. Civ. P. 9(c); cf. Eisenmann Corp. v. General Motors Corp. 2000 WL 140781, at *17 (Del. Super. 2000) ("As a general rule on a contract obligation, at some point in the litigation, the Plaintiff must allege the occurrence of conditions precedent in the contract."); *see generally* Reserves Development LLC v. R.T Properties, L.L.C. 2011 WL 4638799, at *6 (Del. Super. Sept. 21, 2011) ("A contractual condition has been defined as 'an event, not certain to occur, which must occur, unless its non-occurrence is excused, before performance under a contract becomes due.'") (quoting Restatement (Second) of Contracts § 224).
249. Ajax Rubber Co., Inc. v. Gam, 151 A. 828, 829 (Del. Super. 1923).
250. Ajax v. Gam, 151 A. 828, 829, 830 (Del. Super. 1923); Ajax v. Gam, 151 A. 831, 832, 833 (Del. Super. 1924).
251. Reserves Development LLC v. R.T Properties, L.L.C. 2011 WL 4638799, at *6 (Del. Super. Sept. 21, 2011); *see, e.g.,* Gaylords, Inc. v. Tollins, at *2 (Del. Super. 1984).
252. *See* Gaylords, Inc. v. Tollins, at *2 (Del. Super. 1984); *see also* 38 Am. Jur. 2d *Guaranty* § 59 ("A guarantor may insist that he or she is bound to the extent, in the manner, and under the circumstances stated in the obligation and no further.")
253. *See* Sunrise Ventures, LLC v. Rehoboth Canal Ventures, LLC, C.A. No. 4119-VCS, 2010 WL 363845, at *13 n.73 (Del. Ch. Jan. 27, 2010) (noting that a "lender must strictly follow the specific provisions of the guaranty agreement on how, when and where to demand payment" from the guarantor); Fed. Deposit Ins. Corp. v. Bloom, No. 29 C.A. 1977, 1986 WL 221, at * 6 (Del. Super. May 21, 1986) (noting that a "guarantee ... contract must be strictly construed"); *see also* 38 Am. Jur. 2d *Guaranty* § 59.
254. *See* Del. Ch. R. Civ. P. 9(c); Del. Super. R. Civ. P. 9(c); *see also* Levine v. Smith, Civil Action No. 8833, 1989 WL 150784, at *6 n.4 (Del. Super. Nov. 27, 1989).

7.3.2 *Modification of the Guaranty*

Contracts of guaranty are modifiable by the parties like any other contract.[255] An oral or written modification of a contract of guaranty "must be based on [mutual] assent and consideration," or it will be unenforceable.[256]

There is authority for the proposition that a Delaware court will enforce a contractual provision requiring modifications to be made in writing.[257] However, the Delaware Chancery Court has recently noted the "cognitive dissonance" created by Delaware authority that "provisions deeming oral modifications unenforceable can be waived orally or by a course of conduct just like any other contractual provision."[258] The same is true for provisions requiring waiver to be in writing.[259] However, the party claiming that an oral modification or waiver has occurred must satisfy a "high evidentiary burden" rather than proving it by a preponderance of the evidence.[260]

7.3.3 *Failure to Pursue Primary Obligor*

Whether the obligee's failure to pursue the primary obligor provides a defense to the guarantor's liability turns upon the intent of the parties.[261] As discussed *supra*, in the case of absolute guaranties, including guaranties of payment, there is no requirement that the obligee demonstrate due diligence in obtaining satisfaction from the primary obligor prior to seeking satisfaction from the guarantor.[262] Conversely, the parties to a contract of guaranty, as in the

---

255. *See* 38A C.J.S. *Guaranty* § 38 (providing that a contract of guaranty may be modified "[i]n accordance with the rules relating to the modification of contracts in general"); see generally Egan & Sons Air Conditioning Co. v. General Motors Corp., 1988 WL 47314, 8 (Del. Super. April 27, 1988) ("Like *any other contract*, a release can be modified, rescinded or waived by the parties' agreements, acts or conduct. Consent and consideration are needed to modify an agreement.") (emphasis added).

256. Klehr, Harrison, Harvey, Bransburg & Ellers, LP v. Mosaica Educ., Inc., C.A. No. 07C-08-227-JEB 2009 WL 5177144, at *3 (Del. Super. Dec. 14, 2009); Continental Insurance Co. v. Rutledge & Co., Inc., 750 A.2d 1219, 1232 (Del. Ch. 2000) ("Any amendment to a contract, whether written or oral, relies on the presence of mutual assent and consideration."); De Checcis v. Evers, 174 A.2d 463, 464 (Del. Super. 1961) see also 38A C.J.S. *Guaranty* § 38; but see 6 Del. C. § 2A-208(1); 6 Del. C. § 2-209(1) (binding modifications of agreements governed by Article 2 and Article 2A of Delaware's Uniform Commercial Code are permitted without additional consideration).

257. Continental Insurance Co. v. Rutledge & Co., Inc., 750 A.2d 1219, 1228-29 (Del. Ch. 2000) ("The Agreement does, in fact, speak to modifications. It requires the parties to amend its terms in writing....The defendants have not come forward with any writings under either of these sections. Accordingly, this Court will not recognize the unwritten alleged amendment to the Agreement.").

258. Eureka VIII LLC v. Niagara Falls Holdings LLC, 899 A.2d 95, 109-10 (Del. Ch. 2007); *see also* Pepsi-Cola Bottling Co. of Asbury Park v. Pepsico Inc., 297 A.2d 28, 33 (Del. 1972).

259. Eureka VIII LLC v. Niagara Falls Holdings LLC, 899 A.2d 95, 109-10 (Del. Ch. 2007).

260. Development LLC v. Severn Sav. Bank, FSB, 2007 WL 4054231, at *8 (Del. Ch. Nov. 9, 2007); *see also* Continental Insurance Co. v. Rutledge & Co., Inc., 750 A.2d 1219, 1230 (Del. Ch. 2000) ("A party asserting an oral modification must prove the intended change with "specificity and directness as to leave no doubt of the intention of the parties to change what they previously solemnized by formal document."); Eureka VIII LLC v. Niagara Falls Holdings LLC, 899 A.2d 95, 109-10 (Del. Ch. 2007) (indicating that "clear and convincing evidence" is required in the waiver context).

261. *See* Gaylords, Inc. v. Tollins, at *2 (Del. Super. 1984); *see also* Ajax Rubber Co., Inc. v. Gam, 151 A. 828, 829 (Del. Super. 1923).

262. Ajax Rubber Co., Inc. v. Gam, 151 A. 828, 829 (Del. Super. 1923); *see also* A.G. Barr v. Agribusiness Partners Int'l, 2003 WL 1873848, *2 n11 (Del. Super. April 14, 2003). ("The general rules of pleading in contract actions govern the pleadings of the parties in an action to enforce a contract of guaranty. To state a valid claim on an unconditional guaranty of payment, a creditor must allege the existence of the guaranty delivered to the creditor securing repayment of a debt which is in default.") (quoting 38 Am. Jur. *Guaranty* § 114); 38 Am. Jur. *Guaranty* §§ 15, 88 ("An obligation that is absolute or unconditional becomes fixed when the principal debt matures, and the guarantor of payment is not entitled to require that the creditor first proceed or exhaust remedies against the principal debtor.").

case of a guaranty of collection, may provide that the obligee must prove due diligence in pursuing the primary obligor (or proffer an adequate excuse for not doing so) as a precondition to the liability of the guarantor.[263] Whether a contract of guaranty is absolute or conditional, and if so which preconditions to the guarantor's liability are imposed, is determined by the shared objective intent of the parties, looking to the contract as a whole.[264]

7.3.4 Statute of Limitations

Under Delaware law, a guarantor may plead the running of the statute of limitations as an affirmative defense to liability on a guaranty.[265] Generally, Delaware law imposes a three-year statute of limitations on unsealed contracts of guaranty.[266] However, the Delaware Supreme Court affirmed the application of the six-year statute of limitations period applicable to "bills and notes" where the guarantor guaranteed a promissory note.[267] Absent tolling, the statute of limitations begins to run when the cause of action accrues to the plaintiff.[268] "A cause of action for breach of contract accrues at the time of the breach."[269] In the case of a guaranty, it is when the guarantor becomes liable to the obligee.[270]

---

263. *See* Ajax Rubber Co., Inc. v. Gam, 151 A. 828, 830 (Del. Super. 1923); *see* Gaylords, Inc. v. Tollin, No. Civ. A. 80C-JN23, 1984 WL 547850, at *2 (Del. Super. Jan. 31, 1984); *see also* A.G. Barr v. Agribusiness Partners Int'l, 2003 WL 1873848, *2 n11 (Del. Super. April 14, 2003). ("When the guaranty is conditional, such as a guaranty of collection, the creditor should also allege the occurrence or waiver of all conditions to the contract of guaranty.") (quoting 38 Am. Jur. Guaranty § 114); 38 Am. Jur. Guaranty § 89 ("Since liability under a guaranty of collection is conditioned on the creditor attempting to collect from the debtor without success, the creditor usually must proceed against the debtor before resorting to a remedy against the guarantor.").

264. *See* Ajax Rubber Co., Inc. v. Gam, 151 A. 828, 829 (Del. Super. 1923) ("There is nothing in the guaranty to indicate that [the guarantor's] liability was conditioned upon failure of the [obligee] to collect from the principal debtor."); Gaylords, Inc. v. Tollin, No. Civ. A. 80C-JN23, 1984 WL 547850, at *2 (Del. Super. Jan. 31, 1984) (finding "the prosecution of the civil claims against the [primary obligor] or the determination that there was no reasonable hope of recovery were conditions precedent to [the guarantor's] liability"); *see generally* Wilmington & Northern R. Co. v. Delaware Valley Ry. Co., Inc., No. 97C-09-297-WTQ, 1999 WL 463705, at *5 (Del. Super. Mar. 30, 1999) ("In Delaware, guaranty contracts should be governed by the basic consideration that the intent of the parties must prevail.").

265. *See* Brossman v. Fed. Deposit Ins. Corp., 510 A.2d 471, 473-74 (Del. 1986); Cooling v. Springer, 30 A.2d 466, 472 (Del. Super. 1943); *see generally* Abdi v. NVR, Inc., 945 A.2d 1167 (Table), at *1 (Del. Mar. 25, 2008) ("We have held that [the Superior Court] Rules require a defendant to plead the limitations affirmative defense in its answer to the complaint and that failure to do so constitutes a waiver of the right to assert that defense."). It should be noted that "[a] statute of limitations period at law does not automatically bar an action in equity because actions in equity are time-barred only by the equitable doctrine of laches." Whittington v. Dragon Group, L.L.C., 991 A.2d 1, 9 (Del. 2009). "Unlike a statute of limitations, which inherently focuses on the passage of time, laches depends on more than a showing of delay. A party must also prove that he has suffered actual prejudice or injury as a result of the plaintiff's unreasonable delay." Johnston v. Pedersen, 28 A.3d 1079, 1092 (Del. Ch. 2011). That being said "absent a tolling of the limitations period, a party's failure to file within the analogous period of limitations will be given great weight in deciding whether the claims are barred by laches." Whittington v. Dragon Group, L.L.C., 991 A.2d 1, 9 (Del. 2009).

266. 10 Del. C. § 8106; *see also* Sunrise Ventures, LLC v. Rehoboth Canal Ventures, LLC, C.A. No. 4119-VCS, 2010 WL 363845, at *13 n.72 (Del. Ch. Jan. 27, 2010).

267. Brossman v. Fed. Deposit Ins. Corp., 510 A.2d 471, 473-74 (Del. 1986) (applying a six-year statute of limitations provided for in 10 Del. C. § 8109 where defendant guarantied a promissory note).

268. Certainteed Corp. v. Celotex Corp., No. Civ. A. 471, 2005 WL 217032, at *7 (Del. Ch. Jan. 24, 2005); *see also* Wal-Mart Stores, Inc. v. AIG Life Ins. Co., 860 A.2d 312, 319 (Del. 2004).

269. Nardo v. Guido DeAscanis & Sons, Inc., 254 A.2d 254, 256 (Del. Super. 1969); *see* Certainteed Corp. v. Celotex Corp., 2005 WL 217032, at * 7 (Del. Ch. 2005); *see also* U.S. Cellular Inv. Co. of Allentown v. Bell Atlantic Mobile Systems, Inc., 667 A.2d 497, 503 (Del. 1996).

270. *See* Brossman v. Fed. Deposit Ins. Corp., 510 A.2d 471, 472-73 (Del. 1986); Cooling v. Springer, 30 A.2d 466, 471 (Del. Super. 1943).

Parties to unsealed contracts of guaranty may contractually shorten the limitations period to bring a claim.[271] But the contractual limitations period must not be unreasonably short.[272] A recent law review article analyzing the Delaware case law on contractual limitations has noted that the test for "reasonableness" in this context seems easy to satisfy, noting that Delaware courts have on several occasions upheld limitations periods as short as one year and that in one instance a federal court applying Delaware law upheld a six-month limitations period.[273]

Delaware law does not permit parties to an unsealed contract to contractually lengthen the statute of limitations period.[274] However, practically speaking, the parties can lengthen the statute of limitations by making the contract of guaranty under seal.[275] Recent Delaware cases, including a published decision of the Delaware Supreme Court, have referred to the limitations period of a contract under seal as "20 years."[276] This may not be technically correct, as the cases cited in these opinions support the traditional rule that sealed contracts are "exempt[] ... from the applicable statute of limitations."[277] The reference to the "20 year" limitations period may be shorthand for the traditional rule that after 20 years, there is a presumption of satisfaction.[278]

7.3.5 Statute of Frauds

A contract that obliges one to "answer for the debt ... of another" is governed by Delaware's statute of frauds.[279] Consequently, with an exception discussed *infra*, a contract of guaranty is only enforceable if it is (1) "reduced to writing"

271. GRT, Inc. v. Marathon GTF Technology, Ltd., Civil Action No. 5571-CS, 2011 WL 2682898, at *3 (Del. Ch. July 11, 2011); *see* Rumsey Elec. Co. v. Univ. of Delaware, 358 A.2d 712, 714 (Del. 1976) ("[I]n the absence of express statutory provision to the contrary, a statute of limitations does not proscribe the imposition of a shorter limitations period by contract."); *see generally Repose vs. Freedom: Delaware Prohibition on Extending the Statute of Limitations by Contract: What Practitioners Should Know*, Melissa DiVicenzo.

272. Shaw v. Aetna Life Ins. Co., 395 A.2d 384, 386 (Del. Super. 1978); *see generally Repose vs. Freedom: Delaware Prohibition on Extending the Statute of Limitations by Contract: What Practitioners Should Know,* Melissa DiVicenzo.

273. *See generally Repose vs. Freedom: Delaware Prohibition on Extending the Statute of Limitations by Contract: What Practitioners Should Know,* Melissa DiVicenzo.

274. Shaw v. Aetna Life Ins. Co., 395 A.2d 384, 387 (Del. Super. 1978); GRT, Inc. v. Marathon GTF Technology, Ltd., Civil Action No. 5571-CS, 2011 WL 2682898, at *6 (Del. Ch. July 11, 2011) ("Shortening statutes of limitations, as opposed to lengthening them, does not conflict with the legislatively determined limitations period and, in fact, has been seen as being harmonious with the public policy purposes served by statutes of limitations in general."); *See generally Repose vs. Freedom: Delaware Prohibition on Extending the Statute of Limitations by Contract: What Practitioners Should Know*, Melissa DiVicenzo.

275. *See* Sunrise Ventures, LLC v. Rehoboth Canal Ventures, LLC, C.A. No. 4119-VCS, 2010 WL 363845, at *11 n.63 (Del. Ch. Jan. 27, 2010).

276. *See, e.g,* Whittington v. Dragon Group, L.L.C., 991 A.2d 1, 10 (Del. 2009); Sunrise Ventures, LLC v. Rehoboth Canal Ventures, LLC, C.A. No. 4119-VCS, 2010 WL 363845, at *11 n.63 (Del. Ch. Jan. 27, 2010) ("Without the guaranty agreements, it cannot be determined whether the guarantys are sealed documents that are entitled to the protection of a twenty year statu[t]e of limitations[.]"); Clarkson v. Goldstein, C.A. No. 04C-03-109 MMJ, 2007 WL 914635, at *4 (Del. Super. Feb. 28, 2007).

277. Monroe Park v. Metro. Life Ins. Co., 457 A.2d 734, 737 (Del. 1983) (citing Leiter v. Carpenter, 22 A.2d 393 (Del. Ch. 1941) (dealing with a contract of guaranty made under seal).

278. Garber v. Whittaker, 2 A.2d 85, 88 (Del. Ch. 1938) (cited with approval in Whittington v. Dragon Group, L.L.C., 991 A.2d 1, 10 (Del. 2009)).

279. 6 Del. C. § 2714; *see* Chestnut Hill Plaza Holdings Corp. v. Parkway Cleaners, Inc., C.A. No. N10C–09–161 DCS, 2011 WL 1885256, at *5 (Del. Super. May 17, 2011); Borish v. Graham, 655 A.2d 831, 833 (Del. Super. 1994) ("The personal guarantee of the defendants was clearly a promise to answer for the debt of the corporation; thus it is within the statute of frauds.").

and (2) "signed by the party to be charged therewith."[280] The writing must "contain on its face enough to show that the person signing it was assuming liability."[281] Under Delaware law, the statute of frauds can be satisfied by "multiple writings," only one of which need be signed by the alleged guarantor, so long as the writings taken as whole "(a) reasonably identify the subject matter of the contract, (b) indicate that a contract has been made between the parties or an offer extended by the signing party and (c) state with reasonable certainty the essential terms of the unperformed promises in the contract."[282]

Under Delaware law, where a guarantor "gains personal benefit for assuming liability for the debt, the statute of frauds does not apply, and the guarantor may be personally liable" without a signed writing.[283] The test is whether the guarantor has *personally* "improved [its] status or benefited" from obligee's performance with respect to the agreement creating the underlying obligation.[284] This test is not satisfied simply by virtue of the guarantor's status as director, officer, or shareholder of the primary obligor.[285] However, that a guarantor is also a director, officer, or shareholder of the primary obligor will not necessarily lead to the conclusion that the guarantor did not personally benefit.[286]

Additionally, there are circumstances in which an alleged guarantor may be estopped from asserting the statute of frauds as a defense.[287] For example, promissory estoppel may be available to an obligee as a defense to a guarantor's assertion of the statute of frauds where the obligee relied to its detriment or changed its position based on an oral promise of guaranty by the alleged guarantor.[288]

---

280. *See* 6 Del. C. § 2714; Chestnut Hill Plaza Holdings Corp. v. Parkway Cleaners, Inc., C.A. No. N10C–09–161 DCS, 2011 WL 1885256, at *5 (Del. Super. May 17, 2011); Borish v. Graham, 655 A.2d 831, 833 (Del. Super. 1994).
281. Borish v. Graham, 655 A.2d 831, 833 (Del. Super. 1994); Woodcock v. Udell, 97 A.2d 878, 881 (Del. Super. 1953).
282. *See* Olson v. Halvorsen, 982 A.2d 286, 293 (Del. Ch. 2008) (discussing the rule generally); ROI, Inc. v. E. I. du Pont de Nemours & Co., Inc., 1989 WL 135717, at *5 (Del. Super. Oct. 19, 1989) ("In order to satisfy the Statute of Frauds, it is not necessary that the required writing be reflected in a single document. Several documents may be considered even though only one may be signed.").
283. Chestnut Hill Plaza Holdings Corp. v. Parkway Cleaners, Inc., C.A. No. N10C–09–161 DCS, 2011 WL 1885256, at *5 (Del. Super. May 17, 2011); *see* Borish v. Graham, 655 A.2d 831, 834 (Del. Super. 1994); Woodcock v. Udell, 97 A.2d 878, 881 (Del. Super. 1953).
284. Chestnut Hill Plaza Holdings Corp. v. Parkway Cleaners, Inc., C.A. No. N10C–09–161 DCS, 2011 WL 1885256, at *5 (Del. Super. May 17, 2011); *see* Borish v. Graham, 655 A.2d 831, 834 (Del. Super. 1994); Econofreeze v. Int'l Pipefreezing Inc., C.A. No. 84C-JL-14, 1985 Del. Super. LEXIS 1077, at *6 (Del. Super. Apr. 22, 1985) (finding the exception inapplicable and noting "in particular there is no showing that [alleged personal guarantor's] loans or investment [in the primary obligor] had a better status as a result of plaintiff's deliveries to the corporation"); Woodcock v. Udell, 97 A.2d 878, 881 (Del. Super. 1953).
285. Chestnut Hill Plaza Holdings Corp. v. Parkway Cleaners, Inc., C.A. No. N10C–09–161 DCS, 2011 WL 1885256, at *5 (Del. Super. May 17, 2011); *see* Borish v. Graham, 655 A.2d 831, 834 (Del. Super. 1994); Woodcock v. Udell, 97 A.2d 878, 881 (Del. Super. 1953).
286. Chestnut Hill Plaza Holdings Corp. v. Parkway Cleaners, Inc., C.A. No. N10C–09–161 DCS, 2011 WL 1885256, at *6 (Del. Super. May 17, 2011) ("[I]t is still necessary to consider whether the Ciccarones have benefitted personally from the 1999 lease, even if their capacity as corporate officers has been reinstated."); Borish v. Graham, 655 A.2d 831, 834 (Del. Super. 1994); Woodcock v. Udell, 97 A.2d 878, 881 (Del. Super. 1953) (denying defendants' motion for summary judgment concluding that "it could be found that [the defendants, who were shareholders, and one of whom was president of each of the primary obligors] had such a personal interest in the subject matter" that the statute of frauds did not apply).
287. *See* Borish v. Graham, 655 A.2d 831, 834-35 (Del. Super. 1994).
288. *Id.* at 831, 835.

It seems that individuals who claim to have signed a contract solely in their corporate capacity may not be able to successfully argue as a matter of law that their signatures did not satisfy Delaware's statute of frauds where the contract (i) identifies the signatories as guarantors and (ii) sets forth their liability as such.[289] In *Chestnut Hill Plaza Holdings Corp.*, the individual defendants, who were co-owners and officers of the corporate defendant that defaulted on its lease obligations, signed the lease once as officers of the corporation.[290] Nevertheless, the Delaware Superior Court denied the individual defendants' motion to dismiss on the basis that the lease did not satisfy the statute of frauds with respect to the alleged guaranty finding the plaintiff had "satisfied its burden of presenting a conceivable set of circumstances under which" the lease could be read as a whole to establish the individual defendant's liability "in satisfaction of the statute of frauds."[291]

However, the statute of frauds will not permit admission of parol evidence to prove an oral guaranty to explain the appearance of an individual's signatures on a loan to a business entity.[292]

7.3.6 Defenses Particular to Guarantors that are Natural Persons and Their Spouses

Delaware law does not provide for defenses particular to guarantors who are natural persons.

This is also the case with spouses of guarantors.[293] As noted *supra* in the discussion of agency law, Delaware follows the general rule that "only a party to a contract may be sued for breach of that contract."[294] This is no less applicable in the case of a spouse of a guarantor. One spouse does not become liable for the debt of the other—whether these debts are incurred before or after the marriage—simply by virtue of being the debtor's spouse.[295] Rather, this spouse, like any other individual, must specifically assume liability for these debts in compliance with general principles of contract law, e.g., the statute of frauds.[296]

Where a guarantor purports to secure a debt with property that the guarantor does not exclusively own apart from the guarantor's spouse this may present

---

289. *See* Chestnut Hill Plaza Holdings Corp. v. Parkway Cleaners, Inc., C.A. No. N10C–09–161 DCS, 2011 WL 1885256, at *5 (Del. Super. May 17, 2011).
290. *Id.* at *1-2.
291. *Id.* at *5.
292. Woodcock v. Udell, 97 A.2d 878, 881 (Del. Super. 1953) ("A mere signature upon a paper which contains mutual promises of two other persons cannot be supplemented by parol testimony to prove that the third person intended to be surety for one or the other[.]"); *see* Borish v. Graham, 655 A.2d 831, 833 (Del. Super. 1994).
293. The Equal Credit Opportunity Act imposes certain restrictions on requiring a spouse to guaranty the obligations of the other spouse. *See, e.g.,* County Banking & Trust Co. v. Lacey, No. C.A. 146-MRT-90, 1993 WL 390274 (Del. Super. Sept. 16, 1993) (noting that its implementing regulations "provide that creditors may not require the signature of an applicant's spouse ..., other than a joint applicant on any credit instrument, if the applicant qualifies under the creditor's standards of creditworthiness for the amount and the terms of the credit requested.").
294. Wallace ex rel. Cencom Cable Income Partners II, Inc., L.P. v. Wood, 752 A.2d 1175, 1180 Del.Ch. 1999).
295. *See, e.g.,* Trader v. Wilson, No. Civ.A. 01A-06-002, 2002 WL 499888, at *4-6 (Del Super. Feb. 1, 2002); Kent General Hospital, Inc. v. Russell, No. 96-06C-04-009, 1997 WL 524079, at *2-3 (Del. Super. July 14, 1997).
296. *Id.*

difficulties for the obligee seeking to enforce the guaranty.[297] However, we are aware of no Delaware case which discusses the intersection of the enforcement of a guaranty and marital property law. Obviously, this problem is not specific to married couples and might arise any time a guarantor purports to secure a debt which is allegedly owned by another, in whole or in part.[298]

7.4 Right of Set-off

As noted *supra*, in *Anguilla RE, LLC*, the Delaware Superior Court recited as the general rule that a guarantor may generally not set-off "a principal's independent claim against the creditor's claim," but noted that courts have recognized three exceptions set forth in 7.1.[299] However, even in these circumstances "the guarantor may not recover affirmatively."[300] Otherwise, a Delaware court should apply the general principles of set-off applicable to contract claims in a claim for a breach of guaranty.

§ 8 Waiver of Defenses by the Guarantor

8.1 Defenses that Cannot be Waived

Certain waivers of statutory rights are not permitted under Delaware law. For example, Article 9 of the Delaware Uniform Commercial Code ("Delaware UCC") defines "obligor" and "secondary obligor" to include a guarantor of an obligation secured by either a "security interest in or agricultural lien on" collateral.[301] Section 9-602 of the Delaware UCC provides that an obligor may not waive or vary the rules in certain sections of Article 9.

Otherwise there does not appear to be any Delaware authority particular to guaranties limiting the ability of a guarantor to waive its defenses by contract.[302] Further, it should be noted that the Delaware Supreme Court has upheld the entry of judgment against a guarantor pursuant to a warrant to confess judgment contained in a guaranty.[303] With certain caveats to preserve a debtor's due

297. *See, e.g.*, Fischer v. Fischer, 864 A.2d 98, 103 ("Tenancy by the entireties is based on the legal fiction that the husband and wife are one and "neither [spouse] without the consent of the other can [alienate], encumber, or in any way impair the estate with respect to the other.").
298. *See, e.g.*, Stornawaye Capital LLC v. Smithers, C.A. No. 18845-VCN, 2010 WL 673291, at *2 (Del Ch. Feb. 12, 2010) (entering judgment against the guarantor but granting the guarantor's sister's motion to intervene to argue that the property guarantor mortgaged to secure the debt was not properly conveyed to guarantor by their mother).
299. Anguilla RE, LLC v. Lubert-Adler Real Estate Fund IV, L.P., C.A. No. N11C-10-061 MMJ CCLD, 2012 WL 1408857, at *4 (Del. Super. Mar. 28, 2012).
300. *Id.*
301. 6 Del. C. § 9-102(a)(59), (71).
302. *Cf.* Pellaton v. Bank of New York, 592 A.2d 473, 477 (Del. 1991); Wilmington Trust Co. v. Keith, No. C.A. 00C-11-016, 2002 WL 1748622, at *4 (Del. Super. June 26, 2002); First Federal Savings Bank v. CPM Energy Systems Corp., C.A. No. 88C-MY-249, 1991 WL 35689, at * 2 (Del. Super. Mar. 12, 1991).
303. Pellaton v. Bank of New York, 592 A.2d 473, 477 (Del. 1991) (affirming the Delaware Superior Court's entry of judgments against a guarantor pursuant to warrants to confess judgment contained in two contracts of guaranty); *cf.* Architectural Cabinets, Inc. v. Gaster, 291 A.2d 298, 299 (Del. Super. 1971) ("The use of confession of judgment clauses is an established practice in commercial dealings in Delaware.").

process rights, a warrant to confess judgment essentially "permit[s] a creditor to obtain judgment without trial of defenses."[304]

Despite Delaware's strong policy in favor of freedom to contract, as noted *supra*, Delaware courts will not enforce contractual provisions that are illegal or that violate public policy.[305] It should be noted that the following waivers or exculpations will not be enforceable under Delaware law: (1) "A party may not protect itself against liability for its own fraudulent act or bad faith".[306] (2) A party cannot waive its right to discharge in bankruptcy its debt arising out of the contract prior to filing a bankruptcy action.[307] (3) As noted *supra*, party cannot anticipatorily waive the statute of limitations in a contract of guaranty not under seal.[308] (4) Additionally, a waiver contained in an otherwise unenforceable contract is generally unenforceable.[309]

8.2 "Catch-all" Waivers

It is common for a guaranty to provide for the waiver of many, if not all, of the guarantor's defenses through broad waivers, waivers of a litany of defenses, or a combination of the two. Although we know of no case when a Delaware court has refused to enforce a waiver on a guaranty, there are multiple instances in which Delaware cases recite fairly broad waivers either without negative comment or for narrower propositions, e.g., intent of the parties to enter into

---

304. *See generally* Cheidem Corp. v. Farmer, 449 A.2d 1061, 1062 (Del. Super. 1982) ("A confession of judgment is the written authority of the debtor and a direction for entry of judgment against him. *It cuts off all defenses and right of appeal.* Such devices have been recognized in Delaware statutes since the Code of 1852.") (emphasis added) (internal citations omitted).

305. Bunting v. Citizens Financial Group, Inc., No. C.A. 05C-03-013-ESB, 2007 WL 2122137, at *5 (Del. Super. 2007); *see* Lincoln Nat. Life Ins. Co. v. Joseph Schlanger 2006 Ins. Trust, 28 A.3d 436, 441 (Del. 2011); Della Corp. v. Diamond, 210 A.2d 847, 849-50 (Del. 1965).

306. J. A. Jones Const. Co. v. City of Dover, 372 A.2d 540, 545 (Del.Super. 1977).

307. *See* Klingman v. Levinson, 831 F.2d 1292, 1296 n.3 (7th Cir. 1987) ("For public policy reasons, a debtor may not contract away the right to a discharge in bankruptcy."); In re Madison, 184 B.R. 686, 690 (E.D.Pa. 1995) ("[A]n agreement not to file for bankruptcy is unenforceable because it violates public policy."); In re Ethridge, 80 B.R. 581, 586 (Bankr. M.D.Ga. 1987); *see also* Collier on Bankruptcy § 301.08 ("As a matter of public policy, courts will not enforce a promise not to file a bankruptcy petition made eligible to file such a petition.").

308. Shaw v. Aetna Life Ins. Co., 395 A.2d 384, 387 (Del. Super. 1978); GRT, Inc. v. Marathon GTF Technology, Ltd., Civil Action No. 5571-CS, 2011 WL 2682898, at *6 (Del. Ch. July 11, 2011) ("Shortening statutes of limitations, as opposed to lengthening them, does not conflict with the legislatively determined limitations period and, in fact, has been seen as being harmonious with the public policy purposes served by statutes of limitations in general."); *See* generally Repose vs. Freedom: Delaware Prohibition on Extending the Statute of Limitations by Contract: What Practitioners Should Know, Melissa DiVicenzo.

309. Cf Della Corp. v. Diamond, 210 A.2d 847, 849-50 (Del. 1965) (making clear that Delaware courts will not enforce "any term of the illegal agreement" nor will they aid either party in enforcing their rights under it); Eisenman v. Seitz, 25 A.2d 496, 498 (Del. Ch. 1942); Keystone Fuel Oil Co. v. Del-Way Petroleum, Inc., 364 A.2d 826, 829 (Del. Super. 1976) ("A consent judgment is basically an agreement which the Court turns into a judgment. It is similar to a contract between the parties. This means that the Court should not allow a party to free himself from the judgment unless there is some theory in operation which would free him from a contract.") (Internal citations omitted); *see, e.g.,* Architectural Cabinets, Inc. v. Gaster, 291 A.2d 298, 301 (vacating a confessed judgment concluding that the "confessed judgment clause [caused] unfair surprise in the manner that it appears" and thus was unconscionable).

an "absolute" contract of guaranty.[310] There is, at minimum, authority for the proposition that a guarantor can "waive ... any defense ... the principal may have regarding the enforcement of the obligation so long as the waiver is clear and unequivocal."[311]

Moreover, it would seem to follow from the enforceability of confession of judgments provisions in contracts of guaranty that so-called "catch-all" waivers should be enforceable with respect to those defenses that may be waived, as their permissibility would seem to vitiate any argument that use of a general waiver violated Delaware's public policy sufficient to set aside Delaware's strong policy in favor of the freedom to contract.[312] To the extent there is concern that overbreadth of such a "catch-all" waiver would render the waiver itself unenforceable insofar as it covers nonwaiveable defenses, the parties might include the caveat "to the fullest extent permitted by law," which the Delaware Court of Chancery has indicated "arguably precludes an interpretation of the provision that would run afoul of Delaware law."[313]

8.3 Use of Apecific Waivers

Generally, there appears to be no authority for the proposition under Delaware contract law generally for the superiority of a series of specific waivers over a catch-all waiver of one's defenses. Delaware courts have repeatedly noted that in the case of guaranties, the "intent of the parties must prevail."[314] Common sense dictates that a clause specifically waiving a defense, e.g., notice of default by the primary obligor, more clearly evinces the intent of the parties to waive *that* defense than, for example, a waiver of all "suretyship defenses." However, given the limited Delaware case law on "suretyship defenses," including a specific enumeration of them, there may be some practical difficulty in fully listing all those defenses that would come within the coverage of a

310. *See, e.g.*, Addy v. Piedmonte, Civil Action No. 3571-VCP, 2009 WL 707641, at *16 (Del. Ch. Mar. 18, 2009) (The guaranty at issue provided the guarantor's liability "shall not be affected by any circumstance other than ... payment in full of the [underlying obligation]" and further waived, *inter alia*, "any defenses arising by reason of the incapacity, lack of authority or any disability or other defense of [primary obligor]"); *see also* Daystar Const. Management, Inc. v. Mitchell, C.A. No. 04C-05-175-JRS, 2006 WL 2053649, at *3 (Del. Super. July 12, 2006) (The guaranty at issue provided that the guarantor "unconditionally and irrevocably waives all defenses which, under principles of guarantee or suretyship law, may otherwise operate to impair or diminish the liability of [guarantor] hereunder."); Wilmington Trust Co. v. Keith, No. C.A. 00C-11-016, 2002 WL 1748622, at *4 (Del. Super. 2002) ("Guarantor also waives any and all rights or defenses arising by reason of ... any defenses given to guarantors at law or in equity other than actual payment and performance of the indebtedness.").

311. *See* First Federal Savings Bank v. CPM Energy Systems Corp., C.A. No. 88C-MY-249, 1991 WL 35689, at * 2 (Del. Super. Mar. 12, 1991). In this case the defendants-guarantors asserted counterclaims against the plaintiff-obligee arising out of the relationship between plaintiff-obligee and the primary obligor. *Id.* Before the Superior Court was the plaintiff-obligee's motion to dismiss these counterclaims based on a waiver provision in the unconditional guaranty which purported to waive "all defenses available to Borrower or Guarantor at law or in equity." *Id.* At one point in the opinion, it seems that the Court indicates that the defendants-guarantors "did .... waive[] ... the right to assert any defense against the enforcement of [the underlying] obligation." *Id.* This would be at most *dicta*. However, without explication, the Court continued its analysis to see whether "there exists sufficient reason to ignore the language" of the guaranty, and ultimately concluded that the defendants-guarantors had waived their right to assert the principal's counter claims against the obligee. *Id.* at *2-3.

312. Cheidem Corp. v. Farmer, 449 A.2d 1061, 1062 (Del. Super. 1982) ("A confession of judgment is the written authority of the debtor and a direction for entry of judgment against him. It cuts off all defenses and right of appeal.").

313. Wayne County Employees' Retirement System v. Corti, Civil Action No. 3534-CC, 2009 WL 2219260, at *19 (Del. Ch. July 24, 2009).

314. Cooling v. Springer, 30 A.2d 466, 469 (Del. Super. 1943).

"catch-all" waiver. Consequently, it would seem preferable to use a catch-all waiver coupled with specific waivers, carving out where necessary defenses that the guarantor did not wish to waive.

§ 9 Third-party Pledgors—Defenses and Waiver Thereof

As discussed above, a court applying Delaware law will determine whether a contract is a contract of guaranty, and whether a party to it is a guarantor, looking to the objective intent of the contracting parties.[315] Whether the contract itself uses the terms "guarantor" or "guaranty" is not itself determinative.[316] Consequently, a Delaware court may find that a party which pledges collateral to secure the debt of another is a guarantor irrespective of the phraseology used to describe the agreement or the party. In this circumstance the pledgor could avail itself of the defenses set forth in Section 7, to the extent it has not waived these defenses consistent with Section 8.

§ 10 Jointly and Severally Liable Guarantors—Contribution and Reduction of Obligations Upon Payment by a Co-obligor

Guarantors who are jointly and severally liable are presumed to share the secondary obligation equally. The creditor is not obliged to seek full payment from more than one such guarantor.

10.1 Contribution

6 *Del. C.* § 2701 provides that "[a]n obligation or written contract of several persons shall be joint and several, unless otherwise expressed." A guarantor has a right to contribution against its coguarantors "upon being compelled to pay more than [its] just proportion of the principal's debt."[317] The right to contribution is mutually exclusive of the right to indemnification.[318] The guarantor is entitled to proportional reimbursement from its coguarantors for

315. *See* Chestnut Hill Plaza Holdings Corp. v. Parkway Cleaners, Inc., C.A. No. N10C–09–161 DCS, 2011 WL 1885256, at *5 (Del. Super. May 17, 2011); Citizens Bank v. Gupta, No. Civ.A.02J-05-068, 2004 WL 1965924, at *2 (Del. Super. Aug. 26, 2004).
316. W. T. Rawleigh Co. v. Warrington, 199 A. 666, 670 (Del. Super. 1938); *see also* Chestnut Hill Plaza Holdings Corp. v. Parkway Cleaners, Inc., C.A. No. N10C–09–161 DCS, 2011 WL 1885256, at *5 (Del. Super. May 17, 2011).
317. Collins v. Throckmorton, 425 A.2d 146, 149-150 (Del. 1980); *see* Levy v. HLI Operating Co., Inc., 924 A.2d 210, 220 (Del. Ch. 2007) ("An equitable right of contribution arises when one of several obligors liable on a common debt discharges all, or greater than its share, of the joint obligation for the benefit of all the obligors.").
318. Levy v. HLI Operating Co., Inc., 924 A.2d 210, 221 (Del. Ch. 2007).

the amount paid in excess of its share of the principal's debt.[319] The right to contribution rests on "general principles of equity" rather than on contract.[320] Consequently, the coguarantor cannot assert a claim for contribution where it "aids in the commission of a default by the principal, either by [its] negligence or [its] active misconduct."[321]

10.2 Reduction of Obligations Upon Payment of Co-obligor

Generally, damages for breach of a contract of guaranty are measured "by the same rules of law by which the liability of one who has broken an ordinary contract is determined."[322] "The standard remedy in Delaware, as elsewhere, 'for breach of contract is based upon the reasonable expectations of the parties *ex ante.* This principle of expectation damages is measured by the amount of money that would put the promisee in the same position as if the promisor had performed the contract.'"[323] Unless a party specifically contracts for it, "double recovery" is not permitted.[324] Thus, for example, where a guarantor has guaranteed the repayment of a loan, the obligee should not be able to recover the full loaned amount from a guarantor (or coguarantor) where the primary obligor (or some party on its behalf, e.g., a coguarantor) has already paid a portion of it. However, as is evident from the discussions of subrogation *infra* and contribution *supra*, payment of the underlying obligation by a guarantor (or coguarantor) does not discharge the primary obligor's (or coguarantor's) obligation to compensate the party which has paid the primary obligor on its behalf.

§ 11 Reliance

Absent a specific contract provision, reliance is not required to claim under a guaranty.

Unless the parties to a contract of guaranty provide for conditions precedent to the liability of the guarantor (or one is implied by law), the liability of the guarantor is "governed by the same rules of law by which the liability of one who has broken an ordinary contract is determined."[325] Consequently, an

319. Collins v. Throckmorton, 425 A.2d 146, 149-150 (Del. 1980); *see* De Paris v. Wilmington Trust Co., 104 A. 691, 695 (Del. 1918) ("The law of contribution as between two-guarantors is well settled. If one pays the whole of the principal debt he may compel the other to pay one-half thereof.").
320. *See* Collins v. Throckmorton, 425 A.2d 146, 151-152 (Del. 1980); *see also* Chamison v. Health Trust, Inc. – The Hospital Co., 735 A.2d 912, 918 (Del. Ch. 1999).
321. Collins v. Throckmorton, 425 A.2d 146, 149 (Del. 1980).
322. *See* Ajax Rubber Co. v. Gam, 151 A. 831, 832 (Del.Super. 1924).
323. Pharmathene, Inc. v. Siga Technologies, Inc., 2011 WL 4390726, at *31 (Del. Ch. 2011) (quoting Duncan v. Theratx, Inc., 775 A.2d 1019, 1022 (Del. 2001) (citing Restatement (Second) of Contracts § 347 cmt. a).
324. *See* Aveta Inc. v. Cavallieri, 23 A.3d 157, 182 (Del. Ch. 2010) ("As Aveta recognizes, it cannot obtain a double recovery, and therefore any recovery from Bengoa should be taken into account."); *but see* State Farm Mut. Auto. Ins. Co. v. Nalbone, 569 A.2d 71, 75 (Del. 1989) ("There is no reason why a risk-averse insured should not be permitted to contract for a double recovery. If a person pays both auto and health insurance premiums, he has paid the expected value of loss due to injury in an automobile accident twice.").
325. *See* Ajax Rubber Co. v. Gam, 151 A. 831, 832 (Del. Super. 1924).

obligee need not prove reliance upon a validly formed contract of guaranty in order to get relief for breach.[326]

§ 12 Subrogation

Subrogation is an equitable remedy that generally requires total satisfaction of the underlying obligation to the obligee prior to its exercise.

Under Delaware law, "in the absence of other controlling equities, the surety or guarantor who pays the creditor's debt is ordinarily subrogated to all of his rights and remedies, of every nature, against the principal, for its collection."[327] The guarantor succeeds to the rights of the satisfied obligee so long as the following are satisfied: "(1) payment must have been made by the subrogee to protect his or her own interest; (2) the subrogee must not have acted as a volunteer; (3) the debt paid must have been one for which the subrogee was not primarily liable; (4) the entire debt must have been paid; and (5) subrogation must not work any injustice to the rights of others."[328]

"[S]o far as the primary debtor is concerned, the surety or guarantor making the payment, and who relies on the right of subrogation, is regarded as a purchaser, and the equitable assignee of the debt."[329] While this entitles the guarantor to exercise the obligee's contract rights against the primary obligor vis-à-vis the underlying obligation, the guarantor's subrogation rights are equitable in nature, "growing out of the relation existing between the parties, rather than upon any semblance of contract rights."[330] Consequently, even though the guarantor seeks money damages, this form of equitable relief must be sought in the Delaware Court of Chancery.[331] Thus laches rather than the statute of limitations determines whether an action exercising the guarantor's subrogation rights are "time barred."[332]

326. *See* Guttridge v. Iffland, 889 A.2d 283 (Table), at *4 (Del. 2005) (noting that "breach of contract [is] a cause of action for which reliance is not an element.") (citing VLIW Tech., LLC v. Hewlett-Packard Co., 840 A.2d 606, 612 (Del. 2003).
327. Leiter v. Carpenter, 22 A.2d 393, 395 (Del. Ch. 1941) (also noting that "precisely the same principles apply to a guarantor" as to a surety).
328. Reserves Development LLC v. Severn Sav. Bank, FSB, Civil Action No. 2502-VCP, 2007 WL 4054231, at *17 (Del. Ch. Nov. 9, 2007) (citing 73 Am. Jur. 2d Subrogation § 5 (2007).
329. Leiter v. Carpenter, 22 A.2d 393, 396 (Del. Ch. 1941).
330. Leiter v. Carpenter, 22 A.2d 393, 396 (Del. Ch. 1941); *see* Miller v. Stout, 1878 WL 2216, at *2 (Del. Ch. Sept. 1878) ("When a surety or guarantor pays a debt of a principal, equity substitutes him in the place of a creditor, as a matter of course, without any special agreement to that effect.").
331. *See* Ocwen Loan Servicing, LLC v. SFJV-2002-1, LLC, C.A. No. N10C–09–071 CLS, 2011 WL 2175995, 2 (Del. Super. May 25, 2011) ("The remedy of equitable subrogation is an equitable remedy only available in the Court of Chancery."); Clark v. Teeven Holding Co., 625 A.2d 869, 878 (Del. Ch. 1992) ("Certain forms of restitutionary relief, such as the imposition of a constructive trust, the imposition of an equitable lien, or a decree of subrogation, are available only in equity.").
332. *See* Leiter v. Carpenter, 22 A.2d 393, 396 (Del. Ch. 1941) (concluding that the guarantor's action against the primary obligor seven years after satisfying the underlying obligation was not barred by laches); *see generally* Petroplast Petrofisa Plasticos S.A. v. Ameron Intern. Corp., Civil Action No. 4304-VCP, 2011 WL 2623991, at *14 (Del. Ch. July 1, 2011) (noting that "a court of equity ... generally analyzes questions of time bars and undue delay under the doctrine of laches").

Generally, a subrogee's rights have priority over creditors whose rights are created by contract.[333] However, if a creditor has a perfected security interest, this "takes priority over the surety's right of subrogation."[334] Because "rights to equitable subordination" are not covered by Article 9 of the Delaware UCC, "a surety does not need to file a financing statement to perfect its right to equitable subrogation."[335]

§ 13 Triangular Set-off in Bankruptcy

Triangular set-off is not available in bankruptcy petitions filed in the U.S. Bankruptcy Court for the District of Delaware. It is unclear whether a functional equivalent might be achieved by use of a series of guaranties.

An example of triangular set-off in the context of a corporate group is as follows: a corporation having contracts with more than one affiliate in a corporate group ("Contractor") attempts to set-off its debt to bankrupt parent corporation ("Parent") against debt owed to Contractor by Parent's bankrupt wholly owned subsidiary ("Sub").[336]

11 U.S.C. § 553 ("Section 553") governs a creditor's right to set-off in bankruptcy.[337] It "preserves for the creditor's benefit any set-off right that it may have under applicable nonbankruptcy law," so long as these debts are "mutual, prepetition debts."[338] Triangular set-offs, whether or not they involve corporate affiliated debtors, are generally not permitted under Section 553 for failure to satisfy its mutuality requirement.[339] In particular, "[a]bsent a piercing of the corporate veil, 'a subsidiary's debt may not be set off against the credit of a parent or other subsidiary, or vice versa.'"[340]

As a result of a recent decision of the U.S. Bankruptcy Court for the District of Delaware (the "Bankr. D. Del."), it is now clear that a "contract exception" to Section 553's bar on triangular set-off is not recognized by the Bankr. D. Del.[341] According to *Collier on Bankruptcy*, it was thought that "if the parties all agree in a prepetition contract that a setoff may be taken between A, B and C, then the agreement may be enforced in bankruptcy to the extent it

333. *See* Hartford Acc. & Indem. Co. v. Long, 245 A.2d 800, 804 (Del. Ch. 1968) ("The right of the contractor's surety to be subrogated with respect to unpaid funds is usually regarded as superior to the claims of general creditors, the contractor or his receiver or trustee the assignee of funds due under the contract, and various other persons.").
334. United Pacific Insurance Co v. Ripsom, No. 7056, 1984 WL 8269, at *2 (Del. Ch. Sept. 25, 1984).
335. *Id.*
336. *See* 5 Colliers on Bankruptcy § 553.03[3][b][i].
337. 11 U.S.C. § 553.
338. In re Semcrude, L.P., 399 B.R. 388, 393 (Bankr. D. Del. 2009), *aff'd*, 428 B.R. 590 (D.Del. 2010).
339. 5 Colliers on Bankruptcy § 553.03[3][b][i]; In re Semcrude, L.P., 399 B.R. 388, 393 (Bankr. D. Del. 2009), *aff'd*, 428 B.R. 590 (D.Del. 2010) (noting that bankruptcy courts have "routinely" found this to be the case).
340. In re Semcrude, L.P., 399 B.R. 388, 393-94 (Bankr. D. Del. 2009) *aff'd*, 428 B.R. 590 (D.Del. 2010); 5 Colliers on Bankruptcy § 553.03[3][b][i].
341. In re Semcrude, L.P., 399 B.R. 388 (Bankr. D. Del. 2009), *aff'd*, 428 B.R. 590 (D. Del. 2010); *see* In re Lehman Bros, Case No. 08-01420 (JMP) (SIPA), slip op. p. 13 (Bankr. S.D.N.Y.) ("The careful analysis in *SemCrude* is persuasive. There simply is no contract exception to section 553(a), because the statute itself does not allow for one."); *but see generally* Colliers on Bankruptcy § 553.03[3][b][ii] ("A narrow exception has been thought to exist with respect to certain [triangular] setoffs that are contractually based.").

is enforceable under the applicable nonbankruptcy law."[342] However, the Bankr. D. Del. in *SemCrude* recently held that Section 553's "mutuality requirement" could not be satisfied by a "multi-party agreement contemplating a triangular set-off."[343] Moreover, it held that the text of Section 553 did not provide for a "contract exception" and that it would be "improper to recognize" one.[344]

It is unclear whether parties could achieve the practical effect of the contractual exception to the mutuality requirement through use of guaranties.[345] That is whether Contractor can offset debt it owes Parent against debt Sub owes Contractor if Parent has guaranteed the obligation of Sub to Customer. Central to the *SemCrude* court's analysis was its "narrow construction" of "mutual debts": "each party must own [its] claim in [its] own right severally, with the right to collect in [its] own name against the debtor in [its] own right and severally."[346] The *SemCrude* court specifically left open the question of whether "an unpaid guarantee can create mutuality for purposes of section 553," simply noting the "split of authority" on this point in other bankruptcy courts.[347]

§ 14 Indemnification—Whether the Primary Obligor has a Duty

The principal obligor has a duty of indemnification so long as the guarantor undertook its obligations at the request of the principal obligor. The extent of this duty can be altered by contract.

"[I]ndemnification ... places the entire burden of a loss upon the party ultimately liable or responsible for it, and by whom the loss should have been discharged initially."[348] "[A]bsent a contractual or special relationship there is no right to indemnity."[349] Where the primary obligor has bound itself by express contract to reimburse or indemnify the guarantor for monies paid to the obligee to satisfy the underlying obligation, the terms of the contract control and will not be enlarged by implication.[350] Under Delaware law, a party

342. Colliers on Bankruptcy § 553.03[3][b][ii].
343. In re Semcrude, L.P., 399 B.R. 388, 397 (Bankr. D. Del. 2009), *aff'd*, 428 B.R. 590 (D. Del. 2010).
344. In re Semcrude, L.P., 399 B.R. 388, 399 (Bankr. D. Del. 2009), *aff'd*, 428 B.R. 590 (D. Del. 2010) ("The Court finds nothing in the language of the Code upon which to base a conclusion that there is a contractual exception to the 'mutual debt' requirement.").
345. In re Semcrude, L.P., 399 B.R. 388, 397 n.7 (Bankr. D. Del. 2009), *aff'd*, 428 B.R. 590 (D. Del. 2010).
346. In re Semcrude, L.P., 399 B.R. 388, 396 (Bankr. D. Del. 2009), *aff'd*, 428 B.R. 590 (D. Del. 2010); *see* Colliers on Bankruptcy § 553.03[3][b][ii].
347. In re Semcrude, L.P., 399 B.R. 388, 397 n.7 (Bankr. D. Del. 2009), *aff'd*, 428 B.R. 590 (D. Del. 2010); compare In re Ingersoll, 90 B.R. 168, 171 (Bankr. W.D.N.C.) (holding that creditor's status as guarantor "does not change the fact that the debts are between different parties in different capacities and thus, not subject to offset"); with Bloor v. Shapiro, 32 B.R. 993, 1001-02 (S.D.N.Y. 1983).
348. Levy v. HLI Operating Co., Inc., 924 A.2d 210, 221 (Del. Ch. 2007).
349. Giery v. Stover Homes, L.L.C., 2009 WL 768559, at * 2 (Del. Super. 2009).
350. Howard, Needles, Tammen and Bergendoff v. Steers, Perini and Pomeroy, 312 A.2d 621, 624 (Del. 1973) ("[W]hen the parties to a contract have entered into a written agreement, expressly setting forth one party's indemnity liability, there is no room for any enlargement of that obligation by implication."); *see* Celotex Corp. v. Certainteed Corp., No. Civ. A. 471, 2005 WL 217032, at * 3 (Del. Ch. Jan. 24, 2005).

seeking indemnification from another with whom it has no contract cannot "sustain a claim for contractual indemnification as a matter of law."[351]

However, Delaware law "recognize[s] a right to implied indemnification."[352] Delaware courts have at times referred to this as a "common law" indemnity right as opposed to a contractual one.[353] For purposes of the following discussion, "indemnification" and "reimbursement" will be used synonymously.[354] The Delaware Court of Chancery has recognized that a guarantor can bring an action at law for reimbursement on a theory of "implied promise to pay the money paid for [the primary obligor's benefit]."[355] This is in addition to the guarantor's subrogation rights.[356] However, there is little or no Delaware authority explicating the reimbursement rights in the guaranty context. Consequently, the general principles of Delaware indemnification law are instructive.

Common law indemnity claims are not ripe until the party seeking indemnification actually pays the debt.[357] However, there is no right to indemnification if the party paying the debt acted as a "volunteer," i.e., paying the creditor that which it could not be compelled to pay out of any legal or contractual obligation.[358] The primary obligor is liable for the amount actually paid.[359]

---

351. Lagrone v. American Mortell Corp., C.A. Nos. 04C-10-116-ASB, 07C-12-019-JRS, 2008 WL 4152677, at *6 (Del. Super. Sept. 4, 2008).
352. *Id.* at *5.
353. *See, e.g.,* Quereguan v. New Castle County, Civil Action No. 20298-NC, 2006 WL 2522214, at *5 (Del. Ch. 2006) ("'[C]ommon law indemnification' … is defined as a general right of reimbursement for debts owed to third parties by the indemnifier as a secondarily liable party[.]"). Levy v. Hayes Lemmerz Intern, Inc., Civ. A. No. 1395-N, at *11 (Del. Ch. April 5, 2006); Celotex Corp. v. Certainteed Corp., No. Civ. A. 471, 2005 WL 217032, at * 3 (Del. Ch. Jan. 24, 2005).
354. Lagrone v. American Mortell Corp., C.A. Nos. 04C-10-116-ASB, 07C-12-019-JRS, 2008 WL 4152677, at *6 (Del. Super. Sept. 4, 2008) ("Indemnity in its most basic sense means reimbursement and may lie when one party discharges a liability which another rightfully should have assumed."); *see also* Quereguan v. New Castle County, Civil Action No. 20298-NC, 2006 WL 2522214, at *5 (Del. Ch. 2006).
355. Leiter v. Carpenter, 22 A.2d 393, 396 (Del. Ch. 1941); *see also* Eastern States Petroleum Co., Inc. v. Universal Oil Products Co., 44 A.2d 365, 374-75 (Del. Ch. 1945); Shah v. Shah, Civ. A. No. 904-K, 1994 WL 586820, at *8 (Del. Ch. 1994) ("Shashi is liable solely as guarantor, but no claim has been asserted against Shashi in that capacity. That Shashi may be contingently liable to Shastri does not give Shashi a present, ripe claim for indemnity against Mahendra.").
356. *See generally* Leiter v. Carpenter, 22 A.2d 393, 396 (Del. Ch. 1941) ("In other words, subrogation in most cases is rather an additional remedy to an action for reimbursement than a mere incidental right.")
357. *See, e.g.,* Quereguan v. New Castle County, Civil Action No. 20298-NC, 2006 WL 2522214, at *5 (Del. Ch. Aug. 18, 2006) ("[A] cause of action for common law indemnification does not accrue until after the party seeking indemnification has made payment to the third party and the dispute with that party is finally concluded."). Levy v. Hayes Lemmerz Intern, Inc., Civ. A. No. 1395-N, at *11 (Del. Ch. April 5, 2006) ("[A] claim for indemnification in the common law sense is defined by reference to a particular action, and becomes legally cognizable when payment is made to a third party on that action specifically"); Celotex Corp. v. Certainteed Corp., No. Civ. A. 471, 2005 WL 217032, at * 3 (Del. Ch. Jan. 24, 2005) (A "cause of action accrues after the party seeking indemnification has made payment to the third party and the dispute with that party is finally concluded.").
358. Lagrone v. American Mortell Corp., C.A. Nos. 04C-10-116-ASB, 07C-12-019-JRS, 2008 WL 4152677, at *6 (Del. Super. Sept. 4, 2008).
359. *See* Levy v. HLI Operating Co., Inc., 924 A.2d 210, 221 (Del. Ch. 2007); Leiter v. Carpenter, 22 A.2d 393, 396 (Del. Ch. 1941).

§ 15 Enforcement of Guaranties

15.1 Limitations on Recovery

15.1a A Guarantor's Payment of the Underlying Obligation May Constitute a Fraudulent Conveyance Under Delaware or Federal Law.

An obligee should consider whether a guarantor's payment of the underlying obligation may be subsequently avoided as a constructive fraudulent transfer under the Bankruptcy Code or the Delaware Uniform Fraudulent Transfers Act ("DUFTA").[360] A guarantor's satisfaction of an underlying obligation is a transfer within the meaning of both.[361] Under the Bankruptcy Code, a trustee may challenge a transfer as constructively fraudulent under "applicable law," e.g., under DUFTA, or under 11 U.S.C. 548(a)(1)(B) ("Section 548(a)(1)(B)").[362] Because DUFTA "essentially tracks" Section 548(a)(1)(B) in pertinent part, courts applying them have identified them as having the same elements in the constructive fraudulent transfer context.[363]

A constructive fraudulent transfer is a transfer in which the challenging party need not prove actual fraud.[364] Rather, a party challenging a transfer as constructively fraudulent must prove that (1) a debtor made a transfer (2) without receiving "reasonably equivalent value," and (3) the debtor was either "(a) insolvent or became insolvent as a result of the transfer; (b) engaged or about to engage in a business or transaction for which its remaining assets were unreasonably small in relation to the business or transaction; or (c) intended to incur, or believed or reasonably should have believed that it

---

360. *See* Allen Ruda, Asset-Based Financing, § 11.07; In re Image Worldwide, Ltd., 139 F.3d 574, 578 (7th Cir. 1998).

361. *See* Allen Ruda, Asset-Based Financing, § 11.07; Collier § 548.03[1]; *see generally* In re Fruehauf Trailer Corp., 444 F.3d 203, 212 (3d Cir. 2006) ("The Bankruptcy Code" defines 'transfer' in the broadest possible terms."); 6 Del. C § 1301(12) (defining "transfer" to mean "every mode, direct or indirect, absolute or conditional, voluntary or involuntary, of disposing of or parting with an asset or an interest in an asset.").

362. *See* Collier § 658.01[2][a].

363. In re USDigital, Inc., 443 B.R. 22, 23 (Bankr. D. Del. 2011); Collier § 548.01[2][a][i] ("For the most part the [Uniform Fraudulent Transfers Act ("UFTA")] tracks Section 548.") *see* Wilmington Savings Fund Soc., FSB v. Kaczmarczyk, No. Civ.A. 1769–N, 2007 WL 704937, at *3 (Del. Ch. Mar. 1, 2007) (citing bankruptcy precedent in the construction of "reasonably equivalent value"); *see also* In re Image Worldwide, Ltd., 139 F.3d 574, 577 (7th Cir. 1998) (noting that "reasonably equivalent value" as used in UFTA is derived from § 548(a)(2)" of the Bankruptcy Code and thus looking to bankruptcy cases and state law cases applying UFTA as adopted in other jurisdictions because Illinois courts had yet to construe this phrase in the pertinent context). Sections 1304(a)(2) and 1305(a) of DUFTA deal with constructive fraudulent transfer. With the exception of noting their "substantial[] similar[ity]" to each other, Delaware cases elaborating these provisions are sparse. *See generally* Wilmington Savings Fund Soc., FSB v. Kaczmarczyk, No. Civ.A. 1769–N, 2007 WL 704937, at *3 (Del. Ch. Mar. 1, 2007) (noting the relative dearth of cases construing DUFTA's constructive fraud provisions); *see, e.g.,* Roseton OL, LLC v. Dynergy Holdings, C.A. No. 6689-VCP, 2011 WL 3275965, at *16, n.111 (describing the sections as "substantially similar").

364. *See generally* Peltz v. Hatten, 279 B.R. 710, 735 (D. Del. 2002) ("To deem such transactions 'fraudulent' is somewhat of a misnomer, as no proof of actual fraud is required."); Collier § 65.05.

would incur, debts beyond its ability to pay as they became due."[365] Some courts refer to the third prong as the "insolvency" prong.[366] However, in this discussion we will only use "insolvency" to refer to actual insolvency.

Whether there has been reasonably equivalent value *received* by the debtor is determined from the perspective of the creditors rather than the party purportedly giving value.[367] The "touchstone is whether the transaction conferred realizable commercial value on the debtor reasonably equivalent to the realizable commercial value of the assets transferred."[368] The Third Circuit has enunciated a two-prong test, which has been applied to Section 548 and DUFTA claims, for whether reasonably equivalent value has been received: (1) "The court must determine if the debtor received any value,"[369] and (2) if some value has been received, the court determines whether it is reasonably equivalent applying a "totality of the circumstances test."[370] The first prong is typically easily met.[371] If some value has been received, the court determines whether it is reasonably equivalent, applying a "totality of the circumstances test."[372] Courts generally consider three factors in determining if the second prong of the Third Circuit's test is met: (1) whether the transaction was at arm's length, (2) whether the transaction was in good faith, and (3) the degree of difference between the fair market value of the assets transferred and the price paid.[373] "Proper application of the totality of the circumstances test requires comparison between the value that was conferred upon the debtor and the fees paid to the transferee."[374] Courts should take into account the indirect, as well as direct, benefits conferred upon a debtor in exchange for the transfer.[375]

---

365. In re USDigital, Inc., 443 B.R. 22, 23 (Bankr. D. Del. 2011); *see also* In re Plassein Int'l Corp., 428 B.R. 64, 67 (D. Del. 2010). For completeness's sake there is an additional instance where fraudulent transfer may be proven under Section 548(a)(1)(B)(ii)(IV), which pertains to transfers for the benefit of insiders made pursuant "to the terms of an employment contract and not in the ordinary course of business." Collier § 65.05. However, this seems unlikely to come up in the guaranty context.
366. *See, e.g.,* Peltz v. Hatten, 279 B.R. 710, 735 (D. Del. 2002) ("[F]raudulent transactions are ... transactions in which the debtor receives less than reasonably equivalent value, at a time when the debtor was insolvent under one of three of the provided insolvency tests" ... within a prescribed period.); Omnicare, Inc. v. Mariner Health Care Mgmt., Co., C.A. No. 3087-VCN, 2009 WL 1515609, at *5 (Del. Ch. May 29, 2009); In re EBC I, Inc., 308 B.R. 348, 355, 359 (Bankr. D. Del. 2008) (recognizing that "insolvent" is a defined term but referring to undercapitalization or inability to pay debts as "alternative" solvency tests). This can be confusing as there are *three* specifically enumerated states dealt with in both DUFTA and the Bankruptcy Code, and *only* the first requires actual insolvency. It is perhaps better understood that transfers may be avoided if a court later determines they were made while the debtor was in a "financially fragile state." Colliers on Bankruptcy § 548.05[2][a]. "Any transaction made by a financially impaired debtor for less than even of exchange of value is vulnerable." Colliers § 548.01.
367. Mellon Bank v. Metro Comm'ns, Inc., 945 F.2d 635, 646 (3d Cir. 1991).
368. *Id.*
369. In re Plassein Int'l Corp., Case No. 03-11489 (KG), 2008 Bankr. LEXIS 1473, at *18 (Bankr. D. Del May 5, 2008).
370. *Id.*
371. Colliers §.
372. In re Plassein Int'l Corp., Case No. 03-11489 (KG), 2008 Bankr. LEXIS 1473, at *18 (Bankr. D. Del May 5, 2008).
373. *Id.*
374. *Id.*
375. *Id.*

15.1b Not all Guaranties are Susceptible to Challenges as Fraudulent Conveyances. Certain Measures can be Taken to Reduce the Risk that Susceptible Guaranties will be Successfully Challenged. However, it is Unclear Whether So-Called "Savings Clauses" will be Upheld.

Generally, "[t]he securing of a loan concurrent with its funding cannot be a fraudulent transfer, even if the amount of the security exceeds the amount of the debt being secured."[376] Likewise, "downstream guaranties by a corporate parent of a solvent subsidiary's debt are not susceptible to attack [as a constructive fraudulent transfer] since a loan to a subsidiary corporation benefits the parent corporation, as owner, to approximately the same degree as the subsidiary."[377] However, "courts generally hold that [the guaranty of another's debt] provides no value to the debtor" providing the guaranty.[378] Nevertheless, cross-stream (subsidiary-to-subsidiary) and upstream (subsidiary-to-parent) guaranties do not necessarily fail to satisfy the reasonably equivalent value" prong.[379] For example, the Third Circuit enunciated that its "reasonably equivalent value" test provided for the consideration of "indirect economic benefits" realized by the debtor in a case of an intra-corporate family guaranty where the guarantor entity did not directly receive any of the proceeds of the guarantied loan.[380] In particular, the Third Circuit noted that "indirect benefits to the [subsidiary] of this guaranty were the ability to obtain substantial credit due to its new association with the [parent's] corporate group and the synergy expected to result" from the corporate affiliation.[381] However, "[u]pstream ... and cross-stream ... guaranties, in addition to guaranties from entities unaffiliated with the principal debtor ... require a substantial benefit from the transaction guarantied in order to successfully defend against an action under the fraudulent conveyance laws."[382]

As lack of reasonably equivalent value is necessary but not sufficient for a constructive fraudulent transfer, it behooves a lender to investigate whether the putative guarantor falls into one of the three "financially fragile" states

---

376. Colliers § 548.03[5].
377. *See* Allen Ruda, Asset-Based Financing, § 11.07; *see, e.g.,* In re Renegade Holdings, Inc., 457 B.R. 441, 444-445 (Bankr. M.D. NC 2001) ("Generally, transfers to a solvent subsidiary are considered to be reasonably equivalent value, because, since the parent is the sole shareholder of the subsidiary corporation, any benefit received by the subsidiary is also a benefit to the parent. This presumption ... is not available if the subsidiary ... whose obligation was guaranteed was insolvent at the time of the transaction.") (internal citation and quotation marks removed).
378. Colliers § 548.05[2][b].
379. Mellon Bank v. Metro Comm'ns, Inc., 945 F.2d 635, 647 (3d Cir. 1991).
380. Mellon Bank v. Metro Comm'ns, Inc., 945 F.2d 635, 647 (3d Cir. 1991) ("Because Metro did not receive the proceeds of the acquisition loan, it did not receive any direct benefits from extending the guaranty and security interest collateralizing that guaranty. However, in evaluating whether reasonably equivalent value has been given the debtor under section 548, indirect benefits may also be evaluated. If the consideration Metro received from the transaction, even though indirect, approximates the value it gave TCI, this can satisfy the terms of the statute.").
381. Mellon Bank v. Metro Comm'ns, Inc., 945 F.2d 635, 647 (3d Cir. 1991).
382. *See* Allen Ruda, Asset-Based Financing, § 11.07.

set forth above.[383] If a lender is not comfortable with the guarantor's financial health, the lender may attempt to restructure the loan as a downstream guaranty.[384] Another option suggested by some commentators is to insert a "savings clause" that caps the guarantor's liability in a way that it is not insolvent or in another financially fragile state by definition.[385] However, it is unclear whether such a provision will be upheld.[386] The Bankr. D. Del. noted that lenders in a 2003 case were unable to point to "any decision in support of the efficacy of [this type of] 'savings clause'" but did not resolve the question of their enforceability.[387] In 2009, in *In re Tousa*, the Bankruptcy Court for the Southern District of Florida held that such "savings clauses" were *per se* invalid as an attempt to "contract around core provisions of the Bankruptcy Code," noting that such a provision would only be implicated "if the transferee has not provided reasonably equivalent value to an otherwise insolvent debtor."[388] Subsequent decisions by the U.S. District Court for the Southern District of Florida and the Eleventh Circuit U.S. Court of Appeals relating to *In re Tousa* have not resolved this question.[389] Albeit in a different context, subsequent to the *In re Tousa* decision the Bankr. D. Del. reiterated the principle that "[s]avings clauses that attempt to contract around core provisions of the Bankruptcy Code are invalid."[390] Consequently, lenders should be wary of relying solely on such a provision. Additionally, assuming its enforceability, the lender should not use such a clause indiscriminately, as it is designed to save the guaranty by capping the amount the guarantor will ultimately be obligated to pay to the obligee.[391]

15.2 Exercising Rights Under a Guaranty Where the Underlying Obligation is also Secured by a Mortgage

Under Delaware law, that a debt is also secured by a mortgage does not affect the duties and obligations of a guarantor of that debt where there is a material

383. *See* Collier § 548.05[3]; Allen Ruda, Asset-Based Financing, § 11.07 ("In light of the problems posed by the fraudulent conveyance law, creditors relying on upstream, cross-stream or nonaffiliated guaranties should be satisfied that the guaranty will not render the guarantor insolvent.").

384. *See* Allen Ruda, Asset-Based Financing, § 11.07; *see e.g.*, In re Renegade Holdings, Inc., 457 B.R. 441, 444-445 (Bankr. M.D. NC 2001).

385. *See* Allen Ruda, Asset-Based Financing, § 11.07[1]; Jacob W. Reby, Banking and Lending Institution Forms with Commentary and Checklists, Form 7A.18 (captioning its form "Subsidiary Guaranty with Limitation to Avoid Fraudulent Conveyance").

386. *See* Robin Russell, John J. Sparacino, and Chasless L. Yancy, 128 Banking Law Journal 439, 442 *District Court Overturns the Touse Fraudulent Transfer Ruling* (May 2011).

387. Official Comm. of Unsecured Creditors v. Credit Suisse First Boston (In re Exide Techs., Inc.), 299 B.R. 732, 748 (Bankr. D. Del. 2003).

388. *In re Tousa*, 422 B.R. 783, 864.

389. *See* Robin Russell, John J. Sparacino, and Chasless L. Yancy, 128 Banking Law Journal 439, 442 *District Court Overturns the Touse Fraudulent Transfer Ruling* (May 2011) ("It is important to note, however, that one issue left open by the district court opinion [reversing *In re Tousa*] is the bankruptcy court's rejection of the fraudulent conveyance savings clause as [*per se*] invalid."); *see* Official Comm. of Unsecured Creditors of TOUSA, Inc. v. Citicorp N. Am., Inc. (In re Tousa, Inc.), No. 11-11071 (11th Cir. May 15, 2012) (reversing the order of the district court without addressing this issue).

390. Burtch v. Seaport Capital, LLC (In re Direct Response Media, Inc.), 2012 Bankr. LEXIS 41 (Bankr. D. Del. Jan. 12, 2012).

391. *See* Allen Ruda, Asset-Based Financing, § 11.07[1].

breach of the guaranty.[392] For example, in *Pellaton*, the defendant was one of three individual limited partners in a limited partnership that owned certain real estate in Delaware.[393] The limited partnership sought to refinance its mortgage by obtaining a loan from the plaintiff.[394] The plaintiff required the limited partners to personally guaranty both (i) the timely payment of interest under the loan and (ii) the principal amount due under the loan.[395] The guaranties signed by the defendant each contained warrants to confess judgment.[396] Despite the defendant's claim not to have been aware of the warrants to confess judgment, the Delaware Supreme Court affirmed the entry of judgment against the defendant applying general principles of contract law.[397]

This is also the case where the guarantor's obligation is secured by a mortgage.[398]

§ 16 Revival and Reinstatement of Guaranties

A Delaware court should uphold a reinstatement provision in a guaranty.

Generally, where a primary obligor fully satisfies the underlying obligation, this discharges the guarantor from liability under the contract of guaranty.[399] However, if the primary obligor "subsequently goes bankrupt, the [obligee] may have to repay amounts that constitute preferences or fraudulent conveyances."[400] Bankruptcy discharges the primary obligor of its personal liability for the debt, but it does not discharge the debt itself.[401] Consequently, an obligee may want to include terms in the contract of guaranty providing for reinstatement of the guarantor's liability for the underlying obligation where the obligee is required to repay all or some of the amount used to satisfy the underlying obligation.[402]

There is no Delaware case that directly addresses whether such a reinstatement clause would be enforced in the case of a guaranty. However, it is

392. Pellaton v. Bank of New York, 592 A.2d 473 (Del. 1991) (enforcing guaranties of a debt secured by a mortgage applying general principles of contract of guaranty enforcement); Fed. Deposit Ins. Corp. v. Bloom, No. 29 C.A. 1977, 1986 WL 221 (Del. Super. May 21, 1986) (same); *see also* 38A C.J.S. Guaranty § 56 ("The nature and extent of liability of a guarantor of a mortgage … is governed by the terms of the guaranty, as construed by the ordinary rules of construction.").
393. Pellaton v. Bank of New York, 592 A.2d 473, 475 (Del. 1991).
394. *Id.*
395. *Id.*
396. *Id.*
397. Pellaton v. Bank of New York, 592 A.2d 473, 476-79 (Del. 1991) (reversing the Superior Court's limitation of the defendant's liability to one-third of the amount of the related the mortgage finding that the guaranties were not ambiguous with respect to the extent of the defendant's liability).
398. *See, e.g.*, Stornawaye Capital LLC v. Smithers, C.A. No. 18845-VCN, 2010 WL 673291, at *1 (Del. Ch. Feb. 12, 2010) (enforcing the "unambiguous Guaranty, Mortgage, and other loan documents … in accordance with their terms"); York Fed. Sav. and Loan Ass'n v. Heflin, No. Civ. A. 94L-08-018, 1996 WL 30241, at *3 (Del. Super. Ct. Jan 5. 1996) (enforcing a mortgage given to secure the defendant's guaranty of a loan pursuant to its terms upon default under the guaranty).
399. 38 Am. Jur. 2d § 65 ("The guarantor's obligation ends when the debtor's obligation has been paid."); 38A C.J.S. § 92; Cf. S & S Builders, Inc. v Di Mondi, 126 A.2d 826, 830 (Del. 1956).
400. Allen Ruda, Asset-Based Financing: A Transactional Guide, § 11.09[5][b].
401. *See* Chrysler Financial Corp. v. Fruit of the Loom, Inc., C.A. 91C-08-108-1-CV, 1993 WL 19659, at * 5 (Del Super. Jan. 12, 1993).
402. Allen Ruda, Asset-Based Financing: A Transactional Guide, § 11.09[5][b].

likely that such a provision would be enforceable under Delaware law. As noted *supra*, Delaware courts will only decline to enforce the terms of a valid contract in extreme circumstances, none of which seem to apply in this case.[403] A contract term providing for the reinstatement of a contract under certain conditions is neither illegal nor violates public policy.[404] Additionally, an *ex ante* agreement to reinstate would seemingly prevent a guarantor from arguing that it has been discharged by taking action to its disadvantage on the erroneous belief that the underlying obligation was discharged.[405] Consequently, the effect on the guarantor would seem to be no different from agreeing to permit the obligee and primary obligor to extend the life of the underlying obligation, which is permissible under Delaware law.[406]

§ 17 Choice of Law

Delaware courts apply general contract choice-of-law principles to contracts of guaranty.[407] "Delaware courts use the 'most significant relationship test' when conducting a contract choice of law analysis."[408] "Delaware courts will generally honor a contractually designated choice of law provision so long as the jurisdiction selected bears some material relationship to the transaction."[409] "However, a foreign jurisdiction's laws may not be used to interpret a contractual provision in a manner repugnant to the public policy of Delaware."[410] "When conducting a choice of law analysis, Delaware courts generally rely on the Restatement (Second) of Conflicts."[411]

403. Libeau v. Fox, 880 A.2d 1049, 1056 (Del. Ch. 2005); State v. Tabasso, 28 A.2d 248, 252 (Del. Gen. Sess. 1942) ("[F]reedom of contract shall not lightly be interfered with. [It] is the rule and restraints on this freedom the exception, and to justify this exception unusual circumstances should exist.").
404. *See* Harris v. New York Life Ins. Co., 33 A.2d 154, 158 (Del. Ch. 1943) (refusing to rescind a "re-instatement contract" made pursuant to a "reinstatement provision" in an insurance contract).
405. *See* S & S Builders, Inc. v Di Mondi, 126 A.2d 826, 830 (Del. 1956) ("[I]f a creditor, even by mistake advises a guarantor that the [underlying obligation] has been paid and the guarantor as a result ... in some other manner changes his position to his disadvantage, the guarantor is thereby released from any liability under the guaranty.").
406. *See* Cooling v. Springer, 30 A.2d 466, 470 (Del. Super. 1943); *see generally* Fed. Deposit Ins. Corp. v. Bloom, No. 29 C.A. 1977, 1986 WL 221, at * 6 (Del. Super. May 21, 1986).
407. Cf. Bonanze Restaurant Co. v. Wink, 2012 WL 1415512, at *2 (Apr. 17, 2012) (discussing whether to apply Texas law to "both sets of contracts" where the latter set were guaranties and citing generally to Delaware authority on choice of law).
408. Deuley v. DynCorp Int'l., Inc., 8 A.3d 1156, 1160 (Del. 2010) (citing to The Restatement (Second) Conflict of Laws).
409. J.S. Alberici Const. Co., Inc. v. Mid-West Conveyor Co., Inc., 750 A.2d 518, 520 (Del.Supr., 2000). Where the parties' choice-of-law provision selects Delaware law and the requirements of 6 Del. C § 2708 are met, such a provision provides "conclusive proof of a 'material and reasonable relationship with this State and shall be enforced whether or not there are other relationships with this State.'" *See, e.g.,* QVT Fund LP v. Eurohypo Capital Funding LLC I, 2011 WL 2672092, at *8 (Del. Ch. 2011).
410. Deuley v. DynCorp Intern., Inc., 8 A.3d 1156, 1161 (Del. 2010).
411. Smith v. Delaware State University, 2012 WL 2583394, at *6 (Del. July 5,2012); Viking Pump, Inc. v. Century Indem. Co., 2 A.3d 76, 87 (Del. Ch. 2009) (noting that where the contract is silent about which state's law should apply, "Delaware law employs the *Restatement (Second) of Conflict of Laws* [approach].").

Florida State Law of Guaranties

Edgel C. Lester
Lauren E. Sembler
Shannon B. Gray
Carlton Fields, P.A.
4221 W. Boy Scout Boulevard
Suite 1000
Tampa, FL 33607-5780
(813) 223-7000
www.carltonfields.com
elester@carltonfields.com

Contents

Florida State Law of Guaranties

Use of certain terms:

"Guarantor" means a person who, by contract, agrees to satisfy an underlying obligation of another to an obligee upon the primary obligor's default on that underlying obligation.

"Guaranty" means the contract by which the guarantor agrees to satisfy the underlying obligation of a primary obligor to an obligee in the event the primary obligor defaults on the underlying obligation.

"Obligee" means the person to whom the underlying obligation is owed. For example, the lender under a loan agreement would be an obligee vis-à-vis the borrower.

"Primary Obligor" means the person who incurs the underlying obligation to the obligee. For example, the borrower under a loan agreement would be a primary obligor.

"Underlying Obligation" means the obligation or obligations incurred by the primary obligor and owed to the obligee. For example, the borrower's obligation to make payments to a lender of principal and interest on a loan constitutes an underlying obligation.

§ 1 Nature of the Guaranty Arrangement

Under Florida law, a guaranty involves three distinct, yet interrelated, obligations: the underlying obligation between the principal obligor and the obligee, the guaranty between the guarantor and the obligee, and the surety between the principal obligor and the guarantor.

1.1 Guaranty Relationships

A guaranty is a contract of "secondary liability" under which the guarantor has an obligation to pay only upon default by the primary obligor.[1] The relationship between the primary obligor and the guarantor arises as a matter of law,

1. Fed. Deposit Ins. Corp. v. Univ. Anclote, Inc., 764 F.2d 804 (11th Cir. 1985); Ulrich v. Ulrich, 603 So. 2d 78 (Fla. Dist. Ct. App. 2d Dist. 1992); New Holland, Inc. v. Trunk, 579 So. 2d 215 (Fla. Dist. Ct. App. 5th Dist. 1991); Dept. of Revenue, State of Fla. v. Sun Bank, 556 So. 2d 1154 (Fla. Dist. Ct. App. 5th Dist. 1990).

and is based on the notion that, while the guarantor is liable to the obligee, it is the principal obligor who is liable in the first instance.[2]

Under Florida law, no "technical words" are needed to create a guaranty obligation; rather, a court will look to substance over form and whether there exists intent to bind a party in the capacity of a guarantor.[3]

1.2 Other Suretyship Relationships

We note that a suretyship relationship may also arise in connection with a pledge of collateral. In this case, a guaranty-type relationship arises, to the extent of the collateral pledged, when a person supplies collateral for a loan in order to induce the creditor to lend to the debtor or where one party mortgages property to a creditor to secure the debt of another.

§ 2 State Law Requirements for an Entity to Enter a Guaranty[a]

Partnerships, limited liability companies, and corporations can all grant guaranties in furtherance of their business activities. Such grants are generally permitted by the appropriate Florida statute. Additionally, corporations, partnerships, and limited liability companies can sometimes grant guaranties even when not in furtherance of their business activities.

2.1 Corporations

Under Florida law, a corporation may, within the scope of its general corporate powers, give a guaranty in furtherance of its corporate purpose, provided that its articles of incorporation do not provide otherwise.[4]

As with Delaware corporate law, Florida law presumes corporate guaranties granted within affiliate relationships are in the course of business.[5] The philosophy behind this provision is that corporations should have the same powers to act as individuals, except to the extent that those powers are limited by a corporation's own articles of incorporation.[6]

---

2. Brunswick Corp. v. Creel, 471 So. 2d 617 (Fla. Dist. Ct. App. 5th Dist. 1985).
3. Goldring v. Thompson, 58 Fla. 248 (1909).
a. For the purposes of this survey, we assume that a guaranty will not constitute "financial guaranty insurance" within the meaning of Chapter 627 of the Florida Statutes (the "Insurance Law"). *See* FLA. STAT. § 627.971 (2011) (defining financial guaranty insurance). Under the Insurance Law, "[a] financial guaranty insurance corporation must be organized and licensed in the manner prescribed in this code for stock property and casualty insurers" except that it may be licensed to transact residual value insurance, surety insurance, credit insurance, or mortgage guaranty insurance. FLA. STAT. § 679.972(1) (2011). In addition, the Insurance Law limits the underlying obligations for which even a licensed corporation may issue financial guaranty insurance. *See* FLA. STAT. § 697.973(2) (2011).
4. FLA. STAT. § 607.0302(7) (2011).
5. *See* DEL. CODE ANN. tit. 8, § 122(13) (LexisNexis 2011).
6. FLA. STAT. ANN. § 607.0302 (West 2011).

A Florida corporation may execute a guaranty to benefit a director if, in the judgment of the board of directors, such guaranty may reasonably be expected to benefit the corporation.[7]

2.2 Partnerships

Florida's Partnership Law[8] neither expressly empowers a partnership to issue a guaranty nor expressly regulates or prohibits such activity.

2.3 Limited Liability Companies

Florida's Limited Liability Company Act[9] generally permits limited liability companies to issue guaranties unless the articles of organization of the particular company provide otherwise.[10] The law permits these guaranties so long as they are in the interests of the company.[11] Florida law deems guaranties issued by a limited liability company to an affiliate as being in the interests of the business.[12]

2.4 Banks and Trust Companies

Florida's Banking Law[13] neither expressly empowers a bank to issue a guaranty nor expressly regulates or prohibits such activity.

Note also that guaranties offered by state banks may also be significantly affected by federal law. First, federal law prohibits a state-chartered bank from engaging in activities in which a national bank may not engage under federal law. The situations under which a national bank may become a guarantor are governed by federal law.[14]

2.5 Individuals

While a business corporation must have "authority" to execute a guaranty, an individual guarantor must have the "capacity" to enter into the guaranty. Incapacity can be a defense against the enforcement of a guaranty issued by an individual.[15]

It is well established Florida law that property held in a tenancy by the entirety cannot be reached to satisfy the individual debt of either spouse.[16]

7. FLA. STAT. § 607.0833 (2011).
8. FLA. STAT. Ch. 620.
9. FLA. STAT. Ch. 608.
10. FLA. STAT. § 608.404(5) (2011).
11. *Id.*
12. *Id.*
13. FLA. STAT. Ch. 655.
14. *See* National Bank as Guarantor or Surety on Indemnity Bond, 12 C.F.R. § 7.1017 (2010).
15. 38 Am. Jur. 2d Guaranty § 25 (2011).
16. Balding v. Fleisher, 279 So. 2d 883 (Fla. Dist. Ct. App. 3d Dist. 1973); France v. Hart, 170 So. 2d 52 (Fla. Dist. Ct. App. 3d Dist. 1964); Crawford v. U.S. Fidelity & Guaranty Co., 139 So. 2d 500 (Fla. Dist. Ct. App. 1st Dist. 1962).

In a divorce, the court will divide jointly owned property (marital assets) between the parties, based on equitable principles and a number of statutory factors.[17] Nonmarital assets include: those acquired by each party prior to marriage, assets acquired by gift, bequest, devise, or descent, income derived from nonmarital assets (unless treated, used, or relied upon by the parties as a marital asset), and those assets specifically excluded by valid written agreement of the parties.[18]

Confusion may arise in the case of corporate officers or directors signing guaranties in closely held corporations or other organizations. In such instances, a case-by-case inquiry determines whether an individual intended to be personally bound or, instead, only issued a guaranty on behalf of a partnership or corporation and thus only in an official employment capacity.[19] When an individual signs his title as well as his name, this is not dispositive proof of an intention not to issue a personal guaranty.[20]

§ 3 Signatory's Authority to Execute a Guaranty

Generally, the obligee has a duty of reasonable inquiry when it has some notice that the individual executing the guaranty does not have authority to bind the guarantor.

3.1 Corporations

A corporation's powers are defined by statute and by its articles of incorporation and are a matter of public notice.[21] A corporation is presumed to act within its corporate authority until the contrary is shown. The burden of proving the contract is outside the scope of that authority is on the party alleging it.[22] Those dealing with a corporation are required to exercise some degree of care to ascertain the powers of the corporation with reference to the transaction; however, if the transaction has some fair relation to the action within the corporation's authority, the defense of ultra vires will not be available.[23]

17. Fla. Stat. § 61.075(1) (2011).
18. Fla. Stat. § 61.075(6)(b) (2011).
19. *See, e.g.*, Lab. Corp. of Am. v. McKown, 829 So. 2d 311 (Fla. Dist. Ct. App. 5th Dist. 2002).
20. *Id.*; *see also* Great Lakes Prods., Inc. v. Wojciechowski, 878 So. 2d 418 (Fla. Dist. Ct. App. 3d Dist. 2004) (where signatory included "President" after his signature, he did not defeat the purpose of the guaranty when the agreement contained provisions for individual liability); Nelson v. Ameriquest Techs., Inc., 739 So. 2d 161 (Fla. Dist. Ct. App. 3d Dist. 1999) (that a guarantor put "V.P." after his signature could not defeat the clear purpose of the guaranty agreement to impose individual liability upon him as signatory); Saada v. Grumman Credit Corp., 583 So. 2d 430 (Fla. Dist. Ct. App. 3d Dist. 1983); Cent. Nat'l Bank of Miami v. Muskat Corp. of Am., Inc., 430 So. 2d 957 (Fla. Dist. Ct. App. 3d Dist. 1983).
21. Bryan v. St. Andrews Bay Cmty. Hotel Corp., 99 Fla. 132 (Fla. 1930).
22. Hitchcock v. Mortg. Sec. Corp., 95 Fla. 147 (Fla. 1928).
23. McQuaig v. Gulf Naval Stores Co., 56 Fla. 505 (Fla. 1908).

3.2 Partnerships

Section 620.8301 of the Florida Statutes grants a partner the authority to bind the partnership when such partner's act is "for apparently carrying on in the ordinary course of partnership business or business of the kind carried on by the partnership," unless such authority has been explicitly held back in the partnership agreement. If a partner's action is not "apparently for carrying on in the ordinary course the partnership business or business of the kind carried on by the partnership," the partner must be authorized by the other partners to bind a partnership.[24] Authority may also be granted under the partnership agreement.[25] Those dealing with partners do not have a duty of inquiry as to whether a signatory has the appropriate authority to bind the partnership so long as they do not have knowledge or are not on notice of the lack of authority.[26]

Under Florida's Revised Limited Partnership Act (applicable to all Florida limited partnerships formed on or after January 1, 2007), a general partner has the same powers as a partner of a general partnership, except as provided otherwise in the partnership agreement or in the Revised Limited Partnership Act.[27]

3.3 Limited Liability Companies (LLCs)

The Florida Limited Liability Company Act provides that, in the case of a member-managed LLC, every member is an agent of that company and can sign instruments pursuant to carrying on in the usual way of business unless that person has no actual authority to act in such way and his counterparty knows that.[28] In the case of a manager-managed LLC, a member is not an agent solely by reason of being a member.[29] Each manager of a manager-managed LLC can bind the LLC if such guaranty is "for apparently carrying on in the ordinary course the limited liability company's business or business of the kind carried on by the company" unless the manager has no actual authority and the counterparty knows of this lack of authority.[30]

Florida law deems guaranties issued among affiliate limited liability companies to be "in the course of business."[31]

24. Fla. Stat. §§ 620.8301(1) and (2) (2011).
25. Fla. Stat. § 620.8301(2) (2011).
26. RNR Invs. Ltd. P'ship v. Peoples First Cmty. Bank, 27 Fla. L. Weekly D728a (Fla. Dist Ct. App. 1st Dist March 28, 2002) (although general partner entering into a mortgage loan on behalf of the limited partnership violated a provision of the limited partnership agreement, such mortgage is still binding unless lender had "knowledge" or "notice" as defined by § 620.8102). Fla. Stat. § 620.8102 defines knowledge as actual knowledge. Fla. Stat. § 620.8102 defines a person with notice as a person who has actual knowledge or notice or has reason to be on notice.
27. Fla. Stat. § 620.1402 (2011).
28. Fla. Stat. § 608.4235(1)(a) (2011).
29. Fla. Stat. § 608.4235(2)(a) (2011).
30. *Id.*
31. Fla. Stat. § 608.404(5) (2011).

3.4 Banks

Generally, a bank is prohibited from issuing guaranties. A bank is authorized to lend its money, but not its credit.[32] A bank "is not permitted to lend its credit to commercial paper which it does not own" and in which it has no beneficial interest.[33] No provision in the Florida Banking Code either expressly or implicitly authorizes banks to guarantee the payment of a debt of a third party expressly for his or her benefit.[34]

If a bank attempts to lend its credit, that transaction is void[35] and parties that are dealing with the bank are charged with notice.[36] However, a bank does have the right to issue letters of credit on behalf of its customers in favor of third parties.[37]

§ 4 Consideration; Sufficiency of Past Consideration and Reliance

Standard contract principles apply to the analysis of consideration for a contract of guaranty. The principal agreement is sufficient consideration for an accompanying guaranty. Past consideration can be sufficient when the guaranty expresses the past consideration in writing.

Consideration is required to create a valid contract of guaranty.[38] The inquiry into sufficient consideration is based on standard contract law principles. The benefit or obligation that forms the consideration need not flow directly to the guarantor from the obligee; the consideration flowing from the obligee to the principal obligor is sufficient to support a contemporaneous guaranty.[39]

While past consideration, under general principles of contract law, will not support a guaranty, some Florida cases have concluded that "a guaranty, though executed subsequently to the creation of the principal obligation, if given in fulfillment of an agreement on the faith of which the principal obligation was created, is deemed contemporaneous in effect, and requires no other consideration."[40] The issue in these cases is not one of timing, but whether there was consideration for the guaranty.[41]

32. Newsom v. Gill, 145 So. 189 (Fla. 1932); Cottondale State Bank v. Oskamp Nolting Co., 59 So. 566 (Fla. 1912); Cent. Sav. Ass'n v. Cent. Plaza Bank & Trust Co., 223 So. 2d 50 (Fla. Dist. Ct. App. 2d Dist. 1969) (holding that the same principles apply to a savings and loan association).
33. Ferguson v. Five Points Nat'l Bank of Miami, 187 So. 2d 45 (Fla. Dist. Ct. App. 3d Dist. 1966).
34. Cottondale State Bank v. Oskamp Nolting Co., 59 So. 566 (Fla. 1912).
35. *Id.*; Newsom v. Gill, 145 So. 189 (Fla. 1932).
36. Perkins v. Fuquay, 143 So. 323 (Fla. 1932); Cottondale State Bank v. Oskamp Nolting Co., 59 So. 566 (Fla. 1912).
37. Fla. Stat. §§ 675.101–675.1181 (2011).
38. Texaco, Inc. v. Giltak Corp., 492 So. 2d 812 (Fla. Dist. Ct. App. 1st Dist. 1986).
39. *Id.*; Marianna Lime Prods. Co. v. McKay, 109 Fla. 275 (1933).
40. Brandon v. Pittman, 117 Fla. 678, 158 So. 443 (1934).
41. Barnett Bank of S. Fla., N.A. v. Univ. Gynecological Assocs., Inc., 638 So. 2d 595 (Fla. Dist. Ct. App. 4th Dist. 1994).

In addition, Florida courts have found that reliance on a guaranty may be sufficient to serve as consideration for a guaranty.[42]

§ 5 Notice of Acceptance

Notice of acceptance may not be required if the contract waives the notice requirement or if the guaranty is absolute.

Mutual assent of the parties is necessary to create a guaranty contract.[43] Therefore, when an offer of guaranty is made, but is rejected, such guaranty is unenforceable.[44]

Under Florida law, the terms of the guaranty itself control whether a creditor must give notice before the guaranty contract is binding.[45] The guarantor may require notice as a condition of acceptance or waive such requirement.[46] Notice of acceptance also will not be required where the guaranty is absolute, unconditional, and continuing.[47]

§ 6 Assignment

Standard contract principles apply to the assignment of a guaranty.

Contract rights may be assigned unless barred by the terms of the contract, unless such an assignment would violate public policy or some statute, or unless the contract deals with obligations of a personal nature.[48] Therefore, a contract of guaranty providing that the obligation would inure to the benefit of a lender, its successors, legal representatives, and assigns, is assignable.[49] However, an assignment does not give the assignee greater rights against the guarantor than those held by the assignor.[50]

Special rules govern whether guaranties may be assigned. The distinction turns on whether the guaranty is "special" or "general."[51] A "general" guaranty is one that is addressed to all persons generally and is enforceable by the holder of the guaranty.[52] A "special" guaranty is one that is addressed to a particular entity and is generally enforceable only by the specifically named promisee

42. Texaco, Inc. v. Giltak Corp., 492 So. 2d 812 (Fla. Dist. Ct. App. 1st Dist. 1986).
43. 38 Am. Jur. 2d Guaranty § 34 (2011).
44. Advanced Marketing Systems Corp. v. ZK Yacht Sales, 830 So. 2d 924 (Fla. Dist. Ct. App. 4th Dist. 2002); Juliana v. Salzman, 181 So. 2d 3 (Fla. Dist. Ct. App. 3d Dist. 1965).
45. *Id.*;38 Am. Jur. 2d Guaranty § 38 (2011).
46. *Id.*
47. Jones v. McConnon & Co., 130 So. 760 (Fla. 1930).
48. 3A Fla. Jur. 2d Assignments § 6 (2011).
49. Kodel v. Beacon Leasing Corp., 422 So. 2d 90 (Fla. Dist. Ct. App. 3d Dist. 1982).
50. Alderman Interior Sys., Inc. v. First National-Heller Factors, Inc., 376 So. 2d 22 (Fla. Dist. Ct. App. 2d Dist. 1979).
51. New Holland, Inc. v. Trunk, 579 So. 2d 215 (Fla. Dist. Ct. App. 5th Dist. 1991).
52. *Id.*; Brunswick Corp. v. Creel, 471 So. 2d 617 (Fla. Dist. Ct. App. 5th Dist. 1985) (a guaranty addressed to all persons generally or "to whom it may concern" is known as a general guaranty).

described in the guaranty.[53] The general rule is that a special guaranty is not assignable,[54] while a general guaranty is assignable.[55]

§ 7 Interpretation of Guaranties

Courts in Florida strictly construe the obligations of the guarantor as long as they are stated in clear and unambiguous terms. In other regards, courts will interpret a guaranty in the same manner by which they would interpret the language of any other contract.

7.1 General Principles

The principle of *strictissimi juris* guides the interpretation of the terms of a guaranty: a Florida court will strictly construe the clear and unambiguous obligations of a guarantor.[56] Of course, a liberal construction might be used to determine the intent of the parties, but after the intent is determined and the contract is free from ambiguity, the guaranty should be construed strictly.[57] As a general matter, the same principles of construction that apply to contracts will generally apply to guaranties.[58]

7.2 Guaranty of Payment versus Guaranty of Collection

A guaranty of payment is an absolute guaranty that promises to satisfy the underlying obligation to the obligee upon default by the primary obligor, which satisfaction is not conditioned upon the obligee's prior attempt to secure satisfaction from the primary obligor.[59]

On the other hand, a guaranty of collection is a conditional guaranty that merely promises to satisfy the underlying obligation only after the creditor has made a "diligent effort" to collect payment from the primary obligor.[60]

53. New Holland, Inc. v. Trunk, 579 So. 2d 215 (Fla. Dist. Ct. App. 5th Dist. 1991); Brunswick Corp. v. Creel, 471 So. 2d 617 (Fla. Dist. Ct. App. 5th Dist. 1985).
54. New Holland, Inc. v. Trunk, 579 So. 2d 215 (Fla. Dist. Ct. App. 5th Dist. 1991); Brunswick Corp. v. Creel, 471 So. 2d 617 (Fla. Dist. Ct. App. 5th Dist. 1985); Lee v. Rubin, 117 So. 2d 230 (Fla. Dist. Ct. App. 2d Dist. 1960) (if a guaranty covers future credit to be extended to a specific individual, that guaranty may not be transferred to another person).
55. New Holland, Inc. v. Trunk, 579 So. 2d 215 (Fla. Dist. Ct. App. 5th Dist. 1991); Brunswick Corp. v. Creel, 471 So. 2d 617 (Fla. Dist. Ct. App. 5th Dist. 1985).
56. Fed. Deposit Ins. Corp. v. Univ. Anclote, Inc., 764 F.2d 804 (11th Cir. 1985); Scott v. City of Tampa, 158 Fla. 712, 30 So. 2d 300 (1947).
57. Scott v. City of Tampa, 30 So. 2d 300 (Fla. 1947); City of Tampa v. W. L. Cobb Constr. Co., 185 So. 330 (Fla. 1938); People's Sav. Bank & Trust Co. v. Landstreet, 87 So. 227 (Fla. 1920).
58. Miami Nat'l Bank v. Fink, 174 So. 2d 38 (Fla. Dist. Ct. App. 3d Dist. 1965).
59. Luckey v. Thornton, 171 So. 2d 410 (Fla. Dist. Ct. App. 3d Dist. 1965); Scott v. City of Tampa, 30 So. 2d 300 (Fla. 1947) (an absolute guaranty of payment may differ from a conditional guaranty against loss as the result of nonpayment of a debt); Fegley v. Jennings, 42 So. 873 (Fla. 1902).
60. Scott v. City of Tampa, 30 So. 2d 300 (Fla. 1947).

7.3 Language Regarding the Revocation of Guaranties

Generally, a guaranty lasts until it is revoked.[61] This is true of a continuing guaranty as well.[62] However, the provisions of a guaranty itself will generally set forth the manner of revocation required.[63] The termination provisions of a guaranty may require written notice to the obligee and written receipt of such notice by the obligee. The effect of revocation is that obligations incurred after the revocation are not subject to the guaranty.

7.4 Continuing

Florida recognizes continuing guaranties.[64] A continuing guaranty covers all transactions, including future transactions.[65] A guaranty is continuing if: (1) it contemplates a future course of dealing during an indefinite period; (2) it is intended to cover a series of transactions or a succession of credits; or (3) its purpose is to give to the principal debtor a standing credit to be used from time to time.[66] Courts in Florida have found that a continuing guaranty is one that covers all transactions, including future transactions, as long as they are within the contemplation of the agreement.[67]

7.5 "Absolute and Unconditional"

See § 9.2 on "catch-all" waivers.

§ 8 Defenses of the Guarantor; Set-off

The defenses that may be available to a guarantor can be grouped into 3 categories: (1) defenses of the primary obligor; (2) guaranty defenses; and (3) other defenses.

---

61. Sanz v. Prof'l Underwriters Ins. Agency, 560 So. 2d 1254 (Fla. Dist. Ct. App. 3d Dist. 1990); Hemisphere Nat'l Bank v. Goudie, 504 So. 2d 785 (Fla. Dist. Ct. App. 3d Dist. 1987).
62. Causeway Lumber Co., Inc. v. King, 502 So. 2d 80 (Fla. Dist. Ct. App. 4th Dist. 1987); Brann v. Flagship Bank of Pinellas, N.A., 450 So. 2d 237 (Fla. Dist. Ct. App. 2d Dist. 1984).
63. In re Chishold, 54 B.R. 52 (Bankr. M.D. Fla. 1985) (oral revocation is inadequate in light of requirement in the guaranty agreement that revocation be in writing).
64. Sheth v. C.C. Altamonte Joint Venture, 976 So. 2d 85 (Fla. Dist. Ct. App. 5th Dist. 2008); U.S. Home Acceptance Corp. v. Kelly Park Hills, Inc., 542 So. 2d 463 (Fla. Dist. Ct. App. 5th Dist. 1989).
65. Sheth v. C.C. Altamonte Joint Venture, 976 So. 2d 85 (Fla. Dist. Ct. App. 5th Dist. 2008).
66. Fidelity Nat'l Bank of S. Miami v. Melo, 366 So. 2d 1218 (Fla. Dist. Ct. App. 3d Dist 1979).
67. *See* Institutional & Supermarket Equip., Inc. v. C & S Refrigeration, Inc., 609 So. 2d 66 (Fla. Dist. Ct. App. 4th Dist. 1992); Causeway Lumber Co., Inc. v. King, 502 So. 2d 80 (Fla. Dist. Ct. App. 4th Dist. 1987); Brann v. Flagship Bank of Pinellas, N.A., 450 So. 2d 237 (Fla. Dist. Ct. App. 2d Dist. 1984); Fidelity Nat'l Bank of S. Miami v. Melo, 366 So. 2d 1218 (Fla. Dist. Ct. App. 3d Dist 1979).

8.1 Defenses of the Primary Obligor

The general rule in Florida is that the guarantor steps into the shoes of the primary obligor and has all the same defenses as the primary obligor.[68] However, a guarantor may waive its right to raise the primary obligor's defenses.[69] Ultimately, "a guarantor's liability is governed by the terms of the contract."[70] A guarantor may show that the obligee failed to perform such that there is a partial or complete failure of consideration.[71] A guarantor may also assert as a defense that there was a breach by the obligee of an underlying loan agreement.[72]

8.2 Guaranty Defenses

8.2.1 Release or Impairment of Security for the Underlying Obligation

When an obligee has a security interest in collateral to secure an underlying obligation that is guarantied by a guarantor, the obligee holds that security interest "in trust" for the guarantor and has an obligation to preserve that security interest.[73] Florida courts have held that the guarantor may be discharged entirely where a bank failed to take due care to secure collateral,[74] where a holder of a promissory note released its liens on collateral securing the note,[75] and where creditors impaired security by reduction of a bond.[76] Also, Florida courts have held that this defense is waivable by the guarantor.[77]

8.2.2 Contract Defenses

A guarantor may defeat an enforcement action by showing that the alleged guaranty was not executed freely and voluntarily or by showing that the guaranty was obtained by fraud or misrepresentation by the creditor.[78]

Furthermore, guarantors may be released from liability if the creditor fails to mitigate its damages.[79] In Florida, a party cannot recover damages which that party could have reasonably avoided.[80]

---

68. Diaz v. Bell MicroProducts-Future Tech, Inc., 43 So. 3d 138 (Fla. Dist. Ct. App. 3d Dist. 2010).
69. *Id.*
70. *Id.*
71. Shaufelberger v. Mister Softee, Inc., 259 So. 2d 175 (Fla. Dist. Ct. App. 4th Dist. 1972).
72. Warner v. Caldwell, 354 So. 2d 91 (Fla. Dist. Ct. App. 3d Dist. 1977) (guaranty itself referred to a certain building loan agreement and court found that it was not an error to allow guarantor to refer to a breach of the building loan agreement as a defense to its liability under the guaranty).
73. Warner v. Caldwell, 354 So. 2d 91 (Fla. Dist. Ct. App. 3d Dist. 1977).
74. Nw. Bank v. Cortner, 275 So. 2d 317 (Fla. Dist. Ct. App. 2d Dist. 1973); Miami Nat'l Bank v. Fink, 174 So. 2d 38 (Fla. Dist. Ct. App. 3d Dist. 1965).
75. Boneh, Inc. v. Daly, 743 So. 2d 542 (Fla. Dist. Ct. App. 3d Dist. 1999).
76. Warner v. Caldwell, 354 So. 2d 91 (Fla. Dist. Ct. App. 3d Dist. 1977).
77. Tropical Jewelers, Inc. v. NationsBank, N.A. (South), 781 So. 2d 381 (Fla. Dist. Ct. App. 3d Dist. 2000).
78. 38 Am. Jur. 2d Guaranty § 54 (2011).
79. Associated Housing Corp. v. Keller Bldg. Prods. of Jacksonville, Inc., 335 So. 2d 362 (Fla. Dist. Ct. App. 1st Dist. 1976).
80. *Id.*

8.3 Other Defenses

8.3.1 Modification of the Underlying Obligation/Guaranty

Generally, a material modification of the original obligation, including a change in identity of the primary obligor, or duty to which the guaranty relates will discharge the guarantor if the guarantor did not consent to such modification either in the original guaranty or pursuant to a separate agreement.[81] Changes to a guaranty that increase a guarantor's risk without his or her consent will release a guarantor from liability.[82] Courts tend to define "material alteration" to be one that is detrimental to the guarantor,[83] so that a change within the scope of a provision of a guaranty authorizing such a change will not discharge a guarantor.[84]

8.3.2 Failure to Pursue Primary Obligor

According to Florida case law, the failure by a creditor to proceed against the primary obligor on a conditional guaranty of collection will discharge the guarantor.[85] In this instance, even if the creditor knows that suit against the primary obligor will be futile, bringing such suit is a condition precedent to his right of action against the guarantor.[86] However, a guarantor who gives an absolute or unconditional guaranty does not have this defense. One who undertakes an absolute guaranty of payment by another becomes liable immediately upon default in payment by the other.[87] There is no requirement that the creditor proceed against the primary obligor.[88]

8.3.3 Statute of Frauds

A contract of guaranty is a promise to answer for the debt of another within the statute of frauds and is generally required to be in writing.[89] However, this rule does not apply to transactions where the promise to pay the debt of another is independent and unconditional and is made for a valuable consideration, which is subsequently paid by the promisee and is of direct pecuniary value to the promisor.[90] The underlying question is whether a particular promise was an actual assumption of the liability of another, or whether it was the primary obligation of the promisor.[91] In the former instance, the promise is within the

81. Equity Title, Inc. v. First Nat'l Bank & Trust, 564 So. 2d 1182 (Fla. Dist. Ct. App. 1st Dist. 1990); Causeway Lumber Co., Inc. v. King, 502 So. 2d 80 (Fla. Dist. Ct. App. 4th Dist. 1987); Bromlow v. Pyne Corp., 490 So. 2d 1027 (Fla. Dist. Ct. App. 1st Dist. 1986).
82. Am. Eagle Credit Corp. v. Select Holding, Inc., 865 F. Supp. 800 (S.D. Fla. 1994).
83. Causeway Lumber Co., Inc. v. King, 502 So. 2d 80 (Fla. Dist. Ct. App. 4th Dist. 1987).
84. In re Clements, 185 B.R. 895 (Bankr. M.D. Fla. 1995).
85. Scott v. City of Tampa, 30 So. 2d 300 (Fla. 1947).
86. *Id.*
87. Anderson v. Trade Winds Enterprises, Corp., 241 So. 2d 174 (Fla. Dist. Ct. App. 4th Dist. 1970).
88. *Id.*
89. Juliana, Inc. v. Salzman, 181 So. 2d 3 (Fla. Dist. Ct. App. 3d Dist. 1965); Fla. Stat. § 725.01 (2011).
90. Weingart v. Allen & O'Hara, Inc., 654 F.2d 1096 (5th Cir. 1981); Moore v. Chapman, 351 So. 2d 760 (Fla. Dist. Ct. App. 1st Dist. 1977).
91. 27 Fla. Jur. 2d Frauds, Statute of § 5 (2011).

statute of frauds,[92] but in the latter instance, the promise is enforceable whether it is in writing or not.[93]

8.4 Right of Set-off

Generally, a guarantor may set off an individual claim that he has against the creditor.[94] We note that, in an action against a guarantor for a deficiency, where the guaranty has a maximum aggregate guaranty amount, the guarantor may not be entitled to off-set the guarantor's liability by the value of the collateral received by the creditor.[95]

§ 9 Waiver of Defenses by the Guarantor

Guarantors may waive many defenses; however, in order to ensure certain defenses are waived, specific waivers should be used instead of general "catch-all" waivers.

9.1 Generally

Florida courts have held that many defenses may be waived.

Courts have held that a guarantor can waive his or her right to notice of dishonor,[96] notice of default, nonpayment, or protest,[97] and notice of presentment.[98]

9.2 "Catch-all" Waivers

The standard catch-all waiver indicates that the guaranty is "absolute and unconditional" or that the guaranty is "given absolutely and unconditionally." In theory, when such a catch-all waiver is included in a guaranty, the guarantor waives almost all defenses and counterclaims potentially available in an action by the creditor arising from an obligation covered by the guaranty.

9.3 Use of Specific Waivers

No defense requires an explicit waiver.

92. *Id.*
93. *Id.*
94. Kim v. Peoples Fed. Sav. & Loan Ass'n of Tarentum, Pennsylvania, 538 So. 2d 867 (Fla. Dist. Ct. App. 1st Dist. 1989).
95. Kim v. Peoples Fed. Sav. & Loan Ass'n of Tarentum, Pennsylvania, 538 So. 2d 867 (Fla. Dist. Ct. App. 1st Dist. 1989) (guarantor had a $3,800,000 limitation of liability and a foreclosure sale netted lender $3,675,000, leaving a deficiency of $918,398.49, which was well within guarantor's $3,800,000 limitation of liability. Guarantor was not entitled to deduct the foreclosure sale amount from its total limit on liability).
96. Bryant v. Food Mach. & Chem. Corp. Niagara Chem. Div., 130 So. 2d 132 (Fla. Dist. Ct. App. 3d Dist. 1961).
97. John S. Barnes, Inc. v. Paducah Box & Basket Co., 2 So. 2d 861 (Fla. 1941).
98. Chris Craft Indus., Inc. v. Van Valkenberg, 267 So. 2d 642 (Fla. 1972).

General waivers may suffice to waive suretyship defenses. However, as a practical matter, specific waivers may be prudent. Presumably the best evidence of such waiver is an explicit statement of waiver.

§ 10 Third-party Pledgors–Defenses and Waiver Thereof

There are no reported cases or statutes in Florida specifically addressing this topic.

§ 11 Coguarantors

Unless coguarantors are jointly and severally liable, coguarantors are liable for their respective portions of the guaranteed liability.

Coguarantors are presumed to be liable for their proportion of liability on the guaranteed obligation.[99] If one of the coguarantors has paid more than his or her proportional share, then he or she is entitled to recover from the other coguarantors.[100]

Where coguarantors are liable jointly and severally, there is a presumption that they each bear full responsibility for the obligation.[101] Thus, a judgment against one will not affect the independent liability of the other.[102]

Release of one coguarantor may not release all other coguarantors.[103] The language of the agreement may indicate that a coguarantor is to remain liable despite the release of other coguarantors.[104] Furthermore, judgment against one coguarantor does not affect the independent liability of other coguarantors.[105]

§ 12 Reliance

There are no reported cases or statutes in Florida specifically addressing this topic.

99. Desrosiers v. Russell, 660 So. 2d 396 (Fla. Dist. Ct. App. 2d Dist. 1995); Curtis v. Cichon, 462 So. 2d 104 (Fla. Dist. Ct. App. 2d Dist. 1985).
100. Desrosiers v. Russell, 660 So. 2d 396 (Fla. Dist. Ct. App. 2d Dist. 1995).
101. Curtis v. Cichon, 462 So. 2d 104 (Fla. Dist. Ct. App. 2d Dist. 1985).
102. Quarngesser v. Appliance Buyers Credit Corp., 187 So. 2d 662 (Fla. Dist. Ct. App. 3d Dist. 1966).
103. U.S. Home Acceptance Corp. v. Kelly Park Hills, Inc., 542 So. 2d 662 (Fla. Dist. Ct. App. 3d Dist. 1966).
104. Bank Atlantic v. Berliner, 912 So. 2d 1260 (Fla. Dist. Ct. App. 4th Dist. 2005).
105. Quarngesser v. Appliance Buyers Credit Corp., 187 So. 2d 662 (Fla. Dist. Ct. App. 3d Dist. 1966).

§ 13 Subrogation

Subrogation is an equitable remedy that generally requires total satisfaction of the underlying obligation to the obligee prior to its exercise. Concern for protecting the creditor's interests affects the secondary obligor's right to subrogation.

A guarantor may invoke the doctrine of subrogation where he or she makes good the default of the principal obligor.[106] However, where a guarantor pays without any legal requirement to do so, the guarantor is acting as a volunteer and has no right of subrogation.[107] In Florida, a guarantor is only allowed to pursue a primary obligor where the guarantor has a legal duty to pay.[108]

§ 14 Triangular Set-off in Bankruptcy

There are no reported cases or statutes in Florida specifically addressing this topic.

§ 15 Indemnification

There are no reported cases or statutes in Florida specifically addressing this topic.

§ 16 Enforcement of Guaranties

16.1 Limitations on Recovery

Fraudulent conveyance caps on recovery under a guaranty (which prevent recovery from exceeding amounts that would render the guaranty obligations void or voidable under the Bankruptcy Code or applicable state law) may be invalid.

If the guarantors were insolvent before signing the guaranty, any liability under that guaranty might be avoidable. If the guarantors became insolvent after signing the guaranty, these type clauses might be unenforceable as ipso facto clauses. Such clauses may also be seen as impermissible attempts to contract around the fraudulent transfer statute of the Bankruptcy Code.

106. 12 Fla. Jur. 2d Contribution, Indemnity, and Subrogation § 58 (2011).
107. Photomagic Indus., Inc. v. Broward Bank, 526 So. 2d 136 (Fla. Dist. Ct. App. 3d Dist. 1988) (a guarantor may pursue the primary obligor only if the guarantor was required to pay that debtor's obligation).
108. *Id.*

16.2 Enforcement of Absolute Guaranties versus Conditional Guaranties

Where a guaranty is absolute, a guarantor becomes liable upon nonpayment by the principal obligor.[109] The guaranteed party has no duty to pursue the principal obligor before pursuing the guarantors.[110] On the other hand, where a guaranty is conditional, a guarantor incurs no liability until after the guaranteed party exercises due diligence to collect the debt from the principal obligor.[111] A guarantor's liability does not begin until the creditor has taken the necessary steps against the principal to recover the amount due.[112] Furthermore, if the guaranteed party fails to proceed against the principal in a conditional guaranty, the guarantor is discharged from his or her obligation.[113]

16.3 Exercising Rights Under a Guaranty Where the Underlying Obligation is also Secured by a Mortgage

Where a guaranty secures a promissory note and that promissory note refers to the underlying mortgage only for terms relating to acceleration of the indebtedness, no other terms or conditions of the mortgage are covered by the guaranty.[114] The guarantor's maximum liability is the original amount of the note, plus interest on the note.[115] An absolute and unconditional guaranty of a promissory note applies only to the original promissory note and not to any additional advances made under the mortgage.[116]

§ 17 Revival and Reinstatement of Guaranties

There are no reported cases or statutes in Florida specifically addressing this topic.

§ 18 Choice of Law

There are no reported cases or statutes in Florida specifically addressing this topic.

109. Mullins v. Sunshine State Serv. Corp., 540 So. 2d 222 (Fla. Dist. Ct. App. 5th Dist. 1989); Rooks v. Shader, 384 So. 2d 681 (Fla. Dist. Ct. App. 5th Dist. 1980); Anderson v. Trade Winds Enter. Corp., 241 So. 2d 174 (Fla. Dist. Ct. App. 4th Dist. 1970).
110. Quarngesser v. Appliance Buyers Credit Corp., 187 So. 2d 662 (Fla. Dist. Ct. App. 3d Dist. 1966).
111. 28 Fla. Jur. 2d Guaranty § 10 (2011).
112. Scott v. City of Tampa, 30 So. 2d 300 (Fla. 1947).
113. 28 Fla. Jur. 2d Guaranty § 43 (2011).
114. Mullins v. Sunshine State Serv. Corp., 540 So. 2d 222 (Fla. Dist. Ct. App. 5th Dist. 1989).
115. *Id.*
116. *Id.*

Georgia State Law of Guaranties

C. Edward Dobbs*
Parker, Hudson, Rainer & Dobbs LLP
1500 Marquis Two Tower
285 Peachtree Center Avenue NE
Atlanta, Georgia 30303
www.phrd.com

Contents

* This paper was edited by C. Edward Dobbs and co-authored by Mitchell M. Purvis, Douglas A. Nail, Bobbi Acord Noland, Eric W. Anderson, Kathleen O. Currey, Harrison J. Roberts, Jack C. Basham, Jason M. Loring, Seth A. Finck, Daniel H. Ennis, and C. Edward Dobbs, all attorneys in the law firm of Parker, Hudson, Rainer & Dobbs LLP.

Georgia State Law of Guaranties

§ 1 Introduction

1.1 Purpose and Scope of this Chapter

- The purpose of this chapter is to provide an overview of statutory provisions and case law in the State of Georgia relating to guaranties and suretyship contracts. The statutory law in Georgia relating to suretyship contracts was first enacted in 1863, and underwent various amendments in 1868, 1873, 1882, 1895, 1910, 1933, and 1981.
- This chapter does not discuss the rights and obligations of endorsers and other accommodation parties under the Uniform Commercial Code (UCC). The statutory law in Georgia relating to guaranties and suretyship contracts makes clear that Article 3 of Georgia's UCC governs the rights and obligations of accommodation parties with respect to negotiable instruments. Nor does this chapter address the potential impact upon the obligations under a guaranty of various other state or federal laws, including fraudulent conveyance laws and consumer protection laws (such as the Equal Credit Opportunity Act and Regulation B promulgated thereunder).
- Finally, this chapter does not deal with provisions of suretyship law that are applicable primarily or exclusively to compensated sureties, such as those providing assurance of payment in connection with payment or performance bonds in public works projects.

1.2 Sureties vs. Guarantors

Prior to 1981, Georgia law drew a distinction between contracts of suretyship and contracts of guaranty. A surety typically was bound in the same document as its principal and as part of the original undertaking and the consideration to support the suretyship contract was required to consist of some benefit flowing only to the primary obligor.[1] A guarantor's agreement, on the other hand, was usually set forth in a separate document and was limited to the payment of the underlying obligation upon the primary obligor's insolvency.[2] Furthermore, the consideration deemed adequate to support a contract of guaranty was a benefit flowing directly to the guarantor.[3]

1. Jackson v. First Bank of Clayton County, 150 Ga. App. 182, 256 S.E.2d 923 (Ga. App. 1979).
2. *See* Griswold v. Whetsell, 157 Ga. App. 800, 278 S.E.2d 753 (Ga. App. 1981).
3. Erbelding v. Noland Co., Inc., 83 Ga. App. 464, 64 S.E.2d 218 (Ga. App. 1951).

- That distinction was eliminated, effective July 1, 1981, by an amendment to O.C.G.A. § 10-7-1.[4] Today, the terms surety and guarantor are used interchangeably. Although Georgia's statutory provisions refer to sureties and suretyship contracts, the decisions since 1981 have generally used the term "guarantor" and "guaranty" to reflect modern-day preferences for those terms.
- In this chapter, the authors will use the terms "guarantor" and "guaranty" in lieu of the terms "surety" and "suretyship contract," despite statutory usage of the latter terms in certain instances, in order to comport with the terminology more recently adopted by the Georgia courts.

§ 2 Defined Terms

As used throughout this chapter, the following terms have the meanings ascribed to them below:

"Guarantor" means a person who, by contract, agrees to satisfy an underlying obligation of another to an obligee.

"Guaranty" means the contract by which the guarantor agrees to pay or perform an obligation of a primary obligor to an obligee.

"Obligee" means the person to whom the underlying obligation is owed (e.g., the lender under a loan agreement would be the obligee of the primary obligor, the borrower).

"Primary Obligor" means the person who has incurred the underlying obligation (e.g., the borrower under a loan agreement).

"Surety" has the same meaning as "guarantor."

"Suretyship contract" has the same meaning as "guaranty."

"Underlying obligation" means the obligation incurred by the primary obligor to the obligee (e.g., the obligation of the borrower under a loan agreement to repay the loan to the lender).

§ 3 Overview

3.1 Guaranty Defined

- The contract guaranty is one whereby a person obligates himself to pay the debt of another "in consideration of a benefit flowing" to the guarantor or in consideration of credit or indulgence or other benefit given to the primary obligor, with the primary obligor in either instance remaining bound on the underlying obligation.[5]

4. *See* Balboa Ins. Co. v. A.J. Kellos Constr. Co., 247 Ga. 393, 276 S.E.2d 599 (Ga. 1981).
5. O.C.G.A § 10-7-1.

- Guarantors are jointly and severally liable with the primary obligor unless the contract provides otherwise.[6]
- There is no distinction under Georgia law between contracts of suretyship and guaranty.[7]

3.2 Distinguished from Indemnities

- An indemnity arrangement is an agreement pursuant to which one party (the indemnitor) agrees to indemnify and save harmless the other party (the indemnitee) from loss or damage.
- An indemnity contract differs from a guaranty in that the former is an original, rather than a collateral, undertaking and generally requires the indemnitor to make good the indemnitee's loss resulting from his liability to another rather than from another's liability to him.[8]

3.3 Distinguished from Codebtors

- Codebtors are primarily, and jointly and severally, liable for the underlying obligation.
- While the liability, defenses, and rights of codebtors may be similar to those of guarantors, the primary distinction between the two is that a guarantor is legally subrogated to the rights of an obligee and entitled to sue on the original indebtedness, while a codebtor is only entitled to contribution.[9]

3.4 Distinguished from Endorser of an Instrument

- A person placing his signature upon an instrument other than as maker, drawer, or acceptor is deemed to be an endorser unless there is a clear indication that the intention is that such person be bound in another capacity.[10]
- If an instrument is dishonored, an endorser is obligated to pay the amount due on the instrument according to the instrument when endorsed or, if such instrument is incomplete, when such instrument is completed.[11]
- Unlike a guarantor, the obligation of an endorser may not be enforced unless the endorser is given notice of dishonor of the instrument or notice of dishonor is excused under O.C.G.A. § 11-3-504(b), which provides that notice of dishonor is excused if (a) by the terms of the instrument, notice of dishonor is not necessary to enforce the obliga-

6. O.C.G.A § 10-7-1.
7. O.C.G.A § 10-7-1.
8. The Nat'l Bank of Monroe v. Wright, 77 Ga. App. 272, 48 S.E.2d 306 (Ga. App. 1948).
9. Johnson v. AgSouth Farm Credit, 267 Ga. App. 567, 600 S.E.2d 664 (Ga. App. 2004).
10. McCarroll v. First Inv. Co., 109 Ga. App. 748, 137 S.E.2d. 319 (Ga. App. 1964).
11. O.C.G.A. § 11-3-415(a).

tion of a party to pay the instrument or (b) the party whose obligation is being enforced waived notice of dishonor.[12]

3.5 Distinguished from Letters of Credit

- A letter of credit creates an obligation of the issuer to the beneficiary that is independent of the contractual obligations between the beneficiary and account party.
- A letter of credit is distinguishable from a guaranty because the issuer is primarily liable and cannot assert defenses available to the account party that arise from a breach of the underlying contract.[13]

3.6 Distinguished from Support Agreement

- It is not uncommon, particularly in financing transactions, for a parent company or significant equity holder to agree to provide "support" to an entity borrower upon the happening of certain events, such as a loss of liquidity or breach of a financial covenant in credit documents. That support may take the form of either a contribution to the equity capital of the borrower or the making of a loan that is subordinated in right of payment to the indebtedness outstanding under the financing transaction. The proceeds of the equity contribution or subordinated loan may either be used in the borrower's business or may be earmarked for reduction in payment of the outstanding loans in the financing transaction.
- A support arrangement differs from a guaranty in that the former is intended to provide needed liquidity to the primary obligor, whereas a guaranty is a security transaction intended to pay all or part of an underlying obligation after the primary obligor's default in payment.

3.7 Compensated vs. Gratuitous Guarantees

Compensated guarantors can be distinguished from gratuitous guarantors in that the rule of strict construction applies only to gratuitous guaranties and not to compensated guaranties.[14] Further, unlike gratuitous guarantors, compensated guarantors are "not favorites of the law."[15]

12. O.C.G.A. § 11-3-503(b).
13. Dibrell Bros. Int'l S.A. v. Banca Nazionale Del Lavoro, 38 F.3d 1571 (11th Cir. 1994).
14. Houston Gen. Ins. Co. v. Brock Constr. Co., Inc., 241 Ga. 460, 246 S.E.2d 316 (Ga. 1978).
15. Sims' Crane Serv., Inc. v. Reliance Ins. Co., 514 F. Supp. 1033 (S.D. Ga. 1981), aff'd, 667 F.2d 30 (11th Cir. 1982).

§ 4 Validity of Contract of Guaranty

4.1 General Contract Rules Apply

- A guaranty is one type of a contract and therefore the law of contracts, including the doctrines of mutual assent and consideration, generally apply.[16]

4.2 Statute of Frauds

- O.C.G.A. § 13-5-30 requires that any agreement pursuant to which one party agrees to be liable for the debt of another must be in writing and signed by the party to be charged.[17]
- However, a promise to pay the debt of another is not subject to the statute of frauds and need not be in writing if the promise is an original undertaking instead of a collateral one (that is, the promisor intends to substitute itself for the original primary obligor).[18]
- To satisfy the statute of frauds, a guaranty must identify the debt,[19] the primary obligor, the guarantor, and the obligee.[20]
- O.C.G.A. § 24-6-3(a) provides that "[a]ll contemporaneous writings shall be admissible to explain each other."[21]

4.3 Capacity of Individual Guarantor to Contract

- To constitute a valid guaranty by an individual, the guarantor must have legal capacity to contract.[22]

16. C.L.D.F., Inc. v. The Aramore, LLC, 290 Ga. App. 271, 659 S.E.2d 695 (Ga. App. 2008).
17. *See* Management Recruiters of Atlanta North, Inc. v. J&B Smith Co., 184 Ga. App. 662, 362 S.E.2d 462 (Ga. App. 1987) (oral promise to guarantee after obligee had rendered service and primary obligor had been charged was a collateral promise, rather than original undertaking, and therefore was unenforceable under the statute of frauds).
18. Pope v. Triangle Chemical Co., 157 Ga. App. 386, 277 S.E.2d 758 (Ga. App. 1981) (when a party "guarantees" another's debts with words indicating responsibility for the debt, and credit is extended in reliance upon such words, a jury could find that the promise was an original undertaking not subject to the statute of frauds); Howard, Weil, Labouisse, Fredericks, Inc. v. Abercrombie, 140 Ga. App. 436, 231 S.E.2d 451 (Ga. App. 1976) (if an agreement of the guarantor is an original undertaking, one that furthers the guarantor's own interests rather than underwriting the debt of another, it is not within the statute of frauds).
19. Patterson v. Bennett St. Properties, 314 Ga. App. 896, 726 S.E.2d 147 (Ga. App. 2012) (guaranty sufficiently identified debt guaranteed as obligation of tenant when described lease that was assigned to an assignee even though actual assignment did not occur until after execution of the guaranty).
20. John Deere Co. v. Haralson, 278 Ga. 192, 193, 599 S.E.2d 164 (Ga. 2004); Roden Electrical Supply v. Faulker, 240 Ga. App. 556, 524 S.E.2d 247 (Ga. App. 1999) (where the guaranty omits the name of the primary obligor, the guarantor, or the obligee, the guaranty may be found to be unenforceable as a matter of law). *See also* Schroeder v. Hunter Douglas, Inc., 172 Ga. App. 897, 898, 324 S.E.2d 746 (Ga. App. 1984) (a guaranty must, either in itself or in connection with other writings, identify the debt that is the subject of the promise, indicate knowledge of both the amount promised to be paid and the time the debt becomes due). *But see* Brzowski v. Quantum Nat'l Bank, 311 Ga. App. 769, 717 S.E.2d 290 (Ga. App. 2011) (execution date of a personal guaranty is not an essential element required to satisfy the statute of frauds).
21. *See* Dabbs v. Key Equip. Finance, Inc., 303 Ga. App. 570, 573, 694 S.E.2d 161 (Ga. App. 2010) (as long as all the necessary terms are contained in signed contemporaneous writings, statutory requirements and purpose of the statute of frauds have been met, whether or not writings are cross-referenced). *See also* O.C.G.A. § 13-5-30(a).
22. O.C.G.A. § 13-3-1.

- In Georgia, the contract of a minor (less than 18 years of age) or a mentally incompetent person is voidable.[23]

4.4 Power of Entities to Guarantee

- Entities formed in Georgia have the statutory power to give guaranties in furtherance of their business interests unless otherwise provided in their governing documents. The power to guarantee is specifically granted to business corporations[24] and not-for-profit corporations,[25] and is part of the inherent general power that general partnerships and limited liability partnerships possess under O.C.G.A. § 14-8-9; limited partnerships possess under O.C.G.A. § 14-9-106(a); limited partnerships formed after February 15, 1952, and before July 1, 1988, possess under O.C.G.A. § 14-9A-21; and limited liability companies possess under O.C.G.A. § 14-11-202, in each case as such general power may be limited in any manner pursuant to the applicable partnership agreement or articles of organization or operating agreement.
- Under current regulations, a national bank may not issue a guaranty unless the bank has a substantial interest in the performance of the underlying obligation or has a segregated deposit from a customer sufficient to secure reimbursement of any amounts the bank is called upon to pay under the bank's guaranty.[26] State-chartered banks also have limited power to grant guaranties.[27]
- Pursuant to the same statutes cited above, Georgia entities with the power to make guaranties generally have the power to secure any of their obligations by mortgage or pledge of any of their properties, unless otherwise provided in their governing documents.[28]

4.5 Authority of Entities to Guarantee

- For any Georgia corporation required to have a board of directors,[29] all corporate powers must be "exercised by or under the authority of, and the business and affairs of the corporation managed under the direction of, its board of directors," subject to any agreement among the shareholders meeting the requirements of O.C.G.A. § 14-2-732, including the articles of incorporation and bylaws, if approved by the shareholders.[30]

---

23. O.C.G.A. §§ 13-3-20 & 13-3-24.
24. O.C.G.A. § 14-2-302.
25. O.C.G.A. § 14-3-302.
26. 12 C.F.R. Ch. 1, § 7.1017 (2010).
27. O.C.G.A. § 7-1-290.
28. *See also* O.C.G.A. § 14-2-1201 ("A corporation may, on the terms and conditions and for the consideration determined by the board of directors . . . [m]ortgage, pledge, dedicate to the repayment of indebtedness, whether with or without recourse, or otherwise encumber any or all of its property whether or not in the usual and regular course of business.").
29. *See* O.C.G.A. § 14-2-801(a).
30. O.C.G.A. § 14-2-801(b). *See also* O.C.G.A. § 14-3-801 (similar rule for Georgia nonprofit corporations).

- To confirm due authorization by an entity, the obligee should require adoption of a resolution by the board of directors or other governing persons for the entity that evidences authorization for the execution, delivery, and performance of the guaranty and should obtain certification of the resolution to the obligee, as well as opinions of guarantor's counsel, where appropriate to the transaction. The inclusion in the authorizing resolution of a reference to the economic benefit inuring to the guarantor entity may be helpful to evidence the business interests of the guarantor furthered by the guaranty. Obtaining such express authorization will avoid the risks of relying on apparent authority of an officer or other representative.[31] Those pitfalls include the issue of establishing that the obligee accepted the guaranty without knowledge of the signer's lack of authority.
- The execution of any contract by a president or vice-president of a Georgia corporation or a foreign corporation doing business in Georgia, attested by the secretary or assistant secretary of the corporation or other officer to whom the bylaws or the directors have delegated the responsibility for authenticating records of the corporation, attests that the execution of the document on behalf of the corporation has been duly authorized and the incumbency and genuineness of the signature of any officer executing the document.[32] The same presumptions arise from the presence of a corporate seal (or facsimile thereof) on a contract, conveyance, or similar document executed by a corporation and attested by the secretary or assistant secretary of the corporation or other officer to whom the bylaws or the directors have delegated the responsibility for authenticating records of the corporation.[33] When the corporate seal (or facsimile thereof) is affixed to any document, or where a document is executed by the president or a vice president of the corporation, and in either case is attested by the secretary or assistant secretary of the corporation or other officer to whom the bylaws or the directors have delegated the responsibility for authenticating records of the corporation, a third party without knowledge or reason to know to the contrary may rely on such document as being what it purports to be.[34] Affixation of the corporate seal is optional and does not impair the validity of the document or any action taken in pursuance thereof or in reliance thereon.[35]
- A statement of partnership signed by all of the partners may be recorded in the office of the clerk of the superior court in any county in Georgia to state any limitations on the authority of, or authority beyond that described in the Georgia Uniform Partnership Act on the

31. *See, e.g.,* Anderton v. Certainteed Corp., 201 Ga. App. 538, 411 S.E.2d 558 (Ga. App. 1991) (vice president had, at least, apparent authority to execute the guaranty on behalf of the corporate guarantor in the president's absence where the corporation had passed a resolution authorizing the president and secretary to sign the guaranty).
32. O.C.G.A § 14-2-151(b).
33. O.C.G.A § 14-2-151(a).
34. O.C.G.A § 14-2-151(c)
35. O.C.G.A § 14-2-151(d).

part of, one or more partners to act on behalf of the other partners or the partnership that the partnership desires to disclose.[36]

- The act of every partner of a Georgia general partnership, every manager of a Georgia limited liability company (LLC) (if the articles of organization provide that management of the LLC is vested in a manager or managers), and every member (in any other Georgia LLC) "for apparently carrying on the in the usual way" the business of the entity binds the entity, unless the person so acting has in fact no authority to act for the entity in the particular matter and the person with whom such actor is dealing has knowledge of the fact that the actor has no such authority.[37] Conversely, an act of a partner, member, or manager, as the case may be, that is not "apparently" for the carrying on of the business of the entity in the usual way does not bind the entity unless authorized by the other partners or in the partnership agreement (in the case of a partnership) or in accordance with a written operating agreement (in the case of a LLC), in each case at the time of the transaction or at any other time.[38] No act of a partner of a general partnership or of a member or manager of a LLC in contravention of a restriction on authority shall bind the respective entity to persons having knowledge of the restriction.[39]
- A general partner of a Georgia limited partnership has the power to act as an agent of the limited partnership to the same extent that a general partner of a Georgia general partnership may act for the general partnership, except as otherwise provided in the limited partnership agreement.[40]
- If the guarantor entity is not "apparently" furthering its business interests by issuing the guaranty, or if the agency of the persons purportedly authorizing the guaranty is not conclusively established, then a best practice would be for the obligee to require consent of all of the holders of the equity interests in the guarantor entity in addition to the governing persons' authorization described above. If action by the equity interest holders is required, the obligee would be well-advised to obtain a certified copy of the consent and an opinion of counsel to the guarantor.
- Even in the absence of express, statutory or apparent authority, the obligee under an entity guaranty may defend its validity by proving the entity's "ratification."[41]

---

36. O.C.G.A. § 14-8-10.1.
37. O.C.G.A § 14-8-9(1) and O.C.G.A § 14-11-301(a) and (b).
38. O.C.G.A §§ 14-8-9(2) & 14-11-301(c).
39. O.C.G.A §§ 14-8-9(4) & O.C.G.A § 14-11-301(d).
40. O.C.G.A. § 14-9-403(a).
41. *See* Holliday Constr. Co. v. Sandy Springs Assocs., Inc., 198 Ga. App. 20, 400 S.E.2d 380 (Ga. App. 1990), quoting Western American Life Ins. Co. v. Hicks, 135 Ga. App. 90, 91, 217 S.E.2d 323 (Ga. App. 1975) ("Where a corporation knowing all of the facts accepts and uses the proceeds of an unauthorized contract executed in its behalf without authority, the corporation may be bound because of ratification."); Lanier Ins. Agency v. Citizen Bank, 168 Ga. App. 424, 309 S.E.2d 419 (Ga. App. 1983) (found ratification of officer's allegedly unauthorized act in signing corporate guaranty).

4.6 Consideration

- To be enforceable, a guaranty must be supported by consideration, but that consideration may take many forms.
- There is no requirement that the consideration flow personally to the guarantor in order to support a binding guaranty.[42]
- A benefit to the guarantor is sufficient as consideration, but not required.[43] Extension of credit or other indulgence given to the primary obligor may suffice.[44]
- Other benefits given to the primary obligor may suffice. For example, sufficient consideration may be found to support a guaranty when the obligee is induced by the guarantor to:
  - release valuable liens securing the underlying obligation;[45]
  - purchase a portion of a business in exchange for extending credit;[46]
  - relinquish a claim against the primary obligor;[47]
  - extend credit after execution of the guaranty;[48]
  - forbearance from suit against the primary obligor for a specific period of time;[49]
  - provide valuable services to the primary obligor.[50]
- A recitation in the guaranty of "value received" by the guarantor does not necessarily establish consideration.[51] However, a recitation of nominal amount has been held to be sufficient.[52]

---

42. First Union Nat'l Bank of Georgia v. Gurley, 208 Ga. App. 647, 431 S.E.2d 379 (Ga. App. 1993).
43. Collins v. Gwinnett Bank & Trust Co., 149 Ga. App. 658, 255 S.E.2d 122 (Ga. App. 1979).
44. Congress Fin. Corp. v. Commercial Technology, 910 F. Supp. 637. (N.D. Ga. 1995). *See also* Steiner v. Handler, 229 Ga. App. 883, 495 S.E.2d 132 (Ga. App. 1997).
45. First Union Nat'l Bank v. Gurley, 208 Ga. App. 647, 431 S.E.2d 379 (Ga. App. 1993), *cert. denied* 1993 Ga. LEXIS 1073 (Ga. Nov. 5, 1993).
46. Growth Properties of Florida, Ltd., IV v. Wallace, 168 Ga. App. 893, 310 S.E.2d 715 (Ga. App. 1983), *cert. denied*; McGarr v. Bank of Pinehurst, 159 Ga. App. 116, 282 S.E.2d 739 (Ga. App. 1981).
47. First Union Nat'l Bank of Georgia v. Gurley, 208 Ga. App. 647, 431 S.E.2d 379 (Ga. App. 1993); *cert. denied* 1993 Ga. LEXIS 1073 (Ga. Nov. 5, 1993).
48. Rohm & Haas Co. v. Gainesville Paint & Supply Co., 225 Ga. App. 441, 482 S.E.2d 888 (Ga. App. 1997).
49. Graphic Prep v. Graphcom, Inc., 206 Ga. App. 689, 426 S.E.2d 183 (Ga. App. 1992), *cert. denied*, 1993 Ga. LEXIS 138; Casgar v. Citizens & S. Nat'l Bank, 188 Ga. App. 234, 372 S.E.2d 815 (Ga. App. 1988) (forbearance by an obligee to collect an obligation otherwise due and payable will constitute sufficient consideration to support a contract); Berry v. Atlanta Outdoor Advertising, Inc., 164 Ga. App. 541, 298 S.E.2d 268 (Ga. App. 1982). *But see* Loewenherz v. Weil, 33 Ga. App. 760, 127 S.E. 883 (Ga. App. 1925) (mere forbearance by plaintiff to prosecute the judgment, without even so much as a request therefor, does not afford consideration for the promise of the defendants to be liable as guarantors).
50. Holtzclaw v. City of Dalton, 189 Ga. App. 650, 377 S.E.2d 196 (Ga. App. 1988).
51. *See* O.C.G.A § 10-7-1, Wolkin v. Nat'l Acceptance Co., 222 Ga. 487, 150 S.E.2d 831 (Ga. 1966); Gwinnett Commercial Bank v. Flake, 151 Ga. App. 578, 260 S.E.2d 523 (Ga. App. 1979) (determining that the phrase "for value received" does not show conclusively that there was consideration).
52. Hornsby v. First Nat'l Bank, 154 Ga. App. 155, 267 S.E.2d 780 (Ga. App. 1980) (finding that recitation of consideration in the guaranty pierced appellants' defense of failure of consideration); Hickok v. Starka Inds., Inc., 154 Ga. App. 589, 269 S.E.2d 84 (Ga. App. 1980) (determining that consideration of $1.00 stated in suretyship agreement of business debts already owing was sufficient and suretyship contract was therefore valid); DOT v. Am. Ins. Co., 268 Ga. 505, 491 S.E.2d 328 (Ga. 1997) (finding that language stating it is "understood and agreed that…in consideration of the sum of One Dollar cash in hand paid, receipt whereof is hereby acknowledged" is sufficient to form a contract supported by adequate consideration).

- Failure to pay the recited consideration is not determinative of whether consideration was provided for the guaranty.[53]
- A guaranty must be founded on some new type of consideration, independent of that flowing to the primary obligor, and flowing directly to the guarantor[54] or in consideration of credit or indulgence or other benefit given to the principal.[55]
- A promise to pay a pre-existing debt of another without any detriment or inconvenience to the obligee or any benefits obtained by the guarantor in consequence of the undertaking is a nullity.[56] Past consideration given to the primary obligor will not support a contract of guaranty.[57] However, the recitation of the guarantor's receipt of $1.00 in a guaranty of business debts that had already been incurred has been held to be sufficient consideration to support the guaranty.[58] Moreover, where the guaranty contains an unconditional promise to pay, no additional consideration is needed to support the guaranty even if the guaranty is for an antecedent debt.[59]

4.7 Effect of Sealed Instrument

- To constitute a "sealed instrument," there must be both a recital in the body of the instrument of an intention to use a seal and the affixing of a seal after the signature.[60]
- A seal includes "impressions on chapter itself, as well as impressions on wax or wafers," and "with the exception of official seals, a scrawl or any other mark intended as a seal shall be held as such."[61] Georgia courts have held that the seal after the signature can be designated by either the word "seal" or the letters "L.S.,"[62] and the words "witness my hand and seal" is a satisfactory recital within the body of the instrument.[63] The phrase "signed, sealed and delivered in the presence of" preceding the name of a witness does not indicate an intention of the parties to create a sealed instrument.[64] A contract may be "under

53. Jolles v. Wittenberg, 148 Ga. App. 805, 253 S.E.2d 203 (Ga. App. 1979) (where a contract contains a recital of the payment of $1 as its consideration, the contract is valid though the sum named was not actually paid but there is an obligation to pay that sum, enforceable by the other party); Southern Bell Tel. & Tel. Co. v. Harris, 117 Ga. 1001, 44 S.E. 885 (Ga. 1903).
54. Jackson v. First Bank of Clayton County, 150 Ga. App. 182, 256 S.E.2d 923 (Ga. App. 1979); Bearden v. Ebcap Supply Co., 108 Ga. App. 375, 133 S.E.2d 62 (Ga. App. 1963); Durham v. Greenwold, 188 Ga. 165, 3 S.E.2d 585 (Ga. 1939); Etheridge v. Rawleigh Co., 29 Ga. App. 698, 116 S.E. 903 (Ga. 1923).
55. O.C.G.A. § 10-7-1; First Union Nat'l Bank of Georgia v. Gurley, 208 Ga. App. 647, 431 S.E.2d 379 (Ga. App. 1993).
56. Helton v. Jasper Banking Co., 311 Ga. App. 363, 715 S.E.2d 765 (Ga. App. 2011).
57. *See* Shropshire v. Alostar Bank of Commerce, 314 Ga. App. 310, 724 S.E.2d 33 (Ga. App. 2012).
58. Hickok v. Starka Inds., Inc., 154 Ga. App. 589, 269 S.E.2d 84 (Ga. App. 1980) (consideration of $1 stated in guaranty of business debts already owing was sufficient and guaranty was therefore valid).
59. American Viking Contractors, Inc. v. Scribner Equipment Co., 745 F.2d 1365 (11th Cir. 1984) (construing O.C.G.A. § 11-3-408, which provides that "want or failure of consideration is a defense...except that no consideration is necessary for an instrument or obligation thereon given in payment of or as security for an antecedent obligation of any kind.").
60. McCalla v. Stuckey, 233 Ga. App. 397, 504 S.E.2d 269 (Ga. App. 1998).
61. O.C.G.A. § 1-3-3 (17).
62. Crosby v. Burkhalter, 50 Ga. App. 610, 179 S.E. 180 (Ga. App. 1935).
63. Scott v. Gaulding, 60 Ga. App. 306, 3 S.E.2d 766 (Ga. App. 1939).
64. Baxley Hardware Co. v. Morris, 165 Ga. 359, 140 S.E. 869 (Ga. 1927).

seal" as to some parties and not as to others. Even though some of the signatures of the parties may be followed by the word "seal," if no such designation accompanies the signatures of other parties, the contract is not under seal as to those parties whose names are not followed by the word "seal."[65]

- A document executed "under seal" is conclusively presumed to be supported by consideration.[66]
- The statute of limitations for enforcement of contracts under seal is 20 years, as opposed to the usual six-year statute of limitations that governs enforcement of simple contracts in writing.[67]

4.8 Notice of Acceptance of Guaranty

- Generally, a valid contract in Georgia must be accepted by the offeree.[68] Acceptance may be made by notice of acceptance or a specific action if the contract permits or contemplates that acceptance may be made by such action.[69]
- With respect to a guaranty, notice of acceptance is required unless performance, such as funding of the loan that is guaranteed by such guaranty, is specified by the guaranty.[70] In the case of an absolute guaranty where the underlying obligation is fixed and the obligation is effective upon the doing or forbearance of a definite occurrence, no notice of acceptance of the guaranty is required to form a binding contract.[71]
- Most well-drafted guarantees in Georgia will contain a waiver of notice of the obligee's acceptance.

---

65. *See* McCalla v. Stuckey, 233 Ga. App. 397, 504 S.E.2d 269 (Ga. App. 1998).
66. *See, e.g.*, Jolles v. Wittenberg, 148 Ga. App. 805, 253 S.E.2d 203 (Ga. App. 1979) (a contract under seal raises a prima facia presumption of consideration and addition of a recital of any nominal consideration makes the presumption conclusive); Smith v. First Nat'l Bank of Atlanta, 199 Ga. App. 858, 406 S.E.2d 519 (Ga. App. 1991) (presumption of consideration with respect to guaranty executed under seal was conclusive, and fact that guarantor did not receive $5 recited was immaterial).
67. *Compare* O.C.G.A. § 9-3-23 (documents under seal) *with* § 9-3-24 (simple contracts in writing).
68. Lamb v. Decatur Fed. Sav. & Loan Ass'n, 201 Ga. App. 583, 411 S.E.2d 527 (Ga. App. 1991), *reconsideration denied*, 411 S.E.2d 527.
69. Upshaw v. S. Wholesale Flooring Co., 197 Ga. App. 511, 398 S.E.2d 749 (Ga. App. 1990).
70. Upshaw v. S. Wholesale Flooring Co., 197 Ga. App. 511, 398 S.E.2d 749 (Ga. App. 1990); Wehle v. Baker, 97 Ga. App. 111, 102 S.E.2d 661 (Ga. App. 1958) (continuing guaranty became effective when plaintiff, in reliance thereon, lent money to primary obligor, without the necessity of plaintiff giving notice of acceptance); Ferguson v. Atlanta Newspapers, Inc., 93 Ga. App. 622, 92 S.E.2d 321 (Ga. App. 1956) (holding that "where an offer of guaranty contemplates acceptance by the actual extension of credit, it is unnecessary for the obligee to notify the guarantors of its acceptance of the guaranty.").
71. Wehle v. Baker, 97 Ga. App. 111, 102 S.E.2d 661 (Ga. App. 1958).

§ 5 Nature and Extent of Guarantor's Obligation

5.1 Nature of Obligation

- The guarantor's obligation is "accessory to" that of the primary obligor.[72] Accessory means that the liability of the guarantor is measured by the liability of the primary obligor and cannot exceed it. Consequently, the guarantor is not liable if the primary obligor is not.[73]
- If the obligation of the primary obligor becomes "extinct," the guarantor's obligation ceases even if has been reduced to judgment.[74] The bankruptcy of the primary obligor does not release the guarantor.[75] Moreover, a guaranty can be enforced against the guarantor even though a recovery on the underlying obligation is barred by statute of limitations. A verdict for the primary obligor, however, discharges the guarantor.[76]
- Unless otherwise provided in the guaranty, a guarantor is jointly and severally liable for the underlying obligation with the primary obligor and with coguarantors.[77] In the absence of any contractual language altering the statutory terms, coguarantors are likely to be found to be several, as well as joint, obligors.[78] A guaranty is not necessarily inconsistent where it limits the amount of the guarantors' liability but still provides that the guarantors are jointly and severally liable for that amount.[79]
- A person who is subject to service of process must be joined as a party in the applicable action if, in his absence, complete relief cannot be afforded among those who are already parties.[80] Where the guarantor and primary obligor are several, as well as joint, obligors, the primary obligor is not an indispensable party in the obligee's suit against the guarantor on the underlying obligation, absent a provision in the guaranty establishing a different relationship.[81]

---

72. O.C.G.A. § 10-7-2; Parker v. Puckett, 129 Ga. App. 265, 199 S.E.2d 343 (Ga. App. 1973) (noting that the "obligation of the surety is assessory to that of his principal, and if the latter from any cause becomes extinct the former shall cease of course, even though it is in judgment. If, however, the original contract of the principal was invalid from a disability to contract, and this disability was known to the surety, he shall still be bound.").
73. Fidelity & Deposit Co. of Maryland v. West Point Const. Co., 178 Ga. App. 578, 344 S.E.2d 268 (Ga. App. 1986).
74. O.C.G.A. § 10-7-2.
75. First Nat'l Bank of Paulding County v. Millender, 149 Ga. App. 65, 253 S.E.2d 417 (Ga. App. 1979) ("[I]t is well settled that the discharge of claims against a debtor in a reorganization case does not discharge or affect the liability of a co-debtor, guarantor, indorser, insurer, or other surety."); Bradley v. Swift & Co., 93 Ga. App. 842, 93 S.E.2d 364 (Ga. App. 1956) (finding that a bankruptcy discharge in favor of the principal from liability under the terms of a contract does not generally operate to discharge the principal's guarantor).
76. Marietta Fertilizer Co. v. Gary, 22 Ga. App. 604, 96 S.E. 711 (Ga. App. 1918); Schlittler & Johnson v. Dearing Harvester Co., 3 Ga. App. 83, 59 S.E. 342 (Ga. App. 1907).
77. O.C.G.A. § 10-7-1; Ford Motor Credit Co. v. Sullivan, 170 Ga. App. 718, 318 S.E.2d 188 (Ga. App. 1984).
78. Floyd Davis Sales, Inc. v. Central Mortgage Corp. of Michigan, 197 Ga. App. 532, 398 S.E.2d 820 (Ga. App. 1990).
79. Twisdale v. Georgia Railroad Bank & Trust Co., 129 Ga. App. 18, 198 S.E.2d 396 (Ga. App. 1973).
80. O.C.G.A. § 9-11-19(a)(1).
81. Floyd Davis Sales, Inc. v. Central Mortgage Corp. of Michigan, 197 Ga. App. 532, 398 S.E.2d 820 (Ga. App. 1990); Sloan v. S. Floridabanc Fed. Sav. & Loan Ass'n, 197 Ga. App. 601, 398 S.E.2d 720 (Ga. App. 1990) ("O.C.G.A. § 9-11-19 has no application where liability is joint and several and the plaintiff has a right of election as to which defendants plaintiff will proceed against.").

5.2 Assignment of Underlying Obligation

- A transfer of the underlying obligation is generally held to operate as an assignment of the guaranty, absent express language to the contrary in the guaranty.[82]
- Where a guaranty runs in favor of the "holder" of the underlying obligation, the transfer of the principal obligation also operates as an assignment of a guarantor's obligation.[83]
- While the transfer of the principal obligation automatically passes the guaranty on to the transferee, the rule applies only where the assignor of the underlying obligation is also the obligee of the guaranty.[84]
- Where a guaranty was assigned by the original obligee to a third party, and the guarantor did not attempt to revoke or terminate the guaranty, the guarantor remains liable not only for the indebtedness in existence at the time of the assignment but also for future extensions of credit made by the assignee after the assignment to the primary obligor.[85]

5.3 Liability for Attorneys' Fees

- The guarantor may be liable for the payment of the obligee's attorneys' fees, either as a result of an inclusion of language to that effect in the guaranty itself or by virtue of having guaranteed all liabilities of the primary obligor which include the obligee's attorneys' fees.[86]
- A guarantor's obligation to pay attorneys' fees has been held to be included in a provision that promises "prompt payment, at maturity, of any and all notes evidencing such advances, all renewals and extensions thereof, and all other indebtedness that is now, or hereafter may be or become owing by Borrower to Lender."[87]
- Under O.C.G.A. § 13-1-11, an obligation to pay attorneys' fees upon any evidence of the indebtedness is valid and enforceable and collectable if such note or other indebtedness is collected by or through an attorney after maturity.[88] If the evidence of the indebtedness provides for attorneys' fees in a specific percent of the principal and interest owing thereon, such provision is enforceable up to

---

82. Ampex Credit Corp. v. Bateman, 554 F.2d 750 (5th Cir. 1977) (citing Georgia law).
83. Hazel v. Tharpe & Brooke, Inc., 159 Ga. App. 415, 283 S.E.2d 653 (Ga. App. 1981); Schroeder v. Hunter Douglas, Inc., 172 Ga. App. 897, 324 S.E.2d 746 (Ga. App. 1984) ("A transfer of the underlying principal obligation operates as an assignment of the guaranty.").
84. Hurst v. Stith Equipment Co., 133 Ga. App. 374, 210 S.E.2d 851 (Ga. App. 1974) (where parent corporation was named as obligor under a lease and subsequently assigned that lease to another party, the parent did not have any benefit under an accompanying guaranty that had been entered into in favor of the parent corporation's subsidiary).
85. Crowe v. Congress Financial Corp. (Southern), 196 Ga. App. 36, 395 S.E.2d 321 (Ga. App. 1990), *cert. denied*, 1990 Ga. LEXIS 618 (Ga. Sept. 4, 1990) (finding that, following the assignment of the principal debt and the guaranty, the guarantor did not attempt to cancel, revoke, or terminate the guaranty, and that the provisions of the guaranty did not limit the guarantor's obligations to the advances made by the original lender).
86. Rohm & Haas Co. v. Gainesville Paint & Supply Co., 225 Ga. App. 441, 483 S.E.2d 888 (Ga. App. 1997), reconsideration denied, March 13, 1997.
87. McGlaun v. Southwest Georgia Production Credit Ass'n., 256 Ga. 648, 352 S.E.2d 558 (Ga. 1987).
88. O.C.G.A. § 13-1-11(a).

an amount not exceeding 15 percent of the principal and interest owing on the note or other indebtedness.[89] If the evidence of the indebtedness provides for the payment of reasonable attorneys' fees without specifying any specific percent, such provision is construed to mean 15 percent of the first $500.00 of principal and interest owing on the note or other indebtedness and 10 percent of the amount of principal and interest owing in excess of $500.00.[90] The holder of the evidence of the indebtedness is required to notify in writing the party to be held liable that the Georgia Code provisions relative to payment of attorneys' fees in addition to the principal and interest will be enforced and that such party has 10 days from the receipt of such notice to pay the principal and interest without the attorneys' fees.[91] The applicable court may hold a hearing to determine the attorneys' fees to award under this section, and the amount of attorneys' fees awarded will be an amount found by the applicable court to be reasonable and necessary for asserting the rights of the party requesting attorneys' fees.[92] If provided for under the guaranty in question, courts have concluded that attorneys' fees may be collected as part of the guaranteed obligations so long as the obligee complies with O.C.G.A. § 13-1-11.[93]

5.4 General vs. Specific Guaranties[94]

- A general guaranty is one that is addressed "to whom it may concern" and any person is authorized to rely upon it in extending credit to the primary obligor.
- A special guaranty is made in favor of a specific party identified in the guaranty and the guaranty does not, absent contrary language, cover underlying obligations incurred to an assignee after assignment of the guaranty.

5.5 Absolute (or unconditional) vs. Conditional Guaranties

- If the liability of the guarantor is fixed by the mere default of the primary obligor, the guaranty is absolute; but if the guarantor's liability depends upon any other event than the nonperformance of

89. O.C.G.A. § 13-1-11(a)(1).
90. O.C.G.A. § 13-1-11(a)(2). Note that if an award of attorneys' fees under O.C.G.A. § 13-1-11(a)(2) is in an amount greater than $20,000.00, the party required to pay such fees can petition the applicable court for a determination as to the reasonableness of such attorneys' fees. O.C.G.A. § 13-1-11(b)(1). The petitioning party is required to submit an affidavit to the applicable court with evidence of attorneys' fees, and the party required to pay such fees may respond to such affidavit. O.C.G.A. § 13-1-11(b)(2).
91. O.C.G.A. § 13-1-11(a)(3).
92. O.C.G.A. § 13-1-11(b)(3).
93. *See* Westinghouse Credit Corp. v. Hall, 144 B.R. 568 (S.D. Ga. 1992); Federal Deposit Ins. Corp. v. Willis, 497 F. Supp. 272 (S.D. Ga. 1980); Groover v. Commercial Bancorp, 220 Ga. App. 13, 467 S.E.2d 355 (Ga. App. 1996); Rodgers v. First Union Nat'l Bank, 220 Ga. App. 821, 470 S.E.2d 246 (Ga. App. 1996).
94. We were unable to find Georgia case law that has adopted the following statements.

the primary obligor, it is a conditional guaranty.[95] "A guaranty of payment, the unconditional or absolute guaranty, is substantially the same as a suretyship obligation. The only precondition to the guarantor's liability is that the principal obligor has not paid the debt when it fell due."[96]
- In the case of an absolute (or unconditional) guaranty, the guarantor is bound to pay without the necessity of providing notice of default or any requirement that the obligee first pursue the primary obligor as a condition to liability.[97]
- An obligee has no statutory duty to mitigate damages when the guaranty is an absolute obligation to pay.[98]
- A guarantor may consent in advance to conduct that would otherwise result in a discharge, and such consent does not affect the absolute and unconditional obligations under the guaranty.[99]

5.6 Payment vs. Collection Guaranties

- Generally, under a guaranty of payment, the guarantor is jointly and severally liable with the primary obligor for payment of the underlying obligation. Under a guaranty of collection, the guarantor is only obliged to pay if the obligee cannot collect from the primary obligor after reasonable collection efforts, which has been held in essence to be a guaranty of the primary obligor's solvency.[100]
- Prior to 1981, Georgia recognized a distinction between a "surety" and a "guarantor," with a surety generally having been considered a guarantor of payment, and a "guarantor" considered a guarantor of collection.[101] In 1981, by statute the Georgia legislature abolished that distinction.[102]

---

95. Williams Valve Co. v. Amorous, 19 Ga. App. 155, 91 S.E. 240 (Ga. App. 1917).
96. Ford Motor Credit Co. v. Sullivan, 170 Ga. App. 718, 318 S.E.2d 188 (Ga. App. 1984); Breedlove v. Hurst, 181 Ga. App. 4, 351 S.E.2d 212 (Ga. App. 1986) (finding that where the facts do not indicate an intention of the parties to condition the guarantor's obligation to pay on the primary obligor's inability to pay, but merely upon the primary obligor's failure to pay, and such failure to pay having been shown, along with the satisfaction of another condition, a binding contract of guaranty was proven, which is enforceable under Georgia law).
97. Thomasson v. Pineco, Inc., 173 Ga. App. 794, 328 S.E.2d 410 (Ga. App. 1985).
98. Boat Ramp Road Partners, LLC v. The First State Bank, Inc., 314 Ga. App. 452, 724 S.E.2d 464 (Ga. App. 2012).
99. Regan v. U.S. Small Business Administration, 926 F.2d 1078 (11th Cir. 1991) (applying Georgia law); Bobbitt v. Firestone Tire & Rubber Co., 158 Ga. App. 580, 281 S.E.2d 324 (Ga. App. 1981) ("A surety or guarantor may consent in advance to a course of conduct which would otherwise result in his discharge.").
100. *See generally* Ford Motor Credit Co. v. Sullivan, 170 Ga. App. 718, 720, 318 S.E.2d 188, 190-91 (Ga. App. 1984).
101. *See generally* Griswold v. Whetsell, 157 Ga. App. 800, 801, 278 S.E.2d 753,755 (Ga. App. 1981) ("The fundamental difference between a contract of suretyship and that of guaranty is that the undertaking in the former is a primary obligation to pay the debt, and in the latter it is a secondary obligation which merely guarantees the solvency of the principal." [citations omitted]).
102. O.C.G.A. § 10-7-1: "The contract of suretyship or guaranty is one whereby a person obligates himself to pay the debt of another in consideration of a benefit flowing to the surety or in consideration of credit or indulgence or other benefit given to his principal, the principal in either instance remaining bound therefor. Sureties, including those formerly called guarantors, are jointly and severally liable with their principal unless the contract provides otherwise. There shall be no distinction between contracts of suretyship and guaranty."

5.7 Limited vs. Unlimited Guaranties

- A guaranty may limit the amount that the obligee may recover from the guarantor or contain no limit.
- When multiple guarantors sign guaranties that are limited to a dollar amount, imprecise drafting may call into question the aggregate amount that may be recovered from the guarantors.[103]

5.8 Continuing vs. Restricted Guaranties

- A guaranty may cover one or more separate obligations, including obligations incurred after the date of the guaranty.[104]
- A guaranty may limit the amount that the obligee may recover from the guarantor or contain no limit.[105]

§ 6 Construction and Interpretation of Guaranties

6.1 Rule of Strict Construction

- Courts strictly construe guaranties and will not extend them by either implication or interpretation.[106] The rule of strict construction applies only to gratuitous sureties and not to compensated sureties.[107] Suretyship contracts of compensated sureties are construed strongly against them.[108]
- Thus, for example:
  - When a guaranty referenced only a business's trade name and the underlying contract referenced a different trade name of the

103. *See, e.g.,* Boat Ramp Road Partners, LLC v. The First State Bank, Inc., 314 Ga. App. 452, 724 S.E.2d 464 (Ga. App. 2012) (because the guaranties were independent of each other, the liability of each guarantor did not exceed the limitations stated in the guaranty signed by such guarantor even though the aggregate of the judgments against all guarantors exceeded the judgment amount against the primary obligor).
104. *See* Brzowski v. Quantum Nat'l Bank, 311 Ga. App. 769, 717 S.E.2d 290 (Ga. App. 2011) (finding that even where the guaranty did not specifically identify the debt covered thereby, the plain meaning of the guaranty, which included all "present and future debt," demonstrated that the guarantor's obligations under the guaranty had no temporal limitation and applied to debts owed by the primary obligor to obligee that were in existence at the time the guaranty was signed as well as any future debts created after the guaranty's execution); Roberson v. Liberty Nat'l Bank & Trust Co., 88 Ga. App. 271, 76 S.E.2d 522 (Ga. App. 1953) (finding a continuing guaranty where the agreement recited, in connection with the granting of loans secured by warehouse receipts and additional collateral, that the guarantor would "guarantee the fulfillment of these transactions in case of any difficulties").
105. *See* Roswell Festival, L.L.L.P. v. Athens Int'l, Inc., 259 Ga. App. 445, 576 S.E.2d 908 (2003) (finding that where, under the terms of the guaranties, the guarantors' obligations ceased on the 42nd month of the lease in question and so default then existed, such guaranties were deemed expired upon the occurrence of such events); Holland v. Holland Heating & Air Conditioning, 208 Ga. App. 794, 432 S.E.2d 238 (Ga. App. 1993) ("[T]he true nature of the guarantor's liability is established by the terms of the guaranty, which may render the guarantor only secondarily liable on the principal's inability to pay, or otherwise condition or limit liability in any number of ways.").
106. O.C.G.A. § 10-7-3.
107. Houston Gen. Ins. Co. v. Brock Constr. Co., Inc., 241 Ga. 460, 246 S.E.2d 316 (Ga. 1978).
108. Growth Properties of Florida, Ltd., IV v. Wallace, 168 Ga. App. 893, 310 S.E.2d 715 (Ga. App. 1983), *cert. denied.*

same business, a court refused to extend the guaranty to debts incurred under the different trade name.[109]

- When a purported guaranty failed to identify the underlying obligation, the primary obligor, or the guarantor, and the obligee was unable to prove that the purported guaranty was executed in the same transaction as the underlying loan agreement without the use of parol evidence, the statute of frauds applied, preventing the use of parol evidence to prove the underlying obligation, the primary obligor, or the guarantor, a court refused to enforce the purported guaranty.[110]

6.2 Minor Errors

- Minor errors, by themselves, will not automatically render a guaranty invalid, meaning the strict construction doctrine will not void the guaranty.[111]
- Thus, for example:
  - A guaranty that mistakenly identified the guaranteed note as being on the reverse side of the guaranty was still enforced, as the court refused to construe language contrary to the manifest intention of the parties.[112]
  - A guaranty that was physically attached to a lease and incorporated by reference was valid and enforceable against the guarantors even though it was made prior to the lease, with the court finding the only reasonable interpretation of the guaranty was that it should apply to the only extant lease between the parties.[113] However, one Georgia court found that a guaranty could not be deemed to refer to a lease where the guaranty and the lease were executed on different days and had materially inconsistent terms.[114]
  - A court corrected a guaranty that erroneously required the "guarantor" to be in default as a precondition of liability under the guaranty, rather than the primary obligor, when the guaranty clearly indicated the guarantors' intent to guarantee credit extended to the primary obligor.[115]
  - The failure of three intended coguarantors to sign a guaranty, which had blanks for their signatures, did not create a

109. PlayNation Play Systems v. Jackson, 312 Ga. App. 340, 718 S.E.2d 568 (Ga. App. 2011), *cert. denied* 2012 Ga. LEXIS 225 (Ga. Feb. 27, 2012).
110. Dabbs v. Key Equip. Finance, Inc., 303 Ga. App. 570, 694 S.E.2d 161 (Ga. App. 2010).
111. Patterson v. Bennett St. Properties, 314 Ga. App. 896, 726 S.E.2d 147 (Ga. App. 2012).
112. Azar v. Fulton County Employees Pension Bd., 148 Ga. App. 865, 253 S.E.2d 251 (Ga. App. 1979).
113. Town Center Associates v. Workman, 233227 Ga. App. 407, 50455, 487 S.E.2d 272624 (Ga. App. 19981997), *cert. denied* 1997 Ga. App. LEXIS 717 (Ga. November 21, 1997).
114. Avec Corp. v. Schmidt, 207 Ga. App. 374, 427 S.E.2d 850 (Ga. App. 1993).
115. Tucker Station, Ltd. v. Chalet I, Inc., 203 Ga. App. 383, 417 S.E.2d 40 (Ga. App. 1992).

condition precedent to relieve the sole guarantor who did sign the guaranty from liability under the guaranty.[116]

- A guarantor that signed a guaranty, intending for remaining blanks in the guaranty to be completed by the other party, is bound by such other party's completion of those blanks so long as the completion followed the manifest intent of the parties.[117] However, a purported guaranty containing blanks for the name of both the primary obligors and the purported guarantor rendered the guaranty unenforceable against purported guarantor.[118]

6.3 Strict Construction against Drafter

- If a construction of a contract (including a guaranty) is doubtful, the unclear or ambiguous term in the contract will be construed more strongly against the party who prepared the document and with any ambiguity resolved in favor of the nondrafting party.[119]
- This general rule may be rebutted where the contract recites that both parties participated in the drafting of the contract.[120]

6.4 Parol Evidence Rule; Effect of Merger Clause

- Parol evidence is generally inadmissible to contradict or vary the terms of a valid written agreement, except to explain ambiguities (whether latent or patent).[121] Nor may parol evidence be admitted to provide a description of that which is wholly omitted from a guaranty.[122] While parol evidence is inadmissible to add to or take from or vary a written contract, such evidence may be introduced to demonstrate fraud, accident, or a mistake in the procurement of the contract.[123]
- Despite the rule of strict construction, the courts have allowed parol evidence to explain some ambiguities or otherwise have taken a common sense approach to contract interpretation to prevent guarantors from evading clearly intended undertakings:
  - A guarantor was liable for lease obligations despite the subject lease being executed on a date after the date of the lease referred

---

116. Ampex Credit Corp. v. Bateman, 554 F.2d 750 (5th Cir. 1977) (applying Georgia law).
117. Fore v. Parnell-Martin Cos., Inc., 192 Ga. App. 851, 386 S.E.2d 723 (Ga. App. 1989).
118. Sysco Food Services, Inc. v. Coleman, 227 Ga. App. 460, 489 S.E.2d 568 (Ga. App. 1997).
119. O.C.G.A. § 13-2-2(5); Auldridge v. Rivers, 263 Ga. App. 396, 587 S.E.2d 870 (Ga. App. 2003).
120. Carlos v. Lane, 275 Ga. 674, 571 S.E.2d 736 (Ga. 2002).
121. O.C.G.A. §§ 24-6-3(b) & 24-6-1. If an ambiguity exists in the written terms of a contract, parol evidence may be used to ascertain intent and to explain the ambiguity. Khamis Enterprises, Inc. v. DoaneBoone, 224 Ga. App. 348, 480 S.E.2d 364 (Ga. App. 1997;); Jordan v. Tri County Ag, Inc., 248 Ga. App. 661, 546 S.E.2d 528 (Ga. App. 2001); Holcim (US), Inc. v. AMDG, Inc., 265 Ga. App. 818, 596 S.E.2d 197 (Ga. App. 2004); Jordan v. Tri County AG, Inc., 248 Ga. App. 661, 546 S.E.2d 528 (Ga. App. 2001).
122. Roden Elec. Supply, Inc. v. Faulkner, 240 Ga. App. 556, 524 S.E.2d 247 (Ga. App. 1999).
123. O.C.G.A. § 13-2-2(1); Dental One Associates, Inc. v. JKR Realty Associates, Ltd., 228 Ga. App. 307, 491 S.E.2d 414 (Ga. App. 1997), aff'd in part, disapproved in part on other grounds, 269 Ga. 616, 501 S.E.2d 497 (Ga. 1998).

to in the guaranty, as the guarantor admitted that he intended to guarantee the subject lease, the subject lease was the only lease entered into between the primary obligor and the obligee, and the guarantor had previously cured defaults by the tenant under the lease pursuant to the terms of the guaranty.[124]

- An incorrect reference to the date of the note in an amended guaranty did not preclude its enforcement when the guaranty specifically stated that the note was the same note guaranteed under the initial guaranty; the initial guaranty referred to the note guaranteed as "mortgage note of even date herewith"; and the same "even date herewith" language was carried forward into the amended guaranty.[125]
- Parties to a guaranty intended for the guaranty to identify the primary obligor (although the name of the primary obligor in the guaranty was blank) because the guaranty would otherwise be devoid of purpose or meaning, and courts could use parol evidence to ascertain the primary obligor in such cases.[126]

- Parol evidence may also be used by a guarantor to prove guarantor's status as such, either before or after judgment.[127]
- One who signs a note as a comaker may be proved to be a guarantor by parol evidence.[128]
- If a written contract, such as a guaranty, contains a merger clause (to the effect that the written contract embodies the entire understanding of the parties), prior and contemporaneous statements that contradict the written contract may not be used to vary the terms of the contract.[129]
- Notwithstanding the foregoing rules, Georgia law authorizes all contemporaneous writings to be admitted to explain each other.[130]

§ 7 Defenses, Release, and Discharge of Guarantor

7.1 Generally

- Georgia statutory and common law provide that a guarantor may be released or discharged from liability under a guaranty for a variety of reasons.

124. Cohen v. Sandy Springs Crossing Associates, L.P., 238 Ga. App. 711, 520 S.E.2d 17 (Ga. App. 1999), *cert. denied* 1999 Ga. LEXIS 859 (Ga. Oct. 22, 1999).
125. Senske v. Harris Trust & Sav. Bank, 227233 Ga. App. 55407, 504 S.E.2d 272 (Ga. App. 1998).
126. James Talcott, Inc. v. Fullerton Cotton Mills, Inc., 208 F.2d 81 (5th Cir. 1953) (applying Georgia law).
127. *See* § 11.8, *infra*.
128. O.C.G.A. § 10-7-45; Benson v. Henning, 50 Ga. App. 492, 178 S.E. 406 (Ga. App. 1935).
129. First Data PLSPOS, Inc. v. Willis, 273 Ga. 792, 546 S.E.2d 781 (Ga. 2001).
130. O.C.G.A. § 14-6-3(a). That rule obtains even if there is no ambiguity in the writings themselves. Harrison v. Distinctive Builders, Inc., 249 Ga. App. 686, 549 S.E.2d 496 (Ga. App. 2001).

- A guarantor may assert all defenses that are available to the primary obligor.[131]
- A guarantor may not assert as a defense certain "personal defenses" that may be asserted by the primary obligor, such as infancy, bankruptcy, or incapacity.[132]
- A discharge of the underlying obligation in a bankruptcy case involving the primary obligor does not discharge the guarantor.[133]
- If the primary obligor waives a defense, the guarantor is not entitled to revive it.[134]
- If the guaranty is unconditional in nature, the guarantor will remain liable under the guaranty despite defenses that may be available to the primary obligor.[135]

7.2 Release of Coguarantor

- The obligee may release or "compound with" (reach a settlement with) a guarantor without releasing the primary obligor, but a release of or compounding with one guarantor discharges a coguarantor.[136]
- The right to assert this defense can be waived in advance by the guarantor.[137]

7.3 Changes in Underlying Contract (Novation)

- A change in the "nature or terms" of the contract governing the underlying obligation, without the guarantor's consent, may result in a "novation" and a discharge of the guarantor's obligation.[138]

---

131. *See* Metter Banking Co. v. Millen Lumber & Supply Co., 191 Ga. App. 634, 382 S.E.2d 624 (Ga. App. 1989) (breach of contract defense may be asserted by guarantor); Jones v. Dixie O'Brien Div., O'Brien Corp., 174 Ga. App. 67, 329 S.E. 256 (Ga. App. 1985) (failure of consideration defense may be asserted by guarantor in the absence of a waiver of such defenses); *Vickers v. Chrysler Credit Corp.*, 158 Ga. App. 434, 280 S.E.2d 842 (Ga. App. 1981) (guarantor may have been entitled to assert defense available to primary obligor—i.e., that obligee failed to dispose of collateral in commercially reasonable manner—but guarantor waived the defense).
132. Metter Banking Co. v. Millen Lumber & Supply Co., 191 Ga. App. 634, 640, 382 S.E.2d 624, 629 (Ga. App. 1989).
133. Growth Props. of Fla., Ltd., IV v. Wallace, 168 Ga. App. 893, 310 S.E.2d 715 (Ga. App. 1983) (citing Phillips v. Solomon, 42 Ga. 192 (Ga. 1871) and White v. Idelson, 38 Ga. App. 612, 144 S.E. 802 (Ga. App. 1928)).
134. Hurst v. Stith Equip. Co., 133 Ga. App. 374, 210 S.E.2d 851 (Ga. App. 1974).
135. *See, e.g.*, Core LaVista, LLC v. Cumming, 308 Ga. App. 791, 795, 709 S.E.2d 336, 340-41 (Ga. App. 2011) (holding that "reditors are entitled to summary judgment in a suit on an unconditional guaranty when the guarantor has waived all of his defenses").
136. O.C.G.A. § 10-7-20.
137. *See* Lothridge v. First Nat'l Bank of Gainesville, 217 Ga. App. 711, 458 S.E.2d 887 (Ga. App. 1995), *cert. denied,* 1995 Ga. LEXIS 1089 (Ga. Oct. 13, 1995) (guarantor waived right to assert defense under O.C.G.A. § 10-7-20 in guaranty providing that the obligee could release any other obligor, guarantor or surety "'without in any way affecting the obligation'" of guarantor); *Baby Days, Inc. v. Bank of Adairsville*, 218 Ga. App. 752, 463 S.E.2d 171 (Ga. App. 1995), *cert. denied*, 1996 Ga. LEXIS 269 (Ga. Jan. 26, 1996) (citing language in the guaranty that "[a]uthority and consent are hereby expressly given [to obligee] from time to time, and without notice of the undersigned, to give and make such ... settlements and compromises as it may deem proper with respect to any of the indebtedness, liabilities and obligations covered by this guaranty….") (emphasis omitted). *But see* Marrett v. Scott, 212 Ga. App. 427, 441 S.E.2d 902 (Ga. App. 1994) (certain guarantors were not released by operation of obligee's settlement agreement with other guarantors, because the respective guarantors were not jointly and severally liable on the guaranty and because the settlement agreement;s covenant not to sue did not constitute a release for purposes of O.C.G.A. § 10-7-20).
138. O.C.G.A. § 10-7-21.

- The changes in the underlying obligation must be material in order for the guarantor to be discharged,[139] but the guarantor may be discharged even by a material change that benefits the guarantor.[140]
- Changes to an underlying obligation that have resulted in a discharge include:
  - an increase in the principal amount of the underlying obligation;[141]
  - a change in payment terms of the underlying obligation by adding an agreement to pay late charges and enforcement expenses;[142]
  - a consolidation of several loans only one of which is the subject of a guaranty (irrespective of whether the change is for the guarantor's benefit);[143]
  - an extension of time for payment of the underlying obligation;[144]
  - an increase in the interest rate on the underlying obligation.[145]
- A consent by the guarantor to subsequent changes to the underlying obligation may operate as a waiver of the guarantor's defenses under O.C.G.A. § 10-7-21.[146]

7.4 Failure to "Deliver Up"

- Any failure of the obligee to "deliver up" to the guarantor the evidence of and collateral security for the guaranteed debt for enforcement by the guarantor against the primary obligor or coguarantors, upon

139. Thomas-Sears v. Morris, 278 Ga. App. 152, 628 S.E.2d 241 (Ga. App. 2006).
140. Brunswick Nursing & Convalescent Ctr., Inc. v. Great Am. Ins. Co., 308 F. Supp. 297 (S.D. Ga. 1970). *See also* Westinghouse Credit Corp. v. Hall, 144 B.R. 568 (S.D. Ga. 1992) ("To constitute a novation...the alteration, in addition to being material, must be without the knowledge or consent of the guarantor, or it must increase the guarantor's risk.").
141. Carpenter v. Cordele Elec. Supply, 220 Ga. App. 548, 469 S.E.2d 799 (Ga. App. 1996); Southeastern Automotive Warehouse, Inc. v. McCurdy, 205 Ga. App. 550, 422 S.E.2d 574 (Ga. App. 1992).
142. Builder Marts of Am., Inc. v. Gilbert, 257 Ga. App. 763, 572 S.E.2d 88 (Ga. App. 2002).
143. Upshaw v. First State Bank, 244 Ga. 433, 260 S.E.2d 480 (Ga. App. 1979). However, the execution of a note for the underlying obligation is not the type of novation that will discharge the guarantor. Columbia Nitrogen Corp. v. Mason, 171 Ga. App. 685, 320 S.E.2d 838 (Ga. App. 1984).
144. Alropa Corp. v. Snyder, 182 Ga. 305, 185 S.E. 352 (Ga. 1936). *But see* Sens v. Decatur Fed. Sav. & Loan Ass'n., 159 Ga. App. 767, 285 S.E.2d 226 (Ga. App. 1981) (mere agreement to allow delay in payment does not constitute a novation, because debtor's promise to pay debt already due creates no additional obligation).
145. Hill v. O'Neill, 101 Ga. 832, 28 S.E. 996 (Ga. 1897). *But see* Citizens & Southern Nat'l Bank v. Scheider, 139 Ga. App. 475, 228 S.E.2d 611 (Ga. App. 1976) (increase in interest rate applicable under renewal note did not constitute a novation where the guaranty provided that the note and "all extensions or renewals thereof" were guaranteed).
146. *See* Core LaVista, LLC v. Cumming, 308 Ga. App. 791, 709 S.E.2d 336 (Ga. App. 2011) (party may consent in advance to future transactions and will not be heard to claim discharge upon the occurrence of such transactions); Steiner v. Handler, 229 Ga. App. 833, 495 S.E.2d 132 (Ga. App. 1997) (citing language in the guaranty that guarantor "hereby consents and agrees that the Bank may at any time without notice to or further consent from the [guarantor], either with or without consideration...extend or renew for any period, whether or not longer than the original period, alter, modify or exchange any of the Obligations or any writing evidencing the Obligations hereunder") (emphasis in original).

tender by the guarantor of the amount of the underlying obligation, operates to discharge the guaranty.[147]

- Such a discharge applies only to a guarantor that is refused tender by the obligee, and not to other guarantors.[148]

7.5 Failure to Collect from Primary Obligor

- The obligee's failure or refusal to proceed to collect the debt from a primary obligor that is located within the jurisdiction of the state, not later than three months after receipt of written notice to do so from the guarantor, operates to discharge the obligation of the guarantor.[149] *See* discussion at §§ 9.1-9.3.

7.6 Statute of Limitations

- A suit on a guaranty may be barred by the applicable statute of limitations. The statute of limitations in Georgia for guaranty agreements and other simple contracts in writing (excluding contracts for the sale of goods under Article 2 of the UCC and negotiable instruments under Article 3) is six years,[150] but the limitations period is 20 years for a guaranty executed under seal.[151]
- A payment or promise by the primary obligor or a coguarantor does not operate to toll the limitations period or extend (or revive) the guarantor's obligation or the remedy of the obligee against the guarantor.[152]

7.7 Revocation or Termination of Guaranty

- A guaranty of a specific, existing obligation may not be revoked.[153] A guaranty is irrevocable if it is given in exchange for consideration, such as a fully funded term loan, all of which passed at the time of execution of the guaranty.[154]
- On the other hand, if a guaranty is continuing and applies to existing and future indebtedness, it is divisible and may be revoked, but only as to future obligations.[155] Upon revocation of a continuing guaranty,

147. O.C.G.A. § 10-7-23.
148. Hall v. First Nat'l Bank, 145 Ga. App. 267, 243 S.E.2d 569 (Ga. App. 1978).
149. O.C.G.A. § 10-7-24.
150. O.C.G.A. § 9-3-24.
151. O.C.G.A. § 9-3-23.
152. O.C.G.A. § 10-7-25.
153. Haynie v. First Nat'l Bank of Atlanta, 117 Ga. App. 766, 162 S.E.2d 27 (Ga. App. 1968).
154. *Id.*
155. *Id.*

the guarantor remains obligated for the underlying obligation that exists at the time of such revocation.[156]

- At common law, a contract of guaranty, though in writing, could be revoked or terminated orally, but where the contract provides otherwise, revocation or termination must be in accordance with its terms.[157]
- Provision in a guaranty that it is the joint and several obligation of the guarantors is sufficient to permit any guarantor to terminate his obligation by giving specific written notice that he was doing so.[158] If one guarantor provides notice of termination or revocation of the guaranty, such notice is effective only as to him and cannot affect the liability of other co-guarantors.[159]
- The notice of revocation or termination must be clearly expressed and "be unqualified, positive and absolute."[160] In order for any termination of future liability under a guaranty to be effective, the notice of termination must be in strict compliance with the terms of the guaranty.[161] A requirement in a guaranty for written notice of revocation is not satisfied merely by the guarantor giving notice of change of status, such as termination of the guarantor's employment with the primary obligor.[162]

7.8 Alteration of Guaranty

- If a post-signing alteration of a guaranty changes a material term, or the change is unauthorized, the guaranty is void.[163]

---

156. Walter E. Heller & Co. v. Aetna Bus. Cred., Inc., 158 Ga. App. 249, 280 S.E.2d 144 (Ga. App. 1981) (a divisible and continuing guaranty may be canceled in the future only); Lothridge v. First Nat'l Bank of Gainesville, 217 Ga. App. 711, 458 S.E.2d 887 (Ga. App. 1995), *cert. denied* 1995 Ga. LEXIS 1089 (Ga. Oct. 13, 1995) (termination of continuing guaranty by guarantor was effective only as to future loans made with reference to the guaranty, and the guaranty was not effectively terminated as to loans that had already been extended to the primary obligor). *But see* American Express Travel Related Servs. Co. v. Berlye, 202 Ga. App. 358, 414 S.E.2d 499 (Ga. App. 1991), *cert. denied,* 1992 Ga. LEXIS 191 (Ga. Feb. 10, 1992) (guarantors are not authorized to terminate unilaterally guaranty agreements that contained no provision for unilateral termination, and obligee's failure to respond to a unilateral termination letter did not amount to implied acceptance of it).
157. Haynie v. First Nat'l Bank of Atlanta, 117 Ga. App. 766, 162 S.E.2d 27 (Ga. App. 1968).
158. *Id.*
159. *Id.*
160. *Id.*
161. Rambo v. Cobb Bank & Trust Co., 146 Ga. App. 204, 245 S.E.2d 888 (Ga. App. 1978). Browning v. Nat'l Bank of Ga., 143 Ga. App. 278, 238 S.E.2d 275 (Ga. App. 1977). Haynie v. First Nat'l Bank of Atlanta, 117 Ga. App. 766, 162 S.E.2d 27 (Ga. App. 1968).
162. Cosby v. A.N. Smyre Mfg. Co., 158 Ga. App. 587, 281 S.E.2d 332 (Ga. App. 1981).
163. *See* James Talcott, Inc. v. Dettelbach, 138 Ga. App. 475, 226 S.E.2d 309 (Ga. App. 1976) (guaranty executed by purported guarantor unenforceable when bank completed blanks in guaranty with name and address of incorrect primary obligor several months after execution of the guaranty). *See also* O.C.G.A. § 13-4-1 (voiding of contracts materially altered with intent to defraud).

- An authorized or immaterial alteration, however, will not release a guarantor.[164]

7.9 Failure of Consideration

- Failure of consideration may be a defense to payment under a guaranty.[165]
- However, the benefit to the guarantor need not be direct. A benefit to the primary obligor, such as an extension of credit, is sufficient to bind the guarantor.[166]

7.10 Disability of Primary Obligor

- If the underlying contract of the primary obligor was invalid as a result of "a disability to contract" and the disability was known to the guarantor, the guarantor remains liable under the guaranty.[167]
- Duress may amount to a disability.[168]

7.11 Set-off

- Unless a guarantor waives the right of set-off in the guaranty, a guarantor may set-off amounts owed under the guaranty against amounts owed by the obligee to the guarantor.[169]

7.12 Fraud in the Inducement

- A guarantor may assert an affirmative defense or counterclaim against the obligee if the guarantor was induced by fraud to execute the guaranty.[170]

---

164. *See* Patterson v. Bennett St. Properties, 314 Ga. App. 896, 726 S.E.2d 147 (Ga. App. 2012) (change made to guaranty after signing of guaranty was not material when change simply provided that guaranty was limited by terms specified in a particular paragraph, as guaranty was already limited by those terms); Cavenaugh v. Peachtree Bank & Trust Co., 175 Ga. App. 842, 334 S.E.2d 730 (Ga. App. 1985) (guarantor held liable under a guaranty notwithstanding her assertion that certain portions of the guaranty had not been completed when she signed it, because she failed to carry burden of proof that bank was unauthorized to complete blanks); Overcash v. First Nat'l Bank, 117 Ga. App. 818, 162 S.E.2d 210 (Ga. App. 1968) (guaranty was enforced notwithstanding bank's change of the date written on the guaranty, where the correct date was readily ascertainable from the instrument itself and guarantor failed to demonstrate intent to defraud).
165. United States v. Blue Dolphin Assocs., Inc., 620 F. Supp. 463, 466 (S.D. Ga. 1985) ("To be enforceable, a guaranty must show consideration flowing to the guarantor.").
166. United States v. Blue Dolphin Assocs., Inc., 620 F. Supp. 463, 465 (S.D. Ga. 1985).
167. O.C.G.A. § 10-7-2, Patterson v. Gibson, 81 Ga. 802, 10 S.E. 9 (Ga. 1888).
168. Patterson v. Gibson, 81 Ga. 802, 10 S.E. 9 (Ga. 1888).
169. *See, e.g.*, Solid Waste Mgt. Auth. v. Transwaste Servs., 247 Ga. App. 29, 30, 543 S.E.2d 98, 99 (Ga. App. 2000) (holding that, although the right to set-off is preserved under Georgia law by statute, O.C.G.A. §§ 13-7-1 et seq., such rights may be waived by contract).
170. Baxter v. Fairfield Fin. Servs., 307 Ga. App. 286, 704 S.E.2d 423 (Ga. App. 2010).

- For the defense of fraud in the inducement to have merit, the guarantor must show that the guarantor justifiably relied upon false representations of the inducing party.[171]

7.13 Breach of Covenant of Good Faith and Fair Dealing

- Every contract implies a covenant or duty of good faith and fair dealing in the performance of the agreement and its enforcement.[172]
- There can be no breach of an implied covenant of good faith where the contract does nothing more or less than what the provisions of the contract expressly give the party the right to do.[173] Although no reported decisions under Georgia law have been located that address an obligee's breach of a duty of good faith and fair dealing in the performance or enforcement of a guaranty, one Georgia decision, applying New York law, held that the obligee's alleged failure to disclose material and unusual facts surrounding a guaranty created a genuine issue of material fact over whether obligee breached its implied duties of good faith and fair dealing in connection with the guaranty.[174]

§ 8 Discharge by Increase of Risk

8.1 General Rule

- Any act of the obligee, either before or after judgment against the primary obligor, that results in injury or increased risk to the guarantor or exposes the guarantor to greater liability, discharges the guarantor.[175] The statute is written in the disjunctive and establishes three separate bases for discharge: (1) injury, (2) increased risk, and (3) exposure to greater liability.[176] This discharge, which can occur even if the act in question occurred after the obligee obtained a judgment, is very broad and nearly subsumes all of the other grounds for discharge.
- Mere failure by the obligee to sue as soon as the law allows or to prosecute "with vigor" the obligee's legal remedies, unless consideration was received to so act, does not release the guarantor.[177] Thus,

---

171. *See* Baxter v. Fairfield Fin. Servs., 307 Ga. App. 286, 704 S.E.2d 423 (Ga. App. 2010) (holding that guarantor did not justifiably rely upon statements made by bank officer where no confidential relationship existed between bank and guarantor).
172. Rotech Healthcare, Inc. v. Chancy, 392 F. Supp. 2d 1372 (N.D. Ga. 2005) (applying Georgia law); Re/Max Executives, Inc. v. Vacalis, 234 Ga. App. 659, 507 S.E.2d 235 (Ga. App. 1998).
173. Nobel Lodging, Inc. v. Holiday Hospitality Franchising, Inc., 249 Ga. App. 497, 548 S.E.2d 481 (Ga. 2001).
174. Crossing Park Props., LLC v. Archer Capital Fund, LP, 311 Ga. App. 177, 715 S.E.2d 444 (Ga. App. 2011), *cert. denied,* 2012 Ga. LEXIS 40 (Ga. Jan. 9, 2012).
175. O.C.G.A. § 10-7-22.
176. W.T. Rawley Co. v. Kelly, 78 Ga. App. 10, 50 S.E.2d 113 (Ga. App. 1948).
177. O.C.G.A. § 10-7-22.

for example, a mere forbearance without more would not discharge the guarantor.[178]

- The defense of discharge as a result of injury to the guarantor or increase of the guarantor's risk has been held to be unavailable to compensated sureties.[179]

8.2 Examples of Increased Risk Discharge

- Failure to perfect lien or loss of collateral.[180]
- Failure to insure.[181]
- Extension of the time of payment or performance of underlying obligation.[182]
- Failure of obligee, as UCC secured party, to give proper notice of obligee's intended disposition of personal property collateral under the UCC and failure to dispose of collateral in a commercially reasonable manner.[183] There is a rebuttable presumption under Georgia law that the value of collateral disposed of by the obligee is equal to the amount of the underlying obligation, but the obligors with respect to the underlying obligation (including the guarantor) remain liable for any deficiency to the extent that the obligee rebuts the presumption by proof that the value of the collateral disposed of was less than the amount of the debt.[184]
- Obligee's impairment of guarantor's subrogation rights.[185]
- Release of a coguarantor. *See* § 7, *supra* (discussing O.C.G.A. § 10-7-20).

178. Hall v. Langford, 18 Ga. App. 73, 88 S.E. 918 (Ga. App. 1916).
179. Walter E. Heller & Co. v. Aetna Bus. Credit, Inc., 158 Ga. App. 249, 280 S.E.2d 144 (Ga. App. 1981).
180. *See* Bank S. v. Jones, 185 Ga. App. 125, 364 S.E.2d 281 (Ga. App. 1987) (obligee's failure to perfect a security interest results in discharge of a guaranty only to the extent the guarantor proves an impairment). *But see* Panasonic Indus. Co. v. Hall et al., 197 Ga. App. 860, 399 S.E.2d 733 (Ga. App. 1990) (reversing trial court's holding that recording a UCC financing statement in the wrong recording office discharged guarantor's obligation, because guarantor waived such defense in the guaranty).
181. *See* Evans v. American Nat'l Bank & Trust Co., 116 Ga. App. 468, 157 S.E.2d 816 (Ga. App. 1967) (bank's failure to insure collateral of bankrupt primary obligor, or to notify guarantor of the lapse in insurance coverage, materially increased guarantor's risk and discharged the guarantor to the extent of the lapsed insurance).
182. *See* Cantrell v. First Tenn. Nat'l Bank Ass'n, 207 Ga. App. 458, 428 S.E.2d 368 (Ga. App. 1993) (extension of maturity date of loans without the consent of purported guarantor increased guarantor's risk because equity securities pledged by primary obligor, which purported guarantor agreed to repurchase from obligee, decreased in value during extended term of loan, resulting in discharge of purported guaranty).
183. O.C.G.A. §§ 11-9-610 & 11-9-611. *See also* Barbree v. Allis-Chalmers Corp., 250 Ga. 409, 297 S.E.2d 465 (Ga. 1982) (overruling prior decisions, such as McNulty v. Cobb, 157 Ga. App. 8, 276 S.E.2d 73 (Ga. App. 1981), holding that guarantors were not entitled to notice of disposition of collateral pledged by the primary obligor, and that predefault waivers of such notice were enforceable). *See generally* O.C.G.A. § 11-9-611(c) (codifying rule in *Barbree* that a guarantor or "secondary obligor" is entitled to notice of disposition of collateral) and O.C.G.A. § 11-9-602(7) (providing that a predefault waiver of such notice is not enforceable against the guarantor).
184. Emmons v. Burkett, 265 Ga. 855, 353 S.E.2d 908 (Ga. 1987).
185. *But see* Jessee v. First Nat'l Bank of Atlanta, 154 Ga. App. 209, 267 S.E.2d 803 (Ga. App. 1980) (failure of an obligee to tender the amount paid on an obligation by a guarantor when the entire obligation has not been repaid does not interfere with the guarantor's subrogation rights); In re Bloomfield, 35 B.R. 459 (Bankr. N.D. Ga. 1983) (alleged impairment of subrogation rights did not give rise to a defense to the guaranty, when guarantor had waived all subrogation rights until the underlying obligation was paid in full).

8.3 Exceptions

- Generally, an obligee's refusal to extend additional credit to the primary obligor should not result in discharge of the guarantor.[186]
- Courts have held that a discharge may not arise when the acts of the obligee alleged to have increased the guarantor's risk are expressly authorized by law, such as the sale of collateral for less than the value of the underlying obligation at foreclosure.[187]
- Some cases suggest that an obligee's acts that injure a guarantor discharge the guarantor only in proportion to the damage caused.[188] However, the *pro tanto* discharge rule is not applicable if the act of the obligee alters the underlying obligation.[189]

8.4 Waivers

- Waivers of the guarantor's right to assert defenses based on novation and increased risk have been held to be enforceable, even when given in advance.[190]

§ 9 Discharge for Failure or Refusal to sue Primary Obligor

9.1 Notice to Obligee to Collect from Primary Obligor

- A guarantor may, at any time after the debt on which the guarantor is liable "becomes due," give notice in writing to the obligee (or to the obligee's agent or any other person having "possession or control" of the obligation) to proceed to collect the underlying obligation from

186. *See* Ga. Invs. Int'l, Inc. v. Branch Banking & Trust Co., 305 Ga. App. 673, 700 S.E.2d 662 (Ga. App. 2010) (stating "[w]e have consistently held that a lender's failure to lend additional sums to a principal does not discharge a guarantor from liability for the amount which was actually advanced by the lender") (citations omitted).
187. United States v. Blue Dolphin Assocs., 620 F. Supp. 463 (S.D. Ga. 1985).
188. *See* Johnson v. Longley, 142 Ga. 814, 83 S.E. 952 (Ga. 1914) (where obligee's delay in enforcing primary obligation despite guarantor's oral requests resulted in increased risk after damage to collateral, guaranty would be partially discharged to the extent of the loss); Alropa Corp. v. Snyder, 182 Ga. 305, 182 S.E. 352 (Ga. 1936) (where a surety suffers injury arising collaterally and not affecting the contract itself, the discharge is only to the extent of the loss or injury).
189. Alropa Corp. v. Snyder, 182 Ga. 305, 182 S.E. 352 (Ga. 1936).
190. Fielbon Development Co., LLC v. Colony Bank of Houston County, 290 Ga. App. 847, 660 S.E.2d 801 (Ga. App. 2008); Underwood v. NationsBanc Real Estate Serv., 221 Ga. App. 351, 471 S.E.2d 291 (Ga. App. 1996) (relying on guarantor's waiver of "any 'legal or equitable discharge' and of any defense based on increase in risk") (citing Overcash v. First Nat'l Bank, 115 Ga. App. 499, 155 S.E.2d 32 (Ga. App. 1967); Bobbitt v. Firestone Tire & Rubber, 158 Ga. App. 580, 281 S.E.2d 324 (Ga. App. 1981); and Dunlap v. C & S DeKalb Bank, 134 Ga. App. 893, 216 S.E.2d 651 (Ga. App. 1975)). *But see* O.C.G.A. § 11-9-602 (limiting enforceability of waivers relating to notice of disposition of collateral and duty to dispose of collateral in a commercially reasonable manner).

the primary obligor or any one of several primary obligors liable therefor.[191] An oral notice is ineffective.[192]

- The notice from the guarantor must specifically state that the obligee will lose the obligee's rights to pursue the guaranty "as well as any co-sureties, co-guarantors or endorsers" if the obligee fails to commence the legal action with three months "after receiving" the notice. If the notice does not state the county in which the primary obligor resides in the State of Georgia, then the notice is not deemed to be in compliance with the law and is therefore ineffective.[193]
- Notice will not be considered sufficient if it is not a positive demand to sue,[194] or does not state the county of the primary obligor's residence.[195]
- However, the fact that a guaranty required the guarantor to make payment to the obligee upon notice from the obligee of the primary obligor's default did not mean that the guarantor was entitled to notice of default and opportunity to cure.[196]

9.2 Obligee's Failure to Commence Action

- If the obligee or holder of the underlying obligation refuses or fails to commence an action within three months after the notice is received (and provided that the primary obligor is within the jurisdiction of the State of Georgia), both the guarantor giving the notice as well as all subsequent endorsers and all coguarantors are discharged.[197]
- A discharge does not result if the primary obligor is not amenable to the jurisdiction of courts in Georgia.[198]
- Discharge under O.C.G.A. § 10-7-24 is in derogation of the common law and strict compliance with its requirements by one claiming the benefit of a discharge is mandatory.[199]

---

191. O.C.G.A. § 10-7-24; Everts v. Century Supply Corp., 264 Ga. App. 218, 590 S.E.2d 199 (Ga. App. 2003) (describing O.C.G.A. § 10-7-24 as "a mechanism to avoid liability on debt by giving creditor notice in writing to proceed to collect debt from principal debtor after debt becomes due").
192. U.S. v. Blue Dolphin Associates, Inc., 620 F.Supp. 463, 467 (S.D. Ga. 1985).
193. *See* Fricks v. J.R. Watkins Co., 88 Ga. App. 276, 76 S.E.2d 518, *rev'd on other grounds*, 210 Ga. 83, 78 S.E.2d 2 (Ga. 1953).
194. Bethune v. Dozier, 10 Ga. 235 (Ga. 1851) (it is a proper question for the jury to decide whether notice given constituted a demand to sue or simply a "request of a favor" in which case the surety may not have been discharged).
195. Motz v. Landmark First Nat'l Bank of Ft. Lauderdale, 154 Ga. App. 858, 270 S.E.2d 81, 83-84 (Ga. App. 1980).
196. Nobel Lodging, Inc. v. Holiday Hospitality Franchising, Inc., 249 Ga. App. 497, 548 S.E.2d 481 (Ga. App. 2001).
197. Motz v. Landmark First Nat'l Bank of Ft. Lauderdale, 154 Ga. App. 858, 270 S.E.2d 81, 83-84 (Ga. App. 1980).
198. *See* U.S. v. Blue Dolphin Assocs., Inc., 620 F. Supp. 463, 467 (S.D. Ga. 1985); Glasser v. Decatur Lumber & Supply Co., 95 Ga. App. 665, 99 S.E.2d 330 (Ga. App. 1957); Fricks v. J.R. Watkins Co., 88 Ga. App. 276, 76 S.E.2d 518 (Ga. App. 1953), *rev'd on other grounds*, 210 Ga. 83, 78 S.E.2d 2 (Ga. 1953) (guarantor entitled to the benefit of statute and discharge where primary obligor was resident of another state but had business in Georgia, guarantor provided primary obligor's Georgia address in notice, and plaintiff effected service on primary obligor, but did not commence suit against the primary obligor within three months of notice).
199. Howard v. Brown, 3 Ga. 523 (Ga. 1847); Glasser v. Decatur Lumber & Supply Co., 95 Ga. App. 665, 99 S.E.2d 330, 335 (Ga. App. 1957).

- The section applies to both compensated and gratuitous guarantors.[200]
- However, the statute does not apply to guaranty agreements relating to negotiable instruments governed by Article 3 of the Uniform Commercial Code. Under former O.C.G.A. § 11-3-416(1), where the words "payment guaranteed" or similar words are added to a negotiable instrument, a signer of that "guaranty" was required to pay the note when due without resort by the holder to any party.[201]
- The discharge provisions of O.C.G.A. § 10-7-24 may apply where the contract sued upon in Georgia was executed in another state.[202]
- The filing of a lawsuit without service does not operate to commence the suit and no suit is pending until the suit has been served, and suing in the wrong county is not compliant with the statute.[203]
- If after the notice from the guarantor is given, but before the expiration of the three months after receipt of the notice by the obligee the primary obligor removes himself from the jurisdiction of the state, no discharge will occur, as the removal of the primary obligor from the jurisdiction of the Georgia was at the risk of the guarantor and not the oblige.[204]
- The mere failure by the obligee to sue as soon as the law allows or to prosecute with vigor its legal remedies does not operate to release the guarantor.[205]

9.3 Waiver by Guarantor

- The benefits of O.C.G.A. § 10-7-24 may be waived in advance by the guarantor.[206]

---

200. Morrison Assur. Co. v. Preston Carroll Co., Inc., 254 Ga. 608, 331 S.E.2d 520 (Ga. 1985), *cert. denied.* 474 U.S. 1060 (1986).
201. In Gunter v. True, 203 Ga. App. 330, 416 S.E.2d 768 (Ga. App. 1992), *cert. denied*, 416 S.E.2d 768 (1992), the guarantor obligated itself by executing the last page of a promissory note, which page included language of guarantee of the debt evidenced by the promissory note. The court held that the guaranty was governed by [former] O.C.G.A. § 11-3-416(1) and that the guarantor was not discharged by failing to sue the primary obligor under O.C.G.A. § 10-7-24. Subsequent to this case, Article 3 of the UCC was amended in Georgia, with some provisions of former Section 11-3-416 being incorporated into O.C.G.A. § 11-3-419 (dealing with "accommodation parties"), though not the specific language referred to in this case from former Section 11-3-416(1). To date, no Georgia court has addressed whether an Article 3 accommodation party may avail itself of the ability to demand that the obligee sue the primary obligor under O.C.G.A. § 10-7-24.
202. J.R. Watkins Co. v. Seawright, 168 Ga. 750, 149 S.E. 45 (Ga. 1929) (Minnesota contract subject to provisions of the statute.).
203. *But see* J.R. Watkins Co. v. Seawright, 168 Ga. 750, 149 S.E. 45, 46 (Ga. 1929) (obligee had already filed suit against primary obligor in the county of primary obligor's residence before guarantors delivered statutory notice, but sheriff in that county made entry on the docket that primary obligor could not be found in the county, court did not require obligee to bring another suit against primary obligor after receipt of guarantors' notice, "as the law never requires the doing of a vain thing").
204. Howard v. Brown, 3 Ga. 523, 532-534 (Ga. 1847).
205. Greenwald v. Columbus Bank & Trust Co., 228 Ga. App. 527, 492 S.E.2d 248 (Ga. App. 1997).
206. J.R. Watkins v. Fricks, 210 Ga. 83, 78 S.E.2d 2, 4 (Ga. 1953); Metter Banking Co. v. Millen Lumber & Supply Co., 191 Ga. App. 634, 382 S.E.2d 624 (Ga. App. 1989), *rehearing* 1989 Ga. App. LEXIS 753 (Ga. Ct. App. May 23, 1989) (finding that the guarantor agreed in the guaranty to waive his right to require the obligee to take action against the principal as required by O.C.G.A. § 10-7-24 "or any other statutory provision of similar import."); *See also* Breedlove v. Hurst, 181 Ga. App. 4, 351 S.E.2d 212 (Ga. App. 1986) (finding that to the extent that the guarantor attempted to benefit from former Code § 103-205 (O.C.G.A. § 10-7-24), the guarantor failed to prove that he gave the obligee the required notice).

- However, the waiver must be specific. A general statement in a guaranty that the obligee need not exhaust remedies against the primary obligor has been held not to be sufficient to constitute a waiver of the guarantor's right to give notice to the obligee to proceed against the primary obligor within three months under O.C.G.A. § 10-7-24.[207]

§ 10 Waivers and Consents by Guarantor

10.1 General Rule

- A guarantor may make a comprehensive waiver of rights and defenses in the guaranty, including the need for prior consent to increases or changes in potential liability.[208] Thus, the protections that are given to a guarantor by O.C.G.A. §§ 10-7-21 and 10-7-22 (relating to discharge by novation or increase of risk) can be waived in advance in the guaranty.[209]
- At least one court has held that an unconditional guaranty of payment acts as a waiver of the right to assert defenses or claims of the primary obligor in discharge of the guaranty.[210]

10.2 Types of Waivers and Consents

- Pre-consent to increase in or creation of new underlying obligation.[211]
- Pre-consent to increase in guarantor's risk.[212]
- Pre-consent to extending the time of payment or performance of the underlying obligation.[213]

---

207. Vol T. Blacknall Co. v. Frazee, 148 Ga. App. 327, 151 S.E.2d 122 (Ga. App. 1978).
208. Underwood v. NationsBanc Real Estate Service, Inc., 221 Ga. App. 351, 471 S.E.2d 291 (Ga. App. 1996).
209. Ramirez v. Golden, 223 Ga. App. 610, 478 S.E.2d 430 (Ga. App. 1996) (guaranty provided that guarantor waived "any other legal or equitable defenses whatsoever to which [g]uarantor might otherwise be entitled," which precluded guarantor from asserting that he was discharged pursuant to O.C.G.A. §§ 10-7-21 or 10-7-22 even though obligee released primary obligor from certain obligations).
210. Bowden v. Russell, 200 Ga. App. 239, 407 S.E.2d 467 (Ga. App. 1991).
211. *See, e.g.,* Anderton v. Certainteed Corp., 201 Ga. App. 538, 411 S.E.2d 558 (Ga. App. 1991) (guarantor liable for full amount of replacement note that was executed by primary obligor in the amount of original note plus amounts added to account since execution of original note, where guaranty contained consent to "extend, renew, modify or waive any terms of the obligations"); Builders Dev. Corp. v. Hughes Supply, Inc., 242 Ga. App. 244, 529 S.E.2d 388 (Ga. App. 2000) (guarantor's pre-consent, in guaranty, to unlimited liability for all sales made by seller to purchaser is enforceable and subsequent increase in risk will not discharge guarantor); Dyna-Comp Corp. v. Selig Enterprises, Inc., 143 Ga. App. 462, 238 S.E.2d 571 (Ga. App. 1977) (lease modification to increase leased square footage and rent liability was consented to as an "extension or modification of any terms of said lease contract"); *see also* General Motors Acceptance Corp. v. Bowen Motors, Inc., 167 Ga. App. 463, 306 S.E.2d 675 (Ga. App. 1983) (even though it was customary in the floorplan finance trade for the obligee to inform guarantors of primary obligor's nonperformance, where guarantor specifically waived any such notice in the guaranty, obligee's failure to so notify guarantor did not give rise to defense of fraud).
212. General Motors Acceptance Corp. v. Bowen Motors, Inc., 167 Ga. App. 463, 306 S.E.2d 675 (Ga. App. 1983) (waiver of release from guaranty arising from increase in liability).
213. Hearn v. C&S Nat'l Bank, 154 Ga. App. 686, 269 S.E.2d 486 (Ga. App. 1980) (guarantor's agreement that obligee can grant primary obligor an extension of time within which primary obligor can satisfy underlying obligation works to prohibit guarantor from "revoking" that consent by delivering notice under O.C.G.A. § 10-7-24 to sue primary obligor immediately) [*see* § 9 above].

- Pre-consent to failure to perfect lien.[214]
- Pre-consent to release of collateral.[215]
- Pre-consent to failure or refusal to sue primary obligor.[216]
- Pre-consent to obligee's failure to adhere to the terms of the underlying contract.[217]
- Pre-consent to release of other guarantors. [218]
- Pre-consent to the addition of new guarantors.[219]

10.3 Effect of Waiver of Defenses

- By consenting in advance to a waiver of "all legal and equitable defenses," a guarantor is foreclosed from asserting a discharge.[220]

10.4 Effect of Unconditional Payment Guaranty

- At least one court has held that where a guaranty states that it is "a guaranty of payment and not of collection" and contains a waiver by the guarantor of any right to require that an action be brought against the primary obligor first, the guarantor may not invoke the benefits of O.C.G.A. § 10-7-24.[221]

---

214. Lothridge v. First Nat'l Bank of Gainesville, 217 Ga. App. 711, 458 S.E.2d 887, 890 (Ga. App. 1995) (guarantor pre-consent to bank releasing collateral and other obligors is enforceable); Panasonic Indus. Co. v. Hall, 197 Ga. App. 860, 399 S.E.2d 733 (Ga. App. 1990) (guarantor's pre-consent to exchange, release, or surrender of collateral held to bind guarantor where obligee filed UCC financing statement improperly, resulting in failure to perfect security interest); Rogers v. C&S Nat'l Bank, 156 Ga. App. 330, 274 S.E.2d 722 (Ga. App. 1980) (where guaranty was "absolute and unconditional" and contained an express waiver of "all diligence in collection or protection of or realization upon . . . any security," obligee's release of collateral did not discharge guarantor).

215. Panasonic Indus. Co. v. Hall, 197 Ga. App. 860, 399 S.E.2d 733 (Ga. App. 1990) (guarantor's pre-consent to exchange, release, or surrender of collateral held to bind guarantor where obligee filed UCC financing statement improperly, resulting in failure to perfect security interest); Carrollton Car Center, Inc. v. Citizens & Southern Nat'l Bank, 202 Ga. App. 429, 430, 414 S.E.2d 674 (Ga. App. 1992) (guaranty's express language that obligee may release collateral without notice to guarantor bars guarantor from asserting defenses based upon release of collateral); Bullard v. Carreras, 183 Ga. App. 539. 359 S.E.2d 429 (Ga. App. 1987) (obligee's failure to obtain collateral contemplated in note did not discharge guarantors who consented in advance to release or surrender of any or all collateral).

216. Goldstein v. GTE Products Corp., 160 Ga. App. 767, 287 S.E.2d 105 (Ga. App. 1982) (guaranty expressly stated that it was a "guaranty of payment and not of collection" and that guarantor waived any right to require obligee to pursue primary obligor or collateral before action could be brought against guarantor).

217. Thurmond v. Georgia R.R. Bank & Trust Co., 162 Ga. App. 245, 290 S.E.2d 126 (Ga. App. 1982) (guaranty contained broad waiver allowing obligee to waive any rights it may have with respect to collateral, and thus where obligee lent money in excess of the loan-to-value ratio set forth in the loan agreement, guarantor was deemed to have waived any defense regarding obligee's noncompliance with the loan documents, even though it may have increased guarantor's risk).

218. Lothridge v. First Nat'l Bank of Gainesville, 217 Ga. App. 711, 458 S.E.2d 887, 890 (Ga. App. 1995) (guarantor pre-consent to bank releasing collateral and other obligors is enforceable); Smith v. Great Southern Federal Savings Bank, 184 Ga. App. 433, 361 S.E.2d 847 (Ga. App. 1987) (where guaranty provided that guarantors consented to obligee's release of other parties primarily or secondarily liable on the underlying obligation, one guarantor could not claim that obligee's release of another guarantor resulted in the discharge of the first guarantor).

219. Dunlap v. Citizens and Southern DeKalb Bank, 134 Ga. App. 893, 896, 216 S.E.2d 651 (Ga. App. 1975) (adding son-in-law as principal obligor in addition to daughter did not discharge guarantor where guarantor agreed that bank could, without notifying guarantor, enter into guaranties of the underlying obligation with additional, new third parties).

220. Ramirez v. Golden, 223 Ga. App. 610, 478 S.E.2d 430 (Ga. App. 1996) (guaranty provided that guarantor waived "any other legal or equitable defenses whatsoever to which [g]uarantor might otherwise be entitled," which precluded guarantor from asserting that he was discharged pursuant to O.C.G.A. §§ 10-7-21 or 10-7-22 even though obligee released primary obligor from certain obligations).

221. *See* Goldstein v. GTE Products Corp., 160 Ga. App. 767, 287 S.E.2d 105 (Ga. App. 1982).

10.5 Defenses that may not be Waived

- Prior to a default, a guarantor may not waive the obligee's duty as secured creditor to act in a commercially reasonable manner in disposing of collateral.[222]
- Georgia law is not clear on the issue of whether a guarantor can waive the requirement under Georgia law that the obligee must obtain confirmation of a real property foreclosure sale prior to pursuit of an action for deficiency from the guarantor. One federal court has suggested that such a waiver may be possible if the guaranty contained an express waiver of the confirmation statute defense.[223] However, that same court recognized that "the Georgia confirmation statute is analogous to the commercial reasonableness requirement in personal property situations."[224] Accordingly, given the Georgia Supreme Court's decision in *Branan v. Equico Lessors, Inc,.*[225] discussed in the immediately preceding section, it is not clear whether a guarantor may, in the guaranty, waive compliance with the Georgia real property confirmation statute.

§ 11 Rights of Guarantor against Primary Obligor

11.1 Prejudgment Rights

- A guarantor is entitled to the process of attachment against the primary obligor before payment of a debt under the same circumstances as any other obligee.[226]

11.2 Reimbursement Right

- If the guarantor pays the underlying obligation that is past due, the guarantor may then proceed directly against the primary obligor for the sum paid, with interest, and all legal costs to which the guarantor may have been subjected by the default of the primary obligor.[227]
  - This section confers upon the guarantor a right of reimbursement, which is different from subrogation by which the guarantor takes the rights of the obligee.[228]

222. Branan v. Equico Lessors, Inc., 255 Ga. 718, 342 S.E.2d 671 (Ga. 1986) (overruling prior inconsistent cases, court holds that a guarantor is considered a "debtor" under O.C.G.A. § 11-9-504(3) and thus may not waive the defense of commercial reasonableness in the disposition of collateral).
223. U.S. v. Yates, 774 F. Supp. 1368, 1375 (M.D. Ga. 1991) (court held that guaranty provision giving the obligee the power to conduct a real property foreclosure "to be exercised only to the extent permitted by law" was not sufficient to constitute a waiver by guarantor of the confirmation statute defense).
224. U.S. v. Yates, 774 F. Supp. 1368, 1375 (M.D. Ga. 1991).
225. Branan v. Equico Lessors, Inc., 255 Ga. 718, 342 S.E.2d 671 (Ga. 1986).
226. O.C.G.A. § 10-7-40.
227. O.C.G.A. § 10-7-41.
228. Fabian v. Dykes, 214 Ga. App. 792, 449 S.E.2d 305 (Ga. App. 1994); *see* O.C.G.A. §§ 10-7-47 & 10-7-56 (regarding subrogation rights of guarantor).

- This section recognizes an independent legal right of the guarantor to recover from the primary obligor. The guarantor can enforce this right even if the obligee has released the primary obligor, as long as the guarantor is not a party to or otherwise consented to the release of the primary obligor.[229]
- If the promissory note paid by the guarantor provides for the recovery of attorneys' fees, these fees may be recovered by the guarantor.[230]

- Even if the guarantor voluntarily pays the underlying obligation, the guarantor is entitled to proceed against the primary obligor for reimbursement.[231]

11.3 Waiver and Subordination of Reimbursement Rights

- The guarantor may waive or subordinate its right of reimbursement. Such a waiver is not contrary to public policy and, therefore, is enforceable.[232]
- A clause in a guaranty that plainly and unambiguously waives claims the guarantor might have against the primary obligor, whether such claims arose in equity, by contract or under statute or common law, is enforceable, even by way of defense by the primary obligor.[233]

11.4 Effect of Post-judgment Payment by Guarantor

- If the guarantor makes payment after judgment is rendered against the guarantor and the primary obligor had notice of the lawsuit pending against the guarantor, the judgment amount is conclusive against the primary obligor as to the amount for which the guarantor is bound.[234]
- This is so even if the guarantor did not raise all available defenses in the prior action.[235]
- If, however, payment is made after judgment is entered but while the judgment is on appeal, then the amount of judgment is subject to change, and the primary obligor can still challenge the amount.[236]

---

229. Fabian v. Dykes, 214 Ga. App. 792, 449 S.E.2d 305 (Ga. App. 1994).
230. Youmans v. Puder, 13 Ga. App. 785, 80 S.E. 34 (Ga. App. 1913).
231. Fabian v. Dykes, 214 Ga. App. 792, 449 S.E.2d 305 (Ga. App. 1994).
232. In re Buckhead Oil Co., 454 B.R. 242 (Bankr. N.D. Ga. 2011) (primary obligor was third-party beneficiary of waiver in guaranty of subrogation claim, and waiver could be basis of objection to guarantor's claim against primary obligor); Brookside Communities, LLC v. Lake Dow North Corp., 268 Ga. App. 785, 603 S.E.2d 31 (Ga. App. 2004) (waiver of right of reimbursement, indemnification, and subrogation enforceable and not contrary to public policy).
233. In re CUA Autofinder, LLC, 387 B.R. 906 (Bankr. M.D. Ga. 2008); Brookside Communities, LLC v. Lake Dow North Corp., 268 Ga. App. 785, 603 S.E.2d 31 (Ga. App. 2004).
234. O.C.G.A. § 10-7-42; *see* Security Life Insurance Co. of America v. St. Paul Fire & Marine Insurance Co., 278 Ga. 800, 606 S.E.2d 855 (Ga. 2004) (the judgment against guarantor is conclusive against primary obligor only if the judgment is final and not being challenged by guarantor on appeal or otherwise).
235. M-Pax, Inc. v. Dependable Insurance Co., 176 Ga. App. 93, 335 S.E.2d 591 (Ga. App. 1985).
236. Security Life Insurance Co. of America v. St. Paul Fire & Marine Insurance Co., 278 Ga. 800, 606 S.E.2d 855 (Ga. 2004).

11.5 Effect of Prejudgment Payment by Guarantor

- If the guarantor makes payment prior to a judgment, the primary obligor may dispute the validity of the payment as to the amount or as to the authority of the person to whom the amount was paid by the guarantor.[237]

11.6 Effect of Payment of Usurious Interest

- The guarantor is authorized to recover from the primary obligor any usurious interest paid by the guarantor unless, prior to the payment, the guarantor had knowledge that the guarantor would be paying a usurious rate of interest.[238]
- If the guarantor knew the contract was usurious when the debt was paid, the guarantor cannot recover it from the primary obligor.[239]
- If the guarantor had notice of the usury and could have raised it, but failed to do so, the guarantor may be estopped to recover it from the primary obligor.[240]

11.7 Guarantor's Recourse to Indemnifying Security

- If the primary obligor grants security to the guarantor to indemnify the guarantor against loss by reason of the guaranty, the guarantor may proceed to foreclose upon the security "as soon as judgment shall be rendered against him on his contract."[241]
- No foreclosure can be had until after there is a judgment against the guarantor.[242]
- This statutory provision does not preclude the parties from stipulating, without reference to the statutory right, that the guarantor may foreclose on any other terms or conditions.[243]

11.8 Guarantor's Proof of Status vis-à-vis Primary Obligor

- If the existence of a guarantor relationship does not appear on the face of the contract, it may be proven by parol evidence, either before

---

237. O.C.G.A. § 10-7-42; Security Life Insurance Co. of America v. St. Paul Fire & Marine Insurance Co., 278 Ga. 800, 606 S.E.2d 855 (Ga. 2004) (primary obligor can still contest the amount of its liability to guarantor, even after a judgment has been rendered against guarantor, when guarantor is appealing the judgment and, therefore, it is not final).
238. O.C.G.A. § 10-7-43.
239. Jones v. Joyner, 8 Ga. 562 (Ga. 1850).
240. Hargraves v. Lewis, 3 Ga. 162 (Ga. 1847).
241. O.C.G.A. § 10-7-44.
242. Jones v. Norton, 136 Ga. 835, 72 S.E. 337 (Ga. 1911); Importers & Traders Bank v. McGhees & Co., 88 Ga. 702, 16 S.E. 27 (Ga. 1892); Conley v. State, 85 Ga. 348, 11 S.E. 659 (Ga. 1890); Burnett v. Gainesville Nat'l Bank, 28 Ga. App. 255, 110 S.E. 753 (Ga. App. 1922).
243. Jones v. Norton, 9 Ga. App. 333, 71 S.E. 687 (Ga. App. 1911).

or after judgment.[244] For example, when a contract for the sale of property is executed by two persons ostensibly as purchasers, parol evidence may be utilized to demonstrate that one person executed the contract as guarantor only and not as a primary obligor.[245]

- However, the obligee may not be delayed in the exercise of the obligee's remedies by that issue between the primary obligor and the guarantor.[246] The obligee was not "delayed in his remedy" when a new trial was granted to allow the guarantor to prove the guarantor relationship when the trial court erroneously denied the guarantor that right.[247]
- This right of the guarantor requires that the guarantor give notice to the primary obligor of the guarantor's intention to make such proof prior to judgment.[248]
- The purpose of this statutory provision is to allow the guarantor to establish the guarantor relationship with the primary obligor, not as a defense to an action brought by the obligee but for the purpose of enforcing the guarantor's rights vis-à-vis the primary obligor.[249]
- The burden is on the guarantor to prove the relationship and the knowledge of the obligee of such relationship.[250]
- The guarantor's pleading should contain an appropriate prayer for independent affirmative relief against the primary obligor.[251]
- The guarantor's pleading setting up the fact of the guarantor relationship and praying that judgment provide accordingly must also show that prior notice was given to the primary obligor of the guarantor's intention to make such proof.[252] However, no notice of an intention to prove a guarantor relationship is required when the fact of this relationship appears upon the face of the contract.[253]
- If a judgment has been rendered without proof of the existence of a guarantor relationship, the guarantor must give at least 10 days' notice to the primary obligor of the guarantor's intention to apply "at the next term of the court where the judgment was entered" to make such proof and to have the fact of the guarantor relationship entered of record. In addition, the guarantor is entitled to an order for the control of the judgment rendered against the guarantor and execution thereon against the primary obligor, subject to payment by the guarantor of the judgment.[254]

---

244. O.C.G.A. § 10-7-45; *see* Levinson v. American Thermex, Inc., 196 Ga. App. 291, 396 S.E.2d 252 (Ga. App. 1990) (statute allows party to show by parol evidence that signed document as guarantor, and not as principal); Wofford v. Waldrip, 80 Ga. App. 562, 56 S.E.2d 816 (Ga. App. 1949) (same).
245. West v. Nottingham, 71 Ga. App. 282, 30 S.E.2d 651 (Ga. App. 1944).
246. O.C.G.A. § 10-7-45.
247. Whitley v. Hudson, 114 Ga. 668, 40 S.E. 838 (Ga. 1902).
248. O.C.G.A. § 10-7-45.
249. Brown v. Merchants Trading Co., 26 Ga. App. 331, 106 S.E. 208 (Ga. App. 1921).
250. Northcutt v. Crowe, 116 Ga. App. 715, 158 S.E.2d 318 (Ga. App. 1967); Bennett v. Danforth, 36 Ga. App. 466, 137 S.E. 285 (Ga. App. 1927).
251. Morrison v. Citizens & Southern Bank, 19 Ga. App. 434, 91 S.E. 509 (Ga. App. 1917).
252. Johnson v. Georgia Fertilizer & Oil Co., 21 Ga. App. 530, 94 S.E. 850 (Ga. App. 1918).
253. Taff v. Larey, 29 Ga. App. 631, 116 S.E. 866 (Ga. App. 1923).
254. O.C.G.A. § 10-7-46.

- A guarantor who makes part payment of a judgment may have that fact put in the record for purposes of establishing rights of contribution against a coguarantor.[255]
- The guarantor must follow this statutory procedure to gain control of the judgment by having the guarantor relationship defined of record.[256]

11.9 Paying Guarantor's Enforcement of Judgment against Primary Obligor

- If a guarantor "shall have paid" or otherwise discharges a judgment or execution "in whole or in part" and has the fact of such payment entered on the execution by the obligee (or his attorney or the collecting officer), the guarantor is afforded control of the execution and the judgment upon which it is founded, to the same extent as if the guarantor were the original obligee. Moreover, such a guarantor is subrogated to all of the rights of the obligee, for the purpose of reimbursing the guarantor from the primary obligor.[257]
- The language "shall have paid" in the cited section applies to involuntary as well as voluntary payments.[258]
- When a guarantor takes control of the execution against the primary obligor, the judgment lien against the primary obligor in the guarantor's hands takes effect from the date of the judgment.[259]
- If the execution does not reflect the guarantor relationship, the guarantor seeking to enforce the execution cannot prove the relationship by parol evidence.[260]
- The guarantor making payment under this statute is entitled to the same protection as the obligee against a fraudulent conveyance by the primary obligor.[261]
- If the guarantor bought the judgment at a discount or otherwise, after levy upon the guarantor's property, obtained control of the judgment by compromise at a price less than the amount due, the guarantor is entitled to enforce the judgment only for the amount necessary to be reimbursed by the primary obligor.[262]
- Part payment of the judgment amount by the guarantor may not provide the guarantor with any right to control the judgment until the full amount of the judgment is paid,[263] but literal wording of O.C.G.A.

255. Cooper v. Chamblee, 114 Ga. 116, 39 S.E. 917 (Ga. 1901).
256. Patterson v. Clark, 101 Ga. 214, 28 S.E. 623 (Ga. 1897).
257. O.C.G.A. § 10-7-47; *see* Cureton v. Cureton, 120 Ga. 559, 48 S.E. 162 (Ga. 1904) (payment must be entered on execution).
258. Ezzard v. Bell, 100 Ga. 150, 28 S.E. 28 (Ga. 1897).
259. Bailey v. Mizell, 4 Ga. 123 (Ga. 1848).
260. Warthen v. Melton, 132 Ga. 113, 63 S.E. 832 (Ga. 1908).
261. Banks v. McCandless, 119 Ga. 793, 47 S.E. 332 (Ga. 1904).
262. Stanford v. Connery, 84 Ga. 731, 11 S.E. 507 (Ga. 1890).
263. Cherry v. Singleton, 66 Ga. 206 (Ga. 1880).

§ 10-7-47 appears to provide that the statute applies when the guarantor pays off or otherwise discharges a judgment "in part."

- If the guarantor is sued separately from the primary obligor and pays a judgment, the guarantor is entitled to control the judgment and execution against the primary obligor the same as if the judgment and execution were joint. If the guarantor does not appear as guarantor in the judgment, the guarantor may give notice and make the proof and obtain the control in the same manner as provided in the case of joint judgments.[264] A guarantor may be sued separately from the primary obligor and the failure to name the primary obligor as a defendant does not affect the validity of the judgment properly obtained against the guarantor.[265]

11.10 Paying Guarantor's Control of Litigation against Primary Obligor

- If during the course of a pending action against the primary obligor and the guarantor (or against the primary obligor alone), the guarantor pays off the underlying obligation, that payment operates only to cause the action to proceed for the benefit of the guarantor, and judgment may be entered in the name of the obligee for the use of the guarantor.[266]

11.11 Rights of Bona Fide Purchaser

- If the guarantor does not appear as such in the judgment and execution, the judgment lien, when controlled by the guarantor, does not interfere with the rights of a bona fide purchaser without notice from the primary obligor whose rights were vested before the order giving control of the judgment to the guarantor is granted.[267] Apparently, no Georgia court has construed this statute, but the statute appears to provide that a bona fide purchaser can take free of the judgment lien when the statutory conditions are met.

11.12 Paying Guarantor's Subrogation Rights

- A guarantor who has paid the underlying obligation is subrogated, both at law and equity, to all rights of the obligee and, in a controversy with other obligees, shall rank in dignity to the same as the obligee whose claim the guarantor paid.[268]
- Subrogation is the substitution of another person in the place of the obligee whose obligation is paid, so that the person in whose favor

264. O.C.G.A. § 10-7-48.
265. Wesley v. Lewis Bros., 33 Ga. App. 783, 127 S.E. 660 (Ga. App. 1925).
266. O.C.G.A. § 10-7-49.
267. O.C.G.A. § 10-7-55.
268. O.C.G.A. § 10-7-56.

it is exercised succeeds to all of the rights of the obligee. The doctrine of subrogation, being equitable in origin, is designed to prevent injustice.[269]

- A guarantor's right of subrogation relates back to the date the guarantor assumed the obligation to the obligee. The guarantor is not required to file under the UCC to preserve the guarantor's priority under the equitable right of subrogation.[270]
- A guarantor's right of subrogation under § 10-7-56 is to be distinguished from the guarantor's right to recoup the payment of the underlying obligation from the primary obligor under § 10-7-41. A guarantor who has paid the underlying obligation can still recover from the primary obligor even though the obligee has released the primary obligor.[271]
- There is a well-recognized distinction between a claim of legal subrogation, which is equitable in nature, and a claim of conventional subrogation, which is based on an agreement between the parties. A claim for conventional subrogation is not governed by equitable principles, and a guarantor asserting conventional subrogation need not show a superior equity in itself to recover.[272]
- As soon as the underlying obligation is satisfied by the guarantor, the guarantor has subrogation rights by virtue of the statute, and those rights are not dependent upon the commencement of any judicial proceedings.[273]
- Where less than the full amount of the underlying obligation is tendered, subrogation is not allowed.[274] This rule prohibits subrogation *pro tanto*, which would operate to place the guarantor who made a partial payment on equal footing with the obligee holding the balance of the debt, with any loss falling proportionately upon the obligee and the guarantor.[275]
- Subrogation authorizes the guarantor to sue upon the underlying obligation, not only against the primary obligor but also against coguarantors.[276]

11.13 Guarantor's Indemnity Rights

- A guarantor is entitled to indemnity from the primary obligor for any loss sustained by virtue of the guaranty.[277]

269. First Nat'l Bank v. American Surety Co., 71 Ga. App. 112, 30 S.E.2d 402 (Ga. App. 1944).
270. Pembroke State Bank v. Balboa Insurance Co., 144 Ga. App. 609, 241 S.E.2d 483 (Ga. App. 1978).
271. Fabian v. Dykes, 214 Ga. App. 792, 449 S.E.2d 305 (Ga. App. 1994).
272. First Nat'l Bank v. American Surety Co., 71 Ga. App. 112, 30 S.E.2d 402 (Ga. App. 1944).
273. Fender v. Fender, 30 Ga. App. 319, 117 S.E. 676 (Ga. App. 1923).
274. Jessee v. First Nat'l Bank, 154 Ga. App. 209, 267 S.E.2d 803 (Ga. App. 1980).
275. *Id.*
276. Dabney v. Brigman Motors Co., 32 Ga. App. 652, 124 S.E. 370 (Ga. App. 1924).
277. United States v. Jones, 155 F. Supp. 52 (M.D. Ga. 1957); In re Whitacre Sunbelt, Inc., 206 B.R. 1010 (Bankr. N.D. Ga. 1997) (primary obligor has duty to pay and to hold guarantor harmless, and, if guarantor pays, guarantor has claim against primary obligor).

11.14 Subrogation with Respect to Obligee's Collateral

- If a guarantor has paid the underlying obligation of the primary obligor, the guarantor is entitled to be substituted in the place of the obligee with respect to "all securities held by" the obligee for the payment of the underlying obligation.[278]
- The statute "clothes" the guarantor with legal title to the security, and upon payment of the underlying obligation by the guarantor, the obligee has no right to withhold the security from the guarantor.[279]
- Although a guarantor does not have any interest in collateral pledged to the obligee as security for an underlying obligation solely by virtue of the contract of guarantor,[280] the guarantor's subrogation rights arise as soon as the underlying obligation is paid by the guarantor, and the guarantor is thereby substituted in place of the obligee to all collateral held by the obligee.[281]

11.15 Effect of Obligee's Release of Primary Obligor

- The guarantor has an independent legal right to collect payment of the underlying obligation from the primary obligor despite the fact that the primary obligor has been released from liability on the underlying obligation by the obligee, provided that the guarantor is not a party to the primary obligor's release on the underlying obligation.[282]

§ 12 Rights of Guarantor against Coguarantors

12.1 Contribution Rights

- In cases where there is more than one guarantor for the same underlying obligation, a guarantor who pays "more than an equal share of the sum" of the underlying obligation may compel contribution from the coguarantors. If one of the coguarantors is insolvent, the deficiency in that coguarantor's share must be borne equally by the solvent coguarantors.[283] This statutory provision is a codification of the principle of contribution under common law, except for the provisions dealing with insolvent coguarantors.[284]
- The liability of coguarantors is several and not joint. A joint obligor who has paid the joint obligation is entitled to judgment against each

278. O.C.G.A. § 10-7-57.
279. Dabney v. Brigman Motors Co., 32 Ga. App. 652, 124 S.E. 370 (Ga. App. 1924); *see* Aultman v. United Bank, 259 Ga. 237, 378 S.E.2d 302 (Ga. 1989) (when guarantor paid underlying obligation, primary obligor not entitled to cancellation of security deed given by primary obligor to secure underlying obligation).
280. Conley v. Kelley, 43 Ga. App. 822, 160 S.E. 532 (Ga. App. 1931).
281. Hull v. Myers, 90 Ga. 674, 16 S.E. 653 (Ga. 1893).
282. Fabian v. Dykes, 214 Ga. App. 792, 449 S.E.2d 305 (Ga. App. 1994).
283. O.C.G.A. § 10-7-50.
284. Higdon v. Bell, 25 Ga. App. 54, 102 S.E. 546 (Ga. App. 1920).

coobligor only for the proportion for which each is liable. Accordingly, judgment should not be entered against any coobligor or all of them jointly for the aggregate amount of the underlying obligation.[285]

- The right of contribution as among coguarantors does not arise when the joint obligation is made but when one guarantor pays more than his share of the liability.[286]
- No right of contribution is enforceable without proof establishing that the paying guarantor paid more than his proportionate share of the underlying obligation.[287]
- A suit for contribution is not a suit on the underlying obligation by way of subrogation to the obligee's remedy. Subrogation is merely a form of action in aid of the right to contribution from coguarantors.[288]
- The general presumption that each guarantor has benefitted in an equal degree, so as to require contribution in equal shares, is subject to rebuttal by proof that there was an inequality of benefits received by the coguarantors.[289]

12.2 Statute of Limitations

- The four-year statute of limitations is generally applicable to claims for the right of contribution filed by one co-obligor against another pursuant to O.C.G.A. § 10-7-50.[290]

12.3 Prejudgment Interest

- A guarantor that recovers a contribution claim against a coguarantor is entitled to prejudgment interest from the time the underlying obligation was paid by the guarantor, which interest is deemed a liquidated demand.[291]

12.4 Indemnity from Primary Obligor

- In a suit for contribution, a guarantor must "first account" for all money or other property received from the primary obligor to indemnify the guarantor against loss.[292]
- If a guarantor has paid the entire debt, the guarantor may compel a coguarantor to transfer any mortgage or other security received from the primary obligor for the protection of the coguarantor,

285. Todd v. Windsor, 118 Ga. App. 805, 165 S.E.2d 438 (Ga. App. 1968).
286. Steele v. Grot, 232 Ga. App. 847, 503 S.E.2d 92 (Ga. App. 1998).
287. Holand v. Holland Heating & Air Conditioning, Inc., 208 Ga. App. 794, 432 S.E.2d 238 (Ga. App. 1993).
288. Todd v. Windsor, 118 Ga. App. 805, 165 S.E.2d 438 (Ga. App. 1968).
289. Steele v. Grot, 232 Ga. App. 847, 503 S.E.2d 92 (Ga. App. 1998); In re Citrico Int'l, Limited, 2009 Bankr. LEXIS 423 (Bankr. N. D. Ga. 2009).
290. Gray v. Currie, 2005 U.S. Dist. LEXIS 31407 (N. D. Ga. 2005).
291. O.C.G.A. § 10-7-51.
292. O.C.G.A. § 10-7-52.

and such transfer will relieve the coguarantor of all liability for contribution.[293]

12.5 Discharging Guarantor's Control of Principal's Litigation

- The provisions of §§ 10-7-40 through 10-7-49 apply to enable a guarantor discharging a joint underlying obligation, in whole or in part and whether pending the action or after joint or several judgments against the primary obligor and the guarantor, to control the lawsuit or the judgment against the coguarantors for the purpose of compelling them to contribute their respective shares of the amount paid by the guarantor.[294]

12.6 Waiver and Subordination of Contribution Rights

- Each coguarantor may waive or subordinate in the guaranty rights of contribution and other rights against coguarantors until the obligee receives payment in full of the underlying obligation.[295]

§ 13 Reaffirmation and Reinstatement

13.1 Reaffirmation

- A party to a contract who reaffirms the contract and obligations thereunder not only reinstates any otherwise extinguished liability under the contract but also waives all known offenses under the contract.[296]

13.2 Reinstatement

- Although we could not locate any Georgia cases on point, courts in other jurisdictions have held that a guaranty that provides that it is reinstated to the extent of any avoidance in a bankruptcy of pre-bankruptcy payments made by the primary obligor to the obligee is enforceable.[297]

---

293. O.C.G.A. § 10-7-52.
294. O.C.G.A. § 10-7-53; Holland v. Holland Heating & Air Conditioning, Inc., 208 Ga. App. 794, 432 S.E.2d 238 (Ga. App. 1993) (the court noted in dicta that a guarantor would be entitled to contribution only upon proof that such guarantor had paid more than his proportionate share of the debt guaranteed).
295. Brookside Communities, LLC v. Lake Dow North Corp., 268 Ga. App. 785, 603 S.E.2d 31 (Ga. App. 2009) (holding that a waiver of subrogation rights against the primary obligor was enforceable, the court upheld a broad waiver in a guaranty, which waiver included a waiver of contribution rights).
296. Highwoods Realty L.P. v. Cmty. Loans of Am., Inc., 288 Ga. App. 226, 653 S.E.2d 807 (Ga. App. 2007).
297. *See, e.g.,* In re Robinson Bros. Drilling, Inc., 6 F.3d 701 (10th Cir. 1993).

§ 14 Jury Trial Waivers

14.1 Not Enforceable in State Court

A jury trial waiver in a contract will not be enforced in a Georgia court.[298] After litigation is commenced, a knowing waiver of a jury trial right will be enforced.[299]

14.2 Possible Enforcement in Federal Court

- If a waiver of jury trial is contained in a contract governed by Georgia law, the waiver will likely not be enforced by a federal court sitting in Georgia.[300]
- The jury trial waiver may be enforced by a federal court in Georgia if the contract is governed by the laws of a state that permits jury trial waivers.[301]

298. Bank S., N.A. v. Howard, 264 Ga. 339, 444 S.E.2d 799 (Ga. 1994).
299. Ekereke v. Obong, 265 Ga. 728, 462 S.E.2d 372 (Ga. 1995).
300. GE Commercial Fin. Bus. Prop. Corp. v. Heard, 621 F. Supp. 2d 1305 (M.D. Ga. 2009).
301. *Id.*

Hawai`i State Law of Guaranties

Janel M. N. Yoshimoto
Deborah Macer Chun
Chun Yoshimoto LLP
737 Bishop Street, Suite 2800
Pacific Guardian Center, Mauka Tower
Honolulu, Hawai`i 96813
(808) 528-4200
Fax: (808) 531-8466
jyoshimoto@chunyoshimoto.com
www.chunyoshimoto.com

chun yoshimoto LLP
a limited liability law partnership

Contents

Hawai`i State Law of Guaranties

Practice Pointer: Hawai`i has no general statute applicable to guaranties exclusively and relatively little case law addressing guaranties. Accordingly, as evidenced by this survey, there is sparse guidance as to a number of issues in guaranty law; however, it is noted that in rendering decisions the Hawai`i courts have tended to rely substantially on secondary sources such as American Jurisprudence and the Restatement of Security.[1] Because of the paucity of Hawai`i law, local practitioners will typically follow what is considered the majority rule in other jurisdictions.

Introductory Note: In order to standardize our discussion of the law of guaranties, we use the following vocabulary to refer to the various parties to a guaranty and their obligations.

"Guarantor" is a person who, by contract, agrees to satisfy a principal obligation of another obligor in the event of nonperformance of such other obligor.

"Guaranty" means a promise by a guarantor which is collateral to a principal obligation of another obligor and which binds the guarantor to performance in the event of nonperformance of such other obligor.[2]

"Obligee" or **"creditor"** means the person to whom the underlying obligation is owed. For example, the lender under a loan agreement would be an obligee vis-à-vis the borrower.

"Primary obligor" means the person who incurs the underlying obligation to the obligee. For example, the borrower under a promissory note would be a primary obligor.

"Underlying obligation" or **"principal obligation"** means the obligation or obligations incurred by the primary obligor and owed to the obligee. For example, the borrower's obligation to make payments to a lender of principal and interest on a loan constitutes an underlying obligation.

---

1. The Restatement of Suretyship and Guaranty, the successor to the Restatement of Security, has not yet been cited as a secondary authority in any Hawai`i reported case as of the time this survey was prepared.
2. *See* Waikiki Seaside, Inc. v. Comito, 3 Haw. App. 103, 106, 641 P.2d 1363, 1365 (1982); Hawai`i Leasing v. Klein, 5 Haw. App. 450, 454, 698 P.2d 309, 312-13 (1985); Liberty Bank v. Shimokawa, 2 Haw. App. 280, 282, 632 P.2d 289, 291 (1981) (*citing* 38 Am. Jur.2d Guaranty § 1 (1968)).

§ 1 Nature of the Guaranty Arrangement

The general rule in Hawai`i is that the contract of guaranty is an enforceable undertaking or promise on the part of one person (i.e., the guarantor) which is collateral to the principal obligation on the part of another person and which binds the guarantor to performance in the event of nonperformance by the principal obligor.[3] A guarantor is not a co-obligor or jointly and/or severally liable with the primary obligor; rather, the guarantor and primary obligor are parties to separate contracts with the obligee.[4] The guaranty provides a separate remedy from the remedies on the underlying obligation; thus, an action against a guarantor may be brought independently of an action against the obligor, and a prior judgment against the obligor does not discharge a guarantor that was not a party to the action.[5]

§ 2 State Law Requirements for an Entity or Individual to Enter a Guaranty

2.1 Entities

Corporations, nonprofit corporations, and limited liability companies registered or organized under the laws of the State of Hawai`i all have the statutory power to grant guarantees, *unless* their articles of incorporation or articles of organization, as applicable, provide otherwise.[6] Banks authorized to operate as such under Hawai`i law also have the power to grant guarantees as a right and power of a corporation organized under Hawai`i law.[7]

While the requirements for a general partnership or a limited partnership to enter into a guaranty are not expressly covered by statute or case law in Hawai`i, it is presumed that such entities do have the power to grant guarantees (like other forms of business entities), unless their governing partnership agreements prohibit it.

2.2 Individuals

Unless a person lacks the legal capacity to enter into a contract, a person may act, serve, and be a surety on all bonds and undertakings required under the laws of the State of Hawai`i.[8] As discussed in Section 6.2 below, a guarantor is a surety. Accordingly, a legally competent individual has the power to enter into a contract of guaranty under the law of Hawai`i.

3. 3 Haw. App. at 106, 641 P.2d at 1365 (1982).
4. Lee v. Yano, 93 Haw. 142, 147-148, 997 P.2d 68, 73-74 (App. 2000).
5. *Id.*
6. *See* Haw. Rev. Stat. §§ 414-42, 414D-52, and 428-111.
7. *See* Haw. Rev. Stat. § 412:5-200.
8. Haw. Rev. Stat. § 572-27.

2.2.1 *Married individuals and Individuals in other Legal Relationships*

Pursuant to Section 572-22, Hawai`i Revised Statutes (HRS), a married person may enter into a contract with his or her spouse and with any other person, in the same manner as if he or she were sole.[9] Marriages are created statutorily in Hawai`i pursuant to the requirements of HRS Chapter 572. Common law marriages are invalid in Hawai`i.[10] Hawai`i law also provides for the creation of civil unions and reciprocal beneficiary relationships between individuals.

The Civil Unions Statute became effective on January 1, 2012, and provides that a "civil union" is a union between two adult individuals legally established pursuant to the requirements of HRS Chapter 572B.[11] There is no requirement that the civil union must be between adults of the same gender; however, two adults who stand in relation to each other as ancestor and descendant of any degree or as siblings are prohibited from establishing a civil union under the law.[12] Partners to a civil union established under HRS Chapter 572B have all the same rights, benefits, protections, and responsibilities under the law as are granted to those who are married under HRS Chapter 572.[13]

A reciprocal beneficiary relationship is created between two adults, who are legally prohibited from marrying one another[14] under HRS Chapter 572 and who meet the other requirements of HRS Chapter 572C.[15] Unlike partners to a civil union, reciprocal beneficiaries do not have all of the rights and obligations of married persons, but only those rights and obligations expressly provided by law to reciprocal beneficiaries[16] (such as being able to hold title to real and personal property as tenants by the entirety).[17] Accordingly, for purposes of this discussion, reference to a married person or a spouse also means a partner of a civil union, and reference to marriage also means a civil union; however, reciprocal beneficiaries and reciprocal beneficiary relationships will be specifically addressed only when applicable to this discussion.

A married person is generally not liable for the debts of a spouse, nor is a married person's property generally liable to be taken in any collection

9. Prior to the Married Women's Act of 1888, a wife alone did not have legal power to create a contract or to alienate or dispose of property without the consent or joinder of her husband on the basis that a woman lost her independent legal identity upon marriage. *See* Dowsett v. Jones, 9 Haw. 543, 544 (1894), and Moore v. Honeywell Info. Sys., Inc., 558 F. Supp. 1229, 1232 (D. Haw. 1983). The Married Women's Act of 1888 (codified in Chapter 573, HAW. REV. STAT.) extended to married women the right to enter into contracts in their individual capacity, "to own their separate property, to sue and be sued, to act as a surety, or to be a personal representative, guardian, or other fiduciary." *Moore,* 558 F. Supp. at 1232 (D. Haw. 1983). The Act did not, however, "free the husband and wife from the restraints of the common law of contracting and conveying to each other." First National Bank v. Gaines, 16 Haw. 731, 732 (1905). In 1987, the Married Women's Act of 1888 was repealed and replaced by new sections of HAW. REV. STAT. Chapter 572, including HAW. REV. STAT. § 572-22, making it legal for spouses to enter into contracts with each other, as well as with other persons.
10. *See* Parke v. Parke, 25 Haw. 297 (1920).
11. HAW. REV. STAT. § 572B-1.
12. HAW. REV. STAT. § 572B-3.
13. HAW. REV. STAT. § 572B-9.
14. The adults need not be of the same sex; any other relationship that would prevent marriage (e.g., parent and child) would also qualify for reciprocal beneficiary status.
15. HAW. REV. STAT. § 572C-4.
16. HAW. REV. STAT. § 572C-6.
17. *See* HAW. REV. STAT. § 509-2 (providing that land or any other type of property or property rights may be conveyed by reciprocal beneficiaries to themselves, as tenants by the entirety (among other variations of conveyances to oneself and to others)).

process against that person's spouse.[18] The only exception to the separation of liability for one spouse's debts is if the debt incurred by a spouse was for necessaries for both spouses, for one another or for their family during marriage, in which case both spouses shall be liable for the debt created by a spouse, unless such liability is contrary to a court order for support and maintenance pending divorce.[19]

Further, under Hawai`i law, there is a rebuttable presumption that all property, both real and personal, acquired in the name of an individual, is the separate property of that individual, regardless of whether the individual was married at the time of the acquisition.[20] Accordingly, the real and personal property acquired in the name of an individual, whether that individual is married or single, may be granted as security for an individual guarantor's obligations under a contract of guaranty without the consent or joinder of the other spouse. It will be the other spouse's burden to prove that the property of the individual guarantor was not separate property.[21]

2.2.2 *Individuals holding Property as Tenants by the Entirety*

It is clear under Hawai`i law that property held in tenancy by the entirety cannot be used to fulfill the liability of a married guarantor, unless both spouses affirmatively pledge their undivided interest in such property. A tenancy by the entirety must be held exclusively by married spouses or by reciprocal beneficiaries, who alone must possess the mutual right of survivorship.[22] The Hawai`i legislature has recently clarified that when two individuals who own property as tenants by the entirety enter into a different legal relationship with each other that also allows them to hold property as tenants by the entirety (e.g., from a reciprocal beneficiary relationship to a civil union), then their ownership as tenants by the entirety shall be continuous if (a) the new legal relationship is simultaneously entered into with the termination of the prior legal relationship; or (b) the new legal relationship is entered into within 90 days after the prior legal relationship has terminated; provided that no liens attached to the property and were perfected during the interim period.[23] Upon a divorce or the termination of a reciprocal beneficiary relationship, a tenancy by the entirety becomes a tenancy in common.[24]

---

18. Haw. Rev. Stat. § 572-23.
19. Haw. Rev. Stat. § 572-24; *see* The Queen's Medical Ctr. V. Kagawa, 88 Haw. 489, 967 P.2d 686 (App. 1998), *cert. denied*, 91 Haw. 124, 980 P.2d 998 (1998) (holding that regardless of the condition of the marriage, until a final disposition of divorce proceeding is entered and absent entry of a court order for support or maintenance, once necessaries (in this case, necessary hospital care for the husband) are provided, "the provider should be compensated for its goods or services by the person benefitted or by the person upon whom the legal obligation to render payment may have legally devolved as the provider historically was reimbursed at common law").
20. *See* Haw. Rev. Stat. §§ 572-21 and 509-2.
21. *See supra* notes 9 and 19.
22. *See* Haw. Rev. Stat. § 509-2 (providing that reciprocal beneficiaries may hold title to property as tenants by the entirety); *and see* Traders Travel Int'l, Inc. v. Howser, 69 Haw. 609, 613, 753 P.2d 244, 246 (1988) (defining a tenancy by the entirety).
23. HB 2569 HD2 SD1 CD1 (reconfirming and clarifying the provisions of Haw. Rev. Stat. Chapter 572B, including adding a new section to Haw. Rev. Stat. Chapter 509 and a new section to Haw. Rev. Stat. Chapter 572B).
24. *See* Traders Travel Int'l, Inc., 69 Haw. at 614, 753 P.2d at 247 (*citing* Vaughan v. Williamson, 1 Haw. App. 496, 621 P.2d 387 (1980)); *see also* Guray v. Tacras, 119 Haw. 212, 194 P.3d 1174 (reaffirming the holding in Chock v. Chock, 39 Haw. 657 (1953), which states that the legal effect of a divorce is that it converts a tenancy by the entirety into a tenancy in common, unless the property was disposed of by the divorce decree).

HRS Section 509-1 provides for the creation of a tenancy by the entirety in land if the conveyance instrument manifestly indicates the intention to create such tenancy. Further, proceeds from the sale of land that was held in tenancy by the entirety shall retain the entirety characteristic, unless both spouses demonstrate a contrary intent.[25] Tenancy by the entirety may also be created for personal property pursuant to HRS Section 509-2, so long as a manifest intent to create such tenancy by the spouses or reciprocal beneficiaries is apparent.[26]

The issue of whether the interest of one spouse in real property, held in tenancy by the entirety, is subject to levy and execution by his or her individual creditors was decided in the Hawai`i Supreme Court case of *Sawada v. Endo.*[27] In *Sawada,* the Hawai`i Supreme Court held that, following passage of the Married Women's Property Act,[28] the interest of a spouse under a tenancy by the entirety estate is not subject to the claims of such individual spouse's creditors during the joint lives of the spouses.

The Married Women's Property Act put the wife's rights to exercise ownership over the whole estate on equal level as her husband's rights—no longer could the husband convey, lease, mortgage, or otherwise deal with the property without the wife's consent. Accordingly, upon creation of a tenancy by the entirety, each spouse is deemed to be seized of the whole estate or interest from the time of creation of the tenancy and neither spouse has a separate divisible interest in the property that can be conveyed or reached by execution, except by joint action of the spouses.[29] It should be noted, however, that Hawai`i courts have decided that the creation of a tenancy by the entirety cannot be used as a means of defrauding existing creditors.[30]

Act 209, Session Laws of Hawai`i 2012, amends HRS Section 509-2 to expressly permit spouses or reciprocal beneficiaries who own land in Hawai`i as tenants by the entirety to retain the same immunity from claims of their separate creditors when such land is conveyed by them in one of two ways: (1) to a joint trust as tenant in severalty for their benefit, if the trust is revocable and amendable by either or both of them during their lifetime; or (2) to their respective separate trusts in equal shares as tenants in common, if each trust is revocable and amendable by the respective grantor to the trust.[31] Such conveyance, however, must comply with certain statutory requirements to memorialize the intent of the grantors to continue to hold the real property

25. In the Matter of the Estate of David Au, 59 Haw. 474, 478, 583 P.2d 966, 970 (1978) (reasoning that because "proceeds from the sale of land held by the entirety are, in effect, a substitute for the land, we presume that these proceeds retain the entirety characteristic that the land itself had").
26. *Supra* note 22; Haw. Rev. Stat. § 509-2 (which provides that "[l]and, or any interest therein, or *any other type of property or property rights or interests or interests therein,* may be conveyed . . . by spouses to themselves, as tenants by the entirety[.] (emphasis added)).
27. 57 Haw. 608, 561 P.2d 1291 (1977).
28. The Married Women's Property Act of 1888 abolished the common law rule which held that a wife had no legal power to make contracts or to alienate property during marriage without the husband's consent and, if the husband gave his consent, the husband shall be liable with his wife for his wife's debts contracted for during marriage if the husband is joined in the creditor's lawsuit. Dowsett v. Jones, 9 Haw. 543 (1894). The Act freed the wife's property from the management, control, debts, and obligations of the husband and, accordingly, the wife could sue and be sued as if she were unmarried. *Id.*
29. *Sawada* at 613, 561 P.2d at 1295.
30. *Id.* at 616, 561 P.2d at 1297; *also cited* in Valvanis v. Milgroom, 529 F. Supp.2d 1206, 1213 (D. Haw. 2007).
31. HB 2623 HD1 SD1 CD1 (2012).

or its proceeds as tenants by the entirety.[32] The immunity from claims of separate creditors remains in effect so long as the spouses remain married (or in a civil union) or a registered reciprocal beneficiary status continues to exist; upon entry of the decree of divorce or annulment or the termination of the reciprocal beneficiary relationship, such immunity terminates and the real property is treated as held in tenancy in common.[33]

§ 3 Consideration; Sufficiency of Past Consideration

As with any other contract, consideration needs to be present to support a contract of guaranty. Where the guaranty is made at the same time as the principal obligation and it becomes an essential inducement to the formation of the primary contract, the consideration for the principal obligation is also the consideration for the contract of guaranty.[34] If the guaranty is given after the primary contract is created, then new and distinct consideration for the guaranty is required (for instance, the obligee's agreement to forbear on the enforcement of a promissory note or to modify credit terms).[35] Accordingly, it is prudent for lawyers documenting a contract of guaranty to recite the consideration that applies (e.g., that the guaranty is an essential inducement to the obligee entering into the primary contract, if the guaranty is given concurrently with the primary contract,[36] or that the guaranty is being given in consideration for the obligee's forbearance to collect on the debt due and agreement to provide future services[37]).

§ 4 Notice of Acceptance

A contract of guaranty can only be made by the mutual assent of the parties. Where the obligee requests the guarantor to sign the guaranty and the guarantor does so, or if the guaranty recites the receipt of consideration, however small, then mutual assent is proven.[38] If the guaranty is signed by the guarantor without any previous request of the obligee, in the absence of the obligee, and for no consideration between the obligee and guarantor other than an agreement by the obligee to make future advances to the debtor, then the guarantor must receive reasonable notice of the obligee's acceptance of the guaranty in order to be bound.[39] Notice of acceptance, however, may be informal and

32. *See* HAW. REV. STAT. 509-2(b) and (c).
33. HAW. REV. STAT. 509-2(c)(1) and (f).
34. Hutchinson v. Keikiohua, 4 Haw. 47, 49 (1877); Metropolitan Cas. Ins. Co. v. Realty Development Co., 32 Haw. 667, 675 (1933).
35. *Metropolitan Cas. Ins. Co.* at 675.
36. *Id.*
37. Lennen & Newell, Inc. v. Clark Enterprises, Inc., 51 Haw. 233, 236-37, 456 P.2d 231, 234-35 (1969).
38. Schweitzer v. Fishel, 13 Haw. 690, 692-93 (1901).
39. *Id.*

may be implied from the circumstances.[40] Further, notice of acceptance may be waived by the terms of the guaranty.[41]

§ 5 Interpretation of Guaranties

5.1 Generally

Guaranties will be construed generally under the law of contracts. Accordingly, Hawai`i courts construe guaranties, as other contracts, so as to give effect to the parties' intentions. In particular, the obligations of the guarantor are strictly construed according to the terms of the guaranty and cannot be altered, extended or enlarged by the obligee or the primary obligor without the guarantor's consent.[42] A guaranty of the obligations of one obligor cannot, without the guarantor's consent, be extended to the obligations of another obligor.[43]

As a general rule, if a guaranty is "complete and not uncertain or ambiguous, the writing will be presumed to contain the entire agreement, and parol or extrinsic evidence is inadmissible to vary the terms of the written instrument."[44] However, there is an exception if the guaranty was procured by fraud, and parol or extrinsic evidence is admissible to prove such fraud.[45]

5.2 Guaranty of Payment versus Guaranty of Collection

A guaranty of payment and a guaranty of collection both obligate the guarantor thereunder to pay the debt of the primary obligor in the event of a default under the primary contract. A guaranty of payment, however, is "absolute" in that payment by the guarantor is due upon the happening of the default whereas a guaranty of collection requires that the obligee first attempt to collect from the primary obligor before proceeding to collect from the guarantor.[46] Under the rules applicable to the construction of contracts, the terms of the guaranty will determine if the guaranty is one of payment versus collection.[47]

---

40. 13 Haw. at 692-93.
41. Liberty Bank v. Shimokawa, 2 Haw. App. at 283, 632 P.2d at 292.
42. *See* State of Hawai`i v. Tradewinds Electrical Svc. & Contracting Inc., 80 Haw. 218, 223, 908 P.2d 1204, 1209 (1995).
43. *Id.*, 908 P.2d at 1209.
44. Honolulu Federal v. Murphy, 7 Haw. App. 196, 200, 753 P.2d 807, 811 (citing 38 Am. Jur. 2d Guaranty § 124 at 1130 (1968)).
45. *Id.*, 753 P.2d at 811.
46. *See* International Trust Co. v. Suzui, 31 Haw. 34, 39-40 (1929) (which provides "[a]s a general rule a guaranty of the payment of an obligation of another is an absolute undertaking imposing liability upon the guarantor immediately upon the default of the principal debtor and regardless of whether any legal proceedings or steps are taken to enforce the liability of the principal debtor, or whether notice of the default is given to the guarantor, and regardless of the solvency or insolvency of the principal debtor").
47. *Id.* (holding that the guaranty is absolute and unconditional and not a mere guaranty of "collectability" (as such term was used by the court), if the contract is without ambiguity).

5.3 "Continuing" Guaranty

A continuing guaranty is a contract of guaranty that contemplates a future course of dealings between the primary obligor and the obligee over an indefinite period of time and guarantees the overall indebtedness of the primary obligor, not a particular note or obligation.[48] The continuing guaranty is interpreted as an ongoing offer by the guarantor that is accepted by the obligee each time it extends credit to the primary obligor. The continuing guaranty thus remains in effect until it is revoked by the guarantor.[49] Where a former spouse had signed a continuing guaranty of her spouse's obligations and failed to revoke the continuing guaranty after the divorce, it was held that lapse of memory was not a valid basis to disprove intent and that the fundamental rules of contract law governed; thus, absent allegations of fraud, mistake, or duress, the failure to read or understand the guaranty contract was not a defense.[50] Likewise, the failure to include a limit on the liability under the continuing guaranty, even though there was a blank for such an amount, did not invalidate the guaranty.[51]

5.4 "Absolute" versus "Conditional"

A guaranty is "absolute" if the guarantor promises to pay to, or perform some act for the benefit of, the obligee upon the principal obligor's default.[52] If, in addition to the principal obligor's default, the guaranty requires, as a condition to the guarantor's liability, the "happening of some contingent event...or the performance of some act on the part of the creditor" (e.g., the requirement that the creditor first sell the collateral securing the indebtedness before proceeding against the guarantor), then a "conditional" guaranty is created.[53]

5.5 Completion Guaranties and other Performance Guaranties

Issues relating specifically to completion guaranties and other kinds of performance guaranties[54] have not yet been address under Hawai`i law.

---

48. Liberty Bank v. Shimokawa, 2 Haw. App. at 282, 632 P.2d at 291.
49. *Id.*, 632 P.2d at 291 (*citing* 38 Am. Jur. 2d Guaranty § 63 (1968)).
50. Liberty Bank v. Shimokawa, 2 Haw. App. at 284, 632 P.2d at 292.
51. *Id.*, 632 P.2d at 293.
52. *Hawaii Leasing*, 5 Haw. App. at 455, 698 P.2d at 313.
53. *Id.*, 698 P.2d at 313 (*citing* 38 Am. Jur. 2d Guaranty § 21 at 1020 (1968)).
54. A guaranty of lease whereby the guarantor thereunder guaranties all obligations of the lessee under the lease, not just the payment of rent, is an example of a kind of performance guaranty.

§ 6 Defenses of the Guarantor

The defenses that may be available to a guarantor can be grouped into three categories: (1) defenses of the primary obligor; (2) "suretyship defenses"; and (3) other defenses.

6.1 Defenses of the Primary Obligor

Defenses of the primary obligor may generally be asserted by the guarantor as a defense to the enforcement of its guaranty.[55] Hawai`i case law has adopted the view that where judgment is given in favor of an obligee against a principal obligor, other than by default or confession, and the obligee subsequently brings an action against the guarantor, proof of such judgment creates the rebuttable presumption of the principal obligor's liability to the obligee.[56] It is then the obligation of the guarantor to prove that judgment should have been entered for the primary obligor, and the means of proving it is a matter to be determined by the laws of evidence.[57]

6.2 "Suretyship" Defenses Generally

Guarantors are sureties under Hawai`i law.[58] Accordingly, it is standard practice for the guaranty governed by Hawai`i law to waive applicable suretyship defenses. While Hawai`i case law has not addressed the enforceability of all waivers of suretyship defenses or even a blanket waiver of all suretyship defenses, Hawai`i courts have upheld the enforceability of provisions expressly waiving notices to the guarantor.[59] Notably, Section 3-605(i) of the Uniform Commercial Code (UCC), which Hawai`i has adopted, permits blanket waivers of suretyship defenses in negotiable notes given to commercial creditors, and the commentary notes that such waivers are a standard practice.[60]

---

55. *See* Joy A. McElroy. D. Inc. v. Maryl Group, Inc., 107 Haw. 423, 114 P.2d 929 (2005).
56. Motion Picture Industry Pension Plan v. Hawai`ian Kona Coast Associates, 9 Haw. App. 42, 53-54, 823 P.2d 752, 758 (1991) (applying the law of sureties to the question of whether the guarantor is bound to the creditor's judgment against the debtor and stating that "[s]ureties may or may not be guarantors, but guarantors are sureties").
57. *Id.*, 923 P.2d at 758.
58. 9 Haw. App. at 53-54, 823 P.2d at 758. *See also* State of Hawai`i, 80 Haw. at 223, 908 P.2d at 1209 (providing that "...a suretyship relationship exists whenever a person becomes responsible for the debt of another. A guarantee is distinguishable from other forms of surety contracts in that it is a separate, independent contract between the guarantor and the creditor-obligee and is collateral to the contractual obligation between the creditor-obligee and the principal-obligor").
59. *See* Section 8, infra.
60. *See* Comment 2, HAW. REV. STAT. § 3-605(i).

While sureties under that Section of the UCC do not include guarantors[61], the courts apply the same policy to guarantors which, as noted above, are also sureties.

6.2.1 *Significant Modification and Impairment of the Obligee's Security for the Primary Obligation*

Hawai`i courts have adopted the general rule that "any action or omission by a creditor in breach of an obligation to the guarantor which injures the guarantor or the rights of the guarantor operates to discharge the guarantor, at least to the extent of the injury."[62] *In U.S. v. Teruya Restaurant, Ltd.*,[63] the U.S. District Court for the District of Hawai`i held that one obligation of a creditor to a guarantor is to protect and preserve the security for payment of the primary obligor's indebtedness. Further, the court noted that, under general law,[64] when the creditor releases or diverts security for an obligation, the guarantor is generally discharged to the extent of the value of the collateral discharged or diverted, and then found that not achieving and then waiving the requirement for security is at least as egregious and, therefore, the rationale for the general rule likewise applied to those circumstances. Thus, when the creditor failed to obtain and perfect the security for the loan contemplated in the loan agreement delivered concurrently with the guarantors' guaranty and then subsequently waived such collateral after the loan agreement was executed without the guarantors' knowledge or consent, the court held that the guarantors were entitled to discharge of their obligations as guarantors at least to the extent of the value of the collateral which was never obtained and/or waived.[65] Because the value of the collateral released exceeded the obligations under the guaranty, the court refused to address whether the failure to obtain and perfect the expected collateral would have resulted in a complete release of the guarantor if the obligation had exceeded the value of the collateral not obtained.

6.3 Other Defenses

6.3.1 *Failure to Fulfill a Condition Precedent*

If the guarantor's liability is conditioned upon the happening of a contingent event (other than the default of the principal obligation) or the performance of

61. Construing prior UCC provisions, Hawai`i courts held that the reference to a guaranty in a promissory note brought the guaranty within the provisions of the UCC and resulted in the impairment of collateral defense under, and as construed by, Article 3 being available to the guarantor. *See Honolulu Federal*, 7 Haw. App. at 207, 750 P.2d at 815 (1988) and Hawaii Broadcasting Co., Inc. v. Hawai`i Radio, Inc., 82 Hawai`i at 117, 919 P.2d at 1030, construing prior HAW. REV. STAT. § 490:3-606(1)(b), which has been replaced by HAW. REV. STAT. § 490:3-605(f). However, the current corresponding provision of the UCC refers to impairment of collateral discharging of the obligation of a party "who is jointly and severally liable with respect to the secured obligation," HAW. REV. STAT. § 490:3-605(f), and a guarantor does not have joint and several liability with the primary obligor. See Section 1, *supra. On that basis, the prior holdings could be distinguished, such that Article 3 of the UCC is not directly applicable, although the concepts could be applied by analogy.*
62. *Hawai`i Leasing*, 5 Haw. App. at 455, 698 P.2d at 313 (citing 38 Am. Jur. 2d Guaranty § 79 at 1086 (1968)).
63. 675 F. Supp. 1216 (1987).
64. *Id.* at 1220 (citing 38 Am. Jur. 2d Guaranty § 84).
65. 675 F. Supp. at 1220-21.

some act by the obligee is first required, then the nonoccurrence of such event or nonperformance of such act would be a defense of the guarantor.[66]

6.3.2 Breach of Obligation of Good Faith and Fair Dealing

As with other contracts, the parties are subject to an obligation of good faith and fair dealing.[67] Thus, for example, where a guarantor's obligation is conditioned on the prior sale of collateral for the loan, good faith performance requires that the creditor sell the collateral in a manner and at a price that are commercially reasonable under the circumstances.[68]

6.3.3 Failure to pursue Primary Obligor

It has been a long standing rule in Hawai`i that, under a contract of guaranty, a guarantor is released from liability to the extent of the guarantor's injury due to the neglect of the obligee to enforce its claim with reasonable diligence against the principal obligor.[69] There have been no published cases in Hawai`i, applying this rule to determine whether to release a guarantor for its injury. Accordingly, it is unclear what constitutes reasonable diligence in enforcing a claim against a principal obligor. The cases stating the rule did not discuss whether the guaranty to which the rule was being applied was only a guaranty of collection, and any language quoted from the guaranties was not specific. However, for this rule to make sense given the distinction between a guaranty of payment versus a guaranty of collection,[70] the guaranty would presumably have to be a guaranty of collection in order for this defense to apply. Thus, if a guaranty of payment is intended by the guarantor and obligee, the intent should be made very clear in the guaranty so as to avoid any presumption of a different intent and to foreclose the application of this defense.

6.3.4 Nondisclosure of Information

Where a guarantor based its defense on nondisclosure by the obligor of information with respect to the entities that were the obligors on the underlying debt, the court found that the information was generally available to the public—a fact not disputed by the guarantors—and that such availability of the information "disproves the bare contention that the creditor failed to disclose or misrepresented" the information.[71]

6.3.5 Disposition of Collateral-UCC Requirements

A number of the provisions of Part Six (default and enforcement) of Article 9 of the UCC apply to "secondary obligors" which are defined in the UCC

66. *See* Hawai`i *Leasing*, 5 Haw. App. at 455, 698 P.2d at 313.
67. *Hawai`i Leasing*, 5 Haw. App. at 456, 698 P.2d at 313.
68. *Id.*
69. *See Schweitzer*, 13 Haw. at 693; *see also Lee*, 93 Haw. at 148, 997 P.2d at 74 (citing the same rule from Schweitzer).
70. *See* Section 5.2, *supra*.
71. *Hawai`i Broadcasting Co.*, 82 Haw. 106, 115, 919 P.2d 1018, 1027 (Haw. App. 1996).

as persons whose obligations are secondary or who have a right of recourse against the debtor or another obligor with respect to the underlying secured debt.[72] This will include guarantors.[73]

Among other matters, the UCC addresses the requirements for the use and operation of collateral held by the secured party, collection of the collateral, notice of disposition, and the commercially reasonable disposition of collateral. The remedies for failure to comply with the requirements are specified, including the inability of a noncompliant secured party to a deficiency unless the secured party can prove that the amount that would have been obtained for the collateral had the secured party complied with the statutory requirements would have been less than the debt owed, in which case the deficiency is only the difference between the debt and that amount that would have been obtained.[74] It should be noted that, if a security agreement covers both real and personal property, and if both types of property are foreclosed under the rules applicable to mortgage foreclosures, the provisions of Part Six of Article 9 will not apply.[75]

6.3.6 Statute of Limitations

By Hawai`i statute, an action for the recovery of any debt founded upon any contract, obligation, or liability must be commenced within six years after the cause of action accrues or will be barred (with some limited exceptions).[76] Accordingly, if an action to collect under a contract of guaranty is brought after the expiration of the six-year statute of limitation, a defense from such action would exist for the guarantor.

6.3.7 Statute of Frauds

The statute of frauds is codified in Chapter 656 of the Hawai`i Revised Statutes. A contract to answer for the debt, default, or misconduct of another is one of the contracts that is not enforceable unless it is in writing and signed by the persons to be charged or by such persons' agent(s), who are authorized in writing to sign.[77] Note, however, that Hawai`i common law recognizes

72. Haw. Rev. Stat. § 490:9-102(a) and Comment 2.a to that Section.
73. *See* Restatement (Third) of Suretyship and Guaranty, Section 1 (1996) and Comment 4(i) to Haw. Rev. Stat. § 490:9-101.
74. Under prior UCC law, the Hawai`i courts had also adopted a rebuttable presumption such that a secured party that failed to comply with notice or commercially reasonable disposition requirements had the burden of rebutting a presumption that the value of the collateral equaled the debt. *See* Liberty Bank v. Honolulu Providoring, Inc., 65 Haw. 273, 650 P.2d 576 (1982) and Bank of Hawai`i v. Davis Radio Sales & Service, Inc., 6 Haw. App. 469, 727 P.2d 419 (1986).
75. Haw. Rev. Stat. § 490:9-604.
76. Haw. Rev. Stat. § 657-1. However, the statute of limitations for an obligation incurred by a minor for certain types of health care does not begin to run until the minor reaches the age of majority and then must be commenced within two years. Haw. Rev. Stat. § 577A-5.
77. Haw. Rev. Stat. § 656-1.

certain exceptions to the statute of frauds, such as where there is part performance or detrimental reliance[78] or where the matter to be proven is fraud in the inducement.[79]

§ 7 Waivers by the Guarantor

7.1 Generally

In each instance where it has been addressed by the Hawai`i courts, a specific waiver by a guarantor has been upheld; e.g., a waiver of notice of default by the primary obligor[80]; waiver of notice of acceptance of the guaranty and notice of execution of a new note guaranteed by a continuing guaranty, the court noting that it "cannot extend the contract beyond its precise and uncontroverted terms";[81] and waiver of a right to trial by jury.[82] However, it can be expected that the waivers will be strictly construed. In *Teruya*, by way of example, the court found that a waiver in the guaranty that allowed the creditor to "substitute, exchange or release" collateral was not sufficient as a waiver of the obligation to obtain the collateral in the first place;[83] the court did not address whether a specific waiver of the actual failure would have been enforceable.

7.2 Defenses that cannot be Waived

While the UCC is generally not applicable to guaranties, as noted above, certain provisions in Part Six of Article 9 related to the creditor's obligations with respect to the collection of secured debts do affect guarantors. Most notably, both under Hawai`i case law interpreting earlier versions of the UCC[84] and under the express terms of the current UCC,[85] the requirements for notification of the sale of collateral and commercial reasonableness in the conduct of the sale cannot be waived prior to default.

---

78 *See, e.g.*, McIntosh v. Murphy, 52 Haw. 29, 469 P.2d 177 (1970), rehearing denied, 52 Haw. 112 (1970); Lopez v. Soy Young, 9 Haw. 117 (1893); and Shannon v. Waterhouse, 58 Haw. 4, 563 P.2d 391 (1977), rehearing denied, 59 Haw. 667 (1978), cert. denied 440 U.S. 911 (1979).

79. *See* Section 5.1, *supra.*

80. *See Waikiki Seaside*, 3 Haw. App. at 106, 641 P.2d at 1365.

81. *See* Liberty Bank v. Shimokawa, 2 Haw. App. at 282, 632 P.2d at 292.

82. *See McElroy*, 107 Haw. at 431; 114 P.2d at 937.

83. *See Teruya*, 675 F. Supp. at 1219.

84. *See* Liberty Bank v. Honolulu Providoring, Inc., 65 Haw. 273, 650 P.2d 576 (1982) and Bank of Hawai`i v. Davis Radio Sales & Service, Inc., 6 Haw. App. 469, 727 P.2d 419 (1986).

85. Haw. Rev. Stat. § 490:9-624.

§ 8 Application of Debtor's Payments to Multiple Matured Debts of the Same Creditor When not all of those Debts are Guaranteed

When a debtor who owes more than one matured debt to a creditor makes payment to the creditor, the payment shall be applied to these debts according to the following priorities: (a) in accordance with the terms of a binding agreement between the debtor and the creditor; (b) in accordance with the instructions of the debtor given to the creditor either prior to or at the time of the payment; (c) as actually applied by the creditor prior to the existence of any controversy with the debtor or the guarantor concerning the application of the payment; or (d) by the court in accordance with the law's notions of justice set forth in the Restatement (Second) of Contracts § 260 (1981).[86] The law's notions of justice set forth in said Restatement provide for the following order of preference with respect to such payment: (1) to a debt that the debtor is under a duty to a third person to pay immediately (such as the general duty of exoneration owed by a debtor to a guarantor or a duty based on contract); (2) to overdue interest rather than principal and to an unsecured or precarious debt (as opposed to a secured debt or one that is certain to be paid); (3) to the earliest matured debt; and (4) ratably among debts of the same maturity.[87]

§ 9 Choice of Law Rules Applicable to Guaranties

9.1 Application in General to Contracts

With regard to contracts generally, the contracting parties' choice of law of a particular state will govern their contractual relationship if the chosen law has some nexus with the parties or the contract so as to protect the justified expectations of the parties.[88] Similarly, the Hawai`i UCC provides generally that the parties to a covered transaction may agree that the law of a particular state governs their rights and duties when the transaction bears a reasonable relationship to the selected state.[89]

86. *See Lee*, 93 Haw. at 144, 997 P. 2d at 69.
87. *Id.* at 152, 997 P.2d at 78.
88. Airgo, Inc. v. Horizon Cargo Transport, Inc., 66 Haw. 590, 670 P.2d 1277, 1281 (1983) (*citing* Restatement (Second) Conflict of Laws (the "Restatement") § 187 (1) (1971)); Hawai`ian Telephone Co. v. Microform Data Systems, Inc., 829 F.2d 919, 922 (9th Cir. 1987); Brown V. KFC Nat'l Mgmt. Co., 82 Haw. 226, 921 P.2d 146, 153 (1996).
89. H.R.S. § 490: 1-301.

9.2 Exceptions to the General Rule

There are several exceptions to the general rule governing when a choice of law provision is enforceable under a contract:

(1) Real property is exclusively governed by the law of the state within which it is situated and, therefore, "all matters concerning taxation of such realty, title, alienation, and the transfer of such realty and the validity, effect and construction which is to be accorded agreements intending to convey or otherwise deal with such realty are determined by the doctrine of *lex loci rei sitae,* that is, the law of the place where the land is located."[90] Accordingly, matters concerning real property securing a contract of guaranty, such as the method of recordation of a security interest, the effects of the failure to record, and foreclosure and collateral protection provisions, will be governed by the law of the situs of the property.

(2) The Hawai`i UCC prescribes generally the rules for determining the law governing perfection, the effect of perfection or nonperfection, and the priority of a security interest in covered collateral.[91]

(3) Hawai`i courts look to the Restatement (Second) of Conflicts of Laws for guidance regarding conflicts of laws.[92] Thus, where a choice of law provision is contained in a contract, Hawai`i courts have been guided by the Restatement (Second) of Conflicts of Laws § 187(1) (1971).[93] Note, however, that the Restatement is not followed with respect to a contract that has no conflict of law provision. In *Mikelson v. United States Auto Ass'n,*[94] the Hawai`i Supreme Court rejected applying the factors set forth in Section 188 of the Restatement relating to the most significant contacts, and instead utilized a flexible "choice-influencing considerations" approach, which looked to the state with the most significant relationship to the parties and the subject matter. "This flexible approach places primary emphasis on deciding which state would have the strongest interest in seeing its laws applied to the particular case. Hence, this court has said that the interests of the states and applicable public policy reasons should determine whether Hawai`i law or another state's law should apply."[95]

---

90. In Re Grayco Land Escrow, Ltd., 57 Haw. 436, 450, 559 P.2d 264 (1977).
91. Haw. Rev. Stat. § 490: 9-301.
92. UARCO Inc. v. Lam, 18 F. Supp. 2nd 1116 (D. Haw. 1998); California Federal Svgs & Loan v. Bell, 6 Haw. App. 597, 735 P.2d 499 (1987).
93. *See supra* note 88.
94. 107 Haw. 192, 111 P.3d 601 (2005).
95. *Id.* at 198, 111 P.3d at 607. *See also* Del Monte Fresh Produce (Hawai`i), Inc. v. Fireman's Fund Ins. Co., 117 Haw. 357, 183 P.3d 734 (2007); and California Fed. Sav. & Loan v. Bell, 6 Haw. App. 597, 735 P.2d 499 (1987).

Idaho State Law of Guaranties

Kenneth C. Howell[1]
Hawley Troxell Ennis & Hawley LLP
877 Main Street, Suite 1000
Boise, Idaho 83702
208.388.4823
fax: 208.954.5226
e-mail address: khowell@hawleytroxell.com
firm web site: www.hawleytroxell.com

HAWLEY TROXELL
ATTORNEYS AND COUNSELORS

Contents

1. The author would like to gratefully acknowledge the research assistance of the firm's summer law clerk Allison Parker in the preparation of this chapter.

Idaho State Law of Guaranties

Introductory Note: In order to standardize our discussion of the law of guaranties, we use the following vocabulary to refer to the various parties to a guaranty and their obligations.

"Guarantor" means a person who, by contract, agrees to satisfy an underlying obligation of another to an obligee upon the primary obligor's default on that underlying obligation. We do not draw a distinction between guarantors and sureties, as the distinction in Idaho between the two is often muddled.

"Guaranty" means the contract by which the guarantor agrees to satisfy the underlying obligation of a primary obligor to an obligee in the event the primary obligor defaults on the underlying obligation.

"Obligee" means the person to whom the underlying obligation is owed. For example, the lender under a loan agreement would be an obligee vis-à-vis the borrower.

"Primary Obligor" means the person who incurs the underlying obligation to the obligee. For example, the borrower under a loan agreement would be a primary obligor.

"Underlying Obligation" means the obligation or obligations incurred by the primary obligor and owed to the obligee. For example, the borrower's obligation to make payments to a lender of principal and interest on a loan constitutes an underlying obligation.

IDAHO LAW HIGHLIGHTS

1. Idaho recognizes that the obligations imposed by guaranty agreements, and the rights and responsibilities of the parties thereto, are inherently contractual. Idaho gives great deference to the parties' ability to contract with respect to those rights (*see* § 6.1 below). Accordingly, the guaranty agreement should clearly define rights including assignability (*see* § 1.1 below), waiver of notice of acceptance (*see* § 5 below), the continuing nature of the guaranty (*see* § 6.4 below) and revival of the guaranty (*see* § 12 below).
2. Idaho is a community property state, and a guaranty given by one member of the marriage will bind only the guarantor's separate property, and community property. The guaranty will not bind separate property of a spouse. To make that separate property available as an asset to satisfy the guaranty, the obligee must obtain a guaranty from the spouse. *See* § 2.5 below.
3. Idaho does not have well-developed law on contribution among multiple guarantors. Idaho appears to follow general equitable principles, but guaranty

agreements under Idaho law should clearly spell out the contribution rights among multiple guarantors to avoid uncertain results. *See* § 10.1 below.

4. Idaho does not have well-developed law on the amount of debt reduction attributable to "credit bids" at foreclosure sales of real estate collateral. Idaho does generally treat such credit bids as the equivalent of cash, but no reported decision confirms this treatment relative to the value of the property obtained by the credit bid. To assure that the guarantor receives only the value of the credit bid as an offset, rather than the valuation of the property purchased by the credit bid, the guaranty should clearly spell out the credit to be applied in a foreclosure sale. *See* § 7.1.3 below.
5. Idaho generally does not enforce, under Idaho law, venue selection clauses that require litigation in a foreign jurisdiction. *See* § 8 below.

Introduction and Sources of Law

This survey discusses Idaho state law applicable to guaranties of commercial credit transactions. Idaho has a considerable body of law on guaranties and related subjects, but there are also many aspects of the guaranty relationship which have not been the subject of reported appellate decisions. Idaho's authority is primarily case law, although there are some statutes that bear on the guaranty relationship.[2] Idaho courts interpreting Idaho law have looked to the Restatement (Third) of Suretyship and Guaranty (1996) (the "Restatement") for guidance on guaranty and suretyship issues, although on a limited basis.[3] More common have been references to the Restatement (First) of Security.[4]

This survey is, by nature, general in scope and meant as a brief overview of the subjects discussed. It should not be relied upon in a specific transaction without specific legal advice tailored to that transaction and updated to include any new authorities issued since the date of this chapter.

---

2. These statutes are typically limited to discrete industries and are designed for the protection of Idaho residents. For example, Idaho Code §§ 28-23-108 and 28-23-109 provide for limitations on the liability of guarantors of farm machinery and equipment dealers as against manufacturers of such equipment by setting a minimum 90 days' notice requirement for changing time and manner of payment of indebtedness among other things, and also limiting the scope of such a guaranty to the guarantor's personal assets.
3. *See* State v. Two Jinn, Inc., 148 Idaho 752 at 757, 228 P.3d 1019 at 1024 (Ct. App., 2010) (referring to Restatement in context of bailman's bond).
4. *See, e.g.,* Hudson v. Cobbs, 118 Idaho 474, 797 P.2d 1322 (1990); Idaho First Nat'l Bank v. Bliss Valley Foods, Inc., 121 Idaho 266, 824 P.2d 841 (1991); Leliefeld v. Johnson, 104 Idaho 357, 659 P.2d 111 (1983); Weinstein v. Prudential Property and Casualty Insurance Co., 149 Idaho 299, 233 P.3d 1221 (2010); Wolford v. Tankersley, 107 Idaho 1062, 695 P.2d 1201 (1984); Cheney v. Palos Verdes Investment Corp., 104 Idaho 897, 665 P.2d 661 (1983). Indeed, there are at least 147 authorities citing to this version.

§ 1 Nature of the Guaranty Arrangement

A guaranty is an undertaking or promise on the part of the guarantor which is collateral to a primary or principal obligation on the part of another and which binds the obligor to performance in event of nonperformance by the other.[5] The guaranty relationship is inherently one arising under contract law, and the principles of contract law largely determine the creation, enforcement, and scope of the guaranty relationship.[6] A contract of continuing guaranty contemplates a future course of dealing covering a series of transactions extending over an indefinite time. While an absolute guaranty is an unconditional undertaking on the part of the guarantor to pay the debt or perform the obligation immediately upon the debtor's default without any necessity to first exhaust recourse against the principal, a conditional guaranty is an undertaking to pay or perform if payment or performance cannot be obtained from the principal obligor by reasonable diligence.[7]

1.1 Guaranty Relationships

A guaranty is a contract of secondary liability distinguishable from the liability of the primary obligor. The liability of the guarantor is in essence an additional form of security for the underlying obligation.

In other words, the guarantor is responsible as security for the debt or obligation of another person. Under a statute which refers to persons who are "primarily" liable for the payment of an obligation, and those who are "secondarily" liable therefor, it is held that the contract of guaranty creates a secondary liability.[8]

This distinction between the primary and secondary liability is substantive; Idaho courts refuse to enforce guaranty agreements when the guarantor is also the primary obligor. See § 6.6.

As with the interpretation and enforcement of all contracts in Idaho, there are no "magic words" that must be invoked to create a guaranty agreement. Idaho courts look to the content of the agreement, rather than its form, to determine if a guaranty exists. To determine if an agreement creates a relationship of guaranty, Idaho courts look to the intent expressed in the document itself.[9]

Guaranties may be assignable together with the guaranteed obligation as may any other contract. This question is one of fact, not law.[10] Mere use of the term "assigns" in the guaranty contract may be sufficient to evidence an intent to allow assignment. "'[T]he generally applicable principle that the use in the agreement of the term 'assigns' indicates (without being conclusive),

5. Commercial Credit Corp. v. Chisholm Bros. Farm Equipment Co., 96 Idaho 194, 196-97, 525 P.2d 976, 978-79 (1974) (internal citations omitted).
6. Gulf Chem. Employees Fed. Credit Union v. Williams, 107 Idaho 890, 894, 693 P.2d 1092, 1096 (Ct. App. 1984).
7. *See* Mack Financial Corp. v. Scott, 100 Idaho 889, 894, 606 P.2d 993, 998 (1980).
8. Hudson v. Cobbs, 115 Idaho 1128, 1131, 772 P.2d 1222, 1225 (1989).
9. Durant v. Snyder, 65 Idaho 678, 687-88, 151 P.2d 776, 785-786 (1944).
10. Sinclair Marketing, Inc. v. Siepert, 107 Idaho 1000, 1003, 695 P.2d 385, 388 (1985).

that the parties intended that the contract rights should be assignable is applicable to contracts of guarant[y].'"[11] The same factual inquiry as to the scope of the agreement determines whether a guaranty can be enforced as to debts incurred after the assignment:

> The guaranties in the present case state that they are "continuing and unconditional" guaranties in order to induce the extension of future credit on the sale of fungible petroleum products. Whether this contractual right could be assigned and enforced for credit extended subsequent to the assignment would be a factual question to be resolved based upon the intentions of the parties.[12]

1.2 Other Suretyship Relationships

While not the focus of this survey, a suretyship relationship can arise because of the pledge of collateral.[13] Where such a pledge is made as a clear inducement to encourage the creditor to lend to the debtor, a guaranty-type relationship arises to the extent of the collateral so pledged.[14]

§ 2 State Law requirements for an Entity to Enter a Guaranty

Corporations, partnerships, limited liability companies, banks, and trust companies can all grant guaranties in furtherance of their business activities. Such grants are expressly permitted by the relevant Idaho statute governing such entities.

2.1 Corporations

Under the Idaho Business Corporations Act, an Idaho corporation is allowed, within the scope of its general corporate powers, to "make contracts and guarantees, incur liabilities, ... and secure any of its obligations by mortgage or pledge of any of its property, franchises or income."[15] This general corporate power may be restricted or eliminated by the provisions of the corporation's articles of incorporation.[16] This general corporate power to make guaranties is not specifically limited by statute to guaranties that are in furtherance of corporate purposes. To the extent that the grant of any such guaranty would "leave the corporation without a significant continuing business activity," shareholder approval is required.[17]

11. Sinclair Marketing, Inc. v. Siepert, 107 Idaho 1000, 1003, 695 P.2d 385, 388 (1985) (quoting Targa Int'l Corp. v. Gross, 112 Misc.2d 688, 447 N.Y.S.2d 384, 385 (1982)).
12. *Id.*
13. *Id.*
14. *Id.*
15. *See* Idaho Code § 30-1-302(7).
16. *See* Idaho Code § 30-1-302.
17. *See* Idaho Code § 30-1-1202(1).

Nonprofit corporations have the same power to make guaranties as do for-profit business corporations.[18] While there is otherwise a considerable difference between business corporations and corporations organized for nonprofit purposes under the Idaho Nonprofit Corporation Act, the power to make guaranties is not a distinguishing factor.

2.2 Partnerships

Idaho's Uniform Partnership Act[19] does not expressly reference a partnership's authority to make guaranties. Such transactions are, however, common in Idaho.

Idaho's Uniform Limited Partnership Act expressly provides that such an entity has the power "to do all things necessary or convenient to carry on its activities...,"[20] which would certainly encompass the power to grant guaranties.

2.3 Limited Liability Companies

Idaho's Uniform Limited Liability Company Act mirrors the Limited Partnership Act's grant of powers to include the right "to do all things necessary or convenient to carry on its activities...."[21]

2.4 Banks and Trust Companies

An Idaho bank may bind itself as a surety or otherwise become a guarantor, but "only if it has a substantial interest in the performance of the transaction involved or has a segregated deposit sufficient in amount to cover the bank's total potential liability."[22] This power and limitation applies regardless of the nature of the bank. Savings banks and other banking-type entities are bound to this same limitation contained in the Idaho Bank Act.[23]

2.5 Individuals

When the facts of a case involve both business entities and individuals, Idaho courts examine the guaranty agreement to determine which obligations are actually guaranteed. "Absent an express agreement to the contrary, a guarantee to repay money advanced to a business or professional organization generally does not cover advances made to individual members of the organization."[24]

For example, in *Johnson Equipment*, at issue was a contract for sale that was "clearly" a corporate obligation, because the principal debtor was a corporation.[25]

---

18. *See* Idaho Code § 30-3-24(7).
19. Idaho Code Title 53, Chapter 3.
20. Idaho Code § 53-2-105.
21. Idaho Code § 30-6-105.
22. Idaho Code § 26-711.
23. *See* Idaho Code § 26-1804 (Savings Bank); § 26-2108(a) (Credit Unions).
24. Johnson Equipment, Inc. v. Nielson, 108 Idaho 867, 871, 702 P.2d 905, 909 (Ct. App. 1985).
25. *Id.*

A "'credit' was allowed on the contract for the 'down payment' charged to [the] personal open account" of the buyer corporation's president. There was no evidence on the record that the open account was created for corporate purchases. Therefore, the open account was deemed not to be part of the corporate buyer's contract obligation. The obligation was thus "outside the scope of [the] guaranty and [the guarantor] is not individually liable for the 'deficiency' judgment. The 'deficiency' is owed by the corporate buyer's president."[26]

Idaho is a community property state, and this distinction affects the ability of an individual to grant a lien on the spouse's separate assets. A full discussion of the implications of community property in Idaho is beyond the scope of this chapter. The fundamental principle applicable to guaranty agreements, however, is that the individual signing the guaranty can only grant the right to pursue his or her personal property, and community personal property. The individual signing the guaranty cannot put at risk the spouses' separate property, and community real estate cannot be made liable to the guaranty unless both spouses execute the guaranty agreement.

Idaho identifies two types of property in the context of a marriage—"separate property" and "community property." Separate property is defined as "all property of either the husband or the wife owned by him or her before marriage, and that acquired afterward by either gift, bequest, devise or descent, or that which either he or she shall acquire with the proceeds of his or her separate property, by way of moneys or other property, shall remain his or her sole and separate property."[27] Similarly, all other property acquired after marriage by either husband or wife is community property. Moreover, the income of all property, separate or community, is community property, unless a written agreement provides that such income will be separate property. Separate property is subject to the management of the spouse owning the property and shall not be liable for the debts of the other member of the community.[28]

Idaho's community property laws do not displace fundamental principles governing individual liability for a debt.[29] Rather, such laws simply affect the property to which creditors may look for satisfaction of the debt.[30]

Idaho has established a rule of coequal management of community assets or property. Essentially, when either member of the community incurs a debt for the benefit of the community, the property held by the marital community becomes liable for such debt and the creditor may seek satisfaction of the unpaid debt from such property.[31] Specifically, Idaho statutes provide that:

Either the husband or the wife shall have the right to manage and control the community property, and either may bind the community property by contract, except that neither the husband nor wife may sell, convey or encumber the community real estate unless the other joins in executing the sale agreement, deed or other instrument of conveyance. . . .[32]

26. *Id.*
27. Idaho Code § 32-903.
28. Idaho Code § 32-906(1).
29. Lowry v. Ireland Bank, 779 P.2d 22, 26 (Ct. App. 1989).
30. Twin Falls Bank & Trust Co. v. Holley, 723 P.2d 893 (1986).
31. Simplot v. Simplot, 526 P.2d 844 (1974).
32. Idaho Code § 29-912.

§ 3 Signatory's Authority to Execute a Guaranty

3.1 Corporations

A guaranty must be executed by an individual with authority to do so. That authority may be actual or apparent. A corporate officer generally has apparent authority to execute contracts on behalf of the corporation.[33] An obligee dealing with a corporate guaranty, however, should out of prudence obtain a corporate authorization verifying not only the authority to enter into the guaranty, but also the authority of the officer executing such guaranty.

3.2 Partnerships

Under Idaho's Uniform Partnership Act, a partner is an agent of the partnership for the purpose of its business. An act of the partner, including the execution of an agreement in the partnership name for apparently carrying on in the ordinary course the partnership business binds the partnership.[34] If the partner had no authority by reason of the partnership agreement, and the obligee knows of that fact, the transaction does not bind the partnership.[35] An act of a partner which is not apparently for carrying on in the ordinary course of the partnership business binds the partnership only if it was authorized by the other partners.[36]

An obligee dealing with a partnership should obtain the signatures of all partners, or should obtain a resolution of the partnership authorizing the guaranty.

3.3 Limited Liability Companies

Mere membership in a limited liability company (LLC) does not give the member agency power to act in the name of the LLC.[37] A LLC can file with the Idaho Secretary of State a specific statement of authority specifying the authority of individuals to act on its behalf.[38] Such a statement is conclusive in favor of a person (i.e., an obligee) giving value in reliance upon it unless actual knowledge of a lack of authority is shown.[39]

3.4 Banks and Trust Companies

The authority of an individual purporting to sign a guaranty for a bank or trust company must be made on a case-by-case basis in examining the company's corporate governance documents.

33. Valley Lumber Company v. Mcgilvery, 16 Idaho 338, 101 P. 94 (1908).
34. Idaho Code § 53-3-301(1).
35. *Id.*
36. *Id.* at subsection (2).
37. Idaho Code § 30-6-301(1).
38. Idaho Code § 30-6-302(1).
39. Idaho Code § 30-6-302(5).

§ 4 Consideration; Sufficiency of Past Consideration

As a contractual relationship, the consideration necessary to support a contract is all that is required to support a contract of guaranty. A guaranty is "supported by consideration if a benefit to the principal debtor, or detriment to the creditor, is shown."[40] "An extension of credit to a debtor is sufficient consideration for a personal guaranty."[41] This is true even if the guaranty was signed and given before the obligation guaranteed is extended.[42]

§ 5 Notice of Acceptance

A guaranty agreement that is absolute and unconditional does not require notice of acceptance. Idaho courts have long decided that the instrument containing a guaranty is not an "offer" which must be met with "acceptance" as though it were a bilateral contract. Rather, the relationship is treated as a unilateral contract. A contract of guaranty is thus an "absolute and unconditional promise of payment."[43] "Where the transaction is not merely an offer of guaranty, but amounts to a direct or unconditional promise of guaranty... all that is necessary to make the promise binding is that the promisee should act upon it and notice of acceptance is not necessary'"[44]

Furthermore, a guarantor may waive notice of acceptance of the guaranty contract. Idaho courts have determined that such waivers are fully enforceable.[45] For example, in *W. T. Rawleigh v. Van Duyn*, the guarantors argued that they were released from liability because the obligee never gave them notice of acceptance of the contract and guaranty. The contract, however, expressly waived notice of acceptance:

In consideration of the W. T. Rawleigh Medical Company extending credit to the above named person we hereby guarantee to it, jointly and severally, the honest and faithful performance of the said contract by him, waiving acceptance and all notice, and agree that any extension of time shall not release us from liability under this guaranty."[46]

Thus, the guarantors waived notice of acceptance and were not released from liability.

40. Bank of Idaho v. Colley, 103 Idaho 320, 325-26, 647 P.2d 776, 781-82 (Ct. App. 1982).
41. Gulf Chem. Employees Fed. Credit Union v. Williams, 107 Idaho 890, 894, 693 P.2d 1092, 1096 (Ct. App. 1984).
42. Bank of Idaho v. Colley, 103 Idaho 320, 325-26, 647 P.2d 776, 781-82 (Ct. App. 1982).
43. New Idea Spreader Co. v. Satterfield, 45 Idaho 753, 758 (1928).
44. *Id.*
45. *See* W. T. Rawleigh Co. v. Van Duyn, 32 Idaho 767, 773, 188 P. 945 (1920).
46. *Id.*

§ 6 Interpretation of Guaranties

6.1 General Principles

In general, Idaho courts interpret contracts of guaranty in the same manner and to the same extent as the interpretation of other contracts. The rights of the guarantor, however, are strictly construed according to the language in the guaranty, and the creditor's rights are not extended by implication. "The rights of a creditor against a guarantor are strictly determined by the terms of the guaranty contract."[47] Furthermore, a "guarantor, like a surety, has been held to be a favorite of the law and his liability is not to be extended by implication beyond the express limits or terms of the instrument, or its plain intent."[48]

When interpreting a guaranty agreement, the court construes it "strongly in favor of the guarantor."[49] When, however, "the language in the guaranty agreement is unequivocal, the agreement must be interpreted as a matter of law according to the language employed therein."[50] Where the terms of the contract are plain and unambiguous, they alone are consulted to ascertain the obligations guaranteed. As a general rule of contract law, the intent of the parties must be derived from the language of an instrument if it is unambiguous.[51]

6.2 Guaranty of Payment versus Guaranty of Collection

Guaranties may be of collection only, or of payment. A guaranty of collection is, under Idaho decisions, a "conditional guaranty" and an obligee must establish the exhaustion of remedy against the principal obligor or collateral in order to collect against the guarantor.[52] No such restrictions apply to a guaranty of payment, which is described by Idaho decisions as an "unconditional guaranty."[53]

6.3 Language Regarding the Revocation of Guaranties

No specific authority in Idaho has addressed revocation of guaranties. As Idaho generally adopts a contractual analysis in determining the obligations and rights of parties to a guaranty agreement, the language of the guaranty will likely determine whether it may be revoked and upon what terms or conditions.

47. Johnson Equipment, Inc. v. Nielson, 108 Idaho 867, 871, 702 P.2d 905, 909 (Idaho Ct. App. 1985).
48. Industrial Investment Corp. v. Rocca, 100 Idaho 228, 233, 596 P.2d 100, 105 (1979).
49. McGill v. Idaho Bank & Trust Co., 102 Idaho 494, 497, 632 P.2d 683, 686 (1981).
50. *Id.*
51. International Engineering Co. v. Daum Industries, Inc., 102 Idaho 363, 630 P.2d 155 (1981).
52. Marshall v. Enns, 39 Idaho 744, 230 P.46 (1924).
53. *Id. See also* Miller v. Lewiston National Bank, 18 Idaho 124, 108 P. 901 (1910).

6.4 "Continuing"

A contract of continuing guaranty contemplates a future course of dealing covering a series of transactions extending over an indefinite time.[54] Deciding what is a continuing guaranty and what is not turns on a contractual analysis. For instance, a guarantor's agreement to guarantee the obligations resulting from the "time to time" sales of collateral was both an absolute guaranty, and, "in a sense," a continuing guaranty.[55] No special language is required, although good practice would certainly dictate that use of the phrase "continuing guaranty" would be appropriate if that is the contractual relationship the parties desire to create.

6.5 "Absolute and Unconditional"

A guarantor makes an unconditional guaranty when it promises to satisfy the obligation upon default, without requiring the obligee to first exhaust its remedies against the obligor.[56] Idaho courts have routinely decided that under an unconditional guaranty, the obligee was not required to take any action against the primary obligor before seeking collection from the guarantor.[57]

The right of an obligee to pursue a guarantor under an unconditional guaranty is without consideration of whether other collateral subject to execution may exist. Where a guarantor is "absolutely and unconditionally liable upon the guaranty and such liability [arises] immediately upon [the obligor's] default, and a right of action immediately accrued" to the obligee against the obligor or against the guarantors, "without notice or demand ... in a case of absolute guaranty the creditor is not obliged to resort to any security he may have."[58]

6.6 "Liable as a Primary Obligor and not Merely as Surety"

In Idaho, "[g]uarantors are secondarily liable in contracts. One cannot be both primarily and secondarily liable on the same contract or contract provision; it is an either/or proposition."[59] A general exception to this rule is the doctrine of estoppel applied when an entity represented to be a corporation is in fact not a de jure entity. Idaho courts have estopped guarantors from denying the corporate status of an obligor entity which was, due to technical defects, not in fact a valid de jure corporation, but was instead at law merely a de facto corporation.[60]

---

54. Commercial Credit Corp. v. Chisolm Bros. Farm Equipment Co., 96 Idaho 194, 196-97, 525 P.2d 976, 978-79 (1974) (internal citations omitted).
55. W.T. Rawleigh Co. v. Atwater, 33 Idaho 399, 401, 195 P. 545, 547 (1921).
56. CIT Financial Services v. Herb's Indoor RV Center, Inc., 118 Idaho 185, 795 P.2d 890 (Ct. App. 1990).
57. Sanger v. Flory, 49 Idaho 177, 182, 286 P. 610 (1930).
58. *Id.*
59. Hudson v. Cobbs, 115 Idaho 1128, 1131, 772 P.2d 1222, 1225 (1989).
60. Marshall-Wells Co. v. Kramlich, 46 Idaho 355, 267 P. 611 (1928).

§ 7 Defenses of the Guarantor; Set-off

Defenses that may be available to a guarantor are generally those available to the primary obligor, general "suretyship" defenses, and several generic "other" defenses.

7.1 Defenses of the Primary Obligor

7.1.1 *General*

7.1.2 *When Guarantor may assert Primary Obligor's Defense*

A fundamental defense available to both the principal obligor and to the guarantor is the amount of liability assumed. "[T]he liability of a guarantor ordinarily cannot exceed the liability of the principal debtor."[61]

7.1.3 *Defenses that may not be raised by Guarantor*

Statutory protections granted to obligors are not extended to guarantors. For example, Idaho's deficiency limitations statute applicable to the foreclosure of deeds of trust[62] does not apply to guarantors, because the "protection in I.C. § 45-1512 is given to the borrower-grantor who gives the security interest described in the deed of trust." Since the guarantor is not the borrower-grantor, the statute does not protect the guarantor.[63]

Idaho unfortunately does not at present have well-developed law on the credit to be given a guarantor where an obligee "credit bids" on real estate collateral at a judicial or nonjudicial foreclosure sale. Idaho generally treats such credit bids as the equivalent of cash,[64] but no reported appellate decision applies this treatment to confirm the liability of the guarantor. If a credit bid is the equivalent of cash, the guarantor is presumably entitled only to a reduction in the primary obligor's indebtedness to the extent of the credit bid, irrespective of the value of the collateral. To avoid uncertainty, the terms of the guaranty should clearly spell out the credit to be received on account of a "credit bid" at a foreclosure sale.

In general, guarantors are not entitled to notice of the obligor's default. "As a general rule a guaranty of the payment of the obligation of another is an absolute undertaking imposing liability upon the guarantor immediately upon the default of the principal regardless of whether notice is given to the guarantor."[65]

Guarantors are also not entitled to have the obligor's payments applied first to guaranteed obligations. "The rights of the guarantor against the

61. Johnson Equipment, Inc. v. Nielson, 108 Idaho 867, 871, 702 P.2d 905, 909 (Ct. App. 1985).
62. Idaho Code § 45-1502.
63. First Security Bank of Idaho v. Gaige, 115 Idaho 172, 174, 765 P.2d 683, 685 (1988).
64. *See* Federal Home Loan Mortgage Corp. v. Appel, 143 Idaho 42, 137 P.3d 429 (2006); *see also* Spencer v. Jameson, 147 Idaho 497, 211 P.3d 106 (2009).
65. Mcconnon & Co. v. Stallings, 44 Idaho 510, 513, 258 P. 527 (1927).

creditor are determined in the first instance by the terms of the guaranty contract. However, beyond those contractual rights, the law imposes on the creditor an obligation not to deal with any security for the debt in such a manner as to harm the interest of the guarantor."[66] Unless another agreement is made, when an obligor owes multiple debts to an obligee, and only some of these debts are guaranteed, the guarantor does not have the right to require that the payments by the primary obligor be applied to the guaranteed debts. If the obligor does not designate where a payment is to be applied when it is made, the obligee can apply it to either the guaranteed or the nonguaranteed debts.[67] The exception to this rule is that the obligee may not apply obligor's payment to a nonguaranteed debt that is not due if a guaranteed debt is due and will not be paid because of the application of the payment to a nonguaranteed debt.[68]

7.1.4 Defenses that may always be raised by Guarantor

7.2 "Suretyship" Defenses

7.2.1 Change in Identity of Principal Obligor

In Idaho, "[w]here the principal is a corporation, a mere change in its name, without a change in its business, does not discharge the guarantor, especially where such change is participated in by the guarantor as a stockholder."[69]

7.2.2 Modification of the Underlying Obligation, including Release

Idaho follows this rule regarding modification of an underlying obligation:

A guarantor is exonerated, except so far as he may be indemnified by the principal, if by any act of the creditor, without consent of the guarantor, the original obligation of the principal is altered in any respect, or the remedies or rights of the creditor against the principal, in respect thereto, in any way impaired or suspended.[70]

"Any act of a creditor which impairs the remedy of a guarantor will discharge the guarantor."[71] An example of such an act that has been found to impair the remedy of a guarantor is the substitution of one conditional sale contract for another without the guarantor's knowledge and consent. Such a change "constituted such an alteration or change of the original obligation, and impaired and suspended their remedies thereunder, as to result in their release and discharge as guarantors of such obligation."[72]

---

66. Industrial Investment Corp. v. Rocca, 100 Idaho 228, 233, 596 P.2d 100, 105 (1979).
67. *Id.*
68. *Id.*
69. Mountain States Telephone and Telegraph v. Lee, 95 Idaho 134, 135, 504 P.2d 807, 808 (1972).
70. Smith v. Steele Motor Co., 53 Idaho 238, 243 (1933).
71. *Id.*
72. *Id.*

In Idaho, the release of the principal obligor does not always release the guarantor. In *Frost v. Harbert*,[73] the principal debtor was released by the obligee from his obligation after the note had matured. The obligee then attempted to recover the obligation from the debt's guarantor. The court held that the release of the principal debtor does not release the guarantor. The court stated that when the principal debtor was released, "the note had matured and the respondent, as guarantor, became obligated to the appellants upon his guaranty absolutely."[74] Thus, "the appellants were not required to pursue the principal debtor any further in the collection of said note, but could resort to the contract of guaranty and enforce the collection against the respondent upon his contract of guaranty."[75]

Release and substitution of the original obligor normally extinguishes the guarantor's liability, but this can be waived. A guarantor can waive its defense of release of the principal debtor. A "contractual provision constituting a full and complete waiver by the guarantor of the defense that the principal debtor had been released is enforceable."[76]

The scope of the guaranty contract may also determine whether releasing the principal obligor constitutes a defense for the guarantor. In circumstances where the contract is broad enough, the absence of a provision explicitly authorizing a lender to "unilaterally releas[e] the principal debtor and substitute another party, unknown to the guarantor and without his consent," is "not dispositive . . . given the sweeping language in the assignment regarding the guarantor's liability."[77] The language of the guaranty in the *McGill v. Idaho Bank & Trust Co.* case was "all-embracing and contemplates that unless there has been full payment resulting in the cessation of the principal debtor's liability, guarantor McGill shall nevertheless remain liable."[78]

7.2.3 Release or Impairment of Security for the Underlying Obligation

In general, unless waived, "a guarantor is discharged by operation of law from liability by any act on the part of the guarantee which extinguishes the principal contract."[79] Indeed, "[w]here the actions of the creditor impair the value of the collateral in its possession which secures an obligation guaranteed by a guarantor, either absolute or conditional, the guarantor will be discharged to the extent of the loss occasioned by the creditor."[80]

73. 20 Idaho 336, 343, 118 P. 1095, 1102 (1911).
74. *Id.*
75. *Id.*
76. *McGill v. Idaho Bank & Trust Co.*, 102 Idaho 494, 498, 632 P.2d 683, 687 (1981).
77. *Id.*
78. *Id.*
79. Mechanics and Metals Nat'l Bank v. Pingree, 40 Idaho 118, 131, 232 P. 5, 28 (1924).
80. Mack Financial Corp. v. Scott, 100 Idaho 889, 894, 606 P.2d 993, 998 (1980).

7.3 Other Defenses

7.3.1 Failure to fulfill a Condition Precedent

Failure to fulfill a condition precedent discharges the guarantor.[81] For example, in *Marshall v. Enns*,[82] the obligee attempted to collect against the guarantor. Their agreement, however, contained the following condition clause:

It is also understood that the undersigned sureties will not be called upon to make good any indebtedness which may be incurred by the salesman under this contract, except only in case that the salesman fails to pay such indebtedness after a reasonable effort has been made by the Company to collect the same from him.[83]

The court determined that the creditor failed to satisfy this condition, and therefore, the guarantor's liability was discharged.

7.3.2 Modification of the Guaranty

As a general contract obligation, a guaranty may be modified as contracts generally may be modified. This contractual analysis also applies to circumstances where blanks are initially left in the guaranty agreement for later completion.

In one case, guarantors argued that when they initially signed the guaranty agreement, the amount of the obligor's indebtedness was left blank. Later, the amount of indebtedness was filled into the contract. The guarantors urged that because the line was initially blank, filling it in later constituted a detrimental, material alteration and voided the agreement.[84] However, the "surety agreement provided that if the amount of indebtedness was blank it could be filled in, without specifying by whom."[85] Because the contract clearly and unambiguously provided for this contingency, the court declined to accept the guarantors' argument. They took "as conclusive that [the] amount was in the contract at the time it was signed or permissibly inserted thereafter…"[86]

7.3.3 Failure to pursue Primary Obligor

See § 6.5.

In general, the obligee is not required to pursue the primary obligor before seeking payment from the guarantor.[87] Given Idaho's treatment of guaranties as a contractual obligation, the parties could certainly contract for a limitation that the liability of the guarantor was conditional and secondary to the primary obligor. Guaranty agreements almost universally expressly provide that the

81. Marshall v. Enns, 39 Idaho 744, 747, 230 P. 46, 49 (Idaho 1924).
82. *Id.*
83. Marshall v. Enns, 39 Idaho 744, 748, 230 P. 46, 50 (Idaho 1924).
84. J.R. Watkins v. Clark, 65 Idaho 504, 507-08, 147 P.2d 348, 351-52 (1944).
85. *Id.*
86. *Id.*
87. Valley Bank v. Larson, 104 Idaho 772, 775, 663 P.2d 653, 656 (1983).

guaranty obligation is independent of that of the primary obligor, and Idaho fully enforces such contractual provisions.[88]

7.3.4 *Statute of Limitations*

Idaho has a five-year statute of limitations for written contracts such as guaranty agreements.[89]

7.3.5 *Statute of Frauds*

In Idaho, guaranty agreements—"a promise to answer for the debt . . . of another"—are required to be in writing to satisfy the statute of frauds.[90] If, however, the agreement goes beyond creating a guaranty of another's debt, but makes the obligation the debt of the guarantor, the agreement is not subject to this limitation of the statute of frauds.[91] Under the statute of frauds, a guaranty may not be orally modified: "[t]o the extent that [the defendant] seeks to argue the evidence as altering the original terms of the guarantee, we note that such an oral modification would be barred under the statute of frauds."[92]

7.3.6 *Defenses particular to Guarantors that are Natural Persons and their Spouses*

See § 2.5 above on community property implications of guaranties.

7.4 Right of Set-off

Set-off is available in Idaho as a defense, provided that it has not been waived, and provided that the legal requirements for set-off are met. If the requirements for set-off under common law are not met, the guarantor is not entitled to claim the defense. For example, one requirement of set-off in Idaho is establishing mutuality of interest. In *First Piedmont Bank and Trust Co. v. Doyle,*[93] the guarantor argued it was entitled to a defense of set-off. The guarantor argued that the obligor had requested that the obligee bank remove a listed authorized signator from the obligor's checking account. The bank failed to remove the signator, and the signator made withdrawals on the account that the bank honored. There was, however, no showing that the obligor suffered any damage due to the bank's honoring the check. Because there was no mutuality of interest in the sense that damage resulted from the amount sought to be offset, the court refused to allow a set-off defense.[94]

---

88. *See* Bank of Idaho v. Colley, 103 Idaho 320, 323, 647 P.2d 776, 779 (Ct. App. 1982).
89. Idaho Code § 5-216.
90. *See* Idaho Code § 9-505(2).
91. *See* Idaho Code § 9-506; *see also* Kelly v. Arave, 41 Idaho 723, 243 P. 366 (1925). Any such agreement would still have to satisfy other aspects of the statute of frauds, such as being able to be performed within one year, etc.
92. USA Fertilizer v. Idaho First Nat'l Bank, 120 Idaho 271, 275, 815 P.2d 469, 473 (Ct. App. 1991).
93. 97 Idaho 700, 551 P.2d 1336 (Idaho 1976).
94. First Piedmont Bank and Trust Co. v. Doyle, 97 Idaho 700, 551 P.2d 1336 (Idaho 1976).

§ 8 Waiver of Defenses by the Guarantor

In Idaho, following the general rule that guaranty agreements are treated as any other contracts, guarantors may waive defenses. A guarantor can waive its defense of release of the principal debtor. The burden of establishing waiver, however, "is on the releasing creditor if he wants to retain his right of recourse against the guarantor."[95]

A guarantor may also waive any right he or she possesses to require creditors to proceed in any particular way upon default of the primary debtor. For example, if the guarantor has a right to require the lender to proceed against the borrower, that right can be expressly waived.[96]

A guarantor may waive any right it has to have the collateral that secures the underlying obligation protected by the obligee.[97]

A guarantor may legally contract to waive a defense provided to the primary obligor, such as deficiency limitation statutes.[98]

Idaho provides, as a matter of contract law, that any condition by which a party is restricted from enforcing its rights under a contract in Idaho tribunals, or which limits the time within which it may enforce contractual rights, is void as against the public policy of Idaho.[99] This has generally been interpreted by case law to express the strong public policy in Idaho to invalidate venue selection clauses which require litigation of disputes in a foreign jurisdiction.[100] Under the *M/S Bremen v. Zapata Off-Shore Co.*[101] U.S. Supreme Court decision and its tri-part test of the validity of a venue selection clause, the "strong public policy" expressed by Idaho Code § 29-110 has been used to invalidate a forum selection clause.[102] No Idaho case has specifically determined whether this limitation on venue selection clauses can be waived, but procedural rules typically require that the defense be raised at the time of answering, or it is waived.[103]

8.1 Defenses that cannot be Waived

Some statutes affirmatively provide that certain defenses cannot be waived. Commercial reasonableness of the disposition of collateral governed by Article 9 of the Uniform Commercial Code, together with notification of such sales after default, generally cannot be waived.[104]

95. McGill v. Idaho Bank & Trust Co., 102 Idaho 494, 497, 632 P.2d 683, 686 (1981).
96. Valley Bank v. Larson, 104 Idaho 772, 775, 663 P.2d 653, 656 (1983).
97. First Security Bank of Idaho v. Mountain View Co., Inc., 112 Idaho 158, 161, 730 P.2d 1078, 1081 (Idaho App. 1986).
98. Valley Bank v. Larson, 104 Idaho 772, 774, 663 P.2d 653, 655 (1983).
99. Idaho Code § 29-110.
100. Cerami-Kote, Inc. v. Energywave Corp, 116 Idaho 56, 773 P.2d 1143 (1989).
101. 407 U.S. 1, 92 S.Ct. 1907, 32 L.Ed.2d 513 (1972).
102. *See* Cerami-Kote, Inc. v. Energywave Corp, 116 Idaho 56, 773 P.2d 1143 (1989).
103. *See, e.g.*, Idaho Rule of Civil Procedure 12(b).
104. Idaho Code § 28-9-611.

8.2 "Catch-all" Waivers

No Idaho authority appears to address "catch-all" waivers. Given Idaho's frequent citation of the Restatement (First) of Security, there is little reason to believe that Idaho would not recognize catch-all waivers consistent with Restatement (Third) of Suretyship and Guaranty § 48(1).

8.3 Use of Specific Waivers

Regardless of Idaho's approval of a catch-all waiver, it is clear that Idaho authorities generally follow a contractual analysis in the enforcement of guaranties. Guaranty contracts in Idaho routinely contain an extensive listing of waivers, and the failure to do so would certainly give rise to an argument that the parties did not intend a particular waiver (not listed) to be part of the contractual relationship. The better practice would thus be to include a specific list of waivers.

§ 9 Third-party Pledgors—Defenses and Waiver Thereof

Idaho has no case law restricting the obligation of third-party pledgors. Indeed, the *W.T. Rawleigh Co. v. Atwater* decision referenced in Section 6.4, supra, and at note 31, seems to make clear that a third-party pledgor is a guarantor. As such, a third-party pledgor would have the same defenses available to it as are available to a surety.

§ 10 Jointly and Severally Liable Guarantors—Contribution and Reduction of Obligations upon Payment by a Co-obligor

A guaranty signed by more than one guarantor is a joint and several obligation of the guarantors.[105]

10.1 Contribution

Reimbursement, or the right of one party who has satisfied a claim to seek repayment from another party, can be pursued on any one of three interrelated common law principles: indemnity, contribution, or subrogation. All of these principles are based on the concept that a party should be held responsible for

105. Miller v. Lewiston Nat'l Bank, 18 Idaho 124, 145, 108 P. 901, 922 (Idaho 1910).

its own wrongs, and if another is compelled to pay damages caused by the wrongdoer, that party is entitled to recover from the wrongdoer.[106]

These concepts are primarily based on equity.[107] Idaho has recognized that these concepts apply to the obligations of guarantors, but has not substantively addressed the specific rights of contribution, having resolved the case on a procedural basis.[108] In both the *Bank of Idaho v. Colley* case and the *Idaho First National Bank v. Wells* case, the appellate courts appeared to recognize a right to contribution among guarantors, but each case avoided a substantive discussion of that right, finding that the trial court's dismissal of the contribution claims on a procedural basis was without error. In both cases, the third-party actions for contribution were found to have been filed too late.[109]

10.2 Reduction of Obligations upon Payment of Co-obligor

Where multiple obligations exist, an obligee may not apply the obligor's payment to a nonguaranteed debt that is not due if a guaranteed debt is due and will not be paid because of the nonguaranteed payment.[110]

§ 11 Reliance

There are no reported cases in Idaho where the determination of the enforceability of a guaranty depended solely on the obligee's reliance on the guaranty, except where such reliance was analyzed as an indication of consideration.[111]

§ 12 Subrogation

See § 10.1 (contribution) above.

106. Chenery v. Agri-Lines Corp., 115 Idaho 281, 766 P.2d 751 (1988).
107. *Id.*
108. *See* Bank of Idaho v. Colley, 103 Idaho 320, 323, 647 P.2d 776, 779 (Ct. App. 1982); Idaho First Nat'l Bank v. Wells, 100 Idaho 256, 596 P.2d 429 (1979).
109. *See also* World Wide Lease, Inc., v. Woodworth, 111 Idaho 880, 728 P.2d 769 (Ct. App. 1986); In that case, a claim for contribution among guarantors was at issue before the trial court, and was described without comment on appeal and no issue on appeal was apparently taken from the trial court judgment granting the contribution claim.
110. Industrial Investment Corp. v. Rocca, 100 Idaho 228, 233, 596 P.2d 100, 105 (1979).
111. *See, e.g.,* New Idea Spreader Co. v. Satterfield, 45 Idaho 753, 265 P. 664 (1928).

§ 13 Indemnification—Whether the Primary Obligor has a Duty

Idaho generally recognizes that the primary obligor has a duty of indemnification.[112] There are relatively few decisions outside of the insurance context, however.

§ 14 Enforcement of Guaranties

14.1 Limitations on Recovery

An obligor that impairs the collateral securing the underlying obligation releases the guarantor for the amount of the impairment. "'[I]t is a fundamental principle of the law of guaranty that, with respect to additional security for the payment of a debt, the creditor stands in the position of a trustee for the guarantor, and, if a creditor surrenders or impairs collateral security without the consent of the guarantor, the latter is released to the extent of such negligent loss, impairment, or surrender.'"[113]

14.2 Exercising Rights under a Guaranty Where the Underlying Obligation is also Secured by a Mortgage

Idaho follows the "single action" rule that requires there be only one action for collection of an obligation secured by a mortgage or a deed of trust.[114] The pursuit of collection under a contract of guaranty is not an action to collect the obligation secured, but is rather the collection of an independent contractual right. Accordingly, there is no bar in Idaho to pursuing a guarantor when the obligor has encumbered real estate as collateral for the underlying obligation.[115]

14.3 Litigating Guaranty Claims; Procedural Considerations

Although an obligee may pursue a guarantor without first resorting to real or personal property collateral, guarantors often raise defenses related to that failure. Trial courts typically will dismiss these defenses as unjustified, but often considerable time and effort are expended responding to these defenses. Accordingly, unless the collateral has become worthless or it is not feasible to pursue, there is some merit in enforcing liens on collateral before litigating claims against the guarantors. Of course, many factors play into this

112. McCormick International USA, Inc. v. Shore, 152 Idaho 920, 277 P.3d 367 (2012).
113. *Universal C.I.T. Credit Corp. v. Whitworth*, 77 Idaho 528, 534, 296 P.2d 712, 716 (1956) (*quoting Mechanics & Metals Nat'l Bank v. Pingree*, 40 Idaho 118, 232 P. 5, 10).
114. *See* Idaho Code § 6-101 and § 45-1501.
115. First Nat'l Bank v. Commercial Union Asurance Co., 40 Idaho 236, 232 P. 899 (1925).

strategic decision, including the exact nature of the obligation involved, the solvency of the guarantor(s), and the likelihood of disposition of assets prior to judgment.

§ 15 Revival and Reinstatement of Guaranties

In Idaho, it is the general rule that payment or satisfaction of a principal obligation discharges a guarantor and being once discharged a revival of the debt in any way will not renew the guarantor's liability.[116] Idaho authorities caution, however, that the rights of the guarantor against the obligee are determined in the first instance by the terms of the guaranty contract, and accordingly this "general rule" can be altered (and almost universally is so altered) by the terms of the agreement.[117] No Idaho reported decision addresses revival of the debt under this general rule in the context of a bankruptcy-avoided preference payment.

116. *See* Industrial Investment Corp. v. Rocca, 100 Idaho 228, 232, 596 P.2d 100, 104 (1979).
117. *Id.* at 233, 596 P.2d at 105.

Illinois State Law of Guaranties

Teresa Wilton Harmon
Donna Baldry
Donovan Borvan
Geoffrey King
Irfan Siddiqui
Sidley Austin LLP
One South Dearborn Street
Chicago, Illinois 60603
Phone: 312/853-7000
Fax: 312/853-7036
www.sidley.com

Contents

Illinois State Law of Guaranties[1]

Introduction: Illinois has a statutory Sureties Act, specific statutory provisions regarding guaranties entered into by Illinois business organizations, and much judicial precedent regarding guarantors and sureties. The following discussion highlights helpful precedent in several key areas, but is not an exhaustive discussion of all available Illinois case law.[2]

Introductory Note: In order to standardize our discussion of the law of guaranties, we use the following vocabulary to refer to the various parties to a guaranty and their obligations.

"Guarantor" means a person who becomes secondarily liable for another's debt or performance.

"Guaranty" means a promise to answer for the payment of some debt or the performance of some obligation.

"Surety" means one who becomes responsible for the debt or default of another.

"Obligee" means the person to whom the obligation is owed.

"Primary Obligor" means the person with primary liability for the underlying obligation.

"Underlying Obligation" means the obligation that is the subject of the guaranty.

ILLINOIS LAW HIGHLIGHTS

THE SURETIES ACT AND JPMORGAN v. EARTH FOODS

While many states do not distinguish between a guaranty and a surety, the Illinois Supreme Court in *JPMorgan Chase Bank, N.A. v. Earth Foods, Inc.*, 939 N.E.2d 487, 498 (Ill. 2010) has stated that "a suretyship differs from a guaranty in that a suretyship is a primary obligation to see that the debt is paid, while a guaranty is a collateral undertaking, an obligation in the alternative to pay the debt if the principal does not." The court, after a detailed analysis of the legislative history of the Illinois Sureties Act (740 ILCS 155/1) held that "the General Assembly did not intend the term 'surety' to include guarantors and, therefore, the protections afforded under this plain language chosen by the legislature in the Sureties Act are not applicable to guarantors." *Id.*

1. The views expressed in this chapter are exclusively those of the authors and do not reflect those of Sidley Austin LLP or its partners.
2. Illinois courts often frequently cite the Restatement (Third) of Suretyship and Guaranty § 14. For additional information on guaranties in Illinois, see also Chapter 6, "Guaranty, Surety and Indemnity Contracts," Illinois Jurisprudence—Business Relationships, Matthew Bender & Co. (2011) and Illinois Law and Practice, 20 Ill. Law and Practice Guaranty Summary.

The Supreme Court in *Earth Foods* went on to note that whether a party was a "guarantor" or "surety" was not to be determined merely by the words of the contract. Instead, the Supreme Court stated that "when viewed as a whole along with any other evidence of the parties' intentions and the circumstances, a written instrument such as the one [the party] signed may be construed to create a suretyship despite its use of the term 'guaranty.'" *Id.* at 499.

The protections afforded by the Illinois Sureties Act are important ones. Under Section 1 of the Sureties Act, a surety who believes its principal is likely to become insolvent or leave the state may protect itself by requiring the obligee in writing to pursue a claim against the principal. If the obligee does not do so in a reasonable period of time, the surety may be discharged. Section 2 of the Sureties Act extends these protections to heirs, executors, and administrators. Section 3 of the Sureties Act provides that a surety may be released after the death of the principal in the event the creditor does not present the credit to the principal's estate through the appropriate representative or court. Section 4 of the Sureties Act provides procedural protections against judgments by default. Guarantors, or sureties concerned that they may be treated like guarantors, who believe these protections should be part of their contracts should consider including them as express provisions, rather than relying on the Sureties Act as a fallback.

§ 1 Nature of the Guaranty Arrangement

Under Illinois law, a guaranty is "a promise to answer for the payment of some debt or the performance of some obligation, on default of such payment or performance, by a third person who is liable or expected to become liable therefor in the first instance."[3]

1.1 Guaranty Relationships

Under Illinois law, "[a] guaranty contract is an agreement between a guarantor and a creditor wherein the guarantor agrees to be secondarily liable to the creditor for a debt or obligation owed to the creditor by a third-party (the debtor)."[4]

A guaranty introduces a third party into the traditional bilateral lending agreement. By doing so, "[a] guaranty reduces the lender's risk by shifting the risk to a party who 'has a comparative advantage in monitoring or enforcement of the debtor's duties, while the lender has a comparative advantage in liquidity.'"[5]

Thus there are three obligations present in any guaranty: the obligation between the debtor and creditor, the obligation between the guarantor and creditor, and the obligation between the debtor and guarantor. With regard to the obligation between the guarantor and the creditor, "a guarantor's

3. CCP Ltd. P'ship v. First Source Fin., Inc., 856 N.E.2d 492, 497 (Ill. App. Ct. 2006).
4. Int'l Supply Co. v. Campbell, 907 N.E.2d 478, 486 (Ill. App. Ct. 2009).
5. *CCP Ltd. P'ship*, 856 N.E.2d 482, 497 (quoting Avery W. Katz, *An Economic Analysis of the Guaranty Contract*, 66 U. Chi. L. Rev. 47, 113 (1999)).

secondary liability is triggered by a default of the debtor on the obligation the debtor owes to the creditor."[6] A contract whereby one prospective guarantor incurs primary liability on the underlying debt is not a guaranty and will not be interpreted under guaranty principles.[7] Such an arrangement would be considered a surety, and Illinois law recognizes a distinction between sureties and guaranties despite the tendency in most states to consider them identical. Under the Illinois Uniform Commercial Code (UCC), however, "surety" includes a guarantor or other secondary obligor.[8]

1.2 Other Suretyship Relationships

Illinois has a statute governing suretyship. The Illinois Sureties Act states, in part, that when a person "...bound, in writing, as surety for another for the payment of money, or the performance of any other contract, apprehends that his principal is likely to become insolvent or to remove himself from the state, without discharging the contract, if a right of action has accrued on the contract, he may, in writing, require the creditor to sue forthwith upon the same..."[9] The Sureties Act goes on to say that unless such creditor commences an action against the principal debtor, the surety shall be discharged.[10] The Sureties Act also states that it applies to heirs, executors, and administrators of the surety as well as the creditors, but that it does not extend to official bonds of public officers, executors, administrators, or guardians.[11] Finally, the act contains sections that discharge the surety if the creditor does not act within six months after the death of the principal maker of any note, bond, bill, or other written instrument, and gives the chance for the principal debtor to tender sufficient counter security before a surety is allowed to confess judgment or allow judgment to be entered by default in a proceeding that will distress the principal.[12]

The interplay between the obligations of the guarantor, creditor, and debtor is particularly important under Illinois law. While many states do not distinguish between a guarantor and a surety, the Illinois Supreme Court in *JPMorgan Chase Bank, N.A. v. Earth Foods, Inc.*,[13] has stated that "a suretyship differs from a guaranty in that a suretyship is a primary obligation to see that the debt is paid, while a guaranty is a collateral undertaking, an obligation in the alternative to pay the debt if the principal does not."[14] The court, after a detailed analysis of the legislative history of the Illinois Sureties Act[15] held that "the General Assembly did not intend the term 'surety' to include guarantors and, therefore, the protections afforded under this plain language chosen by the legislature in the Sureties Act are not applicable to guarantors."[16] The

6. *Int'l Supply Co.*, 907 N.E.2d at 486.
7. *Id.*
8. 810 ILCS 5/1-201(b)(39) (2012).
9. 740 Ill. Comp. Stat. 155/1 (2012).
10. *Id.*
11. 740 Ill. Comp. Stat. 155/2 (2012).
12. 740 Ill. Comp. Stat. 155/3-4 (2012).
13. 939 N.E.2d 487 (Ill. 2010).
14. *Id.* at 498.
15. 740 ILCS 155/1 (2012).
16. *Earth Foods, Inc.*, 939 N.E.2d at 498.

Supreme Court in *Earth Foods* went on to note that whether a party was a "guarantor" or "surety" was not to be determined merely by the words of the contract. Instead, the Supreme Court stated that "when viewed as a whole along with any other evidence of the parties' intentions and the circumstances, a written instrument such as the one [the party] signed may be construed to create a suretyship despite its use of the term 'guaranty'."[17]

In Illinois, it is also important to note that strictly using the term "guarantor" and "guaranty" does not ensure that the obligation will be interpreted by courts as such. "Labeling a document or a promise a 'guaranty' does not automatically make it a guaranty under the law and does not conclusively establish the obligations of the parties involved ... Rather, the obligations of the parties must be determined from the terms of the contract and the circumstances under which the contract was made."[18] Any ambiguity suggesting a joint obligation to the debt would place a guaranty under danger of being considered a surety. It remains to be seen, post *Earth Foods*, what specific factors Illinois courts will look to when distinguishing between guaranties and sureties.

§ 2 State Law Requirements for an Entity to Enter a Guaranty

2.1 Corporations

The Illinois Business Corporation Act of 1983 lists, as one of several powers of an Illinois corporation, the power to "make contracts, including contracts of guaranty and suretyship. . . ."[19] Prior to the inclusion of this language in 1981, a corporate guaranty of the obligations of another corporation or of an individual could have been *ultra vires* unless (i) the articles of incorporation of the guarantor expressly granted the capacity and power to guaranty or (ii) the business purposes and powers expressed in the articles of incorporation, when considered under the circumstances pertaining to the particular guaranty, were construed to imply the capacity and power to execute and deliver the guaranty.[20]

17. *Id.* at 499 (citing Vermont Marble Co., 190 N.E. 291, 293 (Ill. 1934)).
18. *Int'l Supply Co.*, 907 N.E.2d at 478 (citations omitted).
19. 805 Ill. Comp. Stat. 5/3.10(h) (2012).
20. *See, e.g.*, Rothschild v. Sears, Roebuck & Co., 282 Ill. App. 380, 389 (Ill. App. Ct. 1935) ("a corporation has no corporate power to become the mere surety of another or to pledge its property for the payment of the debt of another in which it has no interest or for which it is in no wise responsible and for mere accommodation. Its charter is the measure of its powers, and all power not expressed or fairly to be implied is denied to it."); *see also* Culhane v. Swords Co., 281 Ill. App. 185, 201 (Ill. App. Ct. 1935) ("In the absence of express authority, a corporation has no power to enter into a contract as surety or guarantor for another."); In re Drive-in Development Corp., 371 F.2d 215, 220 (7th Cir. 1966) (holding that the interrelationship between subsidiaries of the same parent provided sufficient justification for a guaranty despite the lack of corporate authorization); Blue Island Brewing Co. v. Fraatz, 123 Ill. App. 26, 29-30 (Ill. App. Ct. 1905) (holding that a guaranty designed to increase customers was within the corporate purposes of "manufacturing and selling beer" despite the "general principal . . . that a corporation cannot guaranty a note or contract for a third person, and such attempted guaranty is *ultra vires* and void . . . [because] a corporation's charter is the measure of its powers, and all power not expressed or fairly to be implied is denied to it").

There are three types of guaranties within a corporate family: upstream (subsidiary guarantees parent debt); downstream (parent guarantees subsidiary debt); and cross-stream (subsidiary guarantees debt of another subsidiary).[21]

The Seventh Circuit, interpreting Illinois law, has recognized that "[i]ntercorporate guaranties are a routine business practice, and their potential voidability creates a risk for unwary lenders."[22] In certain instances, however, guaranties can run the risk of being voided as fraudulent conveyances.[23]

2.2 Partnerships

The Illinois Uniform Partnership Act of 1997 governs the creation and activities of Illinois general partnerships.[24] The Illinois Uniform Partnership Act does not contain a specific discussion of guaranties, but does acknowledge that the "relations among the partners and between the partners and the partnership are governed by the partnership agreement," except as otherwise provided by the Act.[25] The Illinois Uniform Limited Partnership Act of 2001 governs the creation and activities of Illinois limited partnerships. The Illinois Uniform Limited Partnership Act does not contain a specific discussion of guaranties, but does acknowledge that except as otherwise prohibited, "the partnership agreement governs relations among the partners and between the partners and the partnership" and that "[a] limited partnership has the powers to do all things necessary or convenient to carry on its activities..."[26]

2.3 Limited Liability Companies

The Illinois Limited Liability Company Act governs the creation and activities of an Illinois limited liability company (LLC).[27] The Illinois Limited Liability Company Act provides that Illinois LLCs may "make contracts, including contracts of guaranty and suretyship."[28]

2.4 Banks and Trust Companies

The Illinois Banking Act governs the creation and activities of an Illinois bank.[29]

---

21. Leibowitz v. Parkway Bank & Trust Co. (In re Image Worldwide), 139 F.3d 574, 577-78 (7th Cir. 1998).
22. *Id.* at 578.
23. For a discussion of fraudulent conveyance in the context of guaranties, see *Leibowitz*, 139 F.3d 574.
24. 805 Ill. Comp. Stat. 206/100 et seq. (2012).
25. 805 Ill. Comp. Stat. 206/103(a) (2012).
26. 805 Ill. Comp. Stat. 215, 110(a); 805 Ill. Comp. Stat. 215/105 (2012).
27. 805 Ill. Comp. Stat. 180/1 et seq. (2012).
28. 805 Ill. Comp. Stat. 180/1-30(7). (2012).
29. 205 Ill. Comp. Stat. 5/1 et seq. (2012).

2.5 Individuals

As a general matter, general Illinois law principles of contract formation—including capacity and majority, apply to guaranties.[30] A person who has attained the age of 18 years is of legal age for purposes of contracting in Illinois.[31]

Illinois courts have paid particular attention to spousal relationships in interpreting guaranties, particularly with respect to whether consideration supported a spouse's signature on a guaranty. "[W]here there is no evidence that the signature of the wife of a corporate officer was a prerequisite to the extension of credit to her husband's corporation, the guaranty is void for lack of consideration. Thus, whether sufficient consideration flows to a wife for extension of credit to her husband depends upon whether the credit was extended in reliance upon her signature or guaranty."[32] Conversely, another Illinois court has stated that "where the wife is a co-maker of the note paying for the husband's obligations, there is consideration to the wife as she shares in his wealth and his inheritance. The extension of credit was made to her husband on the basis of her signature and she had a direct interest in the extension."[33]

"Sufficient consideration exists for a wife where credit is extended in reliance on her guaranty."[34]

§ 3 Signatory's Authority to Execute a Guaranty

An Illinois court likely would apply standard contract principles in determining whether a signatory had authority to enter into a guaranty. These could include questions of authority, apparent authority, implied authority, and agency. Under Illinois law, a contract may be signed in any manner that indicates an intention of the signing party to be bound by the contract.[35] With respect to corporations, the designation of the name of the corporation accompanied by a signature of an officer or agent will generally be viewed as binding the corporation but not the individual officer or agent; in some instances a signature merely by a corporate officer without designation of his or her corporate affiliation may be deemed to bind the corporation.[36] With respect to partnerships, one

30. *See generally* RESTATEMENT (THIRD) OF SURETYSHIP AND GUARANTY §§ 7-10 (1996).
31. 755 ILCS 5/11-1.
32. Am. Hardware Supply Co. v. White Eagle Lumber and Supply Inc., No. 86C9799, 1989 U.S. Dist. LEXIS 5947, at **8-9 (N.D. Ill. May 17, 1989). Note that federal and state laws, including without limitation the Equal Credit Opportunity Act and Regulation B, limit the ability of a creditor to require a spousal guaranty in some circumstances.
33. State Bank of Arthur v. Sentel, 293 N.E.2d 444, 448 (Ill. App. Ct. 1973).
34. Chrysler Credit Corp. v. Marino, 63 F.3d 574, 580-581 (7th Cir. 1995).
35. 17 Illinois Jurisprudence COMMERCIAL LAW § 1:55.
36. 10 Ill. Jurisprudence BUSINESS RELATIONSHIPS § 8:11 (citing Dunlop v. McAtee, 333 N.E.2d 76 (Ill. App. Ct. 1975)); McCracken &McCracken, P.C. v. Haegele, 618 N.E.2d 577 (Ill. App. Ct. 1993); People ex rel. Prospect Heights v. Wheeling, 498 N.E.2d 601 (Ill. App. Ct. 1986).

partner generally has the authority to bind the partnership to a contract that is in furtherance of the partnership business.[37]

§ 4 Consideration; Sufficiency of Past Consideration

Contract law principles provide the framework for any analysis of consideration for a guaranty in Illinois. "Generally, a guaranty must be supported by consideration just as any other contract would be."[38] "Significantly, the consideration flowing to the guarantor does not have to render a personal benefit to the guarantor."[39] "A promise based on consideration to benefit a third person constitutes sufficient consideration to bind the guarantor."[40] Forbearance by an obligee from pursuing an outstanding amount on a prior transaction can constitute consideration for a new guaranty, because consideration can result from detriment to the promisee, not just from benefit to the promisor.[41] "Typically, the consideration supporting the underlying obligation will also support the guaranty."[42] "In those circumstances, no separate consideration flowing to the guarantor is necessary."[43] "However, where the guaranty is executed after the underlying obligation has been entered into, new consideration becomes necessary to support it."[44]

For a discussion of consideration required to support a spouse's obligations on a guaranty, see Section 2.5, supra.

§ 5 Notice of Acceptance

Illinois law does not require notice of acceptance by the obligee where a guaranty is absolute and unqualified. In such instances, the guaranty is effective as soon as it is acted upon.[45] Notice of acceptance is required where the guaranty is conditioned, unless the terms of the guaranty waive notice of acceptance.

37. 10 Ill. Jurisprudence BUSINESS RELATIONSHIPS § 13:39, citing Bachewicz v. American Nat'l Bank & Trust Co., 466 N.E.2d 1096 (Ill. App. Ct. 1984), *later proceeding* 482 N.E.2d 95, *and rev'd on other grounds*, 490 N.E.2d 680.

38. Tower Investors, LLC v. 111 East Chestnut Consultants, Inc., 864 N.E.2d 927, 937 (Ill. App. Ct. 2007) (citing Restatement (Third) of Suretyship and Guaranty § 9 (1996)); *see also* A.D.E., Inc. v. Louis Joliet Bank and Trust Co., No. 83-C-268, 1983 U.S. Dist. LEXIS 16324, *3 (N.D. Ill. June 10, 1983) ("Sufficient consideration is also essential to a valid guaranty contract" (citing 20 I.L.P. Guaranty § 14)).

39. *Tower Investors, LLC*, 864 N.E.2d at 938 (citing Restatement (Third) of Suretyship and Guaranty § 9, Illustration 1, at 35 (1996)).

40. *Id.* (citing Lauer v. Blustein, 274 N.E.2d 868, 869-70 (Ill. App. Ct. 1971)).

41. Citibank, N.A. v. Bearcat Tire, A.G., 550 F.Supp. 148, 152 (N.D. Ill. 1982).

42. *Id.* (citing Restatement § 9).

43. *Id.*

44. *Id.* at 937 (citing City Nat'l Bank v. Russell, 615 N.E.2d 1308, 1312 (Ill. App. Ct. 1993); *see also* L.D.S., LLC v. Southern Cross Food, Ltd., 954 N.E.2d 696 (Ill. App. Ct. 2011) (a six-day lag between obligation and guaranty was not fatal given evidence the two were contemporaneous).

45. A.D.E., Inc., v. Louis Joliet Bank and Trust Co., No. 83-C-268, 1983 U.S. Dist. LEXIS 16324, **2-3 (N.D. Ill. June 10, 1983), citing 20 I.L.P. Guaranty § 12, at 520, § 13 at 522; *see also* Frost v. Standard Metal Co., 74 N.E. 139 (Ill. 1905); *see also* Schuman v. Arsht, 249 Ill. App. 562 (Ill. App. Ct. 1928), *cert. denied*, American Exchange Nat. Bank of Chicago v. Seaveras, 121 Ill. App. 450 (Ill. App. Ct. 1905).

§ 6 Interpretation of Guaranties

6.1 General Principles

Illinois courts interpret guaranties much as they interpret other contracts.[46] "The rules of construction applicable to contracts generally apply to contracts of guaranty."[47] "The function of the court is to effectuate, if ascertainable, the intent of the parties to the contract. A guarantor is to be accorded the benefit of any doubt which may arise from the language of the contract, and his liability is not to be varied or extended by construction or implication beyond its precise terms. Where the language of a contract is unequivocal, it must be carried out according to its language, but if it is ambiguous or there is a question of the parties' intentions, subsequent acts of the parties may be considered as evidence of their intentions."[48]

"The meaning of a guaranty agreement is a matter of law to be determined by the court."[49] A guaranty must be "construed according to its terms, so long as they are clear and unambiguous."[50]

Illinois courts have interpreted guaranties using "the principle of strict construction of a guaranty in favor of the guarantor."[51] "[A] guarantor is a favorite of the law. A guarantor is to be accorded the benefit of any doubt which may arise from the language of the contract, and his liability is not to be varied or extended by construction or implication beyond its precise terms. The liability of a guarantor is strictly construed in his favor and against the party in whose favor the guaranty runs."[52]

A guaranty contract that is "unequivocal in its terms speaks for itself and permits no parol evidence in explanation of its language. . . . Furthermore, whatever prior negotiations, understandings and verbal agreements may have been considered before the execution of the guaranty, they must be deemed to have been merged into the written contract and are thereby extinguished."[53]

Surety contracts are also strictly construed under Illinois law.[54] Paid suretyships may be treated as insurance contracts and subject to the rules of construction for insurance contracts.[55]

6.2 Guaranty of Payment versus Guaranty of Collection

Like courts in other states, Illinois courts recognize the distinction between guaranties of payment and guaranties of collection. "Under Illinois law, a

46. Blackhawk Hotel Associates v. Kaufman, 421 N.E.2d 166, 168 (Ill. 1981).
47. State Bank of E. Moline v. Cirivello, 386 N.E.2d 43, 45 (Ill. 1978); *see also* TH Davidson and Co. Inc. v. Eidola Concrete, LLC, 972 N.E.2d 823 (Ill. App. Ct. 2012).
48. McLean County Bank v. Brokaw, 519 N.E.2d 453, 456 (Ill. 1988).
49. *Riley Acquisitions, Inc.* No. 1-10-0880, 2011 Ill. App. LEXIS 187, *12 (Il. App. Ct. Mar. 8, 2011).
50. PNC Bank, Nat' Association v. Djurin, No. 10-C-3785, 2011 U.S. Dist. LEXIS 91831, *8-9 (N.D. Ill. Aug. 16, 2011), citing FDIC v. Rayman, 117 F.3d 994 (7th Cir. 1997).
51. Harris Trust and Savings Bank v. Stephans, 422 N.E.2d 1136, 1138 (Ill. App. Ct. 1981).
52. *Riley Acquisitions, Inc.*, 2011 Ill. App. LEXIS 187, at *12.
53. *Harris Trust and Savings Bank*, 422 N.E.2d at 1142.
54. Newberry Theatre, Inc. v. SBB Theatre, Inc., 422 N.E.2d 152, 153 (Ill App. Ct. 1981).
55. Peoria v. Rausch Koeb, 78 N.E.2d 123, 124 (Ill. App. Ct. 1948).

guaranty of payment requires the payment of a debt immediately when due if the debtor fails to pay, whereas a guaranty of collection requires payment only after the lender first uses all legal means to collect payment from the debtor."[56] Furthermore, "[a] guarantor of payment, as distinguished from a guarantor of collection, cannot avail himself of the defense that the creditor through negligence, or lack of due diligence, lost or dissipated the collateral furnished by the debtor."[57] Illinois courts also recognize guaranties of performance. "While a few cases state that a guarantor's obligation is merely coextensive with that of the principal... it has been held that only guaranties of performance expressly incorporate the terms and conditions of the principal obligation, whereas guaranties of payment are not limited in the same way."[58]

6.3 Language Regarding the Revocation of Guaranties

Illinois courts recognize that guaranties can be revoked, unless expressly stated to be irrevocable. Effective revocation requires notice. When a guaranty is revoked, absent contrary language in the guaranty, the guarantor remains liable for obligations incurred prior to revocation but is not liable for obligations incurred after revocation.[59]

6.4 "Continuing"

Illinois law recognizes both continuing and restricted guaranties. A continuing guaranty covers future borrowings, whereas a restricted guaranty covers specific transactions and does not cover future advances without express language to the contrary in the agreement.[60] In the words of a 2012 Illinois Appellate Court decision, "[a] continuing guaranty is a contract pursuant to which a person agrees to be a secondary obligor for all future obligations of the principal obligor to the obligee."[61] The Illinois Supreme Court has stated that the phrase "whether such indebtedness is now existing or arises hereafter" creates a continuing guaranty for past, present, and future debt.[62] Language regarding a future course of dealing or a succession of credits is viewed by Illinois courts as creating a continuing guaranty.[63]

In Illinois, "[a] guarantor of a continuing guaranty has the right to revoke the guaranty at any time, as long as he provides proper notice to the lender."[64]

---

56. M.S. Distrib. Co. v. Web Records, Inc., No. 00C1436, 2001 U.S. Dist. LEXIS 8472, at *22 (N.D. Ill. June 13, 2001).
57. United States v. Shirman, No. 64 C 1738, 1966 U.S. Dist. LEXIS 7921, **13-14 (N.D. Ill. December 16, 1966).
58. *Roels*, 608 N.E.2d at 415 (citations omitted).
59. *See, e.g.*, City Nat'l Bank v. Reiman, 601 N.E.2d 316 (Ill. App. Ct. 1992); *see also* In re Klink's Estate, 35 N.E.2d 684 (Ill. App. Ct. 1941); *see also* City National Bank of Murphysboro, Ill. v. Reiman, 601 N.E.2d 316 (Ill. App. Ct. 1993); *see also* 17 IL Jurisprudence-Business Relationships (MB) Commercial Law § 6:22.
60. 17 Il Jurisprudence-Business Relationships (MB) Commercial Law § 6:2, citing 38 *AmJur* 2d Guaranty § 23.
61. TH Davidson and Company, Inc., v. Eidola Concrete, LLC, 972 N.E.2d 823 (Ill. App. Ct. 2012), citing Restatement (Third) of Suretyship and Guaranty § 16 (1996).
62. McLean County Bank v. Brokaw, 519 N.E.2d 453, 455 (Ill. 1988).
63. *TH Davidson,* 972 N.E.2d at 823.
64. *CCP Ltd. P'ship*, 856 N.E.2d at 498.

"Unless the contract for a continuing guaranty expressly limits the right to revocation, the guaranty remains subject to the right to revoke."[65]

6.5 "Absolute and Unconditional"

Illinois law recognizes that a guaranty may be stated to be "absolute and unconditional" or that it may be conditional. The Illinois Supreme Court has stated, "[a] guaranty may be absolute or unconditional. A conditional guaranty requires the happening of some contingent event before the guarantor will be liable on his guaranty . . . An absolute guaranty is an unconditional undertaking on the part of the guarantor that the person primarily obligated will pay or otherwise perform. Such guarantor is liable immediately upon default of the principal, without notice. An absolute guaranty, unlike a conditional one, imposes no duty upon the creditor or holder of the obligation to attempt collection from the principal debtor before looking to the guarantor."[66]

An unconditional guaranty does not require a creditor to attempt collection from the principal debtor or collateral before seeking collection from the guarantor.[67]

Illinois courts also recognize that guaranties may be conditional. "Either the creditor or the guarantors may premise the guaranty upon a condition, though typically the condition is imposed by the guarantors. In either case, the condition becomes a part of the guaranty if it is known and agreed upon by the parties."[68] "A conditional guaranty contemplates, as a condition to liability on the part of the guarantor[s], the happening of some contingent event."[69] "A fairly common condition attending guaranties is ... that certain guarantors deliver a signed guaranty subject to the condition that others will also guaranty the debt ... Such a conditional guaranty is unenforceable against those who sign unless the other guarantors sign."[70]

Conditional guaranties that "all or none" sign cannot be waived unilaterally by the guaranty/lender.[71]

6.6 "Liable as a Primary Obligor and not merely as a Surety"

Under Illinois law, a surety is generally viewed as primarily liable under the guaranty contract.[72] Sureties, however, are entitled to certain protections in the Sureties Act. Accordingly, under Illinois law, for parties wishing to

---

65. *Id.*
66. Lawndale Steel Co. v. Joe Appel, 423 N.E.2d 957, 960 (Ill. App. 3d. 1981) (citations omitted).
67. The Northern Trust Co. v. VIII South Michigan Associates, 657 N.E.2d 1095, 1105 (Ill. App. Ct. 1995).
68. *State Bank of E. Moline*, 386 N.E.2d at 45.
69. *Id.*
70. *Id.* (citations omitted).
71. *See id.* at 46-47 ("[T]he condition, though initiated by the bank, contemplated that the guaranty would not become operative unless all 13 limited partners agreed to stand behind the loan. By issuing the loan, the bank materially increased the proportionate liability of those who had signed. . . . When the bank's demand that all 13 limited partners guaranty the loan became a condition to the liability of those who signed the guaranty, it could not be unilaterally waived by the bank.").
72. *See* § 1.2, infra. *See also* Rosewood Care Center, Inc. v. Caterpillar, Inc., 877 N.E.2d 1091 (Ill. 2007).

create pure primary obligor liability, the use of the term "surety" or "guarantor" should be avoided.

§ 7 Defenses of the Guarantor; Set-off

The following describes various defenses that may potentially be available to a guarantor. Note, however, that these defenses may generally be waived in the terms of the guaranty.

7.1 Defenses of the Primary Obligor

7.1.1 General

"Under Illinois law, the liability of a guarantor is limited by and is no greater than that of the principal debtor and if no recovery could be had against the principal debtor, the guarantor would also be absolved of liability."[73] "Although the language of a guaranty agreement ultimately determines a specific guarantor's liability, the general rule is that discharge, satisfaction or extinction of the principal obligation also ends the liability of the guarantor."[74]

7.1.2 When a Guarantor may assert Primary Obligor's Defense

Although the precedent is not uniform, it appears that under Illinois law a guarantor may assert defenses of the underlying debtor.[75] It is clear under Illinois law that, absent express language in a guaranty contract to the contrary, a guarantor is only liable to the extent the underlying primary obligor is liable. In *Riley Acquisitions, Inc. v. Drexler,*[76] the Illinois Appellate Court held that guarantors to a contract were no longer liable under their guaranty because the corporate primary obligors had dissolved and, pursuant to the Illinois Survival Statute, the primary obligors could no longer be held liable. The Court cited prior decisions for the principle that under Illinois law, "the liability of a guarantor is limited by and is no greater than that of the principal debtor and ... if no recovery could be had against the principal debtor, the guarantor would also be absolved of liability."[77]

---

73. Riley Acquisition, Inc. v. Drexler, 946 N.E.2d 957, 963 (Ill. App. Ct. 2011).
74. *Id. quoting* Edens Plaza Bank v. Demos, 660 N.E.2d 1 (Ill. App. Ct. 1995) (citations omitted).
75. Irving Tanning Co., v. American Classic, Inc., 736 F. Supp. 161, 164 n. 2 (N.D. Ill. 1990); *see also* 17 IL. Jurisprudence – Business Relationships (MB) COMMERCIAL LAW § 6:23, citing Schenley Affiliated Brands Corp. v. Mar-Salle, Inc., 703 F. Supp. 744 (N.D. Ill. 1989); Halliburton Co. v. Marlen, 506 N.E.2d 751 (Ill. App. 5th Dist. 1987); *but see* Graff v. Kahn, 18 Ill. App. 485 (Ill. App. Ct. 1886) ("where a surety on a note, bond or other obligation, is sued alone, he can plead as a set-off a demand due to his principal only where he shows that the demand has been assigned to him or that he makes the set-off with the concurrence and consent of his principal, and such concurrence and consent must be evidenced in such manner as to bind the principal").
76. 946 N.E.2d 957 (Ill. App. 2011).
77. *Riley Acquisition, Inc.*, 946 N.E.2d at 963 (citing Edens Plaza Bank v. Demus, 660 N.E.2d 1, 6 (Ill. App. Ct. 1995)).

7.2 "Suretyship" Defenses:

7.2.1 *Change in Identity of Principal Obligor*

"In Illinois, the general principle applies that a guarantor is not released unless the essentials of the original contract have been changed and the performance required of the principal is materially different from that first contemplated."[78] "Unless there is some material change in the business dealings between the debtor and the creditor-guaranty and some increase in the risk undertaken by the guarantor, the obligation of the guarantor is not discharged."[79] "Whether a guarantor is exposed to an increase in the risk it originally undertook is a key variable in determining whether there has been a material change in the guaranty agreement."[80]

In *Jeepers*, the guarantors argued that changes in the identity of the tenants who were the primary obligors under the lease they guaranteed should release them from liability under their guaranty. Although the court may have been sympathetic to the claim in the abstract, it noted that in this instance the guarantors had consented to the specific changes as they happened and that the language of the guaranty specifically provided it was irrevocable, absolute, continuing, and unconditional and that it would remain in effect regardless of changes and modifications in the lease. The *Jeepers* case cites *Bernardi Brothers, Inc. v. Great Lakes Distributing, Inc.*[81] In that case, the primary obligor incorporated and changed its name after its loan obligations were guaranteed by a guarantor. The pool of assets available to satisfy the loan remained unchanged. The *Bernardi Brothers* court refused to release the guarantor because the economic risk of the transaction had not changed.

7.2.2 *Modification of the Underlying Obligation, including Release*

As stated above, "[i]n Illinois, the general principle applies that a guarantor is not released unless the essentials of the original contract have been changed and the performance required of the principal is materially different from that first contemplated."[82] "Unless there is some material change in the business dealings between the debtor and the creditor-guaranty and some increase in the risk undertaken by the guarantor, the obligation of the guarantor is not discharged."[83] "Whether a guarantor is exposed to an increase in the risk it originally undertook is a key variable in determining whether there has been a material change in the guaranty agreement."[84] "A guarantor takes a risk in exchange for a benefit; when events beyond the guarantor's control

78. Chicago Exhibitors Corp. v. Jeepers! Of Ill., Inc., 876 N.E.2d 129, 136 (Ill. App. Ct. 2007). *See generally* 20 Ill. Law and Prac. Guaranty § 26.
79. *Id.*
80. *Id.*
81. 712 F.2d 1205 (7th Cir. 1983).
82. Chicago Exhibitors Corp. v. Jeepers! Of Ill., Inc., 876 N.E.2d 129, 136 (Ill. App. Ct. 2007). *See generally* 20 Ill. Law and Prac. Guaranty § 26.
83. *Id.*
84. *Id.*

dramatically increase the risk, the assumptions upon which the contract was founded are undercut ... The principle that a substantial increase in risk discharges the guaranty rests on the assumption that guarantors would not ordinarily tolerate a substituted increase in risk without seeking something in return."[85]

Illinois courts also may require an obligee to notify a guarantor of material facts that increase the guarantor's risk beyond that intended, or a defense may be available to the guarantor. This ties into the general duty of good faith demanded of contracting parties, including obligees on guaranties, under Illinois law.[86] However, "[t]he failure to disclose a loan as troubled does not constitute the type of fraud that would enable a guarantor to avoid his liability on the guaranty."[87]

Illinois courts may view the execution of a new note as a defense if the new note extends the time for payment or is intended to discharge the original note.[88] The Illinois Supreme Court has viewed an increase in the maximum stated amount of indebtedness as not discharging, or creating a defense under, the guaranty. However, the guarantor was not liable under the guaranty for more than the original amount.[89]

Illinois courts have found "[t]wo exceptions to the rule discharging a guarantor for alteration of the underlying contract . . . First, the rule does not apply where the essentials of the original agreement have not been changed and the performance required of the principal is not materially different from that first contemplated ... Second, the rule has no application where the guarantor has knowledge of and assents, either expressly or by implication, to such change."[90]

"A guarantor may consent to changes to an underlying debt or to releases of security for such a debt by clear language in the guaranty."[91]

Where the guarantor assents to a change in his contract he is not released.[92] Moreover, a change in a guarantor's obligation which can only be beneficial to him does not discharge him.[93] "Under Illinois law, if a guarantor consents to a change in the contract, he will not be released."[94]

The Illinois Supreme Court has also held that the addition of collateral to support the underlying obligation did not materially alter the underlying obligation because possible collateralization had been contemplated.[95]

---

85. *Id.* at 136-37 (citing Roels v. Drew Industries, Inc, 608 N.E.2d 411, 414 (Ill. App. Ct. 1992)); *see also* Grundy County Nat'l Bank v. Cavanaugh, 434 N.E.2d 803 (Ill. App. Ct. 1982) (change in underlying contract dismissed surety); *see also* FDIC v. Rayman, No. 92 C 3688, 1995 U.S. Dist. LEXIS 12180 (N.D. Ill. Aug. 22, 1995) (sale of property and failure to foreclose did not materially increase guarantor's risk).
86. *See* Brzozowski v. Northern Trust Co., 618 N.E.2d 405, 410 (Ill. App. Ct. 1993).
87. *Northern Trust Co.*, 657 N.E.2d at 1102.
88. Corn Belt Bank v. Lincoln Sav. & Loan Association, 456 N.E.2d 150 (Ill. App. Ct. 1983).
89. McLean County Bank v. Brokaw, 519 N.E.2d 453 (Ill. 1988).
90. Lawndale Steel Co. v. Appel, 423 N.E.2d 957, 962 (Ill. App. Ct. 1981) (citations omitted).
91. *Brzozowski*, 618 N.E.2d at 410.
92. U.S. v. McMullen, 222 U.S. 460 (1911).
93. City of Chicago v. Agnew, 106 N.E. 252 (Ill. 1914).
94. Lyon Fin. Serv., Inc. v. Bella Medical Laser Center, Inc., 738 F. Supp. 2d 856, 860 (N.D. Ill. 2010) (citing case law stating that a guarantor can consent to future changes in his obligations).
95. Kramer v. Exchange Nat'l Bank, 515 N.E.2d 57 (Ill. 1987).

7.2.3 Release or Impairment of Security for the Underlying Obligation

The failure of an obligee to preserve collateral, or the release of such collateral, may be a defense under Illinois law depending on the facts.[96] Where the release of collateral or failure to exercise foreclosure remedies does not materially increase the risk to the guarantor, however, the guarantor does not have a defense.[97]

The "impairment of collateral" defense under Section 3-605 of Illinois' UCC is not generally available to a guarantor who signed a stand-alone guaranty, because the defense only applies to instruments.[98]

In addition to the release of security, the release of a coguarantor can also constitute a defense, at least up to the amount of lost contribution rights with respect to the released coguarantor.[99]

7.3 Other Defenses

Fraudulent conveyance law may present a defense to a guaranty under Illinois law particularly with respect to intercompany guaranties. The Seventh Circuit, interpreting Illinois law, has recognized that "[i]ntercorporate guaranties are a routine business practice, and their potential voidability creates a risk for unwary lenders."[100]

7.3.1 Failure to fulfill a Condition Precedent

Failure to satisfy a condition precedent is a defense where the guaranty was conditional upon the satisfaction of such condition precedent.[101]

7.3.2 Modification of the Guaranty

To the extent a guaranty constitutes a contract between a guarantor and an obligee, absent contractual terms to the contrary the guaranty could not be modified without the consent of both parties.[102] As discussed in more detail

96. FDIC v. Hardt, 646 F.Supp. 209 (C.D. Ill. 1986); North Bank v. Circle Inv. Co., 432 N.E.2d 1004 (Ill. App. Ct. 1982); Chicago Bridge & Iron Co. v. Reliance Ins. Co. 264 N.E.2d 134 (Ill. 1970); Watkins Products, Inc. v. Walter, 296 N.E.2d 859 (Ill. App. Ct. 1973).
97. *FDIC v. Rayman*, 1995 U.S. Dist. LEXIS 12180, at *7.
98. See *FDIC v. Rayman*, 1995 U.S. Dist. LEXIS 12180, at *24 (citing Farmers State Bank of Hoffman v. Schulte, 608 N.E.2d 694, 697 (Ill. App. Ct. 1993)); *see also* City National Bank of Murphysboro, Ill. v. Reiman, 601 N.E.2d 316 (Ill. App. Ct. 1993); Addison State Bank v. Nat'l Maintenance Management, Inc., 529 N.E.2d 30, 35, (Ill. App. Ct. 1988) (J. Dunn dissenting); Ishak v. Elgin Nat'l Bank, 363 N.E.2d 159, 161 (Ill. App. Ct. 1977); Federal Deposit Insurance Corp. v. Hardt, 646 F. Supp. 209, 212 (C.D. Ill. 1986) (noting that a guaranty, whether conditional or unconditional, does not contain an "unconditional promise to pay a sum certain" because it is conditioned on nonpayment by the debtor); *but see* Morris v. Columbia Nat'l Bank of Chicago, 79 Bankr. 777, 780-81 (N.D. Ill. 1987) (suggesting that even a guarantor of a nonnegotiable instrument can assert the defense of unjustifiable impairment of collateral).
99. FDIC v. O'Malley, 618 N.E.2d 818, 831 (Ill. App. Ct. 1993); In re Estate of Tiemann, 490 N.E.2d 200 (Ill. App. Ct. 1986); *see also* Oak Brook Bank v. Hawthorne Bank of Wheaton, 413 N.E.2d 491, 495-496 (Ill. App. Ct. 1980) (release of one joint surety releases other co-surety).
100. *Leibowitz*, 139 F.3d at 578. For a discussion of fraudulent conveyance in the context of guaranties, *see id.*
101. *See* § 6.5, *supra.*
102. *See* § 1.1 and 6.1, *infra.*

above, under Illinois law, a material change in a guaranteed obligation—if it increases a guarantor's obligations—is a defense and may discharge the guaranty entirely, unless the guarantor consents. An immaterial change in an underlying guaranteed obligation that does not increase the guarantor's risk generally does not lead to discharge.[103]

7.3.3 Failure to pursue Primary Obligor

Failure of the obligee to pursue the primary obligor can constitute a defense under Illinois law, unless expressly waived.[104]

7.3.4 Statute of Limitations

Section 13-206 of the Illinois Code of Civil Procedure generally provides a 10-year statute of limitations for breach of contract claims.[105] Specifically, it states: "[A]ctions on bonds, promissory notes, bills of exchange, written leases, written contracts, or other evidences of indebtedness in writing, shall be commenced within 10 years next after the cause of action accrued."[106]

In *Travelers Casualty & Surety Company v. Bowman*, the Illinois Supreme Court determined that a breach of contract claim under a performance bond was subject to the 10-year statute of limitations.[107]

The Court emphasized that under Illinois law, "[t]he determination of the applicable statute of limitations is governed by the type of injury at issue, irrespective of the pleader's designation of the action ... [or the] nature of the facts from which the claim arises."[108] On this basis, the court rejected arguments that the claim was based on shorter Illinois statutes of limitations related to construction matters and indemnity/contribution.

Illinois law also has a three-year statute of limitations for claims pursuant to Article 3 of the UCC[109] and a five-year statute of limitations for action on unwritten contracts and all civil actions not otherwise provided by statute.[110]

7.3.5 Statute of Frauds

The statute of frauds for guaranties and suretyships is codified in Illinois law at 740 ILCS 80/1. It clearly requires that covered promises – including promises to pay the debt of another such as a guaranty or suretyship – be in writing.[111]

103. Roels v. Drew Industries, Inc., 608 N.E.2d 411, 414 (Ill. App. Ct. 1992), McLean County Bank v. Brokaw, 519 N.E.2d 453, 457 (Ill. 1988); *see also* 17 IL Jurisprudence-Business Relationships (MB) Commercial Law 6:30.
104. City Nat'l Bank v. Revman, 601 N.E.2d 316, 323 (Ill. App. Ct. 1992).
105. 735 ILCS 5/13-206 (2012).
106. *Id.*
107. 893 N.E.2d 583 (Ill. 2008).
108. *Id.*, citing Armstrong v. Guigler, 673 N.E.2d 290 (Ill. 1996).
109. 810 ILCS 5/3-118(g) (2012).
110. 735 ILCS 5/13-205 (2012); *see also* Kranzler v. Saltzman, 942 N.E.2d 722 (Ill. App. Ct. 2011) (evaluating three and five-year guaranties but ultimately concluding the 10-year provision applies).
111. The surety provision of the Illinois Statute of Frauds provides "No action shall be brought ... whereby to charge the defendant upon any special promise to answer for the debt ... of another person ... unless the promise or agreement ... shall be in writing and signed by the party to be charged therewith, or some other person thereunto by him lawfully authorized." This provision has remained materially unchanged since 1819. Rosewood Care Center, Inc. v. Caterpillar, Inc., 877 N.E.2d 1091, 1095 (Ill. 2007).

The Illinois Supreme Court, in interpreting the surety provision of the statute of frauds, has said "[m]ore certain evidence is required when one promises to pay the debt of another because '[t]here is a temptation for a promisee, in a case where the real debtor has proved insolvent or unable to pay, to enlarge the scope of the promise or to torture mere words of encouragement and confidence into an absolute promise.'"[112]

The Illinois Supreme Court has recently considered two interesting Illinois law questions related to suretyships and guaranties under the statute of frauds. First, the Court evaluated whether the statute of frauds applies where the promise to pay the debt is entered into before the debt is actually incurred. Older Illinois Supreme Court cases had held that under the "Pre-Existing Debt Rule," the statute of frauds only applied where the debt preexisted the guaranty.[113] As recently as 2006, an Illinois Appellate Court concluded it was bound by *stare decisis* to follow this rule, even though the statute of frauds itself did not include it.[114] On appeal from that decision, the Illinois Supreme Court once and for all did away with the preexisting debt rule.[115] The court stated:

"In general, the statute of frauds (740 ILCS 80/1 (West 2004)) provides that a promise to pay the debt of another, i.e., a suretyship agreement, is unenforceable unless it is in writing. However, there is nothing in the plain language of the statute of frauds to indicate that for a writing requirement to apply, the debt must exist prior to the time the promise to pay is made. . . . The plain language of the statute does not require that a debt exist before a promise is made for the promise to fall within the statute."[116] "The plain object of the statute is to require higher and more certain evidence to charge a party, where he does not receive the substantial benefit of the transaction, and where another is primarily liable to pay the debt or discharge the duty; and thereby to afford greater security against the setting up of fraudulent demands, where the party sought to be charged is another than the real debtor, and whose debt or duty, on performance of the alleged contract by such third person, would be discharged."[117]

Second, the Illinois Supreme Court has analyzed the impact of pecuniary interests on the statute of frauds, concluding that Illinois recognizes the "main purpose" or "leading object" exception to the statute of frauds requirement. Under this exception, where the main purpose or leading object of a surety or guarantor is for pecuniary gain or business advantage, the statute of frauds can be ignored.[118]

---

112. Rosewood Care Center, Inc. v. Caterpillar, Inc., 877 N.E.2d 1091, 1096 (Ill. 2007) (citing Davis v. Patrick, 141 U.S. 479, 487-88 (1891)).
113. *See* Williams v. Corbet, 28 Ill. 262 (Ill. 1862); Hartley Bros. v. Varner, 88 Ill. 561 (Ill. 1878).
114. Rosewood Care Ctr., Inc. v. Cook, 852 N.E.2d 540 (Ill. App. 3d Ct. 2006).
115. *See* Rosewood Care Center, Inc. v. Caterpillar, Inc., 877 N.E.2d 1091, 1096 (Ill. 2007).
116. *Id.*
117. *Id.,* citing Eddy v. Roberts, 17 Ill. 504, 505 (Ill. 1856).
118. *Id.* at 1100.

7.3.6 Defenses particular to Guarantors that are Natural Persons and their Spouses

A broad array of federal and state consumer protection laws is applicable to guarantors who are natural persons and their spouses. Because they are too numerous to analyze here, we highlight instead certain consumer protection statutes that have been the subject of relatively recent Illinois Supreme Court decisions.

In *Lee v. Nationwide Cassel, L.P.,* 675 N.E.2d 599 (Ill. 1996), two cosignors on automobile retail installment sales contracts asserted defenses to their obligations under the Motor Vehicle Retail Installment Sales Act, which limits primary liability to consumers who take physical possession of the purchased vehicle and treats cosignors as guarantors of collection. The court concluded that, even though the cosignors had mistakenly signed in the "buyer" and not the "guarantor" signature block, they were at most guarantors of collection under the statute. The court refused, however to accept the co-signors' assertion that the lenders had violated the Illinois Consumer Fraud and Deceptive Business Practices Act or the Sales Finance Agency Act by attempting to enforce the guaranty as a primary obligor, because the law had been unclear. For a discussion of defenses linked to consideration for a spousal guaranty, see § 2.5 infra.

7.3.7. Other Defenses

Other defenses under Illinois law include:

- Failure to provide notice of an event of default,[119]
- Extension of the time for payment without knowledge or consent,[120]
- Increase in risk due to deficiencies in handling collateral.[121] In the *McHenry* case, the lender's failure to perfect a security interest materially increased the guarantor's risk beyond that contemplated by the guaranty. "It is a valid defense to a guaranty contract that the creditor failed to notify the guarantor of facts that materially increased the risk beyond what the creditor has reason to believe the guarantor intended to assume. This does not, however, require the creditor to take unusual steps to inform the guarantor of information that he can assume the guarantor also knows."[122] However, the UCC's impairment of collateral defense may be unavailable to a guarantor who exercises a guaranty that is not a negotiable instrument.[123] In any

119. Juzwik v. Juzwik, 488 N.E.2d 1319, 1322-1323 (Ill. App. Ct. 1986).
120. Lawndale Steel Co. v. Appel, 423 N.E.2d 957, 962 (Ill. App. Ct. 1981); Boulevard Bank Nat'l Association v. Philips Medical Systems Int'l B.V., 15 F.3d 1419, 1425 (7th Cir. 1994).
121. McHenry State Bank v. Y&A Trucking, Inc., 454 N.E.2d 345, 349 (Ill. App. Ct. 1983).
122. Phelps Dodge Corp v. Schumacher Elec. Corp. ,No. 01 C 4305, 2004 U.S. Dist. LEXIS 3724, **18-19 (N.D. Ill. March 9, 2004).
123. *See* Farmers State Bank of Hoffman v. Schulte, 608 N.E.2d 694, 697 (Ill. App. Ct. 1993); *City Nat'l Bank of Murphysboro v. Reiman*, 601 N.E.2d at 322-23.

event, "the defense of impairment of collateral is not available to one who has given an unconditional guaranty of payment."[124]

7.4 Right of Set-off

Illinois courts will generally enforce express contractual rights of set-off between parties and may, depending on the factual circumstances, permit equitable set-off.[125] Equitable set-off requires satisfaction of three conditions: mutuality, maturity, and liquidity.[126] The Illinois Appellate Court, in *Bank of Chicago-Garfield Ridge*, described equitable set-off as available "where the debts are mutual, mature and of such a certain and ascertainable character as to be capable of being applied in compensation of each other."[127] Certain Illinois statutes expressly permit set-off, including the Illinois Insurance Code.[128]

§ 8 Waiver of Defenses by the Guarantor

Illinois courts generally enforce clear and unambiguous waivers of defenses contained in guaranties.[129] "Under Illinois law, a guaranty is regarded as 'a legally enforceable contract that must be construed in accordance according to its terms, so long as they are clear and unambiguous.'"[130] "This remains the case even where a guaranty contains broad statements of guarantor liability, including waivers of all defenses."[131] "The exception to this rule is that every contract, absent express language to the contrary, has an implied covenant of good faith and fair dealing. Thus, courts should take into account public policy concerns in determining the effect and extent of such waivers."[132]

Guaranty agreements containing waivers of all defenses have been upheld as validly binding.[133] While the duty to act in a commercially reasonable manner may be waived, the duty of good faith cannot.[134]

---

124. Istituto Mobiliare Italiano S.p.A. v. Motorola, 689 F. Supp. 812, 817 (N.D. Ill. 1988).
125. Marc Development, Inc. v. Wolin, No. 93 C 2037, 1996 U.S. Dist. LEXIS 8078, at *7 (N.D. Ill. June 10, 1996).
126. *Id.*, citing Bank of Chicago-Garfield Ridge v. Park Nat'l Bank, 606 N.E.2d 72 (Ill. App. Ct. 1992).
127. *Id.*
128. 215 ILCS 5/206.
129. Douglas v. Tonigan, 830 F. Supp. 457, 462 (N.D. Ill. 1993); BA Mortgage & Int'l Realty Corp. v. Am. Nat. Bank & Trust Co., 706 F. Supp 1364, 1376 (N.D. Ill. 1989).
130. Gen. Elec. Bus. Fin. Servs. v. Silverman, 693 F. Supp. 2d 796, 800 (N.D. Ill. 2010) (quoting F.D.I.C. v. Rayman, 117 F.3d 994, 998 (7th Cir. 1997)); *see also* PNC Bank, National Association v. Djurin, No. 10 C 3785, 2011 U.S. Dist. LEXIS 91831 (N.D. Ill. 2011).
131. *Id.* (citing Chem. Bank v. Paul, 614 N.E.2d 436 (Ill. App. Ct. 1993)).
132. *Id.* at 800-01.
133. *Chem. Bank*, 614 N.E.2d at 442.
134. *Id.*; *see also* Bank of Am., N.A. v. 108 N. State Retail LLC, 928 N.E.2d 42 (Ill. App. Ct. 2010) (In contract of guaranty, waiver of all defenses is enforceable under Illinois law; when waivers contained in a guaranty are clear and unambiguous, Illinois courts consistently enforce them.); *but see* AAR Aircraft & Engine Group, Inc. v. Edwards, 272 F.3d 468, 473 (7th Cir. 2001) ("Although we held in other contexts that Illinois law permits absolute waivers to defeat all of a guarantor's defenses, those cases did not involve U.C.C. § 9-501(3)'s express prohibition on waivers of commercial reasonableness ... Because state law prohibits waivers of commercial reasonableness, especially ones drawn up by creditors themselves, the defense survives even guaranties purporting to be absolute and unconditional.") (citations omitted).

§ 9 Third-party Pledgors—Defenses and Waiver Thereof

Whether a pledge of collateral by a third-party constitutes a guaranty as well as a third-party pledge would be a matter of contract interpretation.[135] Pledges of personal property collateral under Illinois law, including third-party pledges, are governed by Article 9 of the UCC, codified at 815 ILCS 5/9-101 et seq.

§ 10 Jointly and Severally Liable Guarantors—Contribution and Reduction of Obligations upon Payment by a Co-obligor

10.1 Contribution

Guarantors have a right to seek contribution from coguarantors. "It is well established that the right to contribution between co-guarantors is based upon principles of equity, although that right may be modified by contract."[136] "The right of contribution is an individual and personal right. It grows out of what the individual himself does. Each one paying is entitled to recover from the others the amount which he has paid in excess of his own proportionate part. His right to recover is dependent upon the excess which he himself pays. In other words, the act is individual, and the right of contribution is individual."[137] "[T]his right to contribution is an inchoate claim which does not ripen into being unless and until [a coguarantor] pays more than her proportionate share to [the creditor]."[138]

However, the right to seek contribution is not absolute. "[A] surety who misleads his co-surety in a respect that prevents the co-surety from protecting himself from loss may be stopped from claiming contribution."[139] "[A] court of law will sustain an action for contribution between two sureties under an implied assumpsit arising from the general principle that equality is equity. But contribution between wrong doers will not be enforced."[140]

Illinois law recognizes that the obligation of the guarantor to contribute does not occur until after the primary debtor defaults on the obligation. "[T] he right to contribution does not arise unless and until there is a default."[141] "Where . . . a guarantor unconditionally guaranties punctual payment of principal and interest and waives a notice of default, a notice of the taking of

135. *See* § 6, *infra.*
136. Trossman v. Philipsborn, 373 Ill. App. 3d 1020, 1047 (Ill. App. Ct. 2007); Harris v. Handmacher, 542 N.E.2d 77, 80 (Ill. App. 1989).
137. *Id.* at 1047-1048.
138. *Id.* at 1048.
139. *Id.* at 1055-1056.
140. *Id.* at 1055 (citations omitted); *see also* State Bank of E. Moline v. Cirivello, 386 N.E.2d 43 (Ill. 1978) (recognizing that guarantors would have had equitable right to contribution). *Harris v. Handmacher*, 542 N.E.2d 77.
141. Trossman v. Philipsborn, 869 N.E.2d 1147, 1168 (Ill. App. Ct. 2007).

any action in connection with the loan, or any other applicable notice, as well as waives presentment and demand, any failure in making timely payments triggers the guarantor's obligations."[142]

10.2 Reduction of Obligations upon Payment of Co-obligor

For a discussion of a reduction of obligations upon release of a co-obligor, see § 7.2.3 infra.

§ 11 Reliance

Reliance by an obligee may play a role in an unwritten suretyship or guaranty.[143]

§ 12 Subrogation

Federal courts sitting in Illinois have recognized that "[w]hen a guarantor pays a debt, he is subrogated to the rights of a creditor against the corporation on whose behalf he paid the debt."[144] While Illinois law recognizes the subrogation rights of a secondary obligor, those rights do not generally arise until the secondary obligor pays its obligations.[145]

§ 13 Triangular Set-off in Bankruptcy

Section 553 of the Bankruptcy Code provides for set-off provided that the debts are mutual and arose prior to the bankruptcy petition.[146] "In order for debts to be mutual they must be in the same right and between the same parties, standing in the same capacity."[147] Given the mutuality requirement, bankruptcy courts have construed Section 553 as prohibiting "triangular"

142. *Id.* at 1169.
143. *Rosewood Care Centers, Inc.*, 877 N.E.2d at 1101.
144. In re Doctors Hosp. of Hyde Park, Inc., 474 F.3d 421, 427 (7th Cir. 2007), citing Weissman v. Weener, 12 F.3d 84, 87 (7th Cir. 1993); Mid-State Fertilizer Co. v. Exch. Nat'l Bank of Chicago, 877 F.2d 1333, 1336 (7th Cir. 1989); *see also* Mut. Serv. Cas. Ins. Co. v. Elizabeth State Bank, 265 F.3d 601, 626 (7th Cir. 2001).
145. Village of Crainville v. Argonaut Ins. Co., 410 N.E.2d 5, 7 (Ill. 1980).
146. In re Communicall Central, Inc., 106 B.R. 540, 545 (Bankr. N.D. Ill. 1989).
147. *Id.* (citations omitted).

set-off, so that one creditor, for example, cannot offset a debt to a debtor against a debt a debtor may owe to another related creditor.[148]

§ 14 Indemnification—Whether the Primary Obligor has a Duty

Illinois law generally recognizes an implied promise by a primary obligor who requests or consents to a guaranty to reimburse the guarantor for amounts paid under the guaranty.[149] However, a guarantor will generally not be entitled to indemnity for amounts paid under a voluntary or unknown guaranty.[150] These general rules can be varied by contract.

§ 15 Enforcement of Guaranties

15.1 Limitations on Recovery

"The meaning of a guaranty is a matter of law to be determined by the trial court."[151] Illinois follows the general rule that "[g]uaranty agreements must be strictly construed in favor of the guarantor."[152] This is deemed to be "especially true where ... the guaranty is on a printed form supplied by the party to whom the guaranty runs," and where "the guarantor is receiving no compensation."[153] "However, where the language of a contract is clear and unambiguous, extrinsic facts are not to be considered."[154]

15.2 Enforcement of Guaranties of Payment versus Guaranties of Performance

Illinois courts recognize guaranties of performance as distinct from guaranties of payment.[155] "While a few cases state that a guarantor's obligation

148. In re Elcona Homes Corp., 863 F.2d 483, 486 (7th Cir. 1988) ("the statute itself speaks of 'a *mutual* debt'... and therefore precludes "triangular" set offs." (citations omitted); *see also* Barber v. Production Credit Servs. (In re KZK Livestock), 221 B.R. 471, 481 (Bankr. C.D. Ill. 1998) ("It fails because...in the triangular situation, mutuality is lacking and triangular setoffs are generally not permitted.").
Although one decision of the Seventh Circuit decided under the former Bankruptcy Act, *In re Berger Steel Co.*, 327 F.2d 401 (7th Cir. 1964), has often been interpreted by bankruptcy courts as permitting triangular set-offs in bankruptcy if the parties entered into a prebankruptcy contract providing for such a set-off, *Berger Steel* did not, in fact, uphold such an arrangement and disallowed such a proposed contractual triangular set-off. Moreover, this reading of *Berger Steel* has been decisively rejected by several recent decisions, albeit none from bankruptcy courts in Illinois. *See, e.g.,* In re Lehman Bros. Inc., 458 B.R. 134, 141-142 (Bankr. S.D.N.Y. 2011); In re Sem-Crude L.P., 399 B.R. 388, 395-396 (Bankr. D. Del. 2009), *aff'd*, 428 B.R. 590 (D. Del. 2010).
149. 20 Ill. Law and Prac. Guaranty § 39, citing Vlahos v. Andrews, 1 N.E.2d 59 (1936).
150. 20 Ill. Law and Prac. Guaranty § 39, citing Schuman v. Arsht, 249 Ill. App. 562 (Ill. App. Ct. 1928).
151. City Nat'l Bank of Murphysboro v. Reiman, 601 N.E.2d 316, 322 (Ill. App. Ct. 1992).
152. *Id.*
153. *Id.*
154. *Id.*
155. *Infra* § 6.2.

is merely coextensive with that of the principal...it has been held that only guaranties of performance expressly incorporate the terms and conditions of the principal obligation, whereas guaranties of payment are not limited in the same way."[156]

15.3 Exercising Rights under a Guaranty Where the Underlying Obligation is also Secured by a Mortgage

Under Illinois law, an action to recover on a guaranty, or a personal judgment on a guaranty, is generally separate from a mortgage foreclosure proceeding.[157] The Illinois Supreme Court has noted that proceedings against real property and personal property may occur simultaneously.[158]

15.4 Litigating Guaranty Claims: Procedural Considerations

An action on a guaranty is generally in the form of an action for breach of contract on the guaranty, not on the underlying obligation.[159] To establish a prima facie case for enforcement of a guaranty under Illinois law, plaintiff must "enter[] proof of the original indebtedness, the debtor's default, and the guaranty."[160] A trier of fact must determine "whether a surety contract exists, the terms and conditions of any such contract, and the parties' intent."[161]

Certain defenses of a guarantor must be specifically pleaded under Illinois law. These include the defense of failure to provide notice of default.[162]

The Illinois Supreme Court has recognized that parol evidence may be admitted on the question of whether an agreement creates a suretyship or guaranty.[163]

Illinois appellate courts are reluctant to overturn findings of fact related to a guaranty. The Illinois Supreme Court has stated "[a] trial court's determination on a guaranty agreement will not be set aside unless contrary to the manifest weight of the evidence."[164]

"Most guaranties are discharged when the borrower pays (or the collateral proves to be sufficient); that's enough to show that claims on the note and guaranty don't rest on the same transaction. Often a claim on a guaranty must wait until other sources of payment have been exhausted, and the

156. *Roels*, 608 N.E.2d at 415 (citations omitted). *See also* Railway Express Agency, Inc. v. Greenberg, No. 92 C 6383, 1995 U.S. Dist. LEXIS 18377, *11 (N.D. Ill. 1995); Newman-Green, Inc. v. Alfonzo-Larrain, 605 F. Supp. 793, 799 (N.D. Ill. 1985).
157. DuQuoin State Bank v. Daulby, 450 N.E.2d 347, 348 (Ill. App. Ct. 1983); Farmer City State Bank v. Champaign Nat'l Bank, 486 N.E.2d 301, 306 (Ill. App. Ct. 1985). *See also* 20 Ill. Law and Prac. Guaranty § 30, citing additional cases.
158. Kramer v. Exchange Nat'l Bank of Chicago, 515 N.E.2d 57, 60-61 (Ill. 1987).
159. 20 Ill. Law and Prac. Guaranty § 30, citing C.J.S. Guaranty § 122.
160. Gen. Elec. Bus. Fin. Serv., Inc. v. Silverman, 693 F.Supp. 2d 796, 799 (N.D. Ill. 2010) (quoting Mid-City Indus. Supply Co. v. Horwitz, 476 N.E.2d 1271, 1277 (Ill. App. Ct. 1985)).
161. Rosewood Care Center, Inc. v. Caterpillar, Inc., 877 N.E.2d 1091, 1101 (Ill. 2007), (citing Howard A. Koop & Associates v. KPK Corp., 457 N.E.2d 66 (Ill. 1983)).
162. Juzwik v. Juzwik, 488 N.E.2d 1319, 1322-1323 (Ill. App. Ct. 1986).
163. *Earth Foods,* 939 N.E.2d at 499 (citations omitted).
164. McLean County Bank v. Brokaw, 519 N.E.2d 453, 456 (Ill. 1988).

deficiency judgment in the foreclosure action resolves how much the guarantor owes."[165]

§ 16 Revival and Reinstatement of Guaranties

Under Illinois law, the general rule is that the liability of the guarantor ends upon the discharge, satisfaction, or extinction of the guaranteed obligation.[166] However, if an obligee must return the payment which satisfied the guaranteed obligation, the guaranty is reinstated.[167]

§ 17 Choice of Law

Illinois courts will generally enforce a contractual choice of law provision in a guaranty even absent a relationship to the State, so long as the contract involves at least $250,000. The Illinois Choice of Law and Forum Act states that "[t]he parties to any contract, agreement or undertaking... in consideration of or relating to any obligation arising out of a transaction covering in the aggregate not less than $250,000... may agree that the law of this State shall govern their rights and duties in whole or in part, whether or not the contract, agreement or undertaking bears a reasonable relation to this state."[168] We note that in at least one instance, a court applying a similar New York statute concluded that application of New York's law to a contract which had no relationship with New York might present constitutional concerns if application of New York's law violated an important public policy of another state.[169]

165. Freedom Mortgage Corp. v. Burnham Mortgage, Inc., 569 F.3d 667, 672 (7th Cir. 2009).
166. Du Quoin State Bank v. Daulby, 450 N.E.2d 347, 348 (Ill. App. Ct. 1983); 17 Illinois Jurisprudence COMMERCIAL LAW § 6:24.
167. Baxter v. Continental Illinois Nat'l Bank and Trust Co. of Chicago, 26 N.E.2d 179, 183 (Ill. App. Ct. 1940); 17 Illinois Jurisprudence COMMERCIAL LAW § 6:24.
168. 735 ILCS 105/5. *See also* Truserv Corp. v. Flegles, Inc., 419 F.3d 584 (7th Cir. 2005) (individual guarantor could not avoid Illinois personal jurisdiction or choice of law where the contract specified Illinois for both, even where there were insufficient contacts; decision focuses primarily on jurisdictional issues).
169. Lehman Bros. Commerc. Corp. v. Minmetals Int'l Non-Ferrous Metals Trading Co., 179 F.Supp. 2d 118 (S.D.N.Y. 2000).

Indiana State Law of Guaranties

Rebecca A. Richardson
Shiv Ghuman O'Neill
John F.W. Fleming
Jennifer A. Pearcy
Dustin R. DeNeal
Kayla D. Britton
Faegre Baker Daniels LLP
300 North Meridian Street, Suite 2700
Indianapolis, Indiana 46204
Telephone: 317.237.0300
Facsimile: 317.237.1000
http://www.faegrebd.com

FAEGRE BAKER DANIELS

Contents

Indiana State Law of Guaranties

INDIANA LAW HIGHLIGHTS

Borrowers and coguarantors may one day be cojudgment debtors. If a coguarantor/ cojudgment debtor buys the creditor's judgment, the judgment is deemed satisfied, and cannot then be enforced against the other cojudgment debtors. Structuring the transaction so the judgment is assigned to a third party strawman will not change the result; if it is found that payment was in fact made by a cojudgment debtor, the judgment will be deemed satisfied.

Waivers of the "impairment of collateral" defense and the "alteration of underlying obligation" defense must be expressly stated to be enforceable against a guarantor. An unconditional guaranty does not operate to waive an impairment of collateral defense. A continuing guaranty that allows modifications of the underlying obligation will not extend to material modifications of the underlying obligation that are not shown to have been within the contemplation of the parties at the time the guaranty was executed, unless the guarantor expressly consents.

Introductory Note: In order to standardize our discussion of the law of guaranties, we use the following vocabulary to refer to the various parties to a guaranty and their obligations.

"Guarantor" means a person who, by contract, agrees to satisfy an underlying obligation of another to an obligee upon the primary obligor's default on that underlying obligation.

"Guaranty" means the contract by which the guarantor agrees to satisfy the underlying obligation of a primary obligor to an obligee in the event the primary obligor defaults on the underlying obligation.

"Obligee" means the person to whom the underlying obligation is owed. For example, the lender under a loan agreement would be an obligee vis-à-vis the borrower.

"Primary Obligor" means the person who incurs the underlying obligation to the obligee. For example, the borrower under a loan agreement would be a primary obligor.

"Underlying Obligation" means the obligation or obligations incurred by the primary obligor and owed to the obligee. For example, the borrower's obligation to make payments to a lender of principal and interest on a loan constitutes an underlying obligation.

Introduction and Sources of Law

In Indiana, case law is the primary source of substantive law governing commercial guaranties. Courts occasionally cite the *Restatement (Third) of Suretyship and Guaranty (1996)*.[1] Statutes governing the rights and remedies of sureties and cosureties may have limited applicability to commercial guaranties.[2]

§ 1 Nature of the Guaranty Arrangement

A guaranty is a conditional promise to answer for the debt, default, or miscarriage of another person who is principally obligated; to be valid, it must be evidenced by a written instrument signed by the guarantor.

1.1 Guaranty Relationships

There are three parties to a guaranty agreement: the primary obligor, the obligee or creditor, and the guarantor.[3] A guaranty is an independent contract by which the guarantor undertakes in writing, upon a sufficient consideration, to be answerable for the debt, or for the performance of some duty, in case of the failure of some other person who is primarily liable to pay or perform.[4] It is collateral to the debt itself, and is a conditional promise whereby the guarantor promises to pay only if the primary obligor fails to pay.[5] Upon default of the primary obligor, the guarantor becomes primarily liable, subject to the type of guaranty executed (conditional or unconditional) and the conditions contained in the guaranty contract.[6] Indiana courts have not distinguished between guaranties of payment of a debt and guaranties of the performance of an obligation (such as completion guaranties) in regard to the rights and obligations of guarantors.

1.2 Other Suretyship Relationships

A "direct undertaking or promise" which is "a promise or undertaking on the part of the person executing it to do a particular thing which another is bound to do," has been characterized as "in the nature of surety."[7] More recent decisions state that Indiana courts recognize the words "guaranty" and "guarantor" as synonyms for "suretyship" and "surety."[8]

---

1. *See* Irish v. Woods, 864 N.E.2d 1117, 1121 (Ind. Ct. App. 2007).
2. *See* Section 15 of this survey.
3. Grabill Cabinet Co., Inc. v. Sullivan, 919 N.E.2d 1162, 1165 (Ind. Ct. App. 2010); S-Mart, Inc. v. Sweetwater Coffee Co., 744 N.E.2d 580, 585 (Ind. Ct. App. 2001).
4. Indianapolis Morris Plan Corp. v. Sparks, 172 N.E.2d 899, 902 (Ind. Ct. App. 1961).
5. *Grabill*, 919 N.E.2d at 1165 (quoting Kordick v. Merch. Nat'l Bank & Trust Co. of Indianapolis, 496 N.E.2d 119, 123 (Ind. Ct. App. 1986)); S-Mart, 744 N.E.2d at 585.
6. McEntire v. Ind. Nat'l Bank, 471 N.E.2d 1216, 1223 (Ind. Ct. App. 1984).
7. *See, e.g.,* Nading v. McGregor, 23 N.E. 283, 284 (Ind. 1890).
8. Yin v. Soc'y Nat'l Bank Ind., 665 N.E.2d 58, 64 (Ind. Ct. App. 1996) (citing Farmers Loan & Trust Co. v. Letsinger, 652 N.E.2d 63, 66 (Ind. 1995)).

§ 2 State Law requirements for an Entity to Enter a Guaranty

Corporations, partnerships, and limited liability companies have the power to make guaranties, subject to limitations imposed in their organizational documents. Banks and trust companies may make guaranties that are necessary, convenient, or expedient to accomplish the purposes for which they were formed.

2.1 Corporations

A corporation formed under the Indiana Business Corporation Law has the same powers as an individual to do all things necessary or convenient to carry out its business and affairs, including the power to "make contracts and guarantees," unless its articles of incorporation provide otherwise.[9] Nonprofit corporations organized under the Indiana Nonprofit Corporation Act of 1991 also have this power.[10] Under prior corporate statutes, guaranties that did not further the business of the corporation were *ultra vires*, unless expressly authorized.[11]

2.2 Partnerships; Limited partnerships

Neither Indiana's Uniform Partnership Act[12] nor the statutes governing limited partnerships[13] expressly authorize or prohibit general partnerships or limited partnerships to guarantee. A limited partner or a general partner of a limited partnership formed under Indiana law may act as a guarantor or surety for the limited partnership, unless the partnership agreement provides otherwise.[14] A limited partner does not participate in the control of the business of a limited partnership, and thereby become liable generally for its obligations, solely as a result of acting as a surety or guarantor for the limited partnership, or guaranteeing one or more specific obligations of the limited partnership.[15]

2.3 Limited Liability Companies

A limited liability company formed under the Indiana Business Flexibility Act has the same powers as an individual to do all things necessary or convenient

9. Ind. Code § 23-1-22-2(7) (West 2011). The Indiana Business Corporation Law applies to all Indiana corporations in existence on July 31, 1987, as well as those incorporated under the Indiana Business Corporation Law.
10. Ind. Code § 23-17-4-2(7) (West 2011). The Indiana Nonprofit Corporation Act of 1991 also applies to domestic corporations in existence on July 31, 1993, and incorporated under Ind. Code § 23-7-1.1 (repealed) or the Indiana general not for profit corporation act of 1935, as well as to certain entities permitted to opt-in to its coverage. Ind. Code § 23-17-1-1 (West 2011).
11. Monsignor Bernard P. Sheridan Counsel No. 6138 Knights of Columbus v. Bargersville State Bank, 620 N.E.2d 732, 734 (Ind. Ct. App. 1993); Crowley v. First Merch. Nat'l Bank of Lafayette, 41 N.E.2d 669, 672 (Ind. Ct. App. 1942).
12. Ind. Code § 23-4-1-1 *et.seq.* (West 2011).
13. Ind. Code § 23-16-1-1 *et.seq.* (West 2011).
14. Ind. Code § 23-16-2-8(a)(3) (West 2011).
15. Ind. Code § 23-16-4-3(b)(3) (West 2011).

to carry out its business and affairs, including the power to "make contracts and guarantees," unless its articles of organization provide otherwise.[16]

2.4 Banks and Trust companies

A bank, trust company, or savings bank chartered under Indiana law has "the capacity to act that is possessed by a natural person" but is authorized to perform only those acts that are "necessary, convenient, or expedient to accomplish the purpose for which it is formed and that are not repugnant to law."[17] The power to "discount, negotiate, sell and guarantee promissory notes, bonds, drafts, acceptances, bills of exchange, and other evidences of debt" is one of the general banking powers granted to state-chartered banks and trust companies[18] and savings banks.[19]

2.5 Individuals

An officer of a corporation who signs a guaranty of corporate debt in the officer's individual capacity, with words indicating the officer's corporate title immediately following, is personally obligated as a guarantor.[20]

A contract executed by a person after reaching the person's eighteenth birthday may not be avoided by the person on the grounds that, at the time the agreement was executed, the person was acting under a legal disability by reason of the person's age, nor can legal disability by reason of age be raised as a defense to the contract.[21]

Married persons have equal right to enter into contracts (including guaranties) and to hold property, separate and apart from their spouses.[22]

A married person may individually acquire real estate, incur debt, and grant a mortgage to secure that debt. The person's spouse has no interest in individually owned real estate, and a mortgage of the real estate is effective without the joinder of the person's spouse.[23] Further, it has been held that under Indiana law, a married person who does not hold title to the marital residence does not acquire an interest in the residence solely by virtue of the fact that it was acquired by the other spouse during the couple's marriage, or by virtue of having resided in it.[24]

When property is held by spouses as tenants by the entireties, both spouses must execute a mortgage in order to create a valid mortgage lien against the

---

16. Ind. Code § 23-18-2-2(6) (West 2011).
17. Ind. Code § 28-1-5-2(a) (West 2010 and Supp. 2011).
18. Ind. Code § 28-1-11-3.1(a) (West 2010 and Supp. 2011).
19. Ind. Code § 28-6.1-6-1 (West 2010 and Supp. 2011).
20. *Kordick*, 496 N.E.2d at 124.
21. Ind. Code § 34-11-6-2 (West 2011 and Supp. 2011).
22. Cooper v. Cooper, 730 N.E.2d 212, 216 (Ind. Ct. App. 2000); Noble County Bank v. Waterhouse, 163 N.E. 119, 120 (Ind. Ct. App. 1928) (wife could not avoid liability on her promise to pay the debt of her husband because statutory prohibitions against married women acting as sureties were abolished).
23. Ind. Code § 29-1-2-3.1 (West 2010); Ind. Code § 31-11-7-2 (West 2008 and Supp. 2011).
24. United States v. Denlinger, 982 F.2d 233 (7th Cir. 1992).

property.[25] There is, strictly speaking, no requirement that both spouses become personally liable for the debt secured. Under Indiana law, a mortgagor does not become personally liable for a debt secured by the mortgage unless the mortgagor executes the debt instrument or undertakes to pay the debt in the mortgage or another agreement.[26] So a married person may execute a mortgage on entireties property to secure a guaranty made by his spouse alone and will not thereby become personally liable upon the obligation secured by the mortgage, unless the mortgage itself (or some other instrument) expresses his promise to pay the secured debt.

Indiana grants certain exemptions to bankruptcy and judgment debtors. When property is exempt, it is "protected from a judicial lien, process, or proceeding to collect a debt."[27] A debtor may claim as exempt real estate or personal property constituting his personal or family residence or the residence of a dependent up to $17,600. This exemption is individually available to joint debtors if they hold the property as tenants by the entireties.[28] Real estate held as tenants by the entireties is exempt, but the exemption does not apply to debts for which the spouses are jointly liable.[29] Real estate on which a debtor has voluntarily granted a lien is not exempt, to the extent of the balance due on the debt secured by the lien. [30]

§ 3 Signatory's Authority to Execute a Guaranty

Generally, agency law determines a signatory's authority to sign a guaranty. If the guaranty is considered a matter arising in the normal course of an entity's business, then a purported agent's execution of the guaranty is generally binding on the entity unless the obligee has knowledge of the signatory's lack of authority.

3.1 Corporations

Unless his or her authority is specially restricted, a general or managing officer or agent may enter into contracts (including guaranties) with respect to matters arising in the ordinary course of the corporation's business, and his or her authority may be presumed.[31] However, if the guaranty falls outside

---

25. Pension Fund of Disciples of Christ v. Gulley, 81 N.E.2d 676, 678 (Ind. 1948) (mortgage of entireties property executed by only one spouse is void).
26. IND. CODE § 32-29-1-2 (West 2002 and Supp. 2011).
27. IND. CODE § 34-6-2-44.3 (West 2011).
28. IND. CODE § 34-55-10-2(c)(1) (West Supp. 2011). The dollar amount of this exemption was established pursuant to rule made by the Indiana Department of Financial Institutions and effective March 1, 2010. 750 I.A.C. 1-11 (West 2010). The dollar amount is to be adjusted every six years based upon changes in the Consumer Price Index for All Urban Consumers. IND. CODE § 34-55-10-2.5(c) (West 2011).
29. IND. CODE § 34-55-10-2(c)(5) (West Supp. 2011).
30. IND. CODE § 34-55-10-2(e) (West Supp. 2011).
31. Blackstone Theatre Corp. v. Goldwyn Distrib. Corp., 146 N.E. 217, 219 (Ind. Ct. App. 1925) ("It is well established that private limitations on the general authority of an agent have no effect on a third person who deals with the agent in good faith, in ignorance of such limitation, and in reliance on the apparent authority under which the agent is clothed.").

the ordinary course of the corporation's business, officers and agents must be given express authority by the board of directors to execute a guaranty.[32]

3.2 Partnerships; Limited Partnerships

"Every partner is an agent of the partnership for the purpose of its business, and the act of every partner, including the execution in the partnership name of any instrument, for apparently carrying on in the usual way the business of the partnership of which he is a member binds the partnership, unless the partner so acting has in fact no authority to act for the partnership in the particular matter, and the person with whom he is dealing has knowledge of the fact that he has no such authority."[33] Therefore, and unless specifically provided otherwise in the partnership agreement, partners in a general partnership are bound by contracts, including guaranties, entered into by one partner in the scope of the partnership's business.[34] Proof that the guaranty was within the authority or apparent authority of a partner is sufficient to establish prima facie that such partner had authority to execute the guaranty for the partnership.[35]

Except as otherwise provided in a "partnership agreement, a general partner of a limited partnership has the rights and powers of, and is subject to the restrictions of, a partner in a partnership without limited partners."[36]

3.3 Limited Liability Companies

The Indiana Business Flexibility Act provides that, in the case of a member-managed limited liability company (LLC), every member is an agent of the LLC and can sign instruments "for apparently carrying on in the usual way the business or affairs of the limited liability company" unless "the acting member does not have authority to act for the limited liability company in the particular matter" and the third party "with whom the member is dealing has knowledge of the fact that the member does not have the authority to act."[37]

If the LLC is manager-managed, a member acting solely as a member is not an agent of the LLC, and so has no authority to sign a guaranty on behalf of the LLC unless such authority is specifically and validly granted to the member.[38] Instead, each manager is an agent of the LLC and can sign instruments "for apparently carrying on in the usual way the business or affairs of

32. Citizens Cas. Co. of N.Y. v. Ready Truck Lines, Inc., 203 F.2d 391, 394 (7th Cir. 1953) (applying Indiana law) (Treasurer's signature on amendment to insurance policy was not within ordinary course of company's business and amendment was therefore invalid because treasurer lacked authority to bind company.).
33. Ind. Code § 23-4-1-9(1) (West 2011).
34. Gallatin Grp. v. Cent. Life Assurance Co., 650 N.E.2d 70, 73 (Ind. Ct. App. 1995) ("It is well established that in a partnership the partners are bound by the contracts of each other when made in the scope of the firm's business.") (citing Bay v. Barenie, 421 N.E.2d 6, 9 (Ind. Ct. App. 1981)).
35. First State Bank of Bourbon v. Binkley (In re Liquidation of Bourbon Banking Co.), 30 N.E.2d 311, 318 (Ind. 1940) ("Generally, proof that the subject matter of a transaction in respect to which a written contract is made is within the authority, or the apparent authority, of an officer of the corporation or of a partner, is sufficient to establish prima facie his authority to execute the written instrument for the corporation or partnership."), *on reh'g*, 31 N.E.2d 52 (Ind. 1941).
36. Ind. Code § 23-16-5-3(a) (West 2011).
37. Ind. Code § 23-18-3-1.1(b) (West 2011).
38. Ind. Code § 23-18-3-1.1(c)(1) (West 2011).

the limited liability company" unless "the manager does not have authority to act for the limited liability company in the particular matter" and the third party "with whom the manager is dealing has knowledge of the fact that the manager does not have the authority to act."[39]

Regardless of whether the LLC is member-managed or manager-managed, a manager or member may not bind the LLC for an act "that is not apparently for the carrying on in the usual way the business of the limited liability company...unless authorized in accordance with a written operating agreement or by the unanimous consent of all members at any time."[40]

3.4 Banks and Trust Companies

Banks and trust companies can be bound by the acts of their officers when acting in the normal course of the bank's business, provided that such actions are not contrary to statute.[41]

§ 4 Consideration; Sufficiency of Past Consideration

Consideration is required to make a guaranty enforceable, and the time of execution of the guaranty is important to determine whether there is consideration.

In Indiana, a guaranty must be supported by sufficient consideration to be enforceable. This prerequisite is similar to the general rules governing all contracts.[42] Lack of consideration is an affirmative defense and the defendant has the burden of proof to plead it[43] or such defense is waived.[44]

It is not necessary for the guarantor to receive any benefit in connection with making the guaranty. Instead, consideration may be in the form of a detriment to the obligee. A guaranty is enforceable if the guarantor entered into the guaranty contemporaneously with the primary obligor entering into the principal contract on the basis that, but for the execution of the guaranty, the obligee would not enter into the principal contract.[45]

Once entered into, a guaranty will support new indebtedness extended by the obligee without additional consideration being given so long as the guaranty contemplated such future extensions of indebtedness.[46] A guaranty executed

39. Ind. Code § 23-18-3-1.1(c)(2) (West 2011).
40. Ind. Code § 23-18-3-1.1(d) (West 2011).
41. *See* Crowe v. Gary State Bank, 123 F.2d 513 (7th Cir. 1941) (applying Indiana law) ("When a contract is made by the president in the name of the corporation, in the usual course of business, and the directors have the power to authorize the making of such contract, the presumption is that the contract is binding on the corporation until the lack of authorization is shown.").
42. Loudermilk v. Casey, 441 N.E.2d 1379, 1383 (Ind. Ct. App. 1982).
43. Ind. Tr. R. 8(c).
44. Willis v. Westerfield, 839 N.E.2d 1179, 1185 (Ind. 2006).
45. Jackson v. Luellen Farms, Inc., 877 N.E.2d 848, 859 (Ind. Ct. App. 2007); Boonville Convalescent Ctr., Inc. v. Cloverleaf Healthcare Srvcs., Inc., 790 N.E. 2d 549, 557 (Ind. Ct. App. 2003); Houin v. Bremen State Bank, 495 N.E.2d 753, 757 (Ind. Ct. App. 1986); *Loudermilk*, 441 N.E.2d at 1385.
46. Fortmeyer v. Summit Bank, 565 N.E.2d 1118, 1122 (Ind. Ct. App. 1991); *Houin*, 495 N.E. 2d at 759.

subsequent to the principal contract, however, cannot rely on the consideration for the prior principal contract unless one of five conditions exists:

(1) The guaranty was executed pursuant to an understanding had before and was an inducement to the execution of the principal contract; or
(2) The guaranty was delivered before any obligation or liability was incurred under the principal contract; or
(3) The guaranty was made pursuant to a contract provision; or
(4) The principal contract does not become operative until the execution of a guaranty; or
(5) The guaranty expressly refers to a previous agreement between the principal debtor and creditor which is executory in its character and embraces prospective dealings between the parties.[47]

If none of these conditions exists, additional consideration is needed or the guaranty will not be enforceable.

§ 5 Notice of Acceptance

The obligee is not required to give notice of acceptance to a guarantor if the guaranty is given contemporaneously with the making of the principal contract or if the guaranty is absolute. One who offers to guaranty an obligation generally is entitled to notice of acceptance, unless the primary obligation already exists and is known to the guarantor.

An offer of guaranty or a proposal to guarantee a debt or obligation that the primary obligor has not yet incurred is not enforceable if the guarantor is not notified that the offer or proposal has been accepted.[48] Unless the offer stipulates that the obligee must give notice of acceptance, notice that the offer of guaranty has been accepted is sufficient if it comes from the primary obligor, or from any source.[49]

However, if the liability under the underlying obligation already exists, and is known to the guarantor, notice of acceptance of an offer of guaranty is not required.[50] Also, notice of acceptance is not required if the principal contract and the guaranty are executed contemporaneously, or if the guaranty is supported by separate consideration that moves between the guarantor and the obligee. [51] A guaranty that is a personal undertaking to pay for goods sold or to be sold to a third person is an "absolute promise or conclusive guaranty" and no notice of acceptance is required.[52]

---

47. Merch. Nat'l Bank & Trust Co. of Indianapolis v. Lewark, 503 N.E.2d 415, 417 (Ind. Ct. App. 1987) (quoting Davis v. B.C.L. Enter., Inc., 406 N.E.2d 1204, 1205-06 (Ind. Ct. App. 1980)); accord Jackson, 877 N.E.2d at 859.
48. Wills v. Ross, 77 Ind. 1, 2 (Ind. 1881).
49. Webster v. Smith, 30 N.E. 139, 140 (Ind. Ct. App. 1892).
50. *Wills*, 77 Ind. at 2.
51. Furst & Bradley Mfg. Co. v. Black, 12 N.E. 504, 506 (Ind. 1887).
52. Wright v. Griffith, 23 N.E. 281, 282 (Ind. 1890).

§ 6 Interpretation of Guaranties

The rules of contract interpretation apply to guaranties. Indiana distinguishes between so-called "strict," "collateral," or "conditional" guaranties on the one hand, and "absolute" or "unconditional" guaranties on the other.

6.1 General Principles

A guarantor is a favorite under the law and is not bound beyond the strict terms of the guarantor's engagement.[53] A guarantor's liability will not be extended by implication beyond the terms of his or her contract. The contract of a guarantor is to be construed based upon the intent of the parties, which is ascertained from the instrument itself read in light of the surrounding circumstances.[54] Writings executed simultaneously and related to the same transaction will be construed together in determining the intent underlying the contracts. That is, the guaranty and any other written agreements it incorporates must be evaluated in conjunction with one another in order to establish the parties' intentions.[55]

The rules of contract interpretation generally apply to guaranties. The terms of a guaranty should neither be so narrowly interpreted as to frustrate the obvious intent of the parties, nor so loosely interpreted as to relieve the guarantor of liabilities fairly within its terms.[56] If there is no ambiguity in the language of the contract, the construction of the guaranty is a question of law.[57] If the court finds that any term is ambiguous, then the parties may introduce extrinsic evidence of its meaning, and the interpretation of that term becomes a question of fact.[58] Ambiguities in a contract are construed against the party who prepared it.[59]

6.2 Guaranty of Payment versus Guaranty of Collection

The nature of a "guaranty of collection" has not been defined in Indiana case law.[60] Indiana courts state that a "strict or collateral guaranty" is one in which the guarantor undertakes to answer for the ability of the primary obligor to perform, but does not assume or engage to perform the underlying obligation if the primary obligor defaults. In a strict guaranty, "the contract of the guarantor is to answer for the default of his principal, if by the use of diligence loss results from such default." In contrast, if the form of the contract is that of

53. *Grabill,* 919 N.E.2d at 1166.
54. *S-Mart,* 744 N.E.2d at 586.
55. TW Gen. Contracting Servs., Inc. v. First Farmers Bank & Trust, 904 N.E.2d 1285, 1288 (Ind. Ct. App. 2009).
56. Paul v. Home Bank SB, 953 N.E.2d 497, 503 (Ind. Ct. App. 2011).
57. Skrypek v. St. Joseph Valley Bank, 469 N.E.2d 774, 777 (Ind. Ct. App. 1984).
58. Goeke v. Merch. Nat'l Bank and Trust Co. of Indianapolis, 467 N.E.2d 760, 765 (Ind. Ct. App. 1984).
59. *Paul,* 953 N.E.2d at 503; *Goeke,* 467 N.E.2d at 770.
60. *See, e.g.,* Hartung v. Architects Hartung/Odle/Burke, Inc., 301 N.E.2d 240, 242 (Ind. Ct. App. 1973) (noting that the obligee had protected itself by obtaining "personal guaranties of payment, as opposed to collection" without explaining the difference or the significance).

an original and absolute undertaking to pay the debt of another, the liability of the promisor is that of a surety; the surety is obligated at once upon his direct engagement to pay.[61] The obligee has no duty to collect or attempt to collect from the primary obligor.[62] The statement "I guaranty the payment of [the underlying obligation]" is a direct and absolute undertaking to pay the debt; the guarantor is not relieved of liability by "laches of the holder of said indebtedness, or failure to collect or attempt to collect the same from the other parties liable for its payment." The fact that the guaranty may state it is a guaranty of "payment and collection" does not change the legal effect of the direct undertaking to pay the debt.[63]

6.3 Language Regarding the Revocation of Guaranties

A continuing guaranty which is for an indefinite period is revocable by the guarantor provided that he does so reasonably. The right of revocation exists absent any provision in the guaranty agreement recognizing it.[64] A guaranty may be revoked orally, unless the guaranty contract calls for written notice.[65] Revocation does not alter existing liability for past transactions that have become binding contracts.[66] The obligor's relationship with the guarantor becomes "fixed or frozen" upon revocation, and the guarantor is released by a subsequent extension of the time for payment, renewal of the underlying obligation, release of collateral, or other alteration of the agreement without notice to or consent of the guarantor.[67]

If a guaranty authorizes extensions of the time of payment of the primary obligation without the guarantor's consent, the guarantor's failure to sign an extension agreement consenting to a specific extension does not constitute an effective revocation.[68]

6.4 "Continuing"

A guaranty may be either continuing or limited, and the rule is that unless the words in which the guaranty is expressed fairly imply that the liability of the guarantor is to be limited, it continues until it is revoked.[69] A continuing guaranty is defined as a guaranty that contemplates a future course of dealings encompassing a series of transactions. A guaranty contract is "continuing" if it contemplates a future course of dealing during an indefinite period, or if it is intended to cover a series of transactions or succession of credits, or if its

61. Furst & Bradley Mfg., 12 N.E. at 507.
62. Metzger v. Hubbard, 54 N.E. 761, 762 (Ind. 1899).
63. *Id.*
64. Vidimos, Inc. v. Vidimos, 456 N.E.2d 455, 458 (Ind. Ct. App. 1983).
65. *Houin,* 495 N.E.2d at 759.
66. *Id.*
67. Franklin Bank and Trust Co. v. Reed, 496 N.E.2d 596, 603-604 (Ind. Ct. App. 1986) *rev'd on other grounds,* 508 N.E.2d 1256 (Ind. 1887). *But see Houin,* 495 N.E.2d at 759 (finding that if the guaranty states that it covers "renewals or substitutions" the guarantor remains liable after revocation for renewals of debts that were covered by the guaranty prior to revocation).
68. Credit Alliance Corp. v. Campbell, 845 F.2d 725, 729 (7th Cir. 1987).
69. *Skrypek,* 469 N.E.2d at 777.

purpose is to give the primary obligor a standing credit to be used from time to time. It covers all transactions, including those arising in the future, which are within the contemplation of the agreement.[70]

Where a continuing guaranty provides that it applies to modifications of the underlying obligation, in the absence of consent by the guarantor to the modification, the continuing guaranty will extend to modifications that were either nonmaterial modifications of the underlying obligation, or material alterations shown to be within the contemplation of the parties at the time the agreement was executed. These are questions of fact that must be analyzed on a case-by-case basis.[71]

6.5 "Absolute and Unconditional"

Guaranties may be either absolute and unconditional, or conditional. An absolute guaranty is an unconditional undertaking that the primary obligor will make payment or will perform, and the guarantor is liable immediately upon default of the primary obligor, without notice. By contrast, a conditional guaranty is an undertaking to pay or perform if payment or performance cannot be obtained from the primary obligor by reasonable diligence.[72] An obligee who receives an absolute guaranty has no duty to attempt to collect from the primary obligor before looking to the guarantor; this is an exception to the general rule that when a contract has been breached, the nonbreaching party must use reasonable diligence to mitigate damages.[73]

6.6 "Liable as a Primary Obligor and not Merely as Surety"

Indiana courts apparently have not construed the meaning or effect of a stipulation in a guaranty to the effect that the guarantor is "liable as a primary obligor" rather than a "surety."

§ 7 Defenses of the Guarantor; Set-off

7.1 Defenses of the Primary Obligor

7.1.1 General

The liability of a guarantor generally is measured by that of the principal, unless a lesser or greater liability is expressly assumed by the guarantor.[74] A guarantor's liability may exceed that of the primary obligor when the guaranty contract so provides; for example, when the guarantor "unconditional and primarily"

70. *Grabill,* 919 N.E.2d at 1165; S-Mart, 744 N.E.2d at 585.
71. *S-Mart,* 744 N.E.2d at 587.
72. *McEntire, 471* N.E.2d at 1225.
73. Bruno v. Wells Fargo Bank, N.A., 850 N.E.2d 940, 948 (Ind. Ct. App. 2006).
74. Smith v. Rogers, 14 Ind. 224, 224 (Ind. 1860).

guarantees payment of a promissory note he is personally liable for even if the primary obligor has no personal liability for payment of the debt.[75]

7.1.2 When Guarantor may assert Primary Obligor's defense

When a guarantor is called upon to pay a deficiency judgment, the guarantor is entitled to assert the defense of lack of commercial reasonableness in the obligee's disposition of collateral securing the underlying obligation.[76]

7.1.3 Defenses that may not be raised by Guarantor

Indiana case law does not identify defenses that a guarantor may not raise.

7.1.4 Defenses that may always be raised by Guarantor

Discharge of the primary obligor from liability for the underlying obligation ordinarily will also discharge the guarantor.[77]

7.2 "Suretyship" Defenses

7.2.1 Change in Identity of Primary Obligor

A change in identity of the primary obligor of the underlying obligation discharges the guarantor's obligations if it causes a "material alteration of the underlying obligation without the consent of the guarantor."[78] A material alteration must be a change that "alters the legal identity of the principal's contract, substantially increases the risk of loss to the guarantor, or places the guarantor in a different position."[79] The assumption of the underlying obligation by a third party does not release the original primary obligor unless there is a novation.[80] Courts have found that the assumption of the underlying obligation without a novation does not change the legal identity of the underlying obligation, substantially increase the risk of loss to the guarantor, or place the guarantor in a different position.[81]

7.2.2 Modification of the Underlying Obligation, including Release

Generally, a guarantor is released when the primary obligor and obligee "cause a material alteration of the underlying obligation without the consent of the guarantor....whether the change is to his injury or benefit for the reason that it

75. *Loudermilk,* 441 N.E.2d at 1384.
76. *McEntire,* 471 N.E.2d at 1226.
77. N. Ind. Steel Supply Co., Inc. v. Chrisman, 204 N.E.2d 668, 671 (Ind. Ct. App. 1965).
78. Kruse v. Nat'l Bank of Indianapolis, 815 N.E.2d 137, 149 (Ind. Ct. App. 2004) (quoting *Yin,* 665 N.E.2d at 64).
79. *Id.*
80. A novation requires "(1) a valid existing contract, (2) the agreement of all parties to a new contract, (3) a valid new contract, and (4) an extinguishment of the old contract in favor of the new one." Modern Photo Offset Supply v. Woodfield Grp., 663 N.E.2d 547, 551 (Ind. Ct. App. 1996) (quoting Winkler v. V.G. Reed & Sons, Inc., 638 N.E.2d 1228, 1233 (Ind. 1994)).
81. *Id.*

is no longer his contract."[82] A material alteration that can cause the discharge of a guarantor must be a change that "alters the legal identity of the principal's contract, substantially increases the risk of loss to the guarantor, or places the guarantor in a different position."[83]

Courts have found that the extension of time for payment or performance of the underlying obligation without the guarantor's consent can discharge the guarantor from further liability.[84] In order to discharge the guarantor, there must be sufficient evidence to demonstrate that the agreement for the extension of time for payment or performance of the underlying obligation "was supported by adequate consideration and constituted a 'new contract.'"[85]

Guarantors may prospectively give consent to material alterations of the underlying obligation in its guaranty,[86] including, without limitation, consent to future extensions of time for the payment or performance of the underlying obligation,[87] consent to the extension of additional loans,[88] and consent to forbearance by the obligee from enforcing payment of the underlying obligation upon a default by the primary obligor.[89]

A release of the primary obligor from the underlying obligation without the consent of the guarantor releases the guarantor from its guaranty.[90]

7.2.3 Release or Impairment of Security for the Underlying Obligation

A guarantor may assert an impairment of collateral defense to attempt to discharge its liability under its guaranty.[91] Under the impairment of collateral defense, the guarantor must "establish that the creditor's conduct unjustifiably impaired the collateral securing the debt."[92] The Indiana Supreme Court has stated that this defense is based on both the guarantor being exposed to greater liability than the guarantor expected when the guaranty was executed, and the impairment of the guarantor's potential subrogation claims against the primary obligor.[93]

The guarantor is released to the extent that such release or impairment of the collateral for the underlying obligation has impaired the collateral.[94] The

82. *Goeke,* 467 N.E.2d at 765.
83. *Kruse,* 815 N.E.2d at 149 (quoting Yin, 665 N.E.2d at 64).
84. Owen County State Bank v. Guard, 26 N.E.2d 395, 399 (Ind. 1940); *Goeke,* 467 N.E.2d at 765.
85. Ind. Univ. v. Ind. Bonding & Sur. Co., 416 N.E.2d 1275, 1281 (Ind. Ct. App. 1981).
86. *Fortmeyer*, 565 N.E.2d at 1122 (citing Carney v. Cent. Nat'l Bank of Greencastle, 450 N.E.2d 1034, 1037-38 (Ind. Ct. App. 1983)).
87. *Yin,* 665 N.E.2d at 64.
88. *Fortmeyer*, 565 N.E.2d at 1122.
89. *Houin*, 495 N.E.2d at 760.
90. *Loudermilk*, 441 N.E.2d at 1386 (citing Lutz v. Frick Co., 181 N.E.2d 14 (Ind. 1962)).
91. Bartle v. Health Quest Realty VII, 768 N.E.2d 912, 922 (Ind. Ct. App. 2002) (citing *Letsinger,* 652 N.E.2d at 66).
92. *Id.* (citing Alani v. Monroe County Bank, 712 N.E.2d 19, 21 (Ind. Ct. App. 1999)).
93. Cole v. Loman & Gray, Inc., 713 N.E.2d 901, 904 (Ind. Ct. App. 1999) (quoting *Letsinger*, 652 N.E.2d at 66).
94. *Id.*, at 904-05 (citing *Letsinger,* 652 N.E.2d at 66; White v. Household Fin. Corp., 302 N.E.2d 828, 833 (Ind. Ct. App. 1973)).

amount of impairment is measured at the time of default by primary obligor under the underlying obligation.[95]

Consent to the release or impairment of collateral by the guarantor in the guaranty waives the impairment of collateral defense.[96]

7.3 Other Defenses

7.3.1 Failure to fulfill a Condition Precedent

An obligee must show compliance with all conditions precedent set forth in the guaranty in order to bring an action against a guarantor.[97] However, "[t]he fact that notice is required of the guarantee does not make the giving of notice a condition precedent" to bringing suit against the guarantor.[98] Instead, any loss that results from failure to give notice is a matter of defense.[99]

7.3.2 Modification of the Guaranty

Modification of a guaranty requires all the elements of a contract, including offer, acceptance, and consideration.[100] A guaranty may be modified by oral or written agreement so long as all elements are met.[101] (*See* § 4 above.)

7.3.3 Failure to pursue Primary Obligor

Indiana law provides that in the case of an absolute guaranty (as opposed to a conditional guaranty), the obligee has no duty to attempt to collect the underlying obligation from the primary obligor prior to seeking collection from the guarantor.[102] Under an absolute guaranty, the guarantor is immediately liable upon default of the primary obligor, whereas under a conditional guaranty (sometimes called a "strict" or "collateral" guaranty) the guarantor is not liable unless the obligee cannot obtain payment or performance from the primary obligor with reasonable diligence.[103] (*See* § 6.2 and § 6.5 above). Thus the guarantor automatically becomes the primary obligor upon default of his principal.[104]

The guarantor may waive in advance any right it may have to require the obligee to first pursue the primary obligor.[105]

---

95. *Cole*, 713 N.E.2d at 904 (citing Rempa v. LaPorte Prod. Credit Ass'n, 444 N.E.2d 308, 313 n.4 (Ind. Ct. App. 1983)).
96. *Letsinger*, 652 N.E.2d at 66 (citing *Carney*, 450 N.E.2d at 1036-37).
97. Knight & Jillson Co. v. Castle, 87 N.E. 976, 980 (Ind. 1909); 14 Ind. L. Ency. *Guaranty* § 32 (2011).
98. Ward v. Wilson, 100 Ind. 52, 58 (Ind. 1885); *see also Castle*, 87 N.E. at 980.
99. 14 Ind. L. Ency. *Guaranty* § 32 (2011).
100. Henthorne v. Legacy Healthcare, Inc., 764 N.E.2d 751, 759 (Ind. Ct. App. 2002).
101. Hamlin v. Steward, 622 N.E.2d 535, 539 (Ind. Ct. App. 1993) (citing Purity Maid Prod. Co. v. Am. Bank & Trust Co., 14 N.E.2d 755, 759 (Ind. Ct. App. 1938)).
102. *Bruno*, 850 N.E.2d at 948 (citing *Kruse*, 815 N.E.2d at 150).
103. *McEntire*, 471 N.E.2d at 1225 (quoting Pavlantos v. Garoufalis, 89 F.2d 203, 206 (10th Cir. 1937); United States v. Willis, 593 F.2d 247 (6th Cir. 1979); Joe Heaston Tractor & Implement Co. v. Sec. Acceptance Corp., 243 F.2d 196 (10th Cir. 1957); U.S.A., Etc. v. Chatlin's Dep't Store, Inc., 506 F.Supp. 108 (E.D. Pa. 1980)).
104. *Id.* at 1225.
105. *Bruno*, 850 N.E.2d at 948; Gemmer v. Anthony Wayne Bank, 391 N.E.2d 1185, 1187 (Ind. Ct. App. 1979).

7.3.4 *Statute of Limitations*

Indiana Code § 34-11-2-9 provides that "an action upon promissory notes, bills of exchange, or other written contracts for the payment of money executed after August 31, 1982, must be commenced within six (6) years after the cause of action accrues."[106] An obligee's action upon a written contract under which the surety/guarantor promised to pay the primary obligor's indebtedness thereafter incurred is an action on a written contract for the payment of money.[107]

7.3.5 *Statute of Frauds*

The Indiana statute of frauds provides that an action may not be brought "charging any person, upon any special promise, to answer for the debt, default, or miscarriage of another" unless the agreement upon which the action is based is in writing and signed by the person charged.[108] A guaranty only needs to be in writing and signed by the guarantor for it to be valid.[109] The obligee's failure to sign the guaranty does not render the guaranty invalid.[110]

7.3.6 *Defenses particular to Guarantors that are Natural Persons and their Spouses*

Guarantors who are natural persons have special defenses that they may raise, including infancy and lack of legal capacity.[111] (*See* § 2.5 above.)

7.3.7 *Right of Set-off*

A guarantor may assert a set-off of only those claims that arise independent of the claim brought by the obligee.[112] A set-off is a "counter-action against the plaintiff and grows out of matter independent of [the plaintiff's] cause of action."[113] Courts look at the facts alleged and the relief sought to determine whether or not the pleading is a set-off.[114]

§ 8 Waiver of Defenses by the Guarantor

Certain defenses cannot be waived before a default occurs. Catch-all waivers are not effective to waive all defenses. Waivers of certain defenses must be expressly stated.

106. Ind. Code § 34-11-2-9 (West 2011 and Supp. 2011).
107. Timberlake v. J. R. Watkins Co., 209 N.E.2d 909, 913 (Ind. Ct. App. 1965).
108. Ind. Code § 32-21-1-1(b)(2) (West 2002 and Supp. 2011).
109. *Grabill,* 919 N.E.2d at 1168.
110. *Id.* at 1166-67.
111. *See* Bowling v. Sperry, 184 N.E.2d 901, 903 (Ind. Ct. App. 1962).
112. Am. Mgmt., Inc. v. MIF Realty, L.P., 666 N.E.2d 424, 432 (Ind. Ct. App. 1996).
113. *Id.* (quoting Sams v. Kern, 98 N.E.2d 920, 921 (Ind. Ct. App. 1951)).
114. *Id.*

8.1 Defenses that cannot be Waived

A guarantor cannot waive the defense of failure to provide notice of disposition of the collateral or the defense of lack of commercial reasonableness in the disposition of the collateral before a default occurs.[115] A guarantor may waive the right to notification of the sale of the collateral only by a post-default agreement.[116]

8.2 "Catch-all" Waivers

Guaranties are interpreted in the same manner as other contracts. In construing a guaranty, a court will give effect to the intentions of the parties and a guarantor cannot be made liable beyond the terms of the guaranty.[117] As a practical matter, the more specific a waiver is, the better evidence it is of the guarantor's intent to waive a particular defense—therefore, catch-all waivers are generally not a best practice. In addition, as set forth below, catch-all waivers are insufficient to waive certain defenses.

8.3 Use of Specific Waivers

Waiver of notice of default must be expressly stated.[118] Language stating that the guarantor waives notice of dishonor on any instrument is not sufficient to waive the guarantor's right to notice of the primary obligor's default.[119] Likewise, waiver of an impairment of collateral defense must be expressly stated—an unconditional guaranty is, by itself, insufficient to waive an impairment of collateral defense.[120] Waiver of the defense of alteration of the underlying obligation also must be expressly stated. Even when a continuing guaranty provides that it applies to modifications of the underlying obligation, in the absence of consent by the guarantors to the modifications, the continuing guaranty will not extend to material modifications of the underlying obligation that were not shown to be within the contemplation of the parties at the time the agreement was executed.[121] (*See also* § 7.2.2 and § 7.2.3 above.)

---

115. Ind. Code § 26-1-9.1-602 (7) (West 2011); Walker v. McTague, 737 N.E.2d 404, 409 n.3 (Ind. Ct. App. 2000); Moore v. Wells Fargo Constr., 907 N.E.2d 1038, 1039 (Ind. Ct. App. 2009).
116. Ind. Code § 26-1-9.1-624 (West 2003 and Supp. 2011).
117. *Kruse,* 815 N.E.2d at 144-45.
118. *Modern Photo,* 663 N.E.2d at 551-552; Bowyer v. Clark Equip. Co., 357 N.E.2d 290, 294 (Ind. Ct. App. 1976).
119. *Bowyer,* 357 N.E.2d at 294.
120. *Letsinger, 652* N.E.2d at 67 n.3.
121. *S-Mart,* 744 N.E.2d at 585.

§ 9 Third-party Pledgors—Defenses and Waiver Thereof

Generally, a pledge of collateral as security for the debt of another results in a surety relationship.[122] As a result, the third-party pledgor can avail itself of the same defenses that are available to a surety.[123]

§ 10 Jointly and Severally Liable Guarantors—Contribution and Reduction of Obligations upon Payment by a Co-obligor

The right to contribution arises when a coguarantor discharges the obligation. Coguarantors with joint and several liability are presumed to be responsible for their proportionate share of the obligation.

10.1 Contribution

Guarantors who are jointly and severally liable are obligated for equal contribution toward the obligation in the absence of an agreement otherwise.[124] The right to contribution arises when a coguarantor discharges the obligation.[125] A coguarantor is entitled to contribution to the extent that the coguarantor's payment exceeded its pro rata share of the underlying obligation.[126]

In determining the rights to contribution, it is important to distinguish between a cosuretyship and a subsuretyship. [127] Cosureties are of equal rank and are entitled to contribution from one another so that each bears an equal burden.[128] In other words, cosureties both guaranteed payment and performance of the underlying obligation and must bear that obligation equally.[129]

Conversely, in a subsuretyship, the "secondary obligors" agree that one (the "principal surety") will bear the cost of payment and performance.[130] If

---

122. *Owen County,* 26 N.E.2d at 398-99 ("One who, with the knowledge of the creditor, furnishes collateral to secure the loan of another stands in the relation of surety to the debtor and such collateral is released by any action of the creditor which would release a surety, such as the extension of the time of payment of the debt, the acceptance of a renewal note, or the release of other security."); Bailey v. Holliday, 806 N.E.2d 6 (Ind. Ct. App. 2004) (discussing role of surety under mechanic's lien statutes); Damler v. Baine, 51 N.E.2d 885, 888 (Ind. Ct. App. 1943) ("Where a pledge is made as security for the obligation of a third-party, the pledgor is a surety to the extent of the pledged collateral"); Eberhart v. Eyre-Shoemaker, Inc., 134 N.E. 227, 228-29 (Ind. Ct. App. 1922) ("One who furnishes collateral as an accommodation to secure the loan of another stands in the relation of surety to the one accommodated.").
123. *Owen County,* 26 N.E.2d at 398-99 (third-party pledgor may assert same defenses as a surety).
124. Cook v. Cook, 92 Ind. 398, 398 (Ind. 1884); Balvich v. Spicer, 894 N.E.2d 235, 240, 245 (Ind. Ct. App. 2008); Fleck v. Ragan, 514 N.E.2d 1287, 1289 (Ind. Ct. App. 1987).
125. *Balvich,* 894 N.E.2d at 243.
126. Small v. Rogers, 938 N.E.2d 18, 23-24 (Ind. Ct. App. 2010); *Balvich,* 894 N.E.2d at 245-47.
127. Sureties and guarantors are generally regarded as synonymous. *Irish,* 864 N.E.2d at 1121 n.4.
128. *Id.* at 1121-22.
129. *Id.*
130. *Id.* at 1122.

the principal surety satisfies the underlying obligation, he is entitled to indemnification from the primary obligor but has no rights to contribution from the subsurety.[131] If the subsurety satisfies the underlying obligation, the subsurety is entitled to indemnification and reimbursement from the principal surety.[132]

A principal surety cannot purchase a defaulted note from the obligee upon the primary obligor's default and thereby create liability for the subsurety who would not otherwise be liable.[133]

10.2 Reduction of Obligations upon Payment of Co-obligor

Payment by a co-obligor satisfies the obligation as to all obligors.[134] If the underlying obligation is partially satisfied, the guarantor is discharged from its secondary obligation pro tanto.[135]

The controlling factor in determining whether the underlying obligation has been satisfied is the payment by a party obligated to pay.[136] An assignment of the underlying obligation is irrelevant.[137] Further, the Indiana Court of Appeals has held that if a strawman is used by a co-obligor to purchase an assignment of the underlying obligation, the underlying obligation is deemed to have been purchased by one of the co-obligors and is satisfied.[138]

10.3 Liability of Parent Guarantors owning less than 100 percent of Primary Obligor

Parent guarantors who own less than 100% of the primary obligor have not been given unique treatment under Indiana case law.

§ 11 Reliance

Indiana courts have not identified the obligee's reliance on the guaranty as a necessary condition to enforceability.

§ 12 Subrogation

Subrogation is an equitable remedy that may be available to a guarantor who pays the primary obligor's debt.

131. *Id.*
132. *Id.*
133. *Id.* at 1124.
134. Tacco Falcon Point, Inc. v. Atlantic Ltd. P'ship XII, 937 N.E.2d 1212, 1220-21 (Ind. Ct. App. 2010).
135. 14 Ind. L. Ency. *Guaranty* § 26 (2004).
136. *Tacco Falcon Point*, 937 N.E.2d at 1221.
137. *Id.* at 1220-21.
138. *Id.* at 1221.

In general, a guarantor who pays a primary obligor's obligation to an obligee may be subrogated to the rights of the obligee as against the primary obligor;[139] however, because subrogation is an equitable remedy, the paying guarantor may only be subrogated to the obligee's rights to the extent equitable.[140]

The Indiana Supreme Court has explained the doctrine of subrogation in Indiana as follows:

> Subrogation is a doctrine of equity long recognized in Indiana. It applies whenever a party, not acting as a volunteer, pays the debt of another that, in good conscience, should have been paid by the one primarily liable. *See, e.g., Loving v. Ponderosa Sys., Inc.*, 479 N.E.2d 531, 536-37 (Ind. 1985). When a claim based on subrogation is recognized, "a court substitutes another person in the place of a creditor, so that the person in whose favor it is exercised succeeds to the right of the creditor in relation to the debt." *Matter of Estate of Devine,* 628 N.E.2d 1227, 1230 n.4 (Ind. Ct. App.1994). It is settled that "[s]ubrogation confers no greater right than the subrogor had at the time the surety or indemnitor became subrogated. The subrogator [sic] insurer stands in the same position as the subrogor, for one cannot acquire by subrogation what another, whose rights he claims, did not have." *American States Ins. Co. v. Williams,* 278 N.E.2d 295, 300 (Ind. Ct. App. 1972). The ultimate purpose of the doctrine, as with other equitable principles such as contribution, is to prevent unjust enrichment. 73 AM.JUR. 2D Subrogation § 4 (1974).[141]

Whereas older Indiana cases on subrogation took the position that subrogation entitles the subrogee to succeed to all of the subrogor's rights,[142] more recent Indiana case law on subrogation holds that a guarantor/subrogee's right of subrogation is really a right of indemnity or contribution with additional rights granted as intended by the parties' intent and equity.[143]

---

139. Ertel v. Radio Corp. of Am., 307 N.E.2d 471, 474 (Ind. 1974) ("The general rule, firmly imbedded in Indiana law, is that a surety, upon satisfaction of a debt, is subrogated to all the rights which the creditor had against the principal debtor prior to satisfaction of the debt."); *see also* Osterman v. Baber, 714 N.E.2d 735, 737 (Ind. Ct. App. 1999) ("[I]f equity permits, the party who has paid the creditor, or subrogee, becomes entitled to the legal rights and security originally held by the creditor."); Am. States Ins. Co. v. Floyd I. Staub, Inc., 370 N.E.2d 989, 995 (Ind. Ct. App. 1978) ("A surety is entitled to a right of subrogation to any rights in collateral that the creditor obtains from the principal debtor.").

140. Neu v. Gibson, 928 N.E.2d 556, 561 (Ind. 2010) (holding that equitable subrogation does not require that the subrogee be entitled to enforce all rights of the subroger and stating, "Nowhere in *Nally* did we state that equitable subrogation always entitles every subrogee to *all* of the rights its subroger possessed. On the contrary, we emphasized that '[t]he key to subrogation is an equitable result.' Nor did we maintain that every party entitled to equitable subrogation is entitled to all the rights the bank held. As the maxim goes, equity supplies what equity demands.") (internal citations omitted) (quoting Bank of N.Y. v. Nally, 820 N.E.2d 644, 653 (Ind. 2005)).

141. Erie Ins. Co. v. George, 681 N.E.2d 183, 186 (Ind. 1997).

142. Opp v. Ward, 24 N.E. 974, 975 (Ind. 1890) ("The doctrine is well established that one who occupies the attitude of a surety will be subrogated to all the rights, remedies, and securities which the creditor had, in case the former has been compelled to pay a debt which in equity and good conscience should have been paid by another. Payment by the surety is equivalent to a purchase from the creditor, and operates as an equitable assignment of the debt, and all incidents, to the former.").

143. *Neu,* 928 N.E.2d at 561; Merch. Nat'l Bank & Trust Co. v. Winston, 159 N.E.2d 296, 304 (Ind. Ct. App. 1959) (analyzing the intent of the parties and finding that "the right of subrogation by the guarantor is one of indemnity only and rests upon an implied promise on the part of the corporation as principal, and the guarantor is not entitled to recover a greater amount than he has paid for the corporation.").

§ 13 Triangular Set-off in Bankruptcy

11 U.S.C. § 553 preserves the right of set-off in bankruptcy, provided that the claimant can show the requisite mutuality of obligations.[144] Generally, however, a "triangular set-off"—as when A attempts to offset an obligation owed to B against B's debt to C—is prohibited because there is no mutuality of obligation. Some courts have held that the requisite mutuality of obligation can exist when, in a formal prepetition agreement, the debtor agrees that a creditor can set-off debts owed by third parties against the debt owed to the creditor.[145]

§ 14 Indemnification—Whether the Primary Obligor has a Duty

The primary obligor has a duty of indemnification once the guarantor's obligation to pay is incurred.

A primary obligor has a duty of indemnification if the guarantor entered into the guaranty agreement at the request of, or with the consent of, the primary obligor and the guarantor paid the underlying obligation.[146] Conversely, the primary obligor has no right of action against the guarantor for contribution.[147]

A guarantor who pays an obligation has rights of reimbursement and subrogation against the primary obligor and may assert a cause of action against the primary obligor accordingly.[148] The guarantor may seek indemnification from the primary obligor in the amount the guarantor paid to discharge the debt.[149] The right to indemnification does not accrue until the guarantor is under an obligation to pay.[150]

---

144. 11 U.S.C. § 553 (2006) ("...this title does not affect any right of a creditor to offset a mutual debt owing by such creditor to the debtor that arose before the commencement of the case under this title against a claim of such creditor against the debtor that arose before the commencement of the case...").
145. *See* Inland Steel Co. v. Berger Steel Co., Inc. (In re Berger Steel Co.), 327 F.2d 401, 405 (7th Cir. 1964) (stating that triangular set-off is allowed when there is a prepetition agreement but holding that set-off was improper because there was no such agreement in the case). *But see* In re SemCrude, L.P., 399 B.R. 388, 392-93 (Bankr. D. Del. 2009) (holding that written prepetition agreement allowing triangular set-off failed to create mutuality of debt required to allow set-off under the Bankruptcy Code).
146. 14 Ind. L. Ency. *Guaranty* § 23 (2004).
147. *See* Ind. Code § 26-1-3.1-419(f) (West Supp. 2011) ("An accommodated party that pays the instrument has no right of recourse against, and is not entitled to contribution from, an accommodation party.").
148. Ind. Code § 26-1-3.1-419(f) (West Supp. 2011) ("An accommodation party who pays the instrument is entitled to reimbursement from the accommodated party and is entitled to enforce the instrument against the accommodated party."); Hendershot v. Charleston Nat'l Bank, 563 N.E.2d 546, 548-49 (Ind. 1990); SPCP Grp. LLC v. Dolson, Inc., 934 N.E.2d 771, 777 (Ind. Ct. App. 2010); 14 Ind. L. Ency. *Guaranty* § 23 (2004).
149. Ross v. Menefee, 25 N.E. 545, 546 (Ind. 1890); Auburn Cordage, Inc. v. The Revocable Trust Agreement of Bryce B. Treadwell, 848 N.E.2d 738, 749 (Ind. Ct. App. 2006).
150. *Balvich,* 894 N.E.2d at 244 (Ind. Ct. App. 2008).

If the obligee releases the primary obligor but reserves its rights against the guarantor, the guarantor is not released and may pay the debt and pursue reimbursement from the primary obligor.[151]

§ 15 Enforcement of Guaranties

15.1 Limitations on Recovery

If a guaranty contract includes an agreement by the guarantor to pay attorneys' fees incurred in connection with the enforcement of the guaranty, the award of attorneys' fees must be reasonable based on evidence presented at trial which fairly tends to prove the amount due.[152]

15.2 Enforcement of Guaranties of Payment versus Guaranties of Performance

See § 6.2 above.

15.3 Exercising Rights under a Guaranty Where the Underlying Obligation is also Secured by a Mortgage

In a foreclosure action, the court must "give a personal judgment against any party to the [foreclosure] suit liable upon any agreement for the payment of any sum of money secured by the mortgage," and must "order the mortgaged premises, or as much of the mortgaged premises as may be necessary to satisfy the mortgage and court costs, to be sold first before the sale of other property of the defendant."[153] A surety is entitled to have the mortgaged property sold in satisfaction of the obligation secured before his own property is made liable.[154]

The mortgagee may not proceed to foreclose the mortgage while pursuing "any other action for the same debt or matter that is secured by the mortgage" or "while the mortgagee is seeking to obtain execution of any judgment in any other action," and may not "prosecute any other action for the same matter while . . . foreclosing the . . . mortgage or prosecuting a judgment of foreclosure."[155]

15.4 Litigating Guaranty claims; Procedural considerations

An action to enforce a guaranty must be brought against the guarantor as a claim for breach of the guaranty contract.[156] If the guaranty is an absolute guaranty, as opposed to a conditional guaranty, there is no requirement that the obligee

151. *Hendershot,* 563 N.E.2d at 548.
152. *Bruno,* 850 N.E.2d at 950-951 (citing Smith v. Kendall, 477 N.E.2d 953, 955 (Ind. Ct. App. 1985)).
153. IND. CODE § 32-30-10-5 (West 2002 & Supp. 2011).
154. *See* Higham v. Harris, 8 N.E. 255, 262 (Ind. 1886).
155. IND. CODE § 32-30-10-10 (West 2002 and Supp. 2011).
156. 14 IND. L. ENCY. *Guaranty* § 32 (2011).

attempt to collect from or bring suit against the primary obligor as a condition precedent to bringing suit against the guarantor.[157] In addition, notice of the primary obligor's default or lack of demand on the guarantor may be defenses to be asserted by the guarantor but are ordinarily not conditions precedent to filing suit unless specifically set forth as such in the guaranty contract.[158]

Under Indiana law, a person who is bound as a surety on a written contract for the payment of debt, or performance of any act, may require the obligee to immediately institute an action on the contract once the right of action has accrued. If the obligee does not bring an action within a reasonable time and prosecute the action to judgment and execution, the surety is discharged from liability.[159] If one codefendant is surety for the others, the surety may, by a written complaint to the court, cause the question of suretyship to be tried and determined at the trial of the original cause, or any time before or after the trial.[160] If that issue is found in favor of the surety, the court must order the judgment to be executed first against the property of the principal, and against the property of the surety only after the property of the principal is exhausted.[161] One whose suretyship status is adjudicated pursuant to the foregoing provisions has statutory subrogation and contribution rights in the event he satisfies, or partially satisfies, the judgment.[162]

§ 16 Revival and Reinstatement of Guaranties

If the obligee surrenders the undertaking of a surety, with the intention of abandoning it and obtaining a new undertaking, the original undertaking is not revived by redelivery thereof to the obligee.[163]

§ 17 Choice of Law

Under Indiana law, parties may stipulate the law that will govern their agreements, and such contractual stipulations generally are favored.[164] If there is no such stipulation, or the court determines that a contractual stipulation should not be honored, the court will apply the "most intimate contacts" test

157. *Kruse*, 815 N.E.2d at 141 n.2 (citing *McEntire,* 471 N.E.2d at 1225); 14 Ind. L. Ency. *Guaranty* § 32 (2011).
158. 14 Ind. L. Ency. *Guaranty* § 32 (2011).
159. Ind. Code §§ 34-22-1-1 (West 2011 and Supp. 2011) and 34-22-1-2 (West 2011 and Supp. 2011). A predecessor version of this statute was held not to apply to an unconditional guaranty, but rather, only to "indorsers and sureties." Sample v. Martin, 46 Ind. 226 (Ind. 1874).
160. Ind. Code § 34-22-1-3 (West 2011 and Supp. 2011).
161. Ind. Code § 34-22-1-4 (West 2011 and Supp. 2011).
162. Ind. Code §§ 34-22-1-5 (West 2011 and Supp. 2011) and 34-22-1-6 (West 2011 and Supp. 2011). *Balvich,* 894 N.E.2d at 247.
163. Stewart v. Knight & Jillson Co., 76 N.E. 743, 747 (Ind. 1906).
164. Kentucky Nat'l Insurance Co. v. Empire Fire and Marine Insurance Co., 919 N.E.2d 565, 575 (Ind. Ct. App. 2010); Hoehn v. Hoehn, 716 N.E.2d 479, 484 (Ind. Ct. App. 1999).

to determine the governing law, considering such factors as (1) the place of contracting, (2) the place of negotiation, (3) the place of performance, (4) the location of the subject matter of the contract, and (5) the domicile, residence, nationality, place of incorporation, and place of business of the parties. However, the court will undertake this analysis only if there is a difference between the relevant laws of the different states.[165]

---

165. *Kentucky Nat'l Insurance Company*, 919. N.E.2d at 575.

Iowa State Law of Guaranties

Thomas L. Flynn
Belin McCormick P.C.
666 Walnut Street, Suite 2000
Des Moines, Iowa 50309
(515) 283-4605 (Telephone)
(515) 558-0605 (Facsimile)
tlflynn@belinmccormick.com
www.belinmccormick.com

Contents

Iowa State Law of Guaranties

INTRODUCTION

This chapter is intended to provide an overview to lawyers and lenders of the laws of the State of Iowa that govern guaranties. It does not attempt to deal with the application of federal law to guaranties, although certain federal statutes may be mentioned. It is, by nature, general in scope and should not be relied on in a specific transaction without legal advice tailored to the transaction.

As a general rule, Iowa courts have routinely adopted or cited with approval to the Restatement (Third) of Suretyship and Guaranty.

Further, as applicable to contracts (and thus guaranties), Iowa courts have followed the Restatement (Second) of Conflicts of Laws. Iowa has no statutory law or case law pertaining to completion guaranties or performance guaranties (i.e., guaranties of obligations other than for the payment of money).

In order to standardize this discussion of the law of guaranties in Iowa, the following terms from relevant statutes and case law are used to refer to the various parties to a guaranty and their obligations.

"Guarantor" means a person who, by contract, agrees to satisfy an underlying obligation of another to an obligee upon the primary obligor's default on that underlying obligation. For the most part, unless specifically addressed, no distinction is drawn between guarantors and sureties, as the distinction in Iowa between the two is often muddled.

"Guaranty" means the contract by which the guarantor agrees to satisfy the underlying obligation of a primary obligor to an obligee in the event the primary obligor defaults on the underlying obligation.

"Obligee" means the person to whom the underlying obligation is owed. For example, the lender under a loan agreement would be an obligee vis-à-vis the borrower.

"Obligor" means the person who incurs the underlying obligation to the obligee. For example, the borrower under a loan agreement would be a primary obligor. The terms "maker" and "principal" are often used interchangeably with "obligor" by the Iowa courts.

IOWA LAW HIGHLIGHTS

1. A guaranty obtained by a lender from a spouse in violation of the Equal Credit Opportunity Act (15 U.S.C. § 1691(a)(1)) is not enforceable even if the statute of limitations by which the guarantor had to bring his/her claim against the lender has expired. See § 2.5 below.
2. A mortgage on homestead property given to secure a guaranty must be signed by both spouses to be enforceable. If the homestead constitutes agricultural land, the mortgage must include a specific homestead exemption waiver executed by both spouses to be enforceable. See § 2.5 below.
3. A guarantor may assert as a defense the statute of limitations that is available to the obligor. If the time for bringing an action against the obligor has expired, the time for bringing an action against the guarantor has similarly expired. See § 7.1.4 below.
4. If a guarantor's debt is secured by agricultural property, the creditor must first obtain a mediation release before seeking to enforce its remedies against the agricultural property. The creditor may obtain a judgment against the guarantor without first obtaining the mediation release, but may not levy on any agricultural property without such release. See § 7.3.1 below.

§ 1 Nature of the Guaranty Agreement

Under Iowa law, a guaranty is a "contract by one party to another party for the fulfillment of a promise of a third party."[1] The nature of a guaranty agreement is to "secure the primary undertaking" between the primary obligor and obligee.[2] The extent of a guarantor's obligation must be determined from the parties' written contract.[3] The same rule is to be applied in the construction of contracts of guaranty as other contracts.[4]

Iowa law establishes an implied promise for the primary obligor to reimburse the guarantor to the full extent of the guarantor's performance to the obligee.[5]

§ 2 State Law Requirements for an Entity to Enter a Guaranty

Corporations, partnerships, limited liability companies, and banks can all grant guaranties in furtherance of their business activities. Such authorization is generally permitted by the Iowa statute applicable to the respective entity.

2.1 Corporations

Under the Iowa Business Corporation Act, an Iowa corporation has the same powers as an individual to do all things necessary or convenient to carry out its business and affairs, including the making of guaranties and the pledging of assets to secure guaranties.[6]

2.2 Partnerships

The Iowa Uniform Partnership Act (Iowa Code Chapter 486A) makes no specific mention of guaranties, but it is presumed that guaranties made in the ordinary course of the partnership's business are valid and binding.

Subject to a contrary statement of partnership authority filed of record pursuant to § 486A.303 of the Iowa Uniform Partnership Act, a partner is an agent of the partnership and may, within the scope of the partnership's business, bind the partnership to a contract of guaranty.[7] An act of a partner which is

---

1. City of Davenport v. Shewry Corp., 674 N.W.2d 79, 86 (Iowa 2004).
2. *Id.* at 87.
3. Bankers Trust Co. v. Woltz, 326 N.W.2d 274, 276 (Iowa 1982).
4. Andrew v. Austin, 213 Iowa 963, 967; 232 N.W. 79, 81 (Iowa 1930).
5. Hills Bank & Trust Co. v. Converse, 772 N.W.2d 764, 772 (Iowa 2009), citing Restatement (Third) of Suretyship and Guaranty § 22, (1996).
6. I.C. § 490.302(7).
7. I.C. § 486A.301(l).

not in the ordinary course of the partnership's business binds the partnership only if the act was authorized by the other partners.[8]

2.3 Limited Liability Companies

The Iowa Revised Uniform Limited Liability Company Act makes no specific mention of guaranties but a limited liability company is empowered to do all things necessary or convenient to carry on its activities.[9]

2.4 Bank and Trust Companies

The Iowa Banking Act (Iowa Code Chapter 524) makes no specific mention of guaranties but allows banks "to contract indebtedness and incur liabilities to effect any and all of the purposes for which the state bank is organized, subject to the provisions of this chapter."[10] However, the Iowa Supreme Court has opined that "it is not within the ordinary functions of a bank to lend its credit . . . . A banking institution is not authorized to become a guarantor, except where this is necessary to protect its rights where the guaranty relates to commercial paper and is an incident to the purchase and sale thereof, or where such guaranty is especially authorized by law."[11] Federal law prohibits a state-chartered bank from engaging in activities in which a national bank may not engage under federal law. The situations under which a national bank may become a guarantor are governed by federal law.[12]

2.5 Individuals

Any individual competent to enter into a contract may issue a guaranty. This requires:

- Mental competence.[13]
- Sufficient age. The age of majority in Iowa is 18 years.[14]

Under Iowa law, a guaranty issued by one spouse does not automatically affect the property or liabilities of the other spouse.[15]

A guaranty obtained by a lender from a spouse in violation of 15 U.S.C. § 1691(a)(1) is not enforceable, even if the statute of limitations has expired by which the guarantor had to bring his/her claim against the lender.[16]

A mortgage on homestead property given to secure a guaranty must be signed by both spouses to be enforceable.[17] If the homestead constitutes

8. I.C. § 486A.301(2).
9. I.C. § 489.105(1).
10. I.C. § 524.801(11).
11. Dewey Column & Monumental Works v. Ryan, 221 N.W. 800, 801 (Iowa 1928).
12. *See* National Bank as Guarantor or Surety on Indemnity Bond, 12 C.F.R. § 7.1017 (2012).
13. *See* Putensen v. Hawkeye Bank of Clay County, 564 N.W.2d 404 (Iowa 1977); *see also* Peoples Bank & Trust Co. v. LaLa, 392 N.W.2d 179, 184 (Iowa 1986) ("[A] contract cannot be set aside on the ground of incompetency unless evidence demonstrates the person lacked sufficient mental capacity to understand the contract.").
14. I.C. § 599.1.
15. I.C. § 597.2 and I.C. § 597.17.
16. Bank of the West v. Kline, 782 N.W.2d 453 (Iowa 2010).
17. I.C. § 561.13(1).

agricultural land, the mortgage must include a specific homestead exemption waiver executed by both spouses to be enforceable.[18]

§ 3 Signatory's Authority to Execute a Guaranty

Generally, a guaranty executed in the ordinary course of business by an entity is enforceable. The obligee has a duty of reasonable inquiry when it has some notice that the person executing the guaranty is not authorized.

3.1 Corporations

A corporate officer must be authorized to enter into a transaction with a third party. Whether a corporate officer has authorization is determined by the extent of his authority, which may be actual or implied:

> "Actual authority to act is created when a principal intentionally confers authority on the agent either by writing or through other conduct which, reasonably interpreted, allows the agent to believe that he has the power to act. Actual authority includes both express and implied authority. Express authority is derived from specific instructions by the principal in setting out duties, while implied authority is actual authority circumstantially proved."[19]

The distinction between actual and implied authority is important, as the source of authority will determine the extent to which the corporation is bound to contracts entered into by agents of the corporation.[20] If a corporate agent acts without authority, he may be personally liable for the responsibilities of the contract.[21]

3.2 Partnerships

The Iowa Uniform Partnership Act provides that all partners have "equal rights in the management and conduct of the partnership business."[22] If a guaranty is considered to be in the ordinary course of business of the partnership, it is binding even if not signed by all partners. "Each partner is an agent of the partnership for the purpose of its business. An act of a partner, including the execution of an instrument in the partnership name for apparently carrying on

18. I.C. § 561.22.
19. Dillon v. City of Davenport, 366 N.W.2d 918, 924 (Iowa 1985); *see also* 6 IA. Prac., Business Organizations § 29:10 (2010 ed.).
20. *See generally* 5 IA. Prac., Business Organizations § 29:10 to 29:13.
21. Kessel v. Murray, 196 N.W. 591 (Iowa 1924); accord W. Branch State Bank v. Farmers Union Exch., 268 N.W. 155, 157 (1936) ("The corporation was their own artificial creation, organized for their own profit. As between themselves and their corporation, the corporation was the principal, and each signing stockholder was severally guarantor of a limited amount, which was proportionate to his interest.").
22. I.C. § 486A.401(6).

in the ordinary course the partnership business or business of the kind carried on by the partnership binds the partnership, unless the partner had no authority to act for the partnership in the particular matter and the person with whom the partner was dealing knew or had received notification that the partner lacked authority."[23] However, a guaranty executed by a partner outside the ordinary course of partnership business would need to be authorized by the other partners.[24]

Partners are "liable jointly and severally for all obligations of the partnership unless otherwise agreed by claimant or provided by law."[25]

3.3 Limited Liability Companies (LLCs)

"A member of a LLC is not an agent of an LLC solely by reason of being a member."[26] Thus, no member of a LLC has authority to make guaranties on behalf of the LLC solely by virtue of being a member. A guaranty deemed not to be in the ordinary course of business for a member-managed LLC must have the consent of all members.[27] Iowa law assumes that members of a LLC will co-manage the company unless the operating agreement expressly states that the company is to be managed by a manager or managers.[28] If the LLC adopts a management structure, managers "decide all matters related to company activities," but decisions outside the ordinary course of business require the consent of all members of the LLC.[29]

3.4 Banks and Trust Companies

Banks are not generally authorized to issue guaranties, "except where this is necessary to protect its rights, where the guaranty relates to commercial paper and is incident to the purchase and sale thereof, or where such guaranty is especially authorized by law."[30]

§ 4 Consideration; Sufficiency of Past Consideration

Standard contract principles apply to the analysis of consideration for a contract of guaranty.

Consideration is required to create a valid contract of guaranty.[31] Whether consideration is sufficient involves application of standard contract law principles. Iowa statutory authority and case law presumes consideration if

23. I.C. § 486A.301(1).
24. I.C. § 486A.301(2).
25. I.C. § 486A.306(1).
26. I.C. § 489.301(1).
27. I.C. § 489.407(2)(d).
28. I.C. § 489.407(1).
29. I.C. § 489.407(2)(d).
30. Dewey Column & Monumental Works v. Ryan, 221 N.W. 800, 801 (1928).
31. Green Bay Lumber Co. v. Fredericksen, 196 N.W. 790, 791-92 (1924) ("A mere naked promise to pay the existing debt of another without any consideration for such promise is not sufficient.").

a contract is in writing and signed by the party to be charged with a debt.[32] The burden is then placed on the guarantor to show the lack of consideration for the guaranty.[33]

A promise of forbearance in exchange for a guaranty also constitutes sufficient consideration for a guaranty contract.[34]

§ 5 Notice of Acceptance

In Iowa, notice of acceptance is not required where the contract of guaranty is absolute and unconditional.

Where a guaranty is absolute and unconditional for the payment of the debt, no notice of acceptance is necessary.[35] If the guaranty is deemed continuous, the acceptance is continuous as well.[36] Notice is not required before each new credit advance in a continuing guaranty unless the contract expressly calls for it.[37]

§ 6 Interpretation of Guaranties

Iowa courts adhere to the principle of "strictissimi juris"—that is, courts will follow contractual language to its letter—when construing the obligations of a guarantor.[38] Aside from this background principle, courts will interpret guaranty contracts by looking to the intent of the parties, which may be discerned from language in the contract itself and the surrounding circumstances of the agreement.[39]

6.1 General Principles

Principles of construction in contract law apply generally to the law of guaranties.[40] Guaranty contracts cannot be enlarged or extended by implication; guarantors can expect courts to construe guaranty contracts strictly according

---

32. I.C. § 537A.2; Boyd v. Miller, 230 N.W. 851, 854 (1930); *see also* Insurance Agents, Inc. v. Abel, 338 N.W.2d 531 (Iowa Ct. App. 1983).
33. *See, e.g.*, North Side State Bank v. Schreiber, 258 N.W. 690, 694 (Iowa 1935).
34. R. J. Watkins Co. v. Peterson, 231 N.W. 489, 490 (1930); Guetzlaff v. First Nat. Bank, 198 N.W. 517, 518 (1924).
35. McKee v. Needles, 98 N.W. 618, 123 Iowa 195 (Iowa 1904).
36. Maresh Sheet Metal Works v. N. R. G., Ltd., 304 N.W.2d 436, 440 (Iowa 1981).
37. *Id.*
38. Schoonover v. Osborne, 79 N.W. 263, 264 (1899).
39. Williams v. Clark, 417 N.W.2d 247, 251 (Iowa Ct. App. 1987), citing Miller v. Geerlings, 128 N.W.2d 207, 211 (1964), and Buser v. Grande Avenue Land Co., 234 N.W. 241, 244 (1931); *see also* Ted Spangenberg Co. v. Peoples Natural Gas., Div. of N. Natural Gas Co., 305 F. Supp. 1129, 1135 (S.D. Iowa 1969) aff'd sub nom. Ted Spangenberg Co. v. Peoples Natural Gas, Div. of N. Natural Gas Co., 439 F.2d 1260 (8th Cir. 1971).
40. Bank of the West v. Michael R. Myers Revocable Trust, 776 N.W.2d 112 (Iowa Ct. App. 2009), citing Andrew v. Austin, 232 N.W. 79, 81 (1930) ("The same rule is to be applied in the construction of contracts of guaranty as other contracts.").

to their terms.[41] Indeed, "[n]o deviation, even for the benefit of the guarantor, will be tolerated."[42]

As such, "care should be taken to hold the party bound to the full extent of his engagement, as the same may be deduced from the language of the contract, read in the light of the surrounding circumstances."[43]

6.2 Guaranty of Payment versus Guaranty of Collection

A guarantor of payment has an absolute obligation to satisfy the underlying promise to the obligee. Such obligation arises

> "immediately upon default of the principal debtor, and regardless of whether any legal proceedings or steps are taken to enforce liability of the principal debtor, or whether notice of default is given to the guarantor, and regardless of the solvency or insolvency of the principal debtor."[44]

In other words, there are no conditions precedent, other than a default, to create liability for a guarantor of payment.[45] A guarantor of payment has a "duty to ascertain whether the note [is] paid or not, and to take any action that he might deem necessary for his own protection."[46]

In contrast, a guarantor of collection only assumes responsibility if, after "due diligence," the obligee is unable to collect from the primary obligor.[47] Typically, what constitutes due diligence is fact-sensitive, but knowledge of a debtor's insolvency standing alone will not suffice to allow the obligee to recover from the guarantor.[48]

6.3 Language Regarding the Revocation of Guaranties

Under Iowa law, a continuing guaranty remains valid "until revoked or terminated by some rule of law."[49] Yet Iowa courts recognize that absent

---

41. Andrew v. Austin, 232 N.W. 79, 81 (1930). Iowa courts have declined to follow contrary authority that suggests guarantor liability extends to successor entities. *Compare* Interstate Elec. Supply Co. v. Blanchard, 682 N.W.2d 81 (Iowa Ct. App. 2004) (declining to extend liability to successor entity), *with* Fehr Bros., Inc. v. Scheinman, 509 N.Y.S.2d 304, 308 (N.Y. 1986) (holding a change in corporate name and operation was not enough to discharge the personal guaranty).
42. Andrews v. Austin, 232 N.W. at 81, citing Schoonover v. Osborne, 79 N.W. 263, 265 (1899).
43. Bridgeport Malleable Iron Co. v. Iowa Cutlery Works, 107 N.W. 937, 938 (1906), quoting Fisk & Co. v. Rickel, 79 N.W. 120 (Iowa 1899).
44. Preferred Inv. Co. v. Westbrook, 174 N.W.2d 391, 395 (Iowa 1970); Cf. Kent Feeds, Inc. v. Manthei, 646 N.W.2d 87, 91 (Iowa 2002) (noting that Iowa courts do not require the creditor to join suits against the obligor and guarantor).
45. Aetna Life Ins. Co. v. Anderson, 848 F.2d 104, 106 (8th Cir. 1988).
46. Granger v. Graef, 212 N.W. 730, 731 (Iowa 1927).
47. Kent Feeds, Inc. v. Manthei, 646 N.W.2d 87, 91 (Iowa 2002); *see also* Cownie v. Dodd, 149 N.W. 904, 905 (Iowa 1914); *Preferred Inv. Co.*, 174 N.W.2d at 395; Schaffer v. Acklin, 218 N.W. 286, 287 (Iowa 1928).
48. Voorhies v. Atlee, 29 Iowa 49, 51-52 (Iowa 1870).
49. *Maresh Sheet Metal Works*, 304 N.W.2d at 440-41 (internal citations omitted).

a specific agreement, a revocation does not typically extend to previously incurred debts.[50]

6.4 "Continuing"

The Iowa Supreme Court has noted that a continuing guaranty "contemplates a future course of dealing during an indefinite period, or it is intended to cover a series of transactions or a succession of credits. ... An offer for a continuing guaranty contract is ordinarily effective until revoked by the guarantor."[51] Use of the word "continuing" is not necessary to establish a continuing guaranty if such an agreement is "sufficiently clear and unambiguous" from the language of the contract.[52]

6.5 "Absolute and Unconditional"

Iowa courts will assume a guaranty is absolute unless there are express terms to the contrary.[53]

If the guaranty is absolute, the guarantor is subject to immediate liability once the principal debtor defaults, regardless of whether the guarantor has notice of the default.[54]

A guaranty for one year by a roofing contractor was deemed enforceable and not violative of any statute to the contrary.[55]

§ 7 Defenses of the Guarantor

The defenses available to a guarantor can be grouped into three categories: (1) defenses of the primary obligor; (2) "suretyship" defenses; and (3) other defenses.

---

50. Union Trust & Savings Bank v. State Bank, 188 N.W.2d 300, 302 (Iowa 1971); *see also* Bank of the West v. Shima, 788 N.W.2d 397 (Iowa Ct. App. 2010) ("It is legally possible, we assume, for a creditor to agree to relieve a guarantor from even preexisting liability, but that would require proof of specific facts supporting such an agreement."); Beal Bank v. Siems, 670 N.W.2d 119, 127 (Iowa 2003), quoting 38 Am.Jur.2d Guaranty § 80 (1990) (noting that "[a] guaranty contract may be abandoned by the creditor so far as it relates to future transactions, so that the guarantor is not liable for future advances to the principal debtor").
51. Bankers Trust Co. v. Woltz, 326 N.W.2d 274, 277 (Iowa 1982), citing 38 Am.Jur.2d, *Guaranty* § 23, § 63 (1968), and Union Trust and Savings Bank v. State Bank, 188 N.W.2d 300, 302 (Iowa 1971); *see also* Wellman Sav. Bank v. Adams, 454 N.W.2d 852, 857 (Iowa 1990) (holding guarantor liable for primary obligor's multiple debts to the bank under a continuing guaranty agreement).
52. *Bankers Trust Co.*, 326 N.W.2d at 277; *see also Maresh Sheet Metal Works*, 304 N.W.2d at 440, citing *Union Trust,* 188 N.W.2d at 302, and 38 Am.Jur.2d Guaranty, § 23 (1968) ("[A guaranty] is restricted if limited to a single transaction or to a limited number of specific transactions. It is continuing if it contemplates a future course of dealing over an indefinite period.").
53. Williams v. Clark, 417 N.W.2d 247, 251 (Iowa Ct. App. 1987).
54. *Id.*
55. Weyerhauser Corp. v. Tamko Roofing Products, Inc., 298 F. Supp.2d, 836 (N.D. Iowa 2003).

7.1 Defenses of the Primary Obligor

7.1.1 General

In Iowa, a guarantor has a complete defense if the primary obligor is not bound to perform the promise because of fraudulent inducement or mistaken representations of the plaintiff.[56] However, a guarantor is not absolved of liability if he fails to read the contents of an instrument that he signs, as a failure to read is not a legally cognizable defense.[57]

The Iowa Code contains a mandatory mediation provision for creditors who wish to enforce a debt against agricultural property;[58] however, the Iowa Supreme Court has declined to extend this provision to actions to secure judgments by creditors against guarantors.[59]

7.1.2 When Guarantor May Assert Primary Obligor's Defense

Typically, the guarantor may raise any defense that is available to the primary obligor.[60] However, there are some exceptions to this rule. One author has suggested a few considerations that may help decide whether a primary obligor's defenses should be available to the guarantor:

> A surety will be permitted to assert a defense of the principal when the circumstances in connection with a particular defense require this result (1) in order to protect properly the principal, (2) in order to protect the surety, if the equities in connection with the defense favor the surety in preference to the creditor, or (3) because both the principal and the surety are entitled to consideration which outweighs that to be accorded the creditor. The creditor's position is important relatively in comparison with the equities of the principal and the surety.[61]

The Iowa Code lists several defenses available to the primary obligor. Whether these defenses are also available to the guarantor depends on a consideration of the different principles listed above.[62]

7.1.3 Defenses that May not be Raised by Guarantor

The guarantor may not assert the insolvency of the primary obligor as a defense unless the guaranty is expressly conditioned on the obligor's solvency.[63]

A dissolving corporation does not absolve guarantors of their obligations on a guaranty of a loan for that corporation.[64]

56. Bennett v. Corey, 34 N.W. 291, 293-294 (1887); Merchants' Nat. Bank of Ocala v. Citizens' State Bank, 61 N.W. 1065, (Iowa 1895).
57. United Suppliers, Inc. v. Schroeder, 683 N.W.2d 126 (Iowa Ct. App. 2004).
58. *See* I.C. § 654A.6(1)(a).
59. *Kent Feeds,* 646 N.W.2d at 90 (declining to extend the mandatory mediation requirement for creditors that deal with agricultural business to judgments against guarantors).
60. First Nat'l Bank v. Drake, 171 N.W. 115, 117 (Iowa 1919).
61. *Note,* Defenses of a Principal Available to a Surety, 27 Iowa L. Rev. 601, 625 (1942).
62. *See* I.C. § 554.3305(1)-(4).
63. Preferred Inv. Co. v. Westbrook, 174 N.W.2d 391 (Iowa 1970).
64. Cownie v. Dodd, 149 N.W. 904, (Iowa 1914).

If an obligee takes possession of collateral from the primary obligor, such possession does not relieve the guarantor from liability.[65]

7.1.4 Defenses that May Always be Raised by Guarantor

The obligations of a guarantor only extend to enforceable promises undertaken by the primary obligor; the guarantor is thus not bound to fulfill any promise that the primary obligor is not legally bound to perform.[66] Payment of the debt "by the principal discharges the guarantor and terminates the obligation."[67]

In Iowa, a guarantor may assert as a defense the statute of limitations that is available to the obligor. If the time for bringing an action against the obligor has expired, the time for bringing an action against the guarantor has similarly expired.[68]

Iowa courts also have suggested they may recognize the insurance law doctrine of reasonable expectations as applied to guaranty contract disputes.[69] The doctrine would allow parties to present extrinsic evidence that they would not have assented to a guaranty contract had they known the exact provisions of the agreement.[70]

A guarantor may raise a defense of promissory estoppel to bar recovery on a guaranty. To establish estoppel, the guarantor must show:

> "(1) a misrepresentation or concealment of material facts by the other party, (2) lack of knowledge of the true facts by the party to whom the misrepresentation is made, (3) an intent to cause reliance on the misrepresentation, and (4) actual reliance on the misrepresentation to the detriment of the party to whom the representation was made."[71]

Delays in enforcing a note will not necessarily release a guarantor from his obligations. The Iowa Supreme Court has indicated in dicta that "[i]t is not clear ... whether a passive failure or delay on the part of the payee will result in the discharge of a comaker."[72] However, absent a guaranty agreement to the contrary, "[a] valid agreement between the payee and the maker of a note to extend time for payment discharges any co-maker who has not consented to the extension."[73]

---

65. Brenton Bank & Trust Co., Clarion v. Beisner, 268 N.W.2d 196, (Iowa 1978), citing 38 Am.Jur.2d Guaranty § 85 ("The fact that the creditor, in order to insure payment of the debt which is due him, has taken additional security thereof does not have the effect of releasing or discharging the guarantor of liability on his contract of guaranty.").
66. Merchants' Nat. Bank of Ocala v. Citizens' State Bank, 61 N.W. at 1065 (Iowa 1895).
67. Decorah State Bank v. Zidlicky, 426 N.W.2d 388, 390 (Iowa 1988).
68. State v. Bi-States Constr. Co., 269 N.W.2d 455, 457 (Iowa 1978); First Nat. Bank, Shenandoah v. Drake, 171 N.W. 115, 117 (1919).
69. Wellman Sav. Bank v. Adams, 454 N.W.2d 852, 856 (Iowa 1990).
    See Rodman v. State Farm Mutual Insurance Co., 208 N.W.2d 903, 906 (Iowa 1973) ("The objectively reasonable expectations of applicants and intended beneficiaries regarding the terms of insurance contracts will be honored even though painstaking study of the policy provisions would have negated those expectations.").
70. Wellman Sav. Bank v. Adams, 454 N.W.2d 852, 856 (Iowa 1990).
71. Int'l Harvester Credit Corp. v. Leaders, 818 F.2d 655, 659 (8th Cir. 1987), citing Grandon v. Ellingson, 144 N.W.2d 898, 903 (Iowa 1966).
72. American State Bank v. Leaver, 153 N.W.2d 348, 351 (Iowa 1967).
73. *Id.* at 351.

7.2 "Suretyship" Defenses

7.2.1 Change in Identity of Principal Obligor

Where guarantors guaranteed the loan of a sole proprietor, who subsequently incorporated his business, guarantors were held not liable for the subsequent loans to the corporation.[74]

7.2.2 Modification of the Underlying Obligation, Including Release

Iowa courts recognize the "established rule that a guarantor is discharged from his obligation by any act on the part of the guarantee which increases the guarantor's risk or in any manner injures his rights or remedies."[75] But, if the terms of the guaranty allow an obligee to make modifications, the defense is not likely viable.[76]

If a lender extends the time for a primary obligor to pay the debt without the guarantor's consent, the guarantor may be discharged from his obligations.[77] In another case, where the guarantor agreed to guarantee debt of $1,500-$2,000, and the obligee extended credit for $3,473, the guarantor was released from all liability.[78]

When a guarantor sold his interest in the business, even though the lender did not prepare a formal, written release or cancellation of the guaranty, where evidence indicated that the lender was aware that a condition of the sale was that the guarantor be released from his guaranty, and loan terms from the lender to the buyer did not mention the guarantor's guaranty, the lender was deemed to have abandoned the guaranty.[79]

But apart from this rule, the court also noted that "the guarantee owes no affirmative duty of diligence to the guarantor of payment,"[80] and even negligence by the primary obligor will not discharge the obligations of the guarantor.[81] The Iowa Supreme Court has indicated that the obligee must do some affirmative act to prejudice the guarantor before the guarantor's obligations are discharged.[82]

---

74. Northwest Bank & Trust Co. v. Witt Express, Inc., 804 N.W.2d 314 (Iowa Ct. App. 2011).
75. Fidelity Savings Bank v. Wormhoudt Lumber Co., 104 N.W.2d 462, 466 (1960), quoting 38 C.J.S. Guaranty § 67.
76. Peoples Bank & Trust Co. of Cedar Rapids v. Lala, 392 N.W.2d 179, 183 (Iowa Ct. App. 1986).
77. Thornton v. Ankeny State Bank, 453 N.W.2d 240, 242 (Iowa 1990); American State Bank v. Leaver, 153 N.W.2d 348, 351 (Iowa 1967).
78. Dewey Column & Monumental Works v. Ryan, 221 N.W. 800, 801 (1928); *see also* Robinson v. Reed, 46 Iowa 219, 220 (Iowa 1877) (attempting to change the wording on a note to make it a surety instead of a guaranty altered the original obligation and released the guarantor from liability).
79. Beal Bank v. Siems, 670 N.W.2d 119 (Iowa 2003).
80. *Id.* (internal citations omitted).
81. *Fidelity Sav. Bank,* 104 N.W.2d at 466, citing Fuller v. Tomlinson Bros., 12 N.W. 127, 128 (Iowa 1882); accord Aetna Life Ins. Co. v. Anderson, 848 F.2d 104, 108 (8th Cir. 1988) (noting that guarantor cannot claim lack of due diligence by the obligee in securing payment from primary obligor because Iowa law imposes no such affirmative duty).
82. Fidelity Sav. Bank v. Wormhoudt Lumber Co., 104 N.W.2d 462, 466 (1960) (noting that an obligee's "affirmative act which diminishe[s] other security which might have been available for payment of the debt, or otherwise injured the guarantor in his rights and remedies … will discharge the latter pro tanto").

7.2.3 Release or Impairment of Security for the Underlying Obligation

In one case, a bank released the land mortgaged by the obligors to secure the debt.[83] However, the release occurred because the obligors did not own the land individually. The court of appeals affirmed the judgment of the trial court that the bank released the collateral for the loan but not the underlying debt and therefore the guarantors remained liable.[84] The court of appeals noted, however, that the burden of proof to show the debt was not extinguished should have been placed on the bank because a release is "prima facie evidence of extinguishment of the debt."[85]

As noted above, Iowa courts draw a distinction between negligence and affirmative acts on the part of the obligee that alter the underlying obligation. In a secured transaction context, if the obligee is negligent in his handling of the collateral, the guarantor will not be discharged.[86]

7.3 Other Defenses

7.3.1 Failure to Fulfill a Condition Precedent

The Iowa Code requires mandatory mediation before a creditor can initiate a proceeding to enforce a debt in an agricultural contract.[87] The Iowa Supreme Court has held, however, that this provision does not require a creditor to participate in mandatory mediation before securing a judgment against a guarantor.[88]

In one case, the Iowa Supreme Court read the words "personal guarantee" to contain no condition precedent. As such, the words "constitute[d] an unconditional guarantee of payment."[89]

Where a lender, as an inducement to an investor to purchase assets of an insolvent company and guarantee a loan to the lender, represented to the investor/guarantor that the lender would collect equally from joint guarantors upon a loan default, but evidence indicated that the lender never intended to seek collection from the other guarantors, the investor/guarantor had a claim against the lender for compensatory and punitive damages.[90]

7.3.2 Modification of the Guaranty

Under Iowa law, unless otherwise provided in the guaranty agreement, material alterations to a guaranty agreement without the guarantor's consent discharge the guarantor from liability.[91] Examples of material alterations include

83. Peoples Bank & Trust Co. of Cedar Rapids v. Lala, 392 N.W.2d 179, 183 (Iowa Ct. App. 1986).
84. *Id.* at 184.
85. *Id.* (citing Watkins v. Watkins, 31 N.W.2d 354, 354 (Iowa 1948)).
86. Fidelity Sav. Bank v. Wormhoudt Lumber Co., 104 N.W.2d 462, 466 (Iowa 1960).
87. I.C. § 654A.6(1)(a).
88. Kent Feeds, Inc. v. Manthei, 646 N.W.2d 87, 89-90 (Iowa 2002).
89. *Preferred Inv. Co.*, 174 N.W.2d at 395.
90. Spreitzer v. Hawkeye State Bank, 779 N.W.2d 726 (Iowa 2009).
91. Lawrence Warehouse Co. v. Menary, 143 F. Supp. 883, 886 (S.D. Iowa 1956) (internal citations omitted).

"increasing the risk by substitution, insertion, and non-deletion of terms" in the guaranty contract.[92]

7.3.3 Failure to Pursue Primary Obligor

The Iowa Code provides a mechanism for guarantors to compel creditors to go after the primary obligor before commencing action against the guarantor.[93] The procedure is only applicable if "the principal is about to become insolvent or remove permanently from the state without discharging the contract."[94] If the creditor refuses to comply with the guarantor's request within 10 days, or else allow the guarantor to pursue the primary obligor, the guarantor is discharged.[95]

7.3.4 Statute of Limitations

In Iowa, a 10-year limitations period applies to the enforcement of guaranty contracts absent specific contractual language to the contrary.[96] However, the statute of limitations commences on the date of default by the obligor, not the date the contract of guaranty is executed.[97]

If the statute of limitations runs against the primary obligor, the guarantor may assert the same defense on his own behalf.[98]

7.3.5 Statute of Frauds

The Iowa Supreme Court has held that parol evidence of a guaranty contract is admissible if the parol agreement created an original contract and was not collateral to an existing obligation.[99] According to the court, such agreements may fall under the "leading object" rule and will fall outside the statute of frauds.[100] The determination is a question of fact.[101] In Iowa, if a guaranty conspicuously includes the language required by Iowa Code Section 535.17(2),[102] any modification to the guaranty must be in writing and signed by the party sought to be bound by the modification.[103]

---

92. *Id.*
93. I.C. §§ 540.1 to 540.3.
94. I.C. § 540.1.
95. I.C. § 540.2
96. I.C. § 614.1(5) (2011).
97. International Harvester Credit Corp. v. Leaders, 818 F.2d 655 (8th Cir. 1987).
98. State v. Bi-States Constr. Co., 269 N.W.2d 455 (Iowa 1978); First Nat. Bank, Shenandoah v. Drake, 171 N.W. 115, 117 (Iowa 1919).
99. *Maresh Sheet Metal Works,* 304 N.W.2d at 438-39, citing 72 Am.Jur.2d, Statute of Frauds, § 226-227 at 749, 752 (1974).
100. *Id.* at 439 ("When the guarantor's purpose is to secure some benefit or business advantage for himself, the matter does not come within the statute of frauds requiring the promise to be in writing.").
101. *Id.* at 440.
102. Section 535.17(2) provides in pertinent part: Unless otherwise expressly agreed in writing, a modification of a credit agreement *which occurs after the person asserting the modification has been notified in writing that the oral or implied modifications to the credit agreement are unenforceable and should not be relied upon,* is not enforceable in contract law by way of action or defense by any party unless a writing exists containing the material terms of the modification and is signed by the party against whom enforcement is sought . . . . I.C.§ 535.17(2) (emphasis added).
103. Beal Bank v. Siems, 670 N.W.2d 119 (Iowa 2003).

It has been suggested that the Iowa statute of frauds provision "does not prevent [a] contract from being established and enforced if the statute is not pleaded affirmatively as a defense by the party sought to be charged."[104] This is in contrast to most states that render an obligation unenforceable if not in writing.[105]

7.3.6 Defenses Particular to Guarantors that are Natural Persons and their Spouses

If the underlying transaction can be classified as providing "consumer credit," a guarantor's obligation is not valid unless the obligee provides notice to the guarantor about the transaction and the guarantor's liability.[106] This provision only applies to persons other than the spouse of the consumer.[107]

7.4 Right of Set-off

Certain defenses of the guarantor may create a set-off against a particular creditor. For instance, in one case, the Iowa Supreme Court noted in dicta that if the guarantors were to adequately plead a defense of promissory estoppel in relying on a bank's assurances that the bank would monitor the disbursement of funds, the guarantors would be entitled to set-off from their obligations the amount of damages stemming from this counterclaim.[108] Other Iowa decisions have recognized the same principle.[109]

The Iowa Code provides that a guarantor may, with the primary obligor's consent, interpose a counterclaim to se-off his indebtedness to the creditor by the amount the creditor owes to the principal.[110]

§ 8 Waiver of Defenses by the Guarantor

A guarantor may waive available defenses.

8.1 Defenses that cannot be Waived

Iowa law follows other states and does not allow guarantors to waive notice *before* default, thereby contracting around statutory protections.[111]

104. Clifford J. Calhoun, *Suretyship for the Iowa Lawyer*, 67 Iowa L. Rev. 219, 230 (1982).
105. *Id.* at note 49.
106. I.C. § 537.3208.
107. *Id.*
108. Union Story Trust & Sav. Bank v. Sayer, 332 N.W.2d at 321-322.
109. *See Fidelity Sav. Bank,* 104 N.W. at 466, and cases cited therein.
110. I.C. § 619.6; *see also* Dolan v. Buckley, 199 N.W. 302, 303 (Iowa 1924).
111. U.S. v. Jensen, 418 N.W.2d 65, 67 (Iowa 1988); *see* I.C. §§ 554.9501(3) and 554.9504(3) (waiver of notice by debtor binding only if signed after default).

8.2 "Catch-all" Waivers

Waivers will be enforced absent some collateral attack on their enforceability.[112] The Eighth Circuit, in interpreting Iowa law, has expressed a willingness to "uphold broad waivers of rights by guarantors."[113]

8.3 Use of Specific Waivers

There is no Iowa law that addresses the subject of use of specific waivers.

§ 9 Third-party Pledgors—Defenses and Waiver Thereof

There is no Iowa law that addresses the subject of third-party pledgors—defenses and waiver thereof.

§ 10 Jointly and Severally Liable Guarantors—Contribution and Reduction of Obligations upon Payment by a Co-obligor

Guarantors who are jointly and severally liable are presumed to share the secondary obligation equally.[114]

The creditor is not obliged to seek full payment from more than one such guarantor. After a guarantor pays the debt, however, he may seek contribution from other coguarantors for their proportional responsibility.[115]

10.1 Contribution

The right of contribution becomes enforceable only after a coguarantor has paid more than his share to the principal. The remaining coguarantors then have a duty of immediate performance to the obligee.[116] The guarantor who has fulfilled his obligation, in contrast, acquires the right to seek payment from the other guarantors through subrogation.[117]

---

112. Aetna Life Ins. Co. v. Anderson, 848 F.2d 104, 107 (8th Cir. 1988) (noting that absent fraudulent or coercive bargaining, a guarantor's waiver of defenses would be enforced).
113. *Id.* at note 10.
114. Mix v. Fairchild, 12 Iowa 351, 351-352 (1861); Marvin v. Adamson, 11 Iowa 371, 372-373 (1860).
115. Hills Bank & Trust Co. v. Converse, 772 N.W.2d 764 (Iowa 2009), adopting the Restatement (Third) of Suretyship and Guaranty.
116. In re Trust of Lunt, 24 N.W.2d 467, 468-69 (Iowa 1946).
117. Restatement of Security, § 141(d).

10.2 Reduction of Obligations upon Payment of Co-obligor

There is no Iowa law that addresses the subject of reduction of obligations upon payment of co-obligor.

10.3 Liability of Parent Guarantors Owning less than 100 percent of Primary Obligor

There is no Iowa law that addresses the subject of liability of parent guarantors owning less than 100 percent of primary obligor.

§ 11 Reliance

Reliance is generally not required to claim under a guaranty.

Under Iowa law, guaranties are governed by the rules generally applicable to contracts. Presumably, then, reliance is not requisite to enforce a guaranty. However, if a guarantor claims his endorsement was ineffective unless signed by coguarantors, an obligee may not assert promissory estoppel in order to enforce the guaranty—unless the obligee was without notice of the condition attached to the guarantor's promise.[118]

§ 12 Subrogation and Reimbursement

"Subrogation" and "reimbursement" are distinguished in Iowa.

Iowa courts distinguish the legal terms "reimbursement" and "subrogation." Reimbursement is a "legal remedy for a guarantor in an implied surety contract between the guarantor and primary debtor in a three-party loan contract."[119] In contrast, subrogation is an "equitable assignment of the creditor's rights to the guarantor, an enforcement mechanism through which the guarantor may be more adequately assured of reimbursement from the primary debtor.[120] In practice, there is little difference between the two concepts, except that a guarantor may assert subrogation only when the debt to the creditor has been fully satisfied, irrespective of any limits on the agreed amount of the guaranty.[121]

118. Furst-McNess Co. v. Kielly, 8 N.W.2d 730, 734 (1943).
119. Spreitzer v. Hawkeye State Bank, 779 N.W.2d 726, 746 (Iowa 2009), citing Restatement (Third) of Suretyship and Guaranty § 22 cmt. *a* (1996).
120. *Id.* at 746, note 7 (Iowa 2009).
121. *Id.*, citing Restatement (Third) of Suretyship and Guaranty at § 27 cmt. *b*.

A guarantor thus has a legal claim for reimbursement against the primary obligor if the guarantor pays the creditor in lieu of the primary obligor.[122] As the Iowa Supreme Court has held:

> Where a guarantor, who has entered into a contract of guaranty at the request of, or with the consent of, the principal obligor, pays or is compelled to pay his principal's debt, the law raises an implied promise, unless there is an express one, on the part of the principal to reimburse the guarantor, and on the payment of the debt the guarantor at once has a right of action against the principal for reimbursement of the amount which he has paid, with interest thereon at the legal rate.[123]
>
> Where the guarantor paid off the loan before it reached maturity, the Iowa Court of Appeals opined that the obligor's obligation to reimburse the guarantor was not due until the maturity date of the loan.[124]

§ 13 Triangular Set-off in Bankruptcy

There is no Iowa law that addresses the subject of triangular set-off in bankruptcy.

§ 14 Indemnification—Whether the Primary Obligor has a Duty

The principal obligor has a duty of indemnification to the guarantor.

As noted above, "where a guarantor, who has entered into a contract of guaranty at the request of, or with the consent of, the principal obligor – pays . . . his principal's debt, the law raises an implied promise . . . on the part of the principal to reimburse the guarantor . . ."[125]

---

122. *Id.* at 744. ("When a creditor bypasses the assets of a debtor and collects the debt from a guarantor under the terms of a personal guaranty, the guarantor may assert the rights of reimbursement against the debtor to recoup the amount paid on the guaranty.").
123. Hills Bank & Trust Co. v. Converse, 772 N.W.2d 764, 772 (Iowa 2009) (internal citations omitted).
124. In re Estate of Stealsmith, 803 N.W.2d 672 (Iowa 2011), citing with approval to Restatement (Third) of Suretyship and Guaranty § 22 cmt. *d,* (1996).
125. Halverson v. Lincoln Commodities, Inc., 297 N.W.2d 518, 522 (Iowa 1980).

§ 15 Enforcement of Guaranties

15.1 Limitations on Recovery

The death of a guarantor does not discharge the guaranty for existing debts, including extensions and renewals of that debt, if such extensions were considered in the initial guaranty agreement.[126] However, no new debt may be attributed to the guaranty.[127]

15.2 Enforcement of Guaranties of Payment versus Guaranties of Performance

There is no Iowa law that addresses the subject of enforcement of guaranties of payment versus guaranties of performance.

15.3 Exercising Rights under a Guaranty Where the Underlying Obligation is also Secured by a Mortgage

There is no Iowa law that addresses the subject of exercising rights under a guaranty where the underlying obligation is also secured by a mortgage.

15.4 Litigating Guaranty Claims: Procedural Considerations

In a suit against the guarantor by the obligee, the guarantor may set off unrelated claims he has against the obligee.[128]

§ 16 Revival and Reinstatement of Guaranties

There is no Iowa law that addresses the subject of revival and reinstatement of guaranties.

126. Brenton Bank & Trust Co., Clarion v. Beisner, 268 N.W.2d 196, 199 (Iowa 1978) ("In effect the guaranty clause covering extensions and renewals is like a clause waiving the defense of extension of time granted the debtor.").
127. *Id.*
128. *See* Iowa R. Civ. P. 30.

Kansas State Law of Guaranties

Christopher J. Rockers
Kevin Zeller
Husch Blackwell LLP
4801 Main Street
Suite 1000
Kansas City, MO 64112
816.983.8000
816.983.8080
christopher.rockers@huschblackwell.com
kevin.zeller@huschblackwell.com
www.huschblackwell.com

HUSCH BLACKWELL

Contents

Kansas State Law of Guaranties

HIGHLIGHTS:

Absent a waiver, if a guaranty is conditional, the obligee must first proceed against the primary obligor before attempting to collect from the guarantor (See § 6.5).

In a Tenth Circuit case interpreting Kansas law in a nonbankruptcy setting, the court permitted triangular set-off (See § 13).

TRAPS:

Subrogation rights do not arise unless and until a guarantor has fully discharged the underlying obligations (See §12).

Introductory Note: In order to standardize our discussion of the law of guaranties, we use the following vocabulary to refer to the various parties to a guaranty and their obligations.

"**Guarantor**" means a person who, by contract, agrees to satisfy an underlying obligation of another to an obligee upon the primary obligor's default on that underlying obligation. Except in limited situations discussed below, this chapter does not draw great distinctions between guarantors and sureties, as there is little difference between the two under Kansas law.

"**Guaranty**" means the contract by which the guarantor agrees to satisfy the underlying obligation of a primary obligor to an obligee in the event the primary obligor defaults on the underlying obligation.

"**Obligee**" means the person to whom the underlying obligation is owed. For example, the lender under a loan agreement would be an obligee vis-à-vis the borrower.

"**Primary Obligor**" means the person who incurs the underlying obligation to the obligee. For example, the borrower under a loan agreement would be a primary obligor.

"**Underlying Obligation**" means the obligation or obligations that the primary obligor owes to the obligee. For example, the borrower's obligation to make payments to a lender of principal and interest on a loan constitutes an underlying obligation.

On at least one occasion, a Kansas court has cited to the Restatement of Suretyship and Guaranty.[1]

1. Baxter State Bank v. Bernhardt, 985 F. Supp. 1259, 1266 (D. Kansas 1997), citing Restatement (Third) of Suretyship and Guaranty, § 16.

§ 1 Nature of the Guaranty Arrangement

Under Kansas law, a guaranty is a "contract between two or more persons, founded upon consideration, by which one person promises to answer to another for debt, default, or miscarriage of a third person, and, in legal sense, has relation to some other contract or obligation with reference to which it is collateral undertaking."[2]

1.1 Guaranty Relationships

The contract of the guarantor is a separate contract. It is in the nature of a warranty by the guarantor that the thing guaranteed to be accomplished by the primary obligor shall be done, and is not an engagement jointly with the primary obligor to do the act. Accordingly, for a guaranty, there must be at least three parties: a guarantor, an obligee, who is the individual to whom the promise is made, and a primary obligor.[3]

Kansas law will not hold a guarantor liable unless an intention to bind itself is "clearly manifested." [4] A guaranty must be in writing, signed by the party to be charged, and state with certainty (1) each party to the contract, (2) the subject matter to which the contract relates, and (3) the terms and conditions of all the promises constituting the contract and by whom and to whom the promises are made.[5]

§ 2 State Law Requirements for an Entity to Enter a Guaranty

2.1 Corporations

A Kansas corporation has the express power to enter into guaranties which are necessary or convenient to the conduct, promotion, or attainment of the business of the corporation. Guaranties with respect to subsidiary, parent, or affiliate corporations are deemed to be "necessary or convenient to the conduct, promotion or attainment of the business of the contracting corporation."[6] Kansas courts have not addressed the "necessary or convenient" language outside the realm of subsidiary, parent, or affiliate corporations. The Kansas statutes are based substantially on Delaware statutes, and the Kansas courts would likely look to any interpretations or guidance provided by Delaware courts.[7]

2. Overland Park Savings and Loan Assn. v. Miller, 763 P.2d 1092, 1098 (Kan. 1988); Bomud Company v. Yockey Oil Company, 299 P.2d 72, 76 (Kan. 1956).
3. Fleetwood Enterprises, Inc. v. The Coleman Co., 161 P.3d 765, 773 (Kan. App. 2007); citing Iola State Bank v. Biggs, 662 P.2d 563 (Kan. 1983).
4. Glencore Grain Limited, 241 F.Supp.2d 1324, 1331 (D. Kansas 2003); citing John S. Britain Dry-Goods Co. v. Yearout, 598 Kan. 684 (Kan. 1898).
5. *Id.*, 241 F.Supp.2d at 1331.
6. K.S.A. § 17-6102(13).
7. *See* Arctic Financial Corp., 38 P.3d 701, 703 (Kan. 2002).

2.2 Partnerships

The Kansas Uniform Partnership Act[8] neither expressly empowers a partnership to issue a guaranty nor expressly regulates or prohibits such activity.

2.3 Limited Liability Companies

Kansas permits a limited liability company (LLC) to carry on any lawful business, purpose, or activity, and to exercise all powers and privileges that are necessary or convenient to the conduct, promotion, or attainment of the business, purposes, or activities of the LLC.[9] Kansas courts have not addressed the "necessary or convenient" language. The Kansas statutes are based substantially on Delaware statutes, and the Kansas courts would likely look to any interpretations or guidance provided by Delaware courts.[10]

2.4 Banks and Trust Companies

Kansas laws and regulations do not expressly permit or prohibit a state chartered bank or trust company to enter into a guaranty agreement. However, an 1897 case, which no court has since cited, stated, "becoming surety upon undertakings is no part of the business of banks."[11]

2.5 Individuals

A case-by-case inquiry is required to determine whether an individual intended to be personally bound, or, instead, only issued a guaranty on behalf of a business entity in his or her official employment capacity. Like other contracts, in interpreting a guaranty, the court will attempt to determine the intent of the parties at the time the contract was entered into.[12] The inclusion of a title next to a person's name is not dispositive in the inquiry, particularly if it would lead to an unreasonable conclusion. For instance, in a situation in which a corporation executed a document as the primary obligor, and an officer executed a document under the heading "Guarantor," the officer was found to have executed as a guarantor, despite the inclusion of his business title after his name. The court held that finding otherwise would render the heading "Guarantor" to an absurdity, as the corporation would not be both the primary obligor of the obligations, and also the guarantor on the same obligations.[13]

With respect to married couples, a spouse's execution of a contract, including a guaranty, does not automatically bind the other spouse, because "neither husband nor wife has the power to act as the other's agent merely by virtue of

8. K.S.A. § 56a-101, *et seq.*
9. K.S.A. § 17-7668.
10. *See* Arctic Financial Corp., 38 P.3d 701, 703 (Kan. 2002).
11. W.D. Long v. Hubbard, 50 P. 968, 969 (Kan. App. 1897).
12. McBride Electric, Inc. v. Putt's Tuff, Inc., 685 P.2d 316, 320 (Kan. App. 1984).
13. *Id.*, 685 P.2d at 321.

the marital relation."[14] However, an express grant of agency is not required, as the court will look at the intent and surrounding actions of the parties.[15]

If only one spouse is bound on a guaranty, the obligee may have difficulty executing on certain of the couple's assets. In Kansas, a spouse's separate property, whether personal or real property, is not subject to the debts of the other spouse.[16] Kansas does not, however, recognize tenancy by the entirety.[17] If a husband and wife jointly own property in Kansas, any execution, levy, and eventual sale or garnishment of such property severs the joint tenancy and converts it into a tenancy in common, the guarantor's portion of which is within the reach of an obligee.[18] Thus, obligees may reach an individual guarantor's assets, despite the failure to obtain the spouse's signature, unless all of the couple's property is held as separate property solely in the name of such nonguarantor spouse.

In certain situations involving a security interest in assets of an unincorporated business, Kansas courts may also deem that a husband and wife intended to create a partnership.[19] In that case, a pledge of business assets signed by only one spouse was effectively a pledge of assets by the partnership, so the entirety of the business assets could be reached by the obligee, rather than solely by the tenant in common interest of the spouse who signed the pledge.[20]

§ 3 Signatory's Authority to Execute a Guaranty

3.1 Corporations

In Kansas, a corporation "is bound by contracts entered into on its behalf by its duly authorized officers or agents acting within the scope of their authority."[21] The scope of authority an officer or agent may have may be actual or apparent.[22] If actual authority, it may be either express or implied.[23] "Apparent agency is based on intentional actions or words of the principal toward third parties which reasonably induce or permit third parties to believe that an agency relationship exists."[24]

There is no bright-line test under Kansas law that a particular office or title imparts actual or apparent authority for a particular action. However, cases do weigh such offices or titles heavily in determining apparent authority under the so-called "powers of position" rule.[25]

14. Grohusky v. Atlas Assurance Co., 408 P.2d 697, 700 (Kan. 1965).
15. *Id.*, 408 P.2d at 700.
16. K.S.A. § 23-201.
17. K.S.A. § 23-201.
18. K.S.A. § 23-201. *See also* Walnut Valley State Bank v. Stovall, 574 P.2d 1382, 1386 (Kan. 1978).
19. In re Oetinger, 49 B.R. 41, 43 (Bkrtcy. D. Kansas 1985).
20. *Id.*, 49 B.R. at 43.
21. Executive Financial Services, Inc. v. Loyd, 715 P.2d 376, 378 (Kan. 1986).
22. Mohr v. State Bank of Stanley, 734 P.2d 1071, 1075 (Kan. 1987).
23. *Id.*, 734 P.2d at 1075.
24. *Id.*, 734 P.2d at 1075.
25. *See* Bucher & Willis Consulting Engineers, Planners and Architects v. Smith, 643 P.2d 1156, 1159 (Kan. App. 1982); Hull v. Manufacturing Co., 141 P. 592 (Kan. 1914); and Western Advertising Co. v. Crawford, 276 P. 813 (Kan. 1929).

3.2 Partnerships

Pursuant to K.S.A. §56a-301, each partner is an agent for the partnership and may execute instruments on behalf of the partnership, provided the instrument is "for apparently carrying on in the ordinary course the partnership business or business of the kind carried on by the partnership." A partner's authority may be explicitly limited by the partnership agreement, a statement of partnership authority filed pursuant to K.S.A. §56a-303, or other means. However, the partnership will be bound by the partner's acts, notwithstanding any limitation, if the act was in the "ordinary course of partnership business" and the person dealing with the partner did not know or had not received notification that the partner lacked authority.[26]

A person dealing with a partner will not be deemed to have knowledge of a limitation or lack of authority based solely on the filing of a statement of authority unless that person has actually seen or has been notified of such statement.[27] If the act is not for carrying on the ordinary course, the act will not be binding on the partnership unless it was authorized by the other partners.[28]

3.3 Limited Liability Companies

If the management of the LLC is vested in the members, each member has the authority to bind the LLC unless such authority is otherwise limited by the operating agreement.[29] If the management of the LLC is vested in one or more managers, the managers have the sole authority to bind the LLC.[30] If any act of either a member or manager, as applicable, is not for "carrying on the usual way of the business or affairs of the LLC," such act is not binding on the LLC unless authorized in accordance with the articles of organization or operating agreement, and absent such language therein, must be approved by a majority, by number, of the members of the LLC.[31]

3.4 Banks and Trust Companies

A case-by-case inquiry of the powers provided for in a bank's or trust company's corporate governance documents is necessary to determine who may validly execute a guaranty on behalf of a bank or trust company.

---

26. K.S.A. § 56a-301(a).
27. K.S.A. § 56a-303(f); provided, however, that with respect to transfers of real estate, a filed statement will be deemed to impart knowledge of a limitation of authority on any person dealing with such partner.
28. K.S.A. 56a-301(b).
29. K.S.A. § 17-7693(a).
30. K.S.A. § 17-7693(a) & (b).
31. K.S.A. 17-7693(c).

§ 4 Consideration; Sufficiency of Past Consideration

Under Kansas law, a guaranty, like any other contract, must be supported by consideration in order to be enforceable. Consideration is defined as some right, interest, profit, or benefit accruing to one party, or some forbearance, detriment, loss, or responsibility given, suffered, or undertaken by the other.[32] The consideration may flow directly. In evaluating the presence of consideration, the same consideration may suffice for both the contract evidencing the underlying obligation as well as the guaranty.[33] Extending the time for payment or forbearance of exercising remedies on an underlying obligation has been held by several Kansas courts to constitute sufficient consideration for a guaranty executed in conjunction therewith.[34]

A valid guaranty may be executed after the contract evidencing the underlying obligation.[35] Generally, as long as the evidence shows that the principal contract and guaranty contract were executed as part of the same transaction, the courts will construe the contracts together to determine consideration, even if they were not executed at precisely the same time.[36]

However, the length of time between the execution of the principal contract and the guaranty may be considered as indicative as to whether the two contracts were "part of the same transaction." A guaranty executed after the fact as a "bare promise" or "afterthought" will not be considered part of the same transaction, such that the two contracts could share the same consideration.[37]

As to the sufficiency of the consideration itself, some cases have recognized that an agreement to forbear from engaging in collection or enforcement activities will not be sufficient consideration if the same are obviously invalid, worthless, or frivolous.[38] However, in one of the same cases, the court held that despite deep insolvency and the presence of other superior creditors, forbearance by an obligee was sufficient consideration because the primary obligor still existed, and it was at least possible that the obligee could be repaid in the future, however unlikely.[39]

---

32. First Specialty Insurance Corp. v. NAIS, Inc., 495 F.Supp.2d 1094, 1100 (D. Kansas 2006); citing Varney Business Servs., Inc. v. Pottroff, 59 P.3d 1003, 1014 (Kan. 2002).
33. Ryco Packaging Corp. of Kansas v. Chapelle Int'l, Ltd., 926 P.2d 669, 676 (Kan. App. 1997); citing 39 Am.Jur.2d, Guaranty § 44, p. 1047.
34. *Ryco Packaging Corp. of Kansas*, 926 P.2d at 677; and First Specialty Insurance Corp. v. NAIS, Inc., 459 F. Supp.2d 1094, 1101 (D. Kansas 2006).
35. *Ryco Packaging Corp. of Kansas,* 926 P.2d at 675.
36. *Id.*, 926 P.2d at 676.
37. *First Specialty Insurance Corp.*, 495 F.Supp.2d at 1101.
38. 495 F. Supp.2d at 1101. *See also Ryco Packaging*, 926 P.2d 669 at 677.
39. *Ryco Packaging*, 926 P.2d 669 at 677.

§ 5 Notice of Acceptance

Kansas courts have explicitly stated that notice of acceptance of a guaranty is not necessary for enforcement.[40] Further, Kansas courts have continually listed the factors required for an enforceable guaranty. As notice of acceptance is not one of the factors listed, the Kansas courts have implicitly confirmed that it is not required in order for a guaranty agreement to be enforceable against a guarantor.[41]

§ 6 Interpretation of Guaranties

In Kansas, "a contract of guaranty is to be construed, as other contracts, according to the intention of the parties, as determined by reasonable interpretation of the language used, in light of the attendant circumstances. After the intention of the parties or the scope of the guarantor's undertaking has been determined by general rules of construction, the obligation is strictly construed and may not be extended by construction or implication."[42]

6.1 General Principles

The rules governing the interpretation and construction of contracts generally apply to the interpretation or construction of a contract of guaranty.[43] The courts will first determine whether the essential terms of a guaranty are present. If the essential terms are present, the court will construe the guaranty within the written terms of the contract, unless a term is ambiguous. If the court finds an ambiguity, it will look to parol evidence to determine the parties' intent at the time the guaranty was executed.[44]

6.2 Limited versus Unlimited Guaranty

Unless the court finds a clear intent to limit liability, either through explicit language, or parol evidence if there is an ambiguity, the guarantor's liability will not be limited.[45]

40. Great Western MFG. Co. v. Porter, 172 P. 1018, 1020 (Kan. 1918).
41. *See* Section 1.1 and *Glencore Grain Limited*, 241 F.Supp.2d at 1331.
42. *Baxter State Bank*, 985 F. Supp. at 1267.
43. Botkin v. Security State Bank, 130 P.3d 92, 97 (Kan. 2006).
44. *Id.*, 130 P.3d at 98.
45. Botkin v. Security State Bank, 111 P.3d 182, 187 (Kan. App. 2005), overturned and remanded for other reasons.

6.3 Language Regarding the Revocation of Guaranties

Guaranties, including continuing guaranties, may be revoked by the guarantor.[46] Any such revocation may be made orally, despite the statute of frauds, unless the guaranty explicitly requires other action to effect the revocation.[47] A revocation will not absolve the guarantor for liabilities existing at the time of the revocation; the valid revocation will only act to extinguish the guarantor's liability for any future debt or obligations incurred by the debtor.[48]

Kansas courts have not addressed whether a provision stating the guaranty is "irrevocable" is enforceable under Kansas law. Further, unless the evidence shows the parties' clear intention to do so, the execution of additional or subsequent guaranty agreements do not extinguish or supersede the prior guaranties.[49]

6.4 "Continuing"

In Kansas, "a guaranty may be either 'continuing' or 'restricted.' The contract is restricted if it is limited to guarantee a single transaction or a number of specific transactions and is not effective for transactions other than those guaranteed. The contract is continuing if it contemplates a future course of dealing during an indefinite period or it is intended to cover a series of transactions or a succession of credits, or if its purpose is to give to the principal debtor a standing credit to be used by him from time to time."[50]

Absent specific language in the guaranty, the courts must look to the facts and nature of the transaction to determine whether the parties intended the guaranty to be limited to a specific transaction, or cover an indefinite period or series of transactions.[51]

6.5 "Absolute and Unconditional"

If a guaranty contract is conditional, the obligee must first proceed against the primary obligor before attempting to collect from the guarantor, while an absolute and unconditional guaranty does not carry this requirement.[52] A guaranty is generally rendered "absolute and unconditional" by the inclusion of the words themselves.[53] At least one Kansas court has held that an "unconditional" guaranty implies the waiver of essentially all defenses. (See § 8.2 below.)

---

46. *Baxter*, 985 F.Supp. at 1266.
47. *Id.*, 985 F.Supp. at 1266.
48. *Id.*, 985 F.Supp. at 1266.
49. *Id.*, 985 F.Supp. at 1266.
50. Iola State Bank v. Biggs, 662 P.2d 563, 568 (Kan. 1983).
51. *Id.*, 662 P.2d at 570.
52. Kansas State Bank & Trust Co. v. DeLorean, 640 P.2d 343, 350 (Kan. App. 1982).
53. Hill Petroleum Co. v. Pathmark Int'l, Inc., 750 F. Supp. 722, 726 (D. Kansas 1991).

6.6 "Liable as a Primary Obligor and not Merely as Surety"

As discussed in § 1, a "guaranty is a contract by which one person promises to answer to another for the debt, default or miscarriage of a third person."[54] A guaranty is in the "nature of a warranty by him that the thing guaranteed to be done by the principal shall be done, and is not an engagement jointly with the principal to do the thing."[55] "When a default occurs on the part of the principal, the guarantor's liability becomes primary and absolute."[56]

By contrast, the "surety's liability is direct, and the surety contracts to perform the principal's obligation."[57] The "direct liability to perform the principal's contract distinguishes a surety from a guarantor in that a guarantor answers only for the consequences of the defaults of the principal."[58]

§ 7 Defenses of the Guarantor; Set-off

7.1 Defenses Generally

7.1.1 General

Subject to numerous exceptions discussed below, a guarantor may be relieved of an obligation to pay if (1) the debt is extinguished, (2) there is a valid release or discharge, (3) a claim against the guarantor is barred by the statute of limitations, (4) there is a change in the original contract between the primary obligor and obligee,[59] (5) the obligee refuses to accept an unconditional proper legal tender made by the primary obligor,[60] or (6) the lender impairs the underlying collateral.[61]

7.1.2 When Guarantor May Assert Primary Obligor's Defense

The guaranty agreement is considered a separate contract, which will be read together, but not necessarily integrated with the underlying credit agreement or promissory note. Because of this, the guarantor is generally not in a position to assert the primary obligor's defenses, unless it relates to the validity of the guaranty itself, such as a lack of consideration, or lack of essential terms in the underlying debt agreement, such that the underlying obligations could not be reasonably determined.

---

54. *Bomud Co.*, 299 P.2d at 76.
55. *Id.*, 299 P.2d at 77.
56. *Id.*, 299 P.2d at 77.
57. Hartford v. Tanner, 910 P.2d 872, 877 (Kan. App. 1996).
58. *Id.*, 910 P.2d at 877.
59. *Iola State Bank*, 662 P.2d at 570.
60. *Hill Petroleum Co.*, 750 F. Supp. at 726.
61. *Kansas State Bank & Trust Co.*, 640 P.2d at 351.

7.1.3 Defenses that May not be Raised by Guarantor

A guarantor may not assert that a guaranty agreement is unenforceable due to an ambiguity as to one of the essential terms (provided the essential term is present), but will instead utilize traditional rules of construction to clarify the ambiguity.[62] Likewise, a guarantor cannot assert a defense based on the guarantor's failure to read the agreement or a misinterpretation of the agreement.[63] The obligee's failure to notify the primary obligor of an assignment of the indebtedness is not a defense that a guarantor may assert to avoid liability,[64] absent any express requirements contained in the note or guaranty agreement.

7.2 "Suretyship Defenses"

7.2.1 Change in Identity of Primary Obligor

Kansas courts have generally addressed the issue of a change in the primary obligor under different theories of discharge. If the transaction has the effect that the new person or entity is now the primary obligor on the debt, and the original person or entity is no longer liable, the court will conclude that the debt was "extinguished" or "released," which are recognized defenses available to the guarantor.[65]

7.2.2 Modification of the Underlying Obligation, Including Release

There are cases that distinguish between "gratuitous or accommodation" guarantors and "compensated" guarantors. The cases state that the gratuitous guarantor is discharged by any modification, whether material or not, and whether or not the guarantor is injured or its risk increases. Conversely, a compensated guarantor is only discharged if the modification is material.[66] Most recent cases have not distinguished between the two types of guarantors, and have simply focused on whether a material modification occurred.[67]

In a few Kansas cases, the court has cited to "surety" cases in which an obligee's deferral or granting of an extension of time to make a payment has been held to be a material modification.[68] However, most modern Kansas courts would likely hold that a payment extension was not a material modification, unless there was an accompanying impairment of collateral.[69] This is consistent with K.S.A. §84-3-605 treatment of "endorsers" or "accommodation parties" with respect to negotiable instruments.

62. Federal Deposit Insurance Corp. v. Neitzel, 769 F. Supp. 346, 349 (D. Kansas 1991).
63. *Id.*, 769 F.Supp. at 350.
64. United States v. M.L.K., Inc., 859 F.Supp. 495, 498 (D. Kansas 1994).
65. *Iola State Bank*, 662 P.2d at 570.
66. *See* F.J. Kutilek v. Union Nat'l Bank of Wichita, 516 P.2d 979, 984; and Fisher v. Pendleton, 336 P.2d 472, 475 (Kan. 1959).
67. First Nat'l Bank of Anthony v. Dunning, 855 P.2d 493, 495 (Kan. App. 1993).
68. *See* Fisher v. Spillman, 118 P. 65 (Kan. 1911); Bank v. Brooks, 67 P. 860 (Kan. 1902); and Stove Works v. Caswell, 29 P. 1072 (Kan. 1892).
69. *First Nat'l Bank of Anthony*, 855 P.2d at 497.

One case has held that if an obligee sells to the primary obligor a greater amount of goods than originally contemplated in the underlying contract to which the guaranty relates, such action will not be deemed a "material modification," but the court will limit the guarantor's liability to the cost of the amount of goods contemplated in the underlying contract.[70]

As discussed in § 8 below, the modification defense may be waived through specific or general waivers.

7.2.3 Release or Impairment of Security for the Underlying Obligation

The common-law rule in Kansas is that impairment of collateral by the beneficiary of a guaranty contract discharges the guarantor's obligations *pro tanto*.[71] However, the general rule is subject to certain exceptions. Guarantors may consent before or after the fact to impairment of collateral. Further, explicit waiver of the impairment defense, or a consent by the guarantor in the contract to a lack of diligence in collection or an impairment of collateral, is an effective waiver of an "impairment" defense.[72] If there is language waiving the defense of waste or deterioration unless caused by the "willful act or willful failure to act by Lender," the guarantor must show a "purpose by the [Lender] to diminish the value of the security in order to intentionally injure the defendants."[73]

If the guarantor signs a promissory note or negotiable instrument directly, Article 3 of the Uniform Commercial Code will apply, and the impairment rule, including the ability to waive, generally mirrors the common-law rules.[74]

In a case where the primary obligor provided no consideration for a release, and there was no change of position in reliance on a release, a mistaken release of underlying collateral will not absolve a guarantor from liability under the guaranty agreement.[75]

At least one Kansas court has held that a guarantor may not assert a third-party claim that an obligee violated its contractual obligations when it failed to perform proper due diligence on the collateral, and failed to obtain a first-priority secured interest on the underlying collateral. However, the particular holding seemed to turn more on the guarantor's express waiver of suretyship defenses and consenting to the obligee's dealing with the collateral in its discretion.[76] It is possible that, absent such waivers, an impairment defense could be raised if the obligee fails to perform proper lien searches and record proper financing statements.

Unless explicitly stated in the guarantor agreement, the obligee is not required to apply the proceeds from the sale of collateral against the

70. *Glencore Grain Limited*, 241 F.Supp.2d at 1334.
71. *Kansas State Bank & Trust Co.*, 640 P.2d at 351.
72. *Id.*, 640 P.2d at 351.
73. United States v. Rook v. Mercantile Bank of Kansas City, 710 F. Supp. 754, 757 (D. Kansas 1989).
74. *See* K.S.A. § 84-3-605.
75. Mid-Continent Lodging Associates, Inc. v. First Nat'l Bank of Chicago, 999 F. Supp. 1443, 1447 (D. Kansas 1998).
76. U.S. v. Healy v. Country Hill Bank, 923 F. Supp. 1424, 1429 (D. Kansas 1996).

guarantor's obligations. For instance, if the guarantor agreed to be liable for up to $1 million of a $3 million underlying obligation, and the obligee forecloses and sells the collateral for $1 million, there are still underlying obligations of $2 million, of which the guarantor will be liable for up to $1 million.[77]

7.3 Other Defenses; Set-off

7.3.1 Failure to Fulfill a Condition Precedent

A guarantor may assert as a defense that an obligee has failed to fulfill a condition precedent in the guaranty contract (or other loan documents, if proper reference or incorporation of such documents is present in the guaranty contract). [78]

7.3.2 Modification of the Guaranty

Subsequently executed guaranty contracts will not be deemed to modify or revoke a previous guaranty contract unless the parties explicitly so intend.[79] General contract principles and the statute of frauds will generally govern other situations involving an alleged modification of a guaranty.

7.3.3 Failure to Pursue Primary Obligor

As discussed in other sections herein, Kansas courts distinguish between a "conditional" and "unconditional" guaranty by the fact a lender must first pursue the primary obligor in a conditional guaranty, while no such requirement exists with respect to an unconditional guaranty.

7.3.4 Statute of Limitations

As a guaranty is a contract in writing, it is governed by K.S.A. § 60-511, which provides for a five-year statute of limitations. A cause of action on a guaranty arises at the time the primary obligor defaults, and the five-year period begins running against the obligee at such time.[80] The guarantor's statute of limitation period runs separate and independently of the primary obligor's period, and the guarantor may remain liable despite the obligee's inability to collect from the primary obligor due to the expiration of the statutory period.[81]

The right to contribution from coguarantors or the primary obligor itself (discussed in §10.1 below), absent express language in a guaranty contract, is an implied agreement at law. Because a claim of contribution would be based on an implied agreement, it will be governed by K.S.A § 60-512, which provides for a three-year statute of limitations. The period begins running against the guarantor on the day which his right to contribution attaches, which is the

77. TMG Life Insurance Co. v. Ashner, 898 P.2d 1145, 1155 (Kan. App. 1995).
78. *Id.*, 898 P.2d at 1163.
79. *Baxter State Bank*, 985 F.Supp. at 1266.
80. Kee v. Lofton, 737 P.2d 55, 59 (Kan. App. 1987). *See also Bomud Co.*, 299 P.2d at 77.
81. *Id.*, 737 P.2d at 59.

day in which the guarantor has contributed more than his or her share of a common obligation.[82]

7.3.5 *Statute of Frauds*

Guaranties are "promises to answer for the debt, default or miscarriage of another," and they are subject to the statute of frauds.[83] Kansas law will not hold a guarantor liable unless an intention to bind itself is "clearly manifested." A guaranty must be in writing, signed by the party to be charged and state with certainty (1) each party to the contract, (2) the subject matter to which the contract relates, and (3) the terms and conditions of all the promises constituting the contract and by whom and to whom the promises are made.[84]

The entire contract must be explained in writing—it cannot rest partly in writing and partly in parol evidence.[85] The three contractual requirements above must be found in the writing, and parol evidence may only be admissible to explain ambiguities.[86] Blanks in a form guaranty agreement with respect to material terms are acceptable, provided that there is default language that may otherwise be relied upon (e.g., "if no amount is stated, the Undersigned shall be liable for all indebtedness without any limitation as to amount").[87]

7.3.6 *Set-off*

A Kansas court has implicitly recognized a guarantor's defense of set-off.[88] We found no cases addressing whether a guarantor's waiver of set-off defenses is enforceable and valid in Kansas.

§ 8 Waiver of Defenses by the Guarantor

8.1 Defenses that cannot be Waived

Based on general contract principles, a guarantor may plead the defenses of lack of consideration, incapacity, and fraud, regardless of any attempt by the obligee to draft language by which the guarantor would waive such defenses.

---

82. *Id.*, 737 P.2d at 59.
83. *Botkin*, 130 P.3d at 96. See K.S.A. § 33-106, which states in part, "No action shall be brought whereby to charge a party upon any special promise to answer for the debt, default or miscarriage of another person... unless the agreement upon which such action shall be brought, or some memorandum or note thereof, shall be in writing and signed by the party to be charged therewith, or some other person thereunto by him or lawfully authorized in writing."
84. *Id.*, 130 P.3d at 97.
85. *Glencore Grain Limited*, 241 F.Supp.2d at 1331.
86. *Id.*, 241 F.Supp.2d at 1331.
87. *See Botkin*, 130 P.3d at 100, and F.J. Kutilek v. Union Nat'l Bank of Wichita, 516 P.2d 979, 983 (Kan. 1973), which contained no default language and which guaranty was held to be void because it lacked essential terms.
88. *See* Ford Motor Credit v. Suburban Ford, 699 P.2d 992, 1000 (Kan. 1985), where the court recognized that the primary obligor's and guarantors' counterclaims, which were contractual in nature, could act as set-offs to the damages sought by the plaintiff from the defendant guarantors.

8.2 "Catch-all" Waivers

A waiver of "any and all defenses available to guarantors, sureties, and other secondary parties at law or in equity," has been held to waive the defense of "modification of the original contract." This is true even if other language in the guaranty agreement states that the guarantor is liable on the underlying note, "as the same may be amended, modified or supplemented with the consent [of the guarantor]."[89]

Further, a Kansas court has held that by agreeing to "unconditionally guaranty" a principal's obligation, the guarantor had waived the defense that full payment had been tendered.[90] Likewise, one Kansas court held that due to the "unconditional nature of [the defendants'] guaranties, [the defendants'] affirmative defenses of waiver and novation fail as a matter of law."[91] The implication of these rulings is that the use of the term "unconditional guaranty" may act as a waiver of most post-execution defenses. Other courts have reached an opposite conclusion, and that the distinction of a guaranty as "unconditional" determines only whether the obligee is required to first proceed against the primary obligor.[92]

8.3 Use of Specific Waivers

Although general waivers, including the simple designation that the contract is an "unconditional guaranty," will waive a great number of defenses, it is still recommended practice to include as many specific waivers as possible. As discussed above, the courts have implicitly allowed a guarantor to assert certain defenses, even in the context of "unconditional guaranties," so the parties should explicitly state the various defenses being waived in order to remove any doubt of the parties' intentions.

§ 9 Third-party Pledgors—Defenses and Waiver Thereof

We have found no evidence that the law as applied to sureties and guarantors would not apply to a third-party pledge.

89. Raytheon Aircraft Credit Corp. v. Pal Air Int'l, Inc., 923 F.Supp. 1408, 1413 (D. Kansas 1996).
90. *Hill Petroleum Co.*, 759 F. Supp. at 726.
91. United States v. Rook v. Mercantile Bank of Kansas City, 710 F. Supp. 754, 756 (D. Kansas 1989); in spite of the quoted language, the court did seem to allow the defendant to raise, although ultimately rejecting, a defense of waste caused by the lender's willful act, due to specific contractual language.
92. *Kansas State Bank & Trust Co.*, 640 P.2d at 350.

§ 10 Jointly and Severally Liable Guarantors–Contribution and Reduction of Obligations Upon Payment of a Co-obligor

Pursuant to K.S.A. § 16-101 and § 16-104, in all cases of joint obligations, which would include coguarantors, the obligations are construed as joint and several, and the suit may be prosecuted against any one or more of the guarantors. Absent specific language, guarantors of a common obligation are presumed to have an implied agreement that if the guaranty is enforced, each guarantor will contribute his or her just proportion of the amount for which he or she might be held liable.[93]

10.1 Contribution

"Contribution must be equally and ratably made. If one or more guarantors are insolvent, the solvent guarantors must each contribute the insolvent guarantor's share in the same proportion."[94] The right to contribution does not arise until, and is contingent until, the guarantor pays more than his or her fair share.

In citing American Jurisprudence, 2d., a Kansas court stated, "It is not necessary that the claimant's payment be made in cash. Its equivalent, as, for example, the negotiable promissory note of the claimant or anything else which the creditor accepts as satisfaction, is generally sufficient. It should be remembered that a note or other negotiable instrument, to be equivalent to payment, must have been accepted by the creditor in satisfaction of the whole or more than the claimant's fair share of the original obligation. If, for example, the original obligation was upon notes and the claimant's note is accepted merely as a renewal, without cancelling the old notes, the claimant is not entitled to contribution until he actually satisfies more than his share of the debt. Whether new notes are merely renewals of the old notes or whether the original notes are paid and discharged by the new ones depends upon the intention of the parties."

10.2 Reduction of Obligations Upon Payment of Co-obligor

As discussed above, coguarantors are jointly and severally liable. Under Kansas law, when two or more debtors are jointly and severally liable on an obligation, the release of one of the debtors discharges the obligation of the other debtor to the extent of the consideration paid for the release.[95]

93. *Kee,* 737 P.2d at 58.
94. *Id.*, 737 P.2d at 58, citing Appleford v. Snake River M.M. & S. Co., 210 P.26 (1922).
95. Oakview Treatment Centers of Kansas, Inc. v. Garrett, 53 F.Supp.2d 1196, 1207 (D. Kansas 1999).

§ 11 Reliance

Kansas courts do not require a showing of "reliance" by an obligee enforcing a guaranty under general contractual theories. However, in asserting an equitable theory of estoppel, the obligee would need to prove reasonable reliance.[96] Estoppel is appropriate where a guarantor attempts to avoid terms of a guaranty agreement, after the obligee has relied upon the enforceability of the guaranty in continuous dealings.[97] In a specific holding, a guarantor was not estopped and had not waived its defense of extinguishment or discharge by failing to request a release of a guaranty at the time the underlying debt was extinguished.[98]

§ 12 Subrogation

In Kansas, "a surety or guarantor, on paying the debt of the principal, is entitled to be subrogated to the rights of the creditor in all or any of the securities, means or remedies which the creditor has for enforcing payment against the principal debtor or against other sureties or guarantors."[99] Partial payments by guarantors will not create a right of subrogation; nor will unsatisfied judgments against guarantors. A guarantor's right to subrogation is predicated on full payment of the primary obligation, not merely an obligation to pay.[100]

§ 13 Triangular Set-off

In a Tenth Circuit case interpreting Kansas law in a nonbankruptcy setting, the court permitted triangular set-off where a third party may set-off payment to a debtor against amounts the debtor owes to an affiliate of the third party, notwithstanding a primary creditor's secured claim to the debtor's accounts receivable. Such triangular right of set-off must have existed prior to the time the primary creditor obtained its rights in the accounts.[101] While not specifically addressed, triangular set-off in a bankruptcy setting would not likely be permitted under Section 553 of the Bankruptcy Code.

96. *Glencore Grain Limited*, 241 F. Supp. 2d at 1336.
97. *Iola State Bank*, 662 P.2d at 571.
98. *Id., 662 P.2d* at 572.
99. Emprise Bank v. Rumisek, 215 P.3d 621, 631 (Kan. App. 2009), citing Haplin v. Frankenberger, 231 P.2d 452 (Kan. 1982).
100. *Id., 215 P.3d* at 631.
101. Commerce Bank, N.A. v. Chrysler Realty Corp., 244 F.3d 777, 784 (10th Cir. 2001).

§ 14 Indemnification

Under Kansas common law, "a guarantor or surety who discharges the obligation of its principal is entitled to be reimbursed by the principal."[102] A contractual indemnity may often exist in the context of stockholders or directors of a corporation and members of an LLC, who may be explicitly indemnified in the organizational documents.

In *Emprise Bank v. Rumisek*, there was a provision in an LLC operating agreement obligating the LLC to hold its members harmless from claims incurred "by reason of the fact that an Indemnitee is or was a Member." In the case, the parties disputed whether such language obligated the LLC to indemnify the members for liabilities suffered due to the members' guaranty of the LLC's debt. In following the Delaware judiciary, the Emprise court held that a "close nexus" between the lawsuit filed and the guarantor's status as a member is all that is necessary to trigger the indemnification, and that members may exercise indemnification rights under an operating agreement, even though their liability to the obligee specifically arose due to their identity as guarantors, and not necessarily due to their membership status.[103]

§ 15 Enforcement of Guaranties

15.1 Exercising Rights Under a Guaranty Where the Underlying Obligation is also Secured by a Mortgage

An obligee may enforce a guaranty in a separate proceeding from the foreclosure proceedings if a mortgage also secures the underlying obligation.[104] However, if the obligee desires to enforce the guaranty in the same proceeding as the foreclosure, the obligee must explicitly petition the court for separate recovery under the guaranty. Simply petitioning to foreclose under the mortgage and attaching the guaranty agreement, without stating a claim on the guaranty, will not suffice if trying to recover against the guarantor in the same proceeding.[105]

In the case of a limited guaranty, absent specific language in the guaranty agreement, proceeds of mortgage foreclosure proceedings need not be applied first against the limited guaranty obligations.[106]

15.2 Litigating Guaranty Claims; Procedural Considerations

In Kansas, procedural considerations for litigation on Guaranty agreements are identical to those regarding litigation on other contract claims. As discussed in

102. U.S. v. Gonzales, 541 F. Supp. 783, 785 (D. Kansas 1982).
103. *Emprise Bank*, 215 P.3d at 633.
104. Sunflower Bank, N.A. v. Airport Red Coach Inn of Wichita, L.L.C., 175 P.3d 883, 885 (Kan. App.).
105. Hoover Equipment Co. v. Smith, 422 P.2d 914, 919 (Kan. 1967).
106. *TMG Life Insurance Co.*, 898 P.2d at 1155.

other sections, there are considerations with respect to the ripeness of claims involving contribution, indemnity, and subrogation, that are somewhat unique to Guaranties. Litigation counsel should also be aware of the dates when various statute of limitation time periods begin to run as they relate to claims against the Guarantor, as well as claims by the Guarantor against the Primary Obligor and Co-Guarantors.

§ 16 Choice of Law

Under Kansas law, Kansas courts apply the law of the place where the contract was made, and a contract is deemed to have been made at such place as the last act necessary for the Guaranty's formation takes place.[107] However, Kansas' choice of law rules permit the court to enforce the law which the contracting parties have chosen in their agreement.[108]

§ 17 Revival and Reinstatement of Guaranties

We found no Kansas cases addressing this topic.

107. Deere & Co. v. K.I. Loy, 872 F. Supp. 867, 870 (D. Kansas 1994).
108. Nat'l Equipment Rental, Ltd. v. Taylor, 587 P.2d 870 (Kan. 1978).

Kentucky State Law of Guaranties

W. P. Wiseman
Mark A. Melvin
Reza A. Rabiee

Bingham Greenebaum Doll LLP
101 S. Fifth Street, Suite 3500
Louisville, Kentucky 40202-3197
Telephone: (502) 589-4200
Facsimile: (502) 587-3695
www.bgdlegal.com

BINGHAM GREENEBAUM DOLL LLP BGD

Contents

Kentucky State Law of Guaranties

KENTUCKY LAW PITFALLS

The Kentucky law of guaranties differs significantly from that of other jurisdictions in that the Commonwealth has a guaranty statute which appears to be unique. Under the terms of the statute, guaranties are valid and enforceable only where either written on or expressly referring to the specific instrument being guaranteed, or where they are in writing, signed by the guarantor, and include provisions specifying the amount of maximum aggregate liability and the date on which the guaranty terminates.[1] The strict requirements imposed under the statute exist for the purpose of protecting guarantors by reducing their risk of exposure to unknown obligations.[2] However, that risk is considered negligible when the guaranty agreement is found on or specifically refers to the instrument being guaranteed. Thus, the statute functions to exempt those forms from the strict statutory requirements.[3]

Under the first accepted alternative, a guaranty agreement was found to expressly reference the instrument it purportedly guaranteed when it included an attachment that laid out the specific promissory note being guaranteed, naming its date of execution and the parties involved.[4] Further, a guaranty was found to not expressly refer to the instrument being guaranteed when it contained only a laundry list of potential present and future obligations of varying types.[5]

Even where the guaranty is not written on or fails to expressly refer to the specific instrument being guaranteed, the statute provides an alternative method to create a valid and enforceable guaranty, but only if certain requirements, referenced above, are met.[6] The statute does not require an instrument to reference or incorporate a separate agreement guaranteeing it. It merely specifies the form that a guaranty agreement must take, in the event that the guaranty agreement does not reference or is not written on the guaranteed instrument.[7]

Although not addressed on appeal, the circuit court in one case determined that a provision stating a month and year as the termination date was sufficiently specific to qualify under the statute's requirements.[8]

The statute generally stands for the proposition that a guarantor should not be subject to an indeterminate and overbroad obligation.[9] However, it also provides that a guaranty may guarantee the payment of interest and other fees, charges, and costs of collection without specifying any particular amounts.[10]

---

1. Kentucky Revised Statutes (KRS) 371.065.
2. Wheeler & Clevenger Oil Co. v. Washburn, 127 S.W.3d 609, 615 (2004).
3. *Id.*
4. Smith v. Bethlehem Sand and Gravel Co., 342 S.W.3d 288, 291 (2011).
5. Brunswick Bowling & Billiards v. Ng-Cadlaon, No. 2010-CA-001844-MR (Nov. 4, 2011).
6. KRS 371.065.
7. *Smith*, 342 S.W.2d at 293.
8. *Id.*, S.W.2d at 292.
9. Wallace Hardware Co. v. Abrams, 223 F.3d 382 (6th Cir. 2000).
10. KRS 371.065.

Introductory Note: In order to standardize this discussion of the law of guaranties in Kentucky, the following terms from relevant statutes and case law are used to refer to the various parties to a guaranty and their obligations.

"Guarantor" means a person who, by contract, agrees to satisfy an underlying obligation of another to an obligee upon the primary obligor's default on that underlying obligation.

"Guaranty" means the contract by which the guarantor agrees to satisfy the underlying obligation of a primary obligor to an obligee in the event the primary obligor defaults on the underlying obligation.

"Obligee" means the person who incurs the underlying obligation to the obligee. For example, the lender under a loan agreement would be an obligee vis-à-vis the borrower.

"Obligor" means the person who incurs the underlying obligation to the obligee. For example, the borrower under a loan agreement would be a primary obligor.

"Underlying Obligation" means the obligation or obligations incurred by the primary obligor and owed to the obligee. For example, the borrower's obligation to make payments to a lender of principal and interest on a loan constitutes an underlying obligation.

Because the statute imposes such stringent requirements, it is necessary to determine whether or not a particular instrument is actually a guaranty and thus subject to those requirements. For example, one court distinguished an indemnity agreement—which involves an indemnitor acting to protect against a loss arising from a liability—as distinct and separate from a guaranty agreement—which involves a guarantor acting to protect against a loss arising from another's failure to carry out an obligation.[11] Of course, where a contract is deemed not a guaranty, it is not subject to the requirements of the guaranty statute. Courts will look to the substance of the agreement regardless of its label in determining whether or not it is in fact a guaranty.[12]

Kentucky law makes a distinction between "guaranty" and "surety" contracts. "The contract of a guarantor is his own separate contract and the fundamental difference between a contract of guaranty and one of suretyship is that the guarantor's contract is collateral to and independent of the contract, the performance of which he guarantees, while that of a surety is an original obligation."[13]

Of note, the statute applies to all guaranty contracts, not just commercial paper.[14]

Introduction and Sources of Law

Kentucky has historically had a limited body of precedent in commercial law, and there is not a large body of precedent in guaranty law. However, with the exception of the provisions of KRS 371.065 highlighted above, Kentucky guaranty law is not notable for quirks or oddities.

11. Intercargo Insurance Co. v. B.W. Farrell, Inc., 89 S.W.3d 422, 426 (2002).
12. Huntington Bank, No. 2001-CA-000505-MR (August 27, 2004).
13. Citizens Fidelity Bank & Trust Co. v. Lamar, 561 S.W.2d 326, 328 (1977).
14. *Wheeler,* 127 S.W.2d at 612.

§ 1 Nature of the Guaranty Arrangement

The rights and obligations of the parties under a contract of guaranty, like any other contract that persons may enter into, depend upon what they contract to do. In the absence of a statute prescribing the duties of creditors and the rights of guarantors, certain rules, which as general rules apply to their duties and rights, can be applied to every contract of guaranty, regardless of what the parties have agreed to and have contracted with each other to do.

A guarantor does not occupy the position of an endorser unless he has contracted to occupy that position. An endorser does not warrant or guarantee the solvency of the principal debtor, and does not undertake to pay the debt unless the debtor does not pay it, and then only if the holder complies with the law relating to demand of the maker of the debt and notice of default in the payment. On the other hand, the debt may be collected if diligent efforts are made, and he may be bound for the payment of a debt, without demand made of the principal debtor, or notice of default, if that is the legal effect of the contract into which he has entered. The obligation of a guarantor may be the same as that of a surety if the contract is such as to require it, and often the liability of a guarantor and surety may be so nearly alike that a distinction between them is clouded, and almost impossible to distinguish.[15]

§ 2 State Law Requirements for an Entity to Enter a Guaranty

Kentucky statutes governing different types of entities generally provide for various powers, included in which is the power to make guaranties.

2.1 Corporations

Under Kentucky's Business Corporations statute, a corporation has the same powers as an individual, including making guaranties, unless its articles of incorporation provide otherwise.[16]

The power of a corporation to act as a guarantor exists whenever it is reasonably necessary in the conduct of its business.[17]

A municipal corporation cannot, without legislative authority, guarantee the bonds or obligations of another, and such authority cannot be deduced from the general and usual powers conferred upon such corporations.[18]

---

15. McGowan v. Wells' Trustee, 184 Ky. 722, 213 S.W.2d 573 (1919).
16. KRS 271B.3-020(g).
17. North Star Company, Inc. v. Howard, 341 S.W.2d 251, 256 (1960).
18. Knepfle's Executrix v. Town of Southgate, 238 S.W. 1051, 1053 (1922).

2.2 Partnerships

Kentucky's Uniform Partnership Act does not act either to empower a partnership to issue guaranties or to prohibit a partnership from issuing guaranties.[19] There are examples in reported cases of partnerships issuing guaranties.[20]

2.3 Limited Liability Companies

Under KRS 275.010, a limited liability company (LLC) is granted the power to do all things necessary or convenient to carry out its business and affairs, unless the articles of organization or operating agreement provide otherwise. Deciding matters connected with the business affairs of the LLC requires the consent of a majority-in-interest of the members in a member-managed LLC and a simple majority of managers in a manager-managed LLC, unless otherwise provided for in the articles or operating agreement.[21]

2.4 Banks and Trust Companies

There is no specific restriction in Kentucky's banking statutes or rules and regulations concerning state banks with regard to the creation of a guaranty by a bank or by a trust company for itself, as opposed to in a trustee capacity; however, the act would have to be one incident to and required by the business or activities for which the bank or trust company is authorized.[22] The scope of permitted activity may, however, be affected by federal law which prohibits a state-chartered bank from engaging in activities not permitted to a national bank. A national bank may become a guarantor within the terms of federal guidelines.[23]

2.5 Individuals

Under Kentucky's agency statutes, "No person shall be bound as the surety of another by the act of an agent unless the authority of the agent is in writing, signed by the principal, or, if the principal does not write his name, then by his sign or mark, made in the presence of at least one creditable attesting witness."[24] This statute "permits an agent to enter into a binding guaranty agreement on behalf of a principal if the principal has given the agent written authority to do so."[25]

When an individual company officer signs his name to a guaranty, a question can arise as to whether the officer has entered into the guaranty in his personal capacity or his representative capacity. The cases have not established a clear rule, and one court has determined that mere inclusion of an officer's

19. KRS Ch. 362.00.
20. *See, e.g.,* Sackett v. Citizens First Bank, No. 2004-CA-001324-MR (August 18, 2006).
21. KRS 275.175.
22. KRS 286.3-180; KRS 286.3-190; KRS 286.3-145; KRS 286.3-146.
23. *See, e.g.,* National Bank as Guarantor or Surety on Indemnity Bank, 12 C.F.R. § 7.1017 (2010).
24. KRS 371.090.
25. Brooks v. United Kentucky Bank, 659 S.W.2d 213, 216 (1983).

title in conjunction with his signature is insufficient to demonstrate that the officer signed in his representative as opposed to personal capacity.[26] When an officer, director, or shareholder acts as an agent of the corporation, that person is protected from personal liability when acting within his authority to bind the principal.[27]

There is very limited authority in Kentucky on the effect upon property owned jointly or as tenants in common where one person, such as a spouse, having an interest in the property is liable on a guaranty on which other interest holders, such as the other spouse, are not liable. The probable result, however, can be deduced from decisions of courts where other types of obligations were undertaken, and the obligor was the holder of an interest in property either jointly or as a tenant in common.

As an example, during the joint lives of a husband and wife, neither may alienate all or any part of a joint interest in a parcel of real estate in which they are tenants by the entirety, but either may alienate all or any part of funds contained in a joint bank account, either with or without survivorship.[28]

In the sale of jointly owned property with survivorship to satisfy a debt, the property would be sold subject to the rights of the nonobligated joint owner.[29]

The above are examples. As it is not the purpose of this chapter to address in detail the liability of property jointly held or held in common for the debts of one interest holder, suffice it to say that Kentucky would be expected to apply the law applicable where other types of obligations are at issue to those instances where a guaranty is involved and property is held jointly or by tenants in common with the usual variations in result where these two different forms of ownership are at issue.

§ 3 Signatory's Authority to Execute a Guaranty

3.1 Corporations

Under Kentucky corporate law, each officer of a corporation has the authority to perform the duties set forth in the bylaws or the duties prescribed by the board of directors, or directed by an officer authorized by the board of directors to prescribe duties of other officers, so long as such duties are consistent with the bylaws.[30]

A person dealing with a person as agent of a corporation is required to use diligence to ascertain the authority of the agent and that person is presumed to know the extent of the agent's authority. [31] However, it is also well established that one asserting and relying on the act of an agent "must establish his

26. Kennedy v. Joy Manufacturing Company, 707 S.W.2d 362, 364 (1986).
27. Smith v. Isaacs, 777 S.W.2d 912, 913 (1989).
28. Barton v. Hudson, 560 S.W.2d 20 (1983).
29. United States v. Winsper, 630 F.3d 482 (6th Cir. 2012).
30. KRS 271B.8-410.
31. Sperti Products, Inc. v. Container Corporation of America, 481 S.W.2d 43, 45 (1972).

authority or prove such facts as will form the basis of a reasonable inference of authority."[32]

3.2 Partnerships

Under Kentucky's Uniform Partnership Act, every partner is granted authority to be an agent for and bind the partnership for acts "apparently carrying on in the usual way the business of the partnership." An act of a partner which is not apparently for the carrying on of the business of the partnership in the usual way will not bind the partnership unless authorized by the other partners. Where the partner has no authority to act for the partnership, and the person with whom he is dealing has knowledge of the fact that he has no authority, then those actions will not bind the partnership. [33]

In the context of a limited partnership, a limited partner will not be liable for the obligations of the limited partnership unless he is also a general partner or he participates in the control of the business.[34] Per KRS 362.437, however, a limited partner will not be deemed to be "participating in the control of the business" solely by acting as a guarantor.

3.3 Limited Liability Companies

Under Kentucky's Limited Liability Companies statute, every member of a LLC is granted the authority to be an agent of the company for the purpose of its business or affairs, and the act of any member "apparently carrying on in the usual way the business or affairs of the limited liability company of which he is a member," shall bind the company.[35] An act of a member which is not apparently for the carrying on in the usual way of the business or affairs of the LLC will not bind the LLC unless the act is authorized in accordance with the operating agreement. Where the member has no authority to act for the LLC, and the person with whom the member is dealing has knowledge or has received notification of the fact the member has no such authority, then those actions will not bind the LLC.[36]

If the LLC is manager-managed, then no member is an agent able to bind the company, but every manager has the same authority as any member in a memberr-managed LLC.[37]

§ 4 Consideration

Consideration is a benefit to the party promising or a loss or detriment to the party to whom the promise is made. A substantial failure of consideration

32. Ritter v. Kentucky-Tennessee Light and Power Company, 151 S.W.2d 435 (1941).
33. KRS 362.190.
34. KRS 362.437.
35. KRS 275.135.
36. *Id.*
37. *Id.*

ordinarily justifies rescission of a contract.[38] A guaranty, as any contract, is subject to this principle and, as a general rule, requires a new and distinct consideration where the underlying obligation has already been entered into.[39] However, sufficient consideration for a guaranty can exist without any new or additional consideration, as distinct from the consideration for the underlying contract or obligation being guaranteed. First, sufficient consideration to sustain the guaranty exists where the guaranty is given before or at the same time the underlying debt or obligation is entered into.[40] Additionally, the guaranty can still be sustained by the consideration of the underlying obligation even if entered into after the original debt is created, so long as the guaranty was part of the inducement to the creation of that original debt.[41] Under Kentucky law, an agreement to continue in ongoing dealings, perhaps by extending future credit, is sufficient consideration to support the guarantor's promise to pay the debtor's past and future indebtedness.[42]

§ 5 Notice of Acceptance

In order for a guaranty to be binding upon the guarantor, the proposed guaranty must be accepted and notice must be given to the guarantors.[43] However, notice of acceptance will not be required where the guarantors have knowledge of the acceptance or where the guarantors waive the giving of notice.[44] Such knowledge or waiver can be considered to have occurred—and thus preclude any requirement to give notice—where, for example, the guaranty is to pay a pre-existing debt (or to pay a debt created at the same time as the guaranty), a guaranty is given to pay a debt at the request of the creditor, a creditor pays a consideration to the guarantors for their obligation, or where the guaranty is an absolute promise, in the nature of a primary liability, to pay a future debt.[45]

Whether notice of acceptance is required to enforce a guaranty can depend on its classification as absolute or conditional. An absolute guaranty is a contract under which "the guarantor promises that if the debtor does not perform his obligation or obligations, the guarantor will perform some acts (such as payment of money) to or for the benefit of the creditor, irrespective of any additional contingencies," whereas a conditional guaranty "contemplates as a condition to the guarantor's liability the happening of some contingent event other than the default of the principal debtor, or the performance of some act on the part of the creditor."[46] Because the nature of a conditional guaranty involves a promise by the guarantor, it is construed as merely an offer

38. Smith, 777 S.W.2d at 293.
39. Walter A. Wood Mowing and Reaping Machine Co. v. Land, 32 S.W. 607, 608 (1895).
40. *Id.*
41. *See Smith,* 777 S.W.2d at 294.
42. *Kennedy*, 707 S.W.2d at 364.
43. McGowan v. Wells' Trustee, 213 S.W. 573, 577 (1919).
44. *Id.*
45. *Id.*
46. APL, Inc. v. Ohio Valley Aluminum, Inc., 839 S.W.2d 571, 573 (1992).

that requires acceptance and notice of such to become effective.[47] Where an absolute guaranty is issued and the terms of the underlying instrument give no indication that the guarantor anticipates notification of acceptance from the creditor, the guaranty is effective, and the guarantor will be liable on the instrument from the time the creditor acts in reliance on it.[48]

§ 6 Interpretation

In reviewing the requirements imposed under KRS 371.065, Kentucky courts will "steadfastly adhere" to a strict construction of the language therein.[49]

In the courts, interpretation of a statute or contract is a question of law for the courts and is subject to de novo review.[50] Interpretation of guaranty contracts stems from basic tenets of contract law.[51]

§ 7 Defenses

The clearest defense a guarantor in Kentucky may raise as to the enforceability of the guaranty arises out of an assertion of a failure to comply under the requirements of Kentucky's guaranty statute. As previously discussed, the statute imposes strict requirements for the validity and enforceability of a guaranty agreement, and the courts will undertake a strict construction of the statute in applying the law. A guarantor can make the claim that the guaranty does not conform with the statute either because it does not specifically refer to or is not written on the underlying obligation being guaranteed.[52] Even if the guaranty is written on or specifically references the underlying contract, the guarantor may still claim nonconformity with the statute if the agreement is not in writing, is not signed by the guarantor, and does not specifically provide for the amount of maximum aggregate liability and the date on which the guaranty terminates.[53]

A potential response to an assertion of one of these defenses is that the agreement is not a guaranty, and thus not subject to the requirements of the statute. For example, an agreement may be an indemnity and not a guaranty at all. (See discussion in § 1).

A guarantor can argue the guaranty never became effective if any requisite consideration or notice of acceptance was never given. (See discussion in §§ 4 and 5).

47. *McGowan*, 213 S.W.2d at 577.
48. *APL, Inc.*, 839 S.W.2d at 573.
49. *Wheeler*, 127 S.W.3d at 614.
50. *Smith*, 777 S.W.2d at 291.
51. *See id.*
52. *See* KRS 371.065.
53. *See id.*

Kentucky's statute of limitations for an action under contract imposes a 15-year limitation period to bring a claim for breach of a guaranty agreement.[54] Parties are permitted to extend the term of a limitations period by contract.[55]

Aside from the express requirement under KRS 371.065 that the guaranty be in writing, a guarantor may claim a defense that an unwritten guaranty agreement is in violation of Kentucky's statute of frauds provision, which applies to "any promise to answer for the debt, default, or misdoing of another."[56]

§ 8 Waiver of Defenses

No Kentucky authority.

§ 9 Third-party Pledgors

No Kentucky authority.

§ 10 Jointly and Severally Liable Guarantors

No Kentucky authority.

§ 11 Reliance

No Kentucky authority.

§ 12 Subrogation

One who is compelled to pay the debt of another is entitled to be subrogated to the rights of the creditor.[57] This doctrine of "subrogation" is founded entirely on principles of equity.[58] A party is entitled to subrogation when it discharges an obligation in performance of a legal duty but for which its liability was subsequent to that of another party.[59] Subrogation cannot be enforced, though,

54. KRS 413.090.
55. KRS 413. 265.
56. KRS 371.010.
57. Lewis Admr. v. U.S. Fidelity & Guaranty Company, 138 S.W. 305, 306 (1911).
58. National Surety Corp. v. First National Bank of Prestonburg, 128 S.W. 766, 769 (1939).
59. *Lewis,* 138 S.W.2d at 306.

until the whole debt is paid to the creditor.[60] Although the entire debt must be extinguished before subrogation can occur, part of the debt can be paid by the guarantor and part can be paid by the principal.[61] In determining whether a guarantor is entitled to subrogation, the question of his inducement to assume the obligation cannot be considered in determining his rights; the only question of import is whether he has been compelled to pay the debt of his principal.[62]

§ 13 Triangular Set-off in Bankruptcy

No Kentucky authority.

§ 14 Indemnification—Primary Obligor's Duty

No Kentucky authority.

§ 15 Enforcement

Under Kentucky law, the terms of a contract will govern the agreement, and a party who can read and has an opportunity to read the contract which he signs must stand by the language of the contract.[63] Enforcement of a guaranty agreement will not be barred by equitable estoppel where the terms of the contract provide otherwise.[64]

§ 16 Revival and Reinstatement

Kentucky law is scant concerning the revival of a guaranty agreement. However, one case does stand for the proposition that if the guarantor pays a guaranteed obligation which is subsequently returned as a result of another legal obligation, then the guarantor's secondary obligation is reinstated.[65]

60. McClure's Executor v. King, 104 S.W. 711, 712 (1907).
61. *Id.*
62. *Lewis,* 138 S.W.2d at 306.
63. *Smith,* 777 S.W.2d at 295.
64. *Id.*
65. *See* Northern Bank of Kentucky v. Farmers' National Bank, 63 S.W. 604, 607 (1901).

§ 17 Choice of Law

There is a very limited body of Kentucky law on the application of choice-of-law principles to guaranties. In most instances, the application of choice-of-law principles to contracts generally would be appropriate. There is, however, one significant decision applying choice-of-law principles where KRS 371.065 was involved. In that matter, involving a guaranty by Kentuckians which by its terms stipulated the application of Tennessee law, the Sixth Circuit reversed the lower federal court and provided its analysis of Kentucky choice-of-law principles.

In a diversity action, the choice-of-law rules of the forum state govern the determination whether to enforce a guaranty's choice-of-law provision.

Under *Restatement (Second) of Conflict of Laws § 187(2)* a choice-of-law clause will be enforced unless either: (a) the chosen state has no substantial relationship to the parties or the transaction and there is no other reasonable basis for the parties' choice, or (b) application of the law of the chosen state would be contrary to a fundamental policy of a state which has a materially greater interest than the chosen state in the determination of the particular issue which, under the rule of *Restatement (Second) of Conflict of Laws § 188*, would be the state of the applicable law in the absence of an effective choice of law by the parties.

In a standard commercial breach-of-contract case, *Restatement (Second) of Conflict of Laws § 187* applies as the analytical framework a Kentucky court would employ for addressing a contractual choice-of-law clause.

Kentucky's enactment of *Ky. Rev. Stat. Ann. § 371.065(1)* is not enough, standing alone, to invalidate the parties' choice of Tennessee law in the parties' guaranty agreement.

The fact that a different result might be achieved if the law of the chosen forum is applied does not suffice to show that the foreign law is repugnant to a fundamental policy of the forum state. Rather, it must be shown that there are significant differences in the application of the law of the two states.[66]

---

66. Wallace Hardware Co. v. Abrams, 223 F.3d 382 (6th Cir., 2000).

Louisiana State Law of Guaranties

R. Marshall Grodner
McGlinchey Stafford, PLLC
301 Main Street
One American Place 14th Floor
Baton Rouge, LA 70825
(225) 383-9000
Fax: (225) 343-3076
www.mcglinchey.com

McGLINCHEY STAFFORD PLLC

Contents

Louisiana State Law of Guaranties

HIGHLIGHTS

- Louisiana does not require "consideration" for a guaranty since it is a unilateral gratuitous promise.
- There should be an agreement (preferably in writing) between the guarantor and the principal obligor that the guarantor can collect attorneys' fees upon exercise of the right to reimbursement against the principal obligor.
- Where there is more than one guarantor and between the guarantors there is an agreement that one or more will be liable for more or less than their equal share, this agreement should be in writing.
- The guaranty agreement and the principal obligation should include language that the principal obligor is "bound with" the guarantor or alternatively that the principal and guarantor are "jointly and severally" and "solidarily" liable.
- The guaranty agreement should contain language stating that the guarantor consents to modification to the principal obligation and changes to the security for the principal obligation.

Introduction

As with much of its other law, Louisiana's law of guaranty follows the civilian tradition. In Louisiana, the law of guaranty is governed by the suretyship articles in the Louisiana Civil Code. Since the suretyship is governed by the Civil Code, the courts generally do not look to the Restatement of Suretyship and Guaranty to interpret Louisiana law. The Louisiana Civil Code articles on suretyship were substantially reworked effective January 1, 1988. This revision changed many of the old rules under the prior articles as well as legislatively overruled some prior jurisprudence. As with most civilian jurisdictions, it is important first to look at the articles in the Civil Code governing suretyship and the comments to such articles. If there are no articles on the specific point, then one must look back at the articles governing more general subjects, such as the articles covering conventional obligations (common law contracts) or obligations in general. Case law may be consulted, but cases prior to 1988 may not be very helpful.

§ 1 Nature and Extent of Suretyship

Article 3035 defines suretyship as follows:

Suretyship is an accessory contract by which a person binds himself to a creditor to fulfill the obligation of another upon the failure of the latter to do so.

It is unilateral, gratuitous, accessory, consensual, and express.

Suretyship is unilateral because only the surety undertakes an obligation to the creditor. The creditor does not undertake any obligations in favor of the surety.[1] It is gratuitous because the surety does not necessarily obtain an advantage in return.[2] Under Louisiana law, a contract does not require consideration, merely a cause—a reason why a person obligates himself.[3] Unlike consideration, there is no necessity for a party to obtain an advantage or benefit in return. Suretyship is accessory since it is made to secure the performance of another obligation (the principal obligation).[4] It also must be express and in writing.[5]

Suretyship can be created for any lawful principal obligation. The principal obligation is not limited to the payment of money, but can be any obligation including performance and completion. The principal obligation, further, may be subject to conditions, may be currently existing, or may arise in the future.[6] Further, there is no requirement that suretyship be accepted by the creditor since acceptance is presumed upon delivery of the writing to the creditor.[7] Last, except for the imperative rules contained in the Louisiana Civil Code (such as the writing requirement), the rules governing suretyship can be modified by contract.[8]

One last rule regarding the nature and extent of suretyship deals with the scenario where a surety ostensibly binds itself as a principal obligor to satisfy the obligation of another. For example, many guaranties state that the guarantor is "solidarily" bound with the principal obligor. Under Louisiana law, the concept of solidarity is similar to joint and several liability in common law. In this case, where the creditor knows that the principal cause of someone's agreement (whether separate or in the principal obligation) is to guarantee the performance of another's obligations, then that someone is considered a surety regardless of what the agreement says, and has all the rights and obligations of surety. If on the other hand, the creditor does not know that one's agreement is to guarantee another's performance, the creditor can treat them as principal obligors in solido (i.e., obligors with joint and several liability) until the creditor clearly knows of the true relationship. In this case, the "guarantor" will not have the rights of a surety.[9]

1. La. Civ. Code art. 1907.
2. La. Civ. Code art. 1910.
3. La. Civ. Code art. 1966.
4. La. Civ. Code art. 1913.
5. La. Civ. Code art. 3038.
6. La. Civ. Code art. 3036.
7. La. Civ. Code art. 3039.
8. La. Civ. Code art. 3040.
9. La. Civ. Code art. 3037.

§ 2 Kinds of Suretyship

Turning next to the types of suretyship, Louisiana recognizes three kinds of suretyship: commercial, legal, and ordinary.[10] First is the commercial suretyship. Commercial suretyship generally arises out of business activity. It is a commercial suretyship where the surety is in the surety business. This type of suretyship also arises when the principal obligor of the surety is a business entity. Commercial suretyship also arises out of a commercial transaction of either the principal obligor or the surety.[11]

Legal suretyship arises pursuant to laws, rules or regulations.[12] Ordinary suretyship is the residual category. Any suretyship that is not a commercial suretyship or a legal suretyship is an ordinary suretyship.[13] These distinctions are important since ordinary suretyship is strictly construed in favor of the surety. This rule indicates implicitly, however, that commercial suretyship and legal suretyship are not strictly construed in favor of the surety.[14]

§ 3 The Effects of Suretyship between the Surety and Creditor

The main legal relationship in suretyship is between the surety and the creditor. The main effect is that a surety, or each surety if there is more than one, is liable to the creditor for the full performance of the principal obligation.[15] This rule, however, may be varied by agreement. Where, for example, there are several sureties, there may be an agreement that each surety is only obligated to perform a certain percentage of the principal obligation or its obligation to perform is limited by a certain dollar amount.[16] Further, the revision of these rules in 1988 eliminated the pleas of division and discussion. Division is a dilatory exception[17] that formerly allowed a surety to point out property of the principal obligor that could satisfy the principal obligation before enforcing the principal obligation against the surety.[18] Division was an affirmative defense[19] that allowed a surety, where there where multiple sureties, to require that the creditor only seek such surety's virile share[20] of the principal obligation. These changes not only allow the creditor to sue either the principal obligor,

10. La. Civ. Code art. 3041.
11. La. Civ. Code art. 3042.
12. La. Civ. Code art. 3043. This chapter will not deal with legal suretyship since its main emphasis is on guaranties. Legal suretyship deals mainly with bonds, such as construction bonds, appeal bonds, and bail bonds.
13. La. Civ. Code art. 3044.
14. La. Civ. Code art. 3044, Comment.
15. La. Civ. Code art. 3045.
16. La. Civ. Code arts. 3040 and 3045, Comment (b).
17. La. Code Civ. Pro. art. 926.
18. La. Code Civ. Pro. art. 5151.
19. La. Code Civ. Pro. art. 1005.
20. Generally, virile share is, for those cases where there is more than one obligor, the amount of the share for which each obligor is responsible. Usually, in contractual situations, it is presumed to be equal shares unless there is an agreement otherwise. See, generally, La. Civ. Code art. 1804.

or one or more of the sureties without joinder of the others,[21] they also allow the creditor to proceed against one of several sureties, seeking to collect the entire amount of the principal obligation against that surety.

The code also provides for defenses that a surety may raise against the claims of the creditor. Generally, a surety may raise any defense against the principal obligation that the principal obligor may assert other than two. The first defense that cannot be asserted by a surety is lack of capacity. Under Louisiana law, every principal obligor must have the capacity to enter into a principal obligation/contract. Persons that are unemancipated minors, interdicts, and persons deprived of reason at the time of contracting lack capacity.[22] Also, it has been held that a principal obligor that has no legal existence (such as a corporation that has not been legally formed) also constitutes a lack of capacity.[23] Thus, the defense that a contract can be rescinded on the grounds of lack of capacity by the principal obligor cannot be raised by a surety.

The other defense that a surety cannot assert is discharge in bankruptcy. Technically, unlike lack of capacity, bankruptcy does not give the principal obligor the right to rescind the contract; it only acts as a bar to the enforcement of the obligation by the creditor. Furthermore, potential insolvency resulting in a discharge in bankruptcy is the main reason that suretyship is required.[24]

Last, there is another action by the creditor that affects the relationship between the surety and the principal obligor. That action is a remission of the principal obligation by the creditor. This action extinguishes the principal obligation. A remission of the debt is similar to a common-law release, but a remission, unlike a release, does not require consideration—it is more of a gratuitous act.[25] A remission of the debt granted to the principal obligor results in the release of any sureties.[26]

§ 4 Effects of Suretyship between the Surety and Principal Obligor

The second relationship governed by the rules of suretyship is the relationship between the surety and the principal obligor. In this relationship, the surety has three rights—the right of subrogation, the right of reimbursement, and the right to require security from the principal obligor.[27]

21. La. Civ. Code art. 3045, Comment (c).
22. La. Civ. Code arts. 1918, et seq.
23. Devoe & Reynolds Co. v. Loup, 129 So. 450 (La. 1930).
24. La. Civ. Code art. 3046, Comment (b).
25. La. Civ. Code art. 1888, Comment (b) and (d).
26. La. Civ. Code art. 1892.
27. La. Civ. Code art. 3047.

4.1 Subrogation

Turning first to subrogation, a surety that pays the principal obligation is subrogated to the rights of the creditor.[28] Generally, subrogation is the substitution of one person to the rights of another.[29] The effect of subrogation is that the obligation remains in favor of the person who performed it, in the present case the surety, and that person may enforce the obligation performed by him against the obligor, in the present case, the principal obligor, as well as against any security given for the obligation so performed.[30] Unlike subrogation created by contract, the rights of a surety when it performs the principal obligation are those of legal subrogation.[31] As a form of legal subrogation, the surety who pays the creditor can only collect the amount paid from the principal obligation, and cannot claim more through conventional subrogation.[32]

There are a couple of important points that arise as the result of applying these subrogation rules. The first is that to the extent the principal obligation is secured by, for example, a mortgage, the subrogation rules allow the surety, upon payment of the principal obligation, to satisfy the principal obligation so paid by enforcement of the mortgage. The second important point is that the surety cannot through an agreement with the creditor claim more, through conventional subrogation, than it paid the creditor on the principal obligation. For example, assume the outstanding amount of the principal obligation is $1,000. The surety pays the creditor $500, and the creditor then contractually assigns the entire principal obligation to the surety. Because of the rules of legal subrogation, even though the surety is the owner of an obligation with an outstanding principal amount of $1,000, the surety can only collect $500 from the principal obligor. The surety is, however, entitled to recover by legal subrogation attorneys' fees and costs that are owed on the principal obligation.[33] It is important to note that in order to recover attorneys' fees and costs, the principal obligation must provide for their collection. As another protection against this legal subrogation limit, there is no reason that in an agreement between the surety and the principal obligor provision cannot be made for the payment of such attorneys' fees and costs, but this would be collected under the right of reimbursement discussed below.

4.2 Reimbursement

A second right that the surety has against the principal obligor is reimbursement. Reimbursement is different from subrogation because subrogation is a derivative right though enforcement of the principal obligation, where reimbursement is a direct right by the surety against the principal obligor. A surety that pays the creditor is entitled to reimbursement from the principal obligor provided, however, if the surety pays prior to the principal obligation being

28. La. Civ. Code art. 3048.
29. La. Civ. Code art. 1825.
30. La. Civ. Code art. 1826.
31. La. Civ. Code arts. 1829(5) and 3048.
32. La. Civ. Code art. 1830.
33. La. Civ. Code art. 3052.

due and payable, the reimbursement may not be recovered until the obligation becomes due and payable.[34] Furthermore, where the principal obligation is owed by solidary (i.e., joint and several) principal obligors, the surety may request reimbursement from any one of the principal obligors for the amount paid to the creditor.[35]

The right of reimbursement may also arise in favor of a surety where the principal obligation has been extinguished (for example, paid) or the principal obligor had a defense to the enforcement of the principal obligation under certain conditions. If the surety in good faith believes that the principal obligation is due and either reasonably tries to notify the principal obligor that the creditor is insisting on payment or if the principal obligor was told that the creditor was insisting on payment, then the surety has a right to reimbursement from the principal obligor. On the other hand, if the principal obligor is notified by either the surety or the creditor that payment is being demanded, and advises the surety that the principal obligor is not liable, the surety may not be entitled to reimbursement. If the surety, however, pays and is not entitled to reimbursement, the surety may still have rights against the creditor.[36]

4.3 Subrogation v. Reimbursement

There are some differences and some similarities between reimbursement and subrogation. The main difference is where the principal obligor has a defense to payment. If there is a defense and the surety pays, there is no subrogation. Under the limited circumstances noted above, however, a surety may still collect by reimbursement even if there is a defense on the principal obligation.[37]

On the other hand, as also previously stated, if the principal obligation provides for attorneys' fees and costs, the surety may collect these items as part of legal subrogation.[38] Through reimbursement, however, attorneys' fees and costs may only be recovered if there is an agreement between the principal obligor and the surety providing for these matters. The reason for this last difference is that subrogation is a derivative action based on the surety stepping into the shoes of the creditor, whereas reimbursement is a direct personal action by the surety against the creditor. The general rule in Louisiana is that attorneys' fees and costs are not recoverable unless the contract so provides. As a derivative action, through subrogation, the surety has the rights of the creditor and if the principal obligation provides for attorneys' fees and costs, the surety has such rights. With reimbursement, however, there is hardly ever a contract between the principal obligor and the surety, much less a contract providing for attorneys' fees and costs.[39]

There is one codal instance where subrogation and reimbursement are indistinguishable. This is the scenario where the surety pays the creditor, but

34. La. Civ. Code art. 3049.
35. *Id.*
36. La. Civ. Code art. 3050 and Comment thereto.
37. *Id.*
38. La. Civ. Code art. 3052.
39. La. Civ. Code art. 3052, Comment (c).

does not warn the principal obligor of the payment and then the principal obligor also pays the creditor. In this case, the surety cannot collect from the principal obligor either through subrogation or reimbursement. The surety, however, may still recover from the creditor.

4.4 Right to Require Security

The last right a surety has in its relationship with the principal obligor is the right to require security for the principal obligor's reimbursement obligations. Such security, for example, can take the form of a mortgage on immovable (real) property, a security interest in movable (personal) property, another suretyship or an escrow deposit.

There are four instances when the surety[40] can require security, and this list is exclusive.[41] The first case is where the surety is being sued by the creditor.[42] The second instance is where the principal obligor is insolvent, unless the principal obligation is such that its performance does not require his solvency.[43]

The third case is where the principal obligor fails to perform an act promised in return for the suretyship.[44] This scenario comes into play where, for example, the principal obligor is paying the surety for the suretyship or where the principal obligor has agreed to obtain the surety's discharge at a certain time. If the principal obligor fails to perform these acts, the surety would have no claim for damages against the principal obligor before the creditor requires payment so it makes sense to allow the surety to require security.

The last instance where the surety can require security is where the principal obligation is due or would have been due except for an extension granted to which consent was not granted by the surety.[45] It is important to note in this instance that if the surety consents to an extension or any extension, this right to require security does not come into play. Thus, most suretyship agreements (guaranties) build in a consent to all extensions of time to pay as part of the agreement's terms.

To enforce any right to require security, the surety must demand in writing that the principal obligor post security. If the principal obligor fails to either post security or obtain the discharge of the surety within 10 days after delivery of the written demand, then the surety has the right to bring an action to require the principal obligor to deposit in the registry of the court an amount sufficient to satisfy his reimbursement obligation.[46]

40. La. Civ. Code art. 3053.
41. La. Civ. Code art. 3053, Comment (b).
42. La. Civ. Code art. 3053(1).
43. La. Civ. Code art. 3053(2).
44. La. Civ. Code art. 3053(3).
45. La. Civ. Code art. 3053(4).
46. La. Civ. Code art. 3054.

§ 5 The Effects of Suretyship among Several Sureties

Turning next to the relationship between sureties where there are multiple sureties who are sureties for the same principal obligation of the same principal obligor (cosureties), there are three interrelated issues. The first deals with the determination of the liability of each cosurety as to the other cosureties. The second deals with the right of contribution from other cosureties. The last is the effect of a remission to (a release of) some, but not all cosureties.

5.1 Liability among Cosureties

First, it is important to determine how cosureties are responsible to each other when the principal obligation is paid by one or more of the sureties. Where there are cosureties, the presumption is that the responsibility is by their number.[47] For example, where there are three sureties each will be responsible for 1/3 of the principal obligation among themselves, even though each is responsible for the whole as to the creditor. This presumption can be varied by agreement among the cosureties, so that, for example, where there are three cosureties, the cosureties could agree that one is responsible for 50 percent and the other two are responsible for 25 percent apiece. Further, it could be contemplated that the surety that bound himself first would be responsible for 100 percent of the debt as to those who become sureties later. This is similar to the general rule under Article 3 of the Uniform Commercial Code that prior indorsers are 100 percent liable to subsequent indorsers who pay a negotiable instrument.[48] If this liability in order of signing is to be proved, the later surety must prove he had knowledge of and relied on the existence of the earlier surety.[49]

A significant point in this context is that the presumption of liability in equal portions is a rebuttable presumption. Parol evidence may be used to rebut this presumption.[50] Consider the following scenario. A closely held corporation has three shareholders. Shareholder A owns 60 percent, shareholder B owns 30 percent and shareholder C owns 10 percent. The corporation borrows $1,000 from creditor. The shareholders guarantee the corporation's debt. The corporation defaults. Shareholder A pays the debt and sues shareholder C for contribution. Although it is presumed that each is liable for 1/3 of the debt as among the sureties, shareholder C may argue that it was contemplated that the virile share was to be based on the percentage of ownership in the corporation, and his virile share is $100. Shareholder C can use parol evidence to try to prove that this was the virile share agreement. Therefore, a careful practitioner may want the agreement among cosureties in this and similar cases be memorialized in writing.

47. La. Civ. Code art. 3055.
48. La. R.S. 10:3-415.
49. La. Civ. Code art. 3055, Comment (c).
50. La. Civ. Code art. 3055, Comment (b).

5.2 Contribution

5.2.1 In general

A surety who pays the creditor has a right to collect directly or by subrogation from the other sureties the share of the principal obligation each is to bear.[51] This right is called contribution. On the other hand, if one of the sureties is insolvent, his portion is to be borne by the other sureties.

5.2.2 Limitations on contribution Rights

The right of contribution has certain limitations. First, a surety who pays more than his share may recover the excess from his cosureties in proportion to the shares of the others.[52] The converse is also true. If a surety pays less than his share, there is no contribution owed by the other sureties.

A second limitation deals with where a surety pays less than the entire amount owed to the creditor and obtains a release for all the cosureties. In that case, any reduction in the amount owed by those released benefits them proportionately.[53]

5.2.3 Release of Cosureties

Another contribution issue arises where a remission of the debt (release) is given to one surety. Such a release operates as a release of the other cosureties to the extent these other sureties had a right of contribution from the released surety. Last, if the creditor grants a remission of the debt to a surety in return for payment, that payment will be imputed to the principal obligation, unless the creditor and the released surety agree otherwise.[54]

5.2.4 Examples

As an example of these rules regarding contribution, its limitations, and release of a surety consider the following examples in a scenario where the principal obligation is $300, and there are three sureties, each responsible for a virile share of 1/3 among each other.

5.2.4.1 One Surety pays less than Virile Share

In the first scenario, one of the sureties pays $90 to the creditor for the release of all the sureties. In this case, the payment is credited to the principal obligation reducing it to $210. The creditor still has a claim of $210 against the principal obligor, but no longer any claim against the sureties because of the release. Furthermore, since the paying surety did not pay any more than its

51. La. Civ. Code art. 3056.
52. La. Civ. Code art. 3057.
53. *Id.*
54. La. Civ. Code art. 1892.

virile share, the paying surety has no claim of contribution against the other sureties.

Similarly, if in that scenario, the paying surety only got a release of himself and not the other sureties, the result would be the same except that the creditor would still have a claim of $200 against either or both of the nonpaying sureties. The reason for the $200 claim is that the release of a surety is deemed to be a release of that surety's virile share by the creditor as to the remaining cosureties, in this case $100, even though the creditor only received $90. So in this case, the principal obligor owes $210 to the creditor, but the remaining sureties can only be required to pay $200. Although there is no case law on the subject, it may be possible for the creditor and a paying surety to agree that the amount paid for the release of the paying surety is for the release of the suretyship obligation and is not to be imputed to the payment of the debt. If this is the case, then the principal obligation would remain at $300, but the creditor's rights against the remaining sureties would still only be for $200.[55]

5.2.4.2 One Surety pays more than Virile Share, but Excess is less than others' Virile Share

In the next scenario, one of the sureties pays $180 to the creditor and obtains a complete release of all the sureties. In this case, the reduction of the amount owed benefits each surety proportionately, so that the amount each nonpaying surety owes the paying surety in contribution is $60. Release of the sureties does not release the principal obligor, but the payment is generally deemed to reduce the principal obligation owed by the principal obligor to the creditor to $120. The paying surety also has a reimbursement or subrogation right for the amount paid against the principal obligor, and so would the nonpaying sureties to the extent they paid their contribution obligations to the paying surety.

Consider the same facts as the previous paragraph, but the paying surety only obtains a release of himself but not the other paying sureties. In this case, the result is the same except in two instances. The surety who paid the creditor paid more than his proportionate share has a different right of contribution. Since the virile share of each is 1/3 of $300, or $100, and the $80 excess paid is not over the virile share of the other sureties, the paying surety can collect against the $80 excess from either or both of the nonpaying sureties. Also, the creditor would still have a claim of $120 against either or both of the nonpaying sureties because they were not released.

5.2.4.3 One Surety pays more than Virile Share and the excess is more than the others' Virile Share

In the last scenario, one of the sureties pays $240 to the creditor and obtains a complete release of all the sureties. The result is similar to the $180 scenario,

55. La. Civ. Code art. 1892, 4th ¶ and Comment (c).

except that the paying surety could claim $80 from each of the other sureties and the principal obligation would generally be deemed reduced to $60.

If in this last scenario, the paying surety only obtained a release of himself, but not the other sureties, the result may be problematic since in this case the excess paid by the paying surety ($140) exceeds the virile share of each surety ($100). In this case, there are two different arguments regarding the contribution rights of the paying surety in this scenario. The first argument is that the paying surety can collect the excess $140 in full from either of the other sureties. The argument here is that because the nonpaying sureties cannot claim division as to the paying surety (i.e., limit the paying surety's claim to the nonpaying sureties' virile share), the paying surety may claim the whole excess against either one (but not both) of the nonpaying sureties. If one of the nonpaying sureties pays, however, it would still have a claim against the other, but it would only be for $40 because its contribution right is limited to the amount over and above its virile share that it paid ($140 payment - $100 virile share = $40 excess).

The other reading of Article 3056 of the Louisiana Civil Code is that the paying surety can only collect the virile share of the each of the remaining sureties. In this case, the paying surety could only collect $70 against each nonpaying surety.

Remember that, as with the other scenarios, the paying surety has reimbursement and subrogation rights against the principal obligor. The creditor, also, still has right as to the $60 remaining on the principal obligation as to the nonreleased sureties and the principal obligor.

§ 6 Termination or Extinction of Suretyship

Last, as to ordinary and commercial suretyship, the Louisiana Civil Code deals with the termination or extinction of suretyship. Generally, when there is an extinction of suretyship, it completely releases the obligation of a surety. In certain circumstances upon termination, however, some of the surety's obligations may survive.

6.1 Extinction

First, generally suretyship can be extinguished in any manner by which a contract can be extinguished.[56] Generally, contracts can be extinguished by performance, impossibility of performance, tender and deposit, novation, remission of the debt (release), compensation (set-off), and confusion (merger).[57]

Second, the extinction of the principal obligation extinguishes the suretyship.[58] This rule only makes sense since suretyship is an accessory obligation, and accessory obligations are dependent on the existence of a principal

56. La. Civ. Code art. 3058.
57. La. Civ. Code arts. 1854 et seq.
58. La. Civ. Code art. 3059.

obligation. Payment of the principal obligation, however, does not affect the right of cosureties among themselves.[59]

Further, suretyship is also extinguished by prescription of the principal obligation.[60] Prescription, in this case specifically liberative prescription, operates in a manner similar to the tolling of a statute of limitations under common law. Liberative prescription is a mode of barring actions as a result of inaction for a period of time.[61] Generally, where the principal obligation is a contract, the action will be considered a personal action, and the right to bring that action prescribes in 10 years.[62] An action on a principal obligation that is a negotiable note, however, prescribes in five years either after its due date (by acceleration or otherwise) or after demand, if a demand note.[63]

There is a specific prescription, also, for the rights of sureties. The right of a surety to bring an action for contribution from his cosureties and to bring an action for reimbursement from the principal obligor prescribes in 10 years.[64]

Prescription can be interrupted, and once interrupted it begins to run again once the interruption ends.[65] The main cause of interruption with regard to the various relationships under suretyship is an acknowledgement of the obligation.[66] Basically, an acknowledgment is an admission that the obligation is owed, and such acknowledgement may be oral or written, formal or informal, and express or tacit.[67] Payment of an obligation constitutes an acknowledgement.[68] Thus, for example, payment by the principal obligor on the principal obligation interrupts prescription on the principal obligation so that the time to bring an action on the surety's obligation to the creditor, as accessory, is also interrupted.[69]

On the other hand, an interruption against a surety is only effective against the principal obligor and other sureties if such parties have agreed to be bound together with such surety. Although generally a guaranty in and of itself arguably constitutes an agreement for the principal obligor and the surety to be bound together and therefore the payment by the surety interrupts prescription as to the principal obligor,[70] a counter argument could be made that if there is no specific language in the principal obligation whereby the principal obligor agrees to be bound together with all sureties or in the suretyship agreement (guaranty) where the surety agrees to be bound together with the principal obligor and all other sureties, then a payment by the surety does not operate as an interruption of prescription on the principal obligation.

An example of this would be as follows: A $100 demand negotiable note with separate guaranty. No "bound with," "solidary," or "joint and several"

59. La. Civ. Code art. 3059, Comment (b).
60. La. Civ. Code art 3060.
61. La. Civ. Code art. 3447.
62. La. Civ. Code art. 3499.
63. La. R.S. 10:3-118.
64. La. Civ. Code art. 3060.
65. La. Civ. Code arts. 3462 et seq.
66. La. Civ. Code art. 3464.
67. La. Civ. Code art. 3463, Comment (e).
68. *See generally* Chaisson v. Chaisson, 690 So.2d 899 (La. App. 2d. Cir. 1997).
69. *See generally* Security National Partners, L.P. v. Baxley, 859 So.2d 890 (La. App. 2d. Cir. 2003).
70. Matter of O'Connor, 153 F.3d 258 (5th Cir. 1998).

language in note or guaranty. Demand is made on July 1, 2007. Surety pays $50 for release on June 30, 2012. Creditor sues principal obligor on July 15, 2012. If the payment by the surety interrupts prescription as to the principal obligor, then the suit is timely as against the principal obligor. If the payment does not interrupt prescription as to the principal obligor, prescription of five years as to the creditor's action on the negotiable note against the principal obligor runs on July 1, 2012, and July 15, 2012 is not timely. The creditor, on the one hand, would argue that the guaranty in and of itself constitutes an agreement to be bound with the principal obligor, the payment by the surety interrupts prescription, and therefore the suit is timely. The principal obligor's counter argument is that the principal obligor was not "bound with" the surety; therefore, payment by the surety does not interrupt prescription as to him.

It is important to point out even if the latter is correct, the surety would still have a reimbursement claim against the principal obligor since prescription on that action is 10 years, but there would be no subrogation claim (i.e., no attorneys' fees and costs), since subrogation is derivative of the creditor's prescribed action. Since there is no dispositive authority on point with regard to these issues, the cautious practitioner may want to include language in the principal obligation that the principal obligor is bound together (or solidarily, and jointly and severally bound) with all sureties and in the suretyship contract that the surety is bound together (or solidarily, and jointly and severally bound) with the principal obligor and all sureties.

6.2 Termination

Next, under the Civil Code, there are really two types of termination. The first is termination by notice or death of the surety. The second is by the actions of the creditor.

6.2.1 Notice; Death

Turning first to termination by notice, the surety has a right to notify the creditor that the suretyship is terminated.[71] This termination does not affect, however, the surety's liability for the principal obligations already incurred, such as the sums the creditor has already lent. It also does not affect liability for obligations which the creditor is bound to permit the principal obligor to incur at the time of the notice, such as where there is a firm commitment to lend money to the principal obligor at the time of the notice. Furthermore, the termination by notice cannot prejudice a creditor who has changed his position in reliance on the suretyship.

Additionally, when a creditor obtains knowledge of the death of a surety, this knowledge has the same effect as a notice of termination.[72] A universal successor of the deceased surety may confirm that the suretyship is not terminated, and this confirmation does not have to be in writing.

71. La. Civ. Code art. 3061.
72. *Id.*

6.2.2 *Modification of the Principal Obligation or Security for the Principal Obligation*

Another way that suretyship can be extinguished is through the dealings between the creditor and principal obligor that make changes to the principal obligation or the security for it without the consent of the surety.[73] Any material modification or amendment by the creditor of the principal obligation or the impairment of real security held for it without the consent of the surety will extinguish an ordinary suretyship. Such actions by the creditor will extinguish a commercial suretyship to the extent the surety is prejudiced. One exception is, in a commercial suretyship where the principal obligation is not for the payment of money and the surety should have contemplated that the creditor would take such action, the commercial suretyship will not be extinguished no matter how prejudicial the action is. Last, it is assumed that the prejudice to the surety is the full amount of the surety's obligation unless the creditor proves otherwise.

There are several important subtexts in the Code in this instance. The first and most important is that the modification or amendment to the principal obligation, or impairment of real security must be "without the consent of the surety." If the surety consents to the changes in the principal obligation or impairment in real security in the contract of suretyship (or subsequently), neither the ordinary suretyship nor the commercial suretyship will be extinguished. Most common guaranty forms have these consents built in, but the careful practitioner should check and make sure these consents are there if the guaranty deals with Louisiana law or Louisiana guarantors.

Another important aspect is that the changes by the creditor must be "material." When it comes to the amendment and modification of the principal obligation, the resolution is relatively simple. If the principal obligation is made more burdensome, then the amendment or modification will be material. Examples of these include extension of time to pay (thereby extending the length of the suretyship), increases in principal amount, increases in interest rates, and other similar changes. On the other hand, changes that make the principal obligations less burdensome are not material. Examples of these sorts of changes are decreases in interest rates and shortening the time to repay.

The materiality of "impairment of real security" is a little more problematic. First, it is important to distinguish personal security and real security under Louisiana law. Personal security generally gives you a right to sue a person other than the principal obligor to enforce the principal obligation. The main example of this is suretyship. Since it is not real security, its impairment does not affect the obligation of the surety under these provision of the code, but it is affected by those provision of the code dealing with the relationship between the creditor and surety, and among cosureties.[74]

Real security, however, is a right to seize and sell a thing (usually a type of property in common law) and apply the proceeds of the sale to the principal obligation. Examples of real security are mortgages in immovables (real prop-

73. La. Civ. Code art. 3062.
74. *See* Sections 3 and 5, *supra*.

erty) and security interests in movables (personal property). In this context, this issue of impairment of real security usually arises in the following general scenario. Creditor lends $1,000 to principal obligor. Creditor secures the loan by a suretyship and a mortgage on two pieces of real property, Property A and Property B. The suretyship agreement does not consent to impairment of real security. In the first derivation of this scenario, surety pays creditor the $1000. Surety is legally subrogated to creditor's rights as to the principal obligation, including the mortgage as an accessory. All things being equal through subrogation, the surety has a right to foreclose on the mortgage and recoup the surety's payment to the creditor.

If one changes the facts a little, a material impairment can be shown. In this fact pattern, suppose Property A and Property B are each worth $750, and the creditor releases Property A from the mortgage. There has been an impairment of real security, and it is material because the principal obligation is $1,000 and the property securing it was originally worth more than the amount of the principal obligation ($1,500), but because of the creditor's action in releasing Property A, the real security is now worth less ($750) than the principal obligation ($1,000). In this case, the ordinary suretyship would be extinguished, but the commercial suretyship would be only to the extent prejudiced. In this simple version, the extent prejudiced would be the difference between what the surety would have been paid if there was no release of real security though exercise of subrogation rights as to the real security—foreclosure on the mortgage on both Property A and Property B ($1,000 as the amount of the principal obligation; the debtor would be entitled to the surplus) and the subrogation right of the surety after release of Property A upon foreclosure ($750). Therefore, the commercial surety would be extinguished as to $250 ($1,000, the principal obligation-$750, the value of remaining Property B) and would still owe the creditor $750 ($1,000, the principal obligation-$250, the amount prejudiced).[75]

An opposite example demonstrates a nonmaterial impairment. Assume the same facts, except that Property A and Property B are each worth $1,500. Creditor releases Property A. Although there has been an impairment of real security it is not material, since the surety has a right to exercise through subrogation its rights against real security in property (Property B) with a value ($1,500) in excess of the value of the principal obligation ($1,000), even after the release of Property A.

§ 7 Choice of Law

Another issue involved in guaranties is what law is to be applied to a guaranty in multistate transactions. The Louisiana Civil Code articles governing suretyship do not provide choice-of-law rules as to what law should be applied to a

75. Of course this is a very simple scenario. In a real case, one would have to take into account the costs of foreclosure and the amount that would have been actually bid at a foreclosure sale, and numerous other factors.

contract of guaranty. Therefore, courts would look to the general Civil Code articles governing conflicts of law. Specifically, the court would look at the articles governing conventional obligations (contracts) under the choice-of-law section of the Civil Code. Generally, the law that the parties expressly chose in their contract or is clearly relied upon by the parties controls issues regarding the contract unless such law contravenes the public policy of the state whose law would otherwise be applicable under the general rule discussed below.[76]

There are two exceptions to this rule deferring to party autonomy. These exceptions are meant to uphold the validity of contracts, including guaranties. The first deals with form. Specifically, if the law of (i) the state where the guaranty is made, (ii) the law of the state where the guaranty is to be performed, (iii) the law of the common state of domicile or place of business of the parties, or (iv) the law chosen or the law applicable under the general rule (as discussed below) would find the form of a guaranty valid, the guaranty is valid as to form under Louisiana choice-of-law rules.[77]

The second exception deals with capacity. A person is capable of entering into a contract, including a guaranty, if the law of either the state of that person's domicile at the time of making the contact or the law of the state applicable under the general rule (as discussed below) provides that the person has the capacity to enter into a contract.[78]

If the parties did not either expressly choose a law or clearly rely upon a law to govern the contract, then there is a general rule applicable to contracts, including guaranties. In that case, the law of the state whose policies would be most seriously impaired if its law were not applied would govern. This law is determined by comparing the relevant policies of the involved states in light of (i) the states where the contract was negotiated, formed, and performed as well as the domicile or place of business of the parties, (ii) the nature and purpose of the contract, and (iii) policies upholding expectations of the parties and promoting multistate commercial transactions.[79]

§ 8 Marital Property

A last and peculiar issue with regard to individual guaranties in Louisiana is the issue of community property where only one spouse guarantees the debt. Generally, this arises where one spouse owns/runs a business (usually an entity), that business gets a loan, and the spouse who runs the business guarantees the loan. The business then fails and the creditor wants to satisfy the debt out of the community property of both spouses.

Although this issue can be very complicated, and most likely will require an in-depth analysis of the particular factual scenario, there are some rules with which a lawyer should be familiar. The first is the difference between separate

76. La. Civ. Code art. 3540.
77. La. Civ. Code art. 3538.
78. La. Civ. Code art. 3538.
79. La. Civ. Code art. 3537.

and community property. Generally, separate property is property which one spouse owns before a marriage or which was acquired by inheritance during a marriage.[80] Community property is any property acquired during the marriage.[81] Each spouse owns a 50 percent undivided interest in community property.[82] Property is presumed to be community.[83] Ultimately, the issue is whether the obligation under a guaranty is community or separate, and can be satisfied out of community property. Obligations are separate if they arose before the community or are not for the common interest of the community.[84]

In the posited scenario, this issue will arise where the business entity is separate property of one of the spouses. Generally, the answer is yes—the obligation can be satisfied out of community property even though the obligation is a separate obligation, but there may be complications regarding reimbursement if the community has been terminated or is being terminated (i.e., a divorce has occurred or is pending).[85] This issue should be recognized by a lawyer for the creditor, but it should not ultimately be an issue for the creditor, particularly if the issue is dealt with at the inception of the guaranty. It may, however, complicate collection.

Conclusion

This chapter deals only generally with Louisiana law of suretyship. Most of the examples are simplified. Most matters arising under these laws are complicated, and should be examined on a case-by-case basis.

80. La. Civ. Code art. 2341.
81. La. Civ. Code art. 2338.
82. La. Civ. Code art. 2336.
83. La. Civ. Code art. 2340.
84. La. Civ. Code art. 2363. If the obligation is a community obligation, there is no issue satisfying it out of community property. Further, there is no issue satisfying a separate obligation out of separate property.
85. La. Civ. Code arts. 2364 and 2366.

Maine State Law of Guaranties

Mark K. Googins
Alistair Y. Raymond
Verrill Dana, LLP
One Portland Square
Portland, ME 04112
207-774-4000
207-774-7499 (Fax)
mgoogins@verrilldana.com
araymond@verrilldana.com
www.verrilldana.com

Verrill Dana LLP
Attorneys at Law

Christopher J. Devlin
Unum
2211 Congress Street, C474
Portland, ME 04122
207-575-4218
207-575-1296 (fax)
cdevlin@unum.com

unum®

Contents

Maine State Law of Guaranties

HIGHLIGHTS

- Maine's Improvident Transfers of Title Act renders potentially avoidable any guaranty given by an elderly (aged 60 or over), dependent person to or for the benefit of a person with whom the elderly person has a confidential or fiduciary relationship. Section 2.5.
- By Maine statute, if the obligated party has been notified of this restriction, no action may be maintained upon any agreement to lend money, extend credit, forbear from collection of a debt, or make any other accommodation for the repayment of a debt for more than $250,000 unless the promise, contract, or agreement on which the action is brought, or some memorandum or note of the promise, contract, or agreement is in writing and signed by the party to be charged, though Maine courts have not had occasion to decide whether the statute benefits guarantors in addition to borrowers. Sections 7.3.2 and 7.3.5.
- Maine's open-end mortgage statute allows a mortgagee to secure and maintain lien priority with respect to guaranty obligations, provided that the maximum amount of the guaranty obligation secured by the mortgage is stated in the mortgage. Section 15.2.

§ 1 Nature of the Guaranty Arrangement

Common law principles apply to guaranties in Maine, and are supplemented or modified, to the extent applicable, by provisions regarding suretyship and accommodation parties under the Maine Uniform Commercial Code (UCC).[1] Maine courts have cited to the RESTATEMENT (THIRD) OF SURETYSHIP AND GUARANTY as an authority for common law principles.[2]

A guaranty is a contract by which the guarantor agrees to be liable to the obligee for the debt of the primary obligor in the event the primary obligor defaults on the debt.[3] A guaranty is a separate and independent contract, distinct from the underlying primary debt.[4] Maine common law generally applies the same rules of construction to guaranties as are applied to other contracts.[5]

1. *See, e.g.*, 11 M.R.S.A. §§ 1-1201(39), 3-1419, 3-1605 (2011). Article 3-A of the Maine U.C.C. (Maine's revised Article 3) governs negotiable instruments, but typically does not apply to guaranties.
2. *See, e.g.*, John Nagle Co. v. Gokey, 2002 ME 101, ¶ 3, 799 A.2d 1225, 1227; MP Associates v. Liberty et al., 2001 ME 22, ¶ 25, 771 A.2d 1040.
3. *See* Guaranty, BLACK'S LAW DICTIONARY (9th ed. 2009).
4. Casco Northern Bank, N.A. v. Moore, 583 A.2d 697, 699 (Me. 1990); International Harvester Co. of America. v. Fleming, 109 Me. 104, 82 A. 843, 845 (1912).
5. Rosenthal v. Means, 388 A.2d 113, 114-15 (Me. 1987).

Consistent with Maine rules of contract construction, all writings that form a part of or pertain to a guaranty are read together to discern the intent of the parties, even if not all such writings are between the same parties.[6]

1.1 Guaranty Relationships

The guaranty is a collateral contract to the principal obligation and binds the parties to the guaranty.[7] Consequently, a creditor's right to enforce a guaranty against the guarantor is usually not contingent upon first bringing suit against the borrower or exercising rights against collateral for the underlying obligation.[8]

1.2 Other Suretyship Relationships

A party extending a guaranty is called a "guarantor" or "surety," and is sometimes referred to as the "secondary obligor" due to the guaranty's nature as a secondary obligation.[9] Although there is a technical distinction between sureties and guarantors (sureties typically share primary liability with the borrower while a guarantor is subject to secondary liability),[10] this distinction is frequently overlooked. Maine's UCC, for example, does not distinguish between the two.[11]

§ 2 State Law Requirements for an Entity to Enter a Guaranty

Business entities, including corporations, nonprofit corporations, limited liability companies (LLCs), and partnerships all may enter into contracts of guaranty or suretyship, provided that these contracts have been properly authorized and are not in violation of the entity's governing documents.

2.1 Corporations

Corporations are authorized to enter into contracts of guaranty or suretyship under the Maine Business Corporation Act, Title 13-C of the Maine Revised Statutes.[12] Maine nonprofit corporations also have statutory authorization to enter into such contracts.[13] These activities are, of course, subject to any restrictions in the corporation's articles of incorporation and bylaws. A guaranty by a corporation for the benefit of a director may be a "director

6. *Id.* at 115.
7. Top Line Distributors, Inc. v. Spickler, 525 A.2d 1039, 1040 (Me. 1987).
8. *See Casco Northern Bank, N.A.*, 583 A.2d at 699; *Top Line Distributors, Inc.*, 525 A.2d at 1040.
9. *MP Associates,* 2001 ME 22, ¶ 14, 771 A.2d 1040.
10. Read v. Cutts, 7 Me. 186, 189 (1831).
11. *See* 11 M.R.S.A. § 1-1201(39) (2011) (defining "surety" to mean a guarantor or other secondary liability).
12. 13-C M.R.S.A. § 302(7) (2011).
13. 13-B M.R.S.A. § 202(1)(K) (2011).

conflicting-interest transaction" under the Maine Business Corporation Act, and therefore subject to special approval requirements by disinterested directors or shareholders.[14]

After a person becomes a beneficial owner of 25 percent or more of the outstanding voting shares of a publicly owned Maine corporation (an "interested shareholder"), the corporation may not guaranty an obligation of the shareholder for five years, except under limited circumstances.[15] An exception is allowed if (i) prior to the date the person becomes an interested shareholder, the obligation is approved by the board of directors, or (ii) subsequent to the date the person becomes an interested shareholder, the obligation is approved by the board of directors and a majority of the voting shares not beneficially owned by the interested shareholder, any affiliate of the interested shareholder, or any person who is a director, officer, or employee of the corporation.[16] A corporation may be exempted from this restriction in its articles of incorporation.[17]

2.2 Partnerships

Maine law regarding the powers of partnerships, limited partnerships, and limited liability partnerships do not specifically authorize a partnership to issue a guaranty, although such authority is evidenced by examples in Maine case law.[18] A creditor may sue the partnership and, to the extent a partner is liable for the obligations of a partnership, a partner.[19] The circumstances under which a judgment creditor may levy execution against a partner's assets for the obligation of the partnership are defined by statute.[20]

2.3 Limited Liability Companies

Although the Maine Limited Liability Company Act does not specifically state the conditions under which an LLC may or may not issue a guaranty, Maine LLCs have the general power to "do all things necessary or convenient to carry on [their] activities."[21] The power of an LLC to issue a guaranty is subject to any restrictions within its operating agreement.

2.4 Maine-chartered Financial Institutions

Maine-chartered financial institutions may be organized as corporations, LLCs, limited partnerships, and limited liability partnerships.[22] Except as otherwise provided in Title 9-B of the Maine Revised Statutes (Maine's "Banking Code"),

14. 13-C M.R.S.A. §§ 871-874 (2011). For nonprofit corporations, *see* 13-B M.R.S.A. § 718 (2011).
15. 13-C M.R.S.A. § 1109 (2011).
16. 13-C M.R.S.A. § 1109(2) (2011).
17. 13-C M.R.S.A. § 1109(3)(B)(2011).
18. *See, e.g., MP Associates,* 2001 ME 22, 771 A.2d 1040.
19. 31 M.R.S.A. § 1035(1) (2011). Pursuant to 31 M.R.S.A. § 1034(1) (2011), partners are generally jointly and severally liable for the obligations of a partnership with specified exceptions.
20. 31 M.R.S.A. § 1035 (2011).
21. 31 M.R.S.A. § 1505 (2011).
22. *See* 9-B M.R.S.A. § 311 (2011).

a Maine-chartered financial institution is subject to the statutory provisions applicable to its form of business entity (e.g., Title 13-C for corporations; Title 31, chapter 21 for LLCs).[23]

The Maine Banking Code imposes restrictions on guaranties issued by financial institutions; these restrictions generally follow their counterparts under federal law. For example, with respect to guaranties issued on behalf of an affiliate, financial institutions are subject to certain market-condition standards, and may not issue a guaranty in excess of 10 percent of the institution's "total capital" for any one affiliate or 20 percent of the institution's total capital for all affiliates.[24] Similarly, a financial institution's liability for a guaranty on behalf of any one person cannot exceed 20 percent of the institution's total capital.[25]

2.5 Individuals

An individual must have legal capacity in order to issue a guaranty; lack of such capacity can be a legal defense against the enforcement of the guaranty.[26] Under the Maine Improvident Transfers of Title Act, a person who is both "elderly" and "dependent on other persons" and who was not represented by independent legal counsel may challenge the enforceability of a previously issued guaranty for the benefit of a primary obligor who is in a "confidential or fiduciary relationship" with the guarantor.[27] The statute defines "elderly" as 60 years old or older.[28] Such a guaranty is presumed to result from undue influence unless the elderly dependent person was represented in the transaction by "independent counsel," which is defined as "an attorney retained by the elderly dependent person to represent only that person's interests in the transfer."[29] If the beneficiary of the guaranty is unable to rebut the presumption of undue influence by a preponderance of the evidence, the elderly dependent person's remedies include rescission of the guaranty.[30]

Minors lack the capacity to enter into a contract under Maine law, and a contract with a minor is unenforceable unless ratified in writing after the minor has attained the age of 18.[31] There is a limited exception for minors who are at least 16 years of age for purposes of furthering a minor's "higher education in the professional, educational, scientific or literary fields."[32]

---

23. 9-B M.R.S.A. § 311 (2011).
24. 9-B M.R.S.A. § 468 (2011) (Maine's counterpart to Regulation W of the Federal Reserve, 12 C.F.R. Part 223).
25. 9-B M.R.S.A. § 439-A (2011); *see* 02-029 C.M.R. ch. 128, § 3(B) (2002).
26. *See, e.g.*, Gorham Sav. Bank v. MacDonald, 1998 ME 97, ¶ 12, 710 A.2d 916.
27. 33 M.R.S.A. §§ 1021-1025 (2011). The statute was amended to include guaranties from elderly persons after the decision in Gorham Savings Bank v. MacDonald, 710 A.2d 916, 921 (Me. 1998), which held that a guaranty made by an elderly person was outside the purview of the act.
28. 33 M.R.S.A. § 1021(2).
29. 33 M.R.S.A. §§ 1022(1), 1021(3).
30. 33 M.R.S.A. §§ 1023. *See* Key Bank v. Sargent, 758 A.2d 528, 536-37 (Me. 2000) (holding that where guaranty and mortgage securing same were alleged to have been obtained in violation of Improvident Transfers of Title Act, remedies included rescission of instrument, imposition of constructive trust, or order enjoining use or commanding return of property, but such remedies could not be granted against employee of bank who was not the transferee of the property, only against the bank that was the actual transferee of the property interest).
31. 33 M.R.S.A. § 52 (2011). Negotiable instruments are specifically identified as unenforceable against a minor. 11 M.R.S.A. § 3-1305 (2011).
32. *Id.*

Maine is not a community property state and assets constituting the property of a married guarantor are generally available to satisfy judgment against that guarantor without need for any spousal consent to the guaranty obligation.[33] Property held in joint tenancy by spouses, however, cannot be reached in its entirety by a judgment creditor. Rather, consistent with common law principles of joint tenancy, the creditor may reach only the debtor's interest in such property.[34]

Marital debts of divorcing spouses may be apportioned between them by a court using the same considerations used to divide marital property.[35] We are not aware of instances in which Maine courts have had occasion to rule on whether these principles would apply to guaranties made by a spouse. However, although a court may allocate responsibility for the payment of debt between spouses in a divorce case, it cannot affect the contractual relationship between the creditor and the spouse or spouses.[36]

§ 3 Signatory's Authority to Execute a Guaranty

3.1 Corporations

A creditor should review a corporation's governing documents (its articles of incorporation and bylaws) and the corporate authorizing resolutions to verify that a signatory is authorized to execute a guaranty on behalf of a corporation. Generally speaking, the authority of a corporation's officers is established by the bylaws, or to the extent consistent with the bylaws, by the board of directors or an officer authorized by the board to prescribe such authority.[37] Unless there is reason to believe otherwise, any person dealing with a corporation's president may assume that the president has authority to execute any contract within the ordinary course of the corporation's business.[38]

3.2 Partnerships

Under Maine's Uniform Partnership Act and Uniform Limited Partnership Act, a general partner acts as the agent of a partnership for purposes of carrying on its business.[39] Generally speaking, each general partner has apparent authority to act on behalf of a partnership in the ordinary course of its business, unless the partner lacked actual authority and the person dealing with the partner was aware of or received notice of such lack of authority.[40] A creditor should

33. *Cf.* Szelenyi v. Miller, 564 A.2d 768 (Me. 1989) (holding that assets that were the sole property of married judgment debtor, including the debtor's proportional ownership of jointly used bank accounts and jointly held real property, were available to satisfy judgment against him).
34. *Id.*
35. Arey v. Arey, 651 A.2d 351, 354 (Me. 1994); *see also* 19-A M.R.S.A. § 953 (2011).
36. Harriman v. Harriman, 1998 ME 108, ¶ 9, 710 A.2d 923 (1998).
37. 13-B M.R.S.A. § 842 (2011).
38. *Id.*
39. 31 M.R.S.A. §§ 1031 (general partnerships), 1352 (limited partnerships).
40. *Id.*

review the partnership agreement and authorizing resolutions when evaluating a partner's authority to bind the partnership.

3.3 Limited Liability Companies

The Maine Limited Liability Company Act was substantially revised in July 2011, with significant changes respecting the apparent authority of members and managers to act on behalf of an LLC. Under the prior Act, the apparent authority of members and managers was established in the articles of organization, with LLCs designated as either "member-managed" or "manager-managed." LLC's are no longer designated as member-managed or manager-managed; the apparent authority of a person to bind an LLC is determined by the existence or absence of a "statement of authority" filed with the Maine Secretary of State.[41]

A creditor should review an LLC's certificate of organization, operating agreement, and authorizing resolutions (to the extent authority is not granted in the operating agreement) to verify the authority of a person to bind the LLC to a guaranty. The authority of a person to act on behalf of an LLC is primarily governed by the LLC's operating agreement.[42] Generally speaking, a person has actual authority to bind an LLC to the extent: (i) authorized as an agent of the LLC, (ii) pursuant to the LLC's operating agreement, and (iii) authorized by the LLC's members.[43] Unless otherwise stated in the operating agreement, the unanimous consent of all members is required to authorize a transaction outside the ordinary course of an LLC's activities.[44]

A statement of authority filed with the Maine Secretary of State gives public notice of a specific person's authority to act for, bind, or otherwise enter into a transaction on behalf of an LLC.[45] Absent the filing of a statement of authority by the LLC, any manager, member, president, or treasurer of the LLC will have apparent authority to bind the LLC.[46] For Maine LLCs in existence on June 30, 2011, the articles of organization are deemed to constitute an LLC's statement of authority until amended by filing a new statement of authority.

3.4 Maine-chartered Financial Institutions

The authority of a person to execute a guaranty on behalf of a Maine financial institution will require a case-by-case analysis of the institution's governing documents. It should be noted, subject to certain exceptions, that guaranties, loans, or extensions of credit in excess of 10 percent of a financial institution's total capital must be approved by the institution's governing body or execu-

41. 31 M.R.S.A. § 1541(4) (2011).
42. 31 M.R.S.A. § 1521 (2011).
43. 31 M.R.S.A. § 1541 (2011).
44. 31 M.R.S.A. § 1556 (2011).
45. 31 M.R.S.A. §§ 1541(3), 1542 (2011). A person may file a "statement of denial" in response to a statement of authority, denying that person's authority to act on behalf of an LLC. M.R.S.A. § 1543 (2011).
46. 31 M.R.S.A. § 1541(4) (2011).

tive committee, and that such transactions with any one person in excess of 20 percent of total capital are prohibited.[47]

§ 4 Consideration; Sufficiency of Past Consideration

Maine generally follows common law contract principles with respect to guaranties, including with regard to the requirement of consideration. A guaranty is an independent contract distinct from the underlying primary obligation with a need for separate consideration.[48] Past consideration is not sufficient for a guaranty after the extension of a loan; some new form of consideration is generally required.[49] Maine case law supports the proposition that, when a guaranty is given at the time credit is extended and is an "essential ground of the credit," no separate consideration is needed other than the extension of credit itself.[50] The recital of "consideration of $1 and other valuable considerations" in the preamble to a guaranty is prima facie evidence that consideration considered sufficient by the guarantor was in fact received.[51]

A guarantor must receive "reasonably equivalent value" in exchange for a guaranty, and the issue of consideration is evident in the case of "upstream guaranties," or guaranties made by a subsidiary to secure a parent's or principal's obligation. Although there is rarely a question of consideration when a parent company or principal guaranties the obligations of a wholly owned subsidiary (a "downstream guaranty"), a fraudulent conveyance claim may arise in connection with an upstream guaranty.[52] A similar concern may arise with the guaranty by a subsidiary of the obligations of a separate subsidiary owned by the same parent (a "sidestream guaranty").

§ 5 Notice of Acceptance

Under guaranty law, generally, the obligee must notify the guarantor of its acceptance of the guaranty within a reasonable time. In Maine, this rule has particular force in the case of continuing guaranties, since acceptance allows the guarantor to ascertain the amount of his liability and to seek indemnification or other security from the primary obligor.[53] Exceptions to this requirement exist when (1) valuable consideration moves directly or indirectly to

---

47. 9-B M.R.S.A. § 439-A (2011); 02-029 C.M.R. ch.128 (1992).
48. *Read,* 7 Me. at 190.
49. Ware v. Adams, 24 Me. 177, 179 (1844).
50. *See, e.g.*, International Harvester Co., 109 Me. 104, 82 A. 843 ; Gillighan v. Boardman, 29 Me. 79 (1848).
51. Pyrofax Gas Corp. v. Consumers Gas Co., 151 Me. 172, 176, 116 A.2d 661, 662-63 (1955).
52. *See* In re Kennebago Corporation, 50 B.R. 153, 157 (Bankr. D. Me. 1985) (determining that note and mortgage executed by subsidiary to secure loan to 90 percent shareholder were void for lack of consideration).
53. Tuckerman v. French, 7 Me. 115, 116-17 (1830) ("There is always an implied condition that notice shall be given by the vendor, who gives credit to a third person on the strength of a guaranty, that such guaranty has been accepted, and such notice must be given in a reasonable time, so that the guarantor may know the fact of his liability.")

the guarantor, (2) the guaranty is made at the creditor's request, or (3) the agreement to accept, or the contract guaranteed, is contemporaneous with the guaranty.[54] What constitutes a reasonable time period for communicating acceptance varies from case to case.[55]

Commonly, the guaranty agreement is drafted to require the guarantor to waive the notification of acceptance requirement.

§ 6 Interpretation of Guaranties

6.1 General Principles

Though earlier Maine decisions indicate that the guarantor is a "favorite of the law" whose contract will be construed in his favor,[56] recent cases, without expressing an intention to depart from the rule of *strictissimi juris*, state that the guaranty is a contract governed by the same rules of construction applicable to other contracts.[57]

The guaranty will be construed together with other instruments that are executed at the same time, by the same contracting parties, for the same purpose, and in the course of the same transaction.[58] However, the undertaking of a guarantor is his own separate and independent contract, distinct from the primary obligor.[59]

6.2 Choice of Law

Maine courts look to Sections 186 to 188 of the RESTATEMENT (SECOND) OF CONFLICT OF LAWS (1971) for purposes of determining a contract's governing law.[60] If a contract contains a choice-of-law provision, pursuant to Section 187(2) of the RESTATEMENT (SECOND), the law chosen by the parties will be given effect unless either:

54. American Agricultural Chemical Co. v. Ellsworth, 109 Me. 195, 83 A. 546, 547 (1912). The case derives these exceptions from Davis v. Wells, 104 U.S. 159, 166 (1881). The first exception to the general rule requiring notice, that valuable consideration moves directly or indirectly to the guarantor, was found present in Westchester Fire Insurance Co. v. Campbell, 55 F.3d 32 (1st Cir. 1995), where the guarantor was found to have benefitted from a surety's execution of the bond that was the subject to the guaranty.
55. Howe v. Nickels, 22 Me. 175, 175 (1842).
56. Foster, State Treasurer v. Kerr & Houston, Inc., 133 Me. 389, 179 A. 297, 300 (1935) (distinguishing between the "individual or voluntary" guarantor, in whose favor all contractual doubts and technicalities are to be resolved, and the compensated surety providing a bond for profit motives, whose guaranty is not to be interpreted under the rule of *strictissimi juris*). *Accord* Carpenter v. Susi, 152 Me. 1, 6, 121 A.2d 336, 338-39 (1956). *But see* Clark v. Anderson, 123 Me. 165, 122 A. 337, 337 (1923) ("[I]n case of ambiguity the language is construed most strongly against the guarantor[.]")
57. Bumila v. Keiser Homes of Maine, Inc., 1997 ME 139, ¶ 12, 696 A.2d 1091(citing Rosenthal v. Means, 388 A.2d 113,114 (Me. 1978)).
58. Handy Boat Service, Inc. v. Professional Services, Inc., 1998 ME 134, ¶ 7, 711 A.2d 1306.
59. *Top Line Distributors,* 525 A.2d at 1040. This means that the obligee is entitled to attachment and other relief against a guarantor without discounting for the value of the collateral provided by the borrower since the borrower collateral secures only the borrower's separate obligation. *Casco Northern Bank, N.A.,* 583 A.2d at 698.
60. State Farm Mut. Auto. Ins. Co. v. Koshy, 2010 ME 44, ¶ 46, 995 A.2d 651, 666.

(a) the chosen state has no substantial relationship to the parties or the transaction and there is no other reasonable basis for the parties' choice, or

(b) the application of the law of the chosen state would be contrary to the fundamental policy of a state which has a materially greater interest than the chosen state in the determination of the particular issue . . . .[61]

In the event a contract does not include a choice-of-law provision, Section 188 of the RESTATEMENT (SECOND) will be used to determine the applicable law. Under Section 188, the rights and obligations of the parties to a contract will be "determined by the local law of the state which, with respect to that issue, has the most significant relationship to the transaction and the parties..."[62] In making this determination, the following factors will be considered according to their relative importance with respect to the particular issue: (a) the place of contracting, (b) the place of negotiation of the contract, (c) the place of performance, (d) the location of the subject matter of the contract, and (e) the domicile, residence, nationality, place of incorporation, and place of business of the parties.[63]

6.3 Guaranty of Payment versus Guaranty of Collection

Maine cases have not spoken in terms of guaranties of payment and collection, but have looked to the guaranty contract to determine whether conditions are imposed on the guarantor's liability. If the guaranty is absolute by its terms, no notice of demand or dishonor[64] and no collection efforts against the primary obligor[65] are necessary to enforcement of the guaranty. In contrast, where the guaranty is drawn to condition the guarantor's liability on the obligee having first undertaken specified collection efforts, those efforts must precede action on the guaranty.[66]

6.4 Language Regarding the Revocation of Guaranties

A guaranty that is by its terms revocable at the guarantor's instance will be construed to give some purpose to the guaranty transaction and to honor the apparent intention of the parties entering into it, and such a guaranty has there-

61. Schroeder v. Rynel, Ltd. Inc., 1998 ME 259, ¶ 8, 720 A.2d 1164, 1166 (adopting Section 187(2) of the RESTATEMENT (SECOND) OF CONFLICT OF LAWS).
62. *State Farm Mut. Auto. Ins. Co.*, 2010 ME 44, ¶ 47, 995 A.2d 651 (citing Section 188 of the RESTATEMENT (SECOND) OF CONFLICT OF LAWS).
63. *Id.*
64. *Read,* 7 Me. at 190-94 (Where underlying debt was fully due at time guaranty was made, and agreement to pay same was expressed as absolute, no demand on the primary obligor or notice to the guarantor of nonpayment were held necessary prior to enforcement of guaranty.).
65. Prentiss v. Garland, 64 Me. 155, 156 (1875).
66. Hills v. Gardiner Savings Institution, 309 A.2d 877, 880 (Me. 1973) (The guarantor's liability is expressly conditioned on obligee applying to underlying obligation proceeds of collateral therefor and on obligee giving guarantor an opportunity to purchase documents evidencing and securing underlying obligation.). *See also Gillighan,* 29 Me. at 82 (1848) (The return of execution as unsatisfied followed by bankruptcy of primary obligor were sufficient, without further action or notice, to satisfy condition that guarantor would be accountable for the underlying obligation if it could not be collected from the primary obligor "after they have obtained execution against him.").

fore been found revocable only as to obligations incurred after revocation, but not as to existing obligations.[67]

Likewise, a "continuing" guaranty (i.e., one that applies to all future obligations of the primary obligor to the obligee) may be terminated with regard to future liability upon notice, but the termination will not be effective as to liabilities incurred by the primary obligor prior to the revocation.[68]

6.5 "Continuing"

Maine courts have not had occasion to construe the term "continuing," but have characterized guaranties as continuing where the guarantor agrees to be a secondary obligor for all future obligations of the primary obligor to the obligee.[69] In doing this, the Maine cases have relied on the definition of continuing guaranty that is contained in the RESTATEMENT (THIRD) OF SURETYSHIP AND GUARANTY § 16.[70] Where, however, the guaranty does not clearly extend to all future liabilities of the primary obligor, no continuing liability will be found.[71]

6.6 "Absolute and Unconditional"

Maine courts have not had occasion to construe the terms "absolute" or "unconditional" in a guaranty agreement. [72]

6.7 "Liable as a Primary Obligor and not Merely as Surety"

Maine courts have not had occasion to construe the phrase "liable as a primary obligor and not merely as surety" in a guaranty agreement.

§ 7 Defenses of the Guarantor; Set-off

The defenses that may be available to a guarantor can be grouped into 3 categories: (1) defenses of the primary obligor; (2) "suretyship defenses"; and (3) other defenses.

67. *Clark*, 123 Me. 165, 122 A. at 337-38 (A guaranty of trade indebtedness and of any notes evidencing same, which allowed for guarantor's withdrawal of his obligation by notice, would be construed to make withdrawal effective only as to renewals of notes made after receipt of notice, but not as to notes then outstanding.).
68. *John Nagle Co.*, 2002 ME 101, ¶ 3, 799 A.2d 1225 (adopting the rule of the RESTATEMENT (THIRD) OF SURETYSHIP AND GUARANTY § 16 (1996)).
69. *John Nagle Co.*, 2002 ME 101, ¶¶ 3-4, 799 A.2d 1225; *accord* Tuckerman, 7 Me. at 117.
70. *John Nagle Co.*, 2002 ME 101, ¶ 3, 799 A.2d 1225.
71. Knowlton v. Hersey, 76 Me. 345, 346 (1884).
72. On a related topic, nineteenth century Maine cases have considered the circumstances under which a guarantor is absolutely liable for the underlying obligation. Irish v. Cutter, 31 Me. 536, 536 (1850) (If the endorser agrees to be "holden" on the endorsed note, he is an absolute guarantor.). *Accord* Blanchard v. Wood, 26 Me. 358, 369-60 (Me. 1846). Guarantors have also been characterized as absolute where no conditions are attached to the effectiveness of their agreement to pay the underlying obligation. *Gillighan,* 29 Me. 79 (1848); *accord Read,* 7 Me. 186 (1831) (The guaranty is absolute where the agreement is framed as an outright agreement to pay an underlying obligation that has already come due at the time the guaranty is given.).

7.1 Defenses of the Primary Obligor

7.1.1 General

While the general rule in Maine is that the guarantor, absent an effective waiver,[73] is not bound to perform if the primary obligor is not bound,[74] a guarantor sued alone may not raise defenses or counterclaims, such as negligence in performance of a contract, that are personal to the primary obligor.[75] If the defense or counterclaim is one that belongs to the primary obligor, it may be adjudicated in an action on the guaranty only if the primary obligor is made a party to the action or has assigned the claim to the guarantor.[76]

7.1.2 When Guarantor may Assert Primary Obligor's Defense

A guarantor may assert the defenses of the primary obligor against the obligee where (1) the guarantor has taken an assignment of the claim or the principal has consented to the surety's use of the claim, (2) both principal and surety are joined as defendants, or (3) the principal is insolvent. [77]

7.1.3 Defenses that may not be Raised by Guarantor

The federal bankruptcy court sitting in Maine has held that confirmation of a reorganization plan under the federal bankruptcy laws, by which the obligations of the primary obligor were restructured, did not cure the primary obligor's default of the underlying obligation so as to constitute a defense against enforcement of the guaranty.[78]

Further, because the guaranty is a separate contract from that giving rise to the underlying obligation, the lapse of the statute of limitations with respect to the underlying obligation will not bar suit on the guaranty.[79]

7.1.4 Defenses that may Always be Raised by Guarantor

Payment of the underlying obligation may be raised by the guarantor as a defense on its guaranty.[80]

---

73. Ford Motor Credit Co. v. Moore, 663 A.2d 30, 32 (Me. 1995) (upholding as valid a waiver of "any defense arising by reason of any disability or other defense of [primary obligor] or by reason of the cessation from any cause whatsoever of the liability of [primary obligor])."
74. Huntress v. Patten, 20 Me. 28, 34 (1841) (Where underling obligation is tainted with usury, guarantor may prove it to be illegal "as well as defective in any other manner to prevent a recovery in part or in the whole.").
75. F.A. Rumery Co. v. Merrill Trust Co., 127 Me. 298, 143 A. 54, 54-55 (1928).
76. *Id.*
77. *Id.* The Maine cases have not developed these rules and the *F.A. Rumery* decision relies in formulating them on cases from other jurisdictions.
78. F.D.I.C. v. LaPierre, 144 B.R. 581, 584-85 (Bankr. D. Me. 1992).
79. *Top Line Distributors,* 525 A.2d at 1040; *accord* Bunker v. Ireland, 81 Me. 519, 17 A. 706 (1889).
80. *Bunker,* 81 Me. 519, 17 A.706 (containing dicta to the effect that payment of note would constitute good defense to guarantor). Acceptance by the creditor of promissory notes from the primary obligor for the latter's trade debt is prima facie evidence of satisfaction of the debt, which may, however, be rebutted by evidence showing a contrary intention. Spitz v. Morse, 104 Me. 447, 72 A. 178, 180 (1908).

7.2 "Suretyship" Defenses

7.2.1 Change in Identity of Primary Obligor

Maine courts have not had occasion to construe the effect of a change in identity of the primary obligor on the guarantor's liability.

7.2.2 Modification of the Underlying Obligation, Including Release

Under Maine law, a material alteration in the underlying obligation, when that alteration is made after the execution of the guaranty contract and without the consent of the guarantor, discharges the guarantor if the material alteration injures the interest of the guarantor.[81] Mere formal changes in the underlying obligation will, however, not operate to relieve a guarantor, particularly when combined with broad waivers of suretyship defenses.[82]

7.2.3 Release or Impairment of Security for the Underlying Obligation

The obligee's surrender or impairment of collateral security without the assent of the guarantor will discharge the guarantor from liability to the extent of the value of the collateral released.[83] This is so because the guarantor is entitled to be subrogated to all the rights and securities of the obligee and such surrender or impairment deprives the guarantor of its means of reimbursement.[84]
The guarantor may waive in advance its defense based on the release or impairment of collateral under Section 3-605 (codified as Section 3-1605) of Maine's UCC.[85]

---

81. Bumila, 1997 ME 139, ¶ 14, 696 A.2d 1091. *See also* Maine Nat. Bank v. Fontaine, 456 A.2d 1273, 1275 (Me. 1983) ("[I]f at the time the surety consents to the extension of time, a creditor knows of facts which the creditor has reason to believe are unknown to the surety, which materially increase the risk beyond the point that the creditor had reason to believe the surety intended to assume, and which the creditor had a reasonable opportunity to communicate to the surety, failure on the part of the creditor to notify the surety of such facts is a defense to the surety.") The modern trend as expressed in *Bumila, supra,* is to relieve only the guarantor who is actually harmed by the modification, but older Maine cases show some inconsistency on the need for injury to the guarantor. *Compare Gillighan,* 29 Me. at 82 ("[A] guarantor is not discharged by proof of negligence and laches, when it appears, that he has not thereby suffered any loss or injury.") *with* Lime Rock Bank v. Mallett, 34 Me. 547, 549 (1852) (Where creditor extends time for payment of principal loan without consent of surety, surety is discharged without proof of prejudice or damage, even where surety agreed to earlier extensions.).
Whether a guarantor consented to a modification is a question of fact. *See* Pokroisky v. Potter, 129 Me. 70, 149 A. 806, 807 (1930); Westbrook Trust Co. v. Timberlake, 121 Me. 64, 115 A. 555 (Me. 1921).
82. *Compare Bumila,* 1997 ME 139, ¶ 15, 696 A.2d 1091 (finding that the change in identity of obligee from individual to his affiliated trust was not a material change resulting in discharge of guarantor) *with* Granite Bank v. Ellis, 43 Me. 367 (1857) (finding that the change in obligee from bank to unrelated private party resulted in discharge of sureties).
83. Cummings v. Little, 45 Me. 183, 188-89 (1858).
84. *Id.* at 187.
85. 11 M.R.S.A. § 3-1605(9)(b). The Federal District Court for the District of Maine also upheld the effectiveness of express waivers of defenses based on release or impairment of collateral under the predecessor section of the Maine UCC, 11 M.R.S.A. § 3-1606. U.S. v. H & S Realty, 647 F. Supp. 1415, 1421-23 (D. Me. 1986), *aff'd* 837 F.2d 1 (1st Cir. 1987) (waiver of release or impairment defense does not violate commercial reasonableness requirement of section 9-504(3)).

7.3 Other Defenses

7.3.1 *Failure to Fulfill a Condition Precedent*

As noted in Section 6.2 above, Maine courts have recognized that no action may lie on a guaranty that places conditions on the guarantor's liability until those conditions have been satisfied.[86] It is a sufficient basis for establishing liability on a guaranty that the condition be satisfied in substance, and literal compliance has not been required.[87]

7.3.2 *Modification of the Guaranty*

Maine statutory law provides that, if the obligated party has been notified of this restriction, no action may be maintained upon any agreement to lend money, extend credit, forbear from collection of a debt, or make any other accommodation for the repayment of a debt for more than $250,000 unless the promise, contract, or agreement on which the action is brought, or some memorandum or note of the promise, contract, or agreement is in writing and signed by the party to be charged,[88] but the statute prohibits such action only by a "borrower," and Maine courts have not had occasion to decide whether the statute applies to guarantors.

7.3.3 *Failure to Pursue Primary Obligor*

Whether the obligee may recover against the guarantor without first pursuing the primary obligor will be determined by the terms of the guaranty, with pursuit being unnecessary where the guaranty is absolute and not conditioned on demand or suit against the primary obligor,[89] and pursuit being required

86. *Gillighan,* 29 Me. at 81-82 (Condition in guaranty that guarantor would be accountable for the underlying obligation if it could not be collected of the primary obligor "after they have obtained execution against him" was satisfied upon proof that execution against the primary obligor was returned unsatisfied and that primary obligor was bankrupt). *Gillighan* distinguished between absolute yet conditional guaranties such as the one there at bar, and those that become binding only upon notice of acceptance by the obligee and of the obligee's extension of credit on the strength of the guaranty. *Id.* Case law in a related context would allow parol evidence of oral conditions to payment of a promissory note. Rogers v. Jackson, 2002 ME 140, 804 A.2d 379. The note at issue in *Rogers* included express payment terms, but the maker claimed that there existed an oral agreement that no payment would be required unless or until he had available cash for that purpose. The Maine Law Court, over a strongly worded dissent, permitted introduction of parol evidence of the oral agreement on the grounds that, even if the note were fully integrated, the oral condition was not inconsistent with the express payment terms of the note since "the condition, as a term of the larger agreement of which the promissory note is but one part, prevents [maker's] payment obligation under the note from coming into effect until such time as he can afford to *pay." Id. at* ¶ 11.

87. Castner v. Slater, 50 Me. 212 (1861) (holding that where guarantor agreed to be accountable for primary obligation upon receipt from the guarantor's attorney of funds representing an inheritance, the condition would be deemed satisfied upon proof that attorney had given guarantor's son a note for the amount of the inheritance in connection with the guarantor's submission of a receipt for the funds to the probate court, since giving the note to the son with the consent of the father as manifested by his receipt was tantamount to payment of inheritance by attorney to guarantor).

88. 10 M.R.S.A. § 1146 (2009).

89. *Read,* 7 Me. at 192 (holding that where note was already due at the time guaranty was given, "nothing was required to be done to perfect the payee's rights against the promissor"); *Prentiss, 64* Me. at 155 (holding that no pursuit of primary obligor was required where bringing of suit against primary obligor was not made a condition precedent to enforcement of guarantor's liability).

where the guarantor's liability is conditioned on the primary obligor's non-performance.[90]

See also sections 6.2 and 7.3.1, above.

7.3.4 Statute of Limitations

Maine statute imposes a six-year statute of limitations on contractual obligations, with certain exceptions.[91] One such exception applies to contracts for the sale of goods that are governed by Article 2 of the Maine UCC, which imposes a four-year statute of limitations,[92] and another is made for contracts or liabilities under seal, to which a 20- year limitations period applies.[93] Maine courts have not had occasion to determine the applicability of either exception to guaranties, though most Maine forms of commercial guaranty recite that they are made under seal. Likewise, Maine cases and statute have not addressed the circumstances under which a contractual waiver of the limitations period applicable to guaranties will be given effect.[94]

7.3.5 Statute of Frauds

Maine statutory law provides that no action shall be maintained to charge any person upon any special promise to answer for the debt, default or misdoings of another unless the promise, contract or agreement on which such action is brought, or some memorandum or note thereof, is in writing and signed by the party to be charged therewith, or by some person thereunto lawfully authorized.[95] Agreements of guaranty are thus within the statute unless removed by an exception.[96]

---

90. Globe Bank v. Small, 25 Me. 366, 369-70 (1845) (Demand on primary obligor is necessary where guarantor's agreement was that primary obligors would "pay as they were bound to do; and not that he himself would pay, without regard to whether they did so or not.").
91. 14 M.R.S.A. § 752 (2011).
92. 11 M.R.S.A. § 2-725 (2011). Of course, a different statute of limitations may apply to loans governed by federal law, such as those guaranteed by the Small Business Administration. *See* United States v. Hanson, 649 F. Supp. 100, 104-105 (D. Me. 1985).
93. The 20-year period applies both to contracts and liabilities under seal and to promissory notes signed in the presence of an attesting witness. The requirements of a seal and attesting witness are disjunctive, so it may be that either feature will earn the 20-year period, though Maine courts have not addressed the issue squarely. *See* Fleet Nat'l Bank v. Liberty, 2004 ME 36, ¶ 2, 845 A.2d 1183 (applying 20-year limitations period to promissory notes on the strength merely of attestation, without discussion of status of notes as sealed instruments). A formula for compliance with the seal requirement is provided by statute. 1 M.R.S.A. §72 (26-B) (Supp. 2011). For a document to be under seal, the seal must be that of the signer of the instrument. Lloyd v. Robbins, 2010 ME 59, ¶ 13, 997 A.2d 733, 739. In *Lloyd*, a deed was delivered that contained no recital as to its status as a sealed document, but only included the word "seal" as part of the notarial block. A notarial seal, the court held, "does not render a document under seal for purposes of 14 M.R.S. §751 because the seal of office belonging to a notary public is not the personal seal of the individual signing the document." *Lloyd*, 2010 ME 59, ¶ 14, 997 A.2d 733.
94. Maine cases have stressed in other contexts the need for any waiver of a limitations period to be a clear and deliberate act, done with full knowledge of the rights waived. *See* Burpee v. Town of Houlton, 156 Me. 487, 496, 166 A.2d 473, 477 (1960) (analyzing whether insurance company's payment of claimant's medical expenses resulted in waiver of limitations period). The statute of limitations is not jurisdictional, but is an affirmative defense that may be waived after the action is commenced. Bellegarde Custom Kitchens v. Leavitt, 295 A.2d 909, 912 (1972).
95. 33 M.R.S.A. § 51 (2011).
96. Todd v. Tobey, 29 Me. 219 (Me. 1848) (holding that a promise to pay debt of another that would normally come under the statute of frauds is removed from statute where promise arises out of new and original consideration moving between the newly-contracting parties).

As noted in Section 7.3.2 above, statute of frauds-type protection is also offered by statute with respect to indebtedness of more than $250,000 if the statutory condition is satisfied, though the statute expressly prohibits action only by a "borrower."

Outside the context of commercial guaranty agreements, the Maine cases have observed that the statute serves primarily an evidentiary function, and that a party may waive the protection of the statute, admit verbal evidence of the contract, and become bound by it.[97] As a result, a party's admission of all the facts necessary to establish an oral agreement will render a contract otherwise within the statute of frauds enforceable against that party.[98]

7.3.6 Defenses Particular to Guarantors that are Natural Persons and their Spouses

As discussed in Section 2.5 above, Maine's Improvident Transfers of Title Act[99] renders potentially avoidable any guaranty given by an elderly, dependent person to or for the benefit of a person with whom the elderly person has a confidential or fiduciary relationship.

Maine courts have invalidated guaranties obtained from a borrower's spouse in violation of the federal Equal Credit Opportunity Act, 15 U.S.C.§1691-1691f (ECOA), which prohibits discrimination on the basis of race, color, national origin, sex, or marital status in any credit transaction.[100] Thus, where a mortgage on the marital home secured both the husband's note and the wife's guaranty that had been obtained in violation of ECOA, the mortgage was held invalid to the extent it secured the spousal guaranty and the mortgagee was allowed to foreclose only on the husband's one-half interest in the property.[101] Maine courts or the federal court sitting in Maine have further held that the two-year statute of limitations applicable to ECOA actions does not apply to defensive use of ECOA in recoupment claims or in making a counterclaim based on ECOA.[102]

---

97. Dehahn v. Innes, 356 A.2d 711, 717-18 (Me. 1976).
98. Mercier v. Town of Fairfield, 628 A.2d 1053, 1055 (Me. 1993) (involving an employment contract); *accord Dehahn*, 356 A.2d at 717-18 (involving a land contract).
99. 33 M.R.S.A. §§ 1021- 1025 (1999 & Supp. 2011).
100. *See also* 12 C.F.R. § 202.7 (2011). Even if a guaranty is obtained in violation of ECOA, however, it does not bar contributions rights among coguarantors who are not "creditors" within the meaning of the act. Spottiswoode v. Levine, 730 A.2d 166, 172-73 (Me. 1999). Maine has a law similar to ECOA that makes unlawful the refusal to extend credit to a person based solely on the person's ancestry, religion, marital status, or sexual orientation. 5 M.R.S.A. § 4595 *et seq.* (2011).
101. Calaska Partners Ltd. v. Corson, 672 A.2d 1099, 1104-05 (Me. 1996).
102. *See, e.g.*, F.D.I.C. v. Notis, 602 A.2d 1164, 1166 (Me. 1992) (excluding recoupment from the bar of statute of limitations); Macias Savings Bank v. Ramsdell, 1997 ME 20, 689 A.2d 595. *See also* Chittenden Trust Co. v. Cabot, 2004 WL 2287763 (D. Me. Oct. 12, 2004) (finding that ECOA may be raised as counterclaim to action on guaranty even after two-year statute of limitations has passed).

7.4 Right of Set-off

Maine law recognizes the defenses of setoff and recoupment generally,[103] but in the context of guaranty agreements has not had occasion to develop parameters to their use, stating only that recoupment may be asserted defensively in an action on a guaranty[104] and cautioning that claims of the primary obligor may not be set-off by the guarantor or recoupment be had in an action against the guarantor unless the principal is also made a party to the action or has assigned its claim to the guarantor.[105]

7.5 Fraud

Fraud in the inducement constitutes a defense on a guaranty even without proof of damage resulting from the fraud.[106] In such a case, the guaranty may be made void at the behest of the guarantor.[107] The misrepresentation by which the guaranty is obtained must, of course, be material.[108]

Even if one coguarantor was induced to join in a guaranty by fraud, such defense will not be available to cosureties unless the signature of the former was a condition by which to obtain that of the latter.[109]

§ 8 Waiver of Defenses by the Guarantor

8.1 Defenses that cannot be Waived

Revised Article 9 of the UCC as enacted in the State of Maine requires that notice of disposition of collateral be given to guarantors of the secured underlying obligation[110] and extends to guarantors the secured party's obligation to conduct a commercially reasonable sale of the collateral.[111] Neither right may be waived in advance of default[112] but post-default waivers of the right to notice of disposition are permitted.[113]

103. *See generally* Inniss v. Methot Buick-Opel, Inc., 506 A.2d 212, 217 (Me. 1986) ("A 'set-off' is a demand that the defendant has against the plaintiff arising out of a transaction extrinsic to the plaintiff's cause of action whereas a 'recoupment' is a reduction of part of the plaintiff's damages because of a right in the defendant arising out of the same transaction.").
104. F.D.I.C. v. Notis, 602 A.2d at 1166 (recognizing availability of recoupment defense based on ECOA in action on guaranty); *accord Machias Savings Bank*, 1997 ME 20, 689 A.2d 595.
105. *F.A. Rumery Co.*, 127 Me. at 298, 143 A. at 54-55 ("[A] claim by the principal for damages for a breach of contract cannot be set off by the guarantor, or a recoupment be had in an action at law against the guarantor alone.")
106. Kuperman v. Eiras, 586 A.2d 1260, 1262 (Me. 1991).
107. *Id.*
108. Franklin Bank v. Stevens, 39 Me. 532, 539 (1855) ("If there be any misrepresentation or concealment in relation to any material part of the transaction to induce the surety to enter into the obligation, the contract will be void.").
109. *Id.*, at 541.
110. 11 M.R.S.A. § 9-1611(3)(b) (Supp. 2011). *See also* Fitallis v. North America v. Hill, 650 A.2d 222 (Me. 1994) (finding that guarantor is entitled to notice of disposition under prerevised Article 9 as accommodation party).
111. 11 M.R.S.A. § 9-1610(2) (Supp. 2011).
112. 11 M.R.S.A. § 9-1602(7) (Supp. 2011).
113. 11 M.R.S.A. § 9-1625(1) (Supp. 2011). The right to commercially reasonable disposition may not be waived, though prerevised Article 9 cases have permitted waiver where the guarantor manifested by written waiver an intent not to rely on the collateral. H & S Realty, 647 F. Supp. at 1421-23.

Maine courts have also expressed the principle that waivers of rights will not be permitted if they violate public policy,[114] but have not found such violations in cases involving guaranties.

8.2 "Catch-all" Waivers

Although Maine courts have not had occasion to determine the general enforceability of blanket waivers of suretyship defenses, they have upheld broad waivers as effective to defeat even defenses that were not addressed with particularity in the waiver.[115] Thus, where guarantors waived, among other matters, "notice of any loans made, extensions granted, or other action taken in reliance hereon" and assented to "renewal, extension or postponement of the time for payment or any other indulgence...." the court held the waiver effective to withstand the claim that the guarantors were discharged by a change in the identity of the obligee on the underlying obligation.[116] The court found that the broad waiver indicated an intention to give the obligee and primary obligor considerable latitude in administering the underlying obligation and that the guaranty would be read to honor these intentions.[117]

8.3 Use of Specific Waivers

Cases decided by Maine courts or federal courts sitting in Maine have given effect to specific waivers of demand and notice[118] and of subrogation rights.[119]

§ 9 Third-party Pledgors—Defenses and Waiver Thereof

Maine courts have not had occasion to directly address whether the law as applied to sureties would also apply to third-party pledgors. However, case law suggests that a pledge of collateral affords the pledgor defenses similar to those of a guarantor,[120] given that, to the extent of the pledge, the pledgor stands in the position of surety to the primary obligor.[121]

114. *Ford Motor Credit Co.*, 663 A.2d at32.
115. *Bumila*, 696 A.2d 1091 (1997). *See also Ford Motor Credit Co.*, 663 A.2d 30 (holding that waiver of defenses arising by reason of disability or other defense of lessee or by reason of the cessation of liability of lessee operated to defeat claim that guarantors were discharged by obligee's failure to accept collateral in satisfaction of underlying obligation).
116. *Bumila*, 696 A.2d at 1094.
117. *Id.*
118. Gilman v. Lewis, 15 Me. 452, 454 (1839).
119. Duhamel v. Turner, 334 B.R. 483, 485-86 (Bankr. D. Me. 2005).
120. *See, e.g.*, Matthews v. Matthews, 128 Me. 495, ¶ 6-9, 148 A. 796 (1930) (holding that a person who furnished collateral to secure the loan of another stands in the relation of surety to the one accommodated and may compel him to exonerate him or his property from liability by payment of the debt); Key Bank, N.A. v. Mott, 1998 ME 151, 712 A.2d 1064 (holding that a wife, as a party to a mortgage with her husband, could avail herself of the affirmative defense of recoupment provided that she had not authorized a post-mortgage note representing the advancement of new funds to her husband).
121. *Cf* True v. Harding, 12 Me. 193 (1853) (characterizing as a guaranty an agreement to secure a note with real estate).

§ 10 Jointly and Severally Liable Guarantors—Contribution and Reduction of Obligations upon Payment by a Co-obligor

The use of "joint and several" language in written guaranties executed by multiple guarantors indicates an intent that the guaranties be considered as one agreement.[122] Guarantors who are jointly and severally liable for an obligation are presumed to share the obligation equally.[123] In enforcing its rights under a guaranty, a creditor may attach the property of each guarantor in the full amount of the obligation, without discounting for the value of property attached from other guarantors.[124]

10.1 Contribution

Absent an express agreement to the contrary, guarantors have a right of contribution against coguarantors, under a theory of implied contract.[125] The right of contribution cannot be waived by implication.[126] There is a presumption that coguarantors have received equal benefit from a guaranty and must therefore contribute equally, although this presumption is subject to rebuttal based on a showing of the inequality of benefits received.[127]

10.2 Reduction of Obligations upon Payment of Co-obligor

Where one of several cosureties has made payment to an obligee, the cosurety may seek reimbursements from nonpaying cosureties and the primary obligor.[128] Although modern Maine cases have not addressed the matter, early Maine cases support the general principle that a nonpaying cosurety is liable to a paying cosurety for his or her proportion, or moiety, of the amount paid, to the extent the paying cosurety has not been reimbursed by the primary obligor.[129]

---

122. Kandlis v. Huotari, 678 A.2d 41, 43 (Me. 1996).
123. *Kandlis*, 678 A.2d at 43; Chase Commercial Corp. v. Hamilton & Son, 473 A.2d 1281 (Me. 1984).
124. *Chase Commercial Corp.*, 473 A.2d at 1284.
125. Spottiswoode v. Levine, 1999 ME 79, ¶ 19, 730 A.2d 166; *Kandlis,* 678 A.2d at 45.
126. *Kandlis*, 678 A.2d at 45.
127. *Spottiswoode,* 1999 ME 79, ¶ 19, 730 A.2d 166.
128. *See, e.g.,* Gould v. Fuller, 18 Me. 364, 366-67 (1841) (Cosurety's payment of the whole obligation resulted in a claim against principal and other cosurety, each for one-half the amount discharged.). It should be noted that the apparent holding in this 1841 case is unusual in that it appears to divide the obligation to reimburse the cosurety equally between the remaining cosureties and the principal obligor. We mention this case only for its discussion of the obligation to reimburse a paying cosurety, without expressing an opinion as to the correctness of its holding.
129. *See, e.g.,* Sargent v. Salmond, 27 Me. 539, 542, 574 (1847) ("[T]he liability of one [co-surety] to the other, to contribute his proportion, in the event that the principals should fail to discharge them, and payment should be made by one, attached at the time the notes were made and passed to the [obligee]."); *Gould,* 18 Me. at 366-67.

10.3 Liability of Parent Guarantors Owning less than 100 Percent of Primary Obligor

We are not aware of Maine case law analyzing downstream guaranties made by parent entities that own less than 100 percent of the subsidiary obligor. Maine cases have, however, addressed rights of contribution between individual coguarantors in the context of guaranties executed by all guarantors,[130] as well as the obligations of a business owner under a continuing guaranty following sale of the business.[131]

§ 11 Reliance

Reliance is a necessary element to bind a principal to the actions of an agent based on the agent's apparent authority.[132]

Reasonable reliance is an essential element of the affirmative defense of fraudulent misrepresentation against enforcement of a guaranty.[133]

§ 12 Subrogation

The rights of a guarantor against the borrower are effectively subrogated to those of the creditor; the guarantor inherits the rights of the creditor, although such rights may not vest until the creditor has been paid in full.[134] As noted in Section 8.3, Maine courts have given effect to contractual waivers by guarantors of the right of subrogation.[135]

§ 13 Triangular Set-off in Bankruptcy

We are not aware of Maine case law regarding "triangular set-offs" in bankruptcy, where a parent guarantor set-offs its obligations to the guaranty's beneficiary against related obligations the beneficiary owes to the primary obligor.

---

130. *See, e.g., MP Associates,* 2001 ME 22, 771 A.2d 1040; *Kandlis*, 678 A.2d 41.
131. *See, e.g., John Nagle Co.*, 2002 ME 101, 799 A.2d 1225 (holding that continuing guaranty remained enforceable against owner absent revocation, notwithstanding sale of the business).
132. MacQuinn v. Patterson, 147 Me. 196, 85 A.2d 183, 186-87 (1951).
133. *See Kuperman*, 586 A.2d at 1261; *see also* Maine Eye Care Associates P.A. v. Gorman, 2008 ME 36, ¶ 12, 942 A.2d 707.
134. Stewart v. Ticonic Nat'l Bank, 104 Me. 578, 72 A. 741, 744 (1908).
135. *See, e.g., Duhamel*, 334 B.R. at 486; Leighton v. Fleet Bank of Maine, 634 A.2d 453, 456 (Me. 1993). In the construction context, Maine courts have recognized the doctrine of equitable subrogation under which a compensated surety has priority over other parties with respect to either unpaid progress payments or retainages of the defaulting subcontractor. Centex-Simpson Co., Inc. v. Fidelity & Deposit of Maryland, 795 F. Supp. 35 (D. Me. 1992); Aetna Casualty & Surety Co.. Eastern Trust & Banking, 156 Me. 87, 161 A.2d 843 (1960).

§ 14 Indemnification—Whether the Primary Obligor has a Duty

Borrowers, as primary obligors, have the obligation to reimburse guarantors for the performance of their obligations under a guaranty.[136]

§ 15 Enforcement of Guaranties

15.1 Enforcement of Guaranties of Payment versus Guaranties of Performance

We are not aware of Maine case law analyzing the enforcement of completion guaranties and other guaranties of performance as a class distinct from other types of guaranties. Such guaranties, however, are used in Maine, for example in the construction industry, and are referenced in Maine cases.[137]

15.2 Exercising Rights Under a Guaranty Where the Underlying Obligation is also Secured by a Mortgage

Foreclosures in Maine are governed by Title 14, Chapter 713 of the Maine Revised Statutes. During the foreclosure process, the mortgagee's acceptance of anything of value applied against a mortgage after the commencement of foreclosure proceedings and before the expiration of the right of redemption may constitute a waiver of the foreclosure.[138]

Title 14, Section 6203-E states that written notice of a mortgagor's intention to foreclose on a mortgage must be timely served on the mortgagor and "its representative in interest" in order to bring an action on a deficiency.[139] There is federal case law interpreting this statute to not extend the notice requirement to guarantors of the mortgage.[140]

Notwithstanding the existence of a mortgage securing the obligations of a primary obligor, a mortgagee may seek to attach property of the guarantor to the full value of the underlying obligation.[141] The attachment is not limited to the difference between the fair market value of the real property and the underlying obligation.[142]

---

136. *MP Associates*, 2001 ME 22, 771 A.2d 1040; *see also* Godfrey v. Rice, 59 Me. 308, 314 (1871).
137. *See, e.g.*, Inhabitants of Richmond v. Johnson, 53 Me. 437 (1866); Hannaford Bros. Co. v. Town of Kennebunk, 2006 WL 522376 (Me. Sup. Ct. Feb. 6, 2006) (holding that performance guaranty for commercial development was required by town ordinance).
138. 14 M.R.S.A. § 6321 (2011). This waiver may be negated by written agreement or by return of the payment within 10 days of receipt.
139. 14 M.R.S.A. § 6203-E (2011).
140. *Hanson*, 649 F. Supp. at 105-06 (declining to impose a requirement to notify guarantors in the absence of Maine authority).
141. *Casco Northern Bank, N.A.*, 583 A.2d at 699.
142. *Id.*

As noted in Section 7.3.6 above, spousal guaranties of a debt secured by a mortgage may give rise to violations under ECOA and Maine courts have allowed ECOA violations to be used defensively against the enforcement of a guaranty even after the expiration of the two-year statute of limitations and to limit a mortgagee's recovery against jointly held real property of a husband and wife.

Although not directly relevant to the situation where the underlying obligation alone is secured by a mortgage, it should be noted that mortgages securing guaranties themselves are specifically contemplated by Maine statute. Maine's open-end mortgage statute[143] allows a mortgagee to secure and maintain lien priority with respect to, among other things, obligations that are not fully mature as of the date of recording and that may never mature into obligations. These latter are called "contingent obligations," and guaranty obligations are named in the statute as an example of them. Contingent obligations have priority from the date of recording of the mortgage, in the full amount of the contingent obligation identified in the mortgage, provided that the maximum amount of the contingent obligation secured by the mortgage is stated in the mortgage.[144]

15.3 Litigating Guaranty Claims: Procedural Considerations

A creditor may seek prejudgment attachment of nonexempt real or personal property in connection with a civil action, unless the debt to be enforced arises out of a consumer credit transaction.[145] Attachment is sought by motion to the court and supporting affidavit. An order for attachment may be granted by the court only if the court finds it more likely than not that the movant will recover a judgment in an amount greater than or equal to the amount of the requested attachment plus any other security or property also subject to attachment. The court must approve a specified amount in its order for attachment. In addition to attachment, trustee process is a remedy (similar to garnishment) available under Maine law.[146] Trustee process may be used to reach money or other property by a process similar to that for attachment.

Following judgment, a creditor may seek a writ of execution from the court.[147] Filing of a writ of execution with the appropriate registry of deeds (for real property) or UCC filing office (for personal property) within one year of the writ's issuance will establish a lien in favor of the creditor.[148] Many assets of a debtor are, to different extents, exempt by statute from seizure by an unsecured creditor, and a creditor's interests may be restricted to maximum values.[149] For example, a debtor may protect up to $47,500 in equity in a residence ($95,000 if the debtor is age 60 or older, physically or mentally

143. 33 M.R.S.A. § 505 (Supp. 2009).
144. 33 M.R.S.A. § 505(1)(A).
145. 14 M.R.S.A. § 4151 (2011); Me. R. Civ. P. 4A.
146. Me. R. Civ. P. 4B.
147. Me. R. Civ. P. 69.
148. 14 M.R.S.A. § 4651-4659 (2011).
149. 14 M.R.S.A. § 4422 (2011).

disabled, or there is a minor dependent).[150] A debtor's interest in tools of trade is limited to not more than $5,000.[151]

Under revised Article 9 of Maine's UCC, obligations arise if a secured party pursues a deficiency judgment against a secondary obligor. If a debtor or secondary obligor raises the issue of whether the secured party's collection, enforcement, disposition, and acceptance activities complied with part 6 of revised Article 9, the secured party will have the burden of proving such compliance.[152] If the secured party fails to meet this burden, in a commercial transaction the debtor or secondary obligor will receive credit against any deficiency for the greater of (i) the actual proceeds from the disposition of collateral, or (ii) the proceeds that would have been realized had the secured party complied.[153] Unless otherwise proven by the secured party, the proceeds that would have been realized are presumed to equal the sum of the secured obligation, plus expenses and attorney's fees.[154]

In a consumer transaction, failure by the secured party to prove compliance will cause the debtor and secondary obligor to have no liability for a deficiency.[155] If collateral is transferred to a secured party, a related party, or a secondary obligor for an amount significantly below the amount that would have been paid by an independent third party, any deficiency will be based on the amount that would have been realized in a sale to an independent third party.[156]

A creditor foreclosing on collateral must provide an "authenticated notification of disposition" to certain affected parties, including any secondary obligor, within a reasonable time before sale of the collateral.[157] Whether the timeliness of the notification is reasonable is a question of fact, except that in a commercial transaction a notification that is sent after default and 10 days or more before disposition is per se reasonable.[158]

§ 16 Revival and Reinstatement of Guaranties

Where a guarantor's obligations to a guaranty's beneficiary have been terminated as a result of a valid defense, a partial payment made by the guarantor on behalf of the principal obligor does not serve to revive the guarantor's obligations.[159]

---

150. 14 M.R.S.A. § 4422(1)(A) (2011).
151. 14 M.R.S.A. § 4422(5) (2011).
152. 11 M.R.S.A. § 9-1626 (2011).
153. *Id.*
154. *Id.*
155. *Id.*
156. 11 M.R.S.A. § 9-1615(6) (2011).
157. 11 M.R.S.A. § 9-1611 (2011).
158. 11 M.R.S.A. § 9-1612 (2011). The content of the notification must also be reasonable under the UCC. *See* 11 M.R.S.A. §§ 9-1613 (2011) (addressing content of notification), 9-1614 (addressing content in consumer transactions) (2011).
159. *See* Lime Rock Bank v. Mallett, 34 Me. 547 (1852).

Maryland State Law of Guaranties

Leslie J. Polt
Adelberg, Rudow, Dorf & Hendler, LLC
7 St. Paul Street, Suite 600
Baltimore, Maryland 21202-1612
(410) 986-0832 (direct)
(410) 539-5195
(410) 539-5834 (fax)
LPolt@AdelbergRudow.com
www.AdelbergRudow.com

Contents

Maryland State Law of Guaranties

Introductory Note: This survey is limited to commercial guaranty undertakings in the context of nonconsumer commercial transactions, and does not cover insurance, credit insurance, surety contracts, or other insurance products regulated under the *Insurance Article* of the Maryland Annotated Code and the Code of Maryland Regulations. The following glossary is provided for ease of uniform reference to the various parties to a guaranty and their obligations:

"Guarantor" means a person who, by contract, agrees to satisfy an underlying obligation of another to an obligee upon the primary obligor's default on that underlying obligation.

"Guaranty" means the contract by which the guarantor agrees to satisfy the underlying obligation of a primary obligor to an obligee in the event the primary obligor defaults on the underlying obligation.

"Obligee" means the person to whom the underlying obligation is owed. For example, the lender under a loan agreement would be an obligee vis-à-vis the borrower.

"Primary Obligor" means the person who incurs the underlying obligation to the obligee. For example, the borrower under a loan agreement would be a primary obligor.

"Underlying Obligation" means the obligation or obligations incurred by the primary obligor and owed to the obligee. For example, the borrower's obligation to make payments to a lender of principal and interest on a loan constitutes an underlying obligation.

§ 1 Nature of the Guaranty Arrangement

Maryland law distinguishes between a contract of suretyship and a contract of guaranty.

1.1 Surety Relationships

A suretyship is a three-party arrangement among the principal obligor, the obligee, and the surety. This contract is a direct and original undertaking under which the surety becomes directly and primarily liable with the principal obligor and therefore is responsible at once if the principal obligor fails to perform. Ultimate liability rests upon the principal obligor rather than the surety, but the creditor has a remedy against both.[1]

1.2 Guaranty Relationships

A contract of guaranty is distinguished from a suretyship by the following: (i) the contract is collateral to and independent of the principal contract; (ii) the guarantor is not a party to the principal obligation; (iii) the guarantor is therefore secondarily liable to the creditor to answer for the debt; (iv) the guarantor's obligation becomes absolute upon default of the principal debt and the satisfaction of all conditions precedent to liability; (v) the guarantor is not bound to take notice of nonperformance, but must first receive notice of default; and (vi) the guaranty is often (but not necessarily) supported by a separate consideration.[2] In practice, however, a well-drafted guaranty will provide for waiver of the conditions precedent to enforcement, such as notice, and of defenses available to a surety.

In determining whether an obligation should be treated as a suretyship rather than a guaranty, the courts disregard the title of the document and look at the substance of the agreement. In doing so, Maryland follows the objective law of contract interpretation and construction. Where the contractual language is clear and unambiguous, and absent fraud, duress, or mistake, parol evidence is not admissible to show the intention of the parties or to contradict the terms of the contract.[3]

As between a principal obligor and its guarantor, the guarantor, being secondarily liable, holds a claim against the principal obligor for indemnification and reimbursement of the full amount paid. A surety, however, being jointly and severally liable with the principal obligor, holds a claim against the principal obligor for contribution but only to the extent it is required to pay a disproportionate share of the obligation. In practice, the distinction between a suretyship and a guaranty can be subtle and may turn on merely one or two words.[4]

---

1. *See* Middlebrook Tech, LLC v. Moore, 849 A.2d 63 (Md. App. 2004), finding the lease guaranty to be a suretyship; Mercy Medical Center, Inc. v. United Healthcare of the Mid-Atlantic, Inc., 815 A.2d 886 (Md. App. 2003) finding the hospital's agreement to stand behind its physician's network obligations to HMOs to be a guaranty. *See also*, Atlantic Contracting & Material Co. v. Ulico, 844 A.2d 460 (2004).
2. *Middlebrook Tech, LLC, supra* at 74.
3. *Middlebrook Tech, LLC, supra* at 78-79, and cases cited therein; Mercy Medical Center, Inc., v. United Healthcare of the Mid-Atlantic, Inc., 815 A.2d 886, 898 (Md. App. 2003). It appears difficult to reconcile the "objective" theory with the following *dicta* in Walton v Washington County Hospital Ass'n, 13 A.2d 627 (1940): "The words of a guaranty should receive a fair and reasonable interpretation to effectuate the intention of the parties, and the circumstances accompanying the transaction may be considered in seeking the intention of the parties. The Court should give the instrument that construction that will best accord with the intention as manifested by the language in the light of all the surrounding circumstances, without stretching the words beyond their import in favor of the creditor, or restricting them in aid of the guarantor."
4. *See, e.g.*, The Mercantile Club, Inc. v. Scherr, 651 A.2d 456 (1995), where the court found the undertaking to be a suretyship: "As appellant correctly points out, appellee did not guarantee the *performance by LJC* of the covenants and conditions set forth in the mortgage; he guaranteed the *performance of LJC's covenants and conditions* as set forth in the mortgage. This distinction establishes a direct and primary promise on the part of appellee to insure the performance of LJC's obligations-payment of the mortgage debt." 651 A.2d at 461. *See also,* Md. Code, Commercial Law Article § 1-201 (40): "Surety includes guarantor," for purposes of the Uniform Commercial Code (UCC).

A suretyship relationship may also arise because of the pledge of collateral.[5] As such, a guaranty-type relationship arises, to the extent of the collateral pledged, when a person supplies collateral for a loan in order to induce the creditor to lend to the debtor or where one party mortgages property to a creditor to secure the debt of another.[6]

Finally, virtually every multiple borrower or multiple debtor transaction presents the possibility that each obligor or debtor stands as surety for the others.[7]

§ 2 State Law Requirements for an Entity to Enter a Guaranty

Partnerships, limited liability companies, corporations, real estate investment trusts, and banks can all grant guaranties in furtherance of their business activities.

2.1 Corporations

A Maryland corporation may, within the scope of its general corporate powers, enter into a guaranty, provided that it is not prohibited or limited by law or its corporate charter.[8] There is no presumption that affiliate guaranties are deemed to be made in the ordinary course of business.

2.2 Partnerships

Maryland's general partnership law neither expressly empowers a partnership to issue a guaranty nor expressly regulates or prohibits such activity. In general, a partner is an agent of the partnership and binds the partnership when dealing with third persons in carrying out the ordinary course of business of the partnership. However, the partnership is not bound if the partner has no authority and the third person knew or had received notice of lack of authority.[9] A partnership is permitted to file a statement of partnership authority expressly stating the authority or limitations on authority of some or all the partners, which constitutes constructive notice.[10]

5. See Restatement (Third) of Suretyship and Guaranty § 1 (noting that a person is a surety when "pursuant to contract . . . an obligee has recourse against [that] person . . . or against that person's property with respect to an obligation . . . of another person . . . to the obligee" (emphasis added)). The Restatement is cited occasionally, but not frequently, as secondary authority in reported Maryland cases (*See, e.g.*, Wetzler v. Cantor, 202 B.R. 573, 576 (USDC Md., 1996); Mercy Medical Center, Inc., supra, note 3).
6. This concept is carried into Secured Transactions provisions of the UCC, which defines "debtor" to include "a person having an interest, other than a security interest or other lien, in the collateral, whether or not the person is an obligor." Md. Code, Commercial Law Article § 9-102 (28).
7. See Restatement (Third) of Suretyship and Guaranty § 3, noting that a suretyship relationship exists when the principal obligor and the secondary obligor are co-obligors.
8. Md. Code, Corporations And Associations Article § 2-103(5).
9. Md. Code, Corporations and Associations Article, § 9A-301.
10. Md. Code, Corporations and Associations Article, § 9A-303.

2.3 Limited Liability Companies

A Maryland limited liability company may, within the scope of its general powers, enter into a guaranty, provided that it is not prohibited or limited by law or its articles of organization.[11]

2.4 Financial Institutions

A commercial bank, trust company, or savings bank, chartered under Maryland law, has all of the general powers granted to Maryland corporations under the General Corporation Law, as set forth in §2.1 above.[12] However, federal banking law may preempt state law in prohibiting state-chartered institutions from engaging in certain activities in which a national bank is barred by federal law. The situations under which a national bank may become a guarantor are governed by federal law. *See National Bank as Guarantor or Surety on Indemnity Bond,* 12 C.F.R. § 7.1017 (2010). The Maryland Code also regulates credit unions, savings and loan associations, small loan companies, and other credit providers, which are somewhat beyond the scope of this compendium.

2.5 Real Estate Investment Trusts

A real estate investment trust may organize either under the general corporate law or under the Real Estate Investment Trust Act (herein, the "REIT Law"). The statutory powers given a REIT under the REIT Law include: "Make contracts, incur liabilities, and borrow money," which language tracks the parallel provision of the general corporation law, with the exception that it omits the phrase "and guarantees" which appears after "make contracts" in the general corporation law. While the editor cannot point to express legislative history or case law support, the general view is that the distinction was inadvertent in the legislation, and that the REIT Law does not prohibit a REIT organized under that law from entering into guaranties. Support for this conclusion may be found in the power given to a REIT to "generally exercise the powers set forth in its declaration of trust which are not inconsistent with law and are appropriate to promote and attain the purposes set forth in its declaration of trust."[13] It is recommended, therefore, that the declaration of trust expressly provide for the power to enter into guaranties.

2.6 Individuals; Spouses

Confusion can sometimes arise in the case of corporate officers or directors signing guaranties in closely held corporations or other organizations. In such instances, a case-by-case inquiry determines whether an individual intended to be personally bound or, instead, only issued a guaranty on behalf of a partner-

11. Md. Code, Corporations and Associations Article, § 4A-203.
12. Md. Code, Financial Institutions Article, §§ 1-201, 3-206, 4-206.
13. Md. Code, Corporations and Associations Article, § 8-301(13).

ship or corporation and thus only in an official employment capacity.[14] When an individual signs his title as well as his name, this is not dispositive proof of an intention not to issue a personal guaranty.[15]

While a business corporation must have "authority" to execute a guaranty, an individual guarantor must have the "capacity" to enter into the guaranty. Incapacity can be a defense against the enforcement of a guaranty issued by an individual.

Spouses executing a guaranty become jointly liable, and therefore the obligee may reach real property held by them as tenants by the entirety, and such property may be reached by a coguarantor who holds an equitable subrogation claim against the spouse/guarantors for contribution.[16] As between themselves, the "pro-rata" distribution is determined by the number of guarantors, not by the interest of each guarantor in the principal obligor.

§ 3 Signatory's Authority to Execute a Guaranty

Generally, the obligee has a duty of reasonable inquiry when it has some notice that the executor of the guaranty does not have authority to bind the guarantor.

3.1 Corporations

For an obligee/creditor to rely on a guaranty, the guaranty must be signed by an officer with actual or apparent authority to act in such capacity. The rights of the obligee are not affected or impaired by any bylaw or resolution setting or limiting the authority of the signer to bind the corporation unless it has knowledge of the bylaw or resolution.[16] Where an obligee-plaintiff invokes the doctrine of apparent authority, that obligee bears a duty of reasonable inquiry.

Generally, an officer of a corporation has authority to act only where: (a) authority has been expressly conferred on him by statute, law, or the act of the directors; (b) the action is properly incidental to the business entrusted to him by the directors; and (c) the action is within his ostensible authority or ratified by proper authority as applicable to contracts of guaranty. If a corporation's guaranty bears some reasonable relationship to the corporation's business, evidence that a signing officer was charged with the general management of the corporation's business can provide apparent authority to execute a guaranty.

---

14. *See, e.g.*, Curtis G. Testerman Co. v. Buck, 667 A.2d 649, 340 Md. 569 (1995), where the court held that an officer is not personally liable on a contract of the corporation where the record is devoid of anything showing intent to assume the obligation, recognizing that where personal as well as corporate liability is demanded, the "nearly universal" practice is to have the officer sign twice, one as an officer and then again as an individual; L&H Enterprises, Inc. v. Allied Bldg. Products Corp., 596 A.2d 672, 88 Md. App. 642 (Md. App. 1991).
15. *Id.*; *see also* Ubom v. SunTrust Bank, 17 A.3d 168, 198 Md. App. 278 (Md. App., 2011), where the managing member of a professional limited liability company was held personally liable as guarantor even though he signed the guaranty line as "Managing Attorney."
16. Wetzler v. Cantor, 202 B.R. 573 (D. Md., 1996).
16. MD. CODE, CORPORATIONS AND ASSOCIATIONS ARTICLE, § 2-414.

3.2 Partnerships

Maryland's Revised Uniform Partnership Act ("RUPA") provides that a partner is an agent of the partnership for purposes of the business, and that the execution of any instrument for the apparent purpose of carrying on the partnership business binds the partnership unless the partner has no authority and the third person knew or had received notice of lack of authority. Authority may also be granted under the partnership agreement. A partnership is permitted to file a statement of partnership authority expressly stating the authority or limitations on authority of some or all the partners, which constitutes constructive notice.[17]

Under RUPA, a general partner of a limited partnership has the same powers as a partner in a general partnership.[18] Since the provisions of RUPA are made applicable to limited partnerships,[19] a limited partnership is permitted to file a statement of partnership authority expressly stating the authority or limitations on authority of some or all the partners, which constitutes constructive notice.

3.3 Limited Liability Companies (LLCs)

The Maryland Limited Liability Company Act[20] provides that every member is an agent of that company and can sign instruments pursuant to carrying on in the usual way of business unless that person has no actual authority to act in such way and his counterparty knows as much. If the articles of organization limit the authority of members to bind the LLC, the members are not agents merely by being members and any third party dealing with a member is presumed to have knowledge of the limitation.[21]

3.4 Banks and Trust Companies

A case-by-case inquiry of the powers provided for in a bank's or trust company's corporate governance documents is necessary to determine who may validly execute a guaranty on behalf of a bank or trust company.

§ 4 Consideration; Sufficiency of Past Consideration

Standard contract principles apply to the analysis of consideration for a contract of guaranty. The principal agreement is sufficient consideration for an accompanying guaranty. A guaranty given after the execution of the principal contract requires new consideration. Special rules apply to instruments under seal.

17. Md. Code, Corporations and Associations Article, § 9A-303.
18. Md. Code, Corporations and Associations Article, § 10-403.
19. Md. Code, Corporations and Associations Article, § 10-108.
20. Md. Code, Corporations and Associations Article, Title 4A.
21. Md. Code, Corporations and Associations Article, § 4A-101.

Consideration is required to create a valid contract of guaranty, but it is not necessary for the consideration to be separately described in the instrument itself.[22] If the guaranty is made contemporaneously with the making of the principal contract, or if the principal contract and the guaranty are part of the same transaction, the consideration which supports the principal contract will also support the guaranty.[23] A guaranty given after execution of the principal contract, and which is not part of the original transaction, requires separate consideration.[24]

A "specialty" is an agreement in writing, sealed and delivered. Merely affixing a corporate seal does not create a specialty; intent to create a sealed instrument must appear on the instrument itself, such as a statement prior to signature: "Whereas, the parties have executed this Agreement, intending that it be construed as an instrument under seal" or "In witness whereof the parties hereto have set their hands and seals the day and year first above written." In addition, the word: "SEAL" must appear at the end of the signature line. Consideration is not necessary for a contract under seal to be valid as a matter of contract law.[25] However, if a contract under seal, including a guaranty, expressly acknowledges that consideration was given or the obligation was incurred in exchange for bargained-for consideration, the obligor may nevertheless raise failure of consideration as a defense as between the parties.[26]

Under general principles of contract law, past consideration, will not support a guaranty.

§ 5 Notice of Acceptance

Notice of acceptance by obligee is a requirement, but generally is waived in a well-drawn guaranty. Notice is not required if the guaranty is "absolute."

Under guaranty law, generally, the obligation commences only after the obligee notifies the guarantor of its acceptance of the guaranty.[27] Notice of acceptance also will not be required where the guaranty is "absolute."[28] Commonly, the guarantor waives the notification of acceptance requirement in the guaranty agreement.[29]

22. Heiston v. National City Bank, 104 A. 281 (1918).
23. Mercy Medical Center, Inc., v. United Healthcare of the Mid-Atlantic, Inc., 815 A.2d 886 (Md. App. 2003); Lutz v. Porter, 112 A.2d 480 (1955).
24. G.M.A.C. v. Daniels, 492 A.2d 1306 (1985). However, a subsequent agreement by the lender to increase the line of credit constitutes consideration for a guaranty given at the time of and as a condition to the additional credit. F.D.I.C. v. Rodenberg, 571 F.Supp.455 (D. Md., 1983).
25. Twining v. National Mortgage Corporation, 302 A.2d 604 (1973).
26. Venners v. Goldberg, 758 A.2d 567 (Md. App. 2000).
27. Art Plate Glass & Mirror Corp. v. Fidelity Construction Corp., 69 A.2d 808 (1949) However, if notice of acceptance is not "required by the terms of the guarantee," the extension of credit by the obligee will "constitute[] acceptance . . . of the guarantor's offer of surety." Stated slightly differently, notice of acceptance is unnecessary "[w]here credit is advanced on the strength of the guaranty . . . ."
28. Greenwell v. American Guaranty Corp., 277 A.2d 70(1971); Eastern Shore Brokerage & Commission Co. v. Harrison; 118 A. 192 (1922).
29. Restatement (Third) of Suretyship & Guaranty § 8 cmt (2006).

§ 6 Interpretation of Guaranties

In construing a guaranty, Maryland follows the objective law of contract interpretation and construction in the same manner by which it would interpret the language of any other contract.

6.1 General Principles

In construing a guaranty, Maryland follows the objective law of contract interpretation and construction. Where the contractual language is clear and unambiguous, and absent fraud, duress, or mistake, parol evidence is not admissible to show the intention of the parties or to contradict the terms of the contract.[30] However, the courts have also stated that: "The words of a guaranty should receive a fair and reasonable interpretation to effectuate the intention of the parties, and the circumstances accompanying the transaction may be considered in seeking the intention of the parties. The Court should give the instrument that construction that will best accord with the intention as manifested by the language in the light of all the surrounding circumstances, without stretching the words beyond their import in favor of the creditor, or restricting them in aid of the guarantor."[31]

6.2 Guaranty of Payment versus Guaranty of Collection

A guarantor of payment promises to satisfy the underlying obligation to the obligee upon default by the primary obligor, which satisfaction is not conditioned upon the obligee's prior attempt to secure satisfaction from the primary obligor.[32] A guarantor may be required to satisfy obligations to an obligee even where the obligee, because of a subordination agreement, cannot collect from the primary obligor.

On the other hand, a guarantor of collection merely promises to satisfy the underlying obligation only after all attempts to obtain payment from the [primary obligor] have failed. A court will look to the intent of the parties as expressed in the guaranty to determine whether it is one of payment or one of collection.

6.3 Language Regarding the Revocation of Guaranties

Under general principles, a guaranty that is "irrevocable" may not be revoked with respect to transactions entered into by the primary obligor prior to the revocation. Where the guarantor is not compensated and the guaranty is for an indefinite period of time, he may revoke the guaranty with regard to future liability upon reasonable notice. Where a guaranty contains language pertain-

30. *Middlebrook Tech, LLC, supra* at 78-79, and cases cited therein; Mercy Medical Center, Inc., v. United Healthcare of the Mid-Atlantic, Inc., 815 A.2d 886, 898 (Md. App. 2003).
31. Walton v. Washington County Hospital Ass'n., 13 A.2d 627 (1940).
32. Steinberg v. Gonzales, 135 A.2d 631 (1957).

ing to revocation or expiration, the language should be considered carefully. In addition, if the guaranty specifies the means by which revocation must be communicated, a noncompliant revocation will be ineffective.

6.4 "Continuing"

A guaranty continues during the time expressly or impliedly provided for in the instrument.[33] While the use of the word "continuing" helps to make clear that a guaranty is meant to be continuing, courts in Maryland have interpreted a guaranty as continuing even where the word "continuing" has not been used.[34]

6.5 "Absolute and Unconditional"

A guaranty is deemed to be absolute rather than conditional, unless its terms impart some condition precedent to the liability of the guarantor.[35]

6.6 "Liable as a Primary Obligor and not Merely as Surety"

There is no reported case interpreting this language or its legal effect, either procedurally or substantively. It is unlikely that a court would construe this language as elevating the status of a guarantor to a primary obligor.

§ 7 Defenses of the Guarantor; Set-off

The defenses that may be available to a guarantor can be grouped into three categories: (1) defenses of the primary obligor; (2) "suretyship defenses"; and (3) other defenses.

7.1 Defenses of the Primary Obligor

7.1.1 General

The general rule is that the guarantor, absent an effective waiver, is not bound to perform if the primary obligor is not bound. A guarantor sued alone may not, in many circumstances, raise defenses or counterclaims that are "personal" to the primary obligor. If the defense is one that belongs to the primary obligor, the primary obligor retains the sole capacity to choose whether to assert it. Such personal defenses include fraud in the inducement, negligence in performance of a contract, and a breach of a warranty contained in the agreement governing the underlying obligation.

33. Art Plate Glass & Mirror Corp. v. Fidelity Construction Corp., 69 A.2d 808 (1949).
34. Gordon v. State National Bank of Bethesda, 239 A.2d 915 (1968).
35. Mercy Medical Center, Inc. v. United Healthcare of the Mid-Atlantic, Inc., 815 A.2d 886, 907 (Md. App. 2003); Hodgson v. Burroughs, 2 A.2d 407 (1938).

7.1.2 *When Guarantor may assert Primary Obligor's defense*

If the guarantor alone is sued, the primary obligor may give its consent to the guarantor's use of the defense or cause of action belonging to the primary obligor. Where the guarantor controls the primary obligor, a court may assume that the primary obligor has consented to the use of the defense or cause of action.

Action by the primary obligor with regard to the defense or claim may permit the guarantor to assert the same defense or claim. For instance, a guarantor may use a fraud in the inducement defense against the obligee if the primary obligor seeks to rescind the underlying obligation on the same basis. A guarantor may raise the defense of limitations.[36]

The illegality of the primary obligation may constitute a defense to the liability of the guarantor.[37]

7.1.3 *Defenses that may not be raised by Guarantor*

The insolvency of the principal obligor is not a defense that the guarantor may raise unless the guaranty is conditioned on the solvency of the primary obligor. A guarantor also may not raise the primary obligor's incapacity as a defense to liability under the guaranty. A guarantor may not raise lack of consideration for the execution of a deed of trust or mortgage on property of the primary obligor.[38]

7.1.4 *Defenses that may always be raised by Guarantor*

A guarantor may show that the obligee failed to perform such that there is a partial or complete failure of consideration.[39] Duress may also be raised as a defense.[40]

7.2 "Suretyship" Defenses

Generally, any act or omission on the part of the creditor or beneficiary of the guaranty in breach of its duty under the guaranty contract which increases the guarantor's risk or otherwise injures the guarantor's rights and remedies discharges the guarantor from liability under the guaranty, at least to the extent of the injury so sustained.[41]

---

36. Henry's Drive-In, Inc. v. Pappas, 287 A.2d 35 (1972).
37. *See* McGinley v. Massey, 525 A.2d 1076 (Md. App., 1987), where the underlying obligation, a stock redemption note, violated the Corporation Code rule against redemptions by an insolvent corporation. The court also rejected the "separate contract" and estoppel arguments.
38. F.D.I.C. v. Rodenberg, 571 F.Supp. 455 (D. Md., 1983).
39. *See* Vennes v. Goldberg, 758 A.2d 567 (Md. App. 2000).
40. Hieston v. National City Bank, 104 A. 281 (1918).
41. United States v. Krochmal, 318 F. Supp. 148 (D. Md. 1970).

7.2.1 Change in Identity of Principal Obligor

Whether a change of the identity of the principal obligor to the underlying obligation discharges the guarantor's obligations depends upon the circumstances. The liability of a guarantor is based on the contract of guaranty, and no change can be made without the guarantor's consent. If the principal contract is changed in a manner not contemplated by the guaranty, without the guarantor's consent, the guarantor might be discharged.[42] However, a technical change in identity of the principal obligor arising from a bankruptcy reorganization would not discharge the guarantor.[43]

7.2.2 Modification of the Underlying Obligation, including Release

Modifications to the underlying obligation may permit the guarantor to raise certain defenses to liability. Because the liability of a guarantor is created by contract, it is strictly confined and limited to the contract, and no change can be made without the guarantor's consent.[44] The Maryland Court of Appeals has stated that "[a] guarantor's obligation cannot be altered without its consent." However, following the Restatement law, an exception to the rule discharging a guarantor for alteration of the underlying contract exists where the guarantor has knowledge of and assents, either expressly or by implication, to such change. In addition, if the guaranty contains a provision that contemplates or authorizes in advance a change in the terms of the principal contract, a change within the scope of that authorization does not discharge the guarantor.[45]

In particular, fundamentally altering the risks faced by the guarantor can impair surety status sufficiently to justify discharge of any of the guarantor's outstanding obligations, while impairing the guarantor's recourse against the primary obligor may have similar results.[46]

However, guarantors will not be relieved of their obligations if they expressly waived notice of any modification or agreed that any extension or modification of the underlying debt would not release the liability of the guarantors.[47]

A release of the principal obligor without the guarantor's explicit or implicit consent releases the guarantor.[48]

---

42. Middlebrook Tech, LLC v. Moore, 849 A.2d 63 (Md. App. 2004).
43. The Mercantile Club, Inc. v. Scherr, 651 A.2d 456 (1995).
44. Mercy Medical Center, Inc. v. United Healthcare of the Mid-Atlantic, Inc., 815 A.2d 886 at 901, and cases cited therein.; *But see* Continental Oil Co. v. Horsey, 9 A.2d 607 (1939), where the guarantor of an overdue open account was not discharged by the creditor taking a promissory note from the primary obligor payable on demand "after date," since the quoted phrase was held not to constitute a one-day extension that would discharge a surety.
45. Mercy Medical Center, Inc. v. United Healthcare of the Mid-Atlantic, Inc., 815 A.2d 886 at 901 (Md. App. 2003).
46. Restatement (Third) of Suretyship & Guaranty § 37. *See* Whalen v. Devlin Lumber & Supply Corp., 246 A.2d 247 (1968), where the court held that guarantors of a general contractor obligated under a supply contract could be released from liability to the extent the supplier applied payment of earmarked funds to nonguaranteed obligations of the contractor.
47. Greenwell v. American Guaranty Corporation, 277 A.2d 70 (1971); United States v. Krochmal, 318 F.Supp. 148 (D. Md., 1970).
48. Chicago Title Insurance Company v. Lumbermen's Mutual Casualty Company, 707 A.2d 913 (Md. App., 1998).

7.2.3 *Release or Impairment of Security for the Underlying Obligation*

While the guarantor may not be required to waive notice of disposition, the failure of the obligee/secured party to conduct a commercially reasonable disposition does not constitute an absolute bar to a deficiency judgment against the guarantor. Maryland adopts the "rebuttable presumption" rule, under which the debt is reduced by the greater of (i) the actual proceeds of disposition or (ii) the amount that would have been realized had the disposition been conducted in a commercially reasonable manner. The creditor retains a claim for any deficiency.[49]

7.3 Other Defenses

7.3.1 *Failure to comply with or Breach of a Condition to the Guaranty*

The guaranty recited that the borrower and guarantor requested that the lender establish a credit for $35,000 and the lender's agreement was conditioned on execution of the guaranty. The guarantor executed a guaranty limited to $35,000 plus collection costs. The lender extended additional credit without the guarantor's knowledge. The recitals in the guaranty did not create an absolute condition to enforceability of the guaranty that credit would not be extended above $35,000, only a limitation on the amount of the guaranty.[50]

7.3.2 *Modification of the Guaranty*

Modifications to a guaranty should not affect its validity even where no new consideration is given for the modification. The State's highest court ruled that the conduct of the parties may constitute a modification of the contract, even if the contract contains an express "non-waiver" clause.[51] In effect, the parties may be found to have waived the nonwaiver clause.

7.3.3 *Failure to pursue Primary Obligor*

An exculpatory provision in a mortgage note relieving the developer-borrower from personal liability does not create an ambiguity or inconsistency with the joint and several unconditional guaranty of several individual guarantors, especially in light of the unconditional nature of the guaranty and the various waivers expressed in the terms of the guaranty instrument.[52]

---

49. CapitalSource Finance, LLC v. Delco Oil, Inc., 608 F.Supp 2d 655 (D. Md., 2009); F.D.I.C. v. Rodenberg, 571 F.Supp.455 (D. Md., 1983); Ruden v. Citizens Band & Trust Co., 638 A.2d 1225 (Md. App., 1994). As to real property, the rule is the same. *See* Walton v. Washington County Hospital Ass'n., 13 A.2d 627 (1940), which also observed that any objection by the guarantor to the adequacy of the price realized at foreclosure must be timely raised or the defense is barred.
50. Equitable Trust Company v. Bratwursthaus Management Corp., 514 F.2d 565 (USCA 4th Cir., 1975, applying Md. Law). *See also* Gordon v. State National Bank of Bethesda, 239 A.2d 915 (1968).
51. Hovnanian Land Investment Group, LLC v. Annapolis Towne Centre at Parole, LLC, 25 A.3d 967 (2011).
52. Kline v. The Chase Manhattan Bank, N.A., 403 A.2d 395 (Md. App., 1979).

7.3.4 Statute of Limitations

A civil action at law shall be filed within three years from the date it accrues unless another provision of the Code provides a different period of time within which an action shall be commenced.[53] If the guaranty or other instrument is under seal and meets the requirement of a "specialty" (see § 4 above), the action must be filed within 12 years after the cause of action accrues.[54] As to the effect of partial performance by the guarantor on the statute of limitations, the Code also provides that any payment of principal or interest on a specialty suspends the 12- year limitation for a period of three years after such payment.[55] In *Allied Funding v. Huemmer,* 626 A.2d 1055 (Md. App. 1993), the lender obtained a guaranty under seal and, after judgment was entered on the defaulted loan, accepted partial payments from the guarantor for eight months. The lender brought suit against the guarantor within 12 years after the last partial payment, but more than 12 years after the judgment. The court held that the action was time-barred, and that the statute does not reset the 12-year limitations period, but is intended only to extend limitations by three years if the partial payment is during the last three years of the 12-year period for specialties (thus assuring the creditor a minimum three-year limitations after partial payment, as with any suit on a simple contract). Otherwise, the three years from partial payment runs concurrently with the 12-year limitations period for specialties.

Statutory exceptions include contracts for the sale of goods that are governed by Article 2 of the Uniform Commercial Code (UCC), and equipment leases under Article 2A of the UCC, both of which impose a four-year statute of limitations.[56]

If the underlying obligation is a lease, for example, governed by the UCC, the four-year statute of limitations would not extend the three-year limitation applicable to a nonspecialty guaranty. By the same token, if the guaranty is under seal, the four-year limitation under the UCC should not result in a reduction of the 12-year limitation to four years. [57]

7.3.5 Statute of Frauds

By statute, an action may not be brought under a guaranty unless the obligation is in writing, signed by the party to be charged.[58] Thus, where an individual executed a deed of trust to secure a third party's loan, but not a personal

53. Md. Code, Courts and Judicial Proceedings Article § 5-101. As to the effect of the bankruptcy of the principal obligor, *see* Alberstadt v. Sovran Bank,/Maryland, 526 A.2d 986 (Md. App. 1987). There, the borrower's payment of the loan on the eve of its bankruptcy was set aside as a preferential transfer under the Bankruptcy Code. The court held that the cause of action against the guarantor accrued not when the creditor first learned that the trustee might try to avoid the payment, but when the bankruptcy court actually entered the order setting aside the payment as a preference, and therefore the suit was not time barred.
54. Md. Code, Courts and Judicial Proceedings Article § 5-102.
55. Md. Code, Courts and Judicial Proceedings Article § 5-102(b).
56. *See* Md. Code, Commercial Law Article §§ 2-725, 2A-506.
57. *See* The Wellington Company, Inc. Profit Sharing Plan and Trust v. Shakiba, 952 A.2d 328 (Md. App., 2007), where a suit on a note was time-barred after three years, but a separate covenant to pay the debt within the deed of trust (mortgage) securing the note, and executed as a sealed instrument, was held to be a separate enforceable contract, governed by the 12-year statute of limitations.
58. Md. Code, Courts & Judicial Proceedings Article, § 5-901(1).

guaranty, the individual was not liable for the deficiency after foreclosure.[59] However, the Maryland courts have also held that if the primary purpose of the guaranty is to further the guarantor's own pecuniary or business interest, the promise is not within the statute of frauds, even if the obligation is couched in the form of a guaranty.[60] Under this rule, a new consideration for the guaranty, as distinct from the underlying debt, would clearly result in an original promise outside of the statute of frauds.

7.3.6 Failure to mitigate Damages

The Maryland Court of Appeals has held that an effective liquidation of damages clause in the underlying debt instrument bars the defense of failure to mitigate damages.[61] While the case did not involve a guarantor, it is unlikely that a guarantor would stand in any different position than the primary obligor. Where the guaranty gives the lender full discretion as to the time, manner, and selection of remedies, and expressly provides that the lender need not exhaust remedies prior to enforcing the guaranty, the failure to conduct a UCC disposition of collateral is not a valid affirmative defense, since the "commercial reasonableness" standard under UCC Article 9 does not apply.[62]

7.3.7 Fraud, Negligent Misrepresentation

A guarantor may raise in defense or counterclaim that the lender fraudulently and without notice to the guarantor inserted a broader guaranty instrument into the execution stack of credit documents than the guarantor anticipated, although under the specific facts the guarantor can be held to have ratified the fraud or waived the counterclaim by remaining silent after the fraud is discovered.[63]

7.3.8 Defenses particular to Guarantors that are Natural Persons and their Spouses

Subject to the normal defenses of legal age, competence, and capacity to enter into contractual obligation, there appear to be no defenses unique to individual, as opposed to entity, guarantors. However, there is no case authority directly on point.

7.4 Right of Set-off

There appears to be no general prohibition on a guarantor's ability to set-off an individual claim that he has against the creditor, regardless of whether the claim is personal to the guarantor or was assigned from the principal obligor. However, there is no reported case law on the subject. However, where a

59. In re Cutaio, 2007 WL 2713390 (Bkrtcy. D. Md., 2007).
60. Kline v. Lightman, 221 A.2d 675 (1966).
61. Barrie School v. Patch, 933 A.2d 382 (2007).
62. CapitalSource Finance, LLC v. Delco Oil, Inc., 608 F. Supp.2d 655 (D. Md. 2009).
63. Ellerin v. Fairfax Savings Association, et. al, 552 A.2d 918 (Md. App. 1989).

guarantor has made an "unconditional" guaranty of payment, there is the risk that it may be barred from asserting set-offs or defenses which arise independently from the underlying guaranteed obligation.

§ 8 Waiver of Defenses by the Guarantor

8.1 Defenses that cannot be Waived

A guarantor is a "secondary obligor" under Article 9 of the UCC. Notification of disposition of collateral must be sent not only to the debtor but also to any secondary obligor. The requirement of notice may not be waived.[64]

However, where the guaranty instrument reserves to the obligee/secured party the right to elect the time, manner, and order of remedies without impairing the guarantor's obligation, and expressly states that it need not exhaust remedies against the collateral, the failure to send notice of disposition or to conduct a commercially reasonable disposition is not a defense to the guarantor's liability.[65] In addition, the notification to guarantor requirement under the UCC does not extend to real property foreclosures, where notice must be given only to the record owner and holders of subordinate interests of record.[66]

8.2 "Catch-all" Waivers

Though catch-all waiver language may be effective, it is advisable for beneficiaries to include waivers to specific suretyship defenses.

The standard catch-all waiver indicates that the guaranty is "absolute and unconditional" or that the guaranty is "given absolutely and unconditionally." In theory, when such a catch-all waiver is included in a guaranty, the guarantor waives almost all defenses and counterclaims potentially available in an action by the creditor arising from an obligation covered by the guaranty. There is no authority in Maryland supporting the notion that a catch-all waiver is effective to constitute a waiver of suretyship defenses. Thus, the inclusion of "absolute and unconditional" language is not always dispositive in creating an absolute and unconditional guaranty.

---

64. *See* Md. Code, Commercial Law Article § 9-602, which provides that a debtor and secondary obligor may not be required to waive notice of disposition of collateral or the requirement that the secured party conduct a commercially reasonable disposition. *See also* Gambo v Bank of Maryland, 648 A.2d 1105 (Md. App., 1994), decided under the pre-2001 recodification of UCC Article 9: "We hold, for purposes of Article 9 of the UCC, as follows: (1) a guarantor is a debtor under § 9-105(1)(d); (2) a guarantor is entitled to the protections provided to a debtor in § 9-504 (3); and (3) § 9-501(3) precludes a guarantor's pre-default waiver of the rights established by § 9-504 (3) and renders any such waiver invalid."
65. CapitalSource Finance, LLC v. Delco Oil, Inc., 608 F. Supp. 2d 655 (D. Md., 2009); Suntrust Equipment Finance & Leasing Corporation v. A & E Salvage, Inc., 2009 WL 3584333 (USDC E.D. TN, 2009, applying Maryland law).
66. Md. Code, Real Property Article, § 7-105.

§ 9 Third-party Pledgors—Defenses and Waiver Thereof

Because the pledgor arguably stands in the relation of a guarantor to the principal obligor to the extent of the pledge, it may most likely avail of the defenses of a guarantor. It may also waive such defenses.

We have found no evidence that the law as applied to sureties would not apply to a third-party pledge. In contrast, the law appears to be that a pledge of collateral results in a surety relationship. It would seem logical, given this state of the law, that the pledgor generally has the same defenses available to it as are available to a surety.

§ 10 Jointly and Severally Liable Guarantors—Contribution and Reduction of Obligations upon Payment by a Co-obligor

Guarantors who are jointly and severally liable are presumed to share the secondary obligation equally. The creditor is not obliged to seek full payment from more than one such guarantor.

Where coguarantors are liable jointly and severally, there is a presumption that they bear the burden equally.[67] Where spouses, along with others, execute a guaranty "as husband and wife," it is presumed that their liability is joint, and not several, for their joint pro rata share, in which case their "entireties" property may be liable for the debt.[68] Moreover, before the creditor obtains judgment, any individual guarantor is obliged to pay the whole debt. Insofar as the guarantor has paid out more than its proportional share of the obligation, only then may it recover from other guarantors proportionate to their liability. Partners and coventurers are deemed to be jointly liable for the obligations of the partnership or joint venture.[69]

§ 11 Subrogation

A guarantor who pays the obligation of the primary obligor is subrogated to the rights of the creditor.

By its payment of the guaranteed obligation, the guarantor acquires an immediate right to be subrogated, to the extent necessary to obtain reimburse-

67. Waitz v. Marram, 366 A.2d 86 (Md. App., 1976).
68. Wetzler v. Cantor, 202 B.R. 573 (D. Md., 1996).
69. Dominion National Bank v. Sundowner Joint Venture, 436 A.2d 501 (Md. App. 1981).

ment, to the rights, remedies, and collateral security which were available to the creditor.[70]

§ 12 Triangular Set-off in Bankruptcy

Triangular set-off has not been approved or rejected.

There is no authority in Maryland suggesting that where a guarantor controls the primary obligor from a business organization's standpoint, the guaranty of the (controlled) primary obligor's obligations to the beneficiary may create "mutuality" such that the guarantor may set-off its obligations to the beneficiary under the guaranty against related obligations that the beneficiary owes to the primary obligor. However, see § 7.14 on the ability of the guarantor to raise contractual defenses of the principal obligor.

§ 13 Indemnification—Whether the Primary Obligor has a Duty

The primary obligor has a duty of indemnification under general principles, although there is no Maryland reported decision on point. An indemnitor is not discharged by an extension of the underlying obligation.

There is no reported case authority discussing the obligation of the primary obligor to indemnify a guarantor, typically because at that point in time the primary obligor is insolvent or judgment-proof. A third-party indemnitor is not discharged by reason of any extension or change in the terms of the underlying obligation.[71]

§ 14 Enforcement of Guaranties

14.1 Applicable Law

In the absence of an effective choice of law provision in the guaranty, the law of the place where the contract was made governs validity, operation, and effect of a guaranty.

A guaranty contract is made in the state where the underlying extension of credit is made, since the extension of credit is that last act to make the guaranty a binding obligation.[72]

70. G.M.A.C. v. Daniels, 492 A.2d 1306 (1985).
71. Rosenbloom v. Feiler, 431 A.2d 102 (1981).
72. Union Trust Co. of New Jersey v. Knabe, 89 A. 1106 (1914).

14.2 Limitations on Recovery

General principles of enforcement apply, although there is little case law support. Courts have placed restrictions on the award of attorney fees.

The guarantor's counterclaims and defenses may reduce or discharge in its entirety the liability of the guarantor. Additionally, the lender is subject to the customary credit and bankruptcy risks associated with collection of a debt. The Maryland courts have not ruled on the legal effect of a fraudulent transfer "savings" clause in the guaranty. [73]

The Maryland Court of Special Appeals recently ruled that a provision for percentage legal fees would not be enforced beyond the fees actually incurred by the lender.[74] Therefore, it is advisable to provide for actual legal fees, in order to avoid a percentage fee becoming a fee cap. The court also held that, under the doctrine of "merger," the contract claim is merged into the judgment for damages. If the amount of the judgment includes attorney fees, the lender will be precluded from recovering additional fees that it subsequently incurs in trying to collect on the judgment (such as lien enforcement, attachment of assets, etc.). Thus, it is imperative that the attorney fee provisions in the guaranty provide nonmerger language to ensure that the lender's right to payment and reimbursement of collection fees, expenses, and costs arising after the entry of judgment (including without limitation costs and expenses to collect the judgment or liquidate and collect collateral) are not extinguished or merged into the judgment but survive the judgment as a claim against the guarantor and any collateral provided by the guarantor.

14.3 Exercising Rights under a Guaranty Where the Underlying Obligation is also Secured by a Mortgage

In *Walton,*[75] a $20,000 mortgage loan was guaranteed "up to $5,000 for whatever part of said mortgage is not collected from the property." The loan went into default and the foreclosure sale was properly advertised. The mortgage holder credit-purchased the property for $17,000, but with taxes, insurance, commissions, and other costs, the deficiency was $7,700. The guarantor asserted that the property's actual market value exceeded the mortgage debt, and therefore the mortgagee suffered no loss. In rejecting that defense, the court held that once the court ratifies the sale, inadequacy of price may not be raised in subsequent or collateral proceedings. Further, for purposes of a deficiency, the price obtained at the sale is conclusive on the issue of market value of the property. Absent fraud, accident, or other extraordinary circumstance, that value would be binding on

73. *See, e.g.,* In re Tousa, Inc., 422 B.R. 783 at 863 (Bkrtcy, S.D. FL, 2011), which rejected a fraudulent transfer savings clause. That holding was not addressed in subsequent appeals. 680 F.3d 1298 (11th Cir. 2012); 444 B.R. 613 (S.D. FL, 2011).

74. SunTrust Bank v. Goldman, 29 A.3d 724 (Md. App., 2011).

75. Kline v. The Chase Manhattan Bank, N.A., 403 A.2d 395 (Md. App, 1979).

the guarantor.[76] The rule extends to any guarantor under an absolute guaranty, even if the guarantor had no notice of default.[77]

As to the effect of an exculpatory provision in a deed of trust or mortgage note on the liability of the guarantor, see § 7.3.3.

§ 15 Revival and Reinstatement of Guaranties

No Maryland jurisprudence

This issue commonly arises when the payment of the guaranteed debt by the primary obligor (which discharges the guaranty by operation of law) is avoided or rescinded as a preferential or constructively fraudulent transfer, and the creditor then asserts a claim under the guaranty. Guaranty agreements frequently provide for automatic revocation of the discharge and reinstatement of the guaranty upon such occurrence. There is no reported Maryland case addressing the conditions under which a guaranty, once discharged, may be reinstated by law or by agreement of the parties.

§ 16 Guaranties of Payment versus Guaranties of Performance

Limited Maryland jurisprudence

There is little reported case law in Maryland on the effect of a performance, as opposed to a credit, guaranty. In an early case,[78] a merchant broker arranged for the purchase by a grocery of a large quantity of tomatoes from a packing house. The buyer questioned the ability of the seller to perform, and the broker responded by letter giving assurances that the packer was good and that the broker had good experience with the packer. In a suit for monetary damages when the packer failed to deliver, the court held that the broker's written assurances, in light of the circumstances, did not amount to a guaranty.

76. The court also held that in the case of a mortgage, taxes, insurance, commissions, counsel fees, and other costs and interest may be considered in determining the amount of the deficiency. 13 A.2d at 630. *See also* Kline v. The Chase Manhattan Bank, N.A., 403 A.2d 395 (Md. App. 1979).

77. Merchants Mortgage Company v. Bogan, 434 F.2d 490 (USDCt. D.C. 1970, applying Maryland law).

78. Kenneweg Co. v. Finney & Robinson, 56 A. 482 (1903).

Massachusetts State Law of Guaranties

Thomas S. Hemmendinger
Brennan, Recupero, Cascione, Scungio & McAllister, LLP
362 Broadway
Providence, RI 02903
(401) 453-2300
fax (401) 453-2345
themmendinger@brcsm.com
www.brcsm.com

Contents

Massachusetts State Law of Guaranties

Traps:

Massachusetts strictly follows traditional common law rules on consideration, so past consideration does not support a guaranty. *See* § 4.

Introductory Note: In order to standardize our discussion of the law of guaranties, we use the following vocabulary to refer to the various parties to a guaranty and their obligations.

"Guarantor" means a person who, by contract, agrees to satisfy an underlying obligation of another to an obligee upon the primary obligor's default on that underlying obligation. Except in limited situations discussed below, this chapter does not draw great distinction between guarantors and sureties, as there is little difference between the two under Massachusetts law.

"Guaranty" means the contract by which the guarantor agrees to satisfy the underlying obligation of a primary obligor to an obligee in the event the primary obligor defaults on the underlying obligation.

"Obligee" means the person to whom the underlying obligation is owed. For example, the lender under a loan agreement would be an obligee vis-à-vis the borrower.

"Primary Obligor" means the person who incurs the underlying obligation to the obligee. For example, the borrower under a loan agreement would be a primary obligor.

"Underlying Obligation" means the obligation or obligations that the primary obligor owes to the obligee. For example, the borrower's obligation to make payments to a lender of principal and interest on a loan constitutes an underlying obligation.

§ 1 Nature of the Guaranty Arrangement

General principles of the common law of suretyship and guaranties apply in Massachusetts. Massachusetts courts authorize broad waivers of suretyship defenses. For purposes of commercial paper, Massachusetts's Uniform Commercial Code (UCC) provisions on endorsers and accommodation parties are identical to the 1990 Official Texts of Articles 3 and 4.

1.1 Guaranty Relationships

A guaranty creates an obligation that is separate and independent from the underlying obligation.[1] The primary obligor is primarily liable on the underlying obligation, and the guarantor agrees to pay it if the primary obligor fails.[2]

The general rules for contract formation apply to guaranties (competent parties, subject matter, a legal consideration, mutuality of agreement, and mutuality of obligation).[3]

Massachusetts law recognizes the following types of guaranties:

- *Absolute guaranty* – where the guarantor promises to pay or perform upon the primary obligor's default, with no other contingencies.[4]
- *Conditional guaranty* – where the guarantor's promise is contingent on one or more conditions other than, or in addition to, the primary obligor's default.[5]
- *Continuing guaranty* – where the guarantor's promise covers both present and future debt.[6]
- *Payment guaranty (or guaranty of payment)* – where the guarantor promises to pay the primary obligor's debt when due.[7]
- *Collection guaranty (or guaranty of collection)* – where the guarantor promises to pay the primary obligor's debt if the obligee cannot collect after exhausting remedies against the primary obligor.[8]
- *Performance guaranty* – where the guarantor promises to perform an act rather than pay a debt.[9]

1.2 Other Suretyship Relationships

While Massachusetts law technically distinguishes between guarantors and sureties, the terms "surety" and "guarantor" are often used interchangeably in the case law, and are nearly identical.

1. SKW Real Estate Ltd. P'ship v. Gold, 428 Mass. 520, 525, 702 N.E.2d 1178, 1182 (1998).
2. Charlestown Five Cents Sav. Bank v. Wolf, 309 Mass. 547, 549-50, 36 N.E.2d 390 (1941).
3. *See* § 6.1 *infra.*
4. *See* § 6.5 *infra. SKW Real Estate v. Gold, supra* note 1.
5. *See* § 7.3.1 *infra.*
6. *See* § 6.4 *infra.*
7. *See* § 6.2 *infra.*
8. *See* § 6.2 *infra.*
9. *See* § 15.2 *infra.*

Both sureties and guarantors are secondarily liable under Massachusetts law. The difference between them lies in the nature of that secondary liability. A surety makes a direct contract with the obligee to pay an obligation for which the surety is secondarily liable.[10] However, a guarantor's promise is collateral to the underlying obligation.[11]

If a codebtor assumes responsibility for the underlying obligation, then the other codebtor becomes a surety on the obligation and has suretyship defenses.[12]

§ 2 State Law Requirements for an Entity to Enter a Guaranty

Entities and associations organized under Massachusetts law can guaranty the obligations of others, only if they have the legal power to do so.

2.1 Corporations

Unless its articles of organization provide otherwise, a Massachusetts business corporation can issue guaranties.[13] The directors must first determine that the guaranty is necessary or convenient to the conduct, promotion, or goals of the corporation's business.[14] There is a safe harbor for guaranties of affiliates—no such determination is necessary if the guarantor and the primary obligor are affiliated through 100 percent ownership.[15] The Massachusetts Business Corporation Act largely eliminates the defense of *ultra vires* as against a commercial lender.[16]

2.2 Partnerships

A general partnership can issue a guaranty only if the parties specifically authorized the guaranty, or if it is in the common course of the partnership's business to issue guaranties.[17] The partnership may ratify an otherwise unau-

10. Welch v. Walsh, 177 Mass. 555, 559, 59 N.E. 440, 442 (1901). *See also* Rhode Island Hospital Tr. Nat'l Bank v. Ohio Cas. Ins. Co., 789 F.3d 74, 78 (1st Cir. 1986).
11. *Welch v. Walsh, supra,* note 10, 177 Mass. at 559, 59 N.E. at 442.
12. Fisher v. Tifft, 127 Mass. 313 (1879).
13. Mass. Gen. Laws Ann. ch. 156D, § 3.02(a)(7) (2012).
14. Mass. Gen. Laws Ann. ch. 156D § 3.02 cmt. (2012).
15. Mass. Gen. Laws Ann. ch. 156D § 3.02(b) (2012) ("Unless its articles of organization provide otherwise, a contract of guarantee or suretyship made by a corporation with respect to the obligation of another entity, (i) all of the equity interest in which is owned, directly or indirectly, by the contracting corporation, or (ii) which owns, directly or indirectly, all of the outstanding stock of the contracting corporation, or (iii) all of the equity interest in which is owned, directly or indirectly, by an entity which owns, directly or indirectly, all of the outstanding stock of the contracting corporation, shall be deemed necessary or convenient to carry out the business and affairs of the contracting corporation.").
16. *See* Mass. Gen. Laws Ann. ch. 156D § 3.04(a) (2012).
17. Mass. Gen. Laws Ann. ch. 108A, § 9 (2012) (part of the 1914 Uniform Partnership Act); Sweetser v. French, 56 Mass. 309, 2 Cush. 309, 48 Am.Dec. 666 (1848) (holding authority of a partner to sign the firm name as guarantor to the debt of another may be implied from the common course of business of the firm or the previous course of dealing between the parties).

thorized guaranty after the fact.[18] The partnership may also be estopped from contesting the guaranty if the partners knew of the guaranty and allowed it to be issued.[19]

2.3 Limited Liability Companies

A Massachusetts limited liability company (LLC) has "the power to make guarantees of the obligations of another person or entity."[20] This power can be limited only by a written operating agreement.[21] Therefore, unless the operating agreement provides otherwise, the guaranty does not have to be in furtherance of the LLC's purpose.

2.4 Banks and Trust Companies

Massachusetts law only indirectly addresses a bank, trust company, or other financial institution's ability to issue a guaranty. Federal law prohibits a state-chartered bank from engaging in activities in which a national bank may not engage under federal law. The situations under which a national bank may become a guarantor are governed by federal law.[22] State-chartered institutions have "incidental powers that may fairly be implied from those expressly conferred and such as are reasonably necessary to enable [them] to exercise fully those powers according to common or accepted banking customs and usages."[23] Therefore, although banks and trust companies can issue letters of credit, it is not clear that they can issue guaranties.[24]

2.5 Individuals

Any individual competent to enter into a contract may issue a guaranty. This requires:

- Mental competence (the party must "understand the nature and quality of the transaction or grasp its significance").[25]
- Sufficient age (18 years).[26]

Under Massachusetts law, a guaranty issued by one spouse does not automatically affect the property or liabilities of the other spouse.[27]

If the guarantor owns real property with his/her spouse as tenants by the entirety, then the guarantor may alienate his/her own interest, but this does not

18. *Sweetser v. French, supra,* note 17.
19. Flagg v. Upham, 27 Mass. 147 (1830).
20. Mass. Gen. Laws Ann. ch. 156C, § 6(b) (2012).
21. Mass. Gen. Laws Ann. ch. 156C, § 6(b) (2012).
22. *See* 12 C.F.R. § 7.1017 (2010) (National Bank as Guarantor or Surety on Indemnity Bond).
23. Mass. Gen. Laws Ann. ch. 168, § 2 (2012) (savings banks). *See also* Mass. Gen. Laws Ann. ch. 170, § 2 (2012) (co-operative banks); and Mass. Gen. Laws Ann. ch. 170, § 1A (2012) (trust companies).
24. Commercial Tr. Co. v. American Tr. Co., 256 Mass. 58, 152 N.E. 104 (1926).
25. Sutcliffe v. Heatley, 232 Mass. 231, 232-233, 122 N.E. 317 (1919); Reed v. Mattapan Deposit & Trust Co., 198 Mass. 306, 314, 84 N.E. 469 (1907). *See also* Meserve v. Jordan Marsh Co., 340 Mass. 660, 662, 165 N.E.2d 905, 906 (1960).
26. Mass. Gen. Laws Ann. ch. 231, § 85P (2012).
27. Mass. Gen. Laws Ann. ch. 209, § 1 (2012); Coraccio v. Lowell Five Cents Sav. Bank, 415 Mass. 145, 151–152, 612 N.E.2d 650, 654–655 (1993).

break the tenancy or encumber the spouse's interest.[28] Individual creditors of the guarantor may attach property held in tenancy by the entirety.[29] However, the creditor cannot levy and sell the property until and unless the guarantor survives the nondebtor spouse.[30] The creditor's interest is wholly defeasible if the nondebtor spouse survives the guarantor.[31]

The protection that tenancy by the entirety provides against creditor claims has several limitations:

- As noted above, if the guarantor survives the nondebtor spouse, then the encumbrance covers the entire fee interest in the property.
- The proceeds of tenants by the entirety property are held as tenants in common, so a creditor of the guarantor can immediately levy on his/her interest in the proceeds.[32]
- Upon divorce, a tenancy by the entirety becomes a tenancy in common.[33]
- In a divorce, the court will assign property between the parties, based on equitable principles and a number of statutory factors.[34]

§ 3 Signatory's Authority to Execute a Guaranty

The individual signing the guaranty as an agent of the guarantor must have the authority to execute the guaranty. The authority must be either express authority or implied (apparent) authority.

One can infer authority from a course of conduct in which the principal acquiesced in previous similar acts and ratified them.[35]

An agent has apparent authority if there are "written or spoken words or any other conduct of the principal which, reasonably interpreted, causes a third person to believe that the principal consents to have the act done on his behalf by the person purporting to act for him."[36]

However, it is better practice to obtain proof of actual authority than to rely on estoppel, ratification, or apparent authority.

28. *Id.*
29. Peebles v. Minnis, 402 Mass. 282, 283, 521 N.E.2d 1372, 1373 (1988).
30. In re Snyder, 231 B.R. 437, 443 (Bankr. D. Mass. 1999), *aff'd as modified*, 249 B.R. 40 (B.A.P. 1st Cir. 2000), *aff'd*, 2 Fed. Appx. 46 (1st Cir. 2001).
31. *Coraccio, supra*, note 27, 415 Mass. At 151-52, 612 N.E.2d at 654-55.
32. Ronan v. Ronan, 339 Mass. 460, 463, 159 N.E.2d 653 (1959).
33. Bernatavicius v. Bernatavicius, 259 Mass. 486, 490, 156 N.E. 685 (1929).
34. Mass. Gen. Laws Ann. ch. 208, § 34 (2012).
35. *See, e.g.*, Philip Morris, Inc. v. Litel, 30 Mass. App. 936 (1991).
36. Nielson v. Malcolm Kenneth Co., 303 Mass. 437, 441, 22 N.E.2d 20 (1939). *See also* Haufler v. Zotos, 446 Mass. 489, 498, 845 N.E.2d 322, 330 n.22 (2006).

3.1 Corporations

Agency principles apply to corporations and other entities.[37] Therefore, the officer signing a guaranty must have actual or apparent authority to bind the corporation.[38]

While courts have occasionally upheld an officer's apparent authority to pay the obligations of a third party,[39] the best practice is to require written evidence of the officer's actual authority to sign a guaranty on behalf of the corporation.[40]

3.2 Partnerships

The 1914 Uniform Partnership Act is still in force in Massachusetts. That law makes each partner an agent of a general partnership "for the purpose of its business" and gives each partner authority to execute "any instrument, for apparently carrying on in the usual way the business of the partnership."[41]

The same rules apply to Massachusetts limited partnerships.[42]

Nevertheless, it is not generally the ordinary business of any organization to issue guaranties. Further, it is not clear that under the common law partnerships had the power to issue guaranties. Therefore, one should not rely on a partner's authority to execute a guaranty on behalf of the partnership without written evidence of actual authority. This evidence should include a provision in the partnership agreement authorizing the partnership to issue guaranties.[43]

3.3 Limited Liability Companies

The Massachusetts limited liability company act distinguishes between manager-managed LLCs and member-managed LLCs.[44] It provides that a manager in a manager-managed LLC is an agent of the LLC and "may execute documents and act for the limited liability company" so long as the manager's act does not contravene any specific operating agreement, the articles of organization, or the Massachusetts LLC act.[45] The same rules apply to a member of a member-managed LLC.[46] Also, members of a manager-managed LLC cannot bind the LLC unless they are also managers.[47]

---

37. Sunrise Properties, Inc. v. Bacon, Wilson, Ratner, Cohen, Salvage, Fialky & Fitzgerald, P.C., 425 Mass. 63, 66, 679 N.E.2d 540, 543 (1997).
38. Doehler Die-Casting Co. v. Bankers' Sec. Corp., 254 Mass. 229, 231-32, 150 N.E. 1, 2 (1926).
39. *See id.*
40. The power to issue "a corporate guaranty of the debt of an unrelated corporation is not within the delegable managerial functions of a corporate officer." Contel Credit Corp. v. Central Chevrolet, Inc., 29 Mass. App. Ct. 83, 86, 557 N.E.2d 77 (1990) (in which the court held that the obligee could rely on an officer's certificate of corporate vote, even though it was a forgery).
41. Mass. Gen. Laws Ann. ch. 108A, § 9 (2012).
42. Mass. Gen. Laws Ann. ch. 109, § 24 (2012).
43. Mass. Gen. Laws Ann. 108A, § 9(2) (2012); *Sweetser v. French, supra,* note 17.
44. Mass. Gen. Laws Ann. ch. 156C, § 24 (2012).
45. Mass. Gen. Laws Ann. ch. 156C, §§ 6, 21, 24 (2012).
46. Mass. Gen. Laws Ann. ch. 156C, § 24 (2012).
47. Mass. Gen. Laws Ann. ch. 156C, § 24 (2012).

If the LLC is member-managed, then "the members shall manage and control the limited liability company."[48]

Further, as noted in § 2.3 *supra*, every Massachusetts LLC has the power to issue guaranties, even if the guaranties are not in furtherance of the LLC's purpose.[49]

However, despite this broad grant of authority, one should require written evidence of a manager's or member's actual authority to sign and issue a guaranty on behalf of the LLC.

3.4 Banks and Trust Companies

One must examine the bank's or trust company's corporate governance documents to determine who may validly execute a guaranty on behalf of the entity.

§ 4 Consideration; Sufficiency of Past Consideration

Consideration sufficient to support a contract in general is sufficient to support a guaranty contract.

Consideration does not necessarily have to flow to the guarantor.[50] A detriment to the obligee is sufficient. The obligee's agreement to extend (or to continue to extend) credit to the primary obligor in exchange for the guaranty is sufficient consideration.[51] It is also sufficient consideration if the obligee agrees to forbear from exercising remedies in exchange for the guaranty.[52]

Past consideration will not support a guaranty. Therefore, if the guarantor issues the guaranty after the underlying obligation has been incurred, then there must be independent consideration for the guaranty.[53]

Based on the case law, if the lender requires the guaranty as a condition to making the loan or as a condition to forbearance after default, the guaranty is supported by adequate consideration.

Consideration for a guaranty does not need to be expressed on the face of the guaranty; it may be inferred from the terms of the guaranty or proved

48. Mass. Gen. Laws Ann. ch. 156C, § 24(b) (2012).
49. Mass. Gen. Laws Ann. ch. 156C, § 6 (2012).
50. Rome v. Gaunt, 246 Mass. 82, 94, 140 N.E. 242, 245 (1923) (holding that the furnishing of credit to a company in reliance on an individual's guaranty of the debt is sufficient consideration for the guaranty even where "no consideration moved directly to the guarantor from the plaintiff").
51. Adams v. Bean, 12 Mass. 137, 140 (1815); Sheraton Service Corp. v. Kanavos, 4 Mass. App. Ct. 851, 851-2, 357 N.E.2d 20 (1976).
52. Packard v. Richardson, 17 Mass. 122, 140-43 (1821). *See also* Atlas Shoe Co. v. Bloom, 209 Mass. 563, 568, 95 N.E. 952 (1911) ("[A] promise by the plaintiff to forbear to press collection of the debt, followed by an actual forbearance for a reasonable time, even if no time was named, . . . would have been a sufficient consideration to support the guaranty."). *Compare* Mecorney v. Stanley, 62 Mass. 85 (1851) (actual forbearance, but without any agreement to forbear, is not sufficient consideration), *with* Merrimack Valley Nat'l Bank v. Baird, 279 Mass. 147, 181 N.E. 219 (1932) (court can infer an agreement to forbear from the parties' conduct).
53. *See* Tenney v. Prince, 21 Mass. (4 Pick.) 385 (1826); Gentzel v. Dodge, 271 Mass. 499, 171 N.E. 454 (1930).

through the use of parol evidence.[54] However, the obligee must prove there was consideration for the guaranty.[55]

If the guaranty was executed under seal, however, consideration is not required.[56] For a document to be executed under seal, it must merely recite that it is so executed—an actual seal is not required.[57]

§ 5 Notice of Acceptance

Whether the obligee must give notice of acceptance of the guaranty depends first on the type of guaranty.

If the guaranty is in the nature of an offer, the guarantor is entitled to know if the obligee accepts it.[58] The obligee's acceptance of a guaranty often manifests itself in the obligee's conducting business with the primary obligor. In such a case, the courts often find that the guarantor is not likely to learn of such acceptance, so notice is required.[59]

Notice of acceptance is not required in the following situations:

- The guaranty is an absolute guaranty that recites the consideration for the guaranty.[60]
- Where notice is inferred from the nature of the transaction.[61]
- Where a valuable consideration flows from the obligee to the guarantor (a compensated guarantor).[62]
- Where the guarantor waives the requirement.[63]

§ 6 Interpretation of Guaranties

Massachusetts courts generally follow the rule of *strictissimi juris*, under which they strictly construe the guarantor's obligations.[64] In other respects,

54. Gloucester Mut. Fishing Ins. Co. v. Boyer, 294 Mass. 35, 40-41, 200 N.E. 557, 561 (1936).
55. *Id.*
56. Mayo v. Bloomberg, 290 Mass. 168, 170, 195 N.E. 99 (1935). *See also* Chem-Lac Products, Inc. v. Gerome, 327 Mass. 394, 395, 99 N.E.2d 61 (1951).
57. Mass. Gen. Laws Ann. ch 4, § 9A (2012); Lawrence H. Oppenheim Co. v. Bloom, 325 Mass. 301, 302, 90 N.E.2d 7 (1950).
58. Black, Starr & Frost v. Grabow, 216 Mass. 516, 104 N.E. 346 (1914); Lane Brothers Co. v. Sheinwald, 275 Mass. 96, 175 N.E. 148 (1931); Paige v. Parker, 74 Mass. (8 Gray) 211, 214 (1857).
59. Bishop v. Eaton, 161 Mass. 496, 499-500, 37 N.E. 665, 667-68 (1894) ("Ordinarily there is no occasion to notify the offerer of the acceptance of such an offer, for the doing of the act is a sufficient acceptance, and the promisor knows that he is bound when he sees that action has been taken on the faith of his offer. But if the act is of such a kind that knowledge of it will not quickly come to the promisor, the promisee is bound to give him notice of his acceptance within a reasonable time after doing that which constitutes the acceptance.").
60. *Mayo v. Bloomberg, supra,* note 56, 290 Mass. at 170-71, 195 N.E. 99. *See also* Gentzel v. Dodge, 271 Mass. 499, 171 N.E. 454 (1930), in which the court ruled for the obligee on a continuing guaranty, based on the guarantor's understanding that the obligee would not work for the primary obligor unless the guarantor guaranteed his compensation.
61. Black, Starr & Frost v. Grabow, 216 Mass. 516, 518, 104 N.E. 346, 346 (1914).
62. *Id.*
63. Cambridgeport Sav. Bank v. Boersner, 413 Mass. 432, 441, 597 N.E.2d 1017, 1013 (1992) (dictum).
64. Warren v. Lyons, 152 Mass. 310, 312, 25 N.E. 721, 722 (1890).

courts will interpret a guaranty according to general principles of contact interpretation.

6.1 General Principles

Generally, courts interpret a guaranty strictly according to general principles of contract construction.[65]

To interpret the language of the guaranty, courts follow general principles of contract construction.[66] They ascertain the liability of a surety or guarantor from the terms of the written instrument, construed according to the usual rules of interpretation in the light of the subject matter, the well-understood usages of business, and the relations of the parties to the transaction.[67] Therefore, if the words are unambiguous, they alone can be examined to determine their meaning.[68]

The courts will look to the guaranty's language, with due consideration to its subject matter, the relative conditions of the parties, and their probable intent.[69] Also relevant are the "conditions under which [the guaranty] was given."[70] This means courts will construe multiple documents (such as the promissory note, the security instruments, and the guaranty) together if they were part of a single transaction, at least if the guarantor had knowledge of the terms of the other documents.[71]

If the language of the guaranty is not clear, then "an interpretation will commonly be adopted which will effectuate a reasonable and enforceable purpose to accomplish a practical and straightforward end."[72] Therefore, in the ordinary case where the obligee drafts the guaranty, an ambiguous term is not construed strictly against the guarantor.[73] This principle is justified by the secondary nature of the guarantor's obligation.[74]

However, if the guarantor is the author of the guaranty, then the normal rules of contract construction apply, and the guaranty will be construed strictly against the guarantor.[75]

In any event, the obligee must show that the guarantor intended to be liable for the underlying obligation. To establish a case upon a guaranty, the plaintiff must prove:

---

65. Zimetbaum v. Berenson, 267 Mass. 250, 255, 166 N.E. 719, 720 (1929) ("No doubt a contract of guaranty is to be construed strictly, and the guarantor is not to be held liable for anything not in accord with the contract."); Davis-Hill Co. v. Wells, 254 Mass. 118, 125, 149 N.E. 693, 695 (1925) ("The guaranty is to be construed strictly, and the [guarantor] is entitled to rely upon its precise terms. . . .").
66. L. Littlejohn & Co. v. Handy, 246 Mass. 370, 374, 141 N.E. 127 (1923).
67. Agricultural Nat'l Bank of Pittsfield v. Brennan, 295 Mass. 325, 327-28, 3 N.E.2d 769, 771 (1936); Zeo v. Loomis, 246 Mass. 366, 368, 141 N.E. 115, 115-16 (1923).
68. Zeo v. Loomis, 246 Mass. 366, 368, 141 N.E. 115, 115-16 (1923).
69. *Agricultural Nat'l Bank of Pittsfield v. Brennan, supra,* note 67, 295 Mass. at 327-28, 3 N.E.2d at 771.
70. Callender, McAuslan & Troup Co. v. Flint, 187 Mass. 104, 108, 72 N.E. 345, 346 (1904) (in which the court concluded that a guaranty covered only a single transaction and was not a continuing guaranty).
71. Charlestown Five Cents Sav. Bank v. Zeff, 275 Mass. 408, 411, 176 N.E. 191 (1931) (the documents were executed at the same time for the same purpose in the same transaction); *Davis-Hill Co. v. Wells, supra,* note 65, 254 Mass. at 126, 149 N.E. at 696.
72. *Agricultural Nat'l Bank of Pittsfield v. Brennan, supra,* note 67, 295 Mass. at 328, 3 N.E.2d at 771.
73. Keith v. Thomas, 266 Mass. 566, 571, 165 N.E. 679 (1929).
74. *Merrimack Valley Nat. Bank v. Baird, supra,* note 52, 372 Mass. at 724, 363 N.E.2d at 691.
75. *Merrimack Valley Nat. Bank v. Baird, supra,* note 52, 372 Mass. at 724-25, 363 N.E.2d at 691.

- the existence of an underlying obligation[76];
- the guaranty by the defendant in writing, including consideration for the guaranty;[77]
- default of the underlying obligation[78]; and
- that the plaintiff has complied fully with all of the terms of both the original contract and of the guaranty.[79]

The parol evidence rule applies to guaranties.[80] It customarily precludes any resort to extrinsic evidence of prior agreements or negotiations to contradict or alter, even potentially, the terms of an unambiguous and final written contract.[81]

Massachusetts courts recognize the following exceptions to the parol evidence rule:

- Fraud.[82]
- Mutual mistake, allowing either rescission or reformation of the contract.[83]
- Where the guaranty does not state the consideration for the guaranty, the parties may introduce extrinsic evidence on the issue of consideration.[84]
- Where the person executed the guaranty in an ambiguous manner, and the court is called upon to determine the capacity in which he/she signed the guaranty.[85]

6.2 Guaranty of Payment versus Guaranty of Collection

Massachusetts courts distinguish between guaranties of payment and guaranties of collection.[86]

A guaranty based on signing a negotiable instrument (either as accommodation maker or as endorser) constitutes a guaranty of payment, unless the guarantor's signature is "accompanied by words indicating unambiguously that the party is guaranteeing collection rather than payment."[87]

76. Merchants Nat'l Bank v. Stone, 296 Mass. 243, 5 N.E.2d 430 (1936).
77. *Tenney v. Prince*, *supra,* note 53; Tenney v. Prince, 24 Mass. (7 Pick.) 243 (1828).
78. Cumberland Glass Mfg. Co. v. Wheaton, 208 Mass. 425, 433, 94 N.E. 803, 805 (1911).
79. First National Bank of Boston v. Ibarra, 47 Mass. App. Ct. 660, 662-63, 716 N.E.2d 647 (1999).
80. Dwight v. Pomeroy, 17 Mass. 303, 328 (1821).
81. *Id. See also* Amerada Hess Corp. v. Garabedian, 416 Mass. 149, 155 (1993); and Gainsboro v. Shaffer, 339 Mass. 1, 157 N.E.2d 536 (1959) (extrinsic evidence admissible to determine meaning of the ambiguous term "service guarantee" in a building contract).
82. *Dwight v. Pomeroy, supra,* note 80, 17 Mass. at 324-25.
83. Polaroid Corp. v. Travelers Indem. Co., 414 Mass. 747, 756, 610 N.E.2d 912, 917 (1993).
84. *Packard v. Richardson, supra,* note 52.
85. Boston Globe Newspaper Co., v. Folktree Concertmakers, Inc., 1998 Mass. App. Div. 206, 1998 Mass. App. Div. LEXIS 88 . In *Folktree,* the president of the corporate primary obligor put the word "President" after his name on the personal guaranty. The court held that it would violate canons of contractual interpretation and render the guaranty "meaningless" if that meant that the person was signing only in his capacity as president, rather than as an individual. *Accord,* IPP of America, Inc. v. B.K.C. Enters., Inc., 2009 Mass. App. Unpub. LEXIS 1352.
86. D'Annolfo v. D'Annolfo Const. Co., Inc., 39 Mass. App. Ct. 189, 192, 654 N.E.2d 82, 84, n.6 (1995).
87. Mass. Gen. Laws Ann. ch. 106, § 3-419(d), cmt. 4 (2012).

6.3 Language Regarding the Revocation of Guaranties

A guaranty of a single, present debt is irrevocable.[88]

A continuing guaranty may be terminated as to future transactions, but only in accordance with the terms of the guaranty agreement.[89] This requires notice to the obligee.[90] However, the guarantor remains liable for indebtedness incurred before the revocation.[91]

The guarantor's intent to revoke must be clearly inferable from the language the guarantor uses.[92] Further, a continuing guaranty is not automatically terminated or revoked when the guarantor terminates employment with, or sells his/her interest in, the primary obligor.[93]

Most commercial finance transactions involve continuing guaranties, because the primary obligor's debts may arise in the future, as with future advances on revolving lines of credit or future loan transactions. Therefore, lenders should use guaranty language that specifies the revocation notice requirements and the consequences of revocation.[94] For example, the lender should require that the guarantor deliver a revocation notice to a particular department where the account officer will get prompt notice. The guaranty should also provide that the revocation becomes effective only on some fixed future date, such as "XX" days after the lender receives the notice. This will give the lender sufficient time to mitigate its risk if a guarantor revokes.

The death of an individual guarantor revokes a continuing guaranty as to debt incurred after the guarantor dies.[95] The guarantor's estate remains liable for debt incurred before death.[96]

6.4 "Continuing"

If the guaranty, the recitals, or reference to custom or course of dealing show that the guaranty covers future transactions or a succession of transactions, then it is a "continuing" guaranty.[97]

The liability of a guarantor under a continuing guaranty continues until the guarantor gives notice of revocation.[98] However, if the guaranty neither

---

88. *See* Fleet Nat'l Bank v. Phillips, 2006 Mass. App. Div. 107 (Dist. Ct. 2006).
89. Federal Financial Co. v. Savage, 431 Mass. 814, 730 N.E.2d 853 (2000); *Merchants Nat'l Bank v. Stone, supra,* note 76, 296 Mass. at 252, 5 N.E.2d 430; Spring v. Leahy, 254 Mass. 614, 43 A.L.R. 1203, 150 N.E. 843 (1926).
90. *Jordan* v. *Dobbins,* 122 Mass. 168, 170, 171 (1877).
91. *Id.*
92. *Merrimack Valley Nat. Bank v. Baird, supra,* note 52, 372 Mass. 721, 725 n.4, 363 N.E.2d 688.
93. Manufacturers' Fin. Co. v. Rockwell, 278 Mass. 502, 505-06, 180 N.E. 224, 226 (1932).
94. *Federal Financial Co. v. Savage, supra,* note 89.
95. *Jordan v. Dobbins, supra,* note 90, 122 Mass. at 170.
96. *Id.*
97. Bent v. Hartshorn, 42 Mass. 24, 26 (1840). *See also* Celluloid Co. v. Haines, 176 Mass. 415, 417, 57 N.E. 691, 692 (1900) (construing a written guaranty "to pay bills of one month upon the 15th of succeeding month, if not already paid" as a continuing guaranty, and not a guaranty only for one month, based upon terms of guaranty and guarantor's acknowledgment of liability to creditor for an unpaid bill several months after guarantor executed the guaranty). *Cf.* Boston & Sandwich Glass Co. v. Moore, 119 Mass. 435 (1876) (guaranty to pay for goods "purchased by" the primary obligor was construed as a limited guaranty).
98. *Manufacturers' Fin. Co. v. Rockwell, supra,* note 93, 278 Mass. at 504, 180 N.E. at 225.

addresses the duration of the guaranty nor states that it remains in effect until revoked, it will only continue for a reasonable duration.[99]

A court will ascertain whether the instrument is a limited or continuing guaranty by giving effect to the intention of the parties as manifested by the terms of the guaranty read in relation to the circumstances under which it was given.[100] For example, the guarantor's statement that "I hereby guarantee all accounts for purchase of leather from your concern made by" the primary obligor constituted a limited guaranty and did not apply to future purchases.[101] But except in the situation where the court is bound to construe a guaranty against the guarantor (*see* § 6 *supra*), the court will presume that an ambiguous guaranty constitutes a limited guaranty, not a continuing guaranty.[102]

A guaranty can be both absolute and continuing.[103]

6.5 "Absolute and Unconditional"

Massachusetts courts distinguish between absolute guaranties and limited (or conditional) guaranties.[104] A guaranty is "absolute" if the only condition precedent to the guarantor's liability is the primary obligor's default on the underlying obligation.[105]

On the other hand, if the guaranty contains conditions precedent to the guarantor's liability, those conditions must be satisfied unless the guarantor waives them.[106]

6.6 "Liable as a Primary Obligor and not Merely as Surety"

As explained in § 1.2 *supra*, a surety makes a direct contract to pay an obligation for which the surety is secondarily liable, while a guarantor makes a collateral promise regarding the underlying obligation. Therefore, the effect of a guarantor's agreement to be liable as a primary obligor is unclear.

§ 7 Defenses of the Guarantor; Set-off

The defenses that may be available to a guarantor can be grouped into three categories:

- Defenses of the primary obligor
- "Suretyship defenses"
- Other defenses.

---

99. *Zeo v. Loomis, supra,* note 67, 246 Mass. at 368, 141 N.E. at 116. *See also Manufacturers' Fin. Co. v. Rockwell, supra,* note 93, 278 Mass. at 504, 180 N.E. at 225.
100. Standard Plumbing Supply Co. v. La Conte, 277 Mass. 497, 499, 178 N.E. 611, 612 (1931).
101. *Keith v. Thomas, supra,* note 73, 266 Mass. at 571.
102. Sherman v. Mulloy, 174 Mass. 41, 43, 54 N.E. 345, 345 (1899); Cutler v. Ballou, 136 Mass. 337 (1884).
103. Community Nat'l Bank v. Loumos, 6 Mass. App. Ct. 830, 831, 372 N.E.2d 265, 266 (1978).
104. *Standard Plumbing Supply Co. v. La Conte, supra,* note 100, 277 Mass. 499, 178 N.E. at 612.
105. Seabury v. Sibley, 183 Mass. 105, 107, 66 N.E. 603, 603 (1903).
106. *See* § 7.3.1, *infra.*

7.1 Defenses of the Primary Obligor

7.1.1 General

A guarantor may assert most defenses that the primary obligor could assert, but cannot assert so-called "personal defenses" of the primary obligor.

7.1.2 When Guarantor may assert Primary Obligor's Defense

As a general rule, a guarantor is not liable unless the primary obligor is liable.[107] There are, however, exceptions to this rule.[108] For example, the guarantor remains liable if the guarantor's obligation is unconditional.[109] In that situation, the guarantor's only defenses are in equity.[110] Also, the surety on a bond is primarily liable, so it cannot assert the primary obligor's defenses.[111]

A guarantor is not, however, liable if the underlying obligation is based on an illegal contract.[112]

7.1.3 Defenses that may not be raised by Guarantor

As noted in § 7.1.1 *supra*, a guarantor cannot generally raise personal defenses of the primary obligor.[113] For example, a guarantor cannot assert the following defenses:

- The primary obligor's incapacity to enter into the underlying transaction.[114]
- The fact that the statute of limitations had expired against the primary obligor at the time the guarantor issued its guaranty.[115]
- The obligee's inducing the primary obligor to incur the underlying obligation.[116]
- The primary obligor's bankruptcy.[117]

Based on the foregoing, a guarantor probably cannot defend based on a claim that the primary obligor's agent did not have authority to incur the underlying obligation.

A guarantor may not raise the primary obligor's fraud on the guarantor as a defense, if the obligee gives value or materially relies on the guaranty "in good faith and without reason to know of the misrepresentation."[118]

---

107. Mestek, Inc. v. United Pacific Ins. Co., 40 Mass. App. Ct. 729, 732, 667 N.E.2d 292, 294 (1996).
108. *Id.*
109. *SKW Real Estate Ltd. P'ship v. Gold, supra,* note 1, 428 Mass. at 525, 702 N.E.2d at 1182; *Mestek, Inc. v. United Pacific Ins. Co., supra,* note 107, 40 Mass. App. Ct. at 732, 667 N.E.2d at 294-95.
110. *Mestek, Inc. v. United Pacific Ins. Co., supra,* note 107, 40 Mass. App. Ct. at 732, 667 N.E.2d at 294-95.
111. *Welch v. Walsh, supra,* note 10, 177 Mass. at 559, 59 N.E. at 442.
112. Riley v. Jordan, 122 Mass. 231, 233 (1877).
113. *SKW Real Estate Ltd. P'ship v. Gold, supra,* note 1, 428 Mass. at 525, 702 N.E.2d at 1182.
114. Winn v. Sanford, 145 Mass. 302, 303, 14 N.E. 119, 121 (1887).
115. Worcester Mechanics' Sav. Bank v. Hill, 113 Mass. 25, 28 (1873).
116. *Rhode Island Hospital Tr. Nat'l Bank v. Ohio Cas. Ins. Co., supra,* note 10, 789 F.2d at 79 n. 6.
117. *See, e.g., Pemstein v. Stimpson, supra,* note 107, 36 Mass. App. Ct. at 293, 630 N.E.2d at 615 (primary obligor's bankruptcy is not a defense).
118. Eagles v. McCabe, 80 Mass. App. Ct. 1116, 957 N.E.2d 731 (2011) (citing the RESTATEMENT (THIRD) OF SURETYSHIP AND GUARANTY § 12(2) (1996)).

In Massachusetts, a mortgagee may not recover a deficiency against the mortgagor unless it issues a deficiency notice to the mortgagor before the foreclosure sale.[119] However, the antideficiency statute does not apply to a guarantor who is not the mortgagor.[120]

7.1.4 Defenses that may always be raised by Guarantor

A guarantor may show that the obligee failed to perform such that there is a partial or complete failure of consideration.

Fraud in the inducement committed against the guarantor is a defense.[121]

Mutual mistake is a defense.[122]

7.2 "Suretyship" Defenses

7.2.1 Change in Identity of Primary Obligor

If the primary obligor transfers its right and obligations to a third party, then the terms of the guaranty determine the guarantor's liability for the transferee's obligations.

7.2.2 Modification of the Underlying Obligation, including Release

A material change in the underlying obligation discharges the guarantor, unless the guarantor consents to the change.[123] If the underlying obligation is a negotiable instrument, then the guarantor is discharged "to the extent the modification causes loss to the [guarantor] with respect to the right of recourse."[124] In that situation, there is a presumption of complete discharge, which the obligee must rebut.[125]

The consent can be in the guaranty itself.[126] Consent might also be inferred from the guarantor's willing participation in the modification.

If the guaranty is a continuing guaranty, then the language describing the future debts may be broad enough to constitute the guarantor's consent to extension of time for performance.[127]

If the change is beneficial to the guarantor, the guarantor may not be discharged.[128]

---

119. Mass. Gen. Laws Ann. ch. 244 §17B.
120. *SKW Real Estate Ltd. P'ship v. Gold, supra,* note 1, 428 Mass. at 525, 702 N.E.2d at 1182.
121. *Atlas Shoe Co. v. Bloom, supra,* note 52, 209 Mass. at 568.
122. *Polaroid Corp. v. Travelers Indem. Co., supra,* note 83, 414 Mass. at 756, 620 N.E.2d at 917.
123. Germainia Fire Ins. Co. v. Lange, 193 Mass. 67, 78 N.E. 746 (1906); Shawmut Bank v. Wayman, 34 Mass. App. Ct. 20, 23, 606 N.E.2d 925, 927 (1993).
124. Mass. Gen. Laws Ann. ch. 106 § 3-605(d).
125. *Id.*
126. *Manufacturers' Fin. Co. v. Rockwell, supra,* note 93, 278 Mass. at 505-06, 180 N.E. at 226.
127. *Bent v. Hartshorn, supra,* note 97, 41 Mass. at 26.
128. Boston Box Co. v. Rosen, 254 Mass. 331, 333, 150 N.E. 177 (1926) (the modification reduced the guarantor's exposure on the underlying obligation).

Extending the time for the primary obligor to perform also discharges the guarantor,[129] unless the guarantor consents to the extension[130] or the obligee expressly reserves its rights against the guarantor.[131] As with modifications in general, the guarantor's consent may be in the guaranty itself.

However, if the guaranty is a continuing guaranty, then extension of time for performance may not discharge the guarantor.[132]

7.2.3 Release or Impairment of Security for the Underlying Obligation

Ordinarily, the obligee has a duty not to release or impair collateral.[133] Breach of this duty discharges the guarantor to the extent of the release or impairment.[134] If the underlying obligation is a negotiable instrument, the release or impairment discharges the guarantor to the extent of the release or impairment.[135] In that situation, the guarantor has the burden of proving the degree of impairment.[136]

Whatever the nature of the underlying obligation, however, the discharge does not apply if the guarantor consents to the release or impairment. [137] The consent may be contained in the guaranty itself.[138]

Release of collateral may be an integral part of the underlying transaction. For example, in a documentary sale of goods, the letter of credit issuer will release documents of title to the buyer. The guarantor of the buyer's reimbursement obligation to the issuer cannot assert the release of the documents of title as a defense to the guaranty.[139]

7.2.4 Notice of Acceptance of the Guaranty

Except as noted in § 5 *supra*, a guarantor is entitled to notice that the obligee has accepted the guaranty. Where notice is required, and the obligee fails to give the notice within a reasonable time, then equitable defenses may apply.[140]

7.2.5 Notice that the Primary Obligor is incurring Additional Debt

In general, the guarantor is entitled to notice when future debt is incurred, but the guarantor may waive this right in the guaranty. However, there is no right

---

129. Union Tr. Co. v. McGinty, 212 Mass. 205, 206, 98 N.E. 679, 680 (1912); Appleton v. Parker, 81 Mass. 173, 177-8 (1860) (even a three-day extension discharges the guarantor).
130. Stanley v. Ames, 378 Mass. 364, 367, 391 N.E.2d 908, 909-10 (1979).
131. *Manufacturers' Fin. Co. v. Rockwell, supra,* note 93, 278 Mass. at 505-06, 180 N.E. at 226.
132. *See Bent v. Hartshorn, supra,* note 97, 42 Mass. at 26 (a continuing guaranty can cover a series of payments due over an indefinite amount of time).
133. *Merchants Nat'l Bank v. Stone, supra,* note 76, 296 Mass. at 251, 5 N.E.2d at 434. *See also Welch v. Walsh, supra,* note 10, 177 Mass. at 558, 59 N.E. at 441.
134. Gens v. Resolution Trust Corp., 112 F.3d 569, 577-78 (1st Cir. 1997).
135. Mass. Gen. Laws Ann. ch. 106, § 3-605(e) – (g) (2012).
136. *Id.*
137. *Merchants Nat'l Bank v. Stone, supra,* note 76, 296 Mass. at 251, 5 N.E.2d at 434.
138. *Id.*
139. Nowell v. Equitable Trust Co., 249 Mass. 585, 594-5, 144 N.E. 749, 751-2 (1924).
140. Mussey v. Rayner, 39 Mass. 223 (1839) (laches).

to such notice in the case of a continuing guaranty.[141] Generally there is no right to notice in the case of a continuing guaranty or an absolute guaranty.[142] Such notice may also be imputed to the guarantor.[143]

7.2.6 Notice that the Primary Obligor has Defaulted on the Underlying Obligation

As noted in § 5 *supra,* in certain circumstances, notice of acceptance of the guaranty is required. The same is not true per se for notice of the default to the guarantor, unless the guaranty requires such notice.[144] If the obligee fails to give such notice, and the failure causes the guarantor to lose its rights against the primary obligor, then the guarantor is discharged.[145] Further, if the guaranty specifies the manner in which notice is to be given, then the obligee's giving notice in that manner is sufficient, even if the guarantor does not receive the notice.[146]

7.3 Other Defenses

7.3.1 Failure to Fulfill a Condition Precedent

If the Guaranty contains a condition precedent to the guarantor's liability, then the obligee must satisfy that condition before pursuing the guarantor.[147]

7.3.2 Modification of the Guaranty

As a general rule, modification of a contract requires both mutual assent and consideration.[148] An agreement to modify a contract can be either express, or it may be inferred from the attendant circumstances and conduct of the parties.[149]

Massachusetts courts generally give effect to a contract provision requiring all modifications to the contract be in writing, unless the party to be charged has waived the requirement. However, such a provision does not necessarily bar oral modification.[150] In order to support the existence of an oral modifica-

141. *Paige v. Parker, supra,* note 58, 74 Mass. (8 Gray) at 214.
142. *Mayo v. Bloomberg, supra,* note 56, 290 Mass. at 170-71, 195 N.E. 99.
143. *Community Nat'l Bank v. Loumos, supra,* note 103, 6 Mass. App. Ct. at 830, 372 N.E.2d at 266.
144. *Welch v. Walsh, supra,* 177 Mass. at 558, 59 N.E. at 441 ("[I]f the guarantor, in violation of his duty, has slumbered because he supposed that, in the absence of a demand by the creditor the act guarantied had been performed by the principal debtor and has suffered damage from so doing, he has nothing of which he can complain but his own negligence, and is liable to pay the sum which he guarantied should be paid."). *Cf.* Vinal v. Richardson, 95 Mass. (13 Allen) 521, 532-33 (1866) (holding that guarantor can make notice of default an express condition to payment in the guaranty).
145. Clark v. Remington, 52 Mass. 361, 365 (1846). *See also* § 7.3.3 *infra.*
146. Protection Ins. Co. v. Davis, 87 Mass. 54 (1862).
147. Curtis v. Hubbard, 47 Mass. 186 (1843); *First Nat. Bank of Boston v. Ibarra, supra,* note 79, 47 Mass. App. Ct. at 662-63, 716 N.E.2d at 649 (holding that obligee satisfied notice requirement contained in guaranty by strict compliance with terms of the guaranty).
148. *See* Gishen v. Dura Corp., 362 Mass. 177, 183 (1972).
149. A. Leo Nash Steel Corp. v. Southern New England Erection Co., 9 Mass. App. Ct. 377, 383 (1980).
150. *Cambridgeport Sav. Bank v. Boersner, supra,* note 63, 413 Mass. at 439, 597 N.E.2d 1017.

tion, the parol evidence must be of sufficient strength to present an ambiguity between the actual conduct of the parties and the contract.[151]

Modification of the guaranty itself, without the guarantor's consent, voids the guaranty.[152] On the other hand, the obligee can complete a signed but blank guaranty, so long as the insertions comport to the terms of the bargain between the guarantor and the obligee.[153]

7.3.3 Failure to pursue Primary Obligor

Except in the case of a guaranty of collection, both at common law and the UCC, the obligee does not have to pursue the primary obligor.[154] If the underlying obligation becomes due and payable in full, then unless the guaranty provides otherwise, the obligee may pursue the guarantor for the full amount of the obligation, even before foreclosing on the primary obligor's collateral.[155]

Nor does the obligee have a duty to exercise due care in dealing with the primary obligor or in deciding whether to enter into the underlying transaction.[156]

However, unless the guaranty provides otherwise, the obligee does have a duty not to impair the guarantor's subrogation rights.[157] The guarantor bears the burden of proving it suffered prejudice from any delay.[158]

7.3.4 Statute of Limitations

Massachusetts law imposes a general six-year statute of limitations on contractual obligations, with certain exceptions.[159] These exceptions include:

- Contracts under seal (20 years).[160]
- Promissory notes and other evidence of debt issued by a bank (20 years).[161]
- Promissory notes signed in the presence of an attesting witness, if the original payee brings the action (20 years).[162] Under the former version

151. *Id. See also* Wells Fargo Bus. Credit v. Environamics Corp., 77 Mass. App. Ct. 812, 817, 934 N.E.2d 283, 287 (2010).
152. Howe v. Peabody, 68 Mass. (2 Gray) 556, 557 (1854).
153. Ulen v. Kittredge, 7 Mass. 233 (1810); Forum Provisions Co., Inc. v. Tom, 1995 Mass. App. Div. 105, 1995 Mass. App. Div. LEXIS 52.
154. *Seabury v. Sibley, supra,* note 105, 183 Mass. at 107, 66 N.E. at 603; Mass. Gen. Laws Ann. ch. 106, § 3-419(d) (2012).
155. Security Co-operative Bank v. Corcoran, 298 Mass. 156, 157, 158, 10 N.E.2d 57 (1937); *Charlestown Five Cents Sav. Bank v. Zeff, supra,* note 71, 275 Mass. at 411, 176 N.E. 191. However, the guarantor is entitled to a credit for the proceeds of any sale that takes place thereafter.
156. *Shawmut Bank v. Wayman, supra,* note 123, 34 Mass. App. Ct. at 24, 606 N.E.2d at 928.
157. *Welch v. Walsh, supra,* 177 Mass. at 558, 59 N.E. at 440 (Although the obligee does not have to notify the guarantor that the primary obligor has defaulted, the obligee owes a duty "to do no act which affects the rights to which the surety is subrogated on meeting his guaranty either in property held by the creditor as security for the debt guarantied, or to bring suit against the principal debtor.").
158. *Protection Ins. Co. v. Davis, supra,* note 146.
159. Mass. Gen. Laws Ann. ch. 260, § 2 (2012).
160. Mass. Gen. Laws Ann. ch. 260, § 1 (first clause) (2012).
161. Mass. Gen. Laws Ann. ch. 260, § 1 (second clause) (2012).
162. Mass. Gen. Laws Ann. ch. 260, § 1 (third clause) (2012).

of UCC Article 3, the Massachusetts Appeals Court has applied this statute to a guaranty that was inscribed on a promissory note.[163]

- Contracts for the sale of goods that are governed by Article 2 of the Massachusetts UCC (four years).[164]

Therefore, the holder of an unsealed guaranty must commence suit within six years after the cause of action accrues.[165] Some lenders have guarantors execute their guaranties under seal, to gain the benefit of the 20-year statute of limitations.

7.3.5 Statute of Frauds

Massachusetts statute of frauds bars enforcement of guaranties, unless they are in writing.[166]

7.3.6 Defenses particular to Guarantors that are Natural Persons and their Spouses

Generally, except for the individual guarantor's competence or age,[167] Massachusetts law does not recognize defenses unique to individuals. Nor does Massachusetts law give a guarantor's spouse any unique defenses.

In one case discussed in § 7.3.9 *infra*, however, the court applied general equitable principles and the implied covenant of good faith and fair dealing to discharge a guarantor.[168]

A guarantor's estate is liable for the unpaid amount of the underlying obligation as of the guarantor's date of death.[169]

7.3.7 Fraud in the inducement

The guarantor can be discharged if the obligee committed fraud in inducing the guarantor to issue the guaranty.[170] Reliance must be both reasonable and justifiable.[171] Further, the guarantor must establish this by clear and convincing evidence.[172]

---

163. *D'Annolfo v. D'Annolfo Const. Co., Inc., supra,* note 86, 39 Mass. App. Ct. 192-93, 654 N.E.2d at 84.
164. Mass. Gen. Laws Ann. ch. 106, § 2-725(1) (2012).
165. Cadle Co. v. Webb, 66 Mass. App. Ct. 269, 270, 846 N.E.2d 1179, 1181 (2006).
166. Mass. Gen. Laws Ann. ch. 259, § 1 (2012). There is a limited exception for the promise to pay the debt of another person, when the essence of the agreement containing such promise is to obtain a pecuniary benefit by the promisor from the promisee, and when such promise is merely incidental to obtaining that benefit. Hayes v. Guy, 348 Mass. 754, 756 (1965); Colpitts v. L.C. Fisher Co., 289 Mass 232, 234 (1935); Pyburn v. Fishery Products, Inc., 12 Mass. App. Ct. 505, 426 N.E.2d 1169 (1981). However, that exception has no bearing on most guaranties.
167. *See* § 2.5 *supra.*
168. Cadle Co. v. Vargas, 55 Mass. App. Ct. 361, 771 N.E.2d 179 (2002).
169. First Nat'l Bank v. McGowan, 296 Mass. 101, 106, 5 N.E.2d 5 (1936).
170. *Atlas Shoe Co. v. Bloom, supra,* note 52, 209 Mass. at 568, 95 N.E. 952.
171. Shaw v. Victoria Coach Line, Inc., 314 Mass. 262, 266, 267, 50 N.E.2d 27 (1943). *See also* Collins v. Huculak, 57 Mass. App. Ct. 387, 391-92, 783 N.E.2d 834, 839 (2003).
172. *Pemstein v. Stimpson, supra,* note 117, 36 Mass. App. Ct. at 288, 630 N.E.2d 608. *Cf.* First Nat'l Bank v. Bergreen, 11 Mass. App. Ct. 956, 957-958 (1981) (in which the court held that the obligee had not committed fraud).

7.3.8 Application of Payments

If the primary obligor does not designate how a payment should be applied, then the obligee may apply it as the oblige sees fit.[173] This even permits the obligee to apply undesignated payments to debt that the guaranty does not cover.[174]

However, an agreement between the primary obligor and the guarantor or an agreement between the guarantor and the obligee as to application of payments will control.[175]

7.3.9 General Equitable Principles and the Implied Covenant of Good Faith and Fair Dealing

In one case, the Massachusetts Appeals Court voided a guaranty on highly unusual facts, based on common sense, good faith, and fair dealing.[176] The guarantor signed the guaranty solely as an accommodation for her then husband. One year after their divorce, he borrowed funds secured by the guaranty, to fund his divorce settlement with the guarantor. The court held that enforcing such a guaranty would be offensive to common sense, good faith, and fair dealing.[177] The court explained the limited scope of its ruling: "Our decision is limited in its scope, as it is by its justification, to the unusual situation appearing of record. For bank loans with standard guaranties, unaffected by such special conditions, the text of the contracts will of course control, interpreted on conventional lines."[178]

7.4 Right of Set-off

Set-off is an equitable rule that permits a party to apply mutual, matured debts against another.[179] Therefore, unless the guarantor has waived the right of set-off, the guarantor may assert its own claims against the obligee. Massachusetts law is not clear, however, whether an absolute guaranty by its nature bars the guarantor's set-off.

A guarantor cannot assert the primary obligor's claims against the obligee to set-off the guarantor's liability under the guaranty.[180] Nor does it appear that a guarantor can set-off the guarantor's claims against an assignee of the obligee.[181]

---

173. *Merchants Nat'l Bank v. Stone*, *supra*, note 76.
174. *Id.*; and William Filene's Sons Co. v. Lothrop, 243 Mass. 214, 217, 137 N.E. 255 (1922). *But see*, Crompton v. Pratt, 105 Mass. 255, 257 (1870), to the effect that payments shall be applied in the order the debts were incurred.
175. Warren Bros. Co. v. Sentry Ins., 13 Mass. App. Ct. 431, 433, 36-37 N.E.2d 1253, 1255 (1982).
176. *Cadle Co. v. Vargas*, *supra*, note 168.
177. *Id.*
178. *Id.*, 55 Mass. App. Ct. at 367, 771 N.E.2d at 184.
179. Harding v. Broadway Nat'l Bank of Chelsea, 294 Mass. 13, 18, 200 N.E. 386, 389 (1936); Allin v. Georgas, 296 Mass. 70, 73, 5 N.E.2d 27, 28 (1936).
180. *Rhode Island Hospital Tr. Nat'l Bank v. Ohio Cas. Ins. Co.*, *supra*, note 10, 789 F.3d at 78 n. 4; Graham v. Middleby, 213 Mass. 437, 442-443 (1913). *Cf.* Baker v. Briggs, 25 Mass. (8 Pick.) 121, 128-129 (1829) (under its subrogation rights, a guarantor may recover from collateral security that the primary obligor gave to the obligee). *See also* Town Bank & Tr. Co. v. Silverman, 3 Mass. App. Ct. 28, 31, 322 N.E.2d 192, 194 (1975).
181. Nelson v. Harrington, 82 Mass. 139 (1860).

If a bank sets-off against its depositor's account, it must provide prompt notice to the depositor after the fact.[182]

§ 8 Waiver of Defenses by the Guarantor

Massachusetts courts recognize that a guarantor may waive defenses expressly or by implication.[183]

8.1 Defenses that cannot be Waived

Even broad waivers cannot relieve the obligee from liability for bad faith or fraud.[184]

In addition, Article 9 of the UCC limits or prohibits certain waivers in secured transactions. For instance, a guarantor cannot waive the right to require a secured creditor to sell or otherwise dispose of collateral in a commercially reasonable manner.[185] A waiver of the right to challenge impairment of collateral probably does not constitute a waiver of the guarantor's rights under § 9-607(c) of the UCC.

Other nonwaivable Article 9 rights include:

- The right to require the secured party to use or operate collateral in the secured party's possession.[186]
- The right to request an accounting, a list of collateral, and a statement of account.[187]
- The secured party's duty to apply noncash proceeds of collateral.[188]
- The right to require accounting or payment of surplus proceeds of collateral.[189]

Other nonwaivable rights are listed in Mass. Gen. Laws ch. 106 §§ 9-602(6) – (13) (2012).

The following Article 9 defenses can be waived, but only by an authenticated agreement made after the default:

- The guarantor's right to notice of sale or other disposition of collateral.[190]

---

182. Mass. Gen. Laws Ann. ch. 62D, § 9 (2012).
183. *Pemstein v. Stimpson, supra,* note 117 (holding that Massachusetts courts have acknowledged that a clear and unequivocal waiver of the guarantor's rights and defenses in the guaranty can preclude the guarantor from raising a defense to the manner of the foreclosure sale); *Shawmut Bank v. Wayman, supra,* note 123, 34 Mass. App. Ct. at 23, 606 N.E.2d 925.
184. *Pemstein v. Stimpson, supra,* note 117.
185. Mass. Gen. Laws Ann. ch. 106, §§ 9-602 and 9-607(c) (2012). Shawmut Worcester County Bank, N.A. v. Miller, 398 Mass. 273, 496 N.E.2d 625 (1986).
186. Mass. Gen. Laws Ann. ch. 106, §§ 9-207(b)(4) and 9-602(1) (2012).
187. Mass. Gen. Laws Ann. ch. 106, § 9-602(2) (2012).
188. Mass. Gen. Laws Ann. ch. 106 § 9-602(4) (2012).
189. Mass. Gen. Laws Ann. ch. 106 § 9-602(5) (2012).
190. Mass. Gen. Laws Ann. ch. 106 §§ 9-602(3), (7) and 9-624(a) (2012). *See* Shawmut Bank, N.A. v. Chase, 416 Mass. 1008, 624 N.E.2d 541 (1993) (secured party failed to give the required notice, so there was a rebuttable presumption that the value of the collateral equaled the amount of the obligation).

- The guarantor's right to redeem collateral in a commercial transaction.[191]

8.2 "Catch-all" Waivers

Though catch-all waiver language may be effective, it is advisable for beneficiaries to include waivers to specific suretyship defenses.

Massachusetts appellate courts[192] have not specifically ruled on whether a statement that the guaranty is "absolute and unconditional" constitutes a blanket waiver of suretyship defenses, so the better practice is to include specific waivers in the guaranty, along with a general clean-up waiver of suretyship defenses.

In interpreting catch-all waivers, the courts usually look for more specific evidence that a guarantor intended to waive all surety defenses.

8.3 Use of Specific Waivers

It is standard practice to include a waiver of suretyship defenses in notes given to financial institutions or other commercial creditors.[193] Massachusetts courts have generally approved waivers of suretyship defenses in the guaranty.[194] For example, courts have specifically approved the following waivers:

- Impairment of real estate collateral.[195]
- Extension for time of performance.[196]
- Modification of the underlying obligation.[197]
- Notice of future indebtedness.[198]
- Failure to diligently pursue the primary obligor.[199]
- Release of the primary obligor or waiver of claims against the primary obligor.[200]
- Exoneration.[201]

8.4 Jury Trial Waivers

Any waiver of the right to jury trial must be knowing and voluntary.[202]

---

191. Mass. Gen. Laws Ann. ch. 106, §§ 9-623 and 9-624(c) (2012).
192. XL Specialty Ins. Co. v. Commonwealth, 2012 Mass. Super. LEXIS 194, quotes with approval comment (d) to the RESTATEMENT (THIRD) OF SURETYSHIP AND GUARANTY § 48 ("There is no requirement of specificity with respect to the language used to forego discharge. General language indicating that the secondary obligor waives defenses based on suretyship is sufficient. The secondary obligor need not waive separately each ground for discharge, nor must the contract describe them.").
193. Mass. Gen. Laws Ann. ch. 106, § 3-605, cmt. 2 (2012).
194. *Cambridgeport Sav. Bank v. Boersner, supra,* note 63, 413 Mass. at 443-44, 597 N.E.2d 1017.
195. *Pemstein v. Stimpson, supra,* note 117, 36 Mass. App. Ct. at 292, 630 N.E.2d at 613-14.
196. *Manufacturers' Fin. Co. v. Rockwell, supra,* note 93, 278 Mass. at 505-06, 180 N.E. at 226.
197. *See id.*
198. Snelling v. State Street Bank & Tr. Co., 358 Mass. 397, 400, 265 N.E.2d 350, 353 (1970).
199. Sigourney v. Wetherell, 47 Mass. 553, 563 (1842).
200. *Snelling v. State Street Bank & Tr. Co., supra,* note 198, 358 Mass. at 400, 265 N.E.2d at 353.
201. *Id.*
202. Aetna Ins. Co. v. Kennedy, 301 U.S. 389 (1937); Ciummei v. Commonwealth, 378 Mass. 504, 509, 392 N.E.2d 1186, 1189 (1979).

In one case, the Massachusetts Appellate Court held that a guarantor waived the right to a jury trial by virtue of waivers contained only in the loan and security agreement. [203] The court reasoned that all the documents were all executed in the same transaction, and with interrelated purposes, were otherwise sufficiently conspicuous.[204]

However, the best practice is to place the jury trial waiver conspicuously in the guaranty itself.[205]

§ 9 Third-party Pledgors—Defenses and Waiver Thereof

A pledge of collateral to secure another person's obligations makes the pledgor a surety.[206] Therefore, the pledgor has the same defenses as any surety, and the pledgor can waive defenses to the same extent as a guarantor can.

§ 10 Jointly and Severally Liable Guarantors—Contribution and Reduction of Obligations upon Payment by a Co-obligor

Where guarantors are jointly and severally liable, the obligee does not have to join all of the guarantors in a single civil action.[207] Therefore, the obligee does not have to seek full payment from more than one guarantor.

10.1 Contribution and Exoneration

If multiple guarantors are liable jointly and severally, then each has an implied right of contribution against the other coguarantors.[208] The right of contribution is an equitable right governed by equitable principles.[209] Therefore, if one guarantor pays the entire obligation, it may recover a proportional share from each other guarantor.[210] However, the guarantor may not seek contribution from the other guarantors until he or she has paid more than his or her proportionate share of the obligation.[211]

On the other hand, the fact that one guarantor has acquired a personal defense against the creditor does not absolve the guarantor from its duty to

203. Chase Commercial Corp. v. Owen, 32 Mass. App. Ct. 248, 251, 588 N.E.2d 705, 707 (1992).
204. *Id.* at 251-54.
205. *Id.* at 253-54.
206. Cotton v. Atlas Nat'l Bank, 145 Mass. 43, 44, 12 N.E. 850, 851 (1887).
207. President, Directors, etc. of Union Bank v. Willis, 49 Mass. 504 (1844).
208. Nissenberg v. Felleman, 339 Mass. 717, 719-20, 162 N.E.2d 304, 306-07 (1959).
209. *Id.*
210. Quintin v. Magnant, 285 Mass. 450, 451, 189 N.E. 209, 209-10 (1934).
211. *Id.*

contribute which arises upon the payment of the debt by the other guarantor who has no such defense.[212]

In rare situations, exoneration allows one coguarantor to limit its liability to its proportionate share of the underlying obligation.[213] This equitable rule applies when the guarantor can prove that payment of the full debt would "cause financial disaster" for the guarantor, and the guarantor would not be able to collect on a contribution claim against the other guarantors.[214]

10.2 Reduction of Obligations upon Payment of Co-obligor

Unless otherwise agreed, another obligor's partial payment does not reduce the guarantor's liability on its guaranty. In other words, the obligee is entitled to apply a partial payment from another obligor to the unguaranteed portion of the debt.[215]

10.3 Liability of Parent Guarantors owning less than 100 percent of Primary Obligor

Massachusetts law does not impose any particular restrictions on parent guarantors who own less than all of the outstanding equity in the primary obligor. As noted in § 2.1 *supra*, however, if the parent corporation does not own 100 percent of the subsidiary, then the parent's directors must determine that the guaranty is necessary or convenient to the conduct, promotion, or goals of the corporation's business.

§ 11 Reliance

Massachusetts law is not clear on whether the obligee must rely on the guaranty.[216]

Consideration is required,[217] and consideration is usually found in the obligee's requiring the guaranty as a condition precedent to extending credit to the primary obligor.

Reasonable and good faith reliance is necessary in order to bind a principal on the theory of apparent authority.[218]

---

212. *See id.*
213. *Nissenberg v. Felleman, supra,* note 207, 339 Mass. at 721, 162 N.E.2d at 308.
214. *Id.*
215. *See Warren Bros. Co. v. Sentry Ins., supra,* note 175, 13 Mass. App. Ct. at 433, 433 N.E.2d at 1255.
216. *But see* Diversified Mortgage Investors v. Viking Gen. Corp., 16 Mass. App. Ct. 142, 147, 450 N.E.2d 176, 179 (1983) (recognizing that a principal inducement to obligee to make a loan to primary obligor must have been the overriding guaranty); and *Cadle Co. v. Vargas, supra,* note 168 (dictum).
217. *See,* § 4, *supra.*
218. *Haufler v. Zotos, supra,* note 36, 446 Mass. at 498, 845 N.E.2d at 330 n.22 (2006); *Neilson v. Malcolm Kenneth Co., supra,* note 36, 303 Mass. at 441, 22 N.E.2d 20.

Reasonable and justifiable reliance is also an essential element of any claim of fraud in the inducement.[219]

§ 12 Subrogation

If the guarantor fully satisfies the underlying obligation, then the guarantor is subrogated to the rights of the obligee.[220] The right of subrogation arises under equity, and is independent of contract.[221]

The guarantor's subrogation claim is entitled to the same priority or lien status that the underlying obligation had when the guarantor paid it.[222]

§ 13 Triangular Set-off in Bankruptcy

As noted in § 7.4 *supra*, set-off permits one party to apply mutual, matured debts against each other. Further, set-off is an equitable remedy.[223] Therefore, triangular set-off would probably not be permitted absent a contractual right to do so.

§ 14 Indemnification—Whether the Primary Obligor has a Duty

In the absence of contract, a guarantor who pays on the underlying obligation probably does not have an indemnification claim against the primary obligor.[224] Even in the absence of an indemnification claim, however, the guarantor will have a subrogation claim.[225]

---

219. Collins v. Huculak, 57 Mass. App. Ct. 387, 391-92, 783 N.E.2d 834, 839 (2003) (citing *Shaw v.* Victoria *Coach Line, Inc., supra,* note 171, 314 Mass. at 266, 50 N.E.2d 27).
220. *Stanley v. Ames, supra,* note 130, 378 Mass. at 367, 391 N.E.2d at 909-10. *See also* National Shawmut Bank of Boston v. New Amsterdam Gas Co., 411 F.2d 843, 844 (1st Cir. 1969).
221. East Boston Sav. Bank v. Ogan, 428 Mass. 327, 329, 701 N.E.2d 331, 333 (1998).
222. Taylor v. Wilcox, 167 Mass. 572, 574-75, 46 N.E. 115, 116 (1897).
223. *Allin v. Georgas, supra,* note 179, 296 Mass. at 73, 5 N.E.2d at 28.
224. H.P. Hood & Sons, Inc. v. Ford Motor Co., 370 Mass. 69, 77, 345 N.E.2d 683 (1976) (in which the court declined to decide whether an implied right of action for indemnity exists).
225. *See* § 12, *supra.*

§ 15 Enforcement of Guaranties

15.1 Limitations on Recovery

If a guarantor is insolvent or severely undercapitalized when it enters into the guaranty and does not receive reasonably equivalent value for the guaranty, then the guaranty may be avoided under Massachusetts' Uniform Fraudulent Transfer Act.[226]

Massachusetts courts have not ruled on the validity of so-called fraudulent conveyance caps on recovery under a guaranty (which prevent recovery beyond the amount that would render the guaranty void under fraudulent transfer law).

Sometimes, a guarantor will settle with the obligee in exchange for an assignment of the underlying obligation. In that situation, the guarantor's contribution recovery against coguarantors may be limited to the amount that the guarantor paid to the obligee.[227]

An agreement to pay a third party's debts will not include attorneys' fees, unless specifically provided for in the agreement.[228] The same rule applies to punitive damages.[229]

15.2 Exercising Rights under a Guaranty Where the Underlying Obligation is also Secured by a Mortgage

In general, the obligee does not have the duty to liquidate its collateral before pursuing the guarantor.[230]

Procedural complications can arise where the obligee must foreclose judicially, and the guarantor is a party in interest in the foreclosure proceeding.[231]

15.3 Litigating Guaranty Claims: Procedural Considerations

The obligee may use entry of a judgment against the primary obligor as evidence of the underlying debt in the obligee's suit against the guarantor.[232]

226. Mass. Gen. Laws Ann. ch. 109A, §§ 1 *et seq.* (2012).
227. Merchants Discount Corp. v. Federal Street Corp., 300 Mass. 167, 171-72, 14 N.E.2d 155, 157-58 (1938). According to older case law, such a guarantor cannot sue on the underlying obligation at all. *See, e.g.,* Putnam v. Tash, 78 Mass. 121 (1858).
228. Schneider v. Armour & Co., 323 Mass. 28, 30, 80 N.E.2d 34, 36 (1948).
229. C & I Steel, LLC v. Travelers Cas. & Sur. Co., 70 Mass. App. Ct. 653, 658-59, 876 N.E.2d 442 (2007).
230. *See* Lewis v. Blume, 226 Mass. 505, 508, 116 N.E. 271, 272 (1917).
231. *Diversified Mortgage Investors v. Viking General Corp., supra,* note 216 (although the obligee had to join the guarantor in a Florida foreclosure proceeding, it could still sue the guarantor on the underlying debt in Massachusetts, because the guarantor had consented to an independent action on the guaranty in Massachusetts).
232. Clark's Executors v. Carrington, 11 U.S. (7 Cranch) 308, 322 (1813).

Only the obligee or its successors in interest may sue on a guaranty, even if the guaranty benefitted third persons.[233]

If the guaranty is lost "other than through the serious fault of" the obligee, then the obligee can use extrinsic evidence to prove that the guarantor signed the guaranty and to prove contents of the guaranty.[234]

A surety can use res judicata as a defense, where the primary obligor has prevailed against the obligee in another case.[235] Conversely, the obligee can use res judicata against a guarantor who was an officer of the primary obligor and directed the primary obligor's conduct in the prior action.[236]

§ 16 Revival and Reinstatement of Guaranties

A guaranty may be revived or reinstated, depending on the language of the guaranty and any admissible extrinsic evidence of the parties' intent.[237] Therefore, if the obligee wants the guaranty to be reinstated upon certain events, such as the avoidance of payments by a bankruptcy trustee, it should include clear reinstatement provisions in its guaranties.

---

233. Mauran v. Bullus, 41 U.S. 528, 535-36, 10 L. Ed. 1056 (1842); Healthco, Inc. v. Zambelis, 2 Mass. App. Ct. 914, 321 N.E.2d 671 (1975) (the assignee of a promissory note covered by a guaranty could sue on the guaranty, even though the guaranty was not separately assigned). *Cf.*, Flynn v. North American Life Ins. Co., 115 Mass. 449, 449-50 (1874), in which the court held that a contract under seal may be enforced only by the original party, not by an assignee.

234. Capitol Bank & Tr. Co. v. Richman, 19 Mass. App. Ct. 515, 520-21, 475 N.E.2d 1236 (1985). M

235. Putignano v. Treasurer, 55 Mass. App. Ct. 828, 833, 774 N.E.2d 1157 (2002) (citing the RESTATEMENT (THIRD) OF SURETYSHIP AND GUARANTY § 12(2) (1996)); *Mestek, Inc. v. United Pacific Ins. Co., supra,* note 107, 40 Mass. App. Ct. at 732, 667 N.E.2d at 294-95. *See also Rhode Island Hospital Tr. Nat'l Bank* v. Ohio Cas. Ins. Co., *supra,* note 10, 789 F.3d at 81-2.

236. Chapian v. Car Wash Systems, Inc., 1995 Mass. App. Div. 167, 1995 Mass. App. Div. LEXIS 77.

237. *See, e.g.,* Rhode Island Hospital Tr. Nat'l Bank v. Howard Communications, Inc., 980 F.2d 823, 828 (1st Cir. 1992) (upholding a guaranty that provided for its reinstatement upon certain conditions).

Michigan State Law of Guaranties

Robert A. Wright, III
Dawda Mann
39533 Woodward Avenue, Suite 200
Bloomfield Hills, Michigan 48304
(248) 642-3700
Fax: (248) 642-7791
dawdamann.com

DAWDA MANN Counselors At Law
Dawda, Mann, Mulcahy & Sadler, PLC

Contents

Michigan State Law of Guaranties

MICHIGAN LAW HIGHLIGHTS

Creditors of both a husband and a wife can levy on property held by them as tenants by the entirety, but such property is not ordinarily liable for the individual debts of either party. The practical implication for creditors is that a judgment against one spouse may not allow a creditor to levy a judgment on real estate owned by a husband and a wife as tenants in the entirety. However, a debtor may not place his or her assets beyond the reach of creditors by investing individual funds in an estate by the entirety. § 2.5.

Under Michigan law, material changes in the contract relations of the parties will release the guarantor; immaterial alterations in the terms of the contract do not release the guarantors from their obligation under the guaranty. § 7.2.2.

Introductory Note: In order to standardize our discussion of the law of guaranties, we use the following vocabulary to refer to the various parties to a guaranty and their obligations.

"Guarantor" means a person who, by an "independent, collateral agreement," agrees to satisfy an underlying obligation of another to an obligee upon the primary obligor's default on that underlying obligation.[1] The distinction between guarantors and sureties in Michigan is one of liability. The surety assumes the liability of a regular party whereas the guarantor becomes secondarily liable in the event the primary obligor defaults.[2]

"Guaranty" means the contract by which the guarantor agrees to satisfy the underlying obligation of a primary obligor to an obligee in the event the primary obligor defaults on the underlying obligation.[3]

"Obligee" means the person to whom the underlying obligation is owed. For example, the lender under a loan agreement would be an obligee vis-à-vis the borrower.

---

1. Harley J. Robinson Trust v. Ardmore Acres, Inc., 6 F. Supp.2d 640, 646 (E.D. Mich. 1998) (stating that "Michigan law defines a guarantor as a party that enters into independent, collateral agreement of guaranty, becoming only secondarily liable upon the principal obligor's default." On the other hand, "a surety is a party that is obligated with the principal under the primary agreement." (internal citations omitted)).
2. *See, e.g.,* Bandit Indus. v. Hobbs Int'l, Inc. (*After Remand)*, 463 Mich. 504, 507-508 n. 4, 620 N.W.2d 531 (Mich. 2001); *see also* 23 MICH. CIV. JUR., SURETYSHIP § 4 cmt. c (2011) ("[W]hile both the 'surety' and 'guarantor' agree to satisfy the debt in the event of the principal obligor's default, only the surety is obligated with the principal under the primary agreement. The guarantor, on the other hand, enters into an independent, collateral agreement of guaranty, becoming only secondarily liable upon the principal obligor's default.").
3. *See* Wynn Oil Co. v. Sharon, No. 02-10302-BC, 2003 WL 2314219, *3 (Dec. 22, 2003) (citing Angelo Iafrate Co. v. Detroit and N. Sav. and Loan Ass'n, 80 Mich. App. 508, 514, 264 N.W.2d 45, 48 (1978)) ("A guaranty contract is an enforceable undertaking or promise by one person collateral to a primary or principal obligation of another which binds the person making the promise to performance of the primary obligation in the event of nonperformance; the secondary party thus becomes primarily responsible for performance.").

"Primary Obligor" means the person who incurs the underlying obligation to the obligee. For example, the borrower under a loan agreement would be a primary obligor.

"Underlying Obligation" means the obligation or obligations incurred by the primary obligor and owed to the obligee. For example, the borrower's obligation to make payments to a lender of principal and interest on a loan constitutes an underlying obligation.

Introduction and Sources of Law

Michigan courts have cited to the Restatement of the Law (Third) Suretyship and Guaranty and the predecessor provisions of the Restatement of Security.[4]

§ 1 Nature of the Guaranty Arrangement

The guarantor must answer secondarily for the underlining obligation or debt for the primary obligor.

1.1 Guaranty Relationships

A guaranty is a contract of secondary liability under which the guarantor has an obligation to pay only upon default by the primary obligor.[5] It is an agreement by one person to answer to another for the debt, default, or miscarriage of a third person.[6] A guaranty relationship exists when a contract for guaranty has been entered by three parties: the principal, the obligee, and the guarantor.[7] A personal guaranty cannot be implied from language that fails to clearly and unambiguously reflect an intention to assume such a responsibility.[8]

Under Michigan law, a guaranty relationship exists when there is some kind of independent, collateral undertaking which, "he [or she] undertakes to pay the obligation if the primary payor fails to do so."[9]

1.2 Suretyship Relationship

While not the focus of this survey, there is little difference between guaranty and suretyship agreements. A suretyship contract requires three parties: a prin-

4. *See* P R Post Corp. v. Maryland Casualty Co., 403 Mich. 543, 271 N.W.2d 521 (1978) (citing Restatement of Security); Schanz v. The Village Apartments a/k/a The Village Apartments in Wixom et al., 998 F. Supp. 784 (E.D. Mich. 1998); Will H. Hall & Son, Inc. Capital Indemnity Corp., 260 Mich. App. 222, 677 N.W.2d 51 (2003)).
5. *See Bandit Indus., Inc.*, 463 Mich. at 508.
6. *See* Angelo Iafrate Co. v. Detroit and Northern Sav. and Loan Ass'n, 80 Mich. App. 508, 264 N.W.2d 45 (1978).
7. Moore v. Capital Nat'l Bank of Lansing, 274 Mich. 56, 61, 264 N.W. 288 (Mich. 1936).
8. *See Bandit Indus., Inc.*, 463 Mich. at 514.
9. First Nat'l Bank & Trust Co. of Ann Arbor v. Dolph, 287 Mich. 219, 225, 283 N.W. 35 (Mich. 1938).

cipal, an obligee, and a surety.[10] A surety is one who undertakes to pay money or take any other action if the principal fails therein.[11] While both surety and guarantor agree to satisfy the debt in the event of the principal obligor's default, only the surety is obligated with the principal under the primary agreement.[12] Michigan case law is minimal concerning sureties.[13]

§ 2 State Law Requirements for an Entity to Enter a Guaranty

Partnerships, limited liability companies (LLCs), and corporations can all grant guaranties.

2.1 Corporations

Under Section 261 of the Michigan Business Corporation Act ("MBCA"), a corporation may enter into a contract as guarantor if it is reasonably necessary or convenient to the conduct, promotion, or attainment of the business of (a) the guarantor's wholly owned subsidiary corporation or LLC, (b) the guarantor's parent corporation or LLC, if the parent owns all of guarantor's shares or interests and (c) a so-called "sister" corporation or LLC if all of the shares or interests are owned, directly or indirectly, by a corporation that owns, directly or indirectly, all of the outstanding shares or interests of the guarantor.[14] This subsection is known as a type of safe harbor that negates any common law doctrine that would hold that a corporation's guaranty for the benefit of a parent or sister corporation or LLC to be *ultra vires* and therefore unenforceable.

However, the MBCA prohibits a corporation from guaranteeing or securing the deposit of public money.[15]

2.2 Partnerships

A guaranty contract can be executed by a partner on behalf of the partnership if it is within the scope of the partnership business.[16] However, the Uniform Partnership Act does not specifically discuss guaranty agreements.[17]

10. *Will H. Hall & Son, Inc.*, 260 Mich. App. at 222 (citing In re Forfeiture of United States Currency, 172 Mich. App. 790, 792; 432 N.W.2d 442 (1988)).
11. *Id.*
12. *See Bandit Indus., Inc.*, 463 Mich. at 508.
13. *See Will H. Hall & Son, Inc.*, 260 Mich. App. at 222.
14. Nat'l Sec. & Trust Co. v. Niles Invisible Door Check Co., 222 Mich. 510, 193 N.W. 199 (1923).
15. Mich. Comp. Laws Ann. § 450.1261(h) (West 2012).
16. *See* Shambleau v. Hoyt, 265 Mich. 560, 567, 251 N.W. 778 (Mich. 1933).
17. The Uniform Partnership Act , Mich. Comp. Laws Ann. § 449.1-449.48 (West 2012).

2.3 Limited Liability Companies

Under the Michigan Limited Liability Company Act ("MLLCA"), a LLC has all powers necessary or convenient to effect any purpose for which the company was formed.[18] The law specifically grants LLCs all of the powers granted to corporations in Section 261 of the MBCA.[19] *See* § 2.1 above.

2.4 Banks and Trust Companies

The definition of a trust company is, "[a] commercial bank that manages trusts."[20] A Michigan trust company has no power to guaranty the payment of a debt of another person as part of a profit-making venture in which it engages on a regular basis.[21] A Michigan bank may engage in the business of banking and a business related or incidental to banking, including the power to make contracts.[22] Michigan law does not specifically authorize or prohibit a bank from entering into guaranties. A Michigan savings bank may also engage in the business of banking and all powers incidental thereto, including the power to make contracts.[23] In particular, a Michigan savings bank is specifically authorized "[t]o execute and deliver guarantees as may be incidental or usual in carrying on the business of banking."[24]

2.5 Individuals

In Michigan, all the distinguishing characteristics of a contract are necessary for a binding guaranty contract executed by an individual and, therefore, contracts of guaranty need the "essentials of a binding contract."[25] The intent of the parties governs in construing contracts of guaranty.[26] Likewise, contract principles generally apply to determine the capacity of a person to be a legitimate guarantor.[27]

The determination whether an individual signed as an individual guarantor or whether he or she signed for an associated company is determined by agency and corporate law. However, a personal guaranty cannot be implied when the language fails to "clearly and unambiguously reflect an intention to assume such responsibility."[28]

---

18. Mich. Comp. Laws Ann. § 450.4210 (West 2012).
19. *Id.*
20. Webster's II New College Dictionary (1999).
21. 6 Mich. Civ. Jur., Corporations § 304; In re Bankers Trust Co. of Detroit, 15 F. Supp. 21 (E.D. Mich. 1936); Reichert v. Metro. Trust Co., 262 Mich. 123, 247 N.W. 128 (Mich. 1933).
22. Mich. Comp. Laws Ann. § 487.14101(1)(a) (West 2012).
23. Mich. Comp. Laws Ann. § 487.3401(1)(c) (West 2012).
24. Mich. Comp. Laws Ann. § 487.3401(1)(u) (West 2012).
25. "It must present the essentials of a binding contract, reasonably definite as to time and for a valid consideration. Payment of interest in advance is a sufficient consideration." Bedford v. Kelley, 173 Mich. 492, 498-99 (1913) (citing Schnitzler v. Wichita Fourth Nat'l Bank, 1 Kan. App. 674 (Kan. Ct. App. 1895); Sweet v. Newberry, 92 Mich. 515 (Mich. 1892)).
26. 11 Mich. Civ. Jur., Corporations § 11 (citing Jerry McCarthy Foundation v. Winshall, 372 Mich. 389 (Mich. 1964)).
27. *See generally* 5A Mich. Civ. Jur. Contracts § 1.
28. 11 Mich. Civ. Jur., Corporations § 11 (citing *Bandit Indus., Inc.*, 463 Mich. at 504.

Creditors of both a husband and a wife can levy on property held by them as tenants by the entirety, but such property is not ordinarily liable for the individual debts of either party.[29] Likewise, rent from property owned by a husband and a wife as tenants by the entirety is not ordinarily subject to garnishment by individual creditors of either party.[30] In *United States v Craft*,[31] the U.S. Supreme Court ruled that a federal tax lien could attach to the entireties interest of one spouse. This ruling does not change the law as to non-IRS creditors having claims against one spouse in an entireties property situation.

The practical implication for creditors is that a judgment against one spouse does not allow a creditor to levy a judgment on real estate owned by a husband and a wife as tenants in the entirety.[32] However, a debtor may not place his or her assets beyond the reach of creditors by investing individual funds in an estate by the entirety.[33]

In contrast to real property, personal property is generally not held by the entirety, and a right of survivorship in personal property may not be created except by an express act.[34] However, all bonds, stock certificates, mortgages, promissory notes, debentures, and the like that are made payable to husband and wife are held as tenants by the entireties unless a phrase like "as joint tenants and not as tenants by the entirety" is used.[35] If a tenancy by the entirety has been created, the creditor cannot execute on the property.[36]

However, if joint personal property is derived directly from property held in the entirety, the courts are sometimes unwilling to subject the property to levy by creditors of only one of the owners.

§ 3 Signatory's Authority to Execute a Guaranty

Generally, the obligee has a duty of reasonable inquiry when it has some notice that the executor of the guaranty does not have authority to bind the guarantor. Whether or not an officer or agent is able to become a guarantor depends on the general rules of agency and corporations.[37]

3.1 Corporations

Identical to the principle for general contracts, for an obligee to rely on a guaranty, the guaranty must be signed by an officer with actual or apparent

29. *See* Rossman v. Hutchinson, 289 Mich. 577, 286 NW 835 (1939); Kolakowski v. Cyman, 285 Mich. 585, 281 N.W. 332 (1938).
30. American State Trust Co. v. Rosenthal, 255 Mich. 157, 237 N.W. 534 (1931).
31. 535 U.S. 274 (2002).
32. In re Farmers' & Merchants' Bank, 221 Mich. 243, 190 N.W. 698 (1922).
33. Dunn v. Minnema, 323 Mich. 687, 36 N.W.2d 182 (1949); McCaslin v. Schouten, 294 Mich. 180, 292 N.W. 696 (1940).
34. Scholten v. Scholten, 238 Mich. 679, 214 N.W. 320 (1927).
35. Mich. Comp. Laws Ann. § 557.151 (West 2012); DeYoung v. Mesler, 373 Mich. 499, 503-504, 130 N.W.2d 38 (1964).
36. *Id.*
37. *See* 11 MICH. CIV. JUR. GUARANTY § 3.

authority to act in such a capacity.[38] The power to bind a principal to a contract of guaranty exists only if properly delegated to the officer.[39]

Agency law has determined that an officer of a corporation has authority to act only where: (a) authority has been expressly conferred on him or her by statute, law, or by the act of the directors; (b) the action is properly incidental to the business entrusted to him or her by the directors; and (c) the action is within his or her ostensible authority or ratified by proper authority as applicable to contracts of guaranty.[40]

However, unlike the above requirements, agency may not be established by proof of declarations by the supposed agent.[41] Nor may the extent of the authority of an agent be shown by testimony as to his acts and conduct not within the actual or implied scope of the powers granted to him by his principal.[42] Also, authority to bind the principal by contract of guaranty is not implied from the existence of general agency; the contract for guaranty must be incidental to the business entrusted to him or her and he or she must have received express authority to act.[43]

3.2 Partnerships

A guaranty contract executed by a partner on behalf of his or her partnership is valid if it is in the scope of the partnership's business.[44] Also, if the contract for guaranty is subsequently ratified by the partners, it will be upheld in court.[45] A partner has apparent authority to execute a guaranty contract if the guaranty is executed by a partner and is within the scope of the partnership business.[46]

3.3 Limited Liability Companies

The Michigan Limited Liability Company Act ("MLLCA") leaves management of the LLC in the hands of its members unless the articles of organization state that the business is to be managed by or under the authority of managers.[47] The MLLCA provides that every member of a company is an agent of that company and can sign instruments pursuant to carrying on in the usual way of business. However, if that member has no actual authority to act and the counterparty has knowledge of this fact, the guaranty may be void.[48]

---

38. *See id.*
39. *See* Hearst Pub. Co. v. Litsky, 339 Mich. 642, 64 N.W.2d 687 (Mich. 1954).
40. 1 Mich. Civ. Jur., Agency § 61, 65; In re Union City Milk Co., 329 Mich. 506, 46 N.W.2d 361 (Mich. 1951).
41. In re *Union City Milk Co.*, 329 Mich. at 513 (citing Miskiewicz v. Smolenski, 249 Mich. 63, 227 N.W. 789 (Mich. 1929)).
42. *Id.* at 513 (citing Cutler v. Grinnell Bros., 325 Mich. 370, 38 N.W.2d 893 (1949)).
43. *Id.* at 513.
44. 19A Mich. Civ. Jur. Partnership § 88; Bowen v. Mead, 1 Mich. 432 (Mich. 1850).
45. *Shambleau*, 265 Mich. at 572.
46. *Id.*
47. Mich. Comp. Laws Ann. § 450.4401 (West 2012); *See also* MICH. COMP. LAWS ANN. § 450.4402, 450.4203 (West 2012).
48. Mich. Comp. Laws Ann. §§ 450.4401(a), 450.4402(4) (West 2012).

The MLLCA makes explicit that the mangers through their agency authority have the authority to bind the company and authorizes indemnification of managers either in accordance with the operating agreement or a contract.[49]

§ 4 Consideration

Any consideration that is sufficient for an ordinary simple contract is sufficient for a contract of guaranty. Standard contract principles apply to the analysis of consideration for a contract of guaranty.

While sufficient legal consideration is essential to a valid guaranty, any consideration that is sufficient under contract law for an ordinary contract is sufficient for a contract of guaranty.[50] The adequacy of consideration is irrelevant to the enforceability of a note and guaranty.[51] Contemporaneous and subsequent guaranties have the same effect in terms of contract law and differ only as to the sufficiency of the consideration.[52] However, if the contract of guaranty is executed after the principal contract, generally the first contract cannot serve as consideration for the contract of guaranty.[53] Where a guaranty is executed with a prior understanding or induces the execution of the principal contract, then there is adequate consideration.[54] Where the guarantors' personal guaranties are made subsequent to the principal contract, but while the loan being guaranteed is in default, and the personal guaranties state that, in order to induce the obligee to renew or extend the loan, the guarantors guaranty the loan, the guaranties are supported by adequate consideration.[55]

§ 5 Notice of Acceptance

Generally, notice of acceptance of a guaranty by the creditor is not required to be given to the guarantor.[56] Moreover, if consideration is recited on the contract of guaranty, then conclusive evidence is furnished that the guaranty has been made with the assent of the obligee, communicated to the guarantors, and in such cases no notice of acceptance is required.[57] Notice is required where the guaranty indicated that it is only an offer to guaranty and not a conclusive guaranty.[58]

49. Mich. Comp. Laws Ann. § 450.4402(4) (West 2012); *See* MICH. CORP. L. & PRAC. s 11.6 (2011).
50. 11 MICH. CIV. JUR., GUARANTY § 8; *See* Brown v. Spiegel, 156 Mich. 138, 120 N.W. 579 (1909); Young v. Wallace, 327 Mich. 395, 41 N.W.2d 904 (1950); First Nat'l Bank v. Redford Chevrolet Co., 270 Mich. 116, 258 N.W. 221 (1935).
51. Enzymes of Am., Inc. v. Deloitte, Haskins & Sells, 207 Mich. App. 28, 523 N.W.2d 810 (Mich. Ct. App. 1994).
52. 38A C.J.S. GUARANTY § 26; Freeman v. Ellison, 37 Mich. 459 (Mich. 1877).
53. U.S. v. Interlakes Mach. & Tool Co., 400 F. Supp. 59 (E.D. Mich. 1975).
54. *Id.*
55. U.S. v. Brown, 833 F. Supp. 625 (E.D. Mich. 1993).
56. Farmers' & Mechanics' Bank v. Kercheval, 2 Mich. 504 (Mich. 1853).
57. Buhrer v. Baldwin, 137 Mich. 263, 270, 100 N.W. 468 (Mich. 1904).
58. Brown v. Spiegel, 156 Mich. 138, 144, 120 N.W. 579 (Mich. 1909).

Usually, the guarantor waives the notification of acceptance requirement in the guaranty agreement.

§ 6 Interpretation of Guaranties

Courts in Michigan will interpret a guaranty in the same manner by which they would interpret the language of any other contract.

6.1 General Principles

Contracts of guaranty are to be construed like other contracts, and the intent of the parties, as collected from the whole instrument and the subject matter to which it applies, is to govern.[59] A Michigan court will strictly construe the obligations of a guarantor.[60] Furthermore, "...assumption of another's debt is a substantial undertaking, and thus the courts will not assume such an obligation in the absence of a clearly expressed intention to do so."[61] The same principles of construction that apply to contracts apply to guaranties.[62]

Contracts of guaranty are to be construed like other contracts, and the intent of the parties, as collected from the whole instrument and the subject matter to which it applies, is to govern.

6.2 Guaranty of Payment versus Guaranty of Collection

A court will look to the intent of the parties as expressed in the guaranty to determine whether the guaranty is one of payment or one of collection.[63] While the obligee may proceed immediately against the guarantor if it is a guaranty of payment,[64] if it is a guaranty of collection, the obligee must first sue the primary obligor.[65]

6.3 Language Regarding the Revocation of Guaranties

A party's intent to revoke a guaranty must be "in clear and unequivocal language which could not reasonably be misunderstood."[66] The test is not what the party meditated, but what the party declared.[67] Upon termination of a

59. Comerica Bank v. Cohen, 291 Mich. App. 40, 805 N.W.2d 544 (Mich. Ct. App. 2010) (citing *First Nat'l Bank*, 270 Mich. at 121 (quotation marks and citation omitted)).
60. *See Bandit Indus.*, 463 Mich. at 507-508 n. 4; W. Shanhouse Sons v. Gudelsky, 259 Mich. 510, 244 N.W. 145 (Mich. 1932); *see* Brenner Oil Co. v. Crank, No. 243572, 2004 WL 1178429, *1 (Mich. Ct. App. May 27, 2004) (stating that in construing a contract of guaranty, the parties' intentions should govern the contract).
61. *See Bandit Indus., Inc.*, 463 Mich. at 512.
62. *Id.*
63. *Id.*
64. *E.g.*, Rider v. Coyne, 246 Mich. 365, 366, 224 N.W. 332 (Mich. 1929).
65. *See* Bosman v. Akeley, 39 Mich. 710 (Mich. 1878); *See* Brodsky v. Lehigh Valley Indus., Inc., 424 F. Supp. 863, 864-65 (E.D. Mich. 1976).
66. Am. Steel & Wire Co. v. Richardson, 191 Mich. 549, 553-554, 158 N.W. 34 (Mich. 1916).
67. *Id. at 554. See also* Erb Lumber, Inc. v. Mortier, No. 204207, 1999 WL 33455141, *4 (Mich. Ct. App. Jan. 5, 1999).

continuing guaranty, the continuing guarantor remains a secondary obligor with respect to obligations of the principal obligor incurred prior to termination and becomes a secondary obligor with respect to obligations of the principal obligor incurred by extensions of credit to the principal obligor after termination pursuant to a commitment that became binding before termination.[68]

6.4 "Continuing"

When the amount of the guaranty is limited, and the time is not, the contract should be construed as a continuing guaranty.[69] A guaranty given to a bank which stated that it was to continue as to each of guarantors until bank received from him written notice of discontinuance thereof as to him, was held to be continuing guaranty contemplating giving of extensions and renewals.[70]

6.5 Completion and Performance Guaranties

There are apparently no Michigan cases on the subject of completion guaranties or other types of performance guaranties in Michigan.

A federal district court has noted that while there are no Michigan cases which deal with a performance guaranty, those jurisdictions that have considered the matter have concluded that the important consideration is whether a guaranty is conditional or absolute and that an absolute guaranty may be for either performance or payment.[71] The court noted that an absolute guaranty of performance is placed on the same ground and subject to the same rules as a guaranty of payment.[72]

§ 7 Defenses of the Guarantor

Generally, defenses to escape the terms of a plain and positive contract of guaranty will not be allowed. However, a guarantor may assert both the defenses available to the primary obligor regarding the principal obligation on the debt and any personal defenses that arise out of the guaranty obligation.[73]

68. *See* In re Jeffrey and Martha Lipa, 433 B.R. 668; 2010 Bankr. LEXIS 2474 (citing Restatement (Third) of Suretyship and Guaranty § 16); Bedford v. Kelley, 173 Mich. 492, 498-99 (1913).
69. In re Landwehr's Estate, 286 Mich. 698, 282 N.W. 873 (1938).
70. *See* In re *Landwehr's Estate, 286 Mich. at 698*; Mathews v. Phelps, 61 Mich. 327, 28 N.W. 108 (1886); Farmers' Co-op. Creamery Co. v. Huhn, 241 Mich. 23, 216 N.W. 370 (1927) (A bond that was given to secure money deposited in a certain bank "from time to time" was found to be a continuing guaranty.).
71. *Brodsky,* 424 F. Supp. at 865 (citing 38 C.J.S. Guaranty § 7 at 1139).
72. *Id.* (citing 38 C.J.S. Guaranty § 7 at 1139).
73. In re Allied Supermarkets, Inc., 951 F.2d 718, 21 Fed. R. Serv. 329 (6th Cir. 1991).

7.1 Defenses of the Primary Obligor

7.1.1 General

The general rule in Michigan is that the guarantor, absent an effective waiver, is not bound to perform if the primary obligor is not bound.[74] On the other hand, summary judgment against the guarantor is proper where there is no dispute that the guarantor guaranteed the prompt and full payment of all liability by using language indicating an absolute and unqualified guaranty.[75]

7.1.2 Defenses that may be raised by Guarantor

The guarantor may assert both the defenses available to the primary obligor regarding the principal obligation on the debt and any personal defenses that arise out of the guaranty obligation.[76]

7.2 "Suretyship" Defenses

7.2.1 Change in Identity of Principal Obligor

As a general rule, a change in the identity of an obligor is a material alteration that may increase the risk to a guarantor and will therefore serve to release the guarantor from his or her obligation.[77] However, this general rule does not apply where the guarantor consents to such a change or such variations of obligor's contract which under the terms of the original agreement should have been anticipated as a possibility.[78]

7.2.2 Modification of the Underlying Obligation, including Release

Under Michigan law, "material changes in the contract relations of the parties will release the guarantor, immaterial alterations in the terms of the contract do not release the guarantors from their obligation under the guarantee."[79] Any material alteration of a principal debt or obligation generally operates to completely discharge any guaranty of that debt or obligation.[80] An alteration of a principal debt that increases that debt is material.[81] However, if the guarantor anticipates that there would be a modification, through consent

74. Bank of Three Oaks v. Lakefront Properties, 178 Mich. App. 551, 557, 444 N.W.2d 217 (Mich. Ct. App. 1989) (holding that the guarantors cannot be liable for a liability that the principal debtor never incurred).
75. *See* Director of Bureau of Workers' Disability Comp. v. Durant Enterprises, Inc., 195 Mich. App. 626, 629, 491 N.W.2d 584 (Mich. Ct. App. 1992).
76. *See generally In re Allied Supermarkets, Inc.*, 951 F.2d at 718.
77. Farm Credit Services v. Ruggles, No. 209257, 1999 WL 33438842 (Mich. Ct. App. July 16, 1999) (citing Farmers' Cooperative Creamery Co. v. Huhn, 241 Mich. 23, 27, 216 N.W. 370 (1927); Reichert v. State Savings Bank of Royal Oak, 261 Mich. 227, 229, 246 N.W. 95 (1933)).
78. *Id.* (citing In re Bluestone Estate, 121 Mich. App. 659, 667, 329 N.W.2d 446 (1982)).
79. 11 MICH. CIV. JUR. GUARANTY § 27 (citing Greer v. Parks, 300 Mich. 492, 498 (Mich. 1942); Johnson v. Shepard, 35 Mich. 115 (Mich. 1876); Texaco Inc. v. Clifton, 87 Mich. App. 546, 274 N.W.2d 486 (1978)).
80. Harvard Drug Group, LLC v. Linehan, 684 F.Supp.2d 921, 927 (E.D. Mich. 2010).
81. *Id.*

or waiver of notice of alteration of the agreement, then the guarantor is still bound by the guaranty.[82]

7.2.3 *Obligee Misconduct*

Misconduct by the obligee that has a material adverse effect on the rights or obligations of the guarantor voids the guaranty contract.[83] However, the guarantors are barred from raising the obligee's conduct as a defense where the guarantors released the obligee, its successors, and its assigns from any liability arising from the creditor's administration of the loan that it guaranteed.[84]

7.3 Other Defenses

7.3.1 *Duress*

A valid duress defense under Michigan law requires proof that compulsion or coercion was used in some illegal or unlawful manner to force a desired result.[85] A party that merely fears "economic ruin" that does not result from the illegal or unlawful coercion of another does not suffer economic duress.[86]

7.3.2 *Fraudulent Inducement*

In order to state a valid defense of fraudulent inducement, guarantor must show (1) that there was a material misrepresentation to him, (2) that the representation was false, (3) that the party who made the representation knew it was false, or it was made recklessly, without knowledge of its truth and as a positive assertion, (4) that the party who made the representation made it with the intention that guarantor would act on it, (5) that guarantor acted in reliance on the representation and (6) guarantor suffered damage.[87] Additionally, the misrepresentation must be made under circumstances in which the assertions may reasonably be expected to be relied upon and are relied upon.[88]

7.3.3 *Failure to pursue Primary Obligor*

The obligee must exercise reasonable due diligence to collect the debt from the primary obligor before proceeding against the guarantor, if it is a guaranty of collection and not a guaranty of payment.[89] What amounts to reasonable diligence to collect from the principal debtor is determined from the facts of each case.[90]

---

82. *Id.*
83. *See generally In re Allied Supermarkets, Inc.*, 951 F.2d at 718.
84. *See* Federal Deposit Ins. Corp., 777 F.Supp. 539, 541 (E.D. Mich. 1991).
85. *Harvard Drug Group, LLC*, 684 F.Supp.2d at 927.
86. *Id.*
87. Belle Isle Grill v. City of Detroit, 256 Mich. App. 463, 666 N.W.2d 271 (2003).
88. Begola Services v. Wild Bros., 210 Mich. App. 636, 534 N.W.2d 217 (1995).
89. *See* Comerica Bank v. Cohen, 291 Mich. App. 40, 805 N.W.2d 544 (Mich. Ct. App. 2010); Under Michigan law, "whether the guarantee must first sue the primary obligor depends upon the type of guaranty. While the guarantee may proceed immediately against the guarantor if it is a guaranty of payment, if it is a guaranty of collection, the guarantee must first sue the primary obligor." *Brodsky*, 424 F. Supp. at 864-65.
90. Bastian Bros. Co. v. Brown, 293 Mich. 242, 251, 291 N.W. 644, 646 (1940).

7.3.4 *Statute of Limitations*

The statute of limitations for contracts in Michigan is six years.[91] Under Michigan law, filing lawsuit to seek enforcement of acceleration of a guaranteed note triggers the running of the six-year period of limitation with regard to the guaranty contracts.[92]

7.3.5 *Statute of Frauds*

A written agreement signed by authorized parties must be executed for a guaranty to be valid under the Michigan statute of frauds.[93] Also, under the statute of frauds, when a financial institution is involved with the guaranty, the guaranty, modification of the guaranty, or waiver of the guaranty is not enforceable unless it is in writing and signed by an authorized representative of a bank.[94]

When trying to negotiate settlement agreements with banks under a guaranteed mortgage or loan, it will be unenforceable under the statute of frauds if there is no signed, written agreement evidencing a compromise.[95]

7.3.6 *Demand and Notice required*

Where, from the terms of the guaranty, demand and notice was required but not given, the omission can be used as a defense where the guarantor can show that he or she has been prejudiced or damaged.[96]

§ 8 Waiver of Defenses by the Guarantor

8.1 Defenses that cannot be Waived

There are apparently no Michigan cases discussing defenses that cannot be waived; provided, however, a guarantor cannot waive the commercial reasonableness defense regarding the disposition of collateral governed by Article 9 of the Uniform Commercial Code.[97]

8.2 "Catch-all" Waivers

The standard catch-all waiver indicates that the guaranty is "absolute and unconditional" and that the guarantor waives all "rights or defenses it may

91. Mich. Comp. Laws Ann. § 600.5807(8) (West 2012).
92. Diversified Fin. Sys., Inc. v. Schanhals, 203 Mich. App. 589, 592, 513 N.W.2d 210, 211 (1994) (citing Aiton v. Slater, 298 Mich. 469, 299 N.W. 149 (Mich. 1941)).
93. Mich. Comp. Laws Ann. § 566.132(1)(b) (West 2012).
94. Mich. Comp. Laws Ann. § 566.132(2) (West 2012); *See* Cadle Co. II, Inc. v. P.M. Group, Inc., No. 275099, 2007 WL 3119569 (Mich. Ct. App. Oct. 25, 2007).
95. Mich. Comp. Laws Ann. § 566.132(2) (West 2012); Morris v. Comerica Bank, No. 245563, 2004 WL 1801034 (Mich. Ct. App. Aug. 12, 2004).
96. Mac Near v. Malow, 282 Mich. 239, 276 N.W. 433 (Mich. 1937).
97. Mich. Comp. Laws Ann. § 440.9602 (West 2012).

have."[98] When such a catch-all waiver is included in a guaranty, the guarantor waives almost all defenses and counterclaims potentially available in an action by the creditor arising from an obligation covered by the guaranty.[99]

However, one defense that the guarantor does not waive is that the catch-all waiver is against public policy. However, that defense is very difficult to substantiate. In a case before the Michigan Court of Appeals, defendants raised the issue that the requirement in the guaranty that they waive "virtually any and all rights or defenses it may have" were contrary to public policy.[100] The court held that even though the waivers were extensive, defendants did not support their contention that the waivers were "violative of law or policy."[101] The court went on to say that, "[t]he bare assertion of a violation, without more, is insufficient."[102]

8.3 Use of Specific Waivers

Any explicit waiver will be analyzed by the plain meaning of the words. From the perspective of the obligee, it may be beneficial to the guarantor to explicitly state what defenses the parties waive, rather than using a blanket unconditional waiver.[103]

§ 9 Third-party Pledgors—Defenses and Waiver Thereof

We have found no evidence that the law as applied to guaranties would not apply to third-party pledgors.

§ 10 Jointly and Severally Liable Guarantors—Contribution and Reduction of Obligations upon Payment by a Co-obligor

Guarantors may apportion their liability among themselves, although it will have no effect on the liability to the obligee.[104] Guarantors who are jointly and severally liable are presumed to share the secondary obligation

98. *See generally Comerica Bank v. Cohen,* 291 Mich. App. at 40; Farm Credit Services v. Ruggles, No. 209257, 1999 WL 33438842 (Mich. Ct. App. July 16, 1999). *See* Flagstar Bank v. Dilorenzo, No. 289856, 2010 WL 2680122, *6 (Mich. Ct. App. July 6, 2010).
99. *See Flagstar Bank*, 2010 WL 2680122 at *6.
100. *See Flagstar Bank*, 2010 WL 2680122 at *6; Farm Credit Services v. Ruggles, No. 209257, 1999 WL 33438842 (Mich. Ct. App. 1999).
101. *Flagstar Bank*, 2010 WL 2680122 at *6.
102. *Id.*
103. *Id.*
104. Wilmarth v. Hartman, 238 Mich. 20, 24, 213 N.W. 73 (Mich. 1927).

equally.[105] The obligee is not obliged to seek full payment from more than one such guarantor.[106]

Where coguarantors are liable jointly and severally, there is a presumption that they bear the burden equally.[107] Moreover, before the obligee obtains judgment, any individual coguarantor can bring in another coguarantor for contribution if the obligee fails to file suit against it.[108]

§ 11 Reliance

Reliance is ordinarily not required for a claim under a guaranty.

Under Michigan contract law, proof of reliance ordinarily is not necessary to maintain a contract action.[109] However, reliance may be relevant to the proof of the elements of consideration, offer, and acceptance in an action on a contract of guaranty of the financial obligation of another.[110]

§ 12 Subrogation

Subrogation is an equitable remedy that may be available to a guarantor who pays the primary obligor's debt.

Under Michigan law a guarantor acquires rights against a principal debtor by subrogation and that regardless whether subrogation rights arise by contract or by operation of law. A subrogee, upon paying the obligation owed to the subrogor, is substituted for the subrogor, "thereby attaining the same and no greater rights to recover against the third party."[111]

Equitable subrogation is a doctrine that "is broad enough to include every instance in which one party pays the debt for which another is primarily answerable." [112] As one federal district court examining Michigan equitable subrogation law has stated:

> The doctrine of equitable subrogation benefits from the flexibility of application that is characteristic of all equitable remedies. The doctrine is "broad enough to include every instance in which one party pays the debt for which another is primarily answerable." Notions of "equity and good conscience" should guide a court's application of the doctrine. Subrogation is an important device for "placing the economic responsibility for injuries on the party whose fault caused the loss." The doctrine "prevent[s] unjust enrichment by

105. *Id.* at 24 ("The guaranty of indebtedness to the bank put a common burden equally upon all the guarantors.")
106. Tinker & Webb v. McCauley, 3 Mich. 188 (Mich. 1854).
107. *See* Presidential Facility, LLC v. Debbas, No. 09-12346, 2011 WL 204617 (E.D. Mich. Jan. 21, 2011).
108. *Id.*
109. *Angelo Iafrate Co.*, 80 Mich. App. at 515-16.
110. *Id.* at 516.
111. Levin v. Thorn Apple Valley, Inc., 1998 Mich. App. Lexis 850, *20 (Mich. Ct. App. 1998) (citing Citizens Ins Co v American Community Mut Ins Co, 197 Mich. App. 707, 709; 495 NW2d 798 (1992)).
112. *Harley J. Robinson Trust*, 6 F. Supp.2d at 645 (citing Allstate Ins. Co. v. Snarski, 174 Mich. App. 148, 154, 435 N.W.2d 408 (1988)).

assuring that the person who in equity and good conscience is responsible for the debt is ultimately answerable for its discharge." [113]

§ 13 Triangular Set-off in Bankruptcy

There are apparently no Michigan court cases discussing triangular set-off in bankruptcy.

§ 14 Indemnification—Whether the Primary Obligor has a Duty

While there are no Michigan cases that specifically address an obligor's duty of indemnification to a guarantor who paid the obligor's underlying obligation, Michigan does recognize an implied agreement as an identifiably separate area of common-law indemnity relating to allocation of responsibility for loss. [114]

§ 15 Enforcement of Guaranties

Contracts of guaranty are to be construed like other contracts.[115] "[U]nambiguous contracts are not open to judicial construction and must be *enforced as written*."[116] "Where one writing references another instrument for additional contract terms, the two writings should be read together."[117]

§ 16 Revival and Reinstatement of Guaranties

There are apparently no Michigan cases discussing this topic.

§ 17 Choice of Law

In the absence of compelling evidence that Michigan has a materially greater interest than another state, courts will decline to void the parties' express

113. *Id.* at 645 (citing In re Air Crash Disaster, 86 F.3d 498 (6th Cir. 1996) (citations omitted)).
114. *See* Proctor & Schwartz, Inc. v. United States Equipment Co., 624 F.2d 771 (6th Cir. Mich. 1980).
115. Keybank National Association v. Leff, 276 Fed.Appx. 486 (6th Cir. 2008).
116. *Id.* at 487 (internal citations omitted).
117. *Id.* (internal citations omitted).

preference for another state's law to apply.[118] Contracts of guaranty are to be construed like all other contracts, and the intention of the parties is the governing factor, as deduced in the light of the surrounding circumstances.[119] When construing a guaranty agreement, Michigan precedent maintains that the intention of the parties governs; to ascertain the parties' intention, the court shall look at the language of the parties' written agreement first, and only if the terms of the agreement are ambiguous shall the court look to extrinsic facts along with the terms of the agreement to determine the parties' intention.[120]

118. Kirco Realty & Development, Limited and Alan M. Kiriluk v. Bankers Trust Co. et al, 1997 Mich. App. LEXIS 2840 (Mich. Ct. Appeals 1997).
119. 18 M.L.P. 2d Guaranty § 21.
120. Wells Fargo Bank, NA v. MPC Investors, LLC, 705 F. Supp. 2d 728 (E.D. Mich. 2010).

Minnesota Law of Guaranties

David B. Clark
Jeremy R. Harrell*
Faegre Baker Daniels LLP
2200 Wells Fargo Center
Minneapolis, MN 55402-3901
tel: (612) 766-7000
fax: (612) 766-1600
http://www.faegrebd.com

FAEGRE BAKER DANIELS

Contents

* The authors acknowledge the assistance of Michael P. Carlson, Jane E. Maschka, James M. Pfau, Michael R. Stewart, and Charles F. Webber, in preparing and reviewing these materials.

Minnesota Law of Guaranties

Introductory Note: In order to standardize our discussion of the law of guaranties, we use the following vocabulary to refer to the various parties to a guaranty and their obligations.

"Guarantor" means a person who, by contract, agrees to satisfy an underlying obligation of another to an obligee upon the primary obligor's default on that underlying obligation.

"Guaranty" means the contract by which the guarantor agrees to satisfy the underlying obligation of a primary obligor to an obligee in the event the primary obligor defaults on the underlying obligation.

"Obligee" means the person to whom the underlying obligation is owed. For example, the lender under a loan agreement would be an obligee vis-à-vis the borrower.

"Primary Obligor" means the person who incurs the underlying obligation to the obligee. For example, the borrower under a loan agreement would be a primary obligor.

"Underlying Obligation" means the obligation or obligations incurred by the primary obligor and owed to the obligee. For example, the borrower's obligation to make payments to a lender of principal and interest on a loan constitutes an underlying obligation.

Introduction and Sources of Law

In Minnesota, case law is the primary source of substantive law governing commercial guaranties. Courts occasionally cite the *Restatement (Third) of Suretyship and Guaranty* (1996)[1] and the *Restatement of Security*.[2]

1. *See, e.g.,* Nelson v. Woodlands Nat'l Bank, 2006 WL 1529489 (Minn. Ct. App. 2006); Loving and Assocs., Inc. v. Carothers, 619 N.W.2d 782, 786 (Minn. Ct. App. 2000).
2. *See, e.g.,* Estate of Frantz v. Page, 426 N.W.2d 894, 901 (Minn. Ct. App. 1988); Koch v. Han-Shire Investments, Inc., 140 N.W.2d 55, 62 (Minn. 1966).

§ 1 Nature of the Guaranty Arrangement

"[T]he contract of guaranty is an undertaking or promise on the part of one person which is collateral to a primary or principal obligation on the part of another and which binds the [guarantor] to performance in the event of nonperformance by such other, the latter being bound to perform primarily. A guarantor is not a party to the principal obligation."[3] The guaranty is independent of the primary obligation.[4] Where individuals had signed a note in two places, once in a representative capacity and separately without any words of qualification, designation, or guaranty, the individuals were comakers and not guarantors.[5]

1.1 Guaranty Relationships

A contract of guaranty, being a collateral engagement for the performance of an undertaking of another, imports the existence of two different obligations, one being that of the principal debtor and the other that of the guarantor. If a primary or underlying obligation does not exist, there cannot be a contract of guaranty. To constitute a guaranty, there must be a principal debtor or obligor. Without a principal debt there can be no guaranty. The debtor is not a party to the guaranty, and the guarantor is not a party to the underlying obligation. The undertaking of the primary obligor is independent of the promise of the guarantor, and the responsibilities which are imposed by the contract of guaranty differ from those which are created by the contract to which the guaranty is collateral.[6] Minnesota does not have any law on the subject of completion guaranties or other types of performance guaranties (i.e., guaranties of obligations other than for the payment of money) separate from the law of surety bonds.

1.2 Other Suretyship Relationships

Suretyship relationships are similar to guaranties but not the focus of this survey. A person is a surety when "pursuant to contract . . . an obligee has recourse against [that] person . . . or *against that person's property* with respect to an obligation . . . of another person . . . to the obligee" (emphasis added).[7] "[I]n many instances a contract of guaranty so clearly resembles a contract of suretyship that the authorities, in determining the rights and liabilities of the parties, apply the same rules of law to both relations."[8]

---

3. Clark v. Otto B. Ashbach & Sons, Inc. 64 N.W.2d 517, 522 (Minn. 1954); Twin City Co-op Credit Union v. Bartlett, 123 N.W.2d 675, 677 (Minn. 1963) (quoting *Clark*, finding that comaker of a promissory note was not a guarantor and could, therefore, assert the defense of usury).
4. *Clark*, 64 N.W.2d at 522.
5. Metropolitan Life Ins. Co. v. Christison, 451 N.W.2d 222, 224 (Minn. Ct. App. 1990).
6. Schmidt v. McKenzie, 9 N.W.2d 1, 7 (1943) (discharging guarantor who did not consent to the obligee's agreement not to enforce the underlying obligation according to its terms).
7. *See* RESTATEMENT (THIRD) OF SURETYSHIP AND GUARANTY § 1.
8. *Schmidt*, 9 N.W.2d at 7; accord Premier Bank v. Becker Development, 767 N.W.2d 691, 696 (Minn. Ct. App. 2009) (reversed on other grounds).

§ 2 State Law Requirements for an Entity to Enter a Guaranty

Partnerships, limited liability companies (LLCs), and corporations can all grant guaranties in furtherance of their business activities. Additionally, corporations, partnerships, and LLCs can sometimes grant guaranties even when not in furtherance of their business activities.

2.1 Corporations

Under the Minnesota Business Corporation Act,[9] a Minnesota business corporation may give a guaranty if approved by the majority of directors present and the guaranty

(a) is in the usual and regular course of business of the corporation;

(b) is with or for the benefit of a related organization, an organization in which the corporation has a financial interest, an organization with which the corporation has a business relationship, or an organization to which the corporation has the power to make donations;

(c) is for the benefit of an officer or other employee of the corporation or a subsidiary, including an officer or employee who is a director of the corporation or a subsidiary, and the board of directors reasonably believes will also benefit the corporation; or

(d) if otherwise approved by either the holders of two-thirds of the voting power of the shares entitled to vote which are owned by disinterested persons, or the unanimous affirmative vote of the holders of all outstanding shares, whether or not entitled to vote.[10]

A guaranty so authorized may be secured in any manner.[11] Minnesota nonprofit corporations have similar abilities but more restrictions are placed on guaranties in favor of officers, directors, and employees.[12]

2.2 Partnerships

Minnesota law neither expressly empowers a partnership to issue a guaranty nor expressly regulates or prohibits such activity.[13] Minnesota's enactment of the Uniform Limited Partnership Act of 2001 gives limited partnerships general powers to do all things necessary or convenient to carry on their activities.[14] Minnesota courts have enforced guaranty obligations against partnerships.[15]

9. Minn. Stat. § 302A.001 et seq. (2012).
10. Minn. Stat. § 302A.501 subd. 1 (2012); Minn. Stat. § 302A.161 subd. 20 (2012).
11. Minn. Stat. § 302A.501 subd. 2 (2012).
12. Minn. Stat. § 317A.501 (2012).
13. Uniform Partnership Act of 1994, Minn. Stat. Chapter 323A (2012); Uniform Limited Partnership Act of 2001, Minn. Stat. Chapter 321 (2012); 1919 Uniform Limited Partnership Act, Minn. Stat. Chapter 322 (2012).
14. Minn. Stat. § 321.0105 (2012).
15. *See, e.g.*, Ed Herman & Sons v. Russell, 535 N.W.2d 803 (Minn. 1995) (mortgage by general partnership on agricultural land to secure a corporation's debt was a guaranty and not protected by Minnesota's election-of-remedies statute); BA Mortgage and Int'l Realty Corp. v. 7100 Northland Circle, 1992 WL 203237 (Minn. Ct. App. 1992) (enforcing guaranty executed by limited partnership).

2.3 Limited Liability Companies

Minnesota law permits LLCs to issue guaranties if approved by the majority of governors present and the guaranty:

(a) is in the usual and regular course of business of the LLC;

(b) is with or for the benefit of a related organization, an organization in which the LLC has a financial interest, an organization with which the LLC has a business relationship, or an organization to which the LLC has the power to make donations;

(c) is with or for the benefit of a member who provides services to the LLC, or a manager or other employee of the LLC or a subsidiary, including a member, manager, or employee who is a governor of the LLC or a subsidiary, and the board of governors reasonably believes will also benefit the LLC; or

(d) if otherwise approved by either the owners of two-thirds of the voting power of disinterested persons, or the unanimous affirmative vote of members.[16]

A guaranty so authorized may be secured in any manner.[17]

2.4 Banks and Trust Companies

Minnesota's banking statutes neither specifically authorize nor prohibit state-chartered banks from issuing guaranties. However, Minnesota's banking statutes do refer to the issuance of guaranties by banks:

> "No officer or employee of a bank or trust company shall have power or authority to borrow money, execute guaranties ... unless the power and authority shall have been given the officer or employee by the board of directors and a written record thereof made in the minute book of the bank and a certified copy of the record delivered to the creditor, guarantee, pledgee, or endorsee of the note, bond, guaranty, or other obligation."[18]

A guaranty not so executed is void.[19] Minnesota law also places severe restrictions on the abilities of state banks to pledge assets.[20]

Note also that guaranties offered by state banks may also be significantly affected by federal law. First, federal law prohibits a state-chartered bank from engaging in activities in which a national bank may not engage under federal law. The situations under which a national bank may become a guarantor are governed by federal law. *See* National Bank as Guarantor or Surety on Indemnity Bond, 12 C.F.R. § 7.1017 (2010).

---

16. Minn. Stat. Chapter 322B (2012); Minn. Stat. § 322B.693 subd. 1 (2012).
17. Minn. Stat. § 322B 693 subd. 2 (2012).
18. Minn. Stat. § 48.17 (2012).
19. "Any note, endorsement, guaranty, pledge, hypothecation, lien or other obligation given contrary to the provisions of sections 48.16 to 48.18 shall be null and void." Minn. Stat. § 48.20 (2012).
20. Minn. Stat. §§ 48.16, 48.18, 48.20 (2012).

2.5 Individuals

An individual must be mentally competent to enter into a guaranty. The standard for determining whether a person is mentally capable of entering into a guaranty or any other contract is whether she has the ability to understand to a reasonable extent the nature and effect of what she is doing.[21]

Minnesota does not have special signature requirements when a guaranty is signed by one spouse but not the other. Except for certain medical and household expenses, a spouse is not liable for the debts of the other spouse unless, in a divorce proceeding, the court apportions the debt between the spouses.[22]

In Minnesota, a debtor's property is subject to levy and execution unless an exemption applies.[23] The debtor must establish the exemption.[24] Minnesota's garnishment statute[25] provides that all nonexempt indebtedness, money, or other property due or belonging to the debtor and owing by the garnishee or in the possession or under the control of the garnishee is attachable by garnishment.[26]

A judgment creditor may serve a garnishment summons on a garnishee, attaching funds in a joint account to satisfy the debt of an account holder, even though not all of the account holders are judgment debtors.[27] Under Minnesota's Multi-Party Accounts Act,[28] funds in a joint account[29] belong to the parties in proportion to their net contributions. For purposes of a creditor serving a garnishment summons and a garnishee initially retaining funds in a joint account, the debtor is initially, but rebuttably, presumed to own all of the funds in a joint account, but any account holder may rebut that presumption upon a preponderance of evidence of ownership.[30] The account holders to a joint account bear the burden of establishing net contributions to the account in a garnishment proceeding.[31] If the presumption is not rebutted, all of the funds in the account are subject to garnishment.[32] Where one party has contributed all the money in a joint account, a creditor may not garnish the account to satisfy

21. State Bank of Cologne v. Schrupp, 375 N.W.2d 48, 51 (Minn. Ct. App. 1985) (remanding to determine competency of 78-year-old guarantor who had a "fainting spell" the day she signed the guaranty and could not recall doing so).
22. Minn. Stat. § 519.05(a) (2012); Luginbill v. Luginbill, 2011 WL 2982095 *3 (Minn. Ct. App. 2011) (upholding trial court's refusal to apportion husband's liability on a guaranty of student loans of the divorcing couple's child when husband signed guaranty over wife's objection).
23. Minn. Stat. §§ 550.10, 550.37 (2012). Russell's AmericInn, LLC v. Eagle General Contractors, LLC, 772 N.W.2d 81, 83 (Minn. Ct. App. 2009).
24. *Id.*
25. Minn. Stat. §§ 571.71-.932 (2012). *See* Savig v. First Nat'l Bank of Omaha, 781 N.W.2d 335, 338-39 (Minn. 2010), for an overview of the garnishment process.
26. Minn. Stat. § 571.73 subd. 3(2) (2012).
27. *Savig*, 781 N.W.2d at 341.
28. Minn. Stat. § 524.6-201 - 6-214 (2012).
29. The Minnesota Multi-Party Accounts Act defines "account" as "a contract of deposit of funds between a depositor and a financial institution, and includes a checking account, savings account, certificate of deposit, share account and other like arrangement," and defines "financial institution" as any organization authorized to do business under state or federal laws relating to financial institutions, including, without limitation, banks and trust companies, savings banks, savings associations, and credit unions. Minn. Stat. § 524.6-201 subd. 2, subd. 3 (2012). The term "account" does not include an investment account with a brokerage firm, Berg v. D.D.M., 603 N.W.2d 361, 364 (Minn. Ct. App. 1999), nor jointly held stock. In re Setterberg, 2001 WL 32848 *1 (Minn. Ct. App. 2001).
30. *Savig*, 781 N.W.2d at 344-45.
31. *Id.* at 347.
32. *Id.* at 348.

a debt belonging to a noncontributing party unless the creditor provides clear and convincing evidence that the depositor intended to confer ownership of the funds on the debtor.[33]

When a judgment is docketed, it becomes a lien on all of the debtor's real property within the county.[34] If the debtor owns real estate as a joint tenant, the lien attaches to the debtor's interest in the property and his interest in the proceeds from the sale of the property. The creditor's interest in such property and its proceeds is no greater than the interest of the debtor.[35]

Minnesota's homestead statute[36] defines the homestead of a debtor and the debtor's family as the house owned[37] and occupied by the debtor as the debtor's dwelling place, together with the land upon which it is situated to the amount of an area of up to 160 acres and a value periodically adjusted.[38] The homestead is exempt from seizure of sale under legal process on account of any debt not lawfully charged thereon in writing.[39] If the debtor is married, the homestead title may be vested in either spouse, and the exemption extends to the debts of either or of both spouses.[40] If the premises claimed as the homestead exceeds the value limitation, an attachment or execution may be levied on the whole.[41] In order to sell the property, the executing creditor must obtain a court order which the court must issue if there is no nondebtor with a valid homestead interest in the property and the fair market value of the property exceeds the sum of the homestead exemption limit and any encumbrances.[42]

When spouses hold the homestead in joint tenancy, however, neither spouse can dispose of his or her right of joint tenancy without the consent of the other. Because a judgment creditor cannot acquire more property rights in a property than those held by the debtor, the creditor of one spouse cannot unilaterally sever and sell a homestead held in joint tenancy even when the unencumbered value of the homestead exceeds the amount of the homestead exemption.[43]

---

33. Enright v. Lehmann, 735 N.W.2d 326, 331 (Minn. 2007). In *Enright*, the Minnesota Supreme Court construed Minnesota's garnishment statute as describing the process by which creditors in Minnesota may satisfy judgments while Minn. Stat. § 524.6-203 of the Minnesota Multi-Party Accounts Act is a specific substantive statute defining the ownership of funds in a joint account. The Court held that Minn. Stat. § 524.6-203 abrogates the rule of Park Enterprises v. Trach, N.W.2d 194 (1951) Park Enterprises followed the "contract" theory to determine ownership of funds in joint accounts and allowed garnishment of all funds in a joint account to satisfy debts of one of the account holders because the account agreement made all funds in the joint account the property of the depositors with right of survivorship.
34. Minn. Stat. § 548.09 subd. 1 (2012).
35. Gibson v. Trustees of the Minnesota State Basic Building Trades Fringe Benefits Funds, 703 N.W.2d 864, 867-69 (Minn. Ct. App. 2005). *Gibson* also upheld the district court's award of sanctions. That portion of the opinion was later vacated. Gibson v. Trustees of the Minnesota State Basic Building Trades Fringe Benefits Funds, 2005 WL 6240753 (Minn. 2005).
36. Minn. Stat. § 510 (2012).
37. Any interest in the land, whether legal or equitable, constitutes ownership. Minn. Stat. § 510.04 (2012).
38. Minn. Stat. § 510.01-.02 (2012). The value limitations are currently $390,000 for nonagricultural property and $975,000 for agricultural property. Minnesota Register volume 36, page 1218 (April 16, 2012).
39. Minn. Stat. § 510.01 (2012). Except for child support obligations, proceeds from the sale of the homestead are also exempt to the same extent as the homestead for a period of one year after sale. Minn. Stat. § 510.07 (2012).
40. Minn. Stat. § 510.04 (2012).
41. Minn. Stat. § 510.08(b) (2012).
42. Minn. Stat. § 550.175 subd. 1 (2012).
43. Minn. Stat. §§ 500.19 subd. 4, 507.02 (2012); Kipp v. Sweno, 683 N.W.2d 259, 262-66 (Minn. 2004); O'Hagan v. United States, 86 F.3d 776, 780 (8th Cir. 1996).

§ 3 Signatory's Authority to Execute a Guaranty

3.1 Corporations

Minnesota law requires a corporation to approve each guaranty by the majority of directors present.[44] The requirement for board approval makes reliance on the doctrine of apparent authority risky.[45]

3.2 Partnerships

Traditionally, Minnesota courts have held that partners must have authority to execute guaranties. "The mere partnership relation does not authorize a partner to use the partnership name for the accommodation of or as surety for another."[46] The obligee has the burden of establishing that the partner had authority and that the guaranty was given for a partnership purpose.[47]

Minnesota's enactments of the Uniform Partnership Act (1994)[48] and the Uniform Limited Partnership Act 2001[49] provide that an act of a partner[50] for apparently carrying on in the ordinary course the partnership business or business of the kind carried on by the partnership binds the partnership unless the partner had no authority to act with respect to the particular matter and the counterparty knew or had received notice that the partner lacked authority,[51] in which case the partner would have personal liability but the partnership would not be bound.[52] However, if the act is not apparently for carrying on in the ordinary course the partnership's activities or activities of the kind carried on by the partnership, the partnership is not bound unless the act was approved by all the other partners.[53] A general partnership may also file a statement of partnership authority which is conclusive in favor of a person who gives value without knowledge to the contrary and absent a filed limitation on that authority.[54] Limited partners do not have authority to bind a limited partnership.[55]

---

44. Minn. Stat. § 302A.501 subd. 1 (2012); Minn. State. § 302A.161 subd. 20 (2012).
45. B.B. & D. Investments, Inc. v. WinHoldCo Corp., 1992 WL 3665 (Minn. Ct. App. 1992) (reversing grant of summary judgment enforcing guaranty when obligee provided no evidence of actual authority of guarantor's executive vice president to sign guaranty nor any evidence of apparent authority from the guarantor).
46. Van Dyke v. Seelye, 52 N.W. 215, 216 (1892).
47. *Id.* at 216.
48. Minn. Stat. § 323A (2012).
49. Minn. Stat. § 321 (2012). Under the 1919 Uniform Limited Partnership Act, Minn. Stat. § 322 et seq. (2012), a general partner generally has all the rights and powers and is subject to all the restrictions and liabilities of a partner in a partnership without limited partners. Minn. Stat. § 322.09 (2012).
50. A general partner in the case of a limited partnership.
51. Minn. Stat. § 323A.0301(1) (2012) (general partnerships); Minn. Stat. § 321.0402(a) (limited partnerships).
52. Minn. Stat. § 323A.0308(a) (2012).
53. Minn. Stat. § 323A.0301(2) (2012) (general partnerships); Minn. Stat. § 321.0402(b) (limited partnerships).
54. Minn. Stat. § 323A.0303(d)(1) (2012). Statements are filed with the Minnesota Secretary of State. Minn. Stat. § 323A.0105(a) (2012).
55. Minn. Stat. § 321.0302 (2012).

3.3 Limited Liability Companies

Minnesota statutes requires a LLC to approve each guaranty by the majority of governors present.[56]

3.4 Banks and Trust Companies

A case-by-case inquiry of the powers provided for in a bank's or trust company's corporate governance documents is necessary to determine who may validly execute a guaranty on behalf of a bank or trust company.

§ 4 Consideration; Sufficiency of Past Consideration

A guaranty agreement, like any other contract, must be supported by a valid consideration. But unlike other contracts, there does not need to be a transfer from the promisee to the promisor.[57]

4.1 Corporations

If the guaranty is with or for the benefit of a related organization,[58] an organization in which the corporation has a financial interest, an organization with which the corporation has a business relationship, or an organization to which the corporation has the power to make donations, such a relationship constitutes sufficient consideration for the guaranty.[59]

4.2 Partnerships

Minnesota's partnership statutes do not expressly address consideration for guaranties.

4.3 Limited Liability Companies

If the guaranty is with or for the benefit of a related organization,[60] an organization in which the LLC has a financial interest, an organization with which the LLC has a business relationship, or an organization to which the LLC has the power to make donations, such a relationship constitutes sufficient consideration for the guaranty.[61]

---

56. Minn. Stat. § 322B.693 subd. 1 (2012).
57. O'Neil v. Dux, 101 N.W.2d 588, 594 (Minn. 1960).
58. "Related Organization" is defined in Minn. Stat. § 302A.011 Subd. 25 (2012) and includes direct and indirect parent and subsidiary corporations and LLCs and sister corporations and LLCs.
59. Minn. Stat. § 302A.501 subd. 1(b) (2012).
60. "Related Organization" is defined in Minn. Stat. § 322B.03 subd. 41 (2012) and includes parent, subsidiary, and sister organizations.
61. Minn. Stat. 322B.693 subd. 1(2) (2012).

4.4 Individuals

If, at the time a loan is made, there is an agreement between the primary obligor and the obligee that an additional guaranty will be obtained, that agreement is sufficient consideration for a guaranty that is provided later even though the guarantor is not bound by that agreement. In providing the guaranty, the guarantor is conclusively presumed to have intended to carry out the agreement.[62]

4.5 Sufficiency of Consideration

A guaranty given after the underlying obligation is incurred must be supported by consideration other than detrimental reliance. A preexisting debt is not sufficient consideration for a third-party guaranty.[63] Where a promissory note is given for a previously existing and past-due debt and is payable at a future date, the extension of time is a sufficient consideration to support a guaranty of payment made by third parties before delivery of the note. Forbearing from exercising remedies and extending additional credit to the primary obligor are both sufficient consideration to support a guaranty even though no consideration flows to the guarantor.[64]

Forbearance must be of reasonable duration. Seven days is not enough.[65] Eighty days was not enough in the context of one shareholder's claims that a second shareholder had guaranteed loans the first shareholder made to the corporation without the required consent of the second shareholder.[66]

The Minnesota statute of frauds requires a writing signed by the guarantor expressing the consideration in order to enforce a guaranty.[67] The phrase "credit given and to be given" is a sufficient expression of consideration.[68]

§ 5 Notice of Acceptance

Notice of acceptance of a guaranty is not required to make the contract effective "where the terms of a guaranty unequivocally anticipate the extension of credit to a third person, and the guarantor can reasonably anticipate that the [obligee] will act in reliance thereon.[69]

---

62. Bowen v. Thwing, 57 N.W. 468 (Minn. 1894); First Nat'l Bank of Hopkins v. Int'l Machines Corp., 156 N.W.2d 86, 88-89 (1968) (discussed at note 168).
63. Baker v. Citizens State Bank, 349 N.W.2d 552, 557 (Minn. 1984).
64. *Schrupp*, 375 N.W.2d at 53.
65. *Baker*, 349 N.W.2d at 559 (forbearance period of seven days was insufficient consideration for guaranty where bank agreed to allow borrower time to reorganize and reduce corporation to a manageable size).
66. Brooksbank v. Anderson, 586 N.W.2d 789, 795 (Minn. Ct. App. 1998) (finding that forbearance period of less than 80 days was not reasonable consideration for guaranty).
67. Minn. Stat. § 513.01 (2012). *See* § 7.3.4.
68. Bartley v. BTL Enterprises, Inc., 490 N.W.2d 664, 667 (Minn. Ct. App. 1992).
69. Southdale Center, Inc. v. Lewis, 110 N.W.2d 857, 863 (Minn. 1961). *See also Schrupp*, 375 N.W.2d at 53 (finding the issue of guarantor's reasonable anticipation of bank's reliance to be a question of fact for the jury along with guarantor's competency).

§ 6 Interpretation of Guaranties

6.1 General Principles

Minnesota courts interpret guaranties as they do all other contracts.[70] Minnesota courts "appl[y] general contract principles when construing the nature and terms of a . . . guaranty."[71] Because a guaranty is a contract, its terms must be understood in light of the parties' intentions and the circumstances under which the guaranty was given. Further, "unambiguous contract language must be given its plain and ordinary meaning." Minnesota courts may not enlarge the terms of the guaranty "beyond the fair and natural import of [its] terms."[72] A guarantor has the right to "insist that he is bound to the extent, in [the] manner, and under the circumstances pointed out in his obligation, and no further."[73] "[A] guaranty is construed the same as any other contract, the intent of the parties being derived from the commonly accepted meaning of the words and clauses used, taken as a whole. The guaranty is not to be unduly restricted by technical interpretation nor enlarged beyond the fair and natural import of its terms. However, once the intent of the parties has been ascertained, the guarantor has the right to insist upon strict compliance with the terms of his obligation."[74] The recitals to a guaranty, like any other contract, are not part of the contract but may be used to resolve ambiguity in the operative provisions of the contract because they indicate the parties' intent.[75] A promise to personally see that the debtor will get paid is not a personal guaranty of payment.[76]

6.2 Guaranty of Payment versus Guaranty of Collection

"A contract of guaranty may be either conditional or absolute. If the guaranty is absolute, the obligor becomes liable merely upon the failure of performance by the debtor. A conditional guarantor, on the other hand, is liable only upon the happening of the stated contingency, such as, for example, suit against the principal debtor, exhaustion of security, or the like. In the absence of language clearly indicating that the guaranty is conditional, it is usually treated as absolute."[77]

---

70. *See, e.g.*, Henning v. Mainstreet Bank, 538 F.3d 975, 978 (8th Cir. 2008); Winthrop Resources Corp. v. Stanley Works, 259 F.3d 901, 905 (8th Cir. 2001).
71. City of Maple Grove v. Marketline Construction Capital, LLC, 802 N.W.2d 809, 815 (Minn. Ct. App. 2011).
72. *Winthrop Resources*, 259 F. 3d at 905 (citing *Loving*, 619 N.W.2d at 786).
73. *Premier Bank*, 767 N.W.2d at 696 (reversing summary judgment due to question of fact as to parties' intentions regarding identity of primary obligor) (reversed on other grounds) (citing Marquette Trust Co. v. Doyle, 224 N.W. 149, 151 (1929), Minneapolis Pub. Hous. Auth. v. Lor, 591 N.W.2d 700, 704 (Minn. 1999), *Schmidt*, 9 N.W.2d at 5).
74. American Tobacco v. Chalfen, 108 N.W.2d 702, 704 (1961).
75. Construction Mortgage Investors Co. v. Farr, 2010 WL 3119443 at *4 (Minn. Ct. App. 2010) (upholding unambiguous "operative" language in a guaranty that was inconsistent with the recitals) (citing Berg v. Berg, 275 N.W. 836, 842 (1937)).
76. Zweber v. Morrison, 1990 WL 105946 *2 (Minn. Ct. App. 1990) (citing Froelich v. Aspenal, Inc., 369 N.W.2d 37, 39 (Minn. Ct. App.1985)); *but see* Martin v. Fee, 226 N.W. 203, 204-05 (1929) (finding the words "we approve of this agreement and will see that the same is carried out" is equivalent to guaranteeing performance of the contract).
77. Dahmes v. Industrial Credit Co., 110 N.W.2d 484, 488-89 (1961) (citations omitted).

Absolute guaranties are also known as "guaranties of payment," and conditional guaranties that require exhaustion of remedies against the primary obligor are also known as "guaranties of collection." "A guaranty of payment is absolute and binds the guarantor to pay at maturity upon default of the principal debtor. A guaranty of collection is conditional and binds the guarantor to pay upon the condition that the guarantee or creditor has prosecuted the debtor without success."[78]

Whereas unconditional guaranties impose liability to the guarantors upon failure of performance by the primary obligor, conditional guaranties state a contingency that must occur before guarantors can be held to account.[79]

6.3 Language Regarding the Revocation of Guaranties

A guarantor's right to revoke a continuing guaranty will be enforced as will the conditions for delivering any required notice of revocation. Where a guaranty permits the guarantor to terminate at any time, the reasonable time limitation[80] does not apply.[81]

6.4 "Continuing"

Depending on the specific language used in a continuing guaranty, a guarantor may become liable for debts incurred by the primary obligor after the date of the guaranty. If the terms of the guaranty itself do not provide a time limit, Minnesota courts invoke a reasonableness standard: "Termination of a guaranty after a reasonable time may be implied if the contract does not contain any time limitation."[82] The court will limit enforcement to a reasonable time based on the facts and circumstances.[83] But when a guaranty contains a right of revocation,[84] it is not ambiguous or unclear as to its duration and the reasonable

78. Holbert v. Wermerskirchen, 297 N.W. 327, 328 (1941) (an agreement to endorse and guaranty a note is a promise to guaranty payment not just collection; upon breach of a contract to guarantee a debt, the party entitled to the guaranty may recover the amount of the debt remaining past due and unpaid).

79. *Dahmes*, 110 N.W.2d at 488-89; Kittson County v. River Ridge Dairy, LLP, 2008 WL 5215988 (Minn. Ct. App. 2008) (obligee's loan to underlying obligor did not satisfy conditions of guaranty).

80. *See* § 6.4.

81. Borg Warner Acceptance Corp. v. Shakopee Sports Ctr., Inc., 431 N.W.2d 539, 541 (Minn. 1988). In *Borg Warner*, a finance company provided credit to a company backed by the guaranties of the shareholders. The guaranties permitted the guarantors to terminate their guaranties by giving notice to the finance company. A shareholder sold his stock in the borrower but neglected to provide notice of termination of his guaranty. The finance company continued to provide credit to the borrower under a new agreement and required the remaining shareholders to sign new guaranties. Two years after the guarantor had sold his stock in the borrower, the borrower defaulted on the credit facility and eventually filed for bankruptcy. The Minnesota Supreme Court, reversing the court of appeals, found that the guarantor was liable under the plain language of the guaranty for credit extended to the borrower.

82. Currie State Bank v. Schmitz, 628 N.W.2d 205, 210-11 (Minn. Ct. Ap. 2001); *see also Borg Warner*, 431 N.W.2d at 541.

83. Continental Can Co. v. Lanesboro Canning Co., 230 N.W. 121, 122 (1930) (finding guarantors liable for amounts owed for goods shipped to primary obligor during the second year of a three-year contract under a guaranty signed during the term of a prior three-year contract). Several Minnesota courts have found three years to be a reasonable time. Tri-State Bank of Ortonville v. Golf Properties, Inc., 395 N.W.2d 409, 412 (Minn. Ct. App. 1986); accord Residential Funding Corp. v. McCord, 2006 WL 2975302, *2 (D. Minn. 2006).

84. *See* § 6.3 regarding revocation.

time rule does not apply.[85] Minnesota courts have enforced guaranties containing revocation language signed 10 years before the debt was incurred.[86]

6.5 "Absolute and Unconditional"

See § 6.2, Guaranty of payment versus guaranty of collection. *See* § 8.2 on "Catch-all" waivers.

6.6 "Liable as a Primary Obligor and not Merely as Surety"

This language, taken literally, seems to conflate the concepts of guarantor and primary obligor. While a guarantor may be a "guarantor of payment" from whom the obligee can seek payment even without pursuing the primary obligor, the guarantor does not become a primary obligor.

§ 7 Defenses of the Guarantor; Set-off

7.1 Defenses of the Primary Obligor

7.1.1 General

In seeking to evade liability for their guaranties, guarantors are generally not entitled to raise the defenses of the primary obligor. This is because Minnesota courts treat the underlying obligation and the guaranty as separate and distinct contracts: "The debtor is not a party to the guaranty, and the guarantor is not a party to the principal obligation."[87] The parties' responsibilities are different, and the conditions of the formation of the agreements are different.[88] A guarantor, therefore, cannot raise the so-called personal defenses of the primary obligor—such as fraudulent inducement or breach of warranty. A guarantor is generally a "total stranger" to the underlying contract and its formation.[89]

7.1.2 Guarantor May Waive Primary Obligor's Defenses

A guarantor may effectively waive any right to assert defenses available to the primary obligor.[90]

85. *Borg Warner*, 431 N.W.2d at 541.
86. F.D.I.C. v. Dynamic Growth, Inc., 1989 WL 80619 *1 (Minn. Ct. App. 1989).
87. *Schmidt*, 9 N.W.2d at 4.
88. *Id.* at 6-8.
89. *Id.* at 8.
90. AEI Income & Growth Fund 24, LLC v. Parrish, 2005 WL 713629 *6 (D. Minn. 2005) (where guarantors "unconditionally and absolutely waive[ ] ... any failure, neglect or omission on the part of Lessor to realize or protect the Leased Premises or any security given therefore," guarantors waived any right to assert the defense of failure to mitigate damages following a breach and termination of a lease even though that defense remained available to the lessor-primary obligor).

7.1.3 Defenses that May not be Raised by Guarantor

Insolvency of the primary obligor will not extinguish a guarantor's obligation, as long as some deficiency remains on the underlying obligation.[91] Provided that the language of the guaranty contains an unconditional promise by the guarantor, Minnesota courts will enforce this rule even in the face of a statute that waives a mortgagee's right to a deficiency judgment against the mortgagor if the mortgagee buys the disputed property at the foreclosure sale.[92]

Guarantors may also not escape their liability to the obligee even when the guaranty was the result of fraud between the primary obligor and the guarantor.[93] As one court put it, "Misrepresentations by the principal do not release a surety from his contractual obligations to the assured obligee."[94]

7.1.4 Defenses that May Always be Raised by Guarantor

Under the common law, any release or discharge of the principal debtor also discharges the guarantor unless the creditor expressly reserves its right of recourse against the guarantor in the contract releasing the debtor, or in the guaranty contract itself.[95]

A guarantor may escape liability upon a showing that the obligee failed to perform her portion of the underlying agreement.[96] In that case, the guarantor is discharged in an amount equivalent to the obligee's failure to perform.[97]

A guarantor is also released from her obligation when the security for the underlying obligation is released or the underlying obligation is otherwise satisfied, absent an effective waiver.[98] As long as no deficiency remains on the underlying agreement, a guarantor cannot be held liable for the primary obligor's debt once the collateral is released or the debt is paid in full. A contrary outcome would create a windfall for the primary obligee, according to Minnesota courts.[99]

7.2 Suretyship Defenses

7.2.1 Change in Identity of Principal Obligor; Modification of the Underlying Obligation, Including Release

Minnesota courts recognize that modifications of the underlying obligation—including changes to the identity of the primary obligor—can release the guarantor, but there are limitations to this rule.[100] First, the modification must

91. *See* State Bank of Young America v. Fabel, 530 N.W.2d 858, 862 (Minn. Ct. App. 1995); *see also* National City Bank v. Lundgren, 435 N.W.2d 588, 592 (Minn. Ct. App. 1989).
92. *See* Victory Highway Village, Inc. v. Weaver, 480 F. Supp. 71, 76 (D. Minn.) (cited by *State Bank of Young America*, 530 N.W.2d at 862). *See* § 15.3.
93. *See* Watkins Products, Inc. v. Butterfield, 144 N.W.2d 56, 57 (Minn. 1966).
94. *Id.*
95. *National City Bank*, 435 N.W.2d at 592.
96. *See* State Bank of Monticello v. Lauterbach, 268 N.W. 918 (Minn. 1936).
97. *Id.*
98. *See State Bank of Young America*, 530 N.W.2d at 861-62.
99. *State Bank of Young America*, 530 N.W.2d at 862.
100. *See* Dewey v. Henry's Drive-Ins, Inc., 222 N.W.2d 553, 555 (Minn. 1974); *Schmidt*, 9 N.W.2d at 5.

materially affect the interest of the guarantor.[101] Second, the modification to the underlying agreement must have occurred after the execution of the guaranty.[102] Finally, the modification must adversely affect the guarantor's interests.[103]

In the absence of express language in the guaranty that disclaims or assumes liability for the obligations of a successor entity, Minnesota courts review changes to the primary obligor on a case-by-case basis. "The guaranty's enforceability depends on whether the merger changed the identity of the [primary obligor] and imposed on the [guarantor] without his consent an obligation that differed materially from the obligation he undertook when he signed the guaranty."[104] "Changes that allow the [primary obligor] to survive as an independent entity and do not affect the guarantor's original undertaking do not discharge a guaranty."[105] "Other relevant factors include whether [the guarantor] participated in effecting the merger or otherwise assented to it, whether he could reasonably have anticipated a material increase in the risk he assumed under the guaranty, whether [the obligee] had notice of the change before performing, and whether [the guarantor] opted to revoke the guaranty."[106]

Minnesota courts are hesitant to find instances of the required material adverse changes, requiring a change of "sufficient magnitude to justify releasing a guarantor."[107] Courts have not released guarantors in instances of, e.g., a merger between the principal debtor and another corporation, an increase in the financing limit for the principal obligor, and the conversion of the principal obligor's business into a different kind of enterprise, as long as the new enterprise bears some resemblance to the previous one.[108] The key inquiry is whether the change to the principal obligor substantially increases the guarantor's liability or exposes the guarantor to greater risk than what she bargained for.[109] In this regard, the waiver language of the guaranty is central.

However, extension of the principal obligor's time for payment without the guarantor's consent will constitute a modification providing for the guarantor's release and discharge.[110]

---

101. *Dewey* at 555.
102. *Id.*
103. *Id.*
104. *Loving* & Assocs., 619 N.W.2d at 787.
105. *Id.*
106. *Id.*
107. *Id.*
108. *See* Business Bank v. Hanson, 2008 WL 4705172 *7 (Minn. Ct. App. 2008) (reversed on other grounds).
109. *Loving & Assocs.*, 619 N.W. at 788. In *Loving & Assocs.*, the Minnesota Court of Appeals found that the primary obligor continued to operate the same business, under the same name, at the same address, under substantially the same management as before the merger, and that the obligee continued to treat the primary obligor in the same manner and under the same terms as before the merger. The court also rejected the guarantor's argument that his risk increased because the successor corporation was larger, pointing out that a bigger business does not necessarily increase a guarantor's risk.
110. *See Currie State Bank*, 628 N.W.2d at 209.

7.2.2 *Release or Impairment of Security for the Underlying Obligation*

In the absence of an enforceable waiver,[111] a creditor has the duty to preserve the collateral held as security for the benefit of the surety.[112] Consequently, if an obligee impairs the value of the collateral securing the underlying agreement, the guarantor is discharged to the extent the obligee impairs the ability of the surety to recover the value of the collateral.[113] In fact, the value of the discharge in the guarantor's obligation is equivalent to the value of the impairment or release of the collateral.[114] At the same time, while the obligee must deal in good faith with the guarantor, the obligee is not required to look after the interest of the guarantor by, e.g., ensuring the primary obligor fulfills her contractual duty.[115]

7.3 Other Defenses

7.3.1 *Failure to Fulfill a Condition Precedent*

Guarantors may raise the defense of a failure to fulfill a condition precedent, but Minnesota courts generally disfavor this defense.[116] In resolving doubts about whether there is a condition preceding a guarantor's duty, courts will seek an interpretation of the guaranty that reduces the obligee's risk of nonpayment, unless the event is clearly within the obligee's control or if the obligee expressly assumed the risk.[117] In other words, a condition precedent to performance of an obligation will not be inferred unless the contract's language unequivocally establishes the existence of a condition precedent.[118] Absent a requirement in the guaranty, Minnesota law does not require the obligee to notify the guarantor that the primary obligor has defaulted.[119]

7.3.2 *Modification of the Guaranty*

As with any contract, modification of a guaranty will not affect its validity, even in the absence of new consideration. As long as parties mutually assent to a new guarantee, there does not need to be new consideration—courts view such a modification as a substitution for the previous agreement.[120]

111. *See* §§ 8.2 and 8.3.
112. Nelson v. Woodlands Nat'l Bank, 2006 WL 1529489, *2-*3 (Minn. Ct. App. 2006).
113. *Id.*; *see also* Manchester Sav. Bank v. Lynch, 186 N.W. 794, 795-96 (Minn. 1922).
114. *Id.*
115. MacKenzie v. Summit Nat'l Bank of St. Paul, 363 N.W.2d 116, 120 (Minn. Ct. App.1985).
116. *See* Mrozik Constr., Inc. v. Lovering Assocs., 461 N.W.2d 49, 51-52 (Minn. Ct. App. 1990).
117. *Id.* at 51-52 (citing Restatement (Second) of Contracts § 227).
118. Schneider v. U.S.G. Interiors, Inc., 1999 WL 171499 (Minn. Ct. App. 1999) (citing Mrozik, 461 N.W. at 52).
119. *Dewey*, 222 N.W.2d at 556.
120. *See* Olson v. Penkert, 90 N.W.2d 193 (Minn. 1958); Wilson v. Hayes, 42 N.W. 467 (Minn. 1889).

7.3.3 Failure to Pursue Primary Obligor

A guaranty of collection requires the obligee to exhaust his remedies against the primary obligor before pursuing the guarantor; a guaranty of payment does not.[121]

Delay by the obligee in attempting to collect a debt from the primary obligor does not discharge the guarantor if the guarantor cannot show an agreement by the obligee to pursue the primary obligor.[122]

7.3.4 Statute of Limitations

Minnesota's six-year statute of limitations for contracts[123] applies to guaranties. "Where one guarantees the debt of another, the statute of limitations does not commence to run until the debt is due and payable."[124] "The limitations period begins to run when a cause of action accrues, not when the guaranty is executed."[125] Because a guaranty is a separate obligation, the obligation under a guaranty does not expire because the statute of limitations has run on the underlying obligation.[126]

Partial payment of an obligation before the statute of limitations runs tolls the running of the statute on the theory that it amounts to a voluntary acknowledgment of the existence of the debt from which a promise to pay the balance is implied.[127] Partial payment of the underlying obligation by the primary obligor, however, does not toll the statute of limitations with respect to enforcement of the guaranty absent evidence that the guarantor ratified the payment or voluntarily acknowledged the debt.[128]

7.3.5 Statute of Frauds

Minnesota's statute of frauds[129] is similar to those found in other states. Minnesota courts will enforce guaranties that fail to comply with the statute of frauds if the guarantor has a direct interest in the performance of the underlying obligation.[130] Minnesota courts also distinguish between "original promises," which fall outside the statute and are therefore enforceable, and "collateral promises," which require a writing to be enforceable. Whether a promise is

121. Midland Nat'l Bank v. Security Elevator Co., 200 N.W. 851, 853 (1924); *Holbert*, 297 N.W. at 328.
122. *Estate of Frantz*, 426 N.W.2d at 899.
123. Minn. Stat. § 541.05 (2012).
124. Nelson v. Hacking, 29 N.W.2d 888, 890 (Minn. 1947); Home Lumber Co., Inc. v. McClavy, 1997 WL 600656 *1-2 (Minn. Ct. App. 1997).
125. *Dynamic Growth, Inc.*, 1989 WL 80619 at *1 (Minn. Ct. App. 1989) (upholding enforcement action begun within two years after default on primary obligation even though the guaranty was signed 10 years before the date of the note evidencing the primary obligation).
126. Trapp v. Hancuh, 1997 WL 396234 *4 (Minn. Ct. App. 1997).
127. Bernloehr v. Fredrickson, 7 N.W.2d 328, 329 (1942).
128. *Home Lumber*, 1997 WL 600656 at *2 (partial payment by primary obligor owned by two guarantors did not toll statute of limitations as to guarantors where there was no evidence that guarantors voluntarily acknowledged the debt or ratified the payments).
129. Minn. Stat. §§ 513.01 and 513.33 (2012).
130. *See Bartley*, 490 N.W.2d at 667 n.1.

original or collateral depends upon the mutual understanding of the parties.[131] A promise to pay the existing debt of another, which promise arises out of a new transaction and for which there is a fresh consideration, is an original undertaking and is not within the statute of frauds.[132]

7.3.6 Fraud in the Execution

Minnesota courts recognize the defense of fraud in the execution, a defense available in any contractual dispute and not particular to guaranties.[133] As a version of common-law fraud, fraud in the execution requires proof that 1) a party[134] knowingly misrepresented essential terms of a contract; 2) the party intended the misrepresentation to induce contract formation; 3) the other party either did not know or could not have known of the essential information; and 4) the misrepresentation caused the formation of the guaranty contract.[135] An example of fraud in the execution includes the secret substitution of one contract for another.[136] To assert this defense, however, the fraud must have been made on the guarantor herself, and often this arises in situations in which the guarantor is related to the primary obligor and was actively involved in the transaction. A guarantor cannot assert this defense if it belongs solely to the primary obligor.

The burden of proving fraud in the execution is steep. Courts closely scrutinize the reasonableness of guarantor's actions to determine whether the person claiming fraud had a reasonable opportunity to learn the essential characteristics and terms of the contract, or whether the claimant acted unreasonably in failing to learn the essential terms of the contract.[137] For instance, a guarantor cannot evade her obligation by claiming simply that she did not know she was signing a personal guaranty—as opposed to a corporate guaranty—if she had an opportunity to review the document before signing it, regardless of oral representations made before signing.[138]

7.3.7 Mistake

Minnesota courts recognize other defenses available in contractual disputes such as mutual mistake of fact and unilateral mistake.[139]

131. Mitchell Feed & Seed, Inc. v. Mitchell, 413 N.W.2d 847, 849 (Minn. Ct. App. 1987) (father's alleged oral promise to "stand behind" his son's feed bill was within the statute of frauds when father only incidentally benefitted by the provision of feed and father's primary purpose was to accommodate his son).

132. Marckel Co. v. Raven, 242 N.W. 471, 472-73 (Minn. 1932) (promise to pay underlying obligation if obligee refrained from garnishment or retaking goods sold was not a collateral undertaking).

133. BankCherokee v. Insignia Development, LLC, 779 N.W.2d 896, 899 (Minn. Ct. App. 2010) (outlining the cause of action in the context of guaranties).

134. The fraud must be by a party or a party's agent. Lyon Financial Services, Inc. v. Hearyman, 2009 WL 1515598 *4 (Minn. Ct. App. 2009), (enforcing a guaranty where fraud was committed by a party unrelated to the obligee) (citing, State v. Bucholz, 210 N.W. 1006, 1006 (Minn. 1926)). *Watkins Products,* 144 N.W.2d at 57 (misrepresentation by the primary obligee to induce the guarantor to sign the guaranty does not release the guarantor).

135. *BankCherokee,* 779 N.W.2d at 899.

136. *Id.*

137. *Id.* (citing, e.g., Minneapolis, St. Paul & Sault Ste. Marie Ry. v. Chisholm, 57 N.W. 63, 64 (1893); Davis v. G.N. Mortgage Corp., 396 F.3d 869, 877 (7th Cir. 2005)).

138. *BankCherokee,* 779 N.W.2d at 900-01.

139. *Farr,* 2010 WL 3119443 at *5.

7.3.8 *Fraudulent Inducement*

To prevail on a claim of fraudulent inducement, the guarantor must prove that

> (1) there was a false representation by a party of a past or existing material fact susceptible of knowledge; (2) made with knowledge of the falsity of the representation or made as of the party's own knowledge without knowing whether it was true or false; (3) with the intention to induce another to act in reliance thereon; (4) that the representation caused the other party to act in reliance thereon; and (5) that the party suffer[ed] pecuniary damage as a result of the reliance.[140]

To establish the fourth element, a plaintiff must prove both actual and reasonable reliance. The party receiving a representation of a past or existing material fact generally does not have an obligation to investigate and, thus, may "reasonably rely on a representation unless the falsity of the representation is known or obvious to the listener." Reasonable reliance is determined in reference to the particular individual, not the average person.[141] A guarantor alleging fraud may not prove reasonable reliance on an alleged oral representation if the oral representation was "directly contradictory to the terms of" a written agreement. Courts will examine each misrepresentation to determine if it is "directly contradictory" to the written agreement, that is, if the guarantor could accept as true both the oral statement and the written statement without inconsistency.[142]

7.3.9 *Failure to Disclose Material Facts*

When a bank transacts business with a depositor or other customer, it has no special duty to counsel the customer and inform him of every material fact relating to the transaction—including the bank's motive, if material, for participating in the transaction—unless special circumstances exist, such as where the bank knows or has reason to know that the customer is placing his trust and confidence in the bank and is relying on the bank so to counsel and inform him.[143]

"Although one party to a business transaction generally has no duty to disclose material facts to the other party, such a duty may arise if the parties stand in a fiduciary relationship or one party has special knowledge of material facts to which the other party does not have access. If a party conceals

---

140. *Hanson*, 2008 WL 4705172 at *3 (citations omitted).
141. *Id.*
142. *Id.* at *6 (citations omitted) (rejecting obligee's argument that clause in guaranty stating that guarantor's obligations would not be affected by obligee's taking or failure to take, or its failure to perfect a security interest in or lien on, any collateral rendered "irrelevant" obligee's oral statement that it was oversecured when it considered the underlying obligation undersecured).
143. Klein v. First Edina National Bank, 196 N.W.2d 619 (Minn. 1972) (no evidence in the record to indicate that defendant bank ought to have known that guarantor was placing her trust and confidence in bank and was depending on bank to look out for her interests).

these facts, knowing that the other party acts on the presumption that no such fact[s] exist, nondisclosure may constitute fraud."[144]

7.3.10 Lack of Mutual Assent

As with all contracts, mutual assent or a "meeting of the minds" as to the essential terms of the contract is required. If a guaranty lacks an essential term, no assent occurs and the guaranty is unenforceable.[145]

7.4 Right of Set-off

Minnesota recognizes both an equitable right of set-off and a contractual right of set-off. Depending on its terms, a contractual right of set-off may be exercised even if the equitable right of set-off may not.[146]

A guarantor is not entitled to a set-off for the fair market value of the collateral when the bankruptcy court avoids the obligee's lien as a preference and the guaranty contains a waiver with regard to obligee's errors and omissions in perfecting security interests.[147]

In the absence of an agreement to the contrary, an obligee in exercising set-off against assets of the primary obligor is not required to apply the amount set-off in the manner most beneficial to the guarantors.[148]

§ 8 Waiver of Defenses by the Guarantor

8.1 Defenses that Cannot Be Waived

Minnesota courts are willing to uphold broad waivers of guarantors' rights (*see* § 8.2 below), but there are some defenses that cannot be waived. A defense of fraud cannot be waived in advance, although it must be proved that the fraud existed at the time the guaranty was executed.[149] Unconscionability is another defense that cannot be waived. Minnesota courts generally look unfavorably on contracts that reflect drastically unequal bargaining power.[150]

---

144. Grace Capital LLC v. Mills, 2010 WL 3396817 *6 (Minn. Ct. App. 2010) (citations omitted) (remanding to trial court to determine if obligees owed guarantor a duty of care to disclose material facts about a fraudulent investment scheme to prevent misleading guarantor in his decision to execute a guaranty of an unrelated obligation).
145. AgStar Financial Services, FLCA v. HJR Farms, LLC, 2012 WL 2078194 *5 (Minn. Ct. App. 2012) (upholding trial court's findings that guaranties were unenforceable because of ambiguity and lack of mutual assent as to a material term (the percentage liability of the guarantor) when the statement "The liability of the Guarantor is limited to _____% of all present and future obligations of Borrower to Lender." was left incomplete).
146. Minnesota Voyageur Houseboats, Inc. v. Las Vegas Marine Supply, Inc., 708 N.W.2d 521 (Minn. 2006) (upholding bank's contractual right to exercise set-off against debtor's bank account upon occurrence of a default under loan documents when equitable right of set-off could not be exercised because debt had not been accelerated and so was not due and owing).
147. Cessna Finance Corp. v. Dwire, 377 N.W.2d 45 (Minn. Ct. App. 1985).
148. Midway Nat'l Bank v. Gustafson, 165 N.W.2d 218, 223 (Minn. 1968).
149. National Equip. Corp. v. Volden, 252 N.W. 444, 445 (1934).
150. Lyon Financial Services, Inc. v. Protech Plumbing & Heating, Inc., 2004 WL 376966 *3 (Minn. Ct. App. 2004).

8.2 "Catch-all" Waivers

Because Minnesota courts will enforce a guaranty according its terms,[151] catch-all waivers take on great importance. These waivers include language providing for "absolute and unconditional" promises to pay, or "irrevocable" promises to pay. By making such promises, guarantors "waive defenses and make themselves unconditionally liable for the indebtedness at issue."[152] As one court has held, by agreeing to these catch-all waivers guarantors can effectively "contract away practically every right that they may later attempt to claim as a defense."[153]

Minnesota courts not only enforce these catch-all waivers, but also will generally uphold these waivers as clear and unambiguous on summary judgment. Coupled with evidence of nonpayment, the existence of catch-all waivers entitles the obligee to recovery on summary judgment.[154]

8.3 Use of Specific Waivers

Minnesota courts enforce specific waivers[155] but those waivers will be scrutinized and "[a] party who makes fraudulent representations to induce another to make a contract cannot escape liability for his fraud by incorporating a disclaimer of fraud in the contract."[156]

A guarantor's waiver of rights with respect to collateral is not a waiver of any right to receive notice of a foreclosure sale.[157]

§ 9 Third-party Pledgors—Defenses and Waiver Thereof

Minnesota courts treat third-party pledgors similarly to guarantors and uphold the same obligations[158] and defenses.[159]

151. *See, e.g.*, Milliken & Co. v. Eagle Packaging Co., Inc., 295 N.W.2d 377, 382 n.3 (Minn. 1980); *McCord*, 2006 WL 2975302 at *2.
152. BA Mortgage v. 7100 Northland Circle, 1992 WL 203237 *2 (Minn. Ct. App. 2002) (citing, e.g., *Gustafson*, 165 N.W.2d at 222).
153. *Gustafson*, 165 N.W.2d at 222.
154. *See id.*; *Parrish*, 2005 WL 713629 at *4-*6.
155. *See, e.g., Cessna Finance*, 377 N.W.2d at 48 (enforcing specific waiver regarding errors or omissions concerning security interests when obligee's security interest in airplane was deemed a preference) (citing *Gustafson*).
156. *Hanson*, 2008 WL 4705172 at *4 *(quoting Volden*, 252 N.W. at 445 and also finding waiver language in guaranty not broad enough to cover a fraud claim).
157. Chemlease Worldwide Inc., v. Brace, 338 N.W.2d 428, 433 (Minn. 1983).
158. McNeill v. Dakota County State Bank, 522 N.W.2d 381 (Minn. Ct. App. 1994) (enforcement of third-party pledge).
159. *Koch*, 140 N.W.2d at 62-63 (obligee's rescission of contract creating underlying obligation without reservation of rights against pledged collateral acted as a discharge of the underlying obligation entitling third-party pledgor to the return of his collateral).

§ 10 Jointly and Severally Liable Guarantors—Contribution and Reduction of Obligations upon Payment by a Co-obligor

10.1 Contribution

"Contribution is the remedy securing the right of one who has discharged more than his fair share of a common liability or burden to recover from another who is also liable the proportionate share which the other should pay or bear."[160] "Contribution rests upon principles of equity."[161]

"Where the parties are guarantors by separate instruments, they are liable for contribution only if the debt for which they are liable is the same. If the guaranties are of separate obligations, although arising out of the same transaction, the guarantors are not cosureties and have no right to contribution. Obligations are separate where the guarantors are bound for different portions of the same debt."[162]

Generally, a coguarantor is not liable for more than his pro-rata share of the debt, absent an agreement to the contrary or any other coguarantor's inability to pay its fair share.[163]

Minnesota courts will not construe a guaranty that does not reference contribution or otherwise explicitly address the guarantors' obligations to each other to include an intent to address coguarantors' contribution rights when such an agreement is immaterial to the obligee, for whose benefit the guaranty is intended.[164]

A contribution action is ripe when a coguarantor has paid more than 50 percent of the original judgment even though neither party has paid 50 percent of the amended judgment.[165]

10.2 Reduction of Obligations upon Payment of Co-obligor

A third party's loss-sharing agreement to reimburse the obligee for a portion of the losses sustained by the obligee on the underlying obligation does not reduce the guarantor's obligations under his guaranty on the basis of overcompensation of the obligee when the obligee is required to pay over the amount recovered from the guarantor to such third party.[166]

---

160. Hendrickson v. Minnesota Power & Light Co., 104 N.W.2d 843, 846 (Minn. 1960), *overruled in part on other grounds by* Tolbert v. Gerber Indus., 255 N.W.2d 362, 368 n.11 (Minn. 1977).
161. *Hendrickson,* 258 Minn. at 370, 104 N.W.2d at 846.
162. General Mills, Inc. v. Wallner, 628 F. Supp. 1573, 1575 (D. Minn. 1986) (citations omitted).
163. *Estate of Frantz,* 426 N.W.2d at 902 (holding, among other things, that trial court erred in determining coguarantors' percentage liability under joint and several guaranties without determining each coguarantor's ability to pay).
164. United Properties Investment, LLC v. Richfield Motors, Inc., 2010 WL 3306906, *4 (Minn. Ct. App. 2010).
165. Senn v. Youngstedt, 589 N.W.2d 314, 316 (Minn. Ct. App. 1999).
166. Ford Motor Credit Co. v. Wintz Cos., 184 F.3d 778 (8th Cir. 1999).

10.3 Liability of Parent Guarantors Owning Less than 100 percent of Primary Obligor

See §§ 2.1 and 2.3.

§ 11 Reliance

Reliance by the obligee on the guaranty is a sufficient[167] but not a necessary condition[168] for consideration. *See* § 5.

§ 12 Subrogation

"The doctrine of subrogation is of purely equitable origin and nature. Whether a case for its application arises in favor of a surety as against third persons depends upon the balance of equities between them and the surety. It does not arise where the result would be prejudicial to innocent purchasers. The object of subrogation is to place the charge where it ought to rest, by compelling the payment of the debt by him who ought in equity to pay it. It will never be enforced when the equities are equal or the rights not clear. The right may be modified or extinguished by contract."[169] Even when the right to subrogation arises by virtue of an agreement, the terms of the subrogation will nonetheless be governed by equitable principles, unless the agreement clearly and explicitly provides to the contrary.[170]

Full payment of the underlying obligation is required before a guarantor may seek equitable subrogation.[171]

A surety is entitled to be subrogated to the rights of the creditor upon payment of the debt and to equitable assignment of the security.[172]

Where a guaranty's very broad impairment clause clearly contemplates a complete loss of the collateral, a guarantor may not assert subrogation claims when the underlying obligation is assigned to a creditor whose debt is not guaranteed but is secured by the same collateral and the assignee creditor elects to apply the proceeds of the collateral to the unguaranteed obligation. The guarantor was effectively guaranteeing a potentially unsecured loan.[173]

167. *Southdale Center*, 110 N.W.2d at 863-64.
168. *First Nat'l Bank v. Int'l Machines Corp.*, 156 N.W.2d at 88-89. In *First National Bank*, two of the four directors of a corporation had guaranteed loans from the bank. When the corporation needed funds again, one of the guarantor directors insisted on the remaining two directors also executing guaranties even though the bank did not require the additional guaranties to make the new loan. The loan was made before the two additional guaranties were executed and delivered but with the understanding that they would be delivered afterwards.
169. Westendorf v. Stasson, 330 N.W.2d 699, 703 (Minn. 1983) (quoting Northern Trust Co. v. Consolidated Elevator Co., 171 N.W. 265, 268 (Minn. 1919)).
170. *Id.*
171. Feltl v. Greenblat, 2005 WL 221872 *2 (Minn. Ct. App. 2005) (citing *Westendorf*, 330 N.W.2d at 703).
172. Leroy v. Marquette Nat'l Bank, 277 N.W.2d 351, 355 (Minn. 1979).
173. West Central Steel, Inc. v. Pick, 1994 WL 71399 *2 (Minn. Ct. App. 1994).

§ 13 Triangular Set-off in Bankruptcy

As of drafting time, no Minnesota courts have addressed this issue.

§ 14 Indemnification—Whether the Primary Obligor has a Duty

The guarantor's payment of the underlying obligation is a necessary condition to a cause of action against the primary obligor for indemnification.[174] *See* § 12.

§ 15 Enforcement of Guaranties

15.1 Limitations on Recovery

See § 6.1.

15.2 Enforcement of Guaranties of Payment Versus Guaranties of Performance

See Section 6.2.

15.3 Exercising Rights under a Guaranty Where the Underlying Obligation Is also Secured by a Mortgage

Minnesota's antideficiency statute,[175] which provides that "[t]he amount received from foreclosure sale [by advertisement] is full satisfaction of the mortgage debt"[176] (with certain exceptions related to the length of redemption periods and agricultural property), does not protect guarantors. A guarantor remains liable for any deficiency regardless of the length of the redemption period.[177] So even though the mortgagor may have no further liability for the deficiency as a result of the foreclosure, a guarantor of the mortgagor's debt remains liable and can be sued for the remaining deficiency. However, having the primary obligor sign a guaranty with respect to the same underlying obligation will not circumvent the antideficiency statute.[178]

If an obligee/mortgagee bids the entire amount of the underlying obligation secured by a mortgage at a foreclosure sale, the underlying obligation is

174. Bennett v. Bennett, 42 N.W.2d 39 (1950).
175. Minn. Stat. § 580.225 (2012).
176. *Id.*
177. *National City Bank,* 435 N.W.2d at 592-93.
178. In re Harstad, 136 B.R. 806 (Bankr. D. Minn. 1992).

extinguished, no deficiency remains, and a guarantor is no longer liable on a guaranty of the underlying obligation. Therefore, the guarantor has no liability if the proceeds from a subsequent sale of the mortgaged property by the obligee/mortgagee are less than the amount of the underlying obligation.[179]

Mortgagees may purchase at a foreclosure sale by advertisement if they do so "fairly and in good faith."[180] Minnesota courts traditionally have determined that price inadequacy is insufficient to invalidate a foreclosure when redemption is available. Redemption, however, does not protect guarantors from the creation of an artificial deficiency due to a low bid. Even if guarantors exercise the right to redeem, they remain liable for the deficiency and their only avenue of recovery is a contribution claim against a mortgagor who may well be insolvent. Accordingly, foreclosure sales must remain "free from fraud or irregularity."[181]

Minnesota's voluntary foreclosure statute[182] which requires the mortgagee to waive any right to a deficiency against the mortgagor, expressly preserves claims against guarantors.[183]

15.4 Litigating Guaranty Claims: Procedural Considerations

When enforcing a guaranty of collection, a single action may be brought against the guarantor and the primary obligor.[184]

Where guaranties are of unlimited duration, Minnesota's parol evidence rule[185] may be used by guarantors to help the court determine the reasonable time limit for the guaranty based on the parties' circumstances. For example, even when a guaranty permitted the obligee to extend the time for payment without notice to the guarantor, parol evidence that the underlying obligations were to be paid from the proceeds of the sale of certain assets of the primary obligors was admissible to help determine the term of a guaranty when the obligee extended the time for payment of the underlying obligations twice without notice to guarantor.[186]

Parol evidence is admissible to show the existence and sufficiency of consideration.[187]

179. *State Bank of Young America*, 530 N.W.2d at 862.
180. Minn. Stat. § 580.11 (2012).
181. Sprague Nat'l Bank v. Dotty, 415 N.W.2d 725, 727 (Minn. Ct. App. 1987) (remanding for a determination as to mortgagee's bad faith in bidding 30-50 percent less than the appraised value and $100,000 less than the loan amount and not honoring promise to inform guarantors that it would bid less than the loan amount).
182. Minn. Stat. § 582.32 (2012).
183. Minn. Stat. § 582.32 Subd. 3(a)(2) (2012).
184. *Security Elevator*, 200 N.W. at 852.
185. Minn. Stat. § 336.2-202 (2012) provides that terms

> set forth in a writing intended by the parties as a final expression of their agreement with respect to such terms as are included therein may not be contradicted by evidence of any prior agreement or of a contemporaneous oral agreement but may be explained or supplemented . . .
>
> (b) by evidence of consistent additional terms unless the court finds the writing to have been intended also as a complete and exclusive statement.

186. *Currie State Bank*, 628 N.W.2d at 211.
187. *Baker*, 349 N.W.2d at 558 (parol evidence admissible to show existence of other bargained-for consideration when stated consideration is insufficient to support guaranty); *Trapp*, 1997 WL 396234 at *5.

§ 16 Revival and Reinstatement of Guaranties

As of drafting time, Minnesota courts have not addressed this issue.

§ 17 Choice of Law

Minnesota traditionally enforces parties' contractual choice-of-law provisions made in good faith and without intent to evade the law.[188] Before a choice-of-law analysis is applied, a court must determine that a conflict exists between the laws of the two forums and that there are sufficient contacts with each forum so that its laws may be constitutionally applied.[189] A conflict exists if the choice of one forum's laws over the other will determine the outcome of the case. If a conflict exists, five factors are reviewed: (1) predictability of results; (2) maintenance of interstate and international order; (3) simplification of the judicial task; (4) advancement of the forum's governmental interest; and (5) application of the better rule of law.[190] With respect to the fourth factor, statutory policy interests may not override Minnesota's historical enforcement of contractual choice-of-law provisions.[191]

188. Hagstrom v. American Circuit Breaker Corp., 518 N.W.2d 46, 48-49 (Minn. Ct. App. 1994); accord Rowlette & Assocs. v Calphalon Corp., 2000 WL 385502 *3.

189. Kolberg-Pioneer, Inc. v. Belgrade Steel Tank Co., ___ N.W.2d _____, 2012 WL 5188055 *2 (Minn. Ct. App. 2012); Allstate Ins. v. Hague, 449 U.S. 302, 312-13, 101 S.Ct. 633, 640, 66 L.Ed.2d 521 (1981).

190. *Kolberg-Pioneer*, ___ N.W.2d _____, 2012 WL 5188055 *3.

191. *Hagstrom*, 518 N.W.2d at 48-49. In *Hagstrom*, the Minnesota Court of Appeals compared the Minnesota Franchise Act, Minn. Stat. § 80C.21(2012), which provides that a choice-of-law provision is void if it has the effect of waiving compliance under the Minnesota Franchise Act, with the Minnesota Termination of Sales Representatives Act, Minn. Stat. § 325E.37 (1992), which did not then contain a similar provision restricting choice- of-law provisions and upheld a choice-of-law clause resulting in enforcement of a termination provision in a sales representative contract in conflict with the Minnesota Termination of Sales Representatives Act. The Minnesota Legislature amended Minn. Stat. § 325E.37 in 2007.

Mississippi State Law of Guaranties

H. Hunter Twiford, III
Stephen F. Schelver
Taylor A. Heck
McGlinchey Stafford PLLC
200 South Lamar Street
City Centre South, Suite 1100
Jackson, MS 39201
(601) 960-8400
Fax: (601) 960-8406

Contents

Mississippi State Law of Guaranties

Introductory Note: In order to standardize this discussion of the law of guaranties in Mississippi, the following terms from relevant statutes and case law are used to refer to the various parties to a guaranty and their obligations.

"**Guarantor**" means a person who, by contract, agrees to satisfy an underlying obligation of another to an obligee upon the primary obligor's default on that underlying obligation. For the most part, unless specifically addressed, no distinction is drawn between guarantors and sureties, as the distinction in Mississippi between the two is often muddled.

"**Guaranty**" means the contract by which the guarantor agrees to satisfy the underlying obligation of a primary obligor to an obligee in the event the primary obligor defaults on the underlying obligation.

"**Obligee**" means the person to whom the underlying obligation is owed. For example, the lender under a loan agreement would be an obligee vis-à-vis the borrower.

"**Obligor**" means the person who incurs the underlying obligation to the obligee. For example, the borrower under a loan agreement would be a primary obligor. The terms "maker" and "principal" are often used interchangeably with "obligor" by the Mississippi courts.

"**Underlying Obligation**" means the obligation or obligations incurred by the primary obligor and owed to the obligee. For example, the borrower's obligation to make payments to a lender of principal and interest on a loan constitutes an underlying obligation.

MISSISSIPPI LAW HIGHLIGHTS:

1. In Mississippi, guaranties are interpreted and enforced like any other contract. See § 6 below.
2. A guarantor's obligations are strictly construed. See § 6 below.
3. Because guaranties are interpreted like contracts, a guarantor may assert typical contract defenses for failure to perform. See § 7 below.

The Mississippi Court of Appeals has cited to the Restatement of Suretyship and Guaranty in *McClatchy v. Anthony Farms*, 936 So. 2d 456, 461-62 (Miss. Ct. App. 2006). Presumably, this Restatement of law is thus at least instructive authority in Mississippi.

§ 1 Nature of the Guaranty Arrangement

1.1 Guaranty Relationships

As a general rule, Mississippi holds firmly to the notion that a guaranty is a contractual agreement that is enforced like any other valid contract. More particularly, "a guaranty is a collateral undertaking by one person to answer for the payment of a debt or the performance of some contract or duty in case of the default of another person who is liable for such payment or performance in the first instance . . . . An agreement providing for the payment of notes executed and to be executed by others in the event of the maker's default in payment is a guaranty."[1]

The terms of the guaranty contract determine the rights and obligations of the parties thereto.[2]

For purposes of interpretation, the four corners of the guaranty contract will govern.[3]

The Mississippi Supreme Court has stated that a guaranty contract possesses the following characteristics: "(1) A guarantor is secondarily liable to the creditor on his contract and his liability is fixed only by the happening of the prescribed conditions at a time after the contract itself is made; (2) the contract of a guarantor is separate and distinct from that of his principal, and his liability arises solely from his own contract, although its accrual depends on the breach or performance of a prior or collateral contract by the principal therein; (3) a guarantor enters into a cumulative collateral engagement, by which he agrees that the principal is able to and will perform a contract which he has made or is about to make, and that if he defaults the guarantor will, on being notified, pay the resulting damages-*i.e.*, a guarantor is an insurer of the ability or solvency of the principal, although this characteristic is not present in an absolute guaranty or a guaranty of payment, but only in a conditional guaranty or a guaranty of collection; and (4) except where the guaranty is absolute, generally the guarantor is entitled to notice of the default of the principal."[4]

1.2 Other Suretyship Relationships

While not the focus of this survey, a suretyship has the following distinguishable attributes from those of a traditional guaranty contract: "(1) A surety is primarily and directly liable to the creditor on his contract from the beginning; (2) the undertaking of a surety is made at the same time and usually jointly

1. Powell v. Sowell, 145 So. 2d 168, 171 (Miss. 1962) (quoting CJS).
2. *See, e.g.*, United States v. Outriggers, Inc., 549 F.2d 337, 339 (5th Cir. 1977) ("It is of course fundamental that the starting point for analysis of the rights and duties of the parties to a guaranty agreement is the instrument itself."); Bank of McLain v. Pascagoula Nat'l Bank, 150 Miss. 738, 747 (Miss. 1928) ("The same rules of construction are applied to a warranty or guaranty as to any other contract . . . ").
3. *See, e.g.*, Zumwalt v. Jones County Bd. of Supervisors, 19 So. 3d 672, 685 (Miss. 2009) ("In interpreting contracts, we look first to the four corners of the document in question. 'An instrument that is clear, definite, explicit, harmonious in all its provisions, and is free from ambiguity' will be enforced.") (citations omitted).
4. Brent v. Nat'l Bank of Commerce of Columbus, 258 So.2d 430, 434 (Miss. 1972).

with that of his principal, and binds him jointly to the performance of the very contract under which the liability of the principal accrues; (3) the contract of the surety is a direct original agreement with the obligee that the very thing contracted for shall be done - *i.e.*, the surety is an insurer of the debt or obligation; and (4) a surety is held to know every default of his principal and is liable without notice."[5]

§ 2 State Law Requirements for an Entity to Enter a Guaranty

Corporations and nonprofit corporations can grant guaranties in furtherance of their business activities. Such grants are generally permitted by statute. Similarly, there are no state–law prohibitions against partnerships, limited liability companies, and banks granting guaranties.

2.1 Corporations

Unless its articles of incorporation provide otherwise, every corporation has the power to "make contracts and guarantees, incur liabilities, borrow money, issue its notes, bonds and other obligations (which may be convertible into or include the option to purchase other securities of the corporation), and secure any of its obligations by mortgage or pledge of any of its property, franchises or income, and make contracts of guaranty and suretyship which are necessary or convenient to the conduct, promotion or attainment of the business of (a) a corporation all of the outstanding stock of which is owned, directly or indirectly, by the contracting corporation, or (b) a corporation which owns, directly or indirectly, all of the outstanding stock of the contracting corporation, or (c) a corporation all of the outstanding stock of which is owned, directly or indirectly, by a corporation which owns, directly or indirectly, all of the outstanding stock of the contracting corporation, which contracts of guaranty and suretyship shall be deemed to be necessary or convenient to the conduct, promotion or attainment of the business of the contracting corporation, and make other contracts of guaranty and suretyship which are necessary or convenient to the conduct, promotion or attainment of the business of the contracting corporation . . . ."[6]

2.1.1 Nonprofit Corporations

"Each [non-profit] corporation shall have and exercise all powers necessary or convenient to effect any or all of the purposes for which the corporation is organized including, without limitation, power: . . . (h) To make contracts and guarantees, incur liabilities, borrow money at such rates of interest as the

5. Brent v. Nat'l Bank of Commerce of Columbus, 258 So.2d 430, 434 (Miss. 1972).
6. Miss. Code Ann. § 79-4-3.02(7).

corporation may determine, issue its notes, bonds and other obligations and secure any of its obligations by mortgage or pledge of all or any of its property, franchises and income, and make contracts of guaranty and suretyship."[7]

2.2 Partnerships

Mississippi follows the traditional rule that each partner of a partnership may bind the partnership itself to contracts and other agreements.[8]

2.3 Limited Liability Companies

Limited liability companies are entitled to the same rights and privileges of a traditional corporation or partnership under Mississippi law. No Mississippi law prohibits or otherwise restrains an LLC from executing instruments in the furtherance of its business.

2.4 Banks and Trust Companies

There are no particular restrictions in Mississippi statutory law and/or the rules and regulations governing state banks with regard to a bank or trust company's ability to execute a guaranty on behalf of an obligor.

However, guaranties offered by state banks may be significantly affected by federal law. For example, federal law prohibits a state-chartered bank from engaging in activities in which a national bank may not engage under federal law. A national bank may become a guarantor only under the guidelines provided by federal law.[9]

2.5 Individuals

An individual's guaranty agreement is nothing more than a contract between the guarantor and the obligee. Basic principles of contract law accordingly apply. "It is, of course, a basic principle of the law of contracts that a contract is not formed between the parties absent the essential elements of offer, acceptance, and consideration."[10]

Contracts made by an individual prior to reaching 18 years of age are voidable. MISS. CODE ANN. § 93-19-13 (Supp. 1977) removes the disability of persons 18 years of age or older. Any ratification of a contract signed while

7. MISS. CODE ANN. § 79-11-151.
8. *See* MISS. CODE ANN. § 79-13-301(1) ("Each partner is an agent of the partnership for the purpose of its business. An act of a partner, including the execution of an instrument in the partnership name, for apparently carrying on in the ordinary course the partnership business or business of the kind carried on by the partnership binds the partnership, unless the partner had no authority to act for the partnership in the particular matter and the person with whom the partner was dealing knew or had received a notification that the partner lacked authority.")
9. *See, e.g.,* National Bank as Guarantor or Surety on Indemnity Bond, 12 C.F.R. § 7.1017 (2010).
10. Whiting v. Univ. of S. Miss., 62 So. 3d 907, 915 (Miss. 2011).

in the minority must be in writing and signed by the individual ratifying the obligation.[11]

In Mississippi, parties to a contract have a duty to read the terms of the contract and are likewise held to have knowledge of the terms in the contract. A party may not fail to read the contract and then complain later of its terms, nor may he avoid a written contract simply because he failed to read it.[12] Even a person considered functionally illiterate still has a duty to determine the terms of the contract he/she executes.[13]

"A conveyance, mortgage, deed of trust or other incumbrance upon a homestead exempted from execution shall not be valid or binding unless signed by the spouse of the owner if the owner be married and living with the spouse."[14]

"It is well established that a conveyance or encumbrance of homestead property is void unless at the time of execution there is the contemporaneous assent of the husband and wife and that the conditions existing at the time determine its validity or invalidity."[15]

§ 3 Signatory's Authority to Execute a Guaranty

A search revealed no Mississippi case law dealing specifically with the requirements for a finding that a signatory has the authority to execute a guaranty; however, generally, a signatory that exhibits either actual or apparent authority will bind the obligor, although the obligee has a duty of reasonable inquiry when it has some notice that the signatory does not have actual authority.

It is well settled that an agency relationship can be established through either actual or apparent authority.[16] However, the issue of actual authority need not be reached if an agent acted within his apparent authority.[17]

---

11. Miss. Code Ann. § 15-3-11 (1972) provides, "An action shall not be maintained whereby to charge any person upon any promise made after full age to pay any debt contracted during infancy, or upon any ratification after full age of any promise or contract made during infancy, unless such promise or ratification shall be made by some writing, signed by the person to be charged therewith"; *see* Ray v. Acme Finance Corp. 367 So.2d 186, 187 -188 (Miss., 1978); *See also* Edmunds v. Mister, 58 Miss. 765 (1881) and Watson v. Peebles, 59 So. 881 (1912).
12. MS Credit Ctr., Inc. v. Horton, 926 So. 2d 167, 177 (Miss. 2006).
13. *See* Maryland Casualty Co. v. Adams, 159 Miss. 88, 96 (Miss. 1931) ("of course the suggestion of illiteracy cannot prevail, for the manifest reason that there cannot be two separate departments in the law of contracts, one for the educated and another for those who are not."). *See also* FMC Finance Corp. v. Murphree, 632 F.2d 413 (5th Cir. Ct. App. 1980) ("the concept of conspicuousness is what a reasonable person ought to have noticed and, as an experienced businessman, the guarantor was expected to have read the instrument creating the obligation on which he unconditionally gave his personal guaranty."); Ivy v. Grenada Bank, 401 So.2d 1302 (Miss. 1981) ("fact that he may not have read the [guaranty] instrument or received a copy of it did not absolve him from liability.").
14. Miss. Code Ann. § 89-1-29 (1972).
15. Hudson v. Bank of Leakesville, 249 So. 2d 371, 373-74 (Miss. 1971).
16. Barnes, Broom, Dallas and McLeod, PLLC. v. Estate of Marilyn Cappaert, 991 So. 2d 1209 (Miss. 2008).
17. Christian Methodist Episcopal Church v. S & S Const. Co., Inc. 615 So. 2d 568 (Miss. 1993); Booker ex rel. Certain Underwriters at Lloyd's of London v. Pettey, 770 So. 2d 39 (Miss. 2000).

It has long been held that a corporate seal affixed to a document signifies that the document was properly executed and represents the will of the corporation.[18]

3.1 Apparent Authority and Reliance

The power of an agent to bind his principal is not limited to the authority actually conferred upon the agent, but the principal is bound if the conduct of the principal is such that persons of reasonable prudence, ordinarily familiar with business practices, dealing with the agent might rightfully believe the agent to have the power he assumes to have. The agent's authority as to those with whom he deals is what it reasonably appears to be. So far as third persons are concerned, the apparent powers of an agent are his real powers.[19]

"There are three essential elements to apparent authority: (1) acts or conduct of the principal; (2) reliance thereon by a third person, and (3) a change of position by the third person to his detriment. All must concur to create such authority."[20] "Apparent authority exists when a reasonably prudent person, having knowledge of the nature and usages of the business involved, would be justified in supposing, based on the character of the duties entrusted to the agent, that the agent has the power he is assumed to have."[21]

"Parties are deemed to have sufficient notice of termination of an agent's authority if they have enough facts in their possession to put them on inquiry."[22]

Corporations: Actions of officers with apparent authority to act on behalf of the corporation may bind a corporation.[23]

Partnerships: If a partner acts within the course and scope of actual or apparent authority, then even liability for fraudulent wrongs can be imputed to the partnership.[24]

Limited liability companies: Unless otherwise provided in the operating agreement, "every member is an agent of the limited liability company for the purpose of conducting its business and affairs, and the act of any member, including, but not limited to, the execution in the name of the limited liability company of any instrument for apparently carrying on in the ordinary course the business or affairs of the limited liability company of which the person is a member, binds the limited liability company, unless the member so acting has, in fact, no authority to act for the limited liability company in the particular

18. *See, e.g.*, Allison v. Camp Creek Drainage Dist., 51 So. 2d 743, 744–745 (Miss. 1951) (Citing Chapter 195, Miss. Laws 1912, Code of 1942, Sec. 4678 provision for petitions creating drainage district which stated, as to corporate signatories: "[I]f the signature of any corporation thereto is attested by the corporate seal, the same shall be sufficient evidence of the assent of the corporation to said petition.").
19. Steen v. Andrews, 78 So. 2d 881, 883 (Miss. 1955).
20. Clow Corp. v. J. D. Mullican, Inc., 356 So. 2d 579, 582 (Miss. 1978).
21. Mladineo v. Schmidt, 52 So. 3d 1154, 1167 (Miss. 2010).
22. Lumberman's Underwriting Alliance v. City of Rosedale, 727 So. 2d 710, 714 (Miss. 1998).
23. Slatery v. Northeast Miss. Contract Procurement, Inc., 747 So. 2d 257, 259 (Miss. 1999).
24. Barrett v. Jones, Funderburg, Sessums, Peterson & Lee, *LLC*, 27 So. 3d 363, 374 (Miss. 2009). *See also* Section 2.2, *supra*.

matter and the person with whom the member is dealing has knowledge of the fact that the member has no such authority."[25]

§ 4 Consideration; Sufficiency of Past Consideration

Standard contract principles apply to the analysis of consideration for a contract of guaranty. The principal agreement is sufficient consideration for an accompanying guaranty.

Generally, a guaranty of a preexisting debt or obligation of another is not binding on the guarantor without a new and independent consideration to support it.[26] However, there is an exception to this rule: when the guaranty is connected with, and the inducement to the original credit or obligation, or a result of a previous promise by the guarantor upon the faith of which the credit was obtained, it requires no new or independent consideration, but is a part of the original transaction and the consideration upon which the credit was given.[27]

The personal guarantee of a preexisting promissory note by an individual who was not a party to the original debt was not valid without some new consideration.[28]

"Where the guaranty or promise, though collateral to the principal contract, is made at the same time with the principal contract, and becomes an essential ground of the credit given to the principal debtor, the whole is one original and entire transaction, and the consideration extends and sustains the promise of the principal debtor, and also of the guarantor. No other consideration need be shown, than that for the original agreement upon which the whole debt rested, and that may be shown by parol proof, as not being within the statute."[29]

It is not necessary that the consideration move from the indemnitee to the indemnitor, but it is necessary only that there be a valid consideration to support the agreement.[30]

The forbearance of a bank to sue on a past due note, without a promise to forbear or a request to forbear, was not sufficient consideration for an unlimited guaranty agreement on the note.[31]

25. Miss. Code Ann. § 79-29-307.
26. Morgan v. United States Fidelity & Guaranty Co., 191 So. 2d 917, 923 (Miss. 1966).
27. *Id.*
28. *See* concurring opinion of Southwick P.J., (with five justices concurring) in Murphree v. W.W. Transp., 797 So.2d 268 (Miss. App. 2001).
29. Wren v. Pearce, 12 Miss. 91, 97 (Miss. 1845).
30. Morgan v. United States Fidelity & Guaranty Co., 191 So. 2d 917, 923 (Miss. 1966).
31. First American Nat'l Bank of Iuka v. Alcorn, 361 So.2d 481 (Miss. 1978).

§ 5 Notice of Acceptance

Notice of acceptance is not required if the guaranty is absolute.

Notice of acceptance is not required where the contract of guaranty is absolute and unconditional.[32]

§ 6 Interpretation of Guaranties

General rules of contract construction apply in construing guaranty agreements, and the guarantor's obligations are strictly construed.

6.1 General Principles

"It is the intention of the contracting parties, or the extent of the guarantor's undertaking, which must be determined. By the customary rules of construction, 'from the instrument itself in which it is clearly expressed, or from the instrument and the surrounding circumstances,' after the intention of the parties or the scope of the instrument has been determined, 'the guarantor is entitled to have his undertaking . . . strictly construed and that it cannot be extended by construction or implication beyond the precise terms of his contract; and in this respect a guarantor is said to be, like a surety, a favorite of the law.'"[33]

When construing a guaranty, "if the language employed be uncertain or doubtful in its import, the true intention must be ascertained, by reference to facts and circumstances accompanying the execution of the instrument; and this may be done without a violation of any rule of law in relation to adding to or contradicting written instruments."[34]

Mississippi makes no distinction between collection guaranties and performance guaranties—both are interpreted according to general contract principles.

6.2 Guaranty of Payment versus Guaranty of Collection

Mississippi has recognized that there can be a distinction between a guaranty of payment, as opposed to a guaranty of collection. "A guarantor enters into a cumulative collateral engagement, by which he agrees that the principal is able to and will perform a contract which he has made or is about to make, and that if he defaults the guarantor will, on being notified, pay the resulting damages — *i.e.,* a guarantor is an insurer of the ability or solvency of the principal, although this characteristic is not present in an absolute guaranty

32. McConnon & Co. v. Prine, 90 So. 730, 732 (Miss. 1921).
33. American Oil Co. v. Estate of Wigley, 251 Miss. 275, 285 (Miss. 1964).
34. Hessig-Ellis Drug Co. v. Parks, 150 Miss. 322, 327-28 (1928).

or a guaranty of payment, but only in a conditional guaranty or a guaranty of collection...."[35]

As a practical matter, nearly all guaranty agreements are absolute and a guaranty of payment, and generally, there is little, if any, discernable difference between collection and payment.

6.3 Language Regarding the Revocation of Guaranties

Again, the terms of the contract itself will be determinative in this regard. Nevertheless, guaranties generally fall within two broad classes: first, where the consideration is entire, that is, where it passes wholly at one time; and second, where it passes at different times, and is therefore separable or divisible.[36] The class into which a guaranty falls can determine whether it is revocable. The law is well settled that where the consideration is entire, the guaranty is not revocable by the guarantor, and is not terminated by his death and notice of his death.[37] Where the consideration passes at different times and the contract of guaranty is divisible, however, this latter class of guaranties may be revoked as to subsequent transactions by the guarantor upon notice to that effect and are terminated by his death and notice of that event.[38]

6.4 "Continuing"

When determining whether the guaranty is limited or continuing, the construction should be adopted which "best accords with the intention of the parties, as manifested by the terms of the guaranty, in connection with the subject matter and surrounding circumstances, neither enlarging the words beyond their natural import in favor of the creditor nor restricting them in aid of the surety."[39]

In a case of a continuing guaranty, each advance constitutes a fresh consideration and, when made, is an irrevocable promise on the part of the living guarantor.[40]

6.5 "Absolute and Unconditional"

An absolute guaranty is one by which the guarantor unconditionally promises payment or performance of the principal contract on default of the principal debtor or obligor.[41] Where a guaranty is absolute in its terms and definite as to its amount and extent, no notice to the guarantor is necessary.[42]

35. Brent v. Nat'l Bank of Commerce of Columbus, 258 So. 2d 430, 434 (Miss. 1972).
36. American Oil Co. v. Estate of Wigley, 251 Miss. 275, 285 (Miss. 1964).
37. *Id.* at 286.
38. *Id.*
39. Wingo-Ellett & Crump Shoe Co. v. Naaman, 175 Miss. 468, 474 (Miss. 1936).
40. *American Oil*, 251 Miss. at 288.
41. Brent v. Nat'l Bank of Commerce of Columbus, 258 So. 2d 430, 435 (Miss. 1972).
42. Baker v. Kelly, 41 Miss. 696, 705 (Miss. 1868).

§ 7 Defenses of the Guarantor; Set-off

7.1 Defenses of the Primary Obligor

7.1.1 General

General defenses to contracts in Mississippi include failure of consideration, illegality, violation of the statute of frauds, unconscionability, fraud, and duress.[43]

As the result of the fiduciary overtones of the surety contract, a surety is regarded as in privity with the principal, and is generally bound by the principal's actions. The converse is also true: the surety cannot do that which the principal could not do. And if the principal waives a known right, or by his acts or representations is bound by estoppel, the surety fares likewise. "However, the surety has every right to be protected by the principal. Accordingly, the suretyship relationship, being contractual in nature, is governed generally by the familiar rules of contract law."[44]

7.1.2 When Guarantor may assert Primary Obligor's Defense

A guaranty contract is separate and apart from the contractual obligation of the primary obligor, and as such, the enforcement of the contract is generally not dependent upon the primary obligor's contractual relationship with the lender or any defense related thereto. There is no case law that directly addresses this particular topic in Mississippi; however, it stands to reason that if a defense of the primary obligor seeks to invalidate the underlying primary obligation, i.e., fraudulent inducement or lack of consideration, the guarantor should then be able to avail himself of the defense generally reserved for the primary obligor, because without default by the principal obligor, there can be no liability on the part of the guarantor.

7.1.3 Defenses that may not be Raised by Guarantor

There are specific instances in which a guarantor cannot avoid his obligations on the basis of these types of defenses, including:

- A guarantor cannot escape liability for payment because alcohol was sold on the premises in violation of a statute.[45]
- A guarantor is not released from liability where the guarantor's signature is obtained by fraud of the principal debtor, unless the obligee participates in or has knowledge of the fraud.[46]

43. *See, e.g.*, Transocean Enter. v. Ingalls Shipbuilding, Inc., 33 So. 3d 459, 468-69 (Miss. 2010); Norwest Fin. Miss., Inc. v. McDonald, 905 So. 2d 1187, 1192 (2005).
44. Fidelity & Guaranty Ins. Co. v. Blount, 63 So.3d 453, 460-61 (Miss. 2011).
45. Smith v. Simon, 224 So. 2d 565 (Miss. 1969).
46. Cresap v. Furst & Thomas, 105 So. 848, 849 (Miss. 1925).

- Lack of notice is generally not a valid defense. Where a guaranty is absolute in its terms and definite as to its amount and extent, no notice to the guarantor of nonpayment of the debt is necessary.[47]
- Voluntary payment by a guarantor cannot be recovered. "A voluntary payment within the meaning of the rule is a payment made, without compulsion or fraud, and without any mistake of fact, of a demand which the payor does not owe, and which is not enforceable against him, instead of invoking the remedy or defense which the law affords against such demand, and when there has been no agreement between the parties at the time of payment, that any excess will be repaid. And the stated rule applies to payments made by guarantors and sureties."[48]

7.1.4 Defenses that may always be Raised by Guarantor

There are likewise specific defenses that may be raised by a guarantor, including:

- "Where a principal is known to be insolvent, after the debt has become due, the surety has an immediate right to sue to compel the principal to pay so the surety's position is not further harmed."[49]
- A guarantor is not liable if he is induced to sign a guaranty by false representations that the obligor owed nothing.[50]
- A guarantor's liability is contingent upon the obligor's not paying according to the terms of the note, and thus, no liability will arise unless and until there is a default by the obligor.[51]

7.1.5 Modification of the Underlying Obligation, Including Release

"The guarantor is released or discharged of liability if, without his consent, the contract of obligation by which the principal debtor is bound to the creditor or obligee has been materially altered in respect of its terms or the manner of execution thereof."[52]

7.1.6 Release or Impairment of Security for the Underlying Obligation

"[W]here a creditor releases collateral without authorization, the guarantor is discharged to the extent of the value of the collateral released."[53]

47. Baker v. Kelly, 41 Miss. 696, 705 (Miss. 1868).
48. McLean v. Love, 157 So. 361, 362 (Miss. 1934).
49. Fidelity & Guaranty Ins. Co. v. Blount, 63 So.3d 453, 461 (Miss. 2011).
50. Henry v. W. T. Rawleigh Co., 120 So. 188, 189 (Miss. 1929).
51. Peoples Bank of Mendenhall v. Wyatt, 441 So. 2d 117, 119 (Miss. 1983).
52. Tower Underwriters, Inc. v. Culley, 53 So. 2d 94, 98 (Miss. 1951) (internal citations omitted).
53. United States v. Sims, 586 F.2d 580, 587 (5th Cir. 1978).

7.2 Other Defenses

7.2.1 *Failure to Fulfill a Condition Precedent*

A guarantor's liability is contingent upon the obligor's not paying according to the terms of the note, and thus no liability will arise until there is a default by the obligor.[54]

7.2.2 *Modification of the Guaranty*

The obligation of guarantor may be discharged by oral agreement between the holder and the guarantor, if supported by consideration flowing to the holder seeking to enforce the instrument.[55]

7.2.3 *Failure to Pursue Primary Obligor*

A guarantor may not claim the failure to pursue the obligor as a defense.[56]

It is not necessary to first prosecute the debtor to insolvency before proceeding against the guarantor.[57]

7.2.4 *Statute of Limitations*

The statute of limitations for bringing an action on a contract of guaranty in Mississippi is three years.[58]

The three-year statute of limitations may not be modified, even by agreement of the parties.[59]

7.2.5 *Statute of Frauds*

Generally, there must be a written agreement in order to have an enforceable guaranty under the Mississippi statute of frauds. "An action shall not be brought whereby to charge a defendant or other party: (a) upon any special promise to answer for the debt or default or miscarriage of another person . . . ."[60] "[T]he promise to answer for the debt, default, or miscarriage of another person, for which the other person himself continues liable, is within the statute of frauds."[61]

54. Peoples Bank of Mendenhall v. Wyatt, 441 So. 2d 117, 119 (Miss. 1983).
55. Brannon v. Langston, 375 So. 2d 231 (Miss. 1979).
56. *See* Baker v. Kelly, 41 Miss. 696, 705-06 (Miss. 1868) ("Where one contracts in the form of a guaranty upon the back of a promissory note, he cannot set up in [defense] the want of demand and notice, nor the mere neglect of the holder to sue the maker.") .
57. Wren v. Pearce, 12 Miss. 91, 98 (Miss. 1845).
58. Miss. Code Ann. § 15-1-49. *See also* First Nat'l Bank v. Drummond, 419 So. 2d 154 (Miss. 1982) (In action on a guaranty contract, the general statute of limitations [§ 15-1-49] would be applied rather than the one-year statute of limitations regarding actions following the foreclosure of an installment note.)
59. Miss. Code Ann. § 15-1-5.
60. Miss. Code Ann. § 15-3-1.
61. Harris v. Griffin, 226 Miss. 74, 77 (Miss. 1955).

7.3 Right of Set-off

If a guarantor is owed money from the obligee, the general defense of a request for a set-off is available to the guarantor.

"A set-off is a counterclaim which the defendant has against the plaintiff, but which is extrinsic to the plaintiff's claim."[62] "As a general rule statutes of set-off are construed to allow the right of set-off of all mutual debts and demands between the parties, whether independent and unconnected with plaintiff's cause of action, or springing from, and connected with, the contractual transaction on which plaintiff's claim is based."[63]

§ 8 Waiver of Defenses by the Guarantor

8.1 Defenses that can be Waived

There are no limitations or prohibitions on the waiver of defenses by a guarantor in Mississippi. So long as the contract is clear and unambiguous and the waiver was knowingly and intelligently waived by the guarantor, the waiver should be enforceable.[64]

§ 9 Jointly and Severally Liable Guarantors—Contribution and Reduction of Obligations upon Payment by a Co-obligor

9.1 Contribution

Guarantors jointly executing a guaranty are primarily and equally liable to the obligee.[65]

9.2 Reduction of Obligations upon Payment of Co-obligor

A guarantor's payment to a creditor does not discharge the primary obligor's obligation. The creditor may bring suit against the primary obligor, and if he recovers more than enough to make himself whole, any excess is held by him in trust for the guarantor as a matter of law. Additionally, a guarantor has a right to recover any amount paid from the primary obligor.[66]

---

62. Miller v. Parker McCurley Props., L.L.C., 36 So. 3d 1234, 1243 (Miss. 2010).
63. Gerald v. Foster, 251 Miss. 63, 72 (Miss. 1964).
64. *See, e.g.*, Vice v. Leigh, 670 So. 2d 6, 10 (Miss. 1995) (a party may waive a right to which he would otherwise have been entitled); *see also* Davis Sewing Mach. Co. v. Rosenbaum, 16 So. 340 (" Provisions of a contract of guaranty waiving notice of acceptance thereof on the part of the guarantee, and permitting him to extend time of payment, without notice to the guarantors, are binding.").
65. Enochs & Flowers, Ltd. v. Roell, 170 Miss. 44 (Miss. 1934).
66. *See* Atkinson v. Nat'll Bank of Commerce, 530 So. 2d 163 (Miss. 1988).

§ 10 Reliance

Reliance is only necessary in order to bind a principal to the acts of his agent under the theory of apparent authority.[67]

§ 11 Subrogation

"Payment by a guarantor of another's indebtedness does not extinguish the obligation of the debtor to pay according to his agreement. Whatever may be the relationship in rights of the payee and guarantor, the fundamental scheme of the transaction remains, and that scheme is that the primary obligors . . . are obligated to pay the full measure of the indebtedness provided in their contract."[68]

"There is nothing untoward in a contract of guaranty made without the knowledge of the principal debtor. While there is no implied promise of reimbursement as when the guaranty is entered into at the request of the debtor, subrogation principles still control.[69]

§ 12 Guaranties in Bankruptcy

Although a creditor is not prohibited from relying on a guaranty if the obligor is in bankruptcy, any dividend received through the bankruptcy should be credited upon the debt guaranteed.[70]

§ 13 Indemnification—Whether the Primary Obligor has a Duty

The principal obligor has a duty of indemnification so long as the guarantor undertook his obligations at the request of the principal obligor. The extent of this duty can be altered by contract.

"Where a guarantor, who has entered into a contract of guaranty at the request of, or with the consent of, the principal obligor, pays or is compelled to pay his principal's debt, the law raises an implied promise, unless there is an express one, on the part of the principal to reimburse the guarantor, and on the payment of the debt the guarantor at once has a right of action against the

67. *See* Section 3, *supra*.
68. Atkinson v. Nat'l Bank of Commerce, 530 So. 2d 163, 165 (Miss. 1988).
69. *Id.* at 167.
70. Richmond Paper Co. v. Bradley, 76 So. 544, 545 (Miss. 1917).

principal for reimbursement of the amount which he has paid, with interest thereon at the legal rate."[71]

"If the engagement be to make advances on future contingencies, which may or may not happen, in addition to the general notice, of acceptance of the guaranty, and a purpose to act on its faith and credit; it may be necessary also, to advise the guarantor of the occurrence of the contingencies and the advances made, for otherwise, he might not know whether any use were made of the guaranty, and might, because thereof, loose opportunity to obtain indemnity from the principal debtor."[72]

§ 14 Enforcement of Guaranties

14.1 Limitations on Recovery

To the extent that the guaranty agreement expressly limits recovery from a particular guarantor to a specific amount, *e.g.*, guaranty of payment up to $500,000, this type of limitation should be enforceable so long as it otherwise comports with basic contract law. For example, under a guaranty agreement limiting the guarantor's liability to $2,000, the guarantor was liable only for $2,000 even though the total debt was over $5,200.[73] As discussed previously, an obligor's bankruptcy does not affect the guarantor's liability.[74] Otherwise, there are no generally recognized limitations on recovery from a guarantor.

14.2 Litigating Guaranty Claims

Under Mississippi law, a guarantor is entitled to have his undertaking strictly construed, and the contract cannot be extended beyond its precise terms. The person claiming under the guaranty has the burden of showing that the debt whose recovery is sought falls within the contractual terms and that all conditions upon the guarantor's liability have occurred. However, the subjective beliefs and intentions of the parties are relevant to the extent necessary to interpret ambiguities in the written document; and to this end, matters extrinsic to the writing may properly be considered by the trier of the facts.[75]

§ 15 Choice of Law

If Mississippi state law governs in the guaranty contract, a choice of law provision in the guaranty will generally apply. *See Federal Sav. & Loan Ins. Corp. v. Griffin*, 935 F.2d 691, 698 (5th Cir. 1991) ("The choice of law

71. Buckley v. Guilbert, 164 So. 2d 743, 744 (1964).
72. Montgomery v. Kellogg & Sandusky, 43 Miss. 486, 492–93 (Miss. 1870).
73. Ely & Walker Dry Goods Co. v. Powell 124 So. 329 (Miss. 1929).
74. *See* Section 12, *supra*.
75. EAC Credit Corp. v. King, 507 F.2d 1232, 1236 (5th Cir. 1975).

provision in the guaranty addresses which state law applies when state law governs the case. Here, however, federal law provides the rule of decision."); *U.S. Bancorp Equip. Fin., Inc. v. Moak*, 2008 U.S. Dist. Lexis 58998 at *6 (S.D. Miss. July 23, 2008) ("Under Mississippi law, parties may legitimately control the choice of substantive law in a contract dispute as long as the state law selected bears a reasonable relation to the transaction.").

Missouri State Law of Guaranties

Christopher J. Rockers
Kevin Zeller
Husch Blackwell LLP
4801 Main Street
Suite 1000
Kansas City, MO 64112
816.983.8000
816.983.8080
christopher.rockers@huschblackwell.com
kevin.zeller@huschblackwell.com
www.huschblackwell.com

HUSCH BLACKWELL

Contents

Missouri State Law of Guaranties

HIGHLIGHTS:

Absent a waiver, material modifications to the underlying obligations which are made without guarantor's consent will discharge a guarantor whether such modification is beneficial or detrimental to the guarantor (See §7.2.2.)

TRAPS:

As to spouses, there is a presumption that jointly owned property is owned as a tenancy by the entirety, not subject to judgments solely against the other spouse. (See § 2.5.)

Introductory Note: In order to standardize our discussion of the law of guaranties, we use the following vocabulary to refer to the various parties to a guaranty and their obligations.

"**Guarantor**" means a person who, by contract, agrees to satisfy an underlying obligation of another to an obligee upon the primary obligor's default on that underlying obligation. Except in limited situations discussed below, this chapter does not draw great distinctions between guarantors and sureties, as there is little difference between the two under Missouri law.

"**Guaranty**" means the contract by which the guarantor agrees to satisfy the underlying obligation of a primary obligor to an obligee in the event the primary obligor defaults on the underlying obligation.

"**Obligee**" means the person to whom the underlying obligation is owed. For example, the lender under a loan agreement would be an obligee vis-à-vis the borrower.

"**Primary Obligor**" means the person who incurs the underlying obligation to the obligee. For example, the borrower under a loan agreement would be a primary obligor.

"**Underlying Obligation**" means the obligation or obligations that the primary obligor owes to the obligee. For example, the borrower's obligation to make payments to a lender of principal and interest on a loan constitutes an underlying obligation.

We found no Missouri courts interpreting Missouri law that cited to the Restatement of Suretyship and Guaranty. However, a Missouri court interpreting New York law did cite to the Restatement in discussing the definition of a continuing guaranty.[1]

1. Rheem Manufacturing Co. v Progressive Wholesale Co., 28 S.W.3d 333, 339.

§ 1 Nature of the Guaranty Arrangement

Under Missouri law, a guaranty is a collateral agreement for performance of undertaking of another, and imports two different obligations, that of principal debtor and that of guarantor.[2]

1.1 Guaranty Relationships

"A guarantor agrees to become secondarily liable for the obligation of a debtor in the event the debtor does not perform the primary obligation... [A guaranty contract] is a collateral agreement for another's undertaking, and is an independent contract which imposes responsibilities different from those imposed in the agreement to which it is collateral."[3]

§ 2 State Law Requirements for an Entity to Enter a Guaranty

2.1 Corporations

The Missouri General and Business Corporations Laws expressly permit corporations to enter into guaranties without limitation.[4]

2.2 Partnerships

Missouri's Uniform Partnership Law neither expressly empowers a partnership to issue a guaranty nor expressly regulates or prohibits such activity.

2.3 Limited Liability Companies

Missouri permits limited liability companies to carry on any lawful business, purpose, or activity, which would include issuing guaranties.[5]

2.4 Banks and Trust Companies

R.S.Mo. § 362.106(3) expressly allows a state-chartered bank or trust company to guarantee the underlying obligations of a subsidiary corporation that owns real property, provided such guaranteed obligations do not exceed 5 percent of such bank or trust company's total assets. Other than the foregoing,

---

2. RTC Mortgage Trust v. Haith, 133 F.3d 574, 577 (8th Cir. 1998).
3. Jamieson-Chippewa Investment Co., Inc. v. McClintock, 996 S.W.2d 84, 87 (Mo.App. 1999).
4. R.S.Mo. § 351.385(7).
5. R.S.Mo. § 347.035.

Missouri laws and regulations do not expressly permit a state-chartered bank or trust company to enter into a guaranty agreement nor do they prohibit a state-chartered bank or trust company from entering into a guaranty agreement.

2.5 Individuals

It is the general rule in Missouri that where a principal is disclosed and the capacity in which the individual signs is evident, the liability is the principal's and not the individual signing for the principal. In order for the individual to be liable in such a case, it must have been both parties' intention to impose individual liability, and the general rule is that the individual should sign twice; once in his corporate capacity and once in his individual capacity.[6] Simply indicating a title, such as Member, is not sufficient disclosure of the "principal" business entity; the entity itself must be referenced somewhere in the guaranty if the individual intends not to be bound in his or her individual capacity.[7]

An individual may expressly authorize another person to execute and bind such individual to guaranty agreements.[8] However, contracts, including guaranties, which are signed by only one spouse, are not automatically binding upon the other spouse, because "there is no agency between a husband and wife merely because of the marital relationship and neither is empowered to act as agent for the other simply because they are married."[9]

If only one spouse is bound on a guaranty, the obligee may have difficulty executing on certain marital assets. In Missouri, a spouse's separate property, whether personal or real property, is not subject to the debts of the other spouse.[10] Further, there is a rebuttable presumption that when spouses jointly own property in Missouri, the property is held as a tenancy by the entirety,[11] and a judgment against one spouse would not constitute a lien on entirety property because neither has a separate interest subject to execution.[12] Finally, if any real estate is pledged or conveyed via a deed of trust in connection with the guaranty, such a conveyance will be deemed to be in fraud of the marital rights of the nonsignatory spouse if such spouse becomes a surviving spouse.[13]

---

6. Cardinal Health 110, Inc. v. Cyrus Pharmaceutical, LLC, 560 F.3d 894, 899 (8th Cir. 2009).
7. Warren Supply Co. v. Lyle's Plumbing, 74 S.W.3d 816, 820 (Mo. App. 2002).
8. Landmark Bank of St. Charles County v. Saettele, 784 F. Supp. 1434, 1440 (E.D. Mo. 1992).
9. Branson Land Co. v. Guilliams, 926 S.W.2d 524, 527 (Mo. App. 1996), citing Mahurin v. St. Luke's Hosp., 809 S.W.2d418, 422 (Mo. App. 1991). While the general rule in Missouri is that there is no deemed agency between husband and wife, the court will look at the prior course of dealing and surrounding circumstances to see if a spouse has implicitly granted general authority to another spouse to act on his or her behalf, as well as whether subsequent actions or inactions ratified such actions. Mark Twain Bank v. Hardesty, 1993 WL 98211 (Mo. App. 1993).
10. R.S.Mo. §§ 451.250 & 451.260.
11. Capital Bank v. Barnes, 277 S.W.3d 781, 782 (Mo. App. 2009).
12. Baker v. Lamar, 140 S.W.2d 31, 35 (Mo. 1940).
13. R.S.Mo. § 474.150.2

§ 3 Signatory's Authority to Execute a Guaranty

3.1 Corporations

"The power of a corporate officer, like that of any other agent, to bind his or her corporation in contract ordinarily rests either upon such officer's actual authority or upon his or her apparent authority."[14] "A corporate officer's actual authority derives, on the one hand, from statute or from the articles and bylaws of the corporation, or on the other hand from the officer's exercise of functions on behalf of the corporation, long tacitly acquiesced in by the board of directors."[15] "Apparent authority comes into existence by the corporation's creation of an appearance of affairs which would cause a reasonable person to believe that the officer had actual authority to do a particular act, upon which appearance a third person relies."[16]

A fact-specific inquiry is necessary to determine if a particular officer or employee of a corporation has the actual or apparent authority to execute a guaranty. However, the general rule in Missouri is that the president of a corporation may, "without any special authority from its board of directors, perform all acts of an ordinary nature which by usage or necessity are incident to his office, and may bind the corporation by contracts in matters arising in the usual course of business."[17] Accordingly, if a guaranty could be deemed to be in the ordinary course of business of a corporation, a president will be deemed to have the authority to execute the guaranty.

This is not true of other officers, including secretaries of corporations, who have no inherent power in Missouri to bind the corporation to obligations for the payment of money.[18] Further, a resolution authorizing a secretary to "negotiate and procure loans" from a lender, did not grant sufficient authority for the secretary to execute a guaranty of a loan made by the obligee to a primary obligor.[19]

3.2 Partnerships

Pursuant to R.S.Mo. §358.090, each partner is an agent for the partnership and may execute instruments on behalf of the partnership, provided the instrument is "for apparently carrying on in the ordinary course the partnership business or business of the kind carried on by the partnership." A partner's authority may be explicitly limited by the partnership agreement or other means. However, the partnership will be bound by the partner's acts, notwithstanding any limitation, if the act was in the "ordinary course of partnership business" and the person dealing with the partner did not know or had not received notification that the partner lacked authority.[20]

---

14. Carter v. St. John's Reg'l Med. Ctr., 88 S.W.3d 1, 9 (Mo. App. 2002).
15. Gaar v. Gaar's Inc., 994 S.W.2d 612, 617 (Mo. App. 1999).
16. Rice v. Bol, 116 S.W.3d 599, 609 (Mo. App. 2003).
17. Nitro Distributing, Inc. v. Dunn, 194 S.W.3d 339, 348 (Mo. 2006).
18. First Nat'l Bank of Clayton v. Frisco Park Realty Co., 510 S.W.2d 59, 61 (Mo. App. 1974).
19. *Id.*, 510 S.W.2d at 62.
20. R.S.Mo. § 358.090(1).

If the act is not for carrying on the ordinary course, the act will not be binding on the partnership unless it was authorized by the other partners.[21]

3.3 Limited Liability Companies

If the management of the limited liability company (LLC) is vested in the members, each member has the authority to bind the LLC unless such authority is otherwise limited by the operating agreement.[22] If the management of the LLC is vested in one or more managers, the managers have the sole authority to bind the limited liability company.[23] If any act of either a member or manager, as applicable, is not for "carrying on in the usual way of the business or affairs of the LLC," such act is not binding on the LLC unless authorized in accordance with the articles of organization or operating agreement.[24] Any act taken by a member or manager which exceeds the scope of authority will not bind the LLC if the person with whom the member or manager is dealing knows the action exceeds such manager or member's authority.[25]

3.4 Banks and Trust Companies

A case-by-case inquiry of the powers provided for in a bank's or trust company's corporate governance documents is necessary to determine who may validly execute a guaranty on behalf of a bank or trust company.

3.5 Individuals

When business entities are involved, including corporations, care must be taken in the execution of the underlying contract and guaranty to ensure the correct parties are named. In *All American Supply Company v. Four Seasons Mechanical, Inc.*, the contract asked for delivery to "Abigail J. Ferrari of Four Seasons Mechanical," as opposed to listing Ferrari on behalf of, or in her capacity as an officer of, Four Seasons Mechanical. Ferrari signed a personal guaranty of the contract, but the court held that the contract was ambiguous because, as written, it could be interpreted that Ferrari was the primary obligor, not Four Seasons Mechanical, and one cannot be both the primary obligor and the guarantor.[26]

§ 4 Consideration; Sufficiency of Past Consideration

"A guaranty is a contract, and, like all contracts, a guaranty must be supported by consideration. However, the consideration need not move only between the

21. R.S.Mo. § 358.090(2).
22. R.S.Mo. 347.065.1.
23. R.S.Mo. 347.065.2.
24. R.S.Mo. 347.065.3.
25. R.S.Mo. 347.065.1 & 347.065.2.
26. All American Supply Co. v. Four Seasons Mechanical, Inc., 152 S.W.3d 884, 887 (Mo. App. 2005).

creditor and guarantor. Benefit to the [principal obligor], or detriment to the creditor is sufficient consideration to support a guaranty, and it is not necessary that the guarantor derive any benefit from either the principal contract or the guaranty."[27] The recitation of "for value received" language in a written guaranty is prima facie evidence of sufficient consideration.[28]

Consideration flowing to the primary obligor will suffice for the guaranty agreement, even if the guaranty agreement is signed at a later date, as long as the two agreements are part of the same underlying loan transaction.[29]

In at least one instance, a court has held that a guaranty was unconscionable because, while recognizing that the benefit may flow to the primary obligor and not the guarantor, there was not sufficient consideration because the preexisting debt being guaranteed was more than four times the new money being loaned to the primary obligor.[30]

The supplying of further goods on credit to the primary obligor and the obligee's agreement to forebear its right to sue for the amount then currently due was deemed to be sufficient consideration for a guaranty.[31]

§ 5 Notice of Acceptance

Notice of acceptance of the guaranty is required unless a) the guaranty was requested by the obligee, b) the offer to guaranty made by the guarantor expressly waived such notice, or c) subsequent actions of the guarantor acknowledging the liability provide an inference of a waiver or constructive notice.[32]

§ 6 Interpretation of Guaranties

6.1 General Principles

A guaranty must contain express conditions of guaranty, specifically stating in the document the liability and obligations of each party, and an agreement not containing the word "guaranty" will likely not be construed as such.[33] The rules of construction applicable to a guaranty are the same as those applied to other contracts. A guarantor's obligation is strictly construed, with no stretching or

27. Mercantile Trust Co. v. H.M. Carp, 648 S.W.2d 920, 923 (Mo. App. 1983)
28. Stewart Title Guaranty Co. v. WKC Restaurants Venture Co., 961 S.W.2d 874, 882 (Mo. App. 1998).
29. Coleman v. Villa Capri Restaurant, 712 S.W.2d 65, 65 (Mo. App. 1986). *See also* Hammons v. Ehney, 925 S.W.2d 843 (Mo. 1996).
30. Smith v. Guaranty State Bank, 15 B.R.691, 693 (Bkrtcy. W.D.Mo. 1981).
31. Nat'l Refining Co. v. McDowell, 201 S.W.2d 342, 348 (Mo. 1947).
32. *See* Industrial Bank & Trust Co. v. Hesselberg, 195 S.W.2d 470, 474 (Mo. 1946); Albert Pipe Supply Co., Inc. v. Sharp Bros. Contracting Co., 416 S.W.2d 237, 240 (Mo. App. 1967); and Riberglass, Inc. v. Giesler, 720 S.W.2d 37, 39 (Mo. App. 1986).
33. Linnenbrink v. First Nat'l Bank of Lee's Summit, 839 S.W.2d 618, 621 (Mo. App. 1992). *See also* Ogilvie v. Ogilvie, 487 S.W.2d 40, 41 (Mo. App. 1972), in which the court held the words "aid and assist" could not be construed as a guaranty.

extension of the terms, and no extensions of liability through implication.[34] However, "a guaranty agreement may be construed together with any contemporaneously executed agreements dealing with the same subject matter, as an aid in ascertaining the intention of the parties."[35]

Further, strict construction and interpretation of a guaranty does not entitle a guarantor to demand an unfair and strained interpretation of the words used in order that it may be released from the underlying obligation that it has assumed.[36]

6.2 Guaranty of Payment versus Guaranty of Collection

An unconditional guaranty of payment, versus a guaranty of collection, is a promise that if the obligation is not paid when due, the guarantor will pay it according to its tenor without resort by the obligee to any other party.[37] "A guaranty of collection, however, is conditional, obligating the guarantor to pay the debt only if the creditor has attempted unsuccessfully but with due diligence to collect the claim from the principal debtor."[38]

6.3 Language Regarding the Revocation of Guaranties

Unless limited by their language, guaranty agreements continue until revoked or terminated by the guarantor.[39] The court will look at the facts and circumstances in determining whether a guarantor complied with the procedures regarding revocation stated in the guaranty agreement.[40] Any oral revocation of a guaranty (if otherwise permitted under the language of the guaranty) must be supported by consideration in order to take effect.[41]

6.4 "Continuing"

A continuing guaranty is one that contemplates guaranteeing a series of possible transactions between the debtor and creditor, rather than only a single such transaction.[42] Further, continuing guaranties may be executed in conjunction with a present extension of credit, and do not need to be limited solely to future activities.[43]

A guaranty of a lease will not be deemed a "continuing" guaranty, and will not apply to future extensions of the lease term, even if such lease extension terms are contemplated in the original lease, unless there is express language in the guaranty indicating as much.[44]

34. *Jamieson-Chippewa Investment Co.*, 996 S.W.2d at 88.
35. *Jamieson-Chippewa Investment Co.*, 996 S.W.2d at 87.
36. Dunn Industrial Group, Inc. v. City of Sugar Creek et al, 112 S.W.3d 421, 434 (Mo. 2003).
37. In the Matter of Clary House, Inc., v. Small Business Administration, 11 B.R. 462, 466 (Bkrtcy. W.D. Mo. 1981).
38. Ulreich v. Kreutz, 876 S.W.2d 726, 729 (Mo. App. 1994); and R.S.Mo. § 400.3-419(d).
39. Lemay Bank and Trust Co. v. Harper, 810 S.W.2d 690, 693 (Mo. App. 1991).
40. Commerce Bank of Lebanon, N.A. v. Berry, 692 S.W.2d 830, 830 (Mo. App. 1985).
41. Farmland Inds., Inc. v. Bittner, 920 S.W.2d 581, 584 (Mo. App. 1996).
42. Savannah Place, Ltd. v. Heidelberg, 122 S.W.3d 74, 82 (Mo. App. S.D. 2003).
43. Ulreich v. Kreutz, 876 S.W.2d at 729.
44. *Jamieson-Chippewa Investment Co.*, 996 S.W.2d at 88.

6.5 "Absolute and Unconditional"

The term "unconditional," particularly when accompanied by additional language indicating the guaranty to be absolute and "not conditioned or contingent on... any other condition or contingency whatsoever," will preclude a defense by the guarantor that the guaranty was conditioned upon the obligee obtaining a first-lien position on the collateral.[45]

6.6 "Specific vs. General"

"A general guaranty is addressed to persons generally and is assignable under the principles of contract law. On the other hand, a special guaranty is addressed to a particular person. As a general rule, a guaranty addressed to a particular person may only be acted upon and enforced by such party."[46] However, the court will look to the intention of the parties in determining whether the guaranty was addressed to a particular person, rather than a strict interpretation of the named obligee.[47]

In practice, most obligees will want the ability to freely assign the guaranty agreement. In addition to explicit language allowing for assignment, it is recommended that the recitals and introductory language are carefully drafted to simply guaranty payment by the guarantors of the primary obligor's obligations owed to the creditor, and that the guaranty is not specifically addressed to the creditor.

Missouri's general rule is that a transfer of the underlying obligation operates as an assignment of a general guaranty, even though there is no specific reference to the guaranty in the assignment.[48]

§ 7 Defenses of the Guarantor

7.1 Defenses Generally

7.1.1 When Guarantor May Assert Primary Obligor's Defense

"The basic rule on the liability... of guarantors is that the ... guarantor is not liable to the creditor unless his principal is liable; thus he may plead the defenses which are available to the principal."[49] "In other words, if the [creditor] has no cause of action against the principal, ... there could be no obligation on the part of the guarantors to pay."[50] Guarantors may present defenses that could have been asserted by the primary obligor, provided that such defenses present a legal reason why the obligee should not be allowed to recover against the primary obligor.[51] However, some courts will hold that an unconditional

45. *Stewart Title Guaranty Co.,* 961 S.W.2d at 881.
46. *Dunn Industrial Group,* 112 S.W.3d at 434.
47. *Id.*, 112 S.W.3d at 434.
48. American First Federal, Inc. v. Battlefield Center, L.P., 282 S.W.3d 1, 6 (Mo. App. 2009).
49. Modern Textile, Inc. v. P.M. Holding Corp., 900 F.2d 1184, 1188 (8th Cir. 1990).
50. Stifel Estate Co. v. Cella, 291 S.W. 515, 519 (Mo. App. 1927).
51. *Id.,* 291 S.W. 515 at 519.

guaranty, accompanied by a waiver of any defenses available to the primary obligor, would preclude a guarantor from defending a claim based on a defense of the underlying obligation, such as unconscionability.[52]

7.1.2 Defenses that May not be Raised by Guarantor

A "failure to read" defense may not be asserted by a guarantor. "Absent fraud, accident or mistake, a party is held to have had knowledge of a contract which he or she had an opportunity to read but did not by reason of indolence, folly or careless indifference to the ordinary and accessible means of information."[53]

In most cases, a guarantor will not be able to assert a defense claiming the primary obligor lacked the authority to execute an underlying credit agreement or promissory note. If the primary obligor is liable for the debt even in the absence of express authority, the guarantor cannot deny liability.[54]

A guarantor may not claim that a lack of ownership, relationship, or other affiliation with the primary obligor should absolve it of liability. Provided there is proper consideration, as discussed above, any relationship, or lack thereof, is immaterial.[55]

If the guarantor waives notice of default, or otherwise has constructive notice of such default, through its role in the primary obligor, the guarantor may not defend a claim based on a lack of notice of the default.[56]

The court will not imply a fiduciary relationship or implied covenant of good faith where one does not exist in the documents.[57]

7.1.3 Defenses that May Always be Asserted

A guarantor's defense of mental incompetency and incapacity to enter into the guaranty agreement may be asserted without requiring that the underlying transaction be unwound, as would be necessary if the underlying transaction were being questioned.[58]

A "fraudulent inducement" defense is generally permitted to be asserted by guarantors. The guarantor must establish: 1) false, material representation by the obligee; 2) knowledge of its falsity or ignorance of its truth by obligee or assignee of obligee; 3) intent that the guarantor act upon the false representations in a manner reasonably contemplated; 4) the guarantor's ignorance of the statement's falsity; and 5) the guarantor's reliance on the statement's truth and a proximate injury.[59]

52. Copelco Leasing Corp. v. Eyerman, M.D., 855 F. Supp. 1049, 1066 (E.D. MO. 1994).
53. *Mercantile Trust Co.*, 648 S.W.2d at 924.
54. *Id.*, 648 S.W.2d at 925.
55. *Id.*, 648 S.W.2d at 923.
56. Lemay Bank and Trust Co., 810 S.W.2d at 693.
57. *Id.*, 810 S.W.2d at 693.
58. Centerre Bank Nat'l Assoc. v. Southern Iron & Supply, Inc., 697 S.W.2d 323, 326 (Mo. App. 1985).
59. *Copelco Leasing Corp.*, 855 F. Supp. at 1062.

7.2 "Suretyship" Defenses

7.2.1 *Change in Identity of Primary Obligor*

In situations where the contract representing the underlying obligation is assigned, such an assignment and change in the primary obligor will not discharge the guarantor, at least in situations where an assignment was contemplated in the underlying contract and the primary obligor was to remain liable upon any such assignment.[60]

7.2.2 *Modification of the Underlying Obligation, Including Release*

Absent a waiver, the general rule in Missouri is that a material alteration of the underlying obligation without guarantor's consent will discharge the guarantor. A material alteration is one that enlarges or lessens liability, and this is true whether the alteration would be to the benefit or detriment of the guarantor.[61] Waivers and consents to modification without notice are enforced by Missouri courts, but they must be explicit and thorough, as one court discharged a guarantor based on a decrease in the interest rate on the underlying debt, even though the guarantor consented to the obligee to make "such extensions, renewals, indulgences, settlements and compromises as it may deem proper."[62]

A failure by the obligee and primary obligor to properly calculate the underlying obligations based on the existing formula was not a modification of the underlying obligation where they did not otherwise amend or change the terms of the underlying agreement.[63] A change in obligee is not a material change allowing for a discharge of the guarantor when the guaranty agreement referred to original obligee and its successors and assigns.[64]

Where a continuing guaranty was executed which guaranteed all loans made or which may be made, the marking of one note as "Paid" does not discharge guarantor's liability under the guaranty for future loans made to the primary obligor, provided the new loan does not exceed the maximum amount stated in the guaranty agreement.[65]

7.2.3 *Release or Impairment of Security for the Underlying Obligation*

While Missouri courts will generally recognize an impairment of collateral defense, it may be waived by the guarantor and become unavailable. When a waiver is present, the Missouri courts will generally conclude that the guarantor

---

60. Nat'l Super Markets, Inc. v. KMSK, Inc., 940 S.W.2d 47, 50 (Mo. App. 1997).
61. DeCota v. J.E.M. Development Corp., 908 S.W.2d 884, 886 (Mo. App. 1995).
62. Wigley v. Capital Bank of Southwest Missouri, 887 S.W.2d 715, 724 (Mo. App. 1994).
63. Bechtle v. Tandy Corp., 77 S.W.3d 689, 693 (Mo. App. 2002).
64. Boatman's Nat'l Bank of St. Louis v. Nangle, 899 S.W.2d 542, 546 (Mo. App. 1995).
65. *Id.*, 899 S.W.2d at 545.

is primarily liable and cannot escape liability by a failure to perfect a security interest, a failure to foreclose on collateral, etc.[66]

Notwithstanding such a waiver, some Missouri courts have said an obligee has a duty to act in good faith and with a reasonable degree of care with respect to the collateral. Most courts have required that the guarantor prove the obligee acted in bad faith and provide evidence of the collateral's value.[67]

7.3 Other Defenses

7.3.1 Failure to Fulfill a Condition Precedent

As guarantors generally cannot be liable where the primary obligor is not liable, a failure to fulfill a condition precedent in the underlying obligation, absolving the primary obligor from performance, also discharges the guarantor.[68]

7.3.2 Modification of the Guaranty

In general, a departure from the terms of the guaranty agreement, if it causes a material alteration of the terms of the agreement, will discharge the guarantor from its obligation. A change is material only if it alters the guarantor's liability. In cases where the guarantor has placed a limit on the amount of obligations it will guarantee, the Missouri courts have held that extensions of credit beyond such limits are not a material alteration of the guaranty by the lender, because the guarantor's liability is still limited to the original amount and was not altered.[69]

7.3.3 Failure to Pursue Primary Obligor

Absent specific language in the guaranty, an obligee does not need to exhaust remedies against the primary obligor prior to pursuing claims against guarantors.[70] However, in situations involving multiple creditors, the court may apply the doctrine of marshaling of assets and cause specific creditors to exhaust remedies against specific obligors.[71]

7.3.4 Statute of Limitations

Guaranty agreements are deemed to be contracts for the payment of money in Missouri, and are subject to the applicable 10-year statute of limitation, rather than the five-year statute of limitation which applies to contracts generally. The statute of limitation begins to run when the obligation to pay arises.[72]

66. ITT Commercial Finance Corp. v. Mid-America Marine Supply Corp., 854 S.W.2d 371, 385 (Mo. 1993). *See also* Mercantile Bank, N.A. v. Loy, 77 S.W.3d 93, 98 (Mo. App. 2002).
67. Boatman's First Nat'l Bank of Kansa City v. P.P.C., Inc., 927 F.2d 394, 397 (8th Cir. 1991).
68. Missouri-Indiana Investment Group v. Shaw, 518 F. Supp. 576, 581 (E.D. Mo. 1981); vacated on other grounds.
69. Spackler v. Boatman's Nat'l Bank of St. Louis, 17 F.3d 1089, 1092 (8th Cir. 1994).
70. Federal Deposit Insurance Corp. v. Indian Creek Warehouse, J.V., 974 F. Supp. 746, 750 (E.D. Missouri 1997).
71. In the Matter of Clary House, 11 B.R. at 466.
72. Mark Twain Bank, N.A. v. Platzelman, 740 S.W.2d 388 (Mo. App. 1987); *see also* St. Louis University v. Belleville, 752 S.W.2d 481 (Mo. App. 1988).

7.3.5 Statute of Frauds

A contract to answer for the debt of another is within the statute of frauds in Missouri, and can be enforced only if there is some memorandum or note thereof in writing signed by the party to be charged therewith.[73]

7.3.6 Defenses Particular to Guarantors that are Natural Persons and their Spouses

There are cases in Missouri involving one spouse's guaranty of the debts of the other spouse where the courts take into account the marital relationship in concluding that a guaranty was unconscionable and not enforceable.[74] The court stated a woman's "relationship with her husband was used to maneuver her into a position in which she would sign a contract which no person in his or her right mind would sign."[75]

7.4 Right of Set-off

A guarantor can generally assert a claim of set-off, but this right is frequently waived in the guaranty agreement, and such a waiver will be enforced in Missouri.[76]

§ 8 Waiver of Defenses by the Guarantor

8.1 "Catch-all" Waivers

An "unconditional" guarantee has been deemed in some cases to be a waiver of most defenses, and broad waivers have been recognized by some courts in Missouri.[77] Notwithstanding such recognition of broad waivers, drafters should include specific and thorough waiver language whenever possible.

8.2 Use of Specific Waivers and Consents

In *Mercantile Bank and Trust Co. v. Eppinger*, the guaranty provided for the waiver of "notice of indebtedness already or hereafter contracted or renewed," and then provided that the guarantor "consents without notice to any and all renewals of any said indebtedness or extension of time for the payment thereof."[78] With respect to "new indebtedness" that was subsequently incurred, the court held that there was no waiver of notice with respect to the indebtedness because, while the waiver provision provided for any "indebtedness... hereafter contracted," the "consent without notice" provision only referred

73. Nat'l Refining Co. v. McDowell, 201 S.W.2d 342, 347 (Mo. 1947).
74. Mercantile Bank and Trust Co. v. Eppinger, 61 B.R. 89, 95 (Bkrtcy. W.D. Mo. 1986); citing Smith, 15 B.R. at 693.
75. *Id.*, 61 B.R. at 95.
76. *Stewart Title Guaranty Co.*, 961 S.W.2d at 888.
77. *Copelco Leasing Corp. v. Eyerman, M.D.*, 855 F. Supp. at 1066.
78. *Mercantile Bank and Trust Co.*, 61 B.R. at 95.

to "renewals."[79] The court held this to be an ambiguity, construed against the drafter, and allowed for a "lack of notice" defense.[80]

In *Wigley v. Capital Bank of Southwest Missouri*, the guarantor was discharged when the bank lowered the interest rate on the underlying obligation, despite the guarantor consenting for the bank "to give and make such extensions, renewals, indulgences, settlements and compromises as it may deem proper." The court held that such language does not "specifically mention" a change in interest rate, and the guarantor had not waived a defense to such modification.[81]

§ 9 Third-party Pledgors—Defenses and Waiver Thereof

We have found no evidence that the law as applied to sureties and guarantors would not apply to a third-party pledge.

§ 10 Jointly and Severally Liable Guarantors–Contribution

In Missouri, there is a rebuttable presumption that coguarantors received equal benefit from the transaction and must contribute equally to payment of any guaranteed obligations.[82] A guarantor will have a claim for contribution from the other coguarantors upon satisfaction of a debt owed under the guaranty.[83]

§ 11 Reliance

Missouri courts have stated that an obligee must prove it relied on the guaranty agreement in extending credit to the primary obligor as a prima facie element of its claim.[84] However, as the same court later states, the issue of reliance is essentially a question of whether consideration is present, which itself becomes a question as to whether the guaranties are part of the same underlying loan transaction. (See § 4 above.)

79. *Id.*, 61 B.R. at 95.
80. *Id.*, 61 B.R. at 95.
81. *Wigley*, 887 S.W.3d at 724.
82. Betz v. Fagan, 962 S.W.2d 432, 436 (Mo. App. 1998).
83. *Id.*, 962 S.W.2d at 437.
84. *See Stewart Title Guaranty Co.*, 961 S.W.2d at 880; and First State Bank of St. Charles, Missouri v. Frankel, 86 S.W.3d 161 (Mo. App. 2002).

§ 12 Subrogation

The Missouri Supreme Court has stated that when a surety or guarantor pays or extinguishes a judgment against the debtor who is primarily liable, such surety or guarantor is subrogated to all of the rights and remedies of the obligee, even without a formal assignment of the judgment. The same right of subrogation applies to cosureties and coguarantors.[85]

§ 13 Triangular Set-off

Missouri courts have not addressed triangular set-off in a non-bankruptcy setting. While Missouri courts have also not specifically addressed triangular set-off inside of bankruptcy, it would likely be impermissible under Section 553 of the Bankruptcy Code.[86]

§ 14 Indemnification or Reimbursement

Generally, in Missouri, where a guarantor pays the debt of a primary obligor, a promise of reimbursement is implied by law, and an action to recover such reimbursement is based on equitable principles.[87] Missouri also specifically recognizes a common law right to indemnity if a plaintiff can show: (1) the discharge of an obligation by the plaintiff; (2) the obligation discharged by the plaintiff is identical to an obligation owed by the defendant; and (3) the discharge of the obligation by the plaintiff is under such circumstances that the obligation should have been discharged by the defendant, and defendant will be unjustly enriched if the defendant does not reimburse the plaintiff to the extent that the defendant's liability has been discharged.[88]

While an indemnity or reimbursement claim is available in guaranty arrangements as described above, the claim might be fruitless if a defunct business entity is the primary obligor who benefited from the guarantor's payment of the indebtedness. Missouri also recognizes claims for unjust enrichment if the plaintiff can show: (1) that the defendant was enriched by the receipt of a benefit; (2) that the enrichment was at the expense of the plaintiff; and (3) that it would be unjust to allow the defendant to retain the benefit. Accordingly, if the owners of the business entity received any distributions or benefits from the business which could have otherwise gone towards the payment of the underlying indebtedness, the guarantors might have a claim against the

85. *Betz,* 962 S.W.2d at 427, citing Phelps v. Scott, 325 Mo. 711 (Mo. 1930).
86. In re Bridge Information Systems, Inc., 314 B.R. 421, 429 (Bkrtcy. E.D. Mo. 2004).
87. In re Jamison's Estate, 202 S.W.2d 879, 993 (Mo. 1947).
88. Beeler v. Martin, 306 S.W.3d 108, 111 (Mo. App. 2010).

owners under an unjust enrichment theory, even if an indemnity claim against the business entity might fail.[89]

§ 15 Enforcement of Guaranties

In enforcing a guaranty agreement, an obligee generally must show: (1) the guarantors executed the guaranty; (2) the guarantors unconditionally delivered the guaranty to obligees, or, if conditioned, that the condition has been met; (3) the obligee thereafter extended credit or provided consideration; and (4) the underlying obligation is outstanding and owed to the obligee.[90]

15.1 Exercising Rights Under a Guaranty Where the Underlying Obligation is also Secured by a Mortgage

Unless the language in the guaranty agreement otherwise limits liability, a guarantor will generally be liable for a mortgagee's deficiency claim after a foreclosure sale. Further, the obligee has no duty to bid the fair market value of the real estate or the amount owed on the property at the foreclosure sale.[91]

15.2 Litigating Guaranty Claims; Procedural Considerations

Guaranty defenses must be properly pleaded before trial. When there are coguarantors, separate defenses must be backed by separate instructions and evidence at trial.[92]

§ 16 Choice of Law

Procedural issues will be governed by the law of the forum jurisdiction, and the court will otherwise honor choice of law contractual clauses in guaranty agreements.[93]

§17 Revival and Reinstatement of Guaranties

We found no Missouri cases addressing this topic.

---

89. *Id.*, 306 S.W.3d at 112.
90. *Stewart Title Guaranty Co.*, 961 S.W.2d at 880.
91. Boatmen's Bank of Jefferson County v. Community Interiors, Inc., 721 S.W.2d 72, 80 (Mo. App. 1986).
92. Linwood State Bank v. Lientz, 413 S.W.2d 248, 255 (Mo. 1967).
93. Rheem Manufacturing Co., 28 S.W.3d at 339.

Montana Law of Guaranties

Charles W. Hingle
Holland & Hart LLP
401 North 31st Street
Suite 1500
Billings, Montana 59101-1277
Telephone: 406.252-2166
Fax: 406.252.1669
chingle@hollandhart.com
www.hollandhart.com

HOLLAND&HART LLP

Contents

Montana Law of Guaranties

HIGHLIGHTS:

1. The Montana Code Annotated includes a comprehensive statutory framework adopted in the 19th Century.[1] Montana case law is less developed.
2. If a guaranty applying Montana law is entered into at the same time as the principal obligation, no other consideration is necessary. See § 4 below.
3. Alteration of the underlying obligation in any respect without the consent of the obligor may cause exoneration of the guaranty. See § 7.2.1 below.
4. The Montana Supreme Court has not held that rights of exoneration can be effectively waived in the guaranty agreement. See § 8.1 below. Lenders should assume the need for consent to any change in the underlying obligation even if the usual contractual waivers are included in the guaranty.

Introduction and Sources of Law

This survey discusses Montana law applicable to guaranties. Montana law includes a comprehensive, though somewhat archaic, statutory framework adopted from the California version of the "Field Code" in 1895.[2] Case law is much less developed than that of other, more populous states with intermediate appellate courts. The Montana Supreme Court has infrequently cited to the Restatement.[3]

---

1. *See* Mont. Code Ann. Title 28, Ch. 11, Parts 1 and 2. [The Montana Code Annotated is available at http://data.opi.mt.gov/bills/mca_toc/index.htm.]
2. Scott J. Burnham, *Let's Repeal the Field Code!*, 67 Mont. L. Rev. 31 (2006); Gunther A. Weiss, *The Enchantment of Codification in the Common-Law World*, 25 Yale J. Intl. L. 435, 504-05 (2000). One neighboring state still maintains Field Code guaranty statutes very similar to Montana's. *See* N.D. Cent. Code § 22-01-01, *et seq.*
3. Specific citations to the Restatement (First) of Security (1941) ["Restatement"] regarding guaranty relationships are set forth below. The Montana Supreme Court has not cited to the Restatement (Third) of Suretyship and Guaranty (1995) ["Third Restatement"].

§ 1 Nature of the Guaranty

Under Montana law, a guaranty is an obligation separate from that of the principal obligor and the obligee.

1.1 Guaranty Relationship

"A guaranty is the promise to answer for the debt, default, or miscarriage of another person."[4] The guarantor is the person who contracts to satisfy the debt of the primary obligor or "principal."[5] In Montana the obligee or counterparty to the guarantor is sometimes referred to as the "guarantee."[6]

The Montana Supreme Court has characterized the guaranty as "distinct and independent" from the underlying obligation.[7] There is no privity, mutuality, or joint liability between the primary obligor and his guarantor.[8]

1.2 Suretyship and Indemnity

Like the law of guaranty, the Montana Code Annotated includes a comprehensive framework for the law of indemnity and suretyship both of which were also adopted from the Field Code.[9] Guarantors, indemnitors, and sureties play distinct roles under Montana laws.[10] The Montana Supreme Court has maintained the distinction between guaranty and suretyship.[11]

§ 2 State Law requirements for an Entity to Enter a Guaranty

Partnerships, limited liability companies, corporations, and trusts can all grant guaranties in furtherance of their business activities.

2.1 Corporations

Corporations have statutory authority to guarantee the debts of another.[12]

---

4. Mont. Code Ann. § 28-11-101.
5. *See*, e.g., Mont. Code Ann. § 28-11-102.
6. *See*, e.g., Mont. Code Ann. § 28-11-106.
7. Baroch v. Greater Montana Oil Co., 70 Mont. 93, 96, 225 P. 800, 801 (1924).
8. *Id.*
9. *See* Mont. Code Ann. Title 28, Ch. 11, Parts 3 and 4.
10. *See* Mont. Code Ann. § 28-11-301 ("Indemnity is a contract by which one engages to save another from a legal consequence of the conduct of one of the parties or of some other person."); Mont. Code Ann. § 28-11-401 (a surety is one who becomes responsible for the performance by another person of some act in favor of a third person).
11. *See* § 6.7, infra.
12. Mont. Code Ann. § 35-1-115(7).

2.2 Partnerships

Partnerships—general, limited, and limited liability partnerships—are governed by the agreements of the parties creating the partnership.[13] Nothing in Montana law prevents the partnership from conferring the power to guarantee the debt of another.

2.3 Limited Liability Companies

Limited liability companies have the statutory power to guarantee the debts of another person unless such power is restricted by the operating agreement of the company.[14]

2.4 Trusts and Estates

Trustees may guarantee the debts of a beneficiary[15] unless the power to do so is limited by the terms of the trust instrument.[16] Montana law does *not* enumerate the power to guarantee the debts of the estate among those powers that may be exercised by a personal representative of a decedent's estate.[17]

2.5 Individuals

Montana is not a community property state. One spouse may transfer his or her individual assets without the consent of the other spouse;[18] one spouse is not "liable for the debts contracted by the other spouse."[19] Thus, a married guarantor's individual assets are subject to the judgment of the obligee under the terms of the guaranty.

§ 3 Signatory's Authority to Execute a Guaranty

The obligee should make reasonable inquiry that the person executing the guaranty has authority to bind the guarantor.

3.1 Corporations

An officer of a corporation has the authority granted under the bylaws of the corporation, by resolution of the board of directors, or "by continued acquiescence, [by which the board] authorizes or permits the [officer] to exercise all of its powers or functions."[20] If a corporation accepts or retains the benefits

13. Mont. Code Ann. § 35-10-106. *See* McCormick v. Brevig, 322 Mont. 112, 121, 96 P.3d 697, 703 (2004).
14. Mont. Code Ann. § 35-8-107(3); 35-8-107(3), 109.
15. Mont. Code Ann. § 72-34-338.
16. Mont. Code Ann. § 72-34-301.
17. Mont. Code Ann. § 72-3-613.
18. Mont. Code Ann. § 40-2-201.
19. Mont. Code Ann. § 40-2-106(1).
20. Edwards v. Plains Light & Water Co., 49 Mont. 535, 545, 143 P. 962, 964-65 (1914).

of an unauthorized contract, such contract is deemed ratified unless it violates some law or public policy.[21]

3.2 Partnerships

General partners have the authority to bind the partnership when "apparently carrying on in the ordinary course of partnership business" unless the obligee "knows or has received a notification that the partner lacks authority."[22] Acts outside the ordinary course of the partnership's business must be authorized "by the other partners."[23]

3.3 Limited Liability Companies

Acts of a member or manager of a limited liability company "in contravention of a restriction [in the operating agreement] on authority" will not bind the company "to persons having knowledge of the restriction."[24]

§ 4 Consideration

If the guaranty is entered into at the same time as the principal obligation, no other consideration is necessary. Otherwise, standard contract principles apply to the analysis of consideration for a contract of guaranty distinct from the principal agreement.

4.1 Consideration not Required

No separate consideration is required if the guaranty is entered into or accepted by the guarantor at the same time as the underlying obligation is created and "forms with that [underlying] obligation a part of the consideration."[25]

4.2 Consideration Required

If the guaranty is entered into at a different time than the underlying obligation, "there must be a consideration distinct from that of the [underlying] obligation."[26] Renewed guaranties require new consideration.[27] Forbearance to enforce a legal right may be sufficient consideration to support a guaranty.[28]

21. Farmers State Bank of Victor v. Johnson, 188 Mont. 55, 60-61, 610, P.2d 1172, 1174-75 (1980).
22. Mont. Code Ann. § 35-10-301(1).
23. Mont Code Ann. § 35-10-301(2).
24. Mont. Code Ann. § 35-8-301(4).
25. Mont. Code Ann. § 28-11-103. *See* Schauer v. Morgan, 67 Mont. 455, 463-64, 216 P. 347, 351 (1923).
26. *Id.*
27. W.T. Rawleigh Co. v. Miller, 105 Mont. 456, 462, 73 P.2d 552, 554 (1937).
28. Doorly v. Goodman, 71 Mont. 529, 531, 230 P. 779, 781 (1924).

4.3 Consideration need not be Recited

A written guaranty need not recite consideration.[29]

§ 5 Notice of Acceptance

Notice of acceptance is not required if the guaranty is absolute.[30] If required, notice of acceptance may be communicated before or after the extension of credit.[31]

§ 6 Interpretation of Guaranties

Montana courts will interpret a guaranty in the same manner by which they would interpret the language of any other contract, but certain terms typically found in guaranty contracts have the specific meanings set forth in the Montana guaranty statutes.

6.1 General Principles

A guaranty must be in writing and signed by the guarantor,[32] though there are five statutory exceptions to the rule.[33] The Montana Supreme Court has not specified any words of guaranty though certain words provided by statute define the guaranty obligation.[34] The verb "guarantee" should be used in any written guaranty agreement. Montana courts adhere to the basic tenet that

---

29. Mont. Code Ann. § 28-11-104. Consideration need not be pleaded in a complaint against the guarantor. *Doorly, supra,* note 28. The burden to prove or disprove consideration rests on the guarantor. *Schauer, supra,* note 25.
30. Mont. Code Ann. § 28-11-106. *See* Section 6.5, *infra.*
31. Miller v. Walter, 165 Mont. 221, 229, 527 P.2d 240, 245 (1974) (citing Restatement § 86 for the adequacy of acceptance even after repossession).
32. Mont. Code Ann. § 28-11-104.
33. A guaranty need not be in writing in the following cases:
    (1) when the promise is made by one who has received property of another upon an undertaking to apply the property pursuant to the promise or by one who has received a discharge from an obligation, in whole or in part, in consideration of the promise;
    (2) when the creditor parts with value or enters into an obligation in consideration of the obligation in respect to which the promise is made, in terms or under circumstances that render the party making the promise the principal debtor and the person in whose behalf the promise is made the party's surety;
    (3) when the promise, being for an antecedent obligation of another, is made upon a consideration;
        (a) that the party receiving the promise cancels the antecedent obligation, accepting the new promise as a substitute for the antecedent obligation;
        (b) that the party receiving the promise releases the property of another from a levy; or
        (c) beneficial to the promisor, whether moving from either party to the antecedent obligation or from another person;
    (4) when a factor undertakes to sell merchandise for a commission and guarantee the sale;
    (5) when the holder of an instrument in payment of a precedent debt of the holder's own or for a new consideration and in connection with the transfer enters into a promise respecting the instrument.

    Mont. Code Ann. § 28-11-105.
34. *See* "Interpretation of Guaranties," § 6, *infra.*

"[o]ne who executes a written contract is presumed to know the contents of the contract and to assent to those specified terms."[35]

6.2 Guaranty of Payment Versus Guaranty of Collection

A guarantor of "payment" or of "performance" is liable to the obligee immediately upon default of the primary obligor "without demand or notice."[36] A guaranty of collection is a conditional guaranty[37] and enforceable when the primary obligor suffers a judgment on the underlying obligation.[38]

6.3 "Continuing"

A "continuing guaranty" relates to the "future liability" of the principal obligor "under successive transactions."[39] The continuing nature of the transactions may include those that may have "been satisfied" and "from time to time renew[ed]."[40]

6.4 Language Regarding the Revocation of Guaranties

Only continuing guaranties may be revoked and only with respect to future liability of the principal obligor.[41] But even the ability to revoke is restricted if there is "continuing consideration" with respect to that portion of the underlying obligation not subject to the revocation.[42]

6.5 "Absolute and Unconditional"

An "absolute" guaranty is binding upon the guarantor without notice of acceptance.[43] A guaranty is deemed "unconditional" unless its terms include a "condition precedent" to the liability of the principal obligor.[44] A guaranty of collection is an example of a conditional guaranty.

---

35. Quinn v. Briggs, 172 Mont. 468, 476, 565 P.2d 297, 301 (1977); Denton v. First Interstate Bank of Commerce, 333 Mont. 169, 177, 142 P.3d 797, 803 (2006).
36. Mont. Code Ann. § 28-11-205. *See* Gen. Finance Co. v. Powell, 114 Mont. 473, 480, 138 P.2d 255, 258 (1943).
37. Nw. Fire and Marine Ins. Co. v. Pollard, 74 Mont. 142, 150, 238 P. 594, 597 (1926). *See* W. Indus., Inc. v. Chicago Mining Corp., 279 Mont. 105, 109-110, 926 P.2d 727, 740 (1996) (guaranty that "authorized [obligee] to collect individually from me" after first proceeding against the principal obligor was a conditional guaranty).
38. *See* Sherwood & Roberts, Inc. v. First Sec. Bank of Missoula, 209 Mont. 402,412, 682 P.2d 149, 155 (1984).
39. Mont. Code Ann. § 28-11-108(1). *See* Wells Fargo Bank, N.A. v. Pallett, 313 Mont. 421, 63 P.3d 513, 2002 WL 31730858 (2002) (unpublished decision enforcing dragnet clause of guaranty).
40. *Id.*
41. Mont. Code Ann. § 28-11-108(2).
42. *Id.*
43. Mont. Code Ann. § 28-11-106. *See W. Indus., supra,* note 37 (a promise in the guaranty to pursue the primary obligor first makes the guaranty conditional); *Sherwood, supra,* note 38.
44. Mont. Code Ann. § 28-11-107.

6.6 "Good or Collectible"

A guaranty "to the effect that an obligation is good or is collectible" means that the debtor is solvent and "that the demand is collectible by the usual legal proceedings if taken with reasonable diligence."[45]

6.7 "Liable as a Primary Obligor and not Merely as Surety"

These terms are not used in the Montana guaranty or suretyship statutes, nor does the case law require usage of such terminology.[46]

§ 7 Defenses of the Guarantor

The defenses that may be available to a guarantor include (1) the defenses available to the primary obligor and (2) the statutory defenses provided to guarantors. Alteration of the underlying obligation in any respect without the consent of the obligor may cause exoneration of the guaranty.

7.1 Defenses of the Primary Obligor

7.1.1 General

The guarantor's obligation may not exceed that of the primary obligor, in amount or "in other respects," and "if in its terms it exceeds it, it is reducible in proportion to the principal obligation."[47] Acceptance of partial satisfaction by the obligee reduces the guarantor's obligation accordingly.[48]

7.1.2 When Guarantor may assert Primary Obligor's Defense

If the underlying obligation is incomplete, that is, when "the terms of [the underlying obligation] are not then settled," the guarantor shall not be exposed to risks greater than "those terms that are most common in similar contracts"

---

45. Mont. Code Ann. § 28-11-204(1).
46. Indeed, use of the phrase "as surety" may blur the relatively clear distinction between a guaranty and the obligation of a surety under Montana law. *Compare* Mont. Code Ann. § 28-11-101 (definition of guaranty), *with* Mont. Code Ann. § 28-11-401 (definition of surety). The distinction has been addressed by the Montana Supreme Court on several occasions. *See* Cole Mfg. Co. v. Morton, 24 Mont. 58, 61, 60 P. 587, 588 (1900) ("[A] surety is bound with the principal as an original promisor on the same contract, while the guarantor makes his own separate contract"); Stensvad v. Miners & Merchants Bank of Roundup, 183 Mont. 160, 165, 598 P.2d 1083, 1086 (1979) (surety answers for performance of principal; guarantor pays debt upon default). Thus, a guarantor is the primary obligor of a separate obligation, the contract of guaranty, while a surety is bound with the primary obligor to the obligee. *See* El-Ce Storms Trust v. Svetahor, 223 Mont. 113, 118-19, 724 P.2d 704, 707 (1986) (citing the Restatement § 82 for the definition of "suretyship"). Some confusion in inevitable, however, since a surety enjoys the rights of a guarantor under Montana law. Mont. Code Ann. § 28-11-414. *See* Montana Bank of Circle v. Ralph B. Myers & Sons, Inc., 236 Mont. 236, 243, 769 P.2d 1208, 1213 (1989) (every suretyship includes a guaranty). The converse is not true. *Id.* (guarantor exoneration statutes not comparable to surety statutes).
47. Mont. Code Ann. § 28-11-201. *See W. Indus., supra,* note 37 (obligee may only collect from the guarantor the amount of the stipulated judgment of the primary obligor); *Sherwood, supra,* note 38, at 410.
48. Mont. Code Ann. § 28-11-216.

in the place of performance.[49] A guarantor shall not be liable if the primary obligor's contract is "unlawful."[50]

7.2 Guarantor's Defenses

7.2.1 Modification of the Underlying Obligation

A guarantor is exonerated "if by any act of the [obligee] without the consent of the guarantor the original [underlying] obligation of the principal is altered in any respect."[51] Exoneration may result from "any" change in the underlying obligation.[52] Rescission of the alteration does not restore the liability of the guarantor.[53] It is strongly recommended that every modification of the underlying obligation be documented and that the guarantor consent to all modifications in writing.

7.2.2 Release or Impairment of Security for the Underlying Obligation

Impairment or suspension of the rights or remedies available to the obligee against the primary obligor is cause for exoneration of the guarantor.[54] Mere delay in the pursuit of the primary obligor does not result in the exoneration of the guarantor,[55] nor does the discharge of the principal "by operation of law."[56] Notwithstanding any cause for exoneration, a guarantor is liable to the obligee to the extent the guarantor was indemnified by the primary obligor.[57]

7.2.3 Failure to Pursue Primary Obligor

The guarantor of an obligation that is "good or collectible" may not assert that the obligee failed to exhaust remedies against the primary obligor "if no part of the debt could have been collected thereby."[58] The Montana Supreme Court has held that the failure to file a claim against the estate of the primary obligor is cause for exoneration.[59]

---

49. Mont. Code Ann. § 28-11-202.
50. Mont. Code Ann. § 28-11-203. But the guarantor may not assert "any mere personal disability" of the primary obligor. *Id.*
51. Mont. Code Ann. § 28-11-211(1).
52. *See* Sec. Bank, N.A. v. Mudd, 215 Mont. 242, 246, 696 P.2d 458, 460 (1985) (citing Restatement § 124(1)) (obligee's failure to apply proceeds of collateral for the underlying obligation with guarantor's consent materially increased guarantor's risk and resulted in exoneration of guaranty); First Sec. Bank v. Sullivan, 347 Mont. 452, 459, 200 P.3d 39, 45 (2008) (obligee changed underlying obligation from revolving loan to term loan without guarantor's consent); Ace Leasing, Inc. v. Boustead, 311 Mont. 289, 55 P.3d 371 (2002) (failure of lessor/obligee to retain ownership of leased equipment deprived guarantor of right to pay debt and obtain equipment). *But see Stensvad, supra,* note 46, at 414 (alteration of primary obligor's remedies did not exonerate guarantor).
53. Mont. Code Ann. § 28-11-212.
54. Mont. Code Ann. § 28-11-211(1).
55. Mont. Code Ann. § 28-11-213.
56. Mont. Code Ann. § 28-11-214.
57. Mont. Code Ann. § 28-11-215.
58. Mont. Code Ann. § 28-11-204(1), (2). If the principal leaves the state "having no property" with which to satisfy the underlying obligation, insolvency is presumed. Mont. Code Ann. § 28-11-204(3).
59. *See* Nw. Bank of Lewistown v. Estate of Coppedge, 219 Mont. 473, 477, 713 P.2d 523, 526 (1986) (failure to file a creditor's claim against the estate of the primary obligor is cause for exoneration of guarantor).

7.2.4 *Notice of Default*

A guarantor is liable upon the default of the principal obligor "without demand or notice" unless the guaranty requires such notice.[60]

7.2.5 *Statute of Limitations*

The eight-year statute of limitations for written contracts in Montana[61] is applicable to a written guaranty.[62] The obligation of the guarantor is not barred by the running of the statute of limitations applicable to the underlying obligation.[63]

§ 8 Waiver of Defenses by the Guarantor

Contractual waivers of exoneration defenses may not be enforceable.

8.1 Defenses that cannot be Waived

The Montana Supreme Court has held that a surety may contract away rights of exoneration.[64] The Court has made no similar holding in a guaranty case. Thus, it is recommended that one assume the need for consent of the guarantor to alteration of the underlying obligation despite the presence of the usual contractual waivers of rights of exoneration in the guaranty agreement.

8.2 "Catch-all" Waivers

There is no Montana law on this subject. The Montana Supreme Court has never considered the application of Third Restatement § 48(1). Drafters should assume "catch-all" waivers are not enforceable but should include the usual litany of waivers in any guaranty agreement as well as a severability provision.

8.3 Use of Specific Waivers

There is no Montana law on this subject.

60. Mont. Code Ann. § 28-11-205. *But see* Mont. Code Ann. § 30-9A-611(3) (a guarantor is a "secondary obligor" entitled to notice of disposition of collateral under Article 9 of the Montana Uniform Commercial Code).
61. Mont. Code Ann. § 28-2-202(1).
62. Mercury Marine v. Monty's Enterprises, Inc., 270 Mont. 413, 416, 892 P.2d 568, 571 (1995) (citing Restatement § 130).
63. *Id.*
64. *See Montana Bank of Circle, N.A., supra,* note 46.

§ 9 Third-party Pledgors—Defenses and Waiver Thereof

There is no Montana law on this subject.

§ 10 Jointly and Severally Liable Guarantors

Guarantors who are jointly and severally liable are presumed to share the guaranty obligation equally.

10.1 Contribution

Joint and several guarantors who discharge the underlying obligation are entitled to contribution from another guarantor for his or her proportionate share of the underlying obligation.[65]

10.2 Unequal Benefits

It is presumed that, subject to proof of the contrary, joint obligors benefited equally from a common debt.[66] But the right of contribution is "an equitable concept" and one who did not receive benefits equal to other guarantors may not be required to contribute equally.[67]

§ 11 Reliance

There is no Montana law on this subject but, presumably, reliance is not required to enforce a claim under a guaranty.

§ 12 Subrogation

Subrogation is an equitable remedy that generally requires total satisfaction of the underlying obligation to the obligee prior to its exercise.[68] A guarantor of a mortgagor will be subrogated to the rights of the mortgagee only when the underlying obligation is fully satisfied.[69]

65. Citizens Bank v. Bossard, 226 Mont. 75, 78, 733 P.2d 1296, 1298 (1987).
66. *Id.*
67. *Id.*; Bossard v. Sullivan, 206 Mont. 392, 394, 670 P.2d 1389, 1391 (1983) (following In re Daily's Estate, 117 Mont. 194, 159 P.2d 327 (1945)). *See* Sun River Stock & Land Co. v. Montana Trust & Savings Bank, 81 Mont. 222, 262 P. 1039 (1928).
68. *Pollard, supra*, note 37, at 150.
69. *Id.*

§ 13 Indemnification

The principal obligor has a duty of indemnification to the guarantor "up to the amount which he has been required to pay."[70] The guarantor may bring an action against the principal obligor upon payment of his or her guaranty obligation.[71]

§ 14 Enforcement of Guaranties

Guaranties are enforced by suit, together with or independently of any suit to enforce the underlying obligation. It is recommended that a guaranty of an underlying obligation secured by a mortgage be prosecuted in the action to foreclose the mortgage.

14.1 Limitations on Recovery

The guarantor's obligation may not exceed that of the primary obligor.[72]

14.2 Exercising rights under a Guaranty Where the Underlying Obligation is also Secured by a Mortgage

Montana mortgage law includes both "one action" and "no further action" or antideficiency rules.

14.2.1 One-action Rule

Montana is a one-action state; that is, obligations secured by a mortgage may only be enforced with a foreclosure action.[73] In other words, a mortgagee may *not* forego the mortgage and sue on the underlying obligation in most circumstances.[74] There is, however, a specific exception to the one-ction rule for the enforcement of a guaranty prior to foreclosure of the mortgage.[75]

14.2.2 Antideficiency Rule

"[N]o other or further action" may be taken against a guarantor of an obligation secured by a deed of trust or "trust indenture" after a foreclosure

70. Lyon v. Featherman, 80 Mont. 504, 513, 261 P. 268, 272 (1927).
71. *Id.; see* Mont. Code Ann. § 28-11-312, 314(2) (law of indemnity entitled the indemnitor to reimbursement but not without payment of the underlying claim).
72. *See* Section 7.1.1, *supra*.
73. Mont. Code Ann. § 71-1-222(1) ("There is only one action for the recovery of debt or the enforcement of any right secured by a mortgage upon real estate . . . ").
74. *See* Barth v. Ely, 85 Mont. 310, 326, 278 P. 1002, 1011 (1929).
75. "(4) The one-action limitation in this section does not prohibit an act or proceeding: . . . (m) concerning a mortgage securing a debt or right guaranteed, to enforce an agreement with a surety or guarantor of the debt or right by a mortgage on real estate, if the surety or guaranty obligation is not secured by the same mortgage." Mont. Code Ann. § 71-1-222(4)(m).

by advertisement and sale.[76] This statutory rule has been extended by the Montana Supreme Court to a deficiency judgment after foreclosure of a trust indenture by judicial process.[77] The rule does not apply to residences used for commercial purposes.[78] Thus, there can be no suit on a guaranty if a deed of trust secures the underlying obligation, and (i) it is foreclosed nonjudicially or (ii) the subject collateral is the guarantor's primary residence.

14.3 Litigating Guaranty Claims: Procedural Consideration

It is recommended that guaranty claims be alleged in separate counts in an action to collect an underlying obligation secured with a mortgage whenever possible.[79]

14.4 Completion Guaranties

No reported Montana cases discuss completion guaranties. Guaranties of performance are contemplated but not defined by the Montana statutes,[80] but the scant case law on performance guaranties offers little guidance.[81]

14.5 Probate Claims

Claims against estates for amounts due on guaranties must be made within four months of published notice to creditors.[82] "Arrangements for future payment" in the form of a present value payment or a bond or other security may be ordered by the probate court for claims not yet due.[83]

14.6 Choice of Law Rules

Montana has no statutes regarding contractual *choice* of law clauses though Montana law does include a provision governing contractual *conflicts* of law.[84] Montana courts will not enforce a contractual choice of law if "(1) the application of the law of the chosen state would be contrary to a fundamental Montana policy; (2) Montana has a materially greater interest than the chosen state; and (3) [Montana law] would apply pursuant to § 188 [of the Restatement

76. Mont. Code Ann. § 71-1-317.
77. First State Bank of Forsyth v. Chunkapura, 226 Mont. 54, 879 P.2d 1203 (1987); First Fed. Sav. and Loan Ass'n. of Missoula v. Anderson, 238 Mont. 296, 777 P.2d 1281 (1989) (rule of *Chunkapura* applies even if residence is no longer occupied).
78. First Sec. Bank v. Abel, 348 Mont. 313, 184 P.3d 318 (2008).
79. Bozeman Deaconess Found. v. Cowgill, 143 Mont. 98, 100, 387 P.2d 435, 436 (1963) (action against guarantor may be joined with an action to foreclose a mortgage) (overruling, without citation, Butte Mach. Co. v. Carbonate Hill Mining Co., 75 Mont. 167, 170, 242 P. 956, 957 (1926)) guarantor and debtor cannot be sued in the same action.
80. *See* Mont. Code Ann. § 28-11-205 (guarantor of "payment or performance" is liable upon default).
81. *See Miller, supra,* note 31 (performance of a purchase contract deemed acceptance of the guaranty).
82. Mont. Code Ann. § 72-3-801(1).
83. Mont. Code Ann. § 72-3-814(2).
84. Mont. Code Ann. § 28-3-102 (place of performance controls, unless none is indicated, then place of execution controls).

(Second) Conflict of Laws], which governs the choice of law in the absence of an effective choice of law provision."[85]

§ 15 Revival and Reinstatement of Guaranties

Rescission of an alteration of the underlying obligation or the impairment of a remedy "does not restore the liability of a guarantor who has been exonerated" as a result of the original alteration or impairment.[86]

85. Tenas v. Progressive Preferred Ins. Co., 347 Mont. 133, 140-41, 197 P.3d 990, 995 (2008). *See* Keystone, Inc. v. Triad Sys. Corp., 292 Mont. 229, 232, 971 P.2d 1240, 1242 (1998).
86. Mont Code. Ann. § 28-11-212.

Nebraska State Law of Guaranties

Brandon R. Tomjack
Eric J. Adams
Baird Holm LLP
1500 Woodmen Tower
1700 Farnam St
Omaha, NE 68102-2068
402.344.0500 (phone)
402.344.0588 (fax)
btomjack@bairdholm.com
eadams@bairdholm.com
www.bairdholm.com

BAIRDHOLM LLP
ATTORNEYS AT LAW

Contents

Nebraska State Law of Guaranties

NEBRASKA LAW HIGHLIGHTS

1. Under Nebraska law, an obligee must file suit against the primary obligor to collect a deficiency after a nonjudicial foreclosure of real property within three months after the foreclosure sale. However, this three-month statute of limitations does not apply to suits against guarantors to recover the deficiency. *See* § 14.1 below.
2. Generally speaking, a party may not recover its attorneys' fees and expenses in a civil action, including actions to enforce guaranties. *See* § 14.2 below.

Introduction and Sources of Law

This survey discusses Nebraska State law applicable to guaranties of commercial credit transactions. While Nebraska does not have an abundant body of law on guaranties, there are cases that analyze and discuss the law of guaranties and related subjects and there are also some statutes that bear on the guaranty relationship.[1] It does not appear that Nebraska state courts have had the opportunity to look to the *Restatement (Third) of Suretyship and Guaranty* (1996) (the "Restatement") for guidance on guaranty and suretyship issues, but a few federal courts have referred to the Restatement when interpreting Nebraska law.[2]

In order to standardize our discussion of the law of guaranties, we use the following vocabulary to refer to the various parties to a guaranty and their obligations.

"Guarantor" means a person who, by contract, agrees to satisfy an underlying obligation of another to an obligee upon the primary obligor's default on that underlying obligation. We do not draw a distinction between guarantors and sureties, as Nebraska courts have used the terms interchangeably.[3] The Nebraska Uniform Commercial Code provides that the term "surety" includes the term guarantor.[4]

"Guaranty" means the contract by which the guarantor agrees to satisfy the underlying obligation of a primary obligor to an obligee in the event the primary obligor defaults on the underlying obligation.

"Obligee" means the person to whom the underlying obligation is owed. For example, the lender under a loan agreement would be an obligee vis-à-vis the borrower.

1. *See, e.g.*, Neb. U.C.C. § 3-605.
2. *See, e.g.*, Dobson Bros. Construction Co. v. Ratliff, Inc., No. 4:08CV3103, 2009 U.S. Dist. LEXIS 53876 (D. Neb. Feb. 27, 2009).
3. *See, e.g.*, Northern Bank v. Dowd, 562 N.W.2d 378, 379 (Neb. 1997); *see also* State ex rel. Wagner v. Amwest Sur. Ins. Co., 738 N.W.2d 805, 810 (2007).
4. Neb. U.C.C. § 1-201(39).

"Primary Obligor" means the person who incurs the underlying obligation to the obligee. For example, the borrower under a loan agreement would be a primary obligor.

"Underlying Obligation" means the obligation or obligations incurred by the primary obligor and owed to the obligee. For example, the borrower's obligation to make payments to a lender of principal and interest on a loan constitutes an underlying obligation.

§ 1 Nature of the Guaranty

Under Nebraska law, a guaranty is "a contractual relation resulting from an agreement whereby one person, the [guarantor], engages to be answerable for the debt, default, or miscarriage of another, the [primary obligor]."[5]

1.1 Guaranty Relationships

A guaranty is a contract by a person to answer for the payment of a debt or the performance of a contract or duty in the event the primary obligor fails to perform the underlying obligation.[6] The guarantor's obligation is not an original and direct one, but is accessory or collateral to the primary obligor's underlying obligation.[7]

Under Nebraska law, no technical words are needed to create a guaranty obligation. To be binding, a promise to be a guarantor for the performance of an obligation (1) must be in writing, (2) must be signed by the guarantor, and (3) must recite a purported consideration.[8] For consideration to exist, the benefit rendered need not be to the guarantor but may be to anyone else at the guarantor's procurement or request.[9] The Nebraska Supreme Court has rejected the concept of "implied surety" in the absence of a written agreement establishing a guaranty.[10]

---

5. Sawyer v. State Sur. Co., 558 N.W.2d 43, 47 (Neb. 1997) (quoting Niklaus v. Phoenix Indemnity Co., 89 N.W.2d 258, 262-63 (Neb. 1958)).
6. Builders Supply Co, Inc. v. Czerwinski, 748 N.W.2d 645 (Neb. 2008).
7. Niklaus v. Phoenix Indemnity Co., 89 N.W.2d 258, 262 (Neb. 1958).
8. Shipley v. Baillie, 547 N.W.2d 711, 714-15 (Neb. 1996) (citing Spittler v. Nicola, 479 N.W.2d 803 (1992)).
9. Erftmier v. Eickhoff, 316 N.W.2d 754 (Neb. 1982).
10. *Id.*

1.2 Other Suretyship Relationships

While not the focus of this survey, we note that a suretyship relationship may also arise because of the pledge of collateral.[11] As such, a guaranty-type relationship arises, to the extent of the collateral pledged, when a person supplies collateral for a loan in order to induce the creditor to lend to the debtor or where one party pledges property to a creditor to secure the debt of another.[12]

§ 2 State Law Requirements for an Entity to Enter a Guaranty

Corporations, partnerships, limited partnerships, limited liability companies, and banks can all grant guaranties in furtherance of their business activities. Such grants are generally permitted by the appropriate Nebraska statute.

2.1 Corporations

Under Nebraska's Business Corporation Act, a Nebraska corporation has the power to do all things necessary or convenient to carry out its business and affairs and may make contracts and guaranties, unless its articles of incorporation provide otherwise.[13]

2.2 Partnerships

Nebraska's Uniform Partnership Act of 1998[14], does not expressly empower or prohibit a partnership from making a guaranty. Case law indicates that a partnership can be a primary obligor, and there is no authority suggesting a partnership cannot also be a guarantor.[15]

2.3 Limited Partnerships

As is the case regarding partnerships, Nebraska's Uniform Limited Partnership Act[16] does not expressly empower or prohibit a limited partnership from making a guaranty; however, there is no authority suggesting a limited partnership cannot be a guarantor.

---

11. *See* Restatement (Third) of Suretyship and Guaranty § 1 (noting that a person is a surety when "pursuant to contract . . . an obligee has recourse against [that] person . . . *or against that person's property* with respect to an obligation . . . of another person . . . to the Obligee" (emphasis added)).
12. *See, e.g.,* Bock v. Bank of Bellevue, 230 Neb. 908 (1989); *Also see* § 9, *infra*.
13. Neb. Rev. Stat. § 21-2025(7).
14. Neb. Rev. St. § 67-401, et seq.
15. Ravenna Bank v. Custom Unlimited, 223 Neb. 540, 391 N.W.2d 557 (Neb. 1986) ("Applying the foregoing law of partnership to the present case, Custom Unlimited's promissory note was a contract creating a partnership debt owed the bank. The Guaranty was a separate undertaking by Navratil and Pabian, individuals distinct from the partnership entity, that is, an agreement to pay Custom Unlimited's debt on default by that partnership.").
16. Neb. Rev. Stat. § 67-233, et seq.

2.4 Limited Liability Companies

There are currently two Acts applicable to Nebraska limited liability companies (LLCs): the Limited Liability Company Act and the Uniform Limited Liability Company Act.[17] Nebraska is only one of five states to have enacted the Uniform Limited Liability Company Act. The Uniform Limited Liability Company Act currently governs only LLCs formed on or after January 1, 2011, and the Limited Liability Company Act currently governs all LLCs formed before January 1, 2011, that have not filed an election for early treatment under the Uniform Limited Liability Company Act. However, beginning January 1, 2013, the Uniform Limited Liability Company Act will govern all LLCs.[18] Both Acts permit LLCs to do all things necessary or convenient to carry on their activities, including making contracts and guaranties.[19]

2.5 Banks and Trust Companies

Nebraska statutes do not expressly authorize Nebraska banks or trust companies to serve as guarantors. However, Nebraska's "wild card" statute permits banks chartered by the state to exercise the powers authorized to a federally chartered bank doing business in Nebraska, including the exercise of all powers and activities that are permitted for a financial subsidiary of a federally chartered bank.[20] Pursuant to this statute, a state bank may serve as guarantor in those circumstances under which a national banking association or its financial subsidiary doing business in Nebraska may serve as a guarantor.[21]

We are not aware of any comparable authority for a Nebraska trust company to serve as a guarantor.

2.6 Individuals

Individuals can be guarantors in Nebraska. Confusion can sometimes arise in the case of corporate officers or directors of closely held corporations or other organizations signing guaranties. In such instances, courts must conduct a case-by-case inquiry to determine whether an individual intended to be personally bound or, instead, only issued a guaranty as an agent on behalf of a corporation or other entity.[22] The fact that an individual signs his title as well as his name is not dispositive proof that the individual did not intend to make a personal guaranty.[23]

While a corporation must have "authority" to make a guaranty, an individual guarantor must have the "capacity" to make a guaranty. An individual can use incapacity as a defense against the enforcement of a guaranty.[24]

---

17. Neb. Rev. Stat. §§ 21-101, et seq. & 21-2601, et seq.
18. Neb. Rev. Stat. §§ 21-197.
19. Neb. Rev. Stat. §§ 21-105 & 21-2603.
20. Neb. Rev. Stat. 8-1,140.
21. *See* National Bank as a Guarantor or Surety on Indemnity Bond, 12 C.F.R. 7.1017 (2012).
22. 780 L.L.C. v. DiPrima, 611 N.W.2d 637 (Neb. App. 2000).
23. *Id.*
24. Schultz v. Rogers, 171 N.W. 910, 911 (Neb. 1919).

There does not appear to be any Nebraska case law addressing marital property issues in the context of guaranties.

§ 3 Signatory's Authority to Execute a Guaranty

Generally, the obligee has a duty of reasonable inquiry when it has some notice that the executor of the guaranty does not have authority to bind the guarantor.

3.1 Corporations

For an obligee to rely on a guaranty of a corporation, the guaranty must be signed by an officer (i.e., the agent) of the corporation (i.e., the principal) with actual or apparent authority to act in this capacity.[25] A principal is not bound if the agent exceeds the scope of his authority and the absence of authority is known to the person dealing with him or if the third person knows or should know the limitation of the agent's authority. Apparent authority is not limitless; therefore, where an obligee is dealing with a principal's agent and the agent appears to have apparent or ostensible authority to bind the principal, the obligee must use reasonable diligence and prudence to ascertain whether the agent acts within the scope of his powers.[26] An obligee dealing with an agent of a guarantor corporation assumes the risk of lack of authority in the agent, cannot "blindly trust" the agent's assertion of authority, and cannot charge the principal by relying on the agent's assumption of authority which proves to be unfounded.[27]

Generally, an officer of a corporation has authority to act only where: (a) the corporation's bylaws so provide; (b) authority has been expressly conferred on him by statute, law, or the act of the directors; (c) the action is properly incidental to the business entrusted to him by the directors; or (d) the action is within his ostensible authority or ratified by proper authority.[28]

In the absence of restriction by statute, articles of incorporation, or corporate bylaws, the president of a corporation, by the very nature of that office, is the head of the corporation, its general agent, chief executive officer, and general manager of corporate affairs.[29] Generally, there is a presumption that acts of corporate officers pertaining to ordinary corporate business transactions are authorized by the corporation; if, however, a corporate officer acts outside the scope of ordinary business, no presumption of authority arises and the other party to the transaction is required to make an inquiry into the officer's authority.[30]

25. *See* Draemel v. Rufenacht, Bromagen & Hertz, Inc., 392 N.W.2d 759 (Neb. 1986).
26. Nebraska Tractor & Equipment Co. v. Great Lakes Pipe Line Co., 56 N.W.2d 288, 293 (Neb. 1953).
27. *Id.*
28. *See* McGowan Grain, Inc. v. Sanburg, 403 N.W.2d 340, 349 (Neb. 1987).
29. *Id.*
30. Western Fertilizer and Cordage Co., Inc. v. BRG, Inc., 424 N.W.2d 588 (Neb. 1988).

3.2 Partnerships

Under Nebraska's Uniform Partnership Act of 1998, each partner is an agent of the general partnership for the purpose of its business. Accordingly, unless otherwise provided in the partnership's statement of authority—which may identify the authority, or limitations of the authority, of some or all of the partners—any partner may act for the partnership in carrying on the ordinary course of the partnership's business, including executing instruments in the name of the partnership.[31] However, if the partner had no authority to act for the partnership in the particular matter and the person with whom the partner was dealing knew or had received a notification that the partner lacked authority, then the partner's actions will not bind the partnership.[32] An act of a partner which is not apparently for carrying on in the ordinary course the partnership business or business of the kind carried on by the partnership binds the partnership only if the act was authorized by the other partners.[33]

3.3 Limited Partnerships

Under Nebraska's Uniform Limited Partnership Act, a general partner of the limited partnership has the rights and powers, and is subject to the restrictions, of a partner in a partnership without limited partners (i.e., a general partnership).[34] The Uniform Partnership Act of 1998 governs any cases not provided for in the Nebraska Uniform Limited Partnership Act.[35] Accordingly, a general partner may act for the partnership in the ordinary course of business in accordance with the Uniform Partnership Act of 1998 discussed above, which includes executing instruments in the name of the limited partnership.

3.4 Limited Liability Companies

Nebraska's Limited Liability Company Act provides that debt shall not be contracted and liability shall not be incurred by or on behalf of a LLC except by a manager, if management of the LLC has been vested in a manager, or by a member of one or more classes, if management of the LLC is retained by a member of such class.[36]

Under Nebraska's Uniform Limited Liability Company Act, a member of a LLC is not its agent solely by reason of being a member.[37] One should look to the LLC's operating agreement and/or statement of authority—which may identify the authority, or limitations of the authority, of some or all of the members—to determine who has authority to act on behalf of the LLC.[38]

31. Neb. Rev. Stat. § 67-413 – 415.
32. *Id.*
33. *Id.*
34. Neb. Rev. Stat. § 67-256.
35. Neb. Rev. Stat. § 67-294.
36. Neb. Rev. Stat. § 21-2616.
37. Neb. Rev. Stat. § 21-126.
38. Neb. Rev. Stat. §§ 21-110 & 21-127.

A LLC is considered to be member-managed unless the operating agreement provides otherwise.[39] If there is no operating agreement and/or statement of authority, or they do not address the issue, then the default rules under the Uniform Limited Liability Company Act apply.

Generally speaking, under the default rules, it seems that any member or manager could bind the LLC to a contract that is entered into in the ordinary course of the LLC's business, but unanimous consent of all members or managers is required to enter into a contract outside of the LLC's ordinary course of business.[40] The Uniform Limited Liability Company Act was only recently enacted, and there is no case law interpreting a member's or manager's ability to bind a LLC under the default rules.

3.5 Banks and Trust Companies

Executive officers of a Nebraska bank must apply for and obtain from the Nebraska Department of Banking and Finance a license prior to acting as an executive officer of the bank.[41] The authority of an officer of a Nebraska bank is generally determined by reference to the bank's corporate governance documents and the Nebraska Business Corporation Act.

§ 4 Consideration; Sufficiency of Past Consideration

Standard contract principles apply to the analysis of consideration for a guaranty. The underlying obligation is sufficient consideration for an accompanying guaranty. Past consideration can be sufficient if all agreements relate to the same transaction.

A guaranty is interpreted using the same general rules as are used for other contracts; therefore, consideration must exist to create a valid guaranty.[42] Consideration exists if there is a benefit on one side, or a detriment suffered or a service done on the other.[43] The benefit rendered does not have to be to the contracting party, but may be to anyone else at the contracting party's procurement or request.[44] Moreover, the consideration of a contract does not need to move to the promisor, and a disadvantage to the promisee is sufficient although the promisor receives no benefit.[45]

The passage of time between consideration of the underlying obligation and a guaranty does not necessarily invalidate the guaranty.[46] Instruments made in reference to and as a part of the same transaction should be consid-

39. Neb. Rev. Stat. § 21-136.
40. *Id.*
41. *See* Neb. Rev. Stat. 8-139.
42. Bock v. Bank of Bellevue, 434 N.W.2d 310, 314 (Neb. 1989); Nogg Bros. Paper Co. v. Bickels, 446 N.W.2d 729 (Neb. 1989).
43. Erftmier v. Eickhoff, 316 N.W.2d 754, 758 (Neb. 1982).
44. *Id.;* Grady v. Denbeck, 251 N.W.2d 164 (Neb. 1977).
45. *Id.;* Musser v. Zurcher, 146 N.W.2d 559 (Neb. 1966).
46. Home Sav. Bank of Fremont v. Shallenberger, 146 N.W. 993 (Neb. 1914) (principal obligor signed promissory note on December 16, 1902, while guarantor signed personal guaranty on December 30, 1902).

ered and construed together, regardless of whether they were made or dated at different times.[47] Generally, when a guaranty is entered into subsequent to the underlying obligation, the guarantor's promise must be in writing and supported by a consideration which is distinct from that of the underlying obligation.[48] However, it is not an absolute rule that there must be separate and distinct consideration for a guaranty executed subsequent to the underlying obligation.[49] A guaranty made subsequent to the underlying obligation is still founded on consideration if the guarantor gave a promise in connection with the underlying obligation, and the underlying obligation was induced or created on the faith of the guaranty.[50]

§ 5 Notice of Acceptance

Under Nebraska law, no notice of acceptance is required for a guaranty of payment.[51] Moreover, a guaranty typically includes a statement that a guarantor waives the notification of acceptance requirement.

§ 6 Interpretation of Guaranties

Courts in Nebraska are guided by the principle of *strictissimi juris* in determining the effect of a guaranty, strictly construing the guarantor's obligations. In addition, certain terms have become words of art in the context of guaranties. In other regards, courts will interpret a guaranty in the same manner by which they would interpret the language of any other contract.

6.1 General Principles

Nebraska courts adhere to the rule of strict construction of guaranties, and adhere to the rule of *strictissimi juris* in determining the effect of a guaranty.[52] When the meaning of the contract is ascertained, or its terms are clearly defined, the guarantor's liability is controlled absolutely by such meaning and limited to the precise terms.[53] A guarantor's liability is not to be enlarged beyond the strict terms of the guaranty.[54]

---

47. Northland Mortgage Co. v. Royalwood Estates, Inc., 206 N.W.2d (Neb. 1973).
48. Spittler v. Nicola, 479 N.W.2d 803 (Neb. 1992); Neb. Rev. Stat. § 36-202.
49. *Id.*
50. *Id.;* In re Estate of Tynan, 7 N.W.2d 628 (Neb. 1943).
51. *See* Nogg Bros. Paper Co. v. Bickels, 446 N.W.2d 729 (Neb. 1989); *Standard Oil Co. v. Hoese,* 78 N.W. 292 (Neb. 1899); *Lininger v. Wheat,* 68 N.W. 941 (Neb. 1896); *Wilcox v. Draper,* 10 N.W. 579 (Neb. 1881).
52. Federal Deposit Ins. Corp. v. Heyne, 417 N.W.2d 162 (Neb. 1987).
53. *Id.*
54. *Id.;* Furst v. Kruger, 271 N.W. 156 (Neb. 1937).

Outside of this principle, and certain terms of art outlined below, the same principles of construction that apply to contracts generally apply to guaranties.[55]

6.2 Guaranty of Payment versus Guaranty of Collection

Under a "guaranty of payment," a guarantor promises that, if debt owed by the primary obligor is not paid when due, the guarantor will pay it according to its terms without regard to whether the obligee has exhausted all remedies against the primary obligor.[56] On the other hand, under a "guaranty of collection," a guarantor undertakes an obligation to pay the obligee only after the obligee has exhausted all reasonable means of collection against the primary obligor.[57]

Since a guaranty is interpreted using the same general rules as are used for other contracts, a written contract expressed in unambiguous language is not subject to rules of construction, and the intention of the parties regarding whether the guaranty is one of payment or performance must be determined from the contents of the guaranty.[58]

6.3 Language regarding the Revocation of Guaranties

Guaranties are governed and interpreted using the same general rules as are used for other contracts and are strictly construed.[59] Accordingly, while there is no Nebraska case law analyzing language in a guaranty regarding revocation, a guaranty that is "irrevocable" should not be revoked with respect to transactions entered into by the primary obligor prior to the revocation. If the guaranty is for an indefinite period of time, the guarantor should be able to revoke the guaranty with regard to future liability by giving the obligee notice of the revocation.

6.4 "Continuing"

A continuing guaranty is a contract pursuant to which a party agrees to be a secondary obligor for all future obligations of the primary obligor to the obligee.[60] Nebraska courts have interpreted a guaranty as continuing even where the word "continuing" has not been used.[61]

---

55. Spittler v. Nicola, 479 N.W.2d 803 (Neb. 1992).
56. Nogg Bros. Paper Co. v. Bickels, 446 N.W.2d 729 (Neb. 1989).
57. *Id.; Sawyer*, 558 N.W.2d at 47.
58. *Id.;* Aetna Life Ins. Co. v. Anderson, 848 F.2d 104 (8th Cir.1988); First Trust Co. v. Airedale Ranch & Cattle Co., 136 Neb. 521, 286 N.W. 766 (1939).
59. State ex rel. Wagner v. Amwest Sur. Ins. Co., 738 N.W.2d 805 (Neb. 2007); *Heyne*, 417 N.W.2d 162.
60. Restatement (Third) of Suretyship and Guaranty § 16.
61. *See* Murphy v. Stuart Fertilizer Co., Inc., 380 N.W.2d 631 (Neb. 1986).

6.5 "Absolute and Unconditional"

Nebraska courts will strictly enforce provisions in guaranties indicating that the guarantor is absolutely and unconditionally guarantying an underlying obligation.[62] When the guaranty is unambiguous, courts will not vary its terms and limit the guarantor's liability by attempting to construe the meaning of the guaranty with another instrument.[63] The guaranty contains the express conditions of the guarantor's liability and defines the guarantor's and obligee's rights, and the presence of a credit limit in a separate credit agreement does not create a limit in the corresponding guaranty.[64]

§ 7 Defenses of the Guarantor; Set-off

The defenses that may be available to a guarantor can be grouped into three categories: (1) defenses of the primary obligor; (2) "suretyship defenses"; and (3) other defenses.

7.1 Defenses of the Primary Obligor

7.1.1 Defenses that may not be raised by Guarantor

The guarantor cannot use defenses that are personal to the primary obligor as defenses to its obligations pursuant to the guaranty.[65] For example, a primary obligor may assert that the underlying obligation is unenforceable against it because the primary obligor lacked the capacity or authority to enter into the underlying obligation.[66] If the underlying obligation is not void, but is merely unenforceable against the primary obligor because of a defense which is personal to the primary obligor, such as incapacity or lack of authority, the guarantor may still be liable on its guaranty because such defenses were personal to the primary obligor.[67]

7.1.2 Defenses that may be raised by Guarantor

There are other instances where a guarantor steps into the shoes of the primary obligor and has the same defenses of the primary obligor.[68] For example, a guarantor may be able to use the statute of limitations as a defense if that is a defense available to the primary obligor.[69] In addition, when the underlying obligation is a promissory note that has been discharged by a written renunciation or surrendered to the primary obligor, any guaranty of the promissory note

62. *See* Builders Supply Co., Inc. v. Czerwinski, 748 N.W.2d 645 (Neb. 2008).
63. *Id.*
64. *Id.*
65. Dept. of Banking of the State of Nebraska v. Keeley, 160 N.W.2d 206 (Neb. 1968).
66. *Id.*
67. *Id.*
68. City of Lincoln v. Hershberger, 725 N.W.2d 787 (2007).
69. *Id.*

is also discharged and the guarantor may assert the discharge of the underlying obligation as a defense.[70]

7.2 "Suretyship" Defenses

7.2.1 *Change in Identity of Principal Obligor*

Whether a change of the identity/corporate structure of the primary obligor discharges the guarantor's obligations depends on the circumstances and must be determined on a case-by-case basis. In making this determination, Nebraska courts place special emphasis on whether the change materially alters the nature of the guarantor's performance, and an alteration of guarantor's risk is particularly pertinent to the inquiry.[71] For example, if the primary obligor was originally a sole proprietorship and later is incorporated, the guarantor's risk may or may not be altered in such a way as to warrant releasing the guarantor from his or her obligations.[72]

7.2.2 *Modification of the Underlying Obligation*

Under Nebraska law, modifications to the underlying obligation may permit the guarantor to raise certain defenses to liability. The Nebraska Supreme Court has held that any material change in the terms of the underlying obligation, made without the guarantor's consent, will release the guarantor from its obligations under the guaranty.[73] In particular, changing the maturity date of the underlying obligation may be deemed to alter the guarantor's risk sufficiently to justify discharging the guarantor's obligations.[74]

However, guarantors will not be relieved of their obligations if they agree in advance to modifications. Nebraska courts will enforce provisions in guaranties in which the guarantor authorizes the lender to make modifications to the underlying obligation without notice to or consent of the guarantor.[75]

It should also be noted that § 3-605 of the Nebraska Uniform Commercial Code provides statutory defenses to an accommodation party's liability when the obligee modifies the underlying obligation in such a way that the accommodation party's right of recourse against the primary obligor is affected. This can apply to guarantors who, by signing the same instrument as the primary obligor, are deemed to be an accommodation party. Like guarantors in general, accommodation parties will not be relieved of their obligations if they consent to the modifications in advance and/or waive defenses based on suretyship.[76]

---

70. J.J. Schaefer Livestock Hauling, Inc. v. Gretna State Bank, 428 N.W.2d 185 (Neb. 1988).
71. NEBCO, Inc. v. Adams, 704 N.W.2d 777 (2005).
72. *Compare* NEBCO, Inc. v. Adams, 704 N.W.2d 777 (Neb. 2005) with Teledyne Mid-America v. HOH Corp., 486 F.2d 987 (9th Cir. 1973).
73. Bash v. Bash, 244 N.W. 788 (Neb. 1932); Hunter v. Huffman, 189 N.W. 166 (Neb. 1922).
74. *Id.*
75. Hastings State Bank v. Misle, 804 N.W.2d 805 (Neb. 2011).
76. Neb. U.C.C. § 3-605(i).

7.2.3 *Release or Impairment of Security for the Underlying Obligation*

An obligee can act or fail to act in such a manner as to impair collateral securing a guaranty and limit the guarantor's liability *pro tanto*. In Nebraska, the general rule is that a guarantor is entitled to be subrogated to the benefit of all the security and means of payment under the obligee's control and is generally released by an act of the obligee that deprives the guarantor of such right.[77] Where the security interest is impaired, the guarantor's liability is reduced to the extent of the impairment.[78]

Despite this general rule, Nebraska courts recognize that the guarantor's defense of release or impairment of security is not available if the guarantor waives the defense, assents to the obligee's acts, or is otherwise estopped from succeeding on the defense.[79] The guarantor's waiver of the defense can be by an express provision in the guaranty agreement or by the guarantor's conduct.[80]

Again, § 3-605 of the Nebraska Uniform Commercial Code provides statutory defenses to an accommodation party's liability when the obligee impairs collateral securing an underlying obligation, although accommodation parties will not be relieved of their obligations if they consent to the impairment of collateral and/or waive defenses based on suretyship.[81]

7.3 Other Defenses

7.3.1 *Obligee's failure to fulfill its Contractual Obligations*

A guarantor may not be liable on its guaranty when the obligee has breached its obligations related to the guaranty, the underlying obligations, and/or related contracts.[82] For example, the obligee's failure to obtain second mortgages on certain real property, contrary to obligee's obligations set forth in a commitment letter signed by both the obligee and the guarantor, relieved the guarantor from its liability pursuant to the guaranty.[83]

7.3.2 *Modification of the Guaranty*

Subsequent to the execution of a guaranty, the modification of such guaranty by new agreements or statements made between the guarantor and obligee may limit a guarantor's obligations under the guaranty if the modification is of such a nature as would substantially change the guarantor's liability.[84]

77. Custom Leasing, Inc. v. Carlson Staple & Shippers Supply, Inc., 237 N.W.2d 645 (Neb. 1976).
78. Production Credit Ass'n of Midlands v. Schmer, 448 N.W.2d 123 (Neb. 1989).
79. Builders Supply Co., Inc. v Czerwkinski, 748 N.W.2d 645 (Neb. 2008).
80. *Id.*
81. Neb. U.C.C. § 3-605(e) & (i).
82. *See* Nat'l Bank of Commerce Trust & Sav. Ass'n v. Katelman, 266 N.W.2d 736 (Neb. 1978); Custom Leasing, Inc. v. Carlson Stapler & Shippers Supply, Inc., 237 N.W.2d 645 (Neb. 1976).
83. 266 N.W.2d 736.
84. Lease Northwest, Inc. v. Davis, 400 N.W.2d 220 (Neb. 1987).

Modification of a guaranty is an affirmative defense, and must be specifically pled to be considered.[85]

7.3.3 Failure to pursue Primary Obligor

When a guaranty is absolute and unconditional, the obligee may maintain an action against the guarantor immediately upon the primary obligor's default, without demand upon the primary obligor or without first proceeding against the primary obligor.[86] Under an absolute guaranty of payment, the guarantor is obligated to pay the indebtedness according to its terms without regard to whether the obligee has exhausted it remedies against the primary obligor.[87]

If the guaranty is a guaranty of collection, the guarantor is obligated to pay the indebtedness to the obligee only after the obligee has exhausted all reasonable means of collection against the primary obligor.[88]

7.3.4 Statute of Limitations

Under Nebraska law, with limited exceptions not applicable to guaranties, an action upon any agreement, contract, or written promise (including a guaranty) must be brought within five years after a cause of action first accrues.[89] In the absence of provisions to the contrary in the guaranty, a cause of action does not accrue against a guarantor until the guarantor's liability has arisen by virtue of the primary obligor's default.[90]

While a primary obligor's partial payment of an underlying obligation may operate to toll the statute of limitations as to the primary obligor,[91] such partial payment does not toll the statute of limitations as to the guarantor if the partial payment was made without the guarantor's authority or consent.[92]

7.3.5 Statute of Frauds

Nebraska's statute of frauds provides that a guaranty must be in writing and signed by the guarantor to be enforceable.[93] An oral agreement to pay a primary obligor's underlying obligation, without any new consideration moving to the promisor, is within the statute of frauds and is unenforceable.[94]

However, Nebraska common law also recognizes the "leading object exception" to the statute of frauds.[95] Under this exception, a promise to answer for the debt of another will be valid, although not in writing, when the main objective of the party promising to pay the debt is to promote his or her own interests, rather than to become a guarantor, and when the promise is made

85. *Id.;* Columbus Bank & Trust Co. v. High Country Stable, 277 N.W.2d 81 (Neb. 1979).
86. Rodehorst v. Gartner, 669 N.W.2d 679 (Neb. 2003) (citing 38 Am. Jur. 2d Guaranty § 105).
87. *Id.;* Transamerica Commercial Fin. Corp. v. Rochford, 509 N.W.2d (Neb. 1993).
88. *Nogg Bros. Paper Co. v. Bickels*, 446 N.W.2d 729 (Neb. 1989).
89. Neb. Rev. Stat. § 25-205; City of Lincoln v. PMI Franchising, 675 N.W.2d 660 (Neb. 2004).
90. *Id.*
91. *See* Pick v. Pick, 171 N.W.2d 766 (Neb. 1969).
92. W.T. Rawleigh Co. v. Smith, 9 N.W.2d 286 (Neb. 1943).
93. Neb. Rev. Stat. § 36-202.
94. Otto Gas, Inc. v. Stewart, 69 N.W.2d 545 (Neb. 1955).
95. Christian v. Smith, 759 N.W.2d 447 (Neb. 2008).

on sufficient consideration. The consideration must operate to the advantage of the promisor, and must also place him under a pecuniary obligation to the obligee independent of the underlying obligation, which obligation is to be discharged by the payment of the underlying obligation.[96]

7.3.6 Right of Set-off

A guarantor can set off an individual claim that he has against the obligee. A claim which would entitle the guarantor to a set-off must be one which the guarantor could have maintained as an independent action against the obligee.[97] However, when a guarantor's set-off claims arise from payments of the primary obligor's obligations to parties other than the obligee, the guarantor is not entitled to a set-off of that amount against the obligee.[98]

§ 8 Waiver of Defenses by the Guarantor

Nebraska courts will strictly enforce a guarantor's waiver of defenses in a guaranty. For example, a guarantor cannot avail himself to the defense that the obligee improperly extended the time of payment of the underlying obligation when the guaranty contained a provision indicating that the guarantor waives "all defenses by reason of extending the time of payment [of the underlying obligation]."[99] As another example, a guarantor cannot use the obligee's release of collateral securing an underlying obligation when the guaranty contained a provision authorizing the obligee to "give and make such extensions, renewals...settlements and compromises as it may deem proper with respect to the [underlying obligation]...including the taking or releasing of security."[100]

In strictly enforcing waivers, the Nebraska Supreme Court has stated that if it were to disregard a waiver provision in a guaranty, it would effectively be deleting terms from the guaranty, which it is unwilling to do.[101]

§ 9 Third-party Pledgors—Defenses and Waiver Thereof

Nebraska case law suggests that a third party's pledge of collateral to secure a primary obligor's underlying obligation results in a surety relationship.[102] While there is very little case law on the issue, its appears that the pledgor

96. *Id.*
97. First Westroads Bank v. Opstein, 1994 Neb. App. Lexis 211; *(citing* American Gas Construction Co. v. Lisco, 241 N.W. 89 (Neb. 1932)).
98. *First Westroads Bank,* 1994 Neb. App. Lexis 211.
99. First Nat'l Bank, Stromsburg v. Benedict Consolidated Indus., Inc., 402 N.W.2d 259 (Neb. 1987).
100. Myers v. Bank of Niobrara, 336 N.W.2d 608 (Neb. 1983).
101. First Nat'l Bank v. Benedict Consolidated Indus., Inc., 402 N.W.2d 259 (Neb. 1987).
102. McCormack v. First Westroads Bank, 473 N.W.2d 102 (Neb. 1991).

generally has the same defenses available to it as are available to a guarantor, and can also voluntarily waive such defenses pursuant to the terms of the written pledge agreement.[103]

§ 10 Contribution among Jointly and Severally Liable Guarantors

Guarantors who are jointly and severally liable are presumed to share the secondary obligation equally. The obligee is not obliged to seek full payment from more than one such guarantor.

Where coguarantors are liable to the obligee with respect to the same underlying obligation, one of the guarantors who satisfies more than its proportionate share of the underlying obligation is entitled to seek equitable contribution from the other guarantors for their proportionate share.[104] Moreover, the right of contribution exists between coguarantors whether they are designated as guarantors, sureties, accommodation makers, or otherwise, provided they are liable with respect to the same underlying obligation. [105]

§ 11 Reliance

Reliance is probably not required to claim under a guaranty.

Under Nebraska law, guaranties are governed and interpreted using the same general rules as are used for other contracts.[106] Presumably, then, reliance by the obligee is not requisite to enforce a guaranty. However, reliance can be used to bring a claim of promissory estoppel.[107] Reliance is necessary in order to bind a principal on the theory of apparent authority.[108]

§ 12 Subrogation

Subrogation is an equitable remedy and is the substitution of one person in the place of another with reference to a lawful claim, demand, or right, so that the one who is substituted succeeds to the rights of the other in relation to the debt or claim, and its rights, remedies, or securities.

---

103. *Id.*
104. Rodehorst v. Gartner, 669 N.W.2d 679 (Neb. 2003); Exchange Elevator Co. v. Marshall, 22 N.W.2d 403 (Neb. 1946).
105. *Id.;* Rogers v. National Sur. Co., 216 N.W. 182 (Neb. 1927).
106. State ex rel. Wagner v. Amwest Sur. Ins. Co., 738 N.W.2d 805 (Neb. 2007).
107. *See, e.g.,* Cass County Bank v. Dana P'ship, 750 N.W.2d 701 (Neb. 2008).
108. StoreVisions, Inc. v. Omaha Tribe of Neb., 795 N.W.2d 271 (Neb. 2011).

Generally, courts apply the doctrine of subrogation to promote equity and achieve the ends of justice.[109] The doctrine of subrogation applies where a party is compelled to pay the debt of a third person to protect his or her own rights or interest, or to save his or her own property, and applies equally to guaranties of payment and performance.[110] The general rule is that a subrogee is entitled to indemnity to the extent only of the money actually paid by him to discharge the obligation.[111] Generally, subrogation is available when the claim of an obligee has been paid in full.[112] For this reason, there is usually no partial subrogation, although statutory exceptions have been made in the case of automobile insurance policies.[113]

In the context of insurance, the right of subrogation is based on two premises: (1) an insured should not be allowed to recover twice for the same loss, which would be the result if the insured recovers from both the insured's insurer and the tortfeasor, and (2) a wrongdoer should reimburse an insurer for payments that the insurer has made to its insured.[114] Under principles of equity, an insurer is entitled to subrogation only when the insured has received, or would receive, a double payment by virtue of an insured's recovering payment of all or part of those same damages from the tortfeasor. An insurer should not recover sums received by the insured from the tortfeasor until the insured has been fully indemnified.[115]

§ 13 Indemnification—Whether the Primary Obligor has a Duty

Generally, when the guarantor pays the underlying obligation for the primary obligor, the law creates an implied promise on the part of the primary obligor to repay the guarantor.

When a guarantor has entered into a guaranty upon the primary obligor's request or consent and, pursuant to the guaranty, pays or is compelled to pay the underlying obligation, Nebraska law provides for an implied promise on the part of the primary obligor to reimburse the guarantor.[116] As a result of the implied promise, after the guarantor pays the underlying obligation, the guarantor has the immediate right of action against the primary obligor for reimbursement of the amount which he has paid.[117] The implied promise, and the primary obligor's obligation to reimburse the guarantor for any amount

109. Universal Underwriters Ins. Co. v. Farm Bureau Ins. Co. of Nebraska, 498 N.W.2d 333 (Neb. 1993).
110. Tri-Par Investments, L.L.C. v. Sousa, 680 N.W.2d 190 (Neb. 2004); Pearlman v. Reliance Ins. Co., 371 U.S. 132, 139 (1962).
111. *Ehlers v. Perry,* 494 N.W.2d 325 (Neb. 1993).
112. Blue Cross & Blue Shield, Inc. v. Dailey, 687 N.W.2d 689 (Neb. 2004).
113. *Id.;* Neb. Rev. Stat. § 44-3,128.01 Neb. Rev. Stat. allows an automobile liability insurance policy to contain a provision permitting pro rata subrogation in the situation where the insured did not fully recover his or her loss.
114. *Id.*
115. *Id.;* Continental Western Ins. Co. v. Swartzendruber, 570 N.W.2d 708 (Neb. 1997).
116. O.K. Door Co. v. Lincoln Eng. Const. Co., 119 N.W.2d 153 (Neb. 1963).
117. *Id.;* McKeeman v. Commercial Credit Equip. Corp., 320 F.Supp. 938 (D.C. Neb. 1970).

of money the guarantor paid the obligee, may be altered by an express agreement between the parties.[118]

§ 14 Enforcement of Guaranties under Nebraska Law

14.1 Exercising Rights under a Guaranty Where the Underlying Obligation is also Secured by a Deed of Trust

Pursuant to the Nebraska Trust Deeds Act,[119] the obligee must file its lawsuit to collect a deficiency against the primary obligor within three months after the date of the foreclosure sale.[120] A lender may also pursue a deficiency action against any guarantor of the primary obligor's underlying obligation. When pursuing a guarantor for a deficiency, the shortened three-month statute of limitations applicable to the primary obligor does not apply.[121]

14.2 Litigating Guaranty Claims: Attorneys' Fees are not Recoverable

A party may recover attorneys' fees and expenses in a civil action only when a statute permits recovery or when the Nebraska Supreme Court has recognized and accepted a uniform course of procedure for allowing attorneys' fees.[122] On numerous occasions, the Nebraska Supreme Court has held that a contract provision providing for attorneys' fees in connection with a lawsuit to enforce a contract was void as against public policy.[123]

§ 15 Conflict of Laws—Choice of Law

Generally, the law of the place where a contract was made—lex loci contratus—determines the validity of a contract, unless the terms of the agreement expressly violate a statute or positive public policy.[124] If a contract states that the law of a particular jurisdiction is applicable and that state bears some

118. *Id.*
119. Neb. Rev. Stat. § 76-1001 et seq.
120. Neb. Rev. Stat. § 76-1013; *See* Sports Courts of Omaha v. Meginnis, 497 N.W.2d 38 (Neb. 1993).
121. Boxum v. Munce, 751 N.W.2d 657 (Neb. App. 2008). The Nebraska Court of Appeals, noting that it was a case of first impression, held that the three-month statute of limitations does not apply to guarantors. The Nebraska Court of Appeals based its ruling on the language of Neb. Rev. Stat. § 76-1013, which states that the lender may commence an action "to recover the balance due *upon the obligation for which the trust deed was given as security*" within three months after the foreclosure sale (emphasis added). According to the Nebraska Court of Appeals, a guaranty from a third party, unlike a promissory note from the principal obligor, is not an obligation secured by a trust deed; rather, a guaranty is a separate and independent contractual obligation, and is itself further security for the principal obligation, and the five-year statute of limitations on actions on any agreements, contracts, or written promises, Neb. Rev. Stat. § 25-205, applies to deficiency lawsuits against guarantors.
122. Wetovick v. County of Nance, 782 N.W.2d 298 (Neb. 2010).
123. *See, e.g., Id.;* Quinn v. Godfather's Investments, 348 N.W.2d 893 (Neb. 1984).
124. Jaramillo v. Mercury Ins. Co., 494 N.W.2d 335 (Neb. 1993).

relationship to the transaction, if the contract is enforceable, it will be enforced under that state's law.[125] Where a guaranty is executed and to be performed in Nebraska, absent a contractual provision to the contrary, Nebraska courts will apply domestic law to determine the effect of the guaranty.[126]

125. Shull v. Kalman & Quail, Inc., 267 N.W.2d 517 (Neb. 1978); Exchange Bank & Trust Co. v. Tamerius, 265 N.W.2d 847 (Neb. 1978).

126. *See* Dunlop Tire & Rubber Corp. v. Ryan, 108 N.W.2d 84 (Neb. 1961); U.S. v. Ryan, 334 F.Supp. 1345 (D. Neb. 1972).

Nevada State Law of Guaranties

Jim Mace
Leslie Godfrey
Greenberg Traurig, LLP
3773 Howard Hughes Parkway, Suite 400 N
Las Vegas, Nevada 89169
(702) 792-3773
(702) 792-9002
macej@gtlaw.com
godfreyl@gtlaw.com
www.gtlaw.com

GT GreenbergTraurig

Contents

Nevada State Law of Guaranties

Introduction and Sources of Law

This survey discusses Nevada state law applicable to guaranties of commercial credit transactions. Nevada does not have a substantial body of law on guaranties and related subjects. Although Nevada has some statutes that bear on a lender's ability to enforce a guaranty, most of Nevada's law on guaranties is contained within Nevada Supreme Court cases. Nevada courts and federal courts interpreting Nevada law generally apply contract interpretation principles to any type of guaranty.[1] A guarantor's liability is strictly construed and its specific application will not be extended beyond the precise provisions of the guaranty to include a principal other than the one expressly named therein.[2] Only one Nevada case has referred to the Restatement of Suretyship[3], and four Nevada cases refer to the Restatement of Security.[4] Accordingly, it cannot be said that Nevada follows these Restatements on a regular basis.

NEVADA LAW HIGHLIGHTS

1. All Nevada contracts are interpreted using basic principles of contract law. A guarantor's liability is strictly construed based upon the express terms of the contract. *See* § 6 below.
2. A guarantor is entitled to the protections set forth in Nevada's antideficiency statutes. *See* § 11 below.
3. Recent changes to Nevada's antideficiency statutes may ensure that guarantors receive credit for the value of any real property collateral securing the underlying obligation, even if that real property has not been or cannot be foreclosed upon. Appeals to the Nevada Supreme Court are currently in process. *See* § 10.6 below.
4. Recent changes to Nevada's antideficiency statutes may ensure that guarantors are only obligated to pay the difference between the value that a loan purchaser paid to purchase the promissory note and the value of the property securing the debt. Appeals to the Nevada Supreme Court are currently in process. *See* § 10.4 below.

---

1. Dobron v. Del Bunch Jr., 125 Nev. 36, 215 P.3d 35 (Nev. 2009).
2. Adelson v. Wilson & Co., 81 Nev. 15, 398 P.2d 106 (Nev. 1965).
3. Dobron v. Del Bunch Jr., 125 Nev. 36, 215 P.3d 35 (Nev. 2009).
4. American Bonding Co. v. Roggen Enterprises, 109 Nev. 588, 854 P.2d 868 (Nev. 1993); Gearhart v. Pierce Enterprises, Inc., 105 Nev. 517, 779 P.2d 93 (Nev. 2004); Investors of Nevada Realty, Inc. v. Nevada State Bank, 98 Nev. 33, 639 P.2d 554 (Nev. 1982); Zuni Construction Co. v. Great American Insurance Co., 86 Nev. 364, 468 P.2d 980 (Nev. 1970).

Introductory Note: In order to standardize our discussion of the law of guaranties, we use the following vocabulary to refer to the various parties to a guaranty and their obligations.

"Guarantor" means a person who, by contract, agrees to satisfy an underlying obligation of another to an obligee upon the primary obligor's default on that underlying obligation. We do not draw a distinction between guarantors and sureties, as the distinction in Nevada between the two is often muddled.

"Guaranty" means the contract by which the guarantor agrees to satisfy the underlying obligation of a primary obligor to an obligee in the event the primary obligor defaults on the underlying obligation.

"Obligee" means the person to whom the underlying obligation is owed. For example, the lender under a loan agreement would be an obligee vis-à-vis the borrower.

"Primary Obligor" means the person who incurs the underlying obligation to the obligee. For example, the borrower under a loan agreement would be a primary obligor.

"Underlying Obligation" means the obligation or obligations incurred by the primary obligor and owed to the obligee. For example, the borrower's obligation to make payments to a lender of principal and interest on a loan constitutes an underlying obligation.

§ 1 Nature of the Guaranty Arrangement

1.1 Guaranty Relationships

A guaranty is the undertaking to pay indebtedness if the principal does not pay.[5] Indebtedness is defined for purposes of Nevada's statutes relating to guaranties secured by real property as the principal balance of the obligation together with all accrued and unpaid interest, costs, fees, and advances, and other amounts secured by the mortgage or lien on real property.[6] However, in general, Nevada courts would otherwise interpret indebtedness in accordance with the terms of the guaranty itself.[7]

5. Daly v. Del E. Webb Corp., 96 Nev. 359, 609 P.2d 319 (Nev. 1980).
6. Nev. Rev. Stat. 40.465.
7. Spinella v. B-Neva Inc., 94 Nev. 373, 580 P.2d 945 (Nev. 1978).

1.2 Other Suretyship Relationships

Nevada courts also recognize guaranties of insurance policies, lease agreements, or other obligations not specifically relating to the lending of money.[8] Nevada courts have articulated a distinction between a guarantor and a surety.[9] Specifically, the Nevada Supreme Court has held a guarantor is one whose obligations are wholly separate from the principal obligation guaranteed, whereas sureties are co-obligors with the principal debtor.[10] Although both a surety and a guarantor are bound for another person or entity, a surety is usually bound by the same instrument that binds the principal and is a debtor from the beginning.[11] The guarantor's contract is a separate undertaking with the creditor.[12] A surety's liability is limited to that of the principal, but a guarantor's liability is not.[13] Indeed, Nevada courts have held a guarantor liable even though the statute of limitations had run against the principal obligor.[14] Nonetheless, Nevada courts extend the same defenses to deficiency judgments available to the primary obligor equally to sureties and guarantors.[15] Accordingly, for all intents and purposes with regard to loans secured by real property, a guaranty and suretyship are indistinguishable.[16] Nevada has not adopted the Restatement of Surety.

1.3 Performance Guaranties

Nevada courts generally interpret guaranties pursuant to basic contract principles and recognize obligations set forth in performance guaranties.[17] A person may guarantee the debt, performance, or completion of an obligation of another person, so long as that guaranty is set forth in writing.[18]

1.4 Accommodation Parties

An accommodation party is one who signs the instrument in any capacity for the purpose of lending his name to another party to it.[19] An endorser is a secondary party whose liability is subject to the preconditions of presentment and proper notice of dishonor.[20] By endorsing a check as an accommodation party, the person commits that upon dishonor of the check and any necessary notice of the dishonor and protest, that person will pay the instrument according to the tenor at the time of his or her endorsement.[21]

---

8. H.K.H. Co. v. American Mortg. Ins. Co., 685 F.2d 315 (C.A. Nev. 1982).
9. Thomas v. Valley Bank of Nev., 97 Nev. 320, 323, 629 P.2d 1205, 1207 (1981) *overruled in part on other grounds*, First Interstate Bank v. Shields, 102 Nev. 616, 730 P.2d 429 (1986).
10. *Id.*
11. *Id.*
12. *Id.*
13. *Id*, citing Nevada v. Friedman, 82 Nev. 417, 420 P.2d 1 (1966).
14. Nevada v. Friedman, 82 Nev. 417, 420 P.2d 1 (1966).
15. Component Systems Corp. v. District Court, 101 Nev. 76, 692 P.2d 1296 (1985).
16. *Id.*
17. Spinella v. B-Neva Inc., 94 Nev. 373, 580 P.2d 945 (Nev. 1978).
18. Tore, LTD. v. Church, 105 Nev. 183, 772 P.2d 1281 (Nev. 1989).
19. Nev. Rev. Stat. § 104.3415
20. Nev. Rev. Stat. § 104.3102(1)(d), Nev. Rev. Stat. §104.3501(1)(b), and Nev. Rev. Stat. §104.3501(2)(a).
21. Nev. Rev. Stat. § 104.3414(1) cited by Nevada State Bank v. Fischer, 93 Nev. 317, 565 P.2d 332 (Nev. 1977)

§ 2 State Law Requirements for an Entity to Enter a Guaranty

Because Nevada law construes a guaranty as a contract, any corporation, partnership, limited liability company (LLC), or individual may enter into a guaranty, to the same extent that it is entitled to and has the capacity to enter into a contract.[22]

2.1 Corporations, Partnerships, and Limited Liability Companies

Every corporation, by virtue of its existence as such, unless otherwise provided in the articles, is entitled to engage in any lawful activity, including making contracts.[23] Likewise, a LLC has the power to make contracts and guaranties, incur liabilities, borrow money at such rates of interest as the company may determine, issue its notes, bonds, and other obligations, and secure any of its obligations by mortgage or pledge of all or part of its property, franchise, and income.[24] This power may be limited by the terms of the LLC's operating agreement. Beyond this, Nevada law does not have any specific discussion of the rights of corporations, partnerships, or LLCs' capacity to enter into a guaranty.

2.2 Individuals—Capacity to Contract

Confusion can sometimes arise in the case of corporate officers or directors signing guaranties on behalf of organizations. In such instance, a case-by-case inquiry determines whether an individual intended to be personally bound, or instead, only issued a guaranty on behalf of a partnership or corporation and thus, only in an official employment capacity.[25] If the plain language of the agreement demonstrates that a guarantor intended to be personally liable in addition to liability in his or her corporate capacity, that guaranty is valid against the individual.[26]

2.3 Individuals—Community Property of Spouses and Domestic Partners

Generally, a guaranty obligation made during the marriage may encumber or create recourse to marital assets in Nevada, even without first obtaining the

22. Dobron v. Del Bunch Jr., 125 Nev. 36, 215 P.3d 35 (Nev. 2009).
23. Nev. Rev. Stat. §78.060(2)(c) and (g).
24. Nev. Rev. Stat. §86.281 (6).
25. Trump v. Eighth Judicial Dist. Court of State of Nevada. In and For County of Clark, 109 Nev. 687 (Nev. 1993).
26. Threklkel v. Shenanigan's, Inc., 110 Nev. 1088, 881 P.2d 674 (Nev. 1994).

signature of the nonguarantor spouse.[27] However, if the obligation is incurred by one spouse for the benefit of noncommunity assets, community assets cannot be the subject of enforcement.[28] The standard for determining whether a debt is community or separate entails factually discerning the intent of the lender when granting the loan.[29] A presumption exists that the proceeds of a loan acquired during marriage are community property. The presumption is rebuttable upon a showing that the loan was extended on the faith of existing separate property belonging to the borrower/guarantor spouse.[30]

2.4 Trusts

Nevada law does not have any specific cases or statutes that address the question of whether a trust is entitled to enter into contracts and/or guaranties. However, Nevada law provides family trust companies with a broad range of powers, which presumably include the ability to enter into guaranties.[31] A family trust company is a corporation or LLC that acts or proposes to act as a fiduciary; is organized or qualified to do business in the State of Nevada to serve family members; and does not transact trust company business with, propose to act as a fiduciary for, or solicit trust company business from a person who is not a family member.[32]

§ 3 Signatory's Authority to Execute a Guaranty

In general, a guaranty by an entity must be signed by an officer with actual or apparent authority to do so.[33] A party claiming apparent authority of an agent as a basis for contract formation must prove (1) that he or she subjectively believed that the agent had authority to act for the principal, and (2) that his or her subjective belief in the agent's authority was objectively reasonable.[34] Apparent authority is in essence an application of equitable estoppel, of which reasonable reliance is a necessary element.[35] The party who claims reliance must not have ignored the warnings or inconsistent circumstances.[36]

With regard to partnerships, every partner is an agent of the partnership for purposes of its business, and the act of every partner including the execution in the partnership name of any instrument for apparently carrying on in the usual way the business of the partnership binds the partnership, unless the partner so acting has in fact no authority to act for the partnership in the matter,

27. Jones v. Edwards, 49 Nev. 299, 245 P. 292 (Nev. 1926); Randono v. Turk, 86 Nev. 123, 466 P.2d 218 (Nev. 1970).
28. Barry v. Lindner, 119 Nev. 661 (Nev. 2003).
29. Schulman v. Schulman, 92 Nev. 707, 558 P.2d 525 (Nev. 1976).
30. Norwest Financial v. Lawver, 109 Nev. 242, 849 P.2d 324 (Nev. 1993).
31. Nev. Rev. Stat. § 669A, generally.
32. Nev. Rev. Stat. § 669A.080
33. Great American Ins. Co. v. General Builders, Inc., 113 Nev. 346, 934 P.2d 257 (Nev. 1997).
34. *Id.* at 352.
35. *Id.* Citing Ellis v. Nelson, 68 Nev. 609, 614, 655 P.2d 996, 998-99 (Nev. 1982).
36. *Id.* Citing Tsouras v. Southwest Plumbing and Heating, 94 Nev. 748, 751, 587 P.2d 1321, 1322 (Nev. 1978).

and the person with whom the partner is dealing has knowledge of that fact.[37] Grant of authority contained in a filed statement of partnership authority is conclusive in favor of a person who gives value without knowledge to the contrary so long as and to the extent that a limitation on that authority is not then contained in another filed statement.[38]

With regard to LLCs, typically, management of a LLC company is vested in its members in proportion to their contribution to its capital, as adjusted from time to time to reflect properly any additional contributions or withdrawals of members.[39] However, if provision is made in the articles of organization, management of the company may be vested in a manager or managers, who may but need not be members.[40] In a manager-managed LLC, only the managers can contract for the LLC debts and incur liabilities on its behalf.[41]

Any contract or conveyance made in the name of a corporation, which is authorized or ratified by the directors, or is done within the scope of authority, actual or apparent, given by the directors, binds the corporation and the corporation acquires rights thereunder, whether the contract is signed or is wholly or in part executory.[42]

§ 4 Consideration; Sufficiency of Past Consideration

Nevada does not have any case law addressing the concept of consideration within the context of a guaranty. However, the U.S. Supreme Court has indicated that valuable consideration, "however small or nominal is given or stipulated for in good faith, is in the absence of fraud, sufficient to support an action on any parol contract including contracts of guaranty."[43] Nevada courts would likely follow the Supreme Court's lead, as it is clear that consideration of some kind is required. Nevada courts have addressed the question of when consideration in general and evidence of consideration is sufficient relative to a promissory note.[44] The Nevada courts have held that:

> [T]he consideration of a note can always be inquired into. If the consideration be embraced in the terms of the notes, so as to constitute a part of the agreement knowingly entered upon, it cannot be disputed or denied that the promise as made was based upon the consideration expressed.[45]

> Nevada courts have ruled on the issue of consideration for the release of a guaranty:

> The release of a guarantor is binding upon the creditor only if the agreement possesses the elements of a contract. Releases, then, must be supported by

37. Nev. Rev. Stat. § 87.090(1).
38. Nev. Rev. Stat. § 87.4327.
39. Nev. Rev. Stat. § 86.291(2).
40. Nev. Rev. Stat. § 86.291(3).
41. Nev. Rev. Stat. § 86.301.
42. Nev. Rev. Stat. § 78.135(3).
43. Davis v. Wells, 104 U.S. 159 (1881).
44. Charleston Hill Nat. Mines, Inc., v. Clough, 79 Nev. 182, 380 P.2d 458 (Nev. 1963).
45. *Id.*

> consideration. To constitute consideration, a performance or return promise must be bargained for. A performance or return promise is bargained for if it is sought by the promisor in exchange for his promise and is given by the promise in exchange for that promise.[46]

§ 5 Notice of Acceptance

Nevada courts have not addressed the question of whether notice of acceptance is required in order for a guaranty to be enforceable. Nonetheless, guaranties often contain waivers of any requirement to notify the guarantor of acceptance of the guaranty.

§ 6 Interpretation of Guaranties

6.1 General Principles

In Nevada, general contract interpretation principles apply to interpret any type of guaranty.[47] A guarantor's liability is strictly construed and its specific application will not be extended beyond the precise provisions of the guaranty to include a principal other than the one expressly named therein.[48]

6.2 Guaranty of Payment versus Guaranty of Collection

Nevada courts have not addressed the distinction between a guaranty of payment and a guaranty of collection.

6.3 Continuing Guaranties

Nevada courts have recognized a continuing guaranty under which a guarantor may contract to be liable for future obligations of the primary obligor.[49] However, a continuing guaranty may be later revoked by the guarantor. Nevada courts have held that revocation of a continuing guaranty must be executed by each guarantor who seeks to revoke it or the revocation will be effective only as to the person who gave the notice.[50] Further, a notice of revocation must be clear in its terms and positive.[51]

---

46. Pink v. Busch, 100 685, 691 P.2d 456 (Nev. 1984).
47. Dobron v. Del Bunch Jr., 125 Nev. 36, 215 P.3d 35 (Nev. 2009).
48. Adelson v. Wilson & Co., 81 Nev. 15, 398 P.2d 106 (Nev. 1965).
49. Tobler & Oliver Const. Corp. v. Nevada State Bank, 89 Nev. 269, 510 P.2d 1364 (Nev. 1973).
50. Brunzell v. Golden Gate Nat'l Bank, 85 Nev. 345, 455 P.2d 31 (Nev. 1969).
51. *Id.*

6.4 Absolute and Unconditional Guaranty

Nevada courts have recognized absolute and unconditional guaranties.[52] However, Nevada courts have not addressed the distinctions between absolute guaranties and conditional guaranties.

6.5 Conflicts and Choice of Law

Nevada courts will recognize a choice of law provision contained within a guaranty, and apply another state's law if the guaranty specifically provides.[53] Nevada law does not contain any language regarding limitations on choice of law with respect to guaranties specifically. However, when Nevada courts generally address conflicts of law issues, Nevada requires at a minimum that the jurisdiction of choice have a substantial relationship to the transaction and must not violate strong public policy of Nevada.[54] Nevada has not adopted the Restatement of Conflicts as a whole, but Nevada courts have referred to it in past cases.[55]

§ 7 Defenses of the Guarantor; Set-off

A body of law regarding "suretyship defenses" does not exist in Nevada law. However, several defenses are available to guarantors and sureties alike, as follows:

7.1. Modification of the Underlying Obligation, including Extension of Time and Release

It is well settled law in Nevada that guarantors and sureties are exonerated if the creditor alters the obligation of the principal without the consent of the guarantor or the surety.[56] This is true regardless of whether the guaranty is absolute and unconditional.[57] However, in the case of a real estate secured loan, simply releasing the collateral does not exonerate a guarantor who has waived the one-action rule discussed in more detail below.[58] The substitution of a new obligation for an existing one effects a novation, which thereby discharges the parties from all of their obligations under the former agreement

52. Marion Properties, Ltd. by Loyal Crownover v. Goff, 108 Nev. 946, 840 P.2d 1230 (Nev. 1992); Coker Equipment, Inc. v. Great Western Capital Corp., 110 Nev. 1266, 885 P.2d 1321 (Nev. 1994).
53. Owens-Corning Fiberglass Corp. v. Texas Commerce Bank Nat'l Association, 104 Nev. 556, 763 P.2d 3356 (Nev. 1988); W. Costanzo v. Marine Midland Realty Credit Corp., 101 Nev. 277, 701 P.2d 747 (Nev. 1985); Pentax Corp. v. Boyd, 111 Nev. 1296, 904 P.2d 1024 (Nev. 1995).
54. Hermenson v. Hermenson, 110 Nev. 1400, 887 P.2d 1241 (Nev. 1994).
55. Williams v. United Services Auto Ass'n, 109 Nev. 333 (Nev. 1993); Northwest Pipe Co. v. Eighth Judicial District Court Ex. Rel. County of Clark, 118 Nev. 133 (Nev. 2002); Dictor v. Creative Management Services, LLC, 223 P.3d 332 (Nev. 2010).
56. Marion Properties, Ltd. by Loyal Crownover v. Goff, 108 Nev. 946, 840 P.2d 1230 (Nev. 1992) citing Williams v. Crusader Disc. Corp., 75 Nev. 67, 70-71, 334 P.2d 843, 846 (Nev. 1959).
57. *Id.*
58. Southwest Securities v. AMFAC, Inc., 110 Nev. 1036, 879 P.2d 755 (Nev. 1994).

inasmuch as such obligations are extinguished by the novation.[59] Assent to a modification may be inferred from conduct and other circumstances. If a guarantor has knowledge of a change in terms, with the understanding that a complete novation of the original loan agreement is proposed, failure to object to that novation may be sufficient evidence of the guarantor's assent.[60]

The agreement of a creditor to release a guarantor from liability under a guaranty is binding upon the creditor only if the agreement possesses all the required elements of a binding contract including adequate consideration. To constitute consideration, a bargain for a performance or return promise must be present. A performance or return promise is bargained for if it is sought by the promisee in exchange for its promise and is given by the promisor in exchange for that promise.[61]

7.2 Statute of Frauds

Contracts of guaranty are subject to the statute of frauds.[62] To satisfy the statute of frauds, a contract must contain certain essential elements. A note or memorandum must show on its face or by reference to other writings, first, the names of the parties; second, the terms and conditions of the contract; third, the interest or property affected; and fourth, the consideration to be paid therefor.[63] "Unless the writing considered alone, expresses the essential terms with sufficient certainty to constitute an enforceable contract, it fails to satisfy the statute of frauds."[64]

7.3 Duty of Good Faith

Every contract imposes upon the contracting parties a duty of good faith and fair dealing. A wrongful act committed during the course of a contractual relationship may give rise to both tort and contractual remedies.[65]

7.4 Failure to Pursue the Primary Obligor

Nevada's antideficiency statutes address the conditions under which the lender must pursue the primary obligor and/or collateral securing the loan prior to pursuing a guarantor or surety. This body of law is discussed in detail below.

7.5 Set-off

In Nevada, set-off is an equitable remedy that should be granted when justice so requires to prevent inequity.[66] Set-off is a doctrine used to extinguish the

59. Nevada Bank of Commerce v. Esquire Real Estate, Inc., 86 Nev. 238, 468 P.2d 22 (Nev. 1970).
60. *Id.*
61. Pink v. Busch, 100 Nev. 684, 691 P.2d 456 (Nev. 1984).
62. Nev. Rev. Stat. §111.220(2).
63. Haspray v. Passarelli, 79 Nev. 203, 380 P.2d 919 (Nev. 1963); *see also* Pentax Corp. v. Boyd, 111 Nev. 1296, 904 P.2d 1024 (Nev. 1995).
64. *Id.*
65. Nev. Rev. Stat. §104.1203; Albert H. Wohlers & Co. Bartgis, 114 Nev. 1249, 969 P.2d 949 (Nev. 1998).
66. Aviation Ventures, Inc. v. Joan Morris, Inc., 121 Nev. 113, 110 P.3d 59 (Nev. 2005).

mutual indebtedness of parties who each owe a debt to one another.[67] The claims that give rise to set-off need not arise out of the same transaction; they may be entirely unrelated.[68] The purpose behind the doctrine of set-off is to allow mutually indebted parties to apply the debts of the other so that by mutual reduction everything but the difference is extinguished.[69]

§ 8 Waiver of Defenses by the Guarantor

Other than the waiver of the one-action rule discussed below, it is against public policy for any document [relating to the financing or sale of real property] to waive any of the rights afforded to a borrower, guarantor, or surety with regard to antideficiency protections discussed in Nevada Revised Statutes ("NRS") Chapter 40. The legislature has specifically instructed courts not to enforce such waivers.[70] However, the Nevada Supreme Court has clarified and confirmed guarantors can waive those rights afforded to them beyond the scope of NRS Chapter 40; for example, guarantors can waive the right to a jury.[71] Nevada courts have not specifically addressed whether a guarantor can waive suretyship defenses.

In some circumstances, NRS 40.430, or the one-action rule, may be waived by a guarantor.[72] If the guarantor waives the provisions of NRS 40.430 in the loan documents, an action for the enforcement of that person's obligation to pay, satisfy, or purchase all of the indebtedness or obligation secured by a mortgage or deed of trust may be maintained separately and independently from a lawsuit against the borrower for default of the promissory note, the exercise of any power of sale, any lawsuit to foreclose or otherwise enforce a deed of trust, or any other proceeding against the mortgager or guarantor of a deed of trust.[73] However, the one- action rule cannot be waived if any of the following circumstances apply: (a) the property secures a loan for which the principal obligation was never greater than $500,000; (b) the property secures a loan to a seller of real property for which the obligation was originally extended to the seller for any portion of the purchase price; (c) the property securing the loan is used for the production of farm products as of the date the lien is placed on the property; or (d) the real property securing the loan is the owners' principal residence, and a residential structure with no more than four families residing therein.[74]

67. *Id.*
68. *Id.*
69. *Id.*
70. NRS 40.453.
71. Lowe Enterprises Residential Partners L.P. v. Eighth Judicial District, 118 Nev. 92, 40 P.3d 405 (Nev. 2002).
72. Nev. Rev. Stat. § 40.459(4).
73. Nev. Rev. Stat. § 40.495(2)(a-d).
74. Nev. Rev. Stat. § 40.495(2)(a-d).

§ 9 Third-party Pledgors—Defenses and Waiver Thereof

Nevada law does not address the issue of third-party pledgors. However, a third-party pledgor who pledges collateral to support the primary obligor's obligations to a third party arguably stands in the relation of a guarantor to the primary obligor to the extent of the pledge. It seems logical, therefore, that the pledgor can avail itself of the defenses of a guarantor and may also waive such defenses.

§ 10 Joint Liability and Joint and Several Liability of Guarantors—Contribution and Reduction of Obligations upon Payment by a Co-obligor

Nevada law does not specifically address joint and several liability in regard to guarantors. However, contract interpretation principles generally provide that "where there are no express words to render joint and several the obligation undertaken by two, it is presumed to be a joint liability."[75]

In addition, Nevada has enacted the Joint Obligations Uniform Act.[76] The act applies equally to contract actions and tort actions.[77] It provides that a judgment against one or more of several obligors, or against one or more of joint, or of joint and several obligors, shall not discharge a co-obligor who was not a party to the proceedings wherein the judgment was rendered.[78] The amount or value of any consideration received by the obligee from one or more of several obligors or from one or more joint and several obligors, in whole or in partial satisfaction of their obligations, shall be credited to the extent of the amount received on the obligations of all co-obligors to whom the obligor or obligors giving the consideration did not stand in the relation of a surety.[79] Further, an obligor is entitled to an offset by the amount of the settlement for the same damages between the obligee and a co-obligor.[80] On the death of a joint obligor in contract, the joint obligor's executor or administrator shall be bound as such jointly with the surviving obligor or obligors.[81]

Contribution rights among coguarantors are discussed in Section 13 below.

75. Turley v. Thomas, 31 Nev. 181, 101 P. 568 (Nev. 1909).
76. Nev. Rev. Stat. Chapter 101.
77. Western Technologies, Inc., an Arizona Corporation v. All American Golf Center, Inc., 122 Nev. 869, 139 P.3d 858 (Nev. 2006).
78. Nev. Rev. Stat. §101.030.
79. Nev. Rev. Stat. §101.040.
80. Western Technologies, Inc., an Arizona Corporation v. All American Golf Center, Inc., 122 Nev. 869, 139 P.3d 858 (Nev. 2006).
81. Nev. Rev. Stat. §101.070.

§ 11 Reliance

Nevada law does not specifically hold that reliance upon the presence of a guaranty constitutes sufficient consideration when an obligee extends credit to a primary obligor. However, general contract interpretation principals in Nevada do provide that where traditional consideration is lacking, reliance which is foreseeable, reasonable, and serious, will under the doctrine of promissory estoppel require enforcement if injustice cannot otherwise be avoided.[82]

Reliance may also be an issue if a guarantor raises a defense that the signatory did not have authority to bind the guarantor. A party claiming apparent authority of an agent as a basis for contract formation must prove that he subjectively believed that the agent had authority to act for the principal and that his subjective belief in the agent's authority was objectively reasonable.[83] Apparent authority is an application of equitable estoppel and reasonable reliance is a necessary element; a party who claims reliance must not have closed his eyes to warnings or inconsistent circumstances.[84] Apparent authority, including a third party's reasonable reliance on such authority, is a question of fact.[85]

§ 12 Subrogation

By statute, a guarantor has the right to pursue the full repayment of an indebtedness from the borrower and contribution from any other guarantor once the guarantor has paid the underlying debt in full.[86] The guarantor is entitled to enforce every remedy that the original creditor had against the borrower or guarantor, and is entitled to an assignment from the creditor of all rights that the creditor then has by way of security for the indebtedness.[87] If a guarantor partially satisfies a debt, the guarantor automatically receives, by operation of law and without further action, an interest in the proceeds of the collateral for the indebtedness to the extent of the partial satisfaction, subject only to the creditor's prior right to first be paid in full.[88] A guarantor may waive these rights, but only after the borrower defaults.[89]

Nevada also recognizes the doctrine of equitable subrogation, which "permits a person who pays off an encumbrance to assume the same priority position as the holder of the previous encumbrance."[90] However, the doctrine

82. American Savings and Loan Association v. Stanton-Cudahy Lumber Co., 85 Nev. 350, 455 P.2d 39 (Nev. 1969).
83. Great American Ins. Co. v. General Builders, Inc., 113 Nev. 346, 934 P.2d 257 (Nev. 1997).
84. *Id.*
85. *Id.*
86. Nev. Rev. Stat. § 40.475.
87. *Id.*
88. Nev. Rev. Stat. § 40.485.
89. Nev. Rev. Stat. § 40.495.
90. Houston v. Bank of America Federal Savings Bank, 119 Nev. 485, 488 (2003) citing Mort v. U.S., 86 F.3d 890, 893 (9th Cir. 1996).

applies only in limited circumstances.[91] To determine when circumstances would warrant allowing a payor to succeed to the priority position of the creditor whose obligation it paid, the Nevada Supreme Court has adopted the approach set forth in the *Restatement (Third) of Real Property: Mortgages.* The Nevada Supreme Court notes, "Pursuant to the *Restatement*, a [payor] will be subrogated when it pays the entire loan of another as long as the mortgagee was promised repayment and reasonably expected to receive a security interest in the [property] with the priority of the mortgage being discharged, and if subrogation will not materially prejudice the holders of intervening interests."[92] This analysis typically relates to a new lender who pays off an existing lien. However, it can be applied to a guarantor if equity requires such an application, and the guarantor isn't otherwise protected.

§ 13 Indemnification/Reimbursement

Nevada law does not address whether a guarantor may seek contribution from other guarantors or reimbursement (sometimes referred to as "indemnification") from the primary obligor beyond those rights afforded by the Joint Obligations Uniform Act discussed in Section 10 above. However, if the language of the written agreement between the parties indicates that a guarantor is entitled to contribution or reimbursement, the court would likely uphold such a provision pursuant to general contract interpretation principles.[93]

§ 14 Enforcement of Guaranties

14.1 One-action Rule—Creditor's Failure to Exhaust Secured Collateral

If a debt or other obligation is secured by a deed of trust encumbering real property, absent a valid waiver in the loan documents, the beneficiary must first exhaust its collateral remedy before pursuing a borrower or guarantor. "There may be but one action for the recovery of any debt, or for the enforcement of any right secured by a mortgage or other lien upon real estate."[94] This is typically referred to in Nevada as the "one-action rule." The purpose of the one-action rule is to "compel one who has taken a special lien to secure his debt to exhaust the secured property before having recourse to the general assets of the debtor."[95] It is not a restrictive or preclusive statute, but a vehicle for efficient litigation and prevention of multiplicity of suits.[96] In the absence of

91. *Id.*
92. *Id.* at 490.
93. Dobron v. Del Bunch Jr., 125 Nev. 36, 215 P.3d 35 (Nev. 2009).
94. Nev. Rev. Stat. § 40.430.
95. *United States v. Cail* 746 F. Supp. 1035 (D. Nev. 1990).
96. Nevada Land and Mortgage Co. v. Hidden Wells Ranch, Inc. 435 Nev. 501, 435 P.2d 198 (Nev. 1967).

a valid waiver of the one-action rule, pursuit of a debtor or guarantor before exhausting the collateral violates the one-action rule.[97] If the loss of the security for the loan obligation is due to the beneficiary's own action, the beneficiary cannot then pursue suit upon the obligation or a guaranty of the obligation if the debtor or guarantor raises the one-action rule as a defense.[98]

14.2 Foreclosure and Failure to provide Adequate Notice of Default

In Nevada, a beneficiary may choose either a judicial or nonjudicial foreclosure process to foreclose on real property. If the beneficiary selects the judicial foreclosure process, the beneficiary must file the claim for judicial foreclosure, breach of the note, and breach of the guaranty in one court action. If the beneficiary fails to bring suit against the guarantor for breach of guaranty in that action and ultimately receives a judgment, the beneficiary would be precluded from filing a second suit against the guarantor unless the guarantor waived the one-action rule.[99]

If the beneficiary selects a nonjudicial foreclosure, the beneficiary may proceed with a trustee sale of the property.[100] To initiate the nonjudicial foreclosure, the beneficiary must send a request to the trustee identified in the deed of trust. The trustee will then record a notice of breach and election to sell with the county recorder in the county where the property is located.[101] The trustee must mail the notice with certified return receipt requested to the record owner of the property, the borrower, and all guarantors and sureties of the loan.

With regard to guarantors, if the address of the guarantor or surety is unknown, the notice must be sent to the address of the trust property. Unless the guarantor has waived this notice requirement in the loan documents,[102] failure to give notice to a guarantor by the beneficiary of a guaranty or a trustee working on the beneficiary's behalf releases the guarantor or surety completely from his or her obligation to the beneficiary.[103] However, failure to provide adequate notice to a guarantor does not affect the validity of the foreclosure sale or the obligation of any guarantor to whom the notice was properly given.[104] Further, a creditor may correct such an error by giving the required notice at least 15 days prior to the expiration of the period of time described in NRS 107.080 during which the borrower is allowed to cure its default.[105] In addition, a guarantor is not released if notice is given at least 15 days prior to any extension of the applicable cure period by the beneficiary. If the beneficiary sends the notice with a statement that the period for the

97. Bonicamp v. Vazquez, 120 Nev. 377, 91 P.3d 584 (Nev. 2004).
98. Keever v. Nicholas Beers Co., 96 Nev. 509, 611 P.2d 1079 (Nev. 1980).
99. Nev. Rev. Stat. § 40.430.
100. Nev. Rev. Stat. § 107.080
101. Nev. Rev. Stat. § 107.080.
102. McDonald v. D.P. Alexander & Las Vegas Boulevard, LLC, 121 Nev. 812, 123 P.3d 784 (Nev. 2005).
103. Nev. Rev. Stat. § 107.095.
104. Nev. Rev. Stat. § 107.095.
105. Nev. Rev. Stat. § 107.095 Section (3)(a)(1).

borrowers, guarantors, or any other interested party to cure the default on the loan has been extended, the guarantor's obligations to the beneficiary are not extinguished.[106] The guarantor's obligations are also not extinguished if the beneficiary rescinds the notice of default and election to sell before the sale is actually advertised.[107]

14.3 Deficiency Actions

In general, the guarantor may assert any legal or equitable defenses provided by NRS 40.451 through 40.463, inclusive. Guarantors enjoy the protection of Nevada's antideficiency legislation,[108] which governs deficiency actions against borrowers and guarantors regarding loans secured by real property.

On June 10, 2011, the Nevada Legislature passed Assembly Bill 273 ("A.B. 273"), codified within NRS 40.451 through 40.463 inclusive. The specific provisions of A.B. 273 are discussed in more detail below; however, it substantially altered the law regarding deficiency limitations. The change in law has resulted in significant disputes among parties to guaranties. Many are arguing that A.B. 273 is unconstitutional, and Nevada district court judges have made various competing rulings. As of January 1, 2012, at least three matters have been submitted to the Nevada Supreme Court for appeal. Nevada awaits the Nevada Supreme Court's interpretation on the breadth and applicability of A.B. 273. In the meantime, it is to be expected that significant litigation will surround any deficiency action by a beneficiary against a borrower or guarantor.

14.4 New Limitations on Calculating the Deficiency

Once a foreclosure of the real property occurs, guarantors and borrowers are entitled to an evidentiary hearing to determine whether the fair market value of the property on the date of the foreclosure sale is a greater amount than the foreclosure bid.[109] Under Nevada law, where the beneficiary is the original beneficiary or is a beneficiary who purchased the interest in the promissory note for par value, a deficiency judgment in favor of the beneficiary is limited to the lesser of (a) the difference between the loan balance and the market value of the property at time of sale with interest from the date of sale, or (b) the difference between the loan balance and the amount for which the property was actually sold plus interest.[110] This calculation also applies to any deficiency judgment entered prior to June 10, 2011.

Pursuant to A.B. 273, if a beneficiary purchased the note from a prior beneficiary for less than par value, the deficiency is limited to the lesser of (a) the difference between the amount for which the current beneficiary purchased the note and the fair market value of the property, or (b) the difference

106. Nev. Rev. Stat. §107.095 Section (3)(a)(3).
107. Nev. Rev. Stat. §107.095 Section (3)(b).
108. First Interstate Bank of Nevada v. Shields, 102 Nev. 616, 730 P.2d 429 (Nev. 1986).
109. Nev. Rev. Stat. § 40.457.
110. Nev. Rev. Stat. § 40.459.

between the amount for which the current beneficiary purchased the loan and the amount for which the property sold. This change became effective on June 10, 2011, and A.B. 273 does not expressly restrict its application to loans purchased after its effective date. Borrowers and guarantors are arguing that this provision applies retroactively to all loan obligations, whether made prior to, or after June 10, 2011. On the other hand, beneficiaries are arguing that it only applies to those loans entered into or purchased after June 10, 2011. The outcome of these disputes is still pending. This change applies equally to commercial and residential loans.

14.5 Calculating a Judgment against a Guarantor if Property is not Sold

Prior to the enactment of A.B. 273, if a guarantor of a loan secured by real property had waived the one-action rule, or the borrower had entered into bankruptcy and sale of the property was stayed, the beneficiary could directly sue the guarantor for the entire outstanding balance of the loan.[111] The deficiency limitations only applied if a foreclosure sale had occurred, except that the beneficiary could not later recover in excess of the amount due and owing if the property was later foreclosed.[112]

A.B. 273 now provides that a guarantor must get credit for the value of the property even if the guarantor has waived the one-action rule and even if the property is inaccessible to the beneficiary as a result of a bankruptcy stay. A.B. 273 provides that the court must hold a hearing to determine the fair market value of the collateral as of the date the lawsuit commences. The judgment is limited to the lesser of (a) the difference between the loan balance and the market value of the property at time of sale with interest from the date of sale, or (b) if a foreclosure sale occurs prior to judgment being entered, the difference between the loan and the amount for which the property was sold. A.B. 273 is silent as to whether the guarantor receives the benefit of the limitation of deficiency in cases where the beneficiary purchased its interest in the note for less than par value. However, given that guarantor may assert any legal or equitable defenses provided pursuant to the provisions of NRS 40.451 through 40.463, inclusive, the limitation will likely apply. This change applies only to an action brought against a guarantor commenced on or after June 10, 2011. Accordingly, if a lawsuit against a guarantor had already been filed as of June 10, 2011, this change likely does not apply.

14.6 Calculating a Deficiency Judgment if Mortgage Insurance is involved

Previously, Nevada law governing deficiency actions did not address situations in which the proceeds of real property insurance or mortgage insurance had been paid to the beneficiary. For deficiency suits commenced after June

111. Nev. Rev. Stat. § 40.430(i) and 40.495.
112. Nev. Rev. Stat. § 40.455.

10, 2011, A.B. 273 requires that the amount owed by the borrower/guarantor on a debt secured by either a first priority or junior lien on real property shall not include the proceeds of any insurance funds received by or payable to the beneficiary. In circumstances where the beneficiary purchased the note from a prior beneficiary, A.B. 273 is unclear as to whether this provision applies to reduce the gross amount owed on the note or the amount the beneficiary paid to purchase the note.

Significant litigation has resulted from these changes. Nevada awaits the Supreme Court's interpretation on the breadth and applicability of A.B. 273; however, that ruling is not likely to be entered until at least the fall of 2012. The language of A.B. 273 is controversial, and the resulting law may be revised or repealed in Nevada's 2013 legislative session.

14.7 Circumstances in which Deficiency Judgments are Precluded

A deficiency judgment is precluded completely against borrowers and guarantors of loans secured by real property if the beneficiary of the deed of trust is a financial institution, the property is a single-family residence, the borrower was the owner of the property as of the time of the foreclosure sale, the loan was made for purposes of purchasing the property securing the debt after October 1, 2009, the debtor continuously occupied the property as its principal residence, and the loan has never been refinanced.[113]

This provision previously only applied to a beneficiary completing a foreclosure sale, and did not apply to a junior beneficiary that was unable to recover its loans from the proceeds of the senior lienholder's foreclosure sale due to the property's insufficient value. A.B. 273 likely changes this provision to prevent junior beneficiaries from filing a deficiency suit after a foreclosure has occurred on a single-family residence. This provision only applies to a junior loan made on a single-family residence where the borrower was the owner of the property as of the time of the foreclosure sale, the loan was made for purposes of purchasing the property securing the debt after June 10, 2011, the debtor continuously occupied the property as the principal residence, and the loan has never been refinanced. While the language of A.B. 273 indicates this particular change applies only to obligations entered into on or after June 10, 2011, it is being disputed by guarantors based upon other language within the bill.

14.8 Statute of Limitations for Deficiency

In all other circumstances, once a foreclosure sale or a nonjudicial foreclosure of real property is complete, the beneficiary can pursue a deficiency action against the borrowers or the guarantors, but only if it does so within six months of the foreclosure sale.[114] Until June 10, 2011, any junior beneficiary who did

113. Nev. Rev. Stat. § 40.455(3).
114. Nev. Rev. Stat. § 40.455.

not hold the foreclosure sale and whose lien was extinguished as a result of a foreclosure held by a higher priority beneficiary had the full six-year statute of limitations to bring its lawsuit. However, A.B. 273 now provides that a junior lienholder must also file suit within six months of any foreclosure sale or sale in lieu of foreclosure that occurs after July 1, 2011.

In general, all the defenses discussed herein are specifically preserved under NRS 40.495 for the benefit of guarantors.

§ 15 Revival and Reinstatement of Guaranties

Nevada law has not specifically addressed the possibility or process of reviving or reinstating a guaranty.

New Hampshire State Law of Guaranties

Connie Boyles Lane
Orr & Reno PA
One Eagle Square,
P.O. Box 3550
Concord, NH 03302-3550
(603) 224-2381
Fax: (603) 224-2318
clane@orr-reno.com
www.orr-reno.com

Contents

New Hampshire State Law of Guaranties

Introduction: New Hampshire has a somewhat limited body of law regarding guaranties. New Hampshire courts have looked to the Restatement (First) of Security to guide their analysis.[1,2] No cases have cited the more recent Restatement (Third) of Suretyship and Guaranty.

New Hampshire Practice Pointer: N.H. Rev. Stat. Ann. § 399-B is a consumer protection statute that requires any person engaged in the business of extending credit to provide each person to whom credit is extended a disclosure of finance charges. N.H. Rev. Stat. Ann. § 399-B:2. The statute applies to both consumer and commercial transactions. A creditor's failure to provide the required disclosure statement may invalidate the transaction, and result in criminal liability for willful violations. N.H. Rev. Stat. Ann. §§ 399-B:3-4.[3] The statute does not limit the permissible complexity of a financial transaction, as long as the creditor accurately communicates its terms to a borrower.[4] A creditor complying with Federal Reserve Regulation Z, Truth in Lending, satisfies the mandate of N.H. Rev. Stat. Ann. § 399-B. N.H. Rev. Stat. Ann. § 399-B:2-a.

New Hampshire courts have not addressed whether disclosure statements must be provided to guarantors under N.H. Rev. Stat. Ann. § 399-B. However, practitioners would be well advised to provide such disclosures to guarantors to avoid potential criminal liability or cancellation of a transaction. It is the general practice of most transaction attorneys in New Hampshire to provide what is called "The 399-B Disclosure" in commercial transactions that involve New Hampshire property, entities, or individuals. This disclosure is often one of the first things for which the bankruptcy trustee looks in the loan documentation of a debtor.

1. Rice v. Snow, 116 N.H. 69 (1976).
2. C-E Building Products, Inc. v. Seal-Rite Aluminum Products of N.H., Inc., 114 N.H. 150 (1974).
3. Decato Bros. v. Westinghouse Credit Corp., 129 N.H. 504, 509 (1987).
4. Bank of N.H. v. Scanlon, 144 N.H. 505, 507-08 (1999).

§ 1 Nature of the Guaranty Agreement

A guaranty is a legal relationship whereby a guarantor pledges to satisfy the debts of a primary obligor upon the primary obligor's default.

1.1 Guaranty Relationship

A guaranty is a contract whereby the guarantor agrees to pay a debt upon default by the primary obligor.[5] A guarantor's obligation is secondary, meaning that a creditor may not refuse a tender of payment by the primary obligor and then look to the guarantor for payment.[6]

Guaranties made for completion of performance are often referred to as bonds in the construction arena. "A bond is a three-party instrument by which one party (the surety) guarantees or promises a second party (the owner or general contractor) the successful performance of contract obligations owed to the second party by its principal (the contractor or subcontractor)."[7] Three common types of construction bonds are bid bonds, payment bonds, and performance bonds.[8]

A bid bond guarantees that the bidder will enter into the contract for the bid amount.[9] "A payment bond assures the owner that the prime contractor will pay its subcontractors and suppliers, who might otherwise file liens against the owner's property."[10] "A performance bond guarantees to the owner that a prime contractor will perform according to the contract referenced in the bond."[11]

N.H. Rev. Stat. Ann. § 447:16 to 18 govern bonding for public works projects.

Guaranty agreements are subject to standard rules of contract interpretation.[12] To determine the nature of the guaranty relationship, a court will look to the plain meaning of the guaranty's language as reflecting the intentions of the parties.[13]

§ 2 State Law Requirements for an Entity to Enter a Guaranty

New Hampshire business entities may grant guaranties in furtherance of their business activities.

5. Watriss v. Pierce, 32 N.H. 560, 570 (1856).
6. Prime Financial Group, Inc. v. Smith, 137 N.H. 74, 76 (1993).
7. General Insulation Co. v. Eckman Const., 159 N.H. 601, 606 (2010) (internal quotations omitted).
8. *Id.*
9. *Id.*
10. *Id.*
11. *Id.; see also* Rivier College v. St. Paul Fire & Marine Ins. Co., 104 N.H. 398, 401 (1963).
12. Bankeast v. Michalenoick, 138 N.H. 367, 369 (1994).
13. *Id.*

2.1 Corporations

A New Hampshire corporation may make guaranties necessary or convenient to carry out its business affairs, provided that its articles of incorporation do not provide otherwise. N.H. Rev. Stat. Ann. §§ 293-A:3.02(7), 295:6.

Corporations are generally prohibited from guaranteeing obligations of its directors, absent approval by the majority of the outstanding shares (excluding any shares owned by the interested director), or a determination and approval by the board that the guaranty benefits the corporation. N.H. Rev. Stat. Ann. § 293-A:8.32.

2.2 Partnerships

New Hampshire's Uniform Partnership Act does not expressly authorize partnerships to make guaranties, nor does it prohibit such conduct. *See* N.H. Rev. Stat. Ann. § 304-A. For over a century, however, New Hampshire courts have honored partnership surteyships where the guarantor has authority to bind the entity.[14]

2.3 Limited Liability Companies

New Hampshire's Limited Liability Company (LLC) statute permits an LLC to make guaranties necessary or convenient to carry out its business purposes, provided that the operating agreement does not prevent it from doing so. N.H. Rev. Stat. Ann. § 304-C:7(I)(f). Likewise, members of an LLC are permitted to guarantee debts of the company or transact similar business with the entity except where prohibited in the operating agreement. N.H. Rev. Stat. Ann. § 304-C:8.

2.4 Banks and Trust Companies

New Hampshire-chartered banks are generally authorized to engage in any activity that is permitted for a national bank under federal laws and regulations. N.H. Rev. Stat. Ann. § 394-A:4; N.H. Code Admin. R. Ann. Ban. 523.02(a). A national bank's authority to make guarantees is subject to a variety of conditions under federal law, which are not addressed here. *See* 12 C.F.R. § 7.1017 (2010). It should be noted that before a state-chartered bank undertakes an activity in reliance upon federal authority to do so, it must provide notice of the action and the federal authority relied upon to the banking commissioner for approval. N.H. Code Admin. R. Ann. Ban. 523.02(b).

Trust companies are prohibited from guaranteeing the "bonds, mortgage securities, or other choses of action of other persons or corporations issued, sold or negotiated as investments." N.H. Rev. Stat. Ann. § 390:2.

---

14. J. S. Kidder & Co. v. Page & Martin, 48 N.H. 380, 383 (1869).

2.5 Individuals

Because a guaranty is a contract subject to the rules of contract interpretation,[15] any individual that can enter into a contract can issue a guaranty.

Generally, marriage does not make a spouse liable for the other spouse's debts that were acquired prior to the marriage. N.H. Rev. Stat. Ann. § 460:3; *see also* N.H. Const. pt. 1, art. 2 (equal rights provision and prohibition of discrimination on account of sex). However, in divorce, the court can apportion part or all of the liability to the other spouse.[16] Such an order does not give a creditor any additional rights.[17]

In a divorce, the court can assign jointly owned and solely owned property between the spouses based on equitable principles and in consideration of a variety of factors including the value of property acquired prior to the marriage. N.H. Rev. Stat. Ann. § 458:61-a.

§ 3 Signatory's Authority to Execute a Guaranty

For a guaranty to be valid and enforceable, the signatory must have actual or apparent authority to make the guaranty (or the principal must ratify the act).

3.1 Corporations

An officer's execution of a guaranty on behalf of a corporation will bind the corporation if the officer had actual or apparent authority to make the guaranty.[18] A corporate officer has actual authority where statute, bylaws, or director resolution authorizes the transaction.[19] In *New England Merchants National Bank v. Lost Valley Corporation,* a corporate resolution authorized the president or treasurer to execute a guaranty on behalf of the corporation.[20] The treasurer, who also served as clerk, signed the guaranty and listed his title as "clerk."[21] The corporation argued that the guaranty was invalid because the clerk lacked authority to execute it.[22] The court concluded that, "Where an individual holds corporate office in two different capacities and executes a deed or contract, it is presumed that he did so in the capacity which would make the act binding on the corporation."[23] The bank was entitled to an inference that the guaranty was executed by the treasurer in that capacity, notwithstanding the reference to "clerk."[24]

15. *Watriss,* 32 N.H. at 506; *Bank*east, 138 N.H. at 369.
16. Bourdon v. Bourdon, 119 N.H. 518, 520 (1979).
17. *Id.*
18. *See* Daniel Webster Council, Inc. v. St. James Ass'n, Inc., 129 N.H. 681, 683 (1987).
19. *Id.*
20. 119 N.H. 254, 255-56 (1979) (applying Massachusetts law).
21. *Id.* at 258.
22. *Id.*
23. *Id.*
24. *Id.*

Apparent authority is "authority which a reasonably prudent person, induced by the principal's acts or conduct, and in the exercise of reasonable diligence and sound discretion, under similar circumstances with the party dealing with the agent, and with like knowledge, would naturally suppose the agent to have."[25] Apparent authority may only exist where "the principal has either so conducted its business as to give third parties the right to believe that the act in question is one the principal has authorized the agent to do, or that it is one agents in that line of business are accustomed to do."[26]

3.2 Partnerships

Although the New Hampshire Uniform Partnership Act does not expressly address guaranties, a partner's actions apparently in furtherance of the purpose of the partnership's business are generally binding upon the partnership, unless the partner lacks actual authority for the particular transaction and the other party to the transaction knows of that lack of authority. N.H. Rev. Stat. Ann. § 304-A:9. A partner's actions not in furtherance of the partnership's business may bind the partnership if all other partners consent to the act.[27] The acts contemplated in this section do not expressly exclude guaranties. *See* N.H. Rev. Stat. Ann. § 304-A *et seq.*

3.3 Limited Liability Companies

Members of a member-managed LLC are agents of the company and may, by default, enter into guaranties or other contracts on behalf of the company apparently in furtherance of the company's business, unless the member's actual authority to do so is limited and the other party to the transaction knows of that limitation. N.H. Rev. Stat. Ann. § 304-C:26.

The members of a manager-managed LLC, on the other hand, have no agency powers and therefore generally cannot bind the company.[28] Instead, the managers have actual authority as agents to further the business and affairs of the LLC, unless the manager's authority for a particular transaction is limited and the other party to the transaction has knowledge of that limitation.[29] Of course, an LLC agreement may modify the statutory default authority of members and managers. N.H. Rev. Stat. Ann. § 304-C:7.

3.4 Banks and Trust Companies

A case-by-case inquiry into the powers conferred by a bank's corporate governance documents is necessary to determine who is authorized to execute a guaranty on the bank's behalf. In general, as with other business entities, the

25. *Daniel Webster Council, Inc.*, 129 N.H. at 683 (internal quotations omitted).
26. *Id.*
27. *Id.*
28. *Id.*
29. *Id.*

binding effect of a guaranty depends on whether the signatory had actual or apparent authority to act on the bank's behalf.

§ 4 Guaranty Formation; Consideration

In New Hampshire, guaranties are subject to the requirements of ordinary contract formation.[30] To be valid, there must be offer, acceptance, meeting of the minds, and consideration.[31] The guaranty must be in writing. N.H. Rev. Stat. Ann. § 506:2.[32] The extension of credit to the primary obligor may serve as adequate consideration for the guaranty.[33]

§ 5 Notice of Acceptance

Notice of acceptance to the guarantor is generally unnecessary unless his or her obligation is less than absolute.

New Hampshire law regarding notice of acceptance to guarantors is somewhat archaic. Absent a notice provision within a guaranty instrument, case law primarily from the 19th century governs notice requirements. In general, notice of acceptance is required, unless the guaranty is absolute.[34] However, express notice of acceptance is unnecessary where the agreement to accept is contemporaneous with the guaranty, or constitutes consideration for the guaranty.[35] In such cases, notice of acceptance may be implied.[36]

§ 6 Interpretation of Guaranty Agreements

New Hampshire courts construe guaranties as ordinary contracts, by considering the instrument's language as it reflects the intentions of the parties.

Guaranty agreements are subject to standard rules of contract interpretation.[37] To determine the nature of the guaranty relationship, a court will look to the plain meaning of the guaranty's language as reflecting the intentions of the parties.[38]

---

30. Fleet Bank-NH v. Christy's Table, 141 N.H. 285, 287 (1996).
31. *Id.*
32. John A. Connare, Inc. v. Gray, 113 N.H. 125 (1973).
33. Simons v. Steele, 36 N.H. 73, 73, 80, 82 (1858); Van Dorn Retail Management, Inc. v. Jim's Oxford Shop, Inc., 874 F.Supp. 476, 478 n.1 (D. N.H. 1994).
34. Bank of Newbury v. Sinclair, 60 N.H. 100, 108 (1880).
35. *Id.* at 106.
36. *Id.*
37. *Bankeast v. Michalenoick*,138 N.H. 367, 369 (1994).
38. *Id.*

New Hampshire has a limited body of case law interpreting guaranty agreements. In general, the courts apply the principle that "[t]he obligation of a guarantor is that which the fair import of the language used imposes upon him."[39] The extent of a guarantor's obligations hinges on a court's construction of the underlying obligation's terms.[40] Under the plain meaning rule, a court will not impose contradictory obligations from parol evidence onto the parties.[41]

"A choice-of-law provision in a contract governs what substantive law will apply, but it does not control which state's law applies to procedural issues."[42] Absent a choice-of- law provision, a guarantee is governed by the law of the state with which it has the most significant relationship.[43]

§ 7 Guarantor Defenses

7.1 Defenses of Primary Obligor

A guarantor may generally raise any defense available to the primary obligor.[44] These include fraudulent or negligent misrepresentation.[45] Guaranties are generally unenforceable against the guarantor if the underlying contract is invalid.[46] In the mortgage context, a guarantor may assert a mortgagee's breach of fiduciary duty, or defend on the ground of commercial unreasonableness.[47]

A guarantor may intervene in a primary obligor's action against the obligee to modify or amend the terms of the contract on which a guarantor has pledged assistance.[48] A guarantor may also intervene in an action against a primary obligor to protect its financial interests.[49] A guarantor has protection if an obligee takes action against the primary obligor without the guaranty's knowledge. In a later action against the guarantor, the creditor cannot introduce any judgments against the primary obligor as evidence against the guarantor.[50] This allows the guarantor to assert defenses the primary obligor may have failed to raise in the original case.[51]

7.2 Other Defenses

Guaranties are generally subject to a three-year statute of limitations. N.H. Rev. Stat. Ann. § 508:4. However, the guarantor may inadvertently toll this

39. Brown Durrell Co. v. Delisle, 83 N.H. 516, 516 (1929).
40. *Bankeast*, 138 N.H. at 369; Staffing Network, Inc. v. Pietropaolo, 145 N.H. 456, 460 (2000).
41. Nashua Trust Co. v. Weisman, 122 N.H. 397, 399 (1982).
42. Lago & Sons Dairy, Inc. v. H.P. Hood, Inc., 1994 WL 484306, 10 (D. N.H. Sept. 6, 1994).
43. Consolidated Mut. Ins. Co. v. Radio Foods Corp., 108 N.H. 494, 496-97 (1968).
44. C-E Bldg. Prods., Inc. v. Seal-Rite Aluminum Prods. of N.H., Inc., 114 N.H. 150, 152 (1974).
45. *Nashua Trust Co.*, 122 N.H. at 400.
46. McCabe v. Acidy, 138 N.H. 20, 28 (1993).
47. First N.H. Mortgage Corp. v. Greene, 139 N.H. 321, 324 (1995).
48. Lavigne v. Lavigne, 87 N.H. 223, 227 (1935).
49. *See C-E Bldg. Prods.*, 114 N.H. at 151-52.
50. *Id.* at 152.
51. *Id.*

limitations period if he or she acknowledges the obligation and expresses a renewed willingness to pay it.[52] A guarantor may also reduce or eliminate liability upon a successful showing that an obligee, in bad faith, obtained an inadequate price during a foreclosure sale before recovering against a guarantor.[53] A guarantor generally has a right to set off his or her liability by the amount lost from an obligee's breach of the agreement.[54]

An obligee may only pursue a claim against a guarantor upon any default of the obligor.[55] An obligee need not prove insolvency of the obligor to pursue collection from the guarantor.[56] Thus, failure to pursue the primary obligor is not a defense for guarantors at common law in New Hampshire; however, a contract's guaranty provisions can provide otherwise.[57]

In transactions governed by Article 3 of New Hampshire's Uniform Commercial Code (the "UCC"), a guarantor has statutory defenses available.[58] Under the UCC, a guarantor is an "accommodation party" who may raise tender of payment or impairment of collateral as a defense against actions by a creditor.[59] *See also* N.H. Rev. Stat. Ann. §§ 382-A:3-419; 603(b).

§ 8 Waiver of Guarantor Defenses

A guarantor may waive most of its defenses. The exceptions are generally defenses pertaining to intentional wrongdoing or actions that violate the state's public policies.

8.1 Nonwaivable Defenses

A guarantor cannot waive its right to defend against or reduce liability for an obligee's intentional, bad faith, or affirmatively negligent actions.[60] Additionally, a guarantor may not waive a defense against a mortgagor who sells foreclosed property in a commercially unreasonable sale.[61] Generally, New Hampshire courts will not enforce a waiver that violates the state's public policies.[62]

52. Premier Capital, Inc. v. Gallagher, 144 N.H. 284, 286 (1999).
53. *See* Reconstruction Finance Corp. v. Faulkner, 101 N.H. 352, 361 (1958).
54. Numerica Savings Bank F.S.B. v. The Mountain Lodge Inn, Corp., 134 N.H. 505, 509 (1991).
55. *See* Johns-Manville Sales Corp. v. Barton, 118 N.H. 195, 198 (1978).
56. *Id.*
57. *See id.*; *Bankeast*, 138 N.H. at 369.
58. Cole v. Hobson, 143 N.H. 14, 16-17 (1998).
59. *Id.* at 16.
60. *Reconstruction Finance Corp.*, 101 N.H. at 361.
61. *First N.H. Mortgage Corp.*, 139 N.H. at 324. *But see* United States v. Mallett, Civ. No. 84-392-D, 1985 WL 5696 (D.N.H. Apr. 1, 1985) (creditor's release of security without consideration was permissible under guaranty agreement).
62. *First N.H. Mortgage Corp.*, 139 N.H. at 323.

8.2 Waivable Defenses

A guarantor may waive its right to claim a set-off of liability for any breaches by the obligee.[63] New Hampshire also allows guarantors to provide a broad waiver of defenses based on the primary obligee's breach of its fiduciary duty.[64] Such a waiver may only extend to a primary obligee's passive negligence; however, a guarantor may defend against liability because of the obligee's affirmative negligence or bad faith, despite a prior waiver.[65]

§ 9 Third-party Pledgors—Defenses and Waiver Thereof

No cases on point.

§ 10 Jointly and Severally Liable Guarantors—Contribution

Where a coguarantor has paid more than its proportional share of a guaranteed obligation, it may recover from the other guarantors in proportion to their liability.[66] However, a right of contribution arises only if payment was made under a "clear legal duty."[67] A coguarantor is entitled to contribution notwithstanding the existence of a defense to the obligation, as long as the payment was made with a justifiable belief that a duty to pay existed, without knowledge of the defense.[68]

§ 11 Reliance

Reliance is generally unnecessary to pursue claims against a guarantor. Reliance may be required for noncontractual enforcement theories.

Courts in New Hampshire interpret guaranties under the general principles of contract law.[69] Under general contract principles, an obligee need not show reliance to enforce a contractual guaranty.[70] However, reliance is a necessary element to prove fraud or apparent authority.[71]

---

63. *Numerica Savings Bank*, 134 N.H. at 509.
64. *First N.H. Mortgage Corp.*, 139 N.H. at 323.
65. *Id.*
66. Fletcher v. Grover, 11 N.H. 368 (1840).
67. Rice v. Snow, 116 N.H. 69, 71 (1976).
68. *Id.*
69. *Bankeast*, 138 N.H. at 369.
70. *See* Tessier v. Rockefeller, 162 N.H. 324, 339 (2011).
71. Wyle v. Lees, 162 N.H. 406 (2011); Demetracopoulos v. Strafford Guidance Ctr., 130 N.H. 209, 215-16 (1987).

§ 12 Subrogation

New Hampshire recognizes the equitable doctrine of subrogation, allowing a secondary obligor who satisfies a debt to an obligee to seek reimbursement against the primary obligor.

"The doctrine of subrogation has its origins in equity."[72] However, "[a] party's right to subrogation can arise either by contract, statute, or common law or equitable principles."[73] "The purpose behind subrogation 'is to place the responsibility where it ultimately should rest by compelling payment by the one who in good conscience ought to pay it."[74]

Under certain circumstances, the doctrine allows a guarantor who has discharged the debt of another to succeed to the rights and position of the satisfied creditor and recover from the primary obligor.[75] To apply, four elements must be met: "(1) the subrogee cannot have acted as a volunteer; (2) the subrogee must have paid a debt upon which it was not primarily liable; (3) the subrogee must have paid the entire debt; and (4) subrogation may not work any injustice to the rights of others."[76] A "volunteer" is one who pays under no legal obligation or when he has no interest protected by payment.[77]

"[Subrogation] is generally not available against a third party, if the equities in the latter's favor are equal or superior to those favoring the surety in respect to the liability involved."[78]

§ 13 Indemnification

New Hampshire has a very limited body of law regarding indemnification under a guaranty agreement. Generally, "[a] right to indemnity arises where one is legally required to pay an obligation for which another is primarily liable."[79] In cases "[w]hen there is an express contract for indemnity... the rights of the surety are not to be determined by general indemnity principles, but by the letter of the contract for indemnity."[80] Thus, "an indemnitee's unilateral acts of settlement, albeit reasonable and undertaken in good faith, cannot bind the indemnitor."[81] Indemnification is not available to a party who makes a voluntary payment, without legal compulsion to do so.[82]

72. Wolters v. Am. Republic Ins. Co., 149 N.H. 599, 601 (2003).
73. *Id.*
74. *Id.*
75. Chase v. Ameriquest Mortgage Co., 155 N.H. 19, 27 (2007); Watriss v. Pierce, 32 N.H. 560 (1856).
76. *Chase*, 155 N.H. at 27.
77. *Id.*
78. Security Fence Co. v. Manchester Fed. Sav. & Loan Ass'n, 101 N.H. 190, 192 (1957).
79. Coco v. Jaskunas, 159 N.H. 515, 519 (2009).
80. Kessler v. Gleich, 161 N.H. 104, 112 (2010).
81. One Beacon Ins., LLC v. M&M Pizza, Inc., 160 N.H. 638, 643 (2010).
82. *Id.*

§ 14 Enforcing a Guaranty

A creditor need not first seek recovery from the principal or its collateral if it would be entirely fruitless, but instead may proceed directly against the guarantor.[83]

§ 15 Triangular Set-off in Bankruptcy

New Hampshire likely would not recognize triangular set-offs in bankruptcy due to the absence of the requisite mutuality between the assignee and the original debtor.[84] The Supreme Court has stated that "an assignee for purposes of collection cannot set-off his personal debt against the assigned claim because, '[s]ince mutuality is essential, the debtor must be the beneficial owner of the claim or judgment which he seeks to set-off and not merely a trustee on behalf of an assignor who has retained the equitable interest in the thing assigned.'"[85]

§ 16 Revival and Reinstatement of Guaranties

As a general rule, though a debtor has paid a debt in full, the obligation of the debtor's guarantor will revive if the debtor's previous payment is later avoided or disgorged, even if the guaranty is otherwise silent on this issue.[86] Many courts have recognized this principle.[87] While there is no New Hampshire case on this issue, it is probable that a New Hampshire court, in a properly reasoned opinion, would follow the generally prevailing view and adopt this general principle.

83. Colby v. Farwell, 71 N.H. 83 (1901).
84. In re Liquidation of Home Ins. Co., 157 N.H. 543, 549 (2008).
85. *Id.* (quoting Norman v. Berney, 235 Cal.App.2d 424, 434 (1965)).
86. Restatement (Third) of Suretyship and Guaranty, § 70.
87. *See, e.g.*, In the Matter of SNTL Corp., 571 F.3d 826, 835-36 (2009) ("[W]e agree that the return of a preferential payment by a creditor generally revives the liability of a guarantor."); Wallace Hardware Co., Inc. v. Abrams, 223 F.3d 382, 408 (2000) ("[T]he courts have uniformly held that a payment of a debt that is later set aside as an avoidable preference does not discharge a guarantor of his obligation to repay that debt."); In re Robinson Bros. Drilling, Inc. v. Manufacturers Hanover Leasing Corp., 6 F.3d 701, 704 (1993) ("[C]ourts have recognized, without regard to any special guaranty language, that guarantors must make good on their guaranties following avoidance of payments previously made by their principal debtors."); In re Herman Cantor Corp. v. Central Fidelity Bank, N.A., 15 B.R. 747, 750 (1981) ("Although a surety usually is discharged by payment of the debt, he continues to be liable if the payment constitutes a preference under bankruptcy law. A preferential treatment is deemed by law to be no payment at all... The courts agree that payment from a debtor which is later set aside as a preference does not discharge a surety.").

New Jersey State Law of Guaranties

Steven D. Fleissig
Greenberg Traurig, LLP
200 Park Avenue
P.O. Box 677
Florham Park, NJ 07932
973.360.7900
Fax: 973.301.8410
fleissigs@gtlaw.com

Contents

New Jersey State Law of Guaranties

§ 1 Introduction and Restatement of the Law (Third), Suretyship and Guaranty

This memorandum contains a survey of New Jersey's law on guaranties. While New Jersey law generally controls the application and enforcement of guaranties, the New Jersey courts give considerable weight to the Restatement (Third) of Suretyship and Guaranty (1996) ("Restatement") and have adopted the views of the Restatement as the views of the New Jersey courts.[1] For instance, the New Jersey courts have cited to the Restatement in addressing matters such as the liability of a primary obligor to the secondary obligor in the absence of notice, the effect of a modification of the obligation enforced by a guaranty where such obligation increases the guarantor's risk or liability, and the obligation of a creditor to disclose facts about a debtor.[2]

§ 2 Guaranty Relationships

A guaranty is a contract pursuant to which a guarantor guarantees the debt of a primary obligor or the performance of a duty of a primary obligor in the event of a default by such primary obligor.[3]

§ 3 State Law Requirements for an Entity to Enter a Guaranty

New Jersey statutory law specifically addresses the ability of corporations, limited liability companies, and banks to issue guaranties. New Jersey statutory law, however, is silent on the ability of partnerships to issue guaranties.

3.1 Corporations

N.J.S.A. 14A:3-1(1)(g) authorizes a corporation to issue a guaranty, provided that such guaranty is in furtherance of the corporation's corporate purpose.

1. Citibank N.A. v. Estate of Simpson, 290 N.J. Super. 519, 530 (1996).
2. Feigenbaum v. Guaracini, 402 N.J. Super. 7 (2008); Center 48 Lid. P'ship v. The May Dep't Stores Co., 355 N.J. Super. 390, 406 (2002); Economic Dev. v. Pavonia Restaurant, 319 N.J. Super. 435 (1998).
3. Cruz-Mendez v. Isu/Insurance Services, 156 N.J. 556, 568 (1999).

Specifically, the statutory provision allows corporations "to make contracts and guarantees and incur liabilities, borrow money, issue its bonds, and secure any of its obligations by mortgage of or creation of a security interest in all or any of its property, franchises and income."[4]

N.J.S.A. 14A:3-1 authorizes a corporation to issue a guaranty not in furtherance of its direct or indirect business interests, provided that such guaranty was authorized by the requisite vote of shareholders entitled to vote on such matter. Upon authorization, such a guaranty also may be secured by a mortgage of or a security interest in all or any part of, or any interest in, the corporation's property.[5]

3.2 Partnerships

New Jersey's Uniform Partnership Act and New Jersey's Uniform Limited Partnership Law do not expressly authorize a partnership to issue a guaranty, but do not prohibit such activity.[6]

3.3 Limited Liability Companies

The New Jersey Limited Liability Company Act does not expressly authorize a limited liability company (LLC) to issue a guaranty.[7] The New Jersey Limited Liability Company Act, however, states that LLCs may possess and exercise "all the powers and privileges granted by this act or by any other law or by its operating agreement, together with any powers incidental thereto, so far as such powers and privileges are necessary or convenient to the conduct, promotion or attainment of the business, purposes or activities of the limited liability company."[8] Therefore, the New Jersey Limited Liability Company Act indirectly authorizes a LLC's issuance of a guaranty where such issuance is "necessary or convenient to the conduct, promotion or attainment of the business, purposes or activities" of the company.[9]

Where the LLC is managed by its members, unless otherwise provided in the operating agreement of the company, each member has the authority to bind the company to a guaranty.[10]

---

4. N.J.S.A. 14A:3-1(1)(g).
5. N.J.S.A. 14A:3-3. *See also* Local 478 v. Baron Holding Corp., 224 N.J. Super. 485, 491 (1988) (finding that the corporation's execution of a guaranty was within its corporate purpose.); Walder, Sondak, Berkeley & Brogan v. Lipari, 300 N.J. Super. 67 (1997).
6. *See* N.J.S.A. 42:1A-1 *et seq.* and N.J.S.A. 42:2A-1 *et seq.*
7. N.J.S.A. 42:2B-1 *et seq.*
8. N.J.S.A. 42:2B-8.
9. *Id.*
10. *See* N.J.S.A. 42:2B-27(b)(1); Kuhn v. Tumminelli, 366 N.J. Super. 431 (2004).

3.4 Banks

A bank may not issue guaranties.[11] In addition, any guaranty issued by one bank to another bank shall be unenforceable by the bank receiving such guaranty.[12] However, this statutory prohibition is not absolute. A bank may issue letters of credit to effectively guarantee its customer's payment of an obligation.[13] In addition, a bank may make guaranties in the ordinary course of its business, provided that such guaranties are incidental to the disposal of assets owned by the bank that the bank transfers in the ordinary course of its business.[14]

3.5 Individuals

N.J.S.A. 12A:3-401 provides that "a person is not liable on an instrument unless the person signed the instrument, or the person is represented by an agent or representative who signed the instrument and the signature is binding on the represented person" provided that the "signature shows unambiguously that the signature is made on behalf of the represented person who is identified in the instrument."[15] A corporate officer shall not be bound individually on an agreement such as a guaranty, unless the corporate officer executes the agreement twice: once in his or her official capacity and once in his or her personal capacity.[16] Even where the language of the agreement provides that the corporate officer was personally guaranteeing the agreement, in the absence of a dual execution of an agreement, the corporate officer shall not be subject to personal liability.[17]

New Jersey law does not specifically address the ability of a spouse to bind his or her spouse to a guaranty but addresses the ability of a spouse generally to bind the other to a contract pursuant to the "Doctrine of Necessaries."[18] In this limited scenario, a spouse shall be personally liable for the debt incurred by his or her spouse where such debt (i) was for necessary expenses, (ii) the debt was incurred during the marriage, and (iii) such liability only is applicable to debts incurred after July 2, 1980, which is the date of the *Jersey Shore Medical Center-Fitkin Hospital v. Estate of Baum* decision.[19] The "Doctrine of Necessaries" shall be applicable even in the absence of an agreement.[20] For

---

11. N.J.S.A. 17:9A-213.1.
12. New Jersey Bank v. Palladino, 146 N.J. Super. 6 (1976), citing Strickland v. Nat'l Salt Co., 79 N.J. Eq. 182, 192 (E. & A. 1911).
13. N.J.S.A. 17:9A-25(3); New Jersey Bank v. Palladino, 77 N.J. 33, 40 (1978).
14. Federal Deposit Ins. Corp. v. Pioneer State Bank, 155 N.J. Super. 381 (1977) Under N.J.S.A. 17:9A-24(12), a bank has the authority to "exercise all incidental powers, not specifically enumerated in this act, which shall be necessary or convenient to carry on the business of the bank or savings bank."
15. N.J.S.A. 12A:3-402.
16. City of Millville v. Rock, et al., 683 F.Supp. 2d 319, 327 (New Jersey 2010) citing Home Buyers Warranty v. Roblyn Dev. Corp., 2006 WL 2190742 (N.J. App. Div. 2006).
17. City of Millville v. Rock, et al., 683 F.Supp. 2d 319, 327 (New Jersey 2010) citing Am. Furniture Mfg. Inc. v. Value Furniture & Mattress Warehouse, 2009 WL 8922 (N.J.Super. Ct. App. Div. 2008).
18. Jersey Shore Medical Center-Fitkin Hospital v. Estate of Baum, 84 N.J. 137, 141 (1980).
19. Jersey Shore Medical Center-Fitkin Hospital v. Estate of Baum, 84 N.J. 137, 141 (1980); DuBois v. DeLARM, 243 N.J. Super. 175, 185 (1990).
20. Jersey Shore Medical Center-Fitkin Hospital v. Estate of Baum, 84 N.J. 137, 141 (1980).

a debt arising from necessary expenses, a creditor is entitled to the property of both spouses where the creditor does not have an agreement with both spouses and where the financial resources of the spouse incurring the debt is insufficient to satisfy the debt.[21]

§ 4 Signatory's Authority to Execute a Guaranty

4.1 Corporations

An officer of a corporation can bind the corporation where the corporate officer's power to bind the corporation has been authorized expressly: "(a) by the corporate charter, (b) by the by-laws of the corporation, or (c) by the corporate action of the stockholders or board of directors."[22] The officers of the corporation also have the power to bind the corporation, provided that such power is express, implied, or apparent. Specifically, the courts have held that such implied powers may arise "(a) from powers expressly conferred or (b) incidental thereto."[23] Further, a corporation shall be bound by the acts of its officers or agents "within the apparent authority which it knowingly permits the agent to assume, or which it holds the agent out to the public as possessing."[24] Essentially, the corporation has placed its officer or the agent in a situation where a person "with whom its officers or agents have dealt to believe it has conferred upon them."[25]

Partnerships Each partner is considered an agent of the partnership and has the authority to bind the partnership, including executing contracts on behalf of the partnership, provided that such partner's actions are related to the business of the partnership.[26] If the acts of the partner were not for the purpose of carrying out the business of the partnership, such act or acts would bind the partnership if authorized by the other partners.[27] However, a partner may not bind the partnership where the partner does not have any authority to bind the partnership and the affected third party knew the partner was without any such authority.[28]

To limit the authority of its partners to bind the partnership, a partnership may file a "statement of authority" that limits the authority of the partners to "enter into transactions on behalf of the partnership."[29] Such statement of authority protects third parties who rely on the statement of authority to give value to the partnership, without knowledge to the contrary of the information contained in the statement of authority.[30] Further, a statement of

21. *Id.*
22. Silver v. Commonwealth Trust Co., 22 N.J. Super. 604 (Cty. Ct. 1952); Budelman v. White's Express & Transfer Co., Inc., 49 N.J. Super. 511 (1958).
23. Budelman v. White's Express & Transfer Co., Inc., 49 N.J. Super. 511 (1958).
24. Augustine v. Haas, 121 N.J.L. 58, 64 (1938).
25. Budelman v. White's Express & Transfer Co., Inc., 49 N.J. Super. 511 (1958).
26. N.J.S.A. 42:1A-13(a).
27. N.J.S.A. 42:1A-13(b).
28. N.J.S.A. 42:1A-13(a).
29. N.J.S.A. 42:1A-15(d).
30. N.J.S.A. 42:1A-15(f).

authority that provides the name of the partnership but does not contain all of the required information still may limit the authority of the partners to bind the partnership.[31]

4.2 Limited Partnerships

Subject to the provisions of the partnership agreement or the New Jersey Uniform Limited Partnership Law, the general partner of a limited partnership shall have the same rights, and shall be subject to the same restrictions, as a partner in a partnership as set forth in N.J.S.A. 42:1A-1 et seq.[32] On any matter not enumerated in the New Jersey Uniform Limited Partnership Law, the provisions of the New Jersey Uniform Partnership Act shall control.[33]

4.3 Limited Liability Companies

In the absence of contrary provisions in the LLC operating agreement, the New Jersey Limited Liability Company Act controls the authority of the members or the managers of a LLC to bind the company and provides that any member or manager shall have the authority to bind the company.[34] In addition, where the LLC is managed by its members, unless otherwise provided in the LLC agreement, each member of the LLC shall have the authority to bind the company.[35] It is in the execution of the LLC operating agreement that the members of the LLC may structure the company in ways that either restrict or expand "the rights, responsibilities and authority of its managers and members."[36]

§ 5 Consideration

Consideration is required to create an effective guaranty. Otherwise, the guaranty is considered a gratuitous promise.[37] Either a benefit or an inconvenience to the guarantor shall be sufficient consideration.[38] The courts have found that there is sufficient consideration even if there is only a slight benefit or inconvenience to the guarantor.[39]

The guaranty has to be executed at the same time as the contractual obligation (such as an underlying loan); otherwise, there has to be separate consideration given for such guaranty to be considered effective.[40]

31. N.J.S.A. 42:1A-15(c).
32. N.J.S.A. 42:2A-32.
33. N.J.S.A. 42:2A-3.
34. N.J.S.A. 42:2B-27.
35. N.J.S.A. 42:2B-27(b)(1).
36. Kuhn v. Tumminelli, 366 N.J. Super. 431, 501 (2004).
37. Great Falls Bank v. Pardo, 263 N.J. Super. 388, 400 (1993).
38. Ross v. Realty Abstract Co., 141 A.2d 319, 322 (1958).
39. *Id.*
40. Great Falls Bank v. Pardo, 263 N.J. Super. 388, 400-01 (1993); RTC v. Berman Inds., 271 N.J. Super. 56, 61 (1993).

§ 6 Interpretation of Guaranties

6.1 Intent of Parties

The rules governing the construction of contracts generally govern the interpretation of guaranties by New Jersey courts. The guaranty usually is interpreted according to its clear terms so as to effect the objective expectations of the parties.[41] The language of a guaranty agreement must be interpreted against the party that prepared the form and any ambiguity in a guaranty agreement should be construed in favor of the guarantor.[42] This prevents a guarantor from being bound beyond the strict terms of its promise or extending the guarantor's obligation by implication.[43] In the face of ambiguity, the courts try to ascertain the intention of the parties based on the language in the contract, the situation of the parties, the surrounding circumstances, and the goal of the parties.[44] Nevertheless, the courts have held that the terms of a guaranty shall be interpreted in accordance with the reasonable expectations of persons engaged in similar commercial transactions.[45]

"For an instrument to be enforceable as a guaranty, it must show, with reasonable clarity, an intent to be liable on an obligation in case of default by the primary obligor, and the agreement must contain the express conditions of [the] liability and obligations of each party within the four corners of the document."[46] Further, "[i]f the language chosen by the parties indicates an intention to answer for the principal debt or obligation of another person, the writing should be construed as a contract of guaranty."[47]

New Jersey courts also require that the party seeking enforcement of a guaranty must demonstrate each of the following[48]: (1) execution of the guaranty, (2) principal obligation and terms, (3) lender's reliance on guaranty in making the loan, (4) default by the primary obligor, (5) written demand for payment on the guaranty, and (6) failure of guarantor to pay upon written demand.

6.2 Guaranty of Payment versus Guaranty of Collection

A guaranty of collection requires that the guaranteed party must first proceed against the "principal debtor" prior to proceeding against the guarantor to enforce the guaranty. In a guaranty of payment, the guaranteed party is not required to proceed against the "principal debtor" prior to enforcing the guaranty.[49]

41. Sunoco, Inc. (R & M) v. Mx Wholesale Fuel Corp., 565 F. Supp.2d 572, 581 (2008).
42. Josefowicz v. Porter, 32 N.J. Super. 585, 590 (App.Div. 1954).
43. Housatonic Bank and Trust Co. v. Fleming, 234 N.J. Super. 79, 82 (1989).
44. Barr v. Barr, 418 N.J. Super 18, 37-38 (2010).
45. Mount Holly St. Bk. v. Mount Holly Washington Hotel, Inc. 220 N.J. Super. 506, 511 (1987).
46. 38 Am.Jur.2d Guaranty § 5.
47. Sunoco, Inc. (R & M) v. Mx Wholesale Fuel Corp., 565 F. Supp.2d 572, 581 (2008).
48. United States v. DelGuercio, 818 F.Supp. 725, 727-28 (D.N.J. 1993).
49. Connecticut General Life Insurance Co. v. Punia, 884 F.Supp. 148, 153 (D.N.J. 1995); United States Rubber Co. v. Champs Tires, Inc., 73 N.J. Super. 364 (1962).

§ 7 Revocation of Guaranties

Under New Jersey law, courts have enforced the terms of a guaranty and declined to relieve parties of their obligations when the parties voluntarily entered into the agreement understanding its terms, the transaction occurred in a commercial setting, viable alternatives existed, and the parties were not subject to oppression or unlawful surprise.[50]

Courts will allow the revocation of a guaranty prior to the advance of funds to the primary obligor. However, once an advance is made, the offer of guaranty is no longer revocable.[51]

A guarantor remains liable on a continuing guaranty even after revocation for any obligations incurred prior to the revocation. This also includes any renewals of the obligations incurred prior to the revocation.[52] This liability has been enforced in the face of revocation where the guaranty agreement specifically provides that the guaranty is a continuing, absolute, and unconditional guaranty or that the guarantor remains liable after revocation for any prerevocation obligations, or any renewal or extension of such obligations.[53] In addition, this liability has been enforced where the guaranty agreement (i) gives the creditor the right to renew or extend payment of the obligations without notice to or consent of the guarantors and (ii) where the guarantor agrees to remain liable on any transactions completed before revocation.[54]

7.1 "Continuing"

A continuing guaranty is, at its inception, an offer from the guarantor and is accepted by the creditor each time the latter does a specified act (e.g., extending credit to the debtor).[55] The continuing guaranty is not limited to a particular transaction and is intended to cover future transactions.[56]

In addition, where a guaranty agreement gives the creditor the right to renew or extend payment of the obligations without notice to or consent of the guarantors (and when read together with the guarantor's agreement to remain liable on any transactions completed before revocation), such guaranty is a continuing guaranty.[57] A continuing guaranty will not be discharged by virtue of the guarantor's death and the guarantor's estate will remain obligated under the guaranty.[58]

In a continuing guaranty, the inclusion of the provision "hereafter arising" holds the guarantor liable for any future indebtedness. Such continuing guaranty, however, could be revoked to prevent the guarantor's liability for

50. First New Jersey Bank v. F.L.M. Bus. Machines, 130 N.J. Super. 151, 162-63 (1974).
51. Mount Holly St. Bk. v. Mount Holly Washington Hotel, Inc., 220 N.J. Super. 506, 511 (1987).
52. First New Jersey Bank v. F.L.M. Bus Machines, 130 N.J. Super. 151 (1974).
53. First New Jersey Bank v. F.L.M. Bus Machines, 130 N.J. Super. 151 (1974); Mount Holly St. Bk. v. Mount Holly Washington Hotel, 220 N.J. Super. 506 (1987).
54. Housatonic Bank and Trust Co. v. Fleming, 234 N.J. Super. 79, 84 (1989).
55. First New Jersey Bank v. F.L.M. Bus. Machines, 130 N.J. Super. 151, 160 (1974).
56. Swift & Co. v. Smigel, 115 N.J. Super. 391, 394 (1971) (citing Fidelity Union Trust Co. v. Galm, 109 N.J.L. 111, 116).
57. Housatonic Bank and Trust Co. v. Fleming, 234 N.J. Super. 79, 84 (1989).
58. First New Jersey Bank v. F.L.M. Bus. Machines, 130 N.J. Super. 151, 160 (1974).

such future loans or indebtedness, provided that the notice of revocation was provided prior to the future transaction.[59]

Further, under a continuing guaranty, even if a guarantor no longer has any interest in the primary obligor, the guarantor still shall be liable for any future indebtedness incurred by such primary obligor prior to revocation and shall be liable for any indebtedness incurred by such primary obligor at the time of the revocation of the guaranty, including any renewals or extensions of such indebtedness.[60]

7.2 "Absolute and Unconditional"

An unconditional guaranty permits a creditor to move against a guarantor without first acting against either the collateral or the principal debtor.[61] An unconditional guaranty is one whereby the guarantor agrees to pay or perform a contract upon default of the principal without limitation.[62] The guaranty does not need to use the term "unconditional" to be considered unconditional.[63]

§ 8 Defenses of the Guarantor

8.1 Defenses of the Guarantor

8.1.1 Personal Defenses

Provided that a guaranty is clear and unambiguous, the guarantor shall be bound by the terms of the guaranty unless the guarantor can prove defenses that include fraud, duress, or another wrongful act.[64] A guarantor also may raise the additional personal defenses of negligence in performance or breach of warranty.

8.1.2 Mistake

A guaranty contract may be rescinded on the basis of a unilateral or bilateral mistake.

8.1.2.1 Bilateral Mistake

Contract law requires a meeting of the minds in order to validate an agreement. When parties enter into a guaranty agreement based on a mutual mistake as to

59. Mount Holly St. Bk. v. Mount Holly Washington Hotel, Inc., 220 N.J. Super. 506, 511 (1987).
60. *See* Mount Holly St. Bk. v. Mount Holly Washington Hotel, Inc., 220 N.J. Super. 506, 511-12 (1987) (the sale of the guarantors' ownership interest in the primary obligor did not discharge their obligations in connection with further loans extended by the bank to the primary obligor.).
61. Delaware Truck Sales, Inc. v. Wilson, 131 N.J. 20, 33 (1993).
62. Nation Wide, Inc. v. Scullin, 256 F. Supp. 929, 933 (D.N.J. 1966) (citing Joe Heaston Tractor & Imp. Co. v. Securities Accept. Corp., 243 F.2d 196, 199 (10 Cir. 1957)).
63. Interchange State Bank v. Rinaldi, 303 N.J. Super. 239, 248-49 (1997) (Language of guaranty did not use the word "unconditional" but merely stated that the guaranty will continue to be in effect until written notice cancelling the guaranty.).
64. National Westminster Bank USA v Sardi's Inc., 174 A.D.2d 470 (1991).

the nature of the underlying contract and the mistake is such that the parties never mutually agreed to the terms of the guaranty contract, then the guaranty agreement may be rescinded.[65]

8.1.2.2 Unilateral Mistake

While a unilateral mistake by a guarantor as to the nature of the underlying transaction is not a basis for relief and generally does not terminate the guaranty agreement, a guarantor can argue against the enforcement of a guaranty if the guarantor proves special circumstances that show (i) the enforcement of the contract would be unconscionable, (ii) the mistaken fact must be material to the guaranty agreement, (iii) the mistaken party exercised reasonable care, and (iv) the rescission of the guaranty would not be seriously prejudicial to the other party other than such party's loss of the benefit of its bargain.[66] In determining the unconscionability of a contract, the courts weigh the procedural unconscionability (unfairness in the formation of the contract) and the substantive unconscionability (excessively disproportionate terms) of the contract.[67] In addition, the reasonable care of a party, viewed as the level of negligence of the party, is determined on a case-by-case basis, based on the particular circumstances of each case.[68] Finally, the prejudice to the rescinding party is reviewed with consideration based on whether the nonrescinding party is left in a no-worse position than if the contract never happened.[69]

8.1.3 Fraud

The guarantor could argue that facts were concealed that would have prevented the guarantor from obligating himself.

8.2 Change in Obligation

A material modification to the contract underlying the guaranty agreement will result in a discharge of the guarantor, where such alteration or modification injures the guarantor or increases the guarantor's risk of liability.[70]

8.3 Change in Condition to Guaranty

If a creditor fails to comply with a condition upon which a guarantor agrees to become bound under the guaranty agreement, the obligations of the guarantor can be discharged.[71]

---

65. Center 48 Lid. P'ship v. The May Dep't Stores Co., 355 N.J. Super. 390, 406 (2002).
66. Center 48 Lid. P'ship v. The May Dep't Stores Co., 355 N.J. Super. 390, 406 (2002); Intertech Assocs., Inc. v. City of Paterson, 255 N.J. Super. 52, 59-60 (App.Div. 1992).
67. In re Andris, No. 11–10330/JHW, 2011 WL 1743430 (Bankr.D.N.J. Apr. 29, 2011) (citing Delta Funding Corp. v. Harris, 189 N.J. 28, 55 (2006); Sitogum Holdings, Inc. v. Ropes, 352 N.J. Super. 555, 564 (2002).
68. Intertech v. City of Paterson, 255 N.J. Super. 52, 61 (1992).
69. In re Andris, No. 11–10330/JHW, 2011 WL 1743430 (Bankr.D.N.J. Apr. 29, 2011).
70. Center 48 Ltd. P'ship v. May Dep't Stores Co., 810 A.2d 610, 619 (N.J. Super.Ct. App. Div. 2002).
71. *See* Peoples Nat'l Bank of N.J. v. Fowler, 73 N.J. 88, 102-103 (1977) (where the obligations of an uncompensated and gratuitous guarantor under a guaranty agreement were discharged as guarantor entered into the guaranty subject to the condition that the bank would comply with the provisions of a federal regulation and the bank violated such express conditions.).

8.4 Impairment of Collateral

A creditor or a secured party may not unjustifiably impair any collateral.[72] Impairment of the collateral as a result of the creditor's improper action or inaction will terminate the obligation of a guarantor, at least to the extent of the value of the security released or impaired.[73] The termination or reduction in the obligation of the guarantor applies where the creditor releases the collateral.[74]

A guarantor, however, will be precluded from asserting the impairment of collateral as a defense where the guaranty agreement states that it is a continuing, absolute, and unconditional guaranty.[75] Such a guaranty grants the creditor the full discretion and the full rights to deal with the collateral, especially where the language of the guaranty agreement shows that "(a) the [guarantor's] obligations were absolute, continuing, and unconditional, (b) the [creditor] had the right to release, compromise, or settle a claim without affecting the continuing liability of the guarantor, (c) the [creditor] had the right to release, substitute, or fail to protect or insure any part of the collateral without affecting the liability of the guarantor, (d) the [creditor] had the right to fail or delay in exercising any rights or remedies against the [primary obligor] and in the event of default, and (e) in the event of default the [creditor] had the right to proceed directly and without notice against the guarantor without first proceeding against the [primary obligor] or in respect of any collateral held by the [creditor]."[76]

8.3 Third-party Pledgors

A third-party's pledge of his property as security for the obligation of another party makes such third-party pledgor a surety to the extent of the pledged property. In addition, the third-party pledgor shall have standing to raise the defenses of a guarantor.[77]

§ 9 Waiver of Defenses

A guarantor can waive all of the foregoing contractual or statutory rights, including impairment of collateral, in the guaranty agreement, provided that

72. National Westminster Bank N.J. v. Lomker, 277 N.J. Super. 491, 497 (1994).
73. Langeveld v. L.R.Z.H. Corp., 74 N.J. 45, 50-51 (1977).
74. *Id.*
75. Delaware Truck Sales, Inc. v. Wilson, 131 N.J. 20 (1993).
76. Brae Asset Fund, L.P. v. Newman, 327 N.J. Super. 129, 136 (1999).
77. Peoples Nat'l Bank of N.J. v. Fowler, 73 N.J. 88, 98-99 (1977).

such waiver is unequivocal.[78] In addition, a guarantor can waive the defenses of bad faith, fraud, or conspiracy, provided that such waiver is explicit.[79]

§ 10 Coguarantors

10.1 Contribution

A guarantor that is party to an agreement with one or more other guarantors is considered a "principal debtor for the portion of the debt which he ought to pay and a surety for the remainder."[80] Such a coguarantor is entitled to exoneration from the other coguarantors, who are required to pay their pro-rata share of the obligation to the creditor upon the maturity of the "guaranteed debt and before any payment has been made by any guarantor."[81] This duty of exoneration arises because, while a coguarantor is not obligated to contribute to a fellow coguarantor's payment of a portion of a debt until the fellow coguarantor has paid more than its pro-rata share of the debt, in the absence of such a duty, the payment by a coguarantor of more than his pro-rata share of the guaranteed debt could subject the paying guarantor to "inequitable hardship."[82] The duty of exoneration arises either upon demand by the coguarantor, or upon notice of default by the primary obligor with respect to the guaranteed debt.[83] The coguarantor seeking exoneration, however, is required first to pay its proportionate share of the guaranteed debt or to make such payment simultaneously with the other coguarantors.[84]

However, where the obligations of the guarantors to a guaranty agreement are joint and several, the failure of a coguarantor to pay its pro-rata share of the guaranteed debt does not affect the obligations of the other coguarantors to pay the guaranteed debt.[85]

§ 11 Subrogation

Subrogation is an equitable remedy intended to compel the ultimate discharge of an obligation to the obligee by the party who "in good conscience ought

78. Langeveld v. L.R.Z.H. Corp., 74 N.J. 45, 53 (1977); Delaware Truck Sales, Inc. v. Wilson, 131 N.J. 20, 32 (1993) (The guaranty on its face gives broad rights to Royal Bank. It states that it is "a continuing, absolute and unconditional guaranty" and may be enforced "without first resorting to any security or other property or invoking other available rights or remedies." Thus, under the guaranty Royal Bank had virtually uncontrolled discretion to deal with the collateral, including the right to assign it.)
79. *See* Halper V. Halper, 164 F.3d 830, 843 (3rd Cir. 1999) (citing National Westminster Bank NJ v. Lomker, 649 A.2d 1328 (N.J. Super. Ct. App. Div. 1994)).
80. D'Ippolito, et al., v. Castoro, et al., 51 N.J. 584, 591 (1968) (citing Bristol Bank & Trust Co. v. Broderick, 122 Conn. 310 (1939)); Sanderson v. Cicero State Bank, 125 N.J. Eq. 450, 453 (Ch. 1939).
81. D'Ippolito, et al., v. Castoro, et al., 51 N.J. 584, 589-90 (1968).
82. *Id.*
83. D'Ippolito, et al., v. Castoro, et al., 51 N.J. 584, 590 (1968).
84. *Id.*
85. Midstates Resources v. Burgess and Fenmore, 333 N.J. Super. 531, 535 (2000).

to pay the debt."[86] Subrogation permits the "substitution of one person in the place of another with reference to a lawful claim, demand or right, so that he who is substituted succeeds to the rights of the other in relation to the debt or claim, and its rights, remedies or securities."[87] However, the successful application of the equitable remedy of subrogation depends on the merits of the subrogor's claims against the third party and whether the subrogor would have recovered against the third party.[88] Further, subrogation is not available where the enforcement of such doctrine would be "inconsistent with the terms of the contract" or when the contract forbids the application of the doctrine.[89]

§ 12 Triangular Set-off in Bankruptcy

New Jersey does not allow triangular set-off in bankruptcy as, under New Jersey law, there must be mutuality of obligation between the debtor and creditor.[90]

§ 13 Enforcement of Guaranties

New Jersey courts have held that a guaranty will not be enforced against a guarantor in instances that include a mutual mistake, lack of consideration, lender bad faith, and misconduct.[91] See the section above on the defenses of a guarantor.

§ 14 Revival and Reinstatement of Guaranties

See section on revocation of guaranties.

§ 15 Choice of Law

New Jersey courts uphold the choice-of-law clause set forth in a guaranty unless "(a) the chosen state has no substantial relationship to the parties or

86. Feigenbaum v. Guaracini, 402 N.J. Super. 7, 10, 19 (2008).
87. Feigenbaum v. Guaracini, 402 N.J. Super. 7, 10 (2008).
88. *Id.*
89. Feigenbaum v. Guaracini, 402 N.J. Super. 7, 16 (2008).
90. In re Pineview Care Center, Inc. 142 B.R. 677, 683 (1992); In re Eisinore Shore Associates, 67 B.R. 926, 936 (1986).
91. Center 48 Lid. P'ship v. The May Dep't Stores Co., 355 N.J. Super. 390, 406 (2002) ("where a mistake is such that the parties never mutually agreed to the terms of the guarantee contract, then the document will not be enforced against the guarantor"); Great Falls Bank v. Pardo, 263 N.J. Super. 388, 400 (1993); National Westminster Bank USA v. Sardi's Inc., 174 A.D.2d 470 (1991).

the transaction and there is no other reasonable basis for the parties' choice," or "(b) application of the law of the chosen state would be contrary to a fundamental policy of a state which has a materially greater interest than the chosen state in the determination of the particular issue and [which would] be the state of the applicable law in the absence of an effective choice of law by the parties."[92]

New Jersey courts have found that a "substantial relationship" exists with a state when one of the parties is headquartered in that state.[93] In addressing prong "(b)" of the choice-of-law test set forth above, New Jersey courts have found that the application of the law of a chosen state was not contrary to fundamental New Jersey policy and that New Jersey does not have a materially greater interest than the chosen state where New Jersey law and the chosen state's law were substantially similar with respect to most of the disputed issues in the litigation.[94]

---

92. Homa v. Am. Express Co., 558 F.3d 225, 227 (3d Cir. 2009) (citing Instructional Sys., Inc. v. Computer Curriculum Corp., 130 N.J. 324 (1992).

93. Instructional Sys., Inc. v. Computer Curriculum Corp., 130 N.J. 324, 341-42 (1992); *see also* Hertz Corp. v. Friend, 130 S.Ct. 1181, 1192 (2010) (finding "principal place of business" in practice to be the place where the corporation maintains its headquarters, "provided that the headquarters is the actual center of direction, control, and coordination.").

94. Campor, Inc. v. Brulant, LLC (N.J. 4-1-2010) (applying Ohio law instead of New Jersey law as Ohio law's recognition of a claim for breach of the implied covenant of good faith and fair dealing as part of a breach of contract claim rather than as a stand-alone claim does not implicate New Jersey public policy concerns.) Contrast Bergen v. Trailer Leasing Co., 158 N.J. 561, 568-569 (1999) (applying New Jersey law instead of Illinois law, even though one of the parties was headquartered in Illinois, as New Jersey has a strong policy disfavoring shifting of attorneys' fees); Zeckman v. Bush Industries, Inc. (D.N.J. 6-23-2009) (applying New York law instead of New Jersey law because, although New York does not apply the doctrine of promissory estoppel in the employment context, there is no violation of any public policy of New Jersey.).

New Mexico State Law of Guaranties

John P. Burton
Rodey, Dickason, Sloan, Akin & Robb, P.A.
315 Paseo de Peralta
Santa Fe, New Mexico 87501
505.954.3906
fax: 505.954.3942
jburton@rodey.com
www.rodey.com

Contents

New Mexico State Law of Guaranties

HIGHLIGHTS

1. New Mexico has little law relevant to guaranties, so its courts usually fill the gaps with law from the Restatement (Third) of Suretyship and Guaranty (1996).
2. New Mexico courts employ freedom-of-contract principles to uphold extensive waivers of a guarantor's rights which impair or eliminate rights of recourse against collateral and coguarantors.
3. New Mexico is a community property state. Its law is unclear about whether there is recourse against any community property for a guaranty executed by only one spouse. The law may reflect the state's public policy. If it does, the uncertainty may extend to a guaranty governed by the law of another jurisdiction.

Introductory Notes

Terminology: In order to standardize our discussion of the law of guaranties, we use the following vocabulary to refer to the parties to a guaranty and their obligations.

"Guarantor" means a person who agrees to satisfy an underlying obligation of another to an obligee upon a primary obligor's default on that underlying obligation. We do not draw a distinction between a guarantor and a surety, as the terminology in New Mexico has been combined, at least for most purposes.[1]

"Guaranty" means a contract by which a guarantor agrees to satisfy an underlying obligation of a primary obligor to an obligee if the primary obligor defaults on the underlying obligation.

"Obligee" means a person to whom an underlying obligation is owed. For example, a lender under a loan agreement is an obligee vis-à-vis the borrower.

"Primary Obligor" means a person who incurs an underlying obligation to an obligee. For example, a borrower under a loan agreement is a primary obligor.

"Underlying Obligation" means an obligation incurred by a primary obligor and owed to an obligee. For example, a borrower's obligation to make payments to a lender of principal and interest on a loan constitutes an underlying obligation.

1. *See, e.g.*, American Bank of Commerce v. Covolo, 88 N.M. 405, 407, n.3, 540 P.2d 1294, 1296 n.3 (1975) (citing UCC Article 1, now amended and recodified at NMSA 1978, § 55-1-201(b)(39) (2005) ("'Surety' includes a guarantor or other secondary obligor.")); *see also* Restatement (Third) of Suretyship & Guaranty § 1 cmt. c (1996).

Introduction and Sources of Law: New Mexico has little law relevant to guaranties. In the absence of relevant New Mexico authority, New Mexico courts usually, but not always,[2] turn to the Restatement (Third) of Suretyship and Guaranty for guidance.[3] The Restatement provides "authoritative guidance on the common law" of guaranties.[4] Articles 3[5] and 9[6] of the Uniform Commercial Code (UCC), as well as their Official Comments,[7] provide supplemental guidance for the secondary obligations to which they apply. If either Article 3 or 9 applies to a transaction, then the general provisions of Article 1 also come into play.[8]

2. McAlpine v. Zangara Dodge, Inc., 2008-NMCA-064, ¶ 19, 144 N.M. 90, 183 P.3d 975 (Castillo J.) (declining to follow the Restatement (Third) of Suretyship & Guaranty § 67(3) on the effect upon the liability of a surety of a default judgment against the principal).
3. Randles v. Hanson, 2011-NMCA-059, ¶ 14, 150 N.M. 362, 258 P.3d 1154 (Fry, J.).
4. Venaglia v. Kropinak, 1998-NMCA-043, ¶ 12, 125 N.M. 25, 956 P.2d 824 (Hartz, C.J.). Venaglia was the first New Mexico case to provide modern law about guaranties.
5. *Id.* ¶ 11. The guarantors in *Venaglia* signed the note as accommodation parties, bringing Article 3 of the UCC into play. Judge Hartz spent many pages analyzing the differences between the Restatement and Article 3 as it existed then. Article 3 has since been amended. One of the purposes of the amendments was to conform it to the Restatement. *See* Uniform Commercial Code, Drafting Committee to Amend Uniform Commercial Code Articles 3 & 4, Prefatory Note, 2 U.L.A. ¶ 4, at 6 (2004) ("Amendments to UCC §§ 4-419 and 3-605 generally conform those provisions to the rules in the *Restatement of Suretyship and Guaranty.*"). New Mexico enacted these amendments in 2009. NMSA 1978, §§ 55-3-101 to -605 (1992), as amended.
6. Article 9 of the UCC was not mentioned in Venaglia because the guarantors had not pledged any personal property as collateral to support the principal obligor's debt. After Venaglia was decided, Article 9 was completely rewritten. Professor Neil B. Cohen, the reporter for the Restatement of Suretyship and Guaranty, served as a member of the drafting committee to revise Article 9. This cross-membership better assured consistency between the Restatement and revised Article 9. New Mexico, along with every other state, has adopted the revised version of Article 9. NMSA 1978, §§ 55-9-101 to -709 (2001), as amended. Recently, Article 9 has been revised yet again. New Mexico will take up this latest revision in the 2013 session of its legislature.
7. Official Comments are "persuasive," although not "controlling authority." First State Bank v. Clark, 91 N.M. 117, 119, 570 P.2d 1140, 1142 (1977) (interpreting the UCC). Official Comments are especially helpful in New Mexico because of its paucity of reported cases and its complete absence of legislative history.
8. NMSA 1978, § 55-1-102 (2005) ("Chapter 55, Article 1 NMSA 1978 applies to a transaction to the extent that it is governed by another article of the Uniform Commercial Code."). Of relevance to this discussion are the provisions of Article 1 containing the definition of good faith, *see infra* § 6.5, and choice-of-law rules, *see infra* § 17.

§ 1 Nature of the Guaranty Arrangement

Under New Mexico law, a guaranty is a collateral agreement to pay a debt or perform a duty for another in case of default, which may be enforced separately from the primary obligation, and when the guaranty exists, it is not necessary to proceed directly against the primary obligor.[9]

1.1 Guaranty Relationships

A guaranty is a contract of secondary liability under which a guarantor has an obligation to pay an obligee after a default by a principal obligor.[10] The relationship between a primary obligor and a guarantor arises as a matter of law, and it is based in the notion that, while a guarantor is liable to an obligee, it is the principal obligor who ultimately should bear the underlying obligation.[11]

1.2 Other Suretyship Relationships

While not the focus of this discussion, a suretyship relationship may also arise because of a pledge of collateral.[12] As such, a guaranty-type relationship arises to the extent of the collateral pledged when one party grants to a creditor a security interest in property to secure the obligation of another.[13] New Mexico statutes prohibit or regulate certain indemnity agreements in transactions relating to construction; mining; drilling wells for oil, gas, or water; and leasing or renting of equipment.[14] These matters are also beyond the focus of this discussion.

§ 2 State Law Requirements for an Entity to Enter into a Guaranty

A business corporation or a nonprofit corporation can grant a guaranty. A state bank generally cannot. New Mexico has no statutory authority or common law relevant to this issue with respect to a partnerships or a limited liability company.

9. Joe Heaston Tractor & Implement Co. v. Sec. Acceptance Corp., 243 F.2d. 196 (10th Cir. 1957) (applying New Mexico law).
10. *Randles,* 2011-NMCA-059, ¶ 11.
11. NMSA 1978, § 55-3-419(f) (2009); Restatement (Third) of Suretyship & Guaranty § 1 cmt. b.
12. *See* Restatement (Third) of Suretyship and Guaranty § 1(1)(a) (noting that a person is a surety when "pursuant to contract . . . an obligee has recourse against [that] person . . . *or that person's property* with respect to an obligation . . . of another person . . . to that obligee" (emphasis added)).
13. *Compare* NMSA 1978, § 55-9-102(a)(28)(A) (2005) (definition of "debtor" under Article 9 of the UCC, which debtor, among other things not relevant to this discussion, has "an interest other than a security interest or other lien" in the collateral, "whether or not the debtor is an obligor") *with* NMSA 1978, 55-9-102(59)(A) (2005) (definition of "obligor" under Article 9, which obligor, among other things not relevant to this discussion, "owes payment or other performance of the obligation").
14. NMSA 1978, § 56-7-1(2005) (construction); *Id.* § 56-7-2 (2003) (mining; drilling oil, gas, and water wells); *Id.* § 56-7-3 (2007) (equipment leases and rentals).

2.1 Corporations

Under the Business Corporation Act, a New Mexico business corporation may, within the scope of its general corporate powers, "make contracts and guarantees."[15] The Nonprofit Corporation Act grants the same powers to a New Mexico nonprofit corporation.[16]

2.2 Partnerships

New Mexico's Uniform Partnership Act and Uniform Revised Limited Partnership Act[17] neither expressly empower a partnership to issue a guaranty nor expressly regulate or prohibit such an activity. There is no example in the case law of a partnership issuing a guaranty.

2.3 Limited Liability Companies

New Mexico's Limited Liability Company Act[18] neither expressly empowers a limited liability company (LLC) to issue a guaranty nor expressly regulates or prohibits such an activity. There is no example in the case law of an LLC issuing a guaranty.

2.4 Banks and Trust Companies

A New Mexico state-chartered bank may not be a guarantor, except for minor exceptions not relevant to this discussion.[19]

2.5 Subsidiary Guaranties

New Mexico has no law about whether a subsidiary has the corporate or other entity power to guarantee or otherwise become liable for indebtedness incurred by its parent or to encumber its assets to secure this indebtedness, except to the extent that the subsidiary may be determined to have benefited from the incurrence of the indebtedness by its parent, or whether this benefit may be measured other than by the extent to which the proceeds of the indebtedness incurred by the parent are directly or indirectly made available to the subsidiary for its corporate or other entity purposes.[20]

---

15. NMSA 1978, § 53-11-4 (1987).
16. NMSA 1978, § 53-8-5 (1975).
17. NMSA 1978, §§ 54-1A-101 to -1206 (1996), as amended; NMSA 1978, §§ 54-2A-101 to -1206 (2007), as amended.
18. NMSA 1978, §§ 53-19-1 to -74 (1993), as amended.
19. NMSA 1978, § 58-1-31 (1963).
20. *See* Donald W. Glazer et al., Glazer and FitzGibbon on Legal Opinions § 8.3.2, at 245 (3d ed. 2008).

2.6 Individuals

2.6.1 *Individuals versus Corporate Officers*

Confusion can sometimes arise in the case of a corporate officer signing a guaranty in a closely held corporation. In such an instance, a case-by-case inquiry determines whether the individual intended to be personally bound by the guaranty or, instead, issued the guaranty only on behalf of the corporation, and thus only in an official employment capacity.[21] When an individual signs the individual's title as well as the individual's name, these facts are not dispositive of an intention not to issue a personal guaranty.[22]

2.6.2 *Marital Property*

In 1983 a Supreme Court case construed one community property statute and ruled that a guaranty signed by one spouse encumbered only the community property interest of that spouse and not that of the other spouse.[23] Ten years later the case was overruled on this point.[24]

Another New Mexico statute, Section 40-3-4, provides that a "contract of indemnity" that is not signed by both spouses does not "obligate" the community property of either spouse.[25] In 1987 the Supreme Court held that this statute does not apply to a promissory note given as collateral for corporate indebtedness.[26] The court stated in what may be dictum that this statute applies only to "contracts of indemnity with surety companies."[27] New Mexico has no other case construing this statute.

The Sample Opinion of the Opinion Task Force of the Real Property, Probate and Trust Law Section of the State Bar of New Mexico contains an exclusion with respect to this statute. The exclusion states, "no community property shall be liable for any indebtedness incurred as a result of any contract of indemnity, unless both husband and wife sign the contract of indemnity. § 40-3-4"[28] This exclusion is stated in connection with a sample loan transaction involving a guaranty in which no surety company is a party and in which no document is titled an indemnity agreement.

The exclusion may serve as an indication of the concerns that some New Mexico practitioners have about the importance of the statute, the dire consequences of a violation, even inadvertent, and uncertainty about its interpretation.

In view of the subject matter of the statute, it is not completely out of the question that a court could find that it reflects the public policy of New Mexico. If a court should find that it does reflect the public policy of New

21. *See, e.g.*, Ricker v. B-W Acceptance Corp., 349 F.2d 892 (10th Cir. 1965) (applying New Mexico law).
22. *Id.*; Ellis v. Stone, 21 N.M. 730, 158 P. 480 (1916).
23. First State Bank v. Muzio, 100 N.M. 98, 99, 666 P.2d 777, 778 (1983) (construing NMSA 1978, § 40-3-12(A) (1973).
24. Huntington Nat'l Bank v. Sproul, 116 N.M. 254, 264, 861 P.2d 935, 945 (1993).
25. NMSA 1978, §40-3-4 (1965).
26. Lubbock Steel & Supply, Inc. v. Gomez, 105 N.M. 516, 517, 734 P.2d 756, 757 (1987).
27. *Id.* at 518, 734 P.2d 758.
28. Lawyers' Opinions in Mortgage Loan Transactions, Qualification ¶ 18, at 50 (2003).

Mexico, then the court might also apply the statute to a guaranty that chooses the law of another state.[29]

2.6.3 Execution Requirements

New Mexico has no special execution requirements for individual guarantors, married or not.

§ 3 Signatory's Authority to Execute a Guaranty

New Mexico has no law dealing with this issue.

§ 4 Consideration

New Mexico has only two cases dealing with consideration in the context of a guaranty. These cases were tried without questioning the fact that consideration was necessary and applied standard contract principles to the analysis.[30] However, consideration is required for the modification of a guaranty.[31] New Mexico has no cases deciding whether consideration flowing to a borrower is sufficient consideration for a guarantor.

§ 5 Notice of Acceptance

New Mexico has no law dealing with this issue.

§ 6 Interpretation of Guaranties

Courts in New Mexico strictly construe the obligations of the guarantor. In other regards, courts will interpret a guaranty in the same manner by which they would interpret the language of any other contract.

---

29. *See infra* § 17; Piña v. Gruy Petroleum Mgmt. Co., 2006-NMCA-063, ¶ 1, 139 N.M. 619, 136 P.3d 1029 (construing NMSA 1978, § 56-7-2 (2003), an indemnity-limiting statute applicable to oil and gas drilling, holding that the statute reflects the public policy of New Mexico, and applying the statute to a contract that chose the law of Texas).
30. Gonzales v. Gauna, 28 N.M. 55, 206 P. 511 (1922); Valley Bank of Commerce v. Hilburn, 2005-NMCA-004, ¶ 24, 136 N.M. 741, 105 P.3d 294 (filed 2004) (Pickard, J.).
31. *See infra* § 7.3.2.

6.1 General Principles

On one hand, New Mexico courts state that they recognize the principles that a guarantor is a favorite of the law and that the obligations of a guarantor are to be strictly construed.[32] On the other hand, the courts recognize the principle of freedom of contract.[33] The courts apply the latter principle to construe broadly, not strictly, a waiver by a guarantor of the guarantor's suretyship defenses, with the result that the guarantor's liability is actually expanded.[34] Outside of these principles, the same principles of construction that apply generally to contracts also apply to guaranties.[35]

6.2 Absolute Guaranty versus Conditional Guaranty

New Mexico classifies guaranties as either absolute or conditional. An absolute guaranty imposes automatic liability on a guarantor upon the default of an obligor, and an obligee is neither required first to seek payment from a principal nor to notify a guarantor of a default.[36]

On the other hand, a guaranty is conditional when its terms state that a condition precedent must be met before a guarantor is held liable.[37]

6.3 Continuing Guaranty versus Restricted Guaranty

Guaranties are also classified as either continuing or restricted.[38] A continuing guaranty is one in which either the amount of debt or the time for payment remains undefined, such as a line of credit.[39]

On the other hand, a restricted guaranty contemplates either a single transaction or a limited number of transactions.[40]

6.4 Revocation of Continuing Guaranty

An offer to guarantee future obligations in a continuing guaranty may be revoked, absent a contrary provision in the guaranty instrument.[41]

---

32. *See, e.g.*, Sunwest Bank v. Garrett, 113 N.M. 112, 117, 828 P.2d 912, 917 (1992).
33. *See, e.g.*, *American Bank of Commerce*, 88 N.M. at 409-10, 540 P.2d at 1298-99 (provision that permitted obligee bank to release collateral construed to relieve bank from liability to perfect lien on collateral, even though failure was arguably negligent); *infra* § 7.2.
34. *Id.*
35. WXI/Z Sw. Malls Real Estate Liab. Co. v. Mueller, 2005-NMCA-046, ¶ 10, 137 N.M. 343, 110 P.3d 1080 (Fry, J.) (citing Restatement (Third) of Suretyship & Guaranty § 14 (stating that standard contract rules apply to secondary obligations)).
36. *Id.* ¶ 14.
37. *Id.*
38. *Id.* ¶ 15.
39. *Id.*
40. *Id.*
41. FDIC v. Moore, 118 N.M. 77, 79, 879 P.2d 78, 80 (1994).

6.5 Duty of Good Faith

The *American Bank of Commerce* case was the first New Mexico case to address the duty of good faith in connection with a guaranty.[42] It relied primarily upon Articles 3 and 1 of the UCC.[43] The court ruled that the obligee-bank's duties of good faith and reasonableness could not be waived under the UCC, but the parties could determine the standards by which those duties could be met.[44] Following *American Bank of Commerce*, New Mexico courts have allowed the complete waiver of a number of surety defenses under the rubric of freedom of contract.[45]

After *American Bank of Commerce*, the Supreme Court held that there is implied in every New Mexico contract a "duty of good faith and fair dealing upon the parties in the performance and enforcement of the contract."[46] The breach of this covenant requires a showing of bad faith or that one party wrongfully and intentionally used the contract to the detriment of the other party."[47]

This implied covenant of good faith and fair dealing requires that neither party do anything that will injure the rights of the other to receive the benefit of their agreement.[48] This implied covenant applies to guaranties.[49]

New Mexico has no reported cases construing the modern definition of "good faith" in Article 1 of the UCC,[50] or the recent amendments to the suretyship provisions of Article 3,[51] or the suretyship provisions that were added with the 2001 revision of Article 9.[52]

§ 7 Defenses of the Guarantor; Set-off

The defenses that may be available to a guarantor can be grouped into three categories: (1) defenses of the primary obligor; (2) "suretyship defenses"; and (3) other defenses.

7.1 Defenses of the Primary Obligor

New Mexico has no law dealing with this issue.

42. *American Bank of Commerce,* 88 N.M. at 407, n.3, 540 P.2d at 1296, n.3.
43. *Id.* Curiously, the court gave no indication why UCC Articles 3 and 1 might apply to the guaranties in that case. *See supra* n. 5.
44. *Id.*
45. *See infra* § 7.2.
46. Paiz v. State Farm Fire & Cas. Co., 118 N.M. 203, 212, 880 P.2d 300, 309 (1994) (internal quotation marks & citation omitted), limited on other grounds by Sloan v. State Farm Mut. Auto Ins. Co. (In re Sloan), 2004-NMSC-004, ¶ 12, 135 N.M. 106, 85 P.2d 230.
47. *Id.*
48. Planning & Design Solutions v. City of Santa Fe, 18 N.M. 707, 714, 885 P.2d 628, 635 (1994).
49. *WHI/Z Sw. Malls,* 2005-NMCA-046, ¶¶ 24-29.
50. *Compare* NMSA 1978, § 55-1-201 (b)(20) (2005) (defining "good faith" as "honesty in fact and the observance of reasonable commercial standards of fair dealing") *with* NMSA 1978, § 55-1-201(19) (1992) (defining "good faith" as "honesty in fact in the conduct or transaction concerned").
51. *See supra* n. 4.
52. *See supra* n. 5.

7.2 "Suretyship" Defenses

7.2.1 Change in Identity of Principal Obligor

New Mexico has no law dealing with this issue.

7.2.2 Modification of the Underlying Obligation

New Mexico's latest case on point, decided in 1994 before the promulgation of the Restatement, held that a guarantor was completely discharged by a material change in the underlying obligation to which the guarantor had not consented.[53] When presented with the proper case, however, New Mexico courts may adopt the modern rule that such a modification will discharge a guarantor only to the extent that the guarantor would suffer a loss as a result of the modification.[54]

A release of the principal obligor without the guarantor's consent releases the guarantor to the extent that it impairs the guarantor's recourse.[55]

7.2.3 Release or Impairment of Security for the Underlying Obligation

Under the common law, a guarantor may waive in advance its defense based on the release or impairment of collateral.[56] The obligee may, however, be estopped to take advantage of such a waiver, if, for example, the court finds that after the waiver the obligee made an express or implied promise to realize upon the collateral, with reliance by the guarantor upon the promise.[57]

7.2.4 Release of Co-surety

The release of one surety without the consent of a co-surety releases the co-surety from liability to the extent that the co-surety could have claimed contribution from the released surety.[58] The surety may consent in advance to the release of a co-surety, and New Mexico courts will enforce the consent.[59]

7.3 Other Defenses

7.3.1 Failure to Fulfill a Condition Precedent

If a guaranty contains an express condition precedent, which makes it a conditional guaranty, the obligee must perform the condition precedent.[60]

---

53. *FDIC*, 118 N.M. at 81, 879 P.2d at 82.
54. Levenson v. Haynes, 1997-NMCA-020, ¶ 18, 123 N.M. 106, 934 P.2d 300 (citing Restatement (Third) of Suretyship & Guaranty § 41).
55. *Venaglia*, 1998-NMCA-043, ¶ 37.
56. *American Bank of Commerce*, 88 N.M. at 409-10, 540 P.2d at 1298-99.
57. Cadle Co. v. Wallach Concrete, Inc, 120 N.M. 56, 62-63, 897 P.2d 1104, 1110-12 (1995).
58. Western Bank v. Aqua Leisure, Ltd.,105 N.M. 756, 758, 737 P.2d 537, 539 (1987).
59. *Sunwest Bank*, 113 N.M. at 116, 823 P.2d at 916.
60. *See supra* § 6.2.

An obligee must also provide notice to the guarantor of the principal's default in the case of a continuing guaranty.[61] This requirement is imposed because in a continuing guaranty the guarantor may terminate its potentially limitless liability by terminating the guaranty as to future debts.[62]

7.3.2 Modification of the Guaranty

Consideration is required for a modification of a guaranty.[63] Even though the terms of a guaranty instrument may require all changes to be in writing, oral modifications are permitted.[64] An oral modification to a written contract must be proved by clear and convincing evidence.[65]

7.3.3 Statute of Limitations

The statute of limitations applicable to guaranties is the six-year period provided for actions on written contracts in Section 37-1-3(A) of the New Mexico Statutes Annotated.[66] The statute of limitations begins to run when a right of action upon the guaranty accrues.[67] On a demand guaranty the statute of limitations does not begin to run against the guarantor until demand is made upon the guarantor.[68] This rule is the opposite of the rule applicable to promissory notes, where the statute of limitations begins to run against the maker of the note when the note is made.[69]

7.3.4 Statute of Frauds

The English statute of frauds has been adopted as part of the common law of New Mexico.[70] A guaranty is covered by the statute of frauds because it is a promise to answer for the debt of another.[71] Nevertheless, an oral modification of a guaranty is permissible if one of the parties materially changes its position in reliance on that modification.[72]

7.3.5 Defenses particular to Guarantors who are Natural Persons and their Spouses

New Mexico has no law dealing with these issues.

---

61. *WXI/Z Sw. Malls*, 2005-NMCA-046, ¶ 16.
62. *Id.*
63. *Valley Bank of Commerce,* 2005-NMCA-004, ¶ 24.
64. *Id.* ¶ 23.
65. *Id.* ¶ 25.
66. Western Bank v. Franklin Dev. Corp., 111 N.M. 259, 260, 804 P.2d 1078, 1079 (1991).
67. *Id.*
68. *Id.*
69. *Id.*
70. Bassett v. Bassett, 110 N.M. 559, 562, 798 P.2d 160, 163 (1990).
71. *See Valley Bank of Commerce,* 2005-NMCA-004, ¶ 23.
72. *Id.*

7.4 Right of Set-off

New Mexico has no law on these issues.

§ 8 Waiver of Defenses by the Guarantor

8.1 Defenses that cannot be Waived

An obligee's duty of good faith cannot be waived by the guarantor, but the parties can determine the standards by which the performance of their good faith obligations is measured, so long as the standards are not unreasonable.[73]

New Mexico has no cases addressing the prohibitions in UCC Article 9 (as amended in 2001) against predefault waivers by guarantors of rights under Article 9 of the UCC.[74]

8.2 "Catch-all" Waivers

New Mexico has no well-developed body of law providing reliable guidance on general, catch-all waiver language in guaranties.

8.3 Use of Specific Waivers

New Mexico courts routinely enforce specific waivers of rights and defenses by guarantors.[75] The state Supreme Court has enforced the waiver of the homestead exemption[76] and the waiver of the right to a commercially reasonable sale of collateral in cases not involving Article 9.[77]

§ 9 Third-party Pledgors—Defenses and Waiver Thereof

Because a pledgor arguably stands in the relation of a guarantor to the principal obligor to the extent of the pledge, the pledgor may most likely avail itself of the defenses of a guarantor. It may also waive such defenses.

We have found no evidence that the law as applied to sureties would not apply to a third-party pledge. In contrast, the law appears to be that the pledge of collateral results in a surety relationship. It would seem logical, given this

73. *American Bank of Commerce,* 88 N.M. at 408, n.6, 540 P.2d at 1297, n.6.
74. NMSA 1978, §§ 55-9-602, -610, -611, -623, -624 (2001). New Mexico will consider the even newer uniform amendments to UCC Article 9 during the 2013 session of its legislature.
75. *See, e.g., American Bank of Commerce*; *WXI/Z Sw. Malls.*
76. *First State Bank,* 100 N.M. at 99, 666 P.2d at 778.
77. *See, e.g., Sunwest Bank,* 113 N.M. at 117, 823 P.2d at 917.

state of the law, that the pledgor generally has the same defenses available to it as are available to a surety.

§ 10 Jointly and Severally Liable Guarantors—Contribution and Reduction of Obligations upon Payment by a Co-obligor

New Mexico has no law dealing with these issues.

§ 11 Reliance

Reliance is probably not required to claim under a guaranty.

Under New Mexico law, a guaranty is governed by the rules generally applicable to contracts.[78] Presumably, then, reliance is not requisite to enforce a guaranty.

§ 12 Subrogation

The secondary obligor is subrogated to the rights of the obligee if the secondary obligor satisfies the underlying obligation.[79]

§ 13 Triangular Set-off in Bankruptcy

New Mexico has no law dealing with this issue.

§ 14 Indemnification—Whether the Primary Obligor has a Duty

New Mexico has no law dealing with these issues.

78. *WXI/Z Sw. Malls*, 2005-NMCA-046, ¶ 10.
79. *FDIC*, 118 N.M. at 82, 878 P.2d at 83.

§ 15 Enforcement of Guaranties

15.1 Limitations on Recovery—Fraudulent Transfer

New Mexico has no law dealing with these issues.

15.2 Enforcement of Guaranties of Payment versus Guaranties of Performance

New Mexico has no law dealing with these issues.

15.3 Exercising Rights under a Guaranty Where the Underlying Obligation is also Secured

Absent an agreement to the contrary, New Mexico has no law requiring an obligee to proceed first against the collateral for an obligation before proceeding against a guarantor.

15.4 Litigating Guaranty Claims: Procedural Considerations

A party is entitled to a jury trial on issues pertaining to a guaranty, even in a case presenting only other equitable issues, such as in a mortgage foreclosure case.[80]

15.5 One-action Laws and Rules

New Mexico has no one-action rule. Like other states, it does have rules against splitting causes of action and it recognizes principles of res judicata and collateral estoppel, so that if an obligee does commence an enforcement action against a guarantor, it should consider asserting all of its claims against the guarantor in the action.[81]

15.6 Antideficiency Laws

Normally, absent an agreement to the contrary, deficiency judgments are obtainable in cases involving commercial loans. This has long been established by case law for judicial foreclosures[82] and is now provided by statute for nonjudicial foreclosures under the Deed of Trust Act.[83]

---

80. State ex rel. McAdams v. District Court, 105 N.M. 95, 96-97, 728 P.2d 1364, 1365-66 (1986), *overruled in part on other grounds* by Blea v. Fields, 2005-NMSC-029, 138 N.M. 348, 120 P.3d 430.
81. *See, e.g., First State Bank*, 100 N.M. at 101, 666 P.2d at 1000 ("A party cannot by negligence or design withhold issues and litigate them in consecutive actions. He may not split his demands or defenses." (internal quotation marks & citations omitted) (emphasis omitted)).
82. *See, e.g.*, Armijo v. Pettit, 34 N.M. 559, 561, 286 P. 827, 828 (1930).
83. NMSA 1978, § 48-10-17 (2007).

§ 16 Revival and Reinstatement of Guaranties

New Mexico has no law dealing with these issues.

§ 17 Choice of Law Rules

New Mexico has no cases that construe choice-of-law clauses in guaranties, so its courts will apply principles applicable to contracts in order to construe these clauses.[84]

If a contract contains an effective choice-of-law clause, and the contract is governed by the UCC, New Mexico courts will enforce the choice-of-law clause if the transaction bears a reasonable relationship to the state or country designated, unless the application of the chosen law would offend New Mexico public policy or otherwise would violate some "fundamental principle of justice."[85] Some believe that New Mexico would follow the same rule for a contract which contains a choice-of-law clause, but which is outside of the UCC, if the issue were squarely presented.[86]

If a contract does not contain an effective choice-of-law clause, the rules in New Mexico are different for contracts governed by the UCC and for those governed by the common law. If a contract does not contain an effective choice-of-law clause and is governed by the UCC, the New Mexico UCC applies to a transaction "bearing an appropriate relation to [New Mexico]."[87]

If a contract does not contain an effective choice-of-law clause and is not governed by the UCC, then absent a statute to the contrary, the general rule in New Mexico is that contracts are governed by the law of the place where the contract was consummated (i.e., where the last act necessary for its formation was performed).[88] This is the Restatement (First) of Conflict of Laws

84. *See supra* § 6.1.
85. NMSA 1978, § 55-1-301(A) (2005); *see, e.g.*, Fiser v. Dell Computer Corp., 2008-NMSC-046, ¶ 7, 144 N.M. 464, 188 P.3d 1215. *Fiser* relied only upon the choice-of-law rules in the UCC; it did not rely upon any precedents, statutory or common law, outside of the UCC.
86. *See, e.g.* Burge v. Mid-Continent Cas. Co., 1997-NMSC-009, ¶ 11, 123 N.M. 1, 933 P.2d 210 (filed 1996) ("New Mexico law recognizes the validity of choice of law provisions contained in contracts.") Dictum; parties stipulated to the choice of foreign state's law. *Burge* relied upon only two cases for this statement. One case was dictum; the other was decided under the UCC. *Burge* did not overrule prior precedent to the contrary. Stevenson v. Louis Dreyfus Corp., 112 N.M. 97, 98, 811 P.2d 1308, 1309 (1991) ("[P]arties are free to choose by contract a law to govern the performance and enforcement of contractual arrangements between them.") Dictum; contract was not executed by both parties. *Stevenson* relied upon only one case for this statement. That case was decided under the UCC. *Stevenson* did not overrule prior precedent to the contrary. Reagan v. McGee Drilling Corp., 1997-NMCA-014, ¶ 7, 123 N.M. 68, 933 P.2d 867 (Pickard, J.) *Reagan* was decided before the *Burge* opinion was released for publication; the release date was delayed because of pending motions for rehearing. *Reagan* noted that "[o]ur courts have strongly endorsed the view that the rights of parties to a contract are primarily determined by the terms of the contract. This strong endorsement may counsel that, if the issue were squarely presented, New Mexico would likely adopt the Restatement (Second) approach to choice of law under circumstances in which the parties had expressly chosen the law." *Id.* (citations omitted), *limited on other grounds by PiÑA v. Gruy Petroleum Mgmt. Co.*, 2006-NMCA-063, ¶ 20. *Regan* found it unnecessary to decide which Restatement should be applied because the result would be the same under both Restatements. *Reagan* contains an excellent overview of the differences between the First and Second Restatements. *Id.* ¶ 6.
87. NMSA 1978, §§ 55-1-301(B) (2005).
88. *See, e.g.*, State Farm Mut. Ins. Co. v. Conyers, 109 N.M. 243, 246-48, 784 P.2d 986, 989-91 (1989).

rule, which is otherwise followed in New Mexico.[89] Most, if not all, of the many[90] uniform laws enacted by statute in New Mexico that contain a choice-of-law provision are to the contrary.[91] They follow the Restatement (Second) of Conflict of Law rule.[92] That rule generally looks to the jurisdiction with the most significant relationship to an agreement.[93] There is no reason why the New Mexico Supreme Court could not use the legislature's many enactments of the Second Restatement as additional support for the court's own adoption of the Second Restatement as the common law of the state[94] when the issue is squarely presented.[95]

If a contract does not contain an effective choice-of-law provision, then no matter which type of law governs the contract – that is, whether the contract is governed by the UCC, another statute, or the common law – a court may always refuse to apply an out-of-state law if the out of state law "would offend New Mexico public policy."[96]

---

89. *Id.*
90. New Mexico has more uniform laws on its books than any other state. *See* Jurisdictions & Acts Adopted, U.L.A. Directory of Uniform Acts & Codes Tables - Index at 57-58 (2012).
91. *See, e.g.*, NMSA 1978, § 46A-1-107(B) (2011) (part of the Uniform Trust Code; absent a controlling designation in the terms of a trust, the meaning and effect of the trust are determined by the law of the jurisdiction having the "most significant relationship to the matter at issue"). There is no reason why the New Mexico Supreme Court could not use the legislature's many adoptions of the Second Restatement as additional support for the court's adoption of the Second Restatement as the common law of the state when the issue is squarely presented.
92. "Such provisions [as those in the Uniform Trust Code] deferring to the jurisdiction with the most significant relationship to an agreement are a hallmark of uniform laws, which generally follow the Second Restatement approach to conflict of laws. These provisions also stand in stark contrast to the New Mexico rules, which generally follow the First Restatement approach of looking to the place of the last act necessary for the formation of an agreement." Jack Burton & Fletcher Catron, *Uniform Probate Code Amendments Take Effect Jan. 1, 2012*, 50 New Mexico Bar Bulletin 9, 11 (December 21, 2011).
93. *Id.*
94. *See* U.S. Bank Nat'l Assoc. v. Martinez, 2003-NMCA-151 ¶ 5, 134 N.M. 665, 812 N.M. 665, 81 P.3d 608 (using provision of Uniform Statute and Rule Construction Act, NMSA 1978, §§ 12-2A-1 to - 20 (1997), that was inapplicable to issue squarely presented in order to develop common law rule).
95. *See supra* n. 86.
96. *Reagan*, 1997-NMCA-014, ¶ 8; *see supra* § 2.6.2.

New York State Law of Guaranties

Penelope L. Christophorou
Catherine A. Borneo
Mbabazi Kasara
Kathleen O'Neill
Benjamin Snodgrass

Cleary Gottlieb Steen & Hamilton LLP
One Liberty Plaza
New York, New York 10006-1470
(212) 225 2000
Facsimile (212) 225 3999
www.clearygottlieb.com

Contents

New York State Law of Guaranties

Introduction and Sources of Law: This survey discusses New York State law applicable to guaranties. This survey refers to relevant statutes, as well as case law. New York courts and federal courts interpreting New York law have cited to the Restatement of Suretyship and Guaranty,[1] and older cases have cited to the predecessor provisions of the Restatement of Security.[2] These materials are, of necessity, summary in nature and should not be relied on as legal advice.

NEW YORK LAW HIGHLIGHTS:

1. New York corporate law does not automatically assume that guaranties granted within affiliate relationships are in the course of the guarantor's business. *See* § 2.1 below.
2. While past consideration, under general principles of contract law that are applicable to guaranties, will not typically support a guaranty, New York's General Obligations Law Section 5-1105 provides that a promise in writing is effective, so long as such consideration is "expressed in writing," "proved to have been given or performed" and "would be a valid consideration but for the time it was given." *See* § 4 below.
3. In New York, a statement that a guarantor is "liable as a primary obligor" is construed in the context of the relevant transactions "analyzed as an integrated whole" and the Court of Appeals has found a guarantor using such terminology to be a guarantor despite the use of this phrase. *See* § 6.5 below.
4. New York is less forgiving with regard to modifications of underlying obligations that are not consented to by the guarantor than is the position taken by the Restatement (Third) of Suretyship and Guaranty. *See* § 7.2.2 below.
5. In finding a guarantor to be bound to the terms of a guaranty notwithstanding a guarantor defense, New York courts favorably look upon "catch-all waivers" (i.e. waivers that are broadly worded, including that a guaranty is "absolute and unconditional" or that the guaranty is given "absolutely and unconditionally") but also often highlight the specificity in a guaranty of a particular waiver. As a result, it continues to be advisable to include both catch-all and specific waivers to guarantor defenses where possible. *See* § 8.2 below.
6. New York case law applying Section 548 of the U.S. Bankruptcy Code (which is similar to New York State's fraudulent conveyance law) in the context of a continuing guaranty seems to indicate that the issues of fair compensation and solvency of the guarantor must be assessed at the time of each transaction under

1. *See, e.g.*, Louis Dreyfus Energy Corp. v. MG Ref. & Mktg., 812 N.E.2d 936, 941 (N.Y. 2004); Chem. Bank v. Meltzer, 712 N.E.2d 656, 660-61 (N.Y. 1999).
2. *See, e.g.*, Gen. Phoenix Corp. v. Cabot, 89 N.E.2d 238, 243 (N.Y. 1949).

the agreement governing the primary obligation (and not just at the time the guaranty was executed). *See* § 15.1 below.

7. New York's Real Property Actions and Proceedings Law provides that, while an action to recover any part of a mortgage debt is pending or after final judgment for the plaintiff in such an action, leave from the court in which the original action is sought is required to bring any other action to recover any part of such mortgage debt. This statute, referred to as the "one action rule," has been interpreted as barring an action relating to a guaranty where the guaranty is not separate and distinct from the debts underlying the mortgage. *See* § 14.2 below.

Introductory Note: In order to standardize our discussion of the law of guaranties, we use the following vocabulary to refer to the various parties to a guaranty and their obligations.

"**Guarantor**" means a person who, by contract, agrees to satisfy an underlying obligation of another to an obligee upon the primary obligor's default on that underlying obligation. We do not draw a distinction between guarantors and sureties, as the distinction in New York between the two is often muddled.[3]

"**Guaranty**" means the contract by which the guarantor agrees to satisfy the underlying obligation of a primary obligor to an obligee in the event the primary obligor defaults on the underlying obligation.

"**Obligee**" means the person to whom the underlying obligation is owed. For example, the lender under a loan agreement would be an obligee vis-à-vis the borrower.

"**Primary Obligor**" means the person who incurs the underlying obligation to the obligee. For example, the borrower under a loan agreement would be a primary obligor.

"**Underlying Obligation**" means the obligation or obligations incurred by the primary obligor and owed to the obligee. For example, the borrower's obligation to make payments to a lender of principal and interest on a loan constitutes an underlying obligation.

3. *See, e.g.*, Gen. Phoenix, 89 N.E.2d at 241; *see also* Restatement (Third) of Suretyship & Guar. § 1 cmt. c (1996). The New York Uniform Commercial Code provides that the term "surety" includes the term guarantor. N.Y. U.C.C. § 1-201(40) (Consol. 2011). New York Jurisprudence 2d first distinguishes between guarantors and sureties but then notes that the lines are not always clear-cut: "The main distinction between a contract of surety and one of guaranty has been expressed by stating that a surety is primarily and jointly liable with the principal debtor, while a guarantor's liability is collateral and secondary to that of the principal debtor… Even so, under some forms of suretyship contract the surety's liability to the creditor is secondary …" 63 N.Y. Jur. 2d *Guaranty & Suretyship* § 1 (West 2006) (citations omitted).

§ 1 Nature of the Guaranty Arrangement

Under New York law, a guaranty involves three "distinct, yet interrelated, obligations"[4]: the underlying obligation between the primary obligor and the obligee, the guaranty between the guarantor and the obligee, and the surety between the primary obligor and the guarantor.

1.1 Guaranty Relationships

A guaranty is a contract of "secondary liability" under which the guarantor has an obligation to pay only upon default by the primary obligor.[5] The relationship between the primary obligor and the guarantor arises as a matter of law, and it is based on the notion that, while the guarantor is liable to the obligee, it is the primary obligor who ultimately should bear the underlying obligation.[6]

New York courts protect this relationship by refusing to enforce provisions indicating that the guarantor is liable as a primary obligor where the substance of the transaction shows otherwise.[7] *See* § 6.5.

Under New York law, no "technical words" are needed to create a guaranty obligation; rather, a court will look to substance over form and whether there exists an intent to bind a party in the capacity of a guarantor.[8]

Multiple guarantors of the same underlying obligation are sureties of each other, unless the guaranty explicitly states that the guarantors are severally liable. Each guarantor stands "as a principal debtor for his proportion of the debt and a surety for the remainder."[9] Therefore, an obligee may seek payment for the full amount of the underlying obligation from any guarantor that is jointly liable or joint and severally liable on the underlying obligation while a guarantor may seek contribution from other guarantors on any payment to the obligee above such guarantor's share. *See* § 10 below.

1.2 Other Suretyship Relationships

1.2.1 Pledges of Collateral

While not the focus of this survey, a suretyship relationship may also arise solely as a result of a grant of a security interest in real or personal property as collateral for the debt of another person.[10] As such, a guaranty-type relationship arises, to the extent of the collateral granted, when a person supplies collateral for a loan in order to induce the creditor to lend to another or where

4. Meltzer, 712 N.E.2d at 660.
5. Weissman v. Sinorm Deli, Inc., 669 N.E.2d 242, 246 (N.Y. 1996).
6. Meltzer, 712 N.E.2d at 660 (citing Restatement (Third) of Suretyship & Guar. § 1 cmt. b (1996)).
7. *Id.* at 660-61.
8. Meltzer, 712 N.E.2d at 660 (citing Gen. Phoenix, 89 N.E.2d at 241).
9. Falb v. Frankel, 423 N.Y.S.2d 683, 685 (App. Div. 2d Dep't 1980).
10. *See* Restatement (Third) of Suretyship and Guar. § 1 (noting that a person is a surety when "pursuant to contract...an obligee has recourse against [that] person... or that person's property with respect to the obligation... of another person...to that obligee" (emphasis added)).

one party mortgages property to a creditor to secure the debt of another.[11] Accordingly, it is advisable to include waivers of suretyship defenses in such security documents and to be aware that all aspects of suretyship law apply to the relationship so created.

1.2.2 Accommodation Parties

The New York Uniform Commercial Code, in Section 3-415, defines an accommodation party as one who signs a negotiable instrument to lend his name to another party to the same instrument.[12] Accordingly, under Article 3 of the New York Uniform Commercial Code,[13] accommodation parties are sureties[14] and a lack of consideration flowing directly to the guarantor is no defense to their obligations as such.[15] Whether a party is an accommodation party, and treated as a guarantor of a negotiable instrument and treated as a primary obligor of the negotiable instrument, depends upon such party's intent in signing the negotiable instrument. The nature of a signature on a negotiable instrument is, however, often ambiguous. The New York Uniform Commercial Code therefore provides that a signature on a negotiable instrument is an indorsement, rendering the signor a primary obligor, unless the negotiable instrument clearly indicates otherwise.[16] In determining whether a signatory is instead an accommodation party (in which case it has, like any guarantor, a right of subrogation against the primary obligor and suretyship defenses),[17] courts look to whether the signatory received a direct benefit from the transaction. The receipt of a direct benefit suggests that the signatory's purpose in signing the negotiable instrument was not to "lend his name to another party" to that negotiable instrument (and thereby be an accommodation party) but to be a primary obligor.[18]

---

11. 63 N.Y. Jur. 2d *Guaranty & Suretyship* § 22; *see* Champlain Valley Fed. Sav. & Loan Ass'n of Plattsburgh v. Ladue, 316 N.Y.S.2d 19, 21 (App. Div. 3d Dep't 1970) (determining that a surety relationship exists when a wife provided a mortgage to secure the debt of her husband); *see also* Geiger v. ENAP, Inc., 695 N.Y.S.2d 577, 578 (App. Div. 2d Dep't 1999) (assignment of mortgage interests to borrower to use as security for loan created surety relationship in respect of assignor of mortgage interests); Congregation Ohavei Shalom, Inc. v. Comyns Bros., Inc., 507 N.Y.S.2d 28, 29 (App. Div. 2d Dep't 1986) ("It is well settled that one who mortgages his property to secure the debt of another becomes a surety for the debt by operation of law." (citing Dibble v. Richardson, 63 N.E. 829 (N.Y. 1902); Ladue, 615 N.Y.S.2d 19)).
12. N.Y. U.C.C. § 3-415 (McKinney 2001).
13. New York has not adopted the 1990 version of Article 3 of the Uniform Commercial Code, UCC Art. 3, Negotiable Instruments (Uniform Law Commission and the American Law Institute, 1990) or its 2002 amendments, UCC Art. 3, Negotiable Instruments and UCC Art. 4 Bank Deposits (Uniform Law Commission and the American Law Institute, 2002).
14. Marks v. Carrier, No. 90 Civ. 6714 (MBM), 1992 U.S. Dist. LEXIS 14228, at **12-13 (S.D.N.Y. Sept. 21, 1992) (citations omitted).
15. *Id.*
16. N.Y. U.C.C. § 3-402 (McKinney 2001).
17. In re Appliance Packing & Warehousing Corp., 358 F. Supp. 84, 86 (S.D.N.Y. 1972).
18. *See* Dubai Bank v. Rohit Joshi, No. 85 Civ. 5005 (MJL), 1986 U.S. Dist. LEXIS 19424, at **5-7 (S.D.N.Y. Oct. 6, 1986). The predecessor law dealing with accommodation parties, Section 55 of the New York Negotiable Instruments Law, 1897 N.Y. Laws 719, 782, amended by, 1898 N.Y. Laws 973, 977, repealed by 1962 N.Y. Laws 2580, 2766, which has since been superseded by Section 3-415 of New York's Uniform Commercial Code, defined an accommodation party as one who signs an instrument "without receiving value therefor." This language no longer appears in the definition of an accommodation party.

§ 2 State Law Requirements for an Entity to Enter a Guaranty[19]

New York's legal requirements for the entry into guaranties by corporations, partnerships, limited liability companies, banks and trust companies and individuals are set forth below.

2.1 Corporations

Under the New York Business Corporation Law, a New York corporation may, within the scope of its general corporate powers, give a guaranty in furtherance of its corporate purpose, provided that its corporate charter and by-laws do not prevent it from doing so.[20] When a guaranty is not in furtherance of corporate purposes, a New York corporation may still give a guaranty, but only when authorized by two-thirds of all voting shares entitled to vote thereon. The guaranty may be secured by corporate property, "[i]f authorized by a like vote..."[21]

The corporate law in some states, such as Delaware, presumes corporate guaranties granted within affiliate relationships are necessary or convenient to the conduct of the guarantor's business; however, the New York Business Corporation Law makes no such presumption for inter-corporate guaranties.[22] At least one federal court (applying New York law) has noted that it is appropriate to examine, in determining whether a corporate purpose exists, the relationship between the entities, whether they have common shareholders, officers and directors, the reasons behind the guaranty and whether the guarantor expects "beneficial results" from the transaction.[23]

A New York corporation may execute a guaranty to benefit a director if the guaranty is approved by a shareholder vote conducted pursuant to statutory requirements (requiring a quorum comprised of holders of a majority of shares entitled to vote, not including shares held by those benefitted by the guaranty, and majority approval by voting shares constituting the quorum).[24]

---

19. For the purposes of this survey, we assume that a guaranty will not constitute "financial guaranty insurance" within the meaning of Section 6901 of the New York Insurance Law (the "Insurance Law"). *See* N.Y. Ins. Law § 6901 (McKinney 2009) (defining financial guaranty insurance); N.Y. Ins. Law § 1101(b)(1) (McKinney Sup. 2012) (outlining the meaning of "doing an insurance business in" New York). Under the Insurance Law, "[f] inancial guaranty insurance may be transacted in [New York] only be a corporation licensed for such purpose pursuant to [§ 6902 of the New York Insurance Law]." N.Y. Ins. Law § 6904(a) (McKinney 2009). In addition, the Insurance Law limits the underlying obligations for which even a licensed corporation may issue financial guaranty insurance. *See* N.Y. Ins. Law § 6904(b) (McKinney 2009).
20. N.Y. Bus. Corp. Law § 202(a)(7) (McKinney 2003).
21. N.Y. Bus. Corp. Law § 908 (McKinney 2003); *see* Lindenbaum v. Albany Post Prop. Assocs., Inc., 747 N.Y.S.2d 118, 119 (App. Div. 2d Dep't 2002); Chester Nat'l Bank v. Rondout Marine, Inc., 362 N.Y.S.2d 268, 271 (App. Div. 3d Dep't 1974).
22. *See* Del. Code Ann. tit. 8 § 122(13) (LexisNexis 2011); cf. N.Y. Bus. Corp. Law § 202(a)(7).
23. Mfrs. & Traders Trust Co. v. Goldman (In re Ollag Constr. Equip. Corp.), 446 F. Supp. 586, 591 (W.D.N.Y. 1978) (applying New York law), aff'd in part, rev'd in part on other grounds, 578 F.2d 904 (2d Cir. 1978).
24. N.Y. Bus. Corp. Law § 714 (McKinney 2003). Certain corporations existing before 1961 may grant such guaranties without a vote. *Id.*

2.2 Partnerships

New York's Partnership Law[25] neither expressly empowers a partnership to issue a guaranty nor expressly regulates or prohibits such activity. There are, however, examples in the case law of partnerships issuing guaranties.[26]

2.3 Limited Liability Companies

New York's Limited Liability Company Law generally permits limited liability companies to issue guaranties unless the articles of organization of a particular company provide otherwise.[27] The law permits these guaranties so long as they are either in the interests of the company or approved by a majority in interest of voting members or by a specified portion as provided in the company's operating agreement.[28] New York law deems guaranties issued by a limited liability company to an affiliate as being in the interests of the business,[29] which is in contrast to the treatment of affiliate guaranties issued by corporations governed by the New York Business Corporation Law.[30]

2.4 Banks and Trust Companies

Under Section 96(9) of the New York Banking Law, a New York state-chartered bank or New York state-licensed branch has the power "[t]o execute and deliver such guaranties as may be incidental to carrying on the business of a bank or trust company."[31] The New York State Department of Financial Services[32] has interpreted this section as permitting a New York state-chartered bank or a New York state-licensed branch of a foreign bank, which for the purposes of guaranties have similar powers, to guaranty the obligations of an affiliate.[33] The Banking Department has suggested, through interpretive letter, that Section 96(9) permits such a bank or branch in "certain situations" to issue a guaranty

---

25. N.Y. P'SHP. LAW § 20 (McKinney 2006).
26. *See, e.g.*, Riley v. S. Somers Dev. Corp., 644 N.Y.S.2d 784, 785 (App. Div. 2d Dep't 1996).
27. N.Y. LTD. LIAB. CO. LAW § 202(e) (McKinney 2007).
28. *Id.; see, e.g.*, CMI II, LLC v. Interactive Brand Dev., Inc., No. 600589/05, 2006 WL 2770095, at *11 (Sup. Ct. N.Y. Cnty. Sept. 26, 2006). New York's Supreme Court is the state's trial court of general jurisdiction. Appeals from the Supreme Court are heard by the Appellate Division of the Supreme Court, divided geographically into four Judicial Departments whose precedents are not binding upon each other. The state's highest appellate court is the Court of Appeals, whose decisions are binding upon all lower courts.
29. *See* N.Y. LTD. LIAB. CO. LAW § 202(e) (McKinney 2007).
30. *See* Section 2.1 above.
31. N.Y. BANKING LAW § 96(9) (Consol. 2011); N.Y. BANKING LAW § 2001(2)(c) (Consol. 2011). Prior to the enactment of Section 96(9) of the Banking Law, the New York Court of Appeals recognized that a bank "may enter into a contract of guaranty if it is for its own benefit, and not solely for the benefit of the debtor, and is incidental to the banking business." O'Connor v. Bankers Trust Co., 289 N.Y.S. 252, 270 (Sup. Ct. N.Y. Cnty. 1936), aff'd 1 N.Y.S.2d 641 (App. Div. 1st Dep't 1937), aff'd 16 N.E.2d 302 (N.Y. 1938).
32. As of October 3, 2011, the New York State Banking Department was abolished and its authorities assumed by a newly established New York State Department of Financial Services, whose head is the Superintendent of Financial Services, and references in the New York Banking Law to the New York State Banking Department and the Superintendent of Banks were changed to references to the NYDFS and the Superintendent of the NYDFS. N.Y. FIN. SERVS. LAW § 102, 205 (Consol. 2012). Citations to precedents issued prior to October 3, 2011, continue to refer to the Banking Department.
33. Letter from Jay Kane, Assistant Counsel, State of N.Y. Banking Dep't (Jan. 12, 2005), available at http://www.dfs.ny.gov/legal/interpret_opinion/banking/lo050112.htm (note that the letter addressed more specific circumstances, but nonetheless illustrates the general principle).

where it lacks a "substantial interest in" or fails to "derive substantial benefit from" the relevant underlying obligation.[34] In that interpretive letter, the Banking Department opined that a guaranty of a New York-licensed branch of a debt owed to one of the branch's regular customers fell within the ambit of Section 96(9).[35] This interpretation under Section 96(9), added to the New York Banking Law in 1984, takes a more expansive view of a bank's authority than case law that preceded that section.[36]

Bank, trust companies, and New York state-licensed branches should generally treat a guaranty like a loan or other extension of credit for purposes of calculating lending limits and other safety and soundness requirements.[37]

Guaranties offered by state banks may be affected by federal law. In general, federal law prohibits a state-chartered bank whose deposits are insured by the Federal Deposit Insurance Corporation from engaging as principal in activities in which a national bank may not engage as principal under federal law.[38] The situations under which a national bank may become a guarantor are governed by federal law.[39]

2.5 Individuals

2.5.1 Mental Competence and Sufficient Age

In order to be bound by a guaranty, a person must have the legal ability to form a contract. A person who is unable, due to age or mental impairment, to understand what he or she is doing when he or she signs a contract may lack capacity to contract. For example, a person under legal guardianship due to a mental defect completely lacks the capacity to contract, rendering any guaranty signed by such a person void.[40] In other situations, a person's lack of capacity to contract may be partial. In such cases, the contract would be voidable at the option of the party claiming incapacity, if he or she is able to prove the incapacity.[41]

A minor generally cannot form an enforceable contract and, therefore, cannot enter into a guaranty. A contract, such as a guaranty, entered into by a minor may be canceled by the minor or by his or her guardian, but it may

34. Letter from Derrick D. Cephas, Deputy Superintendent & Counsel, State of N.Y. Banking Dep't (Dec. 18, 1984) (on file with Cleary Gottlieb Steen & Hamilton LLP) (suggesting, inter alia, that the guaranty should have a definite term or expiration date, that it should have a stated amount or otherwise determinable limit and that it should require the party on whose behalf the guaranty was issued to reimburse the bank for payments made under the guaranty).
35. *Id.*
36. *See* 9 N.Y. JUR. 2D *Banks & Fin. Insts.* § 191 (West 2004).
37. With regard to New York lending limits, *see* N.Y. BANKING LAW §§ 103, 202-f & 661 (Consol. 2012). The general lending limit is 15% of the bank's "capital stock, surplus fund and undivided profits." Lending limits applicable to a New York state-licensed branch are based on the global capital of the entire bank.
38. *See* 12 U.S.C. § 1831a(a) (2006); 12 C.F.R. Part 362 (2012). A New York state-licensed branch is subject to the same limitation.
39. *See* National Bank as Guarantor or Surety on Indemnity Bond, 12 C.F.R. § 7.1017 (2012).
40. *See* 63 N.Y. JUR. 2D *Guaranty & Suretyship* §159; *see also* Brauer v. Lawrence, 150 N.Y.S. 497, 500 (App. Div. 1st Dep't 1914); In re Romero's Estate, 131 N.Y.S.2d 561, 562 (Sup. Ct. N.Y. Cnty. 1954).
41. *See* Leasing Serv. Corp. v. Vita Italian Rest., Inc., 566 N.Y.S.2d 796, 797 (App. Div. 3d Dep't 1991) ("[A] contract entered into by an infant . . . is voidable.").

not be ratified by a guardian.[42] After reaching the age of majority (age 18 in New York)[43] a person still has a reasonable period of time to cancel a contract entered into as a minor;[44] however, if such contract is not canceled within a reasonable period of time, the contract will be considered ratified and therefore binding and enforceable.[45]

A principal's lack of capacity to contract does not generally relieve the guarantor of liability on a contract.[46] However, there are some limited exceptions to the rule that the guarantor remains liable despite the principal's lack of capacity as well as to the general rules regarding a minor's ability to disaffirm a contract. These include (i) entertainment industry contracts with minors,[47] (ii) contracts for necessities,[48] and (iii) life insurance contracts.[49]

2.5.2 *Death of a Guarantor*

Enforceability Against Decedent's Estate

A guarantor's death generally does not, unless otherwise provided, relieve the guarantor's estate from liability under a guaranty.[50] Nevertheless, as a general practice, guaranties specifically provide that the death of a guarantor will not alter the rights or obligations under the guaranty. Cases suggest that, where consideration passes at different times such that the guaranty is "separable or divisible," the guarantor's death may operate as a termination of any obligations created by subsequent transactions.[51] However, where the entire consideration "passes wholly at one time," the guaranty is not revocable, and the guarantor's estate is liable for defaults occurring after the guarantor's death.[52] This analysis is related to "continuing" guaranties generally.[53]

---

42. *See* Al-Shahrani v. Hudson Auto Traders, Inc., 933 N.Y.S.2d 708, 710 (App. Div. 2d Dep't 2011) ("[C]ontrary to the Supreme Court's determination, the [minor's] mother did not have the right or authority to ratify the [minor's] contract." (citations omitted)).
43. N.Y. GEN. OBLIG. LAW § 1-202 (McKinney 2012).
44. Darlington v. Hamilton Bank of New York City, 116 N.Y.S. 678, 680 (App. Term 1909) (finding that the repudiation made by the former minor about three and one half months after she became of full age as a valid repudiation, especially given that she neither expressly affirmed or ratified it nor benefitted from such contract); Levenberg v. Ludington, 274 N.Y.S. 193, 196 (Cnty. Ct. Monroe Cnty. 1934) (holding that a minor's failure to disaffirm his purchase of corporate stock within three years after he reached his full age constitutes a ratification of the purchase agreement).
45. *See* N.Y. Gen. Oblig. Law 3-101(1); Leasing Serv. Corp., 566 N.Y.S.2d at 797 ("Such a party will be deemed to have ratified the contract . . . by failing to timely disaffirm or repudiate the contract or by acts consistent with an intent to be bound . . . following the end of the disability." (citation omitted)).
46. 63 N.Y. JUR. 2D *Guaranty & Suretyship* § 160; Erwin v. Downs, 15 N.Y. 575, 576 (1857) (holding that by indorsing a note, the guarantor was liable for the debt even though his principals were not capable of contracting); President & Fellows of Harvard Coll. v. Kempner, 116 N.Y.S. 437, 438 (App. Div. 2d Dep't 1909) (holding that the surety was liable for the rent the principal owed, despite the fact that the principal was a minor).
47. *See* N.Y. ARTS & CULT. AFF. LAW § 35.03 (McKinney 2011) (allowing New York courts to approve contracts with minors that are performing artists (such as actors, musicians and dancers) and professional athletes made by minors or a parent or guardian of a minor); see also N.Y. GEN. OBLIG. LAW § 3-107 (McKinney 2011) (providing that, under certain circumstances, a parent or guardian of an infant with respect to whose services a contract is made requiring court approval shall not be liable on the contract either as a party or as a guarantor of its performance unless the contract is approved by a court).
48. *See* 67 NY Jur. 2d *Infants & Other Persons Under Legal Disability* § 20.
49. *See* N.Y. INS. LAW § 3207 (McKinney Supp. 2012).
50. *See* Kernochan v. Murray, 18 N.E. 868, 869 (N.Y. 1888).
51. *See* Am. Chain Co. v. Arrow Grip Mfg. Co., 235 N.Y.S. 228, 233 (Sup.Ct. Warren Cnty. 1938); *see* also Kernochan, 18 N.E. at 869; In re Johnson's Estate, 5 N.Y.S.2d 24, 25-26 (Sur. Ct. Erie Cnty. 1938).
52. Am. Chain Co., 235 N.Y.S. at 233.
53. *See* Section 6.3 below.

New York's General Obligations Law states that, upon the death of a joint obligor, such as a co-guarantor, the deceased obligor's estate is jointly and severally liable with that of the surviving obligor.[54]

Procedures for Enforcement of Guaranty Against Decedent's Estate

Where a matured guaranty claim is to be enforced against the deceased guarantor in the New York Surrogate's Court, the creditor shall present the claim to the executor of the decedent's estate in accordance with Section 1803 of the New York Surrogate's Court Procedure Act ("SCPA"), unless the claim is based upon a court decree or order, or a valid judgment.[55] The creditor should present the claim "at the earliest possible moment to avoid any possibility that the estate will be settled and distributed ... or that its collection will be barred by a statute of limitations."[56]

Further, under SCPA Section 1802, if a creditor does not present a claim (such as a current right to proceed against a guarantor for payment) within seven months from the date that the court appoints an individual as executor of the decedent's estate,[57] the executor of the estate is not personally liable for any good faith distribution of the assets before the presentment of the claim.[58] However, the creditor can, after the seven-month period, seek relief against the executor "in [his or her] representative capacity" if there are assets remaining in the estate, compel an account of the administration of the estate and proceed against the beneficiaries who receive the estate assets or bring an action in law or equity under SCPA Section 1810.[59] Of course, as a practical matter, if an executor has distributed the estate assets to numerous beneficiaries of the estate who may have limited outside resources and may have expended the assets received from the estate, enforcement could be cumbersome. This may be a particular concern if the guaranty received by an individual is unsecured.

On the other hand, where a creditor has a contingent or unliquidated claim against a deceased guarantor who is domiciled in New York at the time of his or her death, such creditor may file an affidavit with the executor of the decedent's estate under the SCPA.[60] The creditor's claim is contingent or unliquidated if the claim is possible, conditioned to further events or not ascertained in amount.[61] To the extent that the amount owed, if any, under the guaranty has not become determinable when the guarantor dies, the creditor is considered to hold a contingent claim against the guarantor's estate, since it is undetermined at the time of an individual's death whether the creditor will ever have a claim against the deceased guarantor. The affidavit shall provide the underlying facts upon which the contingent or unliquidated claim is based and the probable amount of the liability.[62] A creditor could provide in the guaranty

54. N.Y. Gen. Oblig. Law § 15-106 (McKinney 2010); *see also* N.Y. Jur. 2d *Guaranty & Suretyship* § 283.
55. N.Y. Surr. Ct. Proc. Act § 1803(3) (McKinney 2011); 6-71 Warren's Heaton on Surrogate's Court Practice § 71.02.
56. 6-71 Warren's Heaton on Surrogate's Court Practice § 71.02.
57. This date is technically referred to as the date that letters testamentary are issued. N.Y. Surr. Ct. Proc. Act § 1802 (McKinney 2011).
58. N.Y. Surr. Ct. Proc. Act § 1802.
59. Supra note 55, Warren's Heaton on Surrogate's Court Practice § 71.02.
60. N.Y. Surr. Ct. Proc. Act § 1804(1) (McKinney 2011).
61. In re Biel, 479 N.Y.S.2d 740, 744 (App. Div. 2d Dep't 1984).
62. Supra note 55, Warren's Heaton on Surrogate's Court Practice § 71.03.

that the death of a guarantor, particularly in the case of an unsecured guaranty, could be treated as an event of default or accelerate repayment of the debt at the election of the creditor to allow the creditor flexibility to restructure the debt if the guarantor's death raises practical collection issues with respect to enforcement of the guaranty.

Upon the filing of the affidavit, there will be no distribution of the decedent's assets without reservation of such assets as the New York Surrogate's Court shall determine to be adequate.[63] The affidavit does not have binding effect, but the creditor will have no personal relief against the executor without the filing of the affidavit.[64] The New York Surrogate's Court has discretion to determine the amount of the estate's assets to be reserved.[65] It shall make the decision through a special proceeding and with consideration of all relevant facts.[66] After the court determines the amount to be reserved, the executor of the estate has the obligation to retain the estate assets for the contingent or unliquidated claims, and such duty "may not be transferred to a testamentary trustee."[67]

2.5.3 *Spouses and Enforcement of Guaranties*

Enforcement Against a Guarantor's Spouse

Where one spouse is contractually obligated, including as a guarantor, the property of the other spouse generally is not available to satisfy the first spouse's obligations. By statute, New York law provides that a contract made by a married woman does not bind her husband or his property.[68] Other provisions of law provide that a wife's property may not be used to satisfy her husband's debts.[69]

One spouse, acting as agent, may bind the other spouse as a guarantor. A New York court will not infer such an agency relationship solely because of the marriage,[70] although, under a common-law approach, a court might infer it. However, "actual agency may be implied from the conduct of the parties or established by proof of subsequent ratification, and, as to third persons, may arise by estoppel."[71]

In addition, there are certain particular circumstances under which a New York court might find one spouse liable for the other's obligations. For instance, under the common law, a husband may be held liable for necessities purchased by his wife, but may not be liable for necessities purchased after a separation.[72] In addition, while New York law places the obligation for the

63. N.Y. Surr. Ct. Proc. Act § 1804 (1).
64. Supra note 55, Warren's Heaton on Surrogate's Court Practice § 71.03.
65. N.Y. Surr. Ct. Proc. Act § 1804(1).
66. *Id.*; In re Estate of Reid, 300 N.Y.S. 1086, 1086-87 (Sur. Ct. N.Y. Cnty. 1937), aff'd sub nom., In re Bankers Trust Co., 6 N.Y.S.2d 360 (App. Div. 1st Dep't 1938).
67. Supra note 55, Warren's Heaton on Surrogate's Court Practice § 71.03; see Matter of Runals, 328 N.Y.S.2d 966, 973-74 (Sur. Ct. Cattaraugus Cnty. 1972).
68. N.Y. Gen. Oblig. Law § 3-305 (McKinney 2012).
69. N.Y. Dom. Rel. Law § 50 (McKinney 2010).
70. *See* B-Sharp Musical Prods, Inc. v. Haber, 899 N.Y.S.2d 792, 794 (App. Div. 1st Dep't 2010); Kozecke v. Humble Oil & Ref. Co., 362 N.Y.S.2d 272, 274 (App. Div. 3d Dep't 1974).
71. Kozecke, 362 N.Y.S.2d at 274.
72. *See, e.g.*, Roach v. Mamakos, 764 N.Y.S.2d 539 (Sup. Ct. Nassau Co. 2003).

funeral expenses of a deceased spouse on the estate of the decedent, provided there are sufficient funds in the estate,[73] a surviving spouse may be liable for the funeral expenses of a deceased spouse for public policy reasons where the decedent spouse's estate is insufficient to cover such expenses.[74]

Enforcement of Guaranty Against Property Owned by Guarantor's Spouse that was Acquired from Guarantor

As an exception to the general rule that an individual is not liable for a guaranty made by his or her spouse, under New York's General Obligations Law, a husband is liable for his wife's pre-marriage debts to the extent he acquires property of his wife by antenuptial contract or otherwise.[75]

Enforcement of Guaranty Against Property Owned by Spouses as Tenants by the Entirety

In New York, spouses may own real property as tenants by the entirety. A tenancy by the entirety is a form of ownership of real property by a married couple whereby each spouse owns the undivided whole of the property, coupled with a right of the survivor of the spouses to receive the real property at the first to die's death.

During the spouses' lifetimes, each spouse may sell or encumber his or her interest in the real property, but the sold or encumbered interest remains subject to the other spouse's interest in the real property. Where one spouse is bound as a guarantor and the obligee obtains a judgment against that spouse, the spouse's interest in the real property as a tenant by the entirety may be subject to an execution sale. However, the purchaser and the other spouse become tenant in common, subject to that other spouse's right of survivorship.[76]

The New York Marriage Equality Act of 2011[77]

Under the recently enacted New York legislation known as the Marriage Equality Act which took effect on July 24, 2011, all marriages irrespective of whether between same-sex couples or different-sex couples will be afforded identical treatment under all laws of the State of New York.[78] The Marriage Equality Act applies to all legal marriages, regardless of whether the marriage occurred in New York.[79] Accordingly, after the effective date, the rights and obligations of spouses under a guaranty will be the same irrespective of the sexes of the married couple.

---

73. N.Y. Surr. Ct. Proc. Act § 1811(1) (McKinney 2011); *see* Colonial Funeral Home v. Gatto, 521 N.Y.S.2d 378, 379 (N.Y. City Civ. Ct. Richmond Cnty. 1987).
74. *See* Colonial, 521 N.Y.S.2d at 379.
75. N.Y. Gen. Oblig. Law § 3-307 (McKinney 2012).
76. See Hiles v. Fisher, 39 N.E. 337, (N.Y. 1895); Finnegan v. Humes, 299 N.Y.S. 501, 503 (App. Div. 4th Dep't), aff'd, 14 N.E.2d 389 (N.Y. 1938); BNY Fin. Corp. v. Moran, 584 N.Y.S.2d 261, 262 (Sup. Ct. N.Y. Cnty. 1992); Levine v. Carr, 215 N.Y.S.2d 402, 405 (Sup. Ct. Nassau Cnty. 1961).
77. Marriage Equality Act, 2011 N.Y. Laws 749-752 (codified in various sections of N.Y. Domestic Relations Law).
78. N.Y. Dom. Rel. Law §§ 10-a & 10-b (McKinney Supp. 2012).
79. *Id.*

§ 3 Signatory's Authority to Execute a Guaranty

The individual signing the guaranty as an agent of the guarantor must have the authority to execute the guaranty, which authority may be express or implied. Generally, the obligee has a duty of reasonable inquiry when it has some notice that the executor of the guaranty does not have authority to bind the guarantor. Confusion can sometimes arise in the case of corporate officers or directors signing guaranties in closely held corporations or other organizations. In such instances, a case-by-case inquiry determines whether an individual intended to be personally bound or, instead, only issued a guaranty on behalf of a partnership or corporation and thus only in an official employment capacity.[80] When an individual signs his title as well as his name, this is not dispositive proof of an intention not to issue a personal guaranty.[81]

3.1 Corporations

For an obligee to rely on a guaranty, the guaranty must be signed by an officer with actual or apparent authority to act in such capacity.[82] An obligee cannot enforce a guaranty if she had notice that the officer who signed for the corporation lacked authority to do so.[83] Where an obligee-plaintiff invokes the doctrine of apparent authority, that obligee bears a duty of reasonable inquiry.[84]

Generally, an officer of a corporation has authority to act only where: (a) authority has been expressly conferred on him by statute, law or the act of the directors; (b) the action is properly incidental to the business entrusted to him by the directors; and (c) the action is within his ostensible authority or ratified by proper authority as applicable to contracts of guaranty.[85] If a corporation's guaranty bears some reasonable relationship to the corporation's business, evidence that a signing officer was charged with the general management of the corporation's business can provide apparent authority to execute a guaranty.[86] However, under New York law, apparent authority is not limitless; the potential obligee dealing with an agent of a guarantor corporation should "make the necessary effort" to ascertain the agent's actual authority.[87]

80. *See, e.g.*, PNC Capital Recovery v. Mech. Parking Sys., 726 N.Y.S.2d 394, 397 (App. Div. 1st Dep't 2001).
81. *Id.; see also* Chem. Bank v. Masters, 574 N.Y.S.2d 754, 755 (App. Div. 1st Dep't 1991); Wells Fargo Bank, N.A. v. Hooper Home Constr. Corp., No. 103795/08, 2010 WL 2594269, at *2 (Sup. Ct. N.Y. Cnty. June 17, 2010).
82. "One who deals with an agent does so at his peril, and must make the necessary effort to discover the actual scope of authority." Ford v. Unity Hosp., 299 N.E.2d 659, 664 (N.Y. 1973).
83. Aaronson v. David Mayer Brewing Co., 60 N.Y.S. 523, 525-26 (App. Term 1899).
84. Collision Plan Unlimited, Inc. v. Bankers Trust Co., 472 N.E.2d 28, 29 (N.Y. 1984).
85. 63 N.Y. Jur. 2d *Guaranty & Suretyship* § 44.
86. Hall v. Ochs, 54 N.Y.S. 4, 7-8 (App. Div. 2d Dep't 1898).
87. Ford, 299 N.E.2d at 664.

3.2 Partnerships

3.2.1 *General Partnerships*

Section 20 of New York's Partnership Law grants a partner in a general partnership the authority to bind the partnership when such partner's act is "for apparently carrying on in the usual way the business of the partnership," unless such authority has been explicitly held back in the partnership agreement and the person dealing with such partner knows that he or she has no such authority.[88] If the action of such a partner is not "apparently for carrying on of the business of the partnership in the usual way" the partner must be authorized by the other partners to bind the partnership.[89] Authority may also be granted under the partnership agreement.[90] Those dealing with partners have a duty of inquiry as to whether a signatory has the appropriate authority to bind the partnership.[91]

In the particular context of guaranties, courts have found that a partner in a general partnership must have the explicit or implied authority to bind her partners if a guaranty is to bind a partnership; mere partnership is insufficient.[92] Implied authority to provide a guaranty may arise from business usage.[93]

3.2.2 *Limited Partnerships*

Under New York's codification of the Uniform Limited Partnership Act (applicable to a New York limited partnership formed before July 1, 1991, which has neither opted into the Revised Limited Partnership Act nor amended or been required to amend its certificate of limited partnership on or after July 1, 1991),[94] a general partner has the same powers as a partner in a general partnership, except that the general partner lacks authority, absent written consent or ratification by all limited partners, to (among other things) act "in contravention of the certificate" or act in a way that "would make it impossible to carry on the ordinary business of the partnership."[95] Under New York's Revised Limited Partnership Act (applicable to all New York limited partnerships formed on or after July 1, 1991),[96] a general partner has the same

88. N.Y. P'SHIP LAW § 20(1) (Consol. 2011).
89. *Id.* at § 20(2).
90. Chelsea Nat'l Bank v. Lincoln Plaza Towers Assocs., 461 N.Y.S.2d 328, 330 (App. Div. 1st Dep't 1983), aff'd, 462 N.E.2d 130 (N.Y. 1984).
91. Chelsea Nat'l Bank, 461 N.Y.S.2d at 331.
92. First Nat'l Bank v. Farson, 123 N.E. 490, 491(N.Y. 1919) ("As to third persons, the authority to a partner must be found in the actual agreement of the partners, or through implication, in the nature of the business according to the usual and ordinary course in which it is carried on by those engaged in it in the locality which is its seat, or as reasonably necessary or fit for its successful prosecution.").
93. *Id.* at 492 (explaining that, if it is usual to give a guaranty when making a sale of bonds, the authority to sell the bonds "carries with it the power to guarantee" and noting further that generally "the power of an agent to bind the principal in contracts of guaranty and suretyship can only be charged against the principal by necessary implication, where the duties to be performed cannot be discharged without the exercise of such a power, or where the power is a manifestly necessary and customary incident of the authority bestowed upon the agent, and where the power is practically indispensable to accomplish the object in view") (citations omitted).
94. N.Y. P'SHIP LAW §§ 90 et seq. (Consol. 2012).
95. N.Y. P'SHIP LAW § 98 (Consol. 2012).
96. Codified as N.Y. P'SHIP LAW §§ 120-101 et seq. (Consol. 2012).

powers as a partner of a general partnership, except as provided otherwise in the partnership agreement or in the Revised Limited Partnership Act.[97]

Limited partners in a limited partnership differ from general partners in such partnerships in that they are insulated from partnership liability and barred from participating in the partnership's management.[98] The rights of limited partners are fairly circumscribed under the relevant partnership statutes and do not include acting as an agent of the limited partnership.[99]

As noted in Section 3.2.1 above, in the particular context of guaranties, courts have found that a partner in a general partnership must have the explicit or implied authority to bind her partners if a guaranty is to bind a partnership; mere partnership is insufficient. Implied authority to provide a guaranty may arise from business usage.[100]

3.3 Limited Liability Companies

The Limited Liability Company Law provides that, in the case of a member-managed LLC, every member is an agent of that company and can sign instruments pursuant to carrying on in the usual way of business unless that person has no actual authority to act in such way and his counterparty knows as much.[101] In the case of a manager-managed LLC, no member has authority to bind the LLC to a guaranty unless authority has been granted to the member by the manager or managers of the LLC or by operating agreement of the LLC. Each manager of a manager-managed LLC can bind the LLC if such guaranty is "for apparently carrying on in the usual way the business of the [LLC]" unless the manager has no actual authority and the counterparty knows of this lack of authority.[102]

3.4 Banks and Trust Companies

A case-by-case inquiry of the powers provided for in a bank's or trust company's corporate governance documents is necessary to determine who may validly execute a guaranty on behalf of a bank or trust company.

97. N.Y. P'ship Law § 121-403 (Consol. 2012).
98. *See* Goldman, Sachs & Co. v. Michael, 496 N.Y.S.2d 427, 429 (App. Div. 1st Dep't 1985).
99. *See* N.Y. P'ship Law §§ 99 & 121-303.
100. *See* Chelsea Nat'l Bank, 461 N.Y.S.2d at 330 (noting that a general partner's authority to bind the limited partnership as the guarantor of an underlying obligation to a third-party obligee "must be found in the partnership agreement or shown to be inherent in the partnership business").
101. N.Y. Ltd. Liab. Co. Law § 412(a) (McKinney 2007).
102. *Id.* § 412(b) (McKinney 2007).

§ 4 Consideration; Sufficiency of Past Consideration

Consideration is required to create a valid contract of guaranty.[103] It is well established in New York that the benefit or obligation that forms the consideration for a guaranty need not flow directly from the obligee to the guarantor; instead, the consideration flowing from the obligee to the primary obligor is sufficient if the guaranty is entered into concurrently with the principal contract.[104] A number of cases have indicated that the passage of a few days between the execution of the underlying obligation documents and the execution of the guaranty will not impair the guaranty's enforceability.[105] In addition, there is some evidence that the courts may enforce a guaranty that was promised to the obligee at the time the primary obligation was entered into and which promise formed the basis for the obligee's extension of credit to the primary obligor, even where the guaranty was executed significantly later than the date on which the underlying obligation was entered into.[106]

Where a guaranty is not contemporaneous with the entry into the contract governing the underlying obligation, New York's General Obligations Law provides that a promise in writing is effective, so long as such consideration is "expressed in the writing," "proved to have been given or performed" and "would be a valid consideration but for the time it was given."[107] Under the General Obligations Law provision, past consideration will not support a guaranty unless explicitly referenced.[108]

---

103. Burgee v. Patrick, No. 91 Civ. 3023, 1996 U.S. Dist. LEXIS 5943, at *16 n.3 (S.D.N.Y. Apr. 29, 1996) (citing Walcutt v. Clevite Corp., 191 N.E.2d 894 (N.Y. 1963); European Am. Bank & Trust v. Boyd, 516 N.Y.S.2d 714 (App. Div. 2d Dep't 1987)).

104. Movado Grp., Inc. v. Presberg, 687 N.Y.S.2d 116, 116-17 (App. Div. 1st Dep't 1999); Beacon Hotel Corp. v Springer, 11 N.Y.S.2d 48 (App. Div. 1st Dep't 1939); De Reszke v. Duss, 91 N.Y.S. 221, 222-23 (App. Div. 1st Dep't 1904) (citing Cahill Iron Works v. Pemberton, 62 N.Y.S. 944 (App. Div. 2d Dep't 1900), aff'd, 61 N.E. 1128 (N.Y. 1901)); Israel Discount Bank of NY v. NCC Sportswear, Corp., No. 603914/06, 2008 N.Y. Misc. LEXIS 744, at **6-7 (Sup. Ct. N.Y. Cnty. Feb. 21, 2008); CMI II, , 2006 WL 2770095, at *11 (citing Erie County Sav. Bank v. Coit, 11 N.E. 54 (N.Y. 1887)).

105. Burke v. N. Fork Bank & Trust Co., 644 N.Y.S.2d 293, 293 (App. Div. 2d Dep't 1996) (emphasizing, "[n]or would the fact that the guaranty was executed a few days after the loan documents were executed impair its enforceability"); Chester Airport, Inc. v. Aeroflex Corp., 237 N.Y.S.2d 752, 754-55 (Sup. Ct. N.Y. Cnty. 1962) (stating, as dicta, that six days between the principal agreement and a subsequent guaranty did not render the principal agreement and the guaranty non-contemporaneous).

106. McNaught v. McClaughry, 42 N.Y. 22, 25 (1870). (Discussing consideration in the context of a note guaranty, the Court summarized: "If [borrower] had given his note to plaintiff and the same had been accepted in performance of the contract without further condition, and the note was yet unmatured, the obtaining an additional indorser would have been a gratuitous act on the part of [borrower], and the indorser would not be bound. He would not be bound, not merely because there was no direct consideration moving to himself, but because there was no sufficient consideration moving to his principal. On the other hand, if [borrower] had originally agreed with the lender that he would obtain the new indorser, and had obtained the money upon the faith of that promise, then his finding the additional indorser was based upon a valid consideration, and the indorser was held by his signature").

107. N.Y. Gen. Oblig. Law § 5-1105 (McKinney 2010); *see* BAII Banking Corp. v. UPG, Inc., No. 86 Civ. 5544, 1990 U.S. Dist. LEXIS 13765, at *18 (S.D.N.Y. Oct. 15, 1990).

108. *See* Mazzella v. Lupinachi, 333 N.Y.S.2d 775, 777 (Civ. Ct. 1972).

§ 5 Notice of Acceptance

When New York courts discuss whether, under New York law, a obligee must notify the guarantor of its acceptance of the guaranty, they have typically held that the circumstances do not require notice of acceptance. For example, courts have held that, if notice of acceptance is not expressly "required by the terms of the guarantee," the extension of credit by the obligee will "constitute[] acceptance . . . of the guarantor's offer of surety."[109] Stated slightly differently, notice of acceptance is generally unnecessary "[w]here credit is advanced on the strength of the guaranty . . . ."[110] New York courts have also examined whether a guaranty was intended to be "absolute" in its terms, without conditions to make it binding, and, where such a finding is made, determined that notice of acceptance is not required.[111] Where the obligee had been involved in the guarantee negotiations and knew the guarantee was in place, similarly, no notice of acceptance was found to be required. [112]

§ 6 Interpretation of Guaranties

6.1 General Principles

New York courts will strictly interpret the terms of a guaranty in determining the obligations of a guarantor.[113] Outside of this principle, and certain terms of art outlined below, the same principles of construction that apply to contracts generally apply to guaranties.[114]

6.2 Guaranty of Payment versus Guaranty of Collection

A guarantor of payment promises to satisfy the underlying obligation to the obligee upon default by the primary obligor, which satisfaction is not conditioned upon the obligee's prior attempt to secure satisfaction from the primary

---

109. Cinerama, Inc. v. Sweet Music, S.A., 355 F. Supp. 1113, 1120 (S.D.N.Y. 1972), rev'd in part on other grounds, 482 F.2d 66 (2d Cir. 1973), aff'd, 493 F.2d 1397 (2d Cir. 1974). For a general discussion of notice of acceptance, *see* PETER A. ALCES, THE LAW OF SURETYSHIP AND GUARANTY § 3:27 (Thompson West 1996); *see also* Davis v. Wells, 104 U.S. 159, 163 (1881).

110. Doehler Die Casting Co. v. Holmes, 52 N.Y.S.2d 321, 322 (Sup. Ct. N.Y. Cnty. 1944) (citing Am. Woolen Co. v. Moskowitz, 144 N.Y.S. 532 (App. Div. 1st Dep't1913)).

111. Union Bank of La. v. Ex'rs of Coster, 3 N.Y. 203, 212 (1850) ("Where the guaranty is absolute no notice of acceptance is necessary."); *see* also Rachman Bag Co. v. Liberty Mut. Ins. Co., 46 F.3d 230, 238 (2d Cir. 1995); Niles Tool-Works Co. v. Reynolds, 38 N.Y.S. 1028, 1029 (App. Div. 1st Dep't 1896); Whitney & Schuyler v. Groot, 24 Wend. 82 (N.Y. Supr. Ct. 1840).

112. *See* Drucker v. Heyl-Dia, 101 N.Y.S. 796 (Sup. Ct. App. Term 1906).

113. *See* White Rose Food v. Saleh, 788 N.E.2d 602, 603 (N.Y. 2003); People v. Stuyvesant Ins. Co., 413 N.Y.S.2d 843, 846-47 (Sup. Ct. Bronx Cnty. 1979) (citing Nat'l Recreation Prods., Inc. v. Gans, 359 N.Y.S.2d 803, 804 (App. Div. 1st Dep't 1974) and People v. Henry, 308, N.Y.S.2d 245, 246 (App. Div. 2d Dep't 1970)).

114. U.S. Bank Nat'l Assoc. v. Perlmutter (In re S. Side House, LLC), 470 B.R. 659, 675 (Bankr. E.D.N.Y. 2012); Gen. Phoenix, 89 N.E.2d at 241; HSH Nordbank AG N.Y. Branch v. Swerdlow, 672 F. Supp. 2d 409, 417 (S.D.N.Y. 2009) (citing Compagnie Financiere de CIC et de L'Union Europeenne v. Merrill Lynch, Pierce, Fenner & Smith Inc., 188 F.3d 31, 34 (2d Cir. 1999)) (applying New York law).

obligor.[115] A guarantor may be required to satisfy obligations to an obligee even where the obligee, because of a subordination agreement, cannot collect from the primary obligor.[116]

On the other hand, a guarantor of collection merely promises to satisfy the underlying obligation "only after all attempts to obtain payment from the [primary obligor] have failed . . . ."[117]

A court will look to the intent of the parties as expressed in the guaranty to determine whether it is one of payment or one of collection.[118]

6.3 Continuing Guaranties

"The New York Court of Appeals has recognized "that the purpose of a continuing guaranty is to enable parties who enter into contracts to be secure in the knowledge that whatever debts become due them under the contracts will be protected by the guaranty,"[119] and courts in New York have described a continuing guaranty as being "in the nature of a continuing offer to guarantee a series of debts . . . ."[120] A continuing guaranty may, however, cap the liability of the guarantor thereunder.[121]

When interpreting guaranties, courts in New York look for language establishing a continuing obligation.[122] While it is advisable to be explicit in a guaranty that it is "continuing,"[123] courts will interpret a guaranty as continuing even in the absence of the exact term in the guaranty.[124]

A continuing guaranty applies to future obligations,[125] and the Court of Appeals has noted that, as a general matter, "[u]nless the parties to a continuing

115. 63 N.Y. Jur. 2d *Guaranty & Suretyship* § 82. *Cf.* N.Y. Gen. Oblig. Law § 15-701 (McKinney 2010) and discussion infra in Section 7.3.3; N.Y. U.C.C. § 3-416(2).

116. *See* 63 N.Y. Jur. 2d *Guaranty & Suretyship* § 107 (West Supp. 2012) (citing Kinville v. Jarvis Real Estate Holdings, LLC, 833 N.Y.S.2d 773, 775 (App. Div 4th Dep't. 2007)).

117. Gen. Phoenix, 89 N.E.2d at 241.

118. *Id.* (stating, "[i]f he binds himself to pay immediately upon default of the debtor, he becomes a guarantor of payment; if he binds himself to pay only after all attempts to obtain payment from the debtor have failed, he becomes a guarantor of collection.") (citation omitted).

119. Louis Dreyfus, 812 N.E.2d at 941; *see* USI Capital & Leasing, a Div. of USI Credit Corp. v. Chertock, 568 N.Y.S.2d 74, 75 (App. Div. 1st Dep't 1991) (noting that "[p]ersonal guaranties which contain language of a continuing obligation are enforceable and survive payment of the original indebtedness").

120. Oak Beverages, Inc. v. Ehrlich, 637 N.Y.S.2d 758, 759 (App. Div. 2d Dep't 1996) (citing Del. Funds v. Zuckerman-Honickman, Inc., 351 N.Y.S.2d 769 (App. Div. 4th Dep't 1974)).

121. *See* Henry McShane Co. v. Padian, 36 N.E. 880, 880-81 (N.Y. 1894) (finding that, where the guarantor guaranteed payment "for any and all materials which [the obligee] may deliver to [the primary obligor] . . ." and the guaranty stated that the guarantor would not "be liable for any balance exceeding five hundred dollars which may become due . . .", the guaranty was clearly and unambiguously a continuing guaranty limiting the guarantor's liability to $500 and that parol evidence was, therefore, inadmissible); Franklin Nat'l Bank v. Skeist, 373 N.Y.S.2d 869, 873 (App. Div. 1st Dep't 1975).

122. *See* Orix Fin. Servs., Inc. v. McMullen, 879 N.Y.S.2d 131, 132 (App. Div. 1st Dep't 2009) (finding, where a guaranty stated that it was a "continuing guaranty," that "the language of the guaranty unambiguously contemplated future agreements between [the lender] and the borrower"); Skeist, 373 N.Y.S.2d at 872 ("The threshold question is whether the words... are susceptible of differing construction or whether the phrase is, as a matter of law, unambiguous. If the latter, evidence of the circumstances surrounding its execution is inadmissible and the instrument must be accorded its legal intendment."); Trade Bank & Trust Co. v. Goldberg, 330 N.Y.S.2d 69, 71 (App. Div. 1st Dep't 1972).

123. Cf. Skeist, 373 N.Y.S.2d at 872 ("That the guaranty in issue is a continuing one is manifest from the language used therein.").

124. *See* Padian, 36 N.E. at 880-81; Birch v. De Rivera, 6 N.Y.S. 206, 206-07 (Gen. Term 1st Dep't 1889) ("There is no doubt that this is a continuing guaranty. The entire instrument so indicates, and the concluding expression, 'my said guaranty to hold good until canceled,' is conclusive.").

125. *See* USI Capital & Leasing, 568 N.Y.S.2d at 75.

guarantee provide otherwise in the writing, such a guarantee is not limited to the life of the loans executed contemporaneously therewith, and generally cannot expire by mere conduct[,] change of circumstances, or lapse of time."[126]

Where a continuing guaranty is silent on termination by the guarantor, the guarantor may terminate the guaranty by notifying the obligee, thereby "revoking [the guarantor's] liability for obligations that may be incurred subsequent to the notice."[127] In the context of a committed facility, the guarantor has agreed up to be liable for all obligations under the facility in exchange for the obligee's agreement to provide such commitment, which prevents the guarantor from revoking its guaranty obligations during the term of the commitment.[128]

A guaranty may provide for specific methods for termination.[129] If a guaranty provides that it may only be terminated by written notice, the Court of Appeals has stated that oral notice of termination by the guarantor is ineffective.[130]

Where a guaranty contains language pertaining to revocation or expiration, the language should be considered carefully. For instance, in the context of revocation, the Court of Appeals determined that, where a continuing guaranty stated that it would "extend to and cover all renewals of any claims or demands guaranteed" under the guaranty but did not state that it would apply only to renewals occurring prior to revocation, the guarantor was liable for post-revocation renewals of underlying obligations initially incurred before revocation.[131] Similarly, in the context of expiration of a guaranty, the Court of Appeals has held that, where the obligee relied on the credit of a parent guarantor and the guaranty provided that the guarantor would be liable for underlying obligations entered into prior to revocation (but silent as to expiration), the guarantor was

126. Chem. Bank v. Sepler, 457 N.E.2d 714, 716 (N.Y. 1983) (citations omitted). Continuing guaranties are common in the context of revolving credit and other loan facilities, they can, of course, be found in other contexts. *See, e.g.*, Louis Dreyfus, 812 N.E.2d at 941.

127. *See* 27th Street Assocs., LLC v. Lehrer, 772 N.Y.S.2d 28, 30 (App. Div. 1st Dep't 2004) (citations omitted).

128. Cf Chain Co. v. Arrow Grip Mfg. Co., 235 N.Y.S. at 233.

129. *See* Chem. Bank v. Geronimo Auto Parts Corp., 639 N.Y.S.2d 340, 341 (App. Div. 1st Dep't 1996) ("Termination of a continuing personal guaranty requires compliance with the provisions governing termination expressly set forth in the guaranty..."); Nat'l Westminster Bank, U.S.A. v. Bronstein, 558 N.Y.S.2d 33, 33 (App. Div. 1st Dep't 1990) (Where continuing guaranty provided for termination on "written notice delivered to the Bank and duly receipted for by it," mere delivery of written notice, "without a written acknowledgment by the bank, did not terminate the guaranty.").

130. *See* Chem. Bank v. Wasserman, 333 N.E.2d 187, 188 (N.Y. 1975) (citing § 15-301 of New York's General Obligations Law); N.Y. Gen. Oblig. Law § 15-301(4) (McKinney 2010); *see also* note 184 below. In one case, the Appellate Division, Third Department, determined that an uncompensated guarantor revoked an continuing guaranty, under which no obligations had been incurred, by ceasing to be a stockholder and officer of the primary obligor (despite a requirement of written notice of revocation). *See* Bankers Trust Hudson Valley, N.A. v. Christie, 414 N.Y.S.2d 787, 789 (App. Div. 3d Dep't 1979), aff'd on reh'g, 420 N.Y.S.2d 521 (App. Div. 3d Dep't 1979). Subsequently, in Chemical Bank v. Sepler, the Court of Appeals stated that the conduct of the parties could not terminate a guaranty that required written termination. 547 N.E.2d at 716 n.2. The court distinguished the case at hand from Rose v. SPA Realty Associates, in which the Court of Appeals addresses the applicability of subdivision one of Section 15-301 in cases of (i) full or partial performance of an oral agreement to modify a written agreement or (ii) equitable estoppel based on inducement of significant and substantial reliance on an oral modification. *See id.;* Rose v. SPA Realty Associates 366 N.E.2d 1279, 1283 (N.Y. 1977). Christie, which relies on Rose's application of equitable estoppel, did not involve an oral modification, but rather termination by the guarantor's conduct. *See* Christie, 457 N.E.2d at 716. The Third Department, which decided Christie, has itself questioned whether Christie remains good law. *See* Endicott Trust Co. v. Milasi, 572 N.Y.S.2d 524, 525-26 (App. Div. 3d Dep't 1991).

131. *See* Corn Exch. Bank Trust Co. v. Gifford, 197 N.E. 178, 179-80 (N.Y. 1935).

liable for underlying obligations that became binding before, but were not yet due and payable as of, expiration of the guaranty.[132]

6.4 "Absolute and Unconditional"

See § 8.2 on "Catch-All" Waivers.

6.5 "Liable as a Primary Obligor and not Merely as Surety"

This language, which is frequently included in guaranties, seems to conflate the concepts of guarantor and primary obligor and may be included by creditors in an attempt to bypass suretyship defenses. While a guarantor may be a "guarantor of payment" from whom the obligee can seek payment even without pursuing the primary obligor, the guarantor will not become a primary obligor simply by the inclusion of this phrase. To the extent that this language is intended to eliminate suretyship defenses, it should not be relied upon as enforceable in New York; instead, express waivers of suretyship defenses should be included in the guaranty.

In New York, a statement that a guarantor is "liable as a primary obligor" has been construed in the context of the relevant transactions and the Court of Appeals has found a person to be a guarantor despite the use of the phrase in the guaranty.[133]

§ 7 Defenses of the Guarantor; Set-off

The defenses that may be available to a guarantor can be grouped into 3 categories: (1) defenses of the primary obligor; (2) "suretyship defenses"; and (3) other defenses.

7.1 Defenses of the Primary Obligor

7.1.1 General

The general rule in New York is that the guarantor, absent an effective waiver, is not bound to perform if the primary obligor is not bound.[134] In other words, where a primary obligor asserts a defense against an obligee, the guarantor can generally avail itself of the same defenses against the obligee. However, where a guarantor is sued alone, the guarantor may not always be able to raise defenses or counterclaims that could have been raised by (i.e., are "personal" to) the primary obligor if the primary obligor has not raised those defenses

132. *See* Louis Dreyfus, 812 N.E.2d at 941.
133. *See* Meltzer, 712 N.E.2d at 660.
134. Walcutt v. Clevite Corp., 191 N.E.2d 894, 897 (N.Y. 1963).

itself.[135] Such personal defenses include fraud in the inducement of the underlying obligation,[136] negligence in performance of the underlying obligation,[137] and a breach of a warranty contained in the agreement governing the underlying obligation.[138] In such instances, the defenses to the obligation (fraud, negligence, breach of a warranty) are actions belonging to the primary obligor and not the surety.[139] Other defenses that are available to the primary obligor may not be asserted by the guarantor, even if the primary obligor asserts them itself (*see* § 7.1.3 below).

7.1.2 When Guarantor May Assert Primary Obligor's Defense

As described generally above, the guarantor's ability to assert certain defenses to guaranty obligations may depend upon the prior action or consent of the primary obligor. In the most straightforward example, action by the primary obligor with regard to the defense or claim may permit the guarantor to assert the same defense or claim. For instance, a guarantor may use a fraud in the inducement defense against the obligee if the primary obligor seeks to rescind the underlying obligation on the same basis.[140] However, a New York court has held that where an obligee sued a guarantor separately, the guarantor could not raise the defense of negligent performance even when the primary obligor had asserted the cause of action in a separate suit.[141]

If the guarantor alone is sued, it may be sufficient for the primary obligor to give its consent to the guarantor's use of the defense or cause of action belonging to the primary obligor.[142] Where the guarantor controls the primary obligor, a court may assume that the primary obligor has consented to the use of the defense or cause of action;[143] however, where the primary obligor is bankrupt, this assumption may not apply.[144]

---

135. *Id.*; Bank v. Wu-Chang Lai, No. 09-CV-4288 (DLI) (CLP), 2011 U.S. Dist. LEXIS 28205 at *5 (E.D.N.Y. March 3, 2011); But see Durable Grp., Inc. v. De Benedetto, 444 N.Y.S.2d 662, 663 (App. Div. 1st Dep't 1981) (citing, erroneously, Walcutt for the proposition that a guarantor may assert any defense of the primary obligor, including economic duress and coercion).

136. Ettlinger v. Nat'l Sur. Co., 117 N.E. 945, 946 (N.Y. 1917); N.J. Bank, Nat'l Ass'n v. Varano, 502 N.Y.S.2d 35, 36 (App. Div. 2d Dep't 1986).

137. Ralston Purina Co. v. Siegel's Poultry, Inc., 264 N.Y.S.2d 601, 601-02 (App. Div. 3d Dep't 1965).

138. Gillespie v. Torrance, 25 N.Y. 306, 311 (1862).

139. *See* Ettlinger, 117 N.E. at 946 (explaining, in the case of fraud, that because a fraudulently induced contract is voidable, it can only be avoided upon election of the primary obligor; any other result would allow a primary obligor to abide by the contract while allowing the surety to avoid its obligation thereunder).

140. Taylor & Jennings, Inc., 57 A.D.2d at 45 (finding that a guarantor may assert the defense of fraud in the inducement of the primary obligation after the primary obligor has asserted the same defense on its own behalf) (citing Taylor-Fichter Steel Constr. Co. v Fidelity & Cas. Co. of N. Y., 258 App Div 235). *See* also Ettlinger v. Nat'l Surety Co., 221 N.Y. 467 (1917).

141. 63 N.Y. Jur. 2d *Guaranty & Suretyship* § 340 (citing Ralston Purina, 264 N.Y.S.2d at 601-02).

142. *See, e.g.*, Cinema N. Corp. v. Plaza at Latham Assocs., 867 F.2d 135, 139 (2d Cir. 1989) (citing Taylor & Jennings, Inc. v. Bellino Bros. Constr. Co., 57 A.D.2d 42, 45 (N.Y. App. Div. 3d Dep't 1977)); *see generally* 63 N.Y. Jur. 2d *Guaranty & Suretyship* § 339.

143. Cathay Bank, 2011 U.S. Dist. LEXIS 28205 at *5. (E.D.N.Y. March 3, 2011); Bloor v. Shapiro, 32 B.R. 993, 1001 (Bankr. S.D.N.Y. 1983) (citing Walcutt, 191 N.E.2d at 894).

144. *See* First N.Y. Bank for Business v. DeMarco, 130 B.R. 650, 655 (S.D.N.Y. 1991).

7.1.3 Defenses that May not be Raised by the Guarantor

Some defenses that may be asserted by the primary obligor to defend itself against the primary obligation may not be used by the guarantor to defend against its obligations under a guaranty, regardless of whether such defenses are asserted by the primary obligor. The insolvency of the primary obligor is not a defense that the guarantor may raise unless the guaranty is conditioned on the solvency of the primary obligor.[145] A guarantor also may not raise the primary obligor's incapacity as a defense to liability under the guaranty.[146]

7.1.4 Defenses that May Always be Raised by the Guarantor

A guarantor may show that the obligee failed to perform such that there is a partial or complete "failure of consideration."[147] Where a judgment against the primary obligor was obtained by default, the guarantor "remains at liberty to contest its own liability by establishing affirmatively that the [primary obligor] was not liable."[148]

7.2 "Suretyship" Defenses

Guarantors and other sureties have a variety of defenses to payment that are generally not available to the primary obligor.

7.2.1 Change in Identity of Primary Obligor

Whether a change of the identity of the primary obligor to the underlying obligation discharges the guarantor's obligations depends upon the circumstances. Where changes are merely "formalistic," the guarantor is not discharged,[149] and relevant inquiries focus on whether (i) the change in the primary obligor's identity significantly changes the business deal that the guarantor agreed to guaranty and (ii) the changes have a "potentially adverse impact" on the guarantor, particularly with regard to the risk borne by the guarantor.[150]

---

145. *See* Taubes v. Stuart, 181 A.D.2d 669, 670-671 (N.Y. App. Div. 2d Dep't 1992) ("It is well-settled that the liability of a guarantor of a corporate debt is not affected by the institution of bankruptcy proceedings involving the corporation" (citations omitted); *see generally* 63 N.Y. Jur. 2d *Guaranty & Suretyship* § 257.
146. Bernstein v. Friedlander, 296 N.Y.S.2d 409, 415 (Sup. Ct. Kings Cnty. 1968) (citing President & Fellows of Harvard Col. v. Kempner, 116 N.Y.S. 437 (App. Div. 2d Dep't 1909)). There are a few exceptions to this general rule. *See* notes 47-49 above.
147. Walcutt, 191 N.E.2d at 897.
148. S.D.I. Corp. v. Fireman's Fund Ins. Co., 617 N.Y.S.2d 790, 792 (App. Div. 2d Dep't 1994) (citing Firedoor Corp. of Am. v. Merlin Indus., 446 N.Y.S.2d 325, 326 (App. Div. 1st Dep't 1982)).
149. *See, e.g.*, State v. Int'l Fid. Ins. Co., 547 N.Y.S.2d 466, 468 (App. Div. 3d Dep't 1989) (citations omitted); Richardson v. Cnty. of Steuben, 122 N.E. 449 (N.Y. 1919); People v. Backus, 22 N.E. 759 (N.Y. 1889); Fehr Bros. v. Scheinman, 509 N.Y.S.2d 304 (App. Div. 1st Dep't 1986)) (finding that that a corporation's transition from being a "debtor in possession" in a proceeding under Chapter 11 of the U.S. Bankruptcy Code to a corporation that had emerged from bankruptcy did not discharge the guarantor's liability); 95 Lorimer, LLC v. Ins. Co. of the State. of Penn., 789 N.Y.S.2d 833, 837 (Sup. Ct. Kings Cnty. 2004) (finding that substitution of newly formed corporation was more than a mere formalistic change even where the initial and subsequent primary obligor were part of the same corporate structure and shared principals and shareholders).
150. Skrabalak v. Rock, 617 N.Y.S.2d 912, 914 (App. Div. 3d Dep't 1994).

In analyzing whether changes in a primary obligor "have the effect of creating a [primary obligor] with a new identity and one the debtors of which the guarantor never intended to guarantee when he executed the agreement[,]" one court has listed a number of factors that have been taken into account: "changes in business name, form, composition, management, or ownership, the involvement of the guarantor in the business entity; and, whether the guarantor participated in the changes."[151] Similarly, courts have found that changes in the ownership of the primary obligor do not affect the obligations of the guarantor where such changes are within the realm of what could be expected given the structure and business of the primary obligor.[152]

Generally, courts accept the logic that at some point changes pertaining to the primary obligor should affect a guaranty, but, as has been noted, there is no "systematic method of determining the effect changes in the entity, the performance of which is guaranteed, have on the guarantor's obligation."[153]

7.2.2 Modification of the Underlying Obligation

Under New York law, modifications to the underlying obligation may permit the guarantor to discharge its obligations thereunder. The Court of Appeals has stated that "[a] guarantor's obligation cannot be altered without its consent . . ."[154] and that an obligation "is altered when the primary obligor is discharged from the original contract and a new contract is substituted in its place."[155] The traditional rule in New York is that neither the materiality of the change nor the presence of any injury to the guarantor is relevant,[156] although the Court of Appeals has stated that mere "indulgence or leniency" by the obligee in enforcing the underlying obligation does not discharge the guarantor where the obligee may still demand payment in accordance with the original terms of the primary obligation.[157] There is even some support for the proposition that "a surety is discharged by any alteration of the contract of which his guarantee is applied, whether material or not, and the courts will not inquire whether it is or is not to his injury."[158] There are, however, some cases that suggest that only "material" alterations to the primary obligation

151. Fehr Bros., 509 N.Y.S. at 306-07 (citing cases); *see also* Richardson, 122 N.E. at (finding that a guarantor was not discharged based on the change in the partners owning a bank where the guarantor did not inquire into the bank's form of organization and where the guaranty suggested that the intent was to guarantee the bank and not the specific members of the partnership and distinguishing circumstances in which guarantors intended to guarantee the liabilities of individuals); Backus, 22 N.E. at 760-61 (determining that extension of bank's charter and corporate existence did not discharge a guarantor).
152. Richardson v. Cnty. of Steuben, 122 N.E. 449, 452 (N.Y. 1919).
153. Fehr Bros., Inc. v. Scheinman, 509 N.Y.S.2d 304, 306 (App. Div. 1st Dep't 1986).
154. White Rose Food v. Saleh, 788 N.E.2d 602, 603 (2003) (citing Bier Pension Plan Trust v. Estate of Schneierson, 545 N.E.2d 1212 (1989)).
155. Bier, 545 N.E.2d at 1214.
156. *See* Becker v. Faber, 19 N.E.2d 997, 999 (N.Y. 1939); Congregation Ohavei Shalom, Inc. v. Comyns Bros., Inc., 507 N.Y.S.2d 28, 29 (App. Div. 2d Dep't 1986).
157. *Id.* at 1214-1215.
158. Hall & Co. v. Cont'l Cas. Co., 310 N.Y.S.2d 950, 952 (App. Div. 3d Dep't 1970) (citing Becker v. Faber, 19 N.E.2d 997, 998-99 (N.Y. 1939)), aff'd, 280 N.E.2d 890 (N.Y. 1972) . There is even some very old case law in New York that changes favorable to a guarantor, such as a reduction in the rent due under the lease that was the underlying obligation, will discharge the guarantor.

serve as the basis for discharge of a guarantor's obligations.[159] The discharge from liability upon such an alteration may result in a complete release of the guarantor.[160] However, for compensated sureties in the context of construction, the Court of Appeals has stated that "discharging the surety is inappropriate where the purported alteration 'cannot be said to affect the surety adversely or to have any effect whatever upon the contract or the defendant's obligation.'"[161] Stated in an alternate way by the Court of Appeals, a guarantor's liability is discharged if there is a "material alteration of the terms of the [underlying obligation]."[162] Moreover, a material alteration will result in a complete discharge of the guarantor. This is in contrast to the position taken in the Restatement (Third) of Suretyship and Guaranty whereby, if a modification would cause the guarantor a loss (*e.g.*, by increasing the interest rate), in many cases he guarantor is only partially discharged to the extent of the loss.[163]

However, guarantors will not be relieved of their obligations if they agree in advance to modifications: "As a general rule, sureties and guarantors are bound by an anticipatory agreement for an extension or extensions of time for the performance of the principal's obligation under a contract to which their undertaking relates."[164] Consent to modification may also be implied so that a guarantor may not demonstrate lack of consent where it actively participated in bringing about the contested modification.[165]

7.2.3 Release of Primary Obligor or Co-guarantor

A release of a primary obligor or, if there are multiple guarantors, a co-guarantor, may partially release the remaining obligors on the underlying obligation. Under New York General Obligations Law Section 15-104, if an obligee expressly reserves his or her rights against any other obligor of the underlying debt "in writing and as part of the same transaction as the release or discharge" of a primary obligor or co-guarantor, or the other obligor will not be released or discharged.[166] However, if an obligee does not expressly reserve its rights against the remaining obligors, the obligee's may have partially released such obligors. The extent of such release is provided for under New York General Obligations Law Section 15-105 and depends on whether or not the obligee knew (or had reason to know) that the released obligor had

159. *See* Corless v. Leonardo II, 748 N.Y.S.2d 620, 622 (App. Div. 3d Dep't 2002); Midland Steel Warehouse Corp. v. Godinger Silver Art Ltd., 714 N.Y.S.2d 466, 468 (App. Div. 1st Dep't 2000); Cent. Fed. Sav. & Loan Ass'n of Nassau Cnty. v. Pergolis, 570 N.Y.S.2d 170, 172 (2d Dep't 1991).

160. *See, e.g.*, White Rose Food, 788 N.E.2d at 603; United Natural Foods, Inc. v. Burgess, 488 F. Supp. 2d 384, 391 (S.D.N.Y. 2007) (interpreting New York law).

161. Mt. Vernon City School Dist. v. Nova Cas. Co., 968 N.E.2d 439, 445 (N.Y. 2012).

162. St. John's Coll., Fordham v. AEtna Indem. Co., 94 N.E. 994, 996 (N.Y. 1911).

163. *See* RESTATEMENT (THIRD) OF SURETYSHIP & GUAR. § 41.

164. Israel v. Chabra, 537 F.3d 86, 98-99 (2d Cir. 2008) (quoting 63 N.Y. JUR. 2D *Guaranty & Suretyship* § 225); *see also* Am. Bank & Trust Co. v. Koplik, 451 N.Y.S.2d 426, 428 (App. Div. 1st Dep't 1982); Banque Worms v. Andre Cafe Ltd., 583 N.Y.S.2d 438, 439 (App. Div. 1st Dep't 1992).

165. *See* Shire Realty Corp. v. Schorr, 390 N.Y.S.2d 622, 627 (App. Div. 2d Dep't 1977) (noting that the guarantors were the sole shareholders and officers of the primary obligor); *see also* Marine Midland Bank v. Smith, 482 F. Supp. 1279, 1288 (S.D.N.Y. 1979), *aff'd*, 636 F.2d 1202 (2d Cir. 1980). *But see* Mangold v. Keip, 679 N.Y.S.2d 240, 241 (App. Div. 1st Dep't 1998) (distinguishing the Shire Realty case on the grounds that the guarantors in Shire Realty were "alter egos" of the primary obligor corporation).

166. N.Y. GEN OBLIG LAW §15-104 (McKinney 2010).

paid less of the underlying obligation than the obligors had agreed or, based on the relations of the co-obligors, was bound to pay.[167] Therefore, if it is known that a primary obligor is responsible for paying the full amount of an underlying obligation, an obligee that releases such primary obligor without reserving his or her rights against the guarantors may also fully release such guarantors.

Consent to the release of the primary obligor or a co-guarantor is one exception to New York General Obligations Law Section 15-105. If a guarantor has consented to such a release in the guaranty, an obligee will not partially release such guarantor, regardless of whether or not the obligee reserves its rights against such guarantor.[168]

7.2.4 Release or Impairment of Security for the Underlying Obligation

Based on the common law, an obligee that holds security for an obligation that also has the benefit of a guaranty may not affirmatively act in a way that "impair[s] the security and deprive[s] the guarantors of any benefit which they might derive therefrom on payment of their guaranty."[169] In general, the release or impairment of collateral securing the underlying obligation results in a *pro tanto* release of the guarantor of the same obligation.[170] There may, however, be situations in which the release of security alters the guaranty such that the guarantor's obligation is completely discharged as the result of an alteration of the guaranty itself.[171]

The precise nature of the obligee's obligation is not always clear. On the one hand, it has been stated that, absent an obligation to the contrary, the obligee does not have an obligation to the guarantor to preserve collateral.[172] On the other hand, it has been stated that, in a situation in which guarantors have pledged collateral and the guarantors have demanded that the obligee liquidate the collateral, the negligent failure to liquidate the collateral breaches the obligee's duty as a secured party to use reasonable care in the custody and preservation of collateral.[173]

---

167. N.Y. GEN. OBLIG. LAW §15-105 (McKinney 2010).
168. Nat'l. Bank of N. Am. v. Kory, 404 N.Y.S.2d 626, 627 (App. Div. 1st Dep't 1978); First Am. Bank of N.Y. v. Fallova Shredder Co., Inc., 587 N.Y.S.2d 119, 120 (Sup. Ct. Albany Cnty. 1992).
169. Humphrey v. Hayes, 94 N.Y. 594, 600 (1884).
170. *Id.*; *see* New York v. Ins. Co. of the State of Penn., 762 N.Y.S.2d 116, 118 (App. Div. 3d Dep't 2003) (citations omitted); Color Mate, Inc. v Chase Manhattan Bank, N.A., 562 N.Y.S.2d 765, 766 (App. Div. 2d Dep't 1990) ("The proper remedy for an improper disposition of collateral proceeds is to 'lessen' the amount of liability, not to discharge it." (citations omitted)).
171. *See* 63 N.Y. JUR. 2D *Guaranty & Suretyship* § 242 (citing, e.g., a case in which the primary obligor and the obligee agree to impair the collateral and a case in which alteration of a mortgage releasing property from the mortgage lien); *see also* Cent. Fed. Sav. & Loan Ass'n v. Pergolis, 570 N.Y.S.2d 170, 172 (App. Div. 2d Dep't 1991) (finding that changes to mortgage loan and mortgage changed the nature of the agreements); Pell v. Webb, 112 N.Y.S.2d 832, 835-37 (Sup. Ct. N.Y. Cnty 1952) (finding that, where the guaranty and mortgage constituted a single contract, the obligee's release of all but five square feet of a fourteen-acre property from the lien of the mortgage was a sufficient alteration of the contract to fully discharge the guarantor (rather than releasing the guarantor on a *pro tanto* basis). .
172. *See* Marubeni Am. Corp. v. U.S. Fid. & Guar. Co., 721 N.Y.S.2d 6, 7 (App. Div. 1st Dep't 2001).
173. *See* Fed. Deposit Ins. Corp. v. Frank L. Marino Corp., 425 N.Y.S.2d 34, 36 (App. Div. 2d Dep't 1980).

In addition, it is unclear whether the obligee's failure to perfect its interest in collateral will constitute an impairment of collateral that reduces a guarantor's liability.[174] It does appear, however, that failure to perfect a security interest will not discharge a guarantor where the guarantor has agreed in advance to the release of collateral.[175]

The guarantor may generally waive in advance its defense based on the release or impairment of collateral.[176] However, a guarantor may not waive in advance standards of commercial reasonableness under New York's adoption of Article 9 the Uniform Commercial Code.[177]

7.3 Other Defenses

7.3.1 Failure to Fulfill a Condition Precedent

Although guarantors may raise a defense of failure to fulfill a condition precedent, "New York courts are cautious when interpreting a contractual clause as a condition precedent, and they will 'interpret doubtful language as embodying a promise or constructive condition rather than an express condition.'"[178] Indeed, "over time, the law has come to recognize and enforce the use of linguistic conventions to create conditions precedent. For example, the Appellate Division observed that the word 'provided,' placed immediately before a contractual requirement, indicates the creation of a condition."[179]

7.3.2 Modification of the Guaranty

Modifications to a guaranty made in accordance with New York's General Obligations Law should not affect its validity even where no new consideration is given for the modification. New York's General Obligations Law provides that "[a]n agreement, promise or undertaking to change or modify, or to discharge in whole or in part, any contract, obligation, or lease, or any mortgage or other security interest in personal or real property, shall not be invalid because of the absence of consideration, provided that the agreement, promise or undertaking changing, modifying or discharging such contract, obligation, lease, mortgage or security interest, shall be in writing and signed by the party against whom it is sought to enforce the change, modification or discharge, or by his agent."[180]

---

174. *See* 63 N.Y. Jur. 2d *Guaranty & Suretyship* § 249.
175. *See* Exec. Bank of Ft. Lauderdale, Fla. v. Tighe, 411 N.Y.S.2d 939, 944 (App. Div. 2d Dep't 1978), modified, 429 N.E.2d 1054 (1981); The North Face, A Division of UF Outdoor, Inc. v. Carp, 2009 WL 129903, at *3-4 (N.Y. Sup. Ct. Nassau Cnty. Jan. 14, 2009).
176. *See* Indianapolis Morris Plan Corp. v. Karlen, 268 N.E.2d 632, 634-35 (1971); Gateway State Bank v. Winchester Builders, Inc., 670, N.Y.S.2d 518, 520 (App. Div. 2d Dep't 1998); Chem. Bank v. PIC Motors Corp., 452 N.Y.S.2d 41, 44 (App. Div. 1st Dep't 1982).
177. *See* § 8.1 below.
178. Chabra, 537 F.3d at 93 (quoting Oppenheimer & Co. v. Oppenheim, Appel, Dixon & Co., 660 N.E.2d 415, 418 (1995)).
179. Nat'l Fuel Gas Dist. Corp. v. Hartford Fire Ins. Co., 814 N.Y.S.2d 436 (App. Div. 4th Dep't 2006); *see also* Ginett v. Computer Task Grp., 962 F.2d 1085, 1100 (2d Cir. 1992) ("'Parties often use language such as 'if,' 'on condition that,' 'provided that,' 'in the event that,' and 'subject to' to make an event a condition, but other words may suffice.'" (quoting II E. L. Allan Farnsworth, Contracts § 8.2 (1990))); Chabra, 537 F.3d at 93.
180. N.Y. Gen. Oblig. Law § 5-1103 (McKinney 2010).

Generally, contracts made in accordance with New York's General Obligations Law cannot be modified or terminated without a written agreement if such contracts contain a "no oral modifications" or "no oral terminations" clause.[181] However, New York courts have recognized certain exceptions to this rule. Where one party has induced another's substantial and significant reliance upon an oral modification, the first party may be estopped from invoking the statute.[182] Furthermore, where there is full or partial performance of an oral modification, the courts may enforce such changes to the contract if performance is unequivocally referable to the oral modification.[183]

7.3.3 Failure to Pursue Primary Obligor

New York General Obligations Law Section 15-701 provides that "the failure or refusal by a creditor, after a demand by a person bound as a surety, to bring an action against a principal debtor . . . shall not discharge such surety."[184] As a result of this statutory provision, a guaranty is presumed to be a guaranty of payment unless it provides otherwise. However, the statute allows the parties to alter this presumption via a writing.[185] If the parties do so agree in writing, case law from before the enactment of the statute should apply.[186]

---

181. Section 15-301 the General Obligations Law provides, in relevant part:
(1) A written agreement or other written instrument which contains a provision to the effect that it cannot be changed orally, cannot be changed by an executory agreement unless such executory agreement is in writing and signed by the party against whom enforcement of the change is sought or by his agent.
(2) A written agreement or other written instrument which contains a provision to the effect that it cannot be terminated orally, cannot be discharged by an executory agreement unless such executory agreement is in writing and signed by the party against whom enforcement of the discharge is sought, or by his agent, and cannot be terminated by mutual consent unless such termination is effected by an executed accord and satisfaction other than the substitution of one executory contract for another, or is evidenced by a writing signed by the party against whom it is sought to enforce the termination, or by his agent.
(3) a. A discharge or partial discharge of obligations under a written agreement or other written instrument is a change of the agreement or instrument for the purpose of subdivision one of this section and is not a discharge or termination for the purpose of subdivision two, unless all executory obligations under the agreement or instrument are discharged or terminated.
b. A discharge or termination of all executory obligations under a written agreement or other written instrument is a discharge or termination for the purpose of subdivision two even though accrued obligations remaining unperformed at the date of the discharge or termination are not affected by it.
c. If a written agreement or other written instrument containing a provision that it cannot be terminated orally also provides for termination or discharge on notice by one or either party, both subdivision two and subdivision four of this section apply whether or not the agreement or other instrument states specifically that the notice must be in writing.
(4) If a written agreement or other written instrument contains a provision for termination or discharge on written notice by one or either party, the requirement that such notice be in writing cannot be waived except by a writing signed by the party against whom enforcement of the waiver is sought or by his agent.
(5) If executed by an agent, any agreement, evidence of termination, notice of termination or waiver, required by this section to be in writing, which affects or relates to real property or an interest therein as defined in section 5-101 in any manner stated in subdivisions one or two of section 5-703 of this chapter shall be void unless such agent was thereunto authorized in writing.
(6) As used in this section the term "agreement" includes promise and undertaking. N.Y. Gen. Oblig. Law § 15-301(1)-(4) (McKinney 2010).

182. Allen v. Rose, 42 N.Y.2d 338, 348 (N.Y. 1977).
183. *Id.* at 343-44
184. N.Y. Gen. Oblig. Law § 15-701 (McKinney 2010).
185. *Id.*
186. 63 N.Y. Jur. 2d *Guaranty & Suretyship* § 238.

7.3.4 *Statute of Limitations*

New York's Civil Practice Law and Rules (the "CPLR") imposes, with certain exceptions, a six-year statute of limitations on contractual obligations.[187] One such exception applies to contracts for the sale of goods that are governed by Article 2 of the New York Uniform Commercial Code, which imposes a four-year statute of limitations.[188]

However, even where the underlying obligation is a contract for the sale of goods governed by the Uniform Commercial Code, the six-year statute of limitations applicable to contracts generally applies to the guaranty.[189] While in many cases the statutes of limitations for the guaranty and the underlying obligation may lapse concurrently, the New York Court of Appeals has rejected, in dictum, the notion that "if the action against the principal is time-barred the guarantor is automatically discharged."[190]

Under New York's General Obligations Law, one may not waive, extend or agree not to plead the statute of limitations, except in the context of an action for recovery of real property (where different rules apply), unless the waiver complies with the requirements of the General Obligations Law: (1) the promise to waive, to extend or not to plead must be in a writing signed by the promisor or his agent; and (2) the promise must be made after the cause of action has accrued.[191] A waiver that complies with the General Obligations Law will prevent the guarantor from interposing the statute of limitations as a defense, so long as the action brought against the guarantor is commenced "within the [statute of limitations] time that would be applicable if the cause of action had arisen at the date of the promise, or within such shorter time as may be provided in the promise."[192]

7.3.5 *Statute of Frauds*

Pursuant to Section 5-701 of New York's General Obligations Law, a guaranty falls within the statute of frauds as "a special promise to answer for the debt, default or miscarriage of another."[193] If a promisor intends to be primarily liable, this particular aspect of the statute of frauds would be inapplicable.[194] In contrast, if a promisor intends to answer for the debt of another, then the promise falls within the statute of frauds. There are also certain exceptions

---

187. N.Y. C.P.L.R. § 213(2) (Consol. 2011).
188. *See* N.Y. U.C.C. § 2-275(1) (Consol. 2011).
189. Am. Trading Co. v. Fish, 364 N.E.2d 1309, 1312 (N.Y. 1977).
190. *Id.*
191. N.Y. Gen. Oblig. Law § 17-103(1) & (3) (McKinney 2010).
192. *Id.* § 17-103(1).
193. N.Y. Gen. Oblig. Law § 5-701(a)(2).
194. *E.g.*, Lou Atkin Castings, Inc. v. M. Fabrikant & Sons, Inc., 628 N.Y.S.2d 98 (App. Div. 1st Dep't 1995) ("The alleged oral agreement or promise by the plaintiff to guarantee the debt of another is also barred by the Statute of Frauds, since the alleged promise did not represent an independent duty of payment, irrespective of the liability of the principal debtor, ... since the alleged promise lacked any consideration beneficial to the promisor flowing to the plaintiff, and since the plaintiff, as the alleged promisor, had no independent duty to pay the ... debt, regardless of the liability of the original debtor." (citations omitted)).

to the basic rule.[195] Courts have stated that a promise by a guarantor to the primary obligor to guaranty the primary obligor's debt does not fall within the statute of frauds when being enforced by the primary obligor.[196]

If a contract falls within New York's statute of frauds, it must be signed by the party to be charged and must contain all "material or essential terms of the agreement, either expressly or by reasonable implication."[197] The writing "must contain substantially the whole agreement, and all its material terms and conditions, so that one reading it can understand from it what the agreement is."[198]

7.3.6 *Fraud in the Inducement*

When analyzing whether fraudulent inducement is a defense to a guaranty, New York courts generally engage in a fact-specific inquiry.[199] However, fraudulent inducement may be waived by either a specific or general waiver.[200]

7.4 Right of Set-off

A guarantor can set-off an individual claim that he has against the creditor regardless of whether the claim is personal to the guarantor or was assigned from the primary obligor.[201] However, where a guarantor has made "an unconditional guaranty of payment [it] may not assert set-offs or defenses which arise independently from the guarantee."[202]

§ 8 Waiver of Defenses by the Guarantor

8.1 Defenses that cannot be Waived

It seems, generally, that some defenses cannot be waived.

---

195. New York does not follow the "main purpose rule" (otherwise known as the "leading object rule"), although it is accepted in other jurisdictions. Martin Roofing Inc. v. Goldstein, 60 N.Y.2d 262, 269 (App. Div. 4th Dep't 1994). The main purpose rule provides that the purpose of the statute of frauds would be satisfied if some benefit for a promise accrues to the promisor and, therefore, such promises should be enforced regardless of whether it meets the requirements under the statute of frauds. *Id.* at 268-69. However, under New York law, a guaranty would still fall within the statute of frauds regardless of whether the guarantor was motivated by his or her own economic advantage. Warlock Paving Corp. v. Camperlino, 617 N.Y.S.2d 87, 88 (N.Y. 1983).
196. Van Brunt v. Rauschenberg, 799 F. Supp. 1467, 1472 (S.D.N.Y. 1992) (citing Posner v. Minn. Mining & Mfg. Co., 713 F. Supp. 562, 564 (E.D.N.Y. 1989)).
197. HPSC Inc. v. Matthews, 579 N.Y.S.2d 474 (App. Div. 3d Dep't 1992).
198. Kobre v. Instrument Sys. Corp., 387 N.Y.S.2d 617, 618-19 (App. Div. 1st Dep't 1976), *aff'd*, 374 N.E.2d 131, 403 (N.Y. 1978) (quoting Mentz v. Newwitter, 25 N.E. 1044, 1046 (1890)).
199. *See* Millerton Agway Coop. v. Briarcliff Farms, 215 N.E.2d 341, 345 (N.Y. 1966) (reversing the trial court's summary judgment against two guarantors on the ground that there were unresolved factual issues relevant to any judgment whether the guarantors were fraudulently induced into executing the guaranties).
200. *See* Citibank, N.A. v. Plapinger, 485 N.E.2d 974, 974 (N.Y. 1985); *see also* § 8.2 generally regarding "Catch-all" waivers.
201. *See, e.g.*, Wallace v. Merrill Lynch Capital Servs., Inc., 816 N.Y.S.2d 412, 413 (App. Div. 1st Dep't 2006); Bank of U.S. v. Braveman, 181 N.E. 50, 52 (N.Y. 1932); Curtis v. Davidson, 109 N.E. 481, 481 (N.Y. 1915).
202. Medallion Funding Corp. v. Norrito, 708 N.Y.S.2d 617 (App. Div. 1st Dep't 2000) (quoting Marcus Dairy v. Jacene Realty Corp., 638 N.Y.S.2d 779, 780 (App. Div. 2d Dep't 1996)).

Courts have held that a guarantor cannot waive a constitutional or statutory protection where the public interest is implicated[203] or where the relevant statute provides that its violation would render the contract void.[204]

A guarantor may not generally waive certain other duties imposed on a secured party in respect of collateral.[205] For example, a guarantor (whether or not he is himself a pledgor) may not waive a defense of lack of commercial reasonableness in the disposition of collateral governed by Article 9 of the UCC.[206] While a waiver of suretyship defenses may waive the guarantor's right to challenge the impairment of collateral before a default, the waiver does not apply in the post-default context, where Article 9's provisions on commercial reasonableness apply.[207]

8.2 "Catch-all" Waivers

Though catch-all waiver language may be effective, it is advisable for beneficiaries to include waivers to specific suretyship defenses.

The standard catch-all waiver indicates that the guaranty is "absolute and unconditional" or that the guaranty is "given absolutely and unconditionally." In theory, when such a catch-all waiver is included in a guaranty, the guarantor waives almost all defenses and counterclaims potentially available in an action by the creditor arising from an obligation covered by the guaranty.[208] In fact, courts have held that where a guaranty is absolute and unconditional, "establishing the existence of a guaranty and submitting an affidavit of nonpayment" entitles the plaintiff/creditor to summary judgment.[209] Additionally, absolute and unconditional guaranties have been enforced even when the primary obligor escapes liability.[210] However, the enumeration of waivers to various defenses continues to be recommended practice, partially in response to the New York judiciary's inconsistent treatment of broad waiver language, as is discussed below.

---

203. Elliott Assocs., L.P. v. Republic if Peru, 12 F. Supp. 2d 328, 357-58 (S.D.N.Y. 1998) (finding that Section 489 of the New York Judiciary Law could not have been waived under the guaranty as the statute is a penal law directed at the public interest), rev'd sub nom. on other grounds; Elliott Assocs., L.P. v. Banco de la Nacion, 194 F.3d 363 (2d Cir. 1999) (finding no violation of Section 489 of the New York Judiciary Law and declining to address the waiver in the guaranty).

204. Stonehill v. Sec. Nat'l Bank, 68 F.R.D. 24, 34 (S.D.N.Y. 1975) (providing that a guaranty of loans that violate Regulation U would be void under Section 29 of the Securities Exchange Act of 1934, notwithstanding the fact that the guaranty stated that it was absolute and unconditional, and reasoning that "any contractual provision purporting to waive compliance with the Exchange Act or any regulation thereunder shall be void . . .").

205. *See* N.Y. U.C.C. §§ 9-602, 9-611 and 9-624 (Consol. 2011) (not permitting waiver of rules, *e.g.*, dealing with use and operation of collateral, requests for accounting with respect to the collateral, collection and enforcement of collateral , application or payment of noncash proceeds, accounting for surplus, disposing of collateral, including without breaching the peace, calculation of deficiency or surplus or acceptance of collateral in satisfaction of obligation (but waiver permitted in writing after default).

206. *See* N.Y. U.C.C. § 9-602 (Consol. 2011).

207. ESL Fed. Credit Union v. Bovee, 801 N.Y.S.2d 482, 485-86 (Sup. Ct. Monroe Cnty. 2005).

208. European Am. Bank v. Lofrese, 586 N.Y.S.2d 816, 819 (App. Div. 2d Dep't 1992). Note, however, that, under the Restatement (Third) of Suretyship and Guaranty, such language is not effective to waive suretyship defenses. *See* Restatement (Third) of Suretyship & Guar. § 48 cmt. d.

209. South Side House LLC et al., 470 B.R. at 679; Bank of Am., N.A. v. Solow, 874 N.Y.S.2d 48, 48-49 (App. Div. 1st Dep't 2009); N. Fork Bank v. ABC Merch. Servs., Inc., 853 N.Y.S.2d 633 (App. Div. 2d Dep't 2008); Raven Elevator Corp. v. Finkelstein, 636 N.Y.S.2d 292 (App. Div. 1st Dep't 1996).

210. Mfrs. Hanover Trust Co. v. Green, 464 N.Y.S.2d 474, 476 (App. Div. 1st Dep't 1983).

In interpreting catch-all waivers, judges usually look for more specific evidence that a guarantor intended to waive all surety defenses:[211] "[i]n finding waivers of various defenses, the New York courts have relied substantially on specific language in the guaranty agreements at issue even though the agreements contained the phrase 'absolute and unconditional.'"[212] Thus, the inclusion of "absolute and unconditional" language is not always dispositive in creating an absolute and unconditional guaranty. Even when a guaranty contains such language, courts have held that blanket waivers are "not a waiver of every defense to a damages claim, and do[] not foreclose a challenge to the calculation of the amount owed."[213] For example, a more specific waiver can prevent a guarantor from asserting equitable defenses, such as "estoppels, waiver, ratification, laches, and recoupment."[214] Additionally, "[a] guarantor may consent in a guarantee agreement to remain liable for the full amount of the guarantee even if the creditor releases the principal debtor or a co-guarantor from its obligations."[215]

A particular issue that arises is whether the defense of fraud in the inducement is available to a party who has entered into an absolute and unconditional guaranty. New York case law varies on this point.[216] In Plapinger, guarantors who were sophisticated business parties who executed an absolute and unconditional guaranty following extended negotiations were not permitted to raise a defense of fraud in the inducement.[217] The Plapinger court noted that the guaranty stated that it applied "'irrespective of (i) any lack of validity . . . of the . . . [underlying Loan Agreement] . . . or any validity agreement or

---

211. *See, e.g.*, Exp.-Imp. Bank of the U.S. v. Asia Pulp & Paper Co., No. 03 Civ.8554, 2008 U.S. Dist. LEXIS 11324 (S.D.N.Y. Feb. 6, 2008). The putative requirement of specificity seems rooted in a line of New York cases and even there it has been applied inconsistently. Although the Second Circuit in Manufacturers Hanover Trust Company v. Yanakas, 7 F.3d 310, 316 (2d Cir. 1993) (interpreting New York law), declared specificity the "touchstone" of enforceability, other authority has focused on the clarity of the waiver rather than its detail. The court in Citibank, N.A. v. Plapinger found the omission of detail unimportant, deeming it "unrealistic in such circumstances to expect an express stipulation that defendants were not relying on a separate oral agreement." 485 N.E.2d 974, 977 (N.Y. 1985). The Court in Valley National Bank v. Greenwich Insurance Company reached a similar conclusion, distinguishing Yanakas as "less applicable . . . where the drafter and more sophisticated party in the transaction now claims that the disclaimer is too broad." 254 F. Supp. 2d 448, 458 (S.D.N.Y. 2003). Cf. N. Fork Bank v. ABC Merch. Servs., Inc., 853 N.Y.S.2d at 633 and Raven Elevator Corp. v. Finkelstein, 636 N.Y.S.2d at 292 and discussion in Section 7.3.6 supra.
In certain cases, depending on the scope of a guarantor's waivers, summary judgment may be allowed even where a defense of fraudulent inducement is alleged. N. Fork Bank, 853 N.Y.S.2d at 633 (stating that the guarantee was absolute and unconditional, and enforceable regardless of the validity of any other obligation); Raven Elevator Corp., 636 N.Y.S.2d at 292 (waiving "any defenses that the borrower might have against the administrative agent and the lender").
212. Philips Lighting Co. v. Schneider, No. 05 Civ. 4820, 2008 U.S. Dist. LEXIS 77820, at *10 (E.D.N.Y. Sept. 30, 2008), vacated on other grounds, 395 Fed. Appx. 796 (2d Cir. 2010).
213. L&B 57th St., Inc. v. E.M. Blanchard, Inc., 143 F.3d 88, 92 (2d Cir. 1998).
214. *See* Exp.-Imp. Bank, 2008 U.S. Dist. LEXIS 11324, at *14.
215. Philips Lighting, 2008 U.S. Dist. LEXIS 77820, at **8-9; *see also* Companie Financiere, 188 F.3d at 35-36.
216. MBIA Ins. Corp. V. Royal Indem. Co., 426 F.3d 204, 218 (3d Cir. 2005).
217. Plapinger, 485 N.E.2d at 977; *see also* Raven Elevator Corp. v. Finkelstein, 636 N.Y.S.2d 292, 296 (App. Div. 1996). Note that fraud in the inducement had already been held unavailable in the case of an explicit disclaimer of reliance on the counterparty's representations in Danann Realty Corp. v. Harris, 157 N.E.2d 597, 604 (N.Y. 1959).

instrument relating thereto.'" The court held that this language was sufficiently specific to waive the defense of fraud in the inducement.[218]

Courts have cabined the application of this rule in Plapinger in three ways.

- First, they have found that a broad waiver does not bar a guarantor's claim of fraudulent concealment where there is not "a clear indication that the disclaiming party has knowingly disclaimed reliance on the specific representations that form the basis of the fraud claim."[219]
- Second, courts have, in certain instances, highlighted the specificity of the language in the particular guaranty in Plapinger. For example, one court reviewing an unconditional and absolute guaranty permitted a defense of fraud in the inducement because there was not "specific language of disclaimer of reliance" in the guaranty at issue, unlike the guaranty in Plapinger.[220] Similarly, language that a guarantor was "absolutely and unconditionally" liable on a guaranty was not dispositive in precluding a guarantor from introducing proof of such fraud where there was no other indication of waiver of a fraud in the inducement defense.[221]
- Third, judges have focused on the sophistication of the parties to a guaranty when assessing whether a general waiver invalidates the defense of fraud in the inducement or other defense. The more sophisticated the parties were when issuing absolute and unconditional guaranties, the more likely courts are to uphold the waiver of a defense of fraud in the inducement.[222] Such decisions emphasize that the strong language in the guaranties should have alerted sophisticated parties to the extent of their waivers.

8.3 Use of Specific Waivers

No defense requires an explicit waiver.

---

218. Plapinger, 485 N.E.2d at 977. The Plapinger rule has also been held to be applicable in the context of a guaranty of performance of a construction contract; *see* Nat'l Westminster Bank PLC v. Empire Energy Mgmt. Sys., 1998 U.S. Dist. LEXIS 1047 (S.D.N.Y. Feb. 4, 1998). *See also* UBS AG, Stamford Branch v. Healthsouth Corp., 645 F. Supp. 2d 135 (S.D.N.Y. 2008) (finding that the defense that there was no actual or apparent authority of an officer to sign was precluded where "'extended negotiations between sophisticated business people'" occurred and where the guaranty was stated to be "'absolute and unconditional . . . without regard to validty, regularity or enforceability ' . . . or 'any other circumstance whatsoever . . . which constitutes, or might be construed to constitute, an equitable or legal discharge'").

219. MLP U.S.A. Inc. v. Motheral, No. 05 Civ. 10796, 2006 U.S. Dist. LEXIS 58589, at **5-6 (S.D.N.Y. Aug. 17, 2006) (quoting JPMorgan Chase Bank ex rel. Mahonia Ltd. v. Liberty Mut. Ins. Co., 189 F. Supp. 2d 24, 27 (S.D.N.Y. 2002)); *see also* Mitsubishi Power Sys. Ams., Inc. v. Babcock & Brown Infrastructure Grp. US, Inc., No. 4499-VCL, 2010 Del. Ch. LEXIS 11, at **38-40 (Del. Ch. Jan. 22, 2010).

220. GTE Automatic Elec. Inc. v. Martin's Inc., 512 N.Y.S.2d 107, 108 (App. Div. 1st Dep't 1987); a*ccord* Yanakas, 7 F.3d at 316; Philips Lighting Co., 2008 U.S. Dist. LEXIS 77820, at **9-10.

221. Zaro Bake Shop, Inc. v. David, 574 N.Y.S.2d 803, 804 (App. Div. 2d Dep't 1991). *See also* note 213 and Fierro v. Gallucci et al., No. 06-CV-5189 (JFB), 2008 U.S. Dist. LEXIS 38513, at **43-44 (E.D.N.Y. May 12, 2008).

222. South Side House LLC et al., 470 B.R. at 680 (noting, in a context other than fraud in the inducement, the sophistication of the parties to give effect to an "absolute and unconditional" guaranty to grant summary judgment in favor of the obligee; Israel Disc. Bank of N.Y. v. Schwebel, No. 101357/2007, 2009 N.Y. Misc. LEXIS 744, at **6-7 (Sup. Ct. N.Y. Cnty Jan. 13, 2009); WestRM-West Risk Mkts., Ltd. v. Lumbermens Mut. Cas. Co., 314 F. Supp. 2d 229, 236 (S.D.N.Y. 2004) (citing Valley Nat'l Bank, 254 F. Supp. 2d at 458-59). *see also* Mitsubishi Power Sys. Ams., Inc. 2010 Del. Ch. LEXIS 11 at *38.

General waivers may suffice to waive suretyship defenses. However, as a practical matter, the inconsistent application of New York law in this area (particularly as it relates to the defense of fraud in the inducement), suggests that specific waivers may be prudent. Moreover, there can be no waiver without a finding of intent to waive.[223] Presumably the best evidence of such waiver is an explicit statement of waiver.

§ 9 Third-party Pledgors – Defenses and Waiver Thereof

A third-party pledgor who pledges collateral to support the primary obligor's obligations to a third party arguably stands in the relation of a guarantor to the primary obligor to the extent of the pledge. It seems logical, therefore, that the pledgor can avail itself of the defenses of a guarantor and may also waive such defenses. We have found no evidence that the law as applied to sureties would not apply to such a third-party pledge.

§ 10 Joint Liability and Joint and Several Liability of Guarantors—Contribution and Reduction of Obligations Upon Payment by a Co-obligor

Guarantors who are jointly and severally liable are presumed to share the secondary obligation equally. The creditor is not obliged to seek full payment from more than one such guarantor.

Guarantors are presumed to have joint liability unless an agreement exists stating otherwise or there are "words of severance" indicating an intention by the guarantors to be severally or joint and severally liable.[224] For example, guarantors who have co-signed a guaranty that uses the singular form (terms such as "the undersigned", "his", or "himself") have been found to be joint and severally liable as opposed to jointly liable.[225] An important difference between joint liability and joint and several liability is that an obligee may face certain procedural hurdles in commencing an action or enforcing a judgment against guarantors who are jointly liable than they would for guarantors who are joint and severally liable.[226]

223. Extruded Louver Corp. v. McNulty, 234 N.Y.S.2d 902, 904 (App. Div. 2d Dep't 1962) (citing Davison v. Klaess, 20 N.E.2d 744 (N.Y. 1939)).

224. U.S. Printing and Lithograph Co. v. Powers, 233 N.Y. 143, 152 (N.Y. 1922); Nat'l Sur. Co. v. Seaich, 157 N.Y.S. 422, (App. Div. 1st Dep't 1916).

225. Battery Assoc., Inc. v. J&B Battery Supply, 914 F. Supp. 171, 178 (E.D.N.Y. 1996).

226. *See, e.g.*, N.Y. CPLR § 5201(b) (Consol. 2012); 73 N.Y. Jur. 2d *Judgments* § 53 (West 2012) (citing Abramovitz v. Markowitz, 108 N.Y.S. 1044 (App. Term 1908)).

10.1 Contribution

Where co-guarantors are liable jointly liable or joint and severally liable, there is a presumption that they bear the burden equally.[227] The doctrine of contribution (i.e., the right of a surety who pays the creditor to recover a portion of the amount paid from other sureties who are equally liable for the same debt) comes from equity, not from the language of a contract.[228]

Moreover, before the creditor obtains judgment, any individual guarantor is obliged to pay the whole debt.[229] Insofar as the guarantor has paid out more than its proportional share of the obligation, only then may it recover from other guarantors proportionate to their liability.[230] In addition, a New York court has determined that, where two parties agreed to jointly and severally guaranty an underlying obligation, a partial payment by one guarantor that is less than that guarantor's pro rata share does not entitle it to seek any contribution.[231]

10.2 Reduction of Obligations Upon Payment of Co-obligor

Section 15-103 of New York's General Obligations Law provides that, when an obligee receives an amount from a co-obligor (whether primary, several, joint, or joint and several) in respect of an obligation of the co-obligors, the amount received will be credited against the amount owed by all co-obligors, provided that the amount will not be credited to co-obligors for whom the co-obligor giving the value stood as a surety.[232] Therefore, if a guarantor makes a payment to an obligee, the obligation of the primary obligor will not be reduced. However, if the primary obligor makes a payment, the obligation of the guarantor will be reduced accordingly.

§ 11 Reliance

The concept of reliance arises in several different contexts within discussions of guaranties. As discussed in Section 4, consideration is necessary to create a valid contract of guaranty. When an obligee can be shown to have extended credit to a primary obligor in reliance on a guaranty, New York courts have found such reliance to be sufficient consideration for the guaranty. There are no reported cases in New York where the determination of the enforceability

227. Philips Lighting Co. v. Schneider, No. 05 Civ. 4820, 2008 U.S. Dist. LEXIS 77820, at *15; Slutsky v. Left, 609 N.Y.S.2d 528, 530 (Civ. Ct. 1993) (finding that three shareholders who guaranteed a loan to the debtor company were each liable for one third of the company's debt, notwithstanding that one shareholder owned 50% of the stock of the company) .
228. Yawger v. Am. Surety Co., 141 N.Y.S. 491 (App. Div. 1st Dep't 1913).
229. Israel Disc. Bank of N.Y. v. Schwebel, No. 101357/2007, 2009 N.Y. Misc. LEXIS 3743 at *3 (Sup. Ct. N.Y. Cnty. Jan. 13, 2009) (citing Slutsky, 609 N.Y.S.2d at 530).
230. Backman v. Hibernia Holdings, 96 Civ. 9590 (LAP), 1998 U.S. Dist. LEXIS 11571, **17-18 (S.D.N.Y. July 27, 1998), Hard v. Mingle, 99 N.E. 542, 543-4 (N.Y. 1912).
231. *See* 63 N.Y. Jur. 2d *Guaranty & Suretyship* § 490 (citing Falb v. Frankel, 423 N.Y.S.2d 683, 685 (App. Div. 2d Dep't 1980)).
232. N.Y. Gen. Oblig. Law § 15-103 (Consol. 2011).

of a guaranty depended solely on the obligee's reliance on the guaranty, except where such reliance was analyzed as an indication of consideration; however, the U.S. Bankruptcy Court for the Southern District of New York is currently being asked to consider whether a claim based on a parent company's general guaranty of its subsidiary's obligations may be expunged because the obligee did not rely on such guaranty.[233]

Reliance is necessary in order to bind a principal on the theory of apparent authority[234] and reasonable reliance is also an essential element of any claim of fraud in the inducement as a defense to a surety claim.[235]

§ 12 Subrogation

A guarantor who pays an obligation is entitled to be subrogated to the rights of the obligee against the primary obligor.

"[S]ubrogation is not a matter of right but an equitable doctrine, designed to promote justice and is thus dependent on the particular relationship of parties and nature of controversy in each case."[236] Subrogation applies equally to guaranties of payment and performance.[237]

Generally subrogation requires total satisfaction of the underlying obligation to the obligee prior to its exercise.[238] For this reason, there is usually no partial subrogation, although exceptions have been made in the case of insurance companies.[239] The general prohibition of partial subrogation is premised on concern for an obligee's ability to recover in full.[240] Nonetheless, where a guarantor has paid installments of interest, each installment of interest is a claim in full, such that the guarantor has a right of subrogation regarding each of these interest payments.[241]

---

233. In July 2012, debtors' counsel in In re Lehman Brothers Holdings Inc., et al, filed an objection to a claim that was based on a guaranty by Lehman Brothers Holdings Inc. of the obligations of a subsidiary debtor. The objection cites Fed. Deposit Ins. Corp. v. Schuhmacher, 660 F. Supp. 6 (E.D.N.Y. 1984) (quoting, in dicta, Calcot Ass'n Ltd. V. Coast Cotton Mills, 295 P.2d 1 (Cal. Dist. Ct. App. 4th Dist. 1956), a California case that, in turn, cites to American Jurisprudence (first edition), for the proposition that, with respect to general guaranties, "[i]t is, of course, elementary that a creditor's right to enforce a contract of guaranty must be based upon knowledge of the existence of the guaranty and that the credit must be extended in reliance thereof").
234. Songbird Jet Ltd. v. Amax Inc., 581 F. Supp. 912, 919 (S.D.N.Y. 1984).
235. Bogda M.B. Clarke et al., Fraud in the Inducement as a Defense to Fidelity and Surety Claims, 42 Tort Trial & Ins. Practice L.J. 181, 186 (citing Restatement (Second) of Contracts § 164 (1981)).
236. Costello v. Geiser, 647 N.E.2d 1261, 1264 (N.Y. 1995); *see* Meltzer, 712 N.E.2d at 661.
237. Pearlman v. Reliance Ins. Co., 371 U.S. 132, 139 (1962).
238. Meltzer, 712 N.E.2d at 661.
239. Hanlon v. Union Bank of Medina, 160 N.E. 650, 650 (N.Y. 1928).
240. *See id.*
241. Prudential Ins. Co. of Am. v. Liberdar Holding Corp., 85 F.2d 504, 507 (2d Cir. 1936).

§ 13 Exoneration and Indemnification

13.1 Exoneration – Right of a Surety Prior to Satisfaction of the Underlying Obligation

Prior to satisfying an underlying obligation, a guarantor has a claim in equity for exoneration – a right to compel the primary obligor to honor its obligation.[242] In a claim for exoneration, the surety must show that the debt is presently due, the primary obligor is liable for the debt, and the surety will be forced to satisfy the underlying obligation.[243]

13.2 Indemnification or Reimbursement[244] – Rights of a Surety after Satisfaction of the Underlying Obligation

The primary obligor has a duty of indemnification so long as the guarantor undertook its obligations at the request of the primary obligor. The extent of this duty can be altered by contract.

A guarantor cannot recover an indemnity from the primary obligor where it entered upon the guaranty contract as a "volunteer," a term that describes a guarantor who binds itself at the request of the obligee.[245] In this sense, indemnification presents a narrower right available to only some guarantors, in contrast to the rights of subrogation and exoneration, neither of which depend upon who requested the guarantor's promise of guaranty.[246]

However, "when a party agrees to become a guarantor at the behest of the primary obligor, a promise to indemnify – even though not expressly provided for in the contract – is implied by law."[247] Absent an express contract of indemnification which provides otherwise, payment by the guarantor is a condition precedent to its recovery in an action against the primary obligor for reimbursement.[248]

The guarantor is entitled to full indemnity against the primary obligor's default.[249] This includes "reimbursement not only of what [the guarantor] may have been obliged to pay in discharge of the obligation for which he was surety, but also of all reasonable expenses legitimately incurred in consequence of

242. Thompson v. Taylor, 72 N.Y. 32, 34 (1878); Hyde v. Equitable Life Assurance, 61 Misc. 518 (1908).
243. Borey v. Nat'l Union Fire Ins. Co., 934 F.2d 30, 32 (2d Cir. 1991).
244. In New York case law, the terms "indemnification" and "reimbursement" appear to be synonymous. They are both to be distinguished from "restitution" because in the latter recovery is limited to the amount of the primary obligor's enrichment, while the former gives an equitable right to the guarantor's reasonable expenses. *See* RESTATEMENT (THIRD) OF SURETYSHIP & GUAR. § 26 cmt. d. We have not found any New York case law that adopts the Restatement's framework for when a surety can recover based on "restitution" as opposed to "reimbursement." *See Id.* § 26 cmts. b and c.
245. 63 N.Y. JUR. 2D *Guaranty & Suretyship* § 409 (citing Van Shaick v. Lawyers' Title & Guar. Co., 268 N.Y.S. 554 (Sup. Ct. N.Y. Cnty. 1933), *aff'd* 271 N.Y.S. 950 (App. Div. 1st Dep't 1934), *aff'd* 191 N.E. 720 (N.Y. 1934)).
246. *See* Van Shaick, 268 N.Y.S. at 565; Corp. Buying Service v. Lenox Hil Radiology Assocs., 1995 U.S. Dist. LEXIS 15180, n. 1 (S.D.N.Y. 1995).
247. Pro-Specialties, Inc. v. Thomas Funding Corp., 812 F.2d 797, 800 (1987) (quoting Konitzky v. Meyer, 49 N.Y. 571, 576 (1872)).
248. *See, e.g.*, Blanchard v. Blanchard, 94 N.E. 630, 631 (N.Y 1911).
249. Lori-Kay Golf, Inc. v. Lassner, 460 N.E.2d 1097, 1098 (N.Y. 1984).

such default, or for his own protection."[250] Full satisfaction of the underlying obligation is not a condition precedent to an action by the guarantor to enforce reimbursement, but a guarantor who has paid only a portion of the debt is entitled to indemnity for only the amount paid.

§ 14 Enforcement of Guaranties

14.1 Limitations on Recovery

New York's Debtor and Creditor Law allows the avoidance of a transfer if, at the time of the transfer, the debtor was insolvent or unreasonably undercapitalized and did not receive fair consideration in return.[251] New York courts have applied this state law fraudulent conveyance provision in the context of insolvency as a defense to guaranties given for less than fair consideration.[252] New York courts have not ruled on when the test for fraudulent conveyance must be made in the context of guaranties covering a series of transactions; however, in applying Section 548 of the U.S. Bankruptcy Code (which is similar to New York's statutory fraudulent conveyance provisions), the U.S. Court of Appeals for the Second Circuit held that the issues of fair consideration and solvency of the guarantor must be assessed at the time of each draw under the facility (and not just when the guaranty was executed).[253] Because nothing in the New York fraudulent conveyance laws specifies when these tests should be applied, it is possible that New York courts applying New York law would apply the same analysis. As noted in an opinion of the U.S. District Court for the Southern District of Florida, Miami Division, *Rubin* has been rarely cited for this principle and legal commentators have roundly criticized the result.[254] Indeed, the Uniform Fraudulent Transfer Act includes specific language clarifying that an obligation is incurred, if oral, when it becomes effective between the parties or, if written, at the time the executed writing is delivered to or for the benefit of the obligee and the official commentary indicates that this language was specifically added "to resolve uncertainty arising from *Rubin*."[255] The Uniform Fraudulent Transfer Act has been enacted in more than 40 states and the District of Columbia, but has not been adopted by New York, where the state statutory provision is based on the Uniform Fraudulent Conveyance Act, which, like the Bankruptcy Code, does not specify when the test for consideration or capitalization should be applied.[256]

250. Thompson v. Taylor, 72 N.Y. 32, 34 (1878).
251. N.Y. Debt. & Cred. Law, §§ 273, 274 & 275 (McKinney 2012).
252. *See* In re Nirvana Restaurant Inc., 337 B.R. 495, 501-06 (Bankr. S.D.N.Y. 2006).
253. *See* Rubin v. Manufacturers Hanover Trust Co., 661 F.2d 979, 990-91 (2d Cir. 1981).
254. *See* Official Comm. of Unsecured Creditors, Inc. v. Citicorp N. Am., Inc. (In re TOUSA, Inc.), No. 09-60589-CIV-JORDAN, 2011 U.S. Dist. LEXIS 40518, at *15 (S.D. Fla. Mar. 4, 2011).
255. Uniform Fraudulent Transfer Act § 6 cmt. 3 (1984).
256. *See* Uniform Fraudulent Conveyance Act § 4, 5 & 6 (1918). In 1984, the National Conference of Commissioners on Uniform State Laws withdrew its recommendation for enactment of the Uniform Fraudulent Conveyance Act (given the promulgation of the Uniform Fraudulent Transfer Act), 7A U.L.A. 245 (Thompson West 2006).

One way that parties attempt to contract around fraudulent conveyance laws is by adding so-called "savings clauses" to the contracts that purport to modify liabilities to make them enforceable to the maximum extent allowed under applicable law New York courts have not ruled on the enforceability of such caps, but there is some authority that such caps on recovery under a guaranty may not be enforceable,[257] particularly where caps are included in guarantees in favor of different lenders to the same borrower, rendering the cap applicable to each group of lenders difficult or impossible to calculate.[258]

14.2 Exercising Rights Under a Guaranty Where the Underlying Obligation is also Secured by a Mortgage

With regard to mortgages on real property, New York's Real Property Actions and Proceedings Law provides that, "[w]hile an action is pending or after final judgment for the plaintiff therein, no other action shall be commenced or maintained to recover any part of the mortgage debt, without leave of the court in which the former action was brought."[259] Referred to as New York's "one-action rule," this provision has been interpreted to extend to a guaranty of the obligation secured by the mortgage.[260] Another court has found that Section 1301(3) applies to a guaranty where the guaranty does not represent an obligation "separate and distinct from the debts underlying the mortgage" to which the guaranty refers.[261]

New York courts have stated that Section 1301 is inapplicable where the mortgaged property is located outside New York state, even if the transaction documents contain a New York choice-of-law provision.[262]

In addition to the one-action rule, the Real Property Actions and Proceedings Law specifies certain procedures that must be undertaken in order for a creditor to be able to obtain a deficiency judgment following the foreclosure on mortgaged property.[263] Within 90 days "after the date of consummation of the sale by delivery of the proper deed of conveyance by the purchaser, . . ."

---

257. *See* Official Comm. of Unsecured Creditors of Tousa, Inc. v. Citicorp N. Am., Inc. (In re: TOUSA, Inc.), 422 B.R. 783, 858-65 (Bankr. S.D. Fla. 2009), rev'd in part on other grounds, Senior Transeastern Lenders v. Official Comm. of Unsecured Creditors (In re TOUSA, Inc.), 680 F.3d 1298, 1309 (11th Cir. 2012) (noting that, though its analysis is based on the U.S. Bankruptcy Code, its analysis of issues under Section 548 applies also to claims made under New York fraudulent conveyance provisions and finding that guaranties provided by affiliates of the primary obligor who were insolvent at the time the guaranty obligations were incurred were fraudulent conveyances, despite contractual caps on their liability, for a number of reasons, including an analysis that enforcement of the caps would "nullify the protection provided by Section 548(a)(1)(B) and the limits that Section 548(c) places on the ability of transferees to retain property," and concluding that such caps are "a frontal assault on the protections that Section 548 provides to other creditors. They are, in short, entirely too cute to be enforced").

258. *Id.* at 864-65 (explaining that, "[b]ecause of the existence of multiple savings clauses, each of which purports to reduce obligations after accounting for all other obligations, it is utterly impossible to determine the obligations that result from the operation of any particular savings clause . . . In mathematical terms, the value of A can be determined only after knowing the value of B; but the value of B can be determined only after knowing the value of A. The savings clauses create a circular problem that has no answer. It is turtles all the way down. Because of the interaction between the two savings clauses, liabilities under the term loans are inherently indeterminate") (citations omitted).

259. N.Y. Real Prop. Acts. Law § 1303(3) (McKinney 2009).

260. Mfrs. Hanover Trust Co. v. 400 Garden City Assocs., 568 N.Y.S.2d 505, 507 (Sup. Ct. Nassau Cnty. 1991) (citing TBS Enters, Inc. v. Grobe, 114 A.D.2d 445, 445-46 (App. Div. 2d Dep't 1985)).

261. Fed. Home Loan Mortg. Corp. v. Sierra, 641 N.Y.S.2d 291, 292 (App. Div. 1st Dep't 1996).

262. *See* Wells Fargo Bank Minn., N.A. v. Cohn, 771 N.Y.S.2d 649, 649 (App. Div. 1st Dep't 2004).

263. *See* N.Y. Real Prop. Acts. Law § 1371 (McKinney 2009).

the creditor must properly file for a deficiency judgment and provide proper notice to the party against whom the judgment is sought.[264] If the creditor does not seek a deficiency judgment in accordance with Section 1371, the sale proceeds from the foreclosure will be deemed in full satisfaction of the mortgage debt.[265]

14.3 Choice of Law Provisions

As a general matter, New York courts enforce choice-of-law clauses as long as the law chosen bears a reasonable relationship to the parties or the transaction, and the chosen law does not violate public policy.[266] In addition, the particular language of a choice-of-law clause may affect the extent of its applicability.[267]

With certain exceptions, the New York General Obligations Law permits parties to a commercial contract, agreement or undertaking in consideration of or relating to any obligation arising out of a transaction covering in the aggregate at least $250,000 to agree that New York law will govern their rights and duties whether or not such contract, agreement or undertaking bears a reasonable relation to New York state.[268] This provision does "not apply to any contract, agreement or undertaking (a) for labor or personal services, (b) relating to any transaction for personal, family or household services, or (c) to the extent provided in [Section 1-105(2)] of the uniform commercial code."[269] Section 5-1401(1) of the General Obligations Law has been interpreted to render enforceable a New York choice-of-law claim within its ambit, "unless procured by fraud or overreaching, even if, under a traditional choice of law

264. *Id.* § 1371(2).

265. *Id.* § 1371(3); *see* Sierra 641 N.Y.S.2d at 292 ("[T]he guarantees cannot be enforced, plaintiff having sought neither leave from the … court to bring a separate action pursuant to RPAPL 1301(3) nor deficiency judgments pursuant to RPAPL 1371(3)." (citation omitted).

266. *See* Brown Bark III, L.P. v. AGBL Enters., LLC, 924 N.Y.S.2d 571, 573 (App. Div. 2d Dep't 2011) (citing Welsbach Elec. Corp. v. MasTec N. Am., Inc., 859 N.E.2d 498 (N.Y. 2006); Astoria Fed. Mortg. Corp. v. Pellicane, 913 N.Y.S.2d 228, 229 (App. Div. 2d Dep't 2010)). In Lehman Bros. Commercial Corp. v. Minmetals International Non-Ferrous Metals Trading Co., the Federal District for the Southern District of New York, under New York law, refused to enforce a Delaware choice-of-law provision where that choice of law would violate the policy of China, which was a "more-interested jurisdiction." 179 F. Supp. 2d 118, 144-45 (S.D.N.Y. 2000).

267. *See* Pegasus Aviation IV, Inc. v. Aerolineas Austral Chile, S.A., No. 08 Civ. 11371 (NRB), 2012 WL 967301, at *5 (S.D.N.Y. Mar. 20, 2012) (noting that where the subject guaranties "contain choice of law provisions designating New York law as that by which they shall be 'governed' and construed,' … those provisions do not control our determination because the defendants challenge the *validity* of the contracts, not their *interpretation*…"); Kniereimen v. Bache Halsey Stuart Shields Inc., 427 N.Y.S.2d 10, 12-13 (App. Div. 1st Dep't 1980), overruled on other grounds, Rescildo v. R,H. Macy's, 594 N.Y.S.2d 139, 142 App. Div. 1st Dep't 1993) (finding that a choice-of-law clause stating that the "contract shall be governed by the laws of the state of New York" did not extend to causes of action sounding in tort); *see also* Fin. One Plc. v. Lehman Bros. Special Fin. Inc., 414 F.3d 325, 335 (2d Cir. 2005) (reasoning that "[p]resumably a contractual choice-of-law clause could be drafted broadly enough to reach such tort claims" but observing that at the time "no reported New York cases present such a broad clause"); Capital Z Fin. Servs. Fund II, L.P. v. Health Net Inc., 840 N.Y.S.2d 16 (App. Div. 1st Dep't 2007) (subsequently applying contractual choice of law to fraud claims where choice-of-law provision specified that it "govern[ed] all issues concerning" *inter alia* "enforcement of the rights and duties of the parties").

268. N.Y. Gen. Oblig. Law § 5-1401(1) (McKinney 2010); *see* IRB-Brazil Resseguros, S.A. v. Inepar Invs., S.A., 922 N.Y.S.2d 308, 310-11 (App. Div. 1st Dep't 2011), leave to appeal granted, 959 N.E.2d 1024 (N.Y. 2011) (applying New York law, based on choice-of-law provision, to determine enforceability of a guaranty allegedly executed without authority under Brazilian law).

269. *Id.* Section 1-105(2) of New York's Uniform Commercial Code includes a variety of provisions that specify applicable law and which may be varied by agreement only to the extent permitted by law.

analysis, the application of the chosen law would violate fundamental public policy or another, more interested jurisdiction."[270]

Even if the choice of law provision is enforceable in New York, the parties risk having the law of another jurisdiction applied to a dispute arising under the guaranty if such dispute is brought before a court outside of New York because such court will use its own choice of law rules in determining what law it should apply to the dispute. Therefore, if the guaranty has a New York choice of law provision, the parties often provide for New York as the choice of forum pursuant to Section 5-1402 of the General Obligations Law as a New York court will, subject to certain exceptions noted above, apply Section 5-1401(1) of the General Obligations Law. However, in order for the parties to be able to select New York as the choice of forum under Section 5-1402 of the General Obligations Law, the guaranty must be in consideration of, or relate to, any obligation arising out of a transaction covering in the aggregate not less than $1,000,000. Furthermore, any foreign corporation or non-resident must agree to submit to the jurisdiction of the courts of New York State in the contract.

In the absence of an enforceable choice-of-law provision, a court, as an initial matter, looks to whether there is a potential choice-of-law issue by determining whether a potential conflict exists among relevant jurisdictions.[271] In the context of contracts law, the New York Court of Appeals has adopted the "center of gravity" or "grouping of contacts" approach to choice-of-law questions.[272]

14.4 Litigating Guaranty Claims: Procedural Considerations

14.4.1 Long-Arm Jurisdiction

Section 302(a)(1) of New York's CPLR provides, as one of several bases for long-arm jurisdiction, that a New York court may exercise personal jurisdiction over a non-domiciliary if the non-domiciliary "transacts business within the state or contracts anywhere to supply goods and services in [New York state] . . . ."[273] Courts in New York are divided on the question of whether long-arm jurisdiction extends to a non-domiciliary who, by a guaranty executed outside New York, guarantees an obligation to be performed in New York. Some courts, including the Appellate Division's First Department, draw a distinction between guaranties of payment and guaranties of performance and have held that a guaranty of payment to a New York corporation is insufficient to confer long-arm jurisdiction under CPLR 302(a)(1); a guaranty of performance in New York, on the other hand, may be sufficient to confer jurisdiction on a non-domiciliary under CPLR 302(a)(1).[274] Other New York

270. Tosapratt, LLC v. Sunset Props., Inc., 926 N.Y.S.2d 760, 763 (App. Div. 3d Dep't 2011).
271. *See* GlobalNet Financial Com, Inc. v. Frank Crystal & Co.., 449 F.3d 377, 382 (2d Cir. 2006) (citing In re Allstate Ins. Co., (Stolarz), 613 N.E.2d 936 (N.Y. 1993); Zurich Ins. Co. v. Shearson Lehman Hutton, Inc., 642 N.E.2d 1065 (N.Y. 1994)).
272. *See* Zurich Ins., 642 N.E.2d at 1068 (citing Auten v. Auten, 124 N.E.2d 99 (N.Y. 1954)).
273. N.Y. C.P.L.R. § 302(a)(1) (Consol. 2012).
274. *See* Bank of Tokyo-Mitsubishi, 671 N.Y.S.2d at 908; Waldorf Assocs. v. Neville, 533 N.Y.S.2d 182, 185 (Sup. Ct. N.Y. Cnty. 1988), *aff'd*, 547 N.Y.S.2d 556 (App. Div. 1st Dep't 1989).

courts, such as the Appellate Division's Third Department, however, have not drawn a distinction, for purposes of the "contracts anywhere to supply goods and services in the state" language of CPLR 302(a)(1), between guaranties of performance and guaranties of payment and conclude that a guaranty of payment to a New York entity is sufficient to confer personal jurisdiction over a non-domiciliary guarantor.[275]

14.4.2 Summary Judgment in Lieu of Complaint

When an action is "based upon an instrument for the payment of money only . . .", CPLR 3213 permits a plaintiff to serve a motion for summary judgment and supporting papers in lieu of a complaint, and the instrument and evidence of failure to pay constitute a prima facie case for summary judgment in lieu of complaint.[276] An absolute and unconditional guaranty of a note is an "instrument for the payment of money only" within the meaning of CPLR 3213.[277] The fact that a guaranty does not recite a sum certain does not preclude relief under CPLR 3213.[278] However, relief under CPLR 3213 does not extend to situations where more than "simple proof of nonpayment or a similar de minimis deviation from the face of the document" is necessary.[279] In addition, the presence of additional provisions in a guaranty may not bar the availability of CPLR 3213, so long as the additional provisions "do not require additional performance as a condition precedent to repayment, or otherwise alter the defendant's promise of payment."[280] Relief under CPLR 3213 may not, however, be available under a guaranty of both performance and payment.[281]

---

275. *See* Rielly Co. v. Lisa B. Inc., 586 N.Y.S.2d 668, 669 (App. Div. 3d Dep't 1992). For suits in federal court where personal jurisdiction is governed by New York's long-arm statute, the Second Circuit has sided with the Third Department. *See* A.I. Trade Fin., Inc. v. Petra Bank, 989 F.2d 76, 81 (2d Cir. 1993) (noting divided case law in New York's Appellate Division, but "predict[ing] that the New York Court of Appeals would construe a financial guaranty payable in New York as a contract to perform services within the meaning of CPLR 302 (a)(1)).
276. N.Y. C.P.L.R. § 3213 (Consol. 2012); Weissman, 669 N.E.2d at 245.
277. Solow, 874 N.Y.S.2d at 48; Juste v. Niewdach, 809 N.Y.S.2d 563, 564 (App. Div. 2d Dep't 2006).
278. *See* Nissan Motor Acceptance Corp. v. Scialpi, 921 N.Y.S.2d 548, 549 (App. Div. 1st Dep't 2011) (noting that an interest rate "not set forth specifically in a note, but . . . tied to rates announced by certain banks, does not preclude recovery under CPLR 3213"); cf. European Am. Bank v. Cohen, 585 N.Y.S.2d 1017, 1017 (App. Div. 1st Dep't 1992) (note fell within CPLR 3213 where it contained "an unconditional promise to pay on a certain day the current balance in the defendant's line of credit, an amount readily ascertainable from the plaintiff's bank records"); Schwartz v. Turner Holdings, Inc., 527 N.Y.S.2d 229, 230 (App. Div. 1st Dep't 1988), appeal dismissed, 529 N.E.2d 422 (N.Y. 1988) (resort to CPLR 3213 permitted where interest rate was not stated in note but was "readily ascertainable" by reference to bank's rate).
279. Kerin v. Kaufman, 745 N.Y.S.2d 22, 23-24 (App. Div. 1st Dep't 2002) (citation omitted) ("[I]n order for an agreement to qualify for this unique form of accelerated judgment, it must conform to the statutory definition when read immediately upon execution; terms and conditions precedent that remain unresolved within the instrument itself cannot be satisfied by future events requiring proof dehors the agreement.").
280. Bank of Am., N.A. v. Solow, No. 601892/07, 2008 WL 1821877, at *4 (Sup. Ct. N.Y. Cnty. Apr. 17, 2008), *aff'd*, 874 N.Y.S.2d 48 (1st Dep't 2009) (citing cases).
281. *See, e.g.*, Dresdner Bank AG v. Morse/Diesel, Inc., 499 N.Y.S.2d 703, 706 (App. Div. 1st Dep't 1986) ("[S]ince the ... letter agreement includes the guarantee of both payment and performance within its terms, it is not an instrument for the payment of money only and thus may not support a CPLR 3213 motion."); but *see id.* (distinguishing Wickham Constr. Co. v. Gevyn Constr. Corp., 408 N.Y.S.2d 814 (App. Div. 2d Dep't 1978), which permitted resort to CPLR 3213 where agreement at issue contained promises of both payment and performance, because the obligation of payment was contained in a divisible section).

§ 15 Revival and Reinstatement of Guaranties

Many guaranties contain provisions which state that, if guarantied payments made by the primary obligor to the obligee must be returned by the obligee (as may be the case with respect to preferences or fraudulent conveyances under applicable insolvency regimes), the guarantor's obligations in respect of those payments under the guaranty will be reinstated. While there is little New York case law specific to these provisions, some federal courts have mentioned the incidence "claw-back" clauses.[282]

Several older New York state- and federal-court cases cite authority for the proposition that, while payment of an underlying obligation by a primary obligor generally releases the guarantor, the guarantor's liability will be revived under the theory that an invalid payment by the primary obligor does not release the guarantor.[283] The guarantor's involvement in the transactions whereby the guaranty is surrendered or destroyed may be a factor in determining whether or not a New York court will permit reinstatement of the guaranty.[284]

282. *See* 139 Fifth Ave. Corp. v. Giallelis, No. 94 Civ. 7956, 1996 WL 154108 (S.D.N.Y. Apr. 3, 1996); Arctrade Liquidation Trust v. Greenwich Ins. Co. (In re Arctrade Fin. Techs., Ltd.), No. 09-01196 (ALG), 2009 WL 2929440 (Bankr. S.D.N.Y. Sept. 3, 2009) (noting, where surety bonds required surety companies to pay amounts when they "became due or if 'any prior payment made to [the obligee] is recovered from the [obligee] pursuant to the bankruptcy, insolvency or similar law in accordance with an order of [a] court of competent jurisdiction...[,]" that the surety companies' liability would be reinstated upon recovery of payments avoided in a bankruptcy).

283. *See* Wright v. Gansevoort Bank, 103 N.Y.S. 548, 552 (App. Div. 1st Dep't 1907); Perry v. Van Norden Trust Co., 103 N.Y.S. 543, 544 (App. Div. 1st Dep't), rev'd on other grounds, 84 N.E. 804 (N.Y. 1908); Dundee Nat'l Bank v. Strowbridge, 184 N.Y.S. 257, 262-63 (Sup. Ct. Yates Cnty. 1920); *see also* Kolkman v. Mfrs. Trust Co., 27 F.2d 659, 660-61 (2d Cir. 1928); Smith v. Powers (In re Ruddy & Saunders Const. Co.), 255 F. 582, 594 (N.D.N.Y. 1919).

284. *See* Smith v. Powers (In re Ruddy & Saunders Const. Co.), 255 F. at 595-596.

North Carolina State Law of Guaranties

Kenneth M. Greene
Carruthers & Roth, P.A.
235 North Edgeworth Street
Greensboro, North Carolina 27401
Telephone: 336-478-1124
Fax: 336-478-1115
Email: kmg@crlaw.com
www.crlaw.com

Contents

North Carolina State Law of Guaranties

ITEMS OF SPECIAL NOTE

- N.C.G.S. § 26-7 permits any surety or guarantor to give notice to the obligee to use all reasonable diligence to recover against the primary obligor and realize upon any collateral.
- Failure of the obligee to take "appropriate action" shall discharge the surety and the guarantor to the extent they are prejudiced.
- It is common for a North Carolina guaranty to include a specific waiver by the surety and the guarantor of all rights under the statute by adding a phrase similar to the following:

  > "Guarantor waives the benefits of N.C.G.S. §§ 26-7 through 26-9, inclusive, as amended, or any similar law, statute or regulation."
- N.C.G.S. § 22B-10 declares unconscionable and void as a matter of law a provision in any contract waiving the right to a jury trial, but the statute expressly permits arbitration provisions.
- For an obligee that wishes to avoid a jury trial in any guarantor litigation, the alternatives are to provide for arbitration or, if the facts and circumstances warrant, provide that the laws of another state that will enforce a contractual jury trial waiver govern the construction and enforcement of the guaranty.

§ 1 Nature of the Guaranty Arrangement

Under North Carolina law, a guaranty involves three distinct, yet interrelated, obligations: the underlying obligation between the principal obligor and the obligee, the guaranty between the guarantor and the obligee, and the indemnification or reimbursement rights of the guarantor against the principal obligor.

1.1 Guaranty Relationships

A guaranty is a contract of "secondary liability" under which the guarantor has an obligation to pay only upon default by the primary obligor. The relationship between the primary obligor and the guarantor arises as a matter of law, and it is based in the notion that, while the guarantor is liable to the obligee, it is the principal obligor who ultimately should bear the underlying obligation.

North Carolina law protects this relationship by providing that the surety has a statutory right, unless waived by the surety, to compel the obligee to proceed against the primary obligor or the security.[1]

With limited exceptions, under North Carolina law the guaranty must be in writing evidencing the promise to answer for the debt, default or miscarriage of the primary obligor.[2]

1.2 Other Suretyship Relationships

While not the focus of this survey, we note that a suretyship relationship may also arise because of the pledge of collateral. As such, a guaranty-type relationship arises, to the extent of the collateral pledged, when a person supplies collateral for a loan in order to induce the creditor to lend to the debtor or where one party mortgages property to a creditor to secure the debt of another.

§ 2 State Law Requirements for an Entity to Enter a Guaranty

Partnerships, limited liability companies (LLCs), corporations, and banks can all grant guaranties in furtherance of their business activities. Additionally, corporations, partnerships, and LLCs can sometimes grant guaranties even when not in furtherance of their business activities.

2.1 Corporations

Under the North Carolina Business Corporation Act, a North Carolina corporation may make guaranties, and secure any of its obligations under those guaranties by mortgage or pledge of any of its property, unless its articles of incorporation provide otherwise.[3]

When the guaranty is for an obligation of a director, a North Carolina corporation may not issue the guaranty, unless (i) the guaranty is approved by the majority vote of all outstanding voting shares of all classes, voting as a single voting group, excluding the shares owned or controlled by the benefited director, or (ii) the corporation's board of directors determines that the guaranty benefits the corporation and either approves the specific guaranty or a general plan authorizing guaranties.[4]

1. N.C.G.S. § 26-7 *et. seq.*
2. N.C.G.S. §§ 22-1, *et. seq.*
3. N.C.G.S. § 55-3-02(7).
4. N.C.G.S. § 55-8-32.

2.2 Partnerships

North Carolina's partnership law neither expressly empowers a partnership to issue a guaranty nor expressly regulates or prohibits such activity. There are, however, examples in the case law of partnerships issuing guaranties.[5]

2.3 Limited Liability Companies

North Carolina's Limited Liability Company Act generally permits a LLC to issue guaranties, and secure any of its obligations under those guaranties by mortgage or pledge of any of its property, unless the articles of organization provide otherwise.[6] The Act does not contain any prohibition against the LLC's issuance of a guaranty of any obligation of a manager, member, or affiliate.

2.4 Banks and Trust Companies

A North Carolina state-chartered bank has all of the powers conferred by law upon private corporations and, in addition, certain additional powers, including the power to issue, advise, and confirm letters of credit.[7] While that would seem to imply that the power to issue guaranties is included among the bank's powers, it has been held otherwise. The court has held that in the absence of an express grant of authority, a North Carolina banking corporation, as a rule, lacks the power to become the guarantor or surety of the obligation of another person, or to lend its credit to any person.[8] The only exception is where the bank enters into a guaranty for its own advantage as an incident to its business, or where the bank actually receives benefit from one who has relied in good faith upon the guaranty.

Additionally, guaranties offered by state banks may also be significantly affected by federal law. Federal law prohibits a state-chartered bank from engaging in activities in which a national bank may not engage under federal law. The situations under which a national bank may become a guarantor are governed by federal law.[9]

A North Carolina trust company may not engage in business other than "trust business and trust marketing except as necessary to fulfill a fiduciary obligation to a client."[10] It is therefore unlikely that a North Carolina trust company has the power to make a guaranty.

2.5 Individuals

Confusion can sometimes arise in the case of corporate officers or directors signing guaranties in closely held corporations or other organizations. In such

5. Church V. Carter, 94 N.C. App. 286, 380 S.E.2d 167 (N.C. 1989) and North Carolina Nat'l Bank v. Wallens, 31 N.C.App. 721, 230 S.E.2d 690 (N.C. 1976).
6. N.C.G.S. § 55-8-32.
7. N.C.G.S. § 53-43.
8. Indiana Quarries Co. v. Angier Bank & Trust Co., 190 N.C. 277, 129 S.E. 619 (N.C. 1925).
9. Nat'l Bank as Guarantor or Surety on Indemnity Bond, 12 C.F.R. § 7.1017 (2010).
10. N.C.G.S. § 53-345.

instances, a case-by-case inquiry determines whether an individual intended to be personally bound or, instead, only issued a guaranty on behalf of a partnership or corporation and thus only in an official employment capacity. While a business corporation must have "authority" to execute a guaranty, an individual guarantor must have the "capacity" to enter into the guaranty. Incapacity can be a defense against the enforcement of a guaranty issued by an individual.

North Carolina is a common law property state. Marriage does not cause either spouse to "incur liability for any debts owing, or contracts made, or for wrongs done by his or her spouse before the marriage."[11] In addition, a married person's separately owned real and personal property is protected from the debts or obligations of his or her spouse.[12] Thus, a guaranty issued by one spouse does not become a joint liability of both spouses.[13]

North Carolina recognizes ownership of real property by husband and wife as tenants by the entirety.[14] During marriage, neither spouse can individually transfer or encumber entireties property in any manner that would affect or defeat the other spouse's right of survivorship.[15] Moreover, the individual creditors of either spouse cannot reach entireties property upon a judgment procured against one spouse.[16] Only a creditor of both spouses can execute and levy on entireties property.[17] Where a judgment is only procured against one spouse, however, the entireties property can still be reached by the creditor upon obtaining a judgment against the other spouse when the judgments are entered in the same lawsuit and on identical claims.[18]

Upon absolute divorce, entireties property is converted by operation of law to a tenancy in common.[19] Immediately thereafter, a creditor's judgment lien may attach to the spouse's tenant in common interest.[20] Further, the creditor's lien in the spouse's tenant in common interest continues even when the whole of the property is awarded to the other spouse pursuant to an equitable distribution proceeding.[21]

In an equitable distribution proceeding related to the dissolution of marriage, debts must be classified as marital debts or separate debts.[22] Marital debts, which are debts incurred during the marriage by either spouse for their joint benefit, are distributed just as marital assets, whereas separate debts cannot be distributed.[23] Significantly, the court may assign responsibility for marital debts among the parties regardless of whether the debt was incurred by one

---

11. N.C.G.S. § 52-11.
12. N.C. Const. art. X, § 4; N.C.G.S. § 52-1.
13. In re Sisler, 2011 WL 5593055 (Bankr. E.D.N.C. 2011).
14. Moore v. Shore, 208 N.C. 446, 181 S.E. 275 (1935).
15. *Id.*
16. Grabenhofer v. Garrett, 260 N.C. 118, 131 S.E.2d 675 (1963); *see also* In re Knapp, 285 B.R. 176, 179 (Bankr. M.D.N.C. 2002) (holding the filing of a bankruptcy petition by one spouse does not sever tenancy by the entirety).
17. L&M Gas Co. v. Leggett, 273 N.C. 547, 161 S.E.2d 23 (1968).
18. In re Medlin, 229 B.R. 353, 360 (Bankr. E.D.N.C. 1998).
19. Martin v. Roberts, 177 N.C. App. 415, 628 S.E.2d 812, (2006).
20. *Id.*
21. Branch Banking & Trust Co. v. Wright, 74 N.C. App. 550, 328 S.E.2d 840, *disc. rev. allowed*, 314 N.C. 662, 335 S.E.2d 321, *appeal withdrawn*, 318 N.C. 505, 353 S.E.2d 225 (1985).
22. Byrd v. Owens, 86 N.C. App. 418, 358 S.E.2d 102 (1987).
23. *Id.*

or both of the spouses.[24] With respect to personal guaranties, the "court must classify and value a personal guaranty if the parties *present sufficient evidence as to the debt's existence and value*."[25]

§ 3 Signatory's Authority to Execute a Guaranty

Generally, the obligee has a duty of reasonable inquiry when it has some notice that the maker of the guaranty does not have authority to bind the guarantor.

3.1 Corporations

For an obligee to rely on a guaranty, the guaranty must be signed by an officer with actual or apparent authority to act in such capacity. An obligee cannot enforce a guaranty if she had notice that the officer who signed for the corporation lacked authority to do so. Where an obligee-plaintiff invokes the doctrine of apparent authority, that obligee bears a duty of reasonable inquiry.

Generally, an officer of a corporation has authority to act only where: (a) authority has been expressly conferred on him by statute, law, or the act of the directors; (b) the action is properly incidental to the business entrusted to him by the directors; and (c) the action is within his ostensible authority or ratified by proper authority as applicable to contracts of guaranty. If a corporation's guaranty bears some reasonable relationship to the corporation's business, evidence that a signing officer was charged with the general management of the corporation's business can provide apparent authority to execute a guaranty. However, under North Carolina law, apparent authority is not limitless; the potential obligee dealing with an agent of a guarantor corporation should make the effort to ascertain the agent's actual authority.

3.2 Partnerships

Under agency principals, every partner is an agent of the partnership for the purpose of its business and therefore has the power to bind the partnership when such partner's act is "for apparently carrying on in the usual way the business of the partnership," unless such authority has been explicitly held back in the partnership agreement. If a partner's action is not "apparently carrying on of the business of the partnership," the partner must be authorized by the other partners to bind a partnership. Authority may also be granted under the partnership agreement or by consent of the other partners.

Even where a partner does not have actual authority to bind the partnership, a partner may bind the partnership because of such partner's apparent

24. Atkins v. Atkins, 102 N.C. App. 199, 401 S.E.2d 784 (1991).
25. Fox v. Fox, 114 N.C. App. 125, 134, 441 S.E.2d 613, 619 (1994) (noting that guaranties can be difficult to value given the contingent nature of such obligations).

authority to contract based on the third party's reasonable belief that the partner has authority to bind the partnership. However, unless the partnership agreement provides otherwise, a partner cannot assign partnership property for the benefit of creditors without the unanimous consent of all the partners.

Under North Carolina law, a general partner of a North Carolina limited partnership has the same powers as a partner in a general partnership, except as provided otherwise in the partnership agreement or in the limited partnership act.[26]

3.3 Limited Liability Companies

North Carolina limited liability law provides that, in the case of a member-managed LLC, every member is an agent of that company and can sign instruments pursuant to carrying on in the usual way of business unless that person has no actual authority to act in such way and the counterparty knows as much.[27] In the case of a manager-managed LLC, no member has authority to bind the LLC to a guaranty unless authority has been granted to the member by the manager or managers of the LLC or by operating agreement of the LLC.[28] Each manager of a manager-managed LLC can bind the LLC if such guaranty is "for apparently carrying on in the usual way the business of the [LLC]" unless the manager has no actual authority and the counterparty knows of this lack of authority.[29] North Carolina law deems guaranties issued among affiliate LLCs to be in the course of the LLC's business.

3.4 Banks and Trust Companies

As indicated above, it is doubtful that a North Carolina bank or trust company may issue a guaranty.

§ 4 Consideration; Sufficiency of Past Consideration

Standard contract principles apply to the analysis of consideration for a contract of guaranty. When a guaranty is executed independently of the transaction giving rise to the underlying obligation, it must be supported by consideration that is independent of the underlying obligation. However, when a guaranty is executed in connection with, or as part of, a transaction that creates the underlying obligation, the creation of the underlying obligation serves as adequate consideration for both the underlying obligation and the guaranty.

The presence of consideration is necessary to create a valid guaranty contract under North Carolina law. A mere promise, without more, is

26. N.C.G.S. § 59-403.
27. N.C.G.S. § 57C-3-20.
28. *Id.*
29. N.C.G.S. § 57C-3-23.

unenforceable.[30] Standard contract principles apply when determining the sufficiency of consideration for a guaranty. It is not necessary that the consideration be full or adequate. Any legal consideration will be sufficient to support the guaranty.[31] A consideration moving directly to the guarantor is not essential for a guaranty, as the promise is enforceable if a benefit to the primary obligor is shown or if detriment or inconvenience to the obligee is present.

When the guaranty is executed as a part of a transaction that creates the underlying obligation, it is not essential to recovery on the guaranty that the guaranty shall be supported by consideration other than the underlying obligation. The creation of the underlying obligation supplies consideration for both the underlying obligation and the guaranty. When the guaranty is executed independently of the transaction in which the underlying obligation is created, it must be supported by consideration which is independent of the underlying obligation. However, if the guaranty is made after the creation of the underlying obligation, there is sufficient consideration for the guaranty if it is executed pursuant to a previous arrangement since, in that case, the underlying obligation is induced by or created on the faith of the guaranty.[32]

The defense that a guaranty is void for failure of consideration is not rendered moot by the fact that the guaranty was signed under seal, as the effect of a seal is not to preclude analysis of the consideration issue, but only to raise a presumption of consideration which may be rebutted by clear and convincing evidence.[33]

§ 5 Notice of Acceptance

North Carolina courts generally recognize, when the terms of the offer of guaranty are absolute in nature, that at least where the surrounding circumstances are such as to indicate that notice of acceptance was not anticipated by the guarantor, notice of acceptance is unnecessary, and the guarantor will be liable on the guaranty from the time the obligee acts in reliance on it.

Under guaranty law, generally, the obligee must notify the guarantor of its acceptance of the guaranty. At least where the guaranty is conditional in nature, North Carolina courts have recognized that notice of acceptance of the guaranty ordinarily must be communicated to the guarantor by the obligee in order to bind the guarantor, in the absence of special circumstances.[34]

However, North Carolina courts generally recognize, when the terms of the offer of guaranty are absolute in nature, that at least where the surrounding circumstances are such as to indicate that notice of acceptance

30. Investment Properties of Asheville, Inc. v. Norburn, 281 N.C. 191, 188 S.E.2d 342 (1972).
31. Gillespie v. DeWitt, 53 N.C.App. 252, 259, 280 S.E.2d 736, 742 (1981).
32. Branch Banking & Trust Co. v. Morrison, 191 N.C. App. 173, 661 S.E.2d 784 (2008).
33. *Id.*
34. Gregory v. Bullock, 120 N.C. 260 (1897).

was not anticipated by the guarantor, notice of acceptance is unnecessary, and the guarantor will be liable on the guaranty from the time the obligee acts in reliance on it.[35] In one North Carolina case, a letter from the guarantor to the obligee was determined to be an absolute promise by the guarantor to pay for obligations of the primary obligor, and thus was a guaranty as a matter of law as opposed to an offer of guaranty and did not require any communication of acceptance. The words "please accept" contained in the letter were held to be words of courtesy that represented an expression of hope that the guaranty would be viewed as reliable by the obligee.[36]

However, where a guarantor entered into a guaranty addressed to no particular obligee that guaranteed payment of purchases made by the primary obligor from any obligee, a North Carolina court has held that the undertaking was not a guaranty but a mere proposal for a guaranty, and notice of acceptance was necessary in order to bind the guarantor on the guaranty. In the court's view, since the offer of guaranty was not directed to any specific creditor, it was incumbent upon the creditor who delivered the goods to provide notice of acceptance to the guarantor so the guarantor could act accordingly.[37]

§ 6 Interpretation of Guaranties

The nature and extent of a guarantor's liability depends on the terms of the guaranty as construed by general rules of contract construction.

6.1 General Principles

The nature and extent of a guarantor's liability depends on the terms of the contract as construed by general rules of contract construction.[38] A guaranty is subject to the parol evidence rule which prohibits the consideration of evidence as to anything that happened prior to or simultaneously with the making of a contract that would vary the terms of the agreement.[39]

6.2 Guaranty of Payment versus Guaranty of Collection

A guaranty of payment is an absolute promise by the guarantor to pay a debt at maturity if it is not paid by the primary obligor, which obligation is separate and independent of the obligation of the primary obligor, and an obligee's cause of action against the guarantor ripens immediately upon the failure of the primary obligor to pay the debt at maturity.[40] A "guaranty of payment" is an absolute or unconditional promise to pay some particular underlying obligation, if not paid by the primary obligor at maturity, and it is generally held that such a

35. Cowan, McClung & Co. v. Roberts, 134 N.C. 415, 46 S.E. 919 (1904).
36. Clear Fir Sales Co. v. Carolina Plywood Distributors, Inc., 13 N.C. App. 429, 185 S.E.2d 737 (1972).
37. Shewell v. Knox, 12 N.C. 404 (1828).
38. Self-Help Ventures Fund v. Custom Finish, LLC, 682 S.E.2d 746 (N.C. Ct. App. 2009).
39. R.B. Cronland Bldg. Supplies, Inc. v. Sneed, 162 N.C. App. 142, 589 S.E.2d 891 (2004).
40. O'Grady v. First Union Nat'l Bank, 296 N.C. 212, 250 S.E.2d 587 (1978).

guaranty is assignable and enforceable by the same persons who are entitled to enforce the underlying obligation which it is given to secure.[41]

A guaranty is an absolute or unconditional promise to pay a particular underlying obligation if it is not paid by the primary obligor and is immediately enforceable against the guarantor upon the primary obligor's default, without any requirement upon the obligee to seek recovery first from the primary obligor.[42]

On the other hand, a "guaranty of collection" is a promise by a guarantor to pay the underlying obligation on the condition that the obligee first diligently prosecutes collection of the underlying obligation without success.[43]

6.3 Language Regarding Revocation of Guaranties

A guaranty that is "irrevocable" may not be revoked with respect to transactions entered into by the primary obligor prior to the revocation. A guaranty is a continuing obligation until it is revoked by the guarantor or terminated by operation of law.[44] A guarantor is liable to the obligee for items of underlying obligation incurred by the primary obligor before revocation or termination of the guaranty where, under the terms of the guaranty, the guarantor was not released upon termination or revocation for underlying obligation already incurred by the primary obligor.[45]

A guaranty, as opposed to an offer of guaranty, is not revoked by the death of the guarantor. Thus, a guarantor's death does not affect the validity of a guaranty for underlying obligation already incurred and outstanding at the time of the guarantor's death where the guaranty expressly states that it binds the guarantor's heirs, executors, legal representatives, successor, and assigns.[46]

Where a guaranty contains language pertaining to revocation, the language should be considered carefully. For example, in the case of *Love v. Bache & Co., Inc.*,[47] the guaranty provided for a guaranty of the underlying obligation and "all renewals, extensions and modifications" thereof. Subsequent to the death of the guarantor, the obligee renewed and extended the underlying obligation that was outstanding at the time of the guarantor's death without the consent of the guarantor's personal representative. The Court of Appeals rejected the argument that the lack of consent negated liability on the guaranty and held that no consent was required.

6.4 "Continuing"

A continuing guaranty is a guaranty that enables the primary obligor to obtain credit over an extended time and to cover successive transactions.[48] A guaranty

41. Self-Help Ventures Fund v. Custom Finish, LLC, 682 S.E.2d 746 (N.C. Ct. App. 2009).
42. Carolina First Bank v. Stark, Inc., 660 S.E.2d 641 (N.C. Ct. App. 2008).
43. EAC Credit Corp. v. Wilson, 281 N.C. 140, 187 S.E.2d 752 (1972).
44. Carolina First Bank v. Stark, Inc., 660 S.E.2d 641 (N.C. Ct. App. 2008).
45. Symons Corp. v. Quality Concrete Const., Inc., 108 N.C. App. 17, 422 S.E.2d 365 (1992).
46. Love v. Bache & Co., Inc., 40 N.C. App. 617, 253 S.E.2d 351 (1979).
47. *Id.*
48. Hickory Novelty Co. v. Andrews, 188 N.C. 59, 123 S.E. 314 (1924).

that covers a series of extensions of credit, or a succession of transactions, is continuing.[49]

When express terms of a guaranty provide that it is a "continuing guaranty," North Carolina courts are likely to hold that the scope and extent of the guaranty is not confined to underlying obligation incurred prior to the primary obligor's entry into a new contract with the obligee, especially where the guaranty extends to modifications and renewals of the terms of the underlying obligation.[50]

6.5 "Absolute and Unconditional"

Where a guaranty provides that the guaranty obligations are "absolute and unconditional," the guarantor theoretically waives almost all defenses and counterclaims potentially available in an action by the obligee based upon the underlying obligation that is guaranteed by the guaranty. Thus, the North Carolina Court of Appeals has held that, by signing an unconditional continuing guaranty, the guarantor waives the defense of discharge due to an extension of the underlying obligation, where the guaranty allows for extensions of time and other modifications, and provides that extensions and modifications do not discharge the guarantor from liability for any underlying obligation.[51]

6.6 "Liable as Primary Obligor and not Merely as Surety"

This language, taken literally, appears to conflate the concepts of guarantor and primary obligor. A "guaranty" is a promise to answer for payment of a debt or the performance of some duty in the event of failure of another person who is primarily liable for such payment or performance. A "surety," on the other hand, is a person who is primarily liable for payment of debt or performance of obligation of another and is engaged in a direct and original undertaking.[52] While both kinds of promises are forms of security, they differ in the nature of the promisor's liability. A guarantor's duty of performance is triggered at the time of the default of another. On the other hand, a surety is primarily liable for the discharge of the underlying obligation, and is engaged in a direct and original undertaking which is independent of any default.

As a result, North Carolina courts have in some instances interpreted a document which on its face appears to be a guaranty to be a suretyship contract. By so holding, the court avoided as fraudulent a transfer of property made by the obligor on the document and rejected the argument that since the transferor was a guarantor and not primarily liable on the debt, the obligee was not a creditor at the time of the transfer and therefore could not establish any fraudulent intent to defraud creditors.[53]

---

49. O'Grady v. First Union Nat'l Bank, 296 N.C. 212, 250 S.E.2d 587 (1978).
50. Amoco Oil Co. v. Griffin, 78 N.C. App. 716, 338 S.E.2d 601 (1986).
51. First Citizens Bank & Trust Co. v. McLamb, 112 N.C. App. 645, 439 S.E.2d 166 (1993).
52. Branch Banking & Trust Co. v. Creasy, 301 N.C. 44, 269 S.E.2d 117 (1980).
53. *Id.*

§ 7 Defenses of the Guarantor; Set-off

The defenses that may be available to a guarantor can be grouped into three categories: (1) defenses of the primary obligor; (2) "suretyship defenses"; and (3) other defenses.

7.1 Defenses of the Primary Obligor

7.1.1 General; When Guarantor may assert Primary Obligor's Defense

The general rule in North Carolina is that a guarantor may plead any claim or defense which is available to the primary obligor.[54] A guarantor may not counterclaim for damages against a creditor but may assert a claim only by way of set-off. But, a guarantor may not avail himself of a defense which is "personal" to the primary obligor.[55] Nor may the guarantor assert a claim which constitutes an independent claim belonging to the primary obligor when the primary obligor is not joined in the action.[56]

7.1.2 Defenses that may not be raised by Guarantor

While there is no North Carolina case expressly holding that the insolvency of the principal obligor is not a defense that the guarantor may raise unless the guaranty is conditioned on the solvency of the primary obligor, there is a case that held that where the guaranty by its express terms created a "primary obligation" from the guarantor to the obligee, and thus established an absolute promise to pay independent of the obligation of the primary obligor, the primary obligor's discharge in bankruptcy did not terminate the guarantor's liability on the guaranty.[57]

7.1.3 Defenses that may always be raised by Guarantor

In North Carolina, a guarantor may show that the obligee failed to perform such that there is a failure of consideration.[58] An entry of default against the primary obligor does not preclude the guarantor from raising counterclaims and defenses.[59]

54. Spartan Leasing, Inc. v. Pollard, 101 N.C. App. 450, 400 S.E.2d 476 (1991).
55. *Id.*
56. *Id.*
57. Exxon Chemical Americas, Div. of Exxon Chemical Co. v. Kennedy, 59 N.C. App. 90, 295 S.E.2d 770 (1982).
58. Perfecting Service Co. v. Product Development & Sales Co., 261 N.C. 660, 136 S.E.2d 56 (1964).
59. Spartan Leasing Inc. v. Pollard, 101 N.C. App. 450, 400 S.E.2d 476 (1991).

7.2 "Suretyship" Defenses

7.2.1 When Surety may assert Primary Obligor's Defense

When a surety is sued by its obligee, the court, on motion of the surety, may join the primary obligor as an additional party defendant, provided the primary obligor is found to be or can be made subject to the jurisdiction of the court.[60] Upon such joinder, the surety shall have all rights, defenses, counterclaims, and set-offs which would have been available to him if the primary obligor and surety had been originally sued together.

7.2.2 Change in Identity of Principal Obligor

Whether a change of the identity of the primary obligor discharges the guarantor's obligations depends upon the circumstances. The relevant inquiry focuses on whether (i) the change in the principal obligor's identity significantly changes the business deal that the guarantor agreed to guaranty, (ii) the changes have a potentially adverse impact on the guarantor, particularly with regard to the risk borne by the guarantor, and (iii) the degree by which the guarantor helped to bring about the change.

At least one North Carolina court has addressed the general question of whether a change in identity of the primary obligor results in the discharge of the guarantor's obligations. The court has held that the fact that the primary obligor changed from being a national bank to a state bank did not serve to destroy or affect the liability of the guarantor under a guaranty made prior to the change.[61]

60. N.C.G.S. § 26-12.
61. Greene County v. Nat'l Bank of Snow Hill, 193 N.C. 524, 137 S.E. 593 (1927).

7.2.3 Modification of the Underlying Obligation, Including Release

Under North Carolina law, modifications to the underlying obligation may permit the guarantor to raise certain defenses to liability. In fact, the general rule in North Carolina is that material alterations of a contract between a primary obligor and the obligee without the guarantor's consent will operate to discharge the guarantor.[62]

However, there are several exceptions to the general rule. If the guarantor either expressly or impliedly consents to the material alteration, then the guarantor is not discharged from its obligation.[63] Also, not every extension of time for payment without the guarantor's consent discharges the guarantor; the guarantor must be prejudiced by the extension.[64] Nor will guarantors be relieved of their obligations if they agree in advance that they will guarantee all renewals, extensions, and modifications of the underlying obligation.[65]

A guarantor may be discharged from liability under a guaranty by a valid release by the obligee that is enforceable against the obligee under general contract law.[66] However, the mere cancellation of a note does not in and of itself release the guarantor. If the obligee cancels a note on which the guarantor is liable, and a new note for the same obligation is issued by the same primary obligor and an additional obligor, and without notifying the guarantor of the new note or additional obligor, the guarantor remains liable for payment on the new note.[67]

7.2.4 Release or Impairment of Security for the Underlying Obligation

Where the obligee has a security interest in collateral to secure the underlying obligation, and the security interest is impaired, the liability of the guarantor is reduced to the extent of the impairment. However, the guarantor may waive in advance its defense based on the impairment of collateral under common law.[68]

7.3 Other Defenses

7.3.1 Failure to Fulfill a condition Precedent

Under North Carolina law, a guarantor may raise a defense of failure to fulfill a condition precedent. For example, where persons signed a note as sureties on the condition that the signature of another surety would be procured, the failure to procure the other signature absolves the signing sureties from

---

62. First Citizens Bank & Trust Co. v. McLamb, 112 N.C. App. 645, 439 S.E.2d 166 (1993).
63. Sherwin Williams Co. v. ASBN, Inc., 163 N.C. App. 547, 594 S.E.2d 135 (2004).
64. Maxwell v. Southern Fidelity Mut. Ins. Co., 217 N.C. 762, 9 S.E.2d 428 (1940).
65. First Citizens Bank & Trust Co. v. McLamb, 112 N.C. App. 645, 439 S.E.2d 166 (1993).
66. Yamaha Int'l Corp. v. Parks, 72 N.C. App. 625, 325 S.E.2d 55 (1985).
67. First Union Nat'l Bank of North Carolina v. King, 63 N.C. App. 757, 306 S.E.2d 508 (1983).
68. Gillespie v. DeWitt, 53 N.C. App. 252, 280 S.E.2d 736 (1981).

liability.[69] But a failure of the obligee to comply with a contractual requirement to give notice of a claim under a guaranty does not discharge the guarantor from liability unless the guarantor can show that the failure caused actual prejudice, loss, or damage.[70]

7.3.2 *Modification of the Guaranty*

North Carolina law provides that the provisions of a written contract may be modified or waived by a subsequent parol agreement or by conduct which naturally and justly leads the other party to believe the provisions of the contract are modified or waived, even if the contract requires by its terms that all amendments or modifications are unenforceable except in writing and signed by the parties.[71]

7.3.3 *Failure to Pursue Primary Obligor*

Once the underlying obligation becomes due and payable, a guarantor may give written notice to the obligee (with copies to all other guarantors) requiring the obligee to use all reasonable diligence to recover against the primary obligor and to proceed to realize against any collateral that secures the underlying obligation.[72] If the obligee then fails or refuses, within 30 days from the service or receipt of the guarantor's notice, to take "appropriate action pursuant thereto," then the guarantor is discharged to the extent the guarantor is prejudiced.[73]

However, the defense of requiring the obligee to use all reasonable diligence to recover against the principal obligor and to realize upon any collateral for the underlying obligation may be expressly waived pursuant to the language of the guaranty.[74]

7.3.4 *Statute of Limitations*

North Carolina law imposes a three-year statute of limitations for the filing of a suit on a contract of guaranty or suretyship.[75] The three-year period commences at the time the guarantor's liability arises which is at the time of the primary obligor's default on the underlying obligation. However, a guaranty executed under seal is subject to a 10-year statute of limitations.[76] However, that 10-year statute of limitations applies only to guaranties and does not apply to sureties.[77]

---

69. Bank of Benson v. Jones, 147 N.C. 419, 61 S.E. 193 (1908).
70. Kimbrell v. Roberts, 186 N.C. App. 68, 650 S.E.2d 444 (2007).
71. *See* Wellikoff v. Progress Development Corp., ___ N.C. App. ___, 709 S.E.2d 436 (2011).
72. N.C.G.S. § 26-7(a).
73. N.C.G.S. § 26-9.
74. Borg-Warner Acceptance Corp. v. Johnston, 97 N.C. App. 575, 389 S.E.2d 429 (1990).
75. N.C.G.S. § 1-52(1).
76. N.C.G.S. § 1-47.
77. North Carolina Bank & Trust Co. v. Williams, 209 N.C. 806, 185 S.E. 18 (1936).

7.3.5 *Statute of Frauds*

A guaranty must be in writing and signed by the guarantor.[78] Enforcement of an alleged oral guaranty is barred. However, North Carolina has long recognized the rule that the promise to pay the debt of another is outside the statute of frauds and thereby enforceable if the promise is supported by an independent and sufficient consideration running to the guarantor.[79] In other words, if the guarantor has such a direct, immediate, and pecuniary interest in the subject matter of the primary obligor's contract so as to indicate that the guarantor has intended to adopt the original contract as its own, then the statute of frauds is not applicable.[80]

7.3.6 *Defenses Particular to Guarantors that are Natural Persons and their Spouses*

Neither North Carolina statute nor North Carolina case law sets forth any defenses particular to guarantors that are natural persons and their spouses. However, guaranties obtained in violation of the federal Equal Credit Opportunity Act, are void and unenforceable.[81]

7.3.7 *Fraud and Failure to Disclose Facts*

The obligee is not ordinarily under the duty to disclose to the guarantor facts relating to the character of the risk unless the obligee knows a fact of vital importance to the risk and knows that the guarantor will not be able to discover such fact in the exercise of due diligence.[82] Similarly, if an obligee knows, or has reasonable grounds for believing, that the guarantor is being deceived or misled, or that the guarantor is induced to enter into the guaranty in ignorance of facts materially increasing the risk of which the obligee has knowledge, and the obligee has an opportunity, before accepting the guaranty, to inform the guarantor of such facts, good and fair dealing demand that the obligee should make such disclosure to the guarantor. If the obligee accepts the guaranty without doing so, the guarantor may afterwards avoid it.[83]

A guarantor may not counterclaim for damages against an obligee but may assert a claim only by way of setoff.[84]

78. N.C.G.S. § 22-1.
79. Watson Electrical Const. Co. v. Summit Companies, LLC, 160 N.C. App. 647, 587 S.E.2d 87 (2003).
80. Burlington Industries, Inc. v. Foil, 19 N.C. App. 172, 198 S.E.2d 194 (1973).
81. *See generally* In re Westbrooks, 440 B.R. 677 (Bankr. M.D. N.C. 2010).
82. Harris & Harris Const. Co. v. Crain & Denbo, Inc., 256 N.C. 110, 123 S.E.2d 590 (1962).
83. First Union Nat'l Bank v. Brown, 166 N.C. App. 519, 603 S.E.2d 808 (2004).
84. Spartan Leasing Inc. v. Pollard, 101 N.C. App. 450, 400 S.E.2d 476 (1991).

§ 8 Waiver of Defenses by the Guarantor

8.1 Defenses that cannot be Waived

As set forth below in Sections 8.2 and 8.3, a guarantor may waive certain defenses pursuant to the language of the guaranty. However, North Carolina common law and statute have both recognized that certain rights and/or defenses cannot be waived by a guarantor. For example, the fact that a guaranty contains a provision waiving any defense of any surety or guarantor by reason of an extension of the time for payment does not prevent the guarantor from the benefits of N.C.G.S. § 26-9.[85]

There is split authority in North Carolina as to whether a guarantor may waive its defense of lack of commercial reasonableness in the disposition of collateral. For example, in 1992, one North Carolina court held that a pre-default waiver of the protections under N.C.G.S. § 25-9-501(3) by the guarantor as a "debtor" is unenforceable.[86] However, in an earlier decision, the same North Carolina court held that a guarantor could waive its right to a commercially reasonable disposition of collateral.[87]

8.2 "Catch-all" Waivers

The standard catch-all waiver indicates that the guaranty is "absolute and conditional" or that the guaranty is "given absolutely and unconditionally." In theory, when such a catch-all waiver is included in a guaranty, the guarantor waives virtually all defenses and counterclaims potentially available in an action by the obligee arising from the underlying obligation.[88]

8.3 Use of Specific Waivers

As described above in Section 8.2, general waivers are sufficient to waive most, if not all, of the defenses and/or rights of guarantors. Outside of the general waiver context, North Carolina courts have recognized that certain rights and/or defenses of a guarantor may be waived pursuant to an explicit waiver in the guaranty. For example, an explicit waiver of the statute of limitations is effective under the laws of North Carolina.[89] Also, a guarantor may waive in advance its defense based on the impairment of collateral under common law.[90]

Most properly drawn North Carolina guaranties contain a specific waiver of the guarantor's rights under § 26-9 *et. seq.*

---

85. N.C.G.S. § 26-9(b).
86. Gregory Poole Equipment Co. v. Murray, 105 N.C. App. 642, 414 S.E.2d 563 (1992).
87. Borg-Warner Acceptance Corp. v. Johnston, 97 N.C. App. 575, 389 S.E.2d 429 (1990). *See also* Community Bank & Trust Co. v. Copses, 953 F.2d 133 (1991).
88. Community Bank & Trust Co. v. Copses, 953 F.2d 133 (4th Cir. 1991).
89. Musarra v. Bock, 200 N.C. App. 780, 684 S.E.2d 741 (2009).
90. Gillespie v. DeWitt, 53 N.C. App. 252, 280 S.E.2d 736 (1981).

§ 9 Third-party Pledgors—Defenses and Waiver Thereof

When a third party pledges property to secure the debt of a primary obligor, the third party becomes in effect a surety for the payment of the underlying obligation to the extent of the pledge. Thus, a third-party pledgor may generally assert and waive the defenses of a surety.

North Carolina courts have held that a suretyship relationship arises when a third party mortgages his interest in real property to secure the debt of another.[91] The same reasoning would apply to a third-party pledge of personal property. A third-party pledgor stands in the relation of a surety to the primary obligor and has the same defenses available to it as available to a surety. The third-party pledgor's liability, therefore, is dischargeable by anything that would discharge a surety or guarantor.[92]

§ 10 Jointly and Severally Liable Guarantors—Contribution and Reduction of Obligations upon Payment by a Co-obligor

Unless provided otherwise in the guaranty, guarantors are presumptively jointly and severally liable for the underlying obligation and each is liable to the other guarantors for contribution for payment of more than his proportionate share of the underlying obligation.

10.1 Contribution

A coguarantor's liability under a guaranty is determined by the terms of the guaranty. For instance, guarantors have been held individually liable, and not jointly and severally liable, where the guaranty permitted the obligee to pursue the guarantors individually for a specified portion of the underlying obligation.[93]

In the absence of any agreement to the contrary, coguarantors are each liable for an equal share of the underlying obligation. To the extent that a guarantor pays more than his proportional share of the underlying obligation, the paying guarantor has the right to recover from the other guarantors an amount that is proportionate to their respective liability.

N.C.G.S. § 26-5 specifically grants a cosurety that has been compelled to satisfy a principal's obligation the right to "maintain an action against every other surety for a just and ratable portion of the same which may have been paid as aforesaid, whether of principal, interest or cost." The surety's cause

91. *See* Weil v. Thomas, 114 N.C. 197, 19 S.E. 103 (1894).
92. Hinton v. Greenleaf, 113. N.C. 6, 18 S.E. 56 (1893).
93. First-Citizens Bank & Trust Co. v. 4325 Park Road Associates, Ltd., 133 N.C. App. 153, 515 S.E.2d 51 (1999).

of action for contribution, however, does not arise until he has paid more than his proportionate share of the underlying obligation.[94]

10.2 Reduction of Obligations upon Payment of Co-obligor

Under equitable principles, "parties which are equally obligated on a debt are treated alike."[95] As between coguarantors, the amount of property or other security received from one guarantor that constitutes a means of indemnity or immunity from loss inures to the benefit of all guarantors.[96] Thus, a reduction of the underlying obligation by one guarantor inures to the benefit of all guarantors.

10.3 Liability of Parent Guarantors Owning less than 100 percent of Primary Obligor

Under North Carolina law, a parent corporation and its subsidiaries are considered distinct legal entities regardless of whether such subsidiaries are wholly owned by the parent corporation. Moreover, a parent corporation is not liable on contracts entered into by one of its subsidiaries merely by owning all of the stock of such subsidiary. Accordingly, the North Carolina Court of Appeals has held that the subsidiaries of a parent corporation could not enforce a guaranty executed by a guarantor in favor of the parent corporation because there was no direct mention or reference to such subsidiaries in the guaranty.[97] In other words, a parent or subsidiary corporation is not made a party to or a beneficiary of a guaranty solely by being the parent or a subsidiary of a party that is a signatory to or the beneficiary of the guaranty.

§ 11 Reliance

Reliance is probably not required to claim under a guaranty, but may be used to enforce an otherwise unenforceable guaranty.

Reliance is not likely required to enforce a guaranty under North Carolina law. Under certain circumstances, however, an obligee may seek to establish reliance to enforce a guaranty that would otherwise be unenforceable. For instance, a purported guarantor that conditionally signed a guaranty and never authorized its delivery to the obligee was nevertheless held to be liable under the guaranty because the obligee extended credit to the primary obligor in reliance on the purported guarantor's execution of the guaranty.[98]

---

94. Lancaster v. Stanfield, 191 N.C. 340, 132 S.E. 21 (1926).
95. Smith v. Carr, 128 N.C. 150, 38 S.E. 732 (1901).
96. Oroweat Employees Credit Union v. Stroupe, 48 N.C. App. 338, 269 S.E.2d 211 (1980).
97. Palm Beach Inc. v. Allen, 91 N.C. App. 115, 370 S.E.2d 440 (1988) (disapproved on other grounds by Kraft Foodservice, Inc. v. Hardee, 340 N.C. 344, 457 S.E.2d 596 (1995)).
98. Spencer Oil Co., Inc. v. Welborn, 20 N.C. App. 681, 202 S.E.2d 618 (1974), *cert. denied*, 285 N.C. 235, 204 S.E.2d 25 (1974).

§ 12 Subrogation

Subrogation is an equitable remedy that generally requires total satisfaction of the underlying obligation to the obligee prior to its exercise. Concern for protecting the obligee's interests affects the secondary obligor's right to subrogation.

The doctrine of equitable subrogation is available when a surety or guarantor satisfies in full the underlying obligation. The surety or guarantor that satisfies the underlying obligation is generally entitled to all of the rights and remedies which the obligee had against the primary obligor.

N.C.G.S. § 26-3.1 codifies the concept of subrogation by permitting a guarantor, surety, or any other person who has paid a debtor's liability under a written obligation to sue the debtor on such obligation and avail himself of any remedy the obligee may have against the debtor. No assignment of the obligation is necessary.

§ 13 Triangular Set-off in Bankruptcy

In limited circumstances, triangular set-off may be permissible in North Carolina.

North Carolina recognizes the right of set-off only where there is mutuality of the parties.[99] In other words, the right to set-off does not exist where the debts are not due to and from the same persons in the same capacity.[100] A North Carolina bankruptcy court recognized that "a situation can exist where a debtor has formally agreed that two entities may aggregate debts owed to and from the debtor for offset purposes," but denied the set-off after finding there was no formal agreement to set off debts owed by the primary obligor to the obligee against amounts the obligee owed to the guarantor.[101]

§ 14 Indemnification—Whether the Primary Obligor has a Duty

The principal obligor has a duty of indemnification so long as the guarantor undertook its obligations at the request of the primary obligor. The extent of this duty can be altered by contract.

A guarantor that, pursuant to a contractual obligation, pays the underlying obligation has a right of action to recover the amount paid from the primary obligor.[102]

99. In re Battery King Mfg. Co., 240 N.C. 586, 83 S.E.2d 490 (1954).
100. In re Bank of Simpson, 205 N.C. 333, 171 S.E. 436 (1933).
101. In re Ingersoll, 90 B.R. 168 (Bankr. W.D.N.C. 1987).
102. American Nat. Fire Ins. Co. v. Gibbs, 260 N.C. 681, 133 S.E.2d 669 (1963).

However, a person that makes such a payment without the duty to do so or any purpose to protect "some real or supposed right or interest of his own" may not claim such right.[103] Full satisfaction of the underlying obligation is not a condition precedent to an action by the guarantor to enforce reimbursement, but a guarantor who has paid only a portion of the underlying obligation is entitled to indemnity for only the amount paid.[104]

§ 15 Enforcement of Guaranties

15.1 Limitations on Recovery

No North Carolina court has considered the validity of fraudulent conveyance caps on recovery under a guaranty (which prevent recovery from exceeding amounts that would render the guaranty obligations void or voidable under the Bankruptcy Code or applicable state law).

It is uncertain whether, and to what extent, a North Carolina court would hold valid or invalid fraudulent conveyance caps on recovery under a guaranty as a Florida Bankruptcy Court did.[105]

15.2 Enforcement of Guaranties of Payment versus Guaranties of Performance/Collection

North Carolina distinguishes between guaranties of payment and guaranties of collection. A guaranty of payment is "an absolute promise by the uarantor to pay the debt at maturity if it is not paid by the principal debtor . . . [T]he creditor's cause of action against the guarantor ripens immediately upon failure of the principal debtor to pay the debt at maturity."[106] In contrast, a guaranty of collection is "a promise by the guarantor to pay [a] debt on the condition that the creditor 'shall diligently prosecute the principal debtor without success,'" and the oblige must first pursue the primary obligor for payment of the underlying debt before it is entitled to pursue the guarantor under the guaranty.[107] What amounts to reasonable diligence in collection is a question for the court to decide in each case.[108]

15.3 Exercising rights under a Guaranty Where the Underlying Obligation is also Secured by a Mortgage

North Carolina does not have any so-called "one-action" rule. If either the underlying obligation or the guaranty obligation is secured, whether the

103. Jamestown Mut. Ins. v. Nationwide Mut. Ins. Co., 277 N.C. 216, 221, 176 S.E.2d 751, 755 (1970).
104. Raleigh Banking & Trust Co. v. York, 199 N.C. 624, 155 S.E. 263 (1930). *See also* N.C.G.S. § 26-3.
105. In re TOUSA, Inc., 422 B.R. 783 (Bankr. S.D. Fla. 2009), *aff'd in part, rev'd in part*, 444 B. R. 613 (S. D. Fla. 2011), *rev'd* 680 F.3d 1289 (11th Cir. 2012).
106. EAC Credit Corp. v. Wilson, 281 N.C. 140, 145, 187 S.E.2d 752, 755 (1972).
107. *Id.*
108. Jones v. Ashford, 79 N.C. 172 (1878).

security consists of real or personal property, upon default the obligee may proceed against the guarantor under a guaranty of payment without first resorting to the security.[109]

15.4 Litigating Guaranty Claims: Procedural Considerations

Because, as indicated above, there is no "one-action" rule in North Carolina, there are no specific procedural considerations in pursuing a claim under a guaranty. Often, however, if suit is filed against a guarantor under a guaranty of payment before proceeding against the primary obligor or any security pledged by the primary obligor or the guarantor, it is common to include an allegation that the obligee is reserving all of its rights and remedies with respect to the primary obligor or the security to avoid a claim that the obligee is abandoning any of its rights and remedies which is a question of fact.[110]

§ 16 Revival and Reinstatement of Guaranties

As a general rule, though a debtor has paid a debt in full, the obligation of the debtor's guarantor will revive if the debtor's previous payment is later avoided or is disgorged, even if the guaranty is otherwise silent on this issue.[111] Many courts have recognized this principle.[112] While there is no North Carolina case on this issue, there is no reason not to believe that a North Carolina court, in a properly reasoned opinion, would not follow the generally prevailing view and adopt this general principle.

§ 17 Guaranties of Completion

North Carolina does not have any developed case law with respect to completion guaranties or guaranties of obligations other than for the payment of money.

109. *See* Page Trust Co. v. Godwin, 190 N.C. 512, S.E. 323 (1925).
110. *See* State of North Carolina v. West, 293 N.C. 18, 235 S.E.2d 150, 157 (1977) ("an essential element of abandonment is the intent of the owner to relinquish the article permanently").
111. Restatement (Third) of Suretyship and Guaranty, § 70.
112. *See, e.g.,* In the Matter of SNTL Corporation, 571 F.3d 826, 835-36 (2009) ("[W]e agree that the return of a preferential payment by a creditor generally revives the liability of a guarantor."); Wallace Hardware Co., Inc. v. Abrams, 223 F.3d 382, 408 (2000) ("[T]he courts have uniformly held that a payment of a debt that is later set aside as an avoidable preference does not discharge a guarantor of his obligation to repay that debt."); In re Robinson Bros. Drilling, Inc. v. Manufacturers Hanover Leasing Corp., 6 F.3d 701, 704 (1993) ("[C]ourts have recognized, without regard to any special guaranty language, that guarantors must make good on their guaranties following avoidance of payments previously made by their principal debtors."); In re Herman Cantor Corp. v. Central Fidelity Bank, N.A., 15 B.R. 747, 750 (1981) ("Although a surety usually is discharged by payment of the debt, he continues to be liable if the payment constitutes a preference under bankruptcy law. A preferential treatment is deemed by law to be no payment at all....The courts agree that payment from a debtor which is later set aside as a preference does not discharge a surety.").

§ 18 Citations to Restatements

Courts in North Carolina have cited to the Restatement of Suretyship and Guaranty (or the predecessor provisions of the Restatement of Security) in many cases.[113]

§ 19 Choice-of-Law Rules Applicable to Guaranties

The choice-of-law rules applicable to guaranties under North Carolina law typically center around general contract principles. Where a contract expressly provides that the laws of a particular state shall be controlling, the laws of the chosen state govern the validity of the contract, where the contract was executed in the chosen state[114] or where the parties had a reasonable basis for their choice and the laws of the chosen state do not violate a fundamental public policy of the state or otherwise violate applicable law.[115]

As to guaranties executed in connection with transactions governed by North Carolina's Uniform Commercial Code, North Carolina statute provides that if the transaction "bears a reasonable relation" to North Carolina and to another state, the parties may choose either the laws of North Carolina or the other state to control their "rights and duties" which would, of course, include the enforcement of the guaranty.[116]

113. Tripps Restaurants of North Carolina, Inc. v. Showtime Enterprises, Inc., 164 N.C. App. 389, 392, 595 S.E.2d 765, 768 (2004); Forrest v. Spicewood Development, LLC, 2011 WL 1327987, at 4 (W.D.N.C. 2011); Whisnant v. Carolina Farm Credit, ACA, 204 N.C. App. 84, 90, 693 S.E.2d 149, 154 (2010); Lawson v. Toney, 169 F. Supp.2d 455, 466 (M.D.N.C. 2001); Branch Banking & Trust Co. v. Thompson, 107 N.C. App. 53, 57, 418 S.E.2d 694, 697 (1992); REA Construction Co. v. Ervin Co., 33 N.C. App. 472, 476, 235 S.E.2d 418, 420 (1977); First Union Nat'l Bank of North Carolina v. King, 63 N.C. App. 757, 759, 306 S.E.2d 508, 509 (1983); RGK, Inc. v. United States Fidelity & Guaranty Co., 292 N.C. 668, 670, 235 S.E.2d 234, 240 (1977); Hatley v. Johnston, 265 N.C. 73, 80, 143 S.E.2d 260, 265 (1965); and Langston v. Brown, 260 N.C. 518, 521, 133 S.E.2d 180, 181 (1963).

114. Tanglewood Land Co., Inc. v. Byrd, 299 N.C. 260, 261 S.E.2d 655 (1980).

115. Torres v. McClain, 140 N.C. App. 238, 535 S.E.2d 623 (2000).

116. N.C.G.S. § 25-1-301.

North Dakota State Law of Guaranties

Richard P. Olson
Wanda L. Fischer
Olson & Burns P.C.
17 1st Ave. SE
Minot, ND 58702-1180
Telephone: (701) 839-1740
Fax: (701) 838-5315
olsonpc@minotlaw.com
http://www.minotlaw.com

Contents

North Dakota State Law of Guaranties[1]

Practice Pointer: A Lexis search revealed that the North Dakota Supreme Court has cited to the Restatement of Suretyship and Guaranty in a single case, in 1974, and to the Restatement of Security in a single case, in 1975. The court did not refer to these Restatements in its analysis, but in both cases was quoting Ammerman v. Miller, 488 F.2d 1285, 1295 (D.C. Cir. 1973). The Eighth Circuit has three cases on record citing these Restatements, but none of these three involved North Dakota law. It can be ventured, then, that these Restatements are not generally resources of interpretation for our courts.

Note: In order to standardize our discussion of the law of guaranties, we use the following vocabulary to refer to the various parties to a guaranty and their obligations.

"Guarantor" means a person who, by contract, agrees to satisfy an underlying obligation of another to an obligee upon the principal debtor's default on that underlying obligation.

"Guaranty" means a contract by which the guarantor agrees to answer for the debt, default, or miscarriage of another person. North Dakota Century Code (N.D.C.C.) § 22-01-01(2).[2]

"Continuing Guaranty" means a guaranty relating to a future liability of the principal debtor under successive transactions which either continue the liability or from time to time renew it after it has been satisfied. N.D.C.C. § 22-01-01(1).

Classifications: A guaranty may be further classified as one of the following:

a. **"Absolute"**—defined as a contract by which the guarantor has promised that if the debtor does not perform his obligation or obligations, the guarantor will perform some act (such as the payment of money) to or for the benefit of the creditor. As the term indicates, an absolute guaranty means that no matter what happens, the guarantor has agreed absolutely to pay the debt.

b. **"Conditional"**—a guaranty is to be deemed unconditional unless its terms import some condition precedent to the liability of the guarantor. N.D.C.C. § 22-01-09.

---

1. For the purposes of this survey, a "guaranty" does not include the activity, purpose, or function of the "insurance guaranty association" as found within N.D.C.C. Ch. 26.1-42.1 or of the "life and health insurance guaranty association" as found within N.D.C.C. Ch. 26.1-38.1. The purpose of the guaranty association is to protect resident policyholders in the event of an insurance company insolvency. When a member insurer is found to be insolvent and is ordered liquidated, a special deputy receiver takes over the insurer under court supervision and processes the assets and liabilities through liquidation. The task of servicing the insurance company's policies and providing coverage to North Dakota's resident policyholders becomes the responsibility of the guaranty association.
2. Although it may be difficult to distinguish a contract of guaranty from that of surety in some cases, North Dakota has not abolished the distinction between a guarantor and a surety and our statutes and case law define these undertakings in separate and distinct terms. Courts will examine the agreement to determine the nature of the contract—a contract of guaranty creates a secondary liability while the contract of surety creates a primary liability. State Bank v. Porter, 167 N.W.2d 527, 529 Syll.2 (N.D. 1969).

c. **"Continuing"**—future loans and debts are covered under the guaranty.

d. **"Guaranty of Solvency"**—a guaranty to the effect that an obligation that is good or is collectible imports that the debtor is solvent and that the demand is collectible by the usual legal proceedings if they are taken with reasonable diligence. N.D.C.C. § 22-01-08.

e. **"Guaranty of Collection" and "Guaranty of Payment"**—a guaranty of the payment of a debt is distinguished from a guaranty of the collection of a debt. A **guaranty of payment** is absolute and a guaranty of collection conditional. The guaranty of payment binds the guarantor to pay the debt at maturity in the event the money has not been paid by the principal debtor; and upon default by the debtor, the obligation of the guarantor becomes fixed.

The **guaranty of collection** is a promise on the part of the guarantor that if the principal creditor cannot collect the claim with due diligence, generally following suit against the principal debtor, the guarantor will pay the creditor. The attempt to collect is generally the condition precedent to the guarantor's liability.

f. "Unlimited Guaranty"—the guarantor guarantees payment of all debts of the principal debtor, present and past, in addition to the debt that is the subject of the current contract of guaranty.

"Obligee" means the person to whom the underlying obligation is owed; e.g., the lender under a loan agreement would be an obligee vis-à-vis the borrower/ principal debtor.

"Principal Debtor" means the person who incurs the principal obligation to the obligee; e.g., the borrower under a loan agreement would be a principal debtor.

"Principal Obligation" means the obligation or obligations incurred by the principal debtor and owed to the obligee; e.g., the borrower's obligation to make payments to a lender of principal and interest on a loan constitutes an underlying obligation.

"Original Obligation" is a promise to answer for the obligation of another in certain cases and which need not be in writing. N.D.C.C. § 22-01-05.[3]

---

3. 1. When the promise is made by one who has received property of another upon an undertaking to apply it pursuant to such promise, or by one who has received a discharge from an obligation in whole or in part in consideration of such promise.
2. When the creditor parts with value or enters into an obligation in consideration of the obligation in respect to which the promise is made, in terms or under circumstances which render the party making the promise the principal debtor and the person in whose behalf it is made the debtor's surety.
3. When the promise, being for an antecedent obligation of another, is made upon the consideration that the party receiving it shall cancel the antecedent obligation and accept the new promise as a substitute therefor, or upon the consideration that the party receiving it shall release the property of another from a levy under an execution on a judgment obtained upon the antecedent obligation, or upon a consideration beneficial to the promisor, whether moving from either party to the antecedent obligation or from another person.
4. When a factor undertakes, for a commission, to sell merchandise and guarantee the sale.
5. When the holder of an instrument for the payment of money upon which a third person is or may become liable to the holder transfers the instrument in payment of a precedent debt of the holder's, or for a new consideration, and in connection with such transfer, enters into a promise respecting such instrument. *See, e.g.*, Ned Nastrom Motors, Inc. v. Nastrom-Peterson-Neubauer Co., 338 N.W.2d 64 (N.D. 1983) (Holding that where the primary objective of an oral guarantee was to subserve some object of his own, notwithstanding that the effect of such promise was to pay the debt of another, the individual's oral guarantee was an original obligation and not within the statute of frauds.)

§ 1 Nature of the Guaranty Arrangement

Guaranty law in North Dakota has not been greatly litigated; much of the caselaw is more than 70 years old. Under North Dakota law, a contract of guaranty is a separate engagement for the performance of an undertaking of another and there exist two different obligations—one obligation is that of the principal debtor, and the other is that of the guarantor. The debtor is not a party to the guaranty, and the guarantor is not a party to the principal obligation. The undertaking of the debtor is independent of the promise of the guarantor, and the responsibilities imposed by the contract of guaranty differs from those that are created by the contract to which the guaranty is collateral. The fact that both contracts are written on the same paper or instrument does not affect the independence or separateness of the one from the other. *See* Hagan v. Havnvik, 421 N.W.2d 56 (N.D. 1988).

1.1 Guaranty Relationships

A guaranty is a contract of "secondary liability." The contract of a guarantor is his own separate contract; it is in the nature of a warranty by him that the thing guaranteed to be done by the principal shall be done, and is not merely an engagement jointly with the principal to do the thing. A guarantor, not being a joint contractor with his principal, is not bound to do what the principal has contracted to do; rather, the guarantor has to answer for the consequences of his principal's default. *See* State Bank v. Porter, 167 N.W.2d 527 (N.D. 1969).

North Dakota courts review the agreement to determine when the obligation of a guarantor is triggered, such as on default, which would create a secondary liability. If it is a contract of secondary liability, it is a contract of guaranty rather than a contract of surety. *See, e.g.,* Alerus Fin., N.A. v. Marcil Group, Inc., 2011 ND 205, 2011 N.D. Lexis 203.

In *Baker Mfg. Co. v. Kramer Sheet Metal,* 371 N.W.2d 149, 152 (N.D. 1985), the court noted that exact words of guarantee are not essential, where the words and circumstances are sufficient to clearly infer a guarantee. However, "'to charge one person with the debt of another, the undertaking must be clear and explicit.'" Northern Improvement Co. v. Pembina Broadcasting Co., Inc., 153 N.W.2d 97, 103 (N.D. 1967).

1.2 Other Suretyship Relationships

While not the focus of this survey, a suretyship relationship may also arise because of the pledge of collateral. As such, a guaranty-type relationship arises, to the extent of the collateral pledged, when a person supplies collateral for a loan in order to induce the creditor to lend to the debtor or where one party mortgages property to a creditor to secure the debt of another.[4]

§ 2 State Law Requirements for an Entity to Enter a Guaranty

Partnerships, limited liability companies, and corporations can all grant guaranties in furtherance of their business activities. Such grants are generally permitted by the relevant North Dakota statute.

2.1 Corporations

Under the North Dakota Business Corporation Law, a corporation may, within the scope of its general corporate powers, give a guaranty in furtherance of its corporate purpose, provided that its corporate charter and bylaws do not prevent it from doing so.[5] A guaranty may be given in cases, whether or not any separate consideration has been paid or promised to the corporation, when it has been approved by two-thirds of the voting shares entitled to vote and the unanimous affirmative vote of the holders of all outstanding shares, whether or not entitled to vote.[6]

With board approval, a corporation may execute a guaranty to benefit an officer or director or other employee of the corporation or a related organization if it may reasonably be expected, in the judgment of the board, to benefit the corporation.[7]

2.2 Partnerships

North Dakota's Partnership Law[8] neither expressly empowers a partnership to issue a guaranty nor expressly regulates or prohibits such activity. However, there are examples in the case law of partnerships issuing guaranties.[9] Nevertheless, a single partner may not issue a guaranty to a third party to bind the partnership unless it can be shown that the giving of guaranties is necessary

4. *See, e.g.*, First Interstate Bank v. Rebarchek, 511 N.W.2d 235 (N.D. 1994) (Although a conveyance made subject to an existing and specified encumbrance does not alone obligate the grantee to pay the mortgage debt, a grantee who assumes a mortgage debt becomes primarily liable for the debt. Under these circumstances, the assuming grantee, if the original mortgagee assents to the arrangement, becomes the principal, the grantor becomes a surety, and the grantee, upon default, is subject to foreclosure of the property.)
5. N.D.C.C. § 10-19.1-89.
6. N.D.C.C. § 10-19.1-89(d).
7. N.D.C.C. § 10-19.1-89(c).
8. Title 45, North Dakota Century Code.
9. *See, e.g.*, Ag Servs. of Am. v. Midwest Inv. Ltd. P'ship., 585 N.W.2d 571 (N.D. 1998). Generally, every general partner was agent for the partnership in the transaction of its business and had authority to do whatever was necessary to carry on such business in the ordinary manner and for this purpose could bind his copartners by an agreement in writing. Union Nat'l Bank v. Western Bldg. Co., 44 N.D. 336, 175 N.W. 628 (1919). This would necessarily include issuing guaranties. But see N.D.C.C. § 45-15-03(1)(b) (providing that the partnership agreement may limit the partners' authority to enter into transactions on behalf of the partnership.)

for carrying on the business of the firm in the ordinary way; otherwise, that partner has no implied authority to bind the partnership.[10]

2.3 Limited Liability Companies (LLCs)

North Dakota's Limited Liability Company Law generally permits limited liability companies to issue guaranties unless the articles of organization of a particular company prohibit it from doing so.[11] The law permits these guaranties so long as the transaction is approved by the affirmative vote of a majority of the governors present and (1) is in the usual and regular course of business of the LLC; (2) is with or for the benefit of a related organization, an organization in which the LLC has a financial interest, an organization with which the LLC has a relationship in the usual and regular course of its business, or an organization to which the LLC has the power to make donations; (3) is with, or for the benefit of, a member who provides services to the LLC, or a manager or other employee of the LLC or a subsidiary, including a member, manager, or employee who is a governor of the LLC or a subsidiary, and may reasonably be expected, in the judgment of the board, to benefit the LLC. Whether or not separate consideration has been promised to the LLC, a guaranty may be approved by the owners of two-thirds of the voting power of persons other than the interested person(s).[12]

2.4 Banks and Trust Companies

State statutes do not permit state-chartered banks to issue guaranties. However, the North Dakota Supreme Court has held that "a bank has not the power to become the guarantor of the obligations of another unless its *charter* or governing statute expressly permits it."[13] The exception to this rule is that when selling or disposing of loans made upon real estate security, a bank may guaranty the payment or collection of the loans as necessary to sell residential mortgage loans on the secondary market.[14] A guaranty made in violation of this provision is not binding on the bank, but is binding upon the person making the guaranty.

State statute does not authorize trust companies to issue guaranties. N.D.C.C. § 6-05-08 provides a list of things a trust company is empowered to do, and provides that notwithstanding any other provision of law and subject to approval by the state banking board, a trust company may "engage in any fiduciary activity in which a federally chartered financial institution that is granted fiduciary powers may engage." Neither 12 C.F.R. § 9.1(g) nor 12 U.S.C. § 92a grant a federally chartered financial institution with fiduciary powers the authority to issue guaranties, meaning that North Dakota trust companies are not authorized to issue guaranties.

10. Clarke v. Wallace, 48 N.W. 339 (N.D. 1891).
11. N.D.C.C. § 10-32-23(1) & (20).
12. N.D.C.C. § 10-32-97.
13. International Harvester Co. v. State Bank, 166 N.W. 507 (N.D. 1918) (*emphasis added*).
14. N.D.C.C.§ 6-03-06.

2.5 Individuals

Sometimes confusion can arise in the case of corporate officers or directors signing guaranties in closely held corporations or other organizations. In such instances, a case-by-case inquiry determines whether an individual intended to be personally bound or only issued a guaranty on *behalf* of a partnership or corporation only in an official employment capacity.[15] While a corporation must have "authority" to execute a guaranty, an individual guarantor must have the "capacity" to enter into the guaranty. Like any other contract, a party must have the mental capacity to enter into a guaranty.[16] Also, as in any other transaction, incapacity can be a defense against the enforcement of a guaranty issued by an individual.[17]

Another consideration with individual guaranties is marital property. North Dakota is not a community property state and under N.D.C.C. § 14-07-06 each spouse can borrow money to the same extent as if he or she were unmarried. Under North Dakota law, a spouse's earnings are treated as the individual property of that spouse. *See* N.D. Cent. Code § 14-07- 08(2) (1997) ("The earnings of one spouse are not liable for the debts of the other spouse. . . ."). Aside from the duty of mutual support, neither spouse has any interest in the property of the other. *See* N.D.C.C. 14-07-04. Put another way, a creditor does not have recourse to the property of a nonsigning spouse under a guaranty signed by the other spouse.

Regarding signature requirements, both spouses *must* execute a nonpurchase money mortgage of homestead property. Lenders typically require the nonborrowing spouse to waive any homestead exemption or other exemptions to which he or she may be entitled to under applicable law. If property is not homestead and a mortgage will be signed by a married person, lenders generally require that both husband and wife must sign the mortgage or the nonhomestead character of the land must be established by an affidavit of nonhomestead. Other than requiring both spouses to execute a nonpurchase money mortgage, North Dakota does not have special signature requirements for the nonobligor spouse; whatever documents that a nonobligor spouse is asked to sign depends on the lender and may vary.

§ 3 Signatory's Authority to Execute a Guaranty

Generally, the obligee has a duty of reasonable inquiry when it has some notice that the executor of the guaranty does not have authority to bind the guarantor.

15. Ned Nastrom Motors v. Nastrom-Peterson-Neubauer Co., 338 N.W.2d 64, (N.D. 1983); Moen v. Meidinger, 547 N.W.2d 44 (N.D. 1996).
16. N.D.C.C.§ 9-01-02.
17. *See, e.g.*, Estate of Wenzel-Mosset by Gaukler v. Nickels, 575 N.W.2d 425 (N.D. 1998).

3.1 Corporations

For an obligee to rely on a guaranty, the guaranty must be signed by an officer with actual or apparent authority to act in such capacity.[18] An obligee cannot enforce a guaranty if she had notice that the officer who signed for the corporation lacked authority to do so.[19] Where an obligee-plaintiff invokes the doctrine of apparent authority, that obligee bears the burden of proof.[20]

Generally, an officer of a corporation has authority to act only where: (a) authority has been expressly conferred on him by statute, law, or the act of the directors; (b) the action is properly incidental to the business entrusted to him by the directors;[21] and (c) the action is within his authority or ratified by proper authority as applicable to contracts of guaranty.[22] Though no North Dakota cases have addressed this particular issue, if a corporation's guaranty bears some reasonable relationship to the corporation's business and the signing officer has apparent authority to execute a guaranty, that guaranty is binding.[23]

Practice Pointer: A guarantor may want to limit his exposure under a guaranty to a certain percentage of the debt. For example, if a corporation borrows money, a guarantor who owns 25 percent of the outstanding shares of stock of the corporation may want to limit the guaranty to 25 percent of the debt. A prudent lender would prefer an amount limitation rather than a percentage guaranty because the latter is an ever-changing amount. If it is absolutely necessary to use a percentage guaranty, the lender should insist that the guaranty contain language clearly stating that the amount of the guaranty is established as a percentage of the debt amount outstanding at the time of default and is not to be reduced thereafter. In this manner, collections from the borrower, the security, and other guarantors after default will not further reduce the liability of the percentage guarantor. If such a provision is not included in the guaranty, the lender may have difficulty establishing the amount of the guarantor's liability in a legal action against the guarantor, and even after exhausting all other remedies the lender may be left with a deficiency that is not fully collectible from the percentage guarantor.

---

18. The party alleging the existence of agency based upon ostensible authority has the burden of proving agency by clear and convincing evidence. Transamerica Ins. Co. v. Standard Oil Co., 325 N.W.2d 210 (N.D. 1982).
19. Persons who have actual or constructive notice of restrictions upon the agent's authority cannot rely upon the agent's ostensible authority. *See* N.D.C.C.§ 3-02-03.
20. When an agency is denied, the one asserting it must establish it by clear and convincing evidence. Johnson v. Production Credit Ass'n of Fargo, 345 N.W.2d 371 (N.D. 1984).
21. N.D.C.C. § 10-19.1-89.
22. *See, e.g.*, N.D.C.C. § 3-03-03.
23. "It is also well established that 'what third persons are interested in is not the secret processes of the principal's mind, but the visible result of those processes--the character in which the agent is held out by the principal to those who may have occasion or opportunity to deal with him. This character is a tangible, discernible thing, and, so far as third persons are concerned, must be held to be authorized, as it is the only expression and evidence from which the principal intends that they shall determine his purposes and objects. . . . Instructions or limitations which are not disclosed cannot be permitted to affect apparent powers. . . . Although the agent violates his instructions or exceeds the limits set to his authority, he will yet bind his principal to such third persons, if his acts are within the scope of the authority, which the principal has caused or permitted him to appear to possess.'" Michigan Idaho Lumber Co. v. Northern Fire & Marine Ins. Co., 160 N.W. 130 (N.D. 1916*), quoting* Mechem, Agency, §§ 278, 279.

3.2 Partnerships

N.D.C.C. § 45-15-01 grants a partner the authority to bind the partnership when such partner's act is for "apparently carrying on in the ordinary course the partnership business" unless such authority has been explicitly held back in the partnership agreement and the person with whom the partner was dealing knew or had received a notification that the partner lacked authority.[24]

If a partner's act is "not apparently carrying on in the ordinary course the partnership business" the partnership is bound only if the other partners authorized the act.[25] Authority may also be granted under the partnership agreement.[26] Those dealing with partners have a duty of inquiry as to whether a signatory has the appropriate authority to bind the partnership.[27] In the particular context of guaranties, the court has found that a partner must have the explicit or implied authority to bind her partners if a guaranty is to bind a partnership; mere partnership is insufficient.[28] Under North Dakota's codification of the Uniform Limited Partnership Act (applicable to those partnerships described in N.D.C.C. § 45-10.2-03), a general partner has the same powers as a partner in a general partnership.[29]

3.3 Limited Liability Companies (LLCs)

Managers do not have general authority to bind the company. Under North Dakota's Limited Liability Company Act, unless otherwise provided by the articles of organization, member-control agreement, by laws, or resolution adopted by the board, the president/manager shall sign and deliver in the name of the LLC any instruments pertaining to the business of the limited liability company.[30] If he is absent or disabled, then the vice president, if any, or if there is more than one, the vice presidents in the order determined by the board shall perform these duties and exercise the powers of the president.[31] Any other managers and agents of the LLC shall perform the duties in the management of the limited liability company as provided in the articles, a member-control agreement, or the bylaws.[32]

§ 4 Consideration; Sufficiency of Past Consideration

Standard contract principles apply to the analysis of consideration for a contract of guaranty. The original obligation is sufficient consideration for an

24. N.D.C.C. § 45-15-01(1).
25. N.D.C.C. § 45-15-01(2).
26. N.D.C.C. § 45-15-03(1)(b).
27. N.D.C.C. § 45-15-01 may limit the authority of the partners and the lender should request a copy of the partnership agreement.
28. *See, e.g.*, Clarke v. Wallace, 48 N.W. 339 (N.D. 1891).
29. N.D.C.C. § 45-10.2-38;
30. N.D.C.C. 10-32-89(1).
31. N.D.C.C. 10-32-89(2).
32. N.D.C.C. § 10-32-89(5).

accompanying guaranty.[33] Past consideration can be sufficient if the principal obligation was induced by or created on the faith of the guaranty.[34]

Practice Pointer: If a guaranty is executed at a time other than when the primary debt is incurred, separate consideration is required. Granting of consideration can be accomplished by lending additional funds or providing an extension of the loan when the guaranty is obtained. Though case law indicates that a single dollar paid to the guarantor is consideration sufficient to support the guaranty, some doubt exists about whether courts would continue to follow that rule. *See* Union Nat'l Bank v. Schimke, 210 N.W.2d 176, 178 (N.D. 1973).

Consideration is required to create a valid contract of guaranty,[35] and the inquiry into the sufficiency of consideration is based on standard contract law principles. The benefit that forms the consideration need not flow directly to the guarantor from the obligee; the consideration flowing from the obligee to the principal debtor is sufficient to support a contemporaneous guaranty.

§ 5 Notice of Acceptance

Notice of acceptance is not required if the guaranty is absolute.

A mere offer to guaranty is not binding until notice of its acceptance is communicated by the obligee to the guarantor. An absolute guaranty is binding upon the guarantor without a notice of acceptance.[36]

§ 6 Interpretation of Guaranties

In North Dakota, courts will interpret a guaranty in the same manner by which they would interpret the language of any other contract.[37] The basis of North Dakota contract law is found in Title 9 of the Century Code, Contracts and Obligations; North Dakota contract law is similar to that of other states.

6.1 Guaranty of Payment versus Guaranty of Collection

A guaranty of the payment of a debt is distinguished from a guaranty of the collection of a debt. A **guaranty of payment** is absolute and a guaranty of collection conditional. The guaranty of payment binds the guarantor to pay the debt at maturity in the event the money has not been paid by the principal

33. N.D.C.C. § 22-01-03.
34. State Bank v. Porter, 167 N.W.2d 527 (N.D. 1969).
35. *See, e.g.,* First Bank (N.A.) v. Scherbenske, 375 N.W.2d 156 (N.D. 1985).
36. N.D.C.C. § 22-01-06.
37. *See, e.g.,* Citizens State Bank - Midwest v. Symington, 780 N.W.2d 676 N.D. 2010); Dakota Bank & Trust Co. v. Grinde, 422 N.W.2d 813, 817 (N.D. 1988) ("Under North Dakota law, a guaranty is 'a promise to answer for the debt, default, or miscarriage of another person.' § 22-01-01(1), N.D.C.C. It is a contract which, although separate and distinct from the contract imposing obligations on the principal, nevertheless imposes an obligation on the guarantor if the principal defaults in performance or payment.")

debtor; and upon default by the debtor, the obligation of the guarantor becomes fixed. The **guaranty of collection** is a promise on the part of the guarantor that if the principal creditor cannot collect the claim with due diligence, generally following suit against the principal debtor, the guarantor will pay the creditor. A court will look to the intent of the parties as expressed in the plain language of the guaranty to determine whether it is one of payment or one of collection.[38]

6.2 Language Regarding the Revocation of Guaranties

All North Dakota guaranties now require a written revocation, often with specific requirements as to the delivery of the revocation.

6.3 "Continuing"

A continuing guaranty is one that looks to future transactions, relating to a future liability of the guarantor under successive transactions.[39] While the use of the word "continuing" helps to make clear that a guaranty is meant to be continuing, courts in North Dakota have interpreted a guaranty as continuing even where the word "continuing" has not been used.[40]

6.4 "Absolute" and "Unconditional"

An "absolute" guaranty is defined as a contract by which the guarantor has promised that if the debtor does not perform his obligation or obligations, the guarantor will perform some act (such as the payment of money) to or for the benefit of the creditor.[41] A guaranty is "unconditional" unless its terms import some condition precedent to the liability of the guarantor.[42] The guaranty of collection is considered "conditional," obligating the guarantor to make payment only on the condition that the creditor has attempted unsuccessfully but with due diligence to collect the claim from the debtor.

6.5 "Completion" or "Performance" Guaranties

North Dakota recognized the "guaranty of completion" in *First Fed. Sav. & Loan Ass'n v. Compass Inv.*, 342 N.W.2d 214 (N.D. 1983), the only recorded case addressing that type of guaranty.

38. Bank of Kirkwood Plaza v. Mueller, 294 N.W.2d 640, 644 (N.D. 1980) ("It is clear from the underscored language of the guaranty agreement that this is an absolute guaranty, i. e., liability becomes fixed on default of the debtor. It is also a guaranty of payment . . . ."); State Bank v. Porter, 167 N.W.2d 527 (N.D. 1969).
39. *See, e.g.,* Baird v. Foss Inv. Co., 226 N.W. 523 (N.D. 1929).
40. *See, e.g.,* First Nat'l Bank & Trust v. Ashton, 436 N.W.2d 215, 216 (N.D. 1989). Athough the defendants asserted that the guaranties were limited and the case does not refer to the existence of the term "continuing" in the guaranty, the court found that the "language of the guaranty indicated that it was an unconditional, continuing guaranty".
41. State Bank v. Porter, 167 N.W.2d 527 (N.D. 1969).
42. N.D.C.C. § 22-01-09; *See* State Bank v. Porter, 167 N.W.2d 527 (N.D. 1969).

§ 7 When is the Guarantor not Liable?

In the 1989 session, the North Dakota legislature repealed at least four subsections that had often provided defenses for guarantors. However, some defenses still exist.

Note: Lenders should draft a guaranty ensuring that a guarantor waives the defense of discharge by payment in full. Otherwise, if a lender makes a credit bid for the full amount of the indebtedness at a foreclosure sale, the guarantor is discharged because the debt is paid in full. In *First Int'l Bank & Trust v. Peterson,* 2009 ND 207, ¶ 10, 776 N.W.2d 543, the court noted that "Here, the guarantors waived all defenses, except the defense of discharge by payment in full," thereby clearly indicating that the waiver of the defense of discharge *is* permissible. See § 7.5.6.

Practice Pointer: Obligees or lenders should include clauses wherein the guarantor waives every possible or potential right to claim a discharge, including waiving the right to discharge due to changes in the agreement.

7.1 Limitations upon Obligation of Guarantor

The obligation of a guarantor must be neither larger in amount, nor more burdensome, than that of the principal. A stockholder or partner of any entity, including a limited liability company, business corporation, professional corporation, and partnership, may enter into a separate contract of guaranty for the real estate mortgage debt of the entity. If in its terms the obligation exceeds that of the principal, the obligation is reducible in proportion to the principal obligation.[43]

7.2 Nonliability of Guarantor on Unlawful Contract—Personal Disability of Principal

A guarantor is not liable if the contract of the principal is unlawful, but the guarantor is liable notwithstanding any mere personal disability of the principal even though the disability is such as to make the contract void as against the principal.[44] No North Dakota cases discussing the "personal disability" issue are reported.

7.3 Revocation of Continuing Guaranty

A continuing guaranty may be revoked at any time by the guarantor, and revocation affects only those debts incurred by the principal debtor *after* the date of revocation, unless there is a continuing consideration as to such transactions which the guarantor does not renounce. A guarantor is still obligated on debt incurred prior to the date of revocation. If the contract of guaranty signed by

43. N.D.C.C. § 22-01-12.
44. N.D.C.C. § 22-01-13; *see also* State Bank of Towner, Inc. v. Rauh, 288 N.W.2d 299 (N.D. 1980).

the guarantor so states, the revocation must be in writing and delivered to the guarantee. If the contract does not so state, an oral attempt to revoke is not effective if at the time of the oral communication the obligee requests delivery of a written revocation and confirms the request in writing.[45]

7.4 Changes in Terms—When Guarantor Exonerated

If a lender makes an alteration in the loan arrangements with the borrower without the consent of the guarantor, it may unintentionally release the guarantor from liability.[46] This would apply even if the guarantor is ultimately *benefitted* by the changes, such as lowering the interest rate. The law provides as follows:

A guarantor is exonerated, except insofar as the guarantor may be indemnified by the principal, if, by any act of the creditor without the consent of the guarantor:

1. The original obligation of the principal is altered in any respect; or
2. The remedies or rights of the creditor against the principal in respect thereto are impaired or suspended in any manner.[47]

7.4.1 Interpretation of the Contract Rules the Day

Courts look closely at the language of the guaranty agreement to determine liability, and are not willing to exonerate the guarantor easily. In *International Harvester Credit Corp. v. Leaders, 818* F.2d 655 (8th Cir. 1987), the Eighth Circuit, applying Iowa law, ruled that a guaranty of payment, although a contract of adhesion, was not unconscionable and was enforceable. It also stated that although there was a "disparity of bargaining power" between the parties, there was no unfair surprise or substantive unfairness, and it noted that the guarantors had an opportunity to read the contract and to consult an attorney before signing it. *Id.* at 659-60.

In North Dakota, full satisfaction of the principal debtor's debt and the discharge of the principal debtor through release or settlement *ordinarily* relieves the guarantor. However, the North Dakota Supreme Court has determined that satisfaction does not exonerate the guarantor of liability where the

45. N.D.C.C. § 22-01-14. If the guaranty requires a written revocation, that written revocation is *required.* Where a bank subsequently obtained new guaranties from other guarantors, that fact does not show that the new guaranties take the place of the earlier guaranties and is therefore not a substitution or novation. A guaranty expressly requiring written revocation cannot be revoked by other ordinarily legally sufficient means, whether or not an oral notice was also given. First Nat'l Bank & Trust Co. v. Meyer Enters., 427 N.W.2d 328 (N.D. 1988).

46. Moline Plow Co. v. Gilbert, 15 N.W. 1 (Dakota Territory 1882) (If a creditor and principal debtor reached an accounting and settlement that changed the time of payments, proportionate part payable, and the interest rate without the consent of the guarantors, that alteration would release and exonerate the guarantors.)

47. N.D.C.C. § 22-01-15. However, a guaranty may provide that the guarantor will permit alterations and waive the right to claim exoneration under this statute. In Wallwork Lease & Rental Co. v. Decker, 336 N.W.2d 356 (N.D. 1983), the guarantor of a lease waived her right to object to subsequent alterations or modifications of the lease, thereby waiving her right to claim exoneration under N.D.C.C. § 22-01-15 because her guaranty contract contained language making it an absolute guaranty and explicitly providing that guarantor's liability shall not be affected by modification of the lease terms.

right of recourse against the guarantor is expressly *reserved* in the guaranty agreement.[48]

The court has also found that there was no alteration and guarantor was *not* exonerated where a promissory note executed by the debtor in 1975 was different in terms and interest rate than a note executed in 1972 when guarantor had agreed in writing to unconditionally guarantee the payment of *all* notes of the debtor then existing and thereafter arising. Thus, the court found that it was of no consequence that the note sued on is not the same note which was discussed when the guaranty was executed because the guaranty, by its terms, extends to the original note, the note sued on, and all of the *intervening* notes.[49]

7.5 Defenses that May be Raised by Guarantor

A guarantor may show that the obligee failed to perform so that there is a partial or complete failure of consideration. North Dakota courts distinguish failure of consideration from lack of consideration. When there is a lack of consideration, no contract is ever formed. For a failure of consideration, a contract, valid when formed, becomes unenforceable because the performance bargained for has not been rendered.[50]

7.5.1 Failure to Fulfill a Condition Precedent

Guarantors may raise a defense of failure to fulfill a condition precedent and, using the general rules of contract interpretation, the courts will review the guaranty agreement to determine whether the guaranty does indeed require a condition before the guarantor is liable. Obviously, a guaranty of collection implies a condition precedent because the guarantor promises that if the creditor cannot collect the claim with due diligence, generally following suit against the principal debtor, the guarantor will pay the creditor.[51]

7.5.2 Modification of the Guaranty

Whether a modification of the guaranty has occurred is a question of fact, and courts consider whether an "alteration" of a contract has occurred—whether there has been a change in the provisions of a contract. If an alteration or

---

48. General Elec. Credit Corp. v. Larson, 387 N.W.2d 734, 735 (N.D. 1986) (Finding that the guaranty remained enforceable against the guarantor because the guaranty contract contained a waiver of the defense of discharge by satisfaction of the principal debtor's obligation.).

49. First Nat'l Bank & Trust Co. v. Hart, 267 N.W.2d 561(N.D. 1978). This case is also interesting because the guarantor raised the "novel argument" that because he did not read it and because he was not given a copy of the guaranty, he was entitled to rely on his recollection of the oral agreement, and therefore should not be bound by the terms of the signed guaranty contract. *Id.* at 563. That position failed, as did the claim that the guaranty was too broad. In finding that although the guaranty was broad, it was still enforceable, the court opined that "We conclude that the breadth of a contract alone does not invalidate it. Unless the great breadth also contributes to a finding of unenforceability due to unconscionability (§ 41-02-19 (2-302), NDCC), unlawful restraint of business (§ 9-08-06, NDCC), fraud or other disqualification, the courts of North Dakota will enforce a broad contract." *Id.* at 564.

50. Farmers Union Oil Co. v. Maixner, 376 N.W.2d 43, 47 (N.D. 1985) *quoting* First National Bank of Belfield v. Burich, 367 N.W.2d 148, 152 (N.D. 1985).

51. *See, e.g.*, State Bank v. Porter, 167 N.W.2d 527 (N.D. 1969).

modification has occurred, the materiality of an alteration of a principal's obligation is irrelevant; under N.D.C.C. § 22-01-15, a guarantor is exonerated if the creditor alters the principal's original obligation "in any respect" without the guarantor's consent. Once the determination has been made that there is an alteration, it is not necessary to inquire into nor to determine to what extent, if at all, the guarantor was injured or prejudiced by the alteration to the principal contract.[52]

7.5.3 Failure to Pursue Principal Debtor

Only when the guaranty is a guaranty of collection is the creditor obligated to first pursue the principal debtor, and the debtor may raise this defense. If the guaranty is one of payment, the guarantor undertakes unconditionally that the debtor will pay, and the creditor may, upon default, proceed directly against the guarantor without taking any step to collect of the principal debtor.[53]

7.5.4 Statute of Limitations

N.D.C.C. § 28-01-16 imposes, with certain exceptions, a six-year statute of limitations on contractual obligations. One such exception applies to contracts for the sale of goods that are governed by Article 2 of the North Dakota Uniform Commercial Code, which imposes a four-year statute of limitations.[54]

North Dakota courts have not yet considered whether, where the underlying obligation is a contract for the sale of goods governed by the Uniform Commercial Code, the six-year statute of limitations applicable to contracts would apply to the guaranty.

7.5.5 Statute of Frauds

Whether a guaranty falls under the statute of frauds is a question of fact. N.D.C.C. § 22-01-05 sets out situations when a guaranty need *not* be in writing. In general, an oral guarantee is enforceable if it was made to "subserve" some interest of the promisor/guarantor.[55]

52. *See, e.g.*, Ag Servs. of Am. v. Midwest Inv. Ltd. P'ship., 585 N.W.2d 571 (N.D.1998); Tri-Continental Leasing Corp. v. Gunter, 472 N.W.2d 437 (N.D. 1991).
53. State Bank of Burleigh County v. Porter, 167 N.W.2d 527, 533 (N.D. 1969).
54. N.D.C.C. § 41-02-104.
55. State Bank of Towner, Inc. v. Rauh, 288 N.W.2d 299 (N.D. 1980). Thompson and Larson were personal friends as well as partners in a cattle feeding business; due to partnership losses, Larson became personally indebted to Thompson for $250,000, but Thompson agreed not to collect until Larson was financially able to repay. The court found that Thompson genuinely had a $250,000 interest in Larson's economic recovery, and knew that he would not likely be paid if Larson was unable to continue the business. *Id.* at 308. They knew that new sources of capital were needed to operate the business because of Larson's finances; Thompson suggested that Larson borrow money from Rauh and was closely involved in persuading Rauh to furnish the money. The court agreed that the persuasion and influence of Thompson were not just acts of friendship to Larson, but that Thompson was interested because of the money that Larson owed him. *Id.* It concluded that the principal or leading object of Thompson's oral guarantee to Rauh was the protection of Thompson's interest as a creditor in the $250,000 debt of Larson and therefore the oral guarantee was an original obligation and did not come within the statute of frauds. *Id.*

7.5.6 Discharge by Payment in Full

Unless a guarantor waives the defense of discharge by payment in full, the guarantor is discharged when the debt is paid in full. This is an issue when a lender makes a credit bid for the full amount of the indebtedness at a foreclosure sale. The North Dakota Supreme Court has explained that "if a third party had bid the full amount of the indebtedness at the foreclosure sale, the guarantors would have been discharged because the borrower's debt would have been paid in full. The same is true when the lender bids at the foreclosure sale. . . . the lender's bid is 'on the same footing as other bids."[56] If the lender cannot sell the property for the amount owed on the debt, it cannot now pursue the guarantor for the deficiency because the credit bid was a payment in full, thereby discharging the guarantor.

§ 8 Waiver of Defenses by the Guarantor

The North Dakota Supreme Court has shown a strong inclination to enforce waivers contained in guaranties of payment. However, some defenses cannot be waived.

8.1 Defenses that Cannot be Waived

Some rights cannot be waived.

Certain waivers of statutory rights are void under North Dakota law.[57] N.D.C.C. § 9-08-05 provides that stipulations in contracts by which any party is restricted from enforcing rights under the contract by the usual legal proceedings in the ordinary tribunals or which limit the time within which a party may enforce those rights is void, except as otherwise specifically permitted by the laws of North Dakota. Waiver of the right to trial by jury is protected under the North Dakota Constitution and generally cannot be waived in loan documents (though there is no right to a jury in equitable actions, such as foreclosures).

§ 9 Jointly and Severally Liable Guarantors

9.1 Contribution

Guarantors who are jointly and severally liable are presumed to share the secondary obligation equally.[58] What this means is that the creditor is not obliged to seek full payment from more than one such guarantor.

56. First Int'l Bank & Trust v. Peterson, 776 N.W.2d 543, 547 (N.D. 2009).
57. N.D.C.C. § 9-08-05.
58. Collection Ctr., Inc. v. Bydal, 795 N.W.2d 667 (N.D. 2011).

Moreover, before the creditor obtains judgment, any individual guarantor is obliged to pay the whole debt. Insofar as the guarantor has paid out more than its proportional share of the obligation, only then may it recover from other guarantors proportionate to their liability. A party to a joint obligation or to a joint and several obligation that satisfies more than its share of the claim against all obligors may require a proportionate contribution from all the parties joined with it.[59] Statutory language provides a joint obligor may recover only once it satisfies more than its share of the debt, making such satisfaction a prerequisite to contribution.[60]

§ 10 Reliance

As noted earlier, guarantees are creatures of contract.[61] Where a guaranty contract is executed subsequent to the incurring of the principal debt involved, and there are (1) no promises made by the lender to the guarantor at the time the guaranty was signed and (2) there is no reliance by the lender on a promised guaranty at the time the principal obligation was incurred, there is no valid guaranty contract in existence binding the guarantor.[62] Conversely, one who extends credit in reliance upon a guarantee of another may proceed against that guarantor for the debt.[63]

§ 11 Subrogation

Subrogation is an equitable remedy that generally requires total satisfaction of the underlying obligation to the obligee prior to its exercise.

The doctrine of subrogation arises not from contract but from principles of equity.[64] Generally, subrogation is available when the claim of an obligee has been paid in full.[65] Nonetheless, where a guarantor has paid installments of interest, each installment of interest is a claim in full, such that the guarantor has a right of subrogation regarding these interest payments.[66]

59. Hombach v. BioDigestor Indus., 2001 U.S. Dist. LEXIS 18504 (D.N.D. Oct. 15, 2001).
60. N.D.C.C. § 9-01-08.
61. First Int'l Bank & Trust v. Peterson, 776 N.W.2d 543 (N.D. 2009).
62. *See* Union Nat'l Bank v. Schimke, 210 N.W.2d 176 (N.D. 1973).
63. *See* Rheault v. Tennefos Constr. Co., 189 N.W.2d 626 (N.D. 1971).
64. First Nat'l Bank v. Haugen Ford, Inc., 219 N.W.2d 847, 851 (N.D. 1974), *quoting* D. W. Jaquays & Co. v. First Sec. Bank, 419 P.2d 85 (Ariz. 1966).
65. State Bank v. Nester, 385 N.W.2d 95 (N.D. 1986).
66. Rouse v. Zimmerman, 212 N.W. 515 (N.D. 1927).

§ 12 Indemnification

A guarantor cannot recover an indemnity from the principal obligor where it entered upon the guaranty contract as a "volunteer," a term that describes a guarantor who binds itself because it has a legal duty to protect.[67]

§ 13 Enforcement of Guaranties

13.1 Exercising Rights Under a Guaranty Where the Underlying Obligation is also Secured by a Mortgage

There is no requirement in North Dakota that actions to enforce a guaranty accompany actions to foreclose a mortgage.[68] Obviously, creditors prefer to avoid the expensive and time-consuming foreclosure process and a guaranty from a solvent creditor is a way to do that.

13.2 Mortgages and Anti-Deficiency Statutes

Case law has made it clear that guarantors are not within the protection of the general anti-deficiency judgment statute, found at N.D.C.C. § 32-19-06. The North Dakota Supreme Court has noted repeatedly that a guarantor's liability is premised on a separate and distinct contract of guaranty rather than on any obligations imposed by the notes and mortgages subject to a foreclosure action.[69]

§ 14 Litigating Guaranty Claims

Practice Pointer: Under North Dakota law, a creditor cannot collect attorneys' fees from a defaulting borrower.[70] Because a guarantee relates to the payment of debt, attorneys' fees are not collectable and a provision for payment by the guarantor is against public policy and void.[71] However, in North Dakota

67. Grinnell Mut. Reinsurance Co. v. Ctr. Mut. Ins. Co., 2003 ND 50,¶ 41 658 N.W.2d 363. However, one acting in good faith in making payment under a reasonable belief that it is necessary to his protection is entitled to indemnity, or subrogation, even though it develops that he in fact had no interest to protect. *Id.*
68. *See, e.g.,* Alerus Fin., N.A. v. Marcil Group, Inc., 2011 ND 205, 2011 N.D. LEXIS 203 (Oct. 18, 2011); State v. Larsen, 515 N.W.2d 178, 180 (N.D. 1994); Norwest Bank North Dakota, Nat'l Ass'n v. Christianson, 494 N.W.2d 165, 167-68 (N.D. 1992); Norwest Bank N.D., Nat'l Ass'n v. Christianson, 494 N.W.2d 165, 167 n.1 (N.D. 1992) (clarifying, in a discussion of cases addressing guaranties and mortgages, that the court "did not thereby imply that a mortgagee must follow a particular chronological order in which to collect what is due." Where guarantors unconditionally guaranteed the debt and made a promise of repayment, the lender is allowed to sue on the personal guaranties without first foreclosing on the underlying real estate.).
69. First Nat'l Bank & Trust Co. v. Anseth, 503 N.W.2d 568, 572-73 (N.D. 1993); Dakota Bank & Trust Co. v. Grinde, 422 N.W.2d 813, 817 (N.D. 1988); H & F Hogs v. Huwe, 368 N.W.2d 553, 555 (N.D. 1985); Bank of Kirkwood Plaza v. Mueller, 294 N.W.2d 640, 643 (N.D. 1980).
70. N.D.C.C. § 28-06-24.
71. Farmers Union Oil Co. v. Maixner, 376 N.W.2d 43 (N.D. 1985).

an oversecured creditor in a bankruptcy proceeding may collect attorneys' fees incurred during the course of the bankruptcy if the loan documents so provide, so, with an eye toward a possible bankruptcy, lenders often include language for the payment of attorneys' fees incurred in enforcing the agreement, knowing that unless it is an oversecured creditor in a bankruptcy, this language is unenforceable.

Guaranty claims are contract claims and the same procedural considerations apply.

14.1 Choice of Law

In North Dakota, the agreement of the parties establishes what law governs a contract, including a guaranty. "A contract must be so interpreted as to give effect to the mutual intention of the parties as it existed at the time of contracting so far as the same is ascertainable and lawful."[72] In addition, N.D.C.C.§ 9-07-02 provides that "The language of a contract is to govern its interpretation if the language is clear and explicit and does not involve an absurdity." In other words, parties are free to have North Dakota law or that of another state govern interpretation of a guaranty.

How does a court decide what law governs when the parties are from different states and the contract is silent on that issue? In 1973 the North Dakota Legislature repealed the statute providing for "what law" governs a contract, indicating "that the flexibility allowed the courts in determining what law governs in tort actions should also apply in contract matters."[73] Since then, the North Dakota Supreme Court specifically adopted the significant contacts approach in contract cases,[74] and its significant contacts analysis mirrors that of the Second Restatement of Conflict of Laws.[75]

72. N.D.C.C. § 9-07-03.
73. Apollo Sprinkler Co. v. Fire Sprinkler Suppliers & Design, 382 N.W.2d 386, 389 n.2 (N.D. 1986).
74. Plante v. Columbia Paints, 494 N.W.2d 140, 141 (N.D. 1992).
75. The Second Restatement's seven choice of law principles are: (1) the needs of the interstate and international systems; (2) the relevant policies of the forum; (3) the relevant policies of other interested states and the relative interest of those states in the determination of the particular issue; (4) the protection of the justified expectations; (5) the basic policies underlying the particular field of law; (6) certainty, predictability and uniformity of result; and (7) ease in the determination and application of the law to be applied. *See* Restatement (Second) of Conflict of Laws, § 6(2)(a)-(g) (1971).

Ohio State Law of Guaranties

Timothy E. Grady
Amy C. Strang
Porter, Wright, Morris & Arthur LLP
41 South High Street
Columbus, Ohio
614-227-2000
www.porterwright.com

porterwright
PORTER WRIGHT MORRIS & ARTHUR LLP

Contents

Ohio State Law of Guaranties

Introductory Note: This survey focuses on Ohio state law applicable to guaranties of commercial credit transactions. Ohio has a substantial body of law on guaranties and related subjects, including both case law and statutory provisions. Although not the focus of this survey, the Ohio Revised Code contains special requirements for sureties for the performance of nonmonetary obligations, such as those who guarantee the fidelity of those holding places of public or private trust, which are discussed briefly below and do not typically apply to guarantors in commercial credit transactions. Ohio courts and federal courts interpreting Ohio law have looked to the Restatement (Third) of Suretyship and Guaranty (1995) (the "Restatement") for guidance on guaranty and suretyship issues.1

In order to standardize our discussion of the law of guaranties, we use the following vocabulary to refer to the various parties to a guaranty and their respective obligations.

"Guarantor" means a person who by contract agrees to satisfy an underlying obligation of another to an obligee upon the primary obligor's default on that underlying obligation. Although the distinction between guarantors and sureties is sometimes muddled, Ohio retains some legal differences between guarantors and sureties.

"Guaranty" means the contract by which the guarantor agrees to satisfy the underlying obligation of a primary obligor to an obligee in the event the primary obligor defaults on the underlying obligation

"Surety" means a person who undertakes to be primarily and jointly liable on an underlying obligation on the same terms as the primary obligor. Ohio law and the Uniform Commercial Code include a "guarantor or any other secondary obligor" in their definitions of "surety."

"Suretyship" means the contract by which the surety agrees to become primarily and jointly liable on an underlying obligation on the same terms as the primary obligor.

"Obligee" means the person to whom the underlying obligation is owed. For example, the lender under a loan agreement would be an obligee vis-à-vis the borrower.

"Primary Obligor" means the person who incurs the underlying obligation to the obligee. For example, the borrower under a loan agreement would be a primary obligor.

---

1. *See* McWane, Inc. v. Fid. & Deposit Co. of MD, 372 F.3d 798 (6th Cir. 2004); Rose v. Volvo Const. Equipment North America, Inc., 542 F.Supp.2d 751 (N.D.Ohio 2008); Jae Co. v. Heitmeyer Builders, Inc., 2009-Ohio-2851 (Ohio Ct. App. 2009); O'Brien v. Ravenswood Apartments, Ltd., 2006-Ohio-5264 at ¶ 21, 862 N.E.2d 549, 555 (Ohio Ct. App. 2006), *appeal not allowed*, 2007-Ohio-724, 862 N.E.2d 118 (2007).

"Underlying Obligation" means the obligation or obligations incurred by the primary obligor and owed to the obligee. For example, the borrower's obligation to make payments to a lender of principal and interest on a loan constitutes an underlying obligation.

OHIO LAW HIGHLIGHTS

STATUTE OF LIMITATIONS SHORTENED

Ohio recently shortened its statute of limitations for an action upon an agreement, contract, or promise in writing, such as a guaranty, from 15 years to eight years after the cause of action accrues.[2] The effective date of this change to Ohio Revised Code Section 2305.06 is September 28, 2012. For causes of action accrued prior to the effective date of the statute, the period of limitations will be the earlier of eight years from such effective date or the expiration of the period in effect prior to the effective date.

STATUTE OF FRAUDS

In addition to agreements being subject to the statute of frauds, the Ohio Revised Code includes a separate statute providing that no claim can be brought on any loan agreement between a financial institution and a debtor, unless the agreement is in writing and signed by the party against whom such action is brought, or signed by the debtor and accepted by the financial institution.[3] This provision does not apply to loan agreements primarily for personal, household, or family purposes, in which the loan is less than $40,000 or is secured by an interest in the debtor's primary residence. "Debtor" and "loan agreement" are defined broadly in the statute, and would include guarantors and guaranties.[4]

CONFESSION OF JUDGMENT PROVISIONS

The Ohio Revised Code permits creditors to include confession of judgment (warrant of attorney) provisions in commercial guaranties (as well as in other instruments evidencing commercial indebtedness). Such provisions are commonly used in commercial practice in Ohio.[5] Section 15.6, *infra*, discusses these provisions in greater detail. An unreported decision, also discussed in Section 15.6, *infra*, held that a creditor's failure to designate the amount of the indebtedness guaranteed by the guaranty in question was a prima facie reason for the court to refuse to enter a judgment using the confession of judgment provisions of the guaranty.

2. 2012 Am. Sub. S. B. No. 224.
3. Ohio Rev. Code Ann. § 1335.02(B) (West 2011).
4. Ohio Rev. Code Ann. § 1335.02(A)(1), (A)(3) (West 2011).
5. Ohio Rev. Code Ann. §§ 2323.12, 2323.13 (West 2011).

§ 1 Nature of Guaranty Arrangement

1.1 Guaranty Relationships

A guaranty is an undertaking by a guarantor to be answerable for the default of a primary obligor, who remains primarily liable on the obligation.[6] A guarantor's liability under a contract of guaranty arises only upon the primary obligor's default and is secondary to that of the primary obligor.[7] The guarantor and the primary obligor are not joint promisors and are not jointly liable.[8] Furthermore, a contract of guaranty is an ancillary undertaking, separate and distinct from the contract between the primary obligor and the obligee,[9] even if written on the same paper or instrument.[10] No particular technical words are necessary to form a guaranty, and the word "guaranty" need not be included.[11]

1.2 Other Suretyship Relationships

In Ohio, a contract of guaranty is a type of suretyship contract, but differs from other suretyships in that nonguarantor sureties are primarily and jointly liable on the obligation underlying their suretyship on the same terms as the primary obligor, whereas a guarantor's liability is secondary and arises only after the primary obligor has failed to perform.[12] Ohio law has largely eliminated the distinction between guaranties and other suretyships, first by authorizing guaranty companies to act as sureties,[3] and second by accepting the Uniform Commercial Code definition of "surety," which includes guarantors.[13] Some legal differences remain between a contract of guaranty and one of suretyship, however, such as Ohio's statutory requirements to enter into such relationships.

Although guaranty contracts are often used as a means of providing extra assurance to lenders in the issuance of credit to principal borrowers, other types of suretyship contracts are sometimes required on bonds given by public officers or employees, or to guarantee the fidelity of those holding places of public or private trust.[14]

---

6. Galloway v. Barnesville Loan, Inc., 57 N.E. 2d 337 (Ohio 1943); Cincinnati, H. & D. Ry. v. Kleybolte, 88 N.E. 879 (Ohio 1909); Metro. Cas. Ins. Co. v. Soucy, 16 Ohio Law Abs. 538 (Ohio Ct. App. 1934).
7. Jazwa v. Alesci, Nos. 69857, 69881, 1996 WL 517639, at *4 (Ohio Ct. App. Sept. 12, 1996) (citing Madison Nat'l Bank of London, Ohio v. Weber, 158 N.E. 453 (Ohio 1927)).
8. Deming v. Bd. of Trustees of Ohio Agric. & Mech. Coll., 31 Ohio St. 41 (1876); Denton v. Whitney, 31 Ohio St. 89 (1876).
9. Madison Nat'l Bank of London, Ohio v. Weber, 158 N.E. 453 (Ohio 1927).
10. Shatelrow v. Brim, 29 Ohio Op. 121 (Ohio C.P. 1944).
11. *Metro. Cas. Ins. Co.*, 16 Ohio Law Abs. at 538 ("Any form of words expressing an undertaking, upon a consideration to insure the other party against the non-payment or delinquency of a third party, may constitute a guaranty.").
12. St. Paul Fire & Marine Ins. Co. v. Indus. Comm. of Ohio, 506 N.E.2d 202 (Ohio 1987); Galloway v. Barnesville Loan, Inc., 57 N.E. 2d 337 (Ohio 1943); Manor Care Nursing & Rehab. Ctr. v. Thomas, 704 N.E.2d 593 (Ohio Ct. App. 1997), *abrogated on other grounds by* Hooten v. Safe Auto Ins. Co., 2003-Ohio-4829, 795 N.E.2d 648 (2003); Carter v. Bernard, 269 N.E.2d 139 (Ohio C.P. 1971).
13. Ohio Rev. Code Ann. § 1301.201(39) (West 2011); U.C.C. § 1-201 (2001); 52 Ohio Jurisprudence 3d (2007) 326, Guaranty and Suretyship, § 1.
14. Ohio Rev. Code Ann. § 117.32 (West 2011).

1.3 Other Joint Debts

Although not the focus of this survey, various other relationships exist in which one party undertakes to indemnify another against the failure of a third party to perform a legal duty. Such relationships include those formed out of an indemnity contract, a warranty contract, the endorsement of a negotiable instrument, or its execution by a comaker or accommodation party.

§ 2 State Law Requirements to Enter into a Guaranty or Suretyship Relationship

Individuals, corporations, partnerships, limited liability companies, banks, mutual insurance companies and stock insurance companies may all grant guaranties under Ohio law upon meeting certain requirements.

2.1 General

To enter into a contract of guaranty or suretyship, a person or entity must have the same contractual capacity required to enter into any other kind of legal contract.[15] Surety and guaranty contracts, as special promises to answer for the debt or default of another, are within the scope of the statute of frauds, and therefore must be in writing and signed by the party to be charged.[16]

Although not the focus of this survey, the Ohio Revised Code contains special requirements for compensated, nonguarantor sureties.[17] These requirements do not, however, apply to typical guarantors in commercial loan transactions.[18]

2.2 Corporations

Corporations incorporated under Ohio law are expressly authorized to "guarantee or secure obligations of any person," as long as such guaranty is made to carry out the purposes stated in the corporation's articles of incorporation.[19] This authorization is subject to limitations prescribed by law or the corporation's own articles of incorporation.[20]

In determining whether, under Ohio law, the execution of a guaranty carried out the purpose stated in the corporation's articles, the Sixth Circuit

15. 52 Ohio Jurisprudence 3d (2007) 338, Guaranty and Suretyship, § 13.
16. Ohio Rev. Code Ann. § 1335.05 (West 2011).
17. Ohio Rev. Code Ann. § 1341.01 *et seq.* (West 2011).
18. Although the Ohio Revised Code includes the Uniform Commercial Code definition of "surety," which includes "a guarantor or other secondary obligor," the statutory requirements of Ohio Rev. Code Ann. § 1341.01 *et seq.* apply only to nonguarantor sureties. *See* Ohio Savings Association v. Cortell, 495 N.E.2d 33 (Ohio Ct. App. 1985) (holding the definition of surety in the Uniform Commercial Code section of the Ohio Revised Code does not apply to Ohio Revised Code Chapter 1341); Mut. Fin. Co. v. Politzer, 241 N.E.2d 906, 908 (Ohio Ct. App. 1968).
19. Ohio Rev. Code Ann. § 1701.13(F)(6) (West 2011).
20. Ohio Rev. Code Ann. § 1701.13(F) (West 2011).

Court of Appeals has found that the directors of a building company, which was a closely held corporation with articles giving authorization to "exercise all the powers and rights conferred by the laws of Ohio upon corporations," did in fact have the authority to enter into a contract of guaranty in favor of its tenant.[21]

Even if the giving of a guaranty by a corporation is found not to carry out the purposes stated in its articles, Ohio has significantly limited the availability of an ultra vires defense. Only a few limited parties are permitted to assert a lack of corporate authority in any action: (i) the state, in an action by it against the corporation; (ii) the corporation, in an action against a director, officer, or shareholder; (iii) a shareholder, in an action against a director, an officer, or another shareholder; and (iv) a party in an action involving an alleged overissue of shares.[22] Accordingly, even if a corporation exceeds its authority in executing a guaranty contract, neither the corporation nor its other creditors can assert lack of authority as a defense to the enforcement of the guaranty by the obligee.

2.3 Partnerships

Except as otherwise provided in the partnership agreement, an Ohio partnership is authorized "to engage in any activity in which a domestic corporation or a domestic limited liability company may lawfully engage," and so may enter a guaranty to the extent described in Sections 2.2 and 2.4.[23]

2.4 Limited Liability Companies

An Ohio limited liability company (LLC) may "guarantee or secure obligations of any person" in carrying out the purposes stated in the LLC's articles of organization or operating agreement, subject to limitations prescribed by law or by the LLC's articles of organization or operating agreement.[24]

2.5 Individuals

Ohio Revised Code Section 3103.08 provides that "neither husband nor wife, as such, is answerable for the acts of the other."[25] Furthermore, no "community property" exists in Ohio, and apart from dower and support rights, neither spouse has any interest in the property of the other.[26] Thus if a guaranty is made by only one spouse, the obligee will not have recourse against the property of the nonguarantor spouse. Accordingly, for an obligee to have recourse against the property of both spouses, both spouses must execute a guaranty and become guarantors.

---

21. *In re* B-F Bldg. Corp., 284 F.2d 679, 681 (6th Cir. 1960).
22. Ohio Rev. Code Ann. § 1701.13(H) (West 2011).
23. Ohio Rev. Code Ann. § 1776.21(C) (West 2011).
24. Ohio Rev. Code Ann. § 1705.03(10) (West 2011).
25. Ohio Rev. Code Ann. § 3103.08 (West 2011).
26. Ohio Rev. Code Ann. § 3103.04 (West 2011); Matre v. Matre, 6 Ohio Law Abs. 484 (Ohio Ct. App. 1928).

2.6 Ohio Incorporated Banks

Guaranties offered by state banks are significantly affected by federal law, as federal law prohibits a state-chartered bank from engaging in activities in which a national bank may not engage under federal law.[27] A national bank is permitted to act as a guarantor if the bank has a substantial interest in the performance of the transaction involved (for example, a national bank that is a fiduciary may guarantee the faithful performance by a cofiduciary of its duties).[28] Alternatively, a national bank may execute a guaranty for the benefit of a customer if the customer makes a segregated deposit with the bank in an amount sufficient to cover the bank's potential liability on the guaranty.[29] Federal regulations also provide that a national bank may guarantee financial obligations of a customer, subsidiary, or affiliate so long as "the amount of the bank's financial obligation is reasonably ascertainable and otherwise consistent with applicable law."[30] Furthermore, Regulation W of Title 12 of the Code of Federal Regulations, governing transactions between Federal Reserve member banks and their affiliates, considers a guaranty of the debt of an affiliate to be a "covered transaction," and limits the aggregate amount of such covered transactions which any member bank may enter into with affiliates.[31]

If an Ohio bank meets the federal requirements for a national bank to act as guarantor, then within certain limitations and upon meeting certain collateral requirements, Ohio law expressly authorizes this bank to issue guaranties to any person or company, but only on behalf of the bank's affiliates.[32] The following are considered affiliates of a bank: (i) a company that controls the bank and any other company controlled by the company that controls the bank; (ii) a bank subsidiary of the bank; a company that is controlled by shareholders who control the bank or any company that controls the bank; (iii) a company in which a majority of the directors or trustees constitute a majority of the directors or trustees of the bank or any company that controls the bank; (iv) a company that the bank or a subsidiary of the bank sponsors and advises on a contractual basis; (v) an investment company to which the bank or one of its affiliates is an investment advisor; and (vi) a company the superintendent of financial institutions determines to have a relationship with the bank or one of its subsidiaries or affiliates such that certain covered transactions by the bank or its subsidiary with that company may be affected by the relationship to the detriment of the bank or its subsidiary.[33] Any transaction a bank enters into with an affiliate or for the benefit of an affiliate must be on terms and conditions consistent with safe and sound banking practices.[34]

Ohio law requires banks to secure guaranties with collateral, the minimum value of which depends on the character of the collateral, as follows:

---

27. 12 U.S.C. § 1831a(a)(1) (2011).
28. 12 C.F.R. § 7.1017(a)(1) (2011).
29. 12 C.F.R. § 7.1017(a)(2) (2011).
30. 12 C.F.R. § 7.1017(b) (2011).
31. 12 C.F.R. §§ 22.3(h), 22.11-14 (2011).
32. Ohio Rev. Code Ann. § 1109.53 (D)(1)(e) (West 2011).
33. Ohio Rev. Code Ann. § 1109.53(A)(1) (West 2011).
34. Ohio Rev. Code Ann. § 1109.54(C) (West 2011).

- if the collateral is composed of obligations of the United States, obligations guaranteed by the United States, certain notes, drafts, bills of exchange, or bankers' acceptances as described in the Code, or an earmarked deposit account with the bank, then the value of the collateral securing the bank's guaranty must be 100 percent of the amount guaranteed;
- if the collateral is composed of obligations of any state or political subdivision thereof, then the value of the collateral securing the bank's guaranty must be 110 percent of the amount guaranteed;
- if the collateral is composed of other debt instruments, including receivables, then the value of the collateral securing the bank's guaranty must be 120 percent of the amount guaranteed; and
- if the collateral is composed of stock, leases, or other real or personal property, then the value of the collateral securing the bank's guaranty must be 130 percent of the amount guaranteed.[35]

Regardless of the type of collateral used, however, the aggregate amount of guaranties and other covered transactions by the bank with any particular affiliate cannot exceed 10 percent of the bank's capital, and the aggregate amount of covered transactions with all of the bank's affiliates cannot exceed 20 percent of the bank's capital.[36]

2.7 Mutual or Stock Insurance Companies

Mutual and stock insurance companies organized or admitted under Title XXXIX of the Ohio Revised Code are authorized to engage in financial guaranty or suretyship insurance transactions.[37] As a condition of issuance of a certificate of authority to engage in such transactions, stock insurance companies must have and maintain capital and surplus in an amount not less than $5 million, with paid-in capital not less than $1 million and contributed surplus not less than $1 million.[38] Insurance companies other than stock insurance companies must have and maintain surplus in an amount not less than $5 million.[39]

Insurance companies engaging in guaranty or suretyship transactions must also maintain reserves in at least an amount equal to the unearned portions of the gross premiums charged on unexpired policies, an amount estimated to be sufficient to provide for the ultimate payment of all losses or claims for which the company may be liable, and an amount that is estimated to provide for the expenses incurred in adjusting or settling such claims.[40] No stock insurance company may incur liability on a single risk in an amount greater than one-tenth of its paid-up capital and surplus, and no mutual insurance company may incur liability on a single risk in an amount greater than one-tenth of its surplus.[41] Furthermore, any company that is foreign to Ohio and engages in

35. Ohio Rev. Code Ann. § 1109.54(D) (West 2011).
36. Ohio Rev. Code Ann. § 1109.54(A) (West 2011).
37. 12 C.F.R. §§ 22.3(h), 22.11-14 (2011); Ohio Rev. Code Ann. § 3929.01 (West 2011).
38. Ohio Rev. Code Ann. § 3929.011(B)(1) (West 2011).
39. Ohio Rev. Code Ann. § 3929.011(B)(2) (West 2011).
40. Ohio Rev. Code Ann. § 3929.012(A) (West 2011).
41. Ohio Rev. Code Ann. § 3929.02(A) (West 2011).

guaranty or suretyship transactions under Title XXXIX must deposit $50,000 in U.S.or Ohio bonds for the benefit and security of all its policy holders with the superintendent of insurance.[42]

Companies in the business of guaranteeing the fidelity of persons holding places of public or private trust and the performance of contracts, other than insurance policies, have an additional requirement of depositing $200,000 in certain securities with the superintendent of insurance, to be held for the benefit and security of all the policyholders of the company.[43] Any company that acts as surety in such a transaction is estopped from denying its corporate power to assume such liability.[44]

§ 3 Signatory's Authority to Execute a Guaranty

The authority of the executor of a guaranty to bind the guarantor depends on the type of entity of the guarantor, the nature of the entity's business, the nature of the underlying obligation, and the content of the entity's governing documents.

3.1 Corporations

The directors of an Ohio corporation can exercise all the authority of a corporation, including the making of guaranties, unless the law, the articles of incorporation, or the code of regulations require shareholder authorization or action.[45] Section 1701.65 of the Ohio Revised Code specifically provides that a corporation's directors may authorize "any mortgage, pledge, or deed of trust of all or any of the property of the corporation of any description, or any interest therein, for the purpose of securing the payment or performance of any obligation or contract," without shareholder vote or consent, unless otherwise provided in the articles.[46] The directors have the authority to adopt bylaws that are not inconsistent with the articles or regulations, and may use these bylaws to limit the agency power of individual directors to enter into guaranty contracts.[47]

3.2 Partnerships

Under the Ohio Uniform Partnership Act, each partner is an agent of the partnership for the purpose of its business.[48] Every act of a partner that is apparently for the carrying on of the partnership business in the ordinary course, or for the carrying on of business of the kind in which the partnership

42. Ohio Rev. Code Ann. § 3929.01(B) (West 2011).
43. Ohio Rev. Code Ann. § 3929.10 (West 2011).
44. Ohio Rev. Code Ann. § 3929.13 (West 2011).
45. Ohio Rev. Code Ann. § 1701.59 (West 2011).
46. Ohio Rev. Code Ann. § 1701.65 (West 2011).
47. Ohio Rev. Code Ann. § 1701.59(A) (West 2011).
48. Ohio Rev. Code Ann. § 1776.31(A) (West 2011).

engages, will bind the partnership unless both of the following are true: (i) the partner had no authority to act for the partnership in that particular matter, and (ii) the person with whom the partner engaged in the unauthorized act had knowledge of or had received a notification of the partner's lack of authority.[49] A partner's act that does not apparently carry on the partnership business in the ordinary course, or business of the kind in which the partnership engages, does not bind the partnership unless authorized by either all of other partners, or the number or percentage of partners necessary to grant such authority as delineated in the partnership agreement.[50]

A guaranty made in the partnership's name for nonpartnership obligations generally does not constitute carrying on the partnership business in the ordinary course.[51] In such a transaction, usually no benefit to the partnership is present, a fact of which the third party is presumably aware. Because of this, a partner should usually obtain authorization from all the other partners, or the number or percentage of partners necessary to grant such authority as delineated in the partnership agreement, before executing a guaranty in the name of the partnership.[52] There are, however, some situations in which a guaranty is considered to be within the ordinary course of a partnership's business, and therefore binding on the partnership without authorization from the remaining partners, such as when the partnership may benefit in some way from the guaranty (e.g., the partnership is benefitted because it has an interest in the entity whose obligation is guaranteed).[53]

Ohio partnerships may file statements of partnership authority as a limited means of notifying third parties of grants of or limitations on a partner's authority. With regard to grants unrelated to the authority to transfer real property, such as a grant of authority to enter into guaranty contracts, a grant contained in a filed statement of partnership authority is conclusive in favor of anyone who gives value without knowledge to the contrary.[54] To protect third parties who generally are not expected to check such filings in transactions which do not involve the transfer of real property, a filed restriction on a partner's authority to enter into guaranty contracts is not deemed to give notice to a non-partner.[55]

3.3 Limited Liability Companies

Slight distinctions are made in Ohio law regarding the authority of managers or members of an Ohio LLC to enter into guaranty. In a member-managed LLC, much like in a partnership, every member is an agent of the company for the purpose of its business.[56] As such, every act of a member that is apparently for the carrying on of the business of the LLC in the usual way will bind

49. *Id.*
50. Ohio Rev. Code Ann. §§ 1776.03(A), 1776.31(B), 1776.41(J) (West 2011).
51. Alan R. Bromberg & Larry E. Ribstein, Bromberg & Ribstein on Partnership, § 4.03(b)(1) (Little, Brown ed. 2003).
52. Ohio Rev. Code Ann. § 1776.31(B) (West 2011).
53. Bromberg & Ribstein, *supra* note 52.
54. Ohio Rev. Code Ann. § 1776.33(D)(1) (West 2011).
55. Ohio Rev. Code Ann. § 1776.33(F) (West 2011).
56. Ohio Rev. Code Ann. § 1705.25(A)(1) (West 2011).

the LLC, unless both of the following are true: (i) the member had in fact no authority to act for the company in that particular matter, and (ii) the person with whom the member engaged in the unauthorized act had knowledge of the member's lack of authority.[57] A member's acts that are not apparently for the carrying on of the business of the LLC in the usual way do not bind the company, unless authorized by the other members.[58]

The law governing authority of a manager in a manager-managed LLC differs from that governing the authority of a member in a member-managed LLC in one significant way: the operating agreements of a manager-managed LLC may provide for different agency rules, while the statutorily prescribed agency rules are mandatory for a member-managed LLC.[59]

It should be further noted that in a member-managed Ohio LLC, unless authorized by all the other members, one or more, but fewer than all, of the members of a LLC have no authority to execute a confession of judgment provision.[60] In manager-managed Ohio LLCs, unless authorized by other members, or except as provided in the operating agreement, no manager has authority to execute a confession of judgment provision.[61]

3.4 Ohio Incorporated Banks

The board of directors of an Ohio bank can exercise all the authority of a bank, including the making of guaranties, unless the law, the articles of incorporation, or the regulations require shareholder authorization or action.[62] The directors have the authority to adopt bylaws that are not inconsistent with the articles or regulations, and may use these bylaws to limit the agency power of individual directors to enter into guaranty contracts.[63]

3.5 Mutual or Stock Insurance Companies

Any officer, director, or employee of a mutual or stock insurance company organized or admitted under Title XXXIX of the Ohio Revised Code is required to be licensed in accordance with Ohio Revised Code Chapter 3905 in order to sell, solicit, or negotiate insurance in Ohio,[64] which includes the execution of financial guaranty or suretyship contracts.[65] Applicants for licensure must take and pass a written examination.[66] In addition to this licensure requirement, each such signatory must also have the authority required to bind the

57. *Id.*
58. Ohio Rev. Code Ann. § 1701.25(A)(2) (West 2011).
59. *Compare* Ohio Rev. Code Ann. § 1705.25(A) (West 2011), with Ohio Rev. Code Ann. § 1705.25(B) (West 2011).
60. Ohio Rev. Code Ann. § 1705.25(A)(3)(d) (West 2011); *see* discussion of warrant of attorney clauses in Section 15.6, *infra*.
61. Ohio Rev. Code Ann. § 1705.25(B)(3) (West 2011).
62. Ohio Rev. Code Ann. § 1105.01 (West 2011).
63. Ohio Rev. Code Ann. § 1105.07 (West 2011).
64. Ohio Rev. Code Ann. §§ 3905.02, 3905.03 (West 2011).
65. Ohio Rev. Code Ann. §§ 3905.01(C), 3929.01(A) (West 2011).
66. Ohio Rev. Code Ann. § 3905.04 (West 2011).

insurance company, which will vary depending on the organization of the insurance company.

§ 4 Consideration

The consideration principles that are applied to guaranties are the same as those applied to contracts generally. Consideration is not required to be given to the promisor but may be paid to a third party. New consideration is required, however, to sustain a guaranty or suretyship that is entered for a previously contracted obligation.

4.1 Generally

A contract of guaranty requires consideration to be enforceable.[67] Consideration that is sufficient to support other kinds of contracts, such as the forbearance of a party's right to assert a legal claim against another, is sufficient to support a guaranty.[68] If a promise to forbear is used as consideration for the guaranty of a debt, some Ohio courts have held that the time period of forbearance must be definite and fixed,[69] while others have held that an agreement to forbear for a "reasonable time" is sufficient.[70] Consideration supporting the underlying obligation will also support the contract of guaranty if both contracts are entered into simultaneously.[71]

For consideration to exist, the guarantor need not derive any benefit from the undertaking; it does not matter to whom or from whom the consideration flows for purposes of contractual validity.[72]

4.2 Sufficiency of Past Consideration

Where a guaranty is issued to secure a previously contracted obligation, there must be new consideration between the parties to sustain it.[73] Although a guaranty may lack consideration as to past transactions or advances, it is binding and enforceable as to those past transactions if it is supported by consideration arising out of future transactions and advances.[74] Accordingly, a further extension of credit is adequate consideration for a contract binding a guarantor to pay a past indebtedness of the primary obligor.[75]

---

67. Zuckerman v. Gray, 2009-Ohio-1319, at ¶ 18; Warren Paint Co v. Swihart, 27 Ohio Cir. Dec. 283, 285 (1908).
68. Cahill v. Smith, 2 Ohio Dec. 156 (Ohio Ct. App. 1894); 52 Ohio Jurisprudence 3d (2007) 347, Guaranty and Suretyship, § 22.
69. Kellogg-Mackay Co. v. O'Neal, 177 N.E. 778 (Ohio Ct. App. 1931).
70. Banta v. Martin, 38 Ohio St. 534 (1882).
71. Toppan v. Cleveland, C. & C.R. Co., 24 F. Cas. 56 (N.D. Ohio 1862) (applying Ohio law); Medina Supply Co. v. Corrado, 689 N.E.2d at 600.
72. Zuckerman v. Gray, 2009-Ohio-1319, at ¶ 18 (quoting RESTATEMENT (SECOND) OF CONTRACTS (1981)); *Medina Supply Co.*, 689 N.E.2d 600, 604 (Ohio Ct. App. 1996); Cahill v. Smith, 2 Ohio Dec. 156 (Ohio Ct. App. 1894).
73. Toppan, 24 F. Cas. at 56; 52 Ohio Jurisprudence 3d (2007) 346, Guaranty and Suretyship, § 21.
74. Rawleigh Co. v. Fritz, 7 Ohio Law Abs. 452 (Ohio Ct. App. 1928).
75. *Medina Supply Co.*, 689 N.E.2d at 600; *Rawleigh Co.*, 7 Ohio Law Abs. at 452.

Ohio courts have not yet considered a case in which the parties anticipate the execution of a guaranty, but the guaranty is not signed until after the loan transaction is closed. Courts in other jurisdictions, however, have found that a guaranty is indeed founded on consideration where evidence exists that the underlying loan was made in anticipation of the guaranty and would not have been made but for the guarantor's undertaking.[76]

4.3 Fraudulent Transfers

Although consideration need not flow to the guarantor to be effective, creditors should be cautious to ensure that the undertakings of a guarantor are not deemed fraudulent transfers under bankruptcy or state law. For example, on May 15, 2012, the U.S. Court of Appeals for the Eleventh Circuit issued an opinion reinstating a widely criticized decision of the U.S. Bankruptcy Court for the Southern District of Florida in *In re TOUSA, Inc.,* which voided as fraudulent transfers the obligations of a debtor's subsidiaries under an upstream guaranty.[77] Both the Eleventh Circuit and the Bankruptcy Court found that the subsidiaries in question did not receive "reasonably equivalent value" in exchange for undertaking such obligations.[78] In 2011, the U.S. District Court for the Southern District of Florida had overruled the bankruptcy court's order, finding that the subsidiaries received "indirect economic benefits" constituting reasonably equivalent value.[79] The Eleventh Circuit, however, found that the Bankruptcy Court did not clearly err in making its factual conclusion that the subsidiaries did not receive reasonably equivalent value. There are no reported cases involving similar facts in Ohio, but parties entering into a guaranty transaction, especially one involving an upstream guaranty, should carefully assess the benefits to each party in the transaction to ensure that it will not constitute a fraudulent transfer.

§ 5 Notice of Acceptance

Notice of acceptance is generally not required, but it is necessary in the event of an offer to guaranty.

Although acceptance by both the guarantor and the obligee is required to create a valid guaranty, formal notice of the obligee's acceptance is generally not required for guaranties or suretyships.[80] If the guaranty is absolute and is acted on in accordance with its terms, no notice of the acceptance of the guar-

76. *See* United States v. Burgreen, 591 F.2d 291 (5th Cir. 1979); United States v. Lowell, 557 F.2d 70 (6th Cir.1977); United States v. Interlakes Machine & Tool Co., 400 F.Supp. 59 (E.D.Mich.1975); In re Estate of Tynan, 7 N.W.2d 628 (Neb. 1943). *See also* 38 Am.Jur.2d Guaranty § 45 (1968).
77. In re TOUSA, Inc., No. 11–11071 (11th Cir. May 15, 2012); In re TOUSA, Inc., 422 B.R. 783 (Bankr. S.D. Fla. 2009).
78. *Id.*
79. In re TOUSA, Inc., 444 B.R. 613 (S.D. Fla 2011).
80. Wise v. Miller, 14 N.E. 218 (Ohio 1887); Snyder v. Hurdley-Pierce-Anderson Co., 34 Ohio Cir. Dec. 424 (Ohio Ct. App. 1912); Gunther v. Pfaffman, 43 Ohio C.C. 43, (Ohio Ct. App. 1911), *aff'd* 106 N.E. 1072 (Ohio 1913).

anty or action on the guaranty is required,[81] even for a continuing guaranty.[82] Notice of acceptance is, however, necessary if the instrument is a mere offer or proposal to guaranty, rather than an absolute guaranty.[83]

The terms of a guaranty control whether an obligee must give notice of its acceptance, so a guarantor can make notice a condition of acceptance if so desired.[84] The more common practice, however, is for the guarantor to waive any requirement for notification of acceptance.[85]

§ 6 Interpretation of Guaranties

Ohio courts apply the same principles used to interpret contracts generally when interpreting contracts of guaranty. If the language of the contract is ambiguous, a gratuitous guaranty will be interpreted in the guarantor's favor, but a compensated guaranty will be interpreted against the surety and in favor of indemnity. Absent ambiguous language, courts will effectuate the intent of the parties as demonstrated by the plain language of the contract.

6.1 General Principles

The law of the jurisdiction in which the guaranty or suretyship was made governs the contract's nature, construction, and legal effect, regardless of where it is enforced.[86] Under Ohio law, the rules governing the interpretation of guaranties and suretyships are the same as those that govern the interpretation of contracts generally[87] and call for effectuating the parties' intentions as expressed in the contract of guaranty or suretyship.[88] The parties are presumed to have intended to contract in the manner in which they did contract, and the language in the contract should be given its ordinary meaning, taking into account the surrounding circumstances and object to be accomplished.[89] In interpreting the parties' intentions, the provisions of a guaranty must be construed together and in the proper context.[90]

81. *Wise*, 14 N.E. at 218; Birdsall v. Heacock, 32 Ohio St. 177, 179 (1877); Powers & Weightman v. Bumcratz, 12 Ohio St. 273 (1861); *Snyder*, 34 Ohio Cir. Dec. at 424; *Gunther*, 43 Ohio C.C. at 43.
82. Rochford v. Rothschild, 9 Ohio Cir. Dec. 47 (Ohio Ct. App. 1896).
83. *Wise*, 14 N.E. at 221.
84. 52 Ohio Jurisprudence 3d (2007) 342, Guaranty and Suretyship, § 18.
85. Restatement (Third) of Suretyship & Guaranty § 8 cmt. (2006).
86. Indem. Ins. Co. of N. America v. Stamberger Co., 174 N.E. 629 (Ohio Ct. App. 1930); St. Croix Mfg. Co. v. Aetna Cas. & Sur. Co., 6 Ohio L. Abs. 415 (Ohio Ct. App. 1928); 52 Ohio Jurisprudence 3d (2007) 376, Guaranty and Suretyship, § 48.
87. Parkway Bus. Plaza Ltd. P'ship v. Custom Zone, Inc., 2006-Ohio-5255at ¶ 15 (Ohio Ct. App.); Amerisourcebergen Drug Corp. v. Hallmark Pharmacies, Inc., 2006-Ohio-2746, at ¶ 12 (Ohio Ct. App.); G.F. Bus. Equip. v. Liston, 454 N.E.2d 1358 (Ohio Ct. App. 1982).
88. Shifrin v. Forest City Ent., Inc., 597 N.E.2d 499 (Ohio 1992), *syllabus*; Blosser v. Enderlin, 148 N.E. 393, 396 (Ohio 1925); *Parkway Bus. Plaza*, 2006-Ohio-5255; Liquidating Midland Bank v. Stecker, 179 N.E. 504 (Ohio Ct. App. 1930).
89. 52 Ohio Jurisprudence 3d (2007) 371, Guaranty and Suretyship, § 44 (citing Third Nat'l Bank of Cincinnati, Ohio v. Laidlaw, 98 N.E. 1015 (Ohio 1912) and Merchants' Nat'l Bank v. Cole, 93 N.E. 465 (Ohio 1910)).
90. Legler v. U.S. Fid. & Guar. Co., 103 N.E. 897 (Ohio 1913); Clark v. Bradley, 16 Ohio Law Abs. 670 (Ohio Ct. App. 1934).

If a contract is clear and unambiguous, the court may not go beyond the plain language of the contract to determine the parties' rights and obligations.[91] Unambiguous terms that limit the duration or subject matter of a guaranty or the obligation under a suretyship will not be extended by implication.[92]

If the language is ambiguous or uncertain, a guaranty will be interpreted in the guarantor's favor,[93] a departure from the normal rule of contract construction wherein a promise is construed against the promisor.[94] A guarantor may, however, lawfully agree that the contract be liberally interpreted in favor of the obligee.[95] In contrast, an ambiguous compensated suretyship contract will be interpreted against the surety and in favor of indemnity.[96]

6.2 Guaranty of Payment versus Guaranty of Collection

A guaranty of payment is an unconditional and absolute guaranty that does not depend on any condition or contingency in the contract other than the default of the primary obligor.[97] Accordingly, an obligee need not pursue its legal remedies against a primary obligor before suing a guarantor who has given a guaranty of payment.[98] Conversely, a guaranty of collection is a conditional guaranty, dependent upon the obligee's exhaustion of legal remedies against the primary obligor.[99]

Guaranties of payment exist when the guarantor agrees to become responsible for the payment or the language of the guaranty as a whole demonstrates the guarantor's intention to undertake an absolute guaranty; however, the use of the word "absolute" is not required.[100] Such unconditional guaranties are enforceable when the terms are clear and unambiguous.[101]

---

91. Wise v. Miller, 14 N.E. 218, 221 (Ohio 1887); George Banta Co., Inc. v. Huntington Nat'l Bank, No. 86AP-380, 1986 WL 13906, at *3 (Ohio Ct. App. Nov. 25, 1986).
92. Gholson v. Savin, 31 N.E.2d 858 (Ohio 1941); Jules P. Storm & Sons v. Blanchet, 165 N.E. 353 (Ohio 1929).
93. *Liquidating Midland Bank*, 179 N.E. at 519; Lakemore Plaza, Inc. v. Shoenterprise, 188 N.E.2d 203 (Ohio C.P. 1962).
94. Third Nat'l Bank of Cincinnati, Ohio v. Laidlaw, 98 N.E. 1015 (Ohio 1912).
95. Mott v. Fulton, 21 Ohio Law Abs. 366 (Ohio Ct. App. 1935), *aff'd*, 3 N.E.2d 404 (Ohio 1936); 52 Ohio Jurisprudence 3d (2007) 378, Guaranty and Suretyship, § 50.
96. Am. Guar. Co. v. Cliff Wood Coal & Supply Co., 155 N.E. 127 (Ohio 1926); Bryant v. Am. Bonding Co., 82 N.E. 960, 961 (Ohio 1907) (citing Supreme Catholic Knights of America v. Fid. & Cas. Co., 63 F. 48 (1894); Mechanics' Savings Bank & Trust Co. v. Guar. Co., 68 F. 459 (1805); and Cowles v. U. S. Fid. & Guar. Co., 72 P. 1032 (Wash. 1903)); 52 Ohio Jurisprudence 3d (2007) 380, Guaranty and Suretyship, § 52 (citing Cleveland Window Glass & Door Co. v. Nat'l Sur. Co., 161 N.E. 280 (Ohio 1928) and Kornhauser v. National Sur. Co., 150 N.E. 921 (Ohio 1926)).
97. Mihalca v. Malita, No. 19395, 2000 WL 372309, at *4 (Ohio Ct. App. Apr. 12, 2000); Buckeye Fed. Sav. & Loan Ass'n v. Olentangy Motel, No. 90AP-1409, 1991 WL 224486, at *2 (Ohio Ct. App. Aug. 22, 1991); Schottenstein v. Byers, No. 75AP-10, 1975 WL 181814, at *2 (Ohio Ct. App. Oct. 7, 1975).
98. *Mihalca*, 2000 WL 372309 at *4; Eden Realty Co. v. Weather-Seal, Inc., 142 N.E.2d 541 (Ohio 1957); Nesco Sales & Rental v. Superior Elec. Co., 2007-Ohio-844, at ¶ 14 (Ohio Ct. App.).
99. *Nesco*, 2007-Ohio-844 at ¶ 14; *Schottenstein*, 1975 WL 181814 at *2.
100. *Buckeye Federal Sav. & Loan*, 1991 WL 224486, at *2 (holding that the language of the contract, viewed objectively under the circumstances, manifested the intent to guarantee lease payments); George Banta Co., Inc. v. Huntington Nat'l Bank, No. 86AP-380, 1986 WL 13906, at *3 (Ohio Ct. App. Nov. 25, 1986); Snyder v. Hurdley-Pierce-Anderson Co., 34 Ohio Cir. Dec. 424 (Ohio Ct. App. 1912); Gunther v. Pfaffman, 43 Ohio C.C. 43 (Ohio Ct. App. 1911), *aff'd*, 106 N.E. 1072 (Ohio 1913).
101. O'Brien v. Ravenswood Apartments, Ltd., 2006-Ohio-5264 at ¶ 21, 862 N.E.2d 549, 555 (Ohio Ct. App. 2006), *appeal not allowed*, 2007-Ohio-724, 862 N.E.2d 118 (2007).

6.3 Language Regarding the Revocation of Guaranties

A guarantor may revoke a guaranty with sufficient notice, unless the guaranty was made either to cover a specific transaction that is not yet completed or was given as continuing consideration, the benefit of which the guarantor does not or cannot renounce.[102] A surety may revoke its suretyship if it has no definite time to run or if it does have such time but the primary obligor has violated the contract such that the surety may lawfully terminate it on account of the breach.[103]

A continuing guaranty can be effectively revoked only when the guarantor clearly communicates to the obligee, either by words or action, an intent to revoke and no longer be bound by the guaranty.[104] A guarantor who wishes to revoke its guaranty must do so pursuant to the express terms of the agreement, if such a provision exists,[105] and often the provisions of a guaranty provide that the guarantor will remain liable for the underlying obligation existing at the time of such revocation.

Revocation of a guaranty by any guarantor is commonly prescribed as an event of default in the loan documents evidencing the underlying obligation and in the guaranty itself.

6.4 Continuing Guaranties

A continuing guaranty is not limited in time or to a particular or specific transaction, but rather contemplates a future course of dealing that includes a series of transactions, and is effective until revoked.[106] A presumption exists against a continuing guaranty unless the agreement's language does not allow for any other construction.[107] A guaranty will be interpreted to continue indefinitely only if the parties' intentions are clearly manifested beyond a reasonable doubt.[108] If the language in a guaranty can be construed either as a continuing guaranty or a limited guaranty, the limiting construction will be adopted.[109]

---

102. Huntington Nat'l Bank of Columbus v. Symetics Group, Nos. 76AP-690 & 76AP-691, 1977 WL 199846 (Ohio Ct. App. Jan. 18, 1977); Nat'l Liberty Ins. Co. of America v. Meyer, 153 N.E. 162, 163 (Ohio Ct. App. 1926).
103. *Nat'l Liberty Ins. Co. of America*, 153 N.E. at 163.
104. Jae Co. v. Heitmeyer Builders, Inc., 2009-Ohio-2851 (Ohio Ct. App. 2009); *Huntington Nat'l Bank*, 1977 WL 199846, at *2.
105. Cascade Indus., Inc. v. Metro Pools, Inc., No. 41552, 1980 WL 355104, at *3 (Ohio Ct. App. Jun. 19, 1980); *Jae Co.*, 2009 WL 1682005, at *3.
106. Merchants' Nat'l Bank v. Cole, 93 N.E. 465 (Ohio 1910); Beatley v. Izzo, 2009-Ohio-3245 (Ohio Ct. App. 2009); Jae Co. v. Heitmeyer Builders, Inc., 2009-Ohio-2851 at *3 (Ohio Ct. App. 2009); *Huntington Natl. Bank*, 1977 WL 199845, at *2.
107. *Beatley*, 2009 WL 1910960, at *2; Yearling Prop., Inc. v. Tedder, 557 N.E.2d 1231 (Ohio Ct. App. 1988); United Excavating Co. v. Hartford Accident & Indem. Co., No. 78 CA 19, 1978 WL 214856, at *2 (Ohio Ct. App. Mar. 6, 1978); Birdsall v. Heacock, 32 Ohio St. 177 (1877).
108. *Beatley*, 2009 WL 1910960 at *2.
109. *Beatley*, 2009 WL 1910960 at *2; Security Dollar Bank v. J.C. Holding Corp., Inc., No. 94-T-5115, 1995 WL 787454, at *3 (Ohio Ct. App. Sept. 8, 1995).

6.5 Uncompensated Guarantor versus Compensated Surety

In the case of ambiguity, a guaranty will be strictly construed in an uncompensated guarantor's favor,[110] because a guarantor is held only according to the exact terms of its obligation as expressed in the contract.[111] In contrast, compensated suretyships, such as those given to bond public officials in exchange for premium payments, are construed under insurance laws or according to the rules applicable to insurance contracts.[112] If a clause in a compensated suretyship contract can be fairly interpreted in more than one way, it should be interpreted in a manner that affords the greatest indemnity, is most favorable to the beneficiary, and is least favorable to the surety.[113] In either case, however, the interpretation should be consistent with the guaranty's or suretyship's purpose and effectuate the intention of the parties as expressed in the guaranty's or suretyship's language.[114]

§ 7 Defenses of the Guarantor; Set-off

The defenses that may be available to a guarantor fall into three main categories: (1) defenses of the primary obligor, (2) "suretyship" defenses, and (3) other defenses. A right of set-off against its obligation to the obligee is also available to a guarantor that has a valid claim against the obligee arising out of the guaranty. Provisions containing waivers of suretyship defenses are frequently included in guaranties of commercial loans, as discussed in Section 8 below.

7.1 Defenses of the Primary Obligor

7.1.1 When the Guarantor May Assert the Primary Obligor's Defense

In defending a claim based on the underlying obligation, a guarantor may assert all nonpersonal defenses that are available to the primary obligor so long as the guarantor has not waived its right to do so.[115]

Because a guaranty is ancillary to the underlying obligation and a suretyship is a dependent obligation accessory to the underlying obligation,[116] if

110. First Nat'l Bank of Van Wert v. Houtzer, 117 N.E. 383 (Ohio 1917); Bryant v. Am. Bonding Co., 82 N.E. 960 (Ohio 1907).
111. Black v. Alvery, 106 N.E. 38 (Ohio 1914).
112. Nat'l Sur. Corp. v. Seward, 165 N.E. 588 (Ohio 1929); *Bryant,* 82 N.E. at 960.
113. Am. Guar. Co. v. Cliff Wood Coal & Supply Co., 155 N.E. 127 (Ohio 1926); *Bryant,* 82 N.E. at 961 (citing Supreme Catholic Knights of America v. Fid. & Cas. Co., 63 F. 48 (1894); Mechanics' Savings Bank & Trust Co. v. Guar. Co., 68 F. 459 (1805); and Cowles v. U. S. Fid. & Guar. Co., 72 P. 1032 (Wash. 1903)); 52 Ohio Jurisprudence 3d (2007) 380, Guaranty and Suretyship, § 52 (citing Cleveland Window Glass & Door Co. v. Nat'l Sur. Co., 161 N.E. 280 (Ohio 1928) and Kornhauser v. National Sur. Co., 150 N.E. 921 (Ohio 1926)).
114. *Cleveland Window Glass & Door*, 161 N.E. at 280; *Kornhauser*, 150 N.E.at 921.
115. State v. Kuhner, 140 N.E. 344 (Ohio 1923); O'Brien v. Ravenswood Apts., Ltd., 2006-Ohio-5264 at ¶ 21, 862 N.E.2d 549 (Ohio Ct. App. 2006), *appeal not allowed*, 2007-Ohio-724, 862 N.E.2d 118 (2007); Mut. Fin. Co. v. Politzer, 256 N.E.2d 606 (Ohio 1970); 52 Ohio Jurisprudence 3d (2007) 479, Guaranty and Suretyship, § 134.
116. Huntington & McIntyre v. W. M. Finch & Co., 3 Ohio St. 445 (1854).

the principal contract is invalid, void, or illegal, a defense is available to the enforcement of the guaranty or suretyship.[117] For example, if the underlying contract supporting a guaranty is void for lack of consideration, the guaranty is unenforceable unless the guarantor has waived its right to assert such defense.[118]

Contrary to the law of some other states, the Ohio Supreme Court has found it permissible for a surety to plead duress of the primary obligor as a defense to the enforcement of its suretyship.[119] This decision was rendered despite the principle that a guaranty of performance is enforceable if the underlying contract is merely voidable at the election of its makers (as discussed in Section 7.1.2. below).

A guarantor may assert the defense that the underlying contract is usurious, but usury will invalidate the contract only to the extent of the usurious excess of interest, and will not void a contract of suretyship beyond the extent to which it is impaired as to the primary obligor.[120]

7.1.2 Defenses of the Primary Obligor not Available to the Guarantor

Guarantors may not raise personal defenses of the primary obligor, nor may they raise defenses that render the underlying contract merely voidable.[121] Personal defenses include the personal incapacity or insolvency of the primary obligor and the obligee's breach of warranty.[122] Authority is mixed in other states regarding whether fraud in the inducement of the primary obligor to enter into the underlying contract is a personal defense of the primary obligor or whether it may be raised as a defense by a surety, and Ohio courts have not yet considered the issue.[123]

7.2 "Suretyship" Defenses

As a general principle, unless the guarantor waives its suretyship defenses in the guaranty, if the obligee and primary obligor make a material change in the terms of the underlying contract without the consent of the guarantor, it will discharge the guarantor's liability.[124] To avoid the results of this default rule, obligees frequently require guarantors to waive suretyship defenses in guaranties of commercial loans. As discussed in Section 8 below, case law in many states, including Ohio, upholds the contractual waiver of such suretyship defenses.

---

117. State v. Kuhner, 140 N.E. at 348; S. Sur. Co. v. Moores-Coney Co., 163 N.E. 575, 576 (Ohio Ct. App. 1928); Zerkle v. Price, 5 Ohio N.P. 480 (C.P. 1898).
118. Sherwin & Co. v. Brigham, 39 Ohio St. 137 (1883).
119. Zerkle v. Price, 5 Ohio N.P. 480 (C.P. 1898); Hyatt v. Robinson, 15 Ohio 372 (1846).
120. First Nat'l Bank of Columbus v. Garlinghouse, 22 Ohio St. 492 (1872); 52 Ohio Jurisprudence 3d (2007) 492, Guaranty and Suretyship, § 145. *See also* Russell v. Failor, 1 Ohio St. 327 (1853); Preble Cnty. Bank v. Russell, 1 Ohio St. 313 (1853).
121. *Zerkle*, 5 Ohio N.P. 480.
122. 52 Ohio Jurisprudence 3d (2007) 489, Guaranty and Suretyship, § 142; 38 Am. Jur. 2d, Guaranty § 50 (1999).
123. 52 Ohio Jurisprudence 3d (2007) 490, Guaranty and Suretyship, § 143.
124. Iddings v. Kerr, 44 N.E. 139 (1895); 52 Ohio Jurisprudence 3d (2007) 424, Guaranty and Suretyship, § 87.

7.2.1 Release of Primary Obligor, Coguarantor, or Cosurety

Ohio courts have held that a release of liability that precludes the obligee from proceeding against the primary obligor will also extinguish the liability of a surety or guarantor;[125] but a contract of guaranty providing that the continuing liability of a guarantor is unaffected by settlement will be effective despite the common law rule.[126]

Similarly, if the obligee releases one coguarantor or cosurety, unless the others have waived their suretyship defenses, they will be discharged from their liability to the extent of the released obligor's proportionate part of the obligation, as determined from the amount of the obligation and the number of cosureties.[127]

An Ohio statutory provision, effective in August 2008, provides an overlay on these common law rules. Section 2307.30 of the Ohio Revised Code provides that if a joint debtor makes a separate composition or compromise with a creditor, it will discharge that debtor, but shall not discharge, or impair the right of the creditor to proceed against, other joint debtors.[128] Coguarantors and cosureties that have a common liability on the same obligation may be considered joint debtors with one another under this statute, in contrast to a primary obligor and its guarantor, which do not share joint liability.[129] Ohio courts have not yet considered the effect of this statute in the context of coguarantor or cosurety liability, but an obligee may argue that its compromise with one guarantor does not discharge the obligation of the other guarantors. The statute provides, however, that the discharge of the debtor is deemed a payment to the creditor equal to the proportionate liability of the discharged debtor.[130] Consequently, such a deemed payment should discharge the obligation of the other joint debtors to the extent of the released debtor's ratable portion of the debt, leading to the same result as would occur under the common law rule. The statute provides, furthermore, that a separate composition or compromise with one joint debtor does not affect any right the other joint debtors may have against the discharged debtor for contribution or reimbursement.[131]

7.2.2 Modification of Identity of Primary Obligor

A change of the primary obligor generally constitutes a material change in the underlying obligation, which will discharge from liability a guarantor or surety that has not waived its suretyship defenses.[132] This principle includes the substitution of a new party for the primary obligor by novation[133] or the addition of a primary obligor, such as a comaker, after the guarantor or surety

125. Banana Sales Corp. v. Chuchanis, 162 N.E. 274 (Ohio 1928); Ide v. Churchill, 14 Ohio St. 372 (1863).
126. New Market Acquisitions, Ltd. v. Powerhouse Gym, 154 F. Supp.2d 1213 (S.D. Ohio 2001).
127. Walsh v. Miller, 38 N.E. 381 (1894); 52 Ohio Jurisprudence 3d (2007) 544, Guaranty and Suretyship, § 195.
128. Ohio Rev. Code Ann. § 2307.30(B) (West 2011).
129. Deming v. Bd. of Trustees of Ohio Agric. & Mech. Coll., 31 Ohio St. 41 (1876); Denton v. Whitney, 31 Ohio St. 89 (1876).
130. Ohio Rev. Code Ann. § 2307.30(C) (West 2011).
131. Ohio Rev. Code Ann. § 2307.30(D) (West 2011).
132. 52 Ohio Jurisprudence 3d (2007) 467, Guaranty and Suretyship, § 123.
133. People's Ins. Co. v. McDonnell, 41 Ohio St. 650 (1885).

has signed the contract.[134] Unless the death of the primary obligor or extinction of a corporate primary obligor makes the performance of the contract impossible, it will not discharge the liability of a guarantor or surety.[135]

7.2.3 Modification of the Underlying Obligation

If an underlying contract is materially changed without the consent of a guarantor or surety that has not waived its suretyship defenses, the guarantor or surety will be discharged from liability.[136] Generally, a change is material if it changes the nature of the contract or the significance of the surety's obligation or if it puts the surety in a different position than it was in before the change was made.[137] Although a showing of injury to an uncompensated guarantor or surety is not necessary to discharge liability upon a modification of the underlying contract,[138] such an injury is required to discharge the obligations of a compensated guarantor or paid surety.[139]

Ohio law has held that some types of modifications discharge the liability of the guarantor or surety, including a change in the amount of the principal sum of the obligation,[140] a change from a consignment contract to a contract of absolute sale,[141] and the agreement between the obligee and primary obligor to change the time for performance of the underlying obligation[142] (although a reasonable extension of time will not release a compensated surety company from liability[143]). The execution of a novation[144] or the unauthorized substitution of a new agreement for the one the performance of which the surety or guarantor guaranteed[145] will likewise discharge the surety or guarantor from liability, unless the surety or guarantor consents to the alteration or substitution. A mere change in collection methods, however, as opposed to a change in terms of credit, will not discharge the guarantor or surety.[146]

The rescission of a modification which discharges the guarantor's or surety's liability will not restore that liability,[147] even if the obligee brings suit upon the underlying instrument in its original form.[148]

---

134. Wallace v. Jewell, 21 Ohio St. 163, 1871 WL 45 (Ohio); 52 Ohio Jurisprudence 3d (2007) 467, Guaranty and Suretyship, § 123; 3 Ohio Jurisprudence 3d (2007) 544, Alteration of Instruments, § 29.
135. Moore v. Gray, 26 Ohio St. 525 (1875); Eden Realty Co. v. Weather-Seal, Inc., 142 N.E.2d 541 (Ohio Ct. App. 1957). *See also* London & Lancashire Indem. Co. of America v. Board of Com'rs of Columbiana Cnty., 140 N.E. 672 (Ohio 1923).
136. Iddings v. Kerr, 44 N.E. 1139 (1895); 52 Ohio Jurisprudence 3d (2007) 424, Guaranty and Suretyship § 87.
137. 52 Ohio Jurisprudence 3d (2007) 429, Guaranty and Suretyship, § 90.
138. Ide v. Churchill, 14 Ohio St. 372 (1863); Sturges v. Williams, 9 Ohio St. 443 (1859); Clinton Bank of Columbus *ex rel.* Rhodes v. Ayres & Neil, 16 Ohio 282 (1847).
139. Van Wert Nat'l Bank v. Roos, 17 N.E.2d 651 (Ohio 1938); *London & Lancashire Indem. Co.*, 140 N.E. at 672.
140. Portage Cnty. Branch Bank v. Lane, 8 Ohio St. 405 (1858); 52 Ohio Jurisprudence 3d (2007) 430, Guaranty and Suretyship § 92.
141. Poss v. Scholss Bros. & Co., 11 Ohio Law Abs. 196 (Ohio Ct. App. 1931).
142. Hoffmaster v. Junkin, 3 F.2d 220 (6th Cir. 1925); Cambria Iron Co. v. Keynes, 47 N.E. 548 (Ohio 1897).
143. 52 Ohio Jurisprudence 3d (2007) 433, Guaranty and Suretyship, § 94 (citing Am. Fid. Co. v. Metro. Paving Brick Co., 35 Ohio Cir. Dec. 662 (Ohio Ct. App. 1919)).
144. Ridenour v. Haynes, 11 Ohio Law Abs. 131 (Ohio Ct. App. 1931).
145. Bakers' Union of Cincinnati v. Streuve, 3 Ohio Dec. Reprint 110 (Ohio Super. Ct. 1859).
146. Burnside Steel Foundry Co. v. Gen. Metal Prod. Corp., 184 N.E.2d 469 (Ohio Ct. App. 1961).
147. Thompson v. Massie, 41 Ohio St. 307 (1884).
148. McAlpin v. Clark, 11 Ohio C.C. 524 (1896), *aff'd by*, 49 N.E. 1112 (1897).

7.2.4 *Release or Impairment of Security for the Underlying Obligation*

An obligee's release or impairment of collateral or any other security for the payment of the underlying obligation will discharge the liability of the guarantor or surety to the extent of the value of the security impaired, unless the guarantor or surety has consented or has waived its suretyship defenses.[149] The obligee must have had actual power of possession over the released or impaired collateral prior to its relinquishment for this defense of the guarantor or surety to be effective.[150]

7.3 Other Defenses

Guarantors may assert defenses to the enforceability of their guaranties that are generally available in contract actions, such as lack of consideration or other defects in the formation of the guaranty contract, failure to fulfill the conditions of a conditional guaranty or the terms of an absolute guaranty, and the discharge or release of the guarantor from liability.[151]

7.3.1 *Failure to Fulfill a Condition Precedent*

As in any contract action, a guarantor or surety may raise the defense of failure to fulfill a condition precedent to the guarantor or surety's liability. An obligee has no cause of action against a guarantor unless and until the primary obligor breaches the underlying contract, and no right of action against the guarantor can arise prior to the existence of a right against the primary obligor.[152] Some common conditions precedent to liability under a guaranty include the breach of the underlying contract in an absolute guaranty, the pursuit of the primary obligor on a conditional guaranty of collection (see Section 7.3.3 below), or other conditions that may exist in the contract evidencing the underlying obligation.

7.3.2 *Modification of the Guaranty*

Any modification of the contract of guaranty must be supported by both mutual consent and consideration of the parties thereto.[153] Because the guarantor must consent to any modification of the guaranty contract for such modification to be effective, the guarantor may not raise the modification of the guaranty contract as a defense to its enforcement.

---

149. HCRI TRS Acquirer, LLC v. Iwer, 708 F. Supp.2d 687 (N.D. Ohio 2010) (applying Ohio law); Dolak v. City Trust & Sav. Bank, 21 Ohio Law Abs. 409 (Ohio Ct. App. 1936); Woolworth v. Brinker, 11 Ohio St. 593 (1860); 52 Ohio Jurisprudence 3d (2007) 454, Guaranty and Suretyship, § 112.
150. *Woolworth*, 11 Ohio St. at 593.
151. 52 Ohio Jurisprudence 3d (2007) 478, Guaranty and Suretyship, § 134.
152. 52 Ohio Jurisprudence 3d (2007) 519, Guaranty and Suretyship, § 172.
153. GenCorp, Inc. v. American Int'l. Underwriters, 178 F.3d 804 (6th Cir. 1999).

7.3.3 Common Law Failure to Pursue Primary Obligor (Conditional Guaranties)

If the contract of guaranty is a conditional guaranty of collection, an obligee must exhaust all remedies against the primary obligor[154] and the collateral security[155] before bringing a suit against the conditional guarantor. Accordingly, a conditional guarantor may raise, as a defense, any failure on the part of the obligee to pursue the primary obligor or collateral before bringing suit on the guaranty.

In contrast to guaranties of collection, absolute guaranties of payment and surety contracts are unconditional; thus the obligee's failure to sue the primary obligor before bringing an action against the surety or absolute guarantor is typically not a defense to the enforcement of the guaranty.[156] Under Ohio common law, however, guarantors[157] and sureties[158] have the right to request that an obligee commence proceedings against the primary obligor without delay. Unless the primary obligor is insolvent at the time such a request is made,[159] the failure of the obligee to pursue a remedy against the primary obligor without delay will discharge the guarantor or surety.[160]

7.3.4 Statutory Failure to Pursue Primary Obligor (Suretyships)

Separate from the common law rule, Section 1341.04 of the Ohio Revised Code provides that a surety that is bound "in a written instrument for the payment of money or other valuable thing," on which a right of action has accrued, has the right to require its obligee to bring an action against the primary obligor, by notice in writing, "to commence an action on such instrument forthwith against the principal debtor."[161] If a surety provides written notice of such a requirement to its obligee and the obligee fails to comply, the obligee forfeits the right it would otherwise have to demand and receive from the surety the amount due.[162] Such notice must contain an unconditional requirement to bring suit "forthwith" on the instrument on which the surety is bound.[163] Unlike the

---

154. 52 Ohio Jurisprudence 3d (2007) 517, Guaranty and Suretyship, § 170 (citing Lakemore Plaza, Inc. v. Shoenterprise, 188 N.E.2d 203 (Ohio C.P. 1962)).
155. 52 Ohio Jurisprudence 3d (2007) 517, Guaranty and Suretyship, § 170; 38 Am. Jur. 2d, Guaranty § 108 (1999).
156. Mihalca v. Malita, No. 19395, 2000 WL 372309, at *4 (Ohio Ct. App. Apr. 12, 2000); Eden Realty Co. v. Weather-Seal, Inc., 142 N.E.2d 541 (Ohio 1957); Nesco Sales & Rental v. Superior Elec. Co., 2007-Ohio-844, at ¶ 14 (Ohio Ct. App.); 52 Ohio Jurisprudence 3d (2007) 518, Guaranty and Suretyship, § 171 (citing Vilas v. Christopher, 8 Ohio Law Abs 521 (Ohio Ct. App. 1930)).
157. 52 Ohio Jurisprudence 3d (2007) 442, Guaranty and Suretyship, § 103 (citing Jones v. Turner, 6 Ohio Dec. Reprint 1059, 8 Ohio Dec. Reprint 194 (Ohio Super. Ct. 1881)).
158. Bank of Steubenville v. Leavitt, 5 Ohio 207 (1831); 52 Ohio Jurisprudence 3d (2007) 442, Guaranty and Suretyship, § 103.
159. Equitable Nat'l Bank v. Morrison, 5 Ohio N.P. 290 (Super Ct. 1898), *aff'd by* 6 Ohio N.P. 7, *aff'd by* 61 N.E. 1146 (1901).
160. *Bank of Steubenville*, 5 Ohio at 207.
161. Ohio Rev. Code Ann. § 1341.04 (West 2011); Clark v. Osborn, 41 Ohio St. 28 (1884). *See also* Ohio Rev. Code Ann. § 1341.05 (West 2011) (providing parallel rights to executors and administrators of a surety).
162. Ohio Rev. Code Ann. § 1341.04 (West 2011).
163. Porter v. First Nat'l Bank, 43 N.E. 165 (1896); *Clark*, 41 Ohio St. at 28 (1884); Baker v. Kellogg, 29 Ohio St. 663 (1876).

common law rule, the statute requires that an obligee diligently prosecute the action regardless of whether the primary obligor is solvent or insolvent.[164]

The statute does not apply to guarantors,[165] only to sureties that appear on the same instrument under which the primary obligor is liable.[166] In addition, sureties on "bonds required by law to be given by guardians, executors, administrators, trustees of an express trust, public officers, or any bond or undertaking required by law to be given in an action or legal proceeding in any court of this state," have no such right to require the obligee to commence an action against the primary obligor.[167]

7.3.5 Statute of Limitations

Effective September 28, 2012, an obligee must bring an action arising under a guaranty within eight years after the accrual of the action.[168] The statute of limitations begins to run with respect to the obligations of the guarantor only upon the occurrence of all conditions to liability.[169] Accordingly, on absolute guaranties of payment, the statute of limitations begins to run upon the primary obligor's default,[170] and on guaranties of collection, the statute of limitations does not begin to run until the obligee has exhausted its legal remedies against the primary obligor. Some Ohio cases have held that a guarantor cannot successfully assert the defense of laches, or delay by the obligee in enforcing a claim, provided that such action is brought within the statutory period.[171]

7.3.6 Statute of Frauds

Guaranty and suretyship contracts are governed by the statute of frauds, which requires they be in writing and be signed by the party to be charged.[172] Additionally, no claim can be brought on any commercial loan agreement for a loan over $40,000 between a financial institution and a debtor unless the agreement is in writing and signed by the party against whom action is brought, or signed by the debtor and accepted by the financial institution.[173] Therefore, the absence of a guarantor's signature on the guaranty contract, or the absence of a surety's signature on a suretyship contract or underlying contract, is a defense to that guarantor or surety.[174] Case law in Ohio has held

---

164. Meriden Silver Plate Co. v. Flory, 7 N.E. 753, 756 (Ohio 1886).
165. Ohio Sav. Ass'n v. Cortell, 495 N.E.2d 33 (Ohio Ct. App. 1985), *disapproved of on other grounds by* Shore West Constr. Co. v. Sroka, 572 N.E.2d 646 (1991); Galloway v. Barnesville Loan, 57 N.E.2d 337 (Ohio Ct. App. 1943).
166. 52 Ohio Jurisprudence 3d (2007) 474, Guaranty and Suretyship § 130 (citing Equitable Nat'l Bank v. Morrison, 7 5 Ohio N.P. 290 (Super Ct. 1898), *aff'd by* 6 Ohio N.P. 7, *aff'd by* 61 N.E. 1146 (1901) (discussing Ohio Rev. Stat § 5833 (1892), a predecessor to OHIO REV. CODE ANN. § 1341.04 (West 2011)).
167. OHIO REV. CODE ANN. § 1341.06 (West 2011).
168. OHIO REV. CODE ANN. § 2305.06 (West 2011); *see also* Ohio Law Highlights, *supra.*
169. W. Strawboard Co. v. Variety Iron Works Co., 42 Ohio C.C. 112 (Ohio Ct. App. 1910), *aff'd*, 102 N.E. 1134 (Ohio 1912); 52 Ohio Jurisprudence 3d (2007) 482, Guaranty and Suretyship, § 136.
170. 52 Ohio Jurisprudence 3d (2007) 482, Guaranty and Suretyship, § 137.
171. Moore v. Gray, 26 Ohio St. 525 (1875); 52 Ohio Jurisprudence 3d (2007) 483, Guaranty and Suretyship, § 137.
172. OHIO REV. CODE ANN. § 1335.05 (West 2011).
173. OHIO REV. CODE ANN. § 1335.02(B) (West 2011); *see also*, Ohio Law Highlights, *supra.*
174. Richardson v. People's Nat'l Bank, 48 N.E. 1100 (1897).

that this defense is available only if the primary object of the guarantor or surety is to answer for another's debt. A guarantor or surety whose primary object was to serve its own business or pecuniary interests thus cannot assert this defense.[175]

7.3.7 Defenses Particular to Guarantors that are Natural Persons and their Spouses

Neither Ohio statutory law nor Ohio case law sets forth any defenses particular to guarantors that are natural persons and their spouses.

7.4 Right of Set-off

When sued under Ohio law by an obligee on a contract of guaranty, a guarantor that has not waived its right to do so may set off against that obligee any valid claim arising from the guaranty, but not a claim arising from any other transaction.[176] If, however, the parties' mutual demands against one another have been liquidated by judgment or decree, such judgments may be equitably set off upon summary application by motion, regardless from which transactions they arose.[177]

If a guarantor pays the debt of a primary obligor after the primary obligor has become insolvent and a receiver has been appointed, and the receiver partially reimburses the guarantor, the guarantor cannot set off the unreimbursed amount against an unrelated claim brought against the guarantor by the primary obligor.[178]

As a general rule, setoff rights apply only to mutual debts, and a joint debt and an individual debt cannot be set off against one another.[179] An individual debt due from the obligee to the primary obligor alone (and not to the guarantor), however, may be set off against a debt due from both primary obligor and guarantor to the obligee.[180] This principle holds that despite their joint liability, the character of the debt which the primary obligor and guarantor owe is really a joint undertaking for the primary obligor's separate debt.[181]

§ 8 Waiver of Defenses by the Guarantor

No Ohio cases have limited the ability of a guarantor or surety to contractually waive any suretyship defenses, and many cases have enforced such

175. Wilson Floors Co. v. Sciota Park, Ltd., 377 N.E.2d 514 (1978).
176. 38A C.J.S. *Guaranty* § 104 (1996); 52 Ohio Jurisprudence 3d (2001) 485, Guaranty and Suretyship, § 140.
177. Barbour v. Nat'l Exch. Bank of Tiffin, 33 N.E. 542, 543-544 (Ohio 1893).
178. Pugh v. Conklin, 184 N.E. 847 (Ohio Ct. App. 1932).
179. Wagner v. Stocking, 22 Ohio St. 297 (1872).
180. *Id.*
181. *Id.*

waivers.[182] Such a waiver should be interpreted according to the plain meaning of its language.[183] In the case of ambiguity, a waiver in the contract of a compensated surety will be construed strongly against the surety and in favor of the person seeking indemnity.[184] In contrast, a waiver in the contract of a gratuitous guarantor will be construed in the guarantor's favor.[185] A waiver of available defenses by some coguarantors will not waive the defenses of another coguarantor that did not execute an instrument waiving its defenses.[186] A guarantor may even waive certain defenses of the primary obligor that the primary obligor is statutorily forbidden from waiving, provided that the statute forbidding the waiver was designed to protect the primary obligor and not the guarantor.[187]

In commercial guaranties, guarantors routinely waive the right to assert defenses arising from any and all of the following: invalidity in or unenforceability of the underlying obligation or any security therefor; lack of notice of acceptance; failure of the obligee to pursue the primary obligor; failure of the obligee to pursue collateral, security, or other guarantors; reduction, amendment, or extinguishment and subsequent increase or reinstatement of the underlying obligation; lack of presentment, demand, protest, notice of protest and notice of dishonor or other nonpayment of the underlying obligation; lack of notice of sale or other disposition of any collateral or security; extension of time or any other indulgence granted by the obligee to the primary obligor or guarantor; omission or delay on the obligee's part in exercising any right against the primary obligor or guarantor; and release, substitution, or modification of any collateral, security, or other guaranties. In addition, guarantors are also commonly required to waive or subordinate their rights of subrogation and contribution until such time as the underlying obligation is indefeasibly paid in full.

The voluntary payment of an obligation by a guarantor, with knowledge of all the facts that would constitute a valid defense against the claim by the guarantor or primary obligor, will waive the defense and estop the guarantor from enforcing its right of reimbursement against the primary obligor.[188]

§ 9 Third-party Pledgors

A third party pledgor has the position of a surety, and if pledged property is taken to satisfy the underlying debt, the pledgor is subrogated to the right of the obligee.

182. HCRI TRS Acquirer, LLC v. Iwer, 708 F. Supp. 2d 687 (N.D. Ohio 2010); O'Brien v. Ravenswood Apartments, Ltd., 862 N.E.2d 549 (Ohio Ct. App. 2006). *See also* Buckeye Fed. Sav. & Loan Assn. v. Guirlinger, 581 N.E.2d 1352 (Ohio 1991).
183. *HCRI TRS Acquirer,* 708 F. Supp.2d 687. *See also* Wise v. Miller, 14 N.E. 218, 221 (Ohio 1887).
184. *HCRI TRS Acquirer*, 708 F. Supp.2d 687.
185. Liquidating Midland Bank v. Stecker, 179 N.E. 504, 519 (Ohio Ct. App. 1930); Lakemore Plaza, Inc. v. Shoenterprise, 188 N.E.2d 203 (Ohio C.P. 1962).
186. Mut. Fin. Co. v. Politzer, 256 N.E.2d 606 (Ohio 1970).
187. *Id.*
188. *Id*; Hoiles v. Fid. & Deposit Co. of MD, 18 Ohio App. 332 (Ohio Ct. App. 1923).

If a third party pledges or mortgages property to secure another's debt, the property so pledged occupies the position of a surety or guarantor.[189] If the obligee then takes the pledged property to satisfy the primary obligor's obligation, the pledgor is subrogated to the right of the obligee in the collateral security[190] and has a right to indemnity from the primary obligor.[191]

§ 10 Jointly and Severally Liable Coguarantors—Contribution and Reduction of Obligations Upon Payment by a Co-Obligor

Jointly and severally liable coguarantors and cosureties enjoy the right of contribution among themselves to equalize their obligation proportionately.

Coguarantors[192] and cosureties[193] that are jointly and severally liable on the same obligation are each liable for the full amount guaranteed. Accordingly, an obligee may enforce the entire obligation against any one such coguarantor or cosurety and recover and collect the full amount without taking a pro rata judgment against each,[194] in which case such coguarantor or cosurety may bring a contribution action to recover against the others.

10.1 Contribution

Cosureties[195] and coguarantors[196] have the right to contribution, that is, to the proportionate balancing of the obligation among the number of persons who have incurred it.[197] This right is an equitable right, not founded in the suretyship contract[198] or any supposed promise,[199] but rather based on the principle that "where the parties stand in *equali jure*, equity will require that the discharge from the common liability which inures to the benefit of all shall be obtained at their equal expense."[200] To be considered a cosurety or coguarantor with another party, both parties must have a common liability on the same obligation,[201] although it is not essential that they be bound on the same instrument, at the same time, or to the same extent as one another.[202]

---

189. Schuermann v. Twachtman, 27 Ohio Cir. Dec. 273 (Ohio Ct. App. 1916).
190. Advance Thresher Co. v. Hogan, 78 N.E. 436 (1906); Dolak v. City Trust & Sav. Bank, 21 Ohio Law Abs. 409 (Ohio Ct. App. 1936).
191. *Schuermann*, 27 Ohio Cir. Dec. at 273.
192. Wilson v. Rose Clare Lead & Spar Co., 7 Ohio Dec. Reprint 223 (Ohio C.P. 1876).
193. Walsh v. Miller, 38 N.E. 381 (Ohio 1894).
194. *Wilson*, 7 Ohio Dec. Reprint at 223.
195. Frank Lerner & Assoc., Inc, v. Vassy, 599 N.E.2d 734 (Ohio Ct. App. 1991).
196. Steele v. Gonyer, 1 Ohio App. 331 (Ohio Ct. App. 1913); *Wilson*, 7 Ohio Dec. Reprint at 223.
197. 18 Ohio Jurisprudence 3d (2007) 281, Contribution, Indemnity and Subrogation § 1.
198. Assets Realization Co. v. Am. Bonding Co. of Baltimore, 102 N.E. 719 (1913); Robinson v. Boyd, 53 N.E. 494 (1899); Corrigan v. Foster, 37 N.E. 263 (1894).
199. Camp v. Bostwick, 20 Ohio St. 337 (1870).
200. 52 Ohio Jurisprudence 3d (2007) 590, Guaranty and Suretyship § 234 (citing Crouse v. Wagner, 41 Ohio St. 470 (1885) and Hartwell v. Smith, 15 Ohio St. 200 (1864)).
201. *Assets Realization Co.*, 102 N.E. at 719.
202. *Robinson*, 53 N.E. at 494. *See also* Frank Lerner & Assoc., Inc, v. Vassy, 599 N.E.2d 734 (Ohio Ct. App. 1991).

The principle of contribution is reflected in the common law through the inference of an implied promise on the part of any cosurety or coguarantor to pay its share of the loss, upon which an action may be maintained, that results from their joint liability to pay a common obligation.[203] Each surety or guarantor is entitled to an account in order to determine the extent of liability and the equities among the cosureties.[204] Coguarantors and cosureties may, at the time of undertaking their obligation, expressly limit their liability to a certain amount that cannot be exceeded despite the general rule of contribution;[205] however, the adjustment of the rights among the cosureties in respect of contribution is a matter entirely among themselves and will not affect the rights of the obligee.[206]

10.2 Reduction of Obligations Upon Payment of Co-Obligor

A complete payment by one coguarantor or cosurety will discharge the obligation of the other coguarantors or cosureties as against the obligee,[207] but it will not discharge any obligations for contribution among the joint obligors. Similarly, a partial payment by one co-obligor will reduce, by the amount of the payment, the obligation of the other co-obligors to the obligee, but will not reduce any obligation the co-obligors may have for contribution to the paying obligor, to the extent the paying obligor has borne a burden that ought to be shared equally by all.[208]

§ 11 Reliance

No showing of reliance by the obligee on the guaranty is required.

Generally, the obligee is not required to show that it relied upon the guaranty in order to enforce it.[209] To the contrary, to establish an estoppel in favor of the guarantor, such guarantor must show that it relied on and was prejudiced by fraud, bad faith, or gross negligence on the part of the obligee.[210]

§ 12 Subrogation

Subrogation of a guarantor who has paid the underlying obligation to the place of the obligee against the primary obligor allows the guarantor to proceed against the primary obligor for reimbursement.

203. *Assets Realization Co.*, 102 N.E. at 719.
204. McCrory v. Parks, 18 Ohio St. 1 (1868).
205. Conet v. Squair, 17 Ohio Dec. 65 (Super. Ct. 1906); *Frank Lerner & Assoc.*, 599 N.E.2d at 734 (stating general rules of contribution).
206. Walsh v. Miller, 38 N.E. 381 (1894).
207. Commercial Cas. Ins. Co. v. Knutsen Motor Trucking Co., 173 N.E. 241 (Ohio Ct. App. 1930).
208. *McCrory*, 18 Ohio St. at 1.
209. *See generally*, 52 Ohio Jurisprudence 3d (2007) 309-636, Guaranty and Suretyship.
210. Forest City Sav. & Trust Co. v. Campbell, 28 Ohio Cir. Dec. 632 (Ohio Cir. Ct. 1909), *aff'd by* 98 N.E. 115 (1911).

If the primary obligor defaults in its obligation to the obligee and the guarantor is required to pay the obligation, the guarantor is subrogated to the place of the obligee against the primary obligor as well as against other guarantors on the obligation.[211] Once so subrogated, the guarantor may proceed against the primary obligor for reimbursement of any amount that the guarantor was required to pay.[212] The guarantor may not compel reimbursement from the primary obligor, however, if the guarantor and primary obligor have a valid defense against the claim but the payment by the guarantor amounts to a waiver or estoppel from asserting that defense.[213] In many commercial guaranties, the guarantor is required to waive or subordinate to the obligee its right to subrogation until such time as the underlying obligation is paid in full and the primary obligor has no right to request further advances.

§ 13 Triangular Set-off in Bankruptcy

Ohio law generally recognizes the right of setoff only when mutuality exists between the parties.[214] Mutuality is found where the debts to be set off against one another are "to and from the same persons and in the same capacity."[215] The Supreme Court of Ohio has recognized, however, that in certain circumstances where it is the only way to prevent a clear injustice, such as some situations in which a party has become insolvent or entered bankruptcy proceedings, a court may apply the doctrine of equity to allow the setoff of nonmutual debts.[216] See Section 7.4, *supra* for more on setoff in relation to a guarantor's obligations.

§ 14 Indemnification, Whether the Primary Obligor has a Duty

The primary obligor has a duty to indemnify guarantors or sureties that made a payment on the underlying obligation, unless the payment was voluntary and such payment waived a valid defense that the guarantor, surety, or primary obligor had against the claim.

211. Crawford v. Turnbaugh, 98 N.E. 858 (1912); Stone v. Rockefeller, 29 Ohio St. 625 (1876); 18 Ohio Jurisprudence 3d (2007) 349, Contribution, Indemnity, and Subrogation § 65.
212. Assets Realization Co. v. Am. Bonding Co. of Baltimore, 102 N.E. 719 (1913); Camp v. Bostwick, 20 Ohio St. 337 (1870).
213. Mut. Fin. Co. v. Politzer, 256 N.E.2d 606 (1970).
214. Nichols v. Metropolitan Life Ins. Co., 31 N.E.2d 224, 225 (Ohio 1941).
215. *Id.*
216. Union Properties v. Baldwin Bros. Co., 47 N.E.2d 983 (Ohio 1943).

14.1 Guarantors

A guarantor is entitled to full indemnity from the primary obligor for any amount the guarantor was required to pay on the underlying obligation.[217] One Ohio decision, in dictum, stated that the primary obligor can be relieved of this duty to indemnify its surety by entering into a settlement agreement in respect of which (i) the obligee releases the primary obligor from all subsequent obligations, and (ii) the guarantor's right to seek indemnification was not expressly reserved in the settlement agreement.[218] The primary obligor also has no duty to indemnify a guarantor for a payment on guaranteed debt to the extent that the guarantor and primary obligor had a valid defense against the claim for payment, and the guarantor's voluntary payment waived such defense.[219]

14.2 Sureties

The primary obligor has a duty to indemnify the surety for any payment collected from the surety[220] or loss sustained because of the suretyship.[221] This duty is implied between the parties but is as valid as if it were expressly made,[222] and is not fixed until the surety makes a payment on the obligation.[223] For the surety to claim a right to reimbursement, both the surety[224] and primary obligor[225] must have had a legal obligation to pay the obligee at the time the surety pays. Furthermore, the primary obligor has no duty to indemnify a surety that had knowledge of a valid defense against the claim but that did not pursue the defense or give notice to the primary obligor.[226] Unless a statute or express contract provides otherwise, the right to indemnity is available to both compensated and unpaid sureties.[227]

In addition to sureties' right to be indemnified by the primary obligor, Ohio law also provides sureties the right to maintain an action against the primary obligor to compel discharge of the underlying obligation after it becomes due,[228] to file a claim in the primary obligor's estate for the payment of the debt,[229] and to maintain an action to compel parties who are indebted to an insolvent primary obligor to satisfy such debt. [230]

---

217. Gholson v. Savin, 31 N.E.2d 858 (1941); Fed. Deposit Ins. Corp. v. Timbalier Towing Co., Inc., 497 F. Supp 912 (N.D. Ohio 1980); New Market Acquisitions, Ltd. v. Powerhouse Gym, 154 F. Supp. 2d 1213 (S.D. Ohio 2011); *Mut. Fin. Co.*, 256 N.E.2d at 606.
218. *New Market Acquisitions*, 154 F. Supp. 2d at 1213.
219. *Mut. Fin. Co.*, 256 N.E.2d at 606.
220. Easter v. White, 12 Ohio St. 219 (1861); Williams' Adm'rs v. Williams' Adm'rs, 5 Ohio 444 (1832).
221. Second Nat'l Bank of Cincinnati v. Am. Bonding Co. of Baltimore, 113 N.E. 221 (1916); Case v. Hall, 38 N.E. 618 (Ohio 1894); McHenry v. Carson, 41 Ohio St. 212 (1884).
222. McConnel v. Scott, 15 Ohio St. 401 (1846).
223. *In re* Deal's Estate, 46 N.E.2d 643 (Ohio Ct. App. 1942); Yakey v. Strunk, 18 Ohio Dec. 726 (C.P. 1908), *aff'd without opinion by*, 91 N.E. 1143 (1910).
224. *McHenry*, 41 Ohio St. at 222 (1884); Holland v. Lee, 33 Ohio Cir. Dec. 520 (Ohio Ct. App. 1907).
225. *McHenry*, 41 Ohio St. at 222 (1884); Russell v. Failor, 1 Ohio St. 327 (1853).
226. *Russell*, 1 Ohio St. at 327.
227. Nat'l Sur. Corp. v. Seward, 165 N.E. 588 (Ohio Ct. App. 1928), *aff'd by*, 165 N.E. 537 (1929).
228. OHIO REV. CODE ANN. § 1341.19 (West 2011).
229. Stump v. Rogers, 1 Ohio 533 (1824).
230. Still v. Holland, 1 Ohio Dec. Reprint 584 (Ohio C.P. 1853).

§ 15 Enforcement of Guaranties

15.1 Limitations on Recovery

A guarantor may expressly limit its guaranty in amount at the time of the undertaking, in which case, recovery on the guaranty cannot exceed the amount of the indebtedness of the primary obligor or the amount specified in the limited guaranty.[231]

A surety cannot be bound in excess of the amount of the obligation found in the express terms of the suretyship contract.[232]

15.2 Enforcement of Guaranties of Payment versus Guaranties of Collection

Because a guaranty of payment is an unconditional and absolute guaranty that does not depend on any contingency other than the primary obligor's default,[233] an obligee may bring an action against a guarantor to enforce a guaranty of payment without first exhausting its legal remedies against the primary obligor.[234] Many courts have held that a guaranty of payment is simply a suretyship contract, pursuant to which the obligation of the guarantor arises upon the primary obligor's failure to pay.[235]

In contrast, a guaranty of collection is conditioned upon the obligee first exhausting legal remedies against the primary obligor.[236] Once an obligee on a guaranty of collection has used due diligence but failed in an effort to collect the debt from the primary obligor, it has the right to recover from the guarantor.[237]

15.3 "Bad boy" Guaranties

"Bad boy" or "bad acts" guaranties are those in which certain "bad" acts of the primary obligor trigger obligations on the part of the guarantor. Although Ohio courts have not considered the enforceability of these types of guaranties, the New York Supreme Court recently rejected a defendant guarantor's argument that "bad boy" guaranties are against public policy because they cause a conflict of interest between the guarantor's self-interest and its duty to the primary obligor's creditors.[238]

231. Arnold, Constable & Co. v. Wilder, 6 Ohio Dec. Reprint 819 (Ohio C.P. 1879)
232. Gholson v. Savin, 31 N.E.2d 858 (Ohio 1941).
233. Mihalca v. Malita, No. 19395, 2000 WL 372309, at *4 (Ohio Ct. App. Apr. 12, 2000); Buckeye Fed. Sav. & Loan Ass'n v. Olentangy Motel, No. 90AP-1409, 1991 WL 224486, at *2 (Ohio Ct. App. Aug. 22, 1991); Schottenstein v. Byers, No. 75AP-10, 1975 WL 181814, at *2 (Ohio Ct. App. Oct. 7, 1975).
234. *Mihalca*, 2000 WL 372309 at *4; Eden Realty Co. v. Weather-Seal, Inc., 142 N.E.2d 541 (Ohio 1957); Nesco Sales & Rental v. Superior Elec. Co., 2007-Ohio-844, at ¶ 14 (Ohio Ct. App.).
235. Liquidating Midland Bank v. Stecker, 179 N.E. 504 (Ohio Ct. App. 1930).
236. *Nesco*, 2007-Ohio-844 at ¶ 14; *Schottenstein*, 1975 WL 181814 at *2 (Ohio Ct. App. 1975); *Liquidating Midland Bank*, 179 N.E. at 504.
237. Union Nat'l Bank v. First Nat'l Bank, 13 N.E. 884 (1887).
238. UBS Commercial Mortg. Trust 2007-FL1 v. Garrison Special Opportunities Fund LP, No. 652412/2010 (N.Y. Sup. Ct., Mar. 8, 2011).

15.4 Exercising Rights Under a Guaranty, the Underlying Obligation of Which is also Secured by Collateral

In an absolute guaranty of payment[239] or a suretyship,[240] the obligee has no obligation to proceed against any collateral securing the underlying obligation before bringing an action against the guarantor or surety. In such a case, if the surety or guarantor of payment satisfies the obligation by paying the obligee, it becomes subrogated to the rights of the obligee in the collateral security.[241] In contrast, in order for an obligee to exhaust all its remedies against the primary obligor before bringing an action against a guarantor of collection, it must first foreclose on any collateral securing the underlying obligation.[242]

No "one-action" rule exists under Ohio law. An obligee proceeding against a guarantor and proceeding in foreclosure is under no obligation to combine both claims in a single action or to exhaust its security as a condition of obtaining a monetary deficiency judgment against the guarantor personally (unless the obligee is required to do so because the guaranty is one of collection).

15.5 Litigating Guaranty Claims: Procedural Considerations

A complaint against a guarantor must specially set forth an express promise to pay, as the law will not imply a promise to pay another's debt.[243] A complaint in an action to recover on a conditional guaranty of collection should allege demand on the primary obligor for payment and notice of the primary obligor's default to the guarantor,[244] but such allegations are not necessary in an action to recover against a guarantor of payment [245] or a surety.[246] The plaintiff obligee has the burden of proving, by a preponderance of the evidence,[247] the events on which its right of recovery relies,[248] but the guarantor bears the burden of establishing every material allegation that sets up any affirmative defense.[249] Thus, the defendant guarantor has the burden of proving that an allegedly unauthorized alteration of the underlying contract was material[250] or that there was an extension of time without the guarantor's consent,[251] if it raises such claims in defense of its liability.

239. 52 Ohio Jurisprudence 3d (2007) 517, Guaranty and Suretyship § 170.
240. Hochevar v. Maryland Cas. Co., 114 F.2d 948 (6th Cir. 1940); Second Nat'l Bank v. Morrison, 3 Ohio Dec. Reprint 534 (Ohio C.P. 1881).
241. Advance Thresher Co. v. Hogan, 78 N.E. 436 (1906); Dolak v. City Trust & Sav. Bank, 21 Ohio Law Abs. 409 (Ohio Ct. App. 1936).
242. 52 Ohio Jurisprudence 3d (2007) 517, Guaranty and Suretyship § 170.
243. *In re* Method's Estate, 10 Ohio Op. 489, 26 Ohio Law Abs. 209 (Prob. Ct. 1936); 52 Ohio Jurisprudence 3d (2007) 603, Guaranty and Suretyship § 247.
244. Clay v. Edgerton, 19 Ohio St. 549 (1869).
245. Neil v. Bd. of Trustees of Ohio Agric. & Mech. College, 31 Ohio St. 15 (1876); *Clay*, 19 Ohio St. at 549; Reed v. Evans, 17 Ohio 128 (1848).
246. Bush v. Critchfield, 4 Ohio 103 (1829).
247. Koppitz-Melchers Brewing Co. v. Schultz, 67 N.E. 719 (Ohio 1903).
248. Ohio Rev. Code Ann. § 2315.01 (West 2011).
249. Schmidt v. Cordes, 13 Ohio Dec. Reprint 911 (Ohio Super. Ct. 1872).
250. Leonard v. Mowbray, 153 N.E. 197 (Ohio Ct. App. 1926).
251. Bramble v. Ward, 40 Ohio St. 267 (1993); Cone v. Rees, 5 Ohio Cir. Dec. 192 (Ohio Cir. Ct. 1896).

The parol evidence rule applies to guaranty and suretyship contracts.[252] Accordingly, when the parties have reduced their agreement to a complete, unambiguous written contract, the writing is presumed to contain the entire agreement and extrinsic evidence is inadmissible to add to, contradict, or change the terms of the contract.[253] Evidence of the circumstances surrounding the undertaking of the agreement, however, is admissible to show the intention of the parties and to construe the words used in the contract in light of these circumstances, including the determination of which parties are primary obligors and which are sureties.[254]

An obligee may jointly sue both the primary obligor and its surety, and judgment may be rendered against one or both, according to the justice of the case.[255] If the surety had notice and an opportunity to defend a suit against the primary obligor, then a judgment against the primary obligor will be conclusive against the surety[256] in the absence of fraud or mistake.[257] If, however, the surety had no notice of the action against the primary obligor, such judgment is not conclusive and may be opened for inquiry into the merits.[258]

15.6 Confession of Judgment Provisions

As discussed in the *Ohio Highlights* section, *supra*, Ohio law permits a confession of judgment clause, also know as a warrant of attorney, to be included in a commercial guaranty and any other instrument evidencing commercial indebtedness. These provisions authorize an attorney to appear on behalf of the guarantor and to confess a judgment, known as a "cognovit judgment," against the guarantor, without notice, right to trial, or right to an appeal.[259] These provisions thus allow an obligee to obtain an expedited judgment against a guarantor as if its claims were fully litigated and to pursue execution on its judgment immediately thereafter.

The warrant of attorney must be accompanied by a statutorily prescribed warning, appearing more clearly and conspicuously than anything else in the document, and located directly above or below the signature of the party authorizing the cognovit judgment.[260] Ohio courts have no jurisdiction to enter cognovit judgments against obligors unless the purported cognovit instrument complies strictly with this warning requirement.[261]

252. Williamson's Adm'rs v. Hall, 1 Ohio St. 190 (1853); McGovney v. State *ex rel* Lee's Adm'r, 20 Ohio 93 (1851).
253. *Id.*
254. Third Nat'l Bank of Cincinnati, Ohio v. Laidlaw, 98 N.E. 1015 (Ohio 1912); Merchants' Nat'l Bank v. Cole, 93 N.E. 465 (Ohio 1910); Cambria Iron Co. v. Keynes, 47 N.E. 548 (Ohio 1897); Oldham v. Broom, 28 Ohio St. 41 (1875).
255. Bever v. Beardmore, 40 Ohio St. 70 (1883); Clinton Bank of Columbus *ex rel* Rhodes v. Ayers & Neil, 16 Ohio 282 (1847).
256. State *ex rel* Fulton & Co. v. Colerick, 3 Ohio 487 (1828); Am. Bonding Co. v. Bd. of Educ. of Cincinnati, 8 Ohio App. 216 (Ohio Ct. App. 1917).
257. Richardson v. People's Nat'l Bank, 48 N.E. 1100 (1897).
258. State v. Safeco Ins. Co., 396 N.E.2d 794 (Ohio App. Ct. 1978).
259. Ohio Rev. Code Ann. §§ 2323.12, 2323.13 (West 2011).
260. Ohio Rev. Code Ann. § 2323.13(D) (West 2011).
261. *Id.*; Klosterman v. Turnkey-Ohio, L.L.C., 2009-Ohio-2508, ¶ 19 (Ohio Ct. App. 2009); Sky Bank v. Colley, 2008-Ohio-1217, ¶ 9 (Ohio Ct. App. 2008).

If any obligor on the instrument resides within, or signed the instrument within, the territorial jurisdiction of an Ohio municipal court, and the amount due on the instrument is $15,000 or less, the obligee must seek cognovit judgment in that municipal court.[262] Otherwise, judgment may be confessed in any court in the county where any obligor resides or signed the warrant of attorney.[263]

A cognovit judgment can be vacated on the same basis as any other judgment under Rule 60(B) of the Ohio Rules of Civil Procedure. Ohio courts have held that a cognovit judgment may be vacated under Rule 60(B)(5) ("any other reason justifying relief from the judgment") if the motion for relief is timely made and the defendant can establish a meritorious defense.[264]

As discussed *supra* in *Ohio Law Highlights,* an unreported court of appeals decision in Ohio has found that the failure to designate the amount of the underlying obligation in a continuing unlimited guaranty was a prima facie reason for the court to refuse to render a judgment under such confession of judgment provisions.[265] No support for this decision is found in the applicable statute or any other case law, and questions abound regarding the decision.

§ 16 Revival and Reinstatement of Guaranties

As a general rule, even if a primary obligor has paid its underlying obligation in full, the obligation of the guarantor will revive if the primary obligor's previous payment is later avoided or disgorged, regardless of whether the guaranty is otherwise silent on this issue.[266] Many courts have recognized this principle.[267] Although no Ohio case exists on this issue, an Ohio court, in a properly reasoned opinion, in all likelihood, would follow the generally prevailing view and adopt this general principle. In practice, however, creditors commonly include specific language reviving and reinstating such indebtedness in the underlying obligation or such guaranty obligation in the guaranty.

262. Ohio Rev. Code Ann. § 2323.13(A) (West 2011).
263. *Id.*
264. First Merit v. NEBS Fin. Serv, Inc. 2006-Ohio-5260, ¶ 16 (Ohio Ct. App. 2006); BJ Bldg. Co., L.L.C., v. LBJ Linden Co., L.L.C., 2005-Ohio-6825, ¶ 38 (Ohio Ct. App. 2005); Meyers v. McGuire, 610 N.E.2d 542 (Ohio Ct. App. 1992).
265. The Huntington Nat'l Bank of Columbus v. Cinemack Corp., No. 79AP-328, 1979 WL 209409, at *3 (Ohio Ct. App. Oct. 30, 1979).
266. Restatement (Third) of Suretyship and Guaranty, § 70 (1995).
267. *See, e.g.,* In the Matter of SNTL Corporation , 571 F.3d 826, 835-36 (9th Cir. 2009) ("[W]e agree that the return of a preferential payment by a creditor generally revives the liability of a guarantor."); Wallace Hardware Co., Inc. v. Abrams, 223 F.3d 382, 408 (6th Cir. 2000) ("[T]he courts have uniformly held that a payment of a debt that is later set aside as an avoidable preference does not discharge a guarantor of his obligation to repay that debt."); In re Robinson Bros. Drilling, Inc. v. Manufacturers Hanover Leasing Corp., 6 F.3d 701, 704 (10th Cir. 1993) ("[C]ourts have recognized, without regard to any special guaranty language, that guarantors must make good on their guaranties following avoidance of payments previously made by their principal debtors."); In re Herman Cantor Corp. v. Central Fidelity Bank, N.A., 15 B.R. 747, 750 (Bankr. E.D.Va. 1981) ("Although a surety usually is discharged by payment of the debt, he continues to be liable if the payment constitutes a preference under bankruptcy law. A preferential treatment is deemed by law to be no payment at all....The courts agree that payment from a debtor which is later set aside as a preference does not discharge a surety.").

§ 17 Conflict of Laws—Choice of Law

Guaranties, like other contracts, are ordinarily governed in Ohio courts by the laws of the state in which such contract is made or is to be performed.[268] In the absence of an effective choice of law provision included in a guaranty by the parties, Ohio courts will apply the contracts test of the Restatement (Second) of Conflict of Laws in order to determine the rights of parties to a contract.[269] Under the Restatement, "the rights and duties of the parties with respect to an issue in contract are determined by the local law of the state which, with respect to that issue, has the most significant relationship to the transaction and the parties."[270] Accordingly, if the parties to a guaranty have not contracted to apply the laws of a particular state, the law of the state with the "most significant relationship" to the guaranty should be applied.[271]

268. McCluskey v. Rob San Services, Inc., 443 F. Supp 65, 10 Ohio Op. 3d 248 (S.D. Ohio 1977).
269. Libbey-Owens-Ford Co. v. Insurance Co. of North America, 9 F.3d 422, 27 Fed. R. Serv. 3d 531 (6th Cir. 1993); Gries Sports Enter. v. Modell, 15 Ohio St.3d 284, 473 N.E.2d 807 (1984) (adopting Restatement (Second) of Conflicts of Law Sec. 188 (1971)), cert. denied, 473 U.S. 906, 105 S.Ct. 3530, 87 L.Ed.2d 654 (1985).
270. Restatement Second, Conflict of Laws § 188(1) (1971).
271. International Ins. Co. v. Stonewall Ins. Co. 863 F.Supp 599 (S.D. Ohio 1994), judgment aff'd 86 F.3d 601, 1996 FED App. 0173P (6th Cir. 1996).

Oklahoma State Law of Guaranties

J. Mark Lovelace
Eric L. Johnson
Joshua L. Edwards
Phillips Murrah P.C.
Corporate Tower | Thirteenth Floor
101 North Robinson
Oklahoma City, Oklahoma 73102
(405) 235-4100
Fax: (405) 235-4133
www.phillipsmurrah.com

PM PHILLIPS MURRAH P.C.
Attorneys and Counselors at Law

Contents

Oklahoma State Law of Guaranties

Oklahoma Law Highlights

1. Separate consideration is not required for a guaranty if it is entered into contemporaneously with the underlying obligation. See Section 4 of this chapter.
2. Under current Oklahoma case law, waivers of guarantor and suretyship defenses will generally be upheld. See Section 8 of this chapter.
3. Although a mortgagor of real property cannot waive the benefit of Oklahoma's antideficiency statute, a guarantor can effectively waive the right to set off the fair market value of the property. See Sections 7 and 8 of this chapter.

Introduction and Sources of Law

The law on guaranties in Oklahoma is a diverse mixture of statutory and case law. The primary Oklahoma statutes on guaranty and surety are contained in Okla. Stat. tit. 15, §§ 321-344 and 371-385, respectively; they originate from the Field Code and are extensive. There are only a small handful of cases that cite either the Restatement of Suretyship and Guaranty or the predecessor sections of the Restatement of Security, and none to any significant extent.

§ 1 Nature of the Guaranty Arrangement

Under Oklahoma law, a guaranty creates a "complex, tripartite relationship" between creditor, principal obligor, and guarantor involving interrelated but independent and separately enforceable rights and obligations:[1] rights and obligations created as a result of the creditor/debtor relationship between the creditor and principal obligor; independent and separately enforceable collateral rights and obligations created as a result of the guaranty between the creditor and guarantor; and rights and obligations created as a result of the suretyship relationship between the principal obligor and the guarantor.

1.1 Guaranty Relationships

Oklahoma's statutes governing guaranties define a guaranty as "a promise to answer for the debt, default or miscarriage of another person."[2] A contract of guaranty is a collateral undertaking and cannot exist without the presence of a main or substantive liability on the part of a third person, either express

1. Riverside National Bank v. Manolakis, 613 P.2d 438, 441 (Okla. 1980).
2. Okla. Stat. tit. 15, § 321; Oppenheim v. National Sur. Co., 231 P. 1076 (Okla. 1924) (a guaranty contract is a collateral undertaking and presupposes an original contract and creates an obligation to answer for the debt, default, or miscarriage of the other party).

or implied.[3] A guarantor is secondarily liable and therefore its obligation is conditioned on the default of the principal obligor.[4]

The guarantor's undertaking creates a collateral obligation independent and separately enforceable from that of the principal obligor; the obligation of the guaranty is contractual, and therefore the extent of the obligation will be determined from the precise terms of the guarantor's undertaking and the dimension or breadth of the guarantor's covenants.[5] A person may become a guarantor even without the knowledge or consent of the principal obligor.[6] Although a guaranty must be in writing to be enforceable, the guaranty itself does not require any specific or formal language or any particular mode of expression and can be inferred from any language expressing an intent to answer for the debt, default, or miscarriage of another person; in determining from the language used whether a guaranty exists, the language used will be interpreted in favor of the creditor relying on such language.[7]

1.2 Third-Party Pledgors

Third-party pledgors are sureties and have all the rights of a guarantor. See Sections 1.3 and 9 of this chapter.

1.3 Other Suretyship Relationships

Oklahoma's statutes governing sureties define a surety as one who, at the request of another person and for the purpose of securing a benefit to such person, becomes responsible for the performance by such person of some act in favor of a third person, or hypothecates property as security therefor.[8] A surety has all the rights of a guarantor, whether or not the surety becomes personally responsible for the underlying obligation.[9] The Oklahoma Supreme Court has held that a contract of guaranty corresponds with a contract of suretyship, and therefore the distinction between them is merely technical.[10]

§ 2 State Law Requirements for an Entity to Enter a Guaranty

Oklahoma law permits corporations, partnerships, limited liability companies, and banks and trust companies all to grant guaranties in furtherance of their business activities and as otherwise permitted under the applicable act governing each such business organization. Each such business organization may

3. Fischer v. Bashwitz, 5 P.2d 356 (Okla. 1931).
4. Lum v. Lee Way Motor Freight, Inc., 757 P.2d 810, 814 (Okla. 1987).
5. Riverside National Bank v. Manolakis, 613 P.2d 438 (Okla. 1980).
6. Okla. Stat. tit. 15, § 322.
7. Ross v. Russell, 475 P.2d 152 (Okla. 1970).
8. Okla. Stat. tit. 15, § 371.
9. Okla. Stat. tit. 15, § 378.
10. Central Sur. & Ins. Corp. v. Richardson, 80 P.2d 663 (Okla. 1938).

limit the ability of the organization to grant guaranties by including restrictions in the organizational or governing documents of the organization.

2.1 Corporations

Under the Oklahoma General Corporation Act, a corporation has the power to make contracts of guaranty and suretyship which are necessary or convenient to the conduct, promotion, or attainment of corporate business.[11] An Oklahoma corporation may also enter into a guaranty that is given in furtherance of the business interests of (a) a subsidiary corporation, all of the outstanding stock of which is owned, directly or indirectly, by the contracting corporation, (b) a parent corporation which owns, directly or indirectly, all of the outstanding stock of the contracting corporation, and (c) a sister corporation, all of the outstanding stock of which is owned, directly or indirectly, by a corporation which owns, directly or indirectly, all outstanding stock of the contracting corporation.[12]

Additionally, Oklahoma corporations may guarantee any obligation of an officer or employee of the corporation or its subsidiary, including officers or employees who are directors, whenever such guaranty may reasonably be expected to benefit the corporation in the judgment of the board of directors of the corporation.[13] The guaranty of the corporation may also be secured in such manner as the board of directors may approve.[14]

2.2 Partnerships

The Oklahoma Revised Uniform Partnership Act neither expressly empowers a partnership to issue a guaranty nor expressly regulates or prohibits such activity, but Oklahoma case law permits partners to execute a guaranty in the partnership name and such guaranty will be binding on the partnership if the giving of such guaranty is necessary in the transaction of business properly within the scope of the partnership.[15] Additionally, partners may authorize or ratify a guaranty that would not be in the ordinary course of the partnership's business or is otherwise outside the scope of the partnership.[16] With respect to limited partnerships, the Oklahoma Uniform Limited Partnership Act of 2010 grants a limited partnership the power to do all things necessary or convenient to carry on its activities.[17]

2.3 Limited Liability Companies

The Oklahoma Limited Liability Company Act gives limited liability companies (LLCs) broad powers to grant guaranties and to do any other

11. Okla. Stat. tit. 18, § 1016(13).
12. Okla. Stat. tit. 18, § 1016(13).
13. Okla. Stat. tit. 18, § 1029.
14. Okla. Stat. tit. 18, § 1029.
15. McNeal v. Gossard, 50 P. 159, 161–62 (Okla. 1897).
16. Okla. Stat. tit. 54, § 1-301(2).
17. Okla. Stat. tit. 54, § 500-105A.

act not inconsistent with law which is appropriate to promote or attain the purposes of the LLC.[18]

2.4 Banks and Trust Companies

Although the Oklahoma Banking Code does not expressly give banks the power to enter into a guaranty, it does grant banks and trust companies organized under the laws of Oklahoma the power to make contracts and to exercise all such powers as may be necessary or desirable to carry on the banking business.[19] Oklahoma courts have upheld and enforced guaranties given by banks.[20] Additionally, the Oklahoma Banking Code specifically empowers corporate trust companies to give certain guaranties, including the power to guarantee special deposits, to guarantee the performance of persons or corporations holding places of public or private trust, to guarantee or become surety on any bond, and to guarantee the principal or interest of any securities of any kind.[21] A trust company that has accepted such grant of power is thereby authorized to become a guarantor to the same extent as an individual and subject to the general law of guaranty.[22]

2.5 Individuals

An individual's capacity to enter into a guaranty binding on the individual should be determined under principles of law applicable to an individual's capacity to enter into contracts generally. The capacity of an individual acting as an agent to grant a guaranty binding on its principal will be determined under principles of law applicable to agency generally as well as statutes governing the applicable organization and the authority of such organization's agents. Generally, a corporation's directors and officers, acting within the power and purpose of the corporation, who execute a contract on behalf of the corporation are not liable along with the corporation unless they bind themselves individually in the making of the contract or by its terms assume liability.[23] However, if an individual does not have authority to sign a contract of guaranty on behalf of an organization, the signer will be personally bound in his or her individual capacity.[24]

Additionally, an individual's guaranty secured by individually owned property could implicate Oklahoma's homestead laws. Although Oklahoma does not have special signature requirements for a nonguarantor spouse related to a guaranty agreement, Oklahoma does have constitutional and statutory homestead rights which accrue to the benefit of an individual and the indi-

18. Okla. Stat. tit. 18, § 2003(3), (14).
19. Okla. Stat. tit. 6, § 402(2), (10), (11).
20. *See* First Nat'l Bank of Hominy, Okla. v. Citizens & S. Bank of Cobb County, Marietta, Ga., 651 F.2d 696 (10th Cir. 1981); Bennett v. W.A. Gage & Co., 176 P. 744 (Okla. 1918); Oklahoma City Nat'l Bank v. Ezzard, 159 P. 267 (Okla. 1916); Dubuque Packing Co., Inc. v. Fitzgibbon, 599 P.2d 440 (Okla. Civ. App. 1979).
21. Okla. Stat. tit. 6, § 1001(7).
22. Barnett v. Kennedy, 92 P.2d 963, 967 (Okla. 1938).
23. Watkins v. Cotton, 67 P.2d 957, 958 (Okla. 1937); Smoot v. B & J Restoration Services, Inc., 279 P.3d 805 (Okla. Civ. App. 2012).
24. Bonneau v. Strauss Bros., 179 P. 10, 12 (Okla. 1919).

vidual's spouse and which require conveyances of interests in homestead real property to be contained in a single document executed by both the husband and wife.[25] Homestead rights also may not be released or waived.[26] Additionally, if a mortgage on any property is executed by a husband and wife to secure promissory notes executed only by one spouse, the other spouse is a surety for the obligation under Okla. Stat. tit 15, § 371 and therefore is entitled to all the rights of a guarantor and surety.[27]

If the guaranty is executed by a married individual but not by the individual's spouse, the nonguarantor spouse will not be liable for the obligations of the guarantying spouse under the guaranty.[28] Likewise, the creditor obtaining a judgment against the guarantor in such situations will not have any recourse against the separate property of the nonguarantor spouse.[29] With respect to property owned jointly by the guarantor and the nonguarantor spouse, a creditor will have recourse against such jointly owned property only to the extent of the guarantor's actual interest in the property.[30] Again, and as also discussed in Section 7.3.6 of this chapter, a creditor's recourse may also be limited by Oklahoma's homestead and property exemption statutes.

§ 3 Signatory's Authority to Execute a Guaranty

Generally, an organization's organic documents will set forth the requirements and restrictions on a signatory's authority to enter into a guaranty on behalf of the organization. An organization may also be bound by a guaranty agreement executed by an individual without actual authority if the individual had apparent authority or the organization received a benefit as a result of the guaranty and the beneficiary of the guaranty did not have notice of the lack of actual authority on the part of the signatory.

3.1 Corporations

Generally, an officer of a corporation must have received a general or specific grant of authority from the corporation's board of directors to enter into contracts to bind the corporation unless such conduct is ratified by the board of directors.[31] However, an officer may also develop authority to contract simply because he or she has assumed and exercised that power in the past.[32] Apparent authority to make a particular contract may be inferred from a course of conduct or dealing by the corporation with its officers and agents and the

25. Okla. Const. art. XII; Okla. Stat. tit. 31, § 2 and Okla. Stat. tit.16, § 4.
26. Grenard v. McMahan, 441 P.2d 950 (Okla. 1968); Thomas v. James, 202 P. 499 (Okla. 1921).
27. Muskogee Indus. Finance Corp. v. Perkins, 361 P.2d 1065 (Okla. 1961).
28. Okla. Stat. tit. 43, § 208.
29. Okla. Stat. tit. 43, § 208.
30. American National Bank and Trust Company of Shawnee, v. McGinnis, 571 P.2d 1198 (Okla. 1977); Sears, Roebuck and Company v. Cosey, 44 P.3d 582 (Okla. Civ. App. 2002).
31. Henry Bldg. Co. v. Cowman, 363 P.2d 208, 212–13 (Okla. 1961).
32. Quaker Oil & Gas Co. v. Jane Oil & Gas Co., 164 P. 671, 673 (Okla. 1917).

corporation will be bound by contracts of its officers if the other party has relied on such apparent authority.[33]

Additionally, if a contract is made in the ordinary administration of the corporation's business by the corporation's managing officers or contracting agents, a formal vote or resolution of the corporation's board of directors may not be necessary in order to bind the corporation.[34]

3.2 Partnerships

Under the Oklahoma Revised Uniform Partnership Act, each partner is an agent of the partnership for purposes of partnership business and, therefore, a partner has the authority to bind the partnership when the partner executes an agreement in the partnership's name and such agreement appears to be within the ordinary course of the partnership's business.[35] However, if the partner does not have actual authority to bind the partnership to the particular contract and the person with whom the partner was dealing knew or had received a notification that the partner lacked such actual authority, then the partnership will not be bound by the contract.[36] Additionally, if the contract is not within the ordinary course of the partnership's business, or business of the kind carried on by the partnership, then the partnership will only be bound by the contract if it was authorized by the other partners.[37] Although the partnership will not be bound if such a guaranty executed by a partner is not authorized, the partner executing the guaranty will be individually bound.[38]

Likewise under the Uniform Limited Partnership Act of 2010, each general partner of a limited partnership is considered an agent of the limited partnership and has the same authority to bind the limited partnership as does a partner in a general partnership. However, a limited partner does not have the right or the power to execute a contract in the name of the limited partnership or to otherwise bind the limited partnership.[39]

3.3 Limited Liability Companies

In Oklahoma, LLCs may be either member-managed or manager-managed. In a member-managed LLC, the LLC operates without designated managers, and each member will be deemed to be a manager of the company for purposes of the Oklahoma Limited Liability Company Act.[40] A manager-managed LLC operates under the authority of one or more managers who may or may not be members of the company.[41]

---

33. East Central Okla. Elec. Coop., Inc. v. Okla. Gas & Elec. Co., 505 P.2d 1324, 1327 (Okla. 1973); Park Addition Co. v. Bryan, 228 P. 959 (Okla. 1924).
34. East Central Okla. Elec. Coop., Inc. v. Okla. Gas & Elec. Co., 505 P.2d 1324, 1327 (Okla. 1973).
35. Okla. Stat. tit. 54, § 1-301(1).
36. Okla. Stat. tit. 54, § 1-301(1).
37. Okla. Stat. tit. 54, § 1-301(2); *see also* Bonneau v. Strauss Bros., 179 P. 10, 12 (Okla. 1919).
38. Bonneau v. Strauss Bros., 179 P. 10, 12 (Okla. 1919).
39. Okla. Stat. tit. 54, § 500-302A.
40. Okla. Stat. tit. 18, § 2015(A) (1).
41. Okla. Stat. tit. 18, § 2013(A).

Unless otherwise provided in the operating agreement of the LLC, each manager in a manager-managed LLC and each member in a member-managed LLC is an agent of the company for the purpose of carrying on its business, and the act of each such person, including the execution in the name of the company of any instrument for apparently carrying on the business of the company, will bind the company, unless such individual so acting lacks the authority to act for the company in a particular matter, and the person with whom he is dealing has knowledge of the fact that he has no such authority.[42]

3.4 Banks and Trust Companies

Similar to corporations, banks and trust companies act through their directors and officers, and therefore banks and trust companies will be bound by contracts entered into by their officers in the name of the bank or trust company if such acts are authorized by the board of directors or are subsequently ratified by the board of directors.[43] Additionally, a bank or trust company may be bound by a contract executed by an officer on behalf of the bank or trust company if authority to enter into the particular contract is inherent in or implied by the office.[44] A bank or trust company generally will not be bound by a contract executed by its officer outside the scope of the officer's authorization and office.[45] However, even when an agent of a bank or trust company enters into a guaranty on behalf of the bank or trust company without the authority to do so, the guaranty may still be enforceable against the bank or trust company if the beneficiary of the guaranty did not have notice of the lack of authority and the bank or trust company received a benefit as a result of providing the guaranty.[46]

§ 4 Consideration; Sufficiency of Past Consideration

A guaranty entered into contemporaneously with the underlying obligation does not require separate consideration to be enforceable. However, if a guaranty is entered into subsequent to the transaction giving rise to the underlying obligation, past consideration alone is insufficient to support the guaranty and new and independent consideration is required for such subsequently given guaranty to be valid.

Oklahoma provides by statute that "[w]here a guaranty is entered into at the same time with the original obligation, or with the acceptance of the latter by the guarantee, and forms, with that obligation, a part of the consideration to him, no other consideration need exist."[47] However, "[i]n all other cases

42. Okla. Stat. tit. 18, § 2019(A).
43. Bank of Quapaw v. Flint, 223 P. 624 (Okla. 1924); Morton v. Central Nat. Bank of Okmulgee, 43 P.2d 394 (Okla. 1935).
44. Bank of Quapaw v. Flint, 223 P. 624 (Okla. 1924).
45. Wilkin-Hale Bank v. Herstein, 149 P. 1109 (Okla. 1915); Bank of Quapaw v. Flint, 223 P. 624 (Okla. 1924).
46. Bennett v. W.A. Gage & Co., 176 P. 744 (Okla. 1918).
47. Okla. Stat. tit. 15, § 323.

there must be a consideration distinct from that of the original obligation."[48] The statutory requirement that a guaranty not supported by distinct consideration be entered into "at the same time" as the underlying obligation means contemporaneously rather than on the same day and is satisfied if the guaranty agreement and the agreement giving rise to the underlying obligation are part of the same overall arrangement, even though one document may be executed or delivered a few days before the other.[49]

Although a guaranty executed contemporaneously with the underlying obligation does not require separate consideration, if the guaranty is not part of the underlying transaction between the creditor and the primary obligor but is given subsequent to the creation of the underlying obligation, there must be consideration from the creditor distinct from that of the underlying obligation.[50] Past consideration alone is insufficient to support a guaranty.[51] However, if a guaranty expressly governs both past and future obligations, the extension of future credit or transactions by the creditor to the primary obligor is sufficient consideration to support the guaranty of both the future and past obligations.[52] Other examples of sufficient new consideration to support a guaranty of past obligations include an agreement by the creditor not to file a lien,[53] the extension of time for payment of the underlying obligation,[54] forbearance by the creditor,[55] and reopening a credit line.[56]

The guaranty agreement itself is not required to express a consideration.[57] In the event of a guaranty given subsequent to the creation of the underlying obligation, extrinsic evidence will be permitted when necessary to prove the giving of distinct consideration to support the guaranty.[58]

§ 5 Notice of Acceptance

Although generally required, notice of acceptance is not necessary if the guaranty is absolute, given in response to an offer by the creditor, waived by the guarantor, or, in certain circumstances, if the guaranty was a condition precedent to the creditor's performance.

48. Okla. Stat. tit. 15, § 323.
49. McMillan v. Lane Wood & Co., 361 P.2d 487 (Okla. 1961).
50. Misco Leasing, Inc. v. Keller, 490 F.2d 545 (10th Cir. 1974).
51. Ford Motor Credit Co. v. Milburn, 615 F.2d 892 (10th Cir. 1980) (Oklahoma statute requires new consideration for a promise to pay an existing obligation); Davis v. First Nat. Bank, 229 P. 228 (Okla. 1924) (subsequent guaranty must be supported by new and independent consideration to be valid).
52. Maney v. Cherry, 41 P.2d 82 (Okla. 1935) (guaranty covering past and future transactions and supported by consideration arising out of future transactions is good as to both past and future transactions); W.T. Rawleigh Co. v. Walker, 246 P. 417 (Okla. 1926) (where the contract of guaranty expressly governs past and future transactions, and is supported by consideration arising out of future transactions, it is good as to the whole); Ford Motor Credit Co. v. Milburn, 615 F.2d 892 (10th Cir. 1980) (the extension of future credit to a principal debtor in reliance on a guaranty is sufficient consideration for contract of guaranty concerning both past and future obligations, even though benefit to debtor constitutes whole consideration).
53. Harness v. McKee-Brown Lumber Co., 89 P. 1020 (Okla. 1907).
54. Yount v. Bank of Commerce, 44 P. 2d 874 (Okla. 1935).
55. Ross v. Russell, 475 P.2d 152 (Okla. 1970).
56. Ford Motor Credit Co. v. Milburn, 615 F.2d 892 (10th Cir. 1980).
57. Okla. Stat. tit. 15, § 324.
58. Cinco Enterprises, Inc. v. Benso, 890 P.2d 866 (Okla. 1994).

An offer of guaranty is not binding until notice of its acceptance is communicated by the creditor to the guarantor.[59] However, an absolute guaranty is binding on the guarantor without notice of acceptance.[60] Additionally, in certain circumstances, performance by the creditor can be sufficient to constitute acceptance if the guaranty was a condition precedent to the creditor's performance.[61]

The Oklahoma Supreme Court has also held that if a guaranty is made in response to an offer by the creditor, delivery of the guaranty to the creditor completes the contract of guaranty, and notice of its acceptance is not necessary.[62] Lastly, notice of acceptance of the guaranty is unnecessary if the notice was expressly waived in the guaranty.[63]

§ 6 Interpretation of Guaranties

Oklahoma courts will construe the guaranty against the guarantor and in favor of the creditor. Guaranty agreements will otherwise be construed in accordance with general rules of contract construction. Additionally, certain terms of art with respect to guaranties are statutorily prescribed.

6.1 General Principles

Oklahoma courts have consistently ruled that the guaranty contract should be construed against the guarantor and in favor of the creditor as the party who parted with property in reliance on the collateral promise of the guarantor.[64] However, there is a small line of cases that suggest if a guarantor gives a guaranty without compensation or without sharing in the benefits of the underlying transaction, the guaranty will be strictly construed and the guarantor cannot be held beyond the precise terms of the guaranty contract.[65]

Contracts of guaranty are otherwise construed according to the rules of construction generally, many of which are set forth in Title 15 of the Oklahoma Statutes.[66] Therefore, the mutual intent of the parties at the time of contract-

59. Okla. Stat. tit. 15, § 326.
60. Okla. Stat. tit. 15, § 326; Shepherd Mall State Bank v. Johnson, 603 P.2d 1115 (Okla. 1979).
61. Ross v. Russell, 475 P.2d 152 (Okla. 1970); Penner v. International Harvester Co. of America, 41 P.2d 843 (Okla. 1935).
62. Miller v. Oil Well Supply Co., 191 P. 1094 (Okla. 1920); Oklahoma City Nat. Bank v. Ezzard, 159 P. 267 (Okla. 1916).
63. Penner v. International Harvester Co. of America, 41 P.2d 843 (Okla. 1935).
64. Riverside National Bank v. Manolakis, 613 P.2d 438 (Okla. 1980) (the terms of a guaranty agreement should be read in favor of one who has parted with property in reliance on the collateral promise of guarantor); First Nat. Bank v. Cleveland, 260 P. 80 (Okla. 1927); *but see* Okla. Stat. tit. 15, § 373 ("A surety cannot be held beyond the express terms of his contract, and if such contract prescribes a penalty for its breach, he cannot in any case be liable for more than the penalty").
65. Lamm & Co. v. Colcord, 98 P. 355, 356 (Okla. 1908) (the guarantor has the right to prescribe the exact terms of the obligation, and to insist upon a discharge in case the terms are not strictly observed); Fuqua v. Tulsa Masonic Bldg. Ass'n., 263 P. 660, 662 (Okla. 1928); Chowning v. First State Bank of Tuskahoma, 225 P. 715, 716 (1924).
66. INA Life Ins. Co. v. Brandywine Assocs., Ltd. 800 P.2d 1073, 1076 (Okla. Civ. App. 1990); Okla. Stat. tit. 15, § 374 ("In interpreting the terms of a contract of suretyship, the same rules are to be observed as in the case of other contracts."). *See* Okla. Stat. tit. 15, §§ 151 *et seq.*, for statutory rules governing contract interpretation.

ing governs the meaning of the guaranty contract.[67] The intent of the parties to a guaranty contract is to be determined from the whole instrument, and if the language of a contract of guaranty is clear and explicit, the intent of the parties must be ascertained from such language, without resort to extrinsic evidence.[68] Ambiguities in a guaranty contract may by explained through the introduction of extrinsic evidence.[69]

6.2 Guaranty of Payment versus Guaranty of Collection

A guaranty of payment or performance is deemed unconditional unless the terms of the guaranty agreement place a condition precedent on the guarantor's liability.[70] The guarantor is liable to the creditor immediately upon default of the primary obligor without any requirement of demand or notice.[71]

A guaranty of solvency or collection is a guaranty that the primary obligor will be solvent and that the creditor will be able to collect the underlying obligation by the usual legal proceedings, if taken with reasonable diligence.[72] Under a guaranty of collection, the guarantor generally is not liable unless the creditor has not been able to collect the underlying obligation through legal proceedings or the primary obligor is insolvent.[73] A creditor is not required to initiate legal proceedings against the primary obligor on the underlying obligation, or upon any collateral securing its payment, if no part of the underlying obligation could have been collected thereby.[74] Additionally, with respect to a guaranty of solvency, the primary obligor will be deemed insolvent for the purpose of giving rise to the obligations and liability of the guarantor if the primary obligor leaves Oklahoma and there is no property in the state from which the underlying obligation might be satisfied.[75]

6.3 Guaranties of Completion or Other Nonmonetary Obligations

Oklahoma recognizes guaranties of completion and other types of performance guaranties or surety contracts for obligations other than for the payment of money. By far the most common type covered in Oklahoma case law is a construction performance bond in which the obligation of the surety is to perform or finish work agreed upon or to pay for the cost of performing or finishing the work.[76] Outside of the construction context, however, there is little reported Oklahoma case law on the subject of guaranties or other surety contracts covering nonmonetary obligations. Enforcement of guaranties of performance is discussed in Section 15.2 of this chapter.

67. Okla. Stat. tit. 15, §§ 152, 164; Founders Bank & Trust Co. v. Upsher, 830 P.2d 1355 (Okla. 1992).
68. Okla. Stat. tit. 15, § 157; Rucker v. Republic Supply Co., 415 P.2d 951 (Okla. 1966).
69. Lum v. Lee Way Motor Freight, Inc., 757 P.2d 810, 815 (Okla. 1987).
70. Okla. Stat. tit. 15, § 331.
71. Okla. Stat. tit. 15, § 332; First Nat'l Bank & Trust Co. of Vinita v. Kissee, 859 P.2d 502, 507 (Okla. 1993).
72. Okla. Stat. tit. 15, § 328; Crowder State Bank v. American Powder Mills, 148 P. 698 (Okla. 1915).
73. Okla. Stat. tit. 15, § 328; Crowder State Bank v. American Powder Mills, 148 P. 698 (Okla. 1915).
74. Okla. Stat. tit. 15, § 329.
75. Okla. Stat. tit. 15, § 330.
76. American Cas. Co. v. Town of Shattuck, Okla., 228 F.Supp. 834 (W.D. Okla. 1964).

6.4 Language Regarding the Revocation of Guaranties

A guaranty cannot be revoked by the guarantor if the entire consideration from the creditor for the guaranty was wholly given at the time of the guaranty's execution.[77] A continuing guaranty can be revoked by the guarantor at any time with respect to future transactions unless there is a continuing consideration as to such future transactions, as opposed to separate consideration passing at the time of the future transaction and therefore making each transaction divisible or separable.[78] The guarantor under a continuing guaranty has the burden of giving notice in writing to creditor of its revocation as to future transactions.[79] An individual guarantor's death will not ordinarily revoke a guaranty if the guaranty could not be revoked by guarantor himself in his lifetime.[80]

6.5 "Continuing"

A guaranty of future obligations of the primary obligor to the creditor regarding successive transactions is a continuing guaranty, which as stated in Section 6.4 above can be revoked by the guarantor at any time with respect to future transactions unless there is a continuing consideration as to such future transactions.[81] A guaranty will be deemed continuing if it contemplates a future course of dealing, not limited to a single transaction, that will continue for an indefinite period of time or until it is revoked.[82] A continuing guaranty is deemed a repetition of the extension of credit so long as it is in force, and liability under a continuing guaranty will be deemed to have continued until it has been revoked by the guarantor if the guaranty agreement contains no express limitation as to duration of the guarantor's responsibility.[83]

6.6 "Absolute and Unconditional"

An absolute guaranty is binding on the guarantor without notice of acceptance.[84] Furthermore, a guaranty is deemed to be unconditional unless its terms import some condition precedent to the liability of the guarantor.[85] A lack of notice and demand or the insolvency of a primary obligor are not defenses in an action on an unconditional guaranty in the absence of fraud.[86] However, a

---

77. Bennett v. Checotah State Bank of Checotah, 56 P.2d 848 (Okla. 1936).
78. Okla. Stat. tit. 15, §§ 336, 337; Rucker v. Republic Supply Co., 415 P.2d 951, 953 (Okla. 1966).
79. Miller v. National Printing & Engraving Co., 45 P.2d 483 (Okla. 1935).
80. Bennett v. Checotah State Bank of Checotah, 56 P.2d 848 (Okla. 1936).
81. Okla. Stat. tit. 15, §§ 336, 337; Rucker v. Republic Supply Co., 415 P.2d 951, 953 (Okla. 1966).
82. Rucker v. Republic Supply Co., 415 P.2d 951 (Okla. 1966); Hazzard v. General Tire & Rubber Co., 76 P.2d 257 (Okla. 1937) (a continuing guaranty is a guaranty which is not limited to a particular or specific transaction, but which is intended to cover future transactions); First Nat. Bank & Trust Co. of El Reno v. Stinchcomb, 734 P.2d 852 (Okla. Civ. App. 1987) (under clear language of guaranty, which stated that guarantor promised to "pay and discharge all indebtedness upon which Debtor now is or may hereafter, from time to time become obligated to the bank," limited to amount of $20,000, guarantor was liable for debtor's continuing obligations, absent any evidence of actual fraud, and even though guarantor maintained that he did not read the document).
83. Rucker v. Republic Supply Co., 415 P.2d 951 (Okla. 1966).
84. Okla. Stat. tit. 15, § 326; Shepherd Mall State Bank v. Johnson, 603 P.2d 1115 (Okla. 1979).
85. Okla. Stat. tit. 15, § 331.
86. Masters v. Boyes, 145 P. 363 (Okla. 1914).

statement that a guaranty is absolute and unconditional alone is generally not effective to waive the guarantor's suretyship defenses.[87]

6.7 "Liable as a Primary Obligor and Not Merely as Surety"

If an agreement contained the above language obligating the party signing such agreement as a primary obligor rather than a guarantor, Oklahoma courts would most likely respect the intent of the parties and enforce the agreement against the signing party as a primary obligor. Oklahoma courts will determine whether an agreement by one person to answer for the obligation of another person was intended to be a "collateral" obligation, meaning the person will be treated as a guarantor under Oklahoma law, or an "original" obligation, meaning the person will be deemed to be a primary obligor with respect to such agreement. By statute, certain agreements to answer for the obligation of another person will be deemed "original" covenants.[88] The determination as to whether an agreement to answer for the obligation of another person is collateral or original primarily affects whether or not the agreement needs to be in writing to be enforceable, since Oklahoma's guaranty statutes require a guaranty to be in writing.[89]

§ 7 Defenses of the Guarantor; Set-off

Oklahoma law provides for typical common law suretyship defenses for guarantors. In addition, Oklahoma statutes governing guarantors and sureties contain a number of defenses, including the right of set-off.[90] However, as discussed in Section 8 of this chapter, a guarantor may waive the benefit of the defenses in advance under the guaranty agreement, including the set-off rights under Oklahoma's antideficiency statutes, even if such defenses or rights could not be waived by the primary obligor.[91]

7.1 Defenses of the Primary Obligor

7.1.1 General

By statute, the obligation of a guarantor must be neither larger in amount, nor in other respects more burdensome than that of the primary obligor and will be reduced in proportion to the underlying obligation if it exceeds the underlying obligation.[92] However, this statutory requirement has been held to

87. Bank of Okla., N.A. v. Welco, Inc., 898 P.2d 172, 178 (Okla. Civ. App. 1995) (finding that the guarantor was discharged based on Okla. Stat. tit. 15, § 344 in absence of effective waiver language even though the guaranty agreement stated that the guaranty was absolute and unconditional).
88. Okla. Stat. tit. 15, § 325; Reed v. Richards & Conover Hardware Co., 110 P.2d 603 (Okla. 1941).
89. *See* Fischer v. Bashwitz, 5 P.2d 356 (Okla. 1931).
90. Okla. Stat. tit. 15, §§ 321-344 (guaranty) and §§ 371-385 (suretyship).
91. Okla. Stat. tit. 12, § 686, discussed in detail in Section 15.3 of this chapter.
92. Okla. Stat. tit. 15, § 334.

relate to conditions in existence at the time of the execution of the guaranty.[93] Although the guaranty agreement's original obligation may be fixed to assure that the guarantor's obligation does not exceed that of the primary obligor at the time of execution, the guarantor may further agree that, upon the occurrence of some specified event, its liability will remain the same even though the primary obligor's underlying obligation may be decreased.[94]

7.1.2 When Guarantor May Assert Primary Obligor's Defense

In general, a guarantor may assert any defense against the creditor that the primary obligor could assert against the creditor except the defenses of infancy, lack of legal capacity, and discharge in insolvency proceedings.[95] Although a judgment against the primary obligor is at least prima facie evidence in an action against a guarantor brought by the creditor, the guarantor is permitted to defend by showing all matters that might have been asserted by the primary obligor.[96] If the underlying obligation is a conditional obligation, the guarantor's liability is commensurate with that of the primary obligor, and therefore the guarantor cannot be held liable if the condition to the primary obligor's liability has not yet occurred.[97]

7.1.3 Defenses that May not be Raised by Guarantor

A guarantor is liable to the creditor notwithstanding any personal disability of the primary obligor, such as lack of capacity or infancy, even if the disability makes the contract creating the underlying obligation void as against the primary obligor.[98] Additionally, the insolvency of a primary obligor is not a defense in an action on an unconditional guaranty.[99] Further, a guarantor cannot use a defense which the primary obligor has waived or is estopped from raising.[100]

7.1.4 Defenses that May Always be Raised by Guarantor

A guarantor will not be liable if the underlying contract is illegal.[101] In addition, any restriction in a contract preventing a party to the contract from access to tribunals to enforce its rights under the contract or which limits the time to enforce its rights is void.[102] However, an agreement by the guarantor to

93. Founders Bank and Trust Co. v. Upsher, 830 P.2d 1355 (Okla. 1992); please note that there are not yet any reported cases interpreting the enforceability of guaranties under Okla. Stat. tit. 15, § 334 given in connection with loans that are nonrecourse to the principal.
94. Founders Bank and Trust Co. v. Upsher, 830 P.2d 1355 (Okla. 1992).
95. Okla. Stat. tit. 12A, § 3-305(d) and Okla. official cmt. 6; Okla. Stat. tit. 15, § 335.
96. Peery v. Merrill, 179 P. 28 (Okla. 1918).
97. Okla. Stat. tit. 15, § 333.
98. Okla. Stat. tit. 15, § 335.
99. Masters v. Boyes, 145 P. 363 (Okla. 1914).
100. M.S. Cohn Gravel Co. v. Southern Surety Co., 264 P. 206 (Okla. 1927).
101. Okla. Stat. tit. 15, § 335.
102. Okla. Stat. tit. 15, § 216.

waive the right of set-off has been found not to be an unenforceable restriction against access to the courts.[103]

7.2 "Suretyship" Defenses

By statute, any act of the creditor taken without the consent of the guarantor and which alters the underlying obligation of the primary obligor in any respect, or impairs or suspends the remedies or rights of the creditor against the primary obligor in respect thereto, exonerates the guarantor.[104] In practice, however, Oklahoma courts have limited the ability of guarantors to be exonerated. Additionally, in general, a guarantor is not discharged merely because the cause of action against a primary obligor is barred.[105] Furthermore, a guarantor is not exonerated by the discharge of the primary obligor by operation of law, without the intervention or omission of the creditor.[106]

7.2.1 Change in Identity of Principal Obligor

A release of one primary obligor without the consent of the guarantor operates to release the guarantor.[107] Also, the addition of another primary obligor to a note can discharge the guarantor.[108] The replacement of a primary obligor with a receiver does not exonerate the guarantor when the guaranty is continuing and obligatory.[109]

7.2.2 Modification of the Underlying Obligation, Including Release

Oklahoma's guaranty statutes provide that any act of the creditor taken without the consent of the guarantor and which alters the underlying obligation of the primary obligor in any respect, or impairs or suspends the remedies or rights of the creditor against the primary obligor in respect thereto, exonerates the guarantor.[110] This includes an extension of time for repayment by the primary obligor not contemplated in the guarantor's agreement.[111] Additionally, the release of the underlying obligation of the primary obligor will act to discharge the guarantor who can no longer recover against his principal.[112] However, a guarantor who has been indemnified by the primary obligor is liable to the creditor to the extent of the indemnity, notwithstanding that the creditor may

103. Local Federal Bank, F.S.B. v. JICO, Inc., 842 P.2d 368 (Okla. Civ. App. 1992).
104. Okla. Stat. tit. 15, § 338.
105. Apache Lanes, Inc. v. National Educators Life Ins. Co., 529 P.2d 984 (Okla. 1974).
106. Okla. Stat. tit. 15, § 344.
107. Shuttee v. Coalgate Grain Co., 172 P. 780 (Okla. 1918).
108. Bank of Commerce of Sulphur v. Webster, 172 P. 942 (Okla. 1918).
109. F.D.I.C. v. Inhofe, 16 F.3d 371 (10th Cir. 1994).
110. Okla. Stat. tit. 15, § 338; Dynalectron Corp. v. Jack Richards Aircraft Co., 337 F. Supp. 659, 663 (W.D. Okla. 1972).
111. *See* Sawyer v. Bahnsen, 226 P. 344, 345 (Okla. 1924) and Kremke v. Radamaker, 159 P. 475 (Okla. 1916) regarding extensions of time; *but see* Patty v. Price, 304 P.2d 289 (Okla. 1956); *see* First Enterprise Bank v. Be-Graphic, Inc., 149 P.3d 1064 (Okla. Civ. App. 2006) regarding both loan renewals and increases.
112. Shuttee v. Coalgate Grain Co., 172 P. 780, 782 (Okla. 1918).

have modified the contract or released the primary obligor without the consent of the guarantor.[113]

7.2.3 Release or Impairment of Security for the Underlying Obligation

Release or impairment of collateral can constitute a successful suretyship defense to the extent of the value of the collateral.[114] However, a continuing and unconditional guarantor whose agreement is not tied to a specific note or collateral is not entitled to the benefit of the impairment of collateral defense.[115]

7.3 Other Defenses

7.3.1 Failure to Fulfill a Condition Precedent

A guaranty is deemed unconditional unless the guaranty agreement expressly provides for conditions precedent to the liability of the guarantor.[116] At any rate, as a general rule for interpreting contracts, Oklahoma courts do not favor making contracts dependent on future contingencies unless required to do so by the plain, unambiguous language of the contract.[117] However, if a creditor and guarantor have agreed to a condition precedent to the liability of the guarantor or the effectiveness of the guaranty, the failure to fulfill such condition precedent will constitute a defense to the liability of the guarantor under the guaranty.[118]

7.3.2 Modification of the Guaranty

By statute, a contract in writing may be modified by another contract in writing, or by an executed oral agreement, and not otherwise.[119] Additionally, a material physical alteration of a guaranty contract to the guarantor's detriment will extinguish the guarantor's liability.[120]

---

113. Okla. Stat. tit. 15, § 343.
114. Okla. Stat. tit. 12A, § 3-605(f); Smiley v. Wheeler, 602 P.2d 209, 212 (Okla. 1979) (if a creditor loses its security interest in collateral, a surety has also lost its right of recovery against collateral; and such failure to keep security interest alive by creditor is an impairment of collateral warranting discharge of surety, extending the benefit of Okla. Stat. tit. 12A § 3-606, now superseded, to a surety).
115. First City Bank, N.A. v. Air Capitol Aircraft Sales, Inc., 820 F.2d 1127 (10th Cir. 1987).
116. Okla. Stat. tit. 15, § 331.
117. M.J. Lee Construction Co. v. Oklahoma Transp. Authority, 125 P.3d 1205 (Okla. 2005); Dillon v. Dillon, 575 P.2d 127 (Okla. Civ. App. 1977), cited in Meacham v. Oklahoma Bank and Trust Co., 600 P.2d 868 (Okla. Civ. App. 1979), in which the guarantor failed to establish that his liability was subject to conditions precedent.
118. Southern Trust Co. v. Vaughn, 277 F. 145 (8th Cir. 1921) (the failure by the original creditor to record a mortgage, which was expressly made a condition precedent to the obligation of a guarantor, constituted defense to an action brought by a subsequent creditor who acquired the underlying obligation) (applying Oklahoma law); Federal Nat. Bank & Trust Co. of Shawnee v. Shanon Drilling, Inc., 762 P.2d 928 (Okla. 1988) (guaranties that were unconditional by their terms but were found to be subject to an oral agreement made by the creditor creating a condition precedent that the guaranties would not be effective unless condition precedent was fulfilled).
119. Okla. Stat. tit. 15, § 237; *See* KKK Medicine Co. v. Harrington, 201 P. 496 (Okla. 1921) concerning an alteration to a guaranty made without the guarantor's consent.
120. Haines Pipeline Const., Inc. v. Exline Gas Systems, 921 P.2d 955 (Okla. Civ. App. 1996), citing Okla. Stat. tit. 15, § 239.

7.3.3 Failure to Pursue Obligor

Mere delay on the part of a creditor to proceed against the primary obligor, or to enforce any other remedy, does not exonerate a guarantor.[121] Generally, a creditor is not required to first pursue the primary obligor before bringing an action against the guarantor. Further, a showing that the primary obligor had the ability to pay the underlying obligation and the creditor failed to first pursue the primary obligor does not release the guarantor.[122] It is the responsibility of the guarantor to see that the primary obligor pays the underlying obligation when due, and the passive inactivity or delay of the creditor to foreclose on a mortgage or security interest is not a defense "in the absence of a legal demand" by the guarantor.[123] However, if the underlying obligation is secured by a mortgage, the creditor's failure to pursue the primary obligor in accordance with the timeframe in Oklahoma's antideficiency statute, thereby discharging the primary obligor, can result in the discharge of the guarantor absent a waiver of defenses based upon alteration, impairment, or suspension of the underlying obligation.[124]

7.3.4 Statute of Limitations

An action to recover on a guaranty agreement cannot be defended by showing that the claim against the primary obligor has been barred by the statute of limitations.[125] However, an action on the guaranty agreement itself is subject to the five-year statute of limitations applicable to written contracts generally.[126]

7.3.5 Statute of Frauds

A guaranty must be in writing and signed by the guarantor to be enforceable.[127] However, if the covenant is original and not collateral, then the covenant need not be in writing.[128] In determining whether a covenant is "original" or "collateral" so as to be within the statute of frauds as a contract of guaranty, it is immaterial that a third party's obligation will be paid in consequence of the performance of the contract, and immaterial whether the primary obligor remains liable.[129] See Section 6.7 of this chapter for an additional discussion

121. Okla. Stat. tit. 15, § 342.
122. Palmer v. Noe, 150 P. 462 (Okla. 1915).
123. Carver v. Tinker Field Employees Credit Union, 442 P.2d 342 (Okla. 1968).
124. Bank of Okla., N.A. v. Welco, Inc., 898 P.2d 172 (Okla. Civ. App. 1995) (failure of second mortgagee to seek deficiency judgment against mortgagor in first mortgagee's foreclosure action impaired mortgagor's obligation on promissory note and thereby exonerated guarantor's liability, absent language in guaranty agreement waiving guarantor's defenses to liability based upon alteration, impairment, or suspension of original obligation) (citing Apache Lanes, Inc. v. National Educators Life Ins. Co., 529 P.2d 984 (Okla. 1974)).
125. Apache Lanes, Inc. v. National Educators Life Ins. Co., 529 P.2d 984 (Okla. 1974).
126. Okla. Stat. tit. 12, § 95A.1; this should not apply to the six-year statute of limitations applicable to an accommodation party signing an instrument as a guarantor or surety under Article 3 of the Oklahoma UCC, Okla. Stat. tit. 12A, §§ 3-118 and 3-419.
127. Okla. Stat. tit. 15, § 324.
128. Okla. Stat. tit. 15, § 325; Reed v. Richards & Conover Hardware Co., 110 P.2d 603 (Okla. 1941).
129. Reed v. Richards & Conover Hardware Co., 110 P.2d 603 (Okla. 1941).

of "original" versus "collateral" covenants to pay the obligation of another person.

7.3.6 Defenses Particular to Guarantors that are Natural Persons and their Spouses

There do not appear to be any defenses to liability on the guaranty itself that are particular to a guarantor who is a natural person. A nonguarantor spouse is not liable for the obligation of the guarantor spouse.[130] If the guaranty is secured by real property that is the homestead of the individual or his or her spouse, a creditor should be aware that Oklahoma's constitutional and statutory homestead rights which accrue to the benefit of an individual and the individual's spouse may impact the creditor's rights with respect to such property, as also discussed in Section 2.5 of this chapter.[131] Homestead rights may not be released or waived.[132] Furthermore, certain additional personal and business property of an Oklahoma resident is exempt from attachment or execution or any other form of forced sale for the payment of debts.[133]

7.4 Right of Set-off

If a creditor accepts anything in partial satisfaction of the underlying obligation, it reduces the obligation of the guarantor to the same extent as that of the primary obligor.[134] However, although the primary obligor has the right to claim a credit for the fair market value of real property sold at a foreclosure sale, this right can be waived by a guarantor in the guaranty agreement, such that the guarantor will only be able to set off the amount for which the property is actually sold at the foreclosure sale, including the amount of any credit bid by the creditor.[135] Although the principal obligor may set off against the underlying obligation any obligation owed by the creditor to the primary obligor, a guarantor will not be able to do so unless the guarantor shows the insolvency of the primary obligor and the inability to obtain relief either in an action brought by the guarantor or as a defense to an action on the underlying obligation.[136]

§ 8 Waiver of Defenses by the Guarantor

Guarantors may waive suretyship defenses either through consenting to the action of the creditor or through a waiver contained in the guaranty agree-

130. Okla. Stat. tit. 43, § 208.
131. Okla. Const. art. XII; Okla. Stat. tit. 31, § 2.
132. Grenard v. McMahan, 441 P.2d 950 (Okla. 1968); Thomas v. James, 202 P. 499 (Okla. 1921).
133. Okla. Stat. tit. 31, § 1.
134. Okla. Stat. tit. 15, § 341.
135. Founders Bank & Trust Co. v. Upsher, 830 P.2d 1355 (Okla. 1992).
136. Willoughby v. Ball, 90 P. 1017 (Okla. 1907).

ment.[137] Oklahoma's statutory protections for guarantors are default rules that the guarantor may contractually waive.[138] Diligence, presentment, protest, notice of dishonor, demand of payment, extension of time for payment, notice of acceptance, enforcement without resorting to collateral, release or subordination of collateral, partial release of liability, and similar defenses are generally waived in the guaranty agreement and such waivers have been upheld by Oklahoma courts.[139] Furthermore, general waiver language in the guaranty agreement will be sufficient to waive statutory defenses and protections.[140]

8.1 Defenses that cannot be Waived

In analyzing the waiver by a guarantor of its statutory and common law defenses, the Oklahoma Supreme Court has held that, absent illegality, the parties to a guaranty are free to bargain as they see fit, and courts will respect the terms of the bargained-for agreement of the parties.[141] While the Oklahoma Supreme Court has suggested that waiver of statutory guarantor and surety defenses could be unenforceable for public policy reasons, the Court has not elaborated on what types of waivers might violate Oklahoma public policy.[142] Although the results may sometimes be harsh, the Oklahoma Supreme Court has acknowledged that a creditor parting with funds may extract from guarantors terms and conditions less favorable than those afforded by statute.[143] Additionally, any defenses or rights available at law or in equity, other than the defense of satisfaction of the underlying obligation, can be effectively waived, including a right to set off for the fair market value of real property securing the underlying obligation that is sold at a foreclosure sale.[144]

8.2 "Catch-all" Waivers

A statement that the guarantor waives all suretyship defenses should be sufficient under Oklahoma law to waive all suretyship defenses.[145] Additionally, if a guaranty agreement provides that the guarantor waives the benefit of "any" statutory provision limiting the liability of a guarantor, including "without limitation" several specific statutory provisions, the waiver is still effective to waive the benefit of any defenses contained in statutes omitted from the

137. Okla. Stat. tit. 15, § 338; Founders Bank & Trust Co. v. Upsher, 830 P.2d 1355, 1363-64 (Okla. 1992).
138. Founders Bank & Trust Co. v. Upsher, 830 P.2d 1355, 1363-64 (Okla. 1992).
139. *See* Okla. Stat. tit. 12A, § 3-605 Okla. cmt. 31; Riverside Nat'l Bank v. Manolakis, 613 P.2d 438 (Okla. 1980); Black v. O'Haver, 567 F.2d 361 (10th Cir. 1977).
140. Black v. O'Haver, 567 F.2d 361 (10th Cir. 1977) (guarantors of loan agreement were not exonerated from their obligation under law of Oklahoma when loan agreement was amended, since guaranty provided that liability of guarantors was not affected by "any amendment or modification of the provisions of the Building Loan Agreement"); Ford Motor Credit Co. v. Milburn, 615 F. 2d 892, 899 (10th Cir. 1980) (guarantor's promise to pay any existing and future debts of principal sufficient to waive discharge under Okla. Stat. tit. 15, § 338 based on alteration of the original obligation); First National Bank and Trust Co. of Vinita v. Kissee, 859 P.2d 502, 508 (Okla. 1993) (guarantor agreed to renewals or extensions in guaranty agreement and therefore guarantor was not entitled to discharge based on an extension of time for payment of the original obligation by the debtor).
141. Founders Bank & Trust Co. v. Upsher, 830 P.2d 1355, 1362 (Okla. 1992).
142. Founders Bank & Trust Co. v. Upsher, 830 P.2d 1355 (Okla. 1992).
143. JPMorgan Chase Bank, N.A. v. Specialty Restaurants, Inc., 243 P.3d 8 (Okla. 2010).
144. *Id.*
145. Okla. Stat. tit. 12A, § 3-605 Okla. cmt. 31.

specific list.[146] Because Oklahoma courts construe the guaranty agreement against the guarantor and in favor of the creditor, waiver language in the guaranty agreement is typically liberally construed.

8.3 Use of Specific Waivers

With respect to statutory defenses, it is effective to use specific waivers by reference to the type of defense waived or by reference to the statutory provisions by section number.[147]

§ 9 Third-party Pledgors—Defenses and Waiver Thereof

A person who hypothecates property as security for the performance of an act by another person in favor of a third party is a surety.[148] Whenever property of a surety is hypothecated with the property of the primary obligor, the surety is entitled to have the property of the primary obligor first applied to the discharge of the underlying obligation.[149] However, the protection of this suretyship defense, like all provisions under the Oklahoma statutes governing suretyship relations in Oklahoma, may be relinquished by contractual waiver.[150]

§ 10 Jointly and Severally Liable Guarantors—Contribution and Reduction of Obligations Upon Payment by a Co-Obligor

A guarantor, upon satisfying the underlying obligation of the primary obligor, is entitled to require all coguarantors to contribute thereto, without regard to the order of time in which they became guarantors.[151] However, a guarantor does not have a claim for reimbursement or contribution against any other persons, even though such persons may have been benefited by the guarantor's payment of the underlying obligation. Generally, any amount received by the creditor from a guarantor reduces the obligation of any coguarantors.

146. JPMorgan Chase Bank, N.A. v. Specialty Restaurants, Inc., 243 P.3d 8 (Okla. 2010).
147. Riverside National Bank v. Manolakis, 613 P.2d 438 (Okla. 1980); Haines Pipeline Const., Inc. v. Exline Gas Systems, Inc., 921 P.2d 955 (Okla. Civ. App. 1996) (guarantor agreed that his liability would not be "affected or impaired" by failure of lender to protect collection of the indebtedness or the collateral); Local Federal Bank, F.S.B. v. JICO, Inc., 842 P.2d 368 (Okla. Civ. App. 1992) (guarantor waived all set-offs and counterclaim); JPMorgan Chase Bank, N.A. v. Specialty Restaurants, Inc., 243 P.3d 8 (Okla. 2010).
148. Okla. Stat. tit. 15, § 371; Stevens v. First Nat. Bank, 245 P. 567 (Okla. 1925).
149. Okla. Stat. tit. 15, § 384; Harden v. American-First Nat. Bank, 6 P.2d 1060 (Okla. 1931).
150. Founders Bank & Trust Co. v. Upsher, 830 P.2d 1355 (Okla. 1992); *but see* First Enterprise Bank v. Be-Graphic, Inc., 149 P.3d 1064 (Okla. Civ. App. 2006), in which the waiver provisions in the pledgor's mortgage were found insufficient to be deemed consent to an increase in the indebtedness, resulting in exoneration of the mortgage.
151. Okla. Stat. tit. 15, § 382.

10.1 Contribution

If one coguarantor, who is jointly and severally bound, pays the underlying obligation, such guarantor is entitled to contribution from the other coguarantors on a pro rata basis.[152] Although coguarantors are generally deemed to be responsible to each other for equal portions of the underlying obligation, coguarantors may by express contract fix or determine their relative liabilities among themselves, notwithstanding the obligation for equitable contribution arising from the original guaranty agreement.[153] Alternatively, equitable principles may require a different allocation of liability among coguarantors, such as one based on their respective ownership interests in the principal obligor.[154] A guarantor is entitled to the benefit of any collateral securing the performance or repayment of the underlying obligation held by a coguarantor.[155]

If a creditor executes on property of a guarantor in satisfaction of a judgment or a guarantor otherwise pays the judgment amount, the guarantor may compel contribution from the other coguarantors, and such guarantor is entitled to the benefit of the creditor's judgment to enforce such contribution if the guarantor files a notice of its payment and its claim to contribution with the court clerk where the judgment was rendered within 10 days after payment of the judgment.[156] Upon the filing of the notice, the court clerk is directed to make an entry thereof in the margin of the docket.[157]

10.2 Reduction of Obligations Upon Payment of Co-Obligor

The acceptance by a creditor of anything in partial satisfaction of the underlying obligation reduces the obligation of a guarantor in the same measure as that of a primary obligor, but does not otherwise affect it.[158] With respect to a limited guaranty, Okla. Stat. tit. 15, § 341 requires that payment on an obligation operates as a pro rata reduction of the guaranty, unless the guarantor has otherwise agreed in the guaranty agreement.[159]

10.3 Liability of Parent Guarantors Owning Less than 100 percent of Primary Obligor

There does not appear to be Oklahoma case law specific to this issue.

---

152. Strickler v. Gitchel, 78 P. 94 (Okla. 1904).
153. Bank of the Wichitas v. Ledford, 151 P.3d 103 (Okla. 2006); National Printing & Office Supply Co. v. Frank, 343 P.2d 1092 (Okla. 1959); Provine v. Wilson, 80 P.2d 291 (Okla. 1938).
154. Brown v. Goldsmith, 437 P.2d 247 (Okla. 1968).
155. Okla. Stat. tit. 15, § 383.
156. Okla. Stat. tit. 12, § 831.
157. Okla. Stat. tit. 12, § 831.
158. Okla. Stat. tit. 15, § 341.
159. State Capitol Bank of Oklahoma City v. Norick, 550 P.2d 587 (Okla. Civ. App. 1976).

§ 11 Reliance

A showing of reliance by the creditor on a guaranty agreement in order to grant the extension of future credit to the primary obligor can be a sufficient defense by the creditor against an objection that a guaranty not entered into contemporaneously with the underlying transaction was given without valuable consideration.[160] Such reliance on the guaranty prior to extending credit can also result in the guaranty being binding without notice of acceptance.[161] Additionally, a showing of reliance may be necessary for a creditor to enforce a guaranty agreement against an entity guarantor under a theory of apparent authority.[162]

§ 12 Subrogation

A guarantor, upon satisfying the underlying obligation of the primary obligor, is entitled to enforce every remedy which the creditor then has against the primary obligor until the guarantor is fully reimbursed for what it has expended.[163] Although a guarantor acquires all of the rights against the primary obligor that the creditor had upon payment of the underlying obligation through the equitable doctrine of subrogation, the guarantor cannot claim greater rights through subrogation than were possessed by the creditor.[164] A guarantor is entitled to the benefit of any collateral securing the performance or repayment of the underlying obligation held by the creditor, whether acquired at the time of entering into the guaranty agreement or acquired afterwards, and whether the guarantor was aware of the collateral security or not.[165]

If a creditor has executed on property of the guarantor in satisfaction of a judgment or the guarantor otherwise pays the judgment amount, the guarantor may compel repayment from the primary obligor, and the guarantor is entitled to the benefit of the creditor's judgment to enforce such repayment if the guarantor files a notice of its payment and its claim to repayment with the court clerk where the judgment was rendered within 10 days after payment of the judgment.[166] Upon the filing of the notice, the court clerk is directed to make an entry thereof in the margin of the docket.[167]

Oklahoma's statutes governing reimbursement of a guarantor and the guarantor's rights as against the primary obligor and coguarantors do not

160. Okla. Stat. tit. 15, § 322; Penner v. International Harvester Co. of America, 41 P.2d 843 (Okla. 1935); St. Louis & S. F. R. Co. v. Union Const. Co., 182 P. 241 (Okla. 1919).
161. *See* Section 5 of this chapter.
162. *See* Section 3 of this chapter.
163. Okla. Stat. tit. 15, § 382.
164. Moore v. White, 603 P.2d 1119 (Okla. 1979).
165. Okla. Stat. tit. 15, § 383.
166. Okla. Stat. tit. 12, § 831.
167. Okla. Stat. tit. 12, § 831.

abrogate or limit the equitable doctrine of subrogation or the rights available to the guarantor thereunder.[168]

§ 13 Triangular Set-off in Bankruptcy

There does not appear to be Oklahoma case law specific to this issue.

§ 14 Indemnification—Whether the Primary Obligor has a Duty

A guarantor has the right of exoneration and may compel the primary obligor to perform the underlying obligation when it becomes due.[169] Additionally, if a guarantor satisfies the underlying obligation, or any part thereof, whether with or without legal proceedings, the primary obligor is bound to reimburse the guarantor for all amounts the guarantor has disbursed, including necessary costs and expenses.[170] The guarantor's right to be reimbursed by the primary obligor has occasionally been expressed as an implied right to indemnification as well as a claim for restitution.[171]

§ 15 Enforcement of Guaranties

15.1 Limitations on Recovery

A creditor may only receive a single complete satisfaction of its judgment on the underlying obligation.[172] However, the possibility of collecting a judgment's unpaid balance from the primary obligor or coguarantors jointly and severally liable does not diminish a guarantor's present liability for the full amount of the unsatisfied balance.[173] A creditor may attempt to collect the balance of its judgment from any or all coguarantors.[174] In the event a guarantor believes the creditor has engaged in collection activities to obtain amounts exceeding the balance of the judgment, the Oklahoma Civil Procedure Code provides remedies for wrongful execution or garnishment.[175]

168. Maryland Cas. Co. v. King, 381 P.2d 153 (Okla. 1963).
169. Okla. Stat. tit. 15, § 380; Okla. Stat. tit. 12, § 1107.
170. Okla. Stat. tit. 15, § 382.
171. Sparks v. Childers, 2 Ind.T. 187, 47 S.W. 316 (1898) (a guarantor who pays an underlying obligation may sue the primary obligor at law on an implied promise to indemnify the guarantor); Apache Lanes, Inc. v. National Educators Life Ins. Co., 529 P.2d 984 (Okla. 1974) (a guarantor of a note may protect himself by paying the debt and suing the debtor for restitution).
172. Founders Bank & Trust Co. v. Upsher, 830 P.2d 1355, 1365 (Okla. 1992).
173. Founders Bank & Trust Co. v. Upsher, 830 P.2d 1355, 1364-65 (Okla. 1992).
174. Founders Bank & Trust Co. v. Upsher, 830 P.2d 1355, 1365 (Okla. 1992).
175. Okla. Stat. tit. 12, §§ 731 *et seq.* and Okla. Stat. tit. 12, §§ 1170 *et seq.*

15.2 Enforcement of Guaranties of Payment versus Guaranties of Performance

A primary distinction in the enforcement of guaranties of performance as compared to guaranties of payment is the right of third parties other than the specified creditor to enforce the guaranty. The most common performance guaranty covered by Oklahoma case law is a construction performance bond, which can result in actions properly brought against the surety by third parties not named as obligees on the bond, such as subcontractors.[176] A performance bond can also be the basis for repayment of a loan made to the surety's principal upon the principal's failure to perform under its contract.[177] Additionally, if a performance bond has been issued by an insurance company, such bond has been held to constitute an insurance contract, thereby subjecting the surety on the bond to implied duties of good faith and fair dealing, a breach of which could give rise to a successful tort claim.[178]

15.3 Exercising Rights Under a Guaranty Where the Underlying Obligation is also Secured by a Mortgage

Oklahoma's civil procedure statutes require a creditor that wishes to obtain a deficiency judgment against a mortgagor after foreclosure on property securing the obligation to seek a deficiency judgment against the mortgagor within 90 days after the date of the foreclosure sale.[179] In the event the fair market value of the mortgaged property exceeds the purchase price at the foreclosure sale, the mortgagor may assert the market value of the mortgaged property as a set-off against the deficiency amount.[180] The Oklahoma Supreme Court has interpreted the 90-day limitation of Okla. Stat. tit. 12, § 686 to completely extinguish the mortgage debt and discharge the mortgagor from liability.[181] Similar protections for the mortgagor are located in Oklahoma's power of sale statute.[182]

The Oklahoma Supreme Court has held that the protection of Okla. Stat. tit. 12, § 686 applies only to mortgagors and does not, per se, operate to exonerate a guarantor from liability on the underlying obligation deemed satisfied by such statute; rather, the liability of the guarantor for any deficiency deemed satisfied by this statute will depend on the terms of the guaranty agreement.[183] While a waiver of the benefits of § 686 by the mortgagor is not enforceable against the mortgagor, a guarantor may waive the right to set off

176. Byler v. Great Am. Ins. Co., 395 F.2d 273 (10th Cir. 1968) (subcontractors with direct contracts with the general contractor/principal were able to successfully make claims on the performance bond obtained by the owner).
177. Lippert Bros. Inc. v. National Union Fire Ins. Co., 247 F.Supp. 874 (W.D. Okla. 1965) (lender to a subcontractor/principal was a co-obligee on the bond with the general contractor and held a collateral assignment of the subcontract that was not performed).
178. Worldlogics Corp. v. Chatham Reinsurance Corp., 108 P.3d 5 (Okla. Civ. App. 2004).
179. Okla. Stat. tit. 12, § 686.
180. Okla. Stat. tit. 12, § 686.
181. Apache Lanes, Inc. v. National Educators Life Ins. Co., 529 P.2d 984, 986 (Okla. 1974).
182. Okla. Stat. tit. 46, § 43(A)(2).
183. Riverside National Bank v. Manolakis, 613 P.2d 438 (Okla. 1980).

the fair market value of mortgaged property provided under § 686 and such waiver will be enforced.[184]

Absent a waiver by the guarantor in the guaranty agreement, a creditor's failure to seek a timely deficiency judgment under § 686 can result in a discharge of the guarantor based on application of Okla. Stat. tit. 15, §§ 344 and 338.[185] However, a contractual waiver of any right of set-off by the guarantor is sufficient to waive the set-off provided in § 686 for the fair market value of the mortgaged property, regardless of whether or not the creditor has failed to bring an action against the primary obligor within the 90-day limitation contained in the statute.[186]

15.4 Litigating Guaranty Claims: Procedural Considerations

A guarantor may require the creditor to first proceed against primary obligor prior to proceeding against the guarantor unless the guarantor has waived that right in the guaranty agreement.[187] However, Oklahoma case law suggests that this is the exception rather than the rule, and the majority of cases interpreting the statute that is the basis for this right have found that the guarantor has waived or otherwise lost the right to require the creditor to first proceed against the primary obligor.[188]

A creditor may join the guarantor in an action against the primary obligor or bring a separate action against the guarantor prior or subsequent to the action against the primary obligor. Typically, however, when the creditor files a foreclosure suit against property securing the underlying obligation, the creditor will name the guarantors as additional parties to the suit. Once the creditor has received judgment against the primary obligor and multiple coguarantors who are jointly and severally liable, the creditor may pursue all possible avenues of recovery simultaneously until the judgment is satisfied.[189]

---

184. Founders Bank & Trust Co. v. Upsher, 830 P.2d 1355, 1359 n. 4 (Okla. 1992).

185. Apache Lanes, Inc. v. National Educators Life Ins. Co., 529 P.2d 984 (Okla. 1974) (mortgagee who first sought a deficiency judgment by bringing an action against guarantors of mortgage note five years after foreclosure sale had no cause of action against guarantors because the debt had been discharged under Okla. Stat. tit. 15, § 344); Bank of Okla., N.A. v. Welco, Inc., 898 P.2d 172, 178 (Okla. Civ. App. 1995) (finding no waiver and relying on *Apache* to hold that a guarantor was exonerated under § 344 because the creditor failed to pursue a timely deficiency judgment under Okla. Stat. tit. 12, § 686); INA Life Ins. Co. v. Brandywine Assocs., Ltd., 800 P.2d 1073, 1076 (Okla. Civ. App. 1990) (recognizing that *Apache* was based on application of Okla. Stat. tit. 15, §§ 338, 344).

186. Founders Bank & Trust Co. v. Upsher, 830 P.2d 1355, 1363 (Okla. 1992).; Riverside National Bank v. Manolakis, 613 P.2d 438 (Okla. 1980) (a guarantor's agreement that its liability would not be affected or impaired by any failure, neglect, or omission of the creditor to protect the collection of the indebtedness or the security given therefor is sufficient to waive defenses under Okla. Stat. tit. 15, § 344 and therefore the guarantor is not exonerated under Okla. Stat. tit. 12, § 686 through creditor's omission in procuring deficiency judgment); Black v. O'Haver, 567 F.2d 361 (10th Cir. 1977) (provision contained in guaranty agreement wherein guarantors consented to liability notwithstanding "the release of the Borrower from performance or observance of any of the agreements, covenants, terms or conditions contained in [the underlying agreements] by operation of law" operated to deprive guarantors of whatever benefit they might have gained by fictional satisfaction of mortgage debt under law of Oklahoma from proceeds of foreclosure sale of property insofar as items of judgment against guarantors corresponded to debt deemed satisfied by sale).

187. Okla. Stat. tit. 15, § 379.

188. *See, e.g.*, Yell v. Davis, 123 P.2d 681 (Okla. 1942); Gregg v. Oklahoma State Bank of Ada, 179 P. 613 (Okla. 1919).

189. Founders Bank & Trust Co. v. Upsher, 830 P.2d 1355, 1364 (Okla. 1992).

§ 16 Revival and Reinstatement of Guaranties

The rescission of an agreement that alters the underlying obligation of a primary obligor or impairs the remedy of a creditor will not act to restore the liability of a guarantor who has been exonerated by such agreement.[190]

§ 17 Choice of Law in Guaranties

Choice of law issues related to guaranties will be analyzed in accordance with Oklahoma's rules regarding choice of law with respect to contracts generally, and assuming the parties' choice of law provision contained in the guaranty agreement does not violate the public policy of Oklahoma, such choice of law provision should be upheld by an Oklahoma court.[191]

190. Okla. Stat. tit. 15, § 340.
191. Dean Witter Reynolds, Inc. v. Shear, 796 P.2d 296, 298-299 (Okla. 1990); Pate v. MFA Mutual Ins. Co., 649 P.2d 809 (Okla. Civ. App. 1982); Moore v. Subaru of America, 891 F.2d 1445 (10th Cir. 1989).

Oregon State Law of Guaranties

Michael R. Silvey
Lane Powell PC
601 SW Second Avenue, Suite 2100
Portland, OR 97204-3158
503.778.2100
www.lanepowell.com

LANE POWELL
ATTORNEYS & COUNSELORS

Contents

Oregon State Law of Guaranties

OREGON LAW HIGHLIGHTS

1. Oregon has no statutory suretyship defenses so specific and general waivers for such defenses are required.
2. Oregon courts use common law principles relating to suretyship defenses and rely upon Restatement (Third) of Suretyship and Guaranty.
3. Discharge of a guarantor is based upon an analysis of whether the guarantor consented to the change of the underlying obligation and if it did not, then whether the change increased the risk to the guarantor
4. A guarantor after a nonjudicial foreclosure of real property is released from any liability for a deficiency.

Introductory Note: In order to standardize our discussion of the law of guaranties, we use the following vocabulary to refer to the various parties to a guaranty and their obligations.

"Guarantor" means a person who, by contract, agrees to satisfy an underlying obligation of another to an obligee upon the primary obligor's default on that underlying obligation. We do not draw a distinction between guarantors and sureties, as the distinction in Oregon between the two is often muddled.1

"Guaranty" means the contract by which the guarantor agrees to satisfy the underlying obligation of a primary obligor to an obligee in the event the primary obligor defaults on the underlying obligation.

"Obligee" means the person to whom the underlying obligation is owed. For example, the lender under a loan agreement would be an obligee vis-à-vis the borrower.

"Primary Obligor" means the person who incurs the underlying obligation to the obligee. For example, the borrower under a loan agreement would be a primary obligor.

"Underlying Obligation" means the obligation or obligations incurred by the primary obligor and owed to the obligee. For example, the borrower's obligation to make payments to a lender of principal and interest on a loan constitutes an underlying obligation.

---

1. *See, e.g.*, Ochoco Lumber Co. v. Fibrex & Shipping Co., Inc., 164 Or. App. 769, 776, 994 P.2d 793, 797 (2000). The Oregon Uniform Commercial Code provides the term "surety" to include the term "guarantor." ORS 71.2020(mm).

§ 1 Nature of the Guaranty Arrangement

Under Oregon law, a guarantor or surety promises to protect the obligee in case the primary obligor fails to perform and the obligee is entitled to collect from the guarantor or surety only in the event of a default by the primary obligor.[2]

1.1 Guaranty Relationships

A guaranty is a contract of "secondary liability" under which the guarantor has an obligation to pay only upon default by the primary obligor.[3] The relationship between the primary obligor and the guarantor arises as a matter of law, and it is based in the notion that, while the guarantor is liable to the obligee, it is the principal obligor who ultimately should bear the underlying obligation.[4]

Oregon courts should protect this relationship by refusing to enforce provisions indicating that the guarantor is liable as a primary obligor.[5] See § 6.6.

Under Oregon law, no "technical words" are needed to create a guaranty obligation; rather, a court will look to substance over form and whether there exists intent to bind a party in the capacity of a guarantor.[6]

1.2 Other Suretyship Relationships

While not the focus of this survey, we note that a suretyship relationship may also arise because of the pledge of collateral.[7] As such, a guaranty-type relationship arises, to the extent of the collateral pledged, when a person supplies collateral for a loan in order to induce the creditor to lend to the debtor °r where one party mortgages property to a creditor to secure the debt of another.[8]

---

2. Atterbury v. Carpenter, 321 F.2d 921, 923 (9th Cir. 1963), where the court distinguishes between an indemnitor and a surety who has pledged securities for the debt of the primary obligor. *See also* CRM Collateral II, Inc. v. TriCounty Metropolitan Transp. Dist. of Or., 669 F. 3rd, 970 (9th Cir., 2012), holding that an applicant to a standby letter of credit was not a surety and therefore could not raise defenses against the beneficiary of the letter of credit.
3. *Id.*
4. Man-Data, Inc. v. B&A Automotive, Inc., A143845 (ORCA) decided December 29, 2011.
5. No Oregon cases could be found supporting this proposition. *See Black v. Commission,* Note 6 below.
6. Black v. Commission, 1 Or. Tax 614 (1964). *See also* Delsman v. Friedlander, 40 Or. 33, 36, 66 P. 297 (1901), the use of the word "guaranteed" in an endorsement on a note was not construed in its technical sense but as signifying "agreement, promise or undertake." The use of the word "guaranty" in an instrument not alone determines the instrument's character. *See also* Warm Springs Forest Products Industries v. Rimrock Ranch, Inc., 83 Or. App. 175, 178, 730 P.2d 1255, 1257) 1986).
7. *See Atterbury v. Carpenter, supra* 1321 F.2d at 922.
8. *See Atterbury v. Carpenter, supra* at 924.

§ 2 State Law Requirements for an Entity to Enter a Guaranty

Partnerships, limited liability companies, corporations, and banks can all grant guaranties in furtherance of their business activities. Such grants are generally permitted by the appropriate Oregon statute. Additionally, corporations, partnerships, and limited liability companies can sometimes grant guaranties even when not in furtherance of their business activities.

2.1 Corporations

Under Oregon's Private Corporations Law, an Oregon corporation may, within the scope of its general corporate powers, give a guaranty, *provided that* its articles of incorporation do not provide otherwise.[9] If so authorized, the guaranty may be secured by corporate property.[10]

2.2 Partnerships

Oregon's Partnership Law[11] neither expressly empowers a partnership to issue a guaranty nor expressly regulates or prohibits such activity. Partnerships typically do issue guaranties but no Oregon cases were found specifically on point.

2.3 Limited Liability Companies

Oregon's Limited Liability Company Law generally permits limited liability companies to issue guaranties unless the articles of organization of a particular company provide otherwise. If so authorized, the guaranty may be secured by the company's property.[12]

2.4 Banks and Trust Companies

Under ORS 708A.0005, a financial institution (which includes Oregon state-chartered banks and trust companies) has the power to do all things necessary or convenient to carry out its business and affairs, including without limitation certain defined powers.[13] None of the defined powers specifically mention the power to execute and deliver guaranties. Additional powers for banking institutions can be authorized by rules by the Oregon Director of the Department of Consumer and Business Services to exercise any of the powers conferred upon any financial institution that is accepting deposits or transacting trust business in Oregon if the director finds that the exercise of the power (i) services the

9. ORS 60.077(g).
10. ORS 60.077(g).
11. ORS 67.005 et. seq.
12. ORS 63.077(e).
13. ORS 708A.005(1)(b).

public convenience and advantage and (ii) equalizes and maintains the quality of competition between banking institutions and other financial institutions.[14] The director has not issued any rules under this authorization section.

Oregon commercial banks are authorized to engage as principals in those activities in which national banks may engage as principals and to acquire and retain those investments that national banks may acquire and retain, subject to conditions and restrictions that apply to national banks.[15]

Note that guaranties offered by state banks may also be significantly affected by federal law. First, federal law prohibits a state-chartered bank from engaging in activities in which a national bank may not engage under federal law. The situations under which a national bank may become a guarantor are governed by federal law.[16]

2.5 Individuals

Confusion can sometimes arise in the case of corporate officers or directors signing guaranties in closely held corporations or other organizations. In such instances, it is expected that Oregon courts would undertake a case-by-case inquiry to determine whether an individual intended to be personally bound or, instead, only issued a guaranty on behalf of a partnership or corporation and thus only in an official employment capacity. No Oregon cases could be found that were specifically on point.

While a business corporation must have "authority" to execute a guaranty, an individual guarantor must have the "capacity" to enter into the guaranty. Incapacity should be a defense against the enforcement of a guaranty issued by an individual, but no Oregon cases could be found supporting this proposition. Oregon's age of majority for control of the person's own actions and business is at the age of 18 years.[17]

Oregon is not a community property state but rather a separate property state. ORS 108.060 provides that when property is owned by either husband or wife, the other has no interest therein, so their respective property is not liable for the contracts or liabilities of the other except as provided for in ORS 108.040, which relates only to the expenses of the family and the education of the minor children. Accordingly, a creditor generally does not have the right to look to the assets of the spouse of a guarantor in connection with a typical commercial loan transaction. In Oregon, most spouses hold real property as tenants by the entireties, which is similar to joint tenancy by which the surviving spouse has a right of survivorship in the deceased spouse's interest. A creditor can seek to levy execution against the interest of one of the tenants by the entireties, but because of the right of survivorship, and homestead rights, such right has been characterized by one Oregon court of appeal as more theoretical than real.[18] It is possible in Oregon for one tenant by the entirety to

14. ORS 706.795.
15. ORS 708A.010(a).
16. *See* National Bank as Guarantor or Surety on Indemnity Bond, 12 C.F.R. § 7.1017 (2011).
17. ORS 109.510.
18. Stack Const. Co. v. Jackson, 40 Or. App. 249, 255, 594 P.2d 1289, 1292 (1979).

grant a deed of trust encumbering the whole title subject to the other spouse's contingent right of survivorship.[19] If a deed of trust is to be taken as security for the guaranteed obligations, it is best practice to have both tenants by the entireties execute the deed of trust.

§ 3 Signatory's Authority to Execute a Guaranty

Generally, the obligee has a duty of reasonable inquiry when it has some notice that the executor of the guaranty does not have authority to bind the guarantor.

3.1 Corporations

For an obligee to rely on a guaranty, the guaranty must be signed by an officer with actual or apparent authority to act in such capacity.[20]

Generally, an officer of a corporation has authority to act only where: (a) authority has been expressly conferred on him or her by statute, law, or the act of the directors; (b) the action is properly incidental to the business entrusted to him by the directors; and (c) the action is within his ostensible authority or ratified by proper authority as applicable to contracts of guaranty.[21]

3.2 Partnerships

Oregon's Partnership Law grants a partner the authority to bind the partnership when such partner's act is "for apparently carrying on in the ordinary course of partnership business or business of the kind carried on by the partnership, unless the partner had no authority to act for the partnership in the particular matter and the person with whom the partner was dealing knew or had received a notification that the partner lacked authority."[22] The converse is also applied, "An act of a partner that is not for apparently carrying on in the ordinary course the partnership business or business of the kind carried on by the partnership binds the partnership only if the act was authorized by the other partners."[23]

There does not appear to be any Oregon case authority that imposes a duty of inquiry as to whether a signatory has the appropriate authority to bind the partnership.

Under Oregon's Uniform Limited Partnership Act (which is automatically applicable to an Oregon limited partnership existing before July 1, 1986[24]), a

19. *See* Ganoe v. Ohmart, 121 Or. 116, 127, 254 P. 203, 207 (1927).
20. *See* Kotera v. Daioh Intern. U.S.A. Corp., 179 Or. App. 253, 271-72, 40 P.3d 506, 520-21 (2002) which discusses actual agency and apparent authority but not in the context of a guaranty situation, but rather in the context of an asserted loan.
21. No Oregon cases could be found directly on point.
22. ORS 67.090(1).
23. ORS 67.090(2).
24. ORS 70.605.

general partner of a limited partnership has the same powers as a partner in a general partnership.[25]

3.3 Limited Liability Companies

The Limited Liability Company Law provides that, in the case of a member-managed LLC, every member is an agent of the company and can sign instruments for apparently carrying on in the ordinary course of the business of the LLC, or business of the kind carried on by the LLC, unless the member had no authority to act for the LLC in the particular matter and the person with whom the member was dealing knew or had notice that the member lacked authority.[26] Like a general partnership, the converse is also true: an act of a member that is not apparently for carrying on in the ordinary course of business of the LLC, or business of the kind carried on by the LLC, binds the LLC only if the act was authorized by the other members.[27] In a manager-managed LLC, a member is not an agent of the LLC for purposes of its business solely by being a member.[28]

The above authority rules for a member-managed LLC are equally applicable to a manager-managed LLC as to such manager.[29] There are no specific limitation in Oregon's statute on the execution and delivery of guaranties although there are with respect to instruments which transfer or affect the LLC's interests in real property.[30]

3.4 Banks and Trust Companies

A case-by-case inquiry of the powers provided for in a bank's or trust company's corporate governance documents is necessary to determine who may validly execute a guaranty on behalf of a bank or trust company.

§ 4 Consideration; Sufficiency of Past Consideration

Standard contract principles apply to the analysis of consideration for a contract of guaranty. The principal agreement is sufficient consideration for an accompanying guaranty. Past consideration can be sufficient when the guaranty expresses the past consideration in writing.

Consideration is required to create a valid contract of guaranty.[31] The inquiry into sufficient consideration is based on standard contract law principles. The benefit or obligation that forms the consideration need not flow

25. 70.185(1). The only limitations listed in this section are those provided for in Chapter 70 or in the partnership agreement. For example, a provision in Chapter 70 would be that a vote of all the parties is required to approve a merger unless the certificate of limited partnership provides for a lesser vote. ORS 70.530.
26. ORS 63.140(1)(a).
27. ORS 63.140(1)(b).
28. ORS 63.140(2)(a).
29. ORS 63.140(2)(a).
30. ORS 63.140(3).
31. First Nat. Bank of Albany v. Hawkins, 73 Or 186, 189, 144 P. 131, 132 (1914).

directly to the guarantor from the obligee; the consideration flowing from the obligee to the principal obligor is sufficient to support a contemporaneous guaranty.[32] Where the guaranty is not contemporaneous with the loan being guaranteed, there must be a new consideration to support it.[33]

§ 5 Notice of Acceptance

Notice of acceptance may not be required, if credit is extended to the primary obligor based upon the guaranty or if the guaranty is absolute.

Under guaranty law, generally, the obligee must notify the guarantor of its acceptance of the guaranty.[34] Oregon case law requires notice of acceptance before a contract of guaranty was effective, but this seems to be in a situation where the guarantors signed as volunteers and were not principals in the company that received the loan.[35]

Notice of acceptance also will not be required where the guaranty is "absolute."[36] Commonly, the guarantor waives the notification of acceptance requirement in the guaranty agreement in order to avoid this technical formality.

§ 6 Interpretation of Guaranties

As with other contracts, Oregon courts interpret a disputed provision in a guaranty in the context of the document as a whole.[37] Once the guarantor's undertaking has been determined, the rule of strictissimi juris becomes applicable, strictly construing the obligations of the guarantor. In addition, certain terms have become words of art in the context of guaranties. In other regards, courts will interpret a guaranty in the same manner by which they would interpret the language of any other contract.

6.1 General Principles

The principle of *strictissimi juris* guides the interpretation of the terms of a guaranty: an Oregon court will strictly construe the obligations of a guarantor.[38] Outside of this principle, and certain terms of art outlined below, the

32. *Id.*
33. *Id. See also* Tomihiro v. United Hotel Corp., 145 Or 629, 632, 28 P.2d 880, 881 (1934). Execution of guaranty two years after execution of the note required new consideration.
34. Peter A. Alces, The Law of Suretyship and Guaranty § 3:27 (Thomson West 1996).
35. Vancouver Nat. Bank v. McCredie, 135 Or 227, 230, 295 P. 452, 453 (1931).
36. *See* Balfour, Guthrie & Co. v. Knight, 86 Or. 165, 172 (1917), citing Davis v. Wells, 104 U.S. 159 26 L.Ed. 686) where the guaranty was made at the request of the creditor and its delivery to or for the use of the creditor constitutes the communication between them and constitutes a contract. In *Balfour*, the guaranty was solicited by the debtor and delivered by debtor to the creditor, and no showing of agency by the debtor of the guarantor.
37. State of Oregon v. Trident Seafood Corp., 248 Or. App. 664, 671, 274 P.3d. 218, 222 (2012).
38. Nike, Inc. v. Spencer, 75 Or. App. 362, 371, 707 P.2d 589, 595 (1985), citing McElwain Co. v. Primarea, 180 App. Div. 288, 294, 167 N.Y.S. 815 (1917).

same principles of construction that apply to contracts generally apply to guaranties.[39]

6.2 Guaranty of Payment Versus Guaranty of Collection

A guarantor of payment promises to satisfy the underlying obligation to the obligee upon default by the primary obligor, which satisfaction is not conditioned upon the obligee's prior attempt to secure satisfaction from the primary obligor.[40] No Oregon case could be found for the proposition that a guarantor may be required to satisfy obligations to an obligee even where the obligee, because of a subordination agreement, cannot collect from the primary obligor.

A court will look to the intent of the parties as expressed in the guaranty to determine whether it is one of payment or one of guaranty.[41]

6.3 Language Regarding the Revocation of Guaranties

A guaranty that is "irrevocable" may not be revoked with respect to transactions entered into by the primary obligor prior to the revocation.

Where the guarantor is not compensated and the guaranty is for an indefinite period of time, the guarantor may revoke the guaranty with regard to future liability upon reasonable notice.[42]

6.4 "Continuing"

A continuing guaranty is one that looks to future transactions. No Oregon cases could be found that interpreted a continuing guaranty even when the word "continuing" had not been used.

An Oregon court of appeal indicated that a continuing guaranty signed by the wife, even after her divorce, could apply to subsequent loans made to her husband but did not extend to a guaranty by her husband of the debts of their son.[43]

6.5 "Absolute and Unconditional"

See § 8.2 on "catch-all" waivers.

---

39. Western Bank v. Youngs, 274 Or. 213, 217, 545 P.2d 886, 888 (1976). *See also* Bank of Northwest v. Brattain, 73 Or. App. 261, 265, 698 P.2d 536, 538 (1985).
40. Miller v. Northern Brewery Co., 242 F. 164, 166 (D. Or. 1917).
41. Delsman v. Friedlander, 40 Or. 33, 36, 66 P.2 97 (1901).
42. D.N. & E Walter & Co. v. Van Domelen, 246 Or. 275, 279, 425 P.2d 166, 167 (1967), which holds that, where one of two coguarantors terminates its guaranty as to future transactions, such action does not release the other coguarantor.
43. Bank of the Northwest v. Brattain, 73 Or. App. 261, 264, 698 P.2d 536, 538 (1985), reversing summary judgment in favor of the bank.

6.6 "Liable as a Primary Obligor and not Merely as Surety"

This language, taken literally, seems to conflate the concepts of guarantor and primary obligor. While a guarantor may be a "guarantor of payment" from whom the obligee can seek payment even without pursuing the primary obligor, the guarantor does not become a primary obligor.

No cases were found that have construed the language "liable as a primary obligor" but an Oregon court has found that a guarantor is just that and not a primary obligor.[44]

§ 7 Defenses of the Guarantor; Set-off

The defenses that may be available to a guarantor can be grouped into three categories: (1) defenses of the primary obligor; (2) "suretyship defenses"; and (3) other defenses.

7.1 Defenses of the Primary Obligor

7.1.1 General

While the general rule in Oregon is that the guarantor, absent an effective waiver, is not bound to perform if the primary obligor is not bound, a guarantor sued alone may not, in many circumstances, raise defenses or counterclaims that are "personal" to the primary obligor.[45] However, an Oregon court held that "the secondary obligor may raise as a defense to the secondary obligation any defense of the principal obligor to the underlying action" Citing Restatement (Third) of Suretyship and Guaranty § 34(1)(1996).[46]

7.1.2 Defenses that May not be Raised by Guarantor

The insolvency of the principal obligor is not a defense that the guarantor may raise unless the guaranty is conditioned on the solvency of the primary obligor.[47] A guarantor also should not be able to raise the primary obligor's incapacity as a defense to liability under the guaranty, although no Oregon cases could be found on this issue.

---

44. Ebco, Inc. v. Brechtold, 251 Or. 543, 547, 446 P.2d 120, 123 (1968).
45. Weiss v. Northwest Acceptance Corp., 274 Or. 343, 546 P.2d 1065 (1976). Similar situation in which guarantor could not raise fraud imposed on the obligor by the beneficiary of the guaranty, in order to assert a separate fraud claim against the beneficiary of the guaranty.
46. Man-Data, Inc. v. B&A Automotive, Inc., 247, Or. App. 429, 437, 270 P.3d 318, 323 (2011).
47. *See* Eutis v. Park-o-Lator Corp., 249 Or. 194, 199, 435 P.2d 802, 804 (1967), where the principal obligor becomes insolvent and guarantor sought to raise statute of limitations against the obligee, but the court held that the statute of limitations applicable to the note was not applicable to the guaranty because the guaranty was conditioned on the insolvency of the debtor.

7.1.3 Defenses that May Always be Raised by Guarantor

Although Oregon does not appear to have any cases on the issue, a guarantor should be able to show that the obligee failed to perform such that there is a partial or complete failure of consideration.[48]

7.2 "Suretyship" Defenses

7.2.1 Change in Identity of Principal Obligor

Whether a change of the identity of the principal obligor to the underlying obligation discharges the guarantor's obligations depends upon the circumstances in the same fashion as a modification of the underlying obligation. See Section 7.2.2

7.2.2 Modification of the Underlying Obligation, Including Release

Under Oregon law, modifications to the underlying obligation may permit the guarantor to raise certain defenses to liability; a guarantor's obligation cannot be altered without its consent if the change is material and increases the risk of the guarantor.[49] The discharge from liability upon such an alteration may result in a complete release of the guarantor. In one case, an increase in the rent under a lease to $1,600 from $1,430 per month, without notifying the guarantor or obtaining his subsequent ratification of the new amount, fully released the guarantor, even from the lower $1,430 per month rent.[50]

7.2.3 Release or Impairment of Security for the Underlying Obligation

Where the primary obligor and the obligee enter into an agreement that impairs the collateral, the guarantor may be discharged entirely but not if guaranty allows lender to deal in any manner with the obligations or collateral.

The guarantor may waive in advance its defense based on the release or impairment of collateral under common law and under Oregon's Uniform Commercial Code (UCC) pursuant to ORS 73.0605 (applicable to negotiable instruments).

---

48. *See Man-Data, Inc. v. B&A Automotive, Inc., supra* at note 46.

49. Fassett v. Deschutes Enterprises, Inc., 69 Or. App. 426, 686 P.2d 1034, review denied 298 Or. 150, 690 P.2d 506 (1982). *See also* Nike Inc. v. Spencer, 75 Or. App. 362, 707 P.2d 589, review denied, 300 Or. 451, 712 P.2d 110 (1985), where guarantor was not released because change did not increase guarantor's risk as a result of the merger of obligee into another company.

50. *Id.*

7.2.4 Change in Obligee

Where a guaranty has been assigned to a new obligee, the guarantor may be able to claim that there has been a change in the underlying obligation and is therefore released.[51]

7.3 Other Defenses

7.3.1 Failure to Fulfill a Condition Precedent

Guarantors may raise a defense of failure to fulfill a condition precedent.[52]

7.3.2 Modification of the Guaranty

Modifications to a guaranty should not affect its validity even where no new consideration is given for the modification.[53]

7.3.3 Failure to Pursue Primary Obligor

Oregon courts have ruled that a guaranty of a lease was an absolute guaranty so the lessor could sue the guarantor without exhausting remedies against the lessee.[54] On the other hand, a guaranty indemnifying the creditor against any loss on account of money due from the debtor was viewed as a conditional guaranty requiring the creditor to exercise reasonable effort to collect from the debtor.[55] The wording of the guaranty is thus important.

7.3.4 Statute of Limitations

Oregon law imposes, with certain exceptions, a six-year statute of limitations on contractual obligations.[56] One such exception applies to contracts for the sale of goods that are governed by Article 2 of the Oregon UCC, which imposes a four-year statute of limitations.[57]

The fact that the statute of limitations had run on the underlying debt owed by a corporation, did not bar an action against individual defendants who agreed in the event the corporation became insolvent to be personally liable to

---

51. Marc Nelson Oil Products, Inc. v. Grim Logging Co., Inc., 199 Or. App. 73, 82-84, 110 P.3d 120, 125-26. Where the appellate court overturned a summary judgment in favor of the new obligee, because the guarantor was entitled to show that the assignment to a new obligee increased the guarantor's risk.
52. Loomis v. MacFarlane, 50 Or. 129, 134, 91 P. 466, 468 (1905) where condition precedent was satisfied but guarantor was relieved because the condition of reaching a stated amount of earnings had not been reached, and earnings were not construed as "net income."
53. Kiernan v. Kratz, 42 Or. 474, 481, 69 P. 1027, 1031 (1902), which holds that where the holder of a third person's contract transfers it to another, upon consideration moving to himself, his guaranty thereof, made at the same time, and as a part of the same transaction, is not a special promise to answer for the debt or default of another, within the meaning of the statute of frauds and therefore need not be in writing. The court further held since the promise was not subject to the statute of frauds it could be modified by parol, meaning that the original consideration supported the original promise.
54. Miller v. Northern Brewery Co., 242 F. 164, 166 (D. Or. 1917); *see also* Depot Realty Syndicate v. Enterprise Brewing Co, 87 Or. 560, 565, 170 P. 294, 296 (1917).
55. Michelin Tire Co. of California v. Cutler, 116 Or. 217, 220, 240 P. 895, 896 (1925).
56. ORS 12.080.
57. ORS 72.7250.

the plaintiffs on notes executed by the corporation, i.e., a conditional guaranty where liability did not accrue until the corporation became insolvent.[58]

7.3.5 Statute of Frauds

While a guaranty is subject to the statute of frauds as an agreement to answer for the debt of another,[59] an oral settlement agreement reached by the parties on how payment would be made was not subject to the statute of frauds.[60]

7.3.6 Defenses Particular to Guarantors that are Natural Persons and their Spouses

No Oregon cases on this subject.

7.4 Right of Set-off

No Oregon cases on this subject.

§ 8 Waiver of Defenses by the Guarantor

8.1 Defenses that cannot be Waived

It seems, generally, that some defenses cannot be waived.

Oregon does not appear to have any cases on this issue except one court of appeal has indicated that it could simply make a waiver which violates public policy separable without invalidating the entire guaranty.[61] Oregon does not appear to have any specific cases in the context of guaranties or under ORS 79.0602 relating to the waiver of commercial reasonableness in the disposition of collateral.[62]

8.2 "Catch-all" Waivers

Though catch-all waiver language may be effective, it is advisable for beneficiaries to include waivers of specific suretyship defenses.

---

58. Eustis v. Park-O-Lator Corp., 249 Or. 194, 199, 435 P.2d 802, 804 (1967).
59. ORS § 41.580(1)(b)
60. Capital Credit & Collection Service, Inc. v. Armani, 227 Or. App. 574, 578-79, 206 P.3d 1114, 1117-18 (2009), *but see* Sheibani v. Nelson, 92 Or. App. 679, 682-84, 759 P.2d 1135 (1988) upholding a jury's verdict holding defendant liable for an oral guaranty because the defendant's main purpose was to serve his own business advantage, taking it outside the statute of frauds, citing White Stag Mfg. Co. v. Wind Surfing, Inc., 67 Or. App. 456, 486, 679 P.2d 312 (1984).
61. *See* W.J. Seufert Land Co. v. Greenfield, 262 Or. 83, 88-90, 496 P.2d 197, 200-01 (Or. 1972), which discusses public policy issues in connection with the validity of waivers in guaranties.
62. *See* ORS 79.0602. A guarantor would probably be considered an obligor based upon other Oregon statutes that protect obligors after a nonjudicial foreclosure. *See* ORS 86.770(2), where the term "or another person obligated on" the note includes guarantors. *See* Sumner v. Enercon Development Co., 98 Or. App. 18, 21, 779 P.2d 150, 151 (1988).

Since Oregon has no statutory suretyship defenses, the waivers cannot reference Oregon code sections.

The standard catch-all waiver indicates that the guaranty is "absolute and unconditional" or that the guaranty is "given absolutely and unconditionally." In theory, when such a catch-all waiver is included in a guaranty, the guarantor waives almost all defenses and counterclaims potentially available in an action by the creditor arising from an obligation covered by the guaranty. In fact, courts have granted summary judgment where the guaranty is absolute and unconditional.[63] Additionally, absolute and unconditional guaranties have been enforced even when the principal obligor escapes liability. However, the enumeration of waivers of various defenses continues to be recommended practice. Waivers of all defenses have held up as not being against public policy except for ones that violate particular statutes.[64]

In determining whether a guarantor or other surety is discharged by alteration of the underlying contractual obligation, Oregon courts must first ask whether the guarantor consented to the modification. If so, the guarantor is not discharged. If not, the court must determine whether the guarantor is a compensated or uncompensated surety. If the guarantor is uncompensated, a change to the guaranteed contract discharges the guarantor if the change is material, as long as the change is not one that could inure only to the guarantor's benefit. If on the other hand, the guarantor is compensated, an alteration discharges the guarantor only if it materially increases the guarantor's risk on the contract.[65] Accordingly, it is a facts and circumstances test in Oregon.

8.3 Use of Specific Waivers

No defense requires an explicit waiver.

It would appear that general waivers should suffice in waiving suretyship defenses, but as noted in Section 7.7.2 above, if the guarantor has consented to the change, the guarantor will be precluded from asserting the defense based on that change. The best evidence of such consent is to have an explicit statement of waiver.

§ 9 Third-party Pledgors—Defenses and Waiver Thereof

Because the pledgor arguably stands in the relation of a guarantor to the principal obligor to the extent of the pledge, it may most likely avail itself of the defenses of a guarantor. It may also waive such defenses.

We have found no evidence that the law as applied to sureties would not apply to a third-party pledge. In contrast, the law appears to be that a pledge

63. Valley State Bank v. Gibson, 64 Or. App. 385, 388-89, 668 P.2d 459, 461 (1983).
64. W.J. Seufert Land Co. v. Greenfield, 262 Or. 83, 88-89, 496 P.2d 197, 199-200 (1972).
65. Marc Nelson Oil Products, Inc. v. Grim Logging Co. Inc., 999 Or. App. 73, 78-80, 110 P.2d 120, 123-24 (2005).

of collateral results in a surety relationship. It would seem logical, given this state of the law, that the pledgor generally has the same defenses available to it as are available to a surety. We have found no Oregon case which deals directly with this issue. We recommend using the same specific suretyship waivers in any third-party pledges that would be used in a guaranty.

§ 10 Jointly and Severally Liable Guarantors—Contribution and Reduction of Obligations Upon Payment by a Co-Obligor

Guarantors who are jointly and severally liable are presumed to share the secondary obligation equally. The creditor is not obliged to seek full payment from more than one such guarantor.

10.1 Contribution

Where coguarantors are liable jointly and severally, there is a presumption that they bear the burden equally unless otherwise stated, although no Oregon cases could be found confirming this point. Insofar as the guarantor has paid out more than its proportional share of the obligation, only then may it recover from other guarantors proportionate to their liability.[66]

10.2 Release of one Coguarantor Releases All

Oregon follows the common law rule that the release of one co-obligor releases all obligors.[67] Accordingly, a release of one coguarantor will release the other coguarantor unless that defense is waived. A revocation of a continuing guaranty by one of the guarantors did not release the other guarantors where the underlying contract provided that notice of revocation by one guarantor would not affect the liability of the other guarantors. The court held that the contract provision was equivalent to a waiver of the defense that a material change had occurred entitling the guarantor to a complete discharge.[68]

§ 11 Reliance

Reliance is probably not required to claim under a guaranty.

Oregon does not appear to have any cases dealing with the concept of reliance by the obligee before being able to make a claim under the guaranty.

66. Mansfield v. McReary, 263 Or. 41, 45-46, 497 P.2d 654, 656 (1972), modified on rehearing 263 Or. 41, 51, 501 P.2d 69, 70 (1972).
67. Schiffer v. United Grocers, Inc., 143 Or. App. 276, 282-84, 922 P.2d 703, 707-708 (1996).
68. Walter & Co. v. Van Comelen, 246 Or. 275, 279, 425 P.2d 166, 167 (1967).

§ 12 Subrogation

Subrogation is an equitable remedy that generally requires total satisfaction of the underlying obligation to the obligee prior to its exercise. Concern for protecting the creditor's interests affects the secondary obligor's right to subrogation.

Subrogation is not a matter of right but an equitable doctrine, designed to promote justice and is thus dependent on the particular relationship of parties and nature of controversy in each case.[69] Subrogation applies equally to guaranties of payment and performance.

Generally subrogation is available when the claim of an obligee has been paid in full.[70] For this reason, there is usually no partial subrogation, although exceptions have been made in the case of insurance companies. The general prohibition of partial subrogation is premised on concern for an obligee's ability to recover in full. Nonetheless, where a guarantor has paid installments of interest, each installment of interest is a claim in full, such that the guarantor should have a right of subrogation regarding these interest payments, but no Oregon cases could be found on this issue.

§ 13 Triangular Set-off in Bankruptcy

We find no Oregon cases dealing with the issue of the right of a guarantor who controls the primary obligor, which obligor is in bankruptcy to set off defenses that the primary obligor would have against the beneficiary under the guaranty. However, there are Oregon cases which allow the guarantor to raise defenses that the primary obligor would have had against the beneficiary relating to the underlying obligation.[71]

§ 14 Indemnification—Whether the Primary Obligor has a Duty

The principal obligor has a duty of indemnification[72] so long as the guarantor undertook its obligations at the request of the principal obligor. The extent of this duty can be altered by contract.

69. Ochoco Lumber Co. v. Fibrex & Shipping Co., Inc., 164 Or. App. 769, 775-77, 994 P.2d 793, 797-98 (2000).
70. Doty v. First State Bank of Oregon, 71 Or. App. 611, 617, 693 P.2d 1308, 1313 (1985).
71. Man-Data, Inc. v. B&A Automotive, Inc., 247, Or. App. 429, 437, 270 P.3d 318, 323 (2011), where the guarantor was allowed to raise the defense of the validity of legal fees charged to the primary obligor even though a default judgment had been taken against the primary obligor.
72. Rodway v. Arrow Light Truck Parts, Inc., 96 Or. App. 232, 237, 772 P.2d 1349, 1352 (1989) dealing with an indemnity as opposed to a guaranty. *See also* Cottage Grove Lumber Co. v. Lillegren, 227 Or. 24, 32, 360 P.2d 927, 931 (1961).

Oregon case law distinguishes guarantors who are asked to guarantee by the principal obligor from those who are asked to guarantee by the beneficiary, but such distinction is not used to determine whether the guarantor is entitled to indemnification from the principal obligor. Oregon courts are more concerned whether the guarantor is compensated or uncompensated and the impact of that status on the discharge of the guarantor as a result of a change in the guaranteed obligations. See Section 8.2 above.

§ 15 Enforcement of Guaranties

15.1 Exercising Rights Under a Guaranty Where the Underlying Obligation is also Secured by a Deed of Trust.

In Oregon, under ORS 86.770(2)(a), a guarantor (being an obligor) is relieved of any deficiency liability after a nonjudicial foreclosure on a deed of trust, whether the deed of trust is granted by the guarantor or by the primary obligor. If the deed of trust is judicially foreclosed, a deficiency can be secured against both the trustor and the guarantor,[73] and the guarantor will have a claim for indemnity or reimbursement against the underlying obligor except if the deed of trust was a residential deed of trust[74] which is defined in ORS 86.705(5). Since mortgages can only be enforced judicially, a guarantor will have a claim for indemnity or reimbursement against the underlying obligor unless the mortgage was a residential mortgage.

§ 16 Revival and Reinstatement of Guaranties

No Oregon cases on this issue could be found.

73. ORS 86.770(3).
74. ORS 86.770(b).

Pennsylvania State Law of Guaranties

Harvey I. Forman
Claire P. Edwards
Blank Rome LLP
One Logan Square
Philadelphia, Pennsylvania 19103
(215) 569-5500

Contents

Pennsylvania State Law of Guaranties

HIGHLIGHTS

1. All Pennsylvania guaranties are considered to be agreements of suretyship unless the agreement expressly states that it is intended to be a contract of guaranty and is not intended as a contract of suretyship. As a surety, the signer is liable on the same direct and primary basis as the principal obligor and the creditor need not attempt to collect the guaranteed indebtedness from the primary obligor before proceeding against the guarantor. From a best practices perspective, guaranty agreements should specifically state that they are intended to be suretyship agreements. §§ 1.1, 1.2.
2. Spousal property is held in tenancy by the entireties under Pennsylvania law. Accordingly, a guaranty executed by an individual spouse will not be enforceable against the property of the entireties. § 2.5.
3. Under Pennsylvania law, every written promise signed by the person promising shall not be invalid or unenforceable for lack of consideration if it contains a statement that the signer intends to be legally bound. § 4.
4. Pennsylvania has a deficiency judgment statute applicable to foreclosure of real estate. If a mortgage is given by the primary obligor or by any guarantor or a creditor obtains a judgment lien against real property, the creditor is required to comply with the deficiency judgment statute following foreclosure if the foreclosing mortgagee/judgment creditor is the successful bidder at the foreclosure sale. Failure to comply or comply timely with the statute in obtaining a deficiency judgment will bar the mortgagee/creditor from proceeding against the mortgagor/judgment debtor or against any other obligor on the underlying indebtedness for any deficiency claim. § 15.3.

Introductory Note: In order to standardize our discussion of the law of guaranties, we use the following vocabulary to refer to the various parties to a guaranty and their obligations.

"**Guarantor**" means a person who, by contract, agrees to satisfy an underlying obligation of another to an obligee upon the primary obligor's default on that underlying obligation.

"**Guaranty**" means the contract by which a collateral promise is made to answer for the debt or performance of another. Pennsylvania distinguishes between guaranty and suretyship agreements. All agreements are deemed contracts of suretyship unless they expressly state otherwise. Under a contract determined to be a guaranty agreement, the creditor must first attempt to collect the debt from the primary obligor before demanding performance from the guarantor.

"**Obligee**" means the person to whom the underlying obligation is owed. For example, the lender under a loan agreement would be an obligee vis-à-vis the borrower.

"**Primary Obligor**" or "**Principal Obligor**" means the person who incurs the underlying obligation to the obligee. For example, the borrower under a loan agreement would be a primary obligor.

"**Underlying Obligation**" means the obligation or obligations incurred by the primary obligor and owed to the obligee. For example, the borrower's obligation to make payments to a lender of principal and interest on a loan constitutes an underlying obligation.

"**Surety**" means a person who, by contract, agrees to satisfy an obligation of another to an obligee upon the primary obligor's default on the underlying obligation.

"**Suretyship**" means a direct and original contractual undertaking under which the obligor is primarily and jointly liable with the primary obligor. The primary difference between a suretyship and a guaranty is that the creditor can look to the surety for immediate payment upon the default by the primary obligor, without first attempting to collect from the primary obligor.

Introduction and Sources of Law

In Pennsylvania, case law is the primary source of substantive law governing commercial guaranties. Courts occasionally cite the Restatement (Third) of Suretyship and Guaranty (1996).[1]

§ 1 Nature of the Guaranty Arrangement

Under Pennsylvania law, the nature and extent of the guarantor's liability depend on the terms of the contract.[2] A guarantor is liable for all consequences of the failure of its principal to perform under the principal contract,[3] and if the terms and conditions of the contract so state, the guarantor may assume greater liability that that of its principal.[4]

1.1 Guaranty Relationships

A guaranty is a collateral and independent undertaking creating a secondary liability under which the guarantor has an obligation to pay only upon default by the primary obligor.[5] As such, if the arrangement is a "guaranty" and not

1. Kiski v. Mid-State Sur. Corp., 600 Pa. 444, 451 (Pa. 2008).
2. American Acceptance Corp. v. Scott Housing Systems, Inc., 630 F. Supp. 70 (E.D. Pa. 1995).
3. Janes v. Scott, 59 Pa. 178 (1868).
4. Hyster Credit Corp. v. O'Neill, 582 F. Supp. 414 (E.D. Pa. 1983).
5. Keystone Bank v. Flooring Specialists, Inc., 513 Pa. 103, 518 A.2d 1179 (1986).

one of "suretyship," the creditor must first attempt to collect the debt from the principal debtor/obligor before demanding performance from the guarantor.[6] Efforts to collect from the primary obligor must prove to be unavailing before the creditor can proceed against the guarantor.

In Pennsylvania, every written agreement made by one person/entity to answer for the default of another is interpreted as a suretyship, unless the agreement contains in substance the words: "This is not intended to be a contract for suretyship,"[7] or unless each portion of such agreement intended to modify the rights and liabilities of suretyship shall contain in substance the words: "This portion of the agreement is not intended to impose the liability of suretyship."[8]

1.2 Suretyship[9] Relationships

A suretyship is a direct and original undertaking under which the third-party obligor is primarily and jointly liable with the principal.[10] The primary difference between a suretyship agreement and a guaranty agreement is the time at which a creditor can collect (or attempt to collect) from each. With regard to a suretyship, the creditor can look to the surety for immediate payment upon the occurrence of a default by the principal obligor or debtor.[11]

Under the Uniform Commercial Code (UCC), the definition of surety includes guarantor.[12]

§ 2 State Law Requirements for an Entity to Enter a Guaranty[13]

Partnerships, limited liability companies, corporations, and banks can all grant guaranties. Like all contracts generally, a valid guaranty requires there be competent parties, an offer and an acceptance, and valid consideration, as well as a sufficient compliance with the formalities required by law.

6. McIntyre Square Assocs. v. Evans, 829 A.2d 446 (Pa. Super. Ct. 2003).
7. 8 P.S. § 1 (2011). *See* Enters v. Rimmeir (In re Bradstreet), 2002 Bankr. LEXIS 1623 (Bankr. E.D. Pa. Dec. 31, 2002) (noting that the debtors and a third-party guarantor were sureties of the obligations of the partnership to the creditor landlord because § 1 applied to a "lease guaranty" where there was no clear language rejecting the presumption of suretyship and the signatory guaranteed the prompt payment of the rent reserved, the performance of any obligations assumed, and the covenants made therein by the lessee).
8. 8 P.S. § 1; Keystone Bank v. Flooring Specialists, Inc., 513 Pa. 103, 518 A.2d 1179 (1986).
9. For purposes of this survey, any reference to the word "guaranty" is deemed to mean a suretyship obligation unless otherwise provided.
10. Reuter v. Citizens & Northern Bank, 410 Pa. Super. 199; 599 A.2d 673 (1991).
11. McIntyre Square Assocs. v. Evans, 827 A.2d 446 (Pa. Super. Ct. 2003).
12. 13 Pa. C.S. § 1201.
13. For the purposes of this survey, we assume that a guarantor is not an "insurance company" within the meaning of Pennsylvania statute which governs insurance contracts. 15 Pa.C.S. § 3101.

2.1 Corporations

Under the Business Corporation Law, a Pennsylvania corporation may become a guarantor absent any express limitation on corporate action contained in the articles, bylaws, or in a statute restricting this statutory power.[14] Unlike New York corporate law, which requires that the guaranty be given in the furtherance of its corporate purpose, nothing in the Pennsylvania corporate statute connects the corporate purposes of the corporation to the statutory power of a Pennsylvania corporation to enter into a guaranty.[15]

A Pennsylvania corporation's statutory power to make contracts of guaranty or suretyship does not exclude or restrict the power to make upstream and intra-stream guaranties.[16] In contrast, New York corporate law requires affiliate guaranties to further its corporate purpose.[17] Pennsylvania can also be distinguished from Delaware corporate law, which presumes guaranties granted within affiliate relationships are in the ordinary course of business.[18]

2.2 Partnerships

Pennsylvania does not restrict a partnership's ability to enter a guaranty as partnerships are generally permitted, subject to any limitations stated in the partnership agreement, to exercise any right, power, franchise, or privilege as corporations engaged in the same line of business might exercise.[19]

2.3 Limited Liability Companies

Pennsylvania generally permits limited liability companies to issue guaranties unless the articles of organization of a particular company provide otherwise.[20] A limited liability company may exercise any right, power, franchise, or privilege that a domestic or foreign corporation engaged in the same line of business might exercise.[21] The affirmative vote or consent of a majority of the members (or managers in a manager-managed entity) shall be required to act on any matter, except as may be required by the certificate of organization or the operating agreement.[22]

---

14. 15 Pa.C.S. § 1502 (2008), Committee Comment (1988).
15. *See* 15 Pa.C.S. § 1301 (2011).
16. 15 Pa.C.S. § 1502 (2008), Committee Comment (1988).
17. N.Y. Bus. Corp. Law § 202(a)(7) (Consol. 2011).
18. *See* Del. Code Ann. tit. 8 § 122(13) (LexisNexis 2011).
19. 15 Pa.C.S. § 8102.
20. 15 Pa.C.S. § 8102.
21. 15 Pa.C.S. §§ 8921(c), 8102(a)(2).
22. 15 Pa.C.S. § 8942(a).

2.4 Banks and Trust Companies

Pennsylvania bank and trust institutions have wide power to contract within the limits of their purposes, statutory powers,[23] and public policy.[24] Courts have held that this includes the contractual power of banks to make guaranties for the furtherance of their own rights or as an incident to the transaction of their own business.[25] Pennsylvania at one time expressly granted the power of banking institutions to guarantee bonds secured by mortgages under 7 P.S. § 208; however, this provision was repealed by the Act of April 22, 1937, 7 P.S. § 819-1021. Despite a lack of express statutory grant of power, courts continue to enforce guaranties supported by consideration that can be characterized as having been entered into by banks for the "furtherance of their own rights" or as an "incident to the transaction of their own business."[26]

In order to protect authorized loans, a bank is generally permitted to guarantee to its borrower's other creditors that its preexisting or subsequently created loans will be honored.[27] A bank may also guarantee or warrant the quality of goods in order to realize on collateral security already obtained; or guarantee payment of a note which is the obligation of another, if this is necessary to dispose of its own paper and securities; and the guaranty of the liabilities of another bank, if accompanied by a receipt of assets, may be upheld as incidental to the exercise of the power either to purchase and discount paper and securities.[28]

Banks and trust companies are limited from issuing a guaranty for the benefit of any person with an amount in excess of 15 percent of the bank's "capital stock, surplus fund, and undivided profits."[29]

Note also that guaranties offered by state banks may also be significantly affected by federal law. First, federal law prohibits a state-chartered bank from engaging in activities in which a national bank may not engage under federal law. The situations under which a national bank may become a guarantor are governed by federal law.[30]

2.5 Individuals

Confusion can sometimes arise in the case of corporate officers or directors signing guaranties. An officer acting within his or her authority is not liable

23. 7 P.S. §§ 301 et seq. Easton Nat'l Bank & Trust Co. v. Union Nat'l Bank & Trust Co., 237 Pa. Super. 316, 352 A.2d 544 (1975) (noting that "a national bank may lend its credit, bind itself as a surety to indemnify another, or otherwise become a guarantor if it has a substantial interest in the performance of the transaction involved or has a segregated deposit sufficient in an amount to cover the bank's total potential liability").
24. Dunn v. McCoy, 113 F.2d 587 (3d Cir. 1940).
25. *Id.* (noting that Pennsylvania at one time authorized banks to guarantee bonds secured by mortgages on real estate, under 7 P.S. § 208; however, this grant was expressly repealed by 7 P.S. § 819-1021).
26. 4 Michie, Banks and Banking sec. 33; 7 Michie, Banks and Banking sec. 163.
27. Robert Mallery Lumber Corp. v. B. & F. Associates, Inc., 294 Pa. Super. 503, 440 A.2d 579, 1982 Pa. Super. LEXIS 3259, 33 U.C.C. Rep. Serv. (CBC) 642 (1982).
28. Dunn v. McCoy, 113 F.2d 587 (3d Cir. 1940).
29. 7 P.S. § 306(b)(iii).
30. *See* National Bank as Guarantor or Surety on Indemnity Bond, 12 C.F.R. § 7.1017 (2010).

for contracts made on behalf of the corporation as a disclosed principal,[31] but an officer will be held individually liable if personal liability on his or her part was intended by the parties.[32] When individuals sign a guaranty only as an agent or officer of the business, they are not personally liable unless they fail to name the corporation they are representing and circumstances indicate that such signature is not being made in a representative capacity.[33]

Any individual 18 years of age or older has the right to enter into binding and legally enforceable contracts and the defense of minority is not available to such individuals.[34] A signed document gives rise to the presumption that it accurately expresses the state of mind of the signing party.[35] The presumption is rebutted where the challenger presents clear and convincing evidence of mental incompetence. Sufficient evidence must be presented to demonstrate that the individual is unable to understand the nature and consequences of the transaction.[36]

While a business corporation must have "authority" to execute a guaranty, an individual guarantor must have the "capacity" to enter into the guaranty. Incapacity can be a defense against the enforcement of a guaranty issued by an individual.[37]

Spousal property is held in tenancy by the entireties under Pennsylvania law.[38] As such, neither spouse may, *inter alia*, independently dispose of or alienate his or her share in the entirety property.[39] A guaranty issued by an individual spouse will not be enforceable against the entirety.[40] Furthermore, where a guaranty is issued by both spouses, a discharge of an individual spouse's obligation in bankruptcy will not discharge the entirety's obligation.[41] The obligation belongs to the unity and accordingly, the discharge of one spouse cannot discharge the unit.

An obligee may, however, have a potential lien against property held by the entirety, which lien is based upon the obligor spouse's contingent expectancy to survive and to become the sole owner of the property.[42] The obligee's claim to such survivorship interest does not give rise to any right or claim to that property during the lifetime of the non-obligor spouse and the obligee does not have standing to complain of a conveyance which eliminates the obligee's future potential interest on such property.[43]

---

31. Leslie v. Philadelphia 1976 Bicentennial Corp., 332 F. Supp. 83 (E.D. Pa. 1971).
32. Commercial Finance Co. v. de Martelly, 269 Pa. 354, 112 A. 447 (1921).
33. Anchor Hocking Glass Corp. v. Edelman, 36 Pa. D. & C.2d 332 (1965).
34. 23 Pa.C.S.A. § 5101.
35. Shafer v. State Employees' Retirement Bd., 548 Pa. 320, 696 A.2d 1186 (1997).
36. Forman v. Public School Employees' Retirement Bd., 778 A.2d 778 (Pa. Commw. Ct. 2001).
37. Trident Corp. v. Reliance Ins. Co., 350 Pa. Super. 142, 504 A.2d 285 (1986).
38. Gasner v. Pierce, 286 Pa. 529, 134 A. 494 (1926).
39. 26 P.L.E. Husband And Wife § 46.
40. *See* Schweitzer v. Evans, 360 Pa. 552, 63 A.2d 39 (1949).
41. Stone Constr. Co. v. Schubert, 1965 Pa. Dist. & Cnty. Dec. LEXIS 203 (Pa. C.P. 1965).
42. Stop 35, Inc. v. Haines, 374 Pa. Super. 604, 611 (Pa. Super. 1988).
43. *Id.*

§ 3 Signatory's Authority to Execute a Guaranty

Generally, the obligee has a duty of reasonable inquiry when it has some notice that the signatory of the guaranty does not have authority to bind the guarantor.

3.1 Corporations

For an obligee to rely on a guaranty, the guaranty must be signed by an officer with actual or apparent authority to act in such capacity.[44] All powers vested in a business corporation shall be exercised by or under the direction of a board of directors.[45] Officers shall have such authority and perform such duties as are provided in the bylaws or as may be determined pursuant to resolutions of the board of directors.[46] Resolutions of the board should in all events be sought by a creditor seeking confirmation that authority exists for the corporation and individual signatory officers to act. If the officer acts without authority, or exceeds the scope of its authority, the officer is ordinarily individually liable on the theory that the officer has breached an implied warranty of authority.[47]

There are four grounds[48] upon which a principal may be bound by a particular act of a signatory and liable to third parties on the basis thereof: (1) the signatory has express authority directly granted by the principal for the signatory to bind the principal as to certain matters; or (2) implied authority is given to the agent to bind the principal to those acts of the agent that are necessary, proper, and usual in the exercise of the agent's express authority; or (3) the agent holds apparent authority, i.e., authority that the principal has by words, conduct, or position of the agent on behalf of the entity; or (4) authority exists that the principal is estopped to deny.[49]

An admitted agent is presumed to be acting within the scope of its authority where the act is legal and the third party has no notice of the agent's limitation.[50] A third party is entitled to rely upon the apparent authority of the agent when this is a reasonable interpretation of the manifestations of the principal obligor.[51] Principles of apparent authority apply only when action is taken in reliance upon facts giving rise to apparent authority[52] such that a person of

44. Agency principles dictate that an admitted agent is presumed to be acting within the scope of his authority where his act is legal and there is no evidence as to any limitations of his authority. In the absence of notice to the contrary, a third person dealing with a known agent may properly assume that he is acting within the scope of his authority. His authority is presumed to be coextensive with the business entrusted to him and to embrace whatever is necessary or usual in the ordinary course of such business. 3 C.J.S. Agency § 317, p. 256. Apparent authority is such authority as the corporation knowingly permits the officer or agent to assume or which it holds him out as possessing. Wood Co. v. McCutcheon, 136 Pa. Super. 446, 453 (Pa. Super. Ct. 1939).
45. 15 Pa.C.S. § 1721.
46. 15 Pa.C.S. § 1732.
47. McDonald v. Luckenbach, 170 F. 434 (3d Cir. 1961).
48. SEI Corp. v. Norton & Co., 631 F.Supp. 497 (E.D. Pa.1986).
49. Garczynski v. Countrywide Home Loans, Inc., 656 F. Supp. 2d 505, 511 (E.D. Pa. 2009) (Baylson, J.) (quoting SEI Corp. v. Norton & Co., 631 F. Supp. 497, 501 (E.D. Pa. 1986)).
50. Continental-Wirt Electron Corp. v. Sprague Electric Co., 329 F.Supp. 959, 963 (E.D. Pa.1971).
51. Turnway Corp. v. Soffer, 461 Pa. 447, 458, 336 A.2d 871 (1975); Industrial Molded Plastic Products, Inc. v. J. Gross & Son, Inc., 263 Pa.Superior Ct. 515, 521, 398 A.2d 695 (1979).
52. Restatement, Agency 2d § 8, comment a; *see also* Meyer v. Industrial Valley Bank & Trust Co., 1967 Pa. Dist. & Cnty. Dec. LEXIS 59 (Pa. C.P. 1967).

ordinary prudence, diligence, and discretion would believe that the agent was acting within the scope of its/his power.[53] Acts taken by an agent with apparent authority will be imputed to the principal or the corporation.[54]

An obligee cannot rely on the apparent authority of an agent to bind a principal if he has knowledge of the limits of the agent's authority.[55] The burden of proving agency rests on the party asserting that an agency relationship exists.[56]

3.2 Partnerships

Pennsylvania partnership law grants a partner the authority to bind the partnership when such partner's act is "for apparently carrying on in the usual way the business of the partnership," unless such authority has been explicitly restricted by the partnership agreement.[57] If a partner's action is not apparently for carrying on the business of the partnership, the partner must be authorized by the other partners to bind a partnership.[58] Authority may also be granted under the partnership agreement and in all events such agreement should be reviewed to confirm that the partnership and any particular partner have authority to act.

A partner generally may not bind the partnership as guarantor or surety for a third person without the assent or ratification of the other partners.[59] Pennsylvania law generally finds that a contract for a guaranty is not usually given in the ordinary course of a partnership's business. Unless ratification is shown or authorization is proved or to be presumed from the scope and usual course of the partnership's business, a joint promise by all of the partners of guaranty or suretyship must be established.[60]

3.3 Limited Liability Companies

Members (and if applicable managers) derive their authority to execute a guaranty from the provisions of the certificate of organization and operating agreement, although, unless otherwise limited, they will have the authority of general partners in a general partnership.[61]

---

53. Friedman v. Kasser, 332 Pa. Super. 475, 483, 481 A.2d 886, 890 (1984) ("If a man of ordinary prudence would believe that the agent possessed the authority he purported to exercise, then the principal is liable for the acts of the agent."); *see* Murphy v. Beverly Hills Realty Corp., 98 Pa.Super. 183 (1930).
54. The Restatement (Third) of Agency notes that this is, in part, because it is the principal who has selected and delegated responsibility to those agents; accordingly, the doctrine creates incentives for the principal to do so carefully and responsibly. § 5.03 cmt. b (2006).
    Additionally, courts have noted that "[i]mputation also serves to protect those who transact business with a corporation through its agents believing the agents' conduct is with the authority of his principal. Imputation creates incentives for a principal to choose agents carefully and to use care in delegating functions to them. Imputation is founded on the duty of the agent to communicate all material information to his principal, and the assumption that he has done so." Official Comm. of Unsecured Creditors of Allegheny Health Educ. & Research Found. v. PricewaterhouseCoopers, LLP, 605 Pa. 269 (2010).
55. Bolus v. United Penn Bank, 363 Pa. Super. 247, 261-262 (1987).
56. Girard Trust Bank v. Sweeney, 426 Pa. 324, 329 (Pa. 1967).
57. 15 Pa.C.S. § 8321(a).
58. 15 Pa.C.S. § 8321(b).
59. 37 P.L.E. Partnerships § 143. (citing Shaaber v. Bushong & Bro., 105 Pa. 514 (1884)).
60. Jamestown Banking Co. v. Conneaut Lake Dock & Dredge Co., 339 Pa. 26, 14 A.2d 325 (1940).
61. 15 Pa.C.S. § 8904(a).

3.4 Banks and Trust Companies

A case-by-case inquiry of the powers provided for in a bank's or trust company's corporate governance documents (and any applicable resolutions) is necessary to determine who may validly execute a guaranty on behalf of a bank or trust company.

3.5 Individuals

Where an individual signatory enters a guaranty agreement on behalf of a principal, but without authority, the principal may avoid the effect of its ratification if at the time it was ignorant of material facts.[62] However, a principal can ratify the unauthorized act of its agent without full knowledge of all material facts connected to the agreement if the principal intentionally and deliberately does so, knowing that he or she does not possess such knowledge and does not make further inquiry into the matter.[63] In such instances, courts will infer that the principal willingly assumed the risk of facts as to which the principal knew he or she was ignorant.[64]

§ 4 Consideration; Sufficiency of Past Consideration

Consideration is required to create a valid contract of guaranty.[65] Standard contract principles apply to analyzing the sufficiency of consideration. The principal agreement is sufficient consideration for an accompanying guaranty. The benefit or obligation that forms the consideration need not flow directly to the guarantor from the obligee; the consideration flowing to the principal obligor is sufficient to support a contemporaneous guaranty.[66]

While past consideration, under general principles of contract law, will not support a contract for guaranty, where the guaranty is executed subsequently to the principal contract, the original consideration will be sufficient where the principal contract was executed pursuant to the request of the guarantor and upon its promise to make such guaranty.[67]

Under Pennsylvania law, every written promise signed by the person promising shall not be invalid or unenforceable for lack of consideration if it contains a statement that the signer intends to be legally bound.[68]

62. *See, e.g.*, Daley v. Iselin, 218 Pa. 515, 518; Shields v. Hitchman, 251 Pa. 455, 459, 460; Culbertson v. Cook, 308 Pa. 557, 564, 565; Simonin's Sons, Inc. v. American Credit Indemnity Co., 318 Pa. 160, 164.
63. Pollock v. Standard Steel Car Co., 230 Pa. 136, 141.
64. Currie v. Land Title Bank & Trust Co., 333 Pa. 310, 314 (1939).
65. Warner-Lambert Pharmaceutical Co. v. Sylk, 471 F.2d 1137 (3d Cir. 1972) (discussing consideration in regard to the modification of a suretyship contract).
66. Greater Valley Terminal Corp. v. Goodman, 405 Pa. 605, 176 A.2d 408 (1962) (An inference of consideration may be drawn where surety is given contemporaneously with principal obligation.).
67. Paul v. Stackhouse, 38 Pa. 302 (1861).
68. 33 P.S. § 6 (Uniform Written Obligations Act).

§ 5 Notice of Acceptance

Under Pennsylvania law, generally, the obligee must notify the guarantor of its acceptance of the guaranty.[69] Acceptance of an offer to act as guarantor does not need to be made in a formal manner and can be implied from the fact that the offer is acted upon. Where one expressly agrees in writing to be a guarantor for another, he or she is not entitled to notice of acceptance by the creditor or obligee.[70] Likewise, notice of acceptance is not necessary where the agreement to accept the guaranty is contemporaneous with the offer, since the guarantor is present and the agreement to accept is made at the time it is offered.[71]

§ 6 Interpretation of Guaranties

Courts in Pennsylvania are guided by the principle of *strictissimi juris*, strictly construing the obligations of the guarantor. This rule, however, does not apply to compensated guarantors. Generally, courts will interpret a guaranty in the same manner by which they would interpret the language of any other contract, according to the intent of the parties.

6.1 General Principles

A guaranty agreement is a contract and subject to the same rules of interpretation as other contracts. Pennsylvania courts consider the language of the agreement to determine the extent of the guarantor's rights and liabilities.[72] A guaranty must be construed as a whole, with regard to surrounding circumstances, and should not be construed so strictly so as to defeat the manifest intention of the parties.[73]

The rule of construction *strictissimi juris* (strict construction) guides the interpretation of gratuitous guaranties.[74] As such, a contract of guaranty will be strictly construed in favor of a gratuitous guarantor, and will not be extended by implication or construction beyond its clear and absolute terms.[75] This principle does not however apply to compensated guaranty agreements.[76] Where the guaranty is executed by professional guarantors, the rule of strict

69. State Camp of Pennsylvania v. Kelley, 267 Pa. 49, 110 A. 339 (1920); *see also* Cornell & Co. v. First Indem. of Am. Ins. Co. (In re Muratone Co.), 198 B.R. 871 (E.D. Pa. 1996), aff'd without op. sub nom., Cornell & Co. v. Muratone Co. (In re Muratone Co.), 111 F.3d 126 (3d Cir. Pa. 1997) (finding that a suretyship agreement did not exist where there was no acceptance of suretyship agreement).
70. Manufacturers Light & Heat Co. v. Thompson, 54 Pa. Super 558 (1913).
71. Fasco, A.G. v. Modernage, Inc., 311 F. Supp. 161 (W.D. Pa. 1970).
72. Citicorp M. Am. v. Thornton, 198 Pa. Super. 147, 707 A.2d 536 (1998).
73. Miller v. Commercial Electric Constr., Inc., 223 Pa. Super. 216, 297 A.2d 487 (1972) (Surety contracts are to be liberally construed in favor of laborers and materialmen).
74. J.F. Walker Co. v. Excalibur Oil Group, Inc., 792 A.2d 1269, 1274 (Pa. Super. 2002).
75. 46 P.L.E. SURETYSHIP § 53.
76. Fessenden Hall of Pa., Inc. v. Mountainview Specialties, Inc., 2004 Pa. Super 456 (2004).

construction does not apply.[77] Additionally, ambiguous language employed by a guarantor will ordinarily be construed in favor of the obligee.[78]

6.2 Guaranty of Payment versus Guaranty of Collection

If the guaranty agreement is accompanied by words indicating unambiguously that the party is guaranteeing collection rather than payment of the obligation of the primary obligor, the guarantor is obliged to pay the amount due on the instrument to an obligee only if: (1) execution of judgment as to the primary obligor has been satisfied; (2) the other party is insolvent or is in an insolvency proceeding; (3) the other party cannot be served with process; or (4) it is otherwise apparent that payment cannot be obtained from the other party.[79]

6.3 Language Regarding the Revocability of Guaranties

The scope and extent of a surety's liability depends on the language of the contract.[80] An offer to guaranty future obligations may be revoked by the guarantor unless the guaranty agreement states otherwise. Revocation of a continuing guaranty does not affect liability for past transactions which have created a contractual relationship between guarantor and creditor.[81]

Generally, "[t]he death of a guarantor operates as a revocation of the guaranty in all cases where the guarantor might, if living, have revoked by giving notice."[82] Whether a guaranty is revocable in a continuing guaranty depends on the nature of the obligations agreed to in the agreement. For example, where a continuing guaranty contemplates a series of future transactions, as successive loans, for each of which the guarantor becomes responsible and the consideration is divisible, transactions occurring after the death of the guarantor and knowledge or notice thereof to the obligee will fall outside the scope of the guaranty agreement.[83] "[I]f the consideration is entire and has already passed, then the guarantor's estate should not be released by reason of his death, even though the creditor has knowledge thereof; and of course liability may exist at the time of the guarantor's death for which his estate could still be held."[84]

6.4 "Continuing"

In determining the scope of a continuing guaranty, Pennsylvania courts have considered 38 Am.Jur.2d, Guaranty, § 63, which provides that:

> "[a] continuing guaranty contemplates a future course of dealings between the creditor and the principal debtor, usually extending over

77. Magazine Digest Pub. Co. v. Shade, 330 Pa. 487, 199 A. 190 (1938).
78. In re Brock, 312 Pa. 7, 166 A. 778 (1933).
79. 9 P.L.E. COMMERCIAL TRANSACTIONS § 322 (citing 13 Pa.C.S. § 3419(d)).
80. Citicorp N. Am. v. Thornton, 707 A.2d 536. (Pa. Super. Ct. 1998).
81. Robert Mallery Lumber Corp. v. B. & F. Associates, Inc., 294 Pa. Super. 503 (Pa. Super. Ct. 1982).
82. In re Fullmer's Estate, 319 Pa. 360, 366 (1935).
83. Pleasonton & Biddle's Appeal, 75 Pa. 344 (1874).
84. In re Fullmer's Estate, 319 Pa. 360, 367 (Pa. 1935).

an indefinite period of time. In its inception, a continuing guaranty is an offer from the guarantor and is accepted by the creditor each time the creditor performs a specified act (such as extending credit to the debtor). An offer for a continuing guaranty is ordinarily effective until revoked by the guarantor or extinguished by some rule of law. At any period of time, therefore, the legal relation between the guarantor and the creditor involves both a contract (as to transactions between the creditor and principal debtor which have been completed) and an offer (as to future transactions between the creditor and principal debtor). When the continuing guaranty is thus properly analyzed, the offer to guarantee future obligations may be revoked by the guarantor, at least in the absence of a contrary provision in the guaranty instrument with the result that the guarantor will not be liable to the creditor on the latter's extension of credit to the debtor subsequent to the receipt of notice of revocation. However, revocation of the continuing guaranty does not affect liability for past transactions which have created a contractual relationship between guarantor and creditor."[85]

The determination of whether a guaranty is continuing or noncontinuing depends on the language of the contract or the course of dealings of the parties. A guaranty will be construed as continuing where it appears that a future course of dealing for an indefinite time or a succession of credits in contemplated by the parties,[86] but a guaranty will not be construed as continuing beyond the first transaction unless the terms of the contract plainly import such liability.

6.5 "Absolute and Unconditional"

An absolute and unconditional guaranty is one where the guarantor waives its rights to claim the creditor failed to proceed against any collateral. Under an absolute and unconditional guaranty agreement, the creditor need not take any action to preserve the security, and the creditor's failure to do so will not relieve the surety's obligation to pay upon default.[87]

6.6 "Liability as a Primary Obligor and not Merely as Surety"

Absent limitations or restrictions in the suretyship contract, the liability of a surety is coextensive with that of the principal.[88] A surety is obligated to per-

85. Robert Mallery Lumber Corp. v. B. & F. Associates, Inc., 294 Pa. Super. 503 (1982).
86. *Id.*
87. McKeesport Nat'l Bank v. Rosenthal, 355 Pa. Super. 291 (1986) (the guarantor "waived presentment, demand, protest and notice of dishonor of any and all of said instruments . . . and likewise waived demand for payment and notice of nonpayment of any and all loans, advances, credits and other obligations hereinbefore referred to, and promptness in commencing suit against any party thereto or liable thereon and/or in giving any notice to or of making any claim or demand; [and] . . .consented and agreed that [creditor] could at any time . . . in its discretion . . . exchange, release and/or surrender all or any of the collateral security, or any part or parts thereof . . . without notice to or further assent from [guarantor], who . . . agreed to be and remain bound upon this guaranty, irrespective of the existence, value or condition of any collateral and notwithstanding any such change, exchange . . . or release. . .").
88. Downer v. U.S. Fid. & Guar. Co., 46 F.2d 733 (3d Cir. 1931).

form whatever is required of its, his, or her principal.[89] As previously noted, if a contract expressly states it is intended to be a contract of guaranty and not of suretyship, the guarantor will be only secondarily liable.

§ 7 Defenses of the Guarantor

The defenses that may be available to a guarantor can be grouped into three categories: (1) defenses of the primary obligor; (2) guarantor's defenses; and (3) other defenses.

7.1 Defenses of the Primary Obligor

7.1.1 General

A guarantor is only bound to the extent and under the conditions set forth in the guaranty agreement. Subject to the terms of the guaranty agreement, a judgment in favor of the creditor against the principal is not conclusive against the guarantor.[90]

Generally, the liability of the guarantor (as surety) is coextensive with the liability of the principal obligor,[91] absent a provision to the contrary in the guaranty agreement. As such, a guarantor is bound to perform whatever is legally required of the principal and may largely assert any defense that the principal may assert.[92]

7.1.2 When Guarantor May Assert Primary Obligor's Defense

Generally, a guarantor may advance any defense that the principal obligor could advance with the exception of defenses that are purely personal to the principal or those which the principal waived or is estopped from asserting.[93] A guarantor cannot assert the disability of the principal obligor as a defense where the guaranty contract was entered into because the principal was under such disability.[94]

A judgment against a principal obligor may or may not be conclusive as to the guarantor depending on the nature of the guaranty and the terms of the guaranty contract. Where a guarantor submits itself to the act of a principal,[95] or in cases involving official bonds,[96] or bonds to insure the faithful performance or duty,[97] or to secure a proper accounting by persons in fiduciary relations, a

89. N. Am. Specialty Ins. Co. v. Chichester Sch. Dist., 158 F. Supp. 2d 468 (E.D. Pa. 2001).
90. Crawford v. Pyle, 190 Pa. 263, 42 A. 687 (1899).
91. Fayette Title & Trust Co. v. Maryland, P. & W. V. Tel. & Tel. Co., 180 F. 928 (C.C.D. Pa. 1910).
92. Superior Precase, Inc. v. Safe Ins. Co. of Am., 71 F. Supp. 2d 438 (E.D. Pa. 1999).
93. American Bonding Co. v. United States, 223 F. 364 (3d Cir. Pa. 1916).
94. Wiggins' Appeal, 100 Pa. 155 (1882).
95. Commonwealth use of Gettman v. A.B. Baxter & Co., 235 Pa. 179, 84 A. 136 (1912).
96. Pennsylvania Turnpike Com. v. U.S. Fid. & Guar. Co., 412 Pa. 222, 194 A.2d 423 (1963).
97. Commonwealth to Use of Haines v. Fid. & Deposit Co., 224 Pa. 95, 73 A. 327 (1909).

judgment against a principal obligor, absent fraud or collusion, is conclusive as to the guarantor's amount of indebtedness.[98]

The defense of duress can only be advanced by the party upon whom the duress was imposed, but a third-party guarantor may assert a defense that he or she entered into the guaranty agreement without knowledge of the duress.[99] Also, a guarantor of a note may assert a defense that the payee gave the note to defraud creditors of the principal obligor without the guarantor's knowledge.[100]

7.1.3 Defenses that May not be Raised by Guarantor

A guarantor is liable even if the contract is not enforceable against the principal obligor because the principal lacked capacity or qualification to enter the contract.[101]

7.1.4 Defenses that May Always be Raised by Guarantor

A guarantor may show that the obligee failed to perform such that there is a partial or complete "failure of consideration."[102]

A guarantor who is induced to enter the guaranty contract by fraudulent and false statements or representations by the obligee may be discharged of liability on that contract.[103] However, where a guarantor is fraudulently induced to enter into the contract by the principal obligor and the obligee did not have knowledge of the fraud or participate in such fraud, the guaranty agreement may not be avoided.[104] The concealment of a material fact of importance that would influence the determination of the guarantor to enter the agreement is considered fraud upon the guarantor and will vitiate the contract.[105] The obligee is not, however, required to disclose facts that are not directly related to the transaction to which the guaranty attaches or connected to the subject of the contract, unless the guarantor inquires.[106] Likewise, an obligee does not have a duty to disclose information to the guarantor regarding the solvency of the principal obligor unless the guarantor requests such information.[107]

Pennsylvania requires proof of fraud by clear and convincing evidence.[108] A guarantor who fails to read or notice the contents of the agreement is liable even if it did not understand the terms of the instrument.[109]

98. Holmes v. Frost, 125 Pa. 328, 17 A. 424 (1889).
99. Bitner v. Diehl, 61 Pa. Super. 483 (1915).
100. Goodwin v. Kent, 201 Pa. 41, 50 A. 290 (1901).
101. Wiggins' Appeal, 100 Pa. 155 (1882).
102. Dunbar v. Fleisher, 137 Pa. 85, 20 A. 520 (1890).
103. Commonwealth v. Edwards, 14 Pa. Commonw. 276, 322 A. 416 (1974).
104. Hancock Bank v. Orlando, 220 Pa. Super 1, 281 A.2d 466 (1971).
105. Bolz v. Stuhl, 4 Pa. Super. 52 (1897).
106. Donaldson v. Hartford Accident & Indem. Co., 269 Pa. 456, 112 A. 562 (1921).
107. Farmers' & Drovers' Nat'l Bank v. Braden, 145 Pa. 473, 22 A. 1045 (1891).
108. Bayout v. Bayout, 373 Pa. 549 (1953); Laughlin v. McConnel, 201 Pa. Superior Ct. 180 (1963).
109. Johnson v. Patterson, 314 Pa. 398, 6 A. 746 (1886). *See* Union Nat'l Bank & Trust Co. v. Lumish, 1 Phila. 177, 181 (Pa. C.P. 1978) (noting that even though guarantor did not read the guaranty, it was bound as guarantor for the total debt).

7.2 "Suretyship" Defenses

7.2.1 *Change in Identity of Principal Obligor*

A guarantor may be discharged where the contractual relationship between the principal obligor and obligee changes by the substitution of new parties in place of those originally contracting, either by the original party assigning its interest in the contract to another in whole or in part, or by associating new parties by partnership agreements, unless the guarantor consents to such change.[110] However, a change in personnel does not always release a guarantor from liability on a guaranty.[111] A merger of a corporate obligee with another corporation[112] or the incorporation of an obligee may not bring about a guarantor's discharge where the change is not material to the risk assumed by the guaranty agreement.[113]

7.2.2 *Modification of the Underlying Obligation, Including Release*

Under Pennsylvania law, modifications to the underlying obligation made without consent of the guarantor may discharge the guarantor's liability. Where a creditor discharges the principal obligor or increases or decreases the principal obligor's obligation without the guarantor's consent, the guarantor will be discharged.[114] The extent of modification required to effectuate a discharge depends upon whether the guaranty was entered gratuitously or for compensation. Any material alteration or change made to the contract for guaranty, or the obligation as to which the performance is secured by the guaranty, will discharge an uncompensated guarantor if he or she did not have knowledge of, or consent to, the modification.[115]

On the other hand, only material and prejudicial changes which substantially increase the guarantor's risk will release a compensated guarantor.[116] A material modification in the creditor-debtor relationship will not vitiate a guaranty where the guarantor gave prior consent to such modifications.[117]

7.2.3 *Release or Impairment of Security for the Underlying Obligation*

An obligee has a positive duty to preserve the security given for the principal debt for the benefit of the principal obligor's guarantor.[118] The obligee must

110. Pure Oil Co. v. Shlifer, 115 Pa. Super. 319, 175 A. 895 (1934).
111. *See* Supplee v. Jerman, 16 Pa. Super. 45 (1901) (finding that the continued occupancy of the widow after the death of a lessee did not release the guarantor).
112. Pennsylvania & N. W. R. Co. v. Harkins, 149 Pa. 121, 24 A. 175 (1892).
113. State Camp of Pennsylvania v. Kelley, 267 Pa. 49, 110 A. 339 (1920).
114. Commonwealth to Use of Dollar Sav. & Trust Co. v. Picard, 296 Pa. 120, 145 A. 794 (1929).
115. Reliance Ins. Co. v. Penn Paving, Inc., 557 Pa. 439, 734 A. 2d 833 (1999).
116. McIntyre Square Assocs. v. Evans, 827 A.2d 446 (Pa. Super. Ct. 2003).
117. *Id.*
118. 46 P.L.E. § 78 (citing In re Bahara, 219 B.R. 77 (M.D. Pa. 1998) (If a creditor discharges a principal in a manner that prejudices the rights and interests of the surety, the surety will be discharged from performing. Further, where a creditor releases the principal's collateral, the surety is discharged to the extent that such collateral would have reduced his obligation. These general rules apply with equal force to the relationship between cosureties.)).

not be negligent with regard to that security and has an obligation to preserve the security interest for the guarantor.[119] The creditor must not do anything affirmatively that would prejudice the rights of the guarantor to resort to the security when the guarantor fulfills the principal's obligation.[120] Where the security interest is impaired, the liability of the guarantor is reduced to the extent of the impairment.[121] As such, where a creditor releases collateral without his or her consent, the guarantor is released to the extent that the collateral would have produced funds to pay the principal debt[122] or to the extent that the guarantor is injured.[123] Furthermore, even though a guarantor was not in a position to enforce the subrogation at the time the impairment occurs, an impairment of the security for the principal debt will discharge the guarantor pro tanto.[124]

Additionally, in commercial transactions, guarantors may assert a commercial reasonableness defense with regard to the disposition of collateral.[125] Under § 9610 of the UCC, disposition of collateral may be by public or private sale, provided the method, manner, time, place, and terms of the sale are commercially reasonable.[126] The possibility of obtaining a higher price for the collateral at a different time and type of sale is not, by itself, enough to establish commercial unreasonableness.[127] The secured party is also required to give reasonable notification to a guarantor (a secondary obligor under the UCC) of any sale of collateral.[128]

In *Old Colony Trust Co. v. Penrose Industries Corp.*, defendants, after default, attacked the commercial reasonableness of a private sale of stock which had been pledged as collateral to secure their loan. The court articulated the following guidelines for determining whether a sale is commercially reasonable under § 9627 (the former § 9507): "It is commercially reasonable if the [secured] party (1) acts in good faith, (2) avoids loss, and (3) makes an effective realization. Furthermore, the party may obtain court approval if he (4) sells in the usual manner in a recognized market, or (5) sells at the current price in a recognized market, or (6) sells in conformity with reasonable commercial practices among dealers in the type of property."[129] Based on those factors, the court found that the sale was commercially reasonable because a private sale would likely bring the maximum sale price for the stock given the circumstances of that case.

119. Keystone Bank v. Flooring Specialists Inc., 513 Pa. 103, 518 A.2d 1179 (1986). (stating that coguarantors had a right to raise "impairment of collateral" defense because of creditors' release of judgment lien on property belonging to other guarantors).
120. Meyer v. Industrial Valley Bank & Trust Co., 44 Pa. D. & C.2d 295 (1967), aff'd, 428 Pa. 577, 239 A.2d 371 (1968).
121. Denny v. Lyon, 38 Pa. 98 (1861).
122. First Nat'l Bank v. Foster, 291 Pa. 72, 139 A. 609 (1927).
123. First Nat'l Consumer Discount Co. v. McCrossan, 336 Pa. Super 541, 486 A.2d 396 (1984).
124. *Id.*
125. Ford Motor Credit Co v. Lotosky, 549 F. Supp. 996 (E.D. Pa. 1982).
126. 13 Pa.C.S. § 9610 (2011).
127. 13 Pa.C.S. § 9627 (2011).
128. 13 Pa.C.S. § 9611 (2011).
129. 280 F. Supp. 698 (E.D. Pa. 1968), aff'd 398 F. 2d 310 (1968).

Where there are multiple guarantors, a coguarantor bears the burden of demonstrating that the alleged impairment of the collateral has resulted in the coguarantor being liable for more that its pro-rata share.[130]

7.3 Other Defenses

7.3.1 Failure to Fulfill a Condition Precedent

Under an agreement expressly stating it is one of guaranty and not suretyship, there must be a default by the principal obligor and the creditor must first make diligent effort to collect from the principal before the creditor can resort to collection from the guarantor.[131] Further, any conditions of the guarantor's obligation stated in the guaranty agreement must be complied with before the guarantor becomes liable.[132] Failure to comply with the conditions in the guaranty contract will release the guarantor from liability unless the nonperformance is due to no fault on the part of the obligee.[133]

7.3.2 Modification of the guaranty

Any material alteration in the original obligation will release a guarantor from liability under his or her guaranty, unless the guarantor assented to the modification.[134] Where a change is immaterial and does not prejudice a guarantor's rights, a compensated guarantor will not be discharged whereas a gratuitous guarantor may be discharged.[135]

7.3.3 Failure to Pursue Primary Obligor

Where a contract is explicitly for a guaranty and not a suretyship, liability will not attach until there is a default by the principal, the conditions of the guarantor's liability have been met, and the obligee first attempts to collect from the principal.[136] The obligee must make a diligent effort to collect from the principal obligor before he or she can pursue the guarantor.[137] However, an obligee need not make a demand on the principal where doing so would not benefit the guarantor, such as where the principal is insolvent and notice of its default is not necessary to enforce the guarantor's obligation.[138]

Under a suretyship agreement, the creditor obligee may look to the guarantor for immediate repayment upon the principal obligor's default and need not first attempt to collect from the primary obligor before enforcing against the guarantor.[139] Unless required by the contract, no demand or notice of default is necessary to trigger surety's liability and liability commences upon

130. In re Brahara, 219 B.R. 77, 1998 U.S. Dist. LEXIS 3067 (M.D. Pa. 1998).
131. Pattison v. Cobb, 212 Pa. 572, 61 A. 1108 (1905).
132. Funk v. Frankenfield, 71 Pa. 205 (1872).
133. Warner Co. v. North City Trust Co., 311 Pa. 1, 155 A. 1108 (1905).
134. Magazine Digest Pub. Co. v. Shade, 330 Pa. 487 (1938).
135. *Id.*
136. Craftmark Homes, Inc. v Nanticoke Constr. Co., 526 F.2d 790 (3d Cir. 1975).
137. Pattison v. Cobb, 212 Pa. 572, 61 A. 1108 (1905).
138. Janes v. Scott, 59 Pa. 178 (1868).
139. *See* Reuter v. Citizens & Northeastern Bank, 410 Pa. Super. 199, 208 n. 3, 599 A.2d 673, 678 n.3 (1991).

the breach by the principal obligor of the contract.[140] Failure to pursue the primary obligor is not a valid defense.

7.3.4 *Statute of Limitations*

Guaranty agreements are subject to the same statute of limitations period as is applicable to contracts, four years in Pennsylvania.[141]

7.3.5 *Statute of Frauds*

The statute of frauds applies to guaranty contracts. Pennsylvania's Uniform Written Obligations Act provides, "[n]o action shall be brought whereby to charge the defendant, upon any special promise, to answer for the debt or default of another, unless the agreement upon which such action shall be brought, or some memorandum or note thereof, shall be in writing, and signed by the party to be charged therewith, or some other person by him authorized."[142]

Whether a promise is required to be in writing depends upon the object of the promise. If the promise is to answer for the debt or default of another, the statute of frauds applies and the agreement must be in writing to be enforceable. If, on the other hand, the main purpose and object of the promisor is not to answer for another, but to serve some pecuniary or business purpose of its own, involving either a benefit to itself, or damages to the other contracting party, its promise is not within the statute, even though it may be in the form of an obligation to pay the debt of another.[143]

7.3.6 *Defenses Particular to Guarantors that are Natural Persons and their Spouses*

Other than defenses related to infancy and lack of capacity,[144] there is no Pennsylvania law specifically providing defenses particular to guarantors that are natural persons and their spouses.

7.4 Right of Set-off

A guarantor sued alone generally cannot set-off the principal's claim against a creditor unless the principal obligor has assigned its claim to the guarantor or has otherwise assented to its use of the claim as a set-off.[145] In certain circumstances, however, equity will allow a guarantor to a set-off based upon

140. Plummer v. Wilson, 322 Pa. 118, 185 A. 311 (1936).
141. *See* 42 Pa. C.S.A. § 5525 and Osprey Portfolio, LLC v. George Izett, 32 A.3d 793 (2011). However, the Pennsylvania Superior Court held in Leedom v. Spano, 436 Pa. Superior Ct. 18 (1994), that a guaranty of a mortgage was subject to the six-year statute of limitations applicable under 42 Pa. C.S.A. § 5527. It shall also be noted that the Osprey court determined that a guaranty executed under seal qualified as an instrument under seal subject to a 20-year statute of limitations.
142. 33 P.S. § 3.
143. Leonard v. Martling, 174 Pa. Super. 206; 100 A.2d 484 (1953). *See also* Lehigh Valley Hospital v. County of Montgomery, 768 A.2d 1197 (Comwlth. 2001).
144. *See* Section 2.5 of this survey.
145. Clark Car Co. v. Clark, 48 F.2d 169 (3d Cir. 1931).

the principal's claim against the creditor.[146] For example, set-off has been permitted where the principal is insolvent.[147]

Where the guarantor and the principal obligor are jointly and severally liable and the guarantor sues the creditor, the creditor is permitted to use any amount of indebtedness owed by the principal as an offset to any liability it may have.[148]

§ 8 Waiver of Defenses by the Guarantor

8.1 Defenses that Cannot be Waived

A guaranty agreement reducing legal rights which would otherwise exist is strictly construed against the party asserting that such rights were waived.[149] In addition, the rules of construction require that a written instrument be strictly construed against the drafter. Where courts find that there is no meeting of the minds, a waiver of defenses in a guaranty agreement may be stricken as a contract of adhesion.[150]

For example, in *Union Nat'l Bank & Trust Co. v. Lumish,* the guarantor had invested $80,000 to $90,000 in a corporation that needed additional funding.[151] Without reading the document, the guarantor signed plaintiff's form agreement relying upon the representations of the obligee.[152] The court found that "[c]learly, it was not within his contemplation to waive his surety defenses, and he had no reason to believe such a clause was contained in the agreement." The court noted that "he signed the agreement in order to obtain a loan for the corporation which was in financial distress."[153] The court declined to enforce the waivers in the guaranty agreement stating that there was "no meeting of the minds, and the agreement is in effect a mere contract of adhesion, whereby (one) simply adheres to a document which he is powerless to alter, having no other alternative than to reject the transaction entirely."[154]

Additionally, under Pennsylvania law, a guarantor cannot waive a commercial reasonableness defense regarding the disposition of collateral governed by Article 9 of the UCC.[155]

8.2 "Catch-all" Waivers

The standard catch-all waiver indicates that the guaranty is "absolute and unconditional" or that the guaranty is "given absolutely and uncondition-

146. *Id.*
147. *Id.*
148. Domestic Sewing Machine Co. v. Saylor, 86 Pa. 287 (1878).
149. Galligan v. Arovitch, 421 Pa. 301 (1966).
150. *See* Spallone v. Siegel, 239 Pa. Super. 586, 599-600 (1976).
151. 1 Phila. 177, 183-185 (Pa. C.P. 1978).
152. *Id.*
153. *Id.*
154. *See also* Kotwasinski v. Rasner, 436 Pa. 32 (1969); Miller v. National Insurance Co., 70 D. & C. 2d 338 (1975); Care v. Berger, 69 D. & C. 2d 434 (1975).
155. Ford Motor Credit Co. v. Lototsky, 549 F. Supp. 996 (E.D. Pa. 1980). *See* 13 Pa.C.S. § 9602.

ally." A guarantor's obligation upon principal's default in an absolute and unconditional guaranty does not depend upon the obligee's inability to realize satisfaction from the collateral.[156] Thus, the obligee is not required to look to the pledged security before demanding payment from the guarantor.[157]

Where it is clear from the language of the guaranty that it is absolute and unconditional, the creditor is not required to take any action to preserve the collateral[158] and the impairment of collateral defense is not available to the guarantor.[159] As such, the creditor's failure to preserve the guarantor's security interest (otherwise available under the doctrine of subrogation) will not relieve the guarantor's obligation to pay upon default.[160]

8.3 Use of Specific Waivers

We have not located a Pennsylvania case explicitly holding that a simple general waiver of all defenses is enforceable and prudent practice suggests that waivers of specific defenses be utilized especially since it will reinforce the creditor's arguments that intent to waive existed.

§ 9 Third-party Pledgors—Defenses and Waiver Thereof

We have found no evidence that the law as applied to guaranties would not apply to a third party pledge. In contrast, the law appears to be that a pledge of collateral to secure the obligation of another results in a guarantor relationship. It would seem logical, given this state of the law, that a pledgor generally has the same defenses available to it as are available to a guarantor.

§ 10 Jointly and Severally Liable Guarantors—Contribution and Reduction of Obligations Upon Payment by a Co-obligor

Guarantors who are jointly and severally liable are presumed to share the obligation equally. The creditor is not obliged to seek full payment from more than one such guarantor.

156. McKeesport Nat'l Bank v. Rosenthal, 355 Pa. Super. 291, 295 (Pa. Super. Ct. 1986).
157. *Id.*
158. First Nat'l Bank v. Kelly, 2010 Pa. Dist. & Cnty. Dec. LEXIS 630 (Pa. County Ct. 2010).
159. *See* Paul Revere Protective Life Insurance Co. v. Weis, 535 F.Supp. 379 (E.D.Pa. 1981) (noting that because the guaranty agreement was an absolute and unconditional one, and because the contract of guaranty did not require the creditor to take such action to protect guarantor's interest in collateral, the impairment defense had no applicability).
160. Continental Leasing Corp. v. Lebo, 217 Pa.Super. 356, 272 A.2d 193 (1970); Ford Motor Credit Co. v. Lototsky, 549 F.Supp. 996 (E.D.Pa.1982); Paul Revere Protective Life Insurance Co. v. Weis, 535 F.Supp. 379 (E.D.Pa.1981), aff'd, 707 F.2d 1403, 1405 (3d Cir.1982).

10.1 Contribution

Where coguarantors are jointly and severally liable, there is a presumption that each guarantor bears the burden of the liability equally.[161] Where there are several guarantors for the principal's unpaid debt, each guarantor owes to its coguarantors a duty to pay its proportional share of their common debt.[162] Under 13 Pa.C.S. § 3116, a guarantor that is jointly and severally liable with respect to a negotiable instrument and pays more than its proportionate share is entitled to receive contribution from its coguarantors for the excess amount.[163]

As such, if the creditor releases collateral obtained from one of several coguarantors to secure the obligation, such release can impair the other guarantors' right to resort to such collateral to enforce their rights of contribution, and if the release has such an effect, the other coguarantors will be entitled to a pro tanto discharge of their obligations.[164]

10.2 Reduction of Obligations upon Payment of Co-obligor

Each coguarantor is treated, as between itself and its coguarantors, as a principal for the fraction of debt which it ought to pay, and as a guarantor for the remainder of the obligation.[165] An agreement to release a guarantor upon its payment of only a portion of the guaranteed liability is unenforceable for want of consideration.[166]

10.3 Liability of Parent Guarantors Owning Less than 100 percent of Primary Obligor

We have not found any authoritative Pennsylvania precedent dealing with this specific circumstance.

§ 11 Reliance

A guaranty agreement that does not comply with the formalities of contract law may still be enforced under the doctrine of reliance or promissory estoppel.[167] Under this theory, a promise which the promisor should reasonably expect to induce action or forbearance on the part of the promisee and which does induce such action or forbearance is binding if injustice can be avoided

161. 13 Pa.C.S. § 3116(a); In re Bahara, 219 B.R. 77 (M.D. Pa. 1998).
162. Commonwealth ex rel. Schnader v. National Surety Co., 349 Pa. 599, 37 A.2d 753 (1944); In re Bailey's Estate, 156 Pa. 634, 27 A. 560 (1893).
163. *See also* Malone v. Stewart, 235 Pa. 99, 83 A. 607 (1912); Templeton v. Shakley, 107 Pa. 370 (1884).
164. Keystone Bank v. Flooring Specialists, Inc., 513 Pa. 103, 115 (Pa. 1986) (citing Beneficial Finance Co. of Norman v. Marshall, 551 P.2d 315 (Okla. 1976)).
165. *Id.*
166. Klingensmith v. Klingensmith's Ex'r, 31 Pa. 460 (1858).
167. First Valley Bank v. Donatelli, 279 Pa. Super. 521 (1980).

only by enforcing the promise.[168] Where an agreement for guaranty is lacking in consideration, an otherwise unenforceable guaranty agreement may be binding if the obligee can demonstrate reliance.[169]

§ 12 Subrogation

Subrogation is an equitable remedy that generally requires total satisfaction of the underlying obligation to the obligee prior to its exercise. Concern for protecting the creditor's interests affects the secondary obligor's right to subrogation.

Under Pennsylvania law, a guarantor is entitled to be substituted to all claims and liens and other securities which the principal obligor holds where the guarantor pays the debts of its principal.[170] As such, a creditor has a duty not to impair the security in its control which may provide the means for satisfying the primary obligor's debt.[171]

The creditor in such a situation must not prejudice the right of the guarantor to resort to the security when the guarantor pays the debt and becomes entitled to subrogation.[172] Impairment of the collateral discharges the guarantor to the extent that the unimpaired security would have paid the principal debt or to the extent of the guarantor's injury.[173] Furthermore, this principle applies even when the guarantor was not in a position to enforce its subrogation rights when the impairment occurred.[174] If the creditor's acts render the subrogation ineffective, the guarantor is released pro tanto or entirely depending on the case, regardless of whether the creditor had knowledge of the relationship between the guarantor and the principal. The guarantor is thus entitled to be subrogated to the rights of the creditor in regard to additional security, and if the creditor cannot assign the security to the guarantor, the guarantor will be discharged.[175]

§ 13 Triangular Set-off in Bankruptcy

Generally, where a guarantor is sued alone, the guarantor cannot set-off the principal's claim against the creditor unless the principal obligor has assigned its claim to the guarantor or consented to the use of its claim as a set-off.[176]

168. Matarazzo v. Millers Mutual Group. Inc.,927 A.2d 689, 692 (Pa. Cmwith. 2007).
169. Travers v. Cameron County School District, 117 Pa. Commw. 606, 544 A.2d 547 (1988).
170. Jacob Sall Bldg. & Loan Ass'n v. Heller, 314 Pa. 237, 171 A. 464 (1934).
171. Fegley v. McDonald, 89 Pa. 128, 130 (1879).
172. Franklin Savings & Trust Co. v. Clark, 283 Pa. 212, 129 A. 56 (1925).
173. First Nat'l Bank v. Foster, 291 Pa. 72, 75, 139 A. 609 (1927) (payment of debt); Robbins v. Robinson, 176 Pa. 341, 35 A. 337 (1896) (extent of injury); Girard Trust Bank v. O'Neill, 219 Pa. Super. 363, 367, 281 A.2d 670, 672 (1971) (extent of injury).
174. First Nat'l Bank & Trust Co. v. Stolar, 130 Pa. Super. 480, 488, 197 A. 499 (1938).
175. Boschert v. Brown, 72 Pa. 372 (1872).
176. Clark Car Co. v. Clark, 48 F.2d 169 (3d Cir. 1931).

In some situations, such as where the principal is insolvent, equity will allow a guarantor to set off the principal's claim against the creditor.[177]

§ 14 Indemnification—Whether the Primary Obligor has a Duty

The principal obligor has a duty of indemnification so long as the guarantor undertook its obligations at the request of the principal obligor. The extent of this duty can be altered by contract.

In the absence of express agreement in the guaranty agreement, there is an implied contract that the principal obligor will indemnify the guarantor for any payment which the guarantor may make in order to comply with the guaranty agreement.[178] Under common law principles of equity, a guarantor is entitled to indemnification only when the guarantor pays off a debt for which the principal is liable.[179] However, where the guaranty agreement expressly provides for indemnification of the guarantor, the guarantor is entitled to stand upon the letter of the contract.[180]

A guarantor's right to reimbursement is not affected by the fact that the guarantor made payments without the permission of the principal obligor. For example, in *Hall Estate*,[181] a guarantor had an implied right to indemnification from the principal obligor where the guarantor paid off a debt which the principal was liable even though the bank never demanded payment from the principal.

§ 15 Enforcement of Guaranties

15.1 Limitations on Recovery

Fraudulent transfer caps on recovery under a guaranty (which prevent recovery from exceeding amounts that would render the guaranty obligations void or voidable under the Bankruptcy Code or applicable state law) may be invalid.

If the guarantor was insolvent before signing the guaranty or was rendered insolvent by signing the guaranty and did not receive fair value for signing the guaranty, liability under that guaranty may be avoidable under the Uniform Fraudulent Transfer Statute.[182] No reported Pennsylvania case addresses the

177. *Id.*
178. Bishoff v. Fehl, 345 Pa. 539, 29 A.2d 58 (1942).
179. 46 PLE § 131.
180. U.S. Fid. & Guar. Co. v. Feius, 15 F. Supp. 2d 579 (M.D. Pa. 1998) (actual liability was not required to justify guarantor's payments to creditors under the guaranty agreement which plainly stated that liability extended to payments made in good faith, for example, in order to lessen guarantor's liability).
181. 20 Fiduciary 2d 346 (2000).
182. 12 Pa. C.S.A. § 5101 et seq.

validity of a cap on the guarantor's liability preventing a recovery that would exceed an amount that would render the guaranty void or voidable under a fraudulent transfer cause of action. If a guarantor became insolvent after signing the guaranty, the clause might be unenforceable as an ipso facto clause.

15.2 Enforcement of Guaranties of Collection versus Guaranties of Performance

Under Pennsylvania law, all obligations to answer for the debt of another are interpreted as suretyship obligations, unless the agreement contains express language stating that it is not intended to be an agreement for suretyship.

15.3 Exercising Rights Under a Guaranty Where the Underlying Obligation is also Secured by a Mortgage

Pennsylvania does not limit a creditor's ability to pursue a guarantor if the underlying obligation is secured by a mortgage.[183]

15.4 Litigating Guaranty Claims: Procedural Considerations

Whether a judgment against a principal obligor is conclusive as to a guarantor must be determined from the nature of the guarantor's obligation and the language and terms of the guaranty agreement.[184] Where a guarantor's liability is not contingent upon the outcome of litigation in which the principal is involved, a judgment against the principal is not conclusive against the guarantor.[185]

Unless stated otherwise in the guaranty agreement, the liability of a guarantor is no greater than that of the principal.[186] The record of a judgment against a principal is inadmissible in evidence in an action against its guarantor unless it is shown to have been rendered on account of matters connected with the guaranty agreement.[187]

§ 16 Revival and Reinstatement of Guaranties

One Pennsylvania trial court considered whether a guarantor's obligation was revived where the trustee in the debtor's bankruptcy proceeding ordered an accounting of all monies collected from the principal obligor by the creditor and vacated the order.[188] Subsequently, the creditor and the debtor's trustee

183. *See*, however, the Deficiency Judgment Act, 42 Pa. C.S.A. § 8103, which requires specific procedures following a foreclosure on real property either of the primary obligor or of any guarantor in order that the foreclosing mortgagee or judgment creditor (if it is the successful bidder at the foreclosure sale) retain and enforce a deficiency claim against any obligor.
184. Commonwealth to Use of Gettman v. A. B. Baxter & Co., 235 Pa. 179, 84 A. 136 (1912).
185. Giltinan v. Strong, 64 Pa. 242 (1870).
186. McShain v. Indemnity Ins. Co., 338 Pa. 113, 12 A.2d 59 (1940).
187. Herzog v. Des Lauriers Steel Mould Co., 46 F. Supp. 211 (D. Pa. 1942).
188. Fid. America Fin. Corp. v. Elkins, 1981 Pa. Dist. & Cnty. Dec. LEXIS 512 (Pa. C.P. 1981).

entered into a settlement agreement whereby the creditor relinquished certain monies to the trustee in exchange for the release of the estate's claims against the creditor.[189] When the creditor sought to collect against the guarantor for the amount relinquished to the trustee, the court held that the guarantor's obligation was not revived because the creditor was not legally obligated to relinquish the monies to the trustee.[190]

§ 17 Choice of Law

Pennsylvania courts will generally enforce a choice of law provision in a contract.[191] Pennsylvania has adopted Section 187 of the *Restatement (Second) Conflicts of Laws* which provides that a choice of law provision in a contract will be given effect unless: (1) the state whose law is specified in the contract has no substantial relationship with the parties or the transaction, or there is no other reasonable basis for the parties' choice or (2) the application of the state law chosen by the parties would be contrary to the public policy of the state having a materially greater interest than the chosen state in determining the particular issue. Where the chosen jurisdiction is either the principal place of business, place of performance, place of contracting, or the location of the principal place of business of a contracting party, Pennsylvania courts will likely find that a substantial relationship exists and enforce the parties' choice of law provision.[192]

189. *Id.* at 513.
190. The court noted that Restatement, Security § 132 controlled, which provides that "where a creditor has security from the principal and knows of the surety's obligation, the surety's obligation is reduced pro-tanto if the creditor (a) surrenders or releases the security, or (b) willfully or negligently harms it, or (c) fails to take reasonable action to preserve its value at a time when the surety does not have an opportunity to take such action." Supra, at *515 (replaced by Restatement (Third) of Suretyship & Guaranty, § 42). The Restatement (Third) of Suretyship & Guaranty, § 70 also provides that "When a secondary obligation is discharged in whole or part by performance by the principal obligor or another secondary obligor, or by realization upon collateral securing such performance, the secondary obligation revives to the extent that the obligee, under a legal duty to do so, later surrenders that performance or collateral, or the value thereof, as a preference or otherwise." Best practices would include language in the guaranty agreement that provides for revival of the guaranty in applicable circumstances.
191. *See* Smith v. Commonwealth Nat'l Bank, 557 A.2d 775, 777 (Pa. Super. Ct. 1989).
192. *See Id.* at 766-77; Kruzits v. Okume Mach. Tool, Inc. 40 F.3d 52, 55056 (3d Cir. 1994); Schifano v. Schifano, 324 Pa. Super. 281, 471 A.2d 839, 843 n. 5 (Pa. Super. 1984).

Rhode Island State Law of Guaranties

Thomas S. Hemmendinger
Brennan, Recupero, Cascione, Scungio & McAllister, LLP
362 Broadway
Providence, RI 02903
(401) 453-2300
fax (401) 453-2345
themmendinger@brcsm.com
www.brcsm.com

Contents

Rhode Island State Law of Guaranties

Introductory Note: In order to standardize our discussion of the law of guaranties, we use the following vocabulary to refer to the various parties to a guaranty and their obligations.

"Guarantor" means a person who, by contract, agrees to satisfy an underlying obligation of another to an obligee upon the primary obligor's default on that underlying obligation. We do not draw a distinction between guarantors and sureties, as there is little difference between the two under Rhode Island law. The few differences are explained below.

"Guaranty" means the contract by which the guarantor agrees to satisfy the underlying obligation of a primary obligor to an obligee in the event the primary obligor defaults on the underlying obligation.

"Obligee" means the person to whom the underlying obligation is owed. For example, the lender under a loan agreement would be an obligee vis-à-vis the borrower.

"Primary Obligor" means the person who incurs the underlying obligation to the obligee. For example, the borrower under a loan agreement would be a primary obligor.

"Underlying Obligation" means the obligation or obligations that the primary obligor owes to the obligee. For example, the borrower's obligation to make payments to a lender of principal and interest on a loan constitutes an underlying obligation.

TRAPS:

Rhode Island strictly follows traditional common law rules on consideration, so past consideration does not support a guaranty. See § 4.

A third party's assumption of the primary obligor's debt transforms the primary obligor into a surety. See § 1.2.

§ 1 Nature of the Guaranty Arrangement

General principles of the common law of suretyship and guaranties apply in Rhode Island. Rhode Island courts authorize broad waivers of suretyship defenses. For purposes of commercial paper, Rhode Island's Uniform Commercial Code provisions on endorsers and accommodation parties are identical to the 1990 Official Texts of Articles 3 and 4.

1.1 Guaranty Relationships

The guaranty is an agreement "separate and distinct from the [underlying obligation]."[1]

The general rules for contract formation apply to guaranties (competent parties, subject matter, a legal consideration, mutuality of agreement, and mutuality of obligation).[2]

Rhode Island law recognizes the following types of guaranties:

- *Absolute guaranty* – where the guarantor promises to pay or perform upon the primary obligor's default.[3]
- *Conditional guaranty* – where the guarantor's promise is contingent on one or more conditions other than, or in addition to, the primary obligor's default.[4]
- *Continuing guaranty* – where the guarantor's promise covers both present and future debt.[5]
- *Payment guaranty (or guaranty of payment)* – where the guarantor promises to pay the primary obligor's debt when due.[6]
- *Collection guaranty (or guaranty of collection)* – where the guarantor promises to pay the primary obligor's debt upon if the obligee cannot collect after exhausting remedies against the primary obligor.[7]
- *Performance guaranty* – where the guarantor promises to perform an act rather than pay a debt.[8]

1.2 Other Suretyship Relationships

While the law technically distinguishes between guarantors and other sureties, the terms "surety" and "guarantor" are often used interchangeably and are nearly identical.[9]

1. New Bedford Morris Plan Co. v. Hicks, 52 R.I. 74, 76, 157 A. 421, 422 (1931).
2. CIC-Newport Assoc., LP v. Lee, 2010 R.I. Super. LEXIS 184 (citing to the RESTATEMENT (THIRD) SURETYSHIP § 7).
3. *See* § 6.5 *infra*.
4. *See* § 7.3.1 *infra*.
5. *See* § 6.4 *infra*.
6. *See* § 6.2 *infra*.
7. *See* § 6.2 *infra*.
8. *See* § 15.2 *infra*.
9. Rhode Island Hospital Tr. Nat'l Bank v. Ohio Cas. Ins. Co., 789 F.3d 74, 78 (1st Cir. 1986).

A guarantor is secondarily liable on the underlying obligation.[10] However, the surety on a bond joins with the contract between the obligee and the primary obligor and can be sued as a primary obligor.[11]

If a third party assumes the primary obligor's obligations, then the primary obligor becomes a surety for the third party's performance and has suretyship defenses.[12] In the leading case on this point, the maker of a mortgage note conveyed the property to a third party, who assumed the debt and continued to make payments.[13] The maker was discharged when the mortgagee later extended the time for the new owner to pay, without obtaining the maker's consent.

§ 2 State Law Requirements for an Entity to Enter a Guaranty

Entities and associations organized under Rhode Island law can guaranty the obligations of others, only if they have the legal power to do so.

2.1 Corporations

A corporation can issue a guaranty, even if it is not in furtherance of its corporate purposes, so long as the shareholders approve the guaranty.[14] The Rhode Island Business Corporation Act largely eliminates the defense of *ultra vires* as against a commercial lender.[15]

2.2 Partnerships

A partnership can issue a guaranty only if the guaranty accomplishes one of the partnership's stated purposes or where the particular transaction is within the scope of the partnership's business.[16]

2.3 Limited Liability Companies

A limited liability company (LLC) can issue a guaranty, even if the guaranty is "not in furtherance of the limited liability company's purpose."[17] However, the LLC's articles of organization or operating agreement may impose limitations on this power.

10. Ambrosino v. Rhode Island Hospital Tr. Co., 92 R.I. 282, 168 A.2d 165 (1961), reh. den. 92 R.I. 282, 168 A.2d 719.
11. Rhode Island Hospital Tr. Nat'l Bank v. Ohio Cas. Ins. Co., 789 F.3d 74, 77-78 (1st Cir. 1986).
12. Industrial Tr. Co. v. Goldman, 59 R.I. 11, 17, 193 A. 852, 854 (1937).
13. *Id.*
14. R.I. Gen. Laws § 7-1.2-302(b)(20) (2012).
15. R.I. Gen. Laws § 7-1.2-303 (2012).
16. Parker v. Burges & Leavens, 5 R.I. 277, 281 (1858).
17. R.I. Gen. Laws § 7-16-4(3) (2012).

2.4 Banks and Trust Companies

Rhode Island law does not address a bank, trust company, or other financial institution's ability to issue a guaranty. However, federal law prohibits a state-chartered bank from engaging in activities in which a national bank may not engage under federal law. The situations under which a national bank may become a guarantor are governed by federal law.[18]

2.5 Individuals

Any individual competent to enter into a contract may issue a guaranty. This requires:

- Mental competence.[19]
- Sufficient age (18 years).[20]

Under Rhode Island law, a guaranty issued by one spouse does not automatically affect the property or liabilities of the other spouse.

If the guarantor owns real property with his/her spouse as tenants by the entirety, then the creditor may obtain a prejudgment attachment.[21] However, the creditor cannot levy and sell the property unless the guarantor survives his/her spouse.[22] If the judgment debtor dies first, then the attachment becomes null and void.[23]

Where property is held in tenancy by the entirety, the one-year deadline for levy in R.I. Gen. Laws § 9-25-23 is stayed by operation of law and does not begin to run until the death of the nondebtor spouse.[24] If the guarantor files bankruptcy, he/she might be able to exempt the property, but the attachment remains in effect, with levy stayed until one spouse dies.[25]

In a divorce, the court will assign jointly owned property between the parties, based on equitable principles and a number of statutory factors.[26] The court may also assign certain solely owned property, based on the same principles.[27] But certain solely owned property is exempt from such assignment:

- Property that one spouse owned before marriage.[28] However, the income from that property is subject to assignment.[29] Further, appreciation in value of that property due to the other spouse's efforts is also subject to assignment.[30]

---

18. *See* 12 C.F.R. § 7.1017 (2010) (National Bank as Guarantor or Surety on Indemnity Bond).
19. Cundall v. Haswell, 23 R.I. 508,510-11, 51 A. 426, 427 (1908).
20. R.I. Gen. Laws § 15-12-1 (2012);.McGuckian v. Carpenter, 43 R.I. 94, 96-97, 110 A. 402, 403 (1920).
21. Cull v. Vadnais, R.I., 406 A.2d 1241 (1979).
22. Knibb v. Security Insurance Co. of New Haven, 121 R.I. 406, 399 A.2d 1214 (1979).
23. *Id.*
24. In re Gibbons, 459 A.2d 938, 940 (R.I. 1983).
25. In re Furkes, 65 B.R. 232, 236 (D. R.I. 1986).
26. R.I. Gen. Laws § 15-5-16.1(a) (2012).
27. *Id.*
28. R.I. Gen. Laws § 15-5-16.1(b) (2012).
29. *Id.*
30. *Id.*

- Property that one spouse acquired during the marriage by inheritance or by gift before, during, or after the term of the marriage.[31]

Further, nonmarital property generally becomes marital property if one spouse transfers it to the parties jointly.[32]

§ 3 Signatory's Authority to Execute a Guaranty

The individual signing the guaranty as an agent of the guarantor must have the authority to execute the guaranty.[33] The authority must be either express authority or implied (apparent) authority.

An agent has apparent authority only if: (1) the principal has manifestly consented to the agent's exercising such authority or has knowingly permitted the agent to exercise such authority; (2) a third person reasonably and in good faith relied on that manifestation; and (3) because of such reliance, the third person would be injured if the principal is not held to the agent's action.[34] The party relying on apparent authority has a duty to inquire as to the agent's authority.[35]

Therefore, the best practice is to obtain proof of actual authority, rather than to rely on apparent authority, ratification, or estoppel.

3.1 Corporations

Agency principles apply to corporations and other entities.[36] Therefore, the officer signing a guaranty must have actual or apparent authority to bind the corporation.[37]

While courts have occasionally upheld an officer's apparent authority to pay the obligations of a third party,[38] the best practice is to require written evidence of the officer's actual authority to sign a guaranty on behalf of the corporation.

3.2 Partnerships

The 1914 Uniform Partnership Act is still in force in Rhode Island.[39] That law makes each partner an agent of a general partnership "for the purpose of its business" and gives each partner authority to execute "any instrument, for apparently carrying on in the usual way the business of the partnership."[40]

---

31. *Id.*
32. Quinn v. Quinn, 512 A.2d 848 (R.I. 1986).
33. Inleasing Corp. v. Jessup, 475 A.2d 989, 994-95 (R.I. 1984).
34. Calenda v. Allstate Insurance Co., 518 A.2d 624, 628 (R.I. 1986).
35. Ward v. Trustees of New England Southern Conference of the Methodist Episcopal Church, 27 R.I. 262, 61 A. 651 (1905).
36. De Pasquale v. Societa d M.S. Maria, 54 R.I. 399, 173 A. 623 (1934).
37. J.P. Morgan & Co. v. Hall & Lyon Co., 34 R.I. 273, 276-77, 83 A. 113, 114 (1912).
38. *See, e.g.*, Manhattan Web Co. v. Aquidneck Nat'l Bank, 133 F. 76 (C.C. D. R.I. 1904).
39. R.I. Gen. Laws §§ 7-12-12 to 7-12-55 (2012).
40. R.I. Gen. Laws § 7-12-20(a) (2012).

This apparent authority differs from the common law, in that the partner has apparent authority unless the other party "has knowledge of the fact that [the partner] has no authority."[41]

The same rules apply to Rhode Island limited partnerships.[42]

Nevertheless, it is not generally the ordinary business of any organization to issue guaranties. Further, it is not clear that under the common law partnerships had the power to issue guaranties. Therefore, one should not rely on a partner's authority to execute a guaranty on behalf of the partnership without written evidence of actual authority. This evidence should include a provision in the partnership agreement authorizing the partnership to issue guaranties.

3.3 Limited Liability Companies

The Rhode Island limited liability company act distinguishes between manager-managed LLCs and member-managed LLCs. It provides that every manager of a manager-managed LLC "is an agent of the limited liability company for the purpose of its business and affairs," unless the manager's act contravenes the articles of organization or the Rhode Island LLC act, or the manager lacks actual authority and the person dealing with the manager "has knowledge of the fact that the manager has no authority."[43] Further, the members of a manager-managed LLC cannot bind the LLC, unless they are also managers.[44]

If the LLC is member-managed, then each member has the same powers as the manager of a manager-managed LLC.[45]

Further, as noted in § 2.3, *supra*, every Rhode Island LLC has the power to issue guaranties, even if the guaranties are not in furtherance of the LLC's purpose.[46]

However, despite this broad grant of authority, one should require written evidence of a manager's or member's actual authority to issue a guaranty on behalf of the LLC.

3.4 Banks and Trust Companies

One must examine the bank's or trust company's corporate governance documents to determine who may validly execute a guaranty on behalf of the entity.

---

41. R.I. Gen. Laws § 7-12-20(a) (2012).
42. R.I. Gen. Laws §§ 7-12-11 and 7-13-24 (2012).
43. R.I. Gen. Laws § 7-16-20(a) (2012).
44. R.I. Gen. Laws § 7-16-20(b) (2012).
45. R.I. Gen. Laws § 7-16-14 (2012).
46. R.I. Gen. Laws § 7-16-4(3) (2012).

§ 4 Consideration; Sufficiency of Past Consideration

Consideration sufficient to support a contract in general is sufficient to support a guaranty contract.[47]

Consideration does not necessarily have to flow to the guarantor. For example, if a corporate officer guarantees the corporation's debt, consideration flowing to the corporation is sufficient.[48] Consideration also exists if a shareholder guarantees the primary obligor's debts and the primary obligor benefits from obtaining credit from the obligee.[49]

If the guarantor issues the guaranty after the underlying obligation has been incurred, then there must be independent consideration for the guaranty.[50] The obligee's forbearance in exchange for the guaranty is sufficient consideration.[51]

Past consideration will not support a guaranty. Therefore, if the guarantor issues the guaranty after the underlying obligation has been incurred, then there must be independent consideration for the guaranty.

Therefore, if the lender requires the guaranty as a condition to making the loan or as a condition to forbearance after default, the guaranty is supported by adequate consideration.

§ 5 Notice of Acceptance

Whether the obligee must give notice of acceptance of the guaranty depends first on the type of guaranty. If the guaranty is in the nature of an offer, then the guarantor is entitled to know if the obligee accepts it.[52] The obligee's acceptance of a guaranty may manifest itself in the obligee's conducting business with the primary obligor. In such a case, the guarantor is not likely to learn of such acceptance, so notice is required.[53]

There are several exceptions to the general rule:

- Where the guaranty is an absolute guaranty.[54]
- Where notice is inferred from the nature of the transaction.[55]
- Where a valuable consideration flows from the obligee to the guarantor (a compensated guarantor).[56]
- Where the guarantor waives the requirement.

47. Katz v. Prete, 459 A.2d 81, 86 (R.I. 1985); J.P. Morgan & Co. v. Hall & Lyon Co., 34 R.I. 273, 278, 83 A. 113, 114 (1912).
48. Katz v. Prete, 459 A.2d 81, 86 (R.I. 1985).
49. Cozzani v. Fioravanti, 51 R.I. 433, 435, 155 A. 409, 409-10 (1931).
50. New Bedford Morris Plan Co. v. Hicks, 52 R.I. 74, 76, 157 A. 421, 422 (1931).
51. CIC-Newport Assoc., LP v. Lee, 2010 R.I. Super. LEXIS 184 *26-27. *See also* Dockery v. Greenfield, 86 R.I. 464, 136 A.2d 682 (1957) (forbearance may serve as consideration for a contract).
52. Cozzani v. Fioravanti, 51 R.I. 433, 435, 155 A. 409, 409 (1931); King v. Batterson, 13 R.I. 117, 119 (1880).
53. King v. Batterson, 13 R.I. 117, 119 (1880).
54 Cozzani v. Fioravanti, 51 R.I. 433, 435, 155 A. 409, 409 (1931);
55. King v. Batterson, 13 R.I. 117, 119 (1880).
56. Cozzani v. Fioravanti, 51 R.I. 433, 435, 155 A. 409, 409 (1931);

§ 6 Interpretation of Guaranties

Rhode Island courts generally follow the rule of *strictissimi juris*, under which they strictly construe the guarantor's obligations. In other respects, courts will interpret a guaranty according to general principles of contract interpretation.

6.1 General Principles

Generally, courts interpret a guaranty strictly according to the express terms of the guaranty.[57]

To interpret a guaranty, courts will read the text of the contract "in connection with the relative position and general purpose of the parties, to gather from it, if [the court] can, their intent in the questionable particular."[58] This means that the court may also interpret the guaranty together with other documents executed at the same time for the same purpose in the same transaction.[59]

If a term is ambiguous, courts have articulated a number of rules to resolve the ambiguity:

- In the older case law, there is authority for the proposition that the court will resolve the guaranty in the guarantor's favor.[60]
- If one interpretation is more reasonable than the other, then the court will adopt the more reasonable interpretation.[61]
- On the other hand, if both interpretations are equally reasonable, then the court will construe the guaranty against the drafter.[62]

The rule that courts are most likely to follow is to construe any ambiguity against the drafter.[63]

In any event, the obligee must show that the guarantor intended to be liable for the underlying obligation.[64] For example, in one case, the defendant sent the obligee a letter requesting an extension of time for the primary obligor to pay its debts "if you can be assured you are not to suffer by the delay" and

57. Marshall Contractors, Inc. v. Peerless Ins. Co., 827 F. Supp. 91, 94 (D. R.I. 1993) (citing Narragansett Pier R.R. v. Palmer, 70 R.I. 298, 302, 38 A.2d 761, 763 (1944)). *See also* Narragansett Pier Railroad Co. v. Palmer, 70 R.I. 298, 302, 38 A.2d 761, 763 (1944) ("[T]he bond must be strictly construed. In the absence of ambiguity, the extent of the liability of the surety on a common-law bond is determined solely by the language of the bond. Construction by implication, which will extend the surety's liability, is not permissible in such a case.").

58. Deblois v. Earle, 7 R.I. 26, 29-30 (1861). *See also* Allied Plywood Co. v. Pearson, 121 R.I. 72, 395 A.2d 716 (1978).

59. Rotelli v. Catanzaro, 686 A.2d 91, 94 (R.I. 1996); R.I. Depositors Economic Protection Corp. v. Coffey & Martinelli, Ltd., 821 A.2d 222, 226-27 (R.I. 2003) (in which the court held that a guaranty covered future debt, in part because the loan agreement provided that the guaranty would secure future debt); Central Soya Co., Inc. v. Henderson, 208 A.2d 110 (R.I. 1965) (letters were admissible as to the guarantor's intent, the amount of the underlying obligation, and to impeach obligee's witness).

60. Russell v. Clark's Executors, 11 U.S. (7 Cranch) 69, 92 (1812) ("It is the duty of the individual, who contracts with one man on the credit of another, not to trust to ambiguous phrases and strained constructions, but to require an explicit and plain declaration of the obligation he is about to assume.")

61. Bailey & Gallup v. Larchar, 5 R.I. 530 (1856).

62. Deblois v. Earle, 7 R.I. 26, 29-30 (1861);.Bailey & Gallup v. Larchar, 5 R.I. 530 (1856).

63. Hartwell & Richards Co. v. Moss, 22 R.I. 583, 584-85, 48 A. 941, 942 (1901).

64. Russell v. Clark's Executors, 11 U.S. (7 Cranch) 69, 92 (1812); Clark's Executors v. Carrington, 11 U.S. (7 Cranch) 308, 326 (1813); Central Soya Co, Inc. v. Henderson, 99 R.I. 388, 208 A.2d 110 (1965); Williams & Flash Co. v. Carpenter, 32 R.I. 349, 79 A. 821 (1911).

giving "assurance that your interest will be protected." The court held that this did not constitute a guaranty. In another case, relying on "the natural and ordinary meaning" of the language at issue, the court held that a letter stating "I am perfectly willing to guarantee this account" constituted an offer to guarantee, not an actual guaranty.[65]

If the guaranty is a complete (integrated) document, then the Parol Evidence Rule generally bars extrinsic evidence to show that the guarantor's obligation is other than as stated in the guaranty.[66] Rhode Island courts recognize the following exceptions to the Parol Evidence Rule:

- Fraud.[67]
- Mutual mistake.[68]
- Where the guaranty does not state the consideration for the guaranty.[69]

6.2 Guaranty of Payment versus Guaranty of Collection

Rhode Island courts distinguish between guaranties of payment and guaranties of collection.[70]

A guaranty based on signing a negotiable instrument (either as accommodation maker or as endorser) constitutes a guaranty of payment, unless the guarantor's signature is "accompanied by words indicating unambiguously that the party is guaranteeing collection rather than payment."[71]

6.3 Language Regarding the Revocation of Guaranties

A guaranty of a single, present debt is irrevocable.[72]

A continuing guaranty is revocable as to future indebtedness by notice to the obligee.[73] However, the guarantor remains liable for indebtedness incurred before the revocation.[74]

Most commercial finance transactions involve continuing guaranties, because the primary obligor's debts may arise in the future, as with future advances on revolving lines of credit or future loan transactions. Therefore, lenders should use guaranty language that specifies the revocation notice requirements and the consequences of revocation. For example, the lender should require that the guarantor deliver a revocation notice to a particular department where the account officer will get prompt notice. The guaranty should also provide that the revocation becomes effective only on some fixed

---

65. Dondero v. Standard Emblem Co., 45 R.I. 329, 6333, 121 A. 401, 402 (1923).
66. Rhode Island Hospital Tr. Nat'l Bank v. Howard Communications Corp., 980 F.2d 823 (1st Cir. 1992); Inleasing Corp. v. Jessup, 475 A.2d 989, 993 (R.I. 1984); New Bedford Morris Plan Co. v. Hicks, 52 R.I. 74, 76, 157 A. 421, 422 (1931).
67. Fleet National Bank, trustee v. 175 Post Road, LLC, 851 A.2d 267 (R.I. 2004); Supreme Woodworking Co. v. Zuckerberg, 108 R.I. 247, 252, 107 A.2d 287, 290 (1954).
68. Ferla v. Commercial Cas. Ins. Co., 74 R.I. 190, 195, 59 A.2d 714, 716 (1948).
69. *Id.; see also* Inleasing Corp. v. Jessup, 475 A.2d 989, 993 (R.I. 1984).
70. Rhode Island Hospital Tr. Nat'l Bank v. National Health Foundation, 119 R.I. 823, 384 A.2d 301 (1978).
71. R.I. Gen. Laws § 6A-3-419(d) (2012).
72. National Eagle Bank v. Hunt, 16 R.I. 148, 151-52, 13 A. 115, 116-17 (1888).
73. *Id.*
74. Snow v. Horgan, 18 R.I. 289, 291, 27 A. 338 (1893).

future date, such as "XX" days after the lender receives the notice. This will give the lender sufficient time to mitigate its risk if a guarantor revokes.

If the guarantor revokes its guaranty, and the primary obligor incurs further debt not covered by the guaranty, then in the absence of any direction from the guarantor, the obligee may apply the guarantor's payments against the unguaranteed debt.[75]

The death of an individual guarantor revokes a continuing guaranty as to debt incurred post-mortem.[76] Death does not, however, revoke the guaranty as to indebtedness incurred before the guarantor dies.[77]

6.4 "Continuing"

A guaranty may secure future indebtedness.[78] This makes it a "continuing" guaranty.[79] If it is not clear from the words of the guaranty whether it is a continuing guaranty or a limited guaranty, then the court will construe it against the party who drafted the guaranty.[80] In one of the leading cases, the guaranty stated, "I hereby guarantee to be responsible for any account that may be due, or to become due to [the obligee] from [the primary obligor], and to see that such account is paid, to the amount of 500 dollars." The court interpreted this language as a continuing guaranty.[81]

6.5 "Absolute and Unconditional"

The courts distinguish between absolute guaranties and limited guaranties. A guaranty is "absolute" if the only condition precedent to the guarantor's liability is the primary obligor's default on the underlying obligation.[82] However, courts will not construe a document as an absolute guaranty by implication.[83]

If the guaranty contains conditions precedent to the guarantor's liability, those conditions must be satisfied unless the guarantor waives them.[84]

6.6 "Liable as a Primary Obligor and not Merely as Surety"

As explained in § 1.2 *supra*, a surety makes a direct contract to pay an obligation, while a guarantor makes a collateral promise regarding the underlying

75. Burt & Snow v. Butterworth, 19 R.I. 127, 129, 32 A. 167, 168 (1895). *See also* § 7.3.8, *infra.*
76. National Eagle Bank v. Hunt, 16 R.I. 148, 13 A. 115 (1888).
77. *Id.*
78. R.I. Depositors Economic Protection Corp. v. Coffey & Martinelli, Ltd., 821 A.2d 222, 226-27 (R.I. 2003).
79. Hartwell & Richards Co. v. Moss, 22 R.I. 583, 585, 48 A. 941, 942 (1901).
80. *Id.*
81. Hartwell & Richards Co. v. Moss, 22 R.I. 583, 585, 48 A. 941, 942 (1901). *See also* Deblois v. Earle, 7 R.I. 26, 30-31 (1861).
82. Cozzani v. Fioravanti, 51 R.I. 433, 155 A. 409 (1931) (the guarantor's statement that he "therefore stand[s] as guarantor for the [primary obligor]" constitutes an absolute guaranty).
83. Di Fonzo v. Notarianni, 61 R.I. 287, 200 A. 774 (1938). *See also* King v. Batterson, 13 R.I. 117 (1880). *But see Gilbert Congdon & Co. v. Read,* 7 R.I. 576, 578 (1863), where the court construed the dollar limit of a guaranty as applying to the aggregate amount of credit the primary obligor could incur. The primary obligor incurred total debt in excess of that limit and repaid the amount stated in the guaranty. Therefore, the court held that there was no longer any underlying obligation.
84. *See* § 7.3.1, *infra.*

obligation. Therefore, the effect of a guarantor's agreement to be liable as a primary obligor is not clear under Rhode Island law.

§ 7 Defenses of the Guarantor; Set-off

The defenses that may be available to a guarantor can be grouped into three categories:

- Defenses of the primary obligor
- "Suretyship defenses"
- Other defenses.

7.1 Defenses of the Primary Obligor

7.1.1 General

A guarantor may assert most defenses that the primary obligor could assert, but cannot assert so-called "personal defenses" of the primary obligor.

7.1.2 When Guarantor May Assert Primary Obligor's Defense

As a general rule, a guarantor is not liable unless the primary obligor is liable.[85] However, the surety on a bond is primarily liable, so it cannot assert this defense.[86]

7.1.3 Defenses that May not be Raised by Guarantor

A guarantor cannot generally raise personal defenses of the primary obligor. For example, a guarantor may not raise the primary obligor's incapacity as a defense to liability under the guaranty.[87] Nor may the guarantor assert that the obligee fraudulently induced the primary obligor to incur the underlying obligation.[88]

Nor can a guarantor defend based on a claim that the primary obligor's agent did not have authority to incur the underlying obligation.[89]

A guarantor may not raise the primary obligor's fraud on the guarantor as a defense, unless the obligee knew or had reason to know of the fraud or misrepresentation.[90]

---

85. Rhode Island Hospital Tr. Nat'l Bank v. Ohio Cas. Ins. Co., 789 F.3d 74, 78-79 (1st Cir. 1986); Central Soya Co, Inc. v. Henderson, 99 R.I. 388, 395, 208 A.2d 110, 114 (1965).
86. Rhode Island Hospital Tr. Nat'l Bank v. Ohio Cas. Ins. Co., 789 F.3d 74, 78 (1st Cir. 1986).
87. Rhode Island Hospital Tr. Nat'l Bank v. Ohio Cas. Ins. Co., 789 F.3d 74, 78-79 (1st Cir. 1986); Katz v. Prete, 459 A.2d 81, 86 (R.I. 1983).
88. Rhode Island Hospital Tr. Nat'l Bank v. Ohio Cas. Ins. Co., 789 F.3d 74, 78-79 (1st Cir. 1986).
89. *Id.*
90. Shepard Land Co. v. Banigan, 36 R.I. 1, 21, 87 A. 531, 539 (1913); CIC-Newport Assoc., LP v. Lee, 2010 R.I. Super. LEXIS 184.

7.1.4 Defenses that may Always be Raised by Guarantor

A guarantor may show that the obligee failed to perform such that there is a partial or complete failure of consideration.[91] Mutual mistake is a defense.[92]

7.2 "Suretyship" Defenses

7.2.1 Change in Identity of Primary Obligor

If the primary obligor transfers its right and obligations to a third party, then the terms of the guaranty determine the guarantor's liability for the transferee's obligations.[93]

7.2.2 Modification of the Underlying Obligation, Including Release

A material change in the underlying obligation discharges the guarantor, unless the guarantor consents to the change.[94] If the underlying obligation is a negotiable instrument, then the guarantor is discharged "to the extent the modification causes loss to the [guarantor] with respect to the right of recourse."[95] In that situation, there is a presumption of complete discharge, which the obligee must rebut.[96]

The guarantor may consent to the modification in the guaranty itself, even if the guaranty addresses the issue only indirectly.[97] In one case, when the obligee accepted promissory notes payable over time in satisfaction of a short-term open account, a provision that the guaranty would "cover open account or other forms of indebtedness and remain in force until notice to the contrary from me in writing" constituted the guarantor's consent to the modification.[98] In another case, the court went further and held that a guaranty covering "any account that may be due or to become due" was broad enough to encompass subsequent modifications to the underlying obligation.[99]

The consent to modification of the underlying obligation may also be implied from the guarantor's knowledge of the parties' course of dealing at the time the guarantor issued the guaranty.[100] For example, if the guarantor knew when it gave the guaranty that the primary obligor could not make payment on time, the guarantor remains liable based on estoppel.[101]

Extending the time for the primary obligor to perform discharges the guarantor, unless the guarantor consents to the extension[102] or the obligee

91. Central Soya Co, Inc. v. Henderson, 99 R.I. 388, 395, 208 A.2d 110, 114 (1965).
92. Cf. Shepard Land Co. v. Banigan, 36 R.I. 1, 87 A. 531 (1913).
93. Davis v. JT Building and Development, LLC, 2010 R.I. Super. LEXIS 155 *21-22.
94. Shepard Land Co. v. Banigan, 36 R.I. 1, 25, 87 A. 531, 540-41 (1913).
95. R.I. Gen. Laws § 6A-3-605(d) (2012).
96. *Id.*
97. *Jackson Bank v. Irons, 18 R.I. 718, 721, 30 A. 420 (1894), rehearing denied,* 19 R.I. 484, 34 A. 951 (1896).
98. Burt & Snow v. Butterworth, 19 R.I. 127, 32 A. 167 (1895).
99. Hartwell & Richards Co. v. Moss, 22 R.I. 583, 585-86, 48 A. 941, 942 (1901).
100. Hartwell & Richards Co. v. Moss, 22 R.I. 583, 586, 48 A. 941, 942 (1901);
101. Shepard Land Co. v. Banigan, 36 R.I. 1, 25, 87 A. 531, 540-41 (1913).
102. Dondero v. Standard Emblem Co., 45 R.I. 329, 121 A. 401 (1923).

expressly reserves its rights.[103] However, the guarantor may not be discharged in the following cases:

- If the guaranty covers successive payments, and only one is extended, then the guarantor is discharged only for that payment, not for later payments.[104]
- If the description of the underlying obligation in a continuing guaranty is broad enough to encompass modifications to the underlying obligation.[105]

7.2.3 Release or Impairment of Security for the Underlying Obligation

Release of collateral discharges the guarantor according to the value of the collateral that was released.[106]

If the obligee impairs the value of the collateral through "negligence or mistake," then the guarantor is discharged to the extent of the diminution in value.[107] However, mere delay in foreclosing on the collateral does not constitute impairment of the collateral.[108]

7.2.4 Notice of Acceptance of the Guaranty

Except as noted in § 5 above, a guarantor is entitled to notice that the obligee has accepted the guaranty.[109]

7.2.5 Notice that the Primary Obligor is Incurring Additional Debt

Although the guarantor is entitled to notice when new debt is incurred, the guarantor may waive this right in the guaranty.[110] Such notice may be inferred from the nature of the transaction.[111] But unless the transaction is such that it gives the guarantor "all the notice [the guarantor] needs at the proper time, then [the guarantor] shall have distinct notice."[112]

7.2.6 Notice that the Primary Obligor has Defaulted on the Underlying Obligation

As noted in § 5 *supra*, in certain circumstances, notice of acceptance of the guaranty is required. The same is not true per se for notice of the default to the

---

103. Jackson Bank v. Irons, 18 R.I. 718, 721-22, 30 A. 420 (1894), *rehearing denied*, 19 R.I. 484, 34 A. 951 (1896).
104. Shepard Land Co. v. Banigan, 36 R.I. 1, 25, 87 A. 531, 540-41 (1913).
105. Hartwell & Richards Co. v. Moss, 22 R.I. 583, 585, 48 A. 941, 942 (1901); Burt & Snow v. Butterworth, 19 R.I. 127, 32 A. 167 (1895).
106. Otis v. Von Storch, 15 R.I. 41, 42, 23 A. 39 (1885).
107. Hidden v. Bishop, 5 R.I. 29 (1857).
108. R.I. Economic Protection Corp. v. Northern Mortgage Funding, Inc., 1995 R.I. Super. LEXIS 123.
109. Cozzani v. Fioravanti, 51 R.I. 433, 435, 155 A. 409, 409 (1931); King v. Batterson, 13 R.I. 117 (1880).
110. Katz v. Prete, 459 A.2d 81, 86 (R.I. 1985).
111. Wildes v. Savage, 29 F. Cas. 1226 (Cir. D. Mass. 1839); King v. Batterson, 13 R.I. 117, 119 (1880).
112. *Id.*

guarantor, unless the guaranty requires such notice. However, if the obligee fails to give such notice, and the failure causes the guarantor to lose its rights against the primary obligor, then the guarantor is discharged.[113]

7.3 Other Defenses

7.3.1 Failure to Fulfill a Condition Precedent

If the guaranty contains a condition precedent to the guarantor's liability, then the obligee must satisfy that condition before pursuing the guarantor.[114]

In one case,[115] after a letter of credit issuer went insolvent, the beneficiary of a standby letter of credit sought to recover from the account party on its reimbursement agreement to the issuer and from a third party on its guaranty of the reimbursement agreement. The court held that, based on the nature of standby letters of credit and on the language of the guaranty, that neither the account party nor the guarantor were liable on the reimbursement agreement.

7.3.2 Modification of the Guaranty

In general, modification of a contract requires not only a meeting of the minds, but also consideration.[116]

Rhode Island courts generally give effect to a contract provision requiring all modifications to the contract be in writing, unless the party to be charged has waived the requirement.[117]

7.3.3 Failure to Pursue Primary Obligor

Except in the case of a guaranty of collection, the obligee does not have to pursue the primary obligor.[118]

However, unless the guaranty provides otherwise, the obligee does have a duty not to impair the guarantor's subrogation rights.[119] This requires the obligee to give the guarantor notice of nonpayment within a reasonable time, "so as to give [the guarantor] an opportunity to save [itself] from loss."[120] Failure to give such notice discharges the guarantor to the extent of the loss.[121]

---

113. Jackson Bank v. Irons, 18 R.I. 718, 721, 30 A. 420 (1894), *rehearing denied,* 19 R.I. 484, 34 A. 951 (1896). *See also* § 7.3.3 *infra.*
114. Rhode Island Hospital Tr. Nat'l Bank v. Ohio Cas. Ins. Co., 613 F. Supp. 1197 (D. R.I. 1985), *rev'd* 789 F.3d 74 (1st Cir. 1986) (contractual requirement that the obligee first obtain judgment against the primary obligor); New Bedford Morris Plan Co. v. Hicks, 52 R.I. 74, 76, 157 A. 421, 422 (1931).
115. Colonial Courts Apartment Co. v. Proc Associates, Inc., 57 F.3d 119 (1st Cir. 1995).
116. Bourg v. Bristol Boat Co., 705 A.2d 969, 971 (R.I. 1998).
117. Fondedile, S.A. v. C.E. Maguire, Inc., 610 A.2d 87, 92 (R.I. 1992).
118. Brown University v. Laudati, 113 R.I. 299, 320 A.2d 609 (1974) (UCC Article 3 case); Snow v. Horgan, 18 R.I. 289, 291, 27 A. 338 (1893).
119. Jackson Bank v. Irons, 18 R.I. 718, 721, 30 A. 420 (1894), *rehearing denied,* 19 R.I. 484, 34 A. 951 (1896).
120. *Id.*
121. *Id.*

7.3.4 *Statute of Limitations*

Rhode Island law imposes a 10-year statute of limitations on contractual obligations, with certain exceptions.[122] One such exception applies to contracts for the sale of goods that are governed by Article 2 of the Rhode Island Uniform Commercial Code (UCC), which imposes a four-year statute of limitations.[123] Rhode Island courts have not decided whether a guaranty of a contract for the sale of goods is governed by the 10-year general contract statute of limitations or by the four-year UCC statute of limitations.

If the contract is executed under seal, the statute of limitations is 20 years.[124]

7.3.5 *Statute of Frauds*

Rhode Island's statute of frauds bars enforcement of guaranties, unless they are in writing.[125]

7.3.6 *Defenses Particular to Guarantors that are Natural Persons and their Spouses*

Aside from the individual guarantor's competence, Rhode Island law does not recognize defenses unique to individuals. Nor does Rhode Island law give a guarantor's spouse any unique defense.

7.3.7 *Fraud in the Inducement*

The guarantor can be discharged if the obligee committed fraud in inducing the guarantor to issue the guaranty.[126] Reliance must be justifiable.[127] Further, the obligee need not have made a knowingly false representation. So long as the other party believed the statement to be true and was misled into entering into the contract, that party may obtain relief.[128] However, the guarantor must establish its case by clear and convincing evidence.[129] Further, fraud by the primary obligor alone, without the obligee's knowledge or participation, does not discharge the guarantor.[130]

---

122. R.I. Gen. Laws § 9-1-13 (2012).
123. R.I. Gen. Laws § 6A-2-725(1) (2012).
124. R.I. Gen. Laws § 9-1-17 (2012).
125. R.I. Gen. Laws § 9-1-4(4) (2012).
126. *See, e.g.,* Cardoso v. Mendes, 1998 R.I. Super. LEXIS 15.
127. Travers v. Spidell, 682 A.2d 471 (R.I. 1996).
128. LaFazia v. Howe, 575 A.2d 182, 185 (1990); Grand Lodge, A.O.U.W. of R.I. v. Massachusetts Bonding & Ins. Co., 38 R.I. 276, 288, 94 A. 859 (1915). *See also* Cardoso v. Mendes, 1998 R.I. Super. LEXIS 15.
129. Brown University v. Laudati, 113 R.I. 299, 301-02, 320 A.2d 609, 610 (1974).
130. CIC-Newport Assoc., LP v. Lee, 2010 R.I. Super. LEXIS 184 *24-25.

7.3.8 *Application of Payments*

If the primary obligor does not designate how a payment should be applied, then the obligee may apply undesignated payments to debt that the guaranty does not cover.[131]

However, an agreement between the primary obligor and the guarantor or an agreement between the guarantor and the obligee as to application of payments will control.[132]

7.4 Right of Set-off

Set-off permits one party to apply mutual, matured debts against each other.[133] Therefore, unless the guarantor has waived the right of set-off, the guarantor may assert its own claims against the obligee. Rhode Island law is not clear, however, whether an absolute guaranty by its nature bars the guarantor's set-off.

On the other hand, a guarantor cannot assert the primary obligor's claims against the obligee to set-off the guarantor's liability under the guaranty.[134]

§ 8 Waiver of Defenses by the Guarantor

Rhode Island courts recognize that a guarantor may waive defenses expressly or by implication.[135]

The guarantor's waiver may be implied from its conduct.[136]

8.1 Defenses that cannot be Waived

Article 9 of the UCC limits or prohibits certain waivers in secured transactions. For instance, a guarantor cannot waive the right to require a secured creditor to sell or otherwise dispose of collateral in a commercially reasonable manner.[137] A waiver of the right to challenge impairment of collateral probably does not constitute a waiver of the guarantor's rights under § 9-607(c) of the UCC.[138]

In Rhode Island, it is not uncommon for secured creditors to liquidate their collateral through state court receivership proceedings. Such court-approved sales are deemed to be commercially reasonable.[139]

---

131. Burt & Snow v. Butterworth, 19 R.I. 127, 129, 32 A. 167, 168 (1895).
132. Warren Bros. Co. v. Sentry Ins., 13 Mass. App. Ct. 431, 433, 36-37 N.E.2d 1253, 1255 (1982).
133. Brill v. Citizens Trust Co., 492 A.2d 1215 (R.I. 1985); Lees v. Industrial Trust Co., 67 R.I. 316, 23 A.2d 197 (1942); Tobey v. Manufacturers' Nat'l Bank, 9 R.I. 236 (1869).
134. Rhode Island Hospital Tr. Nat'l Bank v. Ohio Cas. Ins. Co., 789 F.3d 74, 78 (1st Cir. 1986).
135. *See, e.g.,* Davis v. JT Building and Development, LLC, 2010 R.I. Super. LEXIS 155 *20-21 (the court inferred the guarantor's consent to a change in the underlying obligation through his participation in the transaction that changed the underlying obligation).
136. Shepard Land Co. v. Banigan, 36 R.I. 1, 87 A. 531 (1913) (unilateral mistake by guarantor is not a defense).
137. R.I. Gen. Laws §§ 6A-9-602(3) and 6A-9-607(c) (2012).
138. R.I. Gen. Laws § 6A-9-607(c) (2012).
139. Rhode Island Hospital Tr. Nat'l Bank v. National Health Foundation, 119 R.I. 823, 384 A.2d 301 (1978) (guarantor cannot collaterally attack a court-approved foreclosure sale, where the guarantor had notice of the proceeding).

Other nonwaivable Article 9 rights include:

- The right to require the secured party to use or operate collateral in the secured party's possession.[140]
- The right to request an accounting, a list of collateral, and a statement of account.[141]
- The secured party's duty to apply noncash proceeds of collateral.[142]
- The right to require accounting or payment of surplus proceeds of collateral.[143]

Other nonwaivable rights are listed in R.I. Gen. Laws § 6A-9-602(6) – (13) (2011).

The following Article 9 defenses can be waived, but only by an authenticated agreement made after the default:

- The guarantor's right to notice of sale or other disposition of collateral.[144]
- The guarantor's right to redeem collateral in a commercial transaction.[145]

8.2 "Catch-all" Waivers

Though catch-all waiver language may be effective, it is advisable for beneficiaries to include waivers to specific suretyship defenses.

While Rhode Island courts have not specifically ruled on whether a statement that the guaranty is "absolute and unconditional" constitutes a blanket waiver of suretyship defenses, the better practice is to include specific waivers in the guaranty, along with a general clean-up waiver of suretyship defenses.

In interpreting catch-all waivers, the courts usually look for more specific evidence that a guarantor intended to waive all surety defenses.

8.3 Use of Specific Waivers

Rhode Island courts and statutes have approved waivers of the following defenses contained in the guaranty:

- Extension of time for payment.[146]
- Notice of further indebtedness.[147]
- Modification of the underlying obligation.[148]
- Demand upon the primary obligor.[149]

140. R.I. Gen. Laws §§ 6A-9-207(b)(4)(iii) and 6A-9-602(1) (2012).
141. R.I. Gen. Laws § 6A-9-602(2) (2012).
142. R.I. Gen. Laws § 6A-9-602(4) (2012).
143. R.I. Gen. Laws § 6A-9-602(5) (2012).
144. R.I. Gen. Laws §§ 6A-9-602(3) and (7) and 6A-9-624(a) (2012).
145. R.I. Gen. Laws §§ 6A-9-623 and 6A-9-624(c) (2012).
146. *Shepard Land Co. v. Banigan*, 36 R.I. 1, 25, 87 A. 531, 540-41 (1913).
147. *Katz v. Prete*, 459 A.2d 81 (R.I. 1983).
148. *Old Stone Bank v. McKenney*, 456 A.2d 266 (R.I. 1983).
149. *First Nat'l Bank of Pawtucket v. Adamson*, 25 R.I. 73, 74, 54 A. 930 (1903).

- Release of the primary obligor or waiver of claims against the primary obligor.[150]
- Release of coguarantors.[151]
- Release of collateral.[152]

8.4 Jury Trial Waivers

Any waiver of the right to jury trial must be knowing and voluntary.[153]

In one case, a federal court upheld a waiver in small print that was not set-off in a separate paragraph.[154]

A jury trial waiver in the documents evidencing the underlying obligation may bind the guarantor.[155]

The best practice is to place the jury trial waiver conspicuously in the guaranty itself.

§ 9 Third-party Pledgors—Defenses and Waiver Thereof

It is not common practice in Rhode Island for creditors to accept a pledge of collateral from a third party, without an accompanying guaranty. However, a pledge of collateral to secure another person's obligations makes the pledgor a surety.[156] Therefore, the pledgor has the same defenses as any surety, and the pledgor can waive defenses to the same extent as a guarantor can.

§ 10 Jointly and Severally Liable Guarantors—Contribution and Reduction of Obligations Upon Payment by a Co-obligor

Where guarantors are jointly and severally liable, the obligee does not have to join all of the guarantors in a single civil action.[157] Therefore, the obligee does not have to seek full payment from more than one guarantor.

150. *Old Stone Bank v. McKenney*, 456 A.2d 266 (R.I. 1983).
151. *Id.*
152. R.I. Gen. Laws § 6A-3-605 (2012).
153. Aetna Ins. Co. v. Kennedy, 301 U.S. 389 (1937).
154. The Connecticut Nat'l Bank v. Smith, 826 F. Supp. 57 (D. R.I. 1993).
155. R.I. Depositors Economic Protection Corp. v. Coffey & Martinelli, Ltd., 821 A.2d 222, 227 (R.I. 2003).
156. United Nat'l Bank v. Tappan, 33 R.I. 1, 31, 79 A. 946, 957 (1911).
157. Whipp v. Casey, 21 R.I. 506, 45 A. 93 (1900).

10.1 Contribution

If multiple guarantors are liable jointly and severally, then each has an implied right of contribution against the other coguarantors.[158] The right of contribution is an equitable right governed by equitable principles.[159]

Therefore, if one guarantor pays the entire obligation, it may recover a proportional share from each other guarantor.[160] However, the guarantor may not seek contribution from the other guarantors until he or she has paid more than his or her proportionate share of the obligation. [161]

On the other hand, an indemnity agreement among the guarantors is independent of their contribution rights.[162]

10.2 Reduction of Obligations Upon Payment of Co-obligor

Unless otherwise agreed, another obligor's partial payment does not reduce the guarantor's liability on its guaranty.[163] In other words, the obligee is entitled to apply a partial payment from another obligor to the unguaranteed portion of the debt.[164]

10.3 Liability of Parent Guarantors Owning less than 100 percent of Primary Obligor

Rhode Island law does not impose any particular restrictions on parent guarantors who own less than all of the outstanding equity in the primary obligor.

§ 11 Reliance

Rhode Island law is not clear on whether the obligee must rely on the guaranty. However, consideration is required (see § 4 above), and consideration is usually found in the obligee's requiring the guaranty as a condition precedent to extending credit to the primary obligor.

Reasonable and good faith reliance is necessary in order to bind a principal on the theory of apparent authority.[165]

As noted in § 7.3.7 *supra*, justifiable reliance is an essential element of any claim of fraud in the inducement.[166]

---

158. Katz v. Prete, 459 A.2d 81, 85 (R.I. 1985).
159. *Id.*
160. *Id.*
161. Thomas v. Jacobs, 751 A.2d 732 (R.I. 2000) (adopting the Restatement of Restitution § 82(1)).
162. R.I. Depositors Economic Protection Corp. v. Coffey & Martinelli, Ltd., 821 A.2d 222, 228 (R.I. 2003) (a settlement between one guarantor and the obligee does not affect the other guarantor's indemnity rights).
163. Burt & Snow v. Butterworth, 19 R.I. 127, 129, 32 A. 167, 168 (1895).
164. *Id.*
165. Calenda v. Allstate Insurance Co., 518 A.2d 624, 628 (R.I. 1986).
166. Travers v. Spidell, 682 A.2d 471 (R.I. 1996).

§ 12 Subrogation

If the guarantor fully satisfies the underlying obligation, then the guarantor is subrogated to the rights of the obligee.[167] The right of subrogation arises under equity, and is independent of contract.[168]

The guarantor's subrogation claim is entitled to the same priority or lien status that the underlying obligation had when the guarantor paid it.[169] Further, the subrogation rights of a surety on a payment bond have priority over all claims for money loaned to the principal obligor.[170]

§ 13 Triangular Set-off in Bankruptcy

As noted in § 7.4 above, set-off permits one party to apply mutual, matured debts against each other. Further, set-off is an equitable remedy.[171] Therefore, triangular set-off would probably not be permitted absent a contractual right to do so.

§ 14 Indemnification—Whether the Primary Obligor has a Duty

In the absence of contract, a guarantor who pays on the underlying obligation does not have an indemnification claim against the primary obligor in the absence of contract.[172] Even in the absence of an indemnification claim, however, the guarantor will have a subrogation claim.[173]

§ 15 Enforcement of Guaranties

15.1 Limitations on Recovery

If a guarantor is insolvent or severely undercapitalized when it enters into the guaranty and does not receive reasonably equivalent value for the guaranty, then the guaranty may be avoided under Rhode Island's Uniform Fraudulent Transfer Act.[174]

---

167. United Nat'l Bank v. Tappan, 33 R.I. 1, 31-32, 79 A. 946, 957-58 (1911).
168. *Id.*
169. Willits v. Jencks Mfg. Co., 54 R.I. 164, 167, 171 A. 234, 235 (1934).
170. United States Fidelity & Guaranty Co. v. Rhode Island Covering Co., 53 R.I. 397, 404, 167 A. 143, 146 (1933).
171. Tobey v. Manufacturers' Nat'l Bank, 9 R.I. 236 (1869).
172. Silva v. Home Indemnity Co., 416 A.2d 664, 666 (R.I. 1980). *See also* R.I. Depositors Economic Protection Corp. v. Coffey & Martinelli, Ltd., 821 A.2d 222 (R.I. 2003).
173. *See* § 12 *supra*.
174. R.I. Gen. Laws §§ 6-16-1 *et seq.*

Rhode Island courts have not ruled on the validity of so-called fraudulent conveyance caps on recovery under a guaranty (which prevent recovery beyond the amount that would render the guaranty void under fraudulent transfer law).

15.2 Exercising Rights Under a Guaranty Where the Underlying Obligation is also Secured by a Mortgage

In general, the obligee does not have the duty to liquidate its collateral before pursuing the guarantor.[175]

15.3 Litigating Guaranty Claims: Procedural Considerations

The obligee may use entry of a judgment against the primary obligor as evidence of the underlying debt in the obligee's suit against the guarantor.[176]

Only the obligee or its successors in interest may sue on a guaranty, even if the guaranty benefitted third persons.[177] Whether a guaranty is assignable with the underlying obligation depends on the terms of the guaranty.[178]

15.4 Enforcement of Guaranties of Payment versus Guaranties of Performance

If the guaranty promises performance, rather than payment, then the obligee may sue for performance, but not for monetary damages.[179]

§ 16 Revival and Reinstatement of Guaranties

A guaranty may be revived or reinstated, depending on the language of the guaranty and any admissible extrinsic evidence of the parties' intent.[180] Therefore, if the obligee wants the guaranty to be reinstated upon certain events, it should include reinstatement provisions in its guaranties.

175. *R*.I. Economic Protection Corp. v. Northern Mortgage Funding, Inc., 1995 R.I. Super. LEXIS 123.

176. Clark's Executors v. Carrington, 11 U.S. (7 Cranch) 308, 322 (1813). *See also* South County Sand & Gravel Co. v. National Bonding & Accident Ins. Co., 1989 R.I. Super. LEXIS 7.

177. Mauran v. Bullus, 41 U.S. (16 Pet.) 528 (1842). Woonsocket Rubber Co. v. Banigan, 21 R.I. 146, 147-48, 42 A. 512 (1899).

178. King v. Batterson, 13 R.I. 117, 119 (1880).

179. Bailey & Gallup v. Larchar, 5 R.I. 530 (1856) (the court interpreted a guaranty of the "return and delivery" of certain cloth as a guaranty of performance, not of payment).

180. *See, e.g.*, Rhode Island Hospital Tr. Nat'l Bank v. Howard Communications, Inc., 980 F.2d 823, 828 (1st Cir. 1992) (upholding a guaranty that provided for its reinstatement upon certain conditions).

South Carolina State Law of Guaranties

Mark S. Sharpe
Warren & Sinkler, LLP
171 Church Street
Suite 340
Charleston, South Carolina 29401
Phone: (843) 577-0660
Fax: (843) 577-6843
Email: msharpe@warren-sinkler.com

Contents

South Carolina State Law of Guaranties

Introductory Note: In order to standardize our discussion of the law of guaranties, we use the following vocabulary to refer to the various parties to a guaranty and their obligations.

"Guarantor" means a person who, by contract, agrees to satisfy an underlying obligation of another to an obligee upon the primary obligor's default on that underlying obligation. Although South Carolina cases recognize that a guarantor is in a general sense a type of surety, South Carolina law does make a distinction between a guarantor and a surety.[1]

"Guaranty" means the contract by which the guarantor agrees to satisfy the underlying obligation of a primary obligor to an obligee in the event the primary obligor defaults on the underlying obligation.

"Obligee" means the person to whom the underlying obligation is owed. For example, the lender under a loan agreement would be an obligee vis-à-vis the borrower.

"Primary Obligor" means the person who incurs the underlying obligation to the obligee. For example, the borrower under a loan agreement would be a primary obligor.

"Underlying Obligation" means the obligation or obligations incurred by the primary obligor and owed to the obligee. For example, the borrower's obligation to make payments to a lender of principal and interest on a loan constitutes an underlying obligation.

Introduction

The South Carolina law of guaranties largely follows the traditional common law rules; there is little statutory guaranty law —apart from minimal statute of frauds provisions[2]—and the South Carolina courts have not adopted the more modern rules of the Restatement of Suretyship and Guaranty or the earlier

1. *See, e.g.*, Rouss v. King, 69 S.C. 168, 48 S.E. 220 (1904). That case distinguishes a guarantor from a surety as follows: "A surety undertakes to pay the debt of another. A guarantor undertakes to pay if the principal debtor does not or cannot. A surety joins in the contract of the principal and becomes an original party with the principal. The guarantor does not join in the contract of his principal, but engages in an independent undertaking. A surety promises to do the same thing the principal undertakes; the guarantor promises that the principal will perform his agreement, and if he does not, then he will do it for him." Id. at 172, 48 S.E. at 221 (quoting Arthur Adelbert Stearns, The Law of Suretyship §10 (1903).
2. *See* the discussion in Section 7.3.4 below.

Restatement (Second) of Security. Likewise, citations in South Carolina case law to those Restatements are infrequent.[3]

South Carolina has not adopted, for example, the Restatement position that a change in the underlying obligation will discharge a guarantor only if that change "fundamentally alters" the risks imposed on the guarantor;[4] rather, South Carolina law continues to apply the rule of *strictissimi juris*, with the result that a material modification of the underlying obligation will discharge an uncompensated guarantor even where there is no injury to the guarantor.[5]

There are several guaranty principles peculiar to South Carolina law. First, although waivers of suretyship defenses are generally enforced,[6] a provision in a guaranty waiving defenses that may arise from "any extension" of the underlying obligation may be deemed to apply only to a single extension, with the result that multiple extensions under a guaranty may discharge the guarantor.[7]

Second, guarantors of mortgage loan indebtedness who are joined with the mortgagor debtor in a judicial foreclosure action[8] may have recourse to the South Carolina antideficiency statute, unless certain required notices are given prior to the transaction and a waiver in a statutorily prescribed form is executed as part of the closing.[9]

There are no South Carolina decisions relating to guaranties of performance as such, although there is an established body of law relating to traditional, compensated surety relationship common in the construction law and fidelity bond context.[10]

Choice of law provisions will generally be honored in South Carolina,[11] unless application of the designated choice of law provision will on the facts presented be contrary to the public policy of South Carolina.[12] Choice of forum

---

3. The principal substantive citation to the Restatements is in Federal Deposit Ins. Corp. v. Fagan, 674 F.2d 302 (4th Cir. 1982). In that case, the Fourth Circuit rejects existing South Carolina precedent set forth in Knotts v. Butler, 31 S.C. Eq. (10 Rich. Eq.) 143 (1858) to the effect that the death of a guarantor does not terminate a guaranty until formal notice of termination is given in accordance with the terms of the guaranty. Instead, the Fourth Circuit relies on the Restatement of Security § 87 for the proposition that death of a guarantor terminates a continuing guaranty as to advances made after the date of death, even absent compliance with any applicable formal termination provisions set forth in the guaranty. See the discussion in Section 6.2 below. Most of the other citations are on peripheral matters or relate to the construction bond and fidelity bond surety context. *See, e.g.,* Bank of Ft. Mill v. Lawyers Title Ins. Corp., 268 F.2d 313 (4th Cir. 1959) (citing the Restatement of Security § 141(c) in a surety bond case for the proposition that a compensated surety has limited equities and thus limited subrogation rights); In re Houston, 409 B.R. 799 (Bankr. D.S.C. 2009) (citing the Restatement (Third) of Suretyship and Guaranty for the proposition that the release by an obligee of security impairs the subrogation rights of the guarantor); Masterclean, Inc. v. Star Ins. Co., 347 S.C. 405, 556 S.E.2d 371 (2001) (citing the Restatement (Second) of Security § 82 cmt. b as to the general rule that a surety has right of indemnification from the principal).
4. Restatement (Third) Suretyship and Guaranty § 37.
5. As to compensated sureties, however, the discharge is limited to the extent of injury to the surety. See the discussion in Section 7.2.2 below.
6. *See* the discussion in Section 8 below.
7. *See* the discussion in Section 6.6 below. The better phrasing would be "each and every extension" or "any and all extensions." *See* Brown v. National Surety Corp., 207 S.C. 462, 36 S.E.2d 588 (1946).
8. With the limited exception of foreclosure of certain timeshare interests, all foreclosures in South Carolina are judicial.
9. *See* the discussion in Section 8.
10. *See, e.g.,* Masterclean v. Star Ins. Co., 347 S.C. 405, 556 S.E.2d 371 (2001).
11. *See, e.g.,* Nucor Corp. v. Bell, 482 F. Supp. 2d 714 (D.S.C. 2007); Team IA, Inc. v. Lucas, 395 S.C. 237, 717 S.E.2d 103 (Ct. App. 2011).
12. *Id.* Where there is no choice of law provision in a guaranty, the law of the place where the guaranty was entered into will govern. *See* Livingston v. Atlantic C. L. R. Co., 176 S.C. 385, 180 S.E. 343 (1935); Team IA, Inc. v. Lucas, 395 S.C. 237, 717 S.E.2d 103 (Ct. App. 2011).

provisions, at least between sophisticated parties, will likewise be upheld, unless the application of the forum selection clause will violate a public policy of the state.[13]

§ 1 Nature of the Guaranty Arrangement

Under South Carolina law, a guaranty is a separate and independent contract between the guarantor and the obligee. For there to be a guaranty, however, there must be a separate, underlying obligation owed by the primary obligor to the obligee. The liability of a guarantor to the obligee under the guaranty is secondary to the liability of the primary obligor to the obligee under the underlying obligation.

1.1 Guaranty Relationships

Under South Carolina law, a guaranty is a contract under which the guarantor promises to answer for the payment of some debt, or the performance of some duty, in case of the failure of another person who is himself in the first instance, liable to such payment or performance.[14] Guaranties may be either guaranties of payment (also referred to as "absolute" or "unconditional" guaranties), or guaranties of collection.

A guaranty is an independent contract between the guarantor and the obligee, separate and distinct from the underlying obligation.[15] The primary obligor is not a party to the guaranty, and the guarantor is not a party to the underlying obligation.[16] Even though the guaranty is a separate contract, in general the liability of the guarantor is measured by that of the primary obligor.[17]

A guaranty is deemed a personal obligation of the guarantor running directly from the guarantor to the obligee.[18] A guaranty is nevertheless a collateral undertaking; for a guaranty to exist there must be someone liable as the primary obligor under a valid contract.[19] A guarantor is secondarily liable for the underlying obligation.

No special words are needed to create a guaranty obligation, so long as the words used manifest the appropriate intention.[20]

---

13. *See, e.g.,* Republic Leasing, Inc. v. Haywood, 329 S.C. 562, 495 S.E.2d 804 (Ct. App. 1998), *vacated on other grounds*, 335 S.C. 207, 516 S.E.2d 441 (1999). *But see* S.C. Code Ann. § 15-7-120 (2005) (providing that a forum selection clause cannot preclude assertion of a cause of action in the South Carolina courts, to the extent those courts would otherwise be an appropriate forum.
14. *E.g.,* McGee v. F. W. Poe Mfg. Co., 176 S.C. 288, 180 S.E. 48 (1935).
15. Citizens & S. Nat'l Bank v. Lanford, 313 S.C. 540, 544, 443 S.E.2d 549, 551 (1994); Rock Hill Nat'l Bank v. Honeycutt, 289 S.C. 98, 344 S.E.2d 875 (Ct. App. 1986).
16. *Id.*
17. Carroll County Sav. Bank v, Strother, 28 S.C. 504, 511; 6 S.E. 313, 315 (1888).
18. AMA Management Corp. v. Strasburger, 309 S.C. 213, 420 S.E.2d 868, 1992 (Ct. App. 1992).
19. Carroll Co. Sav. Bank v. Strother, 22 S.C. 552, 555 (1885); Glidden Coatings & Resins v. Suitt Constr. Co., 290 S.C. 240, 349 S.E.2d 89 (Ct. App. 1986), *overruled on other grounds by* Kennedy v. Columbia Lumber & Mfg. Co., 299 S.C. 335, 384 S.E.2d 730 (1989).
20. *E.g.,* Griffin Bro. & Co. v. Rembert, 2 S.C. 410, 414 (1871).

1.2 Other Suretyship Relationships

A suretyship relationship may also arise from a pledge of collateral by a person other than the primary obligor. For example, a third party who mortgages property as security for a loan to the primary obligor will be deemed a surety to the extent of the property mortgaged.[21]

South Carolina also recognizes traditional surety relationships arising in the context of performance and payment bonds.[22] The South Carolina courts note that this category of suretyship contract is a tri-party agreement, among the surety company, the principal, who has the primary duty of performance, and the obligee.[23]

§ 2 State Law Requirements for an Entity to Enter a Guaranty

Corporations, partnerships, limited liability companies, and banks can all enter into guaranty agreements, provided those agreements are in furtherance of their business. Those entities may likewise enter into guaranty agreements not in furtherance of their business, provided that appropriate consents are obtained from their constituents.

2.1 Corporations

Absent a contrary provision in its articles of incorporation, a corporation is authorized by the South Carolina Business Corporation Act of 1988 to make guaranties as necessary or convenient to carry out its business and affairs.[24] A guaranty of a loan to a director of the corporation, however, requires shareholder approval or specific findings by the board of directors of benefit to the corporation.[25]

2.2 Partnerships

The Uniform Partnership Act as in effect in South Carolina does not directly address the question of whether a partnership may execute and deliver a

21. *E.g.*, Wood v. Babb, 16 S.C. 427 (1882). *But see* Philco Finance Corp. v. Mehlman, 245 S.C. 139, 139 S.E.2d 475 (1964) (holding that an assignment in a subordination agreement of claims by the junior creditor to the senior creditor does not create a suretyship relationship absent a personal obligation on the part of the junior creditor to pay the senior creditor's debt).
22. Masterclean, Inc. v. Star Ins. Co., 347 S.C. 405, 556 S.E.2d 371 (2001).
23. Id. at 409-410, 556 S.E.2d at 373-74.
24. S.C. Code Ann. § 33-3-102 (7) (2006).
25. *See* S.C. Code Ann. § 33-8-320 (2006); Tuller v. Nantahala Park Co., 276 S.C. 667, 281 S.E.2d 474 (1981).

guaranty.[26] South Carolina common law, however, has recognized the authority of a partnership to execute guaranties.[27]

A general partner in a South Carolina limited partnership has the same rights and powers and is subject to the same restrictions as a partner in a limited partnership.[28] As a result, the analysis in the preceding paragraph relating to partnerships is also applicable to limited partnerships.

2.3 Limited Liability Companies

Absent a contrary provision in its articles of organization or its operating agreement, a limited liability company may make guaranties to the extent necessary or convenient to carry out the business or affairs of the company.[29]

2.4 Banks and Trust Companies

South Carolina has no statutory provisions directly addressing the power of state commercial banks to enter into guaranties. At common law, however, a bank has no power to make a guaranty, except as may be incident to the transaction of the bank's own business or for the protection of its own rights.[30]

State chartered banks, savings and loan associations, and credit unions are authorized by statute to engage in any activity in which their federally chartered counterparts may engage,[31] and are likewise given the powers of business corporations generally.[32] Neither of these provisions, however, would appear to override the general limitations on the issuance of guaranties by banking institutions, which require that a guaranty be incident to the bank's own business.

As a practical matter, federal law provides that state-chartered banks insured by the Federal Deposit Insurance Corporation are prohibited from engaging in activities and investments in which national banks may not engage.[33] National banks are permitted to issue guaranties only in limited circumstances.[34]

---

26. The South Carolina Uniform Partnership Act is set forth in S.C. CODE ANN. §§ 33-41-10 to -1330 (2008). The South Carolina Uniform Limited Partnership Act is set forth in S.C. CODE ANN. §§ 33-42-10 to -2140 (2008).
27. *See, e.g.*, Fleming, Ross & Co. v. Prescott, Bishop & Gray, 3 Rich. 307 (1832) (upholding an accommodation endorsement made by one of the partners on behalf of a partnership); Hawes v. Dunton & White, 1 Bailey 146 (1829) (enforcing against a partnership a note executed for the debt of another).
28. S.C. CODE ANN. § 33-42-630 (2006).
29. S.C. CODE ANN. § 33-44-112 (b) (5) (2008).
30. *See, e.g.*, Ayer v. Hughes, 87 S.C. 382, 69 S.E. 657 (1910).
31. *See* S.C. CODE ANN. § 34-1-110(A)(1), (2), & (3).
32. *See* S.C. CODE ANN. §§ 34-28-500 & 34-30-50 (2008).
33. *See* 12 U.S.C. § 1831a; 12 C.F.R. § 362.1.
34. *See* 12 C.F.R. § 7.1017 (2010) (requiring generally that a guaranty by a national bank will be permitted only if, among other things, the bank has a substantial interest in the transaction or obtains a segregated deposit in the amount of the guaranty).

2.5 Individuals

Individuals in South Carolina have the freedom to enter into such contracts as they desire, as long as such contracts are not unlawful.[35] Thus, there are, in general, no restrictions on or special requirements to be met in connection with the execution by an individual of a guaranty.

As is the case with any other contract, however, the party executing the contract must have contractual capacity, which is the "ability to understand, at the time the contract is executed, the nature of the contract and its effect."[36] A contract executed by a party lacking this mental capacity at the time of execution is voidable.[37]

A guaranty executed by a minor is voidable by the minor at his option upon reaching the age of majority, but may in the alternative be reaffirmed by the minor upon majority.[38] If the minor guarantor does not reaffirm the obligation upon reaching the age of majority, then the guaranty obligation is not enforceable.[39]

Where an individual signs a guaranty but does not expressly indicate whether he is signing in a representative capacity on behalf of an entity, or in his individual capacity, the court may determine from the context the intent of the parties, and may as appropriate determine the guaranty to be made in the individual capacity of the signer.[40]

Even where a person unambiguously signs a guaranty as an officer or in a similar representative capacity, that person may be bound individually if the terms of the guaranty contain a provision providing for individual liability on the part of that person.[41] Adding a title such as "president" after the signature of the guarantor does not relieve the guarantor of liability, if the terms of the instrument provide for individual liability.[42]

Under South Carolina law, the interest of one spouse in the property of the other spouse does not attach until the commencement of marital litigation.[43] Further, that spousal interest is not effective against third parties until a notice of pendency of the marital litigation is filed or given.[44] As a result, the interest of the nonguarantor spouse in the guarantor spouse's property will be subordinate to the lien of any judgment against the guarantor spouse obtained prior to the filing of the notice of the marital lien.[45]

A mortgage granted by the spouse of a guarantor as security for the guaranty, and encumbering that spouse's separately titled property, is fully enforceable against that property.[46]

---

35. *E.g.*, Jordan v. Aetna Cas. & Sur. Co., 264 S.C. 294, 297, 214 S.E.2d 818, 820 (1975).
36. Verdery v. Daniels, 344 S.C. 564, 544 S.E.2d 854 (Ct. App. 2001).
37. *E.g.*, Langley v. Cease, 122 S.C. 203, 115 S.E. 230 (1922); Shepard v. First American Mortg. Co., 289 S.C. 516, 347 S.E.2d 118 (Ct. App. 1986).
38. Williams v. Harrison, 11 S.C. 412 (1878).
39. State v. Satterwhite, 20 S.C. 536 (1884).
40. *See, e.g.*, Hope Petty Motors v. Hyatt, 310 S.C. 171, 425 S.E.2d 786 (Ct. App. 1992).
41. Klutts Resort Realty, Inc. v. Down'Round Development Corp., 268 S.C. 80, 232 S.E.2d 20 (1977).
42. *Id.*; J. L. Mott Iron Works v. Clark, 87 S.C. 199, 69 S.E. 227 (1910).
43. S.C. CODE ANN. § 20-3-610 (1976).
44. S.C. CODE ANN. § 20-3-670 (1976).
45. Prosser v. Pee Dee State Bank, 295 S.C. 212, 367 S.E.2d 698 (1988).
46. *E.g.*, Wood v. Babb, 16 S.C. 427 (1882).

§ 3 Signatory's Authority to Execute a Guaranty

Generally, an obligee has a duty to exercise due care to verify the authority of the person executing a guaranty in a representative capacity; the doctrine of apparent authority has not been consistently applied in this area.

3.1 Corporations

In order to bind a corporation, the officer signing the guaranty must as a general rule have actual authority to execute an instrument in the name of a corporation.[47] This is especially so where the instrument is not apparently made in furtherance of the business of the corporation.[48] The party relying on the guaranty must use due care to verify the authority of the signer, and has the burden of proving that authorization.[49]

The directors and not the officer of the corporation have the right to exercise powers of the corporation, and the officers in order to bind the corporation must be granted authority to act by the board of directors.[50] Such authority is, of course, typically granted by way of resolution.[51] A grant of authority by the board of directors to execute a guaranty, however, must be consistent with any special restrictions contained in the bylaws.[52]

An officer of a corporation generally does not have actual authority to execute a guaranty by virtue of his title or office alone.[53] Nevertheless, the grant to an officer of a corporate title may be sufficient to enable him to bind the corporation to contracts under the doctrine of apparent authority, where the corporate officer is acting within the apparent scope of his authority.[54]

Likewise, there may be a presumption of authority with respect to an instrument within the power of the corporation executed by an appropriate officer.[55] Generally, however, the person who deals with the corporation is charged with notice of the purpose for which the corporation was organized, and is obligated to inquire into the power and extent of the authority of the agents or officers with whom that person deals.[56]

---

47. *See, e.g.,* Enterprise Bank v. Carolina Inv. Co., 112 S.C. 52, 99 S.E. 25 (1919).
48. *Id.*
49. Pee Dee Nursing Home v. Florence Gen. Hosp., 309 S.C. 80, 419 S.E.2d 834 (Ct. App. 1992). *But see* Moyer v. East Shore Terminal Co., 41 S.C. 300, 19 S.E. 651 (1894) (a third party contracting with a corporation is not required to examine the bylaws of the corporation to confirm whether the officer with whom it is dealing has actual authority to bind the corporation).
50. Pee Dee Nursing Home v. Florence Gen. Hosp., 309 S.C. 80, 419 S.E.2d 834 (Ct. App. 1992).
51. *See, e.g.,* Palmetto Compress & Warehouse Co. v. Citizens & Southern Nat'l Bank, 200 S.C. 20, 20 S.E.2d 232 (1942).
52. Future Group v. NationsBank, 324 S.C. 89, 478 S.E.2d 45 (1996).
53. Bohumir Kryl Symphony Bank, Inc. v. Allen University, 196 S.C. 173, 12 S.E.2d 712 (1940); Pee Dee Nursing Home v. Florence Gen. Hosp., 309 S.C. 80, 419 S.E.2d 834 (Ct. App. 1992).
54. Thompson v. Shaw Motor Co., 128 S.C. 171, 122 S.E. 669, (1924); WDI Meredith & Co. v. American Telesis, Inc., 359 S.C. 474, 597 S.E.2d 885, 2004 (Ct. App. 2004).
55. Atlanta & C. A. L. R. Co. v. Limestone-Globe Land Co., 109 S.C. 444, 96 S.E. 188 (1918).
56. Hutchison v. Rock Hill Real Estate & Loan Co., 65 S.C. 45, 43 S.E. 295 (1902).

3.2 Partnerships

A partner may bind a partnership to an instrument by actual authority or apparent authority. The scope of this authority depends in part on whether or not the instrument is apparently for carrying the usual business of the partnership.

Every partner under South Carolina law is an agent of the partnership for "execution in the partnership name of any instrument, for apparently carrying on in the usual way the business of the partnership."[57] Under this rule, each partner is deemed to have apparent authority to bind the partnership to agreements apparently in the scope of the partnership's business, and this apparent authority may be relied upon by third parties, unless it is the case both that the partner does not in fact have the authority, and that this lack of authority is known to the third party.[58]

Where the instrument executed by a partner is not, however, apparently for carrying on the business of the partnership in the usual way, the partner does not have apparent authority, and the authorization of the other partners must be obtained.[59]

Historically, the execution of a guaranty has not been viewed as within the scope of business of some partnerships (such as "nontrading" partnerships). As a result, a single partner (or less than all the partners) may, depending on the nature of the business of the partnership, not have the power to bind the partnership.[60] In such cases, the consent or authorization of all of the partners is required.[61] As a result, the better approach is to have all of the partners execute, or authorize the execution of, any guaranty.

3.3 Limited Liability Companies (LLCs)

Members in a member-managed LLC are treated in the same manner as are partners in a partnership. Each member of the company is an agent of the company, with the power to sign instruments in the company's name, provided that the instrument is for "apparently carrying on in the ordinary course of the company's business or business of the kind carried on by the company …."[62] Thus, with respect to acts apparently in furtherance of the company's business, each member can bind the company, unless the third-party dealing with the member had actual knowledge that such member lacked actual authority.[63]

On the other hand, an act by a member not apparently for carrying on in the ordinary course of the company's business will bind the company only if the act was in fact authorized by the other members.[64]

---

57. S.C. CODE ANN. § 33-41-310(1).
58. *Id.*; Hofer v. St. Clair, 298 S.C. 503, 381 S.E.2d 736 (1989).
59. S.C. CODE ANN. § 33-41-310(2).
60. *See, e.g.*, Hull v. Young, 30 S.C. 121, 8 S.E. 695 (1889).
61. *Cf.* Sibley v. Young, 26 S.C. 415, 2 S.E. 314 (1887) (holding execution by one partner of instrument under seal, which at common law was not deemed in the ordinary course of a partnership's business and thus not binding on a partnership, was enforceable where ratified by the other partner); Stroman v. Varn, 19 S.C. 307 (1883) (holding a mortgage of partnership assets by a single partner, not otherwise enforceable as not in furtherance of a partnership's business, to be enforceable where ratified or consented to by all of the partners).
62. S.C. CODE ANN. § 33-44-301 (a) (1).
63. *Id.*
64. S.C. CODE ANN. § 33-44-301 (a) (1).

With respect to a manager-managed LLC, members are not agents of the company solely as a result of their status as a member. Thus, the execution of documents by a member in a manager-managed LLC would require that specific authorization be granted to the member.

Each manager, however, in a manager-managed LLC is deemed an agent of the company, with authority to bind the company with respect to instruments signed apparently in the ordinary course of the company's business.[65] The manager does not have authority, solely by virtue of being a manager, to sign instruments in the name of the LLC that are not apparently within the ordinary course of the LLC's business.[66] In addition, to the extent the execution of the instrument is deemed a breach of the duty of loyalty by the manager, then the consent of all of the members must be obtained, irrespective of any contrary provision in the operating agreement.[67]

3.4 Banks and Trust Companies

The authority issues with respect to persons signing on behalf of banks and trust companies are consistent with those issues as they pertain to corporations generally. In banks, as is the case with other corporate entities, authorization to execute an instrument is typically granted to officers by way of resolution of the board of directors.[68]

§ 4 Consideration; Sufficiency of Past Consideration

With respect to guaranties executed simultaneously with or as part of the same transaction as the underlying obligation, no other consideration is required. New consideration is required, however, with respect to guaranties of preexisting indebtedness. As a general rule, past consideration is not sufficient to support the enforcement of a guaranty.

As is the case with other contracts, a guaranty must be supported by consideration.[69] A guaranty not supported by consideration is not enforceable,[70] and the defense of lack of consideration for the guaranty may be asserted by the guarantor.[71]

The right of a guarantor to assert the defense of the lack of consideration, however, is subject to several limitations tied to the parol evidence rule. First, a guarantor may not assert as a defense failure of consideration based on the breach of an alleged contemporaneous agreement inconsistent with the terms

65. S.C. Code Ann. § 33-44-301 (b) (1).
66. S.C. Code Ann. § 33-44-301 (b) (1).
67. S.C. Code Ann. § 33-44-404 (c) (2).
68. *E.g.*, State v. Duckett, 133 S.C. 85, 130 S.E. 340 (1925).
69. *E.g.*, Lowndes v. McCabe Fertilizer Co., 157 S.C. 371, 154 S.E. 641 (1930); Hope Petty Motors v. Hyatt, 310 S.C. 171, 425 S.E.2d 786 (Ct. App. 1992).
70. Lowndes v. McCabe Fertilizer Co., 157 S.C. 371, 154 S.E. 641 (1930); Hope Petty Motors v. Hyatt, 310 S.C. 171, 425 S.E.2d 786 (Ct. App. 1992).
71. *E.g.*, Branch Banking & Trust Co. v. Carolina Crank & Core, Inc., 362 S.C. 647, 608 S.E.2d 896 (Ct. App. 2005).

of the guaranty itself, as that would effectively be a parol modification of the terms of the guaranty.[72]

Second, where consideration is expressed in the guaranty, parol evidence to contradict the stated consideration is admissible only where such consideration is set forth as a mere recital, or where the consideration expressed is an act or a forbearance, as opposed to a promise or covenant.[73] If the recited consideration is a promise or covenant, then the recital cannot be contradicted.[74] Under these rules, a recital in the form of "for value received" would not preclude parol evidence as to the failure of consideration.[75]

The consideration need not flow to the party granting the guaranty; it is sufficient if there is a benefit to the primary obligor or a detriment to the obligee.[76] Specifically, the guarantor need not derive a benefit from the underlying transaction, where there is a benefit to the primary obligor or a detriment to the obligee.[77]

Where the guaranty is made at the same time as the extension of credit to the primary obligor, the extension of the credit is sufficient consideration.[78] On the other hand, where the guaranty is made after the underlying obligation has been entered into, then new consideration is required.[79] Past consideration is not sufficient to support a guaranty.[80] Note, however, that a promissory note given for an antecedent debt is by law supported by consideration, and thus an endorser of such a promissory note may be liable notwithstanding the lack of new consideration.[81]

An agreement to forbear from exercising legal remedies can constitute consideration for a guaranty.[82] The forbearance agreement must, however, be for a definite period, or otherwise be legally adequate to prevent the obligee from enforcing its remedies for a specific period of time.[83] In fact, in a subsequent action on a guaranty obtained in such circumstances, the obligee may be required to establish that the forbearance did in fact occur, with such forbearance effectively being deemed a condition precedent to the enforcement of the guaranty.[84]

72. *E.g.*, Swift & Co. v. Griggs, 235 S.C. 60, 109 S.E.2d 710 (1959).
73. *E.g.*, Iseman v. Hobbs, 290 S.C. 482, 351 S.E.2d 351 (Ct. App. 1986).
74. *Id.*
75. *Id.*
76. *E.g.*, Fales & Jenks Mach. Co. v. Browning, 68 S.C. 13, 46 S.E. 545 (1903); Crafton v. Brown, 346 S.C. 347, 354, 550 S.E.2d 904, 907 (Ct. App. 2001). *Accord*, Heil Quaker v. Swindler, 255 F. Supp. 445 (D.S.C. 1966).
77. *E.g.*, Branch Banking & Trust Co. v. Carolina Crank & Core, Inc., 362 S.C. 647, 608 S.E.2d 896 (Ct. App. 2005).
78. *E.g.*, Fales & Jenks Mach. Co. v. Browning, 68 S.C. 13, 46 S.E. 545 (1903); Branch Banking & Trust Co. v. Carolina Crank & Core, Inc., 362 S.C. 647, 608 S.E.2d 896 (Ct. App. 2005).
79. *E.g.*, Fales & Jenks Mach. Co. v. Browning, 68 S.C. 13, 46 S.E. 545 (1903).
80. *E.g.*, Henderson v. Skinner, 146 S.C. 281, 143 S.E. 875 (1928); Crafton v. Brown, 346 S.C. 347, 550 S.E.2d 904 (Ct. App. 2001); Hope Petty Motors of Columbia, Inc. v. Hyatt, 310 S.C. 171, 178, 425 S.E.2d 786, 791 (Ct. App. 1992) .
81. *See* Farmers & Merchants Bank v. Fargnoli, 274 S.C. 23, 260 S.E.2d 185 (1979); S.C. Code Ann. section 36-3-303 (a) (3)-303 (b).
82. *E.g.*, Pelzer, Rodgers & Co. v. Campbell & Co., 15 S.C. 581, 587 (1881).
83. Haynsworth v. Bischoff, 6 S.C. 159 (1875).
84. Lowndes v. McCabe Fertilizer Co., 157 S.C. 371, 154 S.E. 641 (1930).

In addition to an agreement to forbear from the exercise of remedies, an agreement to extend the time for payment for a definite period is sufficient consideration for a guaranty.[85]

§ 5 Notice of Acceptance

Notice of acceptance is generally not required if the guaranty is executed contemporaneously with the underlying obligation or if the guaranty is absolute.

The general rule is that every guarantor is entitled to notice of the acceptance of his guaranty, unless the character of the underlying transaction itself provides such notice.[86] Generally, where the proposal to make a guaranty originates with the guarantor, notice of acceptance is required.[87]

There are a number of exceptions to this general requirement of notice. Notice of acceptance is not required where the guaranty is an absolute guaranty, i.e., a guaranty of payment.[88] Notice of acceptance is also not required when the guaranty is executed contemporaneously with the underlying obligation.[89]

Likewise, no notice of acceptance is required where the guarantor proposes to guarantee the payment of a specific, existing debt in a definite amount known to the guarantor at the time he makes the proposal.[90] Finally, notice of acceptance is not required when the obligee has requested the guarantor to make the guaranty, and the guarantor complies with this request.[91]

Where notice of acceptance is required, it is not necessary that the guarantor be given express, personal notice by the obligee; rather, such notice may be implied from the circumstances of the particular transaction.[92]

§ 6 Interpretation of Guaranties

Guaranties are contracts, and are to be construed in accordance with the general rules applicable to the construction of contracts. The principal objective is to ascertain the intent of the parties. Although the terms of a guaranty may not be modified by parol evidence, the terms of a guaranty may be supplemented by the terms of contemporaneously executed documents.

---

85. Pelzer, Rodgers & Co. v. Campbell & Co., 15 S.C. 581, 587 (1881); Crafton v. Brown, 346 S.C. 347, 550 S.E.2d 904 (Ct. App. 2001).
86. Duncan & Shumate v. Heller, 13 S.C. 94 (1880).
87. J. L. Mott Iron Works v. Clark, 87 S.C. 199, 69 S.E. 227 (1910).
88. *E.g.*, Ruberg v. Brown, 71 S.C. 287, 51 S.E. 96 (1905).
89. *E.g.*, Crafton v. Brown, 346 S.C. 347, 550 S.E.2d 904 (Ct. App. 2001).
90. Greene v. Simon Brown's Sons, 128 S.C. 91, 121 S.E. 597 (1924).
91. J. L. Mott Iron Works v. Clark, 87 S.C. 199, 69 S.E. 227 (1910); Duncan & Shumate v. Heller, 13 S.C. 94 (1880).
92. Greene v. Simon Brown's Sons, 128 S.C. 91, 121 S.E. 597 (S.C. 1924); Griffin Bro. & Co. v. Rembert, 2 S.C. 410 (1871).

6.1 General Principles

A guaranty is a contract, and the general principles applicable to the construction of contracts apply to a guaranty.[93] The primary objective is to ascertain the intent of the parties, as set forth in the guaranty itself and in light of the context in which the guaranty arises.[94]

In addition to the general rules of contract construction, South Carolina law provides several rules of construction specific to guaranties. First, unless the terms of a guaranty contain conditions precedent or other terms to the contrary, the guaranty will be viewed as an absolute guaranty, or guaranty of payment.[95] Second, where there are multiple guarantors signing a single guaranty, the liability of those guarantors will be deemed joint and several.[96]

Where the guaranty is unambiguous, extrinsic evidence may not be introduced to contradict, explain, or vary its terms.[97] Thus, for example, a guarantor cannot introduce evidence to establish that the guaranty has been terminated in a manner other than that required by the guaranty itself.[98] Likewise, a guarantor cannot introduce parol evidence to establish that a guaranty was intended to expire after six months, where no such provision was contained in the guaranty itself.[99]

Despite the parol evidence rule, in the absence of the contrary intent of the parties, a guaranty is to be construed together with other instruments executed at the same time.[100]

The construction of an unambiguous guaranty, as is the case with any other written instrument, is a matter of law for the court.[101] Where a guaranty is ambiguous, the guaranty will be construed against the drafter.[102]

Finally, where the guarantor is an individual or otherwise a voluntary or accommodation surety, the guaranty is to be strictly construed in favor of the guarantor.[103] Where the guarantor is a paid surety, i.e., one in the business of acting as a surety or guarantor, the contract will be construed in favor of the obligee. *Id.*

6.2 "Continuing"

A continuing guaranty is one that applies not just to a specific indebtedness, but rather to all indebtedness incurred by the primary obligor during the time

93. *See, e.g.*, Peoples Federal Sav. & Loan Ass'n v. Myrtle Beach Retirement Group, Inc., 300 S.C. 277, 387 S.E.2d 672 (1989).
94. *E.g.*, Peoples Federal Sav. & Loan Ass'n v. Myrtle Beach Retirement Group, Inc., 300 S.C. 277, 387 S.E.2d 672 (1989); McGee v. F. W. Poe Mfg. Co., 176 S.C. 288, 180 S.E. 48 (1935).
95. Georgian Company v. Britton, 141 S.C. 136, 139 S.E. 217 (1927).
96. United States v. Kohn, 243 F. Supp. 293 (W.D.S.C. 293).
97. *See, e.g.*, Bankers Trust of South Carolina v. Collins, 270 S.C. 26, 239 S.E.2d 889 (1977); Crafton v. Brown, 346 S.C. 347, 550 S.E.2d 904 (Ct. App. 2001).
98. *See* Bankers Trust of South Carolina v. Collins, 270 S.C. 26, 239 S.E.2d 889 (1977).
99. Federal Deposit Ins. Corp. v. Waldron, 472 F. Supp. 21 (D.S.C. 1979), *aff'd* 630 F.2d 239 (4th Cir. 1980); Bankers Trust of South Carolina v. Collins, 270 S.C. 26, 239 S.E.2d 889 (1977).
100. Klutts Resort Realty, Inc. v. Down'Round Dev. Corp., 268 S.C. 80, 89, 232 S.E.2d 20, 25 (1977).
101. *See, e.g.*, Stackhouse v. Pure Oil Co., 176 S.C. 318, 180 S.E. 188, (1935).
102. *See, e.g.*, Williams v. Teran, Inc., 266 S.C. 55, 221 S.E.2d 526 (1976).
103. *See, e.g.*, Greenville Airport Com. v. United States Fidelity & Guaranty Co., 226 S.C. 553, 86 S.E.2d 249 (1955).

the guaranty is in effect.[104] In determining whether a guaranty is a continuing guaranty, the South Carolina courts first look to the written Guaranty itself.[105] If the Guaranty provides that it extends to future indebtedness, or to liability arising from future dealings between the parties, then it is a continuing Guaranty.[106]

Generally, a continuing Guaranty remains effective until revoked by the Guarantor or otherwise terminated by operation of law.[107] The general rule is that a continuing Guaranty may be revoked at any time, but revocation does not affect the liability of the Guarantor for advances made to the Primary Obligor prior to the date of termination.[108] A Guarantor under a continuing Guaranty must terminate the Guaranty in accordance with requirements of the Guaranty instrument.[109]

Absent a provision in the guaranty to the contrary, an obligee has no duty to notify the guarantor of additional extensions of credit by the obligee to the primary obligor.[110]

Under existing South Carolina case law, a continuing guaranty will remain effective as to advances made after the death of the guarantor until the personal representative has terminated the guaranty in accordance with the notice and termination provisions in the guaranty.[111] This rule has been criticized by the federal courts for South Carolina, as contrary to the majority rule and the Restatement of Security.[112]

A debtor is not released from his obligations under a continuing guaranty by the discharge and later revival of the underlying obligation that occurs during the term of the guaranty.[113]

6.3 "Absolute and Unconditional"

An "absolute" guaranty, or an "absolute and unconditional guaranty," is a guaranty of payment rather than a guaranty of collection. Under an absolute guaranty, the obligee may maintain an action against the guarantor immediately upon default by the primary obligor; there is no requirement of prior recourse against the primary obligor or against any collateral.[114]

---

104. *See, e.g.*, Anderson v. Trust Co. Bank (In re Southco, Inc.), 168 B.R. 95 (Bankr. D.S.C. 1994); Bankers Trust of South Carolina v. Collins, 270 S.C. 26, 239 S.E.2d 889 (1977).
105. Pee Dee State Bank v. National Fiber Corp., 287 S.C. 640, 340 S.E.2d 569 (Ct. App. 1986).
106. *Id.*; W. T. Rawleigh Co. v. Wilson, 141 S.C. 182, 139 S.E. 395 (S.C. 1927); Furst & Thomas v. Moore, 129 S.C. 223, 123 S.E. 825, (1924).
107. Pee Dee State Bank v. National Fiber Corp., 287 S.C. 640, 340 S.E.2d 569 (Ct. App. 1986).
108. *Id.*
109. Bankers Trust of South Carolina v. Collins, 270 S.C. 26, 239 S.E.2d 889 (1977).
110. PPG Industries, Inc. v. Orangeburg Paint & Decorating Center, Inc., 297 S.C. 176, 375 S.E.2d 331, (Ct. App. 1988).
111. Knotts v. Butler, 31 S.C. Eq. (10 Rich. Eq.) 143 (1858).
112. In *Federal Deposit Ins. Corp. v. Fagan*, 674 F.2d 302 (4th Cir. 1982), the Fourth Circuit held that, notwithstanding the holding of *Knotts v. Butler, supra*, the South Carolina courts would find that a continuing guaranty would not extend to indebtedness incurred after the obligee had notice of the guarantor's death. Rather, the court of appeals determined that the South Carolina courts would, if presented again with the issue, follow the Restatement of Security §87, and hold that death terminated the continuing guaranty as to advance made after the date of death.
113. Anderson v. Trust Co. Bank (In re Southco, Inc.), 168 B.R. 95 (Bankr. D.S.C. 1994); Bankers Trust of South Carolina v. Collins, 270 S.C. 26, 239 S.E.2d 889 (1977).
114. Peoples Federal Sav. & Loan Ass'n v. Myrtle Beach Retirement Group, Inc., 300 S.C. 277, 387 S.E.2d 672 (1989); Southern Bank & Trust Co. v. Harley, 292 S.C. 340, 356 S.E.2d 410 (Ct. App. 1987), modified by Southern Bank & Trust Co. v. Harley, 295 S.C. 423, 368 S.E.2d 908 (1988).

6.4 "Liable as a Primary Obligor and not Merely as Surety"

The use of the language "primary obligor" in a guaranty does not appear to impose additional liabilities on the guarantor or otherwise change the substantive nature of the guaranty. Likewise, such language does not appear to change the relationship between the guarantor and the obligee, or the relationship between the guarantor and the primary obligor. Because a guaranty is an independent obligation, a guarantor will always be a "primary obligor" under his guaranty, and a secondary obligor with respect to the underlying obligation.[115] Under South Carolina law, "there is no practical distinction between the liability of an absolute guarantor and that of a surety."[116]

There is, however, authority that in order for a party paying the indebtedness to be subrogated to the rights of the obligee against the primary obligor, the party must have been "secondarily liable" for the underlying obligation.[117] Arguably, to the extent the referenced language does in fact render a guarantor primarily liable with respect to the underlying obligation, the remedy of subrogation may become unavailable to the guarantor.

6.5 "Construction of Limitations on Liability"

Where a guaranty limits liability to a fixed percentage of the loan amount, that percentage is determined by reference to the original loan amount and not by reference to any deficiency remaining after liquidation of the collateral.[118] Similarly, a dollar limitation in a guaranty is not reduced by proceeds of the collateral if the total indebtedness still outstanding exceeds the limitation amount.[119] A guarantor is entitled to have proceeds of the security applied to reduce the guaranteed debt, but not to reduce the contractual liability limit contained in the guaranty.[120]

6.6 "Construction of Waivers of Suretyship Defenses"

Guaranties are contracts, and will be construed based on the language of the guaranties to give effect to the intention of the parties. Thus, waivers of suretyship defenses will be enforced even where enforcement yields an apparently

115. *Cf.* TranSouth Fin. Corp. v. Cochran, 324 S.C. 290, 478 S.E.2d 63 (Ct. App. 1996) (so construing a guaranty designating the guarantor as a "primary obligor").
116. Georgian Company v. Britton, 141 S.C. 136, 141, 139 S.E. 217, 218 (1927).
117. *See, e.g.,* Dunn v. Chapman, 149 S.C. 163, 146 S.E. 818 (1929).
118. *See, e.g.,* Peoples Federal Sav. & Loan Ass'n v. Myrtle Beach Retirement Group, Inc., 300 S.C. 277, 387 S.E.2d 672 (1989).
119. Southern Bank & Trust Co. v. Harley, 292 S.C. 340, 356 S.E.2d 410 (Ct. App. 1987), *modified by* Southern Bank & Trust Co. v. Harley, 295 S.C. 423, 368 S.E.2d 908 (1988).
120. *Id.*

unfair result.[121] Under these principles, waivers of suretyship defenses have consistently been upheld.[122]

Significantly, a provision in a guaranty waiving any defense that may arise from "any extension" may be deemed to apply only to a single extension, with the result that multiple extensions under a guaranty may discharge the guarantor.[123] The better phrasing would be "each and every extension" or "any and all extensions."[124]

Although waivers of suretyship defenses will be enforced as written, they are not favored, and will be construed as narrowly as possible, consistent with the language of the waiver.[125]

§ 7 Defenses of the Guarantor; Set-off

A guarantor may assert any defense available to the primary obligor, except for those defenses personal to the primary obligor and except certain defenses inconsistent with the independent contractual nature of a guaranty. A guarantor may also assert suretyship defenses, to the extent not waived, and "real" defenses such as fraud in the inducement.

7.1 Defenses of the Primary Obligor

7.1.1 General

The general rule is that a guarantor may assert defenses that would be available to the primary obligor.[126] Nevertheless, a guarantor may not assert defenses that are purely personal to the principal, such as the personal incapacity of the primary obligor.[127] Likewise, because a guaranty is an obligation separate from the underlying obligation, certain defenses available under the terms of the underlying obligation may not be available to the guarantor.[128]

---

121. Anderson v. Trust Co. Bank (In re Southco, Inc.), 168 B.R. 95 (Bankr. D.S.C. 1994).
122. *See, e.g.,* Anderson v. Trust Co. Bank (In re Southco, Inc.), 168 B.R. 95 (Bankr. D.S.C. 1994) (enforcing waivers of defenses based on impairment of collateral); Burwell v. South Carolina Nat'l Bank, 288 S.C. 34, 340 S.E.2d 786 (1986) (enforcing waiver of discharge or impairment claims arising from successive renewals of the underlying obligation); Florentine Corp. v. Peda I, Inc., 287 S.C. 382, 339 S.E.2d 112 (1985) (enforcing consent to any and all modifications of the underlying obligation); Wachovia Bank v. Blackburn, 394 S.C. 579, 716 S.E.2d 454 (Ct. App. 2011) (enforcing waiver of jury trial); Regions Bank v. Schmauch, 354 S.C. 648, 582 S.E.2d 432 (Ct. App. 2003) (enforcing waiver of all notices to which a guarantor might otherwise be entitled); TranSouth Fin. Corp. v. Cochran, 324 S.C. 290, 478 S.E.2d 63 (Ct. App. 1996) (finding waivers of specified, customary suretyship defenses enforceable).
123. Tuten v. Bowden, 173 S.C. 256, 175 S.E. 510 (S.C. 1934).
124. Brown v. National Surety Corp., 207 S.C. 462, 36 S.E.2d 588 (1946).
125. Tuten v. Bowden, 173 S.C. 256, 175 S.E. 510 (1934) (construing waiver of a defense based on "any extension of time" granted to Primary Obligor as limited to a single extension).
126. *See, e.g.,* Smith v. Mandel, 66 F.R.D. 405 (D.S.C. 1975); Carroll County Sav. Bank v. Strother, 28 S.C. 504, 6 S.E. 313 (1888).
127. South Carolina State Highway Dep't v. Ft. Fetterman, 148 F. Supp. 620 (D.S.C. 1956); Carroll County Sav. Bank v. Strother, 28 S.C. 504, 6 S.E. 313 (1888).
128. *See, e.g.,* Citizens & S. Nat'l Bank v. Lanford, 313 S.C. 540, 544, 443 S.E.2d 549, 551 (1994); TranSouth Fin. Corp. v. Cochran, 324 S.C. 290, 478 S.E.2d 63 (Ct. App. 1996) (guarantor may not assert expiration of obligee's judgment against primary obligor as a defense to action by the obligee against the guarantor).

7.1.2 When Guarantor may Assert Primary Obligor's Defense

A guarantor may generally assert defenses of the primary obligor arising under the underlying obligation, irrespective of whether the primary obligor is a codefendant. The primary obligor is not a necessary party to an action against the guarantor on the guaranty.[129]

Where, however, a conclusive judgment has been obtained by the obligee against the primary obligor on the underlying obligation, a guarantor may be precluded from asserting defenses that could have been raised in the action giving rise to the judgment.[130]

7.1.3 Defenses that may not be Raised by Guarantor

Many defenses to the underlying obligation that may not be raised by the guarantor arise from the fact that the guaranty is a separate contract, independent of the underlying obligation. For example, a guarantor may not raise as a defense the insolvency of the primary obligor.[131] Likewise, a guarantor is generally deemed not to be a "party to the instrument" evidencing the underlying obligation with the meaning of Article 3 of the Uniform Commercial Code (UCC). As a result, a guarantor may not assert discharge and impairment of collateral defenses under UCC § 3-605.[132]

Likewise, because the guaranty is a separate contract, a guarantor may not assert as a defense the expiration (and resulting unenforceability) of a judgment obtained by the obligee against the primary obligor on the underlying obligation.[133]

Other defenses unavailable to a guarantor relate to the unconditional nature of a guaranty. Because there is no requirement that an obligee proceed against the collateral for the underlying obligation, a guarantor may not assert as a defense the failure of the obligee to dispose of collateral in its possession prior to bringing the action on the guaranty.[134] For the same reason, a guarantor under an absolute guaranty cannot assert a defense that the obligee, through negligence or lack of diligence, impaired the collateral furnished by the debtor.[135]

Because the obligee has the contractual right under an absolute guaranty to recover from the guarantor the full amount sought, the obligee has no duty to mitigate damages.[136] Thus, a guarantor may not assert a defense of failure to mitigate damages.

---

129. *See, e.g.*, Smith v. Mandel, 66 F.R.D. 405 (D.S.C. 1975).
130. *See, e.g.*, Ward v. Fed. Co., 233 S.C. 561, 106 S.E.2d 169 (1958); Int'l Fid. Ins. Co. v. China Constr. Am. (SC) Inc., 375 S.C. 175, 650 S.E.2d 677 (Ct. App. 2007).
131. AMA Management Corp. v. Strasburger, 309 S.C. 213, 420 S.E.2d 868, 1992 (Ct. App. 1992).
132. S.C. Code Ann. § 36-3-605 (2003). *See, e.g.*, Citizens & S. Nat'l Bank v. Lanford, 313 S.C. 540, 443 S.E.2d 549 (1994); Sunrise S&L Ass'n v. Mariner's Cay Dev. Corp., 295 S.C. 208, 367 S.E.2d 696 (1988).
133. TranSouth Fin. Corp. v. Cochran, 324 S.C. 290, 478 S.E.2d 63 (Ct. App. 1996).
134. Andrews v. Von Elten & Walker, Inc., 315 S.C. 199, 432 S.E.2d 500 (Ct. App. 1993).
135. Anderson v. Trust Co. Bank (In re Southco, Inc.), 168 B.R. 95 (Bankr. D.S.C. 1994).
136. Cisson Constr. v. Reynolds & Assocs., 311 S.C. 499, 429 S.E.2d 847 (Ct. App. 1993).

A guarantor may not raise the defense that the underlying obligation violates the statute of frauds. The protection of the statute of frauds is personal to the parties to an agreement, and may not be raised by a third party.[137]

7.1.4 Defenses that may Always be Raised by Guarantor

There are several defenses of a primary obligor that may be asserted by a guarantor. A guarantor, for example, may assert a defense that the guaranty is invalid because the underlying obligation was executed as part of a contract void as in violation of public policy.[138]

Likewise, a guarantor may assert a defense of usury to the same extent the primary obligor may assert that defense.[139]

Finally, a guarantor may assert a defense based on fraud by the obligee in inducing the primary obligor to incur additional guaranteed indebtedness outside of normal business terms under circumstances likely to result in losses and claims against the guarantors.[140]

7.2 "Suretyship" Defenses

7.2.1 Change in Identity of Principal Obligor

The general rule is that a guarantor may be released from liability by a change in the identity of the primary obligor, absent the guarantor's consent to that change.[141]

Where the guaranty is a continuing one, however, it may survive a change in the identity of the primary obligor, at least where the new primary obligor continues the business of the former primary obligor.[142] Similarly, a continuing guaranty may continue in effect notwithstanding the incorporation of a primary obligor who, at the time the guaranty was executed, was conducting business as a sole proprietorship.[143]

Finally, a continuing guaranty may survive the sale of the business of the primary obligor where the guarantor fails to give proper notice of termination of the guaranty in connection with such sale.[144] A guaranty will, however, terminate to the extent the change in the primary obligor is deemed to be a novation, such that the original underlying obligation has been discharged.[145]

---

137. *See* Hatcher v. Harleysville Mut. Ins. Co., 266 S.C. 548, 225 S.E.2d 181 (1976).
138. *See* Liberty Mut. Ins. Co. v. Gilreath, 191 S.C. 244, 4 S.E.2d 126 (1939). *But see* Wallace v. Lark, 12 S.C. 576 (1880) (mere knowledge on the part of a surety that the proceeds of the loan evidenced by the promissory note were to be used for immoral or illegal purposes does not discharge the surety).
139. *See, e.g.*, Wolfe v. Ebert, 37 B.R. 934 (Bankr D.S.C. 1983).
140. *See* J. R. Watkins Co. v. Jaillette, 202 S.C. 429, 25 S.E.2d 478 (1943); J. R. Watkins Co. v. Stephens, 144 S.C. 125, 142 S.E. 245 (1928).
141. *See, e.g.*, Spencer v. Frontier Ins. Co., 290 Fed. Appx. 571 (4th Cir. 2008); Berry v. Adams, 159 S.C. 472, 157 S.E. 805 (S.C. 1931).
142. *See* Porter Bros., Inc. v. Smith, 284 S.C. 292, 325 S.E.2d 588 (Ct. App. 1985) (continuing guaranty remained effective notwithstanding sale of dealership by one individual to another).
143. *See* In re Coogler, 14 B.R. 124 (Bankr. D.S.C. 1981).
144. Wayne Dalton Corp. v. Acme Doors, Inc., 302 S.C. 93, 394 S.E.2d 5 (Ct. App. 1990).
145. *Id.*

7.2.2 *Modification of the Underlying Obligation, Including Release*

As a general rule, any material alteration in the terms of the underlying obligation may discharge the guarantor.[146] Most South Carolina cases find a guarantor discharged even if there is no injury to the guarantor, provided that the alteration to the underlying obligation is material.[147]

A common example of a material alteration that will discharge a guarantor is an extension of time for payment of the underlying obligation. Such an extension may, under the general rule noted above, discharge a guarantor.[148] The extension of time may, as noted, result in discharge even where there is no injury to the guarantor.[149]

For an extension of time to discharge a guarantor, however, there must be a binding agreement for the extension of the payment terms. A mere indulgence granted to a primary obligor does not discharge a guarantor.[150] And, of course, a guarantor is not discharged if the guarantor consents to the extension.[151]

The rule that an extension of time will result in discharge is relaxed in the case of compensated sureties and in the surety bond context, as to which the discharge is limited to the extent of injury suffered by the surety.[152] The rule that a suretyship contract is to be construed *strictissimi juris* does not apply where the surety is a compensated surety.[153]

Further, in order for a discharge to occur as a result of a modification of the underlying obligation, there must be a binding agreement affecting the underlying obligation. A guarantor is not discharged as a result of an independent contract between the primary obligor and the obligee, even where the subject matter of that independent contract is the same as that to which the guaranty relates.[154] Likewise, the granting by the primary obligor of additional security to the obligee does not discharge the surety.[155]

The foregoing rule that a material alteration in the terms of the underlying obligation may discharge the guarantor even absent injury does not, however, apply where the underlying obligation is a negotiable instrument and the guarantor is a party to the instrument. The common law rule has been displaced by statute; under Section 3-605 of the South Carolina Uniform Commercial

146. *E.g.*, Sloan v. Latimer, 41 S.C. 217, 19 S.E. 491 (1894) (holding that six month extension of time for payment of Underlying Obligation discharged Guarantor).
147. *See Id;* Exchange Bank v. McMillan, 76 S.C. 561, 57 S.E. 630 (1907). *But cf.* Florentine Corp. v. Peda I, Inc., 287 S.C. 382, 339 S.E.2d 112 (1985) (enforcing guaranties after change in Underlying Obligation in part because there was no showing of a material change in the Underlying Obligation or prejudice to the Guarantor).
148. *E.g.*, Providence Mach. Co. v. Browning, 70 S.C. 148, 49 S.E. 325 (1904).
149. Kennedy v. Adickes, 37 S.C. 174, 15 S.E. 922 (1892).
150. *E.g.*, Seven Lakes Inv. Group, Inc. v. Crowe, 297 S.C. 534, 377 S.E.2d 576 (1989).
151. *E.g.*, Sawyer v. Senn, 27 S.C. 251, 3 S.E. 298 (1887).
152. *See, e.g.*, Plyler v. United States Fidelity & Guaranty Co., 144 S.C. 105, 142 S.E. 45 (1928); Lee v. Angelos, 123 S.C. 232, 116 S.E. 447 (1923) (holding paid sureties liable to the extent of the underlying obligation as in effect prior to modification).
153. *See, e.g.*, Greenville Airport Com. v. United States Fidelity & Guaranty Co., 226 S.C. 553, 86 S.E.2d 249 (1955); Walker v. Holtzclaw, 57 S.C. 459, 35 S.E. 754 (1900).
154. *E.g.*, Waddell v. Cary, 155 S.C. 152, 152 S.E. 179 (1930) (holding that a separate agreement between the obligee and the primary obligor for the payment of a higher interest rate does not affect the obligations of the guarantor).
155. Providence Mach. Co. v. Browning, 70 S.C. 148, 49 S.E. 325 (1904).

Code, a guarantor is discharged by an extension of time granted the primary obligor only to the extent of the injury suffered by the guarantor.[156]

The acceptance by the obligee of new promissory notes from the primary obligor will extinguish the liability subject to the guaranty, and thus discharge the guarantor, unless a contrary intent of the parties is shown, such as where the parties contemplated the delivery of the promissory notes at the time of the execution of the guaranty.[157] Likewise, no discharge will occur by the obligee's acceptance of new promissory notes, where the notes were intended as additional security.[158]

Finally, a modification of underlying obligation that has been consented to by the guarantor or is contemplated by the guaranty will not result in the discharge of the guarantor.[159]

7.2.3 Release or Impairment of Security for the Underlying Obligation

A guarantor will be discharged by acts of the obligee that impair the security for the underlying obligation and thus the remedies of the guarantor against the primary obligor; the extent of the discharge, however, is limited to the extent of the value of the collateral or the injury to the surety.[160]

Likewise, where an obligee has control of property of the primary obligor (such as a check made payable jointly to the obligee and the primary obligor, or proceeds of collateral or other funds owed by third parties to the primary obligor), out of which the obligee might satisfy the underlying obligation, but does not, then the surety is discharged.[161]

Where the collateral for the underlying obligation is lost or dissipated as a result of negligence of lack of due diligence on the part of the obligee, the guarantor may not assert such loss or dissipation as a defense.[162] Rather, the acts of an obligee sufficient to discharge a guarantor must be of a positive character, and not a mere omission, and those acts must have caused actual injury to the guarantor.[163] Thus, for example, the misapplication by the obligee of funds of the primary obligor that should have been applied to the underlying obligation will discharge the guarantor.[164] On the other hand, an omission such as failing to record a mortgage may not result in discharge.[165]

---

156. S.C. CODE ANN. § 36-3-605(b)(2) (Cum. Supp. 2011).
157. Providence Mach. Co. v. Browning, 72 S.C. 424, 52 S.E. 117 (1905).
158. *Id.*
159. *E.g.*, Florentine Corp. v. Peda I, Inc., 287 S.C. 382, 339 S.E.2d 112 (1985).
160. *See, e.g.*, Edge v. Klutts Resort Realty, Inc., 276 S.C. 389, 278 S.E.2d 783 (1981); Exchange Bank v. McMillan, 76 S.C. 561, 57 S.E. 630 (1907).
161. *See, e.g.*, Exchange Bank v. McDill, 56 S.C. 565, 35 S.E. 260 (1900); Rosborough v. McAliley, 10 S.C. 235 (1878); Glidden Coatings & Resins, Div. of SCM Corp. v. Suitt Constr. Co., 290 S.C. 240, 349 S.E.2d 89 (Ct. App. 1986).
162. Anderson v. Trust Co. Bank (In re Southco, Inc.), 168 B.R. 95 (Bankr. D.S.C. 1994); Bankers Trust of South Carolina v. Collins, 270 S.C. 26, 239 S.E.2d 889 (1977).
163. *See, e.g.*, Brannon v. Harris, 117 S.C. 423, 109 S.E. 396 (1921).
164. Rosborough v. McAliley, 10 S.C. 235 (1878).
165. Brannon v. Harris, 117 S.C. 423, 109 S.E. 396 (1921); Arthur v. Brown, 91 S.C. 316, 74 S.E. 652 (1912).

If, however, the guarantor has affirmatively requested the obligee to perform the acts left undone, then the failure of the obligee to perform those acts may discharge the guarantor.[166]

Where the guarantor consents to the release of collateral, that release does not result in a discharge of the guarantor.[167] And although the release of collateral by an obligee may discharge a guarantor, the taking of additional collateral will not.[168] Likewise, a guarantor has no right to require an obligee to accept additional security, and thus the failure of the obligee to accept that additional security is not a defense to the guaranty.[169]

A related question to the effect of the release of collateral is the effect of the release of one or more other guarantors. The general rule is that at law the release of one guarantor operates to discharge the other guarantors.[170] In equity, however, the other guarantors will not be released if the intention of the parties was not to effect a release of the other guarantors.[171]

The effect of a composition or settlement between an obligee and less than all the guarantors is governed by statute. Any joint debtor may make a separate composition with the obligee.[172] The term "joint debtor" in the statute is broad, and includes guarantors and sureties, whether jointly liable or jointly and severally liable.[173] Such a composition shall discharge only the guarantor making the composition.[174] The liability of the other guarantors shall continue, but shall be reduced by the amount actually paid (and not by the amount of the debt compounded).[175]

The death of one guarantor will not discharge a coguarantor, and the estate of the deceased coguarantor will be liable for the contractual obligations of the deceased coguarantor. *See Susong v. Vaiden*, 10 S.C. 247 (1878).

7.3 Other Defenses

7.3.1 Failure to Fulfill a Condition Precedent

A guarantor may raise the failure of a condition precedent as a defense to an action on a guaranty.[176] The determination of whether a guaranty incorporates a condition precedent to its enforcement is to be made based upon the terms of the guaranty agreement itself.[177] Phrases and words such as "subject to," "if," "when," and "after" are recognized as frequently indicating an intent to create a condition precedent.[178]

---

166. *E.g.*, Jackson v. Patrick, 10 S.C. 197 (1878).
167. *See, e.g.*, Anderson v. Trust Co. Bank (In re Southco, Inc.), 168 B.R. 95 (Bankr. D.S.C. 1994).
168. *E.g.*, Exchange Bank v. McMillan, 76 S.C. 561, 57 S.E. 630 (1907).
169. Rouss v. King, 69 S.C. 168, 48 S.E. 220 (1904).
170. *E.g.*, Poole v. Bradham, 143 S.C. 156, 141 S.E. 267 (1927).
171. *Id.*
172. S.C. CODE ANN. § 32-9-10 (2007).
173. Meyer v. Bouchier, 107 S.C. 254, 92 S.E. 471 (1917); Symmes v. Cauble, 72 S.C. 330, 51 S.E. 862 (1905).
174. S.C. CODE ANN. § 32-9-10 (2007).
175. S.C. CODE ANN. § 32-9-30 (2007); Meyer v. Bouchier, 107 S.C. 254, 92 S.E. 471 (1917).
176. Buckeye Cotton Oil Co. v. Cheraw Ginning Co., 142 S.C. 247, 140 S.E. 581 (1927).
177. Tri-South Mortgage Investors v. Fountain, 266 S.C. 141, 221 S.E.2d 861 (1976), *rev'd on other grounds, by* SCN Mortgage Corp. v. White, 312 S.C. 384, 440 S.E.2d 868 (1994).
178. *E.g.*, Springs & Davenport, Inc. v. AAG, Inc., 385 S.C. 320, 683 S.E.2d 814 (Ct. App. 2009).

If no condition precedent is set forth in the guaranty, the court will find that it is an absolute guaranty.[179] The courts will not imply a condition precedent when the parties could have expressly provided for one in their agreement.[180]

Generally, under an absolute guaranty there is no condition precedent to the liability of the guarantor, except for the failure of the primary obligor to perform as agreed.[181] Where, however, the guaranty is given in consideration of the obligee's agreement to forbear from action against the primary obligor, subsequent, actual forbearance is a condition precedent to the obligation of the guarantor.[182]

7.3.2 Modification of the Guaranty

A guarantor seeking to rely upon a modification of the guaranty must show both that the modification is embodied in a writing signed by the obligee, and that the modification is supported by consideration. In general, a written contract may be amended by an oral agreement, even if the contract states that any amendment must be in writing.[183] Nevertheless, a modification of a guaranty must be in writing, under the rule that if the original contract is subject to the statute of frauds, and thus required to be in writing, any modification must likewise be in writing.[184]

In addition to the traditional statute of frauds relating to promises to answer for the debt of another, South Carolina has adopted a specific statute of frauds relating to lending transactions.[185] Under this statute, absent a writing signed by the party to be charged, no person may assert a defense based upon failure to perform an alleged agreement to renew, modify, amend, or cancel any provision with respect to the loan of money.[186] Further, the statute specifically precludes remedies based on course of dealing or performance, estoppel, negligent misrepresentation, and, in most cases, part performance.[187] The effect of the statute, together with the traditional statute of frauds, is to effectively preclude reliance by a guarantor on an oral modification of the guaranty as a defense.

Modification of a contract is South Carolina generally requires consideration to be enforceable, and this rule applies to modifications of guaranties.[188] Thus, for example, a guarantor cannot enforce a subsequent agreement by which the guaranty was terminated, unless the guarantor can show consideration for that subsequent agreement.[189] Likewise, a guarantor cannot rely on an

---

179. *E.g.*, McGee v. F. W. Poe Mfg. Co., 176 S.C. 288, 180 S.E. 48 (1935).
180. *E.g.*, Plantation A.D., LLC v. Gerald Builders of Conway, Inc., 386 S.C. 198, 687 S.E.2d 714 (Ct. App. 2009).
181. *E.g.*, Tri-South Mortgage Investors v. Fountain, 266 S.C. 141, 221 S.E.2d 861 (1976), *rev'd on other grounds* by SCN Mortgage Corp. v. White, 312 S.C. 384, 440 S.E.2d 868 (1994).
182. Lowndes v. McCabe Fertilizer *Co.*, 157 S.C. 371, 154 S.E. 641 (1930).
183. *E.g.*, Lazer Constr. Co. v. Long, 296 S.C. 127, 370 S.E.2d 900 (Ct. App. 1988).
184. *E.g.*, Windham v. Honeycutt, 279 S.C. 109, 302 S.E.2d 856 (S.C. 1983).
185. *See* S.C. CODE ANN. § 37-10-107 (2002).
186. *Id.*
187. *Id.*
188. *See, e.g.*, Federal Deposit Ins. Corp. v. Waldron, 630 F.2d 239 (4th. S.C. 1980); Rabon v. State Finance Corp., 203 S.C. 183, 26 S.E.2d 501(1943).
189. Federal Deposit Ins. Corp. V. Waldron, 472 F. Supp. 21 (D.S.C. 1979), *aff'd* 630 F.2d 239 (4th Cir. S.C. 1980).

alleged agreement to extend the payment terms of the underlying obligation, absent consideration for the extension.[190]

7.3.3 Failure to Pursue Primary Obligor

Under an absolute guaranty, the obligee has no obligation to pursue the primary obligor, to give notice of nonpayment to the guarantor, or to use diligence in pursuing the primary obligor.[191]

7.3.4 Statute of Limitations

If the terms of the guaranty establish that it is an instrument under seal, the applicable statute of limitations will be 20 years.[192] Whether or not the guaranty is an instrument under seal, the statute of limitations will be 20 years if the guaranty is secured by a mortgage of real property.[193] The effect of this latter statute is to conform the statute of limitations applicable to an instrument secured by a real estate mortgage with the 20-year general statute of limitations applicable to the enforcement of the mortgage itself.[194]

If the guaranty is not deemed an instrument under seal, then the general statute of limitations applicable to contracts applies; that limitation period is three years.[195] Even if the guaranty lacks a physical seal, it may be determined to be an instrument under seal if "it shall appear from the attestation clause or from any other part … that it was the intention of the party or parties thereto that such instrument should be a sealed instrument …."[196]

A contractual provision purporting to shorten the applicable statute of limitations is not enforceable.[197] The enforceability of a contractual provision purporting to extend the applicable statute of limitations has not been decided, but the South Carolina courts have emphasized the important public policy considerations embodied in the statutes of limitations, and thus the enforceability of such provision is doubtful.[198]

After the expiration of the statute of limitations, the underlying obligation may be revived by part payment made by the primary obligor, or by a written acknowledgment of the indebtedness.[199] This revival by a primary obligor of

190. In re Kash & Karry Wholesale, Inc., 28 B.R. 66 (Bankr. D.S.C. 1982).
191. *E.g.*, Georgian Company v. Britton, 141 S.C. 136, 139 S.E. 217 (1927); Providence Machine Co. v. Browning, 68 S.C. 1, 46 S.E. 550 (1903).
192. S.C. CODE ANN. § 15-3-520 (b) (2005).
193. *See* S.C. CODE ANN. § 15-3-520 (a).
194. *See* S.C. CODE ANN. § 29-1-10 (2007).
195. S.C. CODE ANN. § 15-3-530 (1) (2005).
196. *See* S.C. CODE ANN. § 19-1-160 (1976). *But see* Carolina Marine Handling v. Lasch, 363 S.C. 169, 609 S.E.2d 548 (Ct. App. 2005) (finding the language "the parties have hereunto set their hands and seals" insufficient to establish intent to create a sealed instrument).
197. S.C. CODE ANN. § 15-3-140 (2005).
198. *Cf.* Carolina Marine Handling v. Lasch, 363 S.C. 169, 609 S.E.2d 548 (Ct. App. 2005) ("Statutes of limitations embody important public policy considerations in that they stimulate activity, punish negligence, and promote repose by giving security and stability to human affairs.") (citations omitted).
199. Cross v. Stackhouse, 212 S.C. 100, 46 S.E.2d 668 (1948); Butts v. Georgetown Mut. Bldg. & Loan Ass'n, 142 S.C. 353, 140 S.E. 700 (1927).

the otherwise barred indebtedness does not, however, effect a revival as to a guarantor, who still may rely upon the statute of limitations.[200]

The statute of limitations with respect to the claim by a coguarantor for contribution is three years.[201] The statute does not begin to run, however, until the coguarantor seeking contribution has actually made payment.[202]

7.3.5 Statute of Frauds

If the guaranty is an oral guaranty, the guarantor may raise the defense of the statute of frauds,[203] as a promise to answer for the debt of another must be in writing and signed by the party to be charged.[204] The writing, moreover, must contain all of the essential terms of the contract.[205] The writing need not, however, state the consideration for the guaranty.[206] Where the liability of the guarantor arises by way of endorsement of a promissory note evidencing or comprising the underlying obligation, the endorsement signature itself satisfies the statute of frauds.[207]

There are two principal exceptions to the statute of frauds as it relates to guaranties. First, the statute of frauds does not apply where the main purpose of the alleged guarantor's promise is to benefit the guarantor.[208] Under this exception, for example, a promisor owning substantially all of the stock of the corporation may under certain circumstances be deemed to be acting for his own benefit in agreeing to pay the debts of the corporation.[209]

The court must examine the facts and circumstances of each case in order to determine, based on the intent of the parties, whether an alleged guaranty falls within the "main purpose" or "original undertaking" exceptions to the statute of frauds.[210] Generally, the court must find a direct benefit to the promisor for the promise to come within this exception to the statute of frauds.[211]

Second, the statute of frauds does not apply where the agreement to pay the debt of another is an original undertaking between the promisor and the creditor, and is not collateral to the debt.[212] Under this exception, where a promise is made to pay an existing debt of another, and that promise is based on a new and original consideration consisting of a benefit or detriment

---

200. *See, e.g.*, Butts v. Georgetown Mut. Bldg. & Loan Ass'n, 142 S.C. 353, 140 S.E. 700 (1927).
201. *See* .C. Code Ann. § 15-3-530 (2005).
202. *See, e.g., McCrady v. Jones,* 44 S.C. 406, 22 S.E. 414 (1895)
203. *See, e.g.,* Fort v. Magnolia Mfg. Co. (In re Spartan Int'l) (Bankr. D.S.C. Dec. 16, 2005).
204. S.C. CODE ANN. § 32-3-10 (2) (2007).
205. *See, e.g.*, Fort v. Magnolia Mfg. Co. (In re Spartan Int'l), 2005 Bankr. LEXIS 2740 (Bankr. D.S.C. Dec. 16, 2005); Ruff v. Hudspeth, 122 S.C. 391, 115 S.E. 626 (1923). *But see* Griffin Bro. & Co. v. Rembert, 2 S.C. 410 (S.C. 1871) (Guaranty need not specify the name of the obligee, but may be for the benefit of creditors generally).
206. Griffin Bro. & Co. v. Rembert, 2 S.C. 410 (1871).
207. *See, e.g.*, Sloan v. Gibbes, 56 S.C. 480, 35 S.E. 408 (1900).
208. *E.g.*, General Electric Co. v. Gate, 273 S.C. 88, 254 S.E.2d 305 (1979).
209. De Witt Truck Brokers, Inc. v. W. Ray Flemming Fruit Co., 540 F.2d 681 (4th Cir. 1976); American Wholesale Corp. v. Mauldin, 128 S.C. 241, 122 S.E. 576 (1924). *But see* Turner v. Lyles, 68 S.C. 392, 48 S.E. 301 (1904) (holding unenforceable an oral promise by shareholder holding 499 of 500 outstanding shares of the primary obligor).
210. *E.g.*, General Electric Co. v. Gate, 273 S.C. 88, 254 S.E.2d 305 (1979); Stackhouse v. Pure Oil Co., 176 S.C. 318, 180 S.E. 188, 193 (1935).
211. Fort v. Magnolia Mfg. Co. (In re Spartan Int'l), 2005 Bankr. LEXIS 2740 (Bankr. D.S.C. Dec. 16, 2005).
212. *E.g.*, General Electric Co. v. Gate, 273 S.C. 88, 254 S.E.2d 305 (1979); Williams v. Caldwell, 4 S.C. 100 (1873).

moving between the new promisor and the creditor, then the promise is not within the statute of frauds.[213]

Although generally partial performance may take a contract out of the statute of frauds, this rule does not apply to guaranties. Partial or full performance of a promise to answer for the debt of another does not remove the promise from the scope of the statute of frauds.[214]

As noted above, if a contract is subject to the statute of frauds and thus required to be in writing, as is the case with a guaranty, then under the statute of frauds any modification must be in writing.[215]

Finally, the South Carolina courts view the statute of frauds as remedial, with the result that the applicable statute of frauds in the forum state will be applied, rather than the law of the state that governs the substantive terms of the guaranty.[216]

7.3.6 Defenses Particular to Guarantors that are Natural Persons and their Spouses

A guarantor who is a natural person may assert a defense that the guarantor was incompetent at the time of execution of the guaranty. Instruments executed by persons lacking legal competence are void.[217] There is a presumption, however, of mental competency, and thus the burden of proof as to mental incompetency is upon the one seeking to establish it.[218]

A guarantor who is a natural person may also assert a defense of minority. As noted above, a guaranty executed by a minor is voidable by the minor at his option upon reaching the age of majority, and if not specifically affirmed at that time, will be deemed void.[219]

7.4 Right of Set-off

A guarantor may assert a set-off of his obligations under the guaranty for obligations of the obligee to the guarantor.[220]

7.5 Assignment of Underlying Obligation

Unless the underlying obligation or the guaranty instrument provides to the contrary, the assignment of the underlying obligation does not release a guarantor.[221] The assignment of the principal obligation operates as an assignment of the guaranty.[222]

---

213. American Wholesale Corp. v. Mauldin, 128 S.C. 241, 122 S.E. 526 (1924).
214. Dewitt v. Kelly, 256 S.C. 224, 182 S.E.2d 65 (1971).
215. *E.g.*, Windham v. Honeycutt, 279 S.C. 109, 302 S.E.2d 856 (S.C. 1983). *See* the discussion in Section 7.3.2 above.
216. *See* Cooper v. A.A.A. Highway Express, Inc., 206 S.C. 372, 34 S.E.2d 589 (1945).
217. *E.g.*, Shepard v. First American Mortgage Co., 289 S.C. 516, 347 S.E.2d 118 (Ct. App. 1986).
218. *E.g.*, Lincoln Nat'l Life Ins. Co. v. Parker, 2011 U.S. Dist. LEXIS 76293 (D.S.C. July 13, 2011).
219. State v. Satterwhite, 20 S.C. 536 (1884); Williams v. Harrison, 11 S.C. 412 (1878). *See* the discussion in Section 2.5 above.
220. Ex parte Rice, 161 S.C. 77, 159 S.E. 4 (1931).
221. AMA Management Corp. v. Strasburger, 309 S.C. 213, 420 S.E.2d 868, 1992 (Ct. App. 1992).
222. *Id.*

7.6 Misrepresentation and Fraud in the Inducement

A guarantor may not raise a defense based on misrepresentations by the obligee as to the contents of the guaranty.[223] The South Carolina courts have rejected the position taken by the Restatement of Torts,[224] to the effect that the recipient of a fraudulent misrepresentation may rely on its truth even though its falsity was ascertainable.[225]

The South Carolina courts enforce as a matter of public policy the doctrine that every person signing an instrument has a duty to read the instrument. Thus, a guarantor cannot avoid its guaranty obligations by claiming not to have read the guaranty.[226] Likewise, a guarantor may not avoid the effect of waivers contained in the guaranty by claiming ignorance of its contents.[227]

A guarantor may, however, on other grounds raise a defense of fraud in the inducement relating to the execution of the guaranty. [228]

§ 8 Waiver of Defenses by the Guarantor

Subject to limited exceptions, waivers of defenses made by a guarantor will be enforced as written.

8.1 Defenses that cannot be Waived

Certain waivers are unenforceable as a matter of public policy. A waiver of the benefit of the statute of limitations is likely unenforceable.[229] A waiver of a defense based on the invalidity of the underlying obligation is likely unenforceable, where the invalidity arises from the underlying obligation being part of a contract void as in violation of public policy.[230]

A forum selection clause under which a guarantor waives a right to bring an action in the South Carolina courts that is otherwise within the jurisdiction of those courts may be unenforceable.[231]

A waiver of the right to assert a counterclaim will not be enforceable, to the extent the waiver purports to extend to compulsory counterclaims, on the grounds that such a waiver would impermissibly alter the applicable rules of civil procedure.[232]

---

223. *See, e.g.*, Burwell v. South Carolina Nat'l Bank, 288 S.C. 34, 340 S.E.2d 786 (1986).
224. Restatement (Second) of Torts § 540 (1979).
225. *See* Slack v. James, 364 S.C. 609, 614 S.E.2d 636 (2005).
226. *See, e.g.*, Burwell v. South Carolina Nat'l Bank, 288 S.C. 34, 340 S.E.2d 786 (1986).
227. *See, e.g.*, Wachovia Bank v. Blackburn, 394 S.C. 579, 716 S.E.2d 454 (Ct. App. 2011); Regions Bank v. Schmauch, 354 S.C. 648, 582 S.E.2d 432 (Ct. App. 2003).
228. *See, e.g.*, Collins Music Co. v. FMW Corp., 355 S.C. 446, 586 S.E.2d 128 (2003).
229. Carolina Marine Handling v. Lasch, 363 S.C. 169, 609 S.E.2d 548 (Ct. App. 2005). *See* the discussion in Section 7.3.4 above.
230. *See* Liberty Mut. Ins. Co. v. Gilreath, 191 S.C. 244, 4 S.E.2d 126 (1939).
231. S.C. Code Ann. § 17-7-120(A).
232. *See* Beach Co. v. Twillman, Ltd., 351 S.C. 56, 566 S.E.2d 863 (Ct. App. 2002).

8.2 "Catch-all" Waivers

General waivers of "all suretyship defenses" have been enforced in South Carolina.[233]

8.3 Use of Specific Waivers

Because waivers will be enforced, but strictly construed, it is advisable to use specific waivers in addition to blanket or "catch-all" waivers. Most specific waivers have been enforced, as follows.

Waivers of jury trial are enforceable, but will be strictly construed as to the causes of action deemed to be within the scope of the waiver.[234] For example, a waiver of jury trial as to actions on the guaranty itself may be construed, absent clear and unambiguous language to the contrary, not to apply to counterclaims of the guarantor against the obligee.[235] Further, a waiver of jury trial that is set forth in the underlying obligation, but not in the guaranty, will not be binding on the guarantor.[236]

A waiver of personal service of process and the appointment of an agent for service that is affiliated with the obligee is enforceable.[237] Likewise, an agreement to submit to the jurisdiction of a foreign forum is acceptable, so long as there is a reasonable nexus between that forum and the transaction.[238] Further, forum selection clauses are "prima facie valid and enforceable when made at arm's length by sophisticated business entities, absent a compelling reason for abrogation."[239]

Waivers of the right to invoke the South Carolina antideficiency statute applicable to mortgage foreclosures are enforceable, but the guarantor must be given notice prior to the transaction that the waiver will be required, and during the transaction the guarantor must have executed a waiver of the guarantor's rights under the statute.[240] The required wording and format of the waiver is set forth in that statute.[241]

§ 9 Third-party Pledgors—Defenses and Waiver Thereof

Third-party pledgors of collateral are considered sureties under South Carolina law, and may assert suretyship defenses.

233. *See* Ameris Bank v. Sailing Vessel "Yemaya," 2011 U.S. Dist. LEXIS 95736 (D.S.C. Aug. 25, 2011).
234. *E.g.,* Wachovia Bank v. Blackburn, 394 S.C. 579, 716 S.E.2d 454 (Ct. App. 2011).
235. *Id.*
236. *See* North Charleston Joint Venture v. Kitchens of Island Fudge Shoppe, 307 S.C. 533, 416 S.E.2d 637 (1992).
237. Fin. Fed. Credit, Inc. v. Brown, 384 S.C. 555, 683 S.E.2d 486 (2009).
238. *Id.*
239. *Id.* Republic Leasing Company, Inc. v. Haywood, 329 S.C. 562 at 566, 495 S.E.2d 804 (1998) *vacated on other grounds,* 335 S.C. 207, 516 S.E.2d 441 (S.C. 1999). *But see* S.C. Code Ann. § 15-17-120(A).
240. *See* S.C. Code Ann. § 29-3-680 (2007).
241. *See Id.*

Under South Carolina law, third-party pledgors of collateral are considered sureties, and the discussion above as to waivers of suretyship defenses is applicable to such sureties.[242] Any act that would discharge a surety or guarantor will discharge the pledgor.[243]

§ 10 Jointly and Severally Liable Guarantors—Contribution and Reduction of Obligations upon Payment by a Co-obligor

Guarantors who are jointly and severally liable are, absent an agreement to the contrary, equally liable for the underlying obligation. The allocation of liability among guarantors may, however, be changed by agreement. A guarantor who has paid more than his proportionate share is entitled to contribution from the other guarantors.

10.1 Contribution

A guarantor that has paid the underlying obligation, or a disproportionate share of the underlying obligation, has a right of contribution from his coguarantors.[244] Absent an agreement to the contrary, coguarantors are presumed to have equal liability for the underlying obligation.[245] Where, however, one of the coguarantors is insolvent, the contributions must be in proportion to the number of solvent guarantors.[246]

The coguarantors can alter their respective liabilities by separate agreement.[247] This separate agreement need not be in writing, and may be proved by parol evidence.[248] Where there is such a separate agreement between the coguarantors that specifies the amount for which each will be liable, no guarantor will have a right of contribution until that guarantor has paid more than that guarantor's agreed-upon share.[249]

A composition or settlement and release between the obligee and any one guarantor does not alter these contribution rights and obligations. By statute, an obligee can make a composition with any one of multiple guarantors, under which the obligee agrees to accept a compromise amount from the guarantor in exchange for a release of that guarantor.[250] The noncompounding guarantors remain entitled to seek contribution from the compounding guarantor for the full amount of the compounding guarantor's share of the underlying obligation.

242. *See, e.g.*, Wood v. Babb, 16 S.C. 427 (1882).
243. *Id.*
244. *E.g.*, Babb v. Rothrock, 303 S.C. 462, 401 S.E.2d 418 (1991); In re Rock Hill Cotton Factory Co., 68 S.C. 436, 47 S.E. 728 (1904); Gourdin v. Trenholm, 25 S.C. 362 (1886).
245. *E.g.*, Canaday v. Boliver, 25 S.C. 547 (1886).
246. Sloan v. Gibbes, 56 S.C. 480, 35 S.E. 408 (1900).
247. *See, e.g.*, Gourdin v. Trenholm, 25 S.C. 362 (1886).
248. *See, e.g.*, Sloan v. Gibbes, 56 S.C. 480, 35 S.E. 408 (1900).
249. Gourdin v. Trenholm, 25 S.C. 362 (1886).
250. S.C. Code Ann. § 32-9-10 (2007).

As to claims by the obligee, the noncompounding guarantors are entitled to a credit only for the amount actually paid by the compounding guarantor.[251]

A coguarantor may forfeit the right of contribution, if that coguarantor impairs the security granted to the guarantors.[252]

In addition to the right of contribution, a guarantor has the right of exoneration. If the underlying obligation is due, but the guarantor has not yet made any payment, the guarantor may nevertheless require any coguarantors to contribute toward raising funds sufficient to pay the underlying obligation.[253] Under the same circumstance, a guarantor who holds a mortgage as security for the guaranty may bring an action to foreclose the mortgage even though the guarantor has not yet made payment.[254]

10.2 Reduction of Obligations upon Payment of Co-obligor

The payment made by a guarantor on the underlying obligation reduces the amount recoverable by the obligee from the other guarantors.[255] Where an obligee reaches a settlement with a coguarantor, under which the coguarantor pays less than his pro rata share in return for a release, the other coguarantors are entitled to a reduction of their liabilities in the amount actually paid, and not the settling guarantor's full pro rata share of the indebtedness.[256]

10.3 Liability of Parent Guarantors Owning less than 100 percent of Primary Obligor

There are no South Carolina authorities addressing this topic.

§ 11 Reliance

Reliance is not required to claim under a guaranty.

Under South Carolina law, reliance is not necessary in order to render a guaranty enforceable.

§ 12 Subrogation

Subrogation is an equitable remedy, allowing a guarantor who has paid the underlying obligation in full to exercise the rights and remedies otherwise available to the obligee against the primary obligor.

251. S.C. Code Ann. §§ 32-9-10 to -20 (2007); Meyer v. Bouchier, 107 S.C. 254, 92 S.E. 471 (1917).
252. Butler v. Spencer, 116 S.C. 177, 107 S.E. 154 (1921).
253. *E.g.*, Massey v. Brown, 4 S.C. 85 (1873).
254. *See, e.g.*, Beasley v. Newell, 40 S.C. 16, 18 S.E. 224 (1893); Hellams v. Abercrombie, 15 S.C. 110 (1881).
255. 4 Amigos, LLC v. Carolina Bueno, LLC, 2011 U.S. Dist. LEXIS 54932 (D.S.C. May 20, 2011); Symmes v. Cauble, 72 S.C. 330, 51 S.E. 862 (1905).
256. S.C. Code Ann. §§ 32-9-10 & 20 (2007); Meyer v. Bouchier, 107 S.C. 254, 92 S.E. 471 (1917).

The general rule is that a guarantor who pays the underlying obligation has a right to be subrogated to the claims of the obligee against the primary obligor, as well as all other remedies which the obligee may have against the primary obligor or any other parties liable for the underlying obligation.[257] A guarantor is not entitled to subrogation, however, unless the obligee has been paid in full.[258] Where the obligation of the primary obligor to the obligee has been reduced to judgment, the payment by the guarantor does not satisfy the judgment; rather, the guarantor has the right to be subrogated to the position of the judgment holder.[259]

The right of subrogation, however, is an equitable and not absolute right, and a surety seeking subrogation must have greater equities than the party against whom the right is asserted.[260] Based on this principal, a paid surety—which has fewer equities than a gratuitous surety—may be denied subrogation to the rights of the obligee against a primary obligor.[261]

Generally, the party seeking subrogation must have been "secondarily liable" for the underlying obligation.[262] Arguably, to the extent the guaranty includes language making the guarantor primarily liable for the underlying obligation, and that language is given effect, the remedy of subrogation may become unavailable to the guarantor.

§ 13 Triangular Set-off in Bankruptcy

There are no South Carolina authorities addressing this topic.

§ 14 Indemnification—Whether the Primary Obligor has a Duty

A guarantor that has paid the underlying obligation is entitled to indemnity from the primary obligor. A guarantor may also have a right of exoneration by the primary obligor, even prior to payment by the guarantor.

A guarantor is entitled to indemnity from the primary obligor after the payment by the guarantor of the underlying obligation.[263]

Further, a guarantor may, where the underlying obligation is in default, have a right to exoneration by the underlying obligation, such that the

257. *See, e.g.*, Rivers v. Liberty Nat'l Bank, 135 S.C. 107, 133 S.E. 210 (1926); In re Rock Hill Cotton Factory Co., 68 S.C. 436, 47 S.E. 728 (1904).
258. *E.g.*, Pou v. South Carolina Warehousing Corp., 27 F.2d 418 (D.S.C. 1928).
259. Kinard v. Baird, 20 S.C. 377 (1884).
260. Bank of Ft. Mill v. Lawyers Title Ins. Corp., 268 F.2d 313 (4th Cir. 1959) (applying South Carolina law).
261. *Id. But see* South Carolina Nat'l Bank v. Lake City State Bank, 251 S.C. 500, 164 S.E.2d 103 (1968).
262. *See, e.g.*, Dunn v. Chapman, 149 S.C. 163, 146 S.E. 818 (1929).
263. *E.g.*, National Surety Co. v. Carsten, 159 S.C. 222, 156 S.E. 336 (1931); Hellams v. Abercrombie, 15 S.C. 110 (1881).

guarantor can compel the primary obligor to discharge the debt, even though the guarantor himself has not yet been sued.[264]

§ 15 Enforcement of Guaranties

15.1 Limitations on Recovery

Provisions intended to save guaranties from attack as fraudulent conveyances by limiting the amount that may be recovered under the guaranties have not been addressed by South Carolina law. Remedies under guaranties of performance are likely limited to monetary damages. Guarantors may but need not be joined in foreclosure actions relating to mortgages securing the underlying obligation.

There is no South Carolina authority as to the effectiveness of a provision in a guaranty limiting the liability of the guarantor to that amount which would not cause the guaranty to be a fraudulent transfer. South Carolina law does, however, recognize that a guaranty may be set aside as a fraudulent transfer.[265]

15.2 Enforcement of Guaranties of Payment versus Guaranties of Performance

Notwithstanding that the obligation of a guarantor under a guaranty may be nonmonetary in nature, the principal remedy available to the obligee appears to be damages.[266] Specific performance of the underlying obligation will not be granted if that remedy would require "continuous direction and supervision of the court."[267] Likewise, specific performance will not be granted where damages would be an adequate remedy.[268]

As a general rule, the damages recoverable by an obligee would consist of out-of-pocket costs actually incurred by the obligee as a result of the breach of the guaranty contract, including costs incurred by the obligee in obtaining substitute performance of the obligations of the guarantor, at least to the extent that the cost of substitute performance exceeds the original price for such performance.[269] In addition, the obligee may be entitled to recover lost profits or gain that would have been realized by the obligee had the guarantor performed.[270]

---

264. *E.g.*, Norton v. Reid, 11 S.C. 593 (1867).
265. *See, e.g.*, Future Group v. NationsBank, 324 S.C. 89, 478 S.E.2d 45 (1996) (finding a downstream guaranty unenforceable as a fraudulent transfer).
266. Generally, a guarantor under a guaranty of performance has the option of either performing on-demand, or paying damages for such nonperformance. *See, e.g.*, Chester v. National Surety Co., 91 S.C. 17, 74 S.E. 37 (1912).
267. Time Warner Cable v. Condo Servs., 381 S.C. 275, 672 S.E.2d 816 (Ct. App. 2009) (citations omitted).
268. *Id;* Spears v. Long, 32 S.C. 528, 11 S.E. 332 (1890).
269. Bryce Plumbing & Heating Co. v. Maryland Casualty Co., 21 F. Supp. 854 (D.S.C. 1938); South Carolina Federal Sav. Bank v. Thornton-Crosby Dev. Co., 1990 S.C. App. LEXIS 155 (S.C. Ct. App. Nov. 8, 1990), *aff'd* 310 S.C. 232, 423 S.E.2d 114 (1992).
270. South Carolina Federal Sav. Bank v. Thornton-Crosby Dev. Co., 310 S.C. 232, 423 S.E.2d 114 (1992).

15.3 Exercising Rights Under a Guaranty Where the Underlying Obligation is also Secured by a Mortgage

A guarantor may be joined as a defendant in a judicial foreclosure action[271] against the primary obligor.[272] A guarantor may alternatively be sued separately on his guaranty. A guarantor cannot require foreclosure of the mortgage as a condition of suit against the guarantor, nor can a guarantor require that the guarantor be joined as a party in the foreclosure action.[273] Likewise, once a mortgage foreclosure action has been commenced, the completion of the foreclosure and a determination of the deficiency remaining after application of the South Carolina antideficiency statute are not conditions precedent to the action against the guarantor.[274]

There are potential disadvantages to making a guarantor a party to a judicial mortgage foreclosure action. A mortgage foreclosure itself is an equitable action, and the primary obligor will not be entitled to a jury trial even though a judgment will be obtained on the promissory note.[275] A guarantor may, however, absent a waiver be entitled to a jury trial,[276] and thus joinder of the guarantor in the foreclosure may result in procedural complication and delay.

The second disadvantage to joining a guarantor as a defendant in a mortgage foreclosure action against the primary obligor is the possible application of the South Carolina antideficiency statute. That statute recalculates any deficiency judgment based on a hypothetical market value of the property at the time of the foreclosure sale, as such hypothetical value is determined by a panel of appraisers, and substitutes that hypothetical value for the actual sales price for purposes of determining the final deficiency.[277] This antideficiency statute is available, however, only to a defendant in a foreclosure proceeding.[278] Thus, by the simple expedient of not making a guarantor a party to the foreclosure proceeding itself, the guarantor will have no recourse to this antideficiency statute.[279] In any event, a guarantor may waive its rights under the South Carolina antideficiency statute, provided that the mortgage property is not a dwelling place.[280]

---

271. All foreclosures in South Carolina are judicial foreclosures, with the exception of the foreclosure of certain timeshare interests.
272. *E.g.*, Welborn v. Cobb, 92 S.C. 384, 75 S.E. 691 (1912).
273. Tri-South Mortgage Investors v. Fountain, 266 S.C. 141, 145, 221 S.E.2d 861, 863 (S.C. 1976), *rev'd on other grounds*, SCN Mortgage Corp. v. White, 312 S.C. 384, 386, 440 S.E.2d 868, 869 (S.C. 1994).
274. In re Kirven, 180 B.R. 438 (Bankr. D. S. C. 1995).
275. *E.g.*, Gardner v. Travis, 316 S.C. 315, 318, 450 S.E.2d 54, 56 (S.C. Ct. App. 1994); Rule 71(a), SCRCP.
276. *See, e.g.*, Georgian Co. v. Britton, 141 S.C. 136, 139 S.E. 17 (1927).
277. *See* S.C. Code Ann. § 29-3-680 to 770 (2007).
278. S.C. Code Ann. § 29-3-680(A) (2007).
279. *See, e.g.*, In re Kirven, 180 B.R. 438 (Bankr. D. S. C. 1995); Standard Fed. Sav. Bank v. H & W Builders, 323 S.C. 24, 448 S.E.2d 558 (1994); Anderson Bros. Bank v. Adams, 305 S.C. 25, 406 S.E.2d 173 (1991).
280. *See* S.C. Code Ann. § 29-3-680(B) (2007).

15.4 Litigating Guaranty Claims: Procedural Considerations

An action to enforce a guaranty is an action on a contract independent from the underlying obligation.[281] In order to prevail in an action on a guaranty, however, the obligee must prove that there is a valid underlying obligation.[282]

A guarantor is entitled to trial by jury,[283] but this right to trial by jury may be waived.[284] Any such waiver of jury trial, however, will be strictly construed.[285] For example, waivers of jury trials will not be construed to apply to counterclaims asserted by the guarantor, unless those counterclaims are closely related to the scope of the matters addressed in the waiver.[286]

A waiver of jury trial set forth in the underlying obligation but not in a separate guaranty itself will not be binding on the guarantor.[287]

An obligee may choose to proceed against the primary obligor, any one of the guarantors, or any combination thereof.[288] Under an absolute guaranty, the obligee may bring an action against the guarantor immediately upon default by the primary obligor.[289] Thus, in an action by an obligee against a guarantor, the guarantor may not require that the primary obligor be joined as a defendant, and the primary obligor is not deemed a necessary party.[290] By the same token, a guarantor may not object to joinder of the primary obligor in an action against the guarantor.[291]

To the extent that the terms of the guaranty establish that it is an instrument under seal, the applicable statute of limitations will be 20 years.[292] To the extent that the guaranty is not deemed an instrument under seal, the general statute of limitations applicable to contracts applies. That limitation period is three years.[293]

A waiver of personal service of process in a guaranty will be enforced, as will a provision in the guaranty designating a person related to the obligee as the attorney-in-fact for the guarantor to accept service.[294]

Where the guaranties are attached to the complaint, and no specific denial is made as to the validity of the signature or other affirmative defense raised, then the obligee is entitled to recover on the guaranty.[295]

---

281. Citizens & S. Nat'l Bank v. Lanford, 313 S.C. 540, 544, 443 S.E.2d 549, 551 (1994); Rock Hill Nat'l Bank v. Honeycutt, 289 S.C. 98, 344 S.E.2d 875 (Ct. App. 1986).
282. *E.g.*, Carroll Co. Sav. Bank v. Strother, 22 S.C. 552 (1885).
283. *E.g.*, Georgian Co. v. Britton, 141 S.C. 136, 139 S.E. 17 (1927).
284. *E.g.*, North Charleston Joint Venture v. Kitchens of Island Fudge Shoppe, 307 S.C. 533, 416 S.E.2d 637 (1992); Beach Co. v. Twillman, Ltd., 351 S.C. 56, 566 S.E.2d 863 (Ct. App. 2002).
285. North Charleston Joint Venture v. Kitchens of Island Fudge Shoppe, 307 S.C. 533, 534, 416 S.E.2d 637, 638 (1992); Beach Co. v. Twillman, Ltd., 351 S.C. 56, 64, 566 S.E.2d 863, 866 (Ct. App. 2002).
286. *E.g.*, Wachovia Bank v. Blackburn, 394 S.C. 579, 716 S.E.2d 454 (Ct. App. 2011).
287. *See* North Charleston Joint Venture v. Kitchens of Island Fudge Shoppe, 307 S.C. 533, 416 S.E.2d 637 (1992).
288. *E.g.*, Fin. Fed. Credit, Inc. v. Brown, 384 S.C. 555, 683 S.E.2d 486 (2009).
289. *E.g.*, Peoples Federal Sav. & Loan Ass'n v. Myrtle Beach Retirement Group, Inc., 300 S.C. 277, 387 S.E.2d 672 (1989).
290. *See* Smith v. Mandel, 66 F.R.D. 405 (D.S.C. 1975).
291. *See* Georgian Company v. Britton, 141 S.C. 136, 139 S.E. 217 (1927).
292. *See* S.C. Code Ann. § 15-3-520 (b) (2005).
293. S.C. Code Ann. § 15-3-530 (1) (2005).
294. *See* Fin. Fed. Credit, Inc. v. Brown, 384 S.C. 555, 683 S.E.2d 486 (2009).
295. National Equipment, Ltd. v. David Jones Sales, Trucking Div., Inc., 268 S.C. 551, 235 S.E.2d 125 (1977). *Accord* Branch Banking & Trust v. Riley, 2011 U.S. Dist. LEXIS 7699 (D.S.C. Jan. 25, 2011).

A guaranty that provides for attorneys' fees in an amount equal to a fixed percentage of the guaranteed debt is enforceable.[296] Where, however, the underlying obligation provides for attorneys' fees as a fixed percentage of the debt, but the guaranty only provides for "reasonable" attorneys' fees, the obligee may only collect reasonable attorneys' fees.[297]

Although there appears to be no South Carolina state court case on point, the federal courts for South Carolina have held that attorneys' fees are recoverable under a guaranty that has no attorneys' fee provision, if the promissory note the payment of which is guaranteed provides for attorneys' fees.[298]

§ 16 Revival and Reinstatement of Guaranties

A guaranty may be revived or reinstated if such revival or reinstatement is authorized by the terms of the guaranty.

A continuing guaranty may be revived after payment of the outstanding debt under certain circumstances, provided that the language of the guaranty supports such revival.[299]

296. Citizens & S. Nat'l Bank v. Easton, 310 S.C. 458, 427 S.E.2d 640 (1993).
297. First Savings Bank v. Capital Investors, 318 S.C. 555, 459 S.E.2d 307 (1995).
298. *See* Federal Deposit Ins. Corp. v. Fagan, 674 F.2d 302, 306-07 (4th Cir. 1982).
299. *See* Anderson v. Trust Co. Bank (In re Southco, Inc.), 168 B.R. 95 (Bankr. D.S.C. 1994) (reviving continuing guaranty of previously paid debt to the extent creditor was required to disgorge payments as a result of the bankruptcy of the primary obligor).

South Dakota State Law of Guaranties

Haven L. Stuck
Lynn, Jackson, Shultz & Lebrun, P.C.
909 St. Joseph Street, Suite 800
P.O. Box 8250
Rapid City, SD 57709
Tele: 605-342-2592
Fax: 605-342-5185
Email: hstuck@lynnjackson.com
Web Site: www.lynnjackson.com

Contents

South Dakota State Law of Guaranties

Highlights:

- A guarantor is exonerated if the creditor, without the consent of the guarantor, alters the original obligation of the principal debtor or causes the remedies or rights of the creditor against the principal debtor to be impaired or suspended. See § 7.3.1 below.
- A creditor may not recover attorneys' fees in an action against the guarantor of a note, bond, or other evidence of debt. *See* § 15 below.

The following terms and definitions are from South Dakota statutes and cases; however, their use is not consistent.

"**Guarantor**" means a person who, by contract, agrees to satisfy an original obligation of another to a creditor upon the principal debtor's default on that original obligation.

"**Guaranty**" is a promise to answer for the debt, default, or miscarriage of another person.

"**Creditor**" means the person to whom the original obligation is owed. For example, the lender under a loan agreement would be a creditor.

"**Principal Debtor**" means the person who incurs the original obligation to the creditor. For example, the borrower under a loan agreement would be a principal debtor.

"**Original Obligation**" means the obligation incurred by the principal debtor and owed to the creditor. For example, the borrower's obligation to make payments to a lender of principal and interest on a loan constitutes an original obligation. An original obligation is sometimes referred to as an underlying obligation.

Introduction and sources of law: South Dakota statutes on guaranty and suretyship are found in South Dakota Codified Laws (SDCL), Title 56, Chapters 1 and 2. The Supreme Court of South Dakota has cited to the Restatement of the Law, Security.[1]

1. *See* McLaughlin Elec. Supply v. American Empire Ins. Co., 269 N.W.2d 766, 768 (S.D. 1978).

§ 1 Nature of the Guaranty Arrangement

1.1 Guaranty Relationships

"A guaranty is a promise to answer for the debt, default, or miscarriage of another person." [2] "A guaranty creates nothing more than a contract to pay the debt of another"; a guaranty does not create a fiduciary relationship.[3] "It is a contract on the part of one person which is collateral to the principal obligation of another." [4] "A guaranty creates a secondary liability or responsibility to pay only if another does not." [5]

Use of the term "guaranty" is not conclusive of an intent to enter into a guaranty as opposed to another type of agreement. The writing must be read in light of all the surrounding circumstances to determine whether a guaranty was intended.[6] Each case must be resolved on its particular facts when determining whether a guaranty or another type of agreement was intended.[7]

1.2 Guaranty Requirements

If a guaranty is entered into at the same time as the original obligation or with the acceptance of the original obligation by the creditor[8] and forms, with that obligation, part of the consideration to the guarantor, no other consideration is required. In all other cases there must be consideration distinct from that of the original obligation. [9] A guaranty must be in writing and signed by the guarantor unless an exception applies (see section 7.3.3). The writing does not need to express consideration.[10]

1.3 Suretyship Relationships

"Suretyship is a contract by which one who at the request of another and for the purpose of securing to him a benefit becomes responsible for the performance by the latter of some act in favor of a third person or hypothecates property as security therefor."[11] If a debt is enforced against the surety, the surety is entitled to be indemnified by the person who should have paid the debt before the surety was compelled to do so.[12]

---

2. SDCL § 56-1-1.
3. Taggart v. Ford Motor Credit Co., 462 N.W.2d 493, 500 (S.D. 1990).
4. Robbins & Stearns Lumber Co. v. Thatcher, 453 N.W.2d 613, 615 (S.D. 1990).
5. International Multifoods Corp. v. Mardian, 379 N.W.2d 840, 843 (S.D. 1985) (citing Western Petroleum Co. v. First Bank Aberdeen, 367 N.W.2d 773, 776-77 (S.D.1985)).
6. Miners and Merchants Sav. Bank v. Comer, 140 N.W.2d 390, 391 (S.D. 1966).
7. *Id.* at 390, 393.
8. The actual language of SDCL § 56-1-3 states guarantee rather than creditor. Guarantee is another name for creditor. *See* William Deering & Co. v. Mortell, 21 S.D. 159, 110 N.W. 86 (S.D. 1906).
9. SDCL § 56-1-3.
10. SDCL § 56-1-4.
11. SDCL § 56-2-1.
12. State of Wis. Inv. Bd. v. Hurst, 410 N.W.2d 560, 562-63 (S.D. 1987).

§ 2 State Law Requirements for an Entity to Enter a Guaranty

Partnerships, limited liability companies, and corporations are permitted to be guarantors in furtherance of their business activities.

2.1 Entity Issues

A corporation incorporated in South Dakota has the same powers as an individual to do all things necessary or convenient to carry out its business and affairs including the power to make guaranties. If so authorized, the guaranty may be secured by property of the corporation.[13]

A guaranty by a corporation that is broader than the specific terms of its authorizing corporate resolution will be enforced if signed by all of the shareholders, directors, and officers of the corporation.[14] Such a scenario is more common with a closely held corporation. If not all of the shareholders, directors, and officers of the corporation sign the guaranty, the result is uncertain.[15] Individual officers of a corporation who sign a guaranty with corporate titles after their names are not necessarily immune from individual liability on the guaranty.[16]

2.2 Individuals

Marital Property

South Dakota is not a community property state. A spouse can only encumber his or her interest in property. However, if the property is the homestead and both spouses are residents of South Dakota, a conveyance or encumbrance of the homestead requires both the husband and wife to concur in and execute such conveyance or encumbrance either by joint instrument or by separate instruments.[17]

When dividing property in a divorce action, a guaranty signed by a spouse will be analyzed to ascertain if it is likely the spouse will pay on the guaranty. If it is unlikely the spouse will have to pay on the guaranty, then it will not be considered in the property division.[18]

13. SDCL § 47-1A-302 (7).
14. First Nat. Bank of Beresford v. Nelson, 323 N.W.2d 879, 884-85 (S.D. 1982).
15. *Id.* at 879, 885.
16. In *Rawleigh, Moses & Co. v. Kornberg*, 210 F.2d 176 (C.A.8 1954), individual officers of a South Dakota corporation who signed both a factoring agreement and a guaranty by including their corporate titles after their names were held individually liable on the guaranty because to hold otherwise would render the guaranty a mere formality as opposed to an enforceable agreement.
17. SDCL § 43-31-17; In re Lemme 41 B.R. 829, 831 (Bkrtcy. D.S.D. 1984).
18. Larson v. Larson, 733 N.W.2d 272 (S.D. 2007).

§ 3 Signatory's Authority to Execute a Guaranty

3.1 Corporations

Under South Dakota law, "[u]nless its articles of incorporation provide otherwise, a corporation has . . . the same powers as an individual to do all things necessary or convenient to carry out its business and affairs, including the power to . . . . [e]lect directors and appoint officers, employees, and agents of the corporation . . . [and] define their duties."[19] It is presumed that a president who is active in the management of a corporation has the authority to engage in acts that are necessary to the conduct of the corporation's business unless there is evidence to the contrary.[20]

"Liability of a corporation for the acts of its officers is generally governed by the same principles that make an individual as principal liable for the acts of his agent. . . . Actual authority of an agent may be either express or implied and incidental. Implied authority includes authority to do whatever acts are incidental to or are necessary, usual and proper to accomplish or perform, the main authority granted the agent."[21] A corporation may ratify or acquiesce in the acts of an officer that were in violation of his or her authority.[22] However, "[t]he presumption of authority to conduct the business of the corporation will not act to validate a voidable act where it is clear the corporation neither acquiesced in nor ratified the action in question."[23]

3.2 Partnerships

Partnerships are governed by the Uniform Partnership Act as enacted in South Dakota.[24]

Subject to the effect of a statement of partnership authority under SDCL § 48-7A-303 (which may, for instance, limit the authority of a partner and impute this knowledge to a third party):

Each partner is an agent of the partnership for the purpose of its business.

(1) the signing of an instrument by a partner with actual authority binds the company if the signing of the instrument is for apparently carrying on in the ordinary course the partnership's business or business of the kind carried on by the partnership.

---

19. SDCL § 47-1A-302(11).
20. Aimonetto v. Rapid Gas, Inc., 126 N.W.2d 116, 119 (1964).
21. *Id.* at 116,120 (citations omitted).
22. Contract Materials Co. v. Oahe Land & Cattle Co., Inc., 374 N.W.2d 102, 104 (S.D. 1985) (quoting Engler v. Ipswich Printing Co., 63 S.D. 1, 6, 256 N.W. 132, 134 (1934)) (emphasis omitted).
23. Contract Materials Co. v. Oahe Land & Cattle Co., Inc., 374 N.W.2d 102, 104 (S.D. 1985).
24. SDCL § 48-7A.

(2) the signing of an instrument by a partner without authority binds the partnership if
  (a) the signing of the instrument was for apparently carrying on in the ordinary course the partnership's business or business of the kind carried on by the partnership and
  (b) the person with whom the partner is dealing did not know or did not have notice that the partner lacked authority.
(3) an act of a partner which is not apparently for carrying on in the ordinary course the partnership's business or business of the kind carried on by the partnership binds the partnership only if the act was authorized by the other partners.[25]

Limited partnerships are governed by the Uniform Limited Partnership Act as enacted in South Dakota.[26]

A limited partner is not liable for the obligations of a limited partnership unless:

(1) The limited partner knowingly permits his or her name to be used in the name of the limited partnership (with some exceptions[27]), in which case he or she is liable to creditors who extend credit to the limited partnership without actual knowledge that the limited partner is not a general partner;
(2) The limited partner is also a general partner; or
(3) In addition to the exercise of his or her rights and powers as a limited partner, the limited partner participates in the control of the business, in which case he or she is liable only to persons who transact business with the limited partnership reasonably believing (based on the limited partner's conduct) that the limited partner is a general partner.[28]

A limited partner does not participate in the control of the business by acting as a surety for the limited partnership or guaranteeing or assuming one or more specific obligations of the limited partnership.[29]

A general partner in a limited partnership is subject to the following:

(1) Except as provided by statute or in the partnership agreement, a general partner of a limited partnership has the rights and powers and is subject to the restrictions of a partner in a partnership without limited partners.
(2) Except as provided by statute, a general partner of a limited partnership has the liabilities of a partner in a partnership without limited partners to persons other than the partnership and the other partners.[30]

25. SDCL § 48-7A-301.
26. SDCL § 48-7.
27. SDCL § 48-7-303(d); SDCL § 48-7-102(2).
28. SDCL § 48-7-303(a).
29. SDCL § 48-7-303(b)(3).
30. SDCL § 48-7-403.

3.3 Limited Liability Companies

Limited liability companies (LLCs) are governed by the Uniform Limited Liability Company Act as enacted in South Dakota.[31]

Member-managed LLC: Each member is an agent of the LLC for the purpose of its business.

(1) The signing of an instrument by a member with actual authority binds the company if the signing of the instrument is for apparently carrying on in the ordinary course the company's business or business of the kind carried on by the company.

(2) The signing of an instrument by a member without authority binds the company if:

(a) the signing of the instrument was for apparently carrying on in the ordinary course the company's business or business of the kind carried on by the company; and

(b) the person with whom the member is dealing did not know or did not have notice that the member lacked authority.

(3) An act of a member which is not apparently for carrying on in the ordinary course the company's business or business of the kind carried on by the company binds the company only if the act was authorized by the other members.[32]

Manager-managed LLC: Each manager is an agent of the LLC for the purpose of its business.

(1) The signing of an instrument by a manager with actual authority binds the company if the signing of the instrument is for apparently carrying on in the ordinary course the company's business or business of the kind carried on by the company.

(2) The signing of an instrument by a manager without authority binds the company if:

(a) the signing of the instrument was for apparently carrying on in the ordinary course the company's business or business of the kind carried on by the company; and

(b) the person with whom the manager is dealing did not know or did not have notice that the manager lacked authority.

(3) An act of a manager which is not apparently for carrying on in the ordinary course the company's business or business of the kind carried on by the company binds the company only if the act was authorized by a majority of the managers.[33]

---

31. SDCL § 47-34A.
32. SDCL § 47-34A-301(a).
33. SDCL § 47-34A-301(b).

§ 4 Consideration; Sufficiency of Past Consideration

SDCL § 56-1-3 provides that "[w]here a guaranty is entered into at the same time with the original obligation or with the acceptance of the original obligation by the guarantee [creditor] and forms, with that obligation, a part of the consideration to him, no other consideration need exist. In all other cases there must be a consideration distinct from that of the original obligation." Thus, when a guaranty is entered into at some time other than the time of the original obligation, consideration is required distinct from that of the original obligation.[34]

§ 5 Notice of Acceptance

"A mere offer to guarantee [enter into a guaranty] is not binding until notice of its acceptance is communicated by the guarantee [creditor] to the guarantor, but an absolute guaranty[35] is binding upon the guarantor without notice of acceptance."[36] "The test as to whether an instrument purporting to be a guaranty is merely an offer to become a guarantor, or an absolute contract of guaranty, is whether there has been a mutual meeting of the minds of the parties necessary to constitute such instrument an absolute contract of guaranty. This question may be determined from the surrounding facts and circumstances of the transaction as well as from the instrument itself."[37]

If a guaranty is signed by the guarantor at the request of the creditor, or if the creditor's agreement to accept is contemporaneous with the guaranty, or if the receipt from the creditor of a valuable consideration, however small, is acknowledged in the guaranty, mutual assent is proved, and the delivery of the guaranty to the creditor, or for the creditor's use, completes the contract. But if the guaranty is signed by the guarantor without any previous request of the creditor, and, in the creditor's absence, for no consideration moving between them except future advances to be made to the principal debtor, the guaranty is, in legal effect, an offer or proposal on the part of the guarantor, needing an acceptance by the creditor to complete the contract.[38]

34. Richter v. Industrial Finance Co., Inc., 221 N.W.2d 31, 34 (S.D. 1974).
35. See section 6.3 for definition of absolute guaranty.
36. SDCL § 56-1-10.
37. M.E. Smith & Co. v. Kimble, 31 S.D. 18, 139 N.W. 348, 352 (S.D. 1913). *See also* Hirning v. Jacobsen, 213 N.W. 505, 507 (S.D. 1927) (the question whether or not a writing constitutes an absolute guaranty may be determined from the surrounding facts and circumstances of the transaction, as well as from the instrument itself).
38. William Deering & Co. v. Mortell, 21 S.D. 159, 110 N.W. 86, 87 (1906).

§ 6 Interpretation of Guaranties

6.1 General Principles

"The liability of a guarantor will not be enlarged beyond the plain and certain import of the guaranty contract and any ambiguous or uncertain terms in a guaranty will be interpreted most strictly against the party who prepared it."[39]

6.2 "Continuing Guaranty"

A continuing guaranty is "a guaranty relating to a future liability of the principal [debtor], under successive transactions which either continue his liability or from time to time renew it after it has been satisfied."[40] A continuing guaranty may be revoked at any time by the guarantor, in respect to future transactions, unless there is a continuing consideration as to such transactions which the guarantor does not renounce.[41]

"The rule is well established that, where a guaranty is continuing and absolute, the guarantor is not entitled to notice of each transaction in order to bind him. The statement that the guaranty is unconditional waives notice unless it is specifically provided for in the writing… [T]his is particularly true where the guarantors are officers of the corporation whose debts are guaranteed, as they have opportunity equal to that of the guarantor for information on the subject."[42]

6.3 "Absolute and Unconditional"

An absolute guaranty is simply another word for guaranty. It is used in situations to emphasize that an enforceable guaranty exists—i.e., the document or other evidence under scrutiny is not a mere offer to enter into a guaranty, but rather a consummated guaranty contract.[43]

A guaranty is to be deemed unconditional unless its terms import some condition precedent to the liability of the guarantor.[44]

6.4 "Guaranty that Obligation is Good or Collectible"

A guaranty that an obligation is good or collectible is a representation that the debtor is solvent and that the demand is collectible by the usual legal

39. Robbins & Stearns Lumber Co. v. Thatcher, 453 N.W.2d 613, 615 (S.D. 1990).
40. SDCL § 56-1-20.
41. SDCL § 56-1-21.
42. Hirning v. Jacobsen 51 S.D. 270, 213 N.W. 505, 507 (S.D. 1927) (citations omitted).
43. *See* William Deering & Co. v. Mortell, 110 N.W. 86 (S.D. 1906) (interpreting Rev. Civ. Code. § 1974 which was in existence in 1906 and is the same as current SDCL § 56-1-10) *See also* M.E. Smith & Co. v. Kimble, 139 N.W. 348, 352 (S.D. 1913) (holding that the alleged guaranty under dispute was an offer to guaranty instead of an absolute guaranty); Hirning v. Jacobsen, 213 N.W. 505, 507 (S.D. 1927) (when speaking of absolute guaranty the court cites the case of Davis Sewing-Mach. Co. v. Richards, 115 U.S. 524 (1885) which deals with whether an offer of guaranty or a completed guaranty was in existence).
44. SDCL § 56-1-15.

proceedings if taken with reasonable diligence.[45] Such a guaranty is not discharged by any omission to take proceedings against the principal debtor or upon any collateral security, if no part of the debt could have been collected by such proceedings.[46]

§ 7 Defenses of the Guarantor; Set-off

The defenses that may be available to a guarantor can be grouped into three categories: (1) defenses of the principal debtor, (2) suretyship defenses, and (3) other defenses.

7.1 Defenses of the Principal Debtor (that may be used by the Guarantor)

7.1.1 General

SDCL § 56-1-18 provides, "[t]he obligation of a guarantor must be neither larger in amount nor in other respects more burdensome than that of the principal, and if in its terms it exceeds it, it is reducible in proportion to the principal obligation." SDCL § 56-1-18 "is merely a codification of the common law. . . . Generally, the liability of a guarantor cannot exceed the liability of the principal debtor, and all guaranty contracts are conditioned upon the underlying [original] obligation between the creditor and the principal debtor. In order for a plaintiff to enforce an underlying [original] obligation against a guarantor, the plaintiff must show that the guaranty debt or obligation is due him, and, if for any reason the principal debtor is not bound to make payment to the creditor or plaintiff, the plaintiff may not hold the guarantor liable. The rule is that a guarantor is liable only in the event and to the extent that his principal is liable."[47] Note, however, that "SDCL 56-1-18 applies to the ordinary guaranty and should not be interpreted as preventing the parties to freely assume more of an obligation than that imposed in ordinary circumstances. ... Language of a guaranty can indeed create greater liability on the part of the guarantor..."[48]

There may be some exceptions to the rule stated in SDCL § 56-1-18. It has been pointed out that "[a]s for whether a guarantor can raise the principal's defenses of breach of warranty or failure of consideration, some courts have held the guarantor cannot and some courts have held the guarantor can." [49] In a situation where the principal debtor is a corporation and the guarantors are the officers and sole stockholders of the principal debtor, the guarantors can

45. SDCL § 56-1-12.
46. SDCL § 56-1-14.
47. Richter v. Industrial Finance Co., Inc., 221 N.W.2d 31, 36 (S.D. 1974) (citations omitted). *See also* International Multifoods Corp. v. Mardian 379 N.W.2d 840, 843 (S.D. 1985).
48. International Multifoods Corp. v. Mardian, 379 N.W.2d 840 (S.D. 1985) (citations omitted).
49. *Id.* at 840, 843 (citations omitted). Note that the court is not referring to South Dakota courts when it states that "some courts have held that guarantor cannot and some courts have held that the guarantor can."

assert the principal's defenses of breach of warranty and failure of consideration (unless the guarantors have waived these defenses in the guaranty itself).[50]

7.1.2 When Guarantor May Assert Primary Debtor's Defense

"If the contract between the principal [debtor] and the creditor is unlawful, a guarantor is not liable. SDCL 56-1-19."[51] Similarly, if a contract between the principal debtor and the creditor is invalid because it is against public policy, the guarantor is not liable.[52]

SDCL §56-1-25 provides that "[t]he acceptance by a creditor of anything in partial satisfaction of an obligation reduces the obligation of a guarantor thereof in the same measure as that of the principal, but does not otherwise affect it."[53]

7.1.3 Defenses that May not be Raised by Guarantor

"[N]otwithstanding any mere personal disability of the principal [debtor], under SDCL 56-1-19, the guarantor is liable even though the disability is such so as to make the contract void against the principal [debtor]."[54]

"A guarantor is not exonerated by the discharge of his principal [debtor] by operation of law without the intervention or omission of the creditor."[55] Consequently, a bankruptcy creditor may bring an action against a third person such as a surety or guarantor despite the bankrupt's discharge.[56]

7.2 "Suretyship" Defenses

7.2.1 Surety Rights

"A surety has all the rights of a guarantor whether he becomes personally responsible or not."[57] A surety is entitled to have property of the principal debtor first applied to the discharge of the obligation.[58] A surety may require the creditor to proceed against a principal debtor or to pursue remedies which the surety cannot pursue and which would be a benefit to the surety.[59]

7.2.2 Modification of the Original Obligation, Including Release

A surety is exonerated in like manner as a guarantor.[60]

---

50. International Multifoods Corp. v. Mardian, 379 N.W.2d 840, 843-844 (S.D. 1985).
51. International Multifoods Corp. v. Mardian, 379 N.W.2d 840, 843 (S.D. 1985).
52. Federal Deposit Ins. Corp. v. Stensland, 15 N.W.2d 8, 11 (S.D. 1944).
53. "It is well-settled that the liability of a guarantor cannot exceed that of the principal [debtor]… The acceptance by the creditor of anything in partial satisfaction of an obligation reduces the obligation of the guarantor in the same measure as that of the principal." First Nat. Bank of Minneapolis v. Kehn Ranch, Inc., 394 N.W.2d 709, 716 (S.D. 1986) (citations omitted).
54. International Multifoods Corp. v. Mardian, 379 N.W.2d 840, 843 (S.D. 1985).
55. SDCL § 56-1-28
56. Sioux Valley Hosp. Ass'n v. Lake County, 533 N.W.2d 161, 164 (S.D.1995).
57. SDCL § 56-2-4.
58. SDCL § 56-2-7.
59. SDCL§ 56-2-6.
60. SDCL § 56-2-8; SDCL §§ 56-1-22 to 56-1-28.

7.2.3 Release or Impairment of Security for the Original Obligation

"A surety is exonerated to the extent to which he is prejudiced by any act of the creditor which would naturally prove injurious to the remedies of the surety or inconsistent with his rights or which lessens his security."[61] "A surety is exonerated to the extent to which he is prejudiced by an omission of the creditor to do anything when required by the surety which it is his duty to do."[62]

7.3 Other Defenses

7.3.1 Modification of the Original Obligation

Under SDCL § 56-1-22, a guarantor is exonerated if the creditor, without the consent of the guarantor, alters the original obligation of the principal debtor or causes the remedies or rights of the creditor against the principal debtor to be impaired or suspended.[63] *Mere delay* on the part of a creditor to proceed against the principal debtor or to enforce any other remedy does not exonerate a guarantor.[64] However, "an extension of the time of payment of the principal obligation ... if given as the result of a binding agreement between the creditor and the debtor and not consented to by the guarantor, releases the guarantor from his liability under the guaranty agreement."[65]

It is important to note that SDCL § 56-1-22 does not prevent a guarantor from *consenting* to an act by the creditor that alters the original obligation of the principal debtor or that impairs or suspends the remedies or rights of the creditor against the principal debtor.[66] A guarantor's obligations under the guaranty are no greater than those created by the guaranty document. Once the validity of a guaranty is recognized, *the terms of the guaranty document itself* determine whether alterations to the obligations of the principal debtor are sufficient to exonerate the duty of the guarantor.[67] The rights and protections afforded to the guarantor by SDCL § 56-1-22 may be waived by language in the guaranty.[68]

The rescission of an agreement altering the original obligation of the principal debtor or impairing the remedy of the creditor does not restore the liability of the guarantor who has been exonerated by such agreement.[69]

7.3.2 Statute of Limitations

South Dakota Law provides with limited exceptions a six-year statute of limitations for an action upon a contract obligation or liability.[70]

61. SDCL § 56-2-10.
62. SDCL § 56-2-11.
63. SDCL § 56-1-22.
64. SDCL § 56-1-26 (emphasis added).
65. Lane v. Travelers Indem. Co., 563 N.W.2d 423, 426 (S.D. 1997).
66. SDCL § 56-1-22.
67. Lane v. Travelers Indem. Co., 563 N.W.2d 423, 427 (S.D. 1997).
68. Sunbank of South Dakota v. Precision Specialty Products, 429 N.W.2d 73, 76 (S.D. 1988).
69. SDCL § 56-1-24.
70. SDCL § 15-2-13(1).

7.3.3 *Statute of Frauds*

A guaranty must be in writing and signed by the guarantor unless the guaranty falls into one of the exceptions listed in SDCL § 56-1-5 through SDCL § 56-1-9 inclusive.[71] An example of such an exception is when a promise is disguised as a guaranty.[72]

7.3.4 *Reliance*

A plaintiff's reliance on equities and general principles of law is unpersuasive when his rights and liabilities are fixed by contracts of guaranty.[73]

Even if a creditor promised not to collect from the primary debtor by way of a subordination agreement the creditor signed in favor of another party, the creditor can still look to the guarantor for payment. The guarantor "cannot assert as a defense a contractual obligation made for the benefit of someone else"–i.e., the guarantor cannot assert that the creditor is precluded from collecting from the guarantor simply because the creditor promised a third party not to collect from the debtor.[74]

§ 8 Waiver of Defenses by the Guarantor

Guarantors can waive the right to assert the principal debtor's defenses such as setoff or counterclaim.[75] Guarantors can also waive notice of acceptance if receipt of consideration is recited in the guaranty.[76] In a continuing guaranty, notice of each transaction is waived if there is a statement that the guaranty is unconditional (unless notice is specifically provided for in the writing).[77]

In a secured transaction scenario, a debtor or secondary obligor may waive the right to notification of disposition of collateral and the right to require disposition of collateral only by an agreement to that effect entered into and authenticated after default.[78] Additionally, the right to redeem the collateral may be waived in the same manner unless it is a consumer goods transaction.[79]

71. SDCL § 56-1-4 states: Except as prescribed by §§ 56-1-5 to 56-1-9, inclusive, a guaranty must be in writing and signed by the guarantor; but the writing need not express a consideration.
72. "One who purports to guarantee a debt and does so in such a manner as to make himself the principal debtor, shall be held liable on the debt even though the debt was not guaranteed by a writing. . . [B]y definition a 'guarantor' is one who agrees to answer for the debt of a third person. Furthermore, when a person agrees to accept a debt as his own, it follows that said person is no longer a guarantor but in fact a principal debtor. It further follows logically that when a person is in fact a principal debtor, then semantics aside, he ought not be treated as a guarantor, and that in substance is the meaning of the statute." Cargill, Inc. v. American Pork Producers, Inc. 426 F.Supp. 499, 510 (D.C.S.D. 1977) (interpreting SDCL § 56-1-6).
73. Sunbank of South Dakota v. Precision Specialty Products, Inc. 429 N.W.2d 73, 76 (S.D. 1988).
74. Richter v. Industrial Finance Co., Inc., 221 N.W.2d 31, 35 (S.D. 1974).
75. International Multifoods Corp. v. Mardian, 379 N.W.2d 840, 844 (S.D. 1985).
76. Furst v. Risse, 56 S.D. 418, 229 N.W. 293, 294 (S.D. 1930).
77. Hirning v. Jacobsen 213 N.W. 505, 507 (S.D. 1927).
78. SDCL § 57A-9-624(a)-(b).
79. SDCL § 57A-9-624(c).

§ 9 Third-party Pledgors—Defenses and Waiver Thereof

South Dakota has no statutory or case law that would differentiate the position of a third-party pledgor from a surety and a surety has all the rights of a guarantor whether he or she becomes personally responsible or not.[80]

§ 10 Jointly and Severally Liable Guarantors—Contribution and Reduction of Obligations Upon Payment by a Co-Obligor

An obligation imposed upon several persons is presumed to be joint, and not several.[81] However, this rule does not apply where the parties who unite in a promise receive some benefit from the consideration whether past or present. In that case, their promise is presumed to be joint and several.[82] The acceptance by a creditor of anything in partial satisfaction of an obligation reduces the obligation of a guarantor the same as it reduces the obligation of a principal debtor.[83] "A party to a joint, or joint and several, obligation, who satisfies more than his or her share of the claim against all, may require a proportionate contribution from all the parties joined with him."[84]

§ 11 Indemnification and Subrogation

Generally in South Dakota, one, such as a guarantor, who pays a debt that should have been paid by another has a right to indemnification by the party, such as a principal debtor, that should have paid the debt.[85]

If the duty of the principal debtor to the creditor is satisfied, the surety, to the extent that the surety has contributed to the satisfaction, is subrogated to all rights of the creditor against the principal debtor.[86] However, "a surety may not claim subrogation against an insolvent debtor until the claims of creditors against the debtor have been paid in full."[87]

80. *See generally* Pledges of Personal Property SDCL § 44-10; SDCL § 56-2-4.
81. SDCL § 20-1-5.
82. SDCL § 53-2-4.
83. SDCL § 56-1-25.
84. SDCL § 20-1-6.
85. Weiszhaar Farms, Inc. v. Tobin, 522 N.W.2d 484, 492 (S.D. 1994); *Nat'l Farmers Union Prop. & Cas. Co. v. Farm & City Ins. Co.*, 689 N.W.2d 619, 625 (S.D. 2004); SDCL § 20-1-6.
86. SDCL § 56-2-17.
87. City of Madison v. Bailey-Laffey Const., 495 N.W.2d 95, 97 (S.D. 1993)(citing Wieland v. Westcott, 268 N. W. 904, 905 (S.D. 1936)).

§ 12 Enforcement of Guaranties

South Dakota allows for a suit on a note or guaranty without foreclosing a mortgage securing the note. If the creditor later begins an action for the foreclosure of the mortgage, the complaint shall state that there were prior proceedings for the recovery of the debt secured by such mortgage and whether any part of the debt has been collected.[88]

"A guarantor of payment or performance is liable to the guarantee [creditor] immediately upon the default of the principal [debtor] and without demand or notice."[89]

"Where one guarantees a conditional obligation his liability is commensurate with that of the principal [debtor], and he is not entitled to notice of the default of the principal unless he is unable, by the exercise of reasonable diligence, to acquire information of such default, and the creditor has actual notice thereof."[90]

§ 13 Revival and Reinstatement of Guaranties

"The rescission of an agreement altering the original obligation of a debtor or impairing the remedy of a creditor does not restore the liability of a guarantor who has been exonerated by such agreement."[91]

§ 14 Choice of Law and Venue

"A contract is to be interpreted according to the law and usage of the place where it is to be performed or, if it does not indicate a place of performance, according to the law and usage of the place where it is made."[92] Parties may, however, agree to be bound by the law of a particular place.[93] "[W]hen parties have agreed to be bound by the law of a specific place and the agreement is reasonable and fair, the law of that place may govern."[94]

"Parties 'may contractually specify and consent to a state's jurisdiction over legal actions which arise under a contract.'" [95] Forum-selection clauses in a contract are valid unless enforcement would be unreasonable or against

88. SDCL § 21-49-18; SDCL § 21-47-4.
89. SDCL § 56-1-16.
90. SDCL § 56-1-17.
91. SDCL § 56-1-24.
92. SDCL § 53-1-14; Union Pacific R.R. v. Certain Underwriters at Lloyd's London, 771 N.W.2d 611, 618 (S.D. 2009).
93. Briggs v. United Services Life Ins. Co., 117 N.W.2d 804, 807 (S.D. 1962).
94. Baldwin v. Heinold Commodities, Inc., 363 N.W.2d 191,195 (S.D.1985).
95. O'Neill Farms, Inc. v. Reinert, 780 N.W.2d 55, 58 (S.D. 2010) (quoting Baldwin v. Heinold Commodities, Inc., 363 N.W.2d 191, 194 (S.D.1985)).

a strong public policy or unless the clause was invalid for reasons such as fraud or overreaching.[96]

§ 15 Other

Under South Dakota law, "[a]ny provision contained in any note, bond, mortgage, or other evidence of debt that provides for payment of attorneys' fees in case of default of payment or foreclosure is against public policy and void, except as authorized by specific statute."[97] Consequently, a guarantor of a note, bond, or other evidence of debt is not liable for attorneys' fees since the guaranty agreement is linked to the original obligation.[98] Attorneys' fees are recoverable in a mortgage foreclosure, however, as they are authorized under SDCL § 15-17-38.

Performance guaranties often take the form of performance bonds. Such guaranties are common in construction contracts where work is guaranteed to be completed and persons who provide labor or materials are guaranteed to be promptly paid.[99]

96. O'Neill Farms, Inc. v. Reinert, 780 N.W.2d 55, 58 (S.D. 2010).
97. SDCL § 15-17-39.
98. "In *Midcontinent Broadcasting Co.* v. AVA Corp., 329 N.W.2d at 381, this Court held that a guaranty fell within the meaning of 'other evidence of debt' and reversed an award of attorneys' fees which was based on language in a guaranty which permitted such a recovery… Language in a guaranty permitting recovery of attorneys' fees is against public policy and void as the clear dictate of SDCL 15-17-10 [now SDCL § 15-17-39] demands." International Multifoods Corp. v. Mardian, 379 N.W.2d 840, 845 (S.D. 1985) *See also* Credit Collection Services, Inc. v. Pesicka 721 N.W.2d 474, 477-78 (S.D. 2006).
99. SDCL § 5-21-1; County of Pennington for Use and Benefit of Northwest Pipe, 508 N.W.2d 376 (S.D.,1993); Northwestern Engineering Co. v. Thunderbolt Enterprises, Inc., 301 N.W.2d 421 (S.D. 1981).

Tennessee Law of Guaranties and Sureties

Ernest B. Williams IV
Michael B. Schwegler
Ernest B. Williams IV, PLLC
P.O. Box 159264
Nashville, TN 37215
Phone: (615) 372-0993
Fax: (615) 371-1572
erniewilliams@ewivlaw.com

Contents

Tennessee Law of Guaranties and Sureties

Introductory Note: In order to standardize our discussion of the law of guaranties, we use the following vocabulary to refer to the various parties to a guaranty and their obligations.

While the distinction between guarantors and sureties is largely blurred under Tennessee law and although related terms are often used interchangeably, cases do in fact sometimes make a distinction between these terms, including subsets thereof.

"Absolute Guaranty" as the term is construed by Tennessee case law, is a guaranty of payment as opposed to collection, the former being regarded as "absolute" and the latter as conditional. The guaranty of payment binds the guarantor to pay the debt at maturity in the event the money has not been paid by the principal debtor. Upon default by the latter, the obligation of the guarantor becomes fixed. This term should be interchangeable with "unconditional" guaranty.

"Co-obligor" or **"Co-maker"** means additional persons who directly contract for the underlying obligation as primary obligors.

"Conditional Guaranty" means a guaranty with respect to which exercise by the guarantor of the guaranteed obligations is conditional on a future event, including exhaustion of the obligee's remedies against the primary obligor…such as is a guaranty of collection or what some refer to as a "springing" guaranty.

"Continuing Guaranty" means a guaranty in which the guarantor agrees to guarantee all obligations or debt now or in the future of a primary obligor.

"Cosurety" means one or more "persons" who are jointly equally liable to an "obligee" and have the right of contribution one against another in the event a suretyship (guaranteed) obligation is paid.

"Guaranteed Obligation" means the obligations of a guarantor or surety or payment, collection, performance and like obligations.

"Guarantor" means a person who, by contract, agrees to satisfy an underlying obligation of another to an obligee upon the primary obligor's default on that underlying obligation. The distinction between guarantors and sureties is blurred under Tennessee law; however, some notable decisions attempt to clarify the differences.

"Guaranty." A guaranty is an undertaking to answer for the payment of some debt or the performance of some contract or duty of another in case of the failure of such other to pay or perform, the obligation of the guarantor being collateral, or at least secondary, and not primary and may require that obligee proceed first against the principal (absent contractual provisions to the contrary).[1]

"Limited Guaranty." While this term is not defined under Tennessee Law, it typically means a guaranty that is limited to a certain indebtedness or specified obligation, or a percentage amount of a larger debt.

"Obligee" means the person to whom the underlying obligation is owed. For example, the lender under a loan agreement would be an obligee vis-à-vis the borrower.

"Primary Obligor" means the person who incurs the underlying obligation to the obligee. For example, the borrower under a loan agreement would be a primary obligor. Under Tennessee law, a guarantor's obligation may be made "primary" by guaranty language.

"Subsurety" means a surety who, while obligated to the obligee, either has agreed with other sureties that she/he should not have the responsibility of contribution to other sureties or such may be implied because this surety has no interest in the primary obligor.[2]

"Surety" means a person who is primarily liable for the payments of the debts of another. For instance, a bonding company is a surety and principally liable for the payment or performance of an obligation, if the obligor fails to do so, while a guarantor may require that the obligee proceed against the primary obligor first.

"Underlying Obligation" means the obligation or obligations incurred by the primary obligor and owed to the obligee. For example, the borrower's obligation to make payments to a lender of principal and interest on a loan constitutes an underlying obligation.

"Unlimited Guaranty" means the guaranty is not limited to payment or performance of a single act or one or more debt amounts expressly set forth in the guaranty. To the contrary, it can include all obligations of the primary obligor to the obligee, whether or not these exist or are even known. This term is synonymous with a "continuing" guaranty, according to Tennessee decisions. It may differ from the definitions found in restatements and treatises.

Note: The characterization of any guaranty is entirely dependent on the language of the guaranty itself. Generally, that language is to be construed strongly in favor of the obligee and toward preserving the guaranteed obligation.

1. United States Fidelity and Guaranty Co. v. Booth, 45 S.W.2d 1075, 1076 (Tenn. 1932).
2. Cook v. Crabtree, 733 S.W.2d 67, 69 (Tenn. 1987).

Introduction and Sources of Law

Tennessee has but one statutory scheme directly governing the law of guarantees.[3] There are no statutory provisions governing the content, terms or enforceability of guarantees.[4] Courts interpreting Tennessee law have relied upon the Restatement of the Law, Security,[5] as well as the Restatement of the Law, Third, Suretyship and Guaranty.[6] No Tennessee decision indicates that Tennessee has formally or informally adopted either.

§ 1 Nature of the Guaranty Arrangement

Under Tennessee law, a guaranty involves three distinct, interrelated obligations or varying degrees of dependence, one on another: the underlying obligation between the primary obligor and the obligee, the guaranty between the guarantor and the obligee, and the right of "reimbursement" between the primary obligor and the guarantor.[7]

1.1 Use of Specific Terms of Art

No "technical words" are needed to create a guaranteed obligation.[8] However, as the reader will note *infra*, Tennessee courts have consistently used words to describe the nature and extent of guaranteed obligations in Tennessee and guaranty drafters are advised to draw heavily from applicable case law.

1.2 Guaranty Relationships—Guaranty not a Negotiable Instrument

Guaranties, by their very nature, are conditional promises to pay because guarantors promise to pay only on the condition that the principal debtor fails to pay.[9] Likewise, guaranties, even ones containing a limitation on the guarantor's liability, cannot involve a sum certain because the amount of the guarantor's liability cannot be determined solely from the instrument itself without reference to an outside source.[10] Finally, a guaranty is not payable at

3. Tenn. Code Ann. § 47-12-101 *et seq.* (2012) (discussed *infra*, at § 6.1).
4. Note: Tenn. Code Ann. § 47-12-101 *et seq.* provides certain defenses to enforcement of guaranties in limited circumstances.
5. *See, e.g.,* Cook v. Crabtree, 733 S.W.2d 67, 69 (Tenn. 1987); Hickory Springs Mfg. Co., Inc. v. Mehlman, 541 S.W.2d 97, 99 (Tenn. 1976); Kincaid v. Alderson, 354 S.W.2d 775, 778 (Tenn. 1962).
6. *See, e.g.,* Acuity v. McGhee Eng'g, Inc., 297 S.W.3d 718 (Tenn. Ct. App. 2008); Cumberland Bank v. G & S Implement Co., 211 S.W.3d 223 (Tenn. Ct. App. 2006).
7. Villines v. Parham- Lindsey Grocery Co., 6 Tenn. App. 254 (Tenn. Ct. App. 1927).
8. Bank of Waynesboro v. Ghosh, 576 S.W.2d 759 (Tenn. 1979).
9. Guarantor Partners v. Huff, 830 S.W.2d 73, 76 (Tenn. Ct. App. 1992) (citing FDIC v. Percival, 752 F. Supp. 313, 324 (D. Neb. 1990); FDIC v. Galloway, 613 F. Supp. 1392, 1400-01 (D. Kan. 1985), rev'd on other grounds, 856 F.2d 112 (10th Cir. 1988); Gregoire v. Lowndes Bank, 342 S.E.2d 264, 267 (Tenn. Ct. App. 1992)).
10. Guarantor Partners v. Huff, 830 S.W.2d 73, 76 (Tenn. Ct. App. 1992) (citing Branch Banking & Trust Co. v. Creasy, 269 S.E.2d 117, 122 (N.C. 1980); Goss v. Trinity Savs. & Loan Ass'n, 813 P.2d 492, 497 (Okla. 1991); *Dann v. Team Bank*, 788 S.W.2d 182, 186 (Tex. Ct. App. 1990); Gregoire v. Lowndes Bank, 342 S.E.2d 264, 267 (Tenn. Ct. App. 1992)).

a definite time or on demand since it is payable only when the principal debtor defaults. Continuing guaranties may be payable on numerous occasions.[11]

A guaranty is a contract of "secondary liability" under which the guarantor has an obligation to pay only upon default by the primary obligor. This relationship can be altered by contract under Tennessee law such that the guarantor is made primarily liable.[12]

A guaranty is assignable, like any other contract;[13] and provided its terms do not prohibit assignment the guaranty may be assigned together with the underlying obligation. The rights and liabilities of the parties are governed by the law of contract and guaranty, not by the Uniform Commercial Code ("UCC").

When the guaranty, although on a separate form, is so firmly affixed to a negotiable instrument, it becomes part of the instrument itself.[14] Mere descriptive references in a note to a separate guaranty do not have the same effect.[15] However, under this exception, the guaranty itself is not a separate negotiable instrument. It becomes an undistinguishable part of the negotiable instrument to which it is attached.

Tennessee courts considering whether a continuing guaranty is an "instrument" for the purposes of the shelter rule in Tenn. Code Ann. § 47-3-201(1) have held:

> since the shelter rule can only apply to transferees of "instruments" - that is "negotiable instruments" - the majority rule is equally applicable ... a separate guaranty ... is not a negotiable instrument but rather a separate agreement.[16]

1.3 Distinctions between Types of Guaranties

Tennessee cases clearly distinguish a "continuing" [or unlimited] guaranty from all other types of guaranties, however characterized.[17] Over the past two centuries, the Tennessee judiciary has created labels for guaranties. These designations can be inconsistent. At the least, the distinctions drawn between types of guaranties are murky. One distinction is not: the difference between a "continuing" [or unlimited] guaranty and all other forms of guaranty. A "continuing" guaranty is not limited to a particular transaction or identified

11. Guarantor Partners v. Huff, 830 S.W.2d 73, 76 (Tenn. Ct. App. 1992) (citing Brooks v. United Kentucky Bank, 659 S.W.2d 213, 215 (Ky. Ct. App. 1983); Dann v. Team Bank, 788 S.W.2d 182, 186 (Tex. Ct. App. 1990); Gregoire v. Lowndes Bank, 342 S.E.2d 264, 267 (Tenn. Ct. App. 1992)).
12. Commerce Union Bank v. Burger-In-A-Pouch, Inc., 657 S.W.2d 88, 92 (Tenn. 1983).
13. Guarantor Partners v. Huff, 830 S.W.2d 73, 76 (Tenn. Ct. App. 1992) (citing Smith v. Dickinson, 25 Tenn. (6 Hum.) 261, 263 (1845); FDIC v. Gamaliel Farm Supply, Inc., 726 S.W.2d 709, 712 (Ky. Ct. App. 1987)).
14. Guarantor Partners v. Huff, 830 S.W.2d 73, 76 (Tenn. Ct. App. 1992) (citing Shepherd Mall State Bank v. Johnson, 603 P.2d 1115, 1118 (Okla. 1979)); *see also* Tenn. Code Ann. § 47-3-202(2).
15. Guarantor Partners v. Huff, 830 S.W.2d 73, 76 (Tenn. Ct. App. 1992) (citing Uniwest Mortgage Co. v. Dadecor Condominiums, Inc., 877 F.2d 431, 434 (5th Cir. 1989)); *compare* Taylor v. T&N Office Equipment, Inc., 1997 Tenn. App. LEXIS 352, at *2*10 (Tenn. Ct. App. May 23, 1997).
16. Guarantor Partners v. Huff, 830 S.W.2d 73, 76 (Tenn. Ct. App. 1992).
17. Union Planters Nat'l Bank v. Markowitz, 468 F. Supp. 529, 535 (W.D. Tenn. 1979).

set of transactions, but is intended to cover future transactions, whether or not anticipated.[18]

As courts tend to enforce language as written, a continued or unlimited guaranty might contain this language:

> **Definition of Guaranteed Obligations.** As used in this Guaranty, the "Guaranteed Obligations" shall mean all present and future debts and other obligations of Borrower or any successor thereof to Lender, whether arising by contract, tort, guaranty, overdraft, or otherwise; whether direct or indirect, absolute or contingent; whether arising from an original obligation of Borrower to Lender or from Lender's purchase of an obligation of Borrower or acquisition of or by Lender of or by another lender; whether such debts or obligations are from time to time increased, reduced, or entirely extinguished and/or reincurred; whether or not the advances or events creating such debts or other obligations are presently foreseen or are incurred with or without notice to Guarantor; and regardless of the class of the debts or other obligations, be they otherwise secured or unsecured or arising from commercial, credit card, or consumer transactions. Without limiting the foregoing, the "Guaranteed Obligations" specifically includes all principal, interest, costs and expenses that Borrower may presently or hereafter owe to Lender under any instrument or agreement whatsoever, including the obligations of Borrower evidenced by that Promissory Note of approximate even date herewith made by Borrower in the principal amount of $__________ payable to the order of Lender and the obligations of Borrower under any loan or security agreement executed in connection therewith and all modifications, extensions, refinancings and renewals of any of the above.

1.4 Hypothecation and Insurance (surety bonds)

Hypothecation is the pledge of collateral by a party who is not an obligor to secure an obligation for which the pledgor is not "personally" liable. In such cases, care must be taken to ensure the hypothecation is with consideration.

Surety bonds, performance bonds and other third-party enhancements may be obtained in support of an underlying primary obligation. These are often considered insurance products and are not the subject of this chapter.

18. Third Nat'l Bank v. Friend, 626 S.W.2d 464 (Tenn. App. 1981) (citing Farmers-Peoples Bank v. Clemmer, 519 S.W.2d 801, 805 (Tenn. 1975); Mountain City Mill Co. v. Lindsey, 8 Tenn. App. 337 353 (Tenn. Ct. App. 1928).

§ 2 State Law Requirements for an Entity to Enter into a Guaranty

Partnerships, limited liability companies ("LLCs"), corporations and banks can all grant guaranties in furtherance of their business activities. Such grants are generally permitted by the appropriate Tennessee statute. Additionally, corporations, partnerships and LLCs can sometimes grant guaranties even when not in furtherance of their business activities.

2.1 Corporations

Under the Tennessee Business Corporation Act[19], a Tennessee corporation may execute guaranties provided that its corporate "charter" (and presumably bylaws) does not prevent it from doing so.[20] Equally, a corporation may pledge collateral, including for a guaranteed obligation.

2.2 Partnerships

Although at least one case[21] has held that "a partner cannot also be a surety and guarantor of a partnership debt," practitioners in Tennessee are advised to nonetheless obtain guaranties from partners, because the guaranties will contain representations, warranties and waivers that are critical to defining the relationship.

2.2.1 *General Partnerships*

Tennessee's Revised Uniform Partnership Act[22] neither expressly empowers a partnership to issue a guaranty nor expressly regulates or prohibits such activity. Generally, any partner has the authority to bind the partnership.[23]

Tennessee's partnership law provides that each partner is an agent of the partnership for the purpose of its business. An act of a partner, including the execution of an instrument in the partnership name, for apparently carrying on in *the ordinary course the partnership business or business of the kind carried on by the partnership* binds the partnership, unless the partner had no authority to act for the partnership in the particular matter and the person with whom the partner was dealing knew or had received a notification that the partner lacked authority.[24]

However, an act of a partner *which is not apparently for carrying on the ordinary course the partnership business or business of the kind carried on*

19. Tenn. Code Ann. § 48-11-101, *et seq.* (2012).
20. Tenn. Code Ann. § 48-13-102(7) (2012).
21. Hardy v. Miller, 2001 Tenn. App. LEXIS 898, *12 (Tenn. Ct. App. Dec. 10, 2001).
22. Tenn. Code Ann. § 61-1-101, *et seq.* (2012).
23. Bozeman v. Naff, 5 Tenn. App. 77 (Tenn. Ct. App. 1927).
24. Tenn. Code Ann. § 61-1-301(1) (2012).

by the partnership binds the partnership only if the act was authorized by the other partners.[25]

Apparent authority can be limited or refined by filing a "Statement of Partnership Authority."[26] Such statements, executed by at least two partners and certified, may be filed in the office of the Tennessee Secretary of State and "another office" (perhaps register of deeds).[27] "*Either*" may be effective.[28] Most general partnerships in Tennessee are not registered with the Tennessee Secretary of State.

It is advisable for an obligee to review each partnership agreement and obtain a partnership resolution certified by all partners (or appropriate partners indicated in the partnership agreement) both certifying the accuracy of the partnership agreement and the authority of the executing partner.

2.2.2 Limited Partnerships

Tennessee's Revised Uniform Limited Partnership Act[29] provides that a limited partnership may carry on any business that a [general] partnership without limited partners may carry on, unless otherwise prohibited by law.[30]

2.3 Limited Liability Companies

Tennessee's Revised Limited Liability Company Act[31] expressly permits LLCs to make contracts, including without limitation, contracts of guaranty and suretyship, unless the articles of organization or operating agreement of a particular company provide otherwise.[32]

2.4 Banks and Trust Companies

Pursuant to Tennessee's Banking Act,[33] a Tennessee state-chartered bank has the powers to assume secondary liability as an endorser of negotiable instruments, effectively guaranteeing payment thereof.[34] Section 601 of the Tennessee Banking Act allows a state-chartered bank to engage in any activity permissible for a national bank.[35] Thus, it appears Tennessee state-chartered banks may issue/execute guaranties. The Office of the Comptroller of the Currency has issued an interpretive ruling that the issuance of guaranties is within the powers of national banks.[36]

---

25. Tenn. Code Ann. § 61-1-301(2) (2012).
26. Tenn. Code Ann. § 61-1-303 (2012).
27. Tenn. Code Ann. § 61-1-105 (2012).
28. Tenn. Code Ann. § 61-1-105 (2012).
29. Tenn. Code Ann. § 61-2-101, *et seq.* (2012).
30. Tenn. Code Ann. § 61-2-107 (2012).
31. Tenn. Code Ann. § 48-249-101, *et seq.* (2012).
32. Tenn. Code Ann. § 48-249-104(6) (2012).
33. Tenn. Code Ann. § 45-2-103, *et seq.* (2012).
34. Tenn. Code Ann. § 45-2-612 (2012).
35. Tenn. Code Ann. § 45-2-601 (2012).
36. OCC Interpretive Ruling #1010, October 2004; *see also* National Bank as Guarantor or Surety on Indemnity Bond, 12 CFR § 7.1017 (2012).

2.5 Individuals

Care should be taken to ensure individual guarantors execute guaranties in their individual capacity and not in a corporate, company, or partnership capacity. In such instances, a case-by-case inquiry determines whether an individual intended to be personally bound or, instead, only issued a guaranty on behalf of a partnership or corporation and thus only in an official employment capacity. When an individual signs his or her title as well as name, unreported decisions have indicated that a personal guaranty does not exist.[37] These cases have turned more on diligence, or lack thereof, exercised by the obligee and have not followed the principles of liberal construction in favor of finding a guaranty which is the expressed case law standard in Tennessee.[38]

While a legal entity must have "authority" to execute a guaranty, an individual guarantor must have the "capacity" to enter into the guaranty. Incapacity can be a defense against the enforcement of a guaranty issued by an individual.[39]

2.6 Spousal Relationships and Property Rights

Tennessee is not a community property state. Spouses can own property jointly, as tenants in common, as tenants by the entireties, individually, in partnership, as life tenants, remaindermen or in any other manner. Both real and personal property may be owned by spouses as tenants by the entirety.[40] Real property purchased by a husband and wife is generally deemed to be owned as tenants by the entireties.[41] Under an entireties interest, each spouse holds an indivisible interest in the whole.[42] A lien creditor cannot force partition.[43] The lien creditor's judgment lien will only attach to the survivorship interest. Should the non-guarantor spouse die first, the lien creditor's interest will then extend to the whole (including survivorship interest). Conversely, joint tenancies of real or personal property, with or without the right of survivorship, may allow for partition.[44] Tennessee homestead laws provide marital rights in the homestead to a non-obligor spouse.[45] Homestead interested cannot be attached. An obligee has no *in personam* rights against a spouse who does not execute a guaranty (or other instrument) under Tennessee law. Property pledged as collateral to secure a guaranty is only available to an obligee to the extent of

---

37. *See, e.g.,* Samick Music Group v. Hoy, 2008 Tenn. App. LEXIS 639, *8-*9 (Tenn. Ct. App. Oct. 22, 2008).
38. Hassell-Hughes Lumber Co. v. Jackson, 232 SW.2d 325, 329 (Tenn. Ct. App. 1949) (citing Drummond v. Prestman, 25 U.S. 515 (1827) ("...a guarantor shall be held bound to the full extent of what appears to be his engagements, and the rule in expounding these undertakings is that the words of the guaranty are to be taken as strongly against the guarantor as the sense will admit").
39. Davis v. Bank of Illinois, 561 S.W.2d 144, 147-48 (Tenn. 1978) (Henry, C.J., dissenting) (incapacity can be shown by intoxication).
40. *See, e.g.,* Belch v. Alsup, 1999 Tenn. App. LEXIS 300, at *18 (Tenn. Ct. App. May 11, 1999) (citing Catt v. Catt, 866 S.W.2d 570, 573 (Tenn. App. 1993)).
41. *Id.*
42. Moore v. Cole, 289 S.W.2d 695, 698 (Tenn. 1956).
43. *See, e.g., id.*
44. *See, e.g., id.*; *see also, e.g.,* Tenn. Code Ann. § 45-2-703 (2012) (partition of multiple party deposit accounts).
45. Tenn. Code Ann. § 26-2-301, *et seq.* (2012).

the rights of the guarantor owner. Any interests held by a non-obligor spouse should be separately conveyed or disclaimed.

§ 3 Signatory's Authority to Execute a Guaranty

In addition to the principles outlined above, the fundamental principle is that in the absence of express authority, an individual's authority to execute a guaranty on behalf of another is established through the acts of the principal rather than those of the agent or through the perception of a third party.

Rules governing entities' entering into guaranty agreements are set forth above.[46] Obviously, if an individual executes a guaranty on behalf of an entity, and express proof of authority—like a properly executed resolution[47]—is tendered, absence of authority would be difficult to show.

However, in the absence of such written documentation, even a chief executive officer and president of a closely held corporation may lack the apparent authority to sign, on behalf of the corporation, a guaranty of a different company's indebtedness: In an important case, *Bells Banking Co. v. Jackson Centre, Inc.*, the Tennessee Court of Appeals examined a situation of apparent authority, where the president and CEO of the first corporation executed a guaranty whereby the corporation guaranteed payment of a line of credit extended to a second corporation which had just received an engineering contract from the first corporation.[48] The lender made the loan to the second corporation even after it requested from the first corporation, but did not receive, a corporate resolution authorizing the guaranty.[49] When the CEO was introduced to the lender, the lender's testimony showed uncertainty as to the CEO's actual role and the relationship of the corporate director who introduced the two.[50] The first corporation had "entered into [at least four other] financing arrangements solely upon the signature of the CEO," and other corporate resolutions authorized the CEO to act similarly in other transactions.[51] The board, however, expressly authorized each of these other transactions except one, where the CEO executed a lease without the board's consent, and which met with the board's strong disapproval.[52]

Trial testimony from board members stated that the CEO was required to bring financing proposals to the board for approval.[53] Further, the minutes of a board of directors meeting revealed that the CEO admitted that he had no

46. *See* Sections 2.1 through 2.6, *supra*.
47. *See, e.g.*, Rubio v. Precision Aerodynamics, Inc., 232 S.W.3d 738, 742-43 (Tenn. Ct. App. 2006) (a principal registered agent for service may expressly give actual authority to a subagent in direct terms, either orally or in writing).
48. Bells Banking Co. v. Jackson Centre, Inc., 938 S.W.2d 421, 422-23 (Tenn. Ct. App. 1996).
49. *Id.* at 426.
50. *Id.*
51. *Id.* at 423, 425.
52. *Id.* at 426.
53. *Id.*

authority to execute the corporate guaranty.[54] The CEO's duties were subsequently limited such that he could no longer negotiate financing on behalf of the corporation, and the corporate board sought and received a meeting with the lender, but failed to indicate that the guaranty would not be honored.[55] The corporation never attempted to rescind the guaranty on the basis that the CEO's acts were unauthorized.[56] Tennessee courts most frequently define apparent authority as:

> Such authority as the principal knowingly permits the agent to assume or which he holds the agent out as possessing; such authority as he appears to have by reason of the actual authority which he has; such authority as a reasonably prudent man, using diligence and discretion, in view of the principal's conduct, would naturally suppose the agent to possess.[57]

The cases in Tennessee hold that apparent authority must be established through the acts of the principal rather than those of the agent.[58] Accordingly, the Bells Banking Company Court concluded that the CEO acted outside the scope of his authority, and that the corporation was not bound by the guaranty.[59] Thus, while one might presume an officer of any corporation or LLC, as well as a general partner of a general or limited partnership, possesses apparent authority, actual authority is a factual inquiry in Tennessee.

§ 4 Consideration; Sufficiency of Consideration and Past Consideration

Standard contract principles apply to the analysis of consideration for a contract of guaranty. The principal agreement is sufficient consideration for an accompanying guaranty. Past consideration can be sufficient when the guaranty expresses the past consideration in writing.

4.1 Basic Consideration

As with all contracts, consideration is required to create a valid contract of guaranty.[60]

---

54. *Id.* at 427, n. 4.
55. *Id.* at 423-24.
56. *Id.* at 424, n. 2.
57. Bells Banking Co. v. Jackson Centre, Inc., 938 S.W.2d 424 (Tenn. Ct. App. 1996) (citing Rich Printing Co. v. McKellar's Estate, 330 S.W.2d 361, 376 (Tenn. App. 1959); V. L. Nicholson Co. v. Transcon Inv., 595 S.W.2d 474, 483 (Tenn. 1980)).
58. Bells Banking Co. v. Jackson Centre, Inc., 938 S.W.2d 424 (Tenn. Ct. App. 1996) (citing Franklin Distrib. Co. v. Crush Int'l, 726 S.W.2d 926, 931 (Tenn. App. 1986)).
59. Bells Banking Co. v. Jackson Centre, Inc., 938 S.W.2d 421, 427 (Tenn. Ct. App. 1996).
60. Volunteer State Bank v. Dreamer Productions, Inc., 749 S.W.2d 744, 747 (Tenn. Ct. App. 1987) (citing King v. John A. Denies Sons Co., 404 S.W.2d 580, 588 (1966)).

For instance, courts will find consideration when the guarantors were members or shareholders in the primary obligor.[61] Other Tennessee cases indicate that consideration is found if the primary obligation is advanced or the obligee detrimentally relies on the promise of the guarantor.[62]

4.2 Past Consideration

In a somewhat confusing but often cited opinion, *S.M. Williamson & Co. v. Ragsdale*, the Tennessee Supreme Court adopted—in the guaranty context—the basic rule of contracts that past consideration cannot support a current promise.[63] Importantly, the *S.M. Williamson* Court also explained that sufficient consideration to support the guaranty exists when the execution of the guaranty is a known, material inducement of the contract made between the borrower and the lender: "[a] guaranty, although executed subsequently to the creation of the principal obligation, if given in fulfillment of an agreement on the faith of which the principal obligation was created, is deemed contemporaneous in effect, and requires no other consideration."[64] Thus, the *S.M. Williamson* Court determined that later executed guarantees were nonetheless effective.

4.3 Fraudulent Transfer and Conveyance

The inquiry into sufficiency of consideration may also be tested under fraudulent transfer or conveyance standards, pursuant to the Tennessee Uniform Fraudulent Transfer Act,[65] as well as Section 548 of the U.S. Bankruptcy Code.[66] Fraudulent conveyance laws provide that in the event the guarantor received less than "reasonable equivalent value"[67] or "fair consideration"[68] AND the guarantor was insolvent at the time or rendered insolvent, then the guaranty may be avoided.[69]

For instance, if the guarantor was insolvent when executing the guaranty or, by virtue of incurring the guaranteed obligation, was rendered insolvent, the guaranty might fail in whole or in part or payments thereunder may be avoided. Questions can arise when a subsidiary guarantees the obligations of a parent or individual owner, particularly if the underlying obligation is unrelated to the subsidiary's business activities. This is commonly referred to as an upstream guaranty and is potentially subject to avoidance.

While Tennessee case law presumes that owners or parents receive benefit from the guaranty of a subsidiary's obligations, even a guaranty by a parent

61. Mountain City Mill Co. v. Lindsey, 8 Tenn. App. 337, 351 (Tenn. Ct. App. 1928) (guarantor owners deemed "the ultimate beneficiaries of its expected profits"); *see also* Doud v. Nat'l Park Bank, 54 F. 846, 847 (5th Cir. 1893); Birken v. Tapper, 189 N.W. 698 (S.D. 1922); Bond v. Farwell Co., 172 F. 58, 63 (6th Cir. 1922).
62. Galleria Associates, L.P. v. Mogk, 34 S.W.3d 874, 876 (Tenn. Ct. App. 2000).
63. S.M. Williamson & Co. v. Ragsdale, 95 S.W.2d 922, 924-25 (Tenn. 1936).
64. *Id.* (quoting 12 R. C. L., 1078).
65. Tenn. Code Ann. § 66-3-301, *et seq.* (2012).
66. 11 U.S.C. § 548 (2012) (a lack of "reasonably equivalent" value and "insolvency of the guarantor" must be found to support a fraudulent transfer under bankrupty law).
67. 11 U.S.C. § 548(a)(1)(B) (2012).
68. Tenn. Code Ann. § 66-3-305(2012).
69. 11 U.S.C. § 548(a)(1)(B) (2012); Tenn. Code Ann. § 66-3-305(2012).

or owner who is insolvent can lack consideration if the subsidiary is also insolvent. The theory is that the parent receives benefit because the value of the primary obligor is enhanced and the guarantor is benefited by the primary obligor obtaining the loan. If reasonably equivalent value or fair consideration cannot be found, the guaranty may fail.

In each instance, the obligee should be careful to analyze these issues. Each guaranty should express the solvency. For example:

> **Solvency of Guarantor.** Guarantor warrants to Lender that Guarantor is not insolvent and that Guarantor's execution hereof does not render Guarantor insolvent or with unreasonably small capital to conduct Guarantor's business or engage in anticipated transactions or that Guarantor has incurred debts or intends to incur debts beyond Guarantor's ability to pay such debts as they mature.[70]

Where a guaranty is executed after the primary obligation is incurred, the guaranty should express that the guarantor received substantial benefit by virtue of the guaranty's execution and that benefit constitutes fair consideration and reasonably equivalent value as appropriate, even providing a recitation of the circumstances involved. If the obligee would not have continued lending to the primary obligor but for the guaranty, for reasons such as a default or maturity, then such circumstances should be recited in writing in connection with receiving a guaranty after the primary obligation is already advanced.

§ 5 Notice of Acceptance

Notice of acceptance may not be required, if credit is extended to the primary obligor based upon the guaranty or if the guaranty is absolute.

Tennessee case law explains that a mere offer or proposal of guaranty does not become binding on the proposed guarantor until it is accepted by the person to whom it runs; and, as a general rule, it is essential, in order to bind the one offering the guaranty, that notice of such acceptance be seasonably given.[71] But where the guaranty is given in response to a request for it by the creditor, no notice of acceptance is necessary, for the answer of the guarantor to the request sufficiently shows that he knew he had assumed responsibility, and acceptance of a guaranty is not necessary to charge the guarantors where the guarantors are stockholders and directors in the corporation whose future debts are guaranteed and where the guaranty is delivered and credit thereafter extended on the strength of it.[72]

Indeed, the settled law in Tennessee is that "where the instrument purports to be an absolute engagement, no notice either of the acceptance of the guaranty

70. 11 U.S.C. § 548 (2012) (expression of the measures of insolvency found in the fraudulent transfer portion of the U.S. Bankruptcy Code).
71. Hassell-Hughes Lumber Co. v. Jackson, 232 S.W.2d 325, 332 (Tenn. Ct. App. 1949) (citing Mountain City Mill Co., 8 Tenn. App. 337, 349 (Tenn. Ct. App. 1928)).
72. Hassell-Hughes Lumber Co. v. Jackson, 232 S.W.2d 325, 326-29 (Tenn. Ct. App. 1949).

or of nonpayment by the principal is necessary; that such absolute guaranty takes effect as soon as it is acted upon; and to support an action against the guarantor, nothing more is necessary to be shown than that the party to whom it is addressed acted under it."[73] Tennessee courts have also relied on treatises[74] documenting the rule requiring notice by the obligee of his acceptance of the guaranty applies only where the guaranty is in legal effect an offer or proposal; and where the transaction is not merely an offer of guaranty but amounts to a direct or unconditional promise of guaranty, unless notice of acceptance is made a condition of the guaranty, all that is necessary to make the promise binding is that the promisee should act on it, such that notice of acceptance is not necessary.[75] Although conflict of authority is recognized to exist, the Supreme Court of Tennessee, in the case of *Yancey v. Brown*, stated:

Upon such consideration we have adopted the doctrine of the English authorities upon this subject; and the settled law in this State is now that, where the instrument purports to be an absolute engagement, no notice either of the acceptance of the guaranty or of non-payment by the principal is necessary."[76]

§ 6 Interpretation of Guaranties

Courts in Tennessee are guided by the principle of *strictissimi juris*, strictly construing the obligations of the guarantor. In addition, certain terms have become words of art in the context of guaranties. In other regards, courts will interpret a guaranty in the same manner by which they would interpret the language of any other contract.

6.1 General Principles

The principle of *strictissimi juris* guides the interpretation of the terms of a guaranty: a Tennessee court will strictly construe the obligations of a guarantor. In construing a commercial guaranty, the guarantor will be held to the full extent of his engagements, and the rule in construing guaranties is that the "words of guaranty are to be taken as strongly against the guarantor as sense will admit."[77] This has been the law in Tennessee since at least 1853.[78]

---

73. Hassell-Hughes Lumber Co. v. Jackson, 232 S.W.2d 325, 329-30 (Tenn. Ct. App. 1949) (quoting Yancey v. Brown, 35 Tenn. 89, 96 (Tenn. 1855)).
74. Cook v. Crabtree, 733 S.W.2d 67, 69-70 (Tenn. 1987) (relying upon Restatement of the Law, Security, §§ 144-147 (1941)); Hassell-Hughes Lumber Co. v. Jackson, 232 S.W.2d 325, 328, 330 (Tenn. Ct. App. 1949) (citing 38 C. J. S., Guaranty, Sec. 38c, p. 1177, *et seq.*; 24 Am. Jur. 910, *et seq*. Guar. Sec. 56, 57; 38 C. J. S., Guaranty Sec. 11, p. 1148).
75. Hassell-Hughes Lumber Co. v. Jackson, 232 S.W.2d 325, 329 (Tenn. Ct. App. 1949).
76. Yancey v. Brown, 35 Tenn. 89, 96 (Tenn. 1855).
77. Crossville, Inc. v. Kemper Design Center, Inc., 758 F. Supp.2d 517, 526 (M.D. Tenn. 2010).
78. Bright v. McKnight, 33 Tenn (1 Sneed) 158 (Tenn. 1853).

6.2 Guaranty of Payment versus Guaranty of Collection

Tennessee courts distinguish between the guaranty of payment and the guaranty of collection:

The authorities generally recognize that a guaranty of payment of a debt is materially different from a guaranty of collection thereof, the former being regarded as absolute and the latter as conditional. The guaranty of payment binds the guarantor to pay the debt at maturity in the event the money has not been paid by the principal debtor; and upon default by the latter, the obligation of the guarantor becomes fixed. The guaranty of collection obligates the guarantor to make payment upon the condition that the obligee or creditor has prosecuted the debtor without success. [79]

6.3 Language Regarding the Revocation of Guaranties

Tennessee law is somewhat inconsistent as to revocation of a guaranty. An absolute or continuing guaranty may only be canceled or terminated as specifically stated in the guaranty or by accepting a new guaranty as a replacement for a prior one.[80] A guaranty that is "irrevocable" may not be revoked with respect to transactions entered into by the primary obligor prior to the revocation.[81]

Whether a "continuing" guaranty is revocable may depend on various factors, including: (i) whether the primary obligor has changed; (ii) whether a series of guaranteed obligations was reasonably anticipated by the principal obligor, the guarantor and the obligee; (iii) whether the guaranty can be construed as a series of offers and whether each offer may be revoked before it is accepted.[82]

As with all guaranties, its specific language will control. Any language in a guaranty as to revocation should be carefully considered. All "replacement" guaranties, or guaranties executed upon a renewal, modification or extension should make clear that they do no replace or novate a previous guaranty but rather reaffirm and continue existing guaranteed obligations.

For a construction loan, all advances are required to complete the project. The guaranty therefore should indicate each is required and each is made by the obligee in reliance upon the guaranty. Similar language should be incorporated into guaranties of working capital loans.

79. Hassell-Hughes Lumber Co. v. Jackson, 232 S.W.2d 325, 329 (Tenn. Ct. App. 1949); *see* 24 Am. Jur. 886, Guar., Sec. 17.
80. First American Nat'l Bank v. Hall, 579 SW.2d 864, 868 (Tenn. Ct. App. 1978).
81. Clemmer v. Farmers-Peoples Bank, 548 S.W.2d 661, 663 (Tenn. Ct. App. 1976).
82. *See* Stearns v. Jones, 199 S.W. 400 (Tenn. 1917); *see also* Consumer Credit Union v. Hite, 801 S.W.2d 822, 824 (Tenn. Ct. App. 1990); In re Stalcup's Estate, 627 S.W.2d 364 (Tenn. Ct. App. 1981).

6.4 "Continuing" Guaranties

Tennessee law draws a distinction between a "continuing" and a "limited" guaranty. A limited guaranty guarantees a specific obligation or obligations or a portion thereof. For instance "that promissory note in the principal amount of $100,000 and dated June 1 ..." or "___% of the amounts outstanding under that promissory note ...."

A continuing guarantor can guarantee a particular note, but also guarantees something in addition such as "any and all amounts the primary obligor may owe to the obligee in the future."[83] A continuing guarantor is also typically obliged to pay the debts of the defaulting principal whether those debts are secured by collateral or not.[84] For instance, a continuing guarantor cannot raise defenses such as release or impairment of collateral or release of another party liable for the underlying obligation.[85]

While no specific words are required in Tennessee to create a continuing guaranty, obviously the use of the word "continuing" would have meaning as this term has been expressly recognized by Tennessee courts. Numerous specific provisions have been recognized by courts in determining that a continuing guaranty existed. Clarity that the guaranty covers all existing and future obligations is important. For example, "any and all sums of money that may now, or may at any time hereafter, be owing to you ... by [primary obligor] on the note or notes of said [primary obligor] executed by it to you or either of you and upon notes, bills receivable, drafts, acceptances, checks, and other evidences of indebtedness," was found expressly to create a continuing guaranty in *Suntrust Bank v. Dorrough*.[86] Equally, the obligor's ability to renew, modify or extend the underlying obligation has been found indicative of intent to create a continuing guaranty when the following language exists in the guaranty:

> In such a manner and upon such terms as you or either of you may see fit to renew, extend the time for, or change the manner of, payment of any such sum or sums of money, or any part thereof, without notice to us ...[87]

Also, while the guaranties in *Suntrust Bank v. Dorrough* did not contain specific language consenting to the release of collateral, the guarantors implicitly consented to such changes by the fact that the guaranties at issue were continuing guaranties covering all debts owing to the creditor.[88]

---

83. Stearns v. Jones, 199 S.W. 400, 401 (Tenn. 1917) (a "'continuing guaranty' is one which is not limited to a particular transaction or specific transactions, but which is intended to cover future transactions until revoked. It is generally unlimited as to time, but frequently limited as to the amount of indebtedness to be charged against the guarantor"); Suntrust Bank v. Dorrough, 59 S.W.3d 153, 157 (Tenn. Ct. App. 2001).
84. Suntrust Bank v. Dorrough, 59 S.W.3d 153, 158 (Tenn. Ct. App. 2001) (citing Union Planters Nat'l Bank of Memphis v. Markowitz, 468 F. Supp. 529, 535 (W.D. Tenn. 1979)).
85. Suntrust Bank v. Dorrough, 59 S.W.3d 153, 157-58 (Tenn. Ct. App. 2001).
86. *Id.*
87. *Id.* at 157.
88. *Id.*

6.5 "Absolute and Unconditional" Guaranties

Cases interpreting Tennessee law indicate that a guaranty becomes absolute or unconditional upon default or alternatively upon default and demand for payment.[89] "When the guaranty is absolute, no demand or exhaustion of the maker is required; nor is any notice required of the acceptance or default."[90]

6.6 "Liable as a Primary Obligor and not Merely as Surety"

Tennessee courts enforce the literal language contained in guaranties strongly.[91] "[A]n absolute guaranty is an 'unconditional undertaking on the part of the guarantor that he will pay the debt or perform the obligation immediately upon the debtor's default without any necessity to first exhaust the principal.'"[92]

§ 7 Defenses of the Guarantor

The defenses that may be available to a guarantor can be grouped into four categories: (1) statutory defenses; (2) defenses of the primary obligor; (3) "suretyship defenses"; and (4) other defenses.

7.1 Tennessee Statutory Defenses

7.1.1 Requiring Creditor to sue Primary Obligor

Tennessee Code Annotated Section 47-12-101, entitled "Notice requiring creditor to sue – Creditor's inaction," while subject to some interpretation, provides that a surety [or guarantor]:

> who perceives that the principal [primary obligor] is likely to become insolvent, or to migrate from the state, without previously discharging the debt or obligation, the surety may, if the debt or security be due, by notice in writing, require the creditor forthwith to put it to suit … Unless, within thirty (30) days thereafter, the creditor [obligee] commences an action, and proceeds with due diligence in the ordinary course of law to recover judgment for the debt or obligation, and by execution to make the amount due thereon, the creditor shall forfeit the right which the creditor would otherwise have to recover it from the surety.[93]

---

89. *See, e.g.,* Commerce Union Bank v. Burger-In-A-Pouch, Inc., 657 S.W.2d 88, 93 (Tenn. 1983) (upon default, guarantor/surety becomes primarily liable); Klein v. Kern, 28 S.W. 295 (Tenn. 1894); In re Winters, 2012 Bankr. LEXIS 1030, at *8 (Bankr. E.D. Tenn. Mar. 12, 2012).
90. Elgin City Banking Co. v. Hall, 108 S.W. 1068, 1072 (Tenn. 1907).
91. *See* Samick Music Group v. Hoy, 2008 Tenn. App. LEXIS 639, *8 (Tenn. Ct. App. Oct. 22, 2008) (guarantor completed form guaranteeng the obligations as his own, as opposed to obligations of primary obligor).
92. In re: Winters, 2012 Bankr. LEXIS 1030, *8 (Bankr. E.D. Tenn. Mar. 12, 2012) (citations omitted).
93. Tenn. Code Ann. § 47-2-101 (2012).

There have been no reported decisions interpreting this statute for some time.[94] The surety or guarantor must clearly and unambiguously state the appropriate statutory elements in the notice, the delivery of which upon the obligee must be attested by two witnesses.[95] The statute may be used as a defense to endorsement of an instrument.[96] At least one case indicates that the statute is ineffective and cannot be used to the guarantor's advantage if the principal [primary obligor] lives outside Tennessee and the lawsuit by the obligee would have to be brought outside the state.[97] However, if a non-resident primary obligor has property subject to execution in Tennessee, the creditor must still proceed to suit against the primary obligor within 30 days following the guarantor's statutory notice in order to preserve the guaranteed obligation.

7.1.2 Ineffective against Future Obligations (consumer only)

Tennessee Code Annotated Section 47-12-107 provides that no guaranty "... which guaranties the performance of all present and future obligations shall be enforceable against a surety unless the individual or organization agrees in writing to guaranty the future obligation."[98] The exception is limited to the guaranty of personal obligations and not applicable to commercial obligations.

This provision of the statute is poorly written and unclear.[99] It may be more proper to substitute "consumer obligations" for "personal obligations." Consumer obligations are defined in state and federal law, including truth-in-lending laws, as obligations incurred for personal, family or household purposes and include residential mortgage transactions.

Accordingly, a guaranty of a future obligation in a consumer transaction should be set forth in writing in detail. For instance, "all moneys advanced to complete construction of Jane Doe's new principal residence whether or not covered by the construction promissory note in the amount of $100,000..." might be sufficiently specific. The safer approach is that any unanticipated future advances or new credit must be separately (by amendment, not by novation) guaranteed in consumer transactions in Tennessee.

7.1.3 Violation of Tennessee's Anti-deficiency Statute

In 2010, the Tennessee legislature amended its foreclosure provisions[100] to add a rebuttable presumption that the foreclosing creditor has bid "market value" at each foreclosure sale.[101] In the event the debtor shows by a preponderance of the evidence that the bid amount was materially less than "fair market value,"

94. Apparently, the most recent case that cites this statute is Meredith v. Dibrell, 155 S.W. 163 (Tenn. 1913).
95. Tenn. Code Ann § 47-12-102 (2012).
96. Tenn. Code Ann. § 47-2-104 (2012).
97. Hill v. Planter's Bank, 22 Tenn. 670, 671-72 (Tenn. 1842).
98. Tenn. Code Ann. § 47-12-107 (2012); *see* Tenn. Code Ann. § 29-2-101(2) (statute of frauds).
99. The only known case to cite this statute, *In re: Lemka*, adjudicated the issue before the court without interpreting the statute. 201 B.R. 765, 757 (Bankr. E.D. Tenn. 1996).
100. Tenn. Code Ann. § 35-5-101, *et seq.* (2012).
101. Tenn. Code Ann. § 35-5-118 (2012).

the amount of the deficiency will be reduced by the difference between the bid amount and the fair market value as determined by the court. The statute does not specify how "fair market value" is to be determined.

7.2 Defenses of the Primary Obligor

7.2.1 *Generally*

Defenses available to the primary obligor—such as fraud, duress, and undue influence,[102] negligence,[103] and usury[104]—are also available to the guarantor in Tennessee.

7.2.2 *Purported cancellation of Underlying Obligation*

Cancellation of the underlying obligation may be a defense. If payment of the underlying obligation is avoidable as a bankruptcy preference[105] or fraudulent transfer[106] or is otherwise avoidable under the trustee's "strong arm powers,"[107] is the guaranty reinstated?

While application of bankruptcy law generally specifies that the obligee will retain an unsecured claim against the bankruptcy estate for moneys returned, what happens to the released guaranty is less clear. Accordingly, each guaranty should clarify that the guarantor's obligation to reimburse the obligee for avoided amounts is intended to survive the purported cancellation of the guaranty.

7.3 Defenses available to the Guarantor Exclusive of the Primary Obligor

7.3.1 *Failure of Obligee to Perform and Failure of Consideration*

A guarantor may show that the obligee failed to perform such that there is a partial or complete failure of consideration.[108]

7.3.2 *Modification of the Underlying Obligation, including Release*

Under Tennessee law, modifications to the underlying obligation may permit the guarantor to raise certain defenses to liability.

102. FDIC v. Turner, 869 F.2d 270, 274 (6th Cir. 1989).
103. First Tennessee Bank Nat'l Ass'n v. Barreto, 268 F.3d 319, 329 (M.D. Tenn. 2001).
104. Parker v. Bethel Hotel Co., 34 S.W. 209, 289 (Tenn. 1895).
105. 11 USC § 547 (2012).
106. 11 USC § 548 (2012).
107. 11 USC § 544 (2012).
108. Volunteer State Bank v. Dreamer Productions, Inc., 749 S.W.2d 744, 747 (Tenn. Ct. App. 1987).

First, "a renewal note does not discharge the original note unless all of the parties thereto agree that the renewal will have this effect."[109] However, a Tennessee appellate court reached a different result when it was found that the "renewal" note, in fact, "refinanced" the original note such that the original note was paid off by the new note.[110] In addition "where the renewal note is invalid it does not operate to discharge the original note."[111]

Second, fundamentally increasing the principal due from the borrower in an amount that exceeds a mere "modification" (as that word is defined and has been interpreted by the federal courts[112]) may require execution of a new guaranty, and "once a creditor has applied a payment to a particular debt, it may not unilaterally change the application of that payment, particularly to the detriment of a guarantor."[113] At least one case has held that an obligee' s reliance on guaranties' provision that they applied to "all renewals, extensions and modifications" was insufficient to bind the guaranty of additional principal indebtedness; language specifically stating that the guarantor is guaranteeing repayment of any additional indebtedness incurred by the primary obligor in the future is, therefore, strongly recommended.[114] Likewise, *Bank of Waynesboro v. Ghosh*[115] held that a deceased guarantor's estate was discharged when the creditor and the principal obligor agreed to extend the time for payment of principal without the guarantor's consent, although recent cases[116] suggest that *Ghosh* is no longer good law. Accordingly, express contractual terms applying the guaranty to additional notes, increases in indebtedness, extensions in payment dates, cross-collateralization, and default, as well as extensions in maturity dates, are recommended.[117]

Third, "[u]nder the general principles of suretyship law, a release of the principal also releases the surety to the extent that the principal is released ... [t]he surety is not released, however, if the creditor in the release reserves [its] rights against the surety or if the surety consents to remain liable notwithstanding release of the principal," in which case the surety is preserved.[118] That is, if the terms of the guaranty specifically include that the guarantor remains liable for the full amount of the indebtedness following the creditor's and obligor's settlement or compromise, the guarantor is not discharged from performance of his or her obligations. Courts have ruled that even in the absence of specific language consenting to the release of collateral, guaran-

109. Commerce Union Bank v. Burger-In-A-Pouch, Inc., 657 S.W.2d 88, 90 (Tenn. 1983) (citing First Nat'l. Bank of Sparta v. Yowell, 294 S.W. 1101, 1103-04 (Tenn. 1926)).
110. Cumberland Bank v. G & S Implement Co., 211 S.W.2d 233, 230-32 (Tenn. Ct. App. 2006).
111. First Nat'l Bank of Sparta v. Yowell, 294 S.W. 1101, 1104 (Tenn. 1926).
112. Crossville, Inc. v. Kemper Design Center, Inc., 758 F.Supp.2d 517, 524 (M.D. Tenn. 2010) (citing Weaver v. Ogle, 2 Tenn. App. 563, 579 (Tenn. Ct. App. 1926) (evaluating whether a treble increase in principal was as a mere "modification" of the principal amount)).
113. Crossville, Inc. v. Kemper Design Center, Inc., 758 F.Supp.2d 517, 527 (M.D. Tenn. 2010).
114. Crossville, Inc. v. Kemper Design Center, Inc., 758 F.Supp.2d 517, 524 (M.D. Tenn. 2010).
115. Bank of Waynesboro v. Ghosh, 576 S.W.2d 759, 761-62 (Tenn. 1979).
116. *See, e.g.,* Cumberland Bank v. G & S Implement Co., 211 S.W.3d 223, 232 n. 17 (Tenn. Ct. App. 2006).
117. Sample language provided, *supra*, at § 1.3.
118. Hickory Springs Mfg. Co., Inc. v. Mehlman, 541 S.W.2d 97, 99 (Tenn. 1976) (citing Becker v. Faber, 19 N.E.2d 997, 999 (N.Y. 1939); Continental Bank & Trust Co. v. Akwa, 206 N.W.2d 174, 181 (Wisc. 1973); and Shows v. Steiner, Lobman & Frank, 57 So. 700, (Ala. 1911)).

tors may "implicitly consent" to such changes by executing a properly drafted continuing guaranty.[119]

7.3.3 Release or Impairment of Security [collateral] for the Underlying Obligation

There is a recognized exception to the general rule of discharge upon release of collateral where there is consent to the release.[120] The general rule in Tennessee is that when a creditor has consented to the release of collateral, a guarantor is discharged from his or her obligations.[121] However, this rule is subject to an important exception: the guarantor's consent, as determined by the terms of the guaranty agreement.[122] Similarly, the general rule is that a guarantor is discharged to the extent of any loss caused by a creditor's failure to perfect a security interest.[123] Again, this rule is not unqualified, because the terms of a guaranty, executed by a guarantor "who is not a party to the instrument," are determinative in the cases of unlimited and continuing guaranties.[124]

7.3.4 Failure to notify Guarantor of Article 9 foreclosure

Tennessee's enactment of the UCC defines "debtor" as "a person having an interest, other than a security interest or other lien in the collateral, whether or not that person is an obligor.[125] "Obligor" is defined as a person that … owes payment or other performance of the obligation ... has provided collateral for the obligation … or is otherwise accountable in whole or in part for the obligation.[126] UCC Article 9 requires notice of an impending foreclosure to be sent to the "debtor" and any "secondary obligor."[127] The penalty for failure to provide notice can be the loss of any deficiency and thus the loss of a guaranty.

7.3.5 Failure to hold a Commercially Reasonable Sale of Collateral (Article 9)

One of the most litigated defenses to payment of an obligation and therefore a guaranty is the failure to conduct a "commercially reasonable" sale of collateral under Article 9 of the UCC.[128] Like failure to provide notice to the guarantor,

---

119. Suntrust Bank v. Dorrough, 59 S.W.3d 153, 157 (Tenn. Ct. App. 2001).
120. Suntrust Bank v. Dorrough, 59 S.W.3d 153, 157-58 (Tenn. Ct. App. 2001); *see* Ottenheimer Publishers v. Regal Publishers, Inc., 626 S.W.2d 276, 280 (Tenn. Code Ann. 1981).
121. FDIC v. Associated Nursery Systems, Inc., 948 F.2d 233, 240 (6th Cir. 1991) (citing 38 Am.Jur.2d Guaranty § 84 (1968)); Union Planters Nat'l Bank of Memphis v. Markowitz, 468 F. Supp. 529, 533 (W.D.Tenn.(1979).
122. FDIC v. Associated Nursery Systems, Inc., 948 F.2d 233, 240 (6th Cir. 1991).
123. Union Planters Nat'l Bank of Memphis v. Markowitz, 468 F. Supp. 529, 533-34 (W.D. Tenn. 1979); *see* Tenn. Code Ann. § 47-3-605(e).
124. Union Planters Nat'l Bank of Memphis v. Markowitz, 468 F. Supp. 529, 535 (W.D. Tenn. 1979).
125. Tenn. Code Ann. § 47-9-102(28) (2012).
126. Tenn. Code Ann. § 47-9-102(59) (2012).
127. Tenn. Code Ann. § 47-9-611(c) (2012).
128. Tenn. Code Ann. § 47-9-610(b) (2012).

one penalty for failure of commercial resasonableness is loss of the ability to collect some or all of a deficiency amount.[129]

7.4 Other Defenses

7.4.1 *Modification of the Guaranty/New guaranty*

In one case, the Tennessee Court of Appeals found a later guaranty released the guarantor from former guaranties when it appeared that the later one was accepted as a substitute for the earlier.[130]

7.4.2 *Failure to pursue Primary Obligor*

Since Tennessee courts distinguish between the guaranty of payment and the guaranty of collection, a conditional guaranty, which only guarantees collection, necessarily requires at least a preliminary effort to pursue the primary obligor before pursuing the guarantor.[131] This defense is not, however, available or applicable to unlimited or continuing guaranties.[132]

7.4.3 *Failure to provide Notice of Acceptance or Notice of Default*

When the guarantor makes the mere "offer" to provide the guaranty, the creditor must provide notice of acceptance, and the failure to do so makes the guaranty vulnerable under ordinary contract analysis.[133] However, when it is the creditor who requests the guaranty from the guarantor, notice of acceptance is not necessary and this defense is not available to the guarantor.[134]

Likewise, if a guaranty is absolute or unconditional, in that it guarantees payment and not merely collection, and as is normally the case in a continuing guaranty, notice of the primary obligor's default is not required to activate the guarantor's liability.[135] A defense based on the creditor's failure to provide notice of default is, therefore, generally only available to a guarantor who has executed a conditional guaranty, guaranteeing only collection.[136]

7.4.4 *Statute of Limitations*

The statute of limitations in Tennessee for a suit on a demand note is either six or 10 years: if demand is made, the suit must be brought within six years of demand;[137] if no demand is made, since the maturity date on a demand note

---

129. *See* Tenn. Code Ann. §§ 47-9-610, 615 and 616 (2012).
130. First American Nat'l Bank of Nashville v. Hall, et al., 579 SW.2d 864 (Tenn. Ct. App. 1978) citing, 38 C.J.S. Guaranty § 80 p.1249.
131. Hassell-Hughes Lumber Co. v. Jackson, 232 SW.2d 325, 329 (Tenn. Ct. App. 1949).
132. *Id.* at 325, 330.
133. Hassell-Hughes Lumber Co. v. Jackson, 232 S.W.2d 325, 332 (Tenn. Ct. App. 1949) (citing Mountain City Mill Co., 8 Tenn. App. 337, 349 (Tenn. Ct. App. 1928)).
134. Hassell-Hughes Lumber Co. v. Jackson, 232 SW.2d 325, 332 (Tenn. Ct. App. 1949).
135. *Id.*
136. *Id.*
137. Tenn. Code Ann. § 28-3-109(c); Tenn. Code Ann. § 47-3-118(b).

is also the execution date, the suit must be brought within 10 years of execution date.[138] The statute of limitations for a note bearing a maturity date, or a note whose due date has been accelerated, is six years after the maturity date or date of acceleration.[139] The limitations period may be tolled by the borrower's voluntary partial payment of interest.[140] The cause of action accrues on an installment note upon each installment when it becomes due, and the statutory period begins to run from that moment on that installment; a suit may be brought in successive actions upon each default in an installment for the amount of that defaulted installment.[141]

The limitations period for suits on guaranties and leases is six years from the date of accrual.[142] "When a right exists, but a demand is necessary to entitle the party to an action, the limitation commences from the time the plaintiff's right to make the demand accrues, and not from the date of the demand."[143] The cases are silent as to when a claim on a breach of a written guaranty accrues if demand is not necessary, but case law seems to suggest that the claim accrues either upon the earlier of the gratuitous provision of demand or at the time of the breach.[144]

A waiver in a guaranty[145]—or even in a letter [146]—of the right to plead the statute of limitations as a defense is enforceable, and the statute of limitations may be inapplicable to a properly drafted "continuing, absolute and unconditional" guaranty.[147] Thus, as even a limited guaranty or guaranty of a specific obligation may apply to an underlying obligation payable in installments for more than six years, it is important to provide either a waiver of statutes of limitations within the guaranty or language stating that the statute is applicable for six years following the due date of any obligation, including by acceleration.

7.4.5 Statute of Frauds

While cases recognizing oral promises or ambiguous writings that reflect an intent to stand for the debt of another exist, Tennessee's statute of frauds requires that each guaranty be in writing in order to bring an action on the guaranty.[148]

138. Tenn. Code Ann. § 47-3-118(b) ("if no demand for payment is made to the maker, an action to enforce [a demand] note is barred if neither principal nor interest on the note has been paid for a continuous period of ten (10) years"); Slaughter v. Slaughter, 922 S.W.2d 115 (Tenn. Ct. App. 1995).
139. Tenn. Code Ann. § 47-3-118(a) (2012).
140. Graves v. Sawyer, 588 S.W.2d 542, 544 (Tenn. 1979).
141. Consumer Credit Union v. Hite, 801 S.W.2d 822, 824 (Tenn. Ct. App. 1990) ("In matters of installment notes containing acceleration clauses, the cause of action as to future non-delinquent installments does not accrue until the creditor chooses to take advantage of the clause and accelerate the balance") (citing Farmers & Merchants Bank v. Templeton, 646 S.W.2d 920, 923 (Tenn. Ct. App. 1982)).
142. Tenn. Code Ann. § 28-3-109(a)(3) (2012); First American Bank of Nashville, N.A. v. Woods, 734 S.W.2d 622, 630 (Tenn. Ct. App. 1987).
143. Tenn. Code Ann. § 28-1-102 (2012); FDIC v. Cureton, 842 F.2d 887, 890, n. 3 (6th Cir. 1988).
144. *See* FDIC v. Cureton, 842 F.2d 887, 890, n. 3 (6th Cir. 1988); Beal Bank, S.S.B. v. RBM Co., 1999 Tenn. App. LEXIS 790, *23-26 (Tenn. Ct. App. Nov. 30, 1999) (guarantors not notified of default, with substantive issues resolved under Georgia law, but procedural limitations period decided under Tennessee law); Consumer Credit Union v. Hite, 801 S.W.2d 822, 824 (Tenn. Ct. App. 1990).
145. Hardeman County Bank v. Stallings, 917 S.W.2d 695, 699 (Tenn. Ct. App. 1995).
146. First American Bank of Nashville, N.A. v. Woods, 734 S.W.2d 622, 631 (Tenn. Ct. App. 1987).
147. Hardeman County Bank v. Stallings, 917 S.W.2d 695, 699 (Tenn. Ct. App. 1995) (citing Union Planters Nat'l Bank v. Markowitz, 468 F. Supp. 529, 532 (W.D. Tenn. 1979)).
148. Tenn. Code Ann. § 29-2-101(2) (2012).

§ 8 Waiver of Defenses by the Guarantor

The overriding principle concerning a waiver of defenses in a guaranty is that specificity, whether in boilerplate or otherwise, is determinative. General and nonspecific waivers are less enforceable.

8.1 Defenses that cannot be Waived

Tennessee cases are mostly silent as to what defenses cannot be waived in a guaranty contract. However, as discussed, *infra* at § 7.3, one relatively recent case has indicated that waiver of certain formation-related defenses requires some measure of specificity. Further, a 1979 federal case[149] held that the negligence of a secured creditor obligee can be waived by agreement, including a "duty of reasonable care to preserve collateral," notwithstanding language to the contrary in UCC Article 9.[150] However, a subsequent Sixth Circuit case[151] observed that, "as a matter of federal law, the lack of notice and commercial unreasonableness defenses extend to an unconditional guarantor after the debtor has defaulted," and determined that, if asked, the Tennessee Supreme Court would adopt the rule that guarantors are entitled to step into the shoes of debtors and raise the defense of commercial unreasonableness. The same court also noted that "[t]he trend in state court decisions is to recognize unconditional guarantors as UCC debtors entitled to the nonwaivable defenses,"[152] which is consistent with the UCC, as adopted by Tennessee:

> (T)he obligations of good faith, diligence, reasonableness and care prescribed by chapters 1 through 9 of this title may not be disclaimed by agreement ...[153]

Further, Tennessee Code Annotated § 47-9-602 generally specifies obligations which cannot be waived[154]; the list is applicable to "obligors," which is defined to include guarantors.[155]

8.2 Election of Remedies

A creditor need not dispose of collateral under Article 9 of the UCC (even if the collateral is repossessed and held by the creditor) prior to pursuit of the guarantor if the guaranty provides for the creditor's election of remedies.[156] Equally, Tennessee's antideficiency statute applicable to the foreclosure of real property is inapplicable when the obligee only proceeds to collect the underlying debt and elects not to foreclose on the real property collateral.[157]

149. Union Planters Nat'l Bank v. Markowitz, 468 F. Supp. 529, 535 (W.D. Tenn. 1979).
150. Tenn. Code Ann. § 47-9-207.
151. First Heritage Nat'l Bank v. Keith, 902 F.2d 33 (6th Cir. 1990).
152. *Id.*
153. Tenn. Code Ann. § 47-1-302(b).
154. Tenn. Code Ann. § 47-9-602 (2012).
155. Tenn. Code Ann. § 49-9-102(59) (2012).
156. Suntrust Equip. Fin. & Leasing Corp. v. A&E Salvage, Inc., 2009 U.S. Dist. LEXIS 99561, *13-*14 (E.D. Tenn. Oct. 26, 2009) (applying Maryland's adoption of the UCC).
157. Tenn. Code Ann. § 35-1-118(d)(2) (2012).

8.3 "Catch-all" Waivers

Though catch-all waiver language may be effective, it is advisable for drafters to include waivers to specific suretyship defenses.

Citing older Tennessee case law to the effect that "a guarantor in a commercial transaction shall be held to the full extent of his engagements and ... the words of a guaranty are to be taken as strongly against the guarantor as the sense will admit,"[158] Tennessee cases adopt both the principle that the (ambiguous or "boilerplate") language in a guaranty should be construed strictly against the maker, and the principle that so called "catch-all" waivers may not be enforceable unless stated with specificity.[159] The inherent dichotomy in the law is reflected in *Shelby Electric Company*, where the Tennessee Court of Appeals evaluated an issue of first impression—whether a defense of fraud or fraudulent inducement can be waived under the general waiver of "any defenses" in a guaranty—and explored the reasoning of New York courts in adjudicating boilerplate and nonboilerplate "catch-all" waivers executed by the guarantor.[160] The Tennessee Court of Appeals ruled that the agreement "[to waive] any defenses given to guarantors at law or in equity other than actual payment and performance of the indebtedness" contained in a bank's nonnegotiable form guaranty, and lacking a precise reference to a waiver of the defenses of fraud or fraudulent inducement, was insufficiently specific to waive them.[161] The court did not reach the issue of whether a specific waiver of those defenses would be enforceable.[162]

8.4 Use of Specific Waivers

As stated above, Tennessee case law supports the idea that while "catch-all" waivers may be partially enforceable, express waivers are nonetheless preferred. Further, although implied waivers have been recognized, the confluence of the general observation that all guaranties are evaluated using the language therein with the principle of *strictissimi juris* reveals that including specific waivers in a Tennessee guaranty is always preferable.

158. Farmers-Peoples Bank v. Clemmer, 519 S.W.2d 801, 804-05 (Tenn. 1975).
159. Shelby Elec. Co. v. Forbes, *205 S.W.3d 448, 455 (Tenn. Ct. App. 2005), perm. app. den.* Shelby Elec. Co. v. Forbes, 2006 Tenn. LEXIS 827 (Tenn. Sept. 5, 2006).
160. Shelby Elec. Co. v. Forbes, *205 S.W.3d 448, 453-54 (Tenn. Ct. App. 2005), perm. app. den.* Shelby Elec. Co. v. Forbes, 2006 Tenn. LEXIS 827 (Tenn. Sept. 5, 2006) (*interpreting* Citibank, N.A. v. Plapinger, 485 N.E.2d 974 (N.Y. 1985); and Mfrs. Hanover Trust v. Yanakas, 7 F.3d 310, 316 (2d Cir. 1993)). In *Citibank, N.A. v. Plapinger*, the Court of Appeals of New York determined that the guarantors, sophisticated businesspeople who negotiated the terms of the guaranties, knowingly "denominated their obligation unconditional." 485 N.E.2d 974, 977 (N.Y. 1985). The following "catch-all" language satisfactorily waived the guarantors' defenses of fraud and fraud in the inducement: "absolute and unconditional" nature was "irrespective of (i) any lack of validity ... of the ... [loan agreement] ... or any other agreement or instrument relating thereto," or "(vii) any other circumstance which might otherwise constitute a defense to the guarantee." *Id.* at 975. This reasoning was narrowed in Mfrs. Hanover Trust v. Yanakas, wherein the Second Circuit determined that, because of the absolute vitiation of every contract tainted by fraud, a waiver of the defense of fraudulent inducement also requires language specifically disclaiming the existence of or reliance upon specified representations of the obligee. 7 F.3d 310, 315 (2d Cir. 1993). Accordingly, the following language, contained in a pre-printed, form guaranty, and was unaccompanied by any "disclaimers of the representations that formed the basis of" the fraudulent inducement defense, was insufficient to waive the defense: "[that it is a guaranty of payment] regardless of the validity, enforceability of any of said Obligations or purported Obligations ..." *Id.* at 316.
161. Shelby Elec. Co. v. Forbes, *205 S.W.3d 448, 455 (Tenn. Ct. App. 2005).*
162. *Id.* at *448, 455, n. 4.*

§ 9 Third-party Pledgors—Defenses and Waiver Thereof

Because the pledgor arguably stands in the relation of a guarantor to the principal obligor to the extent of the pledge, it may most likely avail itself of the defenses of a guarantor. It may also waive such defenses.

In addition to the hypothecation discussion set forth above,[163] it appears that the law as applied to sureties would also apply to a third-party pledgor and that a pledgor generally has the same defenses as a surety. A guarantor who pledges certificates of deposit as collateral for a loan is not entitled to additional defenses beyond those available as a guarantor by virtue of the hypothecation.[164]

§ 10 Reliance

If the guaranty was required by the creditor as part of the transaction, reliance is not required to claim under the guaranty.

Tennessee case law outlines a basic rule: notice of such acceptance must be seasonably given.[165] It logically and necessarily follows that reliance is required. However, where the guaranty is provided in response to the obligee's request for one, no notice of acceptance—and therefore no reliance—is necessary. The provision of the executed guaranty itself is proof that the gurantor knew she had assumed responsibility. The body of documents for the closing (or an underlying loan agreement) is typically indicative of the fact that the creditor was relying on the guaranty.[166]

§ 11 Jointly and Severally Liable Guarantors—Contribution and Reduction of Obligations upon Payment by a Co-obligor

There are few cases specifically addressing multiple primary guarantors' joint, several, or joint and several liability for the guaranteed debt, and

163. *See infra*, at § 1.4.
164. Taylor v. T&N Office Equipment, Inc., 1997 Tenn. App. LEXIS 352, *2, *10 (Tenn. Ct. App. May 23, 1997).
165. Hassell-Hughes Lumber Co. v. Jackson, 232 S.W.2d 325, 332 (Tenn. Ct. App. 1949) (citing Mountain City Mill Co., 8 Tenn. App. 337, 349 (Tenn. Ct. App. 1928)).
166. Hassell-Hughes Lumber Co. v. Jackson, 232 S.W.2d 325, 326-29 (Tenn. Ct. App. 1949).

although Tennessee follows the common law[167] with respect to contribution among guarantors, the actual treatment of factual scenarios varies greatly.

Guarantors who are jointly and severally liable are presumed to equally share the secondary obligation, and only discharge of a joint or common—as opposed to a merely several—obligation can give rise to a claim for contribution to others.[168] Likewise, Tennessee law is that the creditor is not obliged to seek full payment from more than one such guarantor. Insofar as one guarantor has paid out more than its proportional share of the obligation, it may recover from the other guarantors proportionate to their liability, as determined by ordinary process under contract, tort, property or even equitable principles.[169] A person is not entitled to contribution until he or she has paid more than his or her fair share of a joint obligation.[170]

In one of the only modern Tennessee cases to address liability among multiple guarantors, *Cook v. Crabtree*, the Tennessee Court of Appeals concluded that a divorced wife whose signature was forged on one guaranty instrument but was genuine on a later guaranty was a mere "sub-surety," who bore no duty of contribution to the principal sureties, three male owners of a borrowing corporation.[171] The *Cook* court[172] relied heavily on the Restatement of the Law, Security § 144, *et seq.* (1941) and the comments thereto, such that following test to distinguish cosureties and subsureties is relied on by courts interpreting Tennessee law:

---

167. Unfortunately, in the context of guaranties, the terms "contribution," "subrogation" and "indemnification" are used confusingly and sometimes synonymously in Tennessee caselaw; nevertheless, when asked to identify the differences, Tennessee courts, as with the common law, will likely recognize the distinction that, unlike the term "contribution," the terms "subrogation" and "indemnification" place the *entire* burden for a loss on the primary guarantor or primary obligor who should have discharged the debt, based on the following definitions:

> Contribution: The right that gives one of several people who are liable on a common debt the ability to *recover proportionately* from each of the others when that one person discharges the debt for the benefit of all; the right to demand that another who is jointly liable for a third party's injury supply part of what is required to compensate the third party.

Black's Law Dictionary 378 (9th ed. 2009) (emphasis added).

> Subrogation: The substitution of one party for another whose debt the party pays, *entitling the paying party to rights, remedies or securities that would otherwise belong to the debtor*. For example, a surety who has paid a debt is, by subrogation, entitled to any security for the debt held by the creditor and the benefit of any judgment the creditor has against the debtor, and may proceed against the debtor as the creditor would.

Black's Law Dictionary 1563-64 (9th ed. 2009) (emphasis added); *see* Blankenship v. Estate of Bain, 5 S.W.3d 647, 650 (Tenn. 1999) (subrogation is defined as "the substitution of another person in the place of a creditor, so that the person in whose favor it is exercised succeeds to the rights of the creditor in relation to the debt").

> Indemnity: A duty to make good *any* loss, damage, or liability incurred by another.

Black's Law Dictionary 837 (9th ed. 2009) (emphasis added). Thus, in a guaranty context, the principal differences between indemnification and subrogation appear to be that (1) although a party entitled to indemnification has a right to demand and receive reimbursement (for its payment of the debt) from the obligor whose duties it performed, a party entitled to indemnification does not necessarily step into the shoes—and thus, unlike a party entitled to subrogation, adopt the security interests—of the creditor whose debt was satisfied; and (2) an obligor seeking indemnification from another obligor does so of its own volition, whereas a subrogee succeeds to another's right to payment.

168. Hardy v. Miller, 2001 Tenn. App. LEXIS 898, *15-*16 (Dec. 10, 2001); *see also* Anderson v. May, 57 Tenn. 84, 87 (Tenn. 1872) (appearing to apply an analysis of joint and several liability to a guaranty situation, but holding that a guarantor was liable to a landlord, regardless of whether the landlord was represented by a partnership or an individual partner).
169. Cook v. Crabtree, 733 S.W.2d 67, 68 (Tenn. Ct. App.1987).
170. Frazier v. Frazier, 430 S.W.2d 655, 660 (1968); Young v. Kittrell, 833 S.W.2d 505, 508 (Tenn. Ct. App. 1992).
171. Cook v. Crabtree, 733 S.W.2d 67, 70 (Tenn. Ct. App.1987).
172. *Id.* at 67, 69-70.

§ 146. Determination of the Relation Between Sureties.

Where there are two or more sureties for the same duty of the principal, the following rules apply to the determination of the relation between themselves:

(a) The sureties may conclusively determine their relation by agreement.
(b) The sureties are cosureties in the absence of agreement or stipulation of either to the contrary or of duties or equities imposing the principal liability on one of them.
(c) A surety is a subsurety if he has so stipulated and is not under a duty to assume a greater liability, except to the extent that his stipulation will inequitably increase the obligation of another surety.

In the comments to Section 146(b) it is said that absent an agreement, where two or more sureties are bound to a common duty, they are assumed to be cosureties "unless there is some positive reason for making one a principal and the other a subsurety."[173][174]

Cook and the Restatement recognize two exceptions to the assumption of co-suretyship: first, that one surety has such a business interest in the transaction that he will be the principal surety; and, second, when the surety assumes his obligation at the request of another surety who is already bound.[175]

Unfortunately, in the 2001 opinion of *Hardy v. Miller*, the Court of Appeals of Tennessee muddied the waters with a different approach.[176] In *Hardy*, a joint venture comprised of 10 individuals borrowed $1.4 million, and each member executed a suretyship agreement guaranteeing payment up to $280,000 per member.[177] The joint venture expelled a member, and the venture subsequently executed a renewal and modification, followed by a forbearance agreement.[178] Three members paid the creditor $280,000 each, and the expelled member paid approximately $23,000, satisfying the debt.[179] The three members filed suit against the expelled debtor for his prorated share of the debt.[180] The trial court ruled that the members of the venture were cosureties, "bound to answer for the same duty of the principal," and ordered the expelled member to pay the others up to his prorated share.[181] The Court of Appeals reversed[182], first holding that "a partner cannot also be a surety or guarantor of partnership debt," and second, that:

> the so-called suretyship agreements executed by [the venture's] members had the legal effect of altering what otherwise would have

173. Cook v. Crabtree, 733 S.W.2d 67, 69 (Tenn. Ct. App.1987) (quoting Restatement of the Law, Security § 146, comment b, § 147(2) (1941)).
174. These issues are now addressed in Restatement of Guaranty and Suretyship (1996) § 53.
175. Cook v. Crabtree, 733 S.W.2d 67, 69-70 (Tenn. Ct. App.1987) (quoting Restatement of the Law, Security § 146, comment b, § 147(2) (1941)).
176. Hardy v. Miller, 2001 Tenn. App. LEXIS 898, *12 (Dec. 10, 2001).
177. *Id.* at *3-*4.
178. *Id.* at *4.
179. *Id.*
180. *Id.*
181. *Id.*
182. *Id.* at *12-*13.

> been each member's unlimited joint and several liability for the joint venture's debts. As a result of these agreements, each member's individual liability was made several only and was capped at $ 280,000. Accordingly, these agreements actually served as "limitation of liability" agreements benefitting the individual members of the joint venture. Because no suretyship was ever created, the trial court erred by classifying the members of [the venture] as "co-sureties" and by basing its decision on suretyship principles.

§ 12 Subrogation

Subrogation is an equitable remedy that generally requires total satisfaction of the underlying obligation to the obligee prior to its exercise, and a paying surety's right to enforce a creditor's lien originates in the contract between the surety and the obligee.

Although traditionally, "a mere volunteer who pays the debt of another is not entitled, without more, to be substituted to liens held by the original creditor,"[183] Tennessee cases recognize a historic expansion of the equitable doctrine of subrogation. [184] The cases are clear that a surety who pays an obligor's indebtedness pursuant to contract steps into the creditor's shoes, and assumes the creditor's rights and remedies, including its security interests and the priority thereof, as against the debtor whose debt the surety paid.[185] The rule is that "if a volunteer pays the debt of a third party, although it is a lien upon property, with the intention of extinguishing the debt, and is not induced thereto by fraud, accident, or mistake, or by contract with the payee, he is not entitled to subrogation."[186] Indeed:

> A surety, by paying the debt of his principal, becomes entitled to be substituted to all the rights of the creditor, and to have the benefit of all the sureties which the creditor had for the payment of the debt, without any exception; and is entitled to all his rights to any fund, lien, or equity, against any other person or property, on account of the debt.[187]

The source of a surety's right to subrogation appears to be contractual, but may also lie in equitable principles of law.[188] Accordingly, a surety—who is not

183. *See, e.g.,* Durant v. Davis, 57 Tenn. 522 (Tenn. 1873).
184. *See, e.g.,* Old Nat'l Bank v. Swearingen, 72 S.W.2d 545, 546 (Tenn. 1934); Harrison v. Harrison, 259 S.W. 906, 907 (Tenn. 1923).
185. Third Nat'l Bank v. Highlands Ins. Co., 603 S.W.2d 730, 733 (Tenn. 1980) (surety on contractor's performance bond had unrecorded right of subrogation that defeats intervening creditors); Old Nat'l Bank v. Swearingen, 72 S.W.2d 545, 547-48 (Tenn. 1934) (bank seeking lien on subrogation theory); Maryland Cas. Co. v. McConnell, 257 S.W. 410, 412 (Tenn. 1923) (surety of state school funds on deposit with liquidated bank, following payment of deposit balance to state, obtained same rights and priority as state depositor initially had).
186. Old Nat'l Bank v. Swearingen, 72 S.W.2d 545, 547-48 (Tenn. 1934).
187. Maryland Cas. Co. v. McConnell, 257 S.W. 410, 412 (Tenn. 1923) (citing Bittick v. Wilkins, 54 Tenn. 307 (Tenn. 1872)).
188. *See* Associates Home Equity Servs., Inc. v. Franklin Nat'l Bank, 2002 Tenn. App. LEXIS 207, *10, *22 (Tenn. Ct. App. Mar. 26, 2002) (refinance mortgagee who records lien after nonrefinance mortgagee records its lien may still be entitled to equitable subrogation in Tennessee, a race-notice state).

a volunteer and is primarily liable for payment of the debt—is induced (indeed obligated) to pay the debt of a third party by virtue of a contact with the payee, regardless of whether the surety intends to "extinguish" the debt or continue collection efforts on its own, and is therefore entitled to subrogation.[189]

The rule is not as clear, however, for an ordinary guarantor who is not made primarily liable under the terms of the guaranty contract,[190] though there is little doubt that a waiver of subrogation rights in a guaranty will divest the guarantor of any rights to step into the lender's shoes and exercise the lender's remedies against the primary obligor.

§ 13 Indemnification—Whether the Primary Obligor or Primary Guarantors have a Duty

The principal obligor has a duty of indemnification to the guarantor when the guarantor undertook its obligations at the request of the principal obligor. The extent of this duty can be altered by contract.

Tennessee recognizes that a primary obligor owes a duty of indemnification to a guarantor who satisfies the obligation at the request of the principal obligor. Likewise, a primary guarantor owes a duty of indemnification to a subsurety who satisfies the obligation.[191] Indeed, as it relates to the indemnification of a subsurety by a primary guarantor:

> The most important incident of the relation is that if the subsurety performs he is entitled to reimbursement from the principal surety. If the principal surety performs, he is not entitled to contribution from the subsurety.[192]

§ 14 Enforcement of Guaranties

There is nothing peculiar in Tennessee law or procedure with respect to litigating liability under a written guaranty.

As in federal courts, a party seeking to enforce payment or performance of an obligor's duties under a written guaranty is advised to attach a copy of the guaranty agreement to the initial pleading, so that the agreement becomes part of the pleading.[193] Although suit can be initiated in either circuit or chancery court, chancery court is the traditional venue for such suits, and the chancellors

189. Old Nat'l Bank v. Swearingen, 72 S.W.2d 545, 547 (Tenn. 1934).
190. Commerce Union Bank v. Burger-In-A-Pouch, Inc., 657 S.W.2d 88, 92 (Tenn. 1983).
191. Cook v. Crabtree, 733 S.W.2d 67, 69 (Tenn. Ct. App.1987) (quoting Restatement of the Law, Security § 146, comment a (1941)).
192. Cook v. Crabtree, 733 S.W.2d 67, 69 (Tenn. Ct. App.1987) (quoting Restatement of the Law, Security § 145, comment a (1941)).
193. Tenn. R. Civ. P. 10.03.

may have a greater understanding of the applicable law than do circuit court judges. Local rules may prefer verified complaints, as well.

§ 15 Revival and Reinstatement of Guaranties

Although a guarantor may argue that cancellation of the underlying obligation relieves the guarantor of her obligations, such guaranty obligations may be revived, reinstated or otherwise survive the cancellation of the underlying obligation; the critical consideration is the language contained in the guaranty.

See discussion set forth at § 7.2.2, *supra*.

§ 16 Choice of Law

A choice-of-law provision in a Tennessee guaranty should be valid if the chosen state has a substantial relationship to the parties or the transaction, there is a reasonable basis for the parties' choice, and application of the law of the chosen state is not contrary to public policy.

This chapter is not intended to provide an extensive analysis of Tennessee conflicts of laws principles, of which there is a long and complex history. There is no specific Tennessee statute governing choice of law respecting guaranties. However, two statutes provide guidance. First, Article 1 of the UCC, as adopted in Tennessee, provides that parties may choose the laws of any state or nation bearing a reasonable relationship to the transaction.[194] Second, Tennessee's General Usury Act[195] provides much the same language in connection with interest rates, noting of course that this provision seems to exclude choice-of-law provisions with respect to matters governed by the Truth in Lending Act[196] and Regulation Z[197] (consumer transactions):

47-14-119. Choice of laws

In any transaction otherwise subject to this chapter which is not subject to the disclosure requirements of the Federal Consumer Credit Protection Act, where the transaction bears a reasonable relationship to this state and also to another state or nation, the parties may agree in the written contract evidencing such transaction that the laws of this state or of any other such state or nation shall govern their rights and duties with respect to interest, loan charges, commitment fees, and brokerage commissions.

An excellent decision regarding the enforceability of a choice-of-law provision in a guaranty agreement is *Wallace Hardware Co. v. Abrams*.[198] In this

194. Tenn. Code Ann. § 47-1-301 (2012).
195. Tenn. Code Ann. § 47-14-119 (2012).
196. 15 U.S.C. § 1601 note (2012).
197. 12 C.F.R. Part 226 (2012).
198. 223 F.3d 382 (6th Cir. 2000).

case, the U.S. Court of Appeals for the Sixth Circuit reversed the district court and upheld the Tennessee choice-of-law clause governing personal guaranties of a commercial debt.[199] Each guarantor was a Kentucky resident, and the transaction bore a stronger relationship to Kentucky than to Tennessee, and the Tennessee guaranties would not have been effective under Kentucky law.[200]

The *Wallace* court adopted § 187 of the Restatement of the Law, Second, Conflict of Laws,[201] indicating that the parties' choice of law should be honored "unless (1) 'the chosen state has no substantial relationship to the parties or the transaction and there is no other reasonable basis for the parties' choice,' or (2) application of the law of the chosen state would be contrary to a fundamental policy of a state which has a materially greater interest than the chosen state."[202] The Sixth Circuit added that there seemed to be a reasonable relationship to Tennessee; each side was represented by counsel; and there appeared to be no inequality in bargaining power between the parties.[203]

Further:

> The choice of law provision must be executed in good faith. The jurisdiction whose law is chosen must bear a material connection to the transaction. The basis for the choice of another jurisdiction's law must be reasonable and not merely a sham or subterfuge. Finally, the parties' choice of another jurisdiction's law must not be "contrary to 'a fundamental policy' of a state having [a] "materially greater interest" and whose law would otherwise govern.[204]

Tennessee has also adopted the maxim that parties may choose the law which will lend validity to the transaction if it is otherwise logical.[205]

One cannot state with certainty that choice-of-law provisions localizing a guaranty agreement outside the state of Tennessee will be enforceable in a consumer transaction. This may be due to a belief that Tennessee might have a materially greater interest than another chosen state in the event Tennessee citizens are involved.[206]

---

199. Wallace Hardware Co. v. Abrams, 223 F.3d 382, 387 (6th Cir. 2000).
200. *Id.* at 391.
201. Restatement of the Law (Second) of Conflict of Laws (1988 Revisions), § 187.
202. Wallace Hardware Co. v. Abrams, 223 F.3d 382, 398-400 (6th Cir. 2000).
203. *Id.*
204. Amtax Holdings 285, LLC v. Opportunity Builders, Inc., 2009 U.S. Dist. LEXIS 10144, at *18 (W.D. Tenn. Feb. 9, 2009) (citing Messer Griesheim Indus., Inc., v. Cryotech of Kingsport, Inc., 131 S.W.3d 457, 474-75 (Tenn. Ct. App. 2003)).
205. *See* Deaton v. Vise, 210 S.W.2d 665, 669 (Tenn. 1948).
206. *See* Tenn. Code Ann. § 47-14-119 (2012).

Texas State Law of Guaranties

Kenneth M. Vesledahl
Patton Boggs LLP
2000 McKinney Avenue
Suite 1700
Dallas, Texas 75201
Phone: 214-758-1570
Fax: 214-758-1550
kvesledahl@pattonboggs.com
www.pattonboggs.com

PATTON BOGGS LLP

Contents

Texas State Law of Guaranties

Practice Pointers

- Under Texas statutory law, unless otherwise provided by its governing documents, a Texas domestic entity (a) can grant guaranties regarding indebtedness of a parent, subsidiary, or affiliate of the entity, and (b) can otherwise grant guaranties if these guaranties may reasonably be expected, directly or indirectly, to benefit the entity, and subject to limited exceptions, a decision by the governing body of such an entity that such a guaranty may reasonably be expected to benefit the entity is conclusive and not subject to attack. The common practice in Texas for a lender is to require evidence that the governing body of the entity has approved such a guaranty and has determined the guaranty benefits the entity.
- Chapter 43 of the Texas Civil Practice and Remedies Code discharges a surety on a contract if, after the surety gives notice to the obligee demanding that the obligee bring suit on the contract, the obligee fails to sue or prosecute the suit to judgment and execution within the timing parameters specified in Chapter 43. The definition of "surety" under Chapter 43 includes a "guarantor." The common practice for Texas lenders is to obtain a specific waiver of the requirements of Chapter 43 of the Texas Civil Practice and Remedies Code.

Introductory Notes:

1. Standard terms used in this survey. In order to standardize our discussion of the law of guaranties, we use the following vocabulary to refer to the various parties to a guaranty and their obligations:

"**Guarantor**" means a person who, by contract, agrees to satisfy an underlying obligation of another to an obligee upon the primary obligor's default on that underlying obligation. Under Texas law, differentiating a surety from a guarantor is generally not a useful exercise for a commercial lender because (i) the statutory definition of "surety" set forth in the Texas Business and Commerce Code includes the term "guarantor" and (ii) most contracts and instruments pursuant to which a person or entity becomes liable for the performance of another will directly address the issues of primary and secondary liability and when performance is due.

"**Guaranty**" means the contract by which the guarantor agrees to satisfy the underlying obligation of a primary obligor to an obligee in the event the primary obligor defaults on the underlying obligation.

"**Obligee**" means the person to whom the underlying obligation is owed. For example, the lender under a loan agreement would be an obligee vis-à-vis the borrower.

"**Primary Obligor**" means the person who incurs the underlying obligation to the obligee. For example, the borrower under a loan agreement would be a primary obligor.

"**Underlying Obligation**" means the obligation or obligations incurred by the primary obligor and owed to the obligee. For example, the borrower's obligation to make payments to a lender of principal and interest on a loan constitutes an underlying obligation.

2. Use of Restatement (Third) of Law of Suretyship and Guaranty in Texas case law. The Restatement (Third) of Law of Suretyship and Guaranty has been rarely cited in Texas cases. In those instances where parties before a Texas court have cited the Restatement (Third) of Law of Suretyship and Guaranty, it has not been met with approval by the court, nor are the authors of this survey aware of any Texas case in which a Texas court has approvingly cited The Restatement (Third) of Law of Suretyship and Guaranty or any specific provision thereof.[1]

§ 1 Nature of the Guaranty Arrangement

For there to be a guaranty, there must be an underlying obligation on the part of the primary obligor to the obligee, the performance of which is guaranteed by the guarantor.[2]

1.1 Guaranty Relationships

A guaranty creates a secondary obligation by which the guarantor promises to answer for the debt of the primary obligor, and which the guarantor may be called upon to perform once the primary obligor has failed to perform.[3]

A guaranty contract exists if the agreement reflects (1) the parties involved, (2) a manifestation of intent to guaranty the underlying obligation, and (3) a description of the underlying obligation.[4]

No special words or form is required to create a guaranty.[5] What is required is that a person or entity clearly intends to be bound as a guarantor of the referenced underlying obligation.[6]

1. *See, e.g.*, Garcia v. State, 292 S.W.3d 146 (Tex. App. 2006) (no Texas cases cited in which the cited provisions of the Restatement were adopted); Rodriguez v. State, 283 S.W.3d 465 (Tex. App. 2009) (no Texas cases cited in which the cited provisions of the Restatement have been adopted).
2. Moore v. Grain Dealers Mut. Ins. Co., 450 S.W.2d 954 (Tex. App. 1970).
3. Nu-Way Energy Corp. v. Delp, 205 S.W.3d 667 (Tex. App. 2006).
4. S&A Rest. Corp. v. Lane, No. 3:06-CV-1550-L, 2007 WL 4403304 (N.D. Tex. Dec. 18, 2007).
5. Hueske v. C.E. Broussard & Co., 55 Tex. 201, 1881 WL 9764 (1881).
6. Armstrong, Cator & Co. v. Snyder, 39 S.W.2d 379 (Tex. App. 1897).

1.2 Other Suretyship Relationships

While not the focus of this survey, we note that a suretyship relationship may also arise because of the pledge of collateral.[7] One who hypothecates property as security for payment of another's debt is to the extent of such person's interest in the property considered to be a surety.[8]

1.3 Completion Guaranties

The authors of this survey are unaware of any Texas case law dealing with the construction or enforcement of completion or performance guaranties. This survey accordingly deals with Texas law as to guaranties of payment.

§ 2 State Law Requirements for an Entity to Enter a Guaranty

Partnerships, limited liability companies, and corporations (1) can all grant guaranties regarding indebtedness of a parent, subsidiary, or affiliate of the entity, and (2) can otherwise grant guaranties if these guaranties may reasonably be expected, directly or indirectly, to benefit the entity. These grants are generally permitted by the appropriate Texas statute, as long as the governing documents of the entity do not provide otherwise.

2.1 Corporations

Under the Texas Business Organizations Code, an organization formed under, or the internal affairs of which are governed by, the Texas Business Organizations Code (a "domestic entity"[9]) has the general power to make guaranties,[10] except as otherwise provided by the Texas Business Organizations Code.[11] A "domestic entity" includes corporations, limited liability companies, and partnerships.[12]

Section 2.104(b) of the Texas Business Organizations Code provides that, unless otherwise provided by its governing documents, a domestic entity may: "(1) make a guaranty on behalf of parent, subsidiary, or affiliate of the entity; or (2) make a guaranty of the indebtedness of another person if the guaranty may reasonably be expected directly or indirectly to benefit the entity."[13] Subject

---

7. *See* Restatement (Third) of Suretyship and Guaranty § 1 (noting that a person is a surety when "pursuant to contract ... an obligee has recourse against [that] person ... *or against that person's property* with respect to an obligation ... of another person ... to the obligee") (emphasis added).
8. Westbrook v. Belton Nat'l Bank, 77 S.W. 942 (Tex. 1904); State Fidelity Mortg. Co. v. Varner, 740 S.W.2d 477 (Tex. App. 1987).
9. Tex. Bus. Org. Code Ann. § 2.101 (2012).
10. Tex. Bus. Org. Code Ann. § 2.101(5) (2012).
11. Tex. Bus. Org. Code Ann. § 2.101 (2012).
12. Tex. Bus. Org. Code Ann. Title 2, Title 3, and Title 4 (2012).
13. Tex. Bus. Org. Code Ann. § 2.104(b) (2012).

to specified statutory exceptions, such as fraud,[14] a decision by the governing body of a domestic entity that a guaranty may reasonably be expected to benefit the entity is conclusive and not subject to attack by any person.[15] Note the reference in the Texas statute to "may reasonably be expected directly or indirectly to benefit the entity" does not apply to a guaranty by a domestic entity of indebtedness of a parent, subsidiary or affiliate.[16]

2.2 Partnerships

See discussion above at § 2.1.

2.3 Limited Liability Companies

See discussion above at § 2.1.

2.4 Banks and Trust Companies

Article XVI, Section 16(c), of the Texas Constitution provides that state banks are granted "the same rights and privileges that are or may be granted to national banks of the United States domiciled in this State."[17] The Texas Department of Banking has interpreted this to mean "that a state bank has the authority to lend its credit ... or otherwise become a guarantor if (1) the bank has a substantial interest in the performance of the transaction involved, or (2) the transaction is for the benefit of a customer and the bank obtains from the customer a segregated deposit that is sufficient in amount to cover the bank's total potential liability."[18] By opinion letter, the Texas Department of Banking has stated that a state bank has a substantial interest in the performance of a transaction to which the bank's operating subsidiary is a party.[19]

2.5 Individuals (Marital Property)

An individual's guaranty can have implications for the guarantor's spouse and marital property. One spouse will not be held personally liable for the guaranty of the other spouse based solely on the marriage relationship and

14. Tex. Bus. Org. Code Ann. § 2.104(c) (2012). These exceptions include (a) enforcement by a person who participated in or had knowledge of a fraud resulting in the making of the guaranty, (b) ability of owner of domestic entity to enjoin a *proposed* guaranty on the ground guaranty cannot reasonably be expected to benefit the entity, and (c) ability of domestic entity to bring suit for damages against managerial officials, owners, or members who authorized guaranty on the ground guaranty could not reasonably be expected to benefit the entity.
15. Tex. Bus. Org. Code Ann. § 2.104(c) (2012).
16. *Compare* Tex. Bus. Org. Code Ann. § 2.104(c)(2) and § 2.104(c)(1) (2012).
17. Tx. Const. art. XVI, § 16, cl. (c); *see also* 27 TexReg 8203 (Finance Commission of Texas repealing former 7 TAC § 11.83(b), which provided that a state bank could serve as a guarantor, noting that the rule had become unnecessary after the 1984 constitutional amendment to Article XVI, § 16(c)).
18. Texas Dep't of Banking, Opinion No. 08-01 (July 10, 2008); *cf.* Texas Dep't of Banking, Opinion No. 96-49 (March 5, 1997) (concluding that a Texas state-licensed branch of a foreign bank may issue guarantees in favor of whollyowned subsidiaries of the bank, pursuant to old 7 TAC § 11.83(b)).
19. Opinion No. 08-01 (noting also that the amended 12 CFR § 7.1017(b) potentially expands national bank guaranty authority and suggesting that a state bank would be authorized to guaranty certain operating subsidiary transactions that are "financial in character" so long as the amount of the anticipated bank obligation is "reasonably ascertainable").

community property laws.[20] Nonetheless, the interest of the spouse who did not provide the guaranty in joint management and control community property is subject to execution to satisfy the guaranty obligations of the spouse who did provide the guaranty regardless of whether the nonguarantying spouse executed the guaranty.[21] It should be noted that whether one spouse is liable for the guaranty obligations of the other spouse is an analysis distinct from determining whether the guaranty obligations can be considered in dividing the community estate.[22]

§ 3 Signatory's Authority to Execute a Guaranty

An obligee that does not ascertain whether the signatory of the guaranty has the appropriate authority to bind the entity does so at its own risk.

3.1 Corporations

The law of agency determines the authority of an officer to bind the corporation to a guaranty with a third party obligee.[23] Under the law of agency, for the corporation to be bound to such a guaranty, the guaranty must be signed by an officer with actual, implied, or apparent authority.[24] A court will not presume that sufficient agency power exists; the party asserting agency has the burden of proving it.[25] An obligee cannot enforce a guaranty if it was aware that the officer who signed on behalf of the corporation lacked the authority to do so.[26]

Express actual authority may be conferred upon an officer by provision of the certificate of formation, the bylaws, or resolution of the board of directors.[27] Implied authority is a form of actual authority that usually denotes the authority a principal intentionally allows the agent to believe he possesses or by want of due care allows the agent to believe he possesses.[28] Implied authority exists when a reasonable person would conclude based on the representations by the principal that the purported agent possesses the authority to

---

20. *See, e.g.*, Nelson v. Citizens Bank & Trust Co. of Baytown, Texas, 881 S.W.2d 128, 128 (Tex. App. 1994) (citing Tex. Fam. Code Ann. § 4.031 (West 1993), which provides that a spouse is personally liable for his or her spouse's debts only if the debt is for necessaries, or if the spouse acts as the other spouse's agent when incurring the debt); Carr v. Houston Bus. Forms, Inc., 794 S.W.2d 849, 852 (Tex. App. 1990).
21. *Id.* at 130–31 (citing Tex. Fam. Code Ann. § 5.61 (West 1993) as the basis for its conclusion that the nonsigning spouse's interest in joint management and control of community property is subject to execution).
22. Bush v. Bush, 336 S.W.3d 722, 740 (Tex. App. 2010); *see also* Inwood Nat'l Bank of Dallas v. Hoppe, 596 S.W.2d 183, 185 (Tex. App. 1980) (holding that characterization and division of property in divorce have no effect on third-party creditor's rights).
23. *See* Ginsberg 1985 Real Estate P'ship v. Cadle Co., 39 F.3d 528, 536 (5th Cir. 1994).
24. *See* 20A Elizabeth S. Miller & Robert A. Ragazzo, West's Texas Practice Series: Business Organizations § 35.5 (3d ed. 2011).
25. IRA Res., Inc. v. Griego, 221 S.W.3d 592, 597 (Tex. 2007); Lifshutz v. Lifshutz, 199 S.W.3d 9, 22 (Tex. App. 2006).
26. *See* Restatement (Third) of Agency §§ 6.10(3), 6.11(1).
27. Miller & Ragazzo, *supra* note 23, § 35.6.
28. 2616 S. Loop L.L.C. v. Health Source Home Care, Inc., 201 S.W.3d 349, 356 (Tex. App. 2006).

effect a particular transaction.[29] Apparent authority is determined "by looking at the acts of the principal and ascertaining whether those acts would lead a reasonably prudent person [in the position of the third party] using diligence and discretion to suppose the agent had the authority to act on behalf of the principal."[30] An obligee that does not ascertain both the fact and scope of the agent's authority does so at its own risk.[31]

3.2 Partnerships

Under the Texas Business Organizations Code, every partner is an agent of the partnership for the purpose of the partnership's business.[32] The act of a partner that is "apparently for carrying on in the ordinary course" the business of the partnership or business of the kind carried on by the partnership binds the partnership unless the partner does not have the authority to act for the partnership in such matter and the third party with whom the partner is dealing knows that the partner lacks authority.[33] An act by the partner that is not "apparently for carrying on in the ordinary course" the business of the partnership does not bind the partnership unless authorized by the other partners.[34] Third parties dealing with partners should ascertain the nature and scope of the partnership's business, as they will have the burden of proving that a partner's act was "apparently for carrying on in the ordinary course" the business of the partnership or business of the kind carried on by the partnership.[35]

A general partner in a limited partnership has the same powers as a partner in a general partnership unless otherwise limited under the Texas Business Organizations Code or the partnership agreement.[36] The general partner of a limited partnership is an agent of the limited partnership for the purpose of the limited partnership's business, and the act of the general partner that is "apparently for carrying on in the ordinary course" the business of the partnership or business of the kind carried on by the partnership binds the limited partnership unless the partner does not have the authority to act for the partnership in such matter and the third party with whom the partner is dealing knows that the partner lacks authority.[37]

3.3 Limited Liability Companies (LLCs)

Each governing person of a LLC, whether a member in a member-managed LLC or manager of a manager-managed LLC, and each officer vested with

29. Miller & Ragazzo, *supra* note 23, § 35.8.
30. *Lifshutz*, 199 S.W.3d at 22; *see also* Gaines v. Kelly, 235 S.W.3d 179, 182 (Tex. 2007) (citing Baptist Mem'l Hosp. Sys. v. Sampson, 969 S.W.2d 945, 948 (Tex. 1998)); Miller & Ragazzo, *supra* note 23, § 35.8 (noting that apparent authority may be created when a third party continues to rely on the appearance of authority where an officer has exercised authority in the past with the consent of the board of directors or where the board of directors is silent or acquiesces when an agent represents that he has authority or takes action without actual authority).
31. *Lifshutz*, 199 S.W.3d at 23.
32. Tex. Bus. Org. Code Ann. § 152.301 (2012).
33. Tex. Bus. Org. Code Ann. § 152.302(a) (2012).
34. Tex. Bus. Org. Code Ann. § 152.302(b) (2012).
35. Miller & Ragazzo, *supra* note 23, § 8.3.
36. *See* Tex. Bus. Org. Code Ann. § 153.152(a) (2012).
37. Tex. Bus. Org. Code Ann. §§ 152.301, 152.302(a) (2012).

actual or apparent authority by the governing authority of the LLC, is an agent of the LLC for purposes of carrying out the LLC's business.[38] A guaranty executed by such governing person or officer on behalf of the LLC will bind the LLC if the act is for the purpose of "apparently carrying out the ordinary course of business" of the LLC unless this person does not have actual authority to act for the LLC and the counterparty has knowledge of the person's lack of actual authority.[39]

§ 4 Consideration; Sufficiency of Past Consideration

A guaranty is a contract which must have consideration to be valid. Written guaranties are presumed to be supported by consideration.

At its core, a guaranty is a contract.[40] As such, an offer, acceptance, and consideration are required to have a valid guaranty.[41] Texas law also requires that guaranties be in writing to withstand the statute of frauds.[42]

Texas courts will not review the adequacy of consideration for a guaranty. Nonetheless, there must be consideration to have a valid guaranty.[43] This requirement may be satisfied by providing consideration to either the primary obligor or the guarantor.[44] The guarantor need not directly receive the consideration.[45] Instead, consideration "usually consists of either the sufferance of a detriment by the creditor or a benefit conferred on the primary obligor."[46] Further, written guaranties are presumed to be supported by consideration.[47]

A guaranty that is entered into independently of the underlying obligation must have new consideration to be valid.[48] However, past consideration is sufficient when the guaranty promise is "given as the result of previous arrangement, the principal obligation having been induced by or created on the faith of the guaranty."[49]

38. Tex. Bus. Org. Code Ann. §§ 152.301, 101.254(a) (2012).
39. *See* Tex. Bus. Org. Code Ann. §§ 152.301, 101.254(b) (2012).
40. Gooch v. Am. Sling Co., Inc., 902 S.W.2d 181, 185 (Tex. App. 1995); Hargis v. Radio Corp. of Am., Elec. Components, 539 S.W.2d 230, 232 (Tex. App. 1976).
41. Terry W. Conner, *Enforcing Commercial Guaranties in Texas: Vanishing Limitations, Remaining Questions*, 12 Tex. Tech L. Rev. 785, 793 (1981).
42. Tex. Bus. & Comm. Code Ann. § 26.01(b)(2) (2012).
43. 68 Tex. Jur. 3D, *Suretyship and Guaranty* § 184 (2012) (citing Green v. Am. Ref. Props., 22 S.W.2d 343 (Tex. App. 1929); Shepard v. Phears, 35 Tex. 763 (1872); Fourticq v. Fireman's Fund Ins. Co., 679 S.W.2d 562, 564 (Tex. App. 1984)) [hereinafter Tex. Jur.].
44. *Fourticq*, 679 S.W.2d at 564; *Hargis*, 539 S.W.2d at 232; McWhorter v. First State Bank of Wylie, 11 S.W.2d 808, 809 (Tex. App. 1928).
45. Dean v. Allied Oil Co., 261 S.W.2d 900, 902 (Tex. App. 1953); Maykus v. Texas Bank & Trust Co. of Dallas, 550 S.W.2d 396 (Tex. App. 1977).
46. *Fourticq*, 679 S.W.2d at 564; *McWhorter*, 11 S.W.2d at 809.
47. *Hargis*, 539 S.W.2d at 232; Simpson v. MBank Dallas, N.A., 724 S.W.2d 102, 107 (Tex. App. 1987); *Maykus*, 550 S.W.2d at 398.
48. *Fourticq*, 679 S.W.2d at 564; First Commerce Bank v. Palmer, 226 S.W.3d 396, 398 (Tex. 2007).
49. *First Commerce Bank*, 226 S.W.3d at 398 (citation omitted); *see Gooch*, 902 S.W.2d at 185.

§ 5 Notice of Acceptance

Notice of acceptance is generally not required.

An obligee must provide notice of acceptance under traditional guaranty law. In practice, however, the guarantor waives notice of acceptance in the guaranty agreement.[50] Texas courts waive this notice requirement when "(1) the guaranty is 'absolute' in nature, (2) the guarantor has received consideration from the creditor, (3) the nature of the guaranty eliminates the need for acceptance, (4) the guaranty is 'completed,' and not in the form of an offer or proposal, or (5) the guaranty contains a statement that notice of acceptance is unnecessary."[51]

§ 6 Interpretation of Guaranties

Courts in Texas are guided by the principle of "strictissimi juris," strictly construing the obligations of the guarantor. While courts will interpret a guaranty in the same manner by which they would interpret the language of any other contract, certain terms have become words of art in the context of guaranties.

6.1 General Principles

Interpretation and construction of guaranties are resolved by the same rules as are generally followed in other contract cases.[52] The primary judicial concern is to ascertain the true intentions of the parties.[53] While the rule of strictissimi juris entitles a guarantor to have his guaranty strictly construed and not extended by construction or implication beyond the precise terms of the guaranty, this rule is applicable only after the terms of the guaranty have been ascertained.[54]

6.2 Guaranty of Payment versus Guaranty of Collection

"Guaranty of payment" is used as the equivalent of the term "absolute guaranty" in reference to the payment of debt, as distinguished from the term "guaranty of collection."[55] See § 6.5 on "Absolute guaranty versus conditional guaranty." A guaranty of payment is also referred to as an "unconditional"

---

50. 2 Robin Russell, *Texas Practice Guide: Financial Transactions* § 9:35 (2011).
51. Conner, *supra* note 40, at 793-94 (citing Cobb v. Texas Distrib., Inc., 524 S.W.2d 342, 345 (Tex. App. 1975); Eastman Oil Well Survey Co. v. Hamil, 416 S.W.2d 597, 604–05 (Tex. App. 1967); Hunsley Paint Mfg. Co. v. Gray, 165 S.W.2d 486, 488–89 (Tex. App. 1942)).
52. North Texas Nat'l Bank v. Thompson, 23 S.W.2d 494 (Tex. App. 1929), *aff'd*, 37 S.W.2d 735 (Tex. Comm'n App. 1931).
53. Hasty v. Keller HCP Partners, L.P., 260 S.W.3d 666 (Tex. App. 2008).
54. Material P'ships, Inc. v. Ventura, 102 S.W.3d 252 (Tex. App. 2003).
55. J.I. Case Co. v. Laubhan, 77 S.W.2d 578 (Tex. Civ. App. Amarillo 1934).

guaranty.[56] A leading commentator on enforcement of commercial guaranties in Texas writes ". . . the guaranty of payment (although still ostensibly a 'secondary obligation') has increasingly been recognized as an undertaking that is enforceable in accordance with its own terms and creates liability almost independent of that of the primary obligor."[57]

When the expression "guaranty of collection" is used it means the guaranty is conditional on the reasonable diligence of the obligee in attempting to collect payment from the primary obligor.[58]

While Texas courts generally allow enforcement of a guaranty of payment without joinder of the primary obligor, joinder of the primary obligor will generally be required in a suit to enforce a guaranty of collection.[59]

6.3 Revocation of Guaranties

A continuing guaranty may be revoked by the guarantor as to future transactions unless the right to revoke is expressly waived by the language of the guaranty.[60]

Subsequent to notice of revocation, the guarantor is liable only for extensions of credit before the revocation and any renewals or extensions of such indebtedness.[61]

Language revoking a guaranty should be clear and explicit.[62]

6.4 "Continuing Guaranty"

A "continuing guaranty" contemplates a future course of dealing between the primary obligor and the obligee and the guaranty applies to additional liabilities as they accrue.[63] A continuing guaranty contemplates a future course of dealing covering a series of transactions and for an indefinite time, unless revoked.[64]

6.5 "Absolute Guaranty versus Conditional Guaranty"

An absolute guaranty is conditioned solely on the failure of the primary obligor to perform the underlying obligation which is guaranteed by the guarantor.[65] An agreement providing that payment of a debt is "unconditionally" guaranteed is treated as an absolute guaranty.[66] No duty is imposed on the obligee

56. McGhee v. Wynnewood State Bank, 297 S.W.2d 876 (Tex. App. 1957).
57. Conner, *supra* note 40, at 789.
58. Austin v. Guar. State Bank of Copperas Cove, 300 S.W. 129, 132 (Tex. App. 1927).
59. Ferguson v. McCarrell, 588 S.W.2d 895 (Tex. 1979); Universal Metals & Mach., Inc. v. Bohart, 539 S.W.2d 874 (Tex. 1976); Wolfe v. Schuster, 591 S.W.2d 926, 931–32 (Tex. App. 1979).
60. Straus-Frank Co. v. Hughes, 156 S.W.2d 519, 520 (Tex. 1941).
61. First Bank of Houston v. Bradley, 702 S.W.2d 683, 685–86 (Tex. App. 1985); Holland v. First Nat'l Bank 597 S.W.2d 406, 408–09 (Tex. App. 1980); Dicker v. Lomas & Nettleton Fin. Corp., 576 S.W.2d 672, 676 (Tex. App. 1978).
62. Casey v. Gibson Prod. Co., 216 S.W.2d 266, 268 (Tex. App. 1948).
63. Beal Bank, SSB v. Biggers, 227 S.W.3d 187, 192 (Tex. App. 2007).
64. *See Straus-Frank Co.*, 156 S.W.2d at 520; Blount v. Westinghouse Credit Corp., 432 S.W.2d 549, 553 (Tex. App. 1968); *Beal Bank, SSB*, 227 S.W.3d at 192.
65. *See McGhee*, 297 S.W.2d at 883.
66. *See* Universal Metals & Mach., Inc., 539 S.W.2d at 877–78; Mid-South Telecomms Co., v. Best, 184 S.W.3d 386, 391 (Tex. App. 2006).

to first try to collect from the primary obligor. A "guaranty of payment" is the equivalent of an absolute guaranty, as distinguished from a guaranty of collection.[67]

A conditional guaranty is contingent on some event in addition to the default of the primary obligor, and often this condition is the requirement that the obligee first use reasonable diligence to collect from the primary obligor before attempting to collect from the guarantor.[68] A guaranty of collection is a conditional guaranty.

6.6 "Limited Guaranty versus Unlimited Guaranty"

A limitation of guarantor liability specified in a guaranty distinguishes it from a general guaranty.[69] The liability of a guarantor can be limited in several ways, including by dollar amount, duration, or transaction.[70] Texas courts have also allowed a guarantor's liability to be limited to (1) only defaulted accounts rather than all accounts of the primary obligor[71] and (2) the balance owed by the primary obligor at the time of foreclosure.[72] It is important to expressly set forth any limitations of liability in the guaranty agreement as a guarantor's liability will otherwise be measured by the primary obligor's liability.[73] The extent of the limitation of the guarantor's liability will be interpreted pursuant to the general principles discussed at § 6.1.[74]

§ 7 Defenses of the Guarantor; Set-off

The defenses that may be available to a guarantor can be grouped into three categories: (1) defenses of the primary obligor; (2) "suretyship defenses"; and (3) other defenses.

67. *J. I. Case Co. v. Laubhan*, 77 S.W.2d at 579.
68. Peck v. Mack Trucks, Inc., 704 S.W.2d 583, 585 (Tex. App. 1986).
69. Tex Jur., *supra* note 42, § 171.
70. Russell, *supra* note 49, § 9:8.
71. Pottorff v. J.D. Adams Co., 70 S.W.2d 745, 747 (Tex. Civ. App. – El Paso 1934, writ ref'd).
72. Commerce Sav. Ass'n of Brazoria County v. GGE Mgmt. Co., 539 S.W.2d 71, 77 (Tex. Civ. App. – Houston [1st Dist.] 1976), judgment modified on other grounds, 543 S.W.2d 862 (Tex. 1976).
73. Western Bank-Downtown v. Carline, 757 S.W.2d 111, 113 (Tex. App. – Houston [1st Dist.] 1988, no writ).
74. The application of such general principles to construction of a limited guaranty is exemplified by the decision of the U.S. Fifth Circuit Court of Appeals in *Haggard v. Bank of Ozarks, Inc.*, No. 11-10154, 2012 WL149779 (C.A. 5-Tex. 01/19/12). In *Haggard*, the guaranty at issue limited the guarantor's liability to $500,000 on a $1,600,000 loan, and contained a provision that the guarantor's liability was "limited to the last to be repaid $500,000 of the principal balance." *Haggard* at 2. The guaranty also provided that in the event of default, the obligee was not required to sue the guarantor or the primary obligor to enforce payment nor was the obligee required to enforce its rights against any security prior to demanding payment from guarantor. The critical issue was whether, under Texas law, payment was immediately due under the guaranty or whether no payment was due until the loan balance was $500,000. The Fifth Circuit held the relevant provisions were ambiguous and accordingly held in favor of the guarantor's position because of the general construction principles under Texas law that a guaranty is strictly construed in favor of the guarantor and if ambiguous, the court must apply the construction most favorable to the guarantor.

7.1 Defenses of the Primary Obligor

7.1.1 General

While the general rule in Texas is that the guarantor, absent an effective waiver, is not bound to perform if the primary obligor is not bound,[75] a guarantor sued alone may not, in many circumstances, raise defenses that are "personal" to the underlying obligor.[76]

7.1.2 When Guarantor May Assert Primary Obligor's Defense

As a general rule, a guarantor may assert ordinary contract defenses to the underlying obligation as a defense to its own liability under a guaranty.[77] Further, if an underlying obligation is unenforceable and the primary obligor has no liability as a matter of law, the guarantor of the underlying obligation likewise has no liability.[78] For example, if an underlying obligation is found to be void for illegality, the guaranty is also unenforceable.[79]

7.1.3 Defenses that May not be Raised by Guarantor

A guarantor may not raise defenses that are "personal" to the primary obligor, such as usury, fraud, duress, incapacity, mistake or unconscionability, as a defense to its own guaranty obligations.[80] Contract defenses which would have the effect of making the underlying obligation voidable at the election of the underlying obligor, but not void, are not available to a guarantor as a defense to its guaranty obligations.[81]

A nonconsensual release of the primary obligor is not a defense available to a guarantor. Accordingly, the bankruptcy of the primary obligor is not a defense to a guaranty obligation.[82] Nor will the imposition of an automatic stay generally prevent an obligee from proceeding to enforce a guaranty against a nondebtor guarantor.[83]

7.1.4 Defenses that May Always be Raised by Guarantor

A guarantor may show that the obligee failed to perform such that there is a partial or complete failure of consideration for the underlying obligation discharging the guaranty.[84] This follows from the rule that the guarantor has no liability if an underlying obligation has not been created.[85] Consideration is necessary to support the creation and enforceability of a guaranty.

75. Tex. Jur., *supra* note 42.
76. Russell, *supra* note 49, § 9:88.
77. *Id.*
78. Smith v. Joplin, 879 F.2d 159, 161 (5th Cir. 1989).
79. Houston Sash & Door Co., Inc. v. Hearner, 577 S.W.2d 217, 222 (Tex. 1979).
80. Russell, *supra* note 49, § 9:88.
81. Tex. Jur., *supra* note 42, § 202.
82. *Id.* at § 78.
83. *See, e.g.*, Wedgworth v. Fireboard Corp., 706 F.2d 541, 544 (5th Cir. 1983).
84. *See* Conner, *supra* note 40.
85. *See* Moore v. Grain Dealers Mut. Ins. Co., 450 S.W.2d 954, 957 (Tex. App. 1970).

Consideration may be established by the conferring of a benefit by the obligee on the guarantor or the primary obligor; therefore, it is not necessary that a benefit be conferred directly to the guarantor to establish sufficient consideration to support an enforceable guaranty.[86] An agreement to secure a guaranty after the underlying obligation was created must be supported by new consideration because it was not an inducement in creating the underlying obligation.[87]

7.2 "Suretyship" Defenses

7.2.1 Change in Identity of Principal Obligor

When a new obligor is substituted in the place of the original primary obligor, it will have the effect of discharging the guaranty if this substitution constitutes a material modification of the underlying obligation and is not consented to by the guarantor.[88] Likewise, the consensual release of the primary obligor by the obligee without the consent of guarantor releases the guarantor because it constitutes a material modification of the underlying obligation.[89]

7.2.2 Modification of the Underlying Obligation

If an underlying obligation is materially modified by the obligee and the primary obligor without the guarantor's consent, a new obligation is created, upon which the guarantor is not obligated.[90] Accordingly, a material modification to the underlying obligation which is to the detriment of the guarantor and is not consented to by the guarantor is a defense that will permit the discharge of the guaranty.[91] In asserting the affirmative defense of material modification, the burden is on the guarantor to prove that a modification was (1) material, (2) to the detriment of the guarantor by enhancing risk of loss and (3) made without the consent of the guarantor.[92] If the modification to the underlying obligation does not go to the primary purpose of the guaranty and does not prejudice the guarantor, the modification is not material.[93] Consequently, when the modification is not material, in that it does not place the guarantor in a position of increased risk of loss, the guarantor will not be discharged.[94] Neither will a guarantor be discharged if it waives in advance the defense of material modification.[95]

---

86. Tex. Jur., *supra* note 42, § 184.
87. *Id.* at § 189.
88. May v. Waniger, 164 S.W. 1106, 1106 (Tex. App. 1914) ("The guarantor can only be held for the debt of his principal, and any release of his principal by substituting another principal, or otherwise, releases the guarantor.")
89. *See Id.*
90. Vastine v. Bank of Dallas, 808 S.W.2d 463, 464 (Tex. 1991).
91. *See, e.g.*, United Concrete Pipe Corp. v. Spin-Line Co., 430 S.W.2d 360, 365 (Tex. 1968).
92. Austin Hardwoods, Inc. v. Vanden Berghe, 917 S.W.2d 320, 326 (Tex. App. 1994); Old Colony Ins. Co. v. City of Quitman, 352 S.W.2d 452, 455–56 (Tex. 1961).
93. Russell, *supra* note 49, § 9:100.
94. Tex. Jur., *supra* note 42, § 204.
95. Sonne v. F.D.I.C., 881 S.W.2d 789, 792 (Tex. App. 1994).

7.2.3 Release or Impairment of Security for the Underlying Obligation

A guarantor that has paid an underlying obligation on account of its guaranty is entitled to be subrogated to the rights of the obligee with respect to any security given for payment of the indebtedness. The guarantor therefore has a legal interest in the security and the obligee is deemed a trustee holding the security for all interested parties. It is therefore the duty of the obligee to exercise ordinary care to protect the value of the security from impairment, waste, loss, injury, or release.[96] The standard of care required of the obligee in perfecting the security is the same as that which would be required of a similarly situated trustee. To the extent the security is impaired by the failure of the obligee to fulfill this duty, the guarantor may be discharged of its obligation to the obligee.[97]

If the obligee releases collateral securing the underlying obligation without the consent of the guarantor, the guarantor may be discharged of its guaranty to the extent of such release.[98] However, a release of collateral to a creditor having a superior lien against such collateral will not discharge the guarantor of any liability.[99] Likewise, if a coguarantor is substituted or released without the consent of the guarantor, but at the insistence or knowledge of the obligee, the guarantor will be discharged if such change is to the detriment of the guarantor.[100]

If the obligee liquidates personal property collateral in a manner that is improper or commercially unreasonable, it can affect the deficiency liability of the guarantor.[101] Under Texas law, a guarantor is entitled to notice of the sale of personal property which is collateral for the underlying obligation.[102] If the obligee exercises its remedies against the collateral in a commercially unreasonable manner or does not deliver proper notice to the guarantor, the guarantor may still be held liable for a deficiency, but the deficiency will be based on the amount of proceeds that would have been realized in a hypothetical complying sale.[103]

A guarantor is not entitled to notice of a real estate foreclosure sale of property securing the underlying obligation.[104] With regard to a deficiency resulting from the nonjudicial or judicial foreclosure of real property, a guarantor may assert a defense to its guaranty obligation if it believes the sale price was less than the fair market value of the property.[105] In such a circumstance, if the court finds the sale price was less than the fair market value of the property, the guarantor is entitled to an offset in the amount of the difference against the deficiency liability owing by the guarantor.[106] The guarantor may waive

96. *See* Conner, *supra* note 40, at 831–32.
97. 2 Russell, *supra* note 49, § 9:101.
98. Darnell v. Dolan, 63 Tex. Civ. App. 386, 389, 132 S.W. 857 (Tex. App. 1910).
99. Meacham v. O'Keefe, 198 S.W. 1000, 1001 (Tex. App. 1917).
100. Tex. Jur., *supra* note 42, § 49.
101. Tex. Bus. & Com. Code Ann. § 9.610(b) (2012).
102. Tex. Bus. & Com. Code Ann. § 9.611 (2012).
103. Tex. Bus. & Com. Code Ann. § 9.626(a)(3) (2012).
104. 2 Russell, *supra* note 49, § 9:87.
105. Tex. Prop. Code Ann. § 51.005 (2012).
106. Tex. Prop. Code Ann. § 51.005 (2012).

in advance its defense based on the release or impairment of collateral, both under the common law and under Section 3.605 of the Texas Business and Uniform Commercial Code.[107]

A guarantor lacks standing to assert a defense due to a guaranty obligation based on impairment of the collateral securing the underlying obligation due to the failure of the obligee to act in exercising its remedies against collateral.[108] Unless the guarantor can prove that the obligee undertook an affirmative act or omitted a legal duty that impaired the collateral or lien, the guarantor's liability will not be discharged to any extent.[109]

7.2.4 Failure of Obligee to Sue Underlying Obligor After Notice from Guarantor

Under Chapter 43 of the Texas Civil Practice and Remedies Code, when a right of action accrues on a contract for the payment of money, a surety on the contact may, by written notice, require the obligee to without delay bring a suit on the contract. The surety will be discharged from all liability under the contract if after receipt of this notice the obligee, unless under a legal disability, fails (1) to sue on the contract during the first term of court after receipt of notice (or during the second term of court if good cause is shown for the delay) or (2) to prosecute the suit to judgment and execution.[110] The definition of "surety" under Chapter 43 of the Texas Civil Practice and Remedies Code includes a "guarantor."[111] The common practice for lenders in Texas is to obtain a specific waiver of the requirements of Chapter 43 of the Texas Civil Practice and Remedies Code.

7.3 Other Defenses

7.3.1 Misrepresentation of Fact

A guarantor's obligation may be discharged completely if the obligee "actively and fraudulently" concealed information that the obligee believed or had reason to believe materially increased the financial risk of the guaranty and the guarantor was not aware of these concealed facts.[112] However, a guarantor may be estopped from asserting such a defense by waiver and ratification of the transaction or if the guarantor subsequently ratifies the guaranty or enters into a new guaranty after learning the relevant facts.[113]

107. Tex. Bus. & Com. Code Ann. § 3.605(f) (2012).
108. F.D.I.C. v. Coleman, 795 S.W.2d 706, 710 (Tex. 1990).
109. Tex. Jur., *supra* note 42, § 71.
110. Tex Civ. Prac. & Rem. Code § 43.002 (2012).
111. Tex Civ. Prac. & Rem. Code § 43.001 (2012).
112. Russell, *supra* note 49, § 9:92.
113. *See* Barclay v. Waxahachie Bank & Trust Co., 568 S.W.2d 721, 724 (Tex. App. 1986).

7.3.2 *Duress*

Duress is an affirmative defense to a guaranty obligation; however, it is often difficult to prove that a threatened action is sufficient to negate the guaranty.[114] The guarantor must prove that the obligee made a threat to take an action which it did not have the legal right to take, which overcame the will of the guarantor and caused the guarantor to enter into the guaranty.[115]

7.3.3 *Failure to Accept Tender of Performance from Primary Obligor*

If an obligee does not accept tender of full performance from the underlying obligor, the obligee is estopped from seeking performance by the guarantor.[116]

7.3.4 *Failure to Fulfill a Condition Precedent*

An obligee cannot enforce a guaranty against a guarantor if the obligee has failed to satisfy the conditions precedent required to the effectiveness of the underlying obligation.[117]

7.3.5 *Failure to Pursue Primary Obligor*

In the case of a guaranty of collection, as opposed to payment, the obligee must first pursue collection from the primary obligor with reasonable diligence before the guaranty will become effective against the guarantor.[118] In such a case, the obligee must show that payment could not be obtained by the obligee from the primary obligor after resorting to available legal remedies.[119]

7.3.6 *Statute of Frauds*

An oral guaranty is unenforceable under the statute of frauds. A guaranty must be in writing and signed by the guarantor.[120] The only exception is the main purpose doctrine, which bars the statute of frauds if the oral promise is made to obtain a direct benefit for the promissor.[121]

7.3.7 *Statute of Limitations and Laches*

The statute of limitations is a defense for the guarantor only to the extent it is operative against the guaranty itself, as distinguished from the underlying obligation.[122] The statute of limitations for suing on a guaranty is four years

---

114. RUSSELL, *supra* note 49, § 9:94.
115. *Id.*
116. Lockhart State Bank v. Baker, 264 S.W. 566, 569 (Tex. App. 1924).
117. Fisher v. Alexander, 137 S.W. 715, 716 (Tex. App. 1911).
118. *Id.* at § 213.
119. Tobin Canning Co. v. Fraser, 81 Tex. 407, 411, 17 S.W. 25 (1891).
120. Haddad v. Wood, 949 S.W.2d 438, 442 (Tex. App. 1997); TEX. BUS. & COM. CODE ANN. §26.01(b)(2) (2012).
121. RUSSELL, *supra* note 49, 9:20.
122. TEX. JUR., *supra* note 42, § 203.

after payment on the guaranty becomes due.[123] The similar equitable defense of laches is often difficult for a guarantor to effectively assert against an obligee under Texas law.[124]

7.4 Right of Set-off

A guarantor who has paid an obligee on a guaranty obligation may set off the guaranty payments against any obligations it otherwise owes to the obligee.[125]

§ 8 Waiver of Defenses by the Guarantor

8.1 Defenses that Cannot be Waived

Some defenses cannot be waived.

A guarantor likely cannot effectively waive or consent to acts which would otherwise render the contract void or to fraudulent misrepresentation by the obligee.[126]

The Texas Business and Commercial Code does not permit the waiver by a guarantor or primary obligor of the requirement that a Uniform Commercial Code foreclosure sale be carried out in a commercially reasonable manner.[127]

8.2 "Catch-all" Waivers

Though catch-all waiver language may be effective, it is advisable for obligees to include waivers of specific suretyship defenses.

With few exceptions, a guaranty defense may be waived either by a guarantor expressly waiving the defense or consenting in advance to the conduct that gives rise to the defense.[128] Determining the scope of a waiver is a matter of contract interpretation.[129] "Consent is determined on an individual basis according to the particular language of the guaranty, and courts have held guarantors to the terms of their consent as stated in a guaranty."[130] Commercial guaranties typically contain a catch-all waiver that the guaranty is "absolute and unconditional."

---

123. Tex. Civ. Prac. & Rem. Code Ann. § 16.004(a)(3) (2012).
124. Russell, *supra* note 49, § 9:90.
125. *In re* Corland Corp., 967 F.2d 1069, 1077 (5th Cir. 1992).
126. *See* Conner, *supra* note 40, at 823-24.
127. Tex. Bus. & Com. Code Ann. § 9.602(7) (2012).
128. Russell, *supra* note 49, § 9:105.
129. *Id.*
130. *Sonne*, 881 S.W.2d at 792.

8.3 Use of Specific Waivers

General waivers likely suffice to waive suretyship defenses. However, as a general practice, most commercial practitioners in Texas continue to use specific waivers out of prudence. It does not necessarily follow, for example, from the fact that a guarantor has committed to "an absolute and unconditional guaranty" that the guarantor is consenting to permit its subrogation right to be derogated by the obligee's acts or omissions with respect to the collateral securing the principal obligation which may negatively impact the value thereof. Therefore, it makes sense to include specific waivers in the guaranty as to any defense the guarantor may have as to the treatment, release, exchange, subordination, or perfection of collateral and specific waivers of other suretyship defenses. Such specific waivers include, as noted in § 7.2.4, a waiver of the requirements of Chapter 43 of the Texas Civil Practice and Remedies Code.

§ 9 Third-party Pledgors—Defenses and Waiver Thereof

Because the pledgor arguably stands in the relation of a guarantor to the primary obligor to the extent of the pledge, it may most likely avail itself of the defenses of a guarantor. It may also waive these defenses.

No evidence has been found that the law as applied to sureties would not apply to a third-party pledge. In contrast, the law appears to be that a pledge of collateral results in a surety relationship. See also § 1.2. It seems logical, given this state of the law, that the pledgor generally has the same defenses available to it as are available to a surety.

§ 10 Jointly and Severally Liable Guarantors—Contribution and Release of Guarantors

Jointly and severally liable guarantors who satisfy the underlying obligation may exercise an equitable remedy of contribution to recover each coguarantor's proportionate share of such debt. A jointly and severally liable guarantor is not entitled to release from the obligation if its coguarantors are released.

10.1 Contribution

Jointly and severally liable guarantors have unlimited liability and are individually liable for the entire underlying obligation.[131] But a coguarantor who

131. Guynn v. Corpus Christi Bank & Trust, 620 S.W.2d 188, 190 (Tex. App. 1981).

has satisfied an underlying obligation generally has an equitable right to contribution from the remaining coguarantors.[132] This right remains even if the underlying obligation and guaranty are assigned to one of the coguarantors.[133] The guarantor's status in relation to the other coguarantors does not change under these circumstances.[134]

Under the equitable remedy of contribution, a contract is implied between coguarantors under which the guarantors are held accountable for their respective share of the underlying obligation if one of the guarantors must satisfy the debt.[135] The coguarantor is only entitled to recoup the shares of the other coguarantors and may not recover the full debt.[136]

10.2 Release of Coguarantors

Where the guarantors are jointly liable, the release of one guarantor without the consent of a coguarantor releases the coguarantor.[137] However, there is no such release where the guarantors are jointly and severally liable.[138]

§ 11 Subrogation

A guarantor who satisfies the primary obligor's underlying obligation may choose to either bring an action against the primary obligor to enforce the underlying obligation itself or seek reimbursement.[139] In doing so, the guarantor takes on all of the original obligee's rights and security against the primary obligor.[140] The guarantor's recovery is limited to the amount the guarantor paid on behalf of the primary obligor.[141]

§ 12 Triangular Set-off in Bankruptcy

Set-off is generally permissible in Texas so long as the debt is mutual and arose pre-petition.

A default on the underlying obligation occurs once the primary obligor files for bankruptcy.[142] Generally, "upon default of the maker of a note in the

132. Lavender v. Bunch, 216 S.W.3d 548, 554 (Tex. App. 2007); Huggins v. Johnston, 35 S.W.2d 688 (1931); Miller v. Miles, 400 S.W.2d 4, 7 (Tex. App. 1966).
133. *Lavender*, 216 S.W.3d at 553 (citing Byrd v. Estate of Nelms, 154 S.W.3d 149, 164 (Tex. App. 2004)).
134. *Id.*
135. *Id.* at 554.
136. *Byrd*, 154 S.W.3d at 164.
137. Conner, *supra* note 40, at 828.
138. Conner, *supra* note 40, at 828 (citing U.S. Gypsum Co. v. Sampson, 496 S.W.2d 687 (Tex. App. 1973); *see also Guynn*, 620 S.W.2d at 190.
139. Fox v. Kroeger, 119 Tex. 511, 517, 35 S.W.2d 679 (1931).
140. *Id.*; Scott Paper Co. v. Johnson, 406 S.W.2d 548, 549 (Tex. App. 1966); Fulton v. South Oak Cliff State Bank, 439 S.W.2d 730, 733 (Tex. App. 1969).
141. Russell, *supra* note 49, § 9:80.
142. *In re Corland Corp.*, 967 F.2d at 1073 (5th Cir. 1992).

payment thereof a guarantor of it becomes liable to the holder and the relationship of debtor and creditor is at once established between the guarantor and the holder of the note."[143] Therefore, any payments made by a guarantor on the underlying obligation, whether or not the guarantor tendered such payments as a result of the obligee's demands for payment, are not property of the estate.[144] Further, any such payments may be offset against other debt the guarantor owes the principal obligor so long as the debts and claims are mutual and pre-petition.[145]

§ 13 Indemnification—Whether the Primary Obligor has a Duty

A guarantor may not recover from a primary obligor who did not assent to the guaranty relationship between the guarantor and the obligee. In these situations, the guarantor's rights are equal to those of a purchaser of the underlying obligation.[146]

§ 14 Enforcement of Guaranties

14.1 Notice to Guarantor of Primary Obligor's Default

An obligee is not required to give a guarantor under an absolute guaranty notice of the primary obligor's default or notice of its intent to accelerate in order to recover against the guarantor.[147] Under a conditional guaranty, it is a condition precedent to a guarantor's liability that notice of the primary obligor's default be given to a guarantor;[148] however, such requirement may be waived by agreement of the parties.[149]

14.2 Recovery Under a Guaranty

In order to recover on a breach of a guaranty agreement, the obligee must prove: "(1) the existence and ownership of the guaranty agreement; (2) the terms of the underlying contract by the holder; (3) the occurrence of the conditions upon which liability is based; and (4) the failure or refusal to perform

143. *Id.* at 1073 (quoting United States v. Select Meat Co., 275 F. Supp. 38, 45 (W.D. Tex. 1967) (quotations omitted).
144. *Id.* at 1076.
145. *Id.* at 1076–77 (citations omitted).
146. Marsalis v. Garre, 391 S.W.2d 522, 527–28 (Tex. App. 1965).
147. Tex. Jur., *supra* note 42, § 211.
148. United States v. Little Joe Trawlers, Inc., 776 F.2d 1249, 1253 (5th Cir. 1985) (citing Ray v. Spencer, 208 S.W.2d 103 (Tex. App. 1947)).
149. *Byrd*, 154 S.W.3d at 159; Tex. Jur., *supra* note 42, § 211.

the promise by the guarantor."[150] The burden of proving the breach of the guaranty is on the obligee.[151]

14.3 Joinder of Proper Parties

Texas statutes[152] provide that an obligor primarily liable as to an obligation, such as a guarantor under an absolute guaranty, may be sued alone, but a guarantor who is not primarily liable, such as a guarantor under a guaranty of collection, may not be sued without joining the primary obligor, except under certain conditions.[153] The primary obligor is not required to be joined in a suit under a guaranty if such obligor is a nonresident or resides in a place where he or she cannot be reached by the ordinary process of law, resides in a place that is unknown and cannot be ascertained by the use of reasonable diligence, is dead, or is actually or notoriously insolvent.[154]

14.4 Limitations on Recovery

Though a guaranty may meet all of the requirements required for an obligee to legally enforce it, the guaranty or payments under the guaranty may be subject to avoidance under state or federal fraudulent transfer laws or as a preference under the U.S. Bankruptcy Code.[155] State and federal law view the execution of a guaranty as a transfer of property[156] which may be subject to avoidance by a trustee or debtor in possession under Section 548 of the U.S. Bankruptcy Code[157] or by a creditor, trustee, or debtor in possession under the

---

150. *Byrd*, 154 S.W.3d at 157 (citing Escalante v. Luckie, 77 S.W.3d 410, 416 (Tex. App. 2002) and Marshall v. Ford Motor Co., 878 S.W.2d 629, 631 (Tex. App. 1994)); 2 RUSSELL, *supra* note 49, § 9:74 (in order for a creditor to recover on underlying debt, it must plead and prove: "(1) the existence of the underlying debt and the guaranty of that debt; (2) the guarantor signed the guaranty; (3) the creditor legally owns or holds the guaranty; and (4) a certain balance remains due and owing."). If the guaranty is on debt resulting from a deficiency from a foreclosure sale, the obligee should also plead and prove the foreclosure sale was properly conducted. 2 RUSSELL, *supra* note 49, § 9:74.
151. TEX. JUR., *supra* note 42, § 224.
152. TEX. CIV. PRAC. & REM. CODE ANN. § 17.001(a) ("[A] judgment may not be rendered against a party not primarily liable unless judgment is also rendered against the principal obligor."); TEX. R. CIV. P. 31 ("No surety shall be sued unless his principal is joined with him . . . ").
153. TEX. JUR., *supra* note 42, § 221. *But see* 2 RUSSELL, *supra* note 49, § 9:78 (noting that because many trial courts view Texas Civil Rule of Procedure 31 and section 17.001 of the Texas Civil Practice and Remedies Code as governing both absolute guaranties and guaranties of collection, unless one of the exceptions to joinder of the principal obligor exists or some other good reason, the guarantor on an absolute guaranty should be joined in a suit against the principal obligor).
154. TEX. CIV. PRAC. & REM. CODE ANN. § 17.001(b) (2012).
155. *See* RUSSELL, *supra* note 49, §§ 9:56 to 9:70.
156. RUSSELL, *supra* note 49, § 9:57.
157. *See* 11 U.S.C.A. § 548(a)(1) (West 2010). Under Section 548 of the Bankruptcy Code, a trustee or debtor in possession may avoid any transfer of the debtor's property or any obligation incurred by the debtor that was made or incurred on or within two years before the date of filing of the bankruptcy petition, if the debtor received less than a reasonably equivalent value in exchange for such transfer or obligation and (1) was or became insolvent as a result of the transfer or obligation; or (2) was engaged in or was about to engage in business for which debtor was left with unreasonably small capital; (3) intended to incur debts, or believed that it would incur, debts that would be beyond its ability to pay as they matured; or (4) made such transfer to or for the benefit of an insider, or incurred such obligation to or for the benefit of an insider, under an employment contract and not in the ordinary course of business. 11 U.S.C.A. § 548(a)(1)(B). The trustee or debtor in possession may also avoid any transfer of the debtor's property or any obligation incurred by the debtor made with the actual intent to hinder, delay, or defraud any entity to which the debtor was or became on or after the date of such transfer or such obligation was incurred, indebted. 11 U.S.C.A. § 548(a)(1)(A).

Texas Uniform Fraudulent Transfer Act.[158] The Texas Uniform Fraudulent Transfer Act is available to avoid transfers by Texas debtors whether or not the debtor is in bankruptcy.[159] Under the U.S. Bankruptcy Code, a trustee or debtor in possession may also rely on state fraudulent transfer law to avoid fraudulent transfers so long as at least one creditor holding an unsecured claim would be able to challenge the transfer under applicable state law.[160] The Texas Fraudulent Transfer Act would permit a trustee or debtor in possession to avoid a fraudulent transfer made as far back as four years.[161]

Under Section 547 of the U.S. Bankruptcy Code, payments made on a guaranty within 90 days of the guarantor's filing of a bankruptcy petition may be voidable by a trustee or debtor in possession as a preference.[162]

§ 15 Choice of Law Provisions

In Texas, contractual choice of law issues are decided by applying Chapter 271 of the Texas Business and Commerce Code.[163] The authors of this survey are unaware of any Texas case which applies these principles in a manner unique to guaranties. While a detailed analysis of the Texas choice-of-law statute is beyond the scope of this survey, it is worth noting, in the broader context of commercial finance transactions, that this statute was amended in 2011 to expand and update existing rules to accommodate syndicated loan and other multilender transactions, which often include guaranties of the relevant indebtedness. The amendment, now codified under Chapter 271 of the Texas Business and Commerce Code, permits the parties to a loan transaction involving more than $25 million in credit and at least three lenders to choose as the governing law of such transaction the law of any jurisdiction in the United States where any party to the transaction has an office.[164]

158. *See* TEX. BUS. & COM. CODE ANN. §§ 24.001 through 24.013 (2012). Under the Texas Uniform Fraudulent Transfer Act, a creditor may avoid the transfer of debtor's property or an obligation incurred if the debtor made the transfer or incurred the obligation without receiving reasonable equivalent value in exchange for the transfer or obligation, and the debtor (1) was engaged in or was about to engage in business for which debtor was left with unreasonably small capital or (2) intended to incur debts, or believed that it would incur, debts that would be beyond its ability to pay as they matured. TEX. BUS. & COM. CODE ANN. § 24.005(a)(2) (2012). The creditor may also avoid any transfer made or obligation incurred if the debtor made the transfer or incurred the obligation with the actual intent to hinder, delay, or defraud any creditor of the debtor. TEX. BUS. & COM. CODE ANN. § 24.005(a)(1) (2012).

159. RUSSELL, *supra* note 49, § 9:56; *See* TEX. BUS. & COM. CODE ANN. §§ 24.005 through 24.006 (2012).

160. *See* 11 U.S.C.A. § 544(b) (2010).

161. *See* TEX. BUS. & COM. CODE ANN. § 24.010 (2012) (the cause of action for a fraudulent transfer extinguishes unless action is brought: under § 24.005(a)(2) or 24.006(a), within four years after the transfer was made or the obligation was incurred and under § 24.006(b), within one year after the transfer was made or the obligation was incurred.)

162. *See* 11 U.S.C.A. § 547(b) (2010). The trustee or debtor in possession may avoid any transfer of an interest in property of the debtor if it is (1) to or for the benefit of a creditor; (2) for or on account of an antecedent debt of debtor; (3) made while the debtor is insolvent (there is a rebuttable presumption that the debtor is insolvent if the transfer is made within 90 days before the filing of the petition); (4) made on or within 90 days before the date of the filing of the petition or, if the creditor is an insider, between 90 days and one year before the date of the filing of the petition; and (4) enables the creditor to receive more than the creditor would receive if the case were a case under Chapter 7 of the Bankruptcy Code, the transfer had not been made, and the creditor received payment of this debt to the extent provided under the Bankruptcy Code. 11 U.S.C.A. § 547(b) (2010).

163. TEX. BUS. ORG. CODE ANN. § 271 (2012).

164. TEX. BUS. & COMM. CODE ANN. § 271.004(b)(2)(A) (2012).

Also of note in connection with commercial finance transactions, this statute provides that as to a "qualified transaction" (essentially a transaction involving at least $1 million in value),[165] subject to certain exceptions, the parties to the transaction may agree in writing that the law of a specific jurisdiction will govern and that choice will be accepted if "the transaction bears a reasonable relation to that jurisdiction,"[166] with the statute providing specific safe-harbors as to transactions which meet such a requirement of reasonable relation, including (1) a party is a resident of that jurisdiction, (2) a party's place of business or, if it has more than one place of business, its chief executive office or office from which it conducted a substantial part of negotiations, is in that jurisdiction, (3) all or part of subject matter is located in that jurisdiction, (4) a party is required to perform in that jurisdiction a substantial part of its obligations, such as delivering payments, or (5) a substantial part of the negotiations occurred in or from such jurisdiction and an agreement relating to the transaction was signed in such jurisdiction by a party.[167]

165. Tex. Bus. & Comm. Code Ann. § 271.001 (2012).
166. Tex. Bus. & Comm. Code Ann. § 271.005(a)(2) (2012).
167. Tex. Bus. & Comm. Code Ann. § 271.004(b)(1)(A-E) (2012).

Utah State Law of Guaranties

Carl W. Barton
Holland & Hart LLP
222 South Main Street, Suite 2200
Salt Lake City, Utah 84101
(801) 799-5831
cbarton@hollandhart.com

HOLLAND&HART LLP

Contents

Utah State Law of Guaranties

HIGHLIGHTS:

1. Utah guaranties are governed by the Utah statute of frauds. See § 1.1 below.
2. Coguarantors should enter into a contribution agreement addressing their respective liabilities to one another if one or more should be called upon to pay the creditor. In the absence of such an agreement, guarantors are liable for contribution among themselves on an equal per capita basis. See § 8 below.
3. Utah's one-action rule and antideficiency statutes effect how a lender should structure loans and how it may recover from a guarantor and a borrower. See § 9 below.

Introduction

This chapter is designed to provide an overview of Utah law with respect to guaranties of loans. We have not attempted to address Utah law governing guaranties in other contexts. This topic is necessarily general in its scope, and lenders should not rely on this chapter for answers to questions involving application of Utah law to specific sets of facts. There are generally three statutes affecting this kind of guaranty in Utah: the statute of frauds,[1] Utah's one-action rule,[2] and Utah's anti-deficiency statute.[3] While some Utah court decisions include occasional references to the Restatement of Suretyship and Guaranty or its predecessor, the Restatement of Security, Utah courts rarely cite to or rely on such sources in analyzing the type of guaranty discussed here.

The following general terms will allow an easier reading and clearer understanding of the information contained in this chapter:

"**Guarantor**" means a person who agrees, by contract, to satisfy an underlying loan obligation of another to a lender upon the primary obligor's default on that underlying obligation.

"**Guaranty**" means the contract under which the guarantor agrees to satisfy the underlying obligation of a primary obligor to a lender, in the event the primary obligor defaults on the underlying obligation.

"**Lender**" means the person to whom the underlying obligation is owed. For example, the lender under a loan agreement would be a lender vis-à-vis the borrower.

1. Utah Code Annotated Section 25, 5-4(1)(b), as amended and now in effect.
2. Utah Code Annotated Section 78B-6-901, as amended and now in effect.
3. Utah Code Annotated Section 57-1-32, as amended and now in effect.

"**Primary Obligor**" or "**Borrower**" means the person who incurs the underlying obligation to the lender. For example, the borrower under a loan agreement would be a primary obligor.

"**Underlying Obligation**" or "**Loan**" means the obligation or obligations incurred by the borrower and owed to the lender. For example, the borrower's obligation to make payments of principal and interest to a lender on a promissory note constitutes an underlying obligation.

§ 1 Nature of the Guaranty

1.1 Guaranty Relationships

Under Utah law, a guaranty is an agreement made in advance to pay the underlying obligation of another. In the context of this chapter, it is the way in which the guarantor provides a lender with a manner to recover on or obtain repayment of a loan on which a borrower defaults.

1.2 Statute of Frauds

The Utah Statute of Frauds requires that the guaranty must be in writing and signed by the guarantor.[4]

1.3 Other Relationships

While not the focus of this chapter, we note that other relationships, such as a suretyship relationship, may also arise because of the pledge of collateral. As such, a guaranty-type relationship arises, to the extent of the collateral pledged, when a person supplies collateral for a loan in order to induce the lender to make a loan to the borrower or where one party mortgages property to a lender to secure the debt of another.

§ 2 State law Requirements for an Entity to Enter Into a Guaranty

2.1 Entities

Partnerships, limited partnerships, general partners of general and limited partnerships, limited liability companies, limited liability partnerships, corporations, and individuals can all grant guaranties. Such grants are generally permitted by Utah law, provided they are made in furtherance of the business

4. Utah Code Annotated Section 25, 5-4(1)(b), as amended and now in effect.

activities of the granting entity.[5] Utah law does not prohibit trusts from entering into a guaranty.

2.2 Individuals

Confusion can sometimes arise in the case of corporate officers or directors signing a guaranty in closely held corporations or other organizations, but Utah law does not prohibit an officer, employee, or owner of a Utah entity from entering into and being bound by a guaranty intended to support his or her entity's or employer's underlying obligation to a lender. In such instances, the individual executes the guaranty in his or her individual capacity and not in his or her capacity as an officer, owner, or employee of the borrower. Utah is not a community property state, and the express terms of the guaranty govern the scope of the liability of each guarantor. Also see § 8 below relative to rights of contribution between coguarantors.

§ 3 Consideration for a Guaranty

Fundamental contract principles apply to the analysis of consideration for entering into a guaranty.

Consideration is required to support and create a valid guaranty contract in Utah.[6] In most circumstances, consideration usually takes the form of the lender's agreement to extend or make a loan to the borrower.[7] The fact that the guarantor did not receive any compensation does not mean the guaranty fails for a lack of consideration.[8] When given as part of the same transaction as the underlying obligation, no separate consideration is necessary aside from the lender's making of the loan itself.[9]

However, where a guaranty is executed and delivered to the lender after the loan closing, questions about the enforceability of the guaranty may arise on grounds of a lack of consideration.[10] Lenders can properly and easily address that concern by including language in the loan documents to the effect that the lender is making the loan in anticipation of and on the condition that the guarantor will execute and deliver the guaranty after closing. The principle of adequate consideration for a guaranty is consistent with the notion in the Utah Uniform Commercial Code that an instrument, such as a promissory note, is issued for value and is, therefore, supported by adequate consideration where a promissory note actually includes a guaranty on its face.[11]

5. *See* Utah Code Annotated Section 16-10a-302(7), as amended and now in effect; Section 48-2c-110, as amended and now in effect; and Section 48-2a-203, as amended and now in effect.
6. Bray Lines, Inc. v. Utah Carriers, Inc., 739 P.2d 1115, 1117 (Utah Ct. App. 1987).
7. *Id.*
8. *Id.*
9. Boise Cascade Corp., Building Materials Distribution Division v. Stonewood Development Corp., 655 P.2d 668, 669 (Utah 1982).
10. Yoho Auto., Inc. v. Shillington, 784 P.2d 1253, 1255 (Utah Ct. App 1989).
11. *See* Utah Code Annotated 70A-3-303, as amended and now in effect.

§ 4 Notice of Acceptance

Notice of acceptance may not be required, if credit is extended to the borrower based upon the guaranty or if the guaranty is absolute. Although there is no Utah statute or case law directly on point, under general principles of guaranty law, the lender must notify the guarantor of its acceptance of the guaranty.

§ 5 Interpretation of Guaranties

Courts in Utah have long followed the principle that a guaranty will be strictly construed against the drafter of that document, which is usually the lender.[12]

5.1 General Principles

Consistent with general contract law in certain circumstances, any uncertainty or ambiguity as to the meaning of language in a guaranty is strictly construed against the party that drafted it.[13]

5.2 Application of Payments on a Guaranty

When a lender accepts payment on an underlying obligation knowing it came from a guarantor, the payment must be applied in satisfaction of the guaranty.[14] However, notice of the guarantor's intent to make payments of the underlying obligation against the amount owed under the guaranty is required. Such notice may be inferred or implied, if the lender has a reasonable basis to know that the guarantor's payments were made in satisfaction of the guaranty obligation.[15] Generally, payments received directly from a guarantor are sufficient to satisfy the notice requirement.[16]

5.3 Guaranty of Payment versus Guaranty of Collection

Upon the occurrence of a default by the borrower under the underlying obligation, a guaranty of payment requires the guarantor to satisfy the underlying obligation, even before the lender seeks to enforce the underlying obligation against the borrower. Such a guaranty of payment is sometimes called an "absolute" guaranty, as opposed to a conditional guaranty, and does not contain words of condition or limitation.[17]

---

12. Valley Bank & Trust Co. v. Rite Way Concrete Forming, Inc., 742 P.2d 105, 110 (Utah Ct. App. 1987).
13. General Appliance Corporation v. Haw, Inc., 516 P.2d 345, 347-248 (Utah 1973).
14. Kang S. Park and Marsha Park v. Gary B. Stanford, 258 P.3d 566, 570-571 (Utah 2011).
15. *Id.*
16. *Id.* at 572.
17. Valley Bank & Trust Co. v. Rite Way Concrete Forming, Inc., 742 P.2d 105, 108 (Utah Ct. App. 1987); Carrier Brokers, Inc. v. Spanish Trail v. C.A. Bailey, 751 P.2d 258,261 (Utah Ct. App. 1988).

A guaranty of collection, on the other hand, requires that the lender seek recourse against the borrower before attempting to enforce the guaranty. Such a guaranty is sometimes called a conditional guaranty in Utah.[18] A conditional guaranty may require a lender to sue the borrower, foreclose on the loan collateral, and exhaust other remedies before the lender may seek recourse against the guarantor under the guaranty. If a guaranty does not contain such limiting or conditional language, it constitutes a guaranty of payment in Utah.[19] Thus, it is important for the language of the guaranty to identify the nature of the guaranty and the extent, if any, to which the lender must pursue the borrower before seeking to enforce the guaranty.[20]

5.4 Subrogation

Upon guarantor's payment of the underlying obligation, guarantor has a right of subrogation to or against any of the collateral pledged by the borrower as security for repayment of the loan.[21] These subrogation rights apply equally to absolute and conditional guaranties, strongly indicating that rights of subrogation apply to both guaranties of payment and collection.[22] From the cases cited below, however, it is not completely clear whether Utah courts will require that the guarantor repay the entire amount of the underlying obligation before it may pursue such right of subrogation. To avoid the confusion that arises if the guarantor has only repaid a portion of the underlying guaranty, it is wise for the lender to include a provision under which the guarantor waives such right of subrogation until the underlying obligation has been repaid in full. As set forth below, such a right of subrogation also allows a guarantor to seek a deficiency against the borrower when the value of real estate collateral is insufficient to satisfy the amount of the underlying obligation.[23]

5.5 "Continuing" Guaranty

A continuing guaranty contemplates a series of transactions or a future course of dealing, rather than a single loan transaction, and such a continuing guaranty remains effective until the guarantor properly revokes it.[24] Thus, a guarantor may revoke a continuing guaranty at any time upon proper notice.[25] However, even if a guarantor does properly revokes a continuing guaranty, the guarantor will remain liable to pay the underlying obligation despite substantial financial changes involving the borrower.[26] Courts have interpreted a guaranty to be continuing from the circumstances surrounding the underlying obligation and the guaranty and not just from the bare language of the agreement.[27]

18. *Id.*
19. Carrier Brokers, Inc. v. Spanish Trail v. C.A. Bailey, 751 P.2d 258,261 (Utah Ct. App. 1988).
20. Strevell-Paterson Co., Inc., v. Francis, 646 _P.2d 741, 743 (Utah 1982).
21. Valley Bank & Trust Co. v. Rite Way Concrete Forming, Inc., 742 P.2d 105, 108-109 (Utah Ct. App. 1987).
22. *Id.*
23. Machock v. Fink, 137 P.3d 779, 783 (Utah 2006).
24. Cessna Finance Corp. v. Meyer, 575 P.2d 1048, 1050-1052 (Utah 1978).
25. Mule-Hide Products Co. Inc. v. White, 40 P.3d 1155, 1159 (Utah Ct. App. 2002).
26. *Id.* at 1160.
27. Cessna Finance Corp. v. Meyer, 575 P.2d 1048, 1050 (Utah 1978).

5.6 A Guarantor may be Bound by Judgments Against the Borrower

In Utah, a guarantor may be bound by a judgment obtained against the borrower in a suit to which the guarantor was a party.[28] The Utah Supreme Court has also suggested that even a guarantor that was not party to a suit may be bound by a judgment against the borrower, if the guarantor had notice of its existence.[29]

5.7 Liability of Guarantor may not be Affected by Release of Lender's Collateral if there is a Nonimpairment Provision in the Guaranty

It is common for a guaranty to include a nonimpairment provision expressly stating that the liability of the guarantor is not affected or reduced by the lender's release or surrender of any or all of the collateral for the loan. Such provisions are enforceable under Utah law.[30] Thus, even though a Utah lender may not meet a duty of reasonable care for such collateral, the guarantor is not released from liability under the guaranty.[31] However, if a guarantor does not consent to such a nonimpairment provision, and if the lender's actions impair the value of the collateral in its possession or control, the guarantor may be relieved or discharged of its obligation under the guaranty to the extent of the lender's impairment of such collateral.[32] However, see the discussion below where there is no nonimpairment provision contained in the guaranty.

§ 6 Defenses of the Guarantor

Certain defenses may be available to a guarantor in Utah.

6.1 Defenses of the Borrower

6.1.1 General

In most states, common law states that the guarantor, absent an effective waiver, is not bound to perform, if the borrower is not bound, and the guarantor, if sued alone, may not raise any defense or counterclaim that is personal to the borrower. There are, however, no cases on point in Utah on this topic. Such personal defenses belonging to the borrower may include fraud in the inducement, negligence in performance of a contract, and breach of a warranty contained in the agreement governing the underlying obligation.

28. Miller Brewing Co. v. Capitol Distributing Co. et al, 77 P.2d 359, 361 (Utah 1938).
29. *Id.*
30. Continental Bank & Trust Co. v. Utah Security Mortgage, Inc., 701 P.2d 1095, 1097-1098 (Utah 1985).
31. *Id.*
32. Valley Bank & Trust Co. v. Rite Way Concrete Forming, Inc., 742 P.2d 105, 108-109 (Utah Ct. App. 1987).

6.1.2 When Guarantor may Assert the Borrower's Defense

In most states, if the guarantor alone is sued, the borrower may grant its consent to the guarantor's use of the defense or cause of action belonging to the borrower. This arrangement is common where the guarantor owns or controls the borrower.

6.1.3 Defenses that may not be Raised by Guarantor

While there are no cases directly on point in Utah, it is well-settled that the insolvency of the borrower is not a defense that a guarantor may raise, unless the guaranty is conditioned on the solvency of the primary obligor. A guarantor may also generally not raise the borrower's incapacity or financial condition as a defense to liability under the guaranty.

6.1.4 Defenses that may be Raised by Guarantor

Common defenses raised by a guarantor include a showing that the lender failed to perform such that there is a partial or complete "failure of consideration" or a showing by the guarantor that the borrower was otherwise not liable to repay the underlying obligation.

6.2 Suretyship Defenses

6.2.1 Modification of the Underlying Obligation, Including Release of Collateral or of Coguarantors

While there is no Utah case directly on point, it is well settled that if a lender materially alters the documents evidencing and constituting the underlying obligation, the guarantor may be discharged and released from its obligations under the guaranty.[33] Courts follow this common law rule on principles of fairness, stating that it would be unfair to require a guarantor to guarantee a different loan risk than the guarantor originally understood and undertook to perform, particularly where the modification increases the guarantor's risk and exposure. Many courts apply this rule to discharge a guarantor, even if the modifications to the loan documents do not harm or prejudice the guarantor. Thus, if a lender reduces the interest rate or the loan amount, the lender should first obtain the guarantor's consent. Lenders, however, can address this concern by including a provision in the guaranty stating that the guarantor's obligations will not be affected or reduced because of modifications to the loan documents or to the amount or terms of the loan. Presumably such a provision is enforceable in Utah, but there are no cases directly on point. For that reason, a prudent lender will not rely on such a provision and will, instead, require the guarantor to execute an acknowledgement of any modifications to the loan documents.

33. Clark v. Walter-Kurth Lumber Co., 689 S.W.2d 275, 278 (Tax App. 1 Dist 1985).

6.2.2 *Release or Impairment of Security for or Coguarantor of the Underlying Obligation*

When a lender has a security interest in collateral to secure repayment of a loan that is also guarantied by a guarantor, the lender may not release or impair such collateral and may not release any coguarantor without discharging the guarantor from its obligations under the guaranty.[34] There is no Utah case on point, but this principle is widely accepted in the courts of the states surrounding the State of Utah. The rationale behind this rule is that a guarantor who pays the borrower's obligation to the lender has subrogation rights against the lender's collateral and contribution rights against coguarantors of the same underlying obligation and would therefore, be unfairly prejudiced by the release of any collateral or co-guarantors. As noted above, the inclusion of a nonimpairment provision in the guaranty eliminates this concern for lenders. Further, the nonimpairment provision can and should clearly allow the lender to release some or all of the loan collateral and any or all of the coguarantors without affecting such lender's right to enforce the guaranty against the remaining guarantors.

6.2.3 *Failure to Fulfill a Condition Precedent*

When a conditional, as opposed to an absolute, guaranty is involved, the guarantor may raise a defense in connection with lender's or borrower's failure to perform a condition expressly set forth in the guaranty.

6.2.4 *Failure to Pursue Borrower is not a Defense in Utah*

In a Utah loan secured by real estate, the lender is not required to seek recourse against the Borrower or the collateral before enforcing a guaranty of payment.[35] That approach is also true for a guaranty of collection.[36] This is so because of Utah's one-action rule.[37] See the discussion below in Section 9.1.

6.2.5 *Statute of Limitations*

In Utah, there is a six-year statute of limitations for a guaranty.[38]

6.2.6 *Statute of Frauds*

As noted in Section 1.2 above, enforceable guaranties must be in writing in Utah.

---

34. Speight, McCue & Associates, P.C. v. Wallop, 153 P.3d 250, 256 (Wyo. 2007).
35. Machock v. Fink, 137 P.3d 779, 783 (Utah 2006).
36. *Id.*
37. Utah Code Annotated Section 78B-6-901, as amended and now in effect.
38. Utah Code Annotated Section 78B-2-309, as amended and now in effect.

§ 7 Waiver of Defenses by the Guarantor

7.1 Defenses that Cannot be Waived

It seems, generally, that some defenses cannot be waived.

Courts have generally held that a guarantor cannot waive a constitutional or statutory protection where the public interest is implicated or where the relevant statute provides that its violation would render the contract void.

7.2 Use of Specific Waivers

In Utah, specific waiver provisions contained in a guaranty are generally enforceable in accordance with general principles of contract law, including provisions: (a) empowering a lender to release or reach a settlement with some but not all guarantors without impairing or affecting the liability of the remaining guarantor(s); (b) allowing a lender to release or otherwise deal with the collateral without impairing or affecting the liability of the guarantor; (c) allowing a lender to materially amend, modify, or alter the underlying obligation, including an increase in the interest rate that was deemed material; (d) allowing a lender to fail, refuse, or omit to enforce any provision of the loan documents; and (d) waiving all defenses given to sureties or guarantors at law or in equity other than actual payment of the underlying obligation.[39]

§ 8 Jointly and Severally Liable Guarantors—Contribution upon Payment by a Coguarantor

Guarantors who are jointly and severally liable are presumed to share the guaranty obligation equally. While the lender is not obliged to seek full payment from more than one of the coguarantors, such coguarantors nonetheless have certain rights.

Utah follows the well-settled rule that a coguarantor cannot bring an action or suit for contribution against any other coguarantor for contribution until the first coguarantor has paid more than his or her share of the underlying obligation.[40] Conversely, a coguarantor has a right to contribution when his or her payment of the underlying obligation exceeds his or her proportionate share of the entire amount of the underlying obligation.[41]

39. *Also see* Utah Code Annotated Section 70A-3-605, as amended and now in effect.
40. Gardner v. Bean, 677 P.2d 1116, 1118 (Utah 1984).
41. *Id.*

§ 9 Enforcement of Guaranties

9.1 Utah One-action Rule and Antideficiency Statute

Utah's one-action rule states that there can only be one action for the recovery of any debt or the enforcement of any right secured solely by mortgage on real estate.[42] The one-action rule requires the lender to seek recourse against the real estate collateral through foreclosure before suing the borrower on the underlying obligation.[43] Utah's one-action rule applies to both mortgages and trust deeds.[44] The one-action rule, however, does not apply to a guaranty of payment or to a guaranty of performance, and a lender may proceed directly against the guarantor without first seeking recourse either to the borrower or against the real property encumbered by a trust deed or mortgage.[45]

Utah law also permits a lender to seek recourse against real estate collateral before making a claim on the guaranty.[46] However, if a lender elects to begin foreclosure against the real property covered by the trust deed before bringing a claim on the guaranty, the lender must conclude the foreclosure sale before it can establish the amount, if any, to be recovered under the guaranty. Thus, a lender has the ability to control the timing and sequencing of seeking recourse against the guarantor and should carefully consider those factors in establishing the strategy, timing, and sequence of starting an action on the guaranty and a foreclosure against the real estate collateral.

If any amount remains due under the underlying obligation, a lender may file a deficiency action against the borrower, but must do so within three months after the date of the foreclosure sale.[47] This requirement, known as Utah's antideficiency statute, also applies to a lender's efforts to collect a deficiency from a guarantor under a guaranty.[48] Thus, a lender must file a deficiency action against the borrower and against any guarantor within three months after the date of the foreclosure sale, if at all.

42. Utah Code Annotated Section 78B-6-901, as amended and now in effect.
43. City Consumer Services, Inc., v. Peters, 815 P.2d 234, 236 (Utah 1991).
44. *Id.*
45. Machock v. Fink, 137 P.3d 779, 783, 785 (Utah 2006).
46. *Id.*
47. Utah Code Annotated Section 57-1-32, as amended and now in effect.
48. Surety Life Insurance Co. v Smith, 892 P.2d 1 (Utah 1995).

Vermont State Law of Guaranties

Afi Ahmadi
Margaret Platzer
Daniel Roberts

Dinse, Knapp & McAndrew, P.C.
209 Battery Street
Burlington, Vermont 05401
Phone: (802) 864-5751
Fax: (802) 864-1603
www.dinse.com

Contents

Vermont State Law of Guaranties

HIGHLIGHTS:

- Vermont law is very protective of the guarantor. The obligee cannot look to the guarantor for performance until the obligee has fully pursued performance from the primary obligor (in contrast to a suretyship, where the obligor and guarantor can be pursued for a remedy simultaneously).
- Generally, if the underlying contract for the principal obligation is modified or altered without the guarantor's consent, the guarantor is released from the obligation. The guarantor is not released when parties are substituted in the performance of an obligation or where an obligor uses other mechanisms to reduce the obligation of the primary obligor.
- If an obligee neglects to act or proceed against a principal within a reasonable amount of time, an action against the guarantor can be prohibited. However, a principal's insolvency when the debt becomes due and the obligee's failure to sue the principal does not discharge the guarantor.

This survey does not contemplate guaranties made by insurance companies governed by Title 8 of Vermont Statutes Annotated. This survey also does not address suretyships which are distinct from guaranties under Vermont law.

Throughout the survey we have used the following terms to refer to the parties and their obligations.

"**Guarantor**" is the party that gives the guaranty and promises to answer for a debt of the obligor.

"**Guaranty**" is the undertaking of a promise by one person to support the obligations of another person in an agreement with a third party.

"**Obligee**" is the party that is owed the performance of the primary obligor that is protected by the guaranty and the party that can look to the guarantor in the event the primary obligor fails to perform under its contract with the obligee.

"**Primary Obligor**" or "**Obligor**" is the party accepting the guaranty and contractually involved with the obligee for some performance that is protected by the guaranty.

§ 1 Nature of the Guaranty Arrangement

A guaranty is an undertaking or promise on the part of one person which is collateral to a primary or principal obligation on the part of another and which binds the guarantor to performance in the event of nonperformance by the primary obligor.[1]

Vermont law contemplates a guaranty when two parties enter into a contractual arrangement whereby one party agrees to have an outside third party guaranty that party's obligations under the agreement. The law is also protective of the guarantor and will not allow the obligee to look to the guarantor for performance until the obligee has fully pursued performance from the primary obligor.[2]

1.1 Guaranty Relationships

The relationship between the guarantor and the primary obligor arises through principles of contract law. There are generally two contracts: the contract between the obligee and the primary obligor and the contract between the primary obligor and the guarantor. Although the guarantor is liable for contractual obligations of the obligor, the obligee must first seek payment from the obligor before pursuing the guarantor and the courts will generally restrict recovery from the guarantor to only the performance specifically guaranteed.[3] Guaranty relationships are created when there is a meeting of the minds of the parties by offer and acceptance.[4]

1.2 Other Suretyship Relationships

Vermont law distinguishes guaranty relationships from surety relationships. Under Vermont law, a guarantor enters into a separate and independent agreement with the obligor that the obligor will perform or have performed a duty to the obligee. An obligee must exhaust all options to collect on the performance of a duty before pursuing the guarantor. In contrast, a surety joins another party in agreeing to perform a duty. Under a suretyship, all parties are directly and primarily obligated for the performance and can be pursued for a remedy simultaneously.[5]

1. Merrimack Sheet Metal, Inc. v. Liv-Mar, Inc., 511 A.2d 992 (Vt. 1986).
2. Vt. Dev. Credit Corp. v. Kitchel, 149 Vt. 421 (1988).
3. Joseph W. Corlies & Co. v. Estes, 31 Vt. 653 (1859).
4. Manly Bros. v. Bush, 169 A. 782 (Vt. 1934).
5. Ricketson v. Lizotte, 90 Vt. 386 (1916).

§ 2 State Law Requirements for an Entity to Enter a Guaranty

Vermont law specifically contemplates corporations, limited liability companies, and banks acting as guarantors.

2.1 Corporations

Vermont law grants powers to corporations to "make contracts, including partnership agreements, and guarantees…"[6] Nonprofit corporations may also make guaranty contracts but are specifically prohibited from guaranteeing obligations of a director or officer.[7]

2.2 Partnerships

Partnerships are not explicitly empowered to enter into guaranties but are not prohibited from doing so under Chapter 11 of Vermont's Statutes Annotated.

2.3 Limited Liability Companies

Limited liability companies are explicitly empowered to enter into guaranties.[8]

2.4 Banks and Trust Companies

Banks and trust companies are granted the same powers as corporations, which include the power to enter into guaranties.[9]

2.5 Individuals

An individual acting in his or her capacity as a director, member, partner, or agent of a corporation, limited liability company, partnership, or bank and trust company may enter into a guaranty on behalf of the corporation or business entity. The courts will look to the agreement to interpret whether the guaranty is a personal guaranty or a guaranty on behalf of the business entity.[10]

6. 11A V.S.A § 3.02(7).
7. 11B V.S.A. § 8.32.
8. 11 V.S.A.§ 3012.
9. 8 V.S.A. § 14102.
10. O'Brien Bros. 'P'ship, LLP v. Plociennik, 940 A.2d 692 (Vt. 2007).

§ 3 Signatory's Authority to Execute a Guaranty

3.1 Corporations

Corporations in Vermont may only enter into guaranty agreements through an agent.[11] Agents of the corporation are generally the officers and directors of the entity. Actual authority to execute guaranties may be specifically authorized by a vote of the board or ratification of acts or implied from the conduct of proper officers.[12] Corporate officers will also be found to have apparent or implied authority if their actions are found to be within the scope of their authority and in furtherance of the corporate business.[13]

3.2 Partnerships

Under partnership law, each partner is considered an agent of the partnership for purposes of executed agreements.[14] This authority extends to transactions related to furthering the purpose of the partnership's business. This authority does not extend to situations where the partner had no authority to act and the person the partner was dealing with knew or had been notified that the partner lacked authority.[15] The law prohibits partner acts that do not carry on the ordinary course of the partnership unless they are specifically authorized by the other partners.[16]

3.3 Limited Liability Companies

Vermont law distinguishes between member or manager authority to execute agreements based on whether a limited liability company (LLC) is managed by the members or the managers. If an LLC is managed by the members, the members have authority to enter into contracts. If the LLC is manager-managed, the members do not have authority to enter into agreements. Rather, the managers have authority. As with partnerships, this authority only extends to the execution of agreements that continue the business purposes of the LLC and can be limited by the company organizational documents.[17]

3.4 Banks and Trust Companies

An officer, director, or employee of a Vermont financial institution is prohibited from corruptly soliciting, demanding, or agreeing to accept a fee, present, benefit, or commission for signing with another as accommodation maker,

11. In re McGrath, 411 A.2d. 1316 (Vt. 1980).
12. Edmunds Bros. v. Smith, 115 A. 187 (Vt. 1921).
13. Howland Bros. & Cave v. Barre Sav. Bank & Trust Co. 89 Vt. 290 (1915); Town of Royalton v. Royalton & W. Tpk. Co., 14 Vt. 311 (1842).
14. 11 V.S.A. § 3221.
15. 11 V.S.A. § 3221(1).
16. 11 V.S.A. § 3221(2).
17. 11 V.S.A. § 3041.

surety, or endorser, or for a loan made.[18] As explained above, surety relationships are distinguishable from guaranty relationships under Vermont law and accommodation-maker arrangements are, in nature, surety agreements.[19] However, signing for a loan made could encompass the power to enter into a guaranty, although there is no case law or regulation further defining the scope of the phrase under Vermont law.

§ 4 Consideration; Sufficiency of Past Consideration

The standard principles of contract law apply to the sufficiency of consideration in a guaranty. Courts will look at the behavior of the parties to determine whether sufficient consideration was received.[20]

§ 5 Notice of Acceptance

Notice of the acceptance of a guaranty is required.[21] Notice from the principal to the guarantor of acceptance is sufficient.[22] Notice of the acceptance must be received within a reasonable amount of time after the offer of guaranty has been made.[23] Whether a guarantor has received notice will be determined from the actions of the parties indicating whether the guarantor was aware of acceptance.[24]

§ 6 Interpretation of Guaranties

6.1 General Principles

Under Vermont law, a guarantor's obligation must be strictly interpreted.[25] Vermont relies on principles of contract law to interpret the party's obligations.

6.2 Guaranty of Payment versus Guaranty of Collection

Under Vermont law, guaranties of payments or collection generally refer to arrangements to support a promissory note. Guaranties of payment are generally considered absolute guaranties for payment of the debts of the obligor by either the obligor or the guarantor without active pursuit on the part of a

18. 8 V.S.A. § 14110(b).
19. Putney Credit Union v. King, 130 Vt. 86 (1971).
20. Roberts v. Griswold, 35 Vt. 496 (1863).
21. Lowry v. Adams, 22 Vt. 160 (1850).
22. *See Id.*
23. Woodstock Bank v. Downer, 27 Vt. 539 (1855).
24. M. Noyes & Co. v. Nichols, 28 Vt. 159 (1855).
25. O'Brien Bros. 'P'ship, LLP v. Plociennik, 940 A.2d 692 (Vt. 2007).

creditor to obtain payment. Notice of nonpayment is not required to be given to the guarantor when a guaranty is absolute.[26]

In contrast, guaranties of collection under Vermont law apply to promissory notes and are conditional guaranties that only bind the guarantor upon the condition that the payee uses due diligence to collect the debt from the maker of the note.[27]

6.3 Language Regarding the Revocation of Guaranties

Vermont case law regarding general revocation of a guaranty dictates that a guaranty may be effectively revoked if the obligee is notified and conveys acceptance.[28]

6.4 "Continuing"

A continuing guaranty is a guaranty that applies to a series of transactions and contemplates future dealings upon which the guarantor agrees to guaranty.[29]

Vermont case law indicates that courts will not interpret a guaranty as a continuing guaranty that would apply to the extensions or renewals of lease obligations unless the continuing obligation to guaranty is expressly stated in the personal guaranty, the original lease, or the subsequent lease agreements.[30]

A conditional guaranty may be terminated by the guarantor on notice to the obligee.[31] Courts will interpret the language of the agreement to determine whether a guaranty was intended to be continuous and will not find a continuing obligation unless it has been expressly stated. For example, in a lease agreement, the continuous nature of the guaranty for subsequent lease agreements must be stated in the original agreement or the subsequent lease agreements.[32]

6.5 "Absolute and Unconditional"

The general rule in Vermont is that a conditional guaranty requires exertion from the obligee to collect the debt of the obligor and give notice to the guarantor that the obligor has defaulted.[33] However, an absolute guaranty is defined as such by the language of the guaranty and it is not necessary to make a demand in order to charge an absolute guarantor for payment.[34]

26. Sylvester v. Downer, 18 Vt. 32 (1843).
27. Bull v. Bliss, 30 Vt. 127 (1857).
28. Metro. Washing-Mach. Co. v. Morris, 39 Vt. 393 (1867).
29. Ricketson v. Lizotte, 90 Vt. 386 (1916).
30. O'Brien Bros.' P'ship, LLP v. Plociennik, 940 A.2d 692 (Vt. 2007).
31. Ricketson v. Lizotte, 90 Vt. 386 (1916).
32. O'Brien Bros.' P'ship, LLP v. Plociennik, 182 Vt. 409 (2007).
33. Sylvester v. Downer, 18 Vt. 32 (1848).
34. Patridge v. Davis, 20 Vt. 499 (1848).

6.6 "Liable as Primary Obligor and not Merely as Surety"

Under Vermont law, if requisite statutory language is included in the obligation, a cosigner to an obligation is equally liable for repayment along with the primary obligor.[35] Accordingly, a guarantor may only be primarily liable if it cosigns the underlying obligation.

§ 7 Defenses of the Guarantor; Set-off

7.1 Defenses of the Primary Obligor

7.1.1 General

Generally, a guarantor will not have contractual privity or standing to assert any of the primary obligor's defenses against the obligee. Vermont has no case law further defining instances where standing or privity was found.

7.1.2 When a Guarantor may Assert Primary Obligor's Defense

There is no specific Vermont law regarding allowing the guarantor to assert defenses available to the primary obligor. Suretyship relationships allow the surety to assert defenses of the principal. However, Vermont law distinguishes between the rights available under a surety relationship and a guaranty relationship and will interpret the express language of a guaranty agreement when determining if the nature of the relationship is of surety or guaranty.[36]

7.1.3 Defenses that may always be Raised by Guarantor

There is no Vermont-specific law on this matter; however, the guarantor has the right to raise general contract defenses that would void the guaranty, such as incapacity, undue influence, mistake, etc.

7.2 "Suretyship" Defenses

7.2.1 Change in Identity of Principal Obligor

See Section 7.2.2.

7.2.2 Modification of the Underlying Obligation, Including Release

As a general rule under Vermont law, if the underlying contract for the principal obligation is modified or altered without the guarantor's consent, the guarantor is released from the obligation.[37]

35. Vt. Dev. Credit Corp. v. Kitchel, 149 Vt. 421 (1988); 9 V.S.A. § 102.
36. Vt. Indus. Dev. Auth. v. Setza, 600 A.2d 302 (Vt. 1991).
37. O'Brien Bros. 'P'ship, LLP v. Plociennik, 940 A.2d 692 (Vt. 2007).

Courts have interpreted a change in the underlying obligation to exclude instances where parties are substituted in the performance of an obligation or where an obligor uses other mechanisms to reduce the obligation of the primary obligor. In these instances, the guarantor is not discharged from his or her obligation.[38]

7.2.3 Release or Impairment of Security for the Underlying Obligation

Vermont has taken the position that the loss of property that would have been used to satisfy a guaranty, through the negligence of a third party, releases the guarantor from the obligation.[39] Vermont also will release a guarantor if the guarantor provides property sufficient to satisfy the obligation but the obligee refuses to take.[40]

7.3 Other Defenses

7.3.1 Failure to Fulfill a Condition Precedent

Vermont courts have protected guarantors from attempts to seek guaranties before exhaustion of other remedies to obtain payment. Vermont prohibits actions against guarantors until all legal remedies against the principal have been exhausted or the principal shows that he or she is insolvent.[41] For example, courts failed to find guarantor liability before the conclusion of a court proceeding to obtain payment from an estate of a deceased obligor.[42] The courts will also require obligors to seek other available security to pay a debt before seeking payment from a guarantor.[43]

Further, courts have held that neglecting to give notice of default to a guarantor cannot be used by the guarantor as a defense unless the negligence resulted in a loss or damage to the guarantor.[44]

7.3.2 Modification of the Guaranty

Vermont follows the general rule that if the guaranty is modified or altered in a material way and without the guarantor's consent, the guarantor is released for the obligation.[45]

7.3.3 Failure to Pursue Primary Obligor

See Section 7.3.1.

---

38. M. Noyes & Co. v. Nichols, 28 Vt. 159 (1855); Joseph W. Corlies & Co. v. Estes, 31 Vt. 653 (1859).
39. Hammond v. Chamberlin, 26 Vt. 406 (1854).
40. Meeker v. Denison, Brayt. 237 (1820).
41. Benton v. Fletcher, 31 Vt. 418 (1859).
42. *Id.*
43. Brainard v. Reynolds, 36 Vt. 614 (1864).
44. Bull v. Bliss, 30 Vt. 127 (1857).
45. O'Brien Bros. 'P'ship, LLC v. Plociennik, 940 A.2d 692 (Vt. 2007).

7.3.4 *Statute of Limitations*

There is no Vermont-specific law addressing the applicable statute of limitations on guaranty actions; however, Vermont's statute of limitations relating to breach of contract is six years.[46]

7.3.5 *Statute of Frauds*

Vermont's statute of frauds requires that arrangements whereby someone agrees to act as a surety are required to be in writing.[47]

7.3.6 *Defenses Particular to Guarantors that are Natural Persons and their Spouses*

Corporate president's participation as a corporate officer in negotiating and executing commercial lease extensions did not serve, as a matter of implied consent or estoppel, to extend her obligations under a personal guaranty that was applicable only to original lease agreement; corporate signature did not establish president's consent to personally pay the debts of the corporation, and president did not affirmatively lead landlord to believe that the personal guaranty applied to lease extensions at the time they were signed.[48]

When a signer, on a letter of credit authorizing another to draw on him a certain amount for a limited period and agreeing to accept the drafts and pay them if not paid by the drawer at maturity, dies, his death revokes all authority to thereafter draw on him, even though the person to whom it was given had no notice of the death and the period for which the authority was given had not expired.[49]

7.4 Right of Set-off

There is no Vermont-specific law on this matter.

§ 8 Waiver of Defenses by the Guarantor

8.1 Defenses that cannot be Waived

There is no Vermont-specific law on this matter; see Section 7.1.3.

8.2 "Catch-all" Waivers

There is no Vermont-specific law on this matter.

46. 12 V.S.A. § 511.
47. 12 V.S.A. § 181(2).
48. O' Brien Bros. 'P'ship, LLP v. Plociennik, 182 Vt. 409 (Vt. 2007).
49. Mich. State Bank v. Leavenworth's Estate, 28 Vt. 209 (1856).

8.3 Use of Specific Waivers

Vermont courts will not perceive a waiver of a defense when a guarantor is aware of his defenses and chooses not to inform the obilgee of his intention to pursue them.[50]

§ 9 Third-party Pledgors—Defenses and Waiver Thereof

There is no Vermont-specific law on this matter.

§ 10 Jointly and Severally Liable Guarantors—Contribution and Reduction of Obligations upon Payment by a Co-obligor

10.1 Contribution

Under Vermont law, the guarantor is not jointly and severally liable with the obligor in a guaranty arrangement. The guarantor is not bound to pay until the obligor has defaulted.[51]

10.2 Reduction of Obligations Upon Payment of Co-obligor

There is no Vermont-specific law on this matter.

10.3 Liability of Parent Guarantors Owning less than 100 percent of Primary Obligor

There is no Vermont-specific law on this matter.

§ 11 Reliance

Although Vermont generally applies contract law to the issues involving guaranties, there is no Vermont-specific law defining how the courts would handle reliance on a guaranty.

50. Russell v. Buck, 14 Vt. 147 (1842).
51. Vt. Dev. Credit Corp. v. Kitchel, 544 A.2d 1165 (Vt. 1988).

§ 12 Subrogation

Vermont does recognize a right of subrogation where a party, that is not the original guarantor, is forced to satisfy an obligor's debt with his or her own funds. In this instance, the third party is entitled to subrogation where the obligee is able to recover from others.[52]

§ 13 Triangular Set-off in Bankruptcy

The statute of limitations bar is removed where a guaranty is given on a note by an individual in bankruptcy proceedings in consideration that the holder will give a receipt for the percentage due under the composition offered by the bankrupt, accepted by a majority of the creditors, and ordered by the court.[53]

§ 14 Indemnification

Vermont law allows a guarantor to seek reimbursement from an obligor. Guarantors are not considered jointly and severally liable with principals and owe no payments until the principal has fully defaulted.[54]

§ 15 Enforcement of Guaranties

15.1 Limitations on Recovery

Neglecting to act or proceed against a principal within a reasonable amount of time can prohibit an action against a guarantor. However, a principal's insolvency when the debt becomes due and the obligee's failure to sue the principal does not discharge the guarantor.[55]

15.2 Enforcement of Guaranties of Payment versus Guaranties of Performance

There is no Vermont-specific law on this matter.

52. Hammond v. Chamberlain, 26 Vt. 406 (1854).
53. Robinson v. Larabee, 58 Vt. 652 (1886).
54. Vt. Dev. Credit Corp. v. Kitchel, 544 A.2d 1165 (Vt. 1988).
55. Bull v. Bliss, 30 Vt. 127 (1857).

15.3 Exercising Rights Under a Guaranty Where the Underlying Obligation is also Secured by a Mortgage

There is no Vermont-specific law on this matter. Nevertheless, Vermont case law indicates that the obligee would have to foreclose on the mortgage before exercising rights on the guaranty.[56]

15.4 Litigating Guaranty Claims: Procedural Considerations

A guarantor cannot raise an affirmative defense of estoppel when it is filed 16 months after the formal answer was filed.[57]

In action by credit extension guarantor who claimed that credit corporation had not properly credited corporate debtor for automotive parts taken by credit corporation from debtor and returned to factory, burden was on guarantor to establish by clear or positive evidence that the taking of parts from the corporate debtor and returning of such parts by credit corporation was to cancel all of its claims against corporate debtors, or was intended to do so.[58]

§ 16 Revival and Reinstatement of Guaranties

There is no Vermont-specific law on this matter.

---

56. *See* Benton v. Fletcher, 31 Vt. 418 (1859).
57. First Nat. Bank of Boston v. Silberdick, 146 Vt. 209 (1985).
58. Anderson v. Knapp, 126 Vt. 129 (1966).

Virginia State Law of Guaranties

Wilson R. Trice
ThompsonMcMullan, PC
100 Shockoe Slip
Richmond, VA 23219
804.649.7545
Fax: 804.780.1813
wtrice@t-mlawcom
www.t-mlaw.com

Contents

Virginia State Law of Guaranties

Introductory Note: In order to standardize our discussion of the law of guaranties, we use the following vocabulary to refer to the various parties to a guaranty and their obligations.

"Guarantor" means a person who, by contract, agrees to satisfy an underlying obligation of the primary obligor to an obligee upon the primary obligor's default on the underlying obligation.

"Guaranty" means the contract by which the guarantor agrees to satisfy the underlying obligation of a primary obligor to an obligee in the event the primary obligor defaults on the underlying obligation.

"Obligee" means the person to whom the underlying obligation is owed. For example, the lender under a loan agreement would be an obligee vis-à-vis the borrower.

"Primary obligor" means the person who incurs the underlying obligation to the obligee. For example, the borrower under a loan agreement would be a primary obligor.

"Underlying obligation" means the obligation or obligations incurred by the primary obligor and owed to the obligee. For example, the borrower's obligation to make payments to a lender of principal and interest on a loan constitutes an underlying obligation.

ITEMS OF SPECIAL NOTE

- Va. Code Ann. §§ 49-25 and 49-26 require the obligee to sue the primary obligor upon written demand by the guarantor. The failure of the obligee to bring an action within 30 days will discharge the guarantee.
- It is customary for a Virginia guaranty to include a specific waiver by the guarantor of all rights under the statute as follows:

  > "Guarantor waives the benefits of Sections 49-25 and 49-26 of the Code of Virginia (1950), as same may be amended."

- Va. Code Ann. § 11-10, as interpreted by Virginia case law, provides that the release of one coguarantor does not release another coguarantor.
- Va. Code Ann. § 8.01-435 requires that the signature of the guarantor on a guaranty containing a confession of judgment provision must be notarized.

§ 1 Nature of the Guaranty Arrangement

In Virginia, a guaranty involves separate, but related, relationships: the relationship created by the underlying obligation between the primary obligor and the obligee; the relationship created by the guaranty between the guarantor and the obligee; and the relationship between the primary obligor and the guarantor, governed primarily by rules of law rather than an express contract.

1.1 Guaranty Relationships

A guaranty is a contract under which the guarantor undertakes, in writing, upon a sufficient consideration, to be answerable for the underlying obligation in case of the failure of the primary obligor to pay or perform it.[1] In addition to the two contracts between (i) the primary obligor and the obligee and (ii) the obligee and the guarantor, there is a third contract, (iii) one of indemnification, based on an implied contract, between the primary obligor and the guarantor.[2]

1.2 Suretyship Principles

A guarantor and a surety are often distinguished by observing that a guarantor has a collateral or contingent obligation to pay or perform the underlying obligation, while a surety is primarily liable with the primary obligor to pay or perform the underlying obligation.[3] In either case, it is the primary obligor that is ultimately responsible for the payment or performance of the underlying obligation. It is this core principle that has given rise to a body of law that governs the relationship among the parties to these arrangements, irrespective of labels, called the law of suretyship.[4]

§ 2 State Law Requirements for an Entity to make a Guaranty

Virginia statutes permit corporations and limited liability companies (LLCs) to make guaranties that are necessary or convenient to carry out their business and affairs. The statutes are silent as to partnerships, but partnerships presumably have the authority to guarantee if the guaranty is made within the scope of the partnership business. Banks may guarantee the obligations of others in the regular course of business.

---

1. Bourne v. Board of Supervisors, 172 S.E. 245 (Va. 1934).
2. Dickerson v. Charles, 4 S.E. 2d 351 (Va. 1939). *See also* Colonial American Nat'l Bank v. Kosnoski, 617 F.2d 1025 (4th Cir. 1980) (dissenting opinion).
3. B.F. Goodrich Rubber Co. v. Fisch, 127 S.E. 187 (Va. 1925).
4. Restatement (Third) of Suretyship and Guaranty §1 cmt. b (1996).

2.1 Corporations

Under the Virginia Stock Corporation Act and the Virginia Nonstock Corporation Act, a corporation has the power to make a guaranty to the extent "necessary or convenient to carry out its business and affairs," unless provided otherwise in its articles of incorporation.[5]

2.2 Partnerships

Virginia's partnership statute is silent on the power of a partnership to make a guaranty. A partnership is generally empowered to engage in any lawful activity unless restricted by its partnership agreement and an agreement of the partnership will be enforced if it is within the scope of the partnership's business.[6]

2.3 Limited Liability Companies

Virginia's limited liability company statute permits a LLC to make a guaranty to the extent "necessary or convenient to carry out its business and affairs," unless its articles of organization provide otherwise.[7]

2.4 Banks

A Virginia state banking corporation may exercise all of the powers permitted to business corporations, which means that a state bank may make a guaranty if it is necessary or convenient to carry out its business, unless restricted by its charter.[8] State banks are expressly authorized to guarantee short-term commercial paper.[9] While there are no Virginia cases directly on point, the Virginia Supreme Court has cited with approval a line of cases holding that it is *ultra vires* for a national bank to guarantee the debt of another.[10]

2.5 Individuals

A guaranty is a contract and, like every contract, each party to it must have the capacity to enter into a contract.[11] Accordingly, an individual must be of sufficient age (18) and with sufficient mental capacity.[12]

Under Virginia law, one spouse cannot bind the other spouse to a guaranty automatically.[13] Moreover, a judgment lien arising from a judgment against

5. Va. Code Ann. §§ 13.1-627 A7, 13.1-826 A6 (2005).
6. *See, generally,* 14A MICHIE'S JURISPRUDENCE, PARTNERSHIPS, §§ 4 and 30 (2008).
7. Va. Code Ann. § 13.1-1009(5) (2006).
8. Va. Code Ann. § 6.2-808 (2010); *See also* Va. Code Ann. §13.1-627(A)(7)(2005).
9. Va. Code Ann. § 6.2-814 (2010).
10. Norton Grocery Co. v. People's National Bank of Abingdon, 144 S.E. 501 (Va. 1928).
11. *See, generally,* 9A Michie's Jurisprudence, Guaranty, § 5 (2010).
12. *See, generally,* 4A Michie's Jurisprudence, Contracts § 24 (2007).
13. *See, generally,* 9B Michie's Jurispurdence, Husband and Wife, §§ 83 and 84 (2005).

one spouse will not attach to property owned by both spouses as "tenants by the entireties" (joint tenants with right of survivorship between spouses).[14]

§ 3 Signatory's Authority to Execute a Guaranty

In Virginia there is a duty of inquiry into the authority of persons making a guaranty on behalf of business entities.

3.1 Corporations

General principles of agency law apply to corporations and their officers.[15] The Virginia Supreme Court has held that persons dealing with corporations are bound to inquire into their authority to act and Virginia law imposes a duty on an obligee to inquire into the authority of a corporate officer executing a guaranty. A corporation will be bound only when the officer acts within the scope of his authority.[16]

3.2 Partnerships

Virginia has adopted the Uniform Partnership Act ("UPA"). The UPA provides that each partner is an agent of the partnership for the purpose of its business. An act of a partner with the apparent purpose of carrying on the partnership business in the ordinary course binds the partnership, unless the partner has no such authority and the person with whom such partner has dealt knows that the partner lacked authority. When an act of a partner is not for the apparent purpose of carrying on the partnership business in the ordinary course, the partnership is bound only if the act was authorized by the other partners.[17] A partnership may record a statement of partnership authority and any limitations on the authority of a partner contained therein are deemed to be notice to third persons of such limits.[18]

3.3 Limited Liability Companies

Virginia's Limited Liability Company Act provides that, unless the company is a manager-managed LLC, each member is an agent of the LLC for purpose of its business. An act of a member with the apparent purpose of carrying on its business in the ordinary course binds the LLC unless the member had no authority to act for the LLC and the person with whom he was dealing knew it. When an act of a member is not for the apparent purpose of carrying on the LLC business in the ordinary course, the LLC is bound only if the act

14. *Id.* at HUSBAND AND WIFE, § 29.
15. *See, generally,* 4B MICHIE'S JURISPRUDENCE, CORPORATIONS § 231 (2007).
16. Silliman v. Fredericksburg, Or. & Charl. R.R. Co., 68 Va. 119 (1876).
17. VA. CODE ANN. § 50-73.91 (1996).
18. VA. CODE ANN. §§ 50-73-93 (2007).

was authorized by the other members by majority vote of the members or as otherwise specified in the LLC articles of organization or operating agreement. In a manager-managed LLC, the same rules apply vis-à-vis a manager and third persons.[19]

§ 4 Necessity of Writing

Virginia's statute of frauds requires that a guaranty must be in writing to be enforceable.[20]

The statute of frauds requires only that the promises be in writing and does not require a recitation of consideration for the promise.[21]

§ 5 Consideration; Sufficiency of Past Consideration

Standard contract principles apply to the analysis of consideration for a contract of guaranty. The consideration for the underlying obligation is sufficient consideration for an accompanying guaranty.

A guaranty must be supported by adequate consideration.[22] The inquiry into sufficient consideration is based on standard contract law principles. The benefit or obligation that forms the consideration for a guaranty need not flow directly to the guarantor from the obligee; the consideration flowing from the obligee to the principal obligor is sufficient to support a contemporaneous guaranty.[23] While past consideration is not consideration, sufficient consideration exists if a lender advances money after a promise to guarantee is made although the guaranty was delivered after the loan was made.[24] If a guaranty is executed under seal, consideration is presumed unless there is evidence to the contrary.[25]

§ 6 Notice of Acceptance

Notice of acceptance of the guaranty to the guarantor from the obligor is not required.

An offer to guarantee must be accepted to become binding. Formal notice of acceptance is not required, and acceptance need not be express. For example,

19. Va. Code. Ann. §13.1-1021.1 (1995).
20. Va. Code Ann. §11-2 (1990).
21. Colgin v. Henley, 33 Va. 85 (1835).
22. Patterson v. Shaver, 182 S.E. 261 (Va. 1935).
23. Moore Lumber Co. v. Walker, 67 S.E. 374 (Va. 1910).
24. United States v. Houff, 202 F. Supp. 471 (W.D. Va.), *aff'd*, 312 F.2d 6 (4th Cir. 1962).
25. Henderson v. U.S. Fidelity and Guaranty Co., 831 F.2d 519 (4th Cir. 1987) (consideration presumed when surety executed an agreement by signing under acknowledgment "signed, Sealed and Dated this ____ day of __________, 19____.")

an obligee's forbearance to enforce the underlying obligation will amount to an acceptance if the guaranty induces the forbearance.[26]

§ 7 Interpretation and Construction of Guaranties

A Virginia court will interpret a guaranty as it would any other contract. The effect of a guaranty will be strictly construed in favor of the guarantor.

7.1 General Principles

The interpretation of a guaranty is governed by rules applicable to other contracts.[27] Virginia courts will place neither a strict nor a liberal construction on the guaranty but will fairly construe it according to the intent of the parties as gathered from all language used and the surrounding circumstances.[28] Once the meaning of a guaranty is determined, the effect of the guaranty will be strictly construed in favor of the guarantor, i.e., the guarantor's liability cannot be enlarged beyond the strict intent of the instrument.[29]

7.2 Guaranty of Payment (absolute guaranty) versus Guaranty of Collection (conditional and collateral guaranty)

An absolute guaranty is one by which the guarantor unconditionally promises payment or performance of the underlying obligation on default of the primary obligor. A guaranty is deemed to be absolute unless its terms indicate some condition precedent to the liability of the guarantor. When the guarantor makes an absolute guaranty, the obligee is not obligated to first endeavor to collect from the debtor. This distinguishes an absolute guaranty from a mere guaranty of collectability.[30] A guaranty of payment is an absolute guaranty whereby the guarantor is bound immediately on the failure of the primary obligor to perform the underlying obligation without recourse to the principal obligor.[31]

7.3 "Continuing" guaranties

Virginia courts will give effect to open-ended guaranties of a series of transactions in the future when the intent of the parties is apparent from the language of the guaranty and the circumstances existing at the time it was made. When no duration is stated, the duration of such a guaranty and the amount of the

26. *Colgin v. Henley*, 33 Va. at 104.
27. *See, generally,* 9A Michie's Jurisprudence, Guaranty §11 (2010).
28. Equitable Trust Co. v. Bratwursthaus Mgt. Corp., 514 F.2d 565 (4th Cir. 1975).
29. William Schluderberger – T.J. Kurdle Co. v. Trice, 92 S.E. 2d 374 (Va. 1956).
30. Ives v. Williams, 129 S.E. 675 (Va. 1925).
31. *United States v. Houff,* 202 F. Supp. at 475.

future obligations guaranteed must be reasonable under the circumstances.[32] Nevertheless, if the guaranty states that it will remain in effect until the guarantor withdraws it or revokes it in writing, there is no reasonable time limitation on the duration of the guaranty. Moreover, when the guarantor did not fill in a blank which would limit his liability to a certain amount, it was reasonable to conclude that the guaranty was unlimited in amount. Finally, where a guaranty clearly covers loans to be made in the future, the guaranty does not fail for want of consideration at the time of execution.[33]

§ 8 Defenses of the Guarantor; Set-off

Unless the guarantor and the obligee agree otherwise, the guarantor is discharged if (i) the obligee does not sue the primary obligor on demand, (ii) the obligee releases the primary obligor from the underlying obligation or (iii) the obligee's actions are prejudicial to the guarantor.

8.1 Forcing Action against Primary Obligor

By statute in Virginia, the failure of the obligee to sue the primary obligor within 30 days of the guarantor's written demand will discharge the guarantor from its guaranty unless the primary obligor is insolvent.[34]

8.2 Modification of Underlying Obligation/Discharge of Primary Obligee

It has been held in Virginia that any change in the underlying obligation, however immaterial, which is made without the consent of the guarantor, discharges the guarantor.[35] Likewise, an extension of the time of payment or a renewal of the underlying obligation by the obligee without the consent of the guarantor will discharge the guarantor.[36]

If the obligee releases the primary obligor from the underlying obligation, the guarantor will be released.[37] In addition, the guarantor may assert as a defense any defense that the primary obligor has to the payment or performance of the underlying obligation, other than a so-called "personal defense" such as infancy or insanity.[38] While there is no holding expressly on point in Virginia, it has been widely held that the discharge of the primary obligor in bankruptcy proceedings will not discharge the guarantor.[39]

32. Pascoe Steel Corp. v. Shannon, 298 S.E. 2d 97 (Va. 1982).
33. Bank of Southside Va. v. Candelario, 385 S.E. 2d 601 (Va. 1989).
34. Va. Code Ann. § 49-26 (1979).
35. Citizen's and Marine Bank of Newport News v. McMurran, 123 S.E. 507 (Va. 1924).
36. Carson v. Mott Iron Works, 84 S.E. 12 (Va. 1915) (extension of the time of payment); Cobb v. Vaughan & Co., 126 S.E. 77 (Va. 1925) (renewal of note).
37. Food Lion, Inc. v. S.L. Nusbaum Ins. Agency, Inc., 202 F.3d 223 (4th Cir. 1999).
38. Kyger v. Sipe, 16 S.E. 627 (Va. 1982).
39. *See, generally,* Restatement (Third) of Suretyship & Guaranty, § 34(1).

8.3 Other Defenses

8.3.1 *Statute of Limitations/Frauds*

The running of the statute of limitations on the primary obligation does not bar an action on the guaranty. The statute of limitations on the guaranty runs from the date the cause of action accrues on the guaranty, which is ordinarily upon default of the underlying obligation.[40] Virginia's statute of limitation on a guaranty is five years from the date the cause of action accrues on the guaranty. [41] It has been held that the statute of limitations on a guaranty of payment subscribed on a demand note is coterminous with the statute of limitations on the note.[42] Virginia's statute of frauds requires that a guaranty be written.[43]

8.3.2 *Obligee's Failure to disclose Information/Fraud*

Fraudulent inducement is a defense to the enforcement of a guaranty in Virginia. If the obligee participates in false representations or fraudulent concealment of facts that induce the making of the guaranty, the guarantor may set up fraud as a defense.[44] The obligee is under no duty to seek out the guarantor and explain the nature and extent of the obligation, nor is the obligee responsible for fraudulent misrepresentations made by the primary obligor, or by a third party, without the obligee's knowledge or consent.[45] Failure to inform the guarantor of a fact which the guarantor could have readily learned by inquiry does not constitute a misrepresentation of a material fact.[46]

8.3.3 *Impairing Recourse to Collateral*

If the obligee releases collateral for the underlying obligation without the consent of the guarantor, the guarantor is discharged to the extent of the value of the collateral released.[47]

8.4 Right of Set-off

The right of set-off of mutual debts is recognized generally in Virginia.[48] It has been held that a guarantor may set-off the amount of the guaranty he has paid against any indebtedness owed by him to the primary obligor.[49] In a

40. McDonald v. Nat'l Enterprises, Inc., 547 S.E. 2d. 204 (Va. 2001).
41. VA. CODE ANN. § 8.01-246(2)(1977).
42. Guth v. Hamlet Associates, 334 S.E. 2d 558 (Va. 1985) (decided under "old" § 3-122 of the Uniform Commercial Code ("UCC"). New UCC § 3A-118(b) now provides that the statute of limitations on a demand note runs for 10 years from the date of the note if demand is not made. If demand is made, the statute of limitations is six years from the date of demand.
43. VA. CODE ANN. §11-2 (1990).
44. Sager v. W. T. Rawleigh Co., 150 S.E. 244 (Va. 1929). (The burden of a guarantor is high. In the *Sager* case, the guarantor was denied relief although he alleged that he was illiterate and was misled by the primary obligor who assured him there was no financial obligation attached to his signing the guaranty.)
45. Atlantic Trust & Deposit Co. v. Union Trust & Title Corp., 67 S.E. 182 (Va. 1909).
46. In re: Decker, 225 F. Supp. 716 (W.D. Va. 1964), *rev'd* on other grounds sub nom. Virginia National Bank v. Woodson, 329 F.2d 836 (4th Cir. 1964).
47. Morton v. Dillon, 19 S.E. 654 (Va. 1894).
48. Allen v. Hart, 59 Va. 722 (1868).
49. Dickenson v. Charles, 4 S.E. 2d 351 (Va. 1939).

bankruptcy proceeding, the guarantor can compel the obligee to assert its set-off rights against an insolvent primary obligor to prevent unjust enrichment of the debtor's estate.[50]

§ 9 Waiver of Defenses by the Guarantor

Waivers of suretyship defenses and consents to actions which might otherwise discharge the guarantor should be given effect by the courts in Virginia in the absence of the obligee's bad faith or willful misconduct.[51]

§ 10 Third-party Pledgors

A person pledging collateral on a loan for which he is not the primary obligor has the same rights and privileges as a guarantor.

The Virginia courts have recognized that persons who pledge their property to secure the debts of others are in a relationship of a surety to the obligee.[52] Accordingly, all of the rights and privileges that apply to guarantors should apply to third-party pledgors.[53]

§ 11 Jointly and Severally Liable Guarantors—Contribution and Reduction of Obligations upon Payment by a Co-obligor

Coguarantors are generally presumed to share proportionately their obligation to pay the underlying obligation. Nevertheless, Virginia recognizes that one or more coguarantors may be subsureties.

11.1 Contribution

A coguarantor who pays more than his proportionate share of the underlying obligation has a right of contribution against the other coguarantor(s) for amounts paid in excess of his proportionate share. When coguarantors each settle separately with an obligee for less than their proportionate shares of the underlying obligation, contribution will be based on the total settlement

50. Merritt Commercial Savings & Loan, Inc. v. Guinee, 766 F.2d 850 (4th Cir. 1985).
51. *United States v. Houff,* 202 F. Supp. 471, 479 (giving effect to language in a guaranty releasing the obligee from a duty to prevent deterioration or waste of collateral); *See also* United States *ex. rel.* Small Bus. Administration v. Andresen, 583 F. Supp. 1084 (W.D. Va. 1984) (giving effect to language in a guaranty waiving a defense based on subordination or release of collateral).
52. Breckinridge v. Breckinridge, 31 S.E. 892 (Va. 1898).
53. Courson v. Simpson, 468 S.E. 2d 17 (Va. 1996) (applying the Virginia statute for relief of sureties, Va. Code Ann. §§ 49-25-26 to third-party pledgor).

amount only if the coguarantor seeking contribution has obtained a release of his coguarantor.[54]

There is a presumption of proportionate shares among coguarantors.[55] Proportionate shares may be allocated by agreement and will be adjusted for absent or insolvent coguarantors. Thus, if one of three coguarantors is insolvent or not amenable to process, then the proportionate share of each of the remaining coguarantors is one-half.[56]

11.2 Subsurety

Virginia law recognizes that by agreement or under the circumstances, one coguarantor ought to be compelled to perform the underlying obligation before the other. In this case, the coguarantor who owes the primary duty to perform the underlying obligation is the principal guarantor and the other coguarantor is a subsurety.[57] If the relationship between coguarantors is one of principal guarantor and subsurety, the subsurety owes no duty of contribution to the principal guarantor.[58] Among multiple guarantors there is a presumption that the guarantors are coguarantors of the same underlying obligation even if they execute different instruments at the same or at different times and with or without knowledge of one another.[59]

11.3 Dealing with Coguarantors

The obligations of coguarantors whose obligations are joint and several may be enforced separately.[60] Each coguarantor owes a duty of full performance of the guaranty.[61]

By statute in Virginia, if an obligee settles with a coguarantor, the other coguarantor is not released.[62] When a co-obligor other than a surety settles with the obligee, the obligee is required to credit the underlying obligation with the full share of the co-obligor. When a coguarantor pays an amount in settlement, the statute requires that the underlying obligation be credited with the amount actually paid on the underlying obligation.[63] The statute does not affect or impair any right of contribution.[64]

---

54. Sacks v. Tavss, 375 S.E. 2d 719 (Va. 1989).
55. Van Winckel v. Carter, 95 S.E. 2d 148 (Va. 1956).
56. Cooper v. Greenberg, 61 S.E. 2d 875 (Va. 1950).
57. Stout v. Vause, 40 Va. 169 (1842) (where a surety who added his name to a bond already undertaken by other sureties was, under the circumstances, a co-surety, not a subsurety or surety for the obligations of the remaining sureties).
58. Harrison v. Lane, 32 Va. 414 (1834); *See also* Johnson v. Guerra, 35 Va. Cir. 67 (Cir. Ct. Fairfax County, 1995) (where the wife of partner A guaranteeing with her husband was deemed to be a subsurety as to partner B, who also guaranteed with his wife).
59. Bourne v. Board of Supervisors of Henrico County, 172 S.E. 245 (Va. 1934). *See also* Colonial American National Bank v. Kosnoski, 617 F.2d 1025 (4th Cir. 1980) (dissenting opinion).
60. VA. CODE ANN. § 8.01-30 (1977).
61. 4A MICHIE'S JURISPRUDENCE, CONTRACTS § 6 (2011).
62. VA. CODE ANN. § 11-10; *See* Yuille v. Wimbish, 77 Va. 308 (1883) (where the predecessor statute was applied to a settlement among cosureties).
63. VA. CODE ANN. § 11-11 (1950).
64. VA. CODE ANN. §11-13 (1950).

§ 12 Reliance

There is no Virginia case law or statute which requires any degree of reliance on the guaranty by the primary obligor or the obligee as a prerequisite to enforcement of the guaranty.

Reliance by the obligee on the guarantor's promise is relevant in the inquiry as to whether or not a sufficient consideration has been bargained for, e.g., whether the promise induced a loan or a forbearance to enforce the underlying obligation.[65] The Supreme Court of Virginia has declined the opportunity to adopt the concept of "promissory estoppel" as articulated in § 90 of the Restatement of Contracts (Second) and to supply consideration and create a contract where none exists.[66] Reliance by the obligee is also relevant to demonstrate that an offer to guarantee has been accepted.[67]

§ 13 Subrogation

The Virginia courts recognize that a guarantor who satisfies the underlying obligation is subrogated to the rights of the obligee with respect to collateral pledged to the obligee to secure the underlying obligation.

The Virginia courts have recognized the equitable remedy of subrogation whereby the guarantor steps into the shoes of the obligee and is able to enforce all of the obligee's rights with respect to security for the underlying obligation. Subrogation is a remedy in support of the guarantor's right to be indemnified by the principal obligor.[68] In Virginia, the equitable remedy of subrogation is supplemented by a statute which confers the remedy on a guarantor compelled to pay "all or part" of the underlying obligation in a legal proceeding.[69] The remedy of subrogation also supports the ability of the guarantor to compel the obligee to set off mutual obligations between the obligor and the primary obligor.[70]

65. *See, e.g., Colgin v. Henley*, 33 Va. at 94-95.
66. Tuomala, et al. v. Regent University, 477 S.E. 2d 501 (Va. 1996).
67. *See* § 6 of this Survey.
68. Aetna Cas. & Surety Co. v. Whaley, 3 S.E. 2d 395 (Va. 1939).
69. Va. Code Ann. § 49-27 (1950).
70. *See* Merritt Commercial Savings & Loan, Inc. v. Guinee, 766 F.2d at 855 (4th Cir 1985).

§ 14 Triangular Set-off in Bankruptcy

As of the date of this survey, there are no reported cases from the Virginia courts addressing the issue of triangular set-offs under the U. S. Bankruptcy Code.

§ 15 Indemnification—Whether the Primary Obligor has a Duty

In Virginia, the primary obligor has an implied duty to indemnify the guarantor to the extent of the guarantor's cost of performing its obligation under the guaranty.

Whenever a guarantor pays the obligee, a right of indemnification in favor of the guarantor from the primary obligor arises based upon an implied contract.[71] In Virginia, the common law right of indemnification is supplemented by a statute which provides a mechanism for the guarantor to enforce its right to be reimbursed by the primary obligor.[72]

§ 16 Enforcement of Guaranties

A guaranty may be set aside as a fraudulent conveyance under § 548 of the U. S. Bankruptcy Code or applicable state law if the guaranty is made when the guarantor is insolvent or if the guaranty renders the guarantor insolvent and a fraudulent or fair equivalent value is not received by the guarantor in exchange for the guaranty. Savings clauses in the guaranty designed to limit the obligee's recovery to amounts that would avoid such a result may not be enforceable.

16.1 Guaranties by Subsidiary Corporations

Guaranties by a subsidiary corporation of its parent corporation debt have been attacked as fraudulent conveyances under § 548 of the Bankruptcy Code and state fraudulent conveyance statutes in instances where the guarantor has not received the direct benefit of the loan proceeds.[73] There are currently no cases from the Virginia bankruptcy courts that have applied these statutes in the context of guarantors.

---

71. Cromer v. Cromer's Adm'sr, 70 Va. 280 (1877).
72. Va. Code Ann. § 49-27(1950) provides for recovery from the primary obligor of the amount of the underlying obligation paid by the guarantor plus interest and liquidated damages equal to 5 percent of such amount. The statute also provides subrogation rights. *See* § 13 of this Survey.
73. *See, e.g.*, Clark v. Security Pac. Business Credit (In re Wes Dor, Inc), 996 F.2d 237 (10th Cir. 1993).

Section 55-81 of the Virginia Code renders voidable as to existing creditors any voluntary transfer of property made without valuable consideration when the transferor is insolvent or would be rendered insolvent by the transfer. Unlike § 548 of the Bankruptcy Code, the statute does not expressly cover the incurring of obligations as well as transfers of property, and there are no reported decisions that extend the statute to guaranties.

There is at least one federal court decision that has rendered unenforceable a savings clause in a loan document designed to limit recovery among joint and several obligors to amounts which would avoid a set aside under § 548 of the Bankruptcy Code.[74] There are no reported cases from state or federal courts in Virginia.

16.2 Pleading Requirements

In an action to enforce the guaranty in Virginia, the obligee's complaint must set forth the consideration for the guaranty.[75] Moreover, the complaint must allege that the primary obligor has not paid the underlying obligation.[76]

16.3 Litigating Guaranty Claims: Procedural Considerations

Virginia courts will honor choice of law provisions in a guaranty.[77] Unless otherwise agreed, the governing law is the law of the state where the last act is done, which is necessary to make the guaranty binding.[78]

To recover on a guaranty in Virginia, the obligee must establish the existence and ownership of the guaranty, the terms of the underlying obligation, the default on that obligation by the primary obligor, and the nonpayment of the amount due from the guarantor.[79]

§ 17 Revival and Reinstatement of Guaranties

Virginia courts have recognized the principle that an obligation of the guarantor which has been discharged by payment of the underlying obligation will be revived if the obligee's payment is recovered as a preference in a case under the Bankruptcy Code.

A preferential payment is deemed to be no payment at all.[80] A payment from a debtor in bankruptcy which later is set aside as a preference does not discharge the guarantor.[81]

---

74. In re Tousa, Inc., 422 B.R. 783 (Bankr. S.D. Fla. 2009) (applying New York law). *rev'd on other grounds sub nom.* 444 B.R. 613 (S.D. Fla. 2011), *rev'd on other grounds sub nom.* 680 F.3d 1298 (11th Cir. 2012).
75. Parker v. Carter, 18 Va. 273 (1814).
76. Pasteur v. Parker, 24 Va. 458 (1825).
77. *See, e.g.,* Western Branch Holding Co. v. Trans Marketing Houston, Inc., 722 F.Supp. 1339 (E.D. Va. 1989).
78. Hogue-Kellog Co. v. G.L. Webster Canning Co., 22 F.2d 384 (4th Cir. 1927).
79. McDonald v. Nat'l Enters., 547 S.E. 2d, 204 (Va. 2001).
80. Horner v. First Nat'l Bank, 141 S.E. 767 (Va. 1928).
81. In re: Herman Cantor Corp., 15 B.R. 747 (Bankr. E.D. Va. 1981).

Washington State Law of Guaranties

Brian D. Hulse
Davis Wright Tremaine LLP
1201 Third Avenue, Suite 2200
Seattle, Washington 98101
(206) 622-3150
brianhulse@dwt.com

Contents

Washington State Law of Guaranties

Highlights:

- All Washington guaranties should include the statutory "no oral agreements" legend required in order to invoke the protection of a special statute of frauds applicable to commercial credit transactions. See § 7.3.4 below.
- Washington has nonuniform versions of Uniform Commercial Code §§ 9-602 and 9-624, which vary from the official text in that they allow secondary obligors (including guarantors) to waive their rights under a number of provisions of Article 9 where such waivers are prohibited by the uniform version. See § 8.2 below.
- Coguarantors should enter into a contribution agreement addressing their respective liabilities to one another if one or more should be called upon to pay the creditor. In the absence of such an agreement, guarantors are liable for contribution among themselves on an equal per capita basis. Often, it is more appropriate that liability be shared in accordance with their respective ownership interests in the primary obligor. See § 10.2 below.
- An individual's guaranty should not state, without more, that the guarantor signs "individually" or in his or her "individual capacity." Such language has been interpreted to mean that the individual is creating recourse to his or her separate property only and that the creditor is not intended to have recourse to the guarantor's community property. See § 2.6 below.
- Neither spouse may make a gift of community property without the express or implied consent of the other. This provision can be a trap for unwary lenders. Because a guaranty of another person's debt may be a gift of community property, both spouses should execute, or give their written consent to, guaranties where there is not a clear benefit to the marital community from the guaranteed debt, if the lender intends to have recourse to the spouses' community property. See § 2.6 below.

Introduction and Sources of Law: This survey discusses Washington State law applicable to guaranties of commercial credit transactions. Washington has a substantial body of law on guaranties and related subjects. It is primarily case law, although there are some statutes that bear on the guaranty relationship.[1] Washington courts and federal courts interpreting Washington law have looked to

1. RCW chapter 19.72, which is titled "Suretyship," is the only statute generally applicable to surety relationships; however, it appears to be intended to deal with suretyship in the context of surety bonds and is not frequently cited in cases dealing with guaranties or other types of financial relationships. The Washington Supreme Court has held that the provisions of RCW 19.72.100 and .101, which statutorily adopt the "*Pain v. Packard* rule," do not apply to guarantors of payment. Amick v. Baugh, 66 Wash. 2d 298, 308, 402 P.2d 342 (1965). Surety insurance is addressed in RCW chapter 48.28.

the *Restatement (Third) of Suretyship and Guaranty* (1996) (the "Restatement") for guidance on guaranty and suretyship issues.[2]

This survey is, by nature, general in scope and meant as a brief overview of the subjects discussed. It should not be relied upon in a specific transaction without legal advice tailored to that transaction.

§ 1 Nature of the Guaranty Arrangement

1.1 Guaranty Relationships

Washington does not have statutory or case law that draws a clear distinction between the concepts of guaranty and suretyship.[3] Washington law is consistent with the Restatement's conclusion that: "Differences between these two mechanisms have been the subject of extended, debate, not all of which is illuminating."[4]

The general nature of the guaranty relationship was set out by the Washington Supreme Court in *Robey v. Walton Lumber Co.*[5]:

> The contract of guaranty is an undertaking or promise on the part of one person which is collateral to a primary or principal obligation on the part of another, and which binds the obligor to performance in the event of nonperformance by such other, the latter being bound to perform primarily. An approved definition of 'guaranty' is a promise to answer for the debt, default, or miscarriage of another person.

---

2. *See, e.g.*, Cosmopolitan Engineering Group, Inc. v. Ondeo Degremont, Inc., 128 Wash. App. 885, 892, 117 P.3d 1147 (2005); The Revocable Living Trust of Harold G. Strand v. Wel-Co Group, Inc., 120 Wash. App. 828, 836, 86 P.3d 818 (2004); Reliance Insurance Co. v. U.S. Bank of Washington, N.A., 143 F.3d 502, 506 (1998). Earlier cases cited to the Restatement's predecessor, the Restatement of Security. *See, e.g.*, Warren v. Washington Trust Bank, 92 Wash. 2d 381, 390, 598 P.2d 701 (1979); Peoples Nat'l Bank of Washington v. Taylor, 42 Wash. App. 518, 526-27, 711 P.2d 1021 (1985).
3. *See, e.g.*, the definition of "surety" in Washington's enactment of the general definitions section of the 2001 version of Article 1 of the Uniform Commercial Code. RCW 62A.1-201(39) ("'Surety' includes a guarantor or other secondary obligor"). Washington adopted the 2001 version of Article 1 in 2012. For the rather confused case law discussing differences between suretyship and guaranty, *see, e.g.*, Amick v. Baugh, 66 Wash. 2d 298, 402 P.2d 342 (1965); McAllister v. Pier 67, Inc., 1 Wash. App. 978, 983, 465 P.2d 678 (1970). *See also* Honey v. Davis, 131 Wash. 2d 212, 217-19, 930 P.2d 908 (1996); In attempting to distinguish the two concepts, the court in *McAllister* stated:

   > A guarantee like a contract of suretyship may be absolute; *i.e.*, matured at the moment the debt is in default; or conditional; *i.e.*, matured when conditions precedent to liability have been satisfied or excused and the debt is in default. The promise of an unconditional guarantor is similar to the promise of a surety. The surety's promise is to do the same thing promised by the principal. The guarantor's promise is to perform if the principal does not. If the principal does not perform and the other conditions precedent to liability are satisfied or excused, the promise of the guarantor becomes absolute. There are other respects in which the relationship is not identical, but those differences are not here material. [Citations omitted.]
4. RESTATEMENT § 1, comment c (citing, among other authorities, *Amick v. Baugh, supra*).
5. 17 Wash. 2d 242, 255, 135 P.2d 95 (1943) (citations and internal quotation marks omitted).

> A contract of guaranty, being a collateral engagement for the performance of an undertaking of another, imports the existence of two different obligations, one being that of the principal debtor and the other that of the guarantor. If a primary or principal obligation does not exist, there cannot be a contract of guaranty. To constitute a guaranty, there must be a principal debtor or obligor. Without a principal debt there can be no guaranty.
>
> The debtor is not a party to the guaranty, and the guarantor is not a party to the principal obligation. The undertaking of the former is independent of the promise of the latter; and the responsibilities which are imposed by the contract of guaranty differ from those which are created by the contract to which the guaranty is collateral. The fact that both contracts are written on the same paper or instrument does not affect the independence or separateness of the one from the other.

Under Washington law, no particular form of words is needed to create a guaranty obligation, so long as the agreement contains an undertaking or promise on the part of one person to perform an obligation if it is not performed by another person.[6] Under certain circumstances, words as vague as the following have been held to create a guaranty: "Tell bank I request them to renew the note....I will arrange things satisfactory to them upon my return to Seattle."[7]

Guaranties are generally subject to the same requirements as other contracts for the formation of a binding obligation, including offer and acceptance, delivery (for a written guaranty), and consideration.[8]

A number of Washington cases discuss the difference between compensated sureties and uncompensated sureties and state that the latter are favorites of the law and entitled to a less burdensome interpretation of their obligations.[9] Insiders of the primary obligor, such as its shareholders and directors, are not considered to be uncompensated sureties when they guarantee its obligations.[10]

1.2 Other Suretyship Relationships

1.2.1 Third-party Pledges and Real Suretyship

A suretyship relationship may arise because of the pledge of collateral where the pledgor does not personally assume to pay the secured debt.[11] As such,

---

6. Sherman Clay & Co. v. Turner, 164 Wash. 257, 261, 2 P.2d 688 (1931); B&D Leasing Company v. Ager, 50 Wash. App. 299, 306, 748 P.2d 652 (1988).
7. Exchange Nat'l Bank of Spokane v. Pantages, 74 Wash. 481, 133 P. 1025 (1913).
8. *See, e.g.*, Wilson Court Limited Partnership v. Tony Maroni's, Inc., 134 Wash. 2d 692, 699, 952 P.2d 590 (1998); Nat'l Bank of Washington v. Equity Investors, 86 Wash. 2d 545, 551-52, 546 P.2d 440 (1976); United States v. Everett Monte Cristo Hotel, Inc., 524 F.2d 127, 139 (9th Cir. 1975) (applying Washington law); Gelco IVM Leasing Co. v. Alger, 6 Wash. App. 519, 522, 494 P.2d 501 (1972).
9. *See, e.g.*, Nat'l Bank of Washington v. Equity Investors, 86 Wash. 2d 545, 552-53, 546 P.2d 440 (1976); Kenney v. Read, 100 Wash. App. 467, 477, 997 P.2d 455 (2000).
10. Peoples Nat'l Bank of Washington v. Taylor, 42 Wash. App. 518, 530, 711 P.2d 1021 (1985); Lutz v. Gatlin, 22 Wash. App. 424, 430, 590 P.2d 359 (1979).
11. *See, e.g.*, Carter v. Curlew Creamery, 20 Wash. 2d 275, 284, 147 P.2d 276 (1944); The Revocable Living Trust of Harold G. Strand v. Wel-Co Group, Inc., 120 Wash. App. 828, 836, 86 P.3d 818 (2004); Norton v. McIntosh, 1 Wash. App. 334, 337, 461 P.2d 348 (1969).

a guaranty-like suretyship relationship arises, to the extent of the collateral pledged, when a person supplies collateral for a loan in order to induce the creditor to lend to the debtor or where one party mortgages property to a creditor to secure the debt of another. This type of arrangement is referred to as "real suretyship" as opposed to "personal suretyship," such as an ordinary recourse guaranty.[12] A similar situation arises where a third party provides a letter of credit to support the underlying obligation and such a party has the rights of a surety.[13] In real suretyship, the principles governing personal suretyship, including suretyship defenses, are applicable.[14]

1.2.2 Accommodation Parties—"Borrowers" Who do not Receive Loan Proceeds

A lender should require a party agreeing to be liable for a loan, but who does not actually receive the loan proceeds or otherwise receive the direct benefit of the loan, to sign a guaranty rather than simply signing the promissory note as a purported primary obligor. Otherwise, such a party, even if that party receives an indirect benefit from the transaction (for example, as a stockholder in the borrower), can be characterized as an accommodation party or surety and may be allowed to take advantage of various suretyship defenses, which are not typically thoroughly waived in promissory notes.[15] A co-maker of a promissory note "may show by extrinsic evidence that he made the note as a surety only, and that it was known to the [creditor] that he was a surety only" in which case such a signer may be treated as a surety with respect to the creditor and not just with respect to other signers of the note who are not sureties.[16]

"[W]hile comakers to a written promissory obligation may sign and appear on the face of the writing as principals, they may in fact, as between themselves, occupy the relation of principal and surety, and, as between themselves, their true relationship may be established by parol or circumstantial evidence."[17]

It is important to note that, if the promissory note signed by the accommodation maker is a *negotiable* instrument governed by Article 3 of the Uniform Commercial Code (UCC), the rules of Article 3 about accommodation

12. *See* City Nat'l Bank and Trust Co., Norman, Oklahoma v. Pyle, 25 Wash. App. 583, 588, 609 P.2d 966 (1980).
13. Kenney v. Read, 100 Wash. App. 467, 997 P.2d 455 (2000).
14. *Id.; see also* Thompson v. Metropolitan Building Co., 95 Wash. 546, 550, 164 P. 222 (1917).
15. *See* Plein v. Lackey, 149 Wash. 2d 214, 67 P.3d 1061 (2003). *See also* Uniform Commercial Code §§ 3-419 and 3-605 (RCW 62A.3-419 and 3-605) regarding accommodation parties to notes and other instruments. The *Plein* case did not discuss earlier authority to the effect that stockholders in the borrower should not be accorded as favorable treatment in this regard as some other sureties. *See* Lutz v. Gatlin, 22 Wash. App. 424, 430, 590 P.2d 359 (1979). *Plein* stated that an accommodation party who pays off a note has the right to enforce the note and has the benefit of any security for the note. 149 Wash. 2d at 224-25.
16. Culbertson v. Wilcox, 11 Wash. 522, 524, 39 P. 954 (1895). *Cf.* RCW 62A.3-419(c) for the rule applicable to accommodation parties to *negotiable* promissory notes subject to UCC Article 3 ("Except as provided in RCW 62A.3-605 [which limits the availability of suretyship defenses to accommodation parties where the creditor lacks notice], the obligation of an accommodation party to pay the instrument is not affected by the fact that the person enforcing the obligation had notice when the instrument was taken by that person that the accommodation party signed the instrument for accommodation").
17. Leuning v. Hill, 79 Wash. 2d 396, 400, 486 P.2d 87 (1971).

parties apply and they can be different from common law rules applicable to other types of obligations.[18]

1.2.3 Transferors of Collateral in Loan Assumption Transactions

Where a third party assumes the borrower's obligations on a loan, the creditor has "definite and specific notice" of the assumption, and the creditor consents to the assumption, the original debtor may become merely a surety for the debt with the panoply of defenses generally available to sureties.[19] Some older cases do not seem to require the consent of the creditor in order for the original primary obligor to become a mere surety.[20] These situations usually occur in connection with a transfer of the collateral for a loan.

In *Hemenway v. Miller*, for example, the buyer of a business executed a promissory note to the seller for a portion of the purchase price. The note was secured by assets of the business. The buyer later sold the business and the collateral to a third party, who assumed liability on the note. When the second buyer defaulted on the loan, the original buyer defended against the original seller's claim on the note on the basis that the original seller had allowed the perfection of its security interest to lapse and had thereby unjustifiably impaired the collateral giving the original buyer a defense to payment of the note under Washington's version of UCC § 3-606.

The lesson of these cases is that, when a lender becomes aware that its collateral has been transferred in violation of the provisions of the loan documents, it should either proceed to enforce its remedies for default immediately or enter into an assumption agreement under which the original borrower agrees to remain fully, unconditionally, and absolutely liable for the loan and waives all suretyship defenses that might otherwise be available to it. It is also helpful if the original loan documents provide that the original borrower waives all suretyship defenses that may arise in the future and will remain primarily liable for the debt notwithstanding any transfer of the collateral.

1.2.4 Lessors in "Subordinated Fee" Financings

The Washington Supreme Court has held that a ground lessor that "subordinates" its fee interest in real estate to a mortgage or deed of trust securing a loan to improve the property obtained by a ground lessee (i.e., by signing the mortgage or deed of trust and encumbering its interest in the property) benefits directly from the loan and is, therefore, not a guarantor or surety with respect to either the lender or the ground lessee.[21] As a result, the lessor may not be entitled to a guarantor's common law rights of reimbursement, subrogation, etc. and should consider seeking similar rights by contract.

---

18. *See* RCW 62A.3-419 and 3-605. Pursuant to RCW 62A.3-104(b), to be an instrument governed by Article 3, the instrument must be a *negotiable* instrument as defined in RCW 62A.3-104(a).
19. Hemenway v. Miller, 116 Wash. 2d 725, 728-29, 807 P.2d 863 (1991).
20. *See, e.g.*, Gillman v. Purdy, 167 Wash. 659, 9 P.2d 1092 (1932); Insley v. Webb, 122 Wash. 98, 209 P. 1093 (1922). *See also* Corkrell v. Poe, 100 Wash. 625, 628, 171 P. 522 (1918) (initial transferee of a mortgaged property did not assume the mortgage, but a transferee from that initial transferee did assume it).
21. Honey v. Davis, 131 Wash. 2d 212, 930 P.2d 908 (1996).

§ 2 State Law Requirements for an Entity to Enter a Guaranty

2.1 Corporations

Under the Washington Business Corporation Act, RCW chapter 23B, a Washington for-profit corporation may, within the scope of its general corporate powers, give a guaranty that can reasonably be expected to benefit the corporation, provided that its articles of incorporation and bylaws do not prevent it from doing so. RCW 23B.03.020(2)(h) provides, with respect to Washington for-profit corporations:

> Unless its articles of incorporation provide otherwise, every corporation has the same powers as an individual to do all things necessary or convenient to carry out its business and affairs, including without limitation, power... [t]o make guarantees respecting the contracts, securities, or obligations of any person; including, but not limited to, any shareholder, affiliated or unaffiliated individual, domestic or foreign corporation, partnership, association, joint venture or trust, if such guarantee may reasonably be expected to benefit, directly or indirectly, the guarantor corporation. As to the enforceability of the guarantee, the decision of the board of directors that the guarantee may be reasonably expected to benefit, directly or indirectly, the guarantor corporation shall be binding in respect to the issue of benefit to the guarantor corporation....

A substantially identical provision applies to most nonprofit corporations.[22] The governing statutes for certain other types of specialized nonprofit corporations contained in RCW title 24 (including corporations sole, fraternal societies, and granges) do not contain provisions expressly addressing guaranties.

The doctrine of *ultra vires* under which a corporate action can be challenged on the basis that it is beyond the corporate powers of the corporation is severely limited by RCW 23B.03.040 (for for-profit corporations) and RCW 24.03.040 (for nonprofit corporations).[23] Actions may be challenged on the ground that the corporation did not act in accordance with its governing documents.[24]

There is no requirement under Washington law that a corporate seal appear on a document executed by a corporation.[25]

2.2 Partnerships

Washington statutes governing general and limited partnerships neither expressly empower a partnership to issue a guaranty nor expressly regulate

22. RCW 24.03.035(15).
23. *See also* Granite Equipment Leasing Corp. v. Hutton, 84 Wash. 2d 320, 327, 525 P.2d 223 (1974); Spokane Concrete Products, Inc. v. U. S. Bank of Washington, N.A., 126 Wash. 2d 269, 277-78, 892 P.2d 98 (1995).
24. Hartstene Point Maintenance Ass'n v. Diehl, 95 Wash. App. 339, 345, 979 P.2d 854 (1999).
25. RCW 60.04.105.

or prohibit such activity.[26] There are, however, examples in the case law of partnerships issuing guaranties.[27]

Three types of partnerships are recognized in Washington: (1) general partnerships; (2) limited partnerships; and (3) registered limited liability partnerships.

RCW chapter 25.05 is Washington's version of the Revised Uniform Partnership Act. It contains the statutory provisions governing general partnerships and limited liability partnerships. Limited liability partnerships are intended primarily for use by those engaged in the practice of the licensed professions; however, they are occasionally used for other business purposes.

RCW chapter 25.10 is the primary statute governing limited partnerships, although the very few limited partnerships that were in existence prior to June 6, 1945, are governed by RCW chapter 25.12.

Partners in a general partnership, as well as general partners in a limited partnership, are individually liable for partnership debts; however, with certain limited exceptions, a creditor is generally required to exhaust its recourse against partnership assets before executing on assets of the general partners. This extra step can be avoided by having the general partners waive the requirement of exhaustion of the partnership assets or by having them separately guarantee the debt.[28]

As of January 2010, a limited partnership may elect to become a limited liability limited partnership ("LLLP") by including a statement to that effect in its certificate of limited partnership.[29] Status as an LLLP provides general partners with a shield from liability for obligations of the LLLP.[30]

2.3 Limited Liability Companies

Washington's limited liability company (LLC) act does not expressly address the ability of an LLC to grant a guaranty, but there is no reason to believe that such guaranties are restricted in any unusual way.

LLCs are governed by RCW chapter 25.15. A Washington LLC may be managed either by its members or by one or more managers.[31] Single-member LLCs are permitted in Washington.

Individual members and managers of an LLC are not liable for its debts unless they have executed appropriate guaranties or are personally liable in tort.[32]

There is not an *ultra vires* statute for LLCs comparable to the one for corporations discussed in § 2.1 above.[33]

---

26. *See* RCW title 25.
27. *See, e.g.*, Nat'l Bank of Washington v. Equity Investors, 86 Wash. 2d 545, 546 P.2d 440 (1976) (limited partnership).
28. *See* RCW 25.05.130(4).
29. RCW 25.10.201(1)(d).
30. RCW 25.10.401(3).
31. RCW 25.15.150.
32. RCW 25.15.125.
33. 1B Washington Practice § 70.10 (4th ed. 2008).

2.4 Individuals—Whether Signature is in Personal vs. Entity Capacity

Confusion can sometimes arise in the case of corporate officers or directors signing guaranties in closely held corporations or other organizations. In such instances, a case-by-case inquiry determines whether an individual intended to be personally bound or, instead, only issued a guaranty on behalf of a corporation, LLC, or partnership binding only the entity. When an individual signs his or her title as well as name, this is not dispositive proof of an intention not to issue a personal guaranty.[34] See § 2.6 below regarding the pitfalls to lenders in using the word "individually" or in an "individual capacity" to describe the manner in which an individual signs a guaranty.

2.5 Individuals—Capacity to Contract

While a business corporation must have "authority" to execute a guaranty, an individual guarantor must have the "capacity" to enter into the guaranty. Incapacity can be a defense against the enforcement of a guaranty issued by an individual.

For example, in general, the age of majority at which a person has the capacity to enter into a binding contract is 18.[35] There are special exceptions for minors married to persons over the age of majority and for certain educational loans entered into by minors over the age of 16. A person who enters into a contract while under the age of majority generally can disaffirm the contract within a reasonable time after reaching the age of majority if he or she restores to the other party all money and property received under the contract that remains within his or her control at any time after reaching the age of majority.[36] There are exceptions to the right to disaffirm where the minor misrepresented his or her age or engaged in business as an adult, or where the other party "had good reason to believe the minor capable of contracting."[37]

2.6 Individuals—Community Property of Spouses and Domestic Partners

Lenders should consider the effects of the Washington community property laws when accepting personal guaranties from married Washington residents. The community property laws are set out in RCW chapter 26.16.

In 2008, the legislature comprehensively revised the community property statutes (and many other statutes) to make them applicable to registered domestic partners as well as to spouses. The changes generally became effective June 12, 2008. Registered domestic partnerships are provided for in RCW chapter 26.60. They may be entered into by two people both of

---

34. *See* Key v. Cascade Packing Co., Inc., 19 Wash. App. 579, 582-83, 576 P.2d 929 (1978) and cases cited therein. *See also* Wilson Court Limited Partnership v. Tony Maroni's, Inc., 134 Wash. 2d 692, 705, 952 P.2d 590 (1998).
35. RCW 26.28.010 and 26.28.015(4).
36. RCW 26.28.030.
37. RCW 26.28.040.

whom are at least age 18 and (a) both of whom are of the same sex or (b) at least one of whom is age 62 or older.[38] Although, for ease of readability, this chapter refers to spouses, the community property concepts described are equally applicable to registered domestic partners. In 2012, Washington law was revised to permit same sex marriages.[39] The new law will also ultimately limit registered domestic partnerships to situations where one of the partners is age 62 or older.[40]

Where individuals live as "committed intimate partners," Washington courts will in appropriate circumstances divide the partners' assets in an equitable manner based on the rights they would have had if they had been married to one another.[41]

Washington has an equal management community property system. Under RCW 26.16.030, each spouse has the full authority, acting alone, to enter into debt obligations binding and obligating any and all present and future community property that may exist between spouses with certain exceptions, including the following of particular interest to lenders accepting guaranties from individuals:

(a) Neither spouse may make a gift of community property without the express or implied consent of the other. This provision can be a trap for unwary lenders. Because a guaranty of another person's debt may be a gift of community property, both spouses should execute, or give their written consent to, guaranties where there is not a clear benefit to the marital community from the guaranteed debt, if the lender intends to have recourse to the spouses' community property.[42]

(b) Neither spouse may sell, convey, or encumber the community real property without the other spouse joining in the execution of the deed or other instrument by which the real estate is sold, conveyed, or encumbered, and such deed or other instrument must be acknowledged by both spouses.

(c) Neither spouse may create a security interest (other than a purchase money security interest) in, or sell, community household goods, furnishings, or appliances, or a community mobile home, unless the other spouse joins in executing the security agreement or bill of sale.

(d) Without the consent of the other, neither spouse may acquire, purchase, sell, convey, or encumber the assets, including real estate, or the good will of a business where both spouses participate in its

38. RCW 26.60.030.

39. RCW 26.04.010, as amended by § 1 of Substitute Senate Bill 6239 (2012), effective June 7, 2012.

40. RCW 26.60.030, as amended by §§ 9 and 18 of Substitute Senate Bill 6239 (2012), effective June 30, 2014.

41. *See, e.g.*, Oliver v. Fowler, 161 Wash. 2d 655, 168 P.3d 348 (2007).

42. *See* Nichols Hills Bank v. McCool, 104 Wash. 2d 78, 701 P.2d 1114 (1985) (finding that neither assisting the signing spouse with typing a financial statement submitted to the lender nor failing to advise the lender of her disapproval of the guaranty constituted implied consent of the nonsigning spouse to the guaranty of a debt of the couple's son). However, where there is an expectation of an economic (as opposed, for example, to a familial) benefit to the community, the guaranty of a family member's debt may not constitute a gift of community property. *See* Warren v. Washington Trust Bank, 19 Wash. App. 348, 361, 575 P.2d 1077 (1978). A general power of attorney from one spouse to the other does not authorize a gift of community property unless it expressly contains such authority. Bryant v. Bryant, 125 Wash. 2d 113, 119, 882 P.2d 169 (1994). If both spouses sign a guaranty, the lender must of course comply with the federal Equal Credit Opportunity Act (15 U.S.C. § 1691 *et seq.*) and Regulation B promulgated thereunder (12 CFR part 202).

management; provided, that where only one spouse participates in such management the participating spouse may, *in the ordinary course of such business*, acquire, purchase, sell, convey, or encumber the assets, including real estate, or the goodwill of the business without the consent of the nonparticipating spouse. It is unclear whether, or to what extent, this rule applies to a business conducted in corporate, partnership, or LLC form.[43] It has been held that the purchase of all the stock of a corporation is subject to the statute and requires the consent of both spouses.[44]

A contract signed by one spouse for the benefit of the marital community creates recourse to all the community assets and to the separate property of the signing spouse.[45] If the contract is not for the benefit of the community, there is recourse only to the signing spouse's separate property. In the latter situation, there is no recourse to *any* of the community property. However, there is an extremely strong presumption of community liability and many transactions that might not generally be thought to provide a community benefit are deemed to provide such a benefit for this purpose.[46] The party seeking to avoid the obligation has the burden of rebutting the presumption of community liability by clear and convincing evidence.[47]

A spouse who does not initially consent to, or join in, a transaction requiring his or her consent or joinder can in appropriate circumstances be precluded from disaffirming it by ratifying it after the fact.[48]

Creditors should be careful about adding words such as "individually" after signatures on guaranties. It has been held that doing so can evidence an intention not to bind the signer's marital community and community property even if the transaction actually benefited the community.[49] Therefore, if the creditor intends to have recourse to both the community property and to the separate property of the signing spouse and wants to add additional description of the capacity in which the signing spouse executes the guaranty to the signature block, it should consider using words along the lines of "individually and on behalf of [his] [her] marital community." Alternatively, a sentence or two could be added to the text of the guaranty to describe the nature of the liability intended to be incurred under the guaranty. However, neither type of such additional description should be necessary.

---

43. *See* Washington State Bar Association, Washington Community Property Deskbook, § 4.6 (3rd ed. 2003); 19 Washington Practice § 12.15 (1997).
44. Consumers Insurance Co. v. Cimoch, 69 Wash. App. 313, 320-21, 848 P.2d 763 (1993).
45. *See generally*, Cross, *The Community Property Law in Washington,* 61 Wash. L. Rev. 13, 114-125 (1986). The rule is different for tort liability, for which a plaintiff has recourse to one-half the community property for satisfaction of a judgment on a separate tort of one spouse if that spouse's separate property is insufficient to satisfy the judgment. de Elche v. Jacobsen, 95 Wash. 2d 237, 622 P.2d 835 (1980); Keene v. Edie, 131 Wash. 2d 822, 935 P.2d 588 (1997).
46. Cross, *The Community Property Law in Washington,* 61 Wash. L. Rev. 13, 120 (1986).
47. Rainier Nat'l Bank v. Clausing, 34 Wash. App. 441, 445, 661 P.2d 1015 (1983); Bank of Washington v. Hilltop Shakemill, Inc., 26 Wash. App. 943, 946, 614 P.2d 1319 (1980).
48. Nichols Hills Bank v. McCool, 104 Wash. 2d 78, 84, 701 P.2d 1114 (1985).
49. Grayson v. Platis, 95 Wash. App. 824, 837, 978 P.2d 1105 (1999). *But, cf.* Losh Family, LLC v. Kerstman, 155 Wash. App. 458, 464, 228 P.3d 793 (2010) (referring to "a long established principle that where an agreement contains language binding the individual signer, 'additional descriptive language added to the signature does not alter the signer's personal obligation'" [citation omitted]).

Generally, community property is not available to satisfy the separate debts of either spouse. There is, however, an exception to that rule for debts incurred prior to the marriage if the debt is reduced to judgment within three years after the marriage.[50] This is to prevent people with no significant assets from shielding their income from creditors' claims by marrying and converting their income to community property.

Where one spouse enters into a transaction requiring the joinder of both spouses, the transaction is voidable rather than void and, unless it is actually rescinded or otherwise avoided, it may remain effective.[51] Where the nonjoining spouse was aware of the transaction and encouraged it, he or she may be estopped to rescind or avoid it.[52] Other types of conduct by the nonjoining spouse may also result in an estoppel, ratification, or authorization having the same effect.[53]

When a marriage is dissolved, the former community property and community debts are divided between the divorcing spouses. Where a debt was contracted by one spouse that, during the marriage was a community debt and the separate debt of the contracting spouse but not the separate debt of the noncontracting spouse (for example, a community guaranty signed by only one spouse), the question arises whether the creditor can execute on the former community property awarded to the noncontracting spouse after dissolution of the marriage. In Washington, the creditor can do so but only up to the value of the property at the time of the dissolution, and it cannot do so to the extent of (i) contributions of the separate property of the noncontracting spouse to the asset or (ii) post-dissolution appreciation in the value of the asset.[54] The allocation of the debt to one of the spouses in the property settlement does not affect the rights of creditors that have become fully binding prior to the dissolution.[55]

Complicated conflict of laws questions relating to marital property issues can arise in multistate credit transactions. Although Washington law is not a model of clarity on these issues, the more recent cases hold that Washington courts will generally apply the law of the state of the spouses' residence when determining the property against which a creditor has recourse to satisfy a loan or other contract debt regardless of the law otherwise governing the contract, especially where only one of the spouses is a signatory to the contract.[56] Conflict of laws issues also arise in determining what marital property laws apply

50. RCW 26.16.200.

51. *See, e.g.*, Sander v. Wells, 71 Wash. 2d 25, 28-29, 426 P.2d 481 (1967).

52. *Id.*

53. Washington State Bar Association, Washington Community Property Deskbook, § 4.7 (3rd ed. 2003); Nichols Hills Bank v. McCool, 104 Wash. 2d 78, 84, 701 P.2d 1114 (1985) (discusses ratification by nonsigning spouse).

54. Watters v. Doud, 95 Wash. 2d 835, 631 P.2d 369 (1981).

55. Baffin Land Corp. v. Monticello Motor Inn, Inc., 70 Wash. 2d 893, 906, 425 P.2d 623 (1967). *See also* 19 Washington Practice § 14.11 (1997 and 2010 pocket part).

56. G.W. Equipment Leasing, Inc. v. Mt. McKinley Fence Co., Inc., 97 Wash. App. 191, 197-98, 982 P.2d 114 (1999); Colorado Nat'l Bank v. Merlino, 35 Wash. App. 610, 620-21, 668 P.2d 1304, rev. den. 100 Wash. 2d 1032 (1983); Potlatch No. 1 Federal Credit Union v. Kennedy, 76 Wash. 2d 806, 813, 459 P.2d 32 (1969). *But see* Pacific Gamble Robinson Co. v. Lapp, 95 Wash. 2d 341, 622 P.2d 850 (1980) (Colorado law applied to marital property issues in action to recover on contract entered into while Washington spouses previously lived in Colorado), and Pacific States Cut Stone Company v. Goble, 70 Wash. 2d 907, 425 P.2d 631 (1967) (Oregon law applied to marital property issues in action by Oregon creditor to recover on contract entered into in Oregon by Washington husband).

where spouses have moved from one state to another during their marriage or where they own property located in multiple states.[57] Generally, the character of personal property, as separate property, community property, or otherwise, is determined by the law of the state of the spouses' domicile at the time of acquisition.[58] The character of real property, however, is determined by the law of the state where the property is located.[59] Of course, the character of property may be affected by a prenuptial agreement, community property agreement, or similar status of property agreement entered into by the spouses.

2.7 Trusts

Washington's basic trust statutes are RCW chapters 11.96A through 11.118.

Generally, when a trustee of a trust enters into a loan or other contract, the trustee "may be held personally liable on the contract, if personal liability is not excluded."[60] Personal liability is deemed to be excluded by the addition of the words "trustee" or "as trustee" after the signature or by the transaction of business as trustee under an assumed name in compliance with RCW chapter 19.80 (similar rules apply to estates and personal representatives of decedents).[61]

Washington has an unusual statute that provides that the trustee of a trust may not enter into a "significant nonroutine transaction" in the absence of a "compelling circumstance" (both terms are defined in the statute) without giving certain notices to the trustors of the trust, if living, and to certain beneficiaries.[62] One of the types of nonroutine transactions described in the statute, which could be argued to apply to certain loan transactions is:

> Any sale, option, lease, or other agreement, binding for a period of ten years or more, dealing with any interest in real estate other than real estate purchased by the trustee or a vendor's interest in a real estate contract, the value of which constitutes twenty-five percent or more of the net fair market value of trust principal at the time of the transaction.[63]

When a lender is making a loan secured by trust property that may be subject to the statute, it is advisable to obtain a certificate from the trustee or trustees stating that the requirements of the statute have been met. The lender is entitled to rely on such a written statement unless it has actual knowledge that it is inaccurate.[64]

In the 2011 legislative session, Washington enacted a statute that generally allows parties dealing with trustees to rely on a certification of the trustees as to the identity of the trustees, their powers, nonrevocation of the trust, etc.[65]

---

57. *See generally* Washington State Bar Association, Washington Community Property Deskbook, ch. 8 (3rd ed. 2003).
58. Pacific States Cut Stone Co. v. Goble, 70 Wash. 2d 907, 910, 425 P.2d 631 (1967).
59. Meng v. Security State Bank of Woodland, 16 Wash. 2d 215, 222, 133 P.2d 293 (1943).
60. RCW 11.98.110(2).
61. *Id.*
62. RCW 11.100.140.
63. RCW 11.100.140(2)(a).
64. RCW 11.100.140(7).
65. RCW 11.98.075.

The statute became effective January 1, 2012, but applies to all trusts regardless of when they were created.[66]

2.8 Estates

A personal representative generally may not sell, lease, or mortgage real or personal property without an order of the court supervising the probate.[67] However, if the personal representative has been granted nonintervention powers by the court, he or she may take these actions, among many others, without court order and without notice, approval, or confirmation.[68]

§ 3 Signatory's Authority to Execute a Guaranty

Washington does not have any unusual requirements for an entity to authorize a particular officer or other person to execute guaranties or other contracts on its behalf. The ordinary diligence used in other states to establish that an authorized person has signed on behalf of the entity should suffice in Washington.

§ 4 Consideration; Sufficiency of Past Consideration

As with other contracts, a guaranty is not binding unless it is supported by legal consideration arising out of an agreement between the parties.[69] However, "[t]he obligation of an accommodation party [under a *negotiable* instrument governed by Article 3 of the Uniform Commercial Code] may be enforced ... whether or not the accommodation party receives consideration for the accommodation."[70]

A recital of consideration in the guaranty raises a presumption of consideration and shifts the burden of proof on the issue to the guarantor arguing that there is no consideration.[71]

There need not be independent consideration flowing to the guarantor, and the consideration to the principal obligor is sufficient consideration for the guaranty if the guaranty is entered into before or simultaneously with the principal obligation.[72] However, if the guaranty is entered into after the principal obligation, there must generally be separate consideration for the guaranty, whether flowing to the guarantor or to the principal obligor, or the

66. *See* note to RCW 11.103.020.
67. RCW 11.56.010
68. RCW 11.68.090.
69. Gelco IVM Leasing Co. v. Alger, 6 Wash. App. 519, 522, 494 P.2d 501 (1972); Northern State Construction Co. v. Robbins, 76 Wash. 2d 357, 361, 457 P.2d 187 (1969).
70. RCW 62A.3-419(b).
71. Rattlemiller v. Stone, 28 Wash. 104, 109, 68 P. 168 (1902).
72. Union Bank v. Kruger, 1 Wash. App. 622, 463 P. 273 (1969).

guaranty must be "the result of a previous arrangement."[73] One court summarized these rules as follows:

> (A) As with other contracts, a contract of guaranty is not binding unless supported by a legal consideration.
> (B) It is not necessary that the consideration for the promise of guaranty be distinct from that of the principal debt, if such promise were made as a part of the transaction which created the principal debt.
> (C) If the guaranty contract is made independently of the main debt, it must have a separate and distinct consideration and, accordingly, a past transaction or executed consideration will generally not support a contract of guaranty.
> (D) However, a guaranty may be supported by the consideration of an earlier contract, the performance of which is allegedly guaranteed if one of three circumstances exist....(1) the guarantor has offered or promised the debtor to guarantee the debt for him, and the debtor communicates this information to the creditor, who executes the principal contract in reliance thereon, (2) or the guarantor makes such promise direct to the creditor with the same result, (3) or the debtor gives the creditor an assurance that, if he later deems the debt insecure, he might look to a certain person, then named by the debtor, to guarantee the debt.[74]

Consideration for a guaranty entered into after the primary obligation can consist of either detriment to the creditor or new consideration to the primary obligor or the guarantor. Extension or other modification of the primary obligation, an agreement to forbear from enforcing remedies for default, the advance of additional credit, and the release of other sureties have all been held to provide sufficient consideration.[75] A detriment to the promisee is as much a consideration as a benefit to the promisor.[76] However, mere forbearance from remedies without an agreement by the creditor to do so is not adequate consideration.[77]

---

73. *See, e.g.,* Universal C.I.T. Credit Corp. v. DeLisle, 47 Wash. 2d 318, 320-22, 287 P.2d 302 (1955).
74. Rainier Nat'l Bank v. Lewis, 30 Wash. App. 419, 421, 635 P.2d 153 (1981), citing Gelco IVM Leasing Co. v. Alger, 6 Wash. App. 519, 522, 494 P.2d 501 (1972).
75. Puget Sound Nat'l Bank of Tacoma v. Olsen, 174 Wash. 200, 203, 24 P.2d 613 (1933) (extension, forbearance, additional credit); Washington Belt & Drive Systems, Inc. v. Active Erectors, 54 Wash. App. 612, 619, 774 P.2d 1250 (1989) (release of other sureties, forbearance); J.R. Watkins Co. v. Brund, 160 Wash. 183, 186-188, 294 P. 1024 (1931) (forbearance, extension of time);
76. A.M. Castle & Co. v. Public Service Underwriters, 198 Wash. 576, 590-91, 89 P.2d 506 (1939); Noyes v. Adams, 76 Wash. 412, 417, 136 P. 696 (1913).
77. Cowles Publishing Co. v. McMann, 25 Wash. 2d 736, 741, 172 P.2d 235 (1946). The court in *Cowles* cited a treatise for the proposition that: "An agreement on the part of the creditor for general indulgence toward the principal, without any definite time being specified, with proof of actual forbearance for a reasonable time, is sufficient...*But in order that forbearance by the creditor towards the principal may be a sufficient consideration, there must be an agreement on the part of the creditor that he will forbear.* " *Id.* (emphasis in original).

§ 5 Notice of Acceptance

Notice of acceptance is required for an offer of a guaranty, but is not required if the guaranty is "absolute."[78] Commonly, the guarantor waives the notification of acceptance requirement in the guaranty agreement. The Washington Supreme Court has stated Washington law on acceptance of guaranties as follows:

> The distinction between an agreement to guarantee and a guaranty itself is plainly set forth in one of the citations of appellants, *viz.*, Brandt, *Sur. & Guar.* (3d Ed.) § 205 *et seq.*, which is quoted to sustain the general rule contended for, that notice should be given, and the reasons for the rule. The author, in closing the paragraph quoted, says: 'Where the contract is admitted to amount only to an offer to guarantee, it is universally held that, in order to charge the party making the offer, he must within a reasonable time be notified that his offer is accepted.' The plain implication there is that, where it is a guaranty itself, the other rule prevails; and the authorities cited by the author quoted sustain this distinction....
>
> In 16 L. R. A. (N. S.) at page 354, notes, the author says: 'When a guaranty is an absolute present guaranty, complete in its terms, fixing the liability of the guarantor, and is not a conditional agreement, it takes effect as soon as acted upon; and notice of acceptance is not essential in order to render it binding. Thus, no notice of acceptance is necessary where the promise made is a conclusive guaranty, and not a mere overture to guarantee.[79]

§ 6 Interpretation of Guaranties

6.1 General Principles

In Washington, guaranties and other "contracts to answer for the debt of another must be explicit and are strictly construed.[80] Ambiguous language in a guaranty will be construed against the party using it.[81] It is, of course, critical that the guaranty accurately describe the obligations that are guaranteed. In one unpublished opinion, the Washington Court of Appeals held that a guaranty of a lease "including any extension and/or renewal thereof, or any addendum or amendment thereto" was insufficient to guarantee amounts owing during the term of a month-to-month holdover tenancy resulting from the landlord's acceptance of rent after the expiration of the lease.[82]

78. Robey v. Walton Lumber Co., 17 Wash. 2d 242, 256-57, 135 P.2d 95, 102 (1943); Bank of California v. Union Packing Co., 60 Wash. 456, 461-62, 111 P. 573 (1910). Absolute guaranties are discussed in § 6.5 below.
79. Bank of California v. Union Packing Co., 60 Wash. 456, 460-62, 111 P. 573 (1910) (citation omitted).
80. Wilson Court Limited Partnership v. Tony Maroni's, Inc., 134 Wash. 2d 692, 705, 952 P.2d 590 (1998).
81. Fischler v. Nicklin, 51 Wash. 2d 518, 523, 319 P.2d 1098 (1958); Old Nat'l Bank of Washington v. Seattle Smashers Corp., 36 Wash. App. 688, 691, 676 P.2d 1034 (1984).
82. VLC One, LLC v. Davis, 2009 WL 297005 (Wash. App. 2009).

Outside of these principles, and certain terms of art discussed below, the same principles of construction that apply to contracts generally apply to guaranties.[83]

6.2 Guaranty of Payment versus Guaranty of Collection

A guarantor of payment promises to satisfy the underlying obligation to the obligee upon default by the primary obligor, which satisfaction is not conditioned upon the obligee's prior attempt to secure satisfaction from the primary obligor.[84] On the other hand, a guarantor of collection incurs no liability capable of judgment "until after, by the use of due and reasonable diligence, the guarantee has become unable to collect the debt from the principal debtor."[85] However, unlike some states, Washington does not require that the creditor prosecute a suit to judgment and obtain the return of an execution unsatisfied before it is entitled to judgment against a guarantor of collection if it is clear that doing so would be an idle act.[86]

A court will look to the intent of the parties as expressed in the guaranty to determine whether it is one of payment or one of collection. A guaranty stating that the guarantor agrees to pay a promissory note "to the same extent and effect as if I were an original maker of said promissory note" has been held to be a guaranty of payment and not of collection.[87]

It has been held that a guaranty given after the maturity of the underlying obligation is deemed to be a guaranty of payment.[88]

6.3 Revocation of Guaranties

The general rule is that a continuing guaranty "is revoked as to subsequent advances by notice of the death of the guarantor, unless there is express provision to the contrary"; however, that rule has been held not to apply with respect to the renewal, after the death of the guarantor, of an obligation covered by the guaranty prior to death.[89] While Washington does not have extensive law on the revocation of guaranties, presumably it would follow the general rule of Restatement § 16 that a continuing guaranty may be terminated as to future transactions by notice to the creditor.

Despite the general rule that extending the time of payment of the principal obligation without the consent of the surety discharges the guarantor, where a guaranty expressly includes renewals or extensions of an original obligation, the guaranty cannot be revoked as to such renewals or extensions.[90]

---

83. Washington Machinery & Supply Co. v. Zucker, 19 Wash. 2d 377, 379, 143 P.2d 294 (1943).
84. Macy v. Inland Empire Land Co., 145 Wash. 523, 524, 260 P. 1073 (1927).
85. *Id.*
86. Kesner v. Inland Empire Land Co., 150 Wash. 1, 4-5, 272 P. 29 (1928).
87. Seattle Discount Corp. v. Hollywood Inv. Co., 184 Wash. 14, 24, 49 P.2d 475 (1935).
88. F.C. Palmer & Co. v. Chaffee, 129 Wash. 408, 412, 225 P. 65 (1924).
89. Exchange Nat'l Bank of Spokane v. Hunt, 75 Wash. 513, 135 P. 224 (1913).
90. Old Nat'l Bank of Washington v. Seattle Smashers Corp., 36 Wash. App. 688, 692, 676 P.2d 1034 (1984).

6.4 "Continuing"

"A continuing guaranty is a contract pursuant to which a person agrees to be a secondary obligor for all future obligations of the principal obligor to the obligee."[91] While the use of the word "continuing" helps to make clear that a guaranty is meant to be continuing, courts in Washington have interpreted a guaranty as continuing even where the word "continuing" has not been used.[92] On the other hand, a Washington court has stated that "in every doubtful case, the presumption should be against a continuing guaranty, especially in the case of an uncompensated surety."[93]

Courts have sometimes narrowly construed continuing guaranties. For example, one court held that a guaranty "of any and all loans or rediscounts made by [the lender] to [the borrower]...will be paid at maturity of each of the said loans" constituted a guaranty only of future loans and not of a past loan that had already matured.[94]

6.5 "Absolute and Unconditional"

A number of Washington cases discuss the effect of a guaranty that is deemed absolute and unconditional. It has been held that "though a loan may be inefficiently managed and with adverse consequences, neither inferior lienors nor absolute guarantors have any recourse against the lender unless it is alleged and proved that the lender acted in bad faith."[95] "An absolute and unconditional guaranty should be and is enforceable according to its terms...with full effect given to its contents, and without reading into it terms and conditions on which it is completely silent."[96] Where a "guaranty is absolute and unconditional and does not require the creditor to take any action to preserve the security, the creditor's failure to do so will not relieve the surety's obligation to pay upon default."[97]

"An absolute guaranty is one by which the guarantor unconditionally promises payment or performance of the principal contract on default of the principal debtor or obligor, the most usual form of an absolute guaranty being that of payment."[98] "A guaranty of the payment of an obligation, without words of limitation or condition, is construed as an absolute or unconditional guaranty."[99] A signature followed by the sole words "guarantor" and "as

---

91. Restatement § 16.
92. *See, e.g.*, Putnam v. Ewart, 132 Wash. 573, 232 P. 277 (1925).
93. Nat'l Surety Co. v. Campbell, 108 Wash. 596, 601, 185 P. 602 (1919).
94. American Security Bank v. Liberty Motor Co., 124 Wash. 678, 214 P. 1062 (1923).
95. Nat'l Bank of Washington v. Equity Investors, 81 Wash. 2d 886, 919, 506 P.2d 20 (1973).
96. *Id.*
97. Century 21 Products, Inc. v. Glacier Sales, 129 Wash. 2d 406, 415, 918 P.2d 168 (1996) (citation and internal quotation marks omitted); Grayson v. Platis, 95 Wash. App. 824, 831, 978 P.2d 1105 (1999). It should be noted, however, that the Restatement's comments take the position that "a statement that a guaranty is absolute or unconditional is ordinarily not sufficient to indicate that the [guarantor] is agreeing to forego discharges based on suretyship status." Restatement § 48, comment d.
98. Sherman Clay & Co. v. Turner, 164 Wash. 257, 261, 2 P.2d 688 (1931).
99. Bellevue Square Managers v. Granberg, 2 Wash. App. 760, 766, 469 P.2d 969 (1970). Accord, Robey v. Walton, 17 Wash. 2d 242, 256, 135 P.2d 95 (1943).

guarantor only" has been held to constitute an absolute and unconditional guaranty.[100]

6.6 "Liable as a Primary Obligor and not Merely as a Surety"

This language, taken literally, seems to conflate the concepts of guarantor and primary obligor. While a guarantor may be a "guarantor of payment" from whom the obligee can seek payment even without pursuing the primary obligor, it seems unlikely that a Washington court would hold that the guarantor under a guaranty with such language would be a primary obligor for all purposes (e.g., for purposes of the guarantor's right of indemnity from the principal obligor). The Restatement suggests that a statement in a guaranty that the guarantor "does not have suretyship status, while inaccurate, is ordinarily sufficient [to waive suretyship defenses], however, because by communicating the absence of that status, it communicates that the incidents of suretyship status, such as discharge resulting from impairment of recourse, are unavailable."[101] One Washington case held that a guaranty stating that the guarantor agrees to pay a promissory note "to the same extent and effect as if I were an original maker of said promissory note" is a guaranty of payment and not of collection.[102]

§ 7 Defenses of the Guarantor; Set-off

The defenses that may be available to a guarantor can be grouped into three categories: (1) defenses of the primary obligor; (2) "suretyship defenses"; and (3) other defenses.

7.1 Defenses of the Primary Obligor

7.1.1 General

There is case law in Washington with broad statements to the effect that the general rule is that the guarantor is not liable to the creditor unless the principal obligor is liable and accordingly the guarantor may plead any defense available to the primary obligor.[103] As discussed in the following subsections, these statements cannot be taken at face value.

7.1.2 When Guarantor May Assert Primary Obligor's Defense

The rule that liability of the principal debtor measures and limits the liability of the surety is subject to several important exceptions. One is that "a guaranty

100. Amick v. Baugh, 66 Wash. 2d 298, 303, 402 P.2d 342 (1965). Accord, Sherman Clay & Co. v. Turner, 164 Wash. 257, 263, 2 P.2d 688 (1931) ("A guaranty is deemed to be absolute and unconditional unless its terms import some condition precedent to the liability of the guarantor").
101. Restatement § 48, comment d.
102. Seattle Discount Corp. v. Hollywood Inv. Co., 184 Wash. 14, 24, 49 P.2d 475 (1935).
103. *See, e.g.,* Security State Bank v. Burk, 100 Wash. App. 94, 98, 995 P.2d 1272 (2000).

of an existing contract may stand by itself although the obligation guaranteed is unenforceable, provided that it can fairly be said that such was the intention of the parties."[104]

"No right exists under a guaranty contract to assert the rights of the principal debtor other than a right to raise defensively the claims of the principal debtor" and "a guarantor may not recover affirmatively on the claims of the principal debtor."[105]

7.1.3 Defenses that May not be Raised by Guarantor

Presumably, a guarantor may not raise the primary obligor's discharge in bankruptcy or incapacity as a defense to liability under the guaranty.[106] It has specifically been held that a guarantor generally cannot avoid its guaranty obligations on the ground that the guaranteed obligation was *ultra vires* as to the primary obligor.[107] The court in the early case of *Backus v. Feeks* stated:

> In treating of the exceptions to the rule that the extent of the liability of the principal debtor measures and limits the liability of the surety, in 20 Cyc. 1421, the following view is announced: 'Important exceptions to the above rule exist which must not be overlooked. They are found in those cases where the defect is not in the contract itself but pertains to those matters which are personal to the principal debtor; or they may arise from causes which originate in the law. A guaranty of an existing contract may stand by itself, although the obligation guaranteed is invalid; and it will usually be found that, where the fact that the supposed principal debtor is not bound is held to be a defense on behalf of the guarantor, such fact has also resulted in a failure of consideration for the contract of guaranty, or that such contract has been brought about by fraud or has been entered into under a mutual mistake. And as the guarantor may by the terms of his contract make himself liable for the principal debt, although it be invalid, the question of whether the liability of a guarantor is to be measured by the liability of the principal debtor is largely a matter of interpretation of the contract of guaranty.'[108]

---

104. A.M. Castle & Co. v. Public Service Underwriters, 198 Wash. 576, 590-91, 89 P.2d 506 (1939), citing, inter alia, Backus v. Feeks, 71 Wash. 508, 129 P. 86 (1914). Accord, Robey v. Walton, 17 Wash. 2d 242, 258, 135 P.2d 95 (1943).
105. Miller v. U.S. Bank of Washington, N.A., 72 Wash. App. 416, 424, 865 P.2d 536 (1994).
106. Restatement § 34.
107. Spokane Concrete Products, Inc. v. U.S. Bank of Washington, N.A. (In re Spokane Concrete Products, Inc.), 126 Wash. 2d 269, 278, 892 P.2d 98 (1995). However, it should be noted that the doctrine of *ultra vires* under which a corporate action can be challenged on the basis that it is beyond the corporate powers of the corporation is severely limited by RCW 23B.03.040 (for for-profit corporations) and RCW 24.03.040 (for nonprofit corporations). Actions may be challenged on the ground that the corporation did not act in accordance with its governing documents. Hartstene Point Maintenance Ass'n v. Diehl, 95 Wash. App. 339, 345, 979 P.2d 854 (1999).
108. 71 Wash. 508, 512-13, 129 P. 86 (1914)

7.1.4 Effect on Guarantor of Default or Confessed Judgment Against Primary Obligor

Where a judgment against the primary obligor was obtained by default or confession, that judgment does not deprive the guarantor of any defenses and is evidence only of the fact of its rendition.[109]

7.2 Suretyship Defenses

Guarantors and other sureties have a variety of defenses to payment that are not generally available to the principal obligor. However, the fact of the suretyship must be known to the creditor or the surety can be held liable as a principal obligor.[110]

7.2.1 Change in Identity of Principal Obligor or of Creditor

Whether a change of the identity of the principal obligor to the underlying obligation discharges the guarantor's obligations depends upon the circumstances. "Ordinarily, a surety who guarantees the debts of a business will not be liable for debts incurred after a change in the firm."[111] It has been held that a continuing guaranty of a partnership's debts does not extend to debts of "another later created partnership, composed of a different membership, though the later created partnership succeeded to the ownership of the business and continued it under the same partnership name....unless it appears from the terms of the instrument that the parties intended the guaranty to be a continuing one, without reference to the composition of the firm" (even though there was some commonality of partners throughout the relevant period of time).[112]

An assignment of the guaranteed debt transfers the assignor's rights against the guarantor.[113] The assignment does not provide the guarantor with a defense to payment and the assignee acquires the same rights against the guarantor that were held by the assignor (but no greater rights, as a guaranty is not a negotiable instrument).[114]

7.2.2 Modification of the Underlying Obligation, Including Extension of Time and Release

Under Washington law, modifications to the underlying obligation may permit the guarantor to raise certain defenses to liability; the Court of Appeals has stated that: "Any material change in a surety's obligation without the surety's

109. Lilenquist Motors, Inc. v. Monk, 64 Wash. 2d 187, 189-90, 390 P.2d 1007 (1964).
110. Hemenway v. Miller, 116 Wash. 2d 725, 729, 807 P.2d 863 (1991).; Kenney v. Read, 100 Wash. App. 467, 475, 477, 997 P.2d 455 (2000).
111. Columbia Bank, N.A. v. New Cascadia Corp., 37 Wash. App. 737, 738, 682 P.2d 966 (1984), citing Lumberman's Bank & Trust Co. v. Sevier, 149 Wash. 118, 270 P. 291 (1928) (change of partners); Tupper v. Hartman, 121 Wash. 142, 208 P. 1103 (1922) (substitution of widow for estate of borrower); Spokane Union Stockyards Co. v. Maryland Cas. Co., 105 Wash. 306, 178 P. 3 (1919).
112. Lumberman's Bank & Trust Co. v. Sevier, 149 Wash. 118, 121, 270 P. 291 (1928).
113. C.I.T. Corp. v. Strain, 178 Wash. 260, 264, 34 P.2d 440 (1934).
114. *Id.*

consent will discharge the surety's obligation."[115] Although such statements suggest that *any* material modification in the underlying obligation will exonerate the guarantor, the Restatement is clear that only modifications that are materially *adverse* to the guarantor or that create a substituted obligation that is not covered by the guaranty will do so.[116]

The taking of a promissory note for an antecedent liability does not constitute a payment of the debt in the absence of an agreement to that effect, or evidence that such was the intention of the parties.[117] Mere silence on the part of a surety when informed of a modification of the primary obligation has been held not to imply consent to the modification so as to avoid a discharge of the guarantor's liability.[118]

A change in the underlying debt should not discharge the guarantor under a continuing guaranty, who is liable for all obligations of the primary obligor to the creditor incurred during the life of the guaranty.[119]

A guarantor is generally released from liability if the creditor, by positive contract, extends the time for payment of the primary obligation without the consent of the guarantor.[120] However, if there is no consideration for the extension of time, it is not binding on the creditor and, therefore, may not discharge the guarantor.[121] Moreover, if the guaranty is a continuing guaranty, an extension of time does not release the guarantor.[122]

A release of the principal obligor without the guarantor's explicit or implicit consent releases the guarantor.[123] Of course, payment of the underlying obligation by the primary obligor discharges the guarantor.[124]

There is authority for the proposition that a principal obligor's exercise of an option contained in the guaranteed documents does not result in discharge of the surety.[125]

---

115. Kenney v. Read, 100 Wash. App. 467, 474, 997 P.2d 455 (2000), quoting State v. French, 88 Wash. App. 586, 598-99, 945 P.2d 752 (1997).
116. RESTATEMENT § 41.
117. SAS America, Inc. v. Inada, 71 Wash. App. 261, 266, 857 P.2d 1047 (1993), citing Exchange Nat'l Bank v. Hunt, 75 Wash. 513, 517, 135 P. 224 (1913).
118. Thompson v. Metropolitan Building Co., 95 Wash. 546, 550, 164 P. 222 (1917).
119. *See* Putnam v. Ewart, 132 Wash. 573,575, 232 P. 277 (1925).
120. Lincoln v. Transamerica Investment Corp., 89 Wash. 2d 571, 574, 573 P.2d 1316 (1978). The *Lincoln v. Transamerica* case and the cases on which it relies contain statements about the effect of a reservation of rights against the guarantor expressed by the creditor at the time it grants the extension. It seems likely that a Washington court would no longer take the same view of such a reservation of rights given the evolution of the law since those cases were decided and the Restatement's disavowal of the reservation of rights doctrine since that time. RESTATEMENT § 38.
121. A.M. Castle & Co. v. Public Service Underwriters, 198 Wash. 576, 591, 89 P.2d 506 (1939); Van de Ven v. Overlook Mining & Development Co., 146 Wash. 332, 334-35, 262 P. 981 (1928).
122. Putnam v. Ewart, 132 Wash. 573,575, 232 P. 277 (1925).
123. Fruehauf Trailer Co. of Canada Limited v. Chandler, 67 Wash. 2d 704, 707, 409 P.2d 651 (1966); Kitsap County Credit Bureau v. Richards, 52 Wash. 2d 381, 382, 325 P.2d 292 (1958).
124. Tupper v. Hartman, 121 Wash. 142, 144, 208 P. 1103 (1922).
125. *See* Glesener v. Balholm, 50 Wash. App. 1, 5, 747 P.2d 475 (1987) (exercise of option to extend lease by assignee of tenant's interest does not release assignor/original tenant from continued liability on the lease).

7.2.3 Release or Impairment of Security for the Underlying Obligation

The general rule is that a surety is discharged from liability to the extent of the value of any security the creditor relinquishes, but only if its suretyship status is impaired.[126] It makes no difference that the security was obtained subsequent to the guaranty and without knowledge of the guarantor.[127]

Washington has *not* adopted the rule of *strictissimi juris*, under which a surety is completely discharged by any impairment of collateral whether or not there has been any loss or prejudice to the surety.[128] Thus, in order for a guarantor to be completely discharged by impairment of collateral, the collateral surrendered or lost must be of a value at least equal to the amount of the guaranteed debt.[129] The burden of proof on the issue of the extent of any impairment of collateral is on the guarantor.[130]

Generally, failure to perfect a security interest in collateral constitutes unjustifiable impairment of collateral.[131]

Notwithstanding the general rule, "where a guaranty is absolute and unconditional, impairment of collateral has no effect on the agreement."[132]

7.3 Other Defenses

7.3.1 Failure to Fulfill a Condition Precedent

A number of Washington cases deal with the situation where a guarantor argues that it was a condition precedent to enforcement of the guaranty that one or more other parties also guarantee the obligation. "Washington law appears to be that if other guarantors were merely contemplated, the signing guarantors are not insulated from liability; the missing signatures must actually have been agreed conditions precedent" and the condition precedent "can be effective against a creditor only if the creditor has knowledge of it."[133] Parol evidence can be considered on the issue.[134] Further, if the guaranty document bears on its face evidence of its incompleteness, such as unsigned signature blocks naming certain parties, such incompleteness is "sufficient to put the obligee upon inquiry and charge him with notice that those who signed may have done so only on condition that the other parties named therein would also sign it, thus opening the door to extrinsic evidence of that fact."[135] However, the mere fact

126. Warren v. Washington Trust Bank, 92 Wash. 2d 381, 390, 598 P.2d 701 (1979); The Revocable Living Trust of Harold G. Strand v. Wel-Co Group, Inc., 120 Wash. App. 828, 837, 86 P.3d 818 (2004).
127. Nat'l Bank of Washington v. Equity Investors, 86 Wash. 2d 545, 556, 546 P.2d 440 (1976).
128. Puyallup Valley Bank v. Mosby, 44 Wash. App. 285, 288, 723 P.2d 2 (1986).
129. Seattle Discount Corp. v. Hollywood Inv. Co., 184 Wash. 14, 24, 49 P.2d 475 (1935).
130. Puyallup Valley Bank v. Mosby, 44 Wash. App. 285, 287, 723 P.2d 2 (1986).
131. *Id.*
132. Century 21 Products, Inc. v. Glacier Sales, 129 Wash. 2d 406, 408, 918 P.2d 168 (1996). *See also* fn. 97, *supra,* and related text.
133. United States v. Everett Monte Cristo Hotel, Inc., 524 F.2d 127, 130 (9th Cir. 1975).
134. *Id.*
135. Williams v. Hitchcock, 86 Wash. 536, 540, 150 P. 1143 (1915). *See also* J.R. Watkins Co. v. Brund, 160 Wash. 183, 191-92, 294 P. 1024 (1931); Young v. Union Sav. Bank & Trust Co., 23 Wash. 360, 365-66, 63 P. 247 (1900).

that a loan application identifies multiple guarantors, not all of whom ultimately sign guaranties, is not sufficient to put the creditor on such notice.[136]

7.3.2 *Failure to Pursue Primary Obligor*

See § 6.2 above regarding the distinction between guaranties of payment and guaranties of collection.

7.3.3 *Statute of Limitation*

The statute of limitation applicable to guaranties, promissory notes, and other written contracts is six years.[137] For negotiable promissory notes that are payable on demand, the six-year period begins to run on the date of demand.[138] If no demand is made on such a note, an action to enforce the note is barred if neither principal nor interest has been paid for a continuous period of 10 years.[139] Prior to 1993, the statute of limitation on a negotiable demand note began to run immediately upon the effectiveness of the note.[140] A similar rule appears still to apply to demand loans that are not evidenced by a negotiable note or other negotiable instrument subject to RCW 62A.3-118.[141] Also note that in order to be subject to that statute (and to UCC Article 3 generally), a promissory note or other instrument must be a *negotiable* instrument.[142]

When a written guaranty, promissory note, or other document has been lost and its contents are proved by parol evidence, it is still a written contract for statute of limitation purposes and is subject to the six-year statute.[143]

Whenever a voluntary payment is made, the period of limitation restarts.[144] However, the payment must be made under such circumstances as to show intentional acknowledgment by the debtor of liability for the whole debt as of the date of payment.[145]

A borrower may raise an otherwise time-barred claim as an affirmative defense to a lender's claim on a debt.[146]

An agreement to waive a statute of limitation is enforceable if it is supported by consideration and is for a definite time.[147] Forbearance to sue on the relevant claim is sufficient consideration.[148] "Generally parties can shorten the applicable statute of limitations by contract unless a shorter time frame is unreasonable or prohibited by statute or public policy."[149] It appears that Washington does not have any law on the enforceability of a waiver of the

136. Merrill v. Muzzy, 11 Wash. 16, 21, 39 P. 277 (1895).
137. RCW 62A.3-118 and 4.16.040.
138. RCW 62A.3-118(b).
139. *Id.*
140. *See* former RCW 62A.3-122.
141. *See, e.g.*, Wallace v. Kuehner, 111 Wash. App. 809, 818-19, 46 P.3d 823 (2002) and cases cited therein.
142. RCW 62A.3-104(b).
143. Lutz v. Gatlin, 22 Wash. App. 424, 427, 590 P.2d 359 (1979).
144. RCW 4.16.270.
145. *See, e.g.*, Easton v. Bigley, 28 Wash. 2d 674, 183 P.2d 780 (1947).
146. Seattle-First Nat'l Bank v. Siebol, 64 Wash. App. 401, 407, 824 P.2d 1252 (1992).
147. Taplett v. Khela, 60 Wash. App. 751, 759, 807 P.2d 885 (1991).
148. J.A. Campbell Co. v. Holsum Baking Co., 15 Wash. 2d 239, 254, 130 P.2d 333 (1942).
149. McKee v. AT&T Corp., 164 Wash. 2d 372, 399, 191 P.3d 845 (2008).

statute of limitation entered into in the loan documents prior to accrual of a cause of action.

State statutes of limitation do not apply in arbitration proceedings under Washington law absent the parties' agreement to the contrary.[150]

The statute of limitation applicable to oral contracts is three years.[151] As discussed in § 11.3.2 below, there is a one-year statute of limitation for actions seeking a deficiency judgment against a guarantor after nonjudicial foreclosure of a deed of trust (in the limited situations where such an action is permitted).[152] See § 10.2 below for a discussion of the statute of limitation applicable to rights of contribution among coguarantors.

7.3.4 Statute of Frauds

General rule

RCW 19.36.010(2) provides that "every special promise to answer for the debt" of another is void unless that promise "or some note or memorandum thereof, be in writing, and signed by the party to be charged therewith, or by some person thereunto by him lawfully authorized."[153] Notwithstanding this statute, Washington law provides that "where the 'primary purpose' or 'leading purpose' of the guaranty is to benefit the guarantor, the promise will be upheld without a writing."[154] This exception has been held to apply where guarantors benefit from the guaranteed transaction personally because of their role as the "sole owners, operators, and shareholders" of the primary obligor.[155]

Where a written guaranty has been lost, but its contents are proved by clear, cogent, and convincing evidence, it is still considered to be a written agreement for statute of frauds purposes.[156]

Accommodation parties under negotiable instruments

"The obligation of an accommodation party [under a *negotiable* instrument governed by Article 3 of the UCC] may be enforced notwithstanding any statute of frauds...."[157]

Special statute re credit agreements

Washington has a special statute of frauds applicable to commercial "credit agreements," which is intended to protect lenders against claims that there were oral agreements that modified the written loan documents.[158] "Credit agreement" is defined to mean "an agreement, promise, or commitment to lend money, to otherwise extend credit, to forbear with respect to the repayment of

---

150. Broom v. Morgan Stanley DW Inc., 169 Wash. 2d 231, 236 P.3d 182 (2010).
151. RCW 4.16.080.
152. RCW 61.24.100.
153. *See* South Sound Nat'l Bank v. Meek, 14 Wash. App. 577, 544 P.2d 25 (1975) for a summary of cases discussing the extent to which this statute applies to guaranties.
154. Century 21 Products, Inc. v. Glacier Sales, 74 Wash. App. 793, 796, 875 P.2d 1238 (1994), *rev'd. on other grounds* at 129 Wash. 2d 406, 918 P.2d 168 (1996). Accord, Washington Belt & Drive Systems, Inc. v. Active Erectors, 54 Wash. App. 612, 617-18, 774 P.2d 1250 (1989) and cases cited therein. This exception is further explained in 25 Washington Practice § 3:8 (2011).
155. *Washington Belt & Drive Systems, Inc. v. Active Erectors, supra*, at 54 Wash. App. 619.
156. Lutz v. Gatlin, 22 Wash. App. 424, 4327-28, 590 P.2d 359 (1979).
157. RCW 62A.3-419(b).
158. RCW 19.36.110 - .120.

any debt or the exercise of any remedy, to modify or amend the terms under which the creditor has lent money or otherwise extended credit, to release any guarantor or cosigner, or to make any other financial accommodation pertaining to a debt or other extension of credit."[159]

Where the statute applies, the lender has the benefit of RCW 19.36.110, which provides:

A credit agreement is not enforceable against the creditor unless the agreement is in writing and signed by the creditor. The rights and obligations of the parties to a credit agreement shall be determined solely from the written agreement, and any prior or contemporaneous oral agreements between the parties are superseded by, merged into, and may not vary the credit agreement. Partial performance of a credit agreement does not remove the agreement from the operation of this section.

In order to have the benefit of the statutory protections, the borrower[160] must be given a statutorily prescribed notice as follows:

ORAL AGREEMENTS OR ORAL COMMITMENTS TO LOAN MONEY, EXTEND CREDIT, OR TO FORBEAR FROM ENFORCING REPAYMENT OF A DEBT ARE NOT ENFORCEABLE UNDER WASHINGTON LAW.

The notice must "be in type that is bold face, capitalized, underlined, or otherwise set out from surrounding written materials so it is conspicuous."[161] For that reason, it is advisable that it be bolded, capitalized, and underlined wherever it appears. The notice need not be put into every loan document in a transaction, but it must be given simultaneously with or before a credit agreement is made.[162] Because the statute does not specify when a "credit agreement is made," it is advisable to provide the notice in the earliest possible communication with the borrower and guarantors. It is also advisable to include it in subordination agreements with other creditors. Lenders in Washington commonly put the notice in loan commitments, promissory notes, guaranties, major security documents, and subsequent modifications.

Once the notice is given, it is "effective as to all subsequent credit agreements and effective against the debtor, and its guarantors, successors, and assigns."[163]

If the lender does not properly invoke the protection of RCW 19.36.110, the loan documents may be subject to the general common law rule that "a contract clause prohibiting oral modifications is essentially unenforceable because the clause itself is subject to oral modifications."[164]

---

159. RCW 19.36.100.
160. The second sentence of RCW 19.36.130 provides that: "Notice, once given to a debtor, shall be effective as to all subsequent credit agreements and effective against the debtor, and its guarantors, successors, and assigns." That provision makes the notice given to the primary obligor effective as to the guarantor as well. However, it is prudent also to give the notice to each guarantor.
161. RCW 19.36.140.
162. RCW 19.36.130.
163. RCW 19.36.130.
164. Pacific Northwest Group A v. Pizza Blends, Inc., 90 Wash. App. 273, 277-78, 951 P.2d 826 (1998); Kelly Springfield Tire Co. v. Faulkner, 191 Wash. 549, 554-56, 71 P.2d 382 (1937).

7.3.5 *Right of Set-off*

Washington law provides that, "where two liabilities are owed by and through the same parties in the same right they are properly the subject of off-set, and that the right of set-off is to be liberally construed."[165] That principle is now embodied in the court rule on counterclaims.[166]

The right of set-off against a contract claim, such as a claim on a guaranty, can be asserted with respect to virtually any claim a guarantor may have against the creditor, including a tort claim[167] or a claim reduced to judgment.[168] An unsecured claim can be asserted against a secured claim.[169] A contingent, unliquidated counterclaim can be pleaded as a set-off unless the other party can show prejudice or the court finds the counterclaim would make the proceedings unwieldy.[170]

An assignee of a claim takes it subject to any rights of set-off existing at the time of the assignment.[171] Such a set-off can diminish or defeat the assignee's claim, but the assignee has no liability in excess of the amount of that claim.[172]

By statute, the defense of set-off must be pleaded in the defendant's answer.[173]

7.3.6 *Application of Payments*

A guarantor is, of course, entitled to defend against a claim on the guaranty on the basis that the guaranteed obligation has been paid by the primary obligor. Where the guarantor has guaranteed some, but not all, of the primary obligor's obligations to the creditor, a question may arise as to whether a payment by the primary obligor can be applied by the creditor against obligations that are not guaranteed rather than to those that are guaranteed.

"It is the general rule that, where a principal owes more than one obligation to a creditor and makes payments out of his own funds, in the absence of agreement or special equities, the creditor is bound to apply the payments in accordance with the principal's directions, and if there are no directions, he may apply the payments as he sees fit."[174]

---

165. Johnson v. California-Washington Timber Co., 161 Wash. 96, 103, 296 P. 159 (1931).
166. Washington Civil Rule 13.
167. Topline Equipment, Inc. v. Stan Witty Land, Inc., 31 Wash. App. 86, 95, 639 P.2d 825 (1982). Earlier cases holding to the contrary with respect to tort claims, such as Golmis v. Vlachos, 34 Wash. 2d 627, 629, 208 P.2d 1204 (1949), were based on a statute limiting counterclaims that has since been repealed and replaced by Washington Civil Rule 13.
168. Edwards v. Surety Finance Co. of Seattle, 176 Wash. 534, 540, 30 P.2d 225 (1934).
169. Topline Equipment, Inc. v. Stan Witty Land, Inc., 31 Wash. App. 86, 95, 639 P.2d 825 (1982).
170. Warren, Little & Lund, Inc. v. Max J. Kuney Co., 115 Wash. 2d 211, 216, 796 P.2d 1263 (1990).
171. Nancy's Product, Inc. v. Fred Meyer, Inc., 61 Wash. App. 645, 650-51, 811 P.2d 250 (1991). *See also* RCW 62A.9A-404(a).
172. *Id. See also* RCW 62A.9A-404(b).
173. RCW 4.32.150.
174. Warren v. Washington Trust Bank, 92 Wash. 2d 381, 384, 598 P.2d 701 (1979), citing, inter alia, Armour & Co. v. Becker, 167 Wash. 245, 9 P.2d 63 (1932); Sturtevant Co. v. Fidelity & Dep. Co., 92 Wash. 52, 158 P. 740 (1916); United States Fid. & Guar. Co. v. E.I. DuPont De Nemours & Co., 197 Wash. 569, 85 P.2d 1085 (1939).

Where a guarantor guarantees only a portion of a primary obligation, "a payment on the account would be upon the unguaranteed portion, unless specific directions were given to apply it upon such guaranty."[175]

An agreement in the guaranty about how payments on the primary obligation are to be applied should be enforceable.[176]

7.3.7 *Duty of Good Faith*

There is an implied duty of good faith and fair dealing imposed on the parties to a contract, which extends to guaranties; however, a party's duty to act in good faith exists only in relation to the performance of specific contract terms and does not obligate the party to accept new obligations that represent a material change in the terms of the contract.[177] "Outside the contract, the major duty which a ... lender owes to any other party is the duty of good faith; though a loan may be inefficiently managed and with adverse consequences, neither inferior lienors nor absolute guarantors have any recourse against the lender unless it is alleged and proved that the lender acted in bad faith."[178]

7.3.8 *Failure to Disclose Information About the Primary Obligor or Obligation*

"Where before the surety has undertaken his obligation [a] the creditor knows facts unknown to the surety that materially increase the risk beyond that which the creditor has reason to believe the surety intends to assume, and [b] the creditor also has reason to believe that these facts are unknown to the surety and [c] has a reasonable opportunity to communicate them to the surety, failure of the creditor to notify the guarantor of such facts is a defense to the guarantor."[179] When the creditor, rather than the debtor, solicits the surety, the creditor has a greater duty of disclosure.[180] If the circumstances warrant disclosure and the creditor fails to disclose, the guarantor is discharged regardless of the creditor's intent in not disclosing.[181] However, the Washington cases emphasize the guarantor's responsibility, at least in the case of a compensated guarantor (including an equity owner in the primary obligor), to inquire about the risk being undertaken.[182] They further hold that, if the creditor is nothing more than negligent in not discovering facts that affect the risk to the guarantor, the guarantor is not discharged.[183]

---

175. Washington Grocery Co. v. Citizens' Bank of Anacortes, 132 Wash. 244, 247, 231 P. 780 (1925).
176. Warren v. Washington Trust Bank, 92 Wash. 2d 381, 384, 598 P.2d 701 (1979).
177. Miller v. U.S. Bank of Washington, N.A., 72 Wash. App. 416, 425, 865 P.2d 536 (1994) and cases cited therein.
178. Nat'l *Bank of Washington v. Equity Investors*, 81 Wash. 2d 886, 920, 506 P.2d 20 (1973).
179. Peoples Nat'l Bank of Washington v. Taylor, 42 Wash. App. 518, 526-27, 711 P.2d 1021 (1985), citing Restatement of Security § 124(1) (1941) (now addressed in Restatement § 12(3)).
180. *Id.* at 42 Wash. App. 527.
181. *Id.*
182. *Id.* at 42 Wash. App. 529-30.
183. *Id.* at 42 Wash. App. 531.

§ 8 Waiver of Defenses by the Guarantor

8.1 In General

Waivers of suretyship defenses in guaranties are generally enforced in Washington.[184] Without such waivers, guarantors and other sureties have a wide range of defenses, as is the case in all states.

8.2 Defenses that Cannot be Waived

Washington does not appear to have any law specifically prohibiting the waiver of any particular defenses by a guarantor. In fact, Washington has nonuniform versions of UCC §§ 9-602 and 9-624, which vary from the official text in that they except secondary obligors (including guarantors) from certain rules that invalidate waivers of some Article 9 rights.[185] The Washington versions of those sections omit the restriction on such waivers by secondary obligors that is contained in the uniform version. This nonuniform provision legislatively overruled pre-Revised Article 9 cases to the extent they held to the contrary.[186] Thus, in Washington, guarantors can waive some Article 9 rights in the guaranty agreement that cannot be waived under other states' laws.

8.3 "Catch-all" Waivers

A guaranty that is intended to be as broad as possible and to waive all possible defenses should state that it is "absolute and unconditional" and should also state that the guarantor intends to "waive all defenses based on suretyship."

There is no Washington law expressly approving catch-all waivers; however, the Restatement says that a guarantor's consent or waiver with respect to actions that would, in the absence of such consent, discharge the guarantor's liability can be express or implied from the circumstances and, if express, may be effectuated either "by specific language *or by general language indicating that the [guarantor] waives defenses based on suretyship.*"[187]

8.4 Use of Specific Waivers

As discussed in § 8.3 above, general waivers should be sufficient to waive suretyship defenses. However, it is traditional for guaranties to contain extensive and specific waivers of suretyship defenses and their absence may lead to an argument that the guarantor did not intend to waive all suretyship defenses. Presumably the best evidence of such an intention is a traditional specific waiver.

---

184. *See, e.g.*, Warren v. Washington Trust Bank, 92 Wash. 2d 381, 598 P.2d 701 (1979); Fruehauf Trailer Co. of Canada Limited v. Chandler, 67 Wash. 2d 704, 409 P.2d 651 (1966); Grayson v. Platis, 95 Wash.App. 824, 978 P.2d 1105 (1999); Franco v. Peoples Nat'l Bank of Washington, 39 Wash. App. 381, 693 P.2d 200 (1984).
185. RCW 62A.9A-602 and -624.
186. *See, e.g.*, Security State Bank v. Burk, 100 Wash. App. 94, 99-100, 995 P.2d 1272 (2000).
187. Restatement § 48(1) (emphasis added).

§ 9 Third-party Pledgors—Defenses and Waiver Thereof

As discussed in Section 1.2 above, the grant of a security interest or other lien by a party other than the party primarily liable for the secured debt often results in a surety relationship. Therefore, such a third-party pledgor generally has the same defenses as are available to a guarantor and the creditor should require a waiver of those defenses to the same extent it would require such a waiver from a guarantor.

§ 10 Reimbursement, Subrogation, and Contribution Rights

10.1 Reimbursement and Subrogation

A guarantor who pays a guaranteed obligation is entitled to reimbursement (also referred to as indemnification) in full by the primary obligor and is entitled to be subrogated to the rights of the lender against the borrower, including its collateral.[188] Similar concepts apply in other types of suretyship situations.[189] The primary obligor's obligation to the creditor and its reimbursement obligation to sureties are separate and distinct obligations and remain distinct even where a surety acquires the primary obligation as well as the reimbursement obligation.[190]

Where there are multiple guarantors, all of whom are equally liable to the common creditor, but one or more of whom are, by agreement or because of the equities of the situation, liable for the full loss as among the guarantors, the guarantors liable for the full loss are considered to be primary sureties and the other guarantors are considered to be subsureties.[191] Subsureties are entitled to full reimbursement from primary sureties and primary sureties are not entitled to reimbursement or contribution from subsureties.[192] "An obligor's suretyship status in relation to a creditor is not necessarily dispositive of its status in relation to a co-obligor."[193]

As between the creditor and a guarantor, the right of subrogation does not arise until the creditor has been paid in full, but that rule cannot be invoked

188. McAllister v. Pier 67, Inc., 1 Wash. App. 978, 985-86, 465 P.2d 678 (1970). *See also* Nat'l Bank of Washington v. Equity Investors, 86 Wash. 2d 545, 556, 546 P.2d 440 (1976); Blewett v. Bash, 22 Wash. 536, 543-44, 61 P. 770 (1900).
189. *See generally* Reliance Insurance Co. v. U.S. Bank of Washington, N.A., 143 F.3d 502 (9th Cir. 1998) (applying Washington law); Hanson v. Hanson, 55 Wash. 2d 884, 887-88, 350 P.2d 859 (1960) (post-divorce, former spouses treated as codebtors with contribution rights as to undisclosed liabilities).
190. Wedell v. Sallie Mae, Inc. (In re Wedell), 329 B.R. 59, 61 (W.D. Wash. 2005).
191. *See* Franco v. Peoples Nat'l Bank, 39 Wash. App. 381, 389-91, 693 P.2d 200 (1984).
192. *Id.*
193. Honey v. Davis, 131 Wash. 2d 212, 221, 930 P.2d 908 (1996).

by the primary obligor.[194] Under Article 9 of the UCC, a guarantor or other secondary obligor that is subrogated to the rights of a secured party acquires the rights and becomes obligated to perform the duties of the secured party.[195]

It is common for guaranties to contain a provision postponing the rights of reimbursement and subrogation until the creditor has been paid in full.

As discussed in § 1.2.4 above, the Washington Supreme Court has held that a ground lessor that "subordinates" its fee interest in real estate to a mortgage or deed of trust securing a loan to improve the property obtained by a ground lessee (i.e., by signing the mortgage or deed of trust and encumbering its interest in the property) benefits directly from the loan and is, therefore, not a guarantor or surety with respect to either the lender or the ground lessee.[196] As a result, the lessor may not be entitled to a guarantor's common law rights of reimbursement, subrogation, etc. and, if appropriate, should consider seeking similar rights by contract.

10.2 Contribution

The right of contribution (i.e., the right of a surety who pays the creditor to recover a portion of the amount paid from other sureties who are equally liable for the same debt) is a purely equitable right unless the parties specifically agree to contribution by contract.[197] Where a surety voluntarily pays the debt of another in a situation where it did not have an enforceable legal obligation to pay that debt, the paying surety cannot obtain contribution from other sureties.[198]

Where multiple owners of a corporation or other entity guarantee the entity's debt, they should seriously consider entering into a contribution agreement providing for how they will share the liability on the guaranty among themselves if they are called upon to pay it. In the absence of such an agreement, the guarantors are liable for contribution among themselves on an equal per capita basis and not pro rata according to their ownership interests in the entity.[199] That is often not the result the guarantors would expect or want.

Guarantors and other cosureties may also want a contribution agreement in order to provide that they are entitled to contribution rights even if one of them settles with the creditor for an amount less than the settling party's full contributive share of the entire debt or in other situations where the payor

194. McAllister v. Pier 67, Inc., 1 Wash. App. 978, 985-86, 465 P.2d 678 (1970). *See also* The Revocable Living Trust of Harold G. Strand v. Wel-Co Group, Inc., 120 Wash. App. 828, 838, 86 P.3d 818 (2004) ("The right of subrogation attaches, however, only *after* the surety has satisfied the underlying debt. Restatement Third § 27(1)").

195. RCW 62A.9A-318.

196. *Honey v. Davis, supra.* The case has very interesting concurring and dissenting opinions, which highlight the uncertainties of the law on reimbursement and subrogation and the desirability of the parties entering into an agreement about their rights among themselves where one of them pays the common obligation.

197. Carpenter v. Remtech, Inc., 154 Wash. App 619, 623, 226 P.3d 159 (2010).

198. Lindblom v. Johnston, 92 Wash. 171, 177, 158 P. 972 (1916).

199. Brill v. Swanson, 36 Wash. App. 396, 674 P.2d 211 (1984); Brooke v. Boyd, 80 Wash. 213, 141 P. 357 (1914). *See also* Sound Built Homes, Inc. v. Windermere Real Estate/South, Inc., 118 Wash. App. 617, 634, 72 P.3d 788 (2003) and cases cited therein.

might not be entitled to contribution under traditional equitable principles.[200] Such contribution agreements should also address the mechanics of enforcement of contribution obligations, the effect of the insolvency of one or more of the guarantors, the rate of interest on contribution obligations and whether the guarantor enforcing the contribution obligations is entitled to recover attorneys' fees and other costs.[201] Absent such an agreement, the guarantor seeking contribution is entitled to interest at the legal rate and is not entitled to recover attorneys' fees and costs.[202]

A party who signs a promissory note as an accommodation party is not liable for contribution to an accommodated party who pays the note.[203]

A guarantor who takes an assignment of the primary obligation from the creditor after paying on its guaranty still has only a right of contribution from other guarantors and does not elevate its rights to the level of those of the original creditor.[204] Further, Article 9 of the UCC imposes certain duties on guarantors and other secondary obligors who receive an assignment of a secured obligation, or a transfer of collateral, from the secured party.[205]

The statute of limitations on a right of contribution is the six-year statute applicable to written contracts because it is an implied agreement arising out of a written instrument.[206]

A right of contribution is assignable.[207]

§ 11 Reliance

Under Washington law, reliance is not a requisite to enforcement of a guaranty.

§ 12 Subrogation

See § 10.1 above.

§ 13 Triangular Set-off in Bankruptcy

There is no Washington law on this subject.

---

200. *See, e.g.*, discussion of *Honey v. Davis* in §§1.2.4 and 10.1, *supra*. *See also* Lestorti v. DeLeo, 4 A.3d 269 (Conn. 2010) where the court denied the paying surety's contribution claim because the amount paid was less than the payor's full contributive share even though the other sureties escaped liability to the creditor.
201. *See* Hulse, *Contribution Agreements Among Guarantors*, The Practical Real Estate Lawyer (January 2009).
202. Appleford v. Snake River Mining, Milling & Smelting Co., 122 Wash. 11, 210 P. 26 (1922).
203. Hendel v. Medley, 66 Wash. App. 896, 833 P.2d 448 (1992).
204. Pioneer Mining & Ditch Co. v. Davidson, 111 Wash. 262, 267-68, 190 P. 242 (1920).
205. RCW 62A.9A-618.
206. *Id.* at 111 Wash. 270; Lindblom v. Johnston, 92 Wash. 171, 174, 158 P. 972 (1916); Caldwell v. Hurley, 41 Wash. 296, 83 P. 318 (1906) (the rule is based on the unusual language in the statute of limitation now codified at RCW 4.16.040(1) relating to "liability express or *implied* arising out of a written agreement" [emphasis added]).
207. *Id.* at 111 Wash. 271.

§ 14 Reimbursement or Indemnification

See § 10.1 above.

§ 15 Enforcement of Guaranties and Limitations Thereon

15.1 Fraudulent Transfer Issues

Washington has adopted the Uniform Fraudulent Transfer Act.[208] In most, but not all, cases, an action to avoid a fraudulent transfer must be brought within four years of the date the relevant transfer is made or obligation is incurred.[209] Washington does not appear to have any case law specifically dealing with situations in which a guaranty has been challenged as a fraudulent transfer.

15.2 Enforcement of Guaranties of Payment versus Guaranties of Performance

See § 6.2 above.

15.3 Death of Guarantor

When a guarantor dies while his or her guaranty remains in effect, in order to have a claim allowed in the probate estate, the creditor generally must file a claim in the probate within four months after the first publication of the notice to creditors.[210] This rule applies even if the guaranty obligation remains contingent at the time of death because the primary obligor has not defaulted.[211] When such a contingent claim is made, it is possible for the probate court to delay the distribution of the estate until appropriate provision is made for the contingent guaranty obligation.[212]

15.4 One-action and AntideficiencyLaws Re Real Property Security

Washington's real property security laws have both so-called "one-action" rules and antideficiency rules.

---

208. Codified at RCW chapter 19.40.
209. RCW 19.40.091.
210. Hines Reit Seattle Design Center, LLC v. Wolf (Estate of Earls), 164 Wash. App. 447, 262 P.3d 832 (2011).
211. *Id.*
212. Andrews v. Kelleher, 124 Wash. 517, 523, 214 P. 1056 (1923).

15.4.1 One-action Rules

Washington's one-action rule is set forth primarily in RCW 61.12.120, which prohibits *judicial* foreclosure of a mortgage or deed of trust while any other action for the same debt is pending or is being executed upon and in RCW 61.24.030(4), which states that one of the prerequisites to exercise of the trustee's power of *nonjudicial* sale under a deed of trust is that:

> . . . no action commenced by the beneficiary of the deed of trust is now pending to seek satisfaction of an obligation secured by the deed of trust in any court by reason of the grantor's default on the obligation secured: PROVIDED, That (a) the seeking of the appointment of a receiver shall not constitute an action for purposes of this chapter; and (b) if a receiver is appointed, the grantor shall be entitled to any rents or profits derived from property subject to a homestead as defined in RCW 6.13.010. If the deed of trust was granted to secure a commercial loan, this subsection shall not apply to actions brought to enforce any other lien or security interest granted to secure the obligation secured by the deed of trust being foreclosed....

It can be argued that, although RCW 61.24.030(4) prohibits the beneficiary of a deed of trust from foreclosing nonjudicially while an action is pending on "an obligation secured by the deed of trust," it does not literally preclude a nonjudicial foreclosure while an action is pending on a guaranty if the guaranty is not secured by the deed of trust. There is no case law on this point although there are Washington cases holding that a borrower's obligation on a loan and the guarantor's obligation on a guaranty of that loan are considered to be separate and distinct obligations.[213]

The Washington Supreme Court has stated in dicta that a judicial foreclosure is permissible after completion of a suit on the note secured by a mortgage or deed of trust and does not violate the one-action rule.[214] If the lender first sues on the note and obtains a judgment, "there may be no levy upon the other real or personal property of the mortgage debtor after initiation of a foreclosure action unless the judgment remains unsatisfied after applying thereon the proceeds of the sale of the mortgaged property."[215] The same procedure is permitted in the nonjudicial foreclosure context.[216] Similarly, "a creditor may pursue a guarantor directly without first proceeding against the security for the debt."[217]

15.4.2 Antideficiency Rules

The antideficiency rule applicable to nonjudicial deed of trust foreclosures is set forth in RCW 61.24.100, which provides in pertinent part:

---

213. *See* Freestone Capital Partners L.P. v. MKA Real Estate Opportunity Fund, 155 Wash. App. 643, 660-61, 230 P.3d 625 (2010) and cases cited therein.
214. American Federal Savings & Loan Ass'n of Tacoma v. McCaffrey, 107 Wash. 2d 181, 189, 728 P.2d 155 (1986).
215. *Id.* at 107 Wash. 2d 192. Accord Hanna v. Kasson, 26 Wash. 568, 571-72, 67 P. 271 (1901).
216. RCW 61.24.100(2); Boeing Employees' Credit Union v. Burns, 167 Wash. App. 265, 272 P.3d 908 (2012).
217. Freestone Capital Partners L.P. v. MKA Real Estate Opportunity Fund I, LLC, 155 Wash. App. 643, 664, 230 P.3d 625 (2010); Warren v. Washington Trust Bank, 92 Wash. 2d 381, 390 n.1, 598 P.2d 701 (1979).

> Except to the extent permitted in this section for deeds of trust securing commercial loans ["commercial loan" is defined in RCW 61.24.005(7) to mean a loan that "is not made primarily for personal, family or household purposes"] a deficiency judgment shall not be obtained on the obligations secured by a deed of trust against any borrower, grantor, or guarantor after a trustee's sale under that deed of trust.

Several rather complex exceptions to the antideficiency rule are set forth in the deed of trust act, which was amended substantially in 1998 to add the exceptions.[218] Most of them apply only to deeds of trust securing commercial loans. The statute does not explicitly address the situation where the deed of trust secures both commercial and noncommercial loans and there is no reported case law dealing with that situation.

One of the exceptions is that an action for a deficiency judgment against a guarantor may be obtained after certain nonjudicial foreclosures. Any action under this provision must be brought within one year after the date of the trustee's sale under the deed of trust (or in the case of multiple trustees' sales under deeds of trust securing the same obligation, the latest of those sales).[219] The one-year period is tolled by the period of any relevant stay in bankruptcy or other insolvency proceedings.[220] The exception for deficiency judgments against guarantors applies only to deeds of trust securing commercial loans and it includes some important limitations on the right to a deficiency judgment against a guarantor:

Fair value limitation. The guarantor has the right to have the court or other adjudicator determine the "fair value" (as defined in RCW 61.24.100(5)) of the property (and of any other previously sold collateral securing the same debt) and to have the deficiency calculated on the basis of the greater of that fair value or the amount bid at the trustee's sale. The statute does not require the guarantor to establish that there were unusual economic conditions at the time of the sale or peculiarities of the mortgaged property as would be the case with a party asking the court to establish an upset price in a judicial foreclosure.[221] The statute provides that this fair value hearing is "in lieu of any right any guarantor would otherwise have to establish an upset price pursuant to RCW 61.12.060 prior to a trustee's sale."[222] That is a rather strange provision because RCW 61.12.060 clearly applies only in a judicial foreclosure.

Secured guaranties. A deficiency judgment is *not* available against a guarantor that is the grantor of a deed of trust to secure the guaranty after the foreclosure of *that* deed of trust except to the extent of any waste or "wrongful retention of any rents, insurance proceeds, or condemnation awards by the borrower or grantor, respectively, that are otherwise owed to the beneficiary" of the deed of trust and then only if the beneficiary or its affiliate buys at the trustee's sale and certain other requirements are met.[223] It appears that such

218. RCW 61.24.100.
219. RCW 61.24.100(4).
220. *Id.*
221. *See* American Federal Savings & Loan Ass'n of Tacoma v. McCaffrey, 107 Wash. 2d 181, 187-88, 728 P.2d 155 (1986).
222. RCW 61.24.100(5).
223. RCW 61.24.100(6).

a guarantor would be subject to a deficiency judgment after nonjudicial foreclosure of a separate deed of trust executed by the borrower, but providing that it secures the guaranty as well as the borrower's note, if no deed of trust executed by the guarantor is foreclosed. The wording of the statute is also open to the interpretation that, if a deed of trust on a guarantor's property states that it secures the borrower's promissory note and does not state that it secures the guaranty, the guarantor may be exposed to a deficiency judgment after a nonjudicial foreclosure of a deed of trust on the guarantor's property. However, there is no case law addressing this argument. Also, in such a case, the lender's ability to obtain a deficiency judgment against the borrower may be impaired by RCW 61.24.100(1).

Homestead right re guaranties secured by principal residence. If the guaranty is secured by a deed of trust on the guarantor's principal residence, the guarantor is entitled to be paid an amount equal to the homestead exemption provided for in RCW 6.13.030 "from the bid at the foreclosure sale."[224] How this provision would be applied in the case of a credit bid by the foreclosing creditor is not specified in the statute and has not been determined by case law. This right to receive the homestead amount should not apply in a judicial foreclosure.[225] However, note the reference to a bid accepted by the sheriff in RCW 61.24.100(6). Presumably, this is an error in the drafting of subsection (6) because the sheriff accepts bids only in a judicial foreclosure.

Notices to guarantor. The right to obtain a deficiency judgment against a guarantor after a nonjudicial foreclosure, in the cases where it is allowed by the statute, is conditioned on the guarantor having been given certain statutorily prescribed notices.[226]

Guarantors' reimbursement and contribution rights. The deed of trust statute does not impair the right of a guarantor against which a deficiency judgment has been obtained from enforcing any right of reimbursement that guarantor may have against the borrower.[227] This provision is applicable to deeds of trust securing noncommercial loans as well as commercial loans. The statute does not address contribution rights among coguarantors nor does it address the question of whether the lender can take a security interest in the guarantor's reimbursement rights and then enforce them against the borrower.

Unsecured obligations. "A trustee's sale under a deed of trust securing a commercial loan does not preclude an action to collect or enforce any

224. RCW 61.24.100(6). This homestead exemption applies in the limited circumstance described even though the homestead exemption generally cannot be claimed ahead of the lien of a secured creditor holding a deed of trust, mortgage, or security agreement on the homestead property (whether a first lien or a junior lien). RCW 6.13.080(2) (exemption does not apply in judicial foreclosure of mortgage or deed of trust); Felton v. Citizens Federal Savings and Loan Ass'n of Seattle, 101 Wash. 2d 416, 679 P.2d 928 (1984) (exemption does not apply in nonjudicial foreclosure of deed of trust on the theory that a nonjudicial trustee's sale is not an "execution or forced sale" within the meaning of RCW 6.13.070 because it is consented to in the deed of trust); Household Finance Industrial Loan Company v. Upton, 102 Wash. App. 220, 6 P.3d 1231 (2000) (dealing with junior lien deeds of trust). *See also* Wells Fargo Bank, N.A. v. Brown, 161 Wash. App. 412, 418-19, 250 P.3d 134 (2011).
225. RCW 61.24.100(8).
226. RCW 61.24.042.
227. RCW 61.24.100(11).

obligation of a borrower or guarantor if that obligation, or the substantial equivalent of that obligation, was not secured by the deed of trust."[228]

§ 16 Revival and Reinstatement of Guaranties

Washington does not appear to have any law specific to the reinstatement of guaranties (for example, in the situation where a guaranty has been discharged by payment in full, but where the payment is later avoided as a preference in bankruptcy and recovered from the creditor); however, there is no reason to believe that Washington would not follow the general rule that the guaranty obligation would be revived in such a case.[229]

§ 17 Guaranties of Less than the Entire Primary Obligation

17.1 Common Types of Limited Guaranties

Guarantors often provide guaranties that are less expansive than the primary obligation. Common examples of such guaranties are (a) guaranties limited to a specified dollar amount or percentage of the primary obligation ("Partial Guaranties"); (b) guaranties of losses to the creditor arising from certain actions of the primary obligor that are prohibited by the loan documents or by law such as misapplication of rents of encumbered property, waste, etc. ("Carveout Guaranties"); (c) springing guaranties under which a loan becomes fully recourse to the guarantor if certain events occur such as a bankruptcy filing by the primary obligor or a prohibited transfer of the financed property ("Springing Guaranties"); and (d) completion guaranties by which the guarantor guarantees a construction lender that the contemplated project will be completed by a specified date, in accordance with approved plans and specifications, with all costs paid, and without liens ("Completion Guaranties"). Washington has little law specifically addressing these types of limited guaranties.

17.2 Partial Guaranties

Where a guarantor guarantees only a portion of a primary obligation, "a payment on the account would be upon the unguaranteed portion, unless specific directions were given to apply it upon such guaranty."[230]

It has been held that, where a Partial Guaranty does not specify a particular interest rate, either directly or by reference, interest on amounts owing under

228. RCW 61.24.100(10). Because of this statutory provision, it is common for certain indemnity obligations of Washington guarantors, such as environmental indemnities, to be made expressly unsecured.
229. *See, e.g.*, In re SNTL Corp., 571 F.3d 826, 835-36 (9th Cir. 2009) and cases cited therein.
230. Washington Grocery Co. v. Citizens' Bank of Anacortes, 132 Wash. 244, 247, 231 P. 780 (1925).

the guaranty will accrue at the legal rate applicable to judgments rather than at the rate applicable to the primary obligation.[231]

17.3 Completion Guaranties

Although it did not deal with a typical Completion Guaranty, one case involved a situation in which a guarantor guaranteed that "all bills for labor and materials will be paid under the terms of the contract."[232] The trial court's ruling was in the nature of a decree of specific performance in that it awarded judgment solely on the basis of the amount of the obligations the guarantor had guaranteed, but failed to pay.[233] The Supreme Court reversed on the ground that the nature of an action on a guaranty "is essentially one for damages for breach of contract" and "the measure of damages is the loss sustained by the guarantee by reason of the guarantor's breach."[234] This suggests that a typical Completion Guaranty might well not be enforced strictly according to its terms by requiring the guarantor to achieve completion of the project, but rather that the guarantor would be subject to a damages claim for the loss to the lender arising from the failure to complete the project in accordance with the contract.[235]

§ 18 Conflict of Laws—Choice of Law

As a general rule, Washington courts will honor an express contractual choice-of-law provision agreed to by the parties to a contract and apply the substantive law of the chosen jurisdiction, unless: (1) Washington law would otherwise apply, the application of the law of the chosen jurisdiction would be contrary to a fundamental policy of the State of Washington, and Washington has a materially greater interest than the chosen jurisdiction in the determination of the particular issue; or (2) the chosen jurisdiction has no substantial relationship to the parties or the transaction and there is no other reasonable basis for the parties' choice.[236] "Since 1967, Washington has followed the most significant relationship test of the *Restatement (Second) Conflict of Laws* (1971) when resolving contractual choice-of-law problems in which the parties did *not* make an express choice of law."[237]

Choice-of-law covenants apply only to substantive law and do not extend to procedural matters. In the absence of a contrary intent, a contractual

231. Seattle First Nat'l Bank v. West Coast Rubber Inc., 41 Wash. App. 604, 608-09, 705 P.2d 800 (1985).
232. Western Construction Co. v. Austin, 3 Wash. 2d 58, 99 P.2d 932 (1940). *See also* Sherman v. Western Construction Co., 14 Wash. 2d 252, 127 P.2d 673 (1942).
233. Western Construction Company v. Austin, supra, at 3 Wash. 2d 60.
234. *Id.*
235. The sparse authority from other jurisdictions on the subject of completion guaranties supports this interpretation. *See* Glendale Federal Savings and Loan Ass'n v. Marina View Heights Development Co., Inc., 66 Cal. App. 3d 101, 135 Cal. Rptr. 802, 814-16 (1977); 1633 Associates v. Uris Buildings Corp., 66 A.D.2d 237, 414 N.Y.S.2d 125, 128 (1979).
236. McKee v. AT&T Corp., 164 Wash. 2d 372, 384, 191 P.3d 845 (2008). Accord Schnall v. AT&T Wireless Services, Inc., 168 Wash. 2d 125, 130-31, 225 P.3d 929 (2010).
237. Erwin v. Cotter Health Centers, 161 Wash. 2d 676, 693, 167 P.3d 1112 (2007).

choice-of-law clause refers only to the local law of a state and not to its conflict-of-laws rules.[238]

Washington has little law specifically addressing the effect of bifurcated governing law situations where, for example, a loan agreement and promissory note are governed by New York law and a deed of trust on a Washington property securing the loan is governed by Washington law. However, in one case, the court held that a promissory note and a guaranty of that note may be governed by the laws of different states.[239] In that case, the guaranty was contained in the same document as the note and the note contained a choice-of-law provision, but the guaranty section of the document did not. Thus, the parties should not assume that the chosen law specified in the loan documents executed by the primary obligor will also apply to the guaranty and should expressly include a choice-of-law clause in the guaranty.

---

238. McGill v. Hill, 31 Wash. App. 542, 547-48, 644 P.2d 680 (1982).
239. Freestone Capital Partners L.P. v. MKA Real Estate Opportunity Fund I, LLC, 155 Wash. App. 643, 230 P.3d 625 (2010).

West Virginia State Law of Guaranties

Charles D. Dunbar
R. Grady Ford
Jackson Kelly PLLC
500 Lee Street, East
Suite 1600
P. O. Box 553
Charleston, WV 25322
Phone: (304) 340-1196
Fax: (304) 340-1080
E-Mail: cdunbar@jacksonkelly.com
Firm Web Site: www.jacksonkelly.com

Contents

West Virginia State Law of Guaranties

HIGHLIGHTS:

At the outset, we note that as a small jurisdiction without an intermediate appellate court, West Virginia lacks case law on certain issues, including certain areas of law related to guaranties. However, West Virginia courts often look to the *Restatements,* including the *Restatement of Suretyship* and *Guaranty*, for guidance in filling gaps in authority.[1]

Introductory Note: In order to standardize our discussion of the law of guaranties, we use the following vocabulary to refer to the various parties to a guaranty and their obligations. However, West Virginia courts often look to the Restatements, including the *Restatement of Suretyship and Guaranty*, for guidance.[2]

"Guarantor" means a person who, by contract, agrees to satisfy an underlying obligation of another (typically the payment of money but sometimes performance of some other obligation) to an obligee upon the primary obligor's default on that underlying obligation. While an in-depth discussion of the distinction between guarantors and sureties is beyond the scope of this article, a distinction exists in West Virginia, but that distinction is sometimes muddled.[3]

"Guaranty" means the contract by which the guarantor agrees to satisfy the underlying obligation of a primary obligor to an obligee in the event the primary obligor defaults on the underlying obligation.

"Obligee" means the person to whom the underlying obligation is owed. For example, the lender under a loan agreement would be an obligee vis-à-vis the borrower.

"Primary Obligor" means the person who incurs the underlying obligation to the obligee. For example, the borrower under a loan agreement would be a primary obligor.

"Underlying Obligation" means the obligation or obligations incurred by the primary obligor and owed to the obligee. For example, the borrower's obligation to make payments to a lender of principal and interest on a loan constitutes an underlying obligation.

---

1. *See, e.g.*, Lowe v. Albertazzie, 516 S.E.2d 258 (W. Va. 1999) (citing the Restatement of Suretyship and Guarantee extensively).
2. *Id.*
3. "A guaranty is [often] distinguished from suretyship, it being a collateral and secondary obligation, while the latter is a primary obligation." Michie's Jur. *Guaranty* § 4 (2010). Nevertheless, the distinction is not always emphasized. *See, e.g.*, Henderson v. Kessel, 116 S.E.68 (W. Va. 1923); *see also* Restatement (Third) of Suretyship & Guar. § 1 cmt. c (1996). The West Virginia Uniform Commercial Code provides that the term "surety" includes the term guarantor. W. Va. Code § 46-1-201(40) (2011).

§ 1 Nature of the Guaranty Arrangement

In West Virginia, a guaranty involves three distinct, yet interrelated, obligations: the underlying obligation between the principal obligor and the obligee, the guaranty between the guarantor and the obligee, and the surety between the principal obligor and the guarantor.

1.1 Guaranty Relationships

A contract of guaranty is "collateral and secondary" under which the guarantor has an obligation to pay only upon default by the primary obligor.[4] The relationship between the primary obligor and the guarantor arises as a matter of law, and it is based in the notion that, while the guarantor is liable to the obligee, it is the principal obligor who ultimately should bear the underlying obligation.[5]

In West Virginia, no "technical words" are needed to create a guaranty obligation; rather, a court will look to substance over form and whether there exists intent to bind a party in the capacity of a guarantor.[6]

1.2 Suretyship Relationships

While not the focus of this survey, we note that a suretyship relationship arises where a guarantor party agrees to be primarily liable in the event of default of the principal obligor. The principal distinction between a guaranty and suretyship is that a guarantor is obliged to pay only in the event of the inability of the principal obligor to pay, but a surety is obliged to pay in the event of default as if he or she was the sole debtor.[7]

§ 2 State Law Requirements for an Entity to Enter a Guaranty

Limited liability companies and corporations can grant guaranties that are necessary or convenient to carrying out their business and affairs. Such grants are permitted by the appropriate West Virginia statute. While no statute expressly authorizes partnerships to grant guaranties, it is likely that they can. Under West Virginia law, banks are not permitted to enter into contracts of guaranty.

---

4. Middle States Loan, Bldg., & Const. Co v. Engle, Syl. Pt. 1, 31 S.E. 921 (W. Va. 1898).
5. RESTATEMENT (THIRD) OF SURETYSHIP & GUAR. § 1 cmt. b (1996); *see also* MICHIE'S JUR. *Guaranty* § 4 (2010).
6. Scyoc v. Holmes, 450 S.E.2d 784, 787 (W.Va. 1994); *see also* MICHIE'S JUR. *Guaranty* § 10 (2010).
7. *See* MICHIE'S JUR. *Guaranty* § 4 (2010).

2.1 Corporations

Under the West Virginia Business Corporation Act, a corporation may, within the scope of its general corporate powers, give a guaranty necessary or convenient to carrying out its business and affairs, Unless its articles of incorporation and bylaws provide otherwise.[8]

Unlike Delaware corporate law, which explicitly presumes corporate guaranties granted within affiliate relationships are in the course of business, West Virginia corporate law is silent on the issue of inter-corporate guaranties.[9] Nevertheless, such power is likely implicit in the power to make guaranties "necessary or convenient to carry out its business and affairs."[10]

2.2 Partnerships

West Virginia's partnership statute neither expressly empowers a partnership to issue a guaranty nor expressly regulates or prohibits such activity, but unless expressly prohibited by the partnership agreement, it is likely a partnership may issue a guaranty. [11]

2.3 Limited Liability Companies

West Virginia's limited liability company statute permits limited liability companies to issue guaranties, unless the articles of organization provide otherwise.[12] The law permits these guaranties so long as they are necessary or convenient to carrying on the company's business or affairs.[13]

2.4 Banks

Under West Virginia's banking law, no West Virginia banking institution "shall become surety or guarantor of any person for the discharge of any duty in any position or the performance of any contract or undertaking."[14]

2.5 Individuals

Any individual competent to enter into a contract may issue a guaranty. This requires mental competence,[15] and sufficient age.[16] As in most other states, the age of majority in West Virginia is 18 years.[17]

---

8. W.VA. CODE § 31D-3-302(7) (2011).
9. *See* DEL. CODE ANN. tit. 8 § 122(13) (LexisNexis 2011).
10. W.VA. CODE § 31D-3-302(7) (2011).
11. *See generally* W.VA. CODE § 47B-1-1, et seq. (2011).
12. W.Va. Code § 31B-1-113(b)(5) (2011).
13. *Id.*
14. W.Va. Code § 31A-8-13 (2011).
15. *See* Bade v. Feay, 63 W.Va. 166, 61 S.E. 348, 350 (1907).
16. *See* Hobbs v. Hinton Foundry Machine & Plumbing Co., 74 W.Va. 443, 82 S.E. 267, 269 (1914) (noting contracts of minors are voidable, not void).
17. W.Va. Code § 2-3-1 (2011).

In some instances, corporate officers or directors signing guaranties can be held personally bound. A case-by-case inquiry determines whether an individual intended to be personally bound or, instead, only issued a guaranty on behalf of a partnership or corporation and thus only in an official employment capacity.[18] When an individual signs his title as well as his name, this is not dispositive proof of an intention not to issue a personal guaranty.[19]

West Virginia case law has not yet considered the effect on marital property of a guaranty issued by only one spouse.

§ 3 Signatory's Authority to Execute a Guaranty

Generally, the obligee has a duty of reasonable inquiry when it has some notice that the executor of the guaranty does not have authority to bind the guarantor.

3.1 Corporations

The general principles of agency law apply to private corporations and their officers.[20] For an obligee to rely on a guaranty, the guaranty must be signed by an officer with actual or apparent authority to act in such capacity.[21] Where an obligee-plaintiff invokes the doctrine of apparent authority, that obligee must demonstrate that it acted in good faith and exercised reasonable prudence.[22]

3.2 Partnerships

West Virginia's partnership law grants a partner the authority to bind the partnership when such partner's act is "for apparently carrying on in the ordinary course the partnership business or business of the kind carried on by the partnership," unless such authority has been explicitly held back in the partnership agreement.[23] If a partner's action is not "apparently for carrying on in the ordinary course the partnership business or business of the kind carried on by the partnership" it binds the partnership only if the act was authorized by the other partners.[24]

3.3 Limited Liability Companies

West Virginia limited liability company (LLC) law provides that, in the case of a member-managed LLC, every member is an agent of that company and can

18. *See* Clendenin Lumber & Supply Co., Inc. v. Volpi, 365 S.E.2d 56 (W.Va. 1987).
19. *Id.*
20. Axelrod v. Premier Photo Serv., Inc., 173 S.E.2d 383, 387 (W.Va. 1970).
21. "One who deals with an individual purporting to be an agent of another is bound at his own peril to know the authority of such alleged agency." Pub. Citizen, Inc. v. First Nat. Bank, 480 S.E.2d 538, 546 (W.Va. 1996).
22. *See* John W. Lohr Funeral Home, Inc. v. Hess & Eisenhardt Co., 166 S.E.2d 141, 148 (W.Va. 1969).
23. W.VA. CODE § 47B-3-1 (2011).
24. *Id.*

sign instruments pursuant to carrying on in the usual way of business unless that person has no actual authority to act in such way and his counterparty knows as much.[25] In the case of a manager-managed LLC, no member has authority to bind the LLC to a guaranty unless authority has been granted to the member by the manager or managers of the LLC or by operating agreement of the LLC. Each manager of a manager-managed LLC can bind the LLC if such guaranty is "for apparently carrying on in the ordinary course the company's business or business of the kind carried on by the company" unless the manager has no actual authority and the counterparty knows of this lack of authority.[26]

§ 4 Necessity of Writing

A guaranty must be in writing because it is required by the statute of frauds.[27]

§ 5 Consideration; Sufficiency of Past Consideration

Standard contract principles apply to the analysis of consideration for a contract of guaranty. The principal agreement is sufficient consideration for an accompanying guaranty.

A guaranty must be supported by adequate consideration.[28] The inquiry into sufficient consideration is based on standard contract law principles. The benefit or obligation that forms the consideration need not flow directly to the guarantor from the obligee; the consideration flowing from the obligee to the principal obligor is sufficient to support a contemporaneous guaranty.[29]

§ 6 Notice of Acceptance

Notice of acceptance may not be required, if credit is extended to the primary obligor based upon the guaranty.

It is essential that the obligee "accept the guarantee, but the acceptance need not be express."[30] Notice of acceptance is generally unnecessary where credit is advanced on the strength of the guaranty.[31]

25. W.VA. CODE § 31B-3-301(a) (2011).
26. *Id.* § 301(b).
27. W.VA. CODE § 55-1-1(d).
28. Scyoc v. Holmes, 450 S.E.2d 784, 786 (W.Va. 1994).
29. Pitrolo v. Cmty. Bank & Trust, Syl. Pt. 1, 298 S.E.2d 853 (W.Va. 1982).
30. MICHIE'S JUR. *Guaranty* § 8 (2010).
31. *See* Davis v. Wells, 104 U.S. 159, 163 (1881).

§ 7 Interpretation of Guaranties

Courts in West Virginia interpret a guaranty in the same manner they do any other contract. In the application of the guaranty, however, courts are typically guided by the principle of *strictissimi juris*, strictly construing the obligations of the guarantor.

7.1 General Principles

The principle of *strictissimi juris* guides the application of contracts of guaranty, not the construction thereof.[32] Outside of this principle, the same principles of construction that apply to contracts generally apply to guaranties.[33]

7.2 Guaranty of Payment (absolute guaranty) versus Guaranty of Collection (conditional and collateral guaranty)

In the case of a guaranty of payment or absolute guaranty (sometimes referred to as a suretyship), the guarantor promises to satisfy the underlying obligation to the obligee upon default by the primary obligor, which satisfaction is not conditioned upon the obligee's prior attempt to secure satisfaction from the primary obligor.[34]

On the other hand, a guaranty of collection or conditional guaranty merely promises to satisfy the underlying obligation in the event that all attempts to obtain payment from the primary obligor prove unsuccessful.[35]

A court will look to the intent of the parties as expressed in the guaranty to determine whether it is one of payment or one of collection.[36]

7.3 "Continuing" Guaranties

A continuing guaranty is one that looks to future transactions.[37] For example, where a guarantor guarantees payment on all goods sold to the primary obligor until the guaranty is revoked, the guaranty is plainly a continuing guaranty. While the use of the word "continuing" helps to make clear that a guaranty is meant to be continuing,[38] courts in West Virginia have interpreted a guaranty as continuing even where the word "continuing" has not been used.[39]

32. L. Schreiber & Sons Co, v. Miller Supply Co., Syl. Pts. 1-2, 87 S.E. 236 (W.Va. 1915).
33. *Id.*
34. Esso Standard Oil Co. v. Kelly, 112 S.E.2d 461, 464 (W.Va. 1960).
35. *Id.*
36. *Id.*
37. Restatement (Third) of Suretyship and Guaranty § 16.
38. *See generally* Loverin & Browne Co. v. Bumgarner, 52 S.E. 1000 (W.Va. 1906).
39. *Id.*

§ 8 Defenses of the Guarantor; Set-off

A guarantor can defend an action of the principal guarantor primarily in two ways: (1) compelling suit against the primary obligor and (2) demonstrating modification of the underlying obligation/discharge of primary obligee without the guarantor's consent.

8.1 Forcing Action against Primary Obligor

A guarantor may, by notice in writing, require the obligee to sue the primary obligor when action has accrued. If the obligee does not sue within a reasonable time and the obligor is not insolvent, the guarantor is discharged.[40]

8.2 Modification of Underlying Obligation/Discharge of Primary Obligee

If an obligee releases or impairs security for primary obligation or extends the time of payment for the principal obligee without the consent of the guarantor, then the guarantor's obligation can be discharged to the extent he was harmed as a result.[41]

Similarly, the general rule is that the discharge of the primary obligor releases the guarantor, but this rule does not apply where the primary obligee is discharged on the basis of incapacity only.[42]

8.3 Other Defenses

8.3.1 Statute of Limitations/Frauds

The statute of limitations on written contracts—all guaranties must be in writing—is 10 years.[43]

8.3.2 Obligee's failure to disclose Information/Fraud

An obligee has a duty to disclose certain facts that it is aware of about the primary obligor if (1) the obligee has reason to believe that certain facts increase the guarantor's risk; (2) the obligee has reason to believe guarantor does not know said facts; and (3) the obligee has a reasonable opportunity to communicate said facts to the guarantor. Failure of the obligee to disclose such material facts to the guarantor can result in the court's refusal to enforce the guaranty.[44]

---

40. W.VA. CODE § 45-1-1, 2 (2011).
41. Gregoire v. Lowndes Bank, 342 S.E.2d 264, 267-68 (W.Va. 1986).
42. Burner v. Nutter, 87 S.E. 359, 360-61 (W.Va. 1915).
43. W.VA. CODE § 55-2-6 (2011).
44. Logan Bank & Trust Co. v. Letter Shop, Inc., Syl. Pt. 3 427 S.E.2d 271 (W.Va. 1993).

8.4 Right of Set-off

West Virginia courts generally recognize the right of set-off, but have not considered the issue in a guaranty-specific setting.[45]

§ 9 Waiver of Defenses by the Guarantor

West Virginia courts have not been called upon to consider whether waivers of certain defenses of guarantors are enforceable.

§ 10 Third-party Pledgors

Because the pledgor arguably stands in the relation of a guarantor to the principal obligor to the extent of the pledge, it may most likely avail of the defenses of a guarantor.

We have found no evidence that the law as applied to sureties would not apply to a third-party pledge. In contrast, the law appears to be that a pledge of collateral results in a surety relationship. It would seem logical, given this state of the law, that the pledgor generally has the same defenses available to it as are available to a surety.

§ 11 Jointly and Severally Liable Guarantors—Contribution and Reduction of Obligations upon Payment by a Co-obligor

Guarantors are generally presumed to share the secondary obligation equally, but West Virginia recognizes subsuretyships. The creditor is not obliged to seek full payment from more than one such guarantor.

Coguarantors are liable jointly and severally, and there is a presumption that they bear the burden equally.[46] Parties may vary this principal by agreement, which can be either express or implied.[47]

When a judgment is obtained on the contract in which a party was a coguarantor, that guarantor may obtain a judgment, by motion, against the coguarantor for its share.[48]

45. *See generally* Nichols v. Nichols, 391 S.E.2d 623 (W.Va. 1990).
46. *See generally* Lowe v. Albertazzie, 516 S.E.2d 258 (W.Va. 1999).
47. Lowe v. Albertazzie, 516 S.E.2d 258, 266-67 (W.Va. 1999).
48. W.Va. Code § 45-1-6 (2011).

§ 12 Reliance

Reliance is probably not required to claim under a guaranty.

In West Virginia, guaranties are governed by the rules generally applicable to contracts. See § 7. Presumably, then, reliance is not requisite to enforce a guaranty. Nevertheless, West Virginia courts have stated that, to bind a guarantor, "it must appear that he was notified of the acceptance of the guaranty and of the reliance upon it, this sufficiently appears where it is shown that he expected and understood that the person guaranteed would continue to render services after the guaranty according to its terms."[49]

§ 13 Subrogation

If a guarantor pays a judgment upon a guaranty, the guarantor may, by motion, obtain a judgment against the primary obligee for the amount paid, plus interest.[50]

§ 14 Triangular Set-off in Bankruptcy

West Virginia courts have not considered this issue.

§ 15 Indemnification—Whether the Primary Obligor has a Duty

The principal obligor generally has an implied duty of indemnification. The extent of this duty can be altered by contract.

West Virginia has very limited case law on point but "equity generally implies a right of indemnification in favor of a surety only when the surety pays off a debt for which his principal is liable."[51] However, where an express indemnity provision exists, it controls.[52]

49. Cooper v. Chaffee, Syl. Pt. 4, 130 S.E. 472 (W.Va. 1925).
50. W.VA. CODE § 45-1-4 (2011).
51. Fidelity and Deposit Co. v. Bristol Steel & Iron Works, Inc., 722 F.2d 1160, 1163 (4th Cir. 1983).
52. *Id.*

§ 16 Enforcement of Guaranties

16.1 Limitations on Recovery

Fraudulent conveyance caps on recovery under a guaranty (which prevent recovery from exceeding amounts that would render the guaranty obligations void or voidable under the Bankruptcy Code or applicable state law) may be invalid.

If the guarantors were insolvent before signing the guaranty, any liability under that guaranty might be avoidable. If the guarantors became insolvent after signing the guaranty, the clauses might be unenforceable as ipso facto clauses. Such clauses may also be seen as impermissible attempts to contract around the fraudulent transfer statute of the Bankruptcy Code.[53]

16.2 Pleading Requirements

In an action to enforce the guaranty of one person to pay the debt of another, the plaintiff must plead a count or counts setting forth the supporting consideration.[54] The count or counts must also allege that the primary obligor is in default and has not paid the debt.[55]

16.3 Litigating Guaranty claims; Procedural considerations

Contracts of guaranty are governed by the law where the last act necessary to make them takes place, sometimes even in the face of a contrary choice of law provision.[56] Generally, the last act necessary to make a contract of guaranty binding is the loan of money under the terms of the underlying obligation.[57] West Virginia courts will not enforce a choice of law provision in a contract of guaranty when the guaranty bears no substantial relationship with the jurisdiction whose laws the parties have chosen to govern the agreement, or where the application of that law would offend the public policy of the state.[58]

§ 17 Revival and Reinstatement of Guaranties

West Virginia courts have not been called upon to address the revival or reinstatement of guaranties.

53. In re TOUSA, INC., 422 B.R. 783, 863-864 (Bankr. S.D. Fla. 2009) (applying New York law).
54. Scycoc v. Holmes, Syl. Pt. 1, 450 S.E.2d 784 (W.Va. 1994).
55. MICHIE'S JUR., *Guaranty* § 24 (2010).
56. Gen. Elec. Co. v. Keyser, 275 S.E.2d 289, 296 (W.Va. 1981).
57. *Id.*
58. *Id.*

Wisconsin Law of Guaranties

Brent A. Stork
Jeffrey M. Barrett
Michael Best & Friedrich LLP
100 East Wisconsin Avenue, Suite 3300
Milwaukee, Wisconsin 53202
Telephone: 414-271-6560
http://www.michaelbest.com

Contents

Wisconsin Law of Guaranties

HIGHLIGHTS:

Under Wisconsin law, a guarantor or a guarantor's spouse may claim certain defenses to enforcement of a guaranty against certain collateral based on the Wisconsin marital property law. To the extent the marital estate does not receive consideration, execution of a guaranty by one spouse might be treated as a gift of marital property in excess of the spouse's right to make such a gift under Wisconsin marital property law. Therefore, the guaranty drafting convention in Wisconsin is to try to include the nonguaranteeing spouse's consent to the guaranty. This means that "both spouses act together" to make the gift of any payment or recovery under the guaranty under the Wisconsin marital property law. In addition, the other guaranty drafting convention in Wisconsin is to obtain a signed family purpose statement in the guaranty which states that the guaranty is incurred in the interest of the marriage or the family.

Introductory Note: In order to standardize our discussion of the law of guaranties, we use the following vocabulary to refer to the various parties to a guaranty and their obligations.

"Guarantor" means a person who, by contract, agrees to satisfy an underlying obligation of another to an obligee upon the primary obligor's default on that underlying obligation.

"Guaranty" means the contract by which the guarantor agrees to satisfy the underlying obligation of a primary obligor to an obligee in the event the primary obligor defaults on the underlying obligation.

"Obligee" means the person to whom the underlying obligation is owed. For example, the lender under a loan agreement would be an obligee vis-à-vis the borrower.

"Primary Obligor" means the person who incurs the underlying obligation to the obligee. For example, the borrower under a loan agreement would be a primary obligor.

"Underlying Obligation" means the obligation or obligations incurred by the primary obligor and owed to the obligee. For example, the borrower's obligation to make payments to a lender of principal and interest on a loan constitutes an underlying obligation.

Introduction and Sources of Law

In Wisconsin, case law is the primary source of substantive law governing commercial guaranties. Wisconsin courts occasionally cite the Restatement (Third) of Suretyship and Guaranty (1996).1

§ 1 Nature of the Guaranty Arrangement

Under Wisconsin law, a guaranty may be one of several types: absolute or conditional, a guaranty of payment or collection, a general, special, or continuing guaranty.[2] Wisconsin law recognizes a distinction between a guarantor and a surety in that a surety is primarily liable and a guarantor is secondarily liable.[3] The focus of this survey is on Wisconsin guaranty law and not Wisconsin surety law.

Under Wisconsin law, a guaranty is a contract of secondary liability under which the guarantor has an obligation to pay upon default by the primary obligor. The relationship between the primary obligor and the guarantor arises as a matter of contract, and it is based on the notion that, while the guarantor is liable to the creditor, it is the primary obligor who ultimately should bear the underlying obligation.[4]

Under Wisconsin law, a guaranty is a contract in which the guarantor agrees to become "...responsible for the fulfillment of an agreement of another, to secure, to answer for the debt, default or miscarriage of another...".[5] Since a guaranty is a contract, no technical words are needed to create a guaranty obligation; instead, a Wisconsin court will look to substance over form and whether there exists intent to create a guaranty.[6]

§ 2 State Law requirements for an Entity to Enter into a Guaranty

Wisconsin corporations, partnerships, limited liability companies, and state banks can all grant guaranties in furtherance of their business activities. Such grants are generally permitted by the appropriate Wisconsin statute.

1. *See, e.g.*, Insurance Co. of North America v. DEC Int'l, 586 N.W.2d 691, 696 (Wis. App. 1998); Grove Holding v. First Wisconsin Nat'l Bank of Sheboygan, 12 F. Supp. 2d 885, 894 (E.D. Wis. 1998).
2. Bank of Sun Prairie v. Opstein, 273 N.W. 2d 279, 282-283 (Wis. 1979).
3. Associates Financial Services v. Eisenberg, 186 N.W.2d 272, 275 (Wis. 1971).
4. *Opstein*, 273 N.W.2d at 282.
5. Mann v. Erie Mfg. Co., 120 N.W.2d, 711, 714 (Wis. 1963).
6. DeWitt Ross & Stevens, S.C. v. Galaxy Gaming & Racing, Ltd. Partnership, 682 N.W.2d 839, 844 (Wis. 2004).

2.1 Corporations

Under the Wisconsin Business Corporation Law, a Wisconsin corporation may, within the scope of its general corporate powers, give a guaranty in furtherance of its corporate purpose, provided that its articles of incorporation or bylaws do not prevent it from doing so.[7]

However, a Wisconsin corporation may not guarantee the obligations of a director of the corporation unless any of the following occurs: (a) the guaranty is approved by a majority of the votes represented by the outstanding voting shares of all classes, voting as a single voting group, except the votes of shares owned by or voted under the control of the benefited director; or (b) the corporation's board of directors determines that the guaranty benefits the corporation and either approves the guaranty or a general plan authorizing guaranties.[8]

2.2 Partnerships

Wisconsin's Uniform Partnership Act does not expressly provide that a partnership can issue a guaranty, nor does it prohibit such activity. However, under Wisconsin law, every partner is an agent of the partnership for the purpose of its business, and the act of every partner, including the execution in the partnership name of any instrument, for apparently carrying on in the usual way the business of the partnership of which the partner is a member, binds the partnership, unless the partner so acting has in fact no authority to act for the partnership in the particular matter, and the person with whom the partner is dealing has knowledge of the fact that the partner has no such authority.[9]

2.3 Limited Liability Companies

Wisconsin's Limited Liability Company law generally permits limited liability companies to issue guaranties unless the operating agreement of a particular company provides otherwise.[10]

Under the Wisconsin Limited Liability Company law, "....the act of any member, including the execution in the name of the limited liability company of any instrument, for apparently carrying on in the ordinary course of business the business of the limited liability company binds the limited liability company unless the member has, in fact, no authority to act for the limited liability company in the particular matter, and the person with whom the member is dealing has knowledge that the member has no authority to act in the matter..."[11] Under the Wisconsin Limited Liability Company law, "...the act of any manager, including the execution in the name of the limited liability company of any instrument, for apparently carrying on in the ordinary course

7. Wisconsin Statutes § 180.0302(7) (2012).
8. Wisconsin Statutes § 180.0832 (2012).
9. Wisconsin Statutes § 178.06 (2012).
10. Wisconsin Statutes § 183.0301 (2012).
11. Wisconsin Statutes § 183.0301(1)(b) (2012).

of business the business of the limited liability company binds the limited liability company unless the manager has, in fact, no authority to act for the limited liability company in the particular matter, and the person with whom the manager is dealing has knowledge that the manager has no authority to act in the matter…"[12] However, there is no Wisconsin case law discussing guaranties under these statutory sections.

2.4 State Banks

Under Section 221.0301 of the Wisconsin banking law, a Wisconsin state-chartered bank has the power to "make contracts necessary and proper to effect its purpose and conduct its business."[13] This includes the authority, in certain limited circumstances, to guarantee obligations.[14]

Note that guaranties offered by state banks may be significantly affected by federal law. First, federal law prohibits a state-chartered bank from engaging in activities in which a national bank may not engage under federal law. The situations under which a national bank may become a guarantor are governed by federal law. *See* National Bank as Guarantor or Surety on Indemnity Bond, 12 C.F.R. § 7.1017 (2010).

2.5 Individuals

Under Wisconsin law, adults, i.e. individuals who are 18 or older, have the capacity to enter into contracts, including a guaranty.[15]

Section 7.3.3 of this survey discusses the ability of married individuals to enter into a guaranty and the special provisions that should be included in a guaranty because of the provisions on the Wisconsin Marital Property Act.[16]

If an individual's guaranty is secured by a mortgage, certain other provisions related to the Wisconsin Marital Property Act will apply. Under Wisconsin's Marital Property Act, a spouse with "management and control" over property has the right to mortgage that property.[17] Management and control of property is determined by how property is "held," i.e., titled.[18] A spouse acting alone may mortgage property that is (a) that spouse's individual property, (b) marital property held in that spouse's name alone, and (c) marital property held in the names of both spouses in the alternative.[19] Marital property held in the names of both spouses other than in the alternative may be mortgaged only if both spouses act together.[20] The requirement that both spouses must sign or join in by separate conveyance any mortgage that alienates any interest of a married person in a homestead except a purchase money mortgage

12. Wisconsin Statutes § 183.0301(2)(b) (2012).
13. Wisconsin Statutes § 221.0301(1) (2012).
14. Banking Commission v. First Wisconsin Nat'l Bank of Milwaukee, 290 N.W. 735, 740 (Wis. 1940).
15. Wisconsin Statutes § 990.01(20) (2012).
16. Wis Stats. § 766 et seq. (2012).
17. Wis. Stats. § 766.01(11) (2012).
18. Wis. Stats. § 766.01(9) (2012).
19. Wis. Stats. § 766.51(1) (2012).
20. Wis. Stats. § 766.51(2) (2012).

is not affected by the management and control provisions of the Wisconsin Marital Property Act.[21]

Wisconsin law grants individuals certain exemptions in bankruptcy and with respect to judgment creditors.[22] An individual may claim as exempt real estate constituting his personal or family residence up to $75,000 or personal property up to $12,000.[23] Real estate on which an individual has voluntarily granted a mortgage lien is not exempt, to the extent of the balance due on the mortgage.

§ 3 Signatory's Authority to Execute a Guaranty

Generally, the beneficiary under a guaranty has a duty of reasonable inquiry when that beneficiary has some notice that the individual executing the guaranty does not have authority to bind the guarantor. These general contract principles apply to all forms of statutorily created entities under Wisconsin law.

For a beneficiary to rely on a guaranty, the guaranty must be signed by an officer of the corporation or other entity with actual or apparent authority to act in such capacity.[24] Under Wisconsin law, there are several cases covering the apparent authority of officers of a corporation or other entity to bind such entity with respect to contracts. These cases are all clear that the position of an officer alone does not give the holder of that office the authority to bind an entity. A possible exception to this limitation is that the president of a corporation may be held to have some inherent authority to bind a corporation, but this is not entirely clear.[25]

An individual's authority to bind an entity must arise from actual authority, apparent authority, or another method. Under Wisconsin law, "it is the well settled rule that if a principal so conducts his business as to lead the public to believe that his agent has authority to contract in the name of the principal, he is bound by the acts of such agent within the scope of his apparent authority as to contracts with persons who, acting in good faith, believe and have reasonable ground to believe that the agent has such authority."[26] Under Wisconsin law, apparent authority may be created as to a third person "by written or spoken words or any other conduct of the principal" that causes the third person to reasonably believe the agent is authorized.[27]

Under Wisconsin law, the general analysis used in determining whether an officer in question had apparent authority was whether the entity permitted the officer for any considerable length of time to act as its agent, either through a grant of general authority or the tacit consent of the entity, and

21. Wis. Stats. § 702.01(f) and Wis. Stats. § 766.51(8) (2012).
22. Wis. Stats. § 815.18, et seq. (2012).
23. Wis. Stats. § 815.20 and § 815.18(d) (2012).
24. Vulcan Last Co. v. State, 217 N.W. 412, 417 (Wis. 1928).
25. Ford v. Hill, 66 N.W. 115, 117 (Wis. 1896).
26. Sickinger v. Raymond, 190 N. W. 93, 94 (Wis. 1922); ABC Outdoor Advertising, Inc. v. Dolhun's Marine, Inc., 157 N. W. 2d 680, 683 (Wis. 1968).
27. Scheuer v. Central States Pension Fund, 358 F.Supp. 1332, 1339 (E.D. Wis. 1973).

whether the entity subsequently ratified the officer's acts.[28] If that is the case, then the Wisconsin courts have typically prevented an entity from denying the officer's authority. If, however, the officer does not have a history of acting as the entity's agent, then the question becomes a more fact-specific inquiry as to whether, due to the actions of the entity, the third party believes the officer has the authority to bind the entity and whether this belief is reasonable.

In addition, Wisconsin law is fairly clear that if an entity enjoys any of the benefits of a transaction entered into by an officer on its behalf, then the entity is later estopped from denying the authority of the officer to enter into the transaction and bind the entity.[29]

§ 4 Consideration and Sufficiency of Past Consideration

Standard contract principles apply to the analysis of consideration for a guaranty. The principal agreement is sufficient consideration for an accompanying guaranty.[30]

Consideration is required to create a valid guaranty.[31] The inquiry into sufficient consideration is based on standard contract law principles.[32] The benefit or obligation that forms the consideration need not flow directly to the guarantor from the obligee; however, the consideration flowing from the obligee to the principal obligor must be contemporaneous to the guaranty.[33] Wisconsin case law has indicated that when there is some length of time between the origination of the underlying obligation and the guaranty, this lapse in time may render such new guaranty invalid because of lack of contemporaneous consideration.[34]

§ 5 Notice of Acceptance

Under Wisconsin guaranty law, the obligee generally must notify the guarantor of its acceptance of the guaranty.[35] However, notice of acceptance of a guaranty may not be required if credit is contemporaneously extended to the primary obligor based upon the guaranty or when the guaranty is absolute.[36]

28. Lamoreux v. Oreck, 686 N.W.2d 722, 735-736 (Wis. Ct. App. 2004); Mared Industries, Inc. v. Mansfield, 690 N.W.2d 835 (2005); Pamperin v. Trinity Memorial Hospital, 423 N.W.2d 848 (1988).
29. Santarsiero v. Green Bay Transport, 24 N.W.2d 123, 126 (Wis. 1946).
30. Gritz Harvestore, Inc. v. A.O. Smith Harvestore Products, Inc., 769 F.2d 1225, 1236 (7th Cir. 1985).
31. Electric Storage Battery Co. v. Black, 134 N.W.2d 481, 484 (Wis. 1965).
32. *Id.*
33. Amato v. Creative Confections Concepts, 97 F. Supp 2d 949, 960 (E.D. Wis. 2000); Int'l Text-Book Co. v. Mabbott, 150 N.W. 429, 434 (Wis. 1915).
34. John A. Tolman & Co. v. Peterson, 175 N.W. 916, 918 (Wis. 1920); In Re Menzner's Estate, 207u N.W. 703 (Wis. 1926).
35. Electric Storage Battery Co. v. Black, 134 N.W.2d 481, 489 (Wis. 1965).
36. Chicago Lock Co. v. Kirchner, 225 N.W. 185, 187 (Wis. 1929); Fond du Lac Skyport, Inc. v. Moraine Airways, Inc., 226 N.W.2d 428, 436 (Wis. 1975).

Commonly in Wisconsin, the guarantor waives the notification of acceptance requirement in the actual guaranty agreement.

§ 6 Judicial Interpretation of a Guaranty

6.1 General Principles

Courts in Wisconsin will interpret a guaranty in the same manner by which they would interpret the language of any other contract.[37] In addition, certain terms have become words of art in the context of guaranties.

6.2 Guaranty of Payment versus Guaranty of Collection

A guarantor of payment promises to satisfy the underlying obligation to the obligee upon default by the primary obligor, which satisfaction is not conditioned upon the obligee's prior attempt to secure satisfaction from the primary obligor. A guarantor may be required to satisfy obligations to an obligee even where the obligee, because of a subordination agreement, cannot collect from the primary obligor. Under Wisconsin law, "with a guaranty of payment, a creditor is not under any legal obligation to first enforce collection from the maker or any other guarantor, or to first resort to securities given by the principal debtor. . . . Under a guaranty of payment, and not merely of collection, plaintiff was entitled to immediate recovery from the sureties, and his right to immediate recovery from them could not be postponed for their benefit until after efforts to recover by foreclosure or otherwise were exhausted."[38]

On the other hand, a guarantor of collection merely promises to satisfy the underlying obligation only after all attempts to obtain payment from the primary obligor have failed.[39]

A Wisconsin court will look to the intent of the parties as expressed in the guaranty to determine whether it is a guaranty of payment or a guaranty of collection. Commonly in Wisconsin, the guaranty agreement specifically includes a phrase stating that the guaranty is a guaranty of payment and not merely of collection.

6.3 Language Regarding the Revocation of a Guaranty

A guaranty may not be revoked with respect to transactions entered into by the primary obligor prior to the revocation.[40] Where a guaranty contains language pertaining to revocation or expiration, the language should be con-

---

37. Grove Holding Corp. v. First Wisconsin Nat'l Bank of Sheboygan, 12 F. Supp 2d 885, 894 (E.D. Wis 1998); Harris v. Metropolitan Mall, 334 N.W. 2d 519, 526 (Wis. 1983).
38. First Wisconsin Nat'l Bank of Oshkosh v. Kramer, 246 N.W.2d 536, 541 (Wis. 1976); Bank of Sun Prairie v. Opstein, 273 N.W.2d 279, 282-283 (Wis. 1979).
39. *Id.*
40. Bay State Milling Co. v. Martin, 916 F.2d 1221, 1228 (7th Cir. 1990).

sidered carefully and the procedure for revocation followed.[41] In addition, if the guaranty specifies the means by which revocation must be communicated, a noncompliant revocation may be ineffective.[42]

6.4 "Continuing"

A continuing guaranty is one that looks to future transactions.[43] While the use of the word "continuing" helps to make clear that a guaranty is meant to be continuing, courts in Wisconsin have interpreted a guaranty as continuing even where the word "continuing" has not been used.[44]

§ 7 Defenses of the Guarantor

The defenses that may be available to a guarantor can be grouped into seven categories: (1) defenses of the primary obligor; (2) other suretyship defenses; (3) statute of limitations; (4) statute of frauds; (5) defenses particular to guarantors and their spouses; (6) set-off; and (7) defenses for individual persons.

7.1 Defenses of the Primary Obligor

The general rule in Wisconsin is that the guarantor, absent an effective waiver, is not bound to perform if the primary obligor is not bound.[45] In addition, a guarantor generally may not, in many circumstances, raise defenses or counterclaims that are personal to or primarily those of the primary obligor.[46] Wisconsin law treats the liability of a guarantor as separate and distinct from the liability of the primary obligor, arising not from the underlying obligation itself but from the terms of the guaranty.[47] Therefore, if the defense is one that belongs to the primary obligor, then the primary obligor retains the capacity to choose whether to assert it.[48] For example, the insolvency of the principal obligor is not a defense that the guarantor may raise unless the guaranty is conditioned on the solvency of the primary obligor. In addition, a guarantor also may not raise the primary obligor's incapacity as a defense to liability under the guaranty. The guarantor may not raise defenses that the obligee "through negligence, or lack of due diligence, lost or dissipated the collateral furnished by the primary obligor."[49]

---

41. *But see* Home Savings Bank v. Gertenbach, 71 N.W.2d 347 (Wis. 1955).
42. *Id.*
43. Klatte v. Franklin State Bank, 248 N.W. 158 (Wis. 1933).
44. Associates Financial Services Co. v. Eisenberg, 186 N.W.2d 272 (Wis. 1971).
45. Continental Bank & Trust Co. v. Akwa, 58 Wis. 2d 376 (Wis. 1973).
46. *Id.*
47. *Id.*
48. Bank Mutual f/k/a First Northern Savings Bank v. S.J. Boyer Construction, Inc., Stephen J. Boyer and Marcy A. Boyer, 785 N.W.2d 462 (Wis. 2010).
49. United States v. Klebe Tool & Die Co., 92 N.W.2d 868 (Wis. 1958).

The Wisconsin Supreme Court recently issued an important decision that limits the rights of a guarantor with respect to certain foreclosures.[50] As background, Wisconsin law allows an obligee to shorten the redemption period on a foreclosure of commercial real estate from six months to three months if the primary obligor agreed in writing to the provisions of Section 846.103(2) of the Wisconsin Statutes.[51] In order to utilize the shortened redemption period, however, the statute requires the obligee to elect in the obligee's foreclosure complaint to waive judgment for any deficiency against "every party who is personally liable for the debt secured by the mortgage." The question before the court was whether the guarantor was "personally liable for the debts secured by the mortgage" and therefore free of the debt too. The Wisconsin Supreme Court ruled that the obligee can elect the three-month redemption period, waive the judgment for deficiency against the primary obligor, and still retain the right to obtain judgment against the guarantor for the full amount of the guaranteed debt.

That said, there are certain defenses that the guarantor may always raise, absent an enforceable waiver. A guarantor may show that the obligee failed to perform such that there is a partial or complete failure of consideration.[52] A guarantor may show that the underlying obligation has been satisfied, thus releasing the guaranty. A guarantor may argue bad faith on the part of the obligee.[53]

The *Boyer* decision did not decide several other issues. The obligee in the case argued that the guarantor was still liable under the express provisions of the guaranty and was not released based on § 846.103(2). However, the Wisconsin Supreme Court stated that it did not need to reach the issue of whether the terms of the applicable guaranty overrode the foreclosure statute since a guarantor does not fall within the foreclosure statute.[54]

7.2 Other Defenses/Suretyship Defenses

7.2.1 Modifications of the Underlying Obligation

Under Wisconsin law, modifications to the underlying obligation may permit the guarantor to raise certain defenses to liability. Under Wisconsin law, a modification of an underlying obligation loan agreement has the effect of discharging the underlying guaranty if the modification is (a) material and (b) injures the interest of the guarantor by increasing the risk to the guarantor.[55] To be material, the change must be "substantial" and not simply varied in "the least particular."[56] In order to avoid the discharge of a guaranty, an obligee must obtain the guarantor's consent to modify the underlying obligation.

---

50. Bank Mutual f/k/a First Northern Savings Bank v. S.J. Boyer Construction, Inc., Stephen J. Boyer and Marcy A. Boyer, 785 N.W.2d 462 (Wis. 2010).
51. Wisconsin Statutes § 846.103 (2012).
52. D. M. Osborne & Co. v. Bryce, 23 F. 171 (C.C.E.D. Wis. 1885).
53. First Nat'l Bank & Trust Co. v. Notte, 293 N.W.2d 530 (Wis. 1980).
54. Bank Mutual f/k/a First Northern Savings Bank v. S.J. Boyer Construction, Inc., Stephen J. Boyer and Marcy A. Boyer, 785 N.W.2d 462 (Wis. 2010).
55. Lakeshore Commercial Finance Corp. v. Drobac, 319 N.W.2d 839 (Wis. 1982).
56. Stephens v. Elver, 77 N.W. 737 (Wis. 1898).

However, the obligee can avoid the need for a contemporaneous consent to a modification if the obligee obtains the guarantor's consent to future loan modifications in the language of the original guaranty.[57] Therefore, under Wisconsin law, one of the most important terms in a guaranty is the guarantor's explicit agreement to waive the right to consent to modifications of the underlying loan documents.

7.2.2 Release or Impairment of Security for the Underlying Obligation

Under Wisconsin law, when an obligee has a security interest in collateral to secure an underlying obligation that is guaranteed by a guarantor, the obligee holds that security interest in trust for the guarantor and has an obligation to preserve that security interest. Where the primary obligor and the obligee enter into an agreement that impairs the collateral, the guarantor may be discharged entirely.[58] The guarantor may waive in advance its defense based on the release or impairment of collateral, both under the common law and under Section 403.606 of the Wisconsin Uniform Commercial Code (UCC).[59]

7.3 Other Defenses

7.3.1 Statute of Limitations

Wisconsin law imposes a six-year statute of limitations on contractual obligations.[60] The six-year statute of limitations also applies to contracts for the sale of goods that are governed by Article 2 of the Wisconsin UCC.[61] Under the Wisconsin UCC, the six-year statute of limitations may be reduced in certain circumstances, but cannot be extended beyond six years.[62]

7.3.2 Statute of Frauds

Under the Wisconsin Fraudulent Contracts statute, a guaranty may be void if it is not in writing or if it fails to express the consideration for the guaranty.[63] If a guaranty includes a provision reciting the consideration for the guaranty, then such provision creates a presumption that consideration exists.[64] Under Wisconsin law, a guaranty must be in writing.[65] This requirement cannot be waived and oral guaranties are not enforceable.[66] However, the consideration

57. John Deere Co. v. Babcock, 278 N.W.2d 885 (Wis. 1979).
58. Crown Life Ins. Co. v. La Bonte, 330 N.W.2d 201 (Wis. 1983).
59. Wisconsin Statutes § 403.606 (2012).
60. Wisconsin Statutes § 893.43 (2012).
61. Wisconsin Statutes § 402.725 (2012).
62. *Id.*
63. Wisconsin Statutes § 241.02 (2012).
64. Amato v. Creative Confections Concept, 97 F. Supp. 949 (E.D. Wis. 2000).
65. Prize Steak Products, Inc. v. Bally's Tom Foolery, Inc., 717 F.2d 367 (7th Cir. 1983).
66. *Id.*

requirement for a guaranty can be satisfied with words such as "for value received" or where the guaranty is noted on the underlying obligation.[67]

7.3.3 Defenses particular to a Guarantor and his/her Spouse

Under Wisconsin law, a guarantor or a guarantor's spouse may claim certain defenses to enforcement of a guaranty against certain collateral based on the Wisconsin marital property law. Section 766.51 of the Wisconsin Marital Property Act relating to management and control of marital property does not provide specific rules for entering into guaranties.[68] Thus, a spouse having management and control of marital property may enter into a guaranty to the same extent that the spouse could incur any other type of credit.[69] However, the issues of whether the guaranty is gratuitous and whether marital property assets are being used for a purpose that is not in the interest of the marriage or the family may still arise between the spouses. In such a case the nonincurring spouse might be able to bring an action to recover those assets under Wis. Stat. § 766.70(6)(a).[70] To the extent the marital estate does not receive consideration, execution of a guaranty by one spouse might be treated as a gift of marital property in excess of the spouse's right to make such a gift under Wis. Stat. § 766.53.[71]

The guaranty drafting convention in the State of Wisconsin is to try to include the nonguaranteeing spouse's consent to the guaranty. This means that "both spouses act together" to make the gift of any payment or recovery under the guaranty under Wis. Stat. § 766.53.[72] In addition, the other guaranty drafting convention in the State of Wisconsin is to obtain a signed family purpose statement (which states that the obligation is incurred in the interest of the marriage or the family and could be included in the guaranty form) from the guarantor. Such a marital purpose statement would be conclusive evidence (with respect to the guarantor) as to the obligee's right to recover marital property.[73] While the obligee would be protected, the family purpose statement would not affect the nonincurring spouse's right to an interspousal remedy under Wis. Stat. § 766.70. Thus, in Wisconsin, either a consent or a family purpose statement should be used to protect the obligee from potentially having to disgorge the recovery as recipient of a gift.

The guaranty of an obligation of a member of the guarantor's immediate family probably has a family purpose under most circumstances. Similarly, there usually would be sufficient family purpose to constitute a family purpose obligation under section Wis. Stat. § 766.55(2)(b) if one spouse guarantees an obligation of a business entity in which a spouse works or owns an interest.[74]

---

67. Matter of Mingez Estate, 235 N.W.2d 296 (Wis. 1975); Scollard v. Bach, 116 N.W. 757 (Wis. 1908); Coxe Brothers & Co. v. Milbrath, 86 N.W. 174 (Wis. 1901).
68. Wisconsin Statutes § 766.51 (2012).
69. Bank One, Appleton, NA v. Reynolds, 500 N.W.2d 337 (Ct. App. Wis. 1993).
70. Wisconsin Statutes § 766.70(6)(a) (2012).
71. Wisconsin Statutes § 766.53 (2012).
72. *Id.*
73. Bank One, Appleton, NA v. Reynolds, 500 N.W.2d 337 (Ct. App. Wis. 1993).
74. Wisconsin Statutes § 766.55(2)(b) (2012); *See, e.g.,* Virginia Lee Homes, Inc. v. Schneider & Felix Constr. Co., 395 P.2d 99 (Wash. 1964).

A family purpose is likely to be present if the business ownership interest is classified as marital property.[75] It may also be present if the business is classified as the guarantor spouse's individual property but generates marital property income.[76] Still, use of a family purpose statement or a spousal consent in a guaranty will avoid the possibility of having to address this issue in the context of collection.

7.4 Right of Set-off

Apart from certain insolvency-related exceptions, a guarantor can exercise a common law right to set-off an individual claim that the guarantor has against the creditor regardless of whether the claim is personal to the guarantor or was assigned from the principal obligor.[77] This right can be waived in a guaranty agreement.

The convention for drafting a guaranty in Wisconsin is to provide that the right to set-off shall not be exercised by the guarantor until such time as the obligee has been paid in full.

7.5 Defenses to Natural Persons

Under Wisconsin law, minors lack the capacity to enter into contracts, including a guaranty.[78] In addition, a guarantor may lack the mental capacity to enter into a guaranty.[79] However, an individual is presumed to be fully competent until someone can prove otherwise.[80]

§ 8 Waiver of Defenses by the Guarantor

8.1 Defenses that cannot be Waived

Certain defenses available to a guarantor cannot be waived. Wisconsin courts have held generally that parties cannot waive a constitutional or statutory protection where the public interest is implicated or where the relevant statute provides that its violation would render the contract void. Under Wisconsin law, a guarantor may not waive a defense of lack of commercial reasonableness in the disposition of collateral governed by Article 9 of the Wisconsin UCC.[81]

75. *Id.*
76. *Id.*
77. Carpenter v. Fulmer, 95 N.W. 403 (Wis. 1903).
78. Wisconsin Statutes § 990.01(20) (2012).
79. French Lumbering Co. v. Theriault, 83 N.W. 927 (Wis. 1900).
80. *Id.*
81. Wisconsin Statute § 409.602 (2012).

8.2 "Catch-all" Waivers

Though catch-all waiver language may be effective in Wisconsin, the guaranty drafting convention in Wisconsin is to include waivers to specific various suretyship defenses, in addition to a standard catch-all waiver that indicates that the guaranty is absolute and unconditional and that the guarantor waives all defenses available at law.

§ 9 Third-party Pledgors—Defenses and Waiver Thereof

Because a pledgor of collateral stands in essentially the same relation as a guarantor to the principal obligor to the extent of the pledge of collateral, Wisconsin law provides that such pledgor may most likely avail itself of the defenses of a guarantor. Such pledgor may also waive the defenses available to a guarantor. We have found no evidence that the law of the State of Wisconsin as applied to guarantors would not apply to a third-party pledgor of collateral. Wisconsin law appears to be that a pledge of collateral results in a surety relationship. Because of this, and given the current state of Wisconsin law, it appears that a pledgor generally has the same defenses available to it as are available to a guarantor.

§ 10 Joint and Several Liability for Guarantors; Rights to Contribution

Guarantors who are jointly and severally liable are presumed to share the secondary obligation equally.[82] The creditor is not obliged to seek full payment from more than one such guarantor.[83]

A guarantor who has contributed more than his "equitable" share is entitled to contribution from any coguarantor.[84] Insofar as the guarantor has paid out more than its proportional share of the obligation, only then may it recover from other guarantors proportionate to their liability.[85]

The convention for drafting a guaranty in Wisconsin is to provide that the right to contribution is waived until such time as the obligee has been paid in full.

82. Bissell v. Wisconsin Tax Commission, 291 N.W. 325 (Wis. 1940).
83. *Id.*
84. In Re Bitker's Estate, 30 N.W.2d 449 (Wis. 1947).
85. Kafka v. Pope, 533 N.W.2d 491 (Wis. 1995).

§ 11 Subrogation

Under Wisconsin law, subrogation is akin to indemnification in that it seeks to recoup the total payment that the party seeking subrogation has made.[86] With respect to a guaranty, subrogation rights may arise in two ways: (1) contractual subrogation; and (2) equitable subrogation.[87] Generally, subrogation is available when the claim of an obligee has been paid in full.[88]

The convention for drafting a guaranty in Wisconsin is to bar the guarantor from exercising subrogation rights against the primary obligor until the obligee is paid in full. This will prevent the guarantor from competing with an obligee's efforts to collect from the primary obligor.

§ 12 Indemnification—Whether the Primary Obligor has a Duty

The principal obligor has a duty of indemnification so long as the guarantor undertook its obligations at the request of the principal obligor. Under Wisconsin case law with respect to guaranties, the courts appear to conflate indemnification and subrogation.[89]

The convention for drafting a guaranty in Wisconsin is to bar the guarantor from exercising indemnification rights against the primary obligor until the obligee is paid in full. This will prevent the guarantor from competing with an obligee's efforts to collect from the primary obligor.

§ 13 Enforcement of Guaranties

13.1 Enforcement of Guaranties of Payment versus Guaranty of Collection

Under Wisconsin law, with respect to a guaranty of payment, the obligee may proceed against the guarantor without having commenced any proceeding against the primary obligor.[90]

However, with respect to a guaranty of collection, an absolute condition precedent to the ability to proceed on the guaranty is that the obligee has diligently prosecuted by all usual legal remedies the obligations of the

86. *Id.*
87. Millers Nat'l Insurance Co. v. City of Milwaukee, 516 N.W.2d 376 (Wis. 1994); Berna-Mork v. Jones, 498 N.W.2d 221 (Wis. 1993).
88. *Id.*
89. Bank One, N.A. v. Concord Apartment Associates, 532 N.W.2d 144 (Wis. Ct. App. 1995).
90. Trailer Rental Co., Inc. v. Buchmeier, 800 F. Supp. 759 (E.D. Wis. 1992).

primary obligor.[91] What constitutes such 'diligent prosecution' has not been well established under Wisconsin law. According to one old Wisconsin case, "[t]he prosecution of legal remedies against the principal to final judgment and execution within a reasonable time after the debt falls due is a condition precedent to the right of recovery against a guarantor, and this condition is not satisfied or done away with by proof that the principal was insolvent and that an action against him would have been fruitless."[92] No arbitrary period of time has been set during which the creditor may delay prosecution of the principal without discharging the guarantor from liability under a guaranty of collection.[93]

13.2 Exercising Rights under a Guaranty Where the Underlying Obligation is also Secured by a Mortgage

The Wisconsin Supreme Court recently issued an important decision that limits the rights of a guarantor with respect to certain foreclosures.[94] As background, Wisconsin law allows an obligee to shorten the redemption period on a foreclosure of commercial real estate from six months to three months if the primary obligor agreed in writing to the provisions of Section 846.103(2) of the Wisconsin Statutes.[95] In order to utilize the shortened redemption period, however, the statute requires the obligee to elect in the obligee's foreclosure complaint to waive judgment for any deficiency against "every party who is personally liable for the debt secured by the mortgage." The question before the court was whether the guarantor was "personally liable for the debts secured by the mortgage" and therefore free of the debt too. The Wisconsin Supreme Court ruled that the obligee can elect the three-month redemption period, waive the judgment for deficiency against the primary obligor, and still retain the right to obtain judgment against the guarantor for the full amount of the guaranteed debt.

§ 14 Revival and Reinstatement of Guaranty

A guaranty may be revived or reinstated. In addition, the parties to a guaranty can arrange for automatic reinstatement of the guaranty in some circumstances.

The convention for drafting a guaranty in Wisconsin is to provide that the guarantor's obligations are reinstated if any payment by the primary obligor is overturned as a bankruptcy preference.

91. Westboro v. Lumber Co., 226 N.W. 313 (Wis. 1929).
92. *Id.*
93. *Id.*
94. *Id.*
95. Wisconsin Statutes § 846.103 (2012).

§15 Choice of Law

Under Wisconsin law, the parties to a contract may expressly agree that the law of a particular jurisdiction will control.[96] Wisconsin courts have acknowledged that parties to a contract may expressly agree that the law of a particular jurisdiction shall control their contractual relations.[97] However, this proposition is qualified by the fact that choice-of-law provisions will not be enforced "at the expense of important public policies of a state whose law would be applicable if the parties' choice of law provision were disregarded."[98]

In situations where the parties to a contractual dispute have not included a valid choice-of-law provision in the contract, Wisconsin courts have generally chosen to adopt portions of the Restatement (Second) of Conflict of Laws to determine what law applies.[99] In deciding choice- of-law questions with respect to contract disputes, the Wisconsin Supreme Court has adopted the grouping-of-contacts approach which closely follows section 188 of the *Restatement (Second) of Conflict of Laws*.[100] Using this analysis, the objective is to determine which state has the most significant relationship with the contract by considering the following factors: (a) the place of contracting; (b) the place of negotiation of the contract; (c) the place of performance; (d) the location of the subject matter of the contract; and (e) the domicil, residence, nationality, place of incorporation, and place of business of the parties.[101]

96. Krider Pharmacy & Gifts, Inc. v. Medi-Care Data Systems, Inc., 791 F. Supp. 221, 225 (E. D. Wis. 1992).
97. Bush v. Nat'l School Studios, 139 Wis. 2d 635, 642, 407 N.W.2d 883, 886 (1987).
98. *Id.*
99. Haines v. Mid-Century Ins. Co. 177 N.W.2d 328, 330 (1970).
100. *Id.*
101. Restatement (Second) of Conflict of Laws § 188 (1971).

Wyoming State Law of Guaranties

Gregory C. Dyekman
Dray, Dyekman, Reed & Healey, P.C.
204 East 22nd Street
Cheyenne WY 82001-3729
(307) 634-8891

Contents

Wyoming State Law of Guaranties

HIGHLIGHTS:

1. Wyoming has little statutory or case law on the subject of guaranty and suretyship. As a result, particular importance is placed by Wyoming courts on the language of the agreement creating the guaranty/suretyship relationship. A strict construction is usually placed on the language of the agreement and guaranties are generally enforced according to their terms.
2. Because of the lack of Wyoming authority, courts generally rely primarily on persuasive authority from other jurisdictions and treatises.
3. The authority that does exist in Wyoming suggests that Wyoming courts are not likely to deviate from "typical" rules followed by the majority of other jurisdictions, nor are they likely to create unusual exceptions to those rules unless peculiar facts warrant such exceptions.

Introductory Note: In order to standardize our discussion of the law of guaranties, we use the following vocabulary to refer to the various parties to a guaranty and their obligations.

"Guarantor" means a person who, by contract, agrees to satisfy an underlying obligation of another to an obligee upon the primary obligor's default on that underlying obligation. We do not draw a distinction between guarantors and sureties, as the distinction in Wyoming between the two is often muddled.

"Guaranty" means the contract by which the guarantor agrees to satisfy the underlying obligation of a primary obligor to an obligee in the event the primary obligor defaults on the underlying obligation.

"Obligee" means the person to whom the underlying obligation is owed. For example, the lender under a loan agreement would be an obligee vis-à-vis the borrower.

"Primary Obligor" means the person who incurs the underlying obligation to the obligee. For example, the borrower under a loan agreement would be a primary obligor.

"Underlying Obligation" means the obligation or obligations incurred by the primary obligor and owed to the obligee. For example, the borrower's obligation to make payments to a lender of principal and interest on a loan constitutes an underlying obligation.

§ 1 Nature of the Guaranty Arrangement

Under Wyoming law, a guaranty creates nothing more than a contract to pay the debt of another, and is secondary to the instrument it guarantees.[1]

A guaranty is a contract in which the guarantor has agreed to pay a creditor any amount not paid by the primary borrower.[2] A guaranty is a contract of "secondary liability" under which the guarantor has an obligation to pay only upon default by the primary obligor. A guarantor is never the principal.[3] The law of guaranty is part of the general contract law.[4]

There is relatively little statutory or case law authority in Wyoming dealing with the law of guaranty/suretyship. Much of the case law that does exist is quite old, but has apparently never been revisited by the Wyoming Supreme Court. However, there is also nothing to suggest that Wyoming courts would depart significantly from the majority rule in other common law jurisdictions in this area of the law. Wyoming courts have generally supported the right of parties to contract with one another, and to have their contracts enforced in accordance with their terms.

While there is no case law directly dealing with conflicts of laws in connection with a guaranty, it should be noted that Wyoming follows a rather typical nexus-based conflict of laws analysis in contract cases,[5] so it would be reasonable to assume that since the Wyoming Supreme Court has characterized guaranties as part of the general contract law, it would apply a nexus-based analysis to a guaranty scenario. Parties have the freedom in Wyoming to contract for forum selection clauses and choice of law clauses.[6]

To date, the Wyoming Supreme Court has not cited to the Restatement of Suretyship and Guaranty, nor has it relied on any other particular source of authority on the subject.

---

1. Belden v. Thorkildsen, 197 P.3d 148 (Wyo. 2008).
2. Lee v. LPP Mortg. Ltd., 74 P.3d 152 (Wyo. 2003).
3. McKenzie v. Neale Const. Co., 294 P.2d 355 (Wyo. 1956).
4. Moorcroft State Bank v. Morel, 701 P.2d 1159 (Wyo. 1985).
5. Resource Technology Corp. v. Fisher Scientific Co., 924 P.2d 972 (Wyo. 1996).
6. Nuhome Investments, LLC v. Weller, 2003 WY 171, 81 P.3d 940.

1.1 Other Suretyship Relationships

While not the focus of this survey, we note that a suretyship relationship may also arise because of the pledge of collateral.[7] As such, a guaranty-type relationship arises, to the extent of the collateral pledged, when a person supplies collateral for a loan in order to induce the creditor to lend to the debtor or where one party mortgages property to a creditor to secure the debt of another.

§ 2 State Law Requirements for an Entity to Enter a Guaranty

Partnerships, limited liability companies (LLCs), corporations, and banks are all authorized to grant guaranties in furtherance of their business activities. Such grants are generally permitted by the appropriate Wyoming statute. Additionally, corporations, partnerships, and LLCs can sometimes grant guaranties even when not in furtherance of their business activities.

2.1 Corporations

Under the Wyoming Business Corporation Act, a Wyoming corporation may, within the scope of its general corporate powers, give a guaranty in furtherance of its corporate purpose, *provided that* its articles of incorporation do not prevent it from doing so.[8] However, the Act prohibits guaranties for the obligations of directors unless the guaranty is approved by the majority of the votes represented by the voting shares of all classes, voting as a single voting group, except the votes of shares owned by or voted under the control of the benefited director;[9] or the corporation's board of directors determines that the guarantie benefits the corporation and either approves the specific guaranty or a general plan authorizing loans and guaranties.[10]

2.2 Partnerships

Wyoming's Uniform Partnership Act[11] neither expressly empowers a partnership to issue a guaranty nor expressly regulates or prohibits such activity. Case law from other jurisdictions makes clear, however, that a partnership can grant a guaranty in carrying out its business.

---

7. *See* Restatement (Third) of Suretyship and Guaranty § 1 (noting that a person is a surety when "pursuant to contract . . . an obligee has recourse against [that] person . . . *or against that person's property* with respect to an obligation . . . of another person . . . to the obligee" (emphasis added)).
8. Wyo. Stat. Ann. § 17-16-302(a)(vi).
9. Wyo. Stat. Ann. § 17-16-832(a)(i).
10. Wyo. Stat. Ann. § 17-16-832(a)(ii).
11. Wyo. Stat. Ann. § 17-21-101 et seq.

2.3 Limited Liability Companies

The Wyoming Limited Liability Company Act simply provides that "A limited liability company has the capacity to sue and be sued in its own name and the power to do all things necessary or convenient to carry on its activities."[12]

2.4 Banks and Trust Companies

Wyoming banking statutes are not specific about the legal power to give a guaranty as part of the bank's business, but banks are given statutory authority to make contracts in their own names.

2.5 Individuals

An individual with the capacity to enter into a contract has the legal authority to give a guaranty.

Wyoming is not a community property state. Real property owned by a married couple as husband and wife in Wyoming is presumed to be held as tenants by the entireties. Under Wyoming law, property held between a husband and wife as tenants by the entireties is not subject to the claims of creditors of only one of those tenants where only that one tenant has signed a guaranty.[13] Wyoming is a marital property state in which property division in dissolution of marriage cases is based on the equitable division of that property in the sound discretion of the court.[14] No generalization can therefore be made with respect to the effect of such a division on the sole spouse who is the obligor on a guaranty.

§ 3 Signatory's Authority to Execute a Guaranty

There is no specific case law in Wyoming concerning this issue, but there is no reason to believe that a Wyoming court would not apply traditional tests relating to agency when determining the authority of a signer on a guaranty.

3.1 Corporations

The Wyoming Business Corporation Act does not specify limits or conditions upon the authority of officers to sign guaranty documents. Presumably, traditional agency principles would apply.

12. Wyo. Stat. Ann. § 17-29-105.
13. Ward Terry & Co., v. Hensen, 75 Wyo. 444, 297 P.2d 213 (1956).
14. Wyo. Stat. Ann. § 20-2-114; Pond v. Pond, 2009 WY 134, 203 P.3d 250.

3.2 Partnerships

Wyoming's Uniform Partnership Act grants a partner the authority to bind the partnership when such partner's act is "for apparently carrying on in the usual way the business of the partnership," unless such authority has been explicitly held back in a statement of partnership authority.[15] The contents of a statement of partnership authority are spelled out in the Act.[16]

Under Wyoming's Uniform Limited Partnership Act, a general partner in a limited partnership has the same powers as a partner of a general partnership, except as provided otherwise in the partnership agreement or in the Act.[17]

3.3 Limited Liability Companies

The Wyoming Limited Liability Company Act provides that a member is not an agent of a LLC solely by reason of being a member.[18] However, a member's conduct can subject him to liability under law other than the Act.[19] In a member-managed LLC, an act outside the ordinary course of the activities of the company (which would presumably usually apply to the giving of a guaranty) may be undertaken only with the consent of all members.[20] In a manager-managed LLC, the consent of all members is required to undertake any other act outside the ordinary course of the company's activities.[21]

3.4 Banks and Trust Companies

A case-by-case inquiry of the powers provided for in a bank's or trust company's corporate governance documents is necessary to determine who may validly execute a guaranty on behalf of a bank or trust company.

§ 4 Consideration; Sufficiency of Past Consideration

Standard contract principles apply to the analysis of consideration for a contract of guaranty. The principal agreement is sufficient consideration for an accompanying guaranty. Past consideration can be sufficient when the guaranty expresses the past consideration in writing.

Consideration is required to create a valid contract of guaranty. The inquiry into sufficient consideration is based on standard contract law principles. Wyoming cases concerning consideration have tended to focus on specific factual circumstances to determine the adequacy of consideration. When a

15. Wyo. Stat. Ann. § 17-21-301(a)(i).
16. Wyo. Stat. Ann. § 17-21-303.
17. Wyo. Stat. Ann. § 17-14-503.
18. Wyo. Stat. Ann. § 17-29-301(a).
19. Wyo. Stat. Ann. § 17-29-301(b).
20. Wyo. Stat. Ann. § 17-29-407(b)(iv).
21. Wyo. Stat. Ann. § 17-29-407(c)(iv)(C).

guarantor is not a part of the original transaction of the principal obligor, his or her promise must be supported by separate consideration.[22]

§ 5 Notice of Acceptance

Notice of acceptance may not be required, if credit is extended to the primary obligor based upon the guaranty or if the guaranty is absolute.

There is no Wyoming case law concerning this topic.

§ 6 Interpretation of Guaranties

Courts in Wyoming strictly construe the obligations of the guarantor. Courts will interpret a guaranty in the same manner by which they would interpret the language of any other contract.

6.1 General Principles

A Wyoming court will strictly construe the obligations of a guarantor. A guaranty agreement is strictly limited to its terms.[23] Except for this, the same principles of construction that apply to contracts generally apply to guaranties. In construing the language of a contract of suretyship, the same rules apply that control in the construction of other contracts. [24]

6.2 Guaranty of Payment versus Guaranty of Collection

While there is no Wyoming case law concerning this distinction, there is no reason to suspect that Wyoming courts would not follow typical authority in other jurisdictions that indicates that a court should determine the intent of the parties to the guaranty agreement as expressed in that agreement to determine which type of guaranty was given.

6.3 Language Regarding the Revocation of Guaranties

There is no Wyoming case law on this point, but the language of the guaranty agreement would presumably govern issues of revocation.

22. Moorcroft State Bank v. Morel, 701 P.2d 1159 (Wyo. 1985).
23. Speight, McCue & Associates, P.C. v. Wallop, 153 P.3d 250 (Wyo. 2007).
24. Wyoming Machinery Co. v. U. S. Fidelity and Guaranty Co., 614 P.2d 716 (Wyo. 1980).

6.4 "Continuing"

There is no Wyoming case law on this point. Presumably, a factual inquiry would have to be made by a court, including consideration of the language of the guaranty agreement.

6.5 "Absolute and Unconditional"

No demand on the principal debtor is necessary to render the guarantor liable on an absolute and unconditional guaranty.[25]

6.6 "Liable as a Primary Obligor and not Merely as Surety"

This language, taken literally, seems to confuse the concepts of guarantor and primary obligor. While a guarantor may be a "guarantor of payment" from whom the obligee can seek payment even without pursuing the primary obligor, the guarantor does not become a primary obligor.

While a surety becomes bound as the principal or original debtor is bound, a guarantor is not bound to do what the principal has contracted to do, but only to answer for the consequences of the default of the principal.[26]

§ 7 Defenses of the Guarantor; Set-off

The defenses that may be available to a guarantor can be grouped into three categories: (1) defenses of the primary obligor; (2) "suretyship defenses"; and (3) other defenses.

7.1 Defenses of the Primary Obligor

7.1.1 General

There is no case law in Wyoming on this topic.

7.1.2 When Guarantor may Assert Primary Obligor's Defense

There is no case law in Wyoming on this topic.

7.1.3 Defenses that may not be Raised by Guarantor

There is no case law in Wyoming on this topic.

7.1.4 Defenses that may Always be Raised by Guarantor

There is no case law in Wyoming on this topic.

25. Speight, McCue & Associates, P.C. v. Wallop, 153 P.3d 250 (Wyo. 2007).
26. Speight, McCue & Associates, P.C. v. Wallop, 153 P.3d 250 (Wyo. 2007).

7.2 "Suretyship" Defenses

7.2.1 Change in Identity of Principal Obligor

There is no case law in Wyoming on this topic.

7.2.2 Modification of the Underlying Obligation, Including Release

Under Wyoming law, modifications to the underlying obligation may permit the guarantor to raise certain defenses to liability. Case law is sparse, however. Any valid agreement between the creditor and the principal debtor for an extension of time of payment of the debt, without the consent of the surety, discharges the surety.[27] However, the rule that an extension of time by a creditor does not release the surety where the creditor has expressly reserved his rights against the surety is followed.[28]

7.2.3 Release or Impairment of Security for the Underlying Obligation

The guarantor may waive in advance its defense based on the release or impairment of collateral, both under the common law and, as to negotiable instruments, under Wyo. Stat. Ann. § 34.1-3-605(j), Wyoming's Uniform Commercial Code. However, in the absence of such a waiver, the other provisions of Wyo. Stat. Ann.§ 34.1-3-605 give an accommodation party or indorser rights to be discharged with respect to obligations under negotiable instruments.

7.3 Other Defenses

7.3.1 Failure to Fulfill a Condition Precedent

Signers of a written guaranty must prove the existence of a condition precedent and the creditor's knowledge thereof to escape liability for its nonfulfillment after manual delivery of the instrument that is complete on its face. A condition precedent to the validity of a written guaranty may be shown by the facts and circumstances.[29]

7.3.2 Modification of the Guaranty

There is no Wyoming case law on this point.

7.3.3 Failure to Pursue Primary Obligor

Wyoming statutes pertaining to sureties provide that a surety has the right to demand in writing that the creditor file suit to obtain performance by the

27. Lawrence v. Thom, 64 P. 339 (Wyo. 1901).
28. Lange v. Valencia, 533 P.2d 304 (Wyo. 1975).
29. McClintock v. Ayers, 253 P. 658 (Wyo. 1927).

principal debtor and to pursue that suit diligently. Failure to diligently pursue the principal debtor results in forfeiture of the right to recover from the surety.[30] This right to demand suit also is available to the administrator or personal representative of the estate of a surety.[31] Generally, whatever discharges the principal releases the surety except in cases of defenses that are not inherent in, or do not concern the debt.[32] These statutes appear to have been applied only in cases involving sureties in commercial settings, and not to guaranties in the borrowing context.

7.3.4 Statute of Limitations

Wyoming law generally establishes a statute of limitation for actions on a written contract of 10 years,[33] and upon an oral contract of eight years.[34] One exception applies to contracts for the sale of goods that are governed by Article 2 of the Wyoming Uniform Commercial Code, which imposes a four-year statute of limitations.[35] There is no Wyoming case law dealing with the question of whether a guaranty is always subject to the longer statute of limitations, even in the case of the sale of goods.

Reasonable provisions limiting the time within which actions may be brought on a building contractor's bonds are valid and will be enforced.[36] A requirement contained in a construction bond that suit be filed within one year after the first publication of notice of final payment of the contract was enforced against a supplier, whose claim was held barred by limitations.[37]

7.3.5 Statute of Frauds

Wyoming law provides that every special promise to answer for the debt, default, or miscarriage of another person must be in writing (or at least a note or memorandum of such must exist), or the agreement is void.[38]

7.3.6 Defenses Particular to Guarantors that are Natural Persons and their Spouses

7.4 Right of Set-off

There is no Wyoming case law on this topic.

30. Wyo. Stat. Ann. § 38-1-101.
31. Wyo. Stat. Ann. § 38-1-102.
32. Roberts v. Bd. of Com'rs of Laramie County, 8 Wyo. 177, 56 P. 915 (1899).
33. Wyo. Stat. Ann. § 1-3-105(a)(i).
34. Wyo. Stat. Ann. § 1-3-105(a)(ii)(A).
35. Wyo. Stat. Ann. § 34.1-2-725(a).
36. McWaters and Bartlett v. U.S. for Use and Benefit of Wilson, 272 F.2d 291 (10th Cir. 1959).
37. Colorado Builders' Supply Co. v. National Fire Ins. Co., 423 P.2d 79 (1967).
38. Wyo. Stat. Ann. § 34.1-23-105(a)(ii).

§ 8 Waiver of Defenses by the Guarantor

8.1 Defenses that cannot be Waived

There is no Wyoming case law on this topic.

8.2 "Catch-all" Waivers

Where not specific, a written waiver of defenses available to a guarantor must employ language which fairly indicates the general class of actions consented to or defenses which are waived.[39] Though catch-all waiver language may be effective, it is advisable for beneficiaries to include waivers to specific suretyship defenses.

8.3 Use of Specific Waivers

Other than the case cited in Section 8.2 above, there is no Wyoming case law on this topic.

§ 9 Third-party Pledgors—Defenses and Waiver thereof

There is no Wyoming case law on this topic. There is no reason to assume that a third-party pledgor could not assert the same defenses as a guarantor.

§ 10 Jointly and Severally Liable Guarantors—Contribution and Reduction of Obligations upon Payment by a Co-obligor

There is no Wyoming statutory or case law specifically on this topic, but it is reasonable to expect that Wyoming courts would follow typical holdings of other courts in this area.

10.1 Contribution

There is no Wyoming case explaining the law as it relates to jointly and severally liable guarantors, but the right of contribution has been recognized.[40]

39. Toland v. Key Bank of Wyoming, 847 P.2d 549 (Wyo. 1993).
40. Bolln v. Metcalf, 6 Wyo. 1, 42 P. 12, 71 Am.St.Rep. 898 (1895).

10.2 Reduction of obligations upon payment of co-obligor

There is no Wyoming case law on this topic.

§ 11 Subrogation

Wyoming law provides a statutory right of subrogation under specified circumstances. The statute provides that, "When the surety on a judgment, who is certified therein to be such, or his personal representative pays the judgment, or any part thereof, he shall, to the extent of such payment, have all the rights and remedies against the principal debtor that the plaintiff had at the time of such payment.[41] It is likely that a Wyoming court would find such a right to exist in other circumstances as well consistent with general suretyship law. Upon performance by a surety, he is entitled to the original evidences of debt held by the creditor, and to any judgment in to which the debt has been merged, as well as to all collateral securities held by the creditor.[42]

§ 12 Indemnification—Whether the Primary Obligor has a Duty

Under Wyoming suretyship statutes, a surety may maintain an action against his principal to obtain indemnity against the debt or liability for which he is bound before it is due whenever any of the grounds exist upon which, by the provisions of this act, an order may be made for arrest, or for an attachment.[43] Clearly, this statutory right is quite limited. There is little Wyoming case law dealing with contractual or common law rights for a guarantor/surety to demand indemnification, but it is clear that an indemnification right exists.[44]

§ 13 Enforcement of Guaranties

13.1 Limitations on Recovery

There is no Wyoming case law on this topic.

41. Wyo. Stat. Ann. § 38-1-104.
42. Newell v. Morrow, 9 Wyo. 1, 59 P. 429 (1899).
43. Wyo. Stat. Ann. § 38-1-108.
44. Insurance Co. of No. America v. Bath, 726 F. Supp. 1247 (D. Wyo. 1989).

13.2 Enforcement of Guaranties of Payment versus Guaranties of Performance

There is no Wyoming case law on this topic.

13.3 Exercising Rights under a Guaranty Where the Underlying Obligation is also Secured by a Mortgage

There is no Wyoming case law on this topic. While there is no authority directly on point, Wyoming power of sale foreclosure statutes provide that a power of sale foreclosure may not be used unless "[N]o suit or proceeding has been instituted at law to recover the debt then remaining secured by such mortgage, or any part thereof, or if any suit or proceeding has been instituted, that the same has been discontinued, or that an execution upon the judgment rendered therein has been returned unsatisfied in whole or in part;...".[45] Presumably, a suit on a guaranty would be considered a suit to recover the debt, and would thus make the statute applicable so that a power of sale foreclosure would not be permitted.

In a case involving a guarantor who also gave a mortgage, it was held that a letter written by a guarantor to a bank in which the guarantor consented to the use of his land for a mortgage did not have the effect of limiting the guarantor's liability on the primary debtor's note to an absolute total of the land value, where the guaranty was clear and unambiguous and demonstrated that it was offered and accepted without limitation.[46]

Wyoming has no antideficiency statute, nor does it have any statute or court-adopted rule limiting or conditioning the lender's rights to pursue a deficiency against a guarantor in accordance with the terms of the guaranty itself.

13.4 Litigating Guaranty Claims: Procedural Considerations

In order for a claim to be made with respect to a surety bond securing the obligations of a personal representative of an estate, there must first be a finding by the court that a default or other breach of duty has occurred and setting the amount of the obligation.[47]

§ 14 Revival and Reinstatement of Guaranties

There is no Wyoming case law on this topic.

45. Wyo. Stat. Ann. 34-4-103(a)(ii).
46. Hayes v. American Nat.l Bank of Powell, 784 P.2d 599 (Wyo. 1989).
47. Werner v. American Sur. Co. of New York, 423 P.2d 86 (Wyo. 1967).

§ 15 Guaranties of Less than the Entire Primary Obligation

There is no Wyoming statutory or case law on this topic.

§ 16 Conflict of Laws—Choice of Law

Wyoming permits the parties to determine choice of law rules for guaranties.[48]

The author wishes to thank Erin K. Murphy for her assistance with this survey.

48. Nuhome Investments, LLC v. Weller, 2003 WY 171, 81 P.3d 940.

District of Columbia Law of Guaranties

Edmund D. Harllee
Jamie W. Bruno
Williams, Mullen, Clark & Dobbins, P.C.
8300 Greensboro Drive, Suite 1100
McLean, Virginia 22102
703-760-5200
703-748-0244
www.williamsmullen.com

Contents

District of Columbia Law of Guaranties[1]

Practice Pointers

1. A Lexis search revealed that the District of Columbia Court of Appeals has cited to the **Restatement (Third) of Suretyship and Guaranty** in several recent cases. In particular, in *Allen v. Yates*, 870 A.2d 39 (D.C. 2005), the court heavily relied on the Restatement, and commented as follows concerning that reliance:

   Because we have relied extensively on the [*Restatement (Third) of Suretyship and Guaranty*], we think it worthwhile to note that, like other Restatements, it was published by the American Law Institute. The Institute is comprised of especially distinguished judges, attorneys and scholars, and 'the Restatement may be regarded both as the product of expert opinion and as the expression of the law by the legal profession.' *Poretta v. Superior Dowel Co., 153 Me. 308, 137 A.2d 361, 373 (1957).*[2]

   Thus, while D.C. courts have not officially adopted the entirety of the Restatement, it can be ventured that the Restatement is generally a resource of interpretation for our courts.

2. Despite this general reverence to the Restatement, in the District of Columbia the power of the parties to negotiate their own agreements under contract ultimately reigns supreme (even if contrary to general Restatement principles).

For purposes of this chapter, the following definitions are used:

"Obligee" — the person to whom the underlying obligation is owed; e.g., the lender or creditor in a commercial loan transaction.

"Principal Obligor" — the original obligor owing the underlying obligation to the obligee; e.g., the borrower.

"Secondary Obligation" — the contract giving rise to suretyship status; e.g., the guaranty agreement given by the guarantor in favor of the lender, guaranteeing the payment and performance obligations of the borrower to the lender.

"Secondary Obligor" — the obligor bound by the secondary obligation; e.g., the guarantor.

"Underlying Obligation" — the original obligation owing by the principal obligor to the obligee, e.g., the indebtedness evidenced by the promissory note made by the borrower payable to the order of the lender and the other loan documents executed in connection therewith.

---

1. For the purposes of this survey, a "guaranty" does not include the activity, purpose, or function of the "Life and Health Insurance Guaranty Association" as found within D.C. Code §§ 31-5401 to -5416 or of the "Property and Liability Insurance Guaranty Association" as found within D.C. Code §§ 31-5501 to -5515. The purpose of the guaranty associations is to protect resident policyholders in the event of an insurance company impairment (life and health only) or insolvency. Generally, if a member insurer becomes impaired or insolvent, the relevant association may become a guarantor of the policies, contracts, and certificates of the insurer.
2. *Id.* at 50 n.11.

§ 1 Nature of the Guaranty Agreement

1.1 Suretyship Law Generally

The concept of suretyship has broad legal applications, all "spring[ing] from the confluence of three factors, a primary commitment, the actual or incipient failure to fulfill that commitment, and the secondary commitment of the surety." Though suretyship principles may apply in multitudinous scenarios, perhaps the most commonplace application is in the context of a financial transaction involving a lender/creditor, a borrower and one or more guarantors.

Guaranty law in the District of Columbia is generally governed by the Restatement, which "firmly adopts the principle that the substance of a transaction, rather than its form" determines whether such transaction falls under the tenets of suretyship law.[3] The Restatement applies to any transaction giving rise to "suretyship status," a three-pronged test requiring: (i) a secondary obligation giving the obligee recourse against the secondary obligor (or his property) with respect to the underlying obligation of the principal obligor, (ii) to the extent that either the underlying obligation or the secondary obligation is performed, the obligee is not entitled to the performance of the other obligation, and (iii) the principal obligor, rather than the secondary obligor, should properly perform the underlying obligation or bear the cost of such performance.[4]

The obligee has recourse against the secondary obligor under general suretyship law when (a) the principal obligor owes a duty to perform the underlying obligation, and (b) under the secondary obligation, (i) the secondary obligor has the duty to perform the underlying obligation, (ii) the obligee has the right to pursue performance by the secondary obligor in the event the principal obligor defaults in the performance of the underlying obligation, or (iii) the obligee may require the secondary obligor to perform the underlying obligation or purchase the underlying obligation from obligee.[5]

1.2 Deference to Contract Law

While D.C. courts look to the Restatement for much of their guidance in resolving guaranty issues, ultimately contract law prevails. The Restatement itself even asserts that suretyship law "defers to that private ordering" that parties may contract among themselves,[6] and the terms and provisions of the secondary obligation are governed by contract law principles. The "requisites of contract formation" also apply to the creating of the contract giving rise to the secondary obligation.[7]

3. *Id.* ch. 1, intro. note.
4. *Id.* § 1(1)(a)-(c).
5. *Id.* § 1(2)(a)-(b).
6. *Id.* § 6 cmt. a.
7. *Id.* § 7.

§ 2 State Law Requirements for an Entity to Enter a Guaranty

With respect to capacity questions regarding the ability to enter into a secondary obligation, "general capacity suffices" and any person or entity with the "capacity to contract has the capacity to become a secondary obligor."[8]

2.1 Corporations

Under the District of Columbia Business Corporation Law, a corporation may, within the scope of its general corporate powers, make contracts or guaranties in furtherance of its corporate purpose, provided that its corporate charter and bylaws do not prevent it from doing so.[9]

2.2 Limited Liability Companies

General limited liability company law in the District of Columbia permits a company to "do all things necessary or convenient to carry on its activities."[10] This broad power allows the company to enter into contracts and be bound by their terms, including, without limitation, guaranty agreements, to the extent not expressly prohibited in its operating agreement.[11]

2.3 Banks and Trust Companies

Though some states do not allow banks or trust companies to issue guaranties, D.C. courts have heard cases in which banks and trust companies acted as guarantors;[12] the courts took no issue with the underlying transaction structure.

2.4 Individuals

An important consideration with individual guaranties is the implications for marital property. The District of Columbia is not a community property state and, under D.C. Code § 46-601, each spouse can borrow money to the same extent as if he or she were unmarried.[13] A spouse can only be held liable for

---

8. *Id.* § 10 cmt. a.
9. D.C. Code § 29-302.02(7) (2012).
10. D.C. Code § 29-801.05 (2012).
11. D.C. Code § 29-801.05 (2012).
12. *See* Fidelity-Bankers Trust Co. v. Helvering, 113 F.2d 14, 15 (D.C. Cir. 1940) ("The party of the second part shall purchase, receive, hold, manage, control, lease, encumber and/or sell such properties, as heretofore described, as a majority of the syndicate owners may, from time to time direct, in writing, and the syndicate shall have the power, right or authority to sell any or all properties belonging to it only upon such terms and at such prices as Fidelity-Bankers Trust Company, the guarantor herein, may agree to in writing."); Commercial Nat'l Bank v. McCandlish, 23 F.2d 986, 988 (D.C. 1928) ("In other words the Commercial National Bank as part consideration for the assets thus transferred to it, became the unconditional guarantor of the obligations owing by the Terminal Bank to its depositors and certain other creditors.").
13. D.C. Code § 46-601(b)(1) (2012).

the other spouse's debts or contracts if the spouse is a party to the debt.[14] Put another way, a creditor does not have recourse to the property of a nonsigning spouse under a guaranty signed by the other spouse.

Practice Pointer: The Equal Credit Opportunity Act prohibits a lender from requiring an individual borrower's spouse from signing a guaranty merely because of their marital relationship.[15]

§ 3 Signatory's Authority to Execute a Guaranty

D.C. courts adhere to the concept of apparent authority in evaluating whether the obligee may rely on the signature of an agent to bind its entity principal obligor, noting that authority issues depend inherently on perception.[16]

3.1 Corporations

Though the D.C. Business Corporation Act does not explicitly specify which officers of a corporation may sign contracts, it does provide that generally "[a]ll corporate powers shall be exercised by or under the authority of the board of directors."[17] Officers of the corporation have the authority to perform "[t]he functions set forth in the bylaws," or "[t]o the extent consistent with the bylaws, the functions prescribed by the board of directors,"[18] making the authority question one that can only be resolved by reviewing the Business Corporation Act in conjunction with the corporation's bylaws and resolutions.[19]

3.2 Limited Liability Companies

Managers do not have a general authority to bind a company under D.C.'s Limited Liability Company Act;[20] rather, this authority is enumerated in the organizational documents for each company on a case-by-case basis. The statement of authority that a limited liability company files may state the authority, or limitations on the authority, of any member to enter into transactions or bind the company.[21]

14. D.C. Code § 46-601(b)(2) (2012).
15. 15 U.S.C. § 1691(a) (2011); Regulation B, 12 C.F.R. § 202.7(d) (2012).
16. *See* Green Leaves Rest., Inc. v. 617 H St. Assocs., 974 A.2d 222 (D.C. 2009) ("Apparent authority depends upon the third-party's perception of the agent's authority. The third party's perception may be based upon written or spoken words or any other conduct of the principal which, reasonably interpreted, causes the third person to believe that the principal consents to have the act done on [his] behalf by the person purporting to act for [him]." (alterations in original)).
17. D.C. Code § 29-306.01(b) (2012).
18. D.C. Code § 29-306.41 (2012).
19. *See Green Leaves*, 974 A.2d at 229 ("Private-sector organizations formed as corporations have a governing body ordinarily known as a board of directors . . . that, by statute, . . . is assigned ultimate supervisory responsibility for the corporation's business and affairs. Directors commonly appoint officers for the corporation. . . . [t]he nature and scope of each officer's authority may be defined by statute, by the corporation's constitutional documents, by specific resolutions adopted by the directors, and by custom associating specific functions with a particular position." (alteration in original)).
20. D.C. Code § 29-803.01(a) (2012).
21. D.C. Code § 29-803.02 (2012).

3.3 Partnerships

Partners are considered agents of the partnership under the District of Columbia's version of the Uniform Limited Partnership Act.[22] Thus, the act of a partner, in the ordinary course of the business of the partnership, binds the partnership unless that partner lacked authority to act for the partnership and the third party with whom the partner was dealing knew or received notice that the partner lacked authority.[23] In the case where the binding partner was not acting in the ordinary course of the partnership business, that partner's actions will only bind the partnership if they were authorized by the other partners,[24] unless the partner was given the authority to so bind the partnership in a statement of partnership authority filed with the city.[25]

§ 4 Consideration; Sufficiency of Past Consideration

As with any contract, in D.C. standard consideration is required for a contract of guaranty.[26] The undertaking of a secondary obligation will not usually pose any consideration issues as long as "the underlying obligation is supported by consideration and the later creation of the secondary obligation was part of the exchange for which the obligee bargained."[27] A statement in the recitals of the guaranty agreement that the guarantor has a direct financial interest in the borrower and therefore the transaction, and will benefit from lender's extension of credit, will easily suffice and protect the lender from any potential consideration headaches in the enforcement of the guaranty.

Practice Pointer: It is critical to understand the distinction between consideration required for contract purposes (the infamous "peppercorn" standard) and consideration required to defeat a fraudulent conveyance challenge in bankruptcy (which relies on the "reasonably equivalent value" standard). For this reason, lenders should carefully consider the nature of the relationship between their borrowers and guarantors, and undertake additional due diligence in situations involving cross-stream or upstream liability under a guaranty.

22. D.C. Code § 29-603.01(1) (2012).
23. D.C. Code § 29-603.01(2) (2012).
24. D.C. Code § 29-603.01(3) (2012).
25. D.C. Code § 29-603.03(a)(2) (2012).
26. *See* Vaccaro v. Andresen, 201 A.2d 26, 28 (D.C. 1964) ("An enforceable contract of guaranty or suretyship requires as do all contracts, a valid consideration, and where the guaranty is given subsequent to the original contract, the guaranty must be supported by a new consideration, separate and independent from the original contract.") (*citing* Bader v. Williams, 61 A.2d 637 (D.C. 1948); McMillan v. Zozier, 257 Ala. 435, 59 So.2d 563 (1952); Pierce v. Wright, 117 Cal. App. 2d 718, 256 P.2d 1049 (1953); Bearden v. Ebcap Supply Co., 108 Ga. App. 375, 133 S.E.2d 62 (1963)).
27. Restatement (Third) of Suretyship and Guaranty § 9(2)(a) (1996).

§ 5 Notice of Acceptance

Unless the terms of the secondary obligation explicitly require notice of acceptance by the obligee to the secondary obligor, if the offer by the secondary obligor permits obligee to accept by merely extending credit to or otherwise contracting with the principal obligor, requirements of notice to the secondary obligor of such acceptance are deemed waived.[28] The verbiage of a standard commercial guaranty would typically satisfy this requirement.

§ 6 Interpretation of Guaranties

Under the Restatement, there is no distinct or "special standard of interpretation for contracts creating secondary obligations,"[29] and as such general contract principles apply.

6.1 Surety versus Guaranty

The Restatement largely speaks in terms of suretyship law; however, generally parties to commercial transactions utilize the "guarantor/guaranty" nomenclature. Though legally distinct principles—sureties are traditionally jointly and severally liable with the principal obligor for the underlying obligation whereas the liability of guarantors is traditionally triggered upon the default of the principal obligor— both "guarantors" and "sureties" fall within the purview of the Restatement if they satisfy the criteria for suretyship status set forth above.

(a) General guaranty

If a party is identified as a "guarantor" in a secondary obligation (or the secondary obligation itself is identified as a "guaranty"), then the guarantor party is considered a secondary obligor; upon default by the principal obligor, the secondary obligor must "satisfy the obligee's claim with respect to the underlying obligation."[30] Unless otherwise specifically provided for by the terms of the secondary obligation, the mere use of the terms "guaranty" and "guarantor" (without further distinction) will give rise to a presumption that the secondary obligation falls into the general guaranty category.[31]

(b) Collection guaranty

If a party is identified as a "guarantor of collection" in a secondary obligation (or the secondary obligation itself is identified as a "guaranty of collection"), then the guarantor is considered a secondary obligor; however, upon default by the principal obligor, the secondary obligor must satisfy the obligee's

28. *Id.* § 8(1)(a).
29. *Id.* § 14 cmt. c.
30. *Id.* § 15(a).
31. *Id.* § 15 cmt. c.

claim only if (i) a "judgment against the principal obligor has been returned unsatisfied"; (ii) the principal obligor is insolvent or subject to an insolvency proceeding; (iii) the principal obligor "cannot be served with process"; or (iv) "it is otherwise apparent that payment cannot be obtained" from the principal obligor.[32] These requirements impose substantial limitations on the ability of a lender to collect from its guarantor in the event of a borrower default, and essentially amount to a marshalling requirement.

Note that in D.C., few cases specifically address the distinction between payment and collection guaranties; the ones that do generally adhere to the Restatement rubric.[33] However, these cases also rely heavily on D.C. Code § 28:3-416 (1991), which distinguished between "payment guaranteed" and "collection guaranteed" concepts but was amended in its entirety in 1995 and no longer addresses the collection guaranty issue.

(c) Surety

If a principal obligor and secondary obligor are both parties to a contract that identifies the secondary obligor as a "surety" (or the contract itself is defined as one of "suretyship"), the secondary obligor has joint and several liability with the principal obligor with respect to the underlying obligation set forth in the contract.[34] The important distinction here between a surety and a guarantor is that a default under the underlying obligation is not a condition precedent for the secondary obligor to be compelled to perform for the obligee's benefit.

Practice Pointer: Though the general rules of interpretation favor the application of general guaranty principles rather than imposing a collection guaranty standard if not specifically prescribed in the contract, the best practice for lenders is to include language in its guaranty affirmatively stating "This is a guaranty of payment and not of collection."

6.2 Continuing Guaranties

If a secondary obligor signs up for a "continuing guaranty," the obligee is permitted to make subsequent extensions of credit to the principal obligor in reliance on the original secondary obligation until the secondary obligor gives notice to the obligee of the termination of such secondary obligation.[35] Even after such termination, the secondary obligor remains liable for any advances made prior to the termination of the continuing guaranty; the termination is only effective with respect to advances made subsequent to the termination.[36]

Practice Pointer: In addition to a broad, all-obligations scope of the guaranteed obligations defined in the guaranty, which may imply a continuing guaranty concept, a prudent lender will include an affirmative statement that the guaranty is a "continuing guaranty."

32. *Id.* § 15(b)(1)-(4).
33. *See, e.g.*, Cusimano v. First Md. Savs. & Loan, 639 A.2d 553 (D.C. 1994).
34. Restatement (Third) of Suretyship and Guaranty § 15(c) (1996).
35. *Id.* § 16.
36. *Id.* § 16 cmt. b.

6.3 "Completion" or "Performance" Guaranties

There are no recorded cases in the District of Columbia addressing "completion" or "performance" guaranties. These guaranties, however, have been contemplated by at least one D.C. administrative agency. In an order establishing rules for evaluating certain utility contracts, the District's Public Service Commission discussed the option of requiring guarantors to enter into performance guaranties as opposed to solely monetary guaranties.[37] While the Commission ultimately rejected the proposal, the reasons for rejection concerned business objectives, and there was no indication that the Commission believed performance guaranties would not be enforced.[38]

§ 7 Defenses of the Guarantor

The Restatement provides for several suretyship defenses that the secondary obligor can raise to avoid liability under the secondary obligation. The rationale for these defenses stems from the concept that, if the obligee "changes the risks" under the secondary obligation, then the secondary obligor may suffer greater "loss" than the secondary obligor originally bargained for with the obligee.[39] Likewise, because the secondary obligor's performance of the secondary obligation gives rise to a cause of action against the principal obligor by its terms, the secondary obligor is likely to be ultimately "saved harmless" even if called upon to perform the secondary obligation (provided the principal obligor remains solvent).[40]

7.1 Suretyship Defenses

If the obligee performs any act that "increas[es] [the secondary obligor's] potential cost of performance or decreas[es] its potential ability to cause the principal obligor to bear the cost of performance," such action amounts to an "impairment of suretyship status."[41] The Restatement adopts a "bifurcated approach" to such impairment by either releasing the secondary obligor from all further performance under the secondary obligation or protecting the secondary obligor from suffering unanticipated loss, depending on the severity of the obligee's interference with the original terms of the underlying obligation.[42]

37. *See* D.C. Pub. Serv. Comm'n, Formal Case No. 1017, In the Matter of the Development and Designation of Standard Offer Service in the District of Columbia, Order No. 13241, at 5 (2004), http://www.dcpsc.org/pdf_files/commorders/orderpdf/ordno_13241.pdf.
38. *See id.* at 5-6 (noting that the Commission accepted the recommendation not to adopt a performance guaranty because, inter alia, "[s]o long as the level of monetary damages is sufficient to enable PEPCO to purchase replacement. . . , then a requirement for specific performance is unnecessary").
39. *Id.* ch. 3, intro. note.
40. *Id.*
41. *Id.* § 37(1).
42. *Id.* § 37 cmt. a.

(a) Full discharge from further performance

Certain acts on behalf of the obligee allow the secondary obligor to void all further performance under the secondary obligation, such as if the obligee either releases the principal obligor from any duty (other than the duty to pay money)[43] or modifies the duties of the principal obligor to such an extent that the modifications give rise to a "substituted contract" status, imposing "fundamentally different" obligations and risks on the secondary obligor.[44]

(b) Partial discharge to prohibit further impairment

The secondary obligor will be able to limit its performance under the secondary obligation to prevent unexpected loss thereunder in the event that the obligee does any of the following acts: releases the principal obligor from any duty to pay money;[45] extends the term of the underlying obligation;[46] makes other modifications to the underlying obligation that do not rise to the level of a substituted contract;[47] releases or otherwise "impair[s] the value of . . . collateral securing the underlying obligation;"[48] allows the statute of limitations to expire;[49] or otherwise does any act (or fails to do any act) that "impairs the principal obligor's duty of performance, . . . duty to reimburse [the secondary obligor], or the secondary obligor's right of restitution or subrogation."[50] **Note:** D.C.'s statute of limitations specifies enforcement periods of 12 years for contracts under seal and three years for all other contracts.[51]

(c) Secondary obligor's remedies

The secondary obligor may have a claim against the obligee regarding any performance by the secondary obligor under the secondary obligation that would have been nullified or otherwise "discharged" due to an impaired suretyship status.[52]

§ 8 Waiver of Defenses by the Guarantor

Despite the protections offered to secondary obligors under the Restatement resulting from the obligee's impairment of suretyship status, due to the Restatement's great deference to contract law, the parties have the ability to bargain away these defenses via a waiver by the secondary obligor in the secondary obligation. An affirmative "consent" to any of obligee's or the principal obligor's acts or a broad "waiver of discharge" on behalf of the secondary obligor will serve as an absolution for any impairment of suretyship status.[53]

43. *Id.* § 37(2)(a).
44. *Id.* § 37(2)(b).
45. *Id.* § 37(3)(a).
46. *Id.* § 37(3)(b).
47. *Id.* § 37(3)(c).
48. *Id.* § 37(3)(d).
49. *Id.* § 37(3)(e).
50. *Id.* § 37(3)(f).
51. D.C. Code § 12-301(6)-(7) (2012).
52. Restatement (Third) of Suretyship and Guaranty § 37(4) (1996).
53. *Id.* ch. 3, intro. note.

Practice Pointer: A standard guaranty agreement should include language akin to the following: "Guarantor hereby waives: (a) any right to require Lender to proceed against Borrower, proceed against or exhaust any security for the Indebtedness, or pursue any other remedy in Lender's power whatsoever; (b) any defense arising by reason of any disability or other defense of Borrower, or the cessation from any cause whatsoever of the liability of Borrower; (c) any defense based on any claim that Guarantor's obligations exceed or are more burdensome than those of Borrower; (d) the benefit of any homestead or similar exemption, state or federal, with respect to its obligations hereunder; (e) presentment, demand, protest, demand, and notice of dishonor; and (f) the benefit of any statute of limitations affecting Guarantor's liability hereunder." In addition, despite including the foregoing general waiver language, a lender should always have all loan document modifications documented in writing and signed by all obligor parties, including all guarantors, to further estop the guarantor from raising a suretyship defense.

§ 9 Third-party Pledgors—Defenses and Waiver Thereof

A pledge of collateral to secure another person's obligations gives rise to suretyship status on the part of such pledgor.[54] Therefore, the pledgor may avail itself of any secondary obligor's defenses (and likewise can waive those defenses to the same extent as any other secondary obligor).

§ 10 Joint and Several Liability

Some additional issues may arise when there is more than one secondary obligor liable under the secondary obligation. The terms of each secondary obligor's duty to the obligee is determined by the contract language contained within the four corners of the secondary obligation, irrespective of the secondary obligors' relationships and rights among each other;[55] provided, however, that the obligee's recovery against the secondary obligors, in the aggregate, "may not exceed the amount of the underlying obligation plus any additional amounts recoverable pursuant to the terms of the secondary obligations" (such as attorneys' fees, costs of collection, environmental liability, etc.).[56] Though the D.C. courts have not directly addressed the concept of joint and several liability in the guaranty context, recent cases do generally uphold the notion of joint and several liability awards.[57]

54. *Id.* § 1(1)(a).
55. *Id.* § 52 cmt. a.
56. *Id.* § 52.
57. *See, e.g.*, Convit v. Wilson, 980 A.2d 1104, 1108 (D.C. 2009).

Practice Pointer: A commercial guaranty should include a provision confirming that the guarantor "individually, jointly, and severally" guaranties payment and performance of the underlying obligation, or—if multiple guarantors execute the same guaranty agreement—language clarifying that "If Guarantor consists of more than one party, the obligations under this Guaranty of each of such parties shall be joint and several."

10.1 Subsuretyship versus Cosuretyship

The Restatement distinguishes between two competing principles when faced with a multiple secondary obligor fact pattern: subsuretyship (when one of the sureties is a "principal surety" and has superior payment or performance duties to the others) and cosuretyship (when each surety bears payment and performance duties to the obligee).[58] In the absence of an agreement between the secondary obligors explaining the nature of their relationship, a presumption of cosuretyship prevails.[59]

Practice Pointer: When faced with a cosuretyship scenario, guarantors will often seek to limit their individual liability under a commercial guaranty agreement to a fixed dollar figure or a percentage of the amount of the underlying obligation. In either instance, the lender should be sure to restrict this limitation to principal only as of a specific date of determination, and preserve the ability to tack on interest, attorneys' fees, costs of collection, environmental liability, and other performance duties on a rolling basis. A guaranty with a true ceiling (for instance, an all-in cap of a hard dollar figure inclusive of all obligations under the guaranty), while the most favorable for guarantors, can leave lenders with a gaping hole in their quiver of remedies.

§ 11 Reliance

Though D.C. law does not specifically address the issue of the obligee's reliance on the secondary obligation, the consideration issues discussed in Section 4, *supra*, may be relevant to an evaluation of any such reliance concerns as being "part of the exchange for which the obligee bargained."[60]

§ 12 Subrogation

The secondary obligor is subrogated to the rights of the obligee upon "total satisfaction" of the underlying obligation, but only to the extent such secondary obligor's performance "contributed to [such] satisfaction."[61]

58. Restatement (Third) of Suretyship and Guaranty § 53 (1996).
59. *Id.* § 53 cmt. f.
60. *Id.* § 9(2)(a).
61. Id. § 27(1).

§ 13 Triangular Set-off in Bankruptcy

D.C. law does not specifically address the issue of triangular setoff in bankruptcy with respect to guaranties or sureties.

§ 14 Indemnification—Whether the Principal Obligor has a Duty

Though the Restatement does not specifically provide for indemnification rights, certain reimbursement obligations may be owed to the secondary obligor by the principal obligor.

(a) Principal obligor's duty to reimburse secondary obligor

It is well recognized that the principal obligor has a "duty . . . to reimburse the secondary obligor" for either the secondary obligor's cost of performance of the underlying obligation or to the extent of the secondary obligor's "settlement with the obligee," in whole or in part, that "discharges the principal obligor."[62] This duty of reimbursement arises upon the secondary obligor's performance or settlement.[63]

(b) Defenses to reimbursement

The principal obligor's duty to reimburse the secondary obligor may be relieved by bankruptcy of the principal obligor,[64] availability of a defense to the principal obligor that was "not available" to the secondary obligor,[65] the principal obligor's "lack of capacity" to enter into the underlying obligation (if contractual),[66] discharge of the principal obligor by the obligee[67] or the secondary obligor's performance of the underlying obligation despite the availability of a defense thereto.[68]

§ 15 Enforcement of Guaranties

Since guaranty law is ultimately governed by contract law, the same procedural considerations apply.

62. *Id.* § 22(1).
63. *Id.* § 22(2).
64. *Id.* § 24(1)(a).
65. *Id.* § 24(1)(c).
66. *Id.* § 24(1)(b).
67. *Id.* § 24(1)(d).
68. *Id.* § 24(1)(e)-(f).

15.1 Choice of Law Rules

In the District of Columbia, the agreement of the parties establishes what law governs a contract.[69] While there are no cases of record specifically concerning choice of law provision in guaranty contracts, there is no reason to believe D.C. courts would not uphold such provisions.[70]

In the event that a court must decide what law governs when the parties are from different states and the contract is silent on the issue, the D.C. Court of Appeals conducts a "governmental interests" analysis to determine which state's law applies.[71] This analysis mirrors that of the *Restatement (Second) of Conflict of Laws*, and includes consideration of several factors, "including: (1) the place of contracting; (2) the place of negotiation of the contract; (3) the place of performance; (4) the location of the subject matter of the contract; (5) the residence and place of business of the parties; and (6) the principal location of the insured risk."[72]

§ 16 Revival and Reinstatement of Guaranties

Although a secondary obligation would typically be discharged upon full performance of the underlying obligation (whether by another obligor, collateral realization, or otherwise), the secondary obligation may be revived to the extent the obligee "surrenders that performance or collateral, or the value thereof [under a legal duty to do so]."[73] This scenario would most often arise in the context of bankruptcy, where such payment or performance may constitute a preference in favor of obligee and, as such, must be returned to the bankruptcy estate.

Practice Pointer: If a lender is dealing with a financially insecure or troubled principal obligor, it may be in the lender's best interest to proceed initially against a sounder, more creditworthy secondary obligor to avoid costly and lengthy procedural delays resulting from such potential bankruptcy and reinstatement complications.

---

69. *See, e.g.*, Rollins v. Rollins, 602 A.2d 1121, 1123 (D.C. 1922).
70. Cf. Restatement (Third) of Suretyship and Guaranty § 14 (1996) ("The standards that apply to interpretation of contracts in general apply to interpretation of contracts creating secondary obligations.").
71. Adolph Coors Co. v. Truck Ins. Exch., 960 A.2d 617, 620 (D.C. 2008).
72. *Id.* (citing Restatement (Second) of Conflict of Laws §§ 188, 193 (1971)).
73. Restatement (Third) of Suretyship and Guaranty § 70 (1996).

Equal Credit Opportunity Act's Restrictions Regarding Guaranties

Laura Hobson Brown
McGlinchey Stafford, PLLC
12th Floor
601 Poydras Street
New Orleans, LA 70130
Phone: (504) 586-1200
Fax: (504) 596-2800
www.mcglinchey.com

Contents

Equal Credit Opportunity Act's Restrictions Regarding Guaranties

While state law defines the nature of the guaranty relationship and the parameters of its operation, federal law provides an individual guarantor of business credit with protections against marital status discrimination. Among other protections provided by the Equal Credit Opportunity Act[1] ("ECOA") and its implementing Regulation B,[2] ECOA establishes the limited circumstances under which a creditor may require its business credit applicant[3] to provide another party, a guarantor, to guarantee the business applicant's performance of its obligations to the creditor. In those circumstances in which requiring a guarantor is permitted, ECOA also restricts the creditor's ability to require the guarantor to be the business applicant's spouse.

§ 1 Equal Credit Opportunity Act

The ECOA and Regulation B establish the circumstances under which a creditor may require an applicant seeking individual business credit to provide a guarantor as a condition of receiving the credit requested. An "applicant" is any person, including a natural person, corporation or other type of legal entity who requests or receives a credit extension from a creditor and includes anyone who is or may become contractually liable for the debt.[4] For purposes of determining when the creditor may require a second person to become personally liable for a borrower's debt, the rules protecting an applicant also apply to guarantors, sureties, endorsers, and similar parties (collectively, a "guarantor").[5]

1.1 General Rule

Generally, a creditor may not discriminate against an individual applicant for business credit on the basis of, among other characteristics, the applicant's marital status.[6] The general rule covers all aspects of a credit transaction, including the application procedure, credit evaluation criteria, and the administration and collection of accounts.[7]

1. 15 U.S.C. §§1691, *et seq.* ECOA is most commonly associated with consumer credit protection. However, ECOA also protects a business credit applicant from various forms of discrimination, including discrimination based on marital status. *See* 15 U.S.C. § 1691a(b), (f).
2. Equal Credit Opportunity Act, 12 C.F.R. pt. 1002. Citations herein reflect Regulation B's codification as a regulation of the Consumer Financial Protection Bureau, effective December 30, 2011. *See* 76 Fed. Reg. 79,442 (Dec. 21, 2011).
3. 12 C.F.R. § 1002.2(e), (g).
4. 12 C.F.R. § 1002.2(e).
5. *Id.*
6. 12 C.F.R. § 1002.2(g); 1003(a), (d).
7. 12 C.F.R. § 1002.4(a). Regulation B Official Staff Commentary, comment 4(a)-1.

1.2 Business Credit

For purposes of these rules, "business credit" is a loan primarily for business or commercial (including agricultural) purposes, excluding credit extensions involving public utilities credit, credit extensions subject to Section 7 of the Securities Exchange Act of 1934 or by a broker or dealer subject to regulation under the Securities Exchange Act of 1934, incidental consumer purpose credit, or credit extended to governments or governmental subdivisions, agencies, or instrumentalities.[8]

§ 2 General Rule Regarding Guarantors

Generally, if a credit applicant is individually qualified for the requested credit, the creditor cannot require another person to guarantee the applicant's debt as a condition of credit.[9] If an individual credit applicant does not meet the creditor's creditworthiness standards, the creditor may require him to provide a creditworthy guarantor; however, the creditor cannot require that guarantor to be the applicant's spouse.[10]

2.1 Exception: Business Credit Guarantors

Applications for some types of business credit are not subject to the general prohibition against requiring an individually qualified credit applicant to provide a guarantor. When a creditor extends credit to a business or closely held corporation, the creditor may require each partner, director, or officer of the business and each shareholder of a closely held corporation to personally guarantee the debt, even if the business or closely held corporation is itself creditworthy.[11]

The creditor's requirement for a partner's, officer's, or shareholder's personal guaranty of the business loan must be based on the relationship between the guarantor and the business or corporation and not on an unrelated basis, such as the guarantor's race, color, religion, national origin, sex, marital status, or age.[12] For example, a creditor cannot require personal guaranties for a business owned by women or minorities, but not for an other business owned by men. Similarly, a creditor may not require only married officers of a business or married shareholders of a closely held corporation to personally guarantee the business' debt.[13]

8. 12 C.F.R. § 1002.2(g); 1002.3.
9. 12 C.F.R. § 1002.7(d)(5).
10. Regulation B Official Staff Commentary, comment 7(d).
11. *Id.* at comment 7(d)(6)-1.
12. *Id.*
13. *Id.*

2.2 Spousal Guarantors of Business Credit

As noted above, ECOA generally prohibits a creditor from automatically requiring the spouse of a married individual applicant to guarantee a loan to that individual. The same rule regarding spousal guaranties applies to credit extended to business entities. While a creditor may require each officer of a closely held business to personally guarantee a loan to the corporation, regardless of the corporation's own creditworthiness, the creditor may not automatically require the spouse of each married officer to also sign (and become personally liable for) the officer's guaranty of the corporate debt.[14]

As is the case with any other applicant, a creditor may evaluate the creditworthiness of an officer or shareholder who is guaranteeing a business or corporate debt. If the creditor concludes that the officer's individual financial circumstances are not sufficiently strong, the creditor may require the officer to provide another qualified individual to support his guaranty of the corporate debt. If the officer's spouse meets the creditor's underwriting requirements and is so inclined, she may volunteer to be the additional guarantor, but the creditor cannot automatically require the officer's spouse to be the coguarantor.[15] In determining whether a coguarantor is needed to support an insider's guaranty of a loan extended to a business or closely held corporation, the creditor must apply the same rules that it would utilize to determine whether another person's personal liability is needed to support a loan requested by an individual.[16]

§ 3 Requiring Additional Signatures

The rules governing when a creditor may require an additional party's personal liability to support a business or corporate officer's guaranty depend on the types of assets on which the guarantor is depending to support the guaranty and on whether the guarantor resides in a community property state.

3.1 Jointly Owned Property

If an officer or shareholder guarantor of a corporation's debt does not own sufficient separate property and is depending on jointly owned property to support his or her corporate guaranty, the creditor must determine the value of the guarantor's interest in the jointly owned property.[17] If the value of the guarantor's interest in that property is sufficient to support his obligation as guarantor, the creditor may not require the joint owner of the property to sign a security agreement encumbering his interest in the jointly owned property.[18] However, if the guarantor's interest in the jointly owned property is insufficient to

14. *Id.* at comment 7(d)(6)-2.
15. 12 C.F.R. § 1002.7(d)(5).
16. Regulation B Official Staff Commentary, comment 7(d)(6)-2.
17. *Id.* at comment 7(d)(2)-1.
18. *Id.*

support his or her guaranty, the creditor has the option of requiring the guarantor to provide another guarantor or requiring the joint owner of the property to sign a security agreement in order to ensure the creditor's access to the guarantor's property in the event of the business borrower's default. However, the security agreement cannot create personal liability for the joint owner.[19]

Some states require both spouses to sign or at least concur in granting any security instrument encumbering certain types of property that the couple owns jointly *(e.g. real estate)* in order to grant a secured party an enforceable security interest in that property. In such a state, a creditor may require a guarantor's spouse to sign any security instrument necessary to establish an enforceable security interest in the couple's jointly owned property that will secure the guarantor's obligations under the guaranty. However, the creditor may not require the spouse to sign a guaranty or any other instrument if signing just the security instrument is sufficient to make the jointly owned property available to satisfy the guaranty in the event of default.[20]

3.2 Reliance on Another Party's Income

If a guarantor of corporate debt is relying on another person's income to support his obligations as guarantor, the creditor may be able to require that other person to become a coguarantor in order to ensure that his income will be available to satisfy the guaranty if the borrower defaults.[21] Depending on the circumstances, the additional party could be the guarantor's spouse or another party on whose income the guarantor is relying.

3.2.1 Residents of Community Property States

If a married guarantor of a business or corporate loan resides in a community property state and is relying on his spouse's future earnings to support his guaranty of that debt, the creditor may require the guarantor's spouse to sign the guaranty under certain circumstances in order to ensure that the spouse's future earnings will be available to satisfy the guarantor's obligations in the event of default. The spouse's signature (and, hence, personal liability) on the guaranty may be required if: (1) pursuant to applicable state law, the guarantor lacks the power to individually manage or control sufficient community property to support the guaranty and (2) the guarantor has insufficient separate property to support the guaranty without regard to his community property.[22] However, even if the guarantor is reigning on his spouse's future earnings to support the guaranty, the creditor has the option to elect not to require the guarantor's spouse to become a coguarantor, even if the creditor would otherwise require the personal liability of any other party on whose income the guarantor relied to support the guaranty.[23]

---

19. *Id.* at comment 7(d)(2)-1(ii).
20. *Id.* at comment 7(d)(4)-1.
21. *Id.* at comment 7(d)(5)-2.
22. *Id.* The following states are currently community property states: AZ, CA, ID, LA, NV, NM, TX, WA, WI.
23. *Id.* at comment 7(d)(5)-2.

Neither ECOA nor Regulation B prescribes the procedures that a creditor should follow in determining whether a guarantor who resides in a community property state is relying on his or her spouse's future earnings to support the guaranty. A "best practice" is for the creditor to have the guarantor affirmatively indicate on an application form reliance on his or her spouse's future earnings. However, even if a guarantor affirmatively indicates on an application form reliance on his or her spouse's future earnings, the creditor may wish to confirm that the guarantor's spouse currently has income or separate assets before requiring the spouse to assume personal liability by signing the guaranty. That is, if a guarantor affirmatively indicates reliance on his spouse's future earnings to support his guaranty of his corporation's debt, but his spouse has no current income or separate assets, the creditor most probably should not require the spouse's signature as coguarantor.

This special spousal signature rule for married residents of community property states highlights the potential impact of a couple's divorce on a creditor's ability to collect credit extended individually to one of the spouses. Under the laws of many community property states, a married credit applicant has the individual ability to encumber the couple's community assets without the other spouse's consent (with exceptions for certain types of property, such as real estate). *See*, for example, La. Civ. Code art. 2346. As long as the community continues to exist (*i.e.*, until the community is terminated by divorce, death, etc.), the earned income of both spouses is a community asset and may be reached to satisfy a community debt incurred individually by either spouse. For example, while the couple remains married, a creditor that extends individual credit to a married man may reach his wife's income if necessary to satisfy the loan obtained individually by the husband, provided that the creditor follows appropriate collection procedures. However, if the spouses divorce and the community terminates before that loan is repaid, the creditor will not be able, following the divorce, to sue the former wife and garnish her earnings to satisfy the loan. Following the couple's divorce, those earnings will be the wife's separate property, rather than a community asset. Because she did not sign the husband's note or guaranty, she has no personal liability for the debt and the creditor would have no ability to reach her separate property (her earnings) to satisfy the former husband's loan.

3.2.2 Residents of Other States

If a married guarantor of corporate debt residing in a separate property state is not individually creditworthy but indicates that he or she is relying on the income of his or her spouse or that of another party to support the guaranty, the creditor may require the signature of the guarantor's spouse or the other party to support the guarantor's obligations under the guaranty.[24]

24. *Id.*

Canadian Law of Guaranties

(All Provinces Except Quebec)

S. Jason Arbuck

Cassels Brock & Blackwell LLP
2100 Scotia Plaza
40 King Street West
Toronto, Ontario M5H 3C2
(416) 860-6889
(416) 644-9364
jarbuck@casselsbrock.com
www.casselsbrock.com

CASSELS BROCK
LAWYERS

Contents

Canadian Law of Guaranties

Special thanks for the contributions made by the following associates and students of Cassels Brock & Blackwell LLP: Anita Kim, Steven Pulver, Azim Remani, Laura Shiner, Carolyn Stroz Peter Sullivan, Jennifer Wasylyk, and Laura Weingarden.

Highlights:

- In both Alberta and Saskatchewan, a guaranty given by an *individual* in certain instances will have no effect unless the guarantor appears before a notary public and the notary public issues a certificate in the prescribed form.
- There are no restrictions on providing financial assistance in four of the twelve Canadian common law jurisdictions. The balance of jurisdictions have restrictions of varying degrees.
- A "continuing" guaranty may be revoked at any time in respect of advances made after the time of the revocation. A guaranty may specify a notice requirement for revocation, but a waiver of the right to revoke a continuing guaranty is not enforceable. It is common in Canada for a guaranty to require a minimum number of days' prior notice for revocation in order to protect the obligee against immediate revocation.
- Specific waivers of defenses by a guarantor are enforceable. It is unclear whether a general waiver of all defenses by a guarantor is enforceable.

Introductory Note: Canada is comprised of ten provinces and three territories, all of which, except Quebec, are governed by a common law legal system. Quebec is governed by a civil law legal system. This survey summarizes the law of guaranties in all provinces and territories, excluding Quebec. The law of guaranties in Canada is generally consistent across the common law provinces and territories, except where noted herein. Any reference to "provinces" within this survey is a reference to all Canadian provinces and territories except Quebec, unless otherwise specified.

References to provisions in provincial statutes in this survey are, in the interest of brevity, limited to references to the Ontario statutes only. In all instances, unless otherwise indicated, the provincial statutes of the other provinces contain substantively similar provisions to those referenced in the Ontario statutes.

In Canada, "guaranty" is typically spelled "guarantee." However, for the sake of consistency, the U.S. spelling is used throughout this survey.

In order to standardize our discussion of the law of guaranties, we use the following vocabulary to refer to the various parties to a guaranty and their obligations.

"**Guarantor**" means a person who, by contract, agrees to satisfy an underlying obligation of a primary obligor to an obligee upon the primary obligor's default on that underlying obligation. We do not draw a distinction between guarantors and sureties, as the distinction between the two in Canada is often muddled and of no consequence to the drafting and enforcement of a guaranty.

"**Guaranty**" means the contract by which the guarantor agrees to satisfy the underlying obligation of a primary obligor to an obligee in the event the primary obligor defaults on such underlying obligation.

"**Obligee**" means the person to whom the underlying obligation is owed. For example, the lender under a loan agreement would be the obligee.

"**Primary obligor**" means the person who incurs the underlying obligation to the obligee. For example, the borrower under a loan agreement would be the primary obligor.

"**Underlying obligation**" means the primary obligation incurred by the primary obligor owed to the obligee. For example, a borrower's obligation to make payments of principal and interest to a lender on a loan constitutes an underlying obligation.

§ 1 Nature of the Guaranty

1.1 Guaranty Relationships

A guaranty is an accessory contract under which the guarantor has an obligation to answer for the debt of, or default by, the primary obligor.[1] An agreement is a guaranty only if it is collateral to a primary obligation to which a primary obligor is subject. Central to the notion of the law of guaranty is that there are two sources which the obligee may look to for performance: the primary obligor and the guarantor.

The underlying obligation must be preexisting or be contemplated at the time the guaranty is given. The underlying obligation is "contemplated" where the surrounding circumstances indicate that the parties contemplated that the obligation would arise. It is not necessary that the underlying obligation be explicitly set out in the contract; it may be determined from the circumstances. For example, a promise to guaranty "any and all indebtedness" where the parties contemplated that the creditor would provide future advances would

1. *Gold v. Rosenberg*, [1997] S.C.J. 93, [1997] 3 S.C.R. 767.

fulfill this requirement. If the underlying obligation is not "contemplated," the promise will not be a guaranty but may still be an enforceable contract.[2]

Under Canadian law, there is no specific language required to create a guaranty obligation.[3] Rather, a court will look to substance over form and the substantive intention exhibited by the parties when creating the agreement.[4]

1.2 Other Guarantor-type Relationships

While not the focus of this survey, we note that a guaranty-type relationship arises when a person pledges collateral as security for a loan in order to induce an obligee to lend to a primary obligor. In certain provinces, the applicable personal property security legislation provides that a person may grant a security interest in its personal property to secure the obligation of another person. This guaranty-type relationship is limited in that it only applies to the extent of the collateral pledged. Since there is no formal guaranty, obligees in these guaranty-type relationships do not receive the benefit of the waiver of certain defenses by the guarantor which are often contained in traditional guaranties and discussed further in § 9 *Third-party pledgors—defenses and waiver thereof* of this survey.

§ 2 Canadian Law Requirements for a Person to Enter a Guaranty

Corporations, partnerships, banks, trusts, unlimited liability corporations, and individuals can all grant guaranties in furtherance of their business activities.

2.1 Corporations

Canadian corporate law statutes provide that a corporation has the capacity, rights, powers, and privileges of a natural person and, accordingly, is able to enter into a guaranty.[5] It is not necessary to pass a bylaw in order to confer any particular power on a corporation or its directors.[6] Unless the articles, bylaws, or a unanimous shareholder agreement provide otherwise, the directors of a corporation may, without authorization of the shareholders, give a guaranty on behalf of the corporation to secure the performance of an obligation of any person.[7] The British Columbia *Business Corporations Act* contains no such provision.[8]

2. Morin v. Hammond Lumber Co., [1923] S.C.R. 140 (S.C.C.).
3. Welford v. Beazley (1747), 3 Atk 503, 26 ER 1090.
4. Central Mortgage & Housing Corp. v. Omega Investments Ltd., [1981] N.B.J. 86 (N.B.C.A.).
5. Ontario Business Corporations Act, R.S.O. 1990, c. B.16, s. 15 [OBCA]; Canada Business Corporations Act, R.S.C. 1985, c. C-44, s. 16 [CBCA].
6. OBCA, s. 17(1).
7. CBCA, s. 189(1)(c); OBCA, s. 184(1)(c).
8. (BC) Business Corporations Act, S.B.C. 2002, c. 57 [BCBCA].

Directors of a corporation owe a fiduciary duty to act in the best interests of the corporation.[9] As a result, a corporation may not enter into a guaranty except where the directors conclude, in good faith, that to do so is in the best interests of the corporation and in furtherance of the corporation's objectives.[10]

In certain cases, it may be in the interest of a corporation to provide a guaranty to its affiliates (i.e., a holding company, subsidiary, or sister company).[11] For example, a corporation may be required to provide a guaranty for the obligations of an affiliate corporation in order for that corporation to obtain financing, which in turn benefits the guarantor or its corporate group in addition to benefitting the obligee.

There are no specific rules on intercorporate guaranties for corporations formed in Ontario or at the federal level, and accordingly, such corporations may provide a guaranty to any member of their corporate group (i.e., a holding corporation, subsidiary, or affiliate corporation) where it is in the best interests of the corporation to do so.[12] The applicable Manitoba and Nova Scotia legislation explicitly provides that corporations formed in these provinces are free to provide a guaranty to secure the performance of an obligation of any person.[13]

However, certain rules or limitations on intercorporate guaranties continue to exist in other jurisdictions. Corporations formed under British Columbia, Alberta, and Saskatchewan legislation may give a guaranty to any person for any purpose if it complies with the financial disclosure requirements contained within each respective statute.[14] Under New Brunswick legislation, a corporation is prohibited from providing a guaranty to any of its shareholders or directors for the direct or indirect purpose of a purchase made, or to be made, of any shares in the corporation by any person.[15]

In the remaining jurisdictions—Prince Edward Island, Newfoundland and Labrador, Yukon, Northwest Territories, and Nunavut— a corporation may give a guaranty to a holding company, subsidiary company, or to the corporation's, or an affiliate's, employees in certain specified circumstances.[16] In addition, no such guaranty may be given where there are reasonable grounds for believing that the guarantor corporation may not be solvent pursuant to the solvency test found within the respective statutes.

---

9. OBCA, s. 134(1)(a); BCE Inc. v. 1976 Debentureholders, 2008 SCC 69.
10. Mark V Developments Ltd. v. Big White Ski Developments Ltd., [1985] B.C.J. 112 (B.C.S.C.).
11. KEVIN P. MCGUINNESS, THE LAW OF GUARANTEE 64 (Carswell 1996) [McGuinness].
12. KEVIN P. MCGUINNESS, HALSBURY'S LAWS OF CANADA: GUARANTEE AND INDEMNITY 359 (LexisNexis, 2010) [HALSBURY].
13. Corporations Act, C.C.S.M. , c. C225, s. 183(1); Companies Act, R.S., c. 81, s. 110A [NSCA].
14. BCBCA, s. 195(1); (AB) Business Corporations Act, R.S.A. 2000, c. B-9, s. 45(1) [ABCA]; (SK) Business Corporations Act, R.S.S. 1978, c. B-10, s. 42(1).
15. (NB) Corporations Act, R.S.N.B. 1973, c. C-24, s. 37(1).
16. (PEI) Companies Act, R.S.P.E.I. 1988, c. C-14, s. 69(2); (NL) Corporations Act, R.S.N.L. 1990, c. C-36, s. 79; (YK) Business Corporations Act, R.S.Y. 2002, c. 20, s. 46(2); Business Corporations Act, S.N.W.T. (Nu), 1996, c. 19, s. 46(2); (NWT) Business Corporations Act, S.N.W.T., 1996, c. 19, s. 46(2).

2.2 Partnerships

Canadian law recognizes two types of partnerships: general partnerships and limited partnerships. The partners of a general partnership are jointly and severally liable, without limitation, for the debts and obligations of the partnership.[17] These obligations include any guaranty given by the partnership, or given by one of the partners on behalf of the partnership. Each partner is an agent of the partnership and, subject to the terms of the partnership agreement, can bind the partnership.[18]

A limited partnership consists of at least one general partner and one limited partner.[19] A general partner has all of the powers and liabilities of a partner in a general partnership. This includes the power to give guaranties on behalf of the partnership. The general partners of a limited partnership will be jointly and severally liable for those guaranties.[20] Limited partners, on the other hand, are only liable for the debts and obligations of the partnership (including guaranties) to the extent of the limited partner's contribution to the partnership.[21] Notwithstanding the foregoing, a limited partner will lose its limited liability status if the limited partner takes part in the management or control of the business of the partnership.[22]

2.3 Banks

The *Bank Act*,[23] which governs all Canadian banks, provides that banks may give guaranties on behalf of any person for the payment or repayment of any sum of money, subject to two restrictions. First, the sum of money guarantied must be a fixed sum of money with or without interest; a bank cannot guaranty the payment of an indefinite amount of money. Second, the primary obligor must provide the bank with an unqualified obligation to reimburse the bank fully for payment or repayment. It is presumed that this unqualified obligation can take any form and may also be secured.[24] This latter restriction does not apply where the primary obligor is a subsidiary of the bank.[25]

2.4 Trusts

Under Canadian law, a trust arises where one entity, the trustee, holds property for the benefit of another entity, the beneficiary. Trusts are typically created through a trust instrument, which is a document setting out the property, purpose, and powers of the trust. The trust instrument may restrict the trust's

17. J. Anthony VanDuzer, The Law of Partnerships and Corporations 80 (Irwin Law, 3rd ed. 2009).
18. *Ibid.* at 54-55.
19. *Ibid.* at 80.
20. Re Lehndorff General Partner Ltd (1993), 17 C.B.R. (3d) 24 (Ont. Gen. Div. [Commercial List]); Lyle R. Hepburn, Limited Partnerships 3-20 (Carswell, looseleaf ed. 2011).
21. Limited Partnerships Act, R.S.O. 1990, c. L.16, s. 9 [LPA].
22. LPA s. 13(1).
23 Bank Act S.C. 1991, c. 46 [Bank Act].
24 M.H. Ogilvie, Canadian Banking Law 326 (Carswell, 1998).
25 Bank Act, ss. 414(1) and (2).

investment powers, including the power to guaranty a loan.[26] In the absence of such a restriction in the trust instrument, however, trustees may provide guaranties.[27]

Provincial legislation does not restrict the ability of a trust to guaranty a loan.[28]

2.5 Unlimited Liability Corporations

In an unlimited liability corporation (a "ULC"), the liability of the corporation's shareholders is not limited. Upon winding up or liquidation, the ULC's shareholders will be jointly and severally liable for the full extent of the corporation's unsatisfied obligations. There are no restrictions in Canadian law on a ULC's ability to provide a guaranty.[29]

Only three Canadian jurisdictions permit the incorporation of ULCs: British Columbia, Alberta, and Nova Scotia. In these jurisdictions, the directors of a ULC may give guaranties on behalf of the corporation without prior shareholder authorization unless the articles of incorporation, bylaws, or a unanimous shareholder agreement provide otherwise.[30]

2.6 Individuals

The rules associated with an individual's capacity to enter into a guaranty are fundamentally the same as those for entering into contracts generally.[31] More specifically, an individual entering into a guaranty must possess the requisite mental capacity and must have attained the age of majority.[32]

An individual's capacity to enter into a guaranty is not affected by his or her status as a spouse. A guaranty given by one spouse does not automatically affect the property or liabilities of the other spouse. However, issues may arise upon marriage breakdown. Provincial family law statutes aim to equally divide the value of net family property between two spouses upon the breakdown of the marriage, rather than dividing the property itself.[33] A spouse is typically permitted to deduct his or her debts and liabilities in calculating the value of his or her net family property.[34] In the case of a guaranty, a deduction will only be allowed where it is shown that there exists a "real risk" that the guarantor will be required to make good on the indebtedness.[35] The value of such a

---

26 *Ibid.* at 956.

27 Granata Family Trust (Trustee of) v. Royal Bank of Canada, [2000] OJ 4239; 40 R.P.R. (3d) 6 (Ont. S.C.J. [Commercial List]).

28 Trustee Act, R.S.O. 1990, c. T.23, ss. 26-29.

29 Re InterTAN Canada Ltd (2008), 49 C.B.R. (5th) 248 (Ont. S.C.J. [Commercial List]).

30 BCBCA, s. 51.3; ABCA, ss. 15.1-15.9; NSCA, s. 12.

31. Halsbury 183.

32. *Ibid.* 184; Beam v. Beatty (No. 2), [1902] O.J. 192 , 4 O.L.R. 554 at 559, per Garrow J.A. (Ont. C.A.).

33. Berdette v. Berdette, [1991] O.J. 788, 3 O.R. (3d) 513 at 524 (Ont. C.A.) at 31; Esther Lenkinksi, Halsbury's Laws of Canada: Family 247 (LexisNexis, 2010) [Lenkinksi].

34. Lenkinksi 308.

35. Drysdale v. Drysdale, [1994] O.J. 2897, 9 R.F.L. (4th) 20 (Ont. U.F.C.).

debt for equalization purposes may be discounted based on the likelihood that recovery will be sought against the spouse.[36]

The matrimonial home is an exception to this treatment of family property. The legislative trend across Canada is to recognize the special position of the matrimonial home in family life.[37] Legislative developments in various jurisdictions include prohibitions on the unilateral disposition or encumbrance of the matrimonial home to a third party except in certain circumstances.[38] These prohibitions render a conveyance or encumbrance of the home made without spousal consent void, unless such conveyance is made for valuable consideration, in good faith, and without notice that the property in question was a matrimonial home.[39]

§ 3 Authority to Enter into a Guaranty

Generally, an obligee has a duty of reasonable inquiry when it has some notice that the executor of a guaranty does not have authority to bind the guarantor.

3.1 Corporations

Corporations must enter into contracts through agents (i.e., directors, officers, or other authorized persons) who have either actual or apparent authority to act on behalf of the corporation. Actual authority exists where the agent is, in fact, authorized by the corporation to enter into an obligation pursuant to the bylaws of the corporation, or a combination of the bylaws and a directors' resolution. Apparent authority is created where an agent represents to a third party that the agent has the authority to bind the corporation.

An agent with actual or apparent authority may bind a corporation under a guaranty. When an agent of a corporation executes and delivers a guaranty on behalf of the corporation to an obligee, the obligee is protected by the "indoor management rule." The rule stipulates that a corporation may not assert that a person who has been held out as a director, officer, or agent of the corporation had not been duly appointed or does not have the authority (actual or apparent) to exercise the powers and perform the duties that are customary in the business of the corporation, or that are usual for such director, officer, or agent. The exception to this rule is where the obligee has or ought to have, by virtue of its relationship to the corporation, knowledge to the contrary. British Columbia's *BCBCA* contains no indoor management provision.[40]

36. Cade v. Rotstein, [2004] O.J. 286 (Ont. C.A.); Poole v. Poole, [2001] O.J. 2154, 16 R.F.L. (5th) 397 (Ont. S.C.J.); Duff v. Duff, [2007] N.B.J. 260 (N.B.Q.B.).
37. Lenkinksi 372.
38. *Ibid.* 185.
39. *Ibid.* 186.
40. OBCA, s. 19; CBCA, s. 18.

3.2 Partnerships

Under provincial partnership statutes, every partner is an agent of the partnership and of the other partners for the purpose of the partnership's business. Any act of a partner, carried out in the course of business customary for the partnership, binds the partnership and all partners. The exception to this rule is when the acting partner has no authority to act for the partnership in the particular matter and the person with whom the partner is dealing with either knows that the partner has no authority, or does not know or believe him or her to be a partner.[41]

Where one partner, on behalf of the partnership, provides a guaranty for a purpose apparently not connected with the partnership's ordinary course of business (i.e., in support of a partner's personal obligations), the partnership is not bound unless such partner is, in fact, specially authorized by the other partners. With the exception of limited partnerships, every partner is jointly liable with the other partners for all debts and obligations of the partnership incurred while that person is a partner.[42] In a limited partnership, the general partners are held jointly liable with the other partners; however, the liability of a limited partner is restricted to the value of the money and other property the limited partner contributes or agrees to contribute to the limited partnership.

3.3 Banks

Subject to the *Bank Act*, directors of a bank are required to manage and supervise the management of the business and affairs of the bank.[43] The directors of a bank may, subject to its bylaws, appoint officers, specify their duties, and delegate to them the power to manage the business and affairs of the bank.[44] An act of a director or an officer, including providing a guaranty on behalf of the bank, is valid notwithstanding a defect in the director's qualification or an irregularity in the director's election or in the appointment of the director or officer.

See § 2.3 *Banks* for a discussion on the restrictions imposed on banks providing guaranties.

§ 4 Consideration

Standard contract principles apply to the analysis of consideration required for a guaranty. A guaranty may support both past and future indebtedness. It is not required that consideration flow directly to the guarantor from the obligee. Forbearance is generally sufficient to constitute consideration.

41. (ON) Partnerships Act, R.S.O. 1990 c. P.5, s. 6 [PA].
42. OBCA, ss. 6-10.
43. Bank Act, s. 157(1).
44. *Ibid.*, s. 197(1).

Consideration is required to create a valid contract of guaranty.[45]

Standard contract law principles provide the basis for the inquiry into what constitutes sufficient consideration for a guaranty. Nominal consideration is adequate support of a guaranty. The benefit or obligation that forms the consideration need not flow directly to the guarantor from the obligee; the consideration flowing from the obligee to the primary obligor is sufficient to support a guaranty.[46]

A guaranty may secure both past and future indebtedness.[47] Where a guaranty relates to past indebtedness, it must be supported by new consideration. Generally, continued performance of one's preexisting contractual obligations does not create consideration for a new contract.[48] However, the act of an obligee refraining from putting a primary obligor into default in exchange for a guaranty constitutes sufficient consideration for a new guaranty.[49] In addition, it may be inferred that a guaranty was given in consideration that the obligee would forbear from taking action with respect to the underlying obligations.[50]

§ 5 Notice of Acceptance, Statute of Frauds; Formal Requirements for Guaranties

Notice of acceptance of a guaranty may not be required in every circumstance.

In most circumstances, guaranties must be written and signed to be enforceable. This requirement is essential for guaranties but does not pertain to indemnities. Alberta and Saskatchewan impose additional requirements on parties entering into guaranties.

5.1 Notice of Acceptance

As with all forms of contracts, a guaranty requires mutual consent of the parties through offer and acceptance of the agreement. When making an offer, the offeror must provide sufficient details regarding the terms of the proposed agreement and it must be made with the intention that it is open for the other party to accept. The offeror is not required to use any formal or specific language—the intention to enter into a guaranty may be inferred and held as sufficient to bind the offeror.[51] Courts will determine if a valid offer has been made by looking at the surrounding circumstances of the transaction from the perspective of a reasonable person in the position of the offeree.

45. Bank of Montreal v. Sperling Hotel Co., [1973] M.J. 88 (Man. Q.B.).
46. Ex p. Minet (1807), 14 Ves. 189, 33 E.R. 493 (L.C.).
47. Chapman v. Sutton (1846), 2 C.B. 634, 133 E.R. 1095 (C.P.).
48. Western Surety Co. v. Hancon Holdings Ltd., [2007] B.C.J. 250 (B.C.S.C.) at 30.
49. Harris v. Venables (1872), L.R. 7 Exch. 235.
50. Royal Bank of Canada v. Kiska, [1967] 2 O.R. 379, 63 D.L.R. (2d) 582 (Ont. C.A.).
51. S.M. Waddams, The Law of Contracts 21 (Canada Law Book, 2005); Macneil v. Dana Canada Corp., [2008] O.J. 2809 at 12 seq., per Sheppard J. (Ont. S.C.J.), rev'd [2009] O.J. 1735 (Ont. C.A.).

Under general contract law, acceptance stands for the willingness of the offeree to enter into an agreement with a specific party on the agreed upon terms. The acceptance must be unconditional, absolute, and given in the manner stated under the terms of the offer.[52]

Within the context of guaranties, there are special issues that arise surrounding the acceptance of an offer. In most cases, a guarantor will make an offer by completing and signing a standard form of guaranty and delivering it to the obligee. Within the terms of the offer (i.e., the standard form of guaranty), notice of acceptance in a traditional manner (e.g., providing verbal or written consent) is often not required.[53] As such, guaranties will often take the form of a unilateral contract whereby the obligee accepts the offer through the performance of the terms of the agreement (e.g., by providing a loan or other means of financial assistance, or by forbearing its rights as a creditor).[54] For example, a guarantor may offer a guaranty so that an obligee will extend credit to a primary obligee. Assuming that the offer did not explicitly require written notice of acceptance, the obligee's advancement of credit will constitute acceptance of the offer.[55]

5.2 Statute of Frauds

In Canada, all common law provinces and territories, except Manitoba,[56] are subject to statute of frauds legislation[57] which requires guaranties to be in writing, or be evidenced in writing, and signed by the guarantor or by a lawfully authorized agent of the guarantor. "Evidenced in writing" means that the terms of a guaranty may be oral as long as there is a signed written note or memorandum evidencing the existence of it. In British Columbia, a guaranty that is not in writing may be enforceable if the alleged guarantor has done an act indicating that a guaranty consistent with that alleged has been made.[58]

Notwithstanding the foregoing, it is prudent and common practice to have the entire guaranty agreement in writing and executed.

The applicable statute of frauds legislation applies only to guaranties and not to contracts of indemnity, except in British Columbia where an indemnity must be in writing, or be evidenced in writing, or accompanied by an act of the alleged indemnitor indicating that the indemnity in question has been made.[59]

52. HALSBURY 217.
53. *Ibid.*
54. R.M. GOODE, LEGAL PROBLEMS OF CREDIT & SECURITY 63 (Sweet & Maxwell, 1982).
55. Jays v. Tatler (1898), 14 T.L.R. 461; Lysaght v. Walker (1831), 6 E.R. 707 (H.L.).
56. (MB) An Act to Repeal the Statute of Frauds, C.C.S.M. c. F158.
57. (ON) Statute of Frauds, R.S.O. 1990, c. S.19; (PEI) Statute of Frauds, R.S.P.E.I., c. S-6; (NS) Statute of Frauds, R.S.N.S. 1989, c. 442; (NB) Statute of Frauds, R.S.N.B. 1973, c. S-14. The remaining jurisdictions, excluding Manitoba, received the Statute of Frauds Amendment Act 1828, 9 Geo. 4 , c. 14 from the U.K.
58. (BC) Law and Equity Act, R.S.B.C. 1996, c. 253, s. 59(6).
59. *Ibid.*

5.3 Other Formal Requirements

The provinces of Alberta and Saskatchewan impose additional requirements on certain parties entering into guaranties.

5.3.1 *Alberta*

In Alberta, a guaranty given by an *individual* will have no effect unless the guarantor (a) appears before a notary public, (b) acknowledges to the notary public that he or she executed the guaranty, and (c) in the presence of the notary public, signs a statement in the prescribed form.[60] The notary public must issue a certificate under the notary public's hand and seal in the prescribed form and such certificate must be attached to, or noted on, the guaranty.[61] The notary public need not be licensed as a notary public in the province of Alberta.[62] The foregoing formalities are required for all guaranties governed by the law of Alberta, irrespective of where the guaranty was executed.[63]
There is no time restriction for obtaining the notary public certificate.[64] A guaranty that has not been acknowledged before a notary public is "ineffective" but, once acknowledged, will become effective.

5.3.2 *Saskatchewan*

In Saskatchewan, a guaranty given by an *individual* in respect of a debt of a farmer in relation to farm land situated in Saskatchewan or other assets used in farming in Saskatchewan will not have effect unless: (a) the guarantor appears before a lawyer or notary public; (b) the guarantor acknowledges to the lawyer or notary public that he executed the guaranty, (c) in the presence of the notary public or lawyer, the guarantor signs a certificate in the prescribed form, and (d) the guaranty specifies the maximum financial obligation in sum certain plus interest from the date of the demand.[65]

The lawyer or notary public must issue a certificate in the prescribed form to be attached to, or noted on, the guaranty.[66] The lawyer or notary public need not be licensed in Saskatchewan. Farm land does not include minerals contained on, in, or under the real property or land used primarily for the purpose of extracting, processing, storing or transporting minerals. Farming includes livestock raising, poultry raising, dairying, tillage of the soil, beekeeping, fur farming, or any other activity undertaken to produce primary agricultural produce and animals.[67]

60. Guarantees and Acknowledgement Act, R.S.A. 2000, c. G-11, s. 3.
61. *Ibid.*, s. 4.
62. *Ibid.*, s. 1(b).
63. Lehndorff Property Management Ltd. v. McGrath, [1984] 3 W.W.R. 187, [1984] B.C.J. 2866 (B.C.S.C.).
64. Westeel-Rosco Ltd. v. Edmonton Tinsmith Supplies Ltd. and Roy, [1984] A.J. 954, 58 A.R. 194 (Alta. Q.B.) at 73.
65. The Saskatchewan Farm Security Act, S.S. 1988-1989, c. S-17.1, s. 31(2).
66. *Ibid.*, s. 31(3).
67. *Ibid.*, ss. 2(1)(f), 2(1)(g).

§ 6 Interpretation of Guaranties

Generally, a guaranty will be interpreted in the same manner as other contracts.

Continuing guaranties are revocable by the guarantor.

In order to create an enforceable contract of indemnity, the language needs to be clear and explicit.

6.1 General Principles

Generally, guaranties are interpreted by courts using the same principles of construction applicable to other types of contracts.[68]

6.2 Guaranty of Payment versus Guaranty of Collection

While the precise terms "guaranty of payment" and "guaranty of collection" are not defined in Canadian legislation nor found in Canadian caselaw, the caselaw is clear that, unless the parties expressly agree otherwise, the obligee need not enforce its claim against the primary obligor before enforcing its claim against the guarantor.[69]

Notwithstanding the foregoing, the terminology of "guaranty of payment" and "guaranty of collection" has worked its way into many Canadian guaranties, likely as a result of cross-border dealings.

6.3 Language Regarding the Revocation of Guaranties

A "continuing" guaranty will continue until notice of cancellation is given to the obligee by the guarantor.[70] An inherent feature of a continuing guaranty is that it may be revoked at any time in respect of advances made after the time of the revocation. A guaranty may specify a notice requirement for revocation, but a waiver of the right to revoke a continuing guaranty will not be enforceable. As a result, it is common in Canada for an obligee to include revocation language in a guaranty specifying that the guaranty is revocable upon the guarantor providing a minimum number of days' notice in order to protect the obligee against immediate revocation of a guaranty in respect of a revolving facility. Revocation does not affect the rights that have accrued to the obligee prior to the time of revocation.[71]

A guaranty in respect of a specified debt is not revocable.[72]

68. Kastner v. Winstanley, [1869] O.J. 169, 20 U.C.C.P. 101 (U.C. Ct. CP.).
69. Bank of Nova Scotia v. Papachristopoulos, 29 A.R. 91 at 7.
70. Ross v. Burton, [1848] O.J. 25, 4 U.C.R. 357 (U.C.Q.B.), per Robinson C.J.
71. Tooke Bros. Ltd. v. Al-Waters Ltd (1934), [1934] B.C.J. 26, [1935] 1 D.L.R. 295 (B.C.C.A.).
72. Halsbury 304; Lloyds Bank v. Harper (1880), 16 Ch.D. 290.

6.4 "Continuing"

Use of the word "continuing" in a guaranty will generally indicate that the guaranty is one that extends to a series of transactions.[73] Courts are hesitant to infer the existence of a continuing guaranty obligation unless it is clear that the guarantor intended to assume continuing liability.[74] If uncertainty exists, the guaranty will be construed against the obligee as the obligee has the onus of drafting a guaranty that provides more expansive protection from the guarantor.[75]

6.5 "Liable as a Primary Obligor and not as Guarantor Only"

The inclusion of this phrase is an attempt to convert a guaranty into an indemnity, thus preserving the liability of the guarantor even if the underlying obligations are void, illegal, *ultra vires,* or otherwise unenforceable.

Whether the "liable as a primary obligor" language constitutes an indemnity or guaranty will turn mainly on the construction of the relevant document and the intention of the parties.[76] The caselaw suggests that unless more explicit language is used, it is not prudent to treat a guaranty as having been effectively converted into an indemnity if the document only contains a phrase similar to "liable as primary obligor and not as guarantor only."[77]

Preferred drafting practice in Canada is to include a separate section in the guaranty entitled "Indemnity" with language that clearly provides for indemnification against losses which may arise by virtue of the underlying obligations being (a) void, voidable, *ultra vires*, illegal, invalid, ineffective, or otherwise unenforceable by the obligee, or (b) released or discharged by operation of law. This approach is considered sufficient to create an enforceable indemnity.

§ 7 Defenses of the Guarantor; Set-off

Regarding a "pure" guaranty (i.e., one that is not characterized as an indemnity), the guarantor is not liable to the obligee unless the primary obligor is liable. All defenses available to the primary obligor are generally also available to the guarantor.

73. Bank of British Columbia v. Houston, [1984] B.C.J. 2963, 57 B.C.L.R. 91 (B.C.S.C.).
74. 911943 Ontario Ltd. v. 407922 Ontario Ltd., [2006] O.J. 2123, 10 P.P.S.A.C. (3d) 25, aff'd (2007), 2007 CarswellOnt 7480 (Ont. C.A.) [*Ontario Ltd.*].
75. Pharmaceutical Supplies Ltd. v. Martin, [2000] N.J. 19 (Nfld. S.C.) per Dunn J. at 26-28.
76. Wilfrid M. Estey, Legal Opinion in Commercial Transactions 299 (LexisNexis Butterworths 1997) [Estey]; *see also* Communities Economic Development Fund v. Canadian Pickles Corp. (1991), 85 D.L.R. (4th) 88 (S.C.C.).
77. Estey at 302.

7.1 General

In the case of a "pure" guaranty (i.e., one that is not characterized as an indemnity), the guarantor is not liable to the obligee unless the primary obligor is liable.[78] Thus, if the underlying obligation is void, illegal, *ultra vires,* or otherwise unenforceable, the guaranty is usually unenforceable as well. All defenses available to the primary obligor are generally also available to the guarantor.[79] The defenses arise by operation of law and equity and, generally, need not be specified in the guaranty itself to be effective. However, all such defenses may be waived by agreement.[80]

7.2 Breach by Obligee

Unless specifically waived by the guarantor, a breach by the obligee of the agreement giving rise to the repudiation of the underlying obligation will generally discharge the guarantor of liability.[81]

Where there is a lesser breach by the obligee of the agreement giving rise to the underlying obligation, the guarantor will likely not be discharged unless such a breach gives rise to a material increase in the guarantor's liability.[82]

Where a breach by the obligee of the agreement giving rise to the underlying obligation does not amount to a discharge of the guarantor's liability, the breach may give rise to a right of counterclaim in favour of the primary obligor and may have the effect of reducing the liability of the guarantor.[83]

7.3 Change in Identity of Principal Obligor

Unless otherwise agreed, a fundamental change to the constitution of the obligee or primary obligor may release the guarantor from future liability under a continuing guaranty.

7.3.1 Change in Constitution of a Partnership

Where the primary obligor is a partnership, in the absence of agreement to the contrary, a continuing guaranty is revoked as to future transactions by any change in the constitution of such partnership. Similarly, where the obligee is a partnership, in the absence of agreement to the contrary, a continuing guaranty is revoked as to future transactions by any change in the constitution of such partnership.[84]

---

78. Kesmat Investment Inc. v. Industrial Machinery co., [1985] N.S.J. 109 (N.S.C.A.) at 13.
79. *Ibid.* at 14-15.
80. Bauer v. Bank of Montreal (1980), 33 C.B.R. (N.S.) 291 (S.C.C.), per McIntyre J [*Bauer*].
81. Transamerica Commercial Finance Corp. Canada v. Northgate RV Sales Ltd., [2006] B.C.J. 3298.
82. National Westminster Bank v. Riley, [1986] B.C.L.C. 268 (Eng. C.A.) per May L.J.
83. HALSBURY 522.
84. PA, s. 19.

7.3.2 *Amalgamations*

In Canada, corporations may be formed by the amalgamation of two or more corporations. The effect of an amalgamation is that the amalgamated or resulting corporation has all the property, rights, liabilities, and obligations of each of the amalgamating corporations. An amalgamation is a "confluence of two streams" rather than the corporate extinction of the predecessor companies and the creation of a wholly new amalgamated corporation.[85] There is no transfer of assets involved in an amalgamation and there is no direct equivalent of a U.S.-style "merger" in Canada.

The amalgamation of a corporate guarantor with one or more other corporations will not impact the effectiveness of the guaranty, as the liabilities of the corporate guarantor flow through to the new (amalgamated) corporation.[86] However, the credit worthiness of the original corporate guarantor may change as a result of its amalgamation with another corporation. For this reason, it is not uncommon for obligees to restrict guarantors from completing amalgamations without the prior consent of the obligee.

The amalgamation of a corporate obligee with one or more other corporations will generally not affect its rights under a guaranty.[87]

There appears to be no caselaw nor legislation addressing the issue of whether or not a guarantor is discharged of its liability under a guaranty when a corporate primary obligor amalgamates with one or more other corporations. However, such an amalgamation may constitute a fundamental change in the nature of the underlying obligations.[88] As such, common law principles would suggest that the guarantor would likely be relieved of its liabilities in respect of the underlying obligations arising after such amalgamation, especially where such amalgamation has increased the guarantor's risk. Accordingly, it is common practice in Canada to obtain a confirmation and acknowledgement from the guarantor with respect to its obligations under the guaranty at the time of an amalgamation, or to ensure that the agreement provides for the survivorship of the guaranty should the primary obligor amalgamate with another corporation.[89]

A mere name change of a corporation will not result in the guarantor being discharged.[90]

7.4 Modification of the Underlying Obligation

A material variation of the agreement giving rise to the underlying obligation will discharge the guarantor's liability where the variation results in an increase in the guarantor's risk.[91]

---

85. R. v. Black & Decker Manufacturing Co. [1975] 1 S.C.R. 411; Witco v. The Corporation of Oakville [1975] 1 S.C.R. 273.
86. OBCA s. 179(b).
87. McGuinness 358; Toronto-Dominion Bank v. Poli Holdings Ltd. [1999] O.J. 1489 (Ont. S.C.J.) at 36.
88 McGuinness 359.
89 McGuinness 359.
90 Wilson v. Craven (1841), 151 E.R. 1171 (Ex. Ch.).
91 Pax Management Ltd. v. Canadian Imperial Bank of Commerce, [1992] S.C.J. 78 (S.C.C.).

In cases where it is evident that the alteration is insubstantial or beneficial to the guarantor, the guarantor may not be discharged. However, if it is not clear that the alteration is insubstantial or beneficial to the guarantor, the guarantor must be the sole judge of whether or not it will consent to remain liable despite the alteration. If the guarantor has not so consented, it will be discharged.[92]

At common law, alterations to the underlying obligation are presumed to be material unless it is established that they are plainly insubstantial or necessarily beneficial to the guarantor.[93] Certain provinces, however, have adopted statutory provisions shifting the onus to the defendant guarantor to prove prejudice.[94]

Unless the guaranty provides otherwise, an enforceable contract to extend the time within which the primary obligor is required to perform the underlying obligation is considered a material alteration which may discharge the guarantor.[95]

Unless the guaranty provides otherwise, a release of the primary obligor without the guarantor's explicit consent will release the guarantor from liability.[96]

A guarantor is entitled to a discharge even where a variation to the underlying obligation has not been acted on. Proof of actual prejudice is not required; it is sufficient if there is potential for prejudice.[97] In any case where a proposed variation has the potential for prejudice to the guarantor, an obligee would be well advised to obtain the consent of the guarantor.

Notwithstanding the foregoing, a material alteration of the underlying obligations in a manner contemplated by the original agreements between the parties will not release the guarantor from its obligations. In other words, if the obligee is acting within the terms of the guaranty and related documents, even if the obligee's action is prejudicial to the guarantor, the guarantor will not be discharged.[98]

A guarantor is not released where the primary obligor seeks protection from its obligees under Canadian bankruptcy legislation (which in Canada includes the *Companies Creditors Arrangements Act*[99] and the *Bankruptcy and Insolvency Act*[100]).

---

92 Bank of Canada v. Conlin (1994), 20 O.R. (3d) 499 (C.A.), aff'd (1996), 139 D.L.R. (4th) 427 (S.C.C.) [*Conlin*]; Bank of Montreal v. Wilder, [1986] 2 S.C.R. 551 (S.C.C.).

93 *[Conlin]*.

94 *For example,* (MB) Mercantile Law Amendment Act, C.C.S.M. c. M120, s. 4; (SK) Queens Bench Act, 1998, c.Q-1.01, s.69.

95 Direct Leasing Limited v. Chu, [1976] 6 W.W.R. 587 (B.C.S.C.) at 12.

96 Griffith v. Wade, [1966] A.J. 86 (Alta. C.A.).

97 Newton v. Chorlton (1853), 68 E.R. 1087 (V.C.).

98 TD Canada Trust v. B & B Enterprises (London) Ltd., [2008] O.J. 2198, 2008 CarswellOnt 3282 (Ont. C.A.); Adelaide Capital Corp. v. Offshore Leasing Inc. (1997), 160 N.S.R. (2d) 16 (N.S.C.A.).

99 Companies Creditors Arrangements Act, R.S.C. 1985, c. C-36.

100 Bankruptcy and Insolvency Act, R.S.C. 1985, c. B-3.

7.5 Release or Impairment of Security for the Underlying Obligation

Because a guarantor is entitled to subrogation against the primary obligor, a security interest held by the obligee in collateral that secures the underlying obligation is held "in trust" for the guarantor. The obligee has an obligation to preserve the security interest. Where the security interest is released or impaired by the actions of the obligee, the liability of the guarantor is reduced to the extent of the release or impairment.[101]

7.6 Modification of the Guaranty

Modifications to a guaranty with the guarantor's consent will not affect its validity even where no new consideration is given for the modification.[102] Consideration is not necessary as the consent confirms an existing obligation rather than creating a new one.

See § 5 *Notice of acceptance, statute of frauds; Formal requirements for guaranties* for a discussion of the formal requirements necessary to enter into a guaranty as such requirements will also apply to the modification of a guaranty.

7.7 Failure to Pursue Primary Obligor

As a general rule, the obligee need not bring action or exhaust recourse against the primary obligor before claiming against the guarantor.[103]

The guarantor has a limited right to compel the obligee to demand payment of the underlying obligation from the primary obligor upon it becoming due, but does not have the right to compel the obligee to sue the primary obligor.[104]

The guarantor is not entitled to be notified of the primary obligor's default prior to the obligee bringing a claim against the guarantor.[105]

Two key qualifications to the general rule set out above are as follows. First, the terms of the guaranty may require the obligee to prosecute the obligee's claim against the primary obligor before claiming against the guarantor.[106] Second, where the primary obligor is liable to pay on demand, the formality of making an actual demand must be followed and the obligee must allow the primary obligor a reasonable amount of time to satisfy the demand prior to making claim against the guarantor.[107]

101 Bauer; Traders Finance Corp. v. Ross, [1942] O.J. 469; [1942] O.R. 618 (Ont. H.C.).
102 741431 Alberta Ltd. v. Devon (Town), [2002] A.J. 1169.
103 Canadian Imperial Bank of Commerce v. Pittstone Developments Ltd, [1985] B.C.J. 3013, 24 D.L.R. (4th) 224 (B.C.S.C.).
104 Great West Life Assurance Co. v. Walker (1909), 14 O.W.R. 95 (Ont. H.C.).
105 I.A.C. Ltd v. United Bus Co. (1954), 36 M.P.R. 1 (Nfld. S.C.).
106 National Bank v. Nadalin, [1986] O.J. 272 (Ont. C.A.).
107 Federal Business Development Bank v. Dunn, [1984] 6 W.W.R. 46 (Sask. Q.B.).

7.8 Limitations Act

As the liability of the guarantor is a contractual obligation, a limitation period will apply in most cases. Applicable limitation periods throughout Canada range from two to six years.[108]

Partial payment by the principal primary obligor does not revive the limitation periods.[109]

7.9 Statute of Frauds

Failure to comply with applicable *statute of frauds* legislation will provide the guarantor with a valid defense. See discussion in §5.2 *Statute of frauds* above.

7.10 Defenses Particular to Guarantors that are Individuals and their Spouses

(1) Spousal guaranties

There is no presumption of undue influence when an individual provides a guaranty for his or her spouse. However, a guarantor may raise a defense of undue influence if he or she can prove the de facto existence of a special relationship of trust and confidence beyond what is generally found between spouses.[110] Furthermore, the guarantor must also prove that the obligee knew or had notice of the undue influence in order for the defense to succeed.[111]

Notwithstanding the foregoing, the obligee is under a duty to inquire into the possibility that such special relationship exists between the spouses, even in the case of what appears to be a normal spousal relationship.[112] The caselaw confirms that an obligee who advises the guarantor to seek independent legal advice and who meets with the guarantor (in the absence of his or her spouse) to inform him or herof the potential liability and risks involved will have met his or her duty. [*Barclays*]. The duty does not extend to insisting that independent legal advice be obtained. A guarantor who does not seek independent legal advice prior to signing the guaranty may still be liable thereunder.[113]

---

108 (AB) Limitations Act, R.S.A. 2000, c. L-12, s. 3(1)(a); (BC) Limitation Act, R.S.B.C. 1996, c. 266, ss. 3(2), 6; (MB) Limitation of Actions Act, C.C.S.M. c. L150, s. 2(1)(g); (NB) Limitation of Actions Act, S.N.B. 2009, c. L-8.5, (ON) Limitations Act, 2002, S.O. 2002, c. 24, Sched B, ss. 4, 5.s. 5; (NL) Limitations Act, S.N.L. 1995, c. L-16.1, ss. 5(b); 13; 14; (NWT) Limitation of Actions Act, R.S.N.W.T. 1988, c. L-8, s. 2(e); (NS) Limitation of Actions Act, R.S.N.S. 1989, c.258, s. 2(1)(e); (NU) Limitation of Actions Act, R.S.N.W.T. 1988, c.L-8, s. 2(e); (PEI) Statute of Limitations, R.S.P.E.I. 1988, c. S-7, s. 2(1)(g); (SK) Limitations Act, S.S. 2004, c. L-16.1; (YK) Limitation of Actions Act, R.S.Y. 2002, c. 139, s. 2(1)(e), (f).

109 *Ibid.*, s. 13(11*)*; Walters v. Meiner, [2004] B.C.J. 585 (B.C.S.C.).

110 Barclays Bank plc. v. O'Brien, [1993] 4 All E.R. 417 (H.L.) [*Barclays*].

111 Bank of Montreal v. Holoboff, [1924] 2 W.W.R. 675 (Sask. C.A.).

112 [HALSBURY 449].

113 Bank of Montreal v. Featherstone, [1989] O.J. 613, 68 O.R. (2d) 541 (Ont. C.A.).

(2) *Non est factum*

A guarantor may, in limited circumstances, invoke the defense of *non est factum.* To be successful, the guarantor must prove that he or she did not know the contents or the character of the documents being signed and that the documents actually signed were fundamentally different from those the guarantor believed were being signed.[114]

If the guarantor chooses not to read the guaranty or inform himself or herself of its contents, then the guarantor will not be able to raise a defense of *non est factum*. As well, a mere misunderstanding of the scope of the guaranty is not sufficient to give rise to this defense.[115]

(3) *Misrepresentation*

A guarantor may raise a defense of misrepresentation where the obligee, or the primary obligor with the knowledge of the obligee, makes a material representation which is found to be untrue, *and* the guarantor is found to have relied upon such statement in providing the guaranty.[116]

(4) *Duress/undue influence*

A guarantor may raise a defense of duress if there was pressure on the guarantor, to such a degree, by either the obligee, or the primary obligor with the obligee having knowledge thereof, such that there was no real consent obtained when the guarantor entered into the guaranty. For the guarantor to be successful in this defense, it must be proven that the will of the guarantor was coerced, and such coercion was illegitimate. The caselaw has held that commercial and/or economic pressure, as well as hard bargaining, are not presumptively illegitimate, in the absence of further factors.[117]

7.11 Right of Set-off

Except where the parties have otherwise agreed, a guarantor may benefit from any right of legal set-off that the primary obligor may have against the obligee.[118] Under legal set-off, each of the obligations must be mutual cross obligations for liquidated sums.[119]

Equitable set-off is available where there is a claim for a money sum, liquidated or unliquidated, and does not require that a debt or mutual obligation exist.[120] The purpose of equitable set-off is to achieve a fair dealing as

114 First Independent v. Proby, [1966] B.C.J. 44 (B.C.S.C.). Custom Motors Ltd. v. Dwinnell, [1975] N.S.J. 384 (N.S.C.A.) at 17.

115 London Trust & Savings Corp. v. Corbett, [1992] O.J. 23, 6 O.R. (3d) 547 (Ont. Gen. Div.).

116 Toronto-Dominion Bank v. Paconiel Investments Inc. [1992] 6 O.R. (3d) 547 (Ont. Gen. Div.) at 552.

117 Pao On v. Lau Yiu Long, [1979] 3 All E.R. 65 (P.C.); Gordon v. Roebuck, [1992] O.J. 1499, 9 O.R. (3d) 1 (Ont. C.A.) at 3.

118. BOC Group plc v. Centeon LLC, [1999] 1 All E.R. (Comm) 53, aff'd [1999] 1 All E.R. (Comm) 970, 63. L.R. 104.

119. Telford v. Holt, [1987] S.C.J. 53, (S.C.C.) [*Telford*].

120. Re Polywheels Inc., [2009] O.J. 2086, 53 C.B.R. (5th) 109 (Ont. S.C.J.) at 27.

between two parties.[121] As such, the guarantor would be required to show some equitable ground for being protected against the obligee's claims.[122]

A guarantor is also entitled to any right of set-off that may exist between the guarantor and the obligee. The same requirements for legal and equitable set-off set out above are applicable where the guarantor is claiming set-off directly against the obligee.[123]

§ 8 Waiver of Defenses by the Guarantor

Specific waivers of defenses by a guarantor are enforceable in Canada. It is unclear whether a general waiver of all defenses by a guarantor will be enforceable as such clauses have been held to be too vague or uncertain.

8.1 Specific Waivers

Specific waivers of the defenses, rights, and remedies of a guarantor are prima facie enforceable in Canada in accordance with their terms, unless such terms are inconsistent with or contradict the provisions of the guarantee.[124]

Canadian courts will give effect to the apparent intent of the parties to a waiver, despite any typographical errors,[125] and interpret the waiver in accordance with its terms.[126]

Despite the ability of a guarantor to waive specific defenses, Canadian courts will strictly construe a waiver against the drafting party (typically the obligee) and apply the *contra proferentum* rule of contractual interpretation.[127]

8.2 General Waivers

In Canada, it is unclear whether a general waiver of all defenses and counterclaims potentially available to a guarantor, when provided in a guaranty, will be enforceable as such clauses may be too vague or uncertain. As a practical matter, it is common for an obligee to require specific waivers in place of, or in addition to, a general waiver clause. As well, it is typical for legal opinions in respect of the enforceability of guaranties to provide a qualification relating to general waiver clauses.[128]

121. *Telford.*
122. *Ibid.*
123. Beeland Co-operative Assn. Ltd. v. Simons, [2008] S.J. 809 (Sask. Q.B.).
124. *Bauer.*
125. Greater Peterborough Business Development Centre Inc. v. Brien, [1995] O.J. 1554 (Ont. Gen. Div).
126. *Bauer.*
127. *Conlin.*
128. ESTEY AT 310.

§ 9 Third-party Pledgors—Defenses and Waiver Thereof

Because the third-party pledgor arguably stands in the same place as a guarantor, to the extent of the pledge, it likely is able to avail itself of the defenses of a guarantor. It may also waive such defenses.

We have found no evidence that the law as applied to sureties would not apply to a third-party pledgor. It would seem logical, given this state of the law, that the third-party pledgor is, in effect, a guarantor and generally has the same defenses available to it as are available to a guarantor in respect of a guaranty.

See §1.2 *Other guarantor-type relationships* for a further discussion of third-party pledges.

§ 10 Jointly and Severally Liable Guarantors—Contribution

Coguarantors have a right to contribution from each other.

10.1 Contribution

Unless there is an agreement to the contrary, all coguarantors (where bound jointly, severally, or jointly and severally) are bound equally. Where one or more of the coguarantors' liability is limited to a specified amount, then the amount of the liability of the coguarantors is ratable and not equal.[129]

Where a coguarantor pays more than its ratable proportion of the underlying obligation, such coguarantor is entitled, at law, to recover contribution from the other coguarantors. Where this right is not varied by agreement, the obligation of each coguarantor is found by dividing the total amount owed by all guarantors by the number of solvent guarantors. Although these principles are based on caselaw, each of the jurisdictions except Yukon, Nunavut, Northwest Territories, Alberta, and Saskatchewan[130] have legislation that codifies these principles. [131]

129. *Ontario Ltd.*

130. (ON) Mercantile Law Amendment Act, R.S.O. 1990, c. M.10, s. 2; (BC) Law and Equity Act, R.S.B.C. 1996, c. 253, ss. 34(1), (2), (3); (MB) Mercantile Law Amendment Act, C.C.S.M. c. M120, ss. 2(1), (2), (3); (NS) Judicature Act, R.S. 1989, c. 240, s. 43(7); (NL) Limitations Act, S.N.L. 1995, c. L-16.1, ss. 27(1), (2), (3), and (4); (NB) Property Act, R.S.N.B. 1973, cP-19, ss. 59(1), (2); (PEI) Statute of Frauds, R.S.P.E.I. 1988, c. S-6, ss. 5(1), (2), and (3).

131. The provinces of Alberta and Saskatchewan have not enacted any legislation; however, the following cases confirm that the Mercantile Law Act, 1856 ch. 97 is still in force: Gerrow v. Dorais [2010] A.J. 999, 2010 ABQB 560 and Imperial Bank of Canada v. Kuszko [1932] S.J. 63, [1932] 3 W.W. R. 159 (Sask. D.C.).

§ 11 Reliance

Reliance is likely not required to claim under a guaranty.

As guaranties are governed by the rules generally applicable to contracts,[132] reliance is not required to enforce a guaranty.

§ 12 Subrogation

Subrogation is an equitable remedy that allows the guarantor the full rights to which the obligee is entitled against the primary obligor.

The primary obligor is required to reimburse the guarantor for amounts paid under the guaranty.[133] A guarantor who performs the primary obligor's obligation is subrogated to the full rights to which the obligee is entitled against the primary obligor.[134] The rights of the obligee to which the guarantor is entitled include any securities held by the obligee in respect of the underlying obligations[135] and to an assignment of any judgment obtained by the obligee against the primary obligor.[136] The guarantor's rights against the primary obligor are independent rights which entitle the guarantor to exercise its remedies against the primary obligor in its own name. Accordingly, these rights are not truly subrogatory. However, where the guarantor has paid the obligee in full, the guarantor will be entitled to exercise the rights of the obligee against other third parties but any such claim must proceed in the name of the obligee.

Although these principles are based on caselaw, each of the jurisdictions except Yukon, Nunavut, Northwest Territories, Alberta, and Saskatchewan[137] have legislation that codifies these principles.[138]

§ 13 Triangular Set-off in Bankruptcy

Not applicable in the Canadian context.

§ 14 Indemnification—Right of Guarantor

The guarantor has a right to be indemnified against the primary obligor for the principal, interest, and legal costs paid.

132. Moschi v. ep Air Services, [1973] A.C. 331 at 346-47, per Lord Diplcok (H.L.).
133. HALSBURY 618.
134. R. v. O'Bryan (1900), 7 Ex. C.R. 19; (ON) Mercantile Law Amendment Act, R.S.O. 1990, c. M.10, s. 2.
135. Drew v. Lockett (1863), 32 Beav. 499, 55 E.R.196.
136. Smith v. Burn, [1880] O.J. 231, 30 U.C.C.P. 630 (Ont. Ct. CP.).
137. *Supra*, note 130.
138. *Supra*, note 131.

See discussion of subrogation in §12 *Subrogation* above.

The guarantor has a right to be indemnified by the primary obligor in respect of the amounts paid by the guarantor under the guaranty.

The guarantor's rights of indemnity are not limited to the principal and interest paid by the guarantor in respect of the underlying obligation, but extend to and include legal costs reasonably incurred by the guarantor in the defense of an action brought by the obligee.[139] However, a guarantor will not be entitled to indemnification of costs that are attributable to the guarantor's own neglect or default,[140] or that may be incurred by the guarantor in respect of frivolous defenses.[141]

The right of indemnification is immediate, subject to the exception that the guarantor cannot accelerate his or her remedy by paying a debt that is the subject of the guaranty before it becomes due.[142] The guarantor can exercise his or her right as soon as amounts become due prior to payment. However, the guarantor cannot be indemnified for voluntary payment of a debt after arrangements have been made between the obligee and primary obligor in respect of the debt which results in relieving the guarantor of liability.[143]

§ 15 Enforcement of Guaranties

Not applicable in the Canadian context.

§ 16 Revival and Reinstatement of Guaranties

See § 6.2 *Language regarding the revocation of guaranties* and § 6.3 *"Continuing"* above for a discussion relating the termination and/or revocation of continuing guaranties.

There is no Canadian law directly discussing the revival or reinstatement of guaranties. Given that a guaranty is a contract, it follows that general principles of contract law would apply to the parties' ability to mutually agree to the reinstatement or revival of a guaranty. Additionally, there is nothing in Canadian law restricting the parties to a guaranty from agreeing that a guaranty would be reinstated upon the occurrence of certain events provided there is compliance with the other requirements relating to the formation of an enforceable guaranty.

139. Whitehouse v. Glass, [1858] O.J. 324, 7 Gr. 45 (U.C. Ct. Chan.); Baxendale v. London Chatham & Dover Railway Co. (1874-75), L.R. 10 Ex. 35 (Ex. Ch.), per Quain J [*Baxendale]*.
140. O'Brien v. Makintosh, [1903] S.C.J. 54, 34 S.C.R. 169 (S.C.C.).
141. *Baxendale*.
142. Drager v. Allison, [1959] S.C.J. 46, [1959] S.C.R. 661 (S.C.C.) [*Drager*].
143. *Drager*.

Quebec Law of Guaranties

Keyvan Nassiry
BCF LLP
1100 René-Lévesque Blvd West
25th floor
Montreal, Quebec H3B 5C9 Canada
(514) 397-8500
(514) 397-8515
keyvan.nassiry@bcf.ca
www.bcf.ca

Contents

Quebec Law of Guaranties

The Province of Quebec is a civil law jurisdiction where most principles of law applicable to private legal relationships, including those applicable to guaranties, are codified in the *Civil Code of Quebec*. Case law serves to interpret the intentions of law-makers. Accordingly, the laws of guaranties applicable in Quebec may include certain principles that may be unfamiliar to practitioners in the rest of Canada and the United States which are common law jurisdictions.

Introductory Note: The Province of Quebec is a civil law jurisdiction where most principles of law applicable to private legal relationships, including those applicable to guaranties and to various other nominate contracts, are codified in the *Civil Code of Quebec* (CCQ).[1] Case law serves to interpret the intentions of lawmakers. Due to this distinctive feature of Quebec law, there exist noticeable differences between the laws of guaranties applicable in Quebec and those applied in the rest of Canada and the United States which are common law jurisdictions.

In order to standardize our discussion of the law of guaranties, we have adapted the language of the CCQ and used the following vocabulary for referring to the various parties to a guaranty and their obligations.

"Guarantor" means a person (called a "surety" in the CCQ) who, by contract, agrees to satisfy an underlying obligation of another to an obligee upon the primary obligor's default on that underlying obligation. Under Quebec law and practice, the terms "surety" and "guarantor" are interchangeable.

"Guaranty" means the contract (called a "suretyship" in the CCQ) by which the guarantor agrees to satisfy the underlying obligation of a primary obligor to an obligee in the event the primary obligor defaults on the underlying obligation.

"Obligee" means the person (called a "creditor" in the CCQ) to whom the underlying obligation is owed. For example, the lender under a loan agreement would be an obligee vis-à-vis the borrower.

"Primary Obligor" means the person (called a "debtor" in the CCQ) who incurs the underlying obligation to the obligee. For example, the borrower under a loan agreement would be a primary obligor.

"Underlying Obligation" means the obligation or obligations incurred by the primary obligor and owed to the obligee. For example, the borrower's obligation to make payments to a lender of principal and interest on a loan constitutes an underlying obligation.

1. S.Q. 1991, chapter 64, hereinafter CCQ.

§ 1 Nature of the Guaranty Arrangement

1.1 Guaranty Relationships

Under Quebec law, a guaranty is a contract by which a person, the guarantor, binds itself toward the obligee, gratuitously or for remuneration, to perform the underlying obligation of the primary obligor if the latter fails to fulfill same.[2] A guaranty may also be imposed by statute or a court order, and would be subject to the rules described herein which govern consensual guaranties.[3]

The guarantor may guaranty the underlying obligation without the order or even the knowledge of the primary obligor.[4]

A guaranty may be contracted only for a valid obligation, but not for an amount in excess of the underlying obligation or under more onerous conditions.[5] Also, the guarantor is bound to fulfill the underlying obligation only if the primary obligor fails to perform it.[6] Moreover, unless the guarantor expressly renounced thereto in advance or bound itself with the primary obligor on a "solidary"[7] basis, it may invoke the "benefit of discussion," thus compelling the enforcing obligee to demand payment from and exhaust its recourses against the primary obligor before seeking performance under the guaranty for any shortfall.[8] Due to all of the foregoing, the obligation of the guarantor is typically referred to as being secondary, or "accessory," and "subsidiary" to the underlying (or "principal") obligation.

In case of several guarantors guarantying the same underlying obligation of the same primary obligor, each guarantor is liable for the entire underlying obligation but may invoke the "benefit of division." The benefit of division contemplates the right of a guarantor, sued for performance of the entire underlying obligation, to compel the obligee to divide and reduce its claim to the pro rata share of such guarantor. The benefit of division is not available if the guarantor renounced it expressly in advance or is otherwise obligated towards the obligee on a solidary basis with the primary obligor.[9]

1.2 Guarantor versus Surety

Unlike certain common law jurisdictions which distinguish between a "guarantor" and a "surety," Quebec practitioners use such terms interchangeably. Under Quebec law, a guarantor that has obligated itself on a solidary basis with the primary obligor would become tantamount to the common law surety.

2. Article 2333 CCQ.
3. Article 2334 CCQ; *see also Commentaires du ministre de la justice*, le *Code civil du Québec : un mouvement de société*, published 1993 by Gouvernement du Québec, Ministère de la justice (hereinafter "Comments of the Minister of Justice") for such Article; for an example of a guaranty imposed by statute, *see* section 155 of the *Bills of Exchange Act* (R.S.C., 1985, c. B-4); for an example of a court-ordered guaranty, *see* section 716 of the *Civil Code of Procedure* (R.S.Q., chapter C-25).
4. Article 2336 CCQ.
5. Articles 2340, 2341 CCQ.
6. Article 2346 CCQ; see also the Comments of the Minister of Justice for such Article.
7. A "solidary" obligation is similar to a joint and several obligation under common law.
8. Articles 2347, 2352 CCQ.
9. Articles 2349, 2352 CCQ.

Like the common law suretyship, solidarity between the guarantor and the primary obligor allows the obligee to proceed against the guarantor at once without making any demand of the primary obligor.

1.3 "Cautionnement Réel"(Third-party Pledge)

Under Quebec law, a third party may pledge collateral in favor of the obligee to secure the primary obligation without becoming personally liable for the primary obligation.[10] Such relationship is called *cautionnement réel*.[11] In a recent decision, the Court of Appeal of Quebec[12] ruled that a *cautionnement réel* would not entitle the third party pledgor to the benefits and defenses typically available to a guarantor pursuant to the rules governing guaranties, and thus placing such relationship squarely under the rules governing hypothecs[13] which are beyond the scope of this survey.

1.4 Performance Guaranties

Quebec law recognizes performance or completion guaranties regarding obligations other than the payment of money. While typically entered into by insurance companies against remuneration to support the completion of construction projects, such guaranties are governed by the same rules applicable to guaranties for payment of money.[14] In this regard, unless the obligee requires for a specific person to be the guarantor, the guarantor must be domiciled in Canada and have and maintain sufficient property in the Province of Quebec to meet the object of the primary obligation.[15]

1.5 Conflict of Laws

Under Quebec private international law, the form of a contract of guaranty is governed by the law of the place where it is made. If the contract of guaranty does not create a security interest, it remains valid if made in the form prescribed by the law of the domicile of the guarantor upon execution.[16] Quebec law imposes no particular form for a guaranty to be valid.

Moreover, basing itself on the *Convention on the Law Applicable to Contractual Obligations* (Rome Convention of 1980), Quebec law recognizes the autonomy of the will of the parties where the designation of the applicable law is concerned.[17] Thus, a contract of guaranty, whether or not containing any foreign element, is governed by the law expressly designated therein

10. Article 2681 CCQ.
11. In French, *cautionnement* means guaranty; *réel* may be roughly translated to the Latin expression *in rem*.
12. Roker v. Prêt relais Capital Inc., 2012 QCCA 1295.
13. Depending on whether it charges personal or real property (as understood in the common law jurisdictions), a "hypothec" is equivalent to a security interest or mortgage.
14. Articles 2111, 2123 CCQ; KARIM Vincent, *Contracts d'Entreprise*, 2nd ed., Montreal, Wilson & Lafleur Ltée, 2011, at para 861; *See* Garantie, Cie d'assurance de l'Amérique du Nord v. Vortek Groupe Conseil Inc., 2005 CanLII 11928 (QC C.S.).
15. Article 2337 CCQ.
16. Article 3109 CCQ.
17. Dell Computer Corp. v. Union des consommateurs, [2007] 2 S.C.R. 801, 2007 SCC 34.

(or the designation of which may be inferred with certainty from the terms thereof).[18]

If no law is designated in the guaranty, Quebec courts would apply the law of the country with which the guaranty is most closely connected, in view of its nature and the attendant circumstances.[19] A guaranty containing no choice of law clause would be presumed to be most closely connected with the law of the jurisdiction where the party who is to perform the prestation which is characteristic of the contract (i.e., the guarantor) resides or, if the guaranty is made in the ordinary course of business of an enterprise of the guarantor, the latter's establishment.[20]

§ 2 Quebec Law Requirements for an Entity to Enter a Guaranty

2.1 Corporations[21]

Under Quebec law, all legal persons, including corporations,[22] have full enjoyment of civil rights and, unless prohibited by law, are capable of exercising all their rights (which include the right to contract).[23] While the *Business Corporations Act* (Quebec) does allow for the articles of the corporation to restrict its "business activity,"[24] it is seldom the case in practice. Moreover, the statute provides that, unless otherwise provided in its bylaws or in a unanimous shareholder agreement, the board of directors of a Quebec corporation may, on behalf of the corporation, enter into a guaranty securing the performance of an obligation of any person.[25]

2.2 Partnerships

Under Quebec law, general partnerships and limited partnerships are not considered to be legal persons and are thus not endowed with juridical personality.[26] However, a partnership has been characterized as an entity separate from its members, with the ability to sue and be sued and the capacity to contract in its own name.[27] Accordingly, since a partnership represents a group of natural or legal persons, the absence of juridical personality would not prevent

18. Article 3111 CCQ.
19. Article 3112 CCQ.
20. Article 3113 CCQ.
21. We have limited this survey to Quebec law corporations. Corporations existing under the *Canada Business Corporations Act* are dealt with in the Canada (All Provinces Except Quebec) Survey.
22. Pursuant to section 10 of the *Business Corporations Act*, R.S.Q., chapter S-31.1, a corporation is a legal person.
23. Articles 301, 303 CCQ.
24. Section 5(9) *Business Corporations Act*, R.S.Q., chapter S-31.1.
25. Section 115(3) *Business Corporations Act*, R.S.Q., chapter S-31.1.
26. Article 2188 CCQ; Laval (Ville de) v. Polyclinique médicale Fabreville, s.e.c., [2007] J.Q. no 2309, EYB 2007-117003 (C.A.).
27. Articles 2221, 2225 CCQ.

a partnership, represented by a duly authorized partner, from entering into a contract of guaranty.

2.3 Limited Liability Companies

Quebec law does not contemplate limited liability companies, but would otherwise recognize a valid guaranty governed by foreign law entered into by such entities.

2.4 Banks,[28] Credit Unions, and Trust Companies

A credit union established in Quebec has the power to enter into a guaranty in favor of third parties for the benefit of its members. If the obligee is the Bank of Canada, the Government of Canada or any Canadian Crown corporation, the guaranty must be authorized by the Minister of Finance at the request of the *Autorité des marchés financiers* (AMF), the body mandated by the government of Quebec to regulate the province's financial markets.[29]

Under Quebec law, every company that is expressly authorized by its articles of incorporation to act as tutor or curator to property, liquidator, syndic, sequestrator, adviser to a person of full age or trustee is a trust company. Every Quebec trust company may, in addition to such activities, carry on any accessory activity or activity related to that of administrator of the property of others or of financial intermediary and, in particular, may enter into a guaranty.[30]

2.5 Individuals

A natural person must be mentally competent[31] and have capacity to enter into any contract, including a guaranty. In Quebec, upon attaining the age of majority at 18 years, a person ceases to be a minor and has the full exercise of all his civil rights which includes entering into contracts.[32] A minor, legally emancipated,[33] may also execute a guaranty. The CCQ also provides for certain rules of capacity applicable to the execution of contracts by persons of full age under protective supervision.[34]

Regardless of his or her matrimonial regime,[35] a spouse may enter into a guaranty without the consent of the other spouse if no hypothec secures the guaranty.[36] The guarantor's matrimonial regime determines whether the writ-

28. Canadian banks are dealt with in the Canada (All Provinces Except Quebec) survey.
29. Sections 5(2), 77, 81.1 *An act respecting financial services cooperatives*, R.S.Q., chapter C-67.3.
30. Sections 1, 170(6) *An act respecting trust companies and savings companies*, R.S.Q., chapter S-29.01.
31. Thibodeau v. Thibodeau, [1961] S.C.R. 285.
32. Article 153 CCQ.
33. Article 172 to 176 CCQ.
34. See the tutorship and curatorship rules set forth in Articles 256 *ff.* CCQ.
35. In Quebec, matrimonial rights of a spouse result from marriage or civil union but do not extend to a de facto spouse. At the time of writing, such exclusion of de facto spouses is being challenged before the Supreme Court of Canada.
36. Article 397 CCQ; unless the spouse enters into a contract for the current needs of the family, it would not bind the noncontracting spouse. However, if the contact is entered into for current family needs, the noncontracting spouse may renounces to any obligations thereunder by so informing the counterparty (i.e., obligee) prior to the execution of the contract.

ten consent of the noncontracting spouse is required in case the guaranty is secured by a hypothec.

There are three major matrimonial regimes governing spouses in Quebec: (1) separation as to property created by marriage or civil union contract,[37] (2) community of property,[38] and (3) partnership of acquests.[39] Regardless of the guarantor's matrimonial regime, the written consent[40] of the noncontracting spouse is always required if the collateral charged by such hypothec includes the immovable property[41] used as family residence. Where the guarantor's matrimonial regime is the separation as to property or the partnership of acquests, the consent of the noncontracting spouse is not required if the hypothec charges any other immovable property.[42] Where the guarantor's matrimonial regime is the community of property, the consent of the noncontracting spouse is generally required if the hypothec charges any immovable forming part of the community.[43]

Upon dissolution of the guarantor's marriage or civil union, an unsecured obligee would have ordinary recourse to the assets of the guarantor regardless of whether such assets are dividable with the noncontracting spouse. In case of dissolution of the marriage or civil union, the net value of the assets of the guarantor may be reduced by compensation (i.e., set-off) against obligations owing by the guarantor to the other spouse. Conversely, such assets may increase if the guarantor holds a claim against the noncontracting spouse. Particular rules are provided in the CCQ for partition of marital assets. For instance, the creditor of a guarantor married in partnership of acquests who waives his rights to partition in prejudice of the creditor's rights may apply to the court to challenge the waiver.[44]

Moreover, it is prohibited under Quebec law to proceed with a gift mortis causa outside a will or a marriage or civil union contract.[45] Therefore, if the guarantor co-owns immovable property with the noncontracting spouse, upon death of the guarantor, the latter's share in such property will be automatically included in the estate and continue to remain subject to recourse by the obligee. The foregoing likely constitutes a distinction with joint tenancy rules in common law jurisdictions.

---

37. Articles 485, 521.8 CCQ.
38. Statutory regime for spouses married before July 1, 1970; Articles 1272-1425i of the *Civil Code of Lower Canada* and Article 492 CCQ.
39. Statutory regime for spouses married since July 1, 1970; Articles 448-484 CCQ.
40. Articles 401 ff. CCQ.
41. "Immovable property" is equivalent to real property under common law. Given the complexity of the rules applicable to each matrimonial regime, we have limited this survey to personal guaranty secured by immovable property and have not dealt with hypothecs over movable property (i.e., personal property). By way of example, subject to some exceptions, an unregistered investment portfolio may be generally pledged by the guarantor without the consent of the noncontracting spouse.
42. Articles 461, 486 CCQ.
43. Article 1292 of the *Civil Code of Lower Canada*.
44. Article 470 CCQ.
45. Article 1819 CCQ.

§ 3 Signatory's Authority to Execute a Guaranty

3.1 Corporations

As a legal person, a corporation is represented by its "senior officers," who bind it to the extent of the powers vested in them by law, the corporation's articles or bylaws.[46] The obligee may presume that a corporation is exercising its powers in accordance with its articles and bylaws and any unanimous shareholder agreement, that its directors and officers validly hold office and lawfully exercise the powers of their office, and that a contract (such as a guaranty) executed by a director, officer, or other mandatary of the corporation has been validly entered into.[47]

3.2 Partnerships

The partners of a general partnership created under Quebec law may appoint one or more fellow partners or even a third party to manage the affairs of the partnership. The manager may execute a guaranty if within its powers.[48] Also, notwithstanding any contrary provision in the partnership agreement, each partner, even if excluded from management duties, is a mandatary of the partnership in respect of third parties in good faith and may bind the partnership for a guaranty signed in its name in the ordinary course of business.[49]

In a limited partnership, only the general partner is authorized to bind the partnership.[50]

3.3 Limited Liability Companies

As indicated above, Quebec law does not contemplate limited liability companies.

3.4 Banks,[51] Credit Unions, and Trust Companies

The obligee may presume that a credit union is pursuing its mission and exercising its powers in accordance with its articles and bylaws, that the officers of the cooperative are validly holding office and lawfully exercising the powers arising therefrom, and that a contract (such as a guaranty) which emanates from an officer is valid and binding.[52]

The obligee may presume that a trust company is exercising its powers in accordance with its articles and bylaws and any unanimous shareholder agreement, that its directors and officers validly hold office and lawfully exercise

---

46. Article 312 CCQ.
47. Section 13(4) *Business Corporations Act*, R.S.Q., chapter S-31.1.
48. Article 2213.CCQ.
49. Article 2219 CCQ.
50. Article 2236 CCQ.
51. Canadian banks are dealt with in the Canada (All Provinces Except Quebec) survey.
52. Section 71 *An act respecting financial services cooperatives*, R.S.Q., chapter C-67.3.

the powers of their office, and that a contract (such as a guaranty) executed by a director, officer, or other mandatary of the trust company has been validly entered into.[53] The directors and officers of a trust company are deemed to be mandataries of the company.[54]

§ 4 Consideration

Unlike the other Canadian jurisdictions where an exchange of sufficient consideration is essential in order to create an enforceable contract, consideration (as understood in most common law jurisdictions) is not required for a contract to be binding under Quebec law. From a civil law perspective, instead of an exchange by the parties of valuable rights, a concurrence of wills is required to form a valid bilateral contract.[55] In the Province of Quebec, the element of contract law that offers some similarity with consideration is the *cause* of the contract.[56] The cause of a contract of guaranty is the lawful reason that motivates the guarantor to enter into such contract and it need not be expressed.[57] For instance, in the case of a guaranty entered into as part of a financing, the guarantor's motivating factor would likely be the direct or indirect benefit drawn from the extension of credit by the lender to the borrower.

§ 5 Notice of Acceptance

As is the case with all contracts, a guaranty obligation is formed when and where acceptance is received by the offeror, regardless of the method of communication used, and even if the parties may have not yet agreed on secondary terms.[58] The exchange of consents is accomplished by the express or tacit manifestation of the will of the obligee to accept a guaranty offered by the guarantor.[59]

53. Sections 5 *An act respecting trust companies and savings companies*, R.S.Q., chapter S-29.01 (which refers to the *Business Corporations Act*, R.S.Q., chapter S-31.1).
54. Section 107 *An act respecting trust companies and savings companies*, R.S.Q., chapter S-29.01.
55. TANCELIN Maurice, *Des obligations en droit mixte du Québec*, 7th ed., Montreal, Wilson & Lafleur Ltée, 2009, para 255 *ff*; *see also* analysis in Royal Institution for the Advancement of Learning v. Hutchison, (1931) 50 B.R. 107, and in Banque canadienne impériale de commerce v. Mallette et Co., [1987] R.J.Q. 96 (C.A.).
56. Other than the cause, the other three Quebec law requirements to form a valid contract are capacity, consent, and object (i.e., juridical operation); Article 1385 CCQ.
57. Articles 1371, 1410 CCQ. Article 984 of the former *Civil Code of Lower Canada* made "a lawful cause or consideration" one of the four requisites to the validity of a contract.
58. Article 1387 CCQ.
59. Article 1386 CCQ.

§ 6 Interpretation of Guaranties

6.1 General Principles

A guaranty must be expressly made through a written or verbal contract, and it may not be presumed.[60] The general principles of interpretation applicable to all contracts (set forth in Articles 1425 to 1432 CCQ) would also apply to a guaranty. In interpreting a guaranty, its nature, the circumstances in which it was formed, the interpretation which has already been given to it by the parties or which it may have received, and usage are all taken into account.[61]

In case of doubt or if the guaranty is a contract of adhesion, Quebec courts apply a rule similar to the common law doctrine of contra proferentem:[62] the guaranty is construed strictly in favor of the guarantor and against the obligee.[63]

6.2 Contract of Adhesion

Under Quebec law, a contract of guaranty in which the essential stipulations were imposed or drawn up by the obligee, on its behalf or upon its instructions, and were not negotiable is a contract of adhesion.[64] An example is the form of guaranty often drawn by a lending institution on a standard form, where the guarantor has little or no part in the negotiation of the agreement.

In a guaranty that is a contract of adhesion, the following types of clauses are generally unenforceable:

(i) an external clause, unless it was expressly brought to the attention of the guarantor on the date of execution of the guaranty, or unless the guarantor otherwise knew of it;[65]

(ii) an illegible or incomprehensible clause that causes damage to the guarantor, unless an adequate explanation of the nature and scope of the clause was given to the guarantor;[66] and

(iii) an abusive clause. A clause is considered abusive if it is excessively and unreasonably detrimental to the guarantor and is therefore not in good faith.[67]

60. Article 2335 CCQ; *see also* the Comments of the Minister of Justice under such Article. The foregoing is contrary to the general principal of Article 1386 CCQ which provides that the exchange of consents may be either express or implied.
61. Article 1426 CCQ.
62. For an application of this doctrine by the Supreme Court of Canada, *see* Manulife Bank of Canada v. Conlin, [1996] 3 S.C.R. 415.
63. Article 1432 CCQ.
64. Article 1379 CCQ.
65. Article 1435 CCQ.
66. Article 1436 CCQ.
67. Article 1437 CCQ.

§ 7 Defenses of the Guarantor

7.1 Defenses of the Primary Obligor

7.1.1 General

Whether or not he is bound on a solidary basis with the primary obligor, the guarantor may assert against the obligee all the defenses of the primary obligor, except those that are purely personal to the primary obligor or that are excluded by the terms of guaranty.[68] The foregoing principle results from the accessory nature of the contract of guaranty.[69]

Accordingly, the defenses dealing with the extinction (or reduction) of the primary obligation are available to both the primary obligor and the guarantor. Extinction of debt may occur by total payment of the underlying obligation,[70] the expiry of an extinctive term,[71] novation,[72] prescription,[73] compensation,[74] confusion,[75] release,[76] impossibility of performance[77] or discharge of the primary obligor.[78]

The guarantor may also raise as a defense the nullity of the guaranty due to the primary obligor's defect of consent[79] upon the formation of the contract of guaranty.

7.1.2 Defenses that may not be Raised by Guarantor

The guarantor may not assert defenses that are purely personal to the primary obligor or that have been excluded by agreement in the guaranty. Defenses that are purely personal to the primary obligor include the incapacity[80] and the bankruptcy of the primary obligor. However, pursuant to Article 2340 CCQ, if the guarantor has knowledge of the incapacity of the primary obligor, it may not

68. Article 2353 CCQ.
69. As indicate above, the guarantor is bound to fulfill the underlying obligation only if the primary obligor fails to perform it.
70. Article 1553 CCQ.
71. Article 1517 CCQ. An obligation with an extinctive term is an obligation which has a duration fixed by law or by the parties and which is extinguished by expiry of the term.
72. Articles 1660 *ff.* CCQ. Pursuant to Article 1665 CCQ, novation effected in respect of the primary obligor generally releases its guarantors.
73. Articles 2875 *ff.* CCQ. "Prescription" is equivalent to statute of limitation under common law. Pursuant to Article 2899 CCQ, a judicial demand or any other act of interruption of prescription against the primary obligor or against a guarantor interrupts prescription with regard to both.
74. Articles 1672 *ff.* CCQ. "Compensation" is equivalent to set-off under common law. Pursuant to Article 1679 CCQ, a guarantor may set up compensation for what the obligee owes to the primary obligor, but the latter may not set up compensation for what the obligee owes to the guarantor. Set-off is discussed in more details under § 13 below.
75. Articles 1683 *ff.* CCQ. Pursuant to Article 1684 CCQ, confusion of the qualities of obligee and primary obligor in the same person avails the guarantor. However, confusion of the qualities of guarantor and creditor or of guarantor and primary obligor does not extinguish the primary obligation.
76. Articles 1687 *ff.* CCQ.
77. Article 1693 CCQ; the defense of impossibility of performance is similar to the defense of force majeur or Act of God.
78. Articles 1695 *ff.* CCQ.
79. Pursuant to Article 1407 CCQ, a person whose consent is vitiated has the right to apply for annulment of the contract.
80. Article 1398 CCQ.

use same in its own defense. The Court of Appeal of Quebec[81] has confirmed that in the absence of a specific provision in the text of the guaranty, Quebec law would not release the guarantor from the performance of the guaranty when the primary obligor is adjudged bankrupt.

7.2 Defenses that may only be Raised by Guarantor

Certain defenses are only available to the guarantor.[82] They include the benefit of discussion, the benefit of division, the death of the guarantor,[83] the nullity of the guaranty contract (e.g., defect of consent), the breach by the obligee of its duty to inform the guarantor, the loss of the guarantor's benefit of subrogation, the breach by the obligee of its duty to act in good faith,[84] and the compensation (set-off) of the obligations of the guarantor with the obligations of the obligee to the primary obligor.

§ 8 Waiver of Defenses by the Guarantor

8.1 Defenses that cannot be Waived

Under Quebec law, the guarantor cannot renounce in advance to its right to be provided with information or to the benefit of subrogation.[85] Given that both such rights are of public order, the guarantor may always raise any violation thereof as a defense in any action for performance of the guaranty.

The first defense relating to the duty to inform is based on the duty of the obligee to act in good faith as confirmed by the Supreme Court of Canada.[86] At the request of the guarantor, the obligee must provide it with any useful information respecting the content and the terms and conditions of the primary obligation and the progress made in its performance.[87] The obligee's duty to inform the guarantor has been often limited by case law to situations where the guarantor is in a vulnerable position as regards information, from which damages may result.[88]

With respect to the second right, if the guarantor can no longer be usefully subrogated to the rights of the obligee as a result of the latter's actions, the

81. St-Michael v. Kutlu, EYB 1994-59180 (C.A.). *See also* section 179 *Bankruptcy and Insolvency Act*, R.S., 1985, c. B-3 providing that an order of discharge does not release a person who at the time of the bankruptcy was a person who was a surety or in the nature of a surety for the bankrupt.
82. For a more detailed description of defenses of the guarantor , *see* POUDRIER-LEBEL, Louise, *La libération de la caution*, Service de la formation permanente du Barreau du Québec, *Développements récents en droit commercial (1996)*: *La réforme du Code civil, rétrospective, deux ans plus tard*, Cowansville (Qc), Yvon Blais, 1996.
83. Article 2361 CCQ.
84. Articles 6, 7 and 1375 CCQ.
85. Article 2355 CCQ.
86. Bank of Montreal v. Bail Ltée, [1992] 2 S.C.R. 554; the court confirmed the general theory of the obligation to inform, based on the duty of good faith in the realm of contracts.
87. Article 2345 CCQ; the principle is also inspired from the decision of the Supreme Court of Canada in National Bank v. Soucisse et al., [1981] 2 S.C.R. 339.
88. Trust La Laurentienne du Canada Inc. v. Losier, EYB 2001-22029 (C.A.).

guarantor may be discharged to the extent of the damages suffered.[89] Subrogation is discussed in § 12 below.

8.2 Defenses that may be Waived

Most forms of guaranties governed by Quebec law provide for the waiver of defenses based on the benefit of discussion, the benefit of division, or the defenses of the primary obligor that are not purely personal to it.

One defense that is surprisingly not waived on a consistent basis in forms of guaranties used in Quebec deals with the guarantor's right to terminate a guaranty attached to the performance of special duties upon cessation of such duties.[90] In *Épiciers Unis Métro-Richelieu Inc., division "Éconogros" v. Collin*,[91] the Supreme Court of Canada ruled that once the guarantor has proven that the guaranty was contracted in connection with the special duties he performed (for example, the duties of a director or officer of the primary obligor), the guaranty would be deemed terminated, without notice to the obligee, as soon as such special duties have ended. A guaranty so terminated would then be limited to the amount of underlying obligations existing at the time of cessation of the special duties of the guarantor.[92] The Court confirmed that the foregoing principle is not of public order and may thus be overridden by contract.

§ 9 Third-party Pledgors—Defenses and Waiver Thereof

As indicated in section 1.3 above, under Quebec law, a third party pledgor is no longer entitled to the benefits and defenses typically available to a guarantor pursuant to the rules governing guaranties.

§ 10 Solidary (joint and severally liable) Guarantors—Contribution and Reduction of Obligations upon Payment by a Co-obligor

Where several persons are solidary guarantors of the same primary obligor for the same debt, each of them is liable for the whole debt and may no longer invoke the benefit of division.[93] Solidarity between co-obligors is presumed

89. Article 2365 CCQ.
90. Article 2363 CCQ.
91. [2004] 3 S.C.R. 257, 2004 SCC 59.
92. Article 2364 CCQ.
93. Article 2352 CCQ; under the benefit of division, a guarantor may require the obligee to divide its claim and to reduce it to the amount of the share and portion of each guarantor.

where the obligation is contracted for the service or carrying on of an enterprise, and it otherwise exists if so stipulated by the parties or imposed by law.[94]

Pursuant to Article 2360 CCQ, where several persons have become guarantors of the same primary obligor for the same debt, the guarantor who has paid the debt has in addition to the action in subrogation,[95] a personal right of action against the other guarantors, each for his share and portion.[96] The personal right of action may only be exercised where the guarantor has paid in one of the cases in which he could take action against the debtor before paying. Where one of the guarantors is insolvent, its insolvency is apportioned by contribution among the other guarantors, including the guarantor who made the payment.

Upon receipt of payment, express release granted by the obligee to one of the guarantors releases the other guarantors to the extent of the remedy they would have had against the released guarantor. Nevertheless, no payment received by the obligee from the guarantor for its release may be imputed to the discharge of the primary obligor or of the other guarantors, except as regards the guarantors, where they have a remedy against the released guarantor and to the extent of that remedy.[97]

§ 11 Reliance

The doctrine of reliance-based estoppels is not recognized under Quebec law. Accordingly, reliance is not required to claim under, or otherwise enforce a guaranty.

§ 12 Subrogation

Under Quebec law, a person who pays in the place of a debtor may be subrogated to the rights of the creditor, but such person may not have more rights than the subrogating creditor.[98] Pursuant to Article 1656(3) CCQ, subrogation takes place by operation of law, in favor of a person (i.e., the guarantor) who pays a debt to which he is bound with others or for others and which he has an interest in paying. Once subrogation has occurred, the guarantor would replace the obligee and is entitled to claim payment of the underlying obligation from the primary obligor (as well as other guarantors).

94. Article 1525 CCQ.
95. Pursuant to Article 1656(3) CCQ, subrogation takes place by operation of law in favor of a person who pays a debt to which he is bound with others or for others and which he has an interest in paying.
96. *See also* Schwitzguebel v. Cadieux, REJB 2002-30735 (C.A.) at para. 31.
97. Article 1692 CCQ; payment made by a guarantor to obtain the release of its guaranty should not be considered payment of the underlying obligation of the primary obligor except for the other guarantors who have a claim against the released guarantor (*see* Comments of the Minister of Justice under Article 1692 CCQ); *see also* Banque Nationale du Canada v. Picard, EYB 2007-123123 (C.S.) at para 10.
98. Article 1651 CCQ.

§ 13 Triangular Set-off in Bankruptcy

Regardless of the affiliation, if any, between the parties, Article 1679 CCQ specifically allows for a triangular set-off by stipulating that a guarantor may compensate (i.e., offset) its obligations under the guaranty with what the obligee owes to the primary obligor. The foregoing is consistent with the underlying principle that the guarantor may raise against the obligee all the defenses of the primary obligor, except those which are purely personal to the primary obligor or that are excluded by the terms of the guaranty.[99]

Instead of referring to the requirements of mutuality under legal set-off or a "close connection" required under equitable[100] set-off as both are understood in common law jurisdictions, compensation under Quebec law is effected if both obligations are certain, liquid, and exigible and the object of both of which is a sum of money or a certain quantity of fungible property identical in kind.[101]

Pursuant to subsection 97(3) of the *Bankruptcy and Insolvency Act*,[102] the law of set-off or compensation applies to all claims made against the estate of the bankrupt and also to all actions instituted by the trustee for the recovery of debts due to the bankrupt in the same manner and to the same extent as if the bankrupt were plaintiff or defendant, as the case may be, except insofar as any claim for set-off or compensation is affected by the provisions of such Act respecting frauds or fraudulent preferences.

§ 14 Indemnification

Since the CCQ stipulates the rules allowing the guarantor to recover an indemnification from the primary obligor, contracts of indemnification are rarely used in the Province of Quebec except in cases involving performance guaranties entered into by insurance companies.[103]

---

99. Article 2353 CCQ.
100. In D.I.M.S. Construction inc. (Trustee of) v. Quebec (Attorney General), [2005] 2 SCR 564, the Supreme Court of Canada put a decisive end to an ongoing debate under Quebec law on the application of the rules of equitable set-off in bankruptcy by ruling that equitable set-off does not apply in Québec.
101. Article 1673 CCQ.
102. R.S.C., 1985, c. B-3; *see also* section 21 of *Companies' Creditors Arrangement Act*, R.S.C., 1985, c. C-36. In the D.I.M.S. decision referred to above, the Supreme Court of Canada found that subsection 97(3) B.I.A. must be applied in Quebec on the basis of civil law and not common law rules (at para, 64 of the decision).
103. *See, for example, Cie d'assurances d'hypothèques du Canada* v. *Construction Sylt et Fortier*, J.E. 88-903 (C.A.).

14.1 Guaranty entered into with the Consent of the Primary Obligor

The guarantor may claim from the primary obligor the amount in capital, interest, and costs paid under a guaranty entered into with the consent of the primary obligor, as well as any damages resulting therefrom.[104]

If such guarantor is sued for payment or the primary obligor is insolvent, or if the primary obligor has undertaken to obtain a termination of the guaranty within a certain time, the guarantor may take action against the primary obligor, even before paying under the guaranty.[105] The same rule applies where the debt becomes payable by the expiry of its term (disregarding any extension granted to the primary obligor by the obligee without the consent of the guarantor), or where, by reason of losses incurred by the primary obligor or of any fault committed by the primary obligor, the guarantor is at appreciably higher risk than at the time the guaranty was entered into. If successful, such action typically results in the primary obligor depositing cash collateral with the court or otherwise granting other security to the guarantor.[106]

14.2 Guaranty entered into without the Consent of the Primary Obligor

Conversely, if the primary obligor did not request or consent to the guaranty, the guarantor may only claim the amount from which the primary obligor actually benefits, namely, the sum which the primary obligor would have been bound to pay to the obligee, including damages, if there had been no guaranty.[107]

14.3 No Remedy available against the Primary Obligor

A guarantor having paid a debt who fails to so inform the primary obligor has no remedy against the primary obligor if the latter pays it subsequently.[108] Also, the guarantor has no remedy if at the time of the payment the primary obligor had defenses that could have enabled it to have the debt declared extinguished. In these circumstances, the guarantor has a remedy only for the sum the primary obligor could have been required to pay, to the extent that the primary obligor could raise other defenses against the obligee to cause the debt to be reduced.

Based on the principle of restitution,[109] the guarantor retains his right of action for recovery against the obligee in all such cases.

104. Article 2356 CCQ.
105. Article 2359 CCQ.
106. BOUSQUET, Jean-Pierre, *Le contrat de cautionnement*, in *Obligations et contrats*, Collection de droit 2010-2011, École du Barreau du Québec, vol. 5, Cowansville, Éditions Yvon Blais, 2010, p. 335.
107. However, the obligee's costs subsequent to indication of the payment are payable by the primary obligor; Article 2356 CCQ.
108. Article 2358 CCQ.
109. Pursuant to Articles 1492 and 1699 CCQ, restitution of payments takes place where a person is bound by law to return to another person the property he has received, either unlawfully or by error, or under a juridical act which is subsequently annulled retroactively or under which the obligations become impossible to perform by reason of superior force.

§ 15 Enforcement of Guaranties

Since the guarantor is bound to fulfill the underlying obligation only if the primary obligor fails to perform it,[110] the only condition to the obligee's enforcement is the occurrence of such default by the primary obligor when the underlying obligation is exigible. The contract of guaranty may create additional conditions, such as receipt of a notice of default by the guarantor.[111]

If the guarantor does not voluntarily pay the amount claimed under the guaranty, the obligee may initiate a personal action by instituting judicial proceedings to cause the property of the guaranty to be seized and sold[112]. If the guaranty is secured by hypothec or other security interest, the obligee may also enforce and realize on its security.[113]

§ 16 Revival and Reinstatement of Guaranties

Although rare, certain forms of guaranty agreements used in the Province of Quebec include a revival or reinstatement clause. While likely valid under Quebec law, a reinstated guaranty may be deemed a new obligation of the guarantor subject to the rules of novation which may find application.[114] Consideration should be given to reserving the hypothec securing the guaranty; otherwise, in case of novation, it may not be transferred to the new obligation.[115]

110. Article 2346 CCQ; *see also* Banque Nationale du Canada v. Notre-Dame-du-Lac (Ville), EYB 1990-63566 (C.A.).
111. *See, for example,* Compagnie d'assurance London Garantie v. Girard et Girard Inc., REJB 2004-53445 (C.A.).
112. Article 2646 CCQ.
113. Article 2748 CCQ.
114. Articles 1660 *ff.* CCQ.
115. Article 1662 CCQ.

Puerto Rico Law of Guaranties

Juan C. Salichs
Salichs Pou & Associates, PSC
Popular Center
209 Muñoz Rivera Avenue, Suite 1434
San Juan, Puerto Rico 00918
Telephone: (787) 449-6000
Facsimile: (787) 474-3892
http://www.salichspou.com
e-mail: jsalichs@splawpr.com

Contents

Puerto Rico Law of Guaranties

Highlights:

- Puerto Rico is governed by the civil law system,[1] and it is considered a mistake to go to the common law to resolve situations regulated by civil law.[2] In appropriate cases, however, it shall be lawful to employ the common law, by way of comparative law[3] or for its persuasiveness to resolve issues not regulated by civil law.[4]
- A guaranty contract should be interpreted liberally, so that any third-party beneficiary's claims may prevail.
- Under Puerto Rico law, a guarantor cannot be compelled to pay a creditor until an application has been previously made of all the property of the debtor. This principle is what makes the contract of guaranty subsidiary, as the liquidation of the estate of the debtor allows the guarantor to avoid paying the creditor until the creditor proves the insolvency of the principal debtor, whether it is full or partial. This does not preclude that the guarantor may be notified of the default simultaneously with the principal debtor; it merely stays the moment that the creditor may collect from the guarantor. To take advantage of this right, the guarantor must inform the creditor, once the creditor demands payment from the guarantor, and point to the creditor sufficient assets of the debtor in Puerto Rico to allow for collection.

Introduction and Sources of Law

The Civil Code of Puerto Rico is the primary source of substantive law governing guaranties and sureties. The Puerto Rico civil law establishes basic principles of law—called "Articles"—that regulate through general rules all aspects of civil relationships and rights. The doctrine of law of the case and its close relative, the theory of *stare decisis*, are characteristic features of the common law, but not civil law. The Supreme Court of Puerto Rico has concluded there is no valid basis for applying to the common law doctrine of law of the case or the doctrine of *stare decisis et non still movere*.[5] In Puerto Rico, the decisions of the Supreme Court of Puerto Rico are a source of law, set precedent, and bind as provided by the doctrine of *stare decisis* in the common law tradition. The Supreme Court has cited the Restatement of Security.[6]

1. Travieso v. Del Toro y Travieso, Int., 74 D.P.R. 1009, 1026 (1953).
2. Dalmau v. Hernández Saldaña, 103 D.P.R. 487, 491 (1975).
3. Valle v. Amer. Inter. Ins. Co., 108 D.P.R. 692, 697 (1979).
4. J.A.D.M. v. Centro Com. Plaza Carolina, 132 D.P.R. 785, 797 (1993).
5. Torres Cruz v. Municipio de San Juan, 103 D.P.R. 217, 222 (1975).
6. Kermit E. Ferrer v. Alliance Company of P.R., Inc. y St. Paul Fire & Marine Insurance Co., 93 D.P.R. 1 (1963); Arsuaga, Inc. v. La Hood Constructors, Inc. y Maryland Casualty Company, 90 D.P.R. 104 (1964).

§ 1 Nature of the Guaranty Contract

Under Puerto Rico law, a guaranty is a contract under which "... a person binds himself to pay or perform for a third person in case the latter should fail to do so."[7] A guaranty cannot exist without a valid obligation. The guaranty is not presumed. The guaranty must be expressed and cannot be extended further than that specified by the parties under the contract.

1.1 General Discussion of Obligations and Contracts

The contract theory that governs Puerto Rico jurisdiction is the principle of freedom of contract or autonomy of the parties.[8] In this legal system, all obligations can be guaranteed. "The obligations arising from contracts have the force of law between the contracting parties, and must be fulfilled [based on the contract provisions]."[9] The principle of *pacta sunt servanda* is included in Article 1207 of the Civil Code of Puerto Rico.[10] The article states that the parties may agree to the terms and conditions as they see fit, provided they are not contrary to law, morals, or public order. Contracts are perfected by mere consent, and from then the parties undertake not only the fulfillment of what is expressly agreed but also to all the consequences which by nature are consistent with good faith, usage, and law.[11] However, the principle of contractual freedom is not unlimited and is subject to court intervention.[12]

As a general rule, contracts affect only the parties and their heirs, except that, as to these, the obligations are otherwise not transferable.[13] This rule is known as the principle of relativity of contracts. It postulates that the conditions of the contract bind only those forced by their terms and to their successors and assigns. Another general principle in Puerto Rico is that contracts have no formal requirements. An exception to that general rule in Article 1232 of the Civil Code[14] requires that certain contractual obligations be reduced to writing through a public deed,[15] and all other contracts, in which the consideration of one or both of the two contracting parties exceeds $300, must be reduced to writing even though they may be private contracts.

7. 31 L.P.R.A. § 4871.
8. Young & Co. v. Vega III, 136 D.P.R. 157, 169-170 (1994).
9. 31 L.P.R.A. § 2994.
10. 31 L.P.R.A. § 3372.
11. 31 L.P.R.A. § 3375.
12. *See* note 5; *See also* Federico Puig Peña, Compendio de Derecho Civil español, Vol. III, 338-42 (3rd ed. 1976). Cooperativa de Ahorro y Crédito Sabañera v. Jesús Casiano Rivera, 184 D.P.R. _____, 2011 T.S.P.R. 207.
13. 31 L.P.R.A. § 3374.
14. 31 L.P.R.A. § 3453; *See also* 10 L.P.R.A. § 1032 regarding mercantile or commercial agreements.
15. The contracts that need to be in public instrument form are (1) acts and contracts the object of which is the creation, conveyance, modification, or extinction of rights on real property; (2) leases of the same property for six or more years, provided they are to the prejudice of third persons; (3) contracts to govern property belonging to the conjugal partnership, and the creation and increase of dowries, whenever it is intended to enforce them against third persons; (4) the assignment, repudiation, and renunciation of hereditary rights or of those of the conjugal partnership; (5) the general power of attorney to institute lawsuits and the special powers of attorney to be presented in suits; the power of attorney to administer property and any other power of attorney, the object of which is an act drafted or which is to be drafted in a public instrument, or which may prejudice a third person; and (6) the assignment of actions or rights arising from an act contained in a public instrument.

The form requirements demanded by Article 1232 are purely evidentiary as opposed to those required in specific cases, which require solemn and strict requirements indispensable to the perfection of the contract. But a written contract is not the only evidence admitted to prove the existence of the contract. The Puerto Rico Supreme Court has stated and reiterated that in the Puerto Rico system of law, verbal contracts, although they should be avoided, are as valid as written contracts.[16] It should be clear that in Puerto Rico verbal contracts are not prohibited. The Puerto Rico Supreme Court has consistently held that Article 1232 does not exclude the testimony as evidence, when it is the testimony of the parties to the contract.[17]

1.2 Joint, Several, and Joint and Several Guarantor

The Civil Code of Puerto Rico provides that in obligations involving multiple persons, the same may be joint or several. However, the Supreme Court of Puerto Rico recognized in *Brockway Motor Truck Corp of Puerto Rico v. Lloréis*,[18] that when an obligation is "joint and several" it would be interpreted as a joint obligation.

The Civil Code of Puerto Rico under its Article 1090[19] provides that "[t]he concurrence of two (2) or more creditors, or of two (2) or more debtors in a single obligation, does not imply that each one of the former has a right to ask, nor that each one of the latter is bound to comply in full with the things which are the object of the same. This shall only take place when the obligation determines it expressly, being constituted as a joint obligation." The joint obligation is characterized by the unity of the credit or debt as if it were one single creditor or debtor.[20]

The terms "several" and "joint" are statutory schemes which are mutually exclusive, since the former involves the division of the credit or debt and the second unity of the credit or debt. There is no relationship between solidarity and severability of the Civil Code of Puerto Rico and the "joint," "several," and "joint and several" of the common law legal system. This implies that these figures in our jurisdiction are not homologous to those of the common law jurisdictions.

But the Puerto Rico Supreme Court made it clear that when "joint and several" is expressed in a document written in English, the responsibility of debtors will be "joint and several," as such term means the obligation is jointly secured under the civil law tradition.[21] While in the Puerto Rico legal system, solidarity and severability is part of the substantive law, the common law doctrine states that "[t]he question of whether two promisors promise the same or separate performances is wholly a question of interpretation, while

16. Méndez v. Morales, 142 D.P.R. 26, 34 (1996); In Re Castro Mesa, 131 D.P.R. 1037 (1992).
17. Freyre v. Blasini, 68 D.P.R. 211 (1948); Díaz v. Vilches, 47 D.P.R. 298 (1934); Rivera v. García, 42 D.P.R. 207 (1931); and Santiago v. Cuebas Padilla, 41 D.P.R. 116 (1930).
18. 45 D.P.R. 123 (1933).
19. 31 L.P.R.A. § 3101; Pauneto v. Nuñez, 115 D.P.R. 591, 596(1984); Colón v. P.R. & Am. Insurance Co., 63 D.P.R. 344, 353 (1944).
20. *Id.*
21. Brockway Motor Truck Corp. of Puerto Rico v. Lloréis, 45 D.P.R. 123 (1933).

the question whether promisors who are promising the same performance are bound by "joint," "several," or "joint and several" remedies and duties is a procedural question."[22]

As for the translation of the words "joint" and "several" when referring to Puerto Rico obligations, it must meet the pronouncements in *Wong v. Key Finance Corporation*.[23] In the *Wong* case, the U.S. District Court for the District of Puerto Rico concluded:

> "The Civil Code of Puerto Rico deals with solidary obligations under Article 1090 (31 L.P.R.A. 3101) and following. There, the term used is "*solidaria*" which has been translated in the English version as "joint." According to Black's Law Dictionary, the term "solidary" is treated as follows: SOLIDARY. A term of civil-law origin, signifying that the right or interest spoken of is joint or common. A "solidary obligation" corresponds to a "joint and several" obligation in the common law; that is, one for which several debtors are bound in such wise that each is liable for the entire amount, and not merely for his proportionate share. But in the civil law the term also includes the case where there are several creditors, as against a common debtor, each of whom is entitled to receive the entire debt and give an acquittance for it. On the other hand, a joint and several obligation or liability is defined as follows: JOINT AND SEVERAL. A liability is said to be joint and several when a creditor may sue one or more of the parties to such liability separately, or all of them together at his option. Dicey, Parties 230. 1 Bouv. Law Dict. Rawle's Third Revision, p. 1702 defines a joint liability in the following manner: A joint liability on choses in action implies that though each person subject to it is liable for the whole, they are all treated in law as together constituting one legal entity and must be sued together or a release to one will operate in favor of all. One who pays the debt is entitled to contribution."
>
> * * *
>
> "Merely from looking at the dictionary definitions given to these terms, it is clear that although the juridical figures they are referring to are somewhat similar, there are fundamental differences between the obligations they refer to, as well as between the rights and actions derived from them. Thus, since the Civil Code of Puerto Rico is controlling on the matters brought up here, and since the Spanish language must prevail on the interpretation of the Civil Code, we shall, in considering the nature of the obligation incurred, be bound by this Code and that language."

1.3 Guaranty Contract

The Civil Code of Puerto Rico governs, among other types of contracts, the contract of guaranty or surety.[24] Article 1721[25] of the Civil Code provides that "[f]or the security [or guaranty] one is obligated to pay or to fulfill an

22. Rosario v. Sandoval, 60 D.P.R.411 (1942).
23. 266 F.Supp. 149 (1967).
24. The provisions regarding surety were based on Article 1822 of the Spanish Civil Code, and the Civil Code of 1902 under article 1723.
25. 31 L.P.R.A. § 4871.

obligation to a third person in the case the latter should fail to do so." The contract of guaranty has three defining characteristics, namely: (1) the obligation of the guaranty is ancillary and subsidiary, (2) is one-sided, because it can be established without the intervention of the debtor and the creditor in whose favor the guaranty is established, and (3) the guarantor is someone other than the debtor, because no one can be personally a guarantor of itself.[26]

Guaranty contracts or assertion of rights are those that "... are intended to ensure compliance with one or more obligations or affirm and clarify main rights that have been controversial."[27] Article 1721 also provides that if the guarantor is jointly and severally liable with the principal debtor, the relationship of solidarity is governed by Articles 1090 to 1101 of the Civil Code of Puerto Rico.[28]

The guaranty is characterized by the incidental nature of the obligation, since, like other surety, the guaranty cannot be conceived but is conditioned by the existence of a principal obligation. Hence it is necessary that the principal obligation exists and that it is valid. The subsidiarity applies where the guarantor undertakes to pay only in the case where the principal debtor fails to meet its obligation. Therefore, the life of the guaranty is dependent and is conditioned upon the existence of a primary obligation.

The guarantor supports the obligations of the debtor to its creditors and becomes liable for compliance. This is an agreement created to cover a pre-existing obligation.[29] If the debtor breaches the obligation, the guarantor must comply. But the guarantor can claim from the debtor the obligation paid to his creditor, with interest payments, expenses and damages, absent an agreement to the contrary.[30]

A personal guaranty contract is usually "an accessory obligation, in a third party's debt guaranteed by the guarantor who assumes and must meet the payment obligation in the absence of compliance with the guaranteed obligation."[31] However, once the obligation is extinguished whose primary assurance is concerned, the guaranty also expires, unless the actions arising from the enforcement of the surety.[32] That is the rule and that is why under the personal guaranty contract and the contract of surety, the guarantor must fulfill the obligation if the principal debtor does not. However, Puerto Rico jurisdiction recognizes the figure of joint and several surety or guarantor.

Based on the contemplation of the Puerto Rico Civil Code Article 1725,[33] the Supreme Court of Puerto Rico has directed that the contract of guaranty "is a personal guaranty in which the guarantor may be bound to less, but never more than the principal debtor, both in quantity and in consideration of the obligation." (Citations omitted).[34]

26. Sucn. María Resto v. Ortiz, 157 D.P.R. 803 (2002).
27. José Castán Tobeñas, Derecho Español, Común y Foral, Tomo IV, 744 (11th ed, Madrid, 1981).
28. 31 L.P.R.A. §§ 3101-3112.
29. José R. Torres Vélez, Derecho de Contratos, 529 (1st ed. Intermerican University of Puerto Rico 1990).
30. Artícles 1737-1742 of the Civil Code, 31 L.P.R.A. §§ 4911-4915.
31. San José Realty S.E. v. El Fénix de P.R., 157 D.P.R. 427, 496 (2002).
32. Article 1746 of the Civil Code, 31 L.P.R.A. § 4951.
33. 31 L.P.R.A. § 4875.
34. Andamios de P.R. v. Newport Bonding, 179 D.P.R.503, 511 (2010).

§ 2 Requirements for an Entity to Enter into a Guaranty

Corporations, partnerships, and limited liability companies have the power to execute and enter into guaranties subject to their incorporating or creative documents. The presumption is that an individual can contract and enter into a guaranty; however, a practitioner must take caution with married individuals, as the execution of a guaranty by one spouse may not bind the conjugal partnership and the assets of the conjugal partnership.

2.1 Corporations

Under the General Corporations Law of 2009, a Puerto Rico corporation may, within its general corporate powers, give a guaranty in furtherance of its corporate purpose, *provided* its articles of incorporation and bylaws do not prevent it from doing so.[35] A corporation may even guarantee loans to officers, directors, employees, or its subsidiaries, provided that the board of directors deems it reasonable to expect that such guaranty would benefit the corporation. The guaranty or assistance may be made without interest or collateral or be secured in a form approved by the board of directors, including, without limitation, the pledge of shares of the corporation.[36]

2.2 Partnerships

2.2.1 General Civil Law Partnerships

General civil law partnerships are governed by Articles 1570 to 1599 of the Civil Code of Puerto Rico.[37] The Civil Code neither prohibits nor forbids a civil law partnership from issuing a guaranty. However, the partners of a civil partnership will not be jointly and severally liable for the partnership's debts, and no partner can hold the other liable for a personal act, if the power to do so has not been conferred on the acting partner by the other partners.[38] The main feature of civil partnership is that every partner is a debtor of the partnership for whatever such partner has promised to contribute to the partnership. The partner is also bound to eviction regarding the specified and determined things the partner may have contributed to the partnership in the same cases and as a seller is bound regarding the purchaser.[39] However, the partnership is not completely independent of its partners, who shall be severally and subordinately

35. 14 L.P.R.A. §§ 3521-3522.
36. 14 L.P.R.A. § 3566.
37. 31 L.P.R.A. §§ 4311-4399.
38. 31 L.P.R.A. § 4372.
39. 31 L.P.R.A. § 4343; Under the Civil Code of Puerto Rico by virtue of the warranty referred to in 31 L.P.R.A. § 3801, the seller shall warrant to the purchaser: (1) The legal and peaceful possession of the thing sold; and (2) that there are no hidden faults or defects therein. 31 L.P.R.A. § 3841.

accountable for the obligations of the partnership with their personal assets.[40] That is, the existence of civil partnership does not exempt from liability the partners in their individual capacity. The partners' liability is unlimited, so they are liable with all their present and future assets.[41]

2.2.2 *Mercantile (Commercial) Partnerships*

The Commerce Code of Puerto Rico regulates mercantile or commercial partnerships under the following contexts:[42]

a. *general civil partnerships*—a partnership in which all the partners collectively, and under a firm name, bind themselves to share the same rights and obligations in the proportion they may establish.

b. *special partnerships*—partnership in which one or several persons contribute a specific amount of capital to the common fund, to share in the results of the firm's transactions carried out exclusively by others under a collective name. A special partnership may be created as a civil partnership or a mercantile partnership or a corporation; however, it must comply with certain requirements under tax law. A special partnership had to be created by and filed its election to be treated as a pass-through entity with the Department of Treasury of the Commonwealth of Puerto Rico before December 31, 2010. A special partnership is a tax pass- through conduit.[43] Although the eligibility of a partnership or corporation for special partnership treatment depends on the nature of the partnership's income, it is the partner/shareholder who is taxed on the ratable portion of the income as if he/she had carried on the business activity. The partners or shareholders of a special partnership have limited liability.[44]

c. *limited liability partnerships*—may be a partnership regulated by Puerto Rico's Limited Responsibility Partnerships Act[45] or by the Civil Code of Puerto Rico,[46] in which the partners shall be liable for corporate liabilities with their contribution or in which they shall be bound to contribute to the company or partnership. One partner of a limited liability partnership created under the Limited Liability Partnership Act shall not be liable with his/her personal assets beyond his/her contribution thereto for the debts and obligations of the partnership or of any other partner or partners that arise because of an error, omission, negligence, incompetence, or illegal act committed

40. Asoc. de Propietarios v. Santa Bárbara Co., 112 D.P.R. 33, 50 (1982).
41. Torruella Serallés v. Crédito e Inversiones San Miguel, 113 D.P.R. 24, 33 (1982).
42. 10 L.P.R.A. § 1347.
43. 13 L.P.R.A. § 3331 et seq.
44. Article 1589 of the Puerto Rico Civil Code, 31 L.P.R.A. § 4372; The Internal Revenue Code for a New Puerto Rico has eliminated the special partnership election available under the Puerto Rico Internal Revenue Code of 1994. Special partnerships under the Internal Revenue Code of 1994 will continue to be subject to the pass-through income tax treatment afforded to them under the Internal Revenue Code of 1994, but the deductibility of 50 percent of their losses by the partners from income derived from any other sources is no longer available.
45. Under Common Law, these limited partnerships are known as "Limited Liability Partnership" or "LLP" and are regulated under the Limited Responsibility Partnership Act 10 L.P.R.A. §§ 1861-1867.
46. Article 1582 of the Civil Code, 31 L.P.R.A.§ 4353 and the conclusions of the Puerto Rico Supreme Court in Descartes v. Tribunal de Contribuciones, 79 D.P.R. 866 (1957).

by another partner or employee, agent, or representative of the partnership. A partner will be liable for the partnership's obligation if at the moment the act was committed, he/she was involved, directly or indirectly, in the activity that caused damages to a third party, or if the partner had notice or knowledge of the act that caused damage to a third party. In professional partnerships, the limited liability of each partner shall not be extended to the obligations arising from exercising the profession. Puerto Rico's Limited Responsibility Partnerships Act neither expressly empowers a limited liability partnership to issue a guaranty nor expressly regulates or prohibits such activity. For a partnership to gain the limited liability, it must file the deed of partnership with the Secretary of State.[47]

d. *mercantile partnerships*—The mercantile partnership is governed by the Puerto Rico Commerce Code and its Article 95[48] defines the concept of partnership as a contract by which two or more persons must pool goods, industry, or any other things for profit. Unlike civil partnership, the mercantile partnership agreement must be executed in a public deed and must be submitted for entry in the Mercantile Registry at the corresponding section of the Registry of the Property of Puerto Rico.[49] A mercantile partnership may be created in one of two ways. One is the regular collective partnership in which all partners in a collective name are committed to participate in the proportions established with the same rights and obligations.[50] In the collective partnership, the partners are jointly and severally liable with all their assets for the results of operations made in the name and for the partnership, under the partnership authority and by the person authorized to use it.[51] In the mercantile limited partnership, one or more persons agree to provide certain capital to be pooled to be bound by the results of the partnership transactions conducted exclusively by the general partner(s).[52] The mercantile limited partnership is known as a *sociedad en comandita* under the laws of Puerto Rico; however, this type of entity is not a limited partnership in the common law sense, but is a juridical person with a personality like that of a corporation.[53] In the *sociedad en comandita*, the general partners are jointly and severally bound with the *sociedad en comandita* and

47. 10 L.P.R.A. § 1862(a).
48. 10 L.P.R.A. § 1341; *See also* Negrón Portillo, *L. Derecho Corporativo Puertorriqueño*, 2nd. ed., San Juan, 1996, page 18.
49. 10 L.P.R.A. § 1032.
50. 10 L.P.R.A. § 1347.
51. 10 L.P.R.A. § 1363.
52. 10 L.P.R.A. § 1347.
53. Its members are not primarily liable for its acts and debts, and its creditors are preferred with respect to its assets and property over the creditors of individual members, although the latter may reach the interests of the individual members in the common capital. 31 L.P.R.A. § 1590; *see* Quintana Bros. & Co. v. Ramirez & Co., 22 D.P.R. 707, 716. Although the members whose participation is unlimited are made contingently liable for the debts of the *socieda en comandita* in the event that its assets are insufficient to satisfy them (*see* Successors of M. Lamadrid & Co. v. Torrens, Mortorell & Co., 28 D.P.R. 824), this liability is of no more consequence than that imposed on corporate stockholders by the statutes of some states. *See* Puerto Rico v. Russell & Co., 288 U.S. 476 (1933) for an explanation of the *sociedad en comandita*.

limited partners are liable only for the funds they have contributed to the *sociedad en comandita*, except for rare exceptions.[54] The limited partners have limited liability, but if they perform acts of administration such partners may lose the limited liability protection.

2.3 Limited Liability Companies

Puerto Rico's General Corporations Law permits limited liability companies to issue guaranties.[55]

2.4 Banks

Banks have the same authority that corporations have under the General Corporations Act of 2009. However, banks are restricted from issuing capital liabilities without approval from the Commissioner of Financial Institutions. In Puerto Rico, a state-chartered bank is subject to federal law and its limitation on guaranties.

2.5 Individuals

An individual guarantor must have the "capacity" to enter into the guaranty. The validity of a guaranty and the consent given by an individual is presumed.[56] As a general rule, in Puerto Rico there is a presumption of mental capacity to act as an individual.[57] Incapacity can be a defense against the enforcement of a guaranty issued by an individual. However, the incapacity must be accredited in a clear and complete manner in order to destroy the presumption of capacity. According to Article 1215 of the Civil Code, unemancipated minors, lunatics, or insane, and the deaf who cannot read or write cannot give consent to an agreement.[58] The Puerto Rico Supreme Court has clarified that the reference to a "lunatic" or "insane" is not considered from the psychiatric point of view, but from the person who has no capacity to understand the transaction, after considering all its aspects.[59]

Individuals who are married have certain restrictions in the administration and disposal of the assets of the conjugal partnership established upon marriage. Under Puerto Rico law, marriage is a civil institution, originating in a civil contract whereby a man and a woman mutually agree to become husband and wife and to discharge toward each other the duties imposed by law.[60]

Under Puerto Rico law, married persons commence a conjugal partnership from the day that the marriage is celebrated.[61] Both spouses are

54. 10 L.P.R.A. § 1394.
55. 14 L.P.R.A. § 3956.
56. Unisys v. Ramallo Brothers, 128 D.P.R. 842, 853 (1991).
57. Jiménez v. Jiménez, 76 D.P.R. 718, 733 (1954). *See also* Pueblo v. Marcano Pérez, 116 D.P.R. 917, 927 (1986).
58. 31 L.P.R.A. § 3402.
59. Rivera v. Succession Luzunaris Diaz, 70 D.P.R. 181, 188 (1949).
60. 31 L.P.R.A. § 221.
61. 31 L.P.R.A. § 3622.

coadministrators of the community assets of the conjugal partnership, except when otherwise stipulated, in which case one of the spouses shall grant a power of attorney to the other to act as administrator of the community property.[62] Either spouse may make purchases with community property when the purchases comprise things or articles for personal or family use in accordance with the social and economic standing of the family. Either of the spouses may make said purchases in cash or on credit. The spouses prior to entering into a marriage may agree by virtue of a prenuptial agreement to choose an economic regime different from the community property regime of the Civil Code.[63]

Article 91 of the Civil Code provides that real property owned as community property by the spouses may not be transferred or encumbered, under penalty of nullity of the transaction, except with the written consent of both spouses.[64] Nevertheless, the husband and wife have the right to manage and freely dispose of their respective separate estates.[65] Either of the spouses may legally represent the conjugal partnership. Any unilateral administrative act of one of the spouses shall bind the conjugal partnership and its community assets and shall be presumed valid for all legal purposes.[66]

In Puerto Rico, since the 1976 Civil Code reform, both spouses are considered administrators of the conjugal assets and have the authority to represent the conjugal partnership.[67] Both Article 91 and Article 93 of the Civil Code create a presumption of validity for unilateral actions of either spouse for all legal purposes. This presumption has the practical effect of giving legitimacy to both spouses to act for the conjugal partnership, which besides favoring a public policy and social position of equality of the sexes, also protects the interest of third parties that contract with the spouses and their conjugal partnership.[68]

Article 1313 of the Civil Code[69] provides that, notwithstanding Article 91,[70] neither of the spouses may donate, transfer, or bind for consideration the personal or real property of the community property without the written consent of the other spouse, excepting things for personal or family use in accordance with the social or economic standing of both spouses. Any act of either spouse regarding the transfer or administration of such property in violation of Article 1313 will not affect the other spouse or his or her heirs. The same article provides that if a spouse is engaged in commerce, industry, or a profession, such spouse may, for good cause, acquire or dispose of personal property used for such purposes without the consent of the other spouse. Such spouse engaged in commerce shall, however, be liable for the damages

62. 31 L.P.R.A. § 284.
63. *See* footnote 62.
64. *See* footnote 62.
65. 31 L.P.R.A. § 285.
66. 31 L.P.R.A. § 286.
67. Act No. 51 of May 21, 1976 (31 L.P.R.A. §§ 284, 286, 3661, 3671-3672 y 3717); Blás v. Hosp. Guadalupe, 146 D.P.R. 267 (1998); Urbino v. San Juan Racing Assoc., Inc., supra; Reyes v. Cantera Ramos, Inc., supra.
68. Professor Migdalia Fraticelli Torres, *Un nuevo acercamiento a los regímenes económicos en el matrimonio: la sociedad legal de gananciales en el Derecho Puertorriqueño*, 29 Rev. Jur. U.I.P.R. 413, 449 (1995).
69. 31 L.P.R.A. § 3672.
70. *See* footnote 62.

he or she may cause by said acts to the community property of the conjugal partnership. This damages action shall be exercised exclusively when the community property is dissolved.

The Supreme Court of Puerto Rico has indicated that both articles (91 and 1313) severely limit the individual capacity of a spouse to dispose of community property. Article 1313 refers to both movable and immovable property, while Article 91 relates only to real property. The fundamental difference between these two articles is that Article 91 establishes the nullity due to the violation of its mandate, while Article 1313 prohibits a spouse from disposing of the property without the permission of the other.[71]

Therefore, in any contract of guaranty it is essential to have the concurrence of both spouses.[72] Thus, unauthorized alienation of property by a spouse becomes a voidable legal transaction.[73] In this regard, in *Pérez Mercado v. Martínez Rondón*,[74] the Puerto Rico Supreme Court clarified that "in the case that a contract is executed by a spouse without the appearance of the other spouse—if the other's consent is indispensable—the only person entitled to challenge the validity of that contract is the spouse who did not execute the contract." Therefore, if a creditor fails to obtain both spouses' signatures in a contract of guaranty, the creditor may be precluded or limited in its future collection action against the conjugal partnership or the community property.

§ 3 Signatory's Authority to Execute a Guaranty

Please Review § 1 Regarding the Contract Formalities.

3.1 Corporations

Absent corporate or other documents precisely stating the powers and authority of a corporate officer, as a general rule, a corporate officer has the implicit authority to perform those functions that fall within the scope of the ordinary business of the corporation.[75] Besides the authority expressly delegated, corporate managers may have an implied authority, either by nature of their positions or how the business of the corporation has been conducted in the past. An officer of a corporation has authority to act as expressly conferred on him by statute, law, or the act of the directors of the corporation. A corporate officer may bind the corporation if the actions are incidental to the business or the corporation; or if the action is within his ostensible authority or ratified by proper authority.

---

71. S.L.G. Sierra v. Rodríguez, 163 D.P.R. 738, 754 (2005).
72. Padró Collado v. Espada, 111 D.P.R. 56 (1981); Int'l Charter Mortgage Corp. v. Registrador, 110 D.P.R. 862, 868 (1981); Silva Ramos v. Registrador, 107 D.P.R. 240 (1978); Aguilú v. Sociedad de Gananciales, 106 D.P.R. 652 (1977).
73. Trabal Morales v. Ruiz Rodríguez, 125 D.P.R. 340, 357 (1990).
74. 130 D.P.R. 134 (1992).
75. Reece Corp. v. Ariela, Inc., 122 D.P.R. 270, 282 (1988).

3.2 Partnerships

Article 1583 of the Civil Code states that an administrative partner, if the articles of copartnership provide such authority "... may execute all administrative acts, notwithstanding the opposition of his partners, unless he should act in bad faith; and his power is irrevocable without legitimate cause."[76] Those dealing with a civil partnership must inquire and obtain the partnership agreement to determine the authority of the administrative partner. Under Puerto Rico law, the partners of a civil partnership shall not be jointly and severally liable for the partnership's debts, and no one can hold the other partner liable for a personal act if the power to do so has not been conferred on the partner who acts even if the business of a partnership is conferred on only one managing partner.[77]

If the management of a partnership is entrusted in two or more partners without their duties having been delimited in the partnership agreement, or without a statement having been made that one of them shall not act without the consent of the others, then each partner may severally exercise all acts of administration, but any of them may oppose the acts of the others before they have produced any legal effect.[78] If a managing partner is not to act without the consent of the other managing partner, the consent of all is necessary for the validity of the guaranty and the absence or incapacity of any one of them cannot be alleged unless there should be imminent danger of a serious or irreparable injury to the partnership.[79]

The civil partnership shall not be held liable to a third party for acts that a partner performed in his own name or without the partnership's authority to do so, but the partnership is liable to the partner in whatever way said acts have resulted in benefit for the partnership.

3.3 Limited Liability Companies

The General Corporations Law of 2009 provides that any member or manager may act as surety, guarantor, and endorser and guarantee or assume one or more obligations of that company unless authority has been granted to another member-manager.[80]

§ 4 Requirements for Validity of Guaranty Contract: Consent, Object, and Cause

Puerto Rico Law Requires Three Essential Conditions for the Validity of a Guaranty.

76. 31 L.P.R.A. § 4354.
77. 31 L.P.R.A. § 4372.
78. 31 L.P.R.A. § 4355.
79. 31 L.P.R.A. § 4356.
80. 14 L.P.R.A. § 3957.

Under Puerto Rico law, Article 1213 of the Civil Code of Puerto Rico[81] sets out three requirements that must be satisfied before a contract exists: (1) the consent of the contracting parties, (2) a definite object which may be the subject of the contract, and (3) the cause for the obligation which may be established. Consent is manifested by the concurrence of the offer and the acceptance upon the object and the cause which are to constitute the contract.[82] Furthermore, Article 1230 of the Civil Code of Puerto Rico[83] provides that contracts shall be binding, whatever may be the form in which they may have been executed, provided that the essential conditions for its validity exists. If consent, object, and cause concur in a contract, then a valid contract of guaranty exists. The inquiry into the three elements for the existence of a guaranty contract is based on standard contract law principles.

Consent is shown by the concurrence of the offer and acceptance of the thing and the cause which are to constitute the contract.[84] Under guaranty law, generally, an acceptance made by letter does not bind the person making the offer, but from the time it came to his knowledge. All things, even future ones, which are not out of the commerce of man, may be objects of contracts and all services not contrary to law or to good morals may be the object of a contract. Finally, in contracts, the promise of a thing or service by the other party is understood as a sufficient consideration for each contracting party. In compensated contracts, the service or benefits remunerated, and in those of pure beneficence, the mere liberality of the benefactor is sufficient consideration.[85] Contracts are binding, whatever the form in which they may have been executed, provided the essential conditions required for their validity exist.[86]

§ 5 Interpretation of Guaranties

Courts in Puerto Rico are Guided by Civil Law Principles.

5.1 General Principles

The Civil Code Article 1726 provides the guaranty is never presumed; it must be express and may not extend to more than what is in it.[87] While Puerto Rico courts have ruled that a contract of guaranty must be interpreted to favor the claims of a third-party beneficiary, such an interpretation cannot be abstracted from the real intention of the parties. It must be addressed in the language of the agreement, viewed in its entirety, and according to the rules of hermeneutics arranged in the Civil Code.[88]

81. 31 L.P.R.A. § 3391.
82. 31 L.P.R.A. § 3401.
83. 31 L.P.R.A. § 3451.
84. 31 L.P.R.A. § 3401.
85. 31 L.P.R.A. § 3431.
86. 31 L.P.R.A. § 3451.
87. 31 L.P.R.A. § 4876; Ulpiano Casal, Inc. v. Totty Mfg. Corp., 90 D.P.R. 739, 744 (1964); Sucn. Belaval v. Acosta, 64 D.P.R.109, 111-112 (1944).
88. Caguas Plumbing, Inc. v. Continental Const. Corp, 155 D.P.R. 744 (2001).

5.2 Types of Guaranty

The guaranty may be conventional, legal or judicial, gratuitous, or for a valuable consideration. It may be constituted not only in favor of the principal debtor, but also in favor of the other surety, either with the consent, ignorance, and even against the opposition of the latter.[89]

In Puerto Rico the legal guaranty or bond is that provided by provision of law.[90] The judicial guaranty or bond is imposed by a decision emanating from the judicial authority, i.e., by court order, also known as procedural guaranty. A guaranty cannot exist without a valid obligation. An obligation, the nullity of which may be claimed by an exception purely personal on the part of the obligor, as that of minority, may be the subject of security.

5.3 Termination of Guaranties

The obligation of the guarantor or surety shall expire with that of the debtor, and for the same causes as all other obligations.[91] The Puerto Rico doctrine regarding termination of guaranties is unanimous in that "the reason or determining cause of someone being forced to pay someone else's debt is in the relationship which exists between the guarantor and the principal debtor."[92] "Unless a clause is negotiated to such effect, the obligations resulting from a guaranty end at moment of the death of the debtor, since at that moment the debtor cannot generate further obligations."[93]

The extinction of the guaranty is regulated by Articles 1746-1752 of the Civil Code.[94] The guaranty expires, among other things, by the acceptance of goods by the creditor in settlement of debt (Article 1748), for the extension granted to the debtor by the creditor without the consent of the guarantor (Article 1750), and by payment of the debtor (Article 1746).

Guarantors are released from their obligations under a contract of guaranty "... whenever by an act of the creditor they cannot be subrogated to the rights, mortgages, and privileges of the same."[95] This rule operates to release the guarantor from liability. However, the Supreme Court of Puerto Rico clarified that this provision is limited by the liberal interpretation given to the contract of guaranty by the rule outlined in *Olazabal v. U.S. Fidelity, Etc.*[96] in that: "As a general rule, the surety shall be relieved of liability to the creditor only to the extent that the actions of the creditor have harmed the interests or rights of the former."

---

89. 31 L.P.R.A. § 4872.
90. Colón v. Porto Rican & American Insurance Co., 63 D.P.R. 344 (1944).
91. 31 L.P.R.A. § 4951.
92. Joseph Puig Brutau, Civil Law, T. II, Vol. II, 594 (2nd ed., Bosch, Barcelona, 1987).
93. Our translation, please *see* the original language in Cámara de Comerciantes Mayoristas P.R. v. Hernández, 140 D.P.R. 325, 329 (1996) – "*Basta concluir que, salvo que se pacte una cláusula al efecto, las obligaciones resultantes de fianza terminan al momento de la muerte del deudor afianzado, ya que ahí cesa su capacidad de generar obligaciones.*"
94. 31 LPRA §§ 4951-4957.
95. 31 L.P.R.A § 4956.
96. 103 D.P.R. 448 (1975).

The extension granted to the debtor by the creditor, without the consent of the guarantor, extinguishes the security.[97] However, in a case of a joint and several guarantor, an extension granted by the creditor to the principal debtor does not release the guarantor from his obligation.[98]

§ 6 Defenses of the Guarantor

6.1 Defenses of the Primary Obligor

Under the statute in the Puerto Rico Civil Code on debt and joint sureties, those jointly and severally bound to a creditor may raise certain defenses or exceptions. This arises from Article 1101 of the Civil Code which provides that a guarantor may assert against the claims of the creditor all defenses arising from the obligation and those personal to the obligor. Those personally pertaining to the others may be employed by the obligor only regarding the share of the debt for which the obligor may be liable.[99] This provision introduces an exception from the principles of the joint and several obligations, because in the joint and several guaranties all the debtors (including the guarantor) are responsible for the totality of the debt. This provision exists to protect the guarantor from any illicit acts by the creditor, who may contract with an incapacitated guarantor or may obtain the consent of the guarantor by deceit, with the innocent guarantor suffering the consequences of the illicit activity of the creditor.

This article welcomes "a deviation from the principles of joint obligations" as Professor José Ramón Vélez Torres poses, to echo the ideas of Castán, as joint and several liability on all debtors are responsible for the entire debt. However, this author finds a "more reasonable commentary [of] Pairó Díaz, who justifies the rule stating that you cannot protect an unlawful action by the creditor who contracted, for example, with an incompetent or obtained the consent by fraud, or claims before the due date, etc., making the innocent cosigner suffer the consequences from the unlawful act."[100]

Under Puerto Rico law the guarantor is not bound to perform if the primary obligor is not bound, except if a waiver occurs. If the defense belongs to the primary obligor, the primary obligor retains the sole capacity to choose whether to assert it. Such personal defenses include fraud in the inducement, negligence in performance of a contract, and a breach of a warranty in the agreement governing the underlying obligation.

97. 31 L.P.R.A. § 4955.

98. National City Bank v. De la Torre, 48 D.P.R. 134 (1935), confirmed in De la Torre v. National City Bank, 91 F.2d 399 (1937), certiorari denied, De la Torre v. National City Bank, 302 U.S. 752; 58 S. Ct. 272; 82 L. E d. 581 (1937).

99. 31 L.P.R.A. § 3112.

100. José Ramón Vélez Torres, Derecho de las Obligaciones, 90 (UIPR 1997).

The guarantor may present against the creditor all the exceptions which pertain to the principal obligor and which may be inherent to the debt, but not those which may be purely personal to the debtor.[101]

If the guarantor pays without informing the debtor, the latter may use against him all the exceptions which he could have set up against the creditor at the time of paying.[102] If the guarantor pays a term debt before it was due, the guarantor cannot require the debtor to reimburse him until the period has expired.[103]

Finally, if the guarantor pays the creditor without notifying the debtor, and the debtor, not knowing of the payment, also pays the debt, the guarantor cannot make a claim to the debtor. The guarantor cannot only make a claim against the creditor.[104]

§ 7 Waiver of Defenses by the Guarantor

7.1 Defenses that Cannot be Waived

A party cannot waive a constitutional or statutory protection where the public interest is implicated or where the statute provides its violation would render the contract void.

§ 8 Subrogation

Article 1738 of the Puerto Rico Civil Code provides that the guarantor is subrogated by payment to the rights which the creditor had against the debtor.[105] When the guarantor pays the debt, the guarantor can demand to be indemnified for the entire debt, statutory interest, charges, and damages, if any, caused to the guarantor.[106] Under Article 1751 of the Puerto Rico Civil Code[107] the guarantor is released from its obligation "if by some act of the creditor the guarantor cannot be subrogated to the rights, mortgages and privileges thereof." We must differentiate between the guarantor and the codebtor. When a codebtor pays, the obligation is extinguished, and the codebtor can only claim from his codebtors the shares pertaining to each one with interest on the amounts advanced.[108] If a codebtor does not fulfill the obligation to repay the other codebtor by reason of his insolvency, then the other codebtors shall make whole the paying codebtor in proportion to the debt of each. On the

101. 31 L.P.R.A. § 4957.
102. 31 L.P.R.A. § 4913.
103. 31 L.P.R.A. § 4914.
104. 31 L.P.R.A. § 4915.
105. 31 L.P.R.A. § 4912; Gil v. C.R.U.V., 109 D.P.R. 551 (1980); Suc. María Resto v. Ortiz Lebrón, 157 D.P.R. 803 (2002).
106. 31 L.P.R.A. § 4911.
107. 31 L.P.R.A. § 4956.
108. 31 L.P.R.A. § 3109.

other hand, a guarantor who pays an obligation of the debtor retains all rights to collect the debt against the debtor, without being subject to the limitations indicated above to a codebtor.[109]

If there are two or more guarantors for the same debtor and for the same debt, the one who has paid the obligation may demand of each of the others, the debtor and the other guarantor, the part which he or they should proportionally have paid. If any one of them should be insolvent, the part of the insolvent guarantor or the debtor shall be paid by all in the same proportion. The payment of the guarantor must have been made by virtue of judicial proceedings or when the principal debtor should have made an assignment or is bankrupt.[110]

§ 9 Indemnification—Whether the Primary Obligor has a Duty

When a guarantor pays the debt, the guarantor can demand indemnification for the entire debt.[111] The guarantor may demand the total amount of the debt, the legal interest on the debt from the day on which the payment may have been communicated to the debtor, even when it did not produce interest for the creditor, the expenses incurred by the guarantor after it informed the debtor that it has been sued for payment, and the losses and damages suffered by the guarantor, when proper.

§ 10 Enforcement of Guaranties

A party seeking to enforce a guaranty must sue for breach of the guaranty contract in the applicable Court of First Instance. Under Puerto Rico law, a guarantor cannot be compelled to pay a creditor until an application has been previously made of all the property of the debtor.[112] This principle is what makes the contract of guaranty subsidiary, as the liquidation of the estate of the debtor allows the guarantor to avoid paying the creditor until the creditor proves the insolvency of the principal debtor, whether it is full or partial. This does not preclude that the guarantor may be notified of the default simultaneously with the principal debtor; it merely stays the moment that the creditor may collect from the guarantor.[113] To take advantage of this right, the guarantor must inform the creditor, once the creditor demands payment from the

109. WRC Props., Inc. v. Santana, 116 D.P.R. 127, 136 (1985).
110. 31 L.P.R.A. § 4931.
111. *See* footnote 91.
112. 31 L.P.R.A. § 4891.
113. 31 L.P.R.A. § 4895.

guarantor, and point to the creditor sufficient assets of the debtor in Puerto Rico to allow for collection.[114]

However, this provision may be waived or rendered inapplicable by: (1) an agreement of the parties, (2) if the guarantor has jointly bound himself with the debtor,[115] (3) in the case of bankruptcy of the debtor, or (4) when the debtor cannot be judicially sued within Puerto Rico.[116]

§ 11 Choice of Law and Choice of Forum

Under Puerto Rico law, parties have freedom to contract; thus, they may stipulate the law that will govern their agreements.[117] The Supreme Court, citing the "Restatement of the Laws (2d.), Conflict of Laws" of 1971, recognized the validity of such clauses when such clauses do not contravene fundamental provisions of public policy, the law, or the morals and the jurisdiction selected has substantial connection with the contract. If those requirements are met, then the selection of choice of law would not be considered unjust or unreasonable. Therefore, any court decision rendered by any of the states of the United States will be enforced in Puerto Rico without need of retrial or re-examination of the merits of the case, provided a Puerto Rico court in an exequatur[118] proceeding finds that the court of such state of the United States (1) had subject matter and in *personam* jurisdiction in the judicial proceeding that resulted in said final judgment and (2) said judgment was issued by a court of competent jurisdiction absent any fraud and in compliance with due process of law.

In the case of federal court judgments, the Supreme Court of Puerto Rico has held that, regardless of the district court where rendered, such judgments will be enforced *ex propio vigore* in Puerto Rican jurisdiction under Rule 69 of the Federal Rules of Civil Procedure.[119]

---

114. 31 L.P.R.A. § 4893.
115. 31 L.P.R.A. § 4871.
116. 31 L.P.R.A. § 4892; F.D.I.C. v. Municipio de Ponce, 904 F.2d 740 (1990); Colon v. Porto Rican & American Insurance Co., *supra*, note 44.
117. Walborg Corporation v. Tribunal Superior, 104 D.P.R. 184 (1975) and Unisys P.R. v. Ramallo Brothers, 128 D.P.R. 842 (1991).
118. An exequatur proceeding is the mechanism by virtue of which foreign and state court judgments are given "full faith and credit" in Puerto Rico.
119. Sosa Hernández v. Borrás Marína, 145 D.P.R. 859 (1998).

Editors and Contributors

Editors

Jeremy S. Friedberg
Leitess Friedberg PC
10451 Mill Run Circle, Suite 1000
Baltimore, MD 21117
www.lf-pc.com

Brian D. Hulse
Davis Wright Tremaine LLP
1201 Third Avenue, Suite 2200
Seattle, Washington 98101
www.dwt.com

James H. Prior
Porter Wright Morris & Arthur LLP
41 S High Street
Suites 2800-3200
Columbus, OH 43215
www.porterwright.com

Contributors

Eric J. Adams (Nebraska)
Baird Holm LLP
1500 Woodmen Tower
1700 Farnam St
Omaha, NE 68102-2068
www.bairdholm.com

Afi Ahmadi (Vermont)
Dinse, Knapp & McAndrew, P.C.
209 Battery Street
Burlington, Vermont 05401
www.dinse.com

S. Jason Arbuck (Canada except Quebec)
Cassels Brock & Blackwell LLP
2100 Scotia Plaza
40 King Street West
Toronto, Ontario M5H 3C2
www.casselsbrock.com

Donna Baldry (Illinois)
Sidley Austin LLP
One South Dearborn Street
Chicago, Illinois 60603
www.sidley.com

Thomas A. Barr (Delaware)
Richards, Layton & Finger PA
One Rodney Square
920 North King Street
Wilmington, Delaware 19801
www.rlf.com

Jeffrey M. Barrett (Wisconsin)
Michael Best & Friedrich LLP
100 East Wisconsin Avenue, Suite 3300
Milwaukee, Wisconsin 53202
http://www.michaelbest.com

Carl W. Barton (Utah)
Holland & Hart LLP
222 South Main Street, Suite 2200
Salt Lake City, Utah 84101

Laura J. Biddy (Alabama)
Johnston Barton Proctor & Rose LLP
Colonial Brookwood Center
569 Brookwood Village, Suite 901
Birmingham, Alabama 35209
www.johnstonbarton.com

Kayla D. Britton (Indiana)
Faegre Baker Daniels LLP
300 North Meridian Street, Suite 2700
Indianapolis, Indiana 46204
http://www.faegrebd.com

Laura Brown (U.S. federal guaranty law)
McGlinchey Stafford, PLLC
12th Floor
601 Poydras Street
New Orleans, LA 70130
www.mcglinchey.com

Jamie W. Bruno (Disctrict of Columbia)
Williams, Mullen, Clark & Dobbins, P.C.
8300 Greensboro Drive, Suite 1100
McLean, Virginia 22102
www.williamsmullen.com

Catherine A. Borneo (New York)
Cleary Gottlieb Steen & Hamilton LLP
One Liberty Plaza
New York, New York 10006-1470
www.clearygottlieb.com

Donovan Borvan (Illinois)
Sidley Austin LLP
One South Dearborn Street
Chicago, Illinois 60603
www.sidley.com

John P. Burton (New Mexico)
Rodey, Dickason, Sloan, Akin & Robb, P.A.
315 Paseo de Peralta
Santa Fe, New Mexico 87501
www.rodey.com

Penelope L. Christophorou (New York)
Cleary Gottlieb Steen & Hamilton LLP
One Liberty Plaza
New York, New York 10006-1470
www.clearygottlieb.com

Deborah Macer Chun (Hawai`i)
Chun Yoshimoto LLP
737 Bishop Street, Suite 2800
Pacific Guardian Center, Mauka Tower
Honolulu, Hawai`i 96813
www.chunyoshimoto.com

David B. Clark (Minnesota)
Faegre Baker Daniels LLP
2200 Wells Fargo Center
Minneapolis, MN 55402-3901
http://www.faegrebd.com

Dustin R. DeNeal (Indiana)
Faegre Baker Daniels LLP
300 North Meridian Street, Suite 2700
Indianapolis, Indiana 46204
http://www.faegrebd.com

Christopher J. Devlin (Maine)
Unum
2211 Congress Street, C474
Portland, ME 04122

C. Edward Dobbs (Georgia)
Parker, Hudson, Rainer & Dobbs LLP
1500 Marquis Two Tower
285 Peachtree Center Avenue NE
Atlanta, Georgia 30303
www.phrd.com

Charles D. Dunbar (West Virginia)
Jackson Kelly PLLC
500 Lee Street, East
Suite 1600
P. O. Box 553
Charleston, WV 25322
www.jacksonkelly.com

Gregory C. Dyekman (Wyoming)
Dray, Dyekman, Reed & Healey, P.C.
204 East 22nd Street
Cheyenne WY 82001-3729

Claire P. Edwards (Pennsylvania)
Blank Rome LLP
One Logan Square
Philadelphia, Pennsylvania 19103

Joshua L. Edwards (Oklahoma)
Phillips Murrah P.C.
Corporate Tower | Thirteenth Floor
101 North Robinson
Oklahoma City, Oklahoma 73102
www.phillipsmurrah.com

Shadi J. Enos (California)
Buchalter Nemer P.C.
55 Second Street, Suite 1700
San Francisco, California 94105-3493
www.buchalter.com

Wanda L. Fischer (North Dakota)
Olson & Burns P.C.
17 1st Ave. SE
Minot, ND 58702-1180
http://www.minotlaw.com

Steven D. Fleissig (New Jersey)
Greenberg Traurig, LLP
200 Park Avenue
P.O. Box 677
Florham Park, NJ 07932
fleissigs@gtlaw.com

John F.W. Fleming (Indiana)
Faegre Baker Daniels LLP
300 North Meridian Street, Suite 2700
Indianapolis, Indiana 46204
http://www.faegrebd.com

Thomas L. Flynn (Iowa)
Belin McCormick P.C.
666 Walnut Street, Suite 2000
Des Moines, Iowa 50309
www.belinmccormick.com

R. Grady Ford (West Virginia)
Jackson Kelly PLLC
500 Lee Street, East
Suite 1600
P. O. Box 553
Charleston, WV 25322
www.jacksonkelly.com

Harvey I. Forman (Pennsylvania)
Blank Rome LLP
One Logan Square
Philadelphia, Pennsylvania 19103

Leslie Godfrey (Nevada)
Greenberg Traurig, LLP
3773 Howard Hughes Parkway, Suite 400 N
Las Vegas, Nevada 89169
www.gtlaw.com

Mark K. Googins (Maine)
Verrill Dana, LLP
One Portland Square
Portland, ME 04112
www.verrilldana.com

Timothy E. Grady (Ohio)
Porter, Wright, Morris & Arthur LLP
41 South High Street
Columbus, Ohio 43215-6194
www.porterwright.com

Shannon B. Gray (Florida)
Carlton Fields, P.A.
4221 W. Boy Scout Boulevard
Suite 1000
Tampa, FL 33607-5780
www.carltonfields.com

Kenneth M. Greene (North Carolina)
Carruthers & Roth, P.A.
235 North Edgeworth Street
Greensboro, North Carolina 27401
www.crlaw.com

R. Marshall Grodner (Louisiana)
McGlinchey Stafford, PLLC
301 Main Street
One American Place 14th Floor
Baton Rouge, LA 70825
www.mcglinchey.com

Timothy W. Grooms (Arkansas)
Quattlebaum, Grooms,
Tull & Burrow PLLC1
111 Center Street, Suite 1900
Little Rock, AR 72201
www.QGTB.com

Brynn Hallman (Arizona)
Greenberg Traurig, LLP
2375 E. Camelback Rd. Suite 700
Phoenix, AZ 85016
www.gtlaw.com

Teresa Wilton Harmon (Illinois)
Sidley Austin LLP
One South Dearborn Street
Chicago, Illinois 60603
www.sidley.com

Edmund D. Harllee
(Disctrict of Columbia)
Williams, Mullen, Clark & Dobbins, P.C.
8300 Greensboro Drive, Suite 1100
McLean, Virginia 22102
www.williamsmullen.com

Jeremy R. Harrell (Minnesota)
Faegre Baker Daniels LLP
2200 Wells Fargo Center
Minneapolis, MN 55402-3901
http://www.faegrebd.com

Taylor A. Heck (Mississippi)
McGlinchey Stafford Pllc
200 South Lamar Street
City Centre South, Suite 1100
Jackson, MS 39201

Thomas S. Hemmendinger
(Massachusetts and Rhode Island)
Brennan, Recupero, Cascione,
Scungio & McAllister, LLP
362 Broadway
Providence, RI 02903
www.brcsm.com

Charles W. Hingle (Montana)
Holland & Hart LLP
401 North 31st Street
Suite 1500
Billings, Montana 59101-1277
www.hollandhart.com

Kenneth C. Howell (Idaho)
Hawley Troxell Ennis & Hawley LLP
877 Main Street, Suite 1000
Boise, Idaho 83702
www.hawleytroxell.com

Brian D. Hulse (Washington)
Davis Wright Tremaine LLP
1201 Third Avenue, Suite 2200
Seattle, Washington 98101

Eric L. Johnson (Oklahoma)
Phillips Murrah P.C.
Corporate Tower | Thirteenth Floor
101 North Robinson
Oklahoma City, Oklahoma 73102
www.phillipsmurrah.com

Haskins W. Jones (Alabama)
Johnston Barton Proctor & Rose LLP
Colonial Brookwood Center
569 Brookwood Village, Suite 901
Birmingham, Alabama 35209
www.johnstonbarton.com

Jeb H. Joyce (Arkansas)
Quattlebaum, Grooms, Tull & Burrow
PLLC1
111 Center Street, Suite 1900
Little Rock, AR 72201
www.QGTB.com

Cynthia D. Kaiser (Delaware)
Richards, Layton & Finger PA
One Rodney Square
920 North King Street
Wilmington, Delaware 19801
www.rlf.com

Mbabazi Kasara (New York)
Cleary Gottlieb Steen & Hamilton LLP
One Liberty Plaza
New York, New York 10006-1470
www.clearygottlieb.com

Geoffrey King (Illinois)
Sidley Austin LLP
One South Dearborn Street
Chicago, Illinois 60603
www.sidley.com

Paul Kyed (Colorado)
Holland & Hart LLP
555 17th Street, Suite 3200
Denver, CO 80202
www.hollandhart.com

Connie Boyles Lane (New Hampshire)
Orr & Reno PA
One Eagle Square,
P.O. Box 3550
Concord, NH 03302-3550
www.orr-reno.com

Erik Lemmon (Colorado)
Holland & Hart LLP
555 17th Street, Suite 3200
Denver, CO 80202
www.hollandhart.com

Edgel C. Lester (Florida)
Carlton Fields, P.A.
4221 W. Boy Scout Boulevard
Suite 1000
Tampa, FL 33607-5780
www.carltonfields.com

J. Mark Lovelace (Oklahoma)
Phillips Murrah P.C.
Corporate Tower | Thirteenth Floor
101 North Robinson
Oklahoma City, Oklahoma 73102
www.phillipsmurrah.com

Jim Mace (Nevada)
Greenberg Traurig, LLP
3773 Howard Hughes Parkway, Suite 400 N
Las Vegas, Nevada 89169
www.gtlaw.com

Michael F. Maglio (Connecticut)
Robinson & Cole LLP
280 Trumbull Street
Hartford, CT 06103-3597
www.rc.com

Mark A. Melvin (Kentucky)
Bingham Greenebaum Doll LLP
101 S. Fifth Street, Suite 3500
Louisville, Kentucky 40202-3197
www.bgdlegal.com

Keyvan Nassiry (Quebec)
BCF LLP
1100 René-Lévesque Blvd West, 25th floor
Montreal, Quebec H3B 5C9 Canada
www.bcf.ca

Richard P. Olson (North Dakota)
Olson & Burns P.C.
17 1st Ave. SE
Minot, ND 58702-1180
http://www.minotlaw.com

Kathleen O'Neill (New York)
Cleary Gottlieb Steen & Hamilton LLP
One Liberty Plaza
New York, New York 10006-1470
www.clearygottlieb.com

Shiv Ghuman O'Neill (Indiana)
Faegre Baker Daniels LLP
300 North Meridian Street, Suite 2700
Indianapolis, Indiana 46204
http://www.faegrebd.com

Garrett Parks (Alaska)
Davis Wright Tremaine LLP
701 West Eighth Avenue, Suite 800
Anchorage, AK 99501
http://www.dwt.com

Jennifer A. Pearcy (Indiana)
Faegre Baker Daniels LLP
300 North Meridian Street, Suite 2700
Indianapolis, Indiana 46204
http://www.faegrebd.com

Margaret Platzer (Vermont)
Dinse, Knapp & McAndrew, P.C.
209 Battery Street
Burlington, Vermont 05401
www.dinse.com

Leslie J. Polt (Maryland)
Adelberg, Rudow, Dorf & Hendler, LLC
7 St. Paul Street, Suite 600
Baltimore, Maryland 21202-1612
www.AdelbergRudow.com

Reza A. Rabiee (Kentucky)
3500 National City Tower
101 South Fifth Street
Louisville, KY 40202

Alistair Y. Raymond (Maine)
Verrill Dana, LLP
One Portland Square
Portland, ME 04112
www.verrilldana.com

Joseph L. Reece (Alaska)
Davis Wright Tremaine LLP
701 West Eighth Avenue, Suite 800
Anchorage, AK 99501
http://www.dwt.com

Rebecca A. Richardson (Indiana)
Faegre Baker Daniels LLP
300 North Meridian Street, Suite 2700
Indianapolis, Indiana 46204
http://www.faegrebd.com

Daniel Roberts (Vermont)
Dinse, Knapp & McAndrew, P.C.
209 Battery Street
Burlington, Vermont 05401
www.dinse.com

Christopher J. Rockers (Kansas and Missouri)
Husch Blackwell LLP
4801 Main Street
Suite 1000
Kansas City, MO 64112
www.huschblackwell.com

Juan C. Salichs (Puerto Rico)
Salichs Pou & Associates, PSC
Popular Center
209 Muñoz Rivera Avenue, Suite 1434
San Juan, Puerto Rico 00918
http://www.salichspou.com

Stephen F. Schelver (Mississippi)
McGlinchey Stafford Pllc
200 South Lamar Street
City Centre South, Suite 1100
Jackson, MS 39201

James C. Schulwolf (Connecticut)
Shipman & Goodwin LLP
One Constitution Plaza
Hartford, CT 06103
www.shipmangoodwin.com

Michael B. Schwegler (Tennessee)
Ernest B. Williams IV, PLLC
P.O. Box 159264
Nashville, TN 37215

Lauren E. Sembler (Florida)
Carlton Fields, P.A.
4221 W. Boy Scout Boulevard
Suite 1000
Tampa, FL 33607-5780
www.carltonfields.com

Mark S. Sharpe (South Carolina)
Warren & Sinkler, LLP
171 Church Street
Suite 340
Charleston, South Carolina 29401

Irfan Siddiqui (Illinois)
Sidley Austin LLP
One South Dearborn Street
Chicago, Illinois 60603
www.sidley.com

Michael R. Silvey (Oregon)
Lane Powell PC
601 SW Second Avenue, Suite 2100
Portland, OR 97204-3158
www.lanepowell.com

R. Jeffrey Smith (Connecticut)
Bingham McCutchen LLP
One State Street
Hartford, CT 06103
www.bingham.com

Benjamin Snodgrass (New York)
Cleary Gottlieb Steen & Hamilton LLP
One Liberty Plaza
New York, New York 10006-1470
www.clearygottlieb.com

Amy C. Strang (Ohio)
Porter, Wright, Morris & Arthur LLP
41 South High Street
Columbus, Ohio 43215-6194
www.porterwright.com

Beat U. Steiner (Colorado)
Holland & Hart LLP
555 17th Street, Suite 3200
Denver, CO 80202
www.hollandhart.com

Brent A. Stork (Wisconsin)
Michael Best & Friedrich LLP
100 East Wisconsin Avenue, Suite 3300
Milwaukee, Wisconsin 53202
http://www.michaelbest.com

Haven L. Stuck (South Dakota)
Lynn, Jackson, Shultz & Lebrun, P.C.
909 St. Joseph Street, Suite 800
P.O. Box 8250
Rapid City, SD 57709
www.lynnjackson.com

Jeremy Syz (Colorado)
Holland & Hart LLP
555 17th Street, Suite 3200
Denver, CO 80202
www.hollandhart.com

Rob Thomas (Colorado)
Holland & Hart LLP
555 17th Street, Suite 3200
Denver, CO 80202
www.hollandhart.com

Brandon R. Tomjack (Nebraska)
Baird Holm LLP
1500 Woodmen Tower
1700 Farnam St
Omaha, NE 68102-2068
www.bairdholm.com

Wilson R. Trice (Virginia)
ThompsonMcMullan, PC
100 Shockoe Slip
Richmond, VA 23219
www.t-mlaw.com

H. Hunter Twiford, III (Mississippi)
McGlinchey Stafford PLLC
200 South Lamar Street
City Centre South, Suite 1100
Jackson, MS 39201

Jeffrey H. Verbin (Arizona)
Greenberg Traurig, LLP
2375 E. Camelback Rd. Suite 700
Phoenix, AZ 85016
www.gtlaw.com

Kenneth M. Vesledahl (Texas)
Patton Boggs LLP
2000 McKinney Avenue
Suite 1700
Dallas, Texas 75201
www.pattonboggs.com

Thomas J. Welsh (Connecticut)
Brown & Welsh, P.C.
530 Preston Avenue, Suite 220
Meriden, CT 06450

Ernest B. Williams IV (Tennessee)
Ernest B. Williams IV, PLLC
P.O. Box 159264
Nashville, TN 37215

W. P. Wiseman (Kentucky)
Bingham Greenebaum Doll LLP
101 S. Fifth Street, Suite 3500
Louisville, Kentucky 40202-3197
www.bgdlegal.com

Robert A. Wright, III (Michigan)
Dawda Mann
39533 Woodward Avenue, Suite 200
Bloomfield Hills, Michigan 48304
dawdamann.com

Janel M. N. Yoshimoto (Hawai`i)
Chun Yoshimoto LLP
737 Bishop Street, Suite 2800
Pacific Guardian Center, Mauka Tower
Honolulu, Hawai`i 96813
www.chunyoshimoto.com

Robert A. Zadek (California)
Buchalter Nemer P.C.
55 Second Street, Suite 1700
San Francisco, California 94105-3493
www.buchalter.com

Kevin Zeller (Kansas and Missouri)
Husch Blackwell LLP
4801 Main Street
Suite 1000
Kansas City, MO 64112
www.huschblackwell.com